THE ULTIMATE
BASEBALL
ROAD TRIP

2ND EDITION

Also by Josh Pahigian and Kevin O'Connell

The Ultimate Baseball Road Trip, 1st edition
Why I Hate the Yankees

Also by Josh Pahigian

101 Baseball Places to See Before You Strike Out
The Seventh Inning Stretch
The Ultimate Minor League Baseball Road Trip
The Red Sox in the Playoffs
Spring Training Handbook

THE ULTIMATE
BASEBALL
R⚾AD TRIP

2ND EDITION

A Fan's Guide to Major League Stadiums

Josh Pahigian and Kevin O'Connell

LYONS PRESS

Guilford, Connecticut

An imprint of Rowman & Littlefield

Lyons Press is an imprint of Rowman & Littlefield.

Distributed by
NATIONAL BOOK NETWORK

Library of Congress Cataloging-in-Publication Data is available on file.

ISBN 978-0-7627-7340-4

Printed in the United States of America

Contents

Introduction

Well, they did it again. For a second time the good folks at the Lyons Press decided it a reasonable investment to send us on the greatest sports road trip ever known to man, woman, or child. And believe us, we're the last ones you'll hear complaining. Truth is, we thought they were a bit crazy the first time around. You know, back in the summer of 2003 when they sent us—two eager but undiscovered writers—into the American Summer to find baseball Nirvana. We got to live out our dream of traveling the entire country to see a game in every big league park. And get this—*they paid for it!*

Is America a great country, or what?

Before you start reading about our *second* journey through the emerald cathedrals of the Major Leagues and before you begin to plan your own epic baseball adventure, we thought we'd tell you a bit more about ourselves and what we were trying to accomplish in writing *The Ultimate Baseball Road Trip* 2.0. We also thought we'd pause to reflect on some of the ways the game and the fans who enjoy it have changed in the years since the book's original publication.

Firstly, though, while it's nice to think that the second edition of the book will attract a bevy of new readers, we feel as though we owe a special debt of gratitude to our *returning* readers. A decade ago when we managed to convince Lyons to fund our fantasy tour of the bigs, we were just two guys fresh out of grad school with a shared passion for the game and a mutual sense of wanderlust. We had never embarked upon anything close to the magnitude of the trip or subsequent book we'd proposed to write. Like many of our readers, we'd always dreamed of a summer spent pursuing a singular kind of bliss—one that seemed as close to the heart of the American Spirit as apple pie, blue jeans, and Fourth of July fireworks. We imagined scurrying after batting practice homers, raising cups of suds with newfound friends, and waking up the next morning and doing it all again. And more than just that, we imagined a future in which we would help others plot their own hardball odysseys. But we never imagined the sort of overflowing reader response our first book would garner.

The letters and e-mails started filling our mailboxes about a month after *The Ultimate Baseball Road Trip* hit the bookstore shelves in 2004. They came from college kids, fathers, grandfathers, wives, and mothers. They included pictures of glowing faces set against ballpark backdrops far and wide. They reflected the same joy we'd come to know during our own trip. Just as we'd been eager to share the story of our trip with readers, now they were sharing their magical moments with us. The veritable deluge gave us goosebumps. Some of the e-mails described multi-generational family pilgrimages. Others recalled the lengths to which fans had gone to carry out their excursions on shoestring budgets. One was from a young

bride who told us about how she and her new husband had used the book to make their honeymoon all it could be. Another was from an elderly gentleman in England, who had always been fascinated by American culture but had never been to a big league park; now, he said, he *felt* as though he had, thanks to the vicarious trip he'd taken by reading our book. Another was from an American soldier deployed in Iraq, who was planning a trip with one of his buddies for the summer after their deployment ended. As soon as they got home, he said, they planned to rent a van and see all thirty yards. Talking about the trip and charting its course was helping them pass the time.

We were amazed and humbled. Our book was playing a meaningful role in real people's lives.

And so, a tad older and hopefully a bit wiser, we set out again into the great expanse of Americana, in search of that perfect night where the air is warm and dry, the ballpark seats are close and cheap, the hot dogs snap with spice, the beer is cold, and the game plays out before us with all the drama and passion of a Shakespearian tragedy.

Kevin: This time around, I knew better than to let you drive.

Josh: And I knew better than to let you buy a tray full of beers at the end of the seventh inning.

Now then, let us offer an important disclaimer. First and foremost, we are baseball fans. The book is written from our perspective as two fans, eager to share our observations, experiences, and suggestions with fellow devotees. Yes, we are *baseball writers,* whatever that means, but we are not beholden to any official or approved points of view. Why does this matter to you? Well, let's just say that while the American ballpark trail presents a path full of magic, majesty, and amazing memories just waiting to be discovered, it isn't perfect. Some of the stadium seats are too pricey or too far from the infield. Some of the foods they shovel at you aren't worth slopping at pigs. Some of the neighborhoods in which the parks reside do little to enhance the game-day experience (we're thinking of *you,* Anaheim!). And we feel you need to know all of this. We're not striving to write a puff piece for the MLB Chamber of Commerce. They're doing just fine without our help. We're offering a frank review of the game's parks. We'll call the statue of Stan the Man outside Busch Stadium what it is: a grotesque distortion of one of the greatest players of all time and a man who in real life, actually looks quite humanoid. We'll spare no punches in calling the much-ballyhooed Dodger Dog a bland disappointment, especially when corners are cut in its preparation. We'll pan the upper level at Miller Park for housing—however ironically—a sea of Uecker Seats. Our goal is to give an honest review of the MLB parks so that you can be as savvy a consumer as possible.

Josh: So, we're kind of like that Rick Steves guy, only for ballparks?

Kevin: And without the Pete Rose bowl-cut.

Now, don't get us wrong. We're not trying to suggest that the ballpark trail is riddled with pitfalls. It's not. But there are some traps along the way and they're easily enough avoided as long as someone gives you a heads-up. And don't forget, there's much to potentially miss about a city's baseball past and present if no one bothers to tell you where to look. That's what we aim to do—to give you all the knowledge you need to enhance your own experiences.

By reading our book you can ensure that you won't miss out on much of anything related to a city's baseball wonders before moving on to your next destination. We know this is a concern for traveling fans because, well, we're a lot like you. We share your obsession with stats, your hunger for baseball lore, and the way the hair always stands up on the back of your neck when you walk up the ramp and lay eyes on the field. We still get chills as batting practice winds down and first pitch approaches. We feel the same craving you do all summer long—that need for your daily fix. We know what it's like to cry yourself to sleep after your fantasy team goes three-for-thirty-two or after your home team blows the lead in the ninth.

Kevin grew up in Seattle listening to radio broadcasts of the Dodgers, because before the Mariners debuted in 1977, Vin Scully's baseball voice was one of the few that could be heard up and down the West Coast. When the Mariners finally arrived, he'd long been rooting for the Giants in the NL and the Red Sox in the AL—though his second favorite team on any night was *whoever was playing the Yankees.* When Edgar Martinez and Ken Griffey Jr. reigned in Seattle and the Mariners became committed to being more than a farm team for the rest of the league, Kevin began to root for the difficult-to-love and much-maligned Mariners. Now that the M's have finally dug themselves out from under the grotesque weight of the baseball tomb that was the Kingdome and while they still search for their first World Series berth, Kevin uses all forms of available technology to happily follow the ups and downs of baseball in the Pacific Northwest from his home in Pittsburgh. While the current Pirates remind him plenty of the hapless Mariners before Junior came to town, his second favorite team remains whoever is playing the Yankees.

Josh grew up in the heart of Red Sox Nation, long before it was fashionable to root for Boston's once-perennial also-rans. Back then, it was inconceivable that the Old Towne Team would one day play in front of what are practically home crowds in far-away cities like Pittsburgh and Anaheim. During Josh's formative baseball years, to be a Red Sox fan meant to embrace a life spent suffering the throes of one baseball catastrophe after another. Back then, even Fenway Park was considered a local disappointment. Many Bostonians viewed it as a run-down relic in desperate need of replacement. Being a Sox fan in those days had its benefits too, though. Josh's father could walk him up to a ticket window on Yawkey Way an hour before first pitch and buy seats in the infield grandstand at face value. And once old Richard Pahigian did even better than that for his wide-eyed baseball-loving son at the Fenway ticket booths, when a ticket attendant handed him two front-row seats, right behind the plate. Oh, how times have changed. . . . These days, Josh follows the Sox from his home in Southern Maine. When he isn't home watching the big league Red Sox on NESN, he's sitting at Hadlock Field in Portland, watching the team's Double-A prospects play. It's a pretty tough life, but he figures someone has to do it.

Kevin: Do you ever get tired of watching baseball?

Josh: Well . . . no, I guess I don't.

Kevin: Me neither.

Since the first edition of our book was published in March 2004, eight new big league parks have opened. And the technical whiz kids from Silicon Valley invented social media, smartphones, tablets, and an amorphous world unto its own known as the blogosphere. We'll get back to the topic of how these latter innovations have changed the ways we fans follow the game in a moment, and tell you how this new and improved version of the book capitalizes on the opportunities they present. But first, we ought to acknowledge how the game itself has changed—and thankfully so—since the first edition of the book. When *The Ultimate Baseball Road Trip* 1.0 came out, the world was just opening its eyes to the full extent of baseball's steroid problem. Home runs were still en vogue and "small-ball" still referred to a style of play that seemed as relevant to modern times as those puffy exterior chest protectors home plate umps used to wield like medieval shields.

Josh: I notice you're not wearing your Bonds jersey this time 'round.

Kevin: And you're not wearing your Clemens jersey.

Josh: Touché.

Part of the reason it took so darned long for the Steroid Era's wool to be lifted from casual observers' eyes was because the sport's pundits largely protected the modern players from scrutiny. Nearly to a person they'll profess otherwise, but, as we said, we prefer to tell it like it is. And we are telling you that the game's most prominent television commentators—most of whom are ex-ballplayers—all had to know something was amok. During their own playing days, these announcers made it their life's work to test the very limits of their unenhanced bodies. The years they spend in the booth are meant to allow them to share their wealth of knowledge with their viewers. When players started doing things on the field they themselves had never come close to doing, well, not one came out and said a thing. They had to know. But down to the last man, they remained silent. Are we to believe that none harbored any suspicions about performance-enhancing drugs? We have an easier time believing the Big Tobacco studies expounding the health benefits of smoking.

As far as we're concerned you can put a black mark next to the name of every scout, general manager, coach, and manager of the era too. They all made a living evaluating talent. Heck, if Josh was onto the juicers—and he was, as a review of the Fenway Park chapter in this book's original edition demonstrates—they were too. But, lots of fans knew . . . and were powerless to do a darned thing about it.

You see, back then, there was no way for fans—the one constituency without a vested interest in keeping the game's big secret hush-hush—to take charge of the conversation. Today, all that has changed. With the rise of the new media, fans play a more active, more direct, and more vital role than ever before in shaping the game's major and minor story lines. And they do so in real time. Being a fan is a far more interactive experience today than it was a decade ago. That's why we've gone to lengths to make this edition of the book as social-media/cyber-friendly as possible. More than just sharing *our* impressions of the ballparks, teams, and fans across the land, we've infused the book with links to the better blogs and Web forums through which each fan base communicates with its members.

In addition, we've included links to the ballpark seating maps and ticketing websites, to the menus of sports bars and restaurants, and to a range of other points of baseball interest worthy of cyber (and real world) exploration by readers.

These new aspects of the book are presented, of course, in addition to all of the favorite features of the book fans enjoyed in the first edition. Like its predecessor, *The Ultimate Baseball Road Trip* 2.0 is part travel manual, part ballpark atlas, part baseball history book, part baseball trivia challenge, part food critique, part city guide, and part epic narrative. It touches all the bases in endeavoring to make your baseball odysseys fulfilling and meaningful. And it does so within a lively prose style that leaves room for a few dollops of humor and a few dribs and drabs of ketchup (or mustard) along the way. After all, your road trip is important to you. It may just be the most soul-affirming, awe-inspiring, life-altering adventure you ever attempt. In any case, it's going to be a blast. So, we want your experience reading our book to be fun too.

Everything you need to plan your trip is here. So order those plane or train tickets. Get that tune-up you've been putting off. Call your college buddies or dad. Plot your itinerary. Pack your bags. Square things with the boss. Have a heart-to-heart with your significant other, who can either come along for the ride or accept this is something you've just got to do. The time is now. One way or another, you're hitting the road. *The Ultimate Baseball Road Trip* 2.0 will be your guide. We'll be your companions. Just keep us in the glove-box, or on your smartphone, or as a link on the personal computing device of your choice. Whichever, we'll be there to help you along.

As for our primary piece of advice, it's to do it all, or to do as much as you physically can. Touch the Green Monster in Boston. Catch a batting practice homer off the B&O Warehouse in Baltimore. Sample the Garlic Fries in San Francisco. Root for the Bratwurst to win the Sausage Race in Milwaukee. Sing "Take Me Out to the Ball Game" three notes off-key in Chicago. Experience all the wonders of the American Game, as you enjoy the most magical summer of your life. Drive safely. Eat heartily. Root for the home team. And keep those e-mails and pictures coming!

BOSTON RED SOX, FENWAY PARK

BOSTON, MASSACHUSETTS
215 MILES TO NEW YORK CITY
310 MILES TO PHILADELPHIA
410 MILES TO BALTIMORE
450 MILES TO WASHINGTON, D.C.

A Little Green Diamond in the Heart of Beantown

Within Boston's hardball cathedral, the grass seems greener, the crack of the bat crisper, and the excitement in the air more palpable than anywhere else. In fact, most of the ballparks that have opened in recent years have been designed with Fenway's old-time charm in mind, as ballpark architects have sought to replicate the nuances of Fenway in much the same way church builders once imitated the Sistine Chapel. "Retro" is the name of the game these days in ballpark design. What's old is new. Baltimore started the trend when it built Oriole Park at Camden Yards to mimic Fenway's set-in-the-city ethos, cozy confines, and asymmetrical field dimensions. Cleveland's Progressive Field offers a nod to Fenway's trademark thirty-seven-foot-high left-field wall with a nineteen-foot Mini-Monster of its own. Rangers Ballpark in Arlington sports a scoreboard built into the outfield fence like at Fenway. And Washington's Nationals Park showcases relief pitchers warming up in home-run-territory bullpens that invoke Fenway's right-field stables.

As the oldest facility in the bigs, Fenway is part ballpark and part time machine. You leave the twenty-first century and enter the 1920s when you ascend the narrow ramps leading from the concourse to the seating bowl and behold the narrow rows of wooden seats, the nooks and crannies created by the zigzagging outfield fence, the slate scoreboard, the green paint, and that looming edifice in left. This living dinosaur has been the stomping grounds of such immortals as Cy Young, Babe Ruth, Jimmie Foxx, Tris Speaker, Ted Williams, and Carl Yastrzemski. It was Boston's field when your grandfather used to listen to games on a radio the size of a coffee table and when *his* father used to follow the American League the only way a fan could, short of holding a ticket, back then—by reliving the previous day's events through elaborate newspaper retellings.

Since those dead-ball days, the world has changed to the point where Great Gramps—were he alive today—might barely recognize it, but Fenway has remained essentially the same. Provided you train your eye to ignore the blinking pitch-speed register above the center-field fence, and the neon advertising above the roof in right, your experience within Boston's ballyard will be pretty close to your granddad's, right down to the sore butt you'll drag home after spending nine innings wedged into the tiny hardwood seats that fill the Grandstand. But you won't mind this slight ass fatigue. Once you've gazed at the mighty Monster, rapped your knuckles against Pesky's Pole, and sat in Teddy Ballgame's "red seat" during batting practice, you'll be a convert. You'll feel like baseball was invented specifically to be played (and watched!) at Fenway. So power down your smart phone, buy a Fenway Frank, and squeeze into that seat.

So where did they come up with the name Fenway Park? No, it wasn't in tribute to some generous beneficiary named John Q. Fenway. Nor were the rights to the stadium's name bought and paid for as if the park were nothing but a cheap, tawdry, street-corner . . . umm . . . billboard. In fact, when this part of Massachusetts was being developed hundreds of years ago, Boston's "fens" were a backwater of the Charles River. The Fens Way was the road that ran through the swamp. Thus, the name "Fenway Park." The Fens were not declared "inhabitable" until 1777, after the completion of a decade-long effort to level the local "tri-mountain" and dump the fill into the 450-acre marsh that became Boston's Fenway District. Fenway Park was built in 1912 after being designed to fit snugly into the confines of a pre-existing city block. That's why the field and stands are so irregularly shaped.

After cleaning out their lockers at their old home, the Huntington Avenue Grounds, the Red Sox opened Fenway with a 2-0 win over Harvard University on April 10, 1912. Then, eight days later, the home team defeated the New York Highlanders 7-6 in the park's first official game. The

1

opening-week exuberance was dampened, however, by the sinking of the *Titanic* in the icy North Atlantic. Fenway took center stage six months later, though, as the Red Sox celebrated a World Series title on the Fenway lawn after downing the New York Giants 3–2 before seventeen thousand fans in the deciding game. With the victory, Boston's American Leaguers (who were also known as the Pilgrims, Americans, and Red Stockings in their early days) claimed the second of five World Championship banners they would raise between 1903 and 1918. They might have had six if John McGraw's Giants hadn't refused to play the Pilgrims in 1904, owing to the feisty manager's disdain for the upstart Junior Circuit.

After laying claim to being the most successful franchise of the first two decades of the Modern Era, the Red Sox sold Babe Ruth to the Yankees for $100,000 in 1920. Thus began a long period of what might best be described as haplessness. Following their victory over the Cubs in the 1918 October Classic, the Red Sox would not taste World Series champagne for a very, very long time. In fact, it was eighty-six years before the Red Sox broke the supposed "Curse of the Bambino," overcoming a three-games-to-none deficit to beat the Yankees in the 2004 American League Championship Series and then sweeping the Cardinals in the World Series. With another Series sweep, this time of

the Rockies in 2007, the Red Sox cemented their claim to being the most successful team of the first decade of the new century.

In between these golden eras of Beantown ball the local rooters experienced their share of heartbreak. The Old Towne Team took its World Series opponents the full seven games in 1946, 1967, 1975, and 1986, only to fall short each time. For at least three generations of New England life there were no "Red Sox fans," only "long-suffering Red Sox fans." But all that has changed. And as a result, Fenway is a more popular destination than ever before. Game after game, the ballpark sells out, as hardcore fans who have followed the team since birth merge with pink-hat-wearing band-wagon-jumping corporate types. This is an annoyance for Beantown seam-heads, but, most agree, a relatively small tradeoff for the privilege of experiencing what many of their fathers and grandfathers never did: a World Series victory parade.

Kevin: I miss the curse.

Josh: Blasphemy! I won't hear it!

Kevin: No, I really miss it. It was one of the most mystical things in all of sports.

Fenway has stood the test of time, to be certain, but not without enduring some brushes with mortality. In 1926 a fire destroyed the left-field bleachers and for seven years thereafter ownership cried poverty while third basemen and shortstops tiptoed into the charred rubble after pop-ups. These were dark days for the Boston Nine. Dark and sooty days. Finally, in 1934, the team installed new seats along the left field line. It was at this time that the Green Monster was erected. "The Wall," as it is known to locals, consists of concrete, and is coated with wood, plated with tin, and covered with green paint. Prior to its construction, a much shorter fence had stood atop "Duffy's Cliff," a ten-foot embankment named after Sox left fielder Duffy Lewis, who was adroit at scaling the hill to catch fly balls.

Other changes have been made to the park through the years too. When Fenway was constructed it was customary for relief pitchers to warm up on the field of play behind the outfielders. Mind you, this was during the Dead Ball Era, when long fly balls were rare and starting pitchers usually went the full nine. As time passed, relievers came to more commonly warm up in foul territory or under the stands. Finally, in 1940, the Red Sox brought in the right-field fence and

Yawkey Way

Photo by Josh Pahigian

The Green Monster

Fans await batting practice long balls atop the Monster.
Photo by Josh Pahigian

Fenway's nostalgic feel. In fact, the Monster Seats are more visually appealing than the ratty old screen into which long fly balls used to settle above the Wall. And they look like they've always been there. Likewise, management's efforts to widen Fenway's concourses, expand its concession areas, and modernize its facilities have dramatically improved the fan experience. It wasn't long ago that male fans had to relieve themselves into trough-style urinals that stood in the middle of each Fenway men's room. We kid you not. And it wasn't long ago that, in the dying days of the Yawkey Trust's stewardship of the team, fans and local radio hosts spoke about the replacement of Fenway with a shiny new retractable-roof ballpark on the South Boston waterfront as if it were a not-too-distant inevitability. For preserving Fenway for future generations of New Englanders to call "home," we tip our caps to John Henry.

Since the arrival of Henry and Co., the Red Sox have added nearly four thousand seats, increasing Fenway's capacity to a bit over thirty-seven thousand for night games and a bit under that for day games. This unusual day/night split exists because several hundred center-field seats are covered with a black tarp during day games to provide a better backdrop for hitters. Once

added twenty-three-foot-deep bullpens in home run territory. It was no coincidence that a sweet-swinging lefty named Ted Williams had burst onto the scene the year before. The pens were dubbed "Williamsburgh" and "The Kid" promptly began dropping homers into the inviting landing strip.

The most obvious modification to Fenway since John Henry's Fenway Sports Group bought the team in 2002 would have to be the addition of nearly three hundred seats atop the Green Monster. Another biggie was the expansion of the manual scoreboard in left to include the National League scores, which it had decades earlier. Other major changes have included the replacement of the glassed-in .406 Club above home plate with an open-air luxury seating area, the addition of right-field roof seats, the installation of two gigantic high-def video screens above the center-field bleachers, a massive food court behind the bleachers in right, and the closing of Yawkey Way on game day so that only ticket holders may partake in the just-outside-the-gates festivities. For the most part your humble authors approve of these changes. We understand that Henry and Co. paid $700 million for the team and must cram as many fannies into Fenway as possible. Fortunately, the renovations have been made with the sensibilities of baseball purists in mind and have not too egregiously compromised

Trivia Timeout

Undergrad: Why is there a solitary red seat in Fenway's bleachers while the rest are green?
Master's: Who are the seven Red Sox whose numbers have been retired?
Ph.D.: What popular Broadway song did fans of the Boston Pilgrims sing to rattle the Pittsburgh Pirates during baseball's first World Series?
Look for the answers in the text.

you factor in the standing room tickets, ballpark capacity settles somewhere around thirty-eight thousand, which gives Fenway one of the smallest "full houses" in the bigs, right there with the Oakland Coliseum, Tropicana Field, and PNC Park. The 38,422 fans the Red Sox drew to a June 2011 game against the Padres was the largest Boston crowd since World War II. That banged-out house also represented the

Red Sox 668th consecutive home sellout. For the record, the biggest Fenway crowd ever to fill the park turned out for a double-header against the Yankees in 1935 to the tune of an official attendance of 47,627. Fans were standing in the aisles, hanging from the rafters, sitting on each other's laps, and otherwise jamming the park to such a ridiculous extent that soon after, fire laws were put in place disallowing the Red Sox from "over-filling" the park.

Getting a Choice Seat

The relatively few number of seats, combined with the fanaticism of the Red Sox faithful, helps explain why the Red Sox sold out every game from May 15, 2003, through this book's publication date. With "the streak," the Red Sox, who passed the seven-hundred-game mark in 2011, demolished the previous record of 455 straight sellouts that the Cleveland Indians established between 1995 and 2001. What does this mean to you as a ballpark traveler? It means if you don't want to pay the scalpers' mark-up you must buy your Red Sox tickets when they go on sale in January. To do this, you must stare at your computer screen in the team's virtual waiting room.

Home Plate and Dugout Boxes

The only seats that position rooters closer to home plate than these are the ones behind the backstop at the new Yankee Stadium. And, as is the case in the Bronx, these seats are extremely hard to come by. And they cost a fortune. Basically, unless you're one of the players' wives or happen to own one of the local companies that advertise at Fenway, these spitting-distance chairs are beyond your reach. For the record, Fenway's backstop is sixty feet from home plate, which means Giant Glass president Dennis Drinkwater—the middle-aged blond guy who has occupied the best seat in the house since 2003—is closer to the catcher than the pitcher is.

Field Boxes (Boxes 9–84)

These infield box seats provide delightfully unobstructed sight lines. Season-ticket holders sit in them, as do folks who spend several hundred dollars per ticket in the secondary market. But don't be discouraged: Fenway offers plenty of great seats that you can afford.

Loge Boxes (Boxes 99–166)

Located above the Field Boxes from which they're separated by a narrow mid-level concourse, these seats are slightly more affordable on the secondary market, especially if you're willing to split from your friends and buy a "single."

Green Monster Seats (Sections M1–M10)

The 274 Green Monster Seats are among the most unusual and coveted seats in baseball. Each is an individual chair that positions fans behind a pavilion-style counter. Unless you're willing to lay down a few thou for an "Ultimate Monster Tour" package, the only way to purchase a Green Monster Seat is by getting lucky in the annual lottery the Red Sox hold in March. You can register online. Then, if your name is plucked from the proverbial E-hat, you have the right to purchase two tickets. But don't get your hopes up.

Right Field Boxes (Boxes 1A, 1–7, 86–97)

Ah, finally we've gotten to the seats that won't cost the equivalent of a mortgage payment for you to acquire. The only problem is that while these Right Field Boxes are within your means of procurement, they don't provide good views. The first few rows (A-F) of Boxes 86 and 87 in home run territory are decent, as are the "tarp alley" Boxes (1A, 1–7) near Pesky's Pole, but the majority of them point fans toward center field rather than home plate. And they're rather distant from the infield for the price. You'll be more satisfied with a smartly selected Grandstand or Bleacher seat. Boxes 89–92 should be especially avoided.

infield

Fenway celebrated its 100th Anniversary in 2012.
Photo by Josh Pahigian

> **Seating Capacity:** 37,402
> **Ticket Office:** http://boston.redsox.mlb.com
> **Seating Chart:** http://boston.redsox.mlb.com/bos/ticketing/seating_pricing.jsp

Kevin: Yes, avoided like burritos before a long stretch on the road.

Josh: It's the first chapter and you're already making bathroom jokes?

Kevin: Hey, that's solid advice.

Infield Grandstand (Sections 11–31)

Compared to the second-tier options at other parks, Fenway's Grandstands are first-rate. They're close to the field and offer exceptional views. But buyers beware: These seats were designed for turn-of-the-century New Englanders who were apparently about five-feet, six-inches tall and had rear ends made of New Hampshire granite. The tiny seats are made of hard wooden slats. If you're a tall man—like Kevin is—or a wide man—like Josh may someday be if he continues to eat four Fenway Sausages each time he visits Fenway—you may prefer the greater comfort of the plastic Bleacher seats.

When considering a Grandstand ticket, also realize that large metal pillars rise up from between the seats to support the Grandstand roof. The team sells "Obstructed View" seats at regular price but does clearly label these tickets "obstructed." Buying one is something of a crapshoot. In some cases, sitting in an Obstructed View seat means you will be straddling one of those pillars for nine innings and seeing little more than peeling green paint. In other cases, it means you'll have a great view of home plate but no view of the pitcher's mound. In other cases, it means you'll have to lean to one side all game but will be able to see pretty much all of the important stuff. So before you buy an Obstructed View seat ask yourself a simple question: Do you feel lucky, punk?

Otherwise, shoot for the first ten rows of the Grandstands, seeing as fans farther back have no guarantee they'll be able to follow the full flight of pop-ups, fly-outs and home runs, owing to the overhang of the roof.

Apart from those disclaimers, we do recommend the Grandstands. Sections 19–22 provide the best view of the batter's box. From Sections 14–17, along the first-base line, the Wall provides a delightfully looming backdrop for the game. Sections 29–31, along the left-field line, are raised and angled nicely, enabling fans to feel like they're sitting right behind the shortstop.

Outfield Grandstand (Sections 1–10, 32–33)

The best seats in this category are found in Sections 32 and 33, out by the Green Monster. Here, there are very few Loge Boxes—or none at all—between the Grandstands and the playing field. Additionally, these seats are angled toward the infield. The only potential drawback is that Sections 32 and 33 comprise Fenway's "Family Section," which means ticket holders are prohibited from drinking beer in these seats. We should also note that Section 33 is the only Grandstand section that is not covered by the roof, which may be a consideration on a rainy night. The upside to Section 33 is that unlike the rest of the seats in the Grandstands, it offers comfortable plastic seats. Apparently, being exposed to the elements caused the old wooden seats to deteriorate prematurely.

Kevin: I still think we should put that part about NO BEER ALLOWED in all caps.

Josh: But they really are great seats for the money.

As for the right field Outfield Grandstands (Sections 1–10), they point occupants squarely toward center field, rather than the infield. As such, fans must peer over their left shoulders and, in many instances, around the roof's support columns to see the pitcher's mound and/or home plate. Seats in Section 10 are worth purchasing, but otherwise, we suggest spending less money for a better view in the Bleachers or more money for a better view in the Infield Grandstands.

Bleachers (Sections 34–43)

As we've already said, quite a few of the Bleacher seats provide better views than the higher-priced seats in the Right Field Boxes and Outfield Grandstands. In addition, these are all comfortable plastic seats. And there are no poles to block the view.

Our favorite Bleacher seats are the ones beside the centerfield camera platform in Sections 34 and 35. This is a great place from which to call balls and strikes while awaiting home run balls.

Section 40, behind the home bullpen, offers the opportunity to both interact with the players and check out the Bleacher groupies as they flock to the screen separating the seats from the middle relievers.

The first fifteen rows of Sections 36–38 are also quite good. As you make your way toward right-field (39–43), however, the distance from the plate steadily increases and the quality of the view diminishes. This is especially true as you climb above Row 30.

The atmosphere in Fenway's Bleachers has changed considerably since the Henry ownership group took charge. What was once a rough-and-tumble beer-swilling part of the park has mellowed to the point where today's Bleachers provide a comfortable climate for families. The college kids are still able to have their fun and the beer still flows, but the ushers are on high-alert for offensive behavior and violators are promptly put on notice or "asked" to leave.

Another recent change involves the steel gate that once stood on the concourse beneath the Bleachers. For generations the barrier prevented bleacher creatures from interacting with the human beings populating the rest of Fenway. Thankfully it has been removed. Today's bleacher-ites may wander into the rest of the park.

Upper Bleachers (Top Rows of Sections 37 and 38)

Unless you enjoy watching a game of baseball from a different postal code than the one in which home plate resides, you should avoid these seats! Some are literally *behind* the JumboTron!

EMC Club/Home Plate Pavilion/Pavilion Box/Left Field Pavilion

It seems like the Red Sox open a new premium seating area on Fenway's narrow upper deck every other season. Unless you have a "connection," you will find these seats hard to come by. But you'd rather sit with the real fans at field level anyway.

Right-field Roof Terrace (Terraces A & B)

We don't recommend these seats in deep right field, way up on the roof . . . unless you're attending Fenway primarily to check out the skyline and catch a nice breeze.

Standing Room

You know a team is doing well when it can charge $20–$35 for standing room and clear most of its inventory. The spots atop the Green Monster are the costliest, but they are well worth the expense. But that could be said of many of the standing areas within Fenway, provided your knees and back can handle the rigor of standing in one place for four hours. In fact, with an Infield Grandstand Standing Room ticket you'll see more of the game and be closer to it than you would have with a seat in the cramped and poorly angled Right Field Boxes and right-field Grandstands. Just don't

SEATING TIP

A risky but sometimes rewarding proposition is to report to Fenway's Gate E on game day where, ninety minutes before the start of each game, the Red Sox release a few hundred tickets. These consist of standing room, obstructed view seats, orphaned single seats and occasionally some pretty posh comp seats that Red Sox VIPs have declined to use and have returned to the box office. Fans are allowed to start lining up five hours before the game and there is a strictly enforced one-ticket-per-person rule. So make sure everyone within your party who needs a ticket is physically present in line.

expect to follow the full flight of fly balls from this standing locale. And don't forget your mittens if you're going to an April game. It can get pretty windy above the first base and home plate seats.

The most important thing to remember for any fan holding a Standing Room ticket is to show up early. Stake out a good spot within your designated standing area and it will be yours all game. Fail to, and you may find yourself peering over the shoulders and between the heads of two or three people who *did* bother to show up when the gates opened.

The Black Market

In a shameless nod to the widespread acceptability of second-hand ticket retailers these days—even after so many years of the sports industry pillorying street-corner scalpers as the scourge of the earth—the Red Sox go so far as to name one such agency the "official on-line ticket re-seller of the Boston Red Sox." But if you're like us, you'd rather haggle in a litter-strewn back alley with a guy who looks like he hasn't shaved in three days and smells like he hasn't bathed in ten.

Kevin: Are you sure about this, Josh?

Josh: Trust me. I know our readers.

Fortunately for Fenway fans, the chance of finding just such an individual presents itself almost immediately upon their stepping out of the Kenmore Square MBTA station. There on the sidewalk, in the shadow of the Hotel Buckminster, fans find a motley crew of hardworking gents who aren't bashful about barking out enticing propositions like "Got two, first base side." Unless the Yankees are in town or a late-season tilt with playoff implications is on the docket, expect to pay double-face for Grandstand and Box seats and triple-face for the still-more-affordable Bleacher seats.

Before/After the Game

Boston's Fenway neighborhood provides much of the housing for the city's collegiate population. Even on game days visitors are apt to observe nearly as many sweatshirts bearing the crests of Boston University, Northeastern, Emerson College and Berklee College of Music as ones bearing Red Sox logos. This is a fun, funky part of town that is safe and welcoming. The bars and nightclubs cater to the twenty-something clientele, combining the expected Red Sox decor with live music and relatively inexpensive cheer.

Getting to Fenway

Built into the footprint of an actual city block at a time before the average American owned an automobile, Fenway's planners never imagined the future benefit a multi-tiered parking garage beside the park might have provided. As such, fans are left at the mercy of private lots in the surrounding blocks. On game days, the gas stations on Boylston Street and even a local McDonald's cordon off parts of their parking lots and charge road trippers exorbitant rates for the privilege of parking within their bounds. These range between $30 and $60 per game. For those who don't mind walking a mile or so, better rates may be had. The Clarendon Garage (100 Clarendon St.) charges $27 on game days, but fans who have ticket stubs upon arriving pay just $9. Similarly, the Prudential Tower (800 Boylston St.) charges a flat rate of $16 for fans who arrive after two o'clock on weekdays. The only catch is that fans must relinquish their ticket stubs (one per car) upon settling up with the Pru parking attendants after the game. Well, there's one other catch too. If the game's rained out, the Pru charges the regular hourly rate. How's that for insult to injury?

Prudential Parking Info: www.prudentialcenter.com/parking/rates.php

Kevin: Hold on there, Sparky. You're telling me first I miss the game, then I get hosed on parking?

Josh: That seems un-American.

Another option is to use one of the oldest subway systems in the country, Boston's MBTA. Follow the Green Line to the recently remodeled Kenmore Station and it's just a short walk to the game.

Subway Map: www.mbta.com/schedules_and_maps/subway/

Outside Attractions

PLAYER PARKING

If you have time to kill before the game, head to Fenway early and stake out a spot on the corner of Yawkey Way and Van Ness Street. Here, you'll find Boston's legendary sausage vendors setting up their carts and better yet, you'll get to rub elbows with the Red Sox players as they arrive. Well, to be more accurate, you'll get to "rub elbows" with their side-view mirrors as they steer their Escalades and Mercedes through the channel of police barriers leading to the player parking lot. When the Sox are doing well and spirits in the home clubhouse are high, players often sign autographs or at least roll down their windows and exchange pleasantries with the fans who await them four or five hours before first pitch.

BYE-BYE BASEBALL . . . HELLO, SOUVENIR

A pregame activity in which slightly later-arriving fans may partake transpires on the other side of the park, behind Fenway's famous left-field Wall. Here, on Lansdowne Street—where, it should be noted, loiterers also get to bask in the aromatic delight of so many sizzling sausages—fans keep their eyes on the sky so as to avoid taking a batting practice homer off the noggin. As batting practice participants take aim at the Green Monster, balls careen into the street with regularity and glove-toting fans scramble to procure them. The best spot is behind the foul pole, in front of the Cask & Flagon. Here, the Wall stands just 310 feet from home plate, whereas farther down Lansdowne, in left-center, it stands 379 feet away.

If you think Lansdowne is crowded with ball hawks and sausage lovers on the day you visit, you may take heart in knowing it could be worse. Such was the case on a July evening in 1999 when Fenway hosted the midsummer Home Run Derby. A day before local hero Pedro Martinez would claim MVP honors in the All-Star Game, ten thousand fans crammed Lansdowne in hopes of snagging a McGwire or Sosa long ball. The juiced-up Red Head hit thirteen dingers in the first round, while the Doping Dominican hit an embarrassing one. In the end, Ken Griffey Jr., a lefty swinger who we'd like to think was "clean," went home the winner.

Kevin: Speaking as a lifelong Mariner fan, I can assure you Junior was clean.

Josh: You could tell me Mother Teresa was clean and I wouldn't believe you if she played baseball in the 1990s.

TEDDY BALLGAME: MEET THE SPLENDID SPLINTER

Believe it or not, there are two statues of Ted Williams outside Fenway's right-field entrance on Van Ness Street. The longer-standing one depicts an aging Williams playfully placing his cap on the head of an awestruck youngster. The

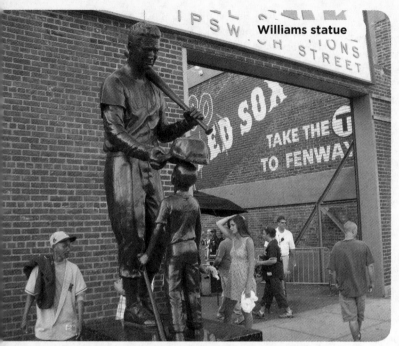

Williams statue

A statue outside Fenway's right-field gate pays homage to franchise icon Ted Williams.
Photo by Josh Pahigian

piece, which was erected in 2004, was inspired by Williams's generous support of the Jimmy Fund, a charitable arm of the Dana-Farber Cancer Institute, which was founded in 1948 and has enjoyed a partnership with the Red Sox since 1953. Thanks to Williams's work back in the early days, through the generations supporting the Jimmy Fund became as much a part of Red Sox fan tradition as eating Yaz Bread and booing umpire Larry Barnett whenever he returned to the Fens after his bad call in the 1975 World Series.

The second Williams rendering exists among a quartet of Red Sox heroes in a sculpture titled "The Teammates." The piece is named after iconic sports historian David Halberstam's 2003 book of the same name. In the sculpture, Williams poses with Dom DiMaggio, Johnny Pesky, and Bobby Doerr. All are portrayed in the prime of youth. In the book, Halberstam told the story of how, as octogenarians, DiMaggio, Pesky, and Doerr embarked on a thirteen-hundred-mile car ride to visit the seriously ill Williams in 2001.

BANNER DECOR
Along Fenway's Van Ness Street façade the Red Sox display several large vertical banners honoring the greatest players

in club history. Included are the names and uniform numbers of old-time stars like Tris Speaker, Lefty Grove, and Rick Ferrell, as well as of more recent ones like Bruce Hurst, Jerry Remy, and Bob Stanley.

Along the same stretch, the Red Sox' retired numbers hang on the stadium's brick exterior. We'll wait to tell you more about these until we get inside, where, of course, the same numbers also appear.

Following the stadium perimeter toward Gate A, fans will encounter bronze plaques mounted on the brick exterior honoring the most influential of Red Sox. These Cooperstown-style tributes celebrate the achievements of former owner Tom Yawkey, former manager Eddie Collins, former "pitcher" George Herman Ruth, and several others.

OLD-TIME TICKET BOOTHS
Back in the days before every game at Fenway was sold out in advance, and before Red Sox management transformed Yawkey Way into part of the inside-the-turnstiles experience, fans would walk up to the park's original ticket booths to buy game passes. These booths still stand today, set just inside the large bay doors that compose Fenway's Gate A. They are unmanned and serve no functional purpose since the fans passing through them already have had their tickets electronically scanned on the street. Still, it's worth visiting these relics, walking through their narrow corridors, and reveling in their charm.

THE YAWKEY WAY STORE
Across the street from Gate A this large souvenir and apparel store hawks the expected assortment of caps, jerseys, and tees, as well as novelty items like the very same "Wally the Green Monster" Bean Bag Buddy that Red Sox commentator Jerry Remy brings to every game, home or away, to join him and fellow NESN announcer Don Orsillo in the booth.

Kevin: Isn't the Rem-Dog a tad old to be playing with dolls?

Josh: Aren't you a tad old to be collecting stadium ice cream helmets?

Kevin: Touché.

THE HOTEL BUCKMINSTER
645 Beacon St.
www.bostonhotelbuckminster.com/

A block from the park, on the other side of the bridge that spans the Mass Pike, stands a harmless-looking triangular building that houses a Pizzeria Uno at ground level and a 94-room hotel upstairs. This is the Hotel Buckminster, which, in fact, has as dark a history as any just-outside-the-park hotel in the bigs. According to Eliot Asinof's account of the 1919 Black Sox scandal, *Eight Men Out,* this is where the conspiracy to fix the World Series took shape. Within the Buckminster, gangster Joe "Sport" Sullivan reputedly met White Sox first baseman Chick Gandil and the two agreed upon the price of $80,000 to put the Series in the proverbial bag. Its history aside, "the Buck" is a classy and convenient place for fans to stay. And hotel staff is happy to field questions related to "the scandal."

THE HUNTINGTON AVENUE BASEBALL GROUNDS
400 Huntington Ave.

Not far from Fenway, on the campus of Northeastern University, a bronze statue depicts Cy Young staring in to read a sign from an imaginary catcher. The statue stands where the pitcher's mound once rose at the Huntington Avenue Grounds, which served the Boston Pilgrims when they hosted the very first World Series in 1903. Young, who delivered the first pitch of the best-of-nine tilt against the Pittsburgh Pirates, lost the first game and his Pilgrims lost three of the first four, before rebounding to win the World Championship in eight games. The next season, Young threw the first perfect game in American League history from the Huntington mound, blanking the Philadelphia A's 3-0.

Watering Holes and Outside Eats

CASK & FLAGON
62 Brookline Ave.
www.casknflagon.com/

Situated behind the Green Monster, "the Cask" displays an impressive collection of historic ballpark and Boston pictures. This is probably your best bet if you want the traditional Red Sox fan experience. There's usually a line at the door but it moves quickly. And the patio allows more patrons to partake than back when the Cask was just an indoor place.

For the record, this is the place where—fueled by a few too many pints and a shared dream—your humble authors drew up the first bullet-point outline of the book proposal that would eventually become *The Ultimate Baseball Road Trip.* As cliché as it sounds, Kevin literally scribbled notes on a cocktail napkin while Josh munched on buffalo wings and greasily imagined a future in which two road tripping

Emerson College grad students would convince a publisher to front their fantasy tour of the big leagues.

Josh: Come to think of it, you scribbled class notes on cocktail napkins at Emerson too.

Kevin: Funny. But for some reason I don't remember that.

BOSTON BEER WORKS
61 Brookline Ave.
www.beerworks.net/home

More upscale and with a larger menu than the Cask, Beer Works boasts an assortment of Fenway- and Red-Sox-named homebrews. Since opening at this location in 1992, it has introduced satellite franchises at Logan Airport, near the Fleet Center, and in the surrounding suburbs. Its beer may be purchased at stores throughout Massachusetts.

WHO'S ON FIRST
19 Yawkey Way

Located across from Gate A, this is a proximate place to grab a quickie before the game. If it's convenience you seek, however, the Cask is just as close and is a better bet, provided the line to get in isn't too long.

Cy Young statue

This statue of Cy Young stands on the campus of Northeastern University where the first World Series game was played.
Photo by Josh Pahigian

BLEACHER BAR
82A Lansdowne St.
http://bleacherbarboston.com

Built right into Fenway's left-center-field façade, Bleacher opened in 2008 in the space where the visiting team's batting cages had resided. This is prime real estate. A massive interior window provides a view that allows patrons to watch batting practice *before* they pass through the turnstiles. Even on off-days, guests enjoy a view of the field that can only be had otherwise by buying a ticket.

GAME ON
82 Lansdowne St.
http://gameonboston.com/

Near the intersection of Lansdowne and Brookline Avenue, Game On occupies the space where there was once—and not long ago—a fully functional bowling alley beneath Fenway Park. As much as we used to enjoy rolling grapefruit-sized balls at the candlepins at Ryan Family Amusement, we have to admit Game On is a better use of the space. Its menu features wood-fired pizzas and steaks, and its festive atmosphere offers a window through which patrons may watch visiting players hit in the batting cages. On off-days and during the off-season, fans may even take a few hacks in these cages (for a price).

THE LANSDOWNE
9 Lansdowne St.
www.lansdownepubboston.com/flash/

This is one of Kevin's favorite spots in the Fenway neighborhood. It melds a classic, more upscale Irish Pub experience with the local sports-crazed ethos.

THE BASEBALL TAVERN
1270 Boylston St.
www.thebaseballtavern.com/

The highlight of this three-story establishment is its roof deck, which looks a lot like the upper right-field concession deck at Fenway. If the game's sold out, this is a solid place to enjoy the night air, the sparkle of the nearby ballpark lights, and the roar of the crowd.

MCGREEVY'S PUB
911 Boylston St.
www.mcgreevysboston.com/

Since its opening as the brainchild of Dropkick Murphys lead vocalist Ken Casey, McGreevy's has become a staple of the Red Sox fan experience. It's the pregame haunt of choice for fans like Kevin who can't get enough bangers and mash or Guinness, and also for fans like Josh who can't get enough local sports history. And it's *the* place for anyone who likes

the Dropkicks, who got their start as a basement band in Quincy in the 1990s before rising to prominence within Red Sox Nation with their 2004 remake of "Tessie," and then gaining further street cred when Red Sox closer Jonathan Papelbon adopted "I'm Shipping Up to Boston" as the blaring anthem to which he would burst from the Fenway bullpen.

To what does the name "McGreevy's" refer, you ask? And what's the significance of this "Tessie" song?

Well, we're going to tell you.

Back in 1903, when the Pilgrims faced the Pittsburgh (spelled "Pittsburg" at the time) Pirates in the first World Series, the Red Sox "Royal Rooters" traveled by rail to the Steel City for the games at Exposition Park. The Rooters were led by Boston Mayor John "Honey Fitz" Fitzgerald—the maternal grandfather of future US President John F. Kennedy—and legendary Boston barkeep Mike "Nuf Ced" McGreevy—who'd earned his nickname by ending turn-of-the-century baseball debates with an authoritative "enough said."

After Boston fell behind three games to one, the tide turned in Pittsburgh when, according to Boston lore, the Rooters arrived at Exposition Park with a band they had commissioned just for the occasion. Throughout the fifth game, they played and sang "Tessie," which was a number from a contemporary theatrical production called *The Silver Slipper*. The Rooters cleverly changed the lyrics to mock Honus Wagner and Pirates pitcher Brickyard Kennedy. Thus harangued, and in their home park no less, the Pirates folded. They lost 11-2 that day and lost the next three games as well.

More than a century later, the Dropkicks released their Irish-punk version of "Tessie" and the 2004 Red Sox promptly proceeded to win the franchise's first World Series in eighty-six years. Coincidence? We think not.

Josh: The ballpark gates open in fifteen minutes. We should get moving.

Kevin: It's still two hours till first pitch.

Josh: Yeah, but you want to catch BP, don't you? Well, don't you???

Kevin: Not as much as I want to have another Guinness.

Josh: They sell Guinness on Fenway's first base concourse now.

Kevin: I am *not* drinking Guinness out of a plastic cup.

JERRY REMY'S SPORTS BAR AND GRILLE
1265 Boylston St.
www.jerryremys.com/

This family-friendly restaurant is a must-visit for anyone who remembers Jerry Remy as the home team's speedy second-sacker in the early 1980s, as well as for anyone who has enjoyed Remy's commentating during the past two decades. Despite his busy NESN schedule and the obligations he bears as President of Red Sox Nation, the Rem-Dog makes time to hobnob with patrons. His signature "Remy Burger" is served on fried dough. We're still awaiting word from the American Heart Association on whether the concoction gets its stamp of approval. We'll let you know as soon as we hear anything.

EL TIANTE'S CUBAN STAND
Yawkey Way
Remy isn't the only favorite son who's parlayed his popularity into a cottage industry. The jovial Luis Tiant may be the best pitcher not in Cooperstown (no offense intended, Jack Morris). He also makes a mean Cuban sandwich and is happy to pose for pictures and recall his exploits on the Fenway mound. Of all the famous former Sox who return to Fenway to watch games, no one garners a larger ovation than "El Tiante" when he tips his hat to the crowd from the team's legends' box on the first base side of the plate.

Kevin: I thought Bob Stanley gets a lot of cheers too.

Josh: That's because he's remembered fondly for popping beach balls in the bullpen.

SAUSAGE VENDORS
No trip to Fenway would be complete without paying a visit to the sausage stands on Lansdowne Street or at the corner of Van Ness and Yawkey Way. You won't find a sandwich this fresh, juicy, and utterly mouth-watering inside the park. Get a sweet sausage "loaded" with sautéed peppers and onions or, if you prefer, order it "naked." Just get one. Among the vendors that rate high on our pork-o-meters are **The Sausage Guy**—whose logo features a half-naked woman straddling a space ship—**The Sausage King,** and **Che-Chi's,** which has the best secret sauce this side of Milwaukee.

Even if you're visiting Boston on a non-game day, you can usually find **The Sausage Guy** stand behind the Monster on Thursday through Saturday, between 9:00 p.m. and 3:00 a.m., catering to the local bar crowd.

Inside the Park

Have you ever seen such wacky field dimensions? Three hundred and two feet down the right-field line. Three hundred and eighty to straightaway right. Four hundred and twenty to right-center. Three hundred and ninety to dead center. Three hundred and seventy-nine to deep left. And just 310

down the left-field line. For years the park was considered a haven for right-handed pull hitters and a graveyard for southpaw hurlers, but through the years lefty swingers have actually enjoyed considerably more success at Fenway than their right-handed counterparts. Think of David Ortiz, Mo Vaughn, Mike Greenwell, Wade Boggs, Fred Lynn, Carl Yastrzemski, Ted Williams, and Babe Ruth as lefties who make the case for this counter-intuitive ballpark effect. According to our theory, this is because the spacious right field leaves plenty of room for safeties to drop and the Wall rewards lefties who can go the other way with even mediocre power. As for those pull-hitting righties who are supposed to be the beneficiaries of the Wall's munificence? There's a saying in Boston: "The wall giveth and the wall taketh away." What does this mean? For every routine fly that settles into the Monster Seats there's at least one rising liner that would have been a homer in any other park but clangs off the Wall for a single. Just ask former Sox like Jack Clark or Mike Lowell, who will be happy to tell you all about it.

Ballpark Features
THE MONSTER
Fenway's signature Wall is an ever-evolving edifice. In fact, when Fenway first opened in 1912 it wasn't even part of the design. Rather, a steep hill rose at the back of the left-field lawn and atop the hill stood a twenty-five-foot-high fence separating the hillcrest from the street outside. With the advent of the lively ball, the Red Sox leveled the hill in 1934 and constructed a two-hundred-foot-long, thirty-seven-foot-high fence, using more than fifteen tons of materials. The manual scoreboard on the Wall debuted in 1934, although the trademark green paint did not appear until 1947. Originally, the Wall was plastered with advertisements for products like Lifebuoy Soap, Gem Razors, Arrow Collars, and other products. Then for decades it was pure and green. Today it is adorned with an ad for the Jimmy Fund and the insignias of several local companies. Because the Henry ownership group has taken care to blend these ads in with the design of the scoreboard, though, locals have not taken much offense at the affront to, or perhaps we should say, *return* to Fenway tradition.

In 1936, a twenty-three-foot-high screen was added atop the Wall to protect pedestrians and motorists on Lansdowne Street. The screen collected homers until 2003 when the Red Sox added the Monster Seats in its place. For old time's sake, the Red Sox left in place the ladder that members of the grounds crew had used for decades to scale the

Wall and retrieve balls out of the screen after batting practice. Today, any batter who hits a ball off the ladder that then bounces out of the park is awarded a ground rule double.

Josh: I've been watching the Sox all my life and I've never seen that.

Kevin: Still, it's nice to know the Sox are prepared.

Upon arriving at Fenway for the first time, we recommend you head out to Section 33 and lean out to rap your knuckles on the Wall. Go ahead. Don't be shy. Touch it. Take a picture too. Then check out the dents and dings that eighty years of batted balls have left. Look closely and you'll see the red marks left by baseball seams.

THE SCOREBOARD

Fenway's scoreboard features a hidden Morse code message that Sox owner Thomas A. Yawkey installed on its face as a love message to his wife, Jeanne R. Yawkey. Look carefully and you should be able to find the dashes and dots. Then brush up on your decoding skills and see if you can figure out what they mean.

More recently, the scoreboard and its narrow doorway entered into Red Sox lore for being the portal through which mascot Wally the Green Monster entered the world of humans and for being the portal through which former Sox left fielder Manny Ramirez would sneak when he needed to umm . . . relieve himself . . . during pitching changes. We should mention that there is *not* a bathroom inside the Wall. Manny was also known to occasionally play left field with a plastic water bottle protruding from his back pants pocket. We will let you figure that one out on your own, or, if you prefer, you may merely chalk it up to "Manny Being Manny," as the saying went until New Englanders finally tired of Manny's circus show.

Josh: Prostate problems are something a lot of men our age wrestle with. We should cut Manny some slack.

Kevin: Speak for yourself. In my book, peeing in the scoreboard is never acceptable.

Josh: I don't have prostate problems.

Kevin: I didn't say you did.

Josh: Oh. Well, I don't. But if I did, I'd appreciate a little understanding.

THE CITGO SIGN

Although it's not technically located inside Fenway, the glowing Citgo sign mounted upon a rooftop in Kenmore Square might as well be. Flashing its familiar red, white, and blue neon, it is the most prominent feature on the left-field skyline and seems to hover just above the Wall. It was originally installed in 1965 to capitalize on the crowds Fenway was attracting. In 1979, Massachusetts Governor Edward King pressured Citgo to turn off the sign as a symbol of energy conservation and it remained dark for four years before the gas company decided to remove it. But a contingent of Fenway residents claimed the sign was a fixture of the local landscape that shouldn't be removed. While the Boston Landmarks Commission debated whether the sign should be declared a historic landmark, Citgo reversed course and decided to refurbish and re-illuminate the sign. It has been lit since 1983, excepting times in 2005 and 2010 when it was briefly dimmed to allow for the installation of more energy-efficient bulbs.

Monsters Aplenty

Aside from spawning backyard Wiffle Ball replicas throughout New England, Fenway's Wall has been copied at several professional fields. The most notable of these from a Red Sox fan's perspective are the facsimiles at **JetBlue Park** in Fort Myers, Florida, where the Red Sox have played their Spring Training games since 2012, **Hadlock Field** in Portland, Maine, where the Red Sox' Double-A prospects play, and **Fluor Field** in Greenville, South Carolina, where the franchise's Single-A prospects play. This is a savvy move. By the time aspiring Sox left-fielders, pitchers, and hitters reach the Show, they already know how a thirty-seven-foot-high fence in left field can change a game.

Although we do so with less enthusiasm, we must also mention that the **Bucky Dent Baseball School** in Delray Beach, Florida, also features a Monster replica. The highlight of Dent's career came in 1978, of course, when he lifted the Yankees to victory in a one-game playoff at Fenway Park to determine the American League East crown. The winning blow came in the seventh inning when Dent lofted a Mike Torrez pitch into the screen for a three-run homer. To this day, Dent is referred to throughout New England as "Bucky F---ing Dent." As for the biggest difference between the real Green Monster and Dent's replica? Rather than featuring a slate scoreboard like the one in Boston, Dent's scoreboard is painted onto the wall and frozen in time to appear exactly as it did after his home run. The line score shows that three runs have just crossed the plate for the Yankees, that number 21 (Torrez) is pitching for the Red Sox, and number 49 (Ron Guidry) is pitching for the Yankees.

THE PRU

On the right-field skyline, the Prudential Tower rises in the distance beyond the Bleachers. You'll be able to see it if your seats are on the third base side. During the 1986 World Series, Boston's corporate types displayed their yankee (with a lower case "y") ingenuity when they turned the Pru into a giant billboard. A coordinated effort signaled "#1" in the form of office lights left on overnight. During the 2004 and 2007 World Series, the strategically illuminated offices read, "Go Sox."

THE RED SEAT

The story of how a solitary red seat came to reside among the sea of green seats in Fenway's Bleachers is a rather colorful one. The seat, which sits in the thirty-seventh row of Section 42, high above the visitors' bullpen, became an unlikely Fenway landmark on a Sunday in June of 1946 when it was the landing spot of the longest home run in Fenway history. A fifty-six-year-old construction worker from Albany, New York, named Joseph Boucher was sitting on one of the actual bleacher benches that filled the Bleachers back then. And he was wearing a big straw hat to keep the late-afternoon sun out of his eyes. He squinted, but he didn't quite see the 502-foot homer Ted Williams hit off Detroit's Fred Hutchinson. Not until the last minute. That's when the incoming projectile punched a hole in Boucher's hat and left him with a bump on his noggin the size of a baseball. To ease Boucher's suffering, Tom Yawkey awarded him season tickets for life. And the lifelong Yankee rooter, according to Red Sox lore anyway, cheered for the Red Sox forever after.

Decades later, when the Red Sox replaced the old benches with chair-backs in the 1970s, they decided to commemorate the spot where Boucher had been sitting. Local fans and sportswriters agreed no one had come close to hitting a ball that high into the bleachers since Williams, and so the newly minted red chair became the official marker of the longest homer in Fenway history. As a testament to Williams's prowess, the seat easily withstood the onslaught of the Steroid Era, even as the admittedly juiced David Ortiz set a Red Sox record with fifty-four home runs in 2006.

RETIRED NUMBERS

According to the official Red Sox guidelines, players need accrue at least ten seasons in a Red Sox uniform and be enshrined in the National Baseball Hall of Fame before the team will consider taking their number out of circulation and hanging it on the green facing above the right field grandstands. For years, the only retired numbers were those of Bobby Doerr (1), Joe Cronin (4), Carl Yastrzemski (8), and Ted Williams (9).

Since the Henry group took over, though, the Red Sox have added three new retired numbers and have loosened the admission requirements a bit, even if the official criteria haven't changed. Carlton Fisk (27) and Jim Rice (14) entered Cooperstown and got their due at Fenway, while "Mr. Red Sox" Johnny Pesky (6) got his due despite not being a member of the National Baseball Hall of Fame. Pesky was allowed this exemption owing to the fact that he had spent fifty-seven of his sixty-nine years in the game with the Red Sox—as a player, manager, and coach—at the time of his number's retirement in 2008.

It remains to be seen whether Wade Boggs (26), who is officially eligible, and Roger Clemens (21), who will be eligible if he is elected to the Hall of Fame despite allegations that he used performance-enhancing drugs, will see their numbers retired in the Fens.

PESKY'S POLE

The right-field foul pole stands just 302 feet from home plate. Since the 1940s it has been called Pesky's Pole thanks to Mel Parnell, who used to joke it was the only place in the majors where the light-hitting shortstop could reach the seats. For the record, Pesky hit six of his seventeen career long balls at Fenway. Today, fans sign their names on the Pole with magic markers as a sort of local tagging ritual. And a bronze plaque at the base of it—in Section 94, Row E—honors Pesky and the unusual landmark that bears his name.

FISK'S POLE

As for the foul pole affixed to the Green Monster, we've always thought it should be named in honor of the walk-off homer Fisk clanged off it in the twelfth inning of Game 6 of the 1975 World Series against the Reds. After all, the footage of Fisk dramatically waving his arms, imploring the ball to stay fair, as he leapt down the first-base line, has ensured the homer's entrenchment within the canon of great baseball moments. And yet, most locals simply refer to it as "the left-field foul pole." For decades after that Series, however, Boston fans never forgot to boo umpire Larry Barnett whenever he returned to Fenway. Barnett was working the plate for Game 3 and failed to cite Cincinnati's Ed Armbrister for runner's interference after he blocked Fisk from fielding a bunt and led Fisk to throw errantly into center field.

SPENCER'S BRICK

As part of Fenway's centennial celebration in 2012, the Red Sox gave fans the chance to purchase inscribed bricks that appear on the concourse between Gates B and C. Josh, of course, is represented. Well, actually, his son Spencer is, courtesy of a gift from proud grandparents Butch and Lynn. See if you can find Spencer's brick. It reads:

> JP & HP #1 Son
> Spencer 3-6-11
> Love Papa & Nan

Kevin: Okay, I think you've talked enough about your kid.

Josh: I just thought our readers would like a little scavenger hunt.

Kevin: Well, you could have told them to find the Joe Cronin plaque or a Jimmy Fund donation box, or something Red Sox related.

Josh: Spencer *is* Red Sox related: He's *my* son.

Stadium Eats

The dining options at Fenway have improved dramatically in the past decade. There are more offerings than at any time previously and the food is of higher quality than when Josh was attending games as a youngster. This pleasant development has been made possible, at least in part, by the continued expansion of concourse space within the ballpark. First, in the early 2000s, the team received permission from the City of Boston to close off a stretch of Yawkey Way so that it becomes, in effect, a vending space within the park on game days. Next, the team widened the concourse beneath the first base seats, added a large vending galley above the left-field Grandstand, and created a spacious Food Court beneath the Right Field Bleachers.

FENWAY FRANK (DOG REVIEW)

It's hard to beat a Fenway Frank topped with ketchup (Josh) or mustard (Kevin). It has a firm, yet supple texture and packs a mild, yet spicy punch. It is meaty, the way a hot dog ought to be. If you fall in love with this frank while visiting the Fens, hit a local supermarket before leaving town and fill a cooler.

FENWAY SAUSAGE (TRADEMARK FOOD)

Once upon a time it was sacrilege to buy a Fenway Sausage from a concession stand within the park, rather than from a vendor outside, but today the disparity between a freshly made, amply topped, Fenway-sanctioned sausage and a sweet Italian on Van Ness or Lansdowne is not as great. So don't despair if you arrive at Fenway having just eaten dinner in the North End and don't get a sausage craving until the fifth inning. The grills inside the park serve a more-than-respectable version of this Fenway treat.

BEST OF THE REST

What would a trip to the crown jewel of the New England sports scene be without a creamy cup of **New England Clam Chowder?** This is a much-appreciated treat on a drizzly April night. And it's real chowda, not that tomato-infused stuff they try to pass off as chowder in Manhattan. Other local favorites include **Dunkin Donuts** coffee, **Lobster Rolls,** and **Steak Tip** sandwiches that come courtesy of the Saugus, Massachusetts, landmark Hilltop Steak House. The deli stands on the concourse offer several kinds of **Sushi** courtesy of Basho, a local restaurant that hand-rolls the day's offerings approximately three hours before each game.

In addition to the aforementioned **Cuban Sandwich** served by former Red Sox right-hander Luis Tiant on Yawkey Way, the stands "outside" offer the only **Pulled Pork Sandwich** at Fenway, **Boars Head Sandwiches,** jumbo **Monster Dogs,** and an array of **Fresh Roasted Nuts** that are superior to the pre-packed nuts sold inside the ballpark proper.

Those seeking healthy options may enjoy the **Fruit** and **Veggie Cups, Fried Dough,** and **Milk Shakes.** That's a joke. Seriously, though, a stand on the third base concourse sells **Veggie Dogs** and **Veggie Burgers.** Fenway offers plenty of options for dessert, highlighted by the traditional Fenway treat—a **Hood Sports Bar** (vanilla ice cream with a chocolate streak down the middle, coated by a thin layer of hard chocolate).

SAY "NO, THANKS," AND WALK AWAY

The seasoned french fries available throughout Fenway fall far short of the hand-cut fries sold at many other parks these days. Plus, they don't tend to be that fresh after they've sat under the heat lamps for a minute or two. Also, you're better off buying your peanuts from one of the vendors outside the park where they really are fresh roasted, not vacuum sealed inside a plastic bag, as are the case with the "fresh" nuts sold inside the park.

The Fenway Experience

More than at any other park, the experience of watching a game in Boston immerses one in the rhythm of the game. The crowd of diehard Red Sox loyalists buzzes with seemingly every pitch. Whether you're attending a game in mid-April or late September, this effect is noticeable. It may take you a few innings to get your Fenway groove on, but don't worry, eventually you will. Sometimes it will be obvious to you why the crowd is groaning or standing or high-fiving in unison, while other times it may not be. For example, if the crowd suddenly breaks into applause or grumbles in the later innings and you can't quite figure out why, that probably means they just changed the Yankee score out on the left-field out-of-town scoreboard.

BRUNCH AT THE BALLPARK

The Red Sox are the only big league team that plays a regularly scheduled morning game each season. This rare breakfast treat occurs on the third Monday of April, which is celebrated by locals as Patriots' Day. This not-too-well-known federal holiday commemorates the events that led to the American Revolution. It falls during school vacation week and also serves as the date of the Boston Marathon. The first pitch is usually slated for 10:30 or 11:00 a.m., which, if the game is played briskly, leaves time for fans to visit Kenmore Square afterwards to watch the runners pass through on their way to the finish line in Copley Square.

Believe it or not, this rare morning game traces its roots back to 1903 when Cy Young's Pilgrims faced the Philadelphia A's in a 10:00 a.m. game at the Huntington Avenue Grounds on the date of the seventh Boston Marathon. In later decades, the Red Sox and National League Boston Braves alternated home dates on Patriots' Day, with the Red Sox usually hosting a doubleheader in even-numbered years and the Braves in odd-numbered years. Since the Braves departed for Milwaukee in 1953, however, this unique game has become a staple of the Red Sox schedule. Memorable mornings include the 2006 affair when a walk-off "Monster Shot" by Mark Loretta gave the Red Sox a come-from-behind win over the Mariners and, on the other end of the spectrum, the 1990 affair, which the Red Sox lost to the Brewers 18-0, in a game that featured the final at-bat of future Red Sox manager Terry Francona's playing career.

FENWAY REALLY IS A TIME MACHINE....

A more recent eccentricity of the Fenway schedule that has been a hit with fans is the annual Futures at Fenway doubleheader that takes place on a summer weekday when the big league Red Sox are out of town. The extravaganza welcomes four of the Red Sox minor league teams to the Fens and pairs them against one another in two exhibition games. Thus, fans enjoy the opportunity to purchase discounted tickets that range from $5.00 Bleacher seats to $30.00 Green Monster seats. This event is not only for the fans, though. It's also for the organization's prospects. The chance to play a game at America's most historic ballpark reminds them of why they're enduring all those eight-hour bus rides and eating all those rest-stop burgers in the Bushes. Fame, fortune, and the chance to play in a great

baseball city are just around the corner if they do their part. The annual Cape Cod League All-Star Game is played at Fenway each July too, so just because the Red Sox are out of town when you're visiting Boston for business or your family vacation, don't automatically assume you won't be able to catch a game at Fenway.

A LYRIC LITTLE BANDBOX

Shortly after arriving in Boston, the John Henry ownership group reinvigorated a long-dormant Fenway tradition: reintroducing a summer concert series. Three decades after Ray Charles and Stevie Wonder brought down the house at Fenway, Bruce Springsteen and the E Street Band breathed new life into Fenway's P.A. system in 2003. Since then, the Red Sox have made a point of welcoming at least one major act per summer at a time when the team is on the road and the ballpark can be transformed into what John Updike once called "a lyric little bandbox." Included among the impressive list of acts to play Fenway recently are the Rolling Stones, the Dave Matthews Band, Jimmy Buffett, Sheryl Crow, Willie Nelson, Phish, Paul McCartney, Aerosmith, and Neil Diamond.

FENWAY FUTBOL, ANYONE?

Current Red Sox ownership has aggressively pursued opportunities to stage other sporting events at Fenway too. In 2010, the ballpark that served as the home grid of the NFL's Boston Patriots in the 1960s opened its gates to football fans of another stripe, welcoming the Sporting Clube de Portugal and Celtic Football for a summer soccer exhibition. The match drew thirty-two thousand fans who watched Celtic prevail 6-5 in a shootout.

Earlier that year, Fenway hosted its first NHL game, welcoming the Philadelphia Flyers and Boston Bruins for a regular season New Year's Day extravaganza. On an unseasonably warm 39-degree day, thirty-eight thousand Boston fans enjoyed a pregame concert by the Dropkick Murphys and then watched the Bruins win 2-1 in overtime.

Kevin: You weren't kidding about the Sox diversifying Fenway's revenue stream.

Josh: No, I was not.

Kevin: Concerts. Hockey. Futbol. What's next, American Revolution re-enactments? Or auto racing?

Josh: Not funny.

Kevin: What did I say?

Josh: You know John Henry owns NASCAR's Roush Racing team, right?

Kevin: I do now.

Josh: He owns the Premier League's Liverpool Football Club too.

Kevin: I actually knew that. They're my favorite football side. Makes me pine for a few pints with the scousers at the Twelfth Man.

Josh: Huh? What?

Kevin: You know, the Spirit of Shankly who rock Anfield when Chelsea's in town.

Josh: Who? What? Are you talking about Chelsea Clinton or Chelsea Handler?

Kevin: You really don't know anything about soccer, do you?

CAROLINE

In the middle of the eighth inning Red Sox fans stand in unison and sing along to the 1970s Neil Diamond hit "Sweet Caroline," shouting out, "So good, so good, so good!" and swaying to the feel-good ditty that blares through the Fenway speakers. And how, you ask, did this unusual ballpark tradition begin? According to a fine bit of investigative reporting the *Boston Globe* did a few years back, it was the brainchild of Amy Tobey, a game-day productions staffer at Fenway who spun the song for the first time at the stadium in 1998 and then periodically afterwards, until 2002 when the Henry group requested she play it during every game.

On Opening Night 2010, Mr. Diamond made a surprise appearance in the Fens in the middle of the eighth. With a microphone in hand, a Red Sox hat on his head, and the words "Keep the Dodgers in Brooklyn" scrawled across his blue blazer, he led the sing-along. Then, the Red Sox finished off a 9–7 win over the Yankees.

Josh: Keep the Dodgers in Brooklyn? Does this guy know what decade this is?

Kevin: Maybe not, but I bet he knows why the Liverpudlians hate Chelsea.

Josh: Are you talking about Chelsea Handler?

Kevin: Never mind.

YANKEES SUCK

No trip to Fenway would be complete without the obligatory impromptu chorus of "Yankees Suck" during the middle innings. This nightly affirmation of shared purpose and understanding among Red Sox fans is as sure to occur when the Red Sox are playing the Yankees as when they're playing the Orioles, Royals, Rays, or . . . well, you get the point.

K-MEN

Look for the K-Men in left-center in Monster Section 10. Whenever a Red Sox pitcher records a strikeout, they post another red K, facing either forward for striking out while swinging or backward for striking out while looking. They also flash signs throughout the game when certain Red Sox players do something notable. For example, they flash A-G-O-N when Adrian Gonzalez hits a homer. This is a tradition that dates back to Roger Clemens's heyday of the 1980s, although back then the K-Men were in the centerfield bleachers and a metal screen was all that could be found atop the Wall.

DIRTY WATER

The Red Sox play a trio of victory songs over the P.A. system on nights when the home team wins. The eclectic set includes the aforementioned "Tessie," the uplifting Three Dog Night tune "Joy to the World," and the anthem "Dirty Water" by the Standells. The water to which the latter song refers is the Charles River, along which the 1960s cult classic informs its listeners they'll find Boston's "lovers, muggers, and thieves." The catchy refrain of "Boston, you're my home!" sends every Red Sox fan home with an oddly pleasant melody reverberating in their eardrums.

Cyber Super-Fans

- **Boston Dirt Dogs**
  http://bostondirtdogs.com/
  This smart, funny site is the Web's best source for gossip about the Sox, as well as for trade rumors and conspiracy theories.
- **Sons of Sam Horn**
  www.sonsofsamhorn.net/
  This site's name honors burly Sox flash-in-the-pan Sam Horn, who later served as a studio analyst on NESN for a while.
- **The Remy Report**
  http://remy.trufan.com/
  This site comes courtesy of former Sox second baseman/NESN color man/tireless entrepreneur/local restaurateur Jerry Remy.

CELEBRITY SUPER-FANS

As a glam team, the Red Sox have some high-profile fans these days. And we're not talking about the guys who paint their chests red in the centerfield bleachers. We're talking about actual celebs who turn out in the Fens to support the home team. Maine author Stephen King is one. He can often be found keeping score in the infield boxes.

Meanwhile, actor Ben Affleck, who has local ties and whose mom still teaches in the Cambridge Public School Department, likes to sit down the third-base line.

Sports in (and around) the City

The Cape Cod League
Barnstable County, Massachusetts
http://v2.capecodbaseball.org/

Each summer the nation's best college players and a few dozen baseball scouts flock to the peninsula that is one of New England's premiere vacation destinations. The players, who arrive on "the Cape" to take part in the invitation-only summer circuit, play a forty-four-game schedule that runs from mid-June through mid-August. They live with local families, work part-time jobs, often in support of the Cape's thriving beach-tourism industry, swim in the warm Cape waters, and bask on the Cape's beaches. And each night they test their skills against other top prospects. For many players, this is the first time they have to use wooden bats instead of the lighter aluminum ones allowed in the college game. And it shows. Pitchers dominate the Cape League.

In recent decades, the Cape's ten fields have served as the proving grounds for up-and-comers like Jeff Bagwell, Albert Belle, Will Clark, Nomar Garciaparra, Todd Helton, Ben Sheets, Frank Thomas, Jason Varitek, and Barry Zito. But those are just a handful of the recent success stories. The Cape League actually dates back to 1885. It was a "town league" in those days, and wouldn't become a college league until 1963. In 1919, though, future Hall of Famer Pie Traynor played for the club in Falmouth. In 1967, Thurman Munson batted .420 for Chatham, a record that would stand until 1976 when Buck Showalter batted .434 for Barnstable.

Today, during a typical Major League season, about two hundred Cape Cod League alumni appear in the bigs, or, to put it another way, one in every seven major leaguers spent a summer on the Cape. And not only do the games on the Cape showcase some of the most highly regarded names on the *Baseball America* top prospects list, but they do so at intimate ballparks that serve as high school fields during the spring. The games begin between 5:00 and 7:00 p.m., and admission is free.

The league's ten fields are all located within fifty miles of one another. For directions and a current schedule, visit the web address above. Oh, and don't forget to pack your bathing suit too!

Doug Flutie, the former Boston College and Canadian Football League legend, who finished his career serving as third-string quarterback for the New England Patriots, often sits down the first-base line. He wears a glove on his left hand and once snagged two foul balls in the same game.

Former General Electric CEO Jack Welch is a Sox diehard too. He usually camps out in one of the posh luxury boxes upstairs.

Aerosmith frontman Steven Tyler has been known to sit right behind home plate near Dennis Drinkwater. As for the guy who sits a few seats to the third base side of Drinkwater behind the plate, wearing the oversized 1980s-style yellow earmuff headphones, that's Red Sox senior baseball advisor Jeremy Kapstein.

While We Were in Boston
We Wrote a Book

During our original trip, we visited most Major League cities for only a few days before piling our junk back into the road trip car and hauling our butts to the next city. And during our second trip, we actually flew around the country in style

(read: discount coach seats), watched one or two games in each city, and then headed back to the airport. In both cases, the road or skies always beckoned. But Boston is where it all began. Josh's home city and Kevin's onetime adoptive home city served as the launching pad for our adventure.

While we were in Boston, Kevin got married, earned a Master's degree, and fell in love with New England clam chowder. Josh got married, earned a Master's degree, and developed a severe food allergy to lobster. Red Sox games were attended. College classes were taken and then, later, taught. Beers and good times were had. But most importantly (with apologies to Meghan and Heather), Boston is where we realized we could parlay our love for baseball and our writing skills into something wonderful. Boston is where *The Ultimate Baseball Road Trip* was born.

Josh had just returned from a brief hardball sojourn during which he and his future wife Heather had visited the ball yards in New York, Philadelphia, and Baltimore, when Kevin popped his head into Josh's office at Emerson College where we were both teaching writing courses. Kevin offered his daily "What's up?"

"Not much," Josh said.

"Hey, how was the baseball trip?"

"It was . . ." Josh began, but then he looked away. "It was . . ." he tried, before pausing and shifting uncomfortably in his seat. Then he lowered his head into his hands and wept like a small child.

"I'll come back in a little while," Kevin said, backing out of Josh's office like a terrified crab. He avoided Josh for the next nine days, before finally stopping in again when he ran out of printer paper. "Recover from the breakdown yet?" he asked, inching his way toward Josh's supply cabinet.

"Sort of," Josh said.

"Something terrible happened during the road trip, didn't it?" Kevin asked.

"Yes," Josh said.

"Wanna talk about it? What happened? Car crash? Another lobster poisoning? Another incident with Canseco?"

"Well," Josh said, his eyes starting to well with tears. "It was pretty bad. I ordered a Philly cheese steak at Veteran's Stadium in Philly and it was . . . it was . . . it was . . . it was bland! And the meat was chewy."

"You ordered a cheese steak at the Vet?" Kevin howled. "Everyone knows the cheese steaks at the Vet are bland and chewy! Why didn't you go to *Pat's* or *Geno's*?"

"Pat's? Geno's?"

"They're steak joints down on 9th Street. That's where I get my fix when I'm catching a game in Philly. I could have told you before you left that it was a mistake to get a cheese steak at the Vet!"

"But you didn't!"

"I didn't think of it. Don't feel bad. I ordered a chewy steak myself the first time I went to the Vet. That's how you learn."

"So every baseball wanderer that visits Philly has to learn his lesson?"

"At least until the Phillies build a new ballpark . . . or at least start selling decent steaks inside the Vet."

"Until then what? Getting one's hopes up and eating a bland cheese steak at the game is just gonna be part of the visiting fan's experience?"

"Exactly."

"That sucks."

"Yeah, kind of. But it's not like there's a baseball bible dedicated to making sure fans get the most out of their ballpark travels . . . making sure they don't waste their time and money on inferior cheese steaks or lousy tickets. You live and learn."

A few days later while sitting in the Cask & Flagon outside Fenway Park, we decided it wasn't right that baseball fans should travel unaware to foreign big league parks and cities. So we vowed to walk blindly one last time into every Major League park, to take careful notes and occasional pictures, and then to share our tips, opinions, and observations with the world. Our goal was to ensure that no (semi-literate) baseball fan afterward would ever buy chewy meat or substandard seats again. We were fired up and ready to go. Then we procrastinated for three and a half years before getting our act together and hitting the road.

NEW YORK METS, CITI FIELD

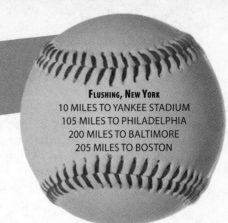

FLUSHING, NEW YORK
10 MILES TO YANKEE STADIUM
105 MILES TO PHILADELPHIA
200 MILES TO BALTIMORE
205 MILES TO BOSTON

A Diamond Fit (and Priced) for a Queen

Citi Field may not be the coziest ballpark built in recent years. And it doesn't reside in anything resembling a fun and festive game-day neighborhood. But we'll give it this: It's a ballpark, not a stadium like the towering Shea Stadium, which had served as the Mets home from 1964 to 2008. The unfortunate reality for the Mets, though, is that since Citi Field's opening during the throes of one of the worst US economic downturns in history, it has been widely panned for offering substandard sight lines at exorbitant prices. It certainly didn't help that the park debuted with the logo of one of the worst culprits of the banking crisis tattooed across its marquee at a time when many American households were still struggling to make ends meet. Citi was one of the largest recipients of TARP, or the Troubled Asset Relief Program, enacted under President George W. Bush. And many people were put off that the banking giant had pocketed $45 billion in taxpayer money, then turned around and paid the most money any company had ever paid to name a sports facility, shelling out $400 million for the naming rights to the new Mets park. But politics aside, Mets fans are still a rabid bunch, and the fact that attendance at their games has fallen from more than forty-five thousand fans per game during the last several seasons at Shea to barely thirty thousand at Citi during 2011, speaks volumes about how New Yorkers have received the new park. It also speaks to the economic reality of the times for fans, as attendance has fallen—though not nearly as dramatically—across MLB.

From the auto-shop-lined streets outside, Citi actually projects a charming old-time façade, even if the towering upper deck rises higher than the regal reddish-brown brick arches that comprise the first few stories. After fans vacate the 7

Train or the spacious parking lots in which they've left their road-trip mobiles and walk past the Big Apple that used to periodically emerge from behind the center-field fence at Shea, they pass through the arches and into a beautiful marble rotunda that was designed as a tribute to the entryway of Brooklyn's old Ebbets Field. In fact, the entire exterior façade, not just the rotunda, was designed to replicate the façade of the ballpark that served the Dodgers from 1913 to 1957. If you Google "Ebbets Field" and refresh your memory of its old façade at the corner of McKeever and Sullivan Place, you'll see what a striking resemblance Citi bears to it. While this may be a nice tip of the cap to old-time Dodgers fans like Mets owner Fred Wilpon, Citi Field has actually been criticized for this. Many modern-day Mets fans, who grew up going to games at Shea, feel as though the park

exterior

Photo by Josh Pahigian

goes overboard honoring a history that has little to do with their own.

Similarly, many Mets fans feel that the Jackie Robinson Rotunda is more a Brooklyn Dodgers homage than a New York Mets one. And they're right. The Rotunda features a big blue No. 42 sculpture, as well as a wealth of Robinson quotes and photos of him with his Dodgers teammates. It does offer entry to an extensive Mets Museum and Hall of Fame that keeps the focus on the home team. But not far away, the Mets Team Store sells not only Mets apparel, but Sandy Koufax jerseys and other pieces of Dodgers gear. And for us, this takes the nostalgia thing a bit too far. While we understand that Mr. Wilpon grew up in Brooklyn and was a childhood friend and teammate of Koufax at Lafayette High School, it struck us as odd to find Dodgers gear on display in the Mets store. We have to agree with the Queens fans that it's a tad goofy for a team with a five-decade-plus history of its own to hitch its wagon so dramatically to another team's legacy.

Despite this Dodgers fixation, and the unfortunate fact that 16,400 of Citi Field's 41,800 seats are on the upper level where we found the views of the field to be pretty poor, we did find many things to like about the park. The open first-level concourse is well done, for example, offering quality views to folks roaming around, except from behind home plate where an in-stadium bar occupies that space. And Citi offers a tremendous range of specialty foods that are available at field level as well as upstairs. At a lot of other parks, the good foods are only sold downstairs. But the Mets made certain to put a top-notch food court on the third level too, and for that we applaud them. We also like the wavy lighting banks high above the upper deck, and the built-in quirks, like the bigger-than-at-Shea Home Run Apple behind the center-field fence, and the distinctive Shea Bridge in right field. Another outfield eccentricity, though, that we were not so keen on: Above the black batter's backdrop in center, an overabundance of massive advertising signs blocks what might have otherwise been a nice view of Flushing Bay. The video board is dwarfed by the signs surrounding it. Now, we know advertising is part of the ballpark experience these days, just as it was in our fathers' and grandfathers' days, but the concept is taken to an absurd extreme when the square footage of the JumboTron pales in comparison to the Budweiser and Geico signs.

Josh: If I peek between the billboards with my binocs, I can see the bay.

Kevin: If you have to try that hard, it doesn't really count as a "view," does it?

Josh: At least you can't see all the chop shops like at Shea.

Citi Field was designed by the noted ballpark architects at Populous (formerly HOK) and built at a cost of $850 million. The funding came from the sale of municipal bonds that will be repaid by the Mets with interest. Construction began in July 2006 in the parking lot behind Shea Stadium's left-field fence, and was completed in time for Opening Day 2009. Before the Mets took the field for the first time, though, the St. John's Red Storm hosted the Georgetown Hoyas for a Big East game on March 29, 2009. The visitors won 6-4 after former Mets closer John Franco tossed out the ceremonial first pitch.

Two weeks later, the Mets hosted the San Diego Padres for the first major league game in Citi history and the home fans went home disappointed: The Friars spoiled the debut with a 6-5 win. Jody Gerut actually led off the game for the Padres with a home run. In the long history of big league baseball, that clout ranks as the first and only leadoff dinger to open a new ballpark.

home view

Photo by Josh Pahigian

Later that April, aging Met Gary Sheffield hit his five hundredth homer at Citi against his original team, the Brewers. Then in June, the Yankees' Mariano Rivera notched his five hundredth career save at Citi. The Mets generously awarded him the pitching rubber from the game and installed a new one for the rest of the season.

Another noteworthy event occurred on August 23, 2009, when Phillies second baseman Eric Bruntlett recorded an unassisted triple play off the bat of Jeff Francoeur to end a 9-7 Phillies win. The fifteenth unassisted trifecta in MLB history was just the second to end a game and the first to do so in NL play. Bruntlett caught Francoeur's line drive, then tagged second base to double off Luis Castillo, and tagged Daniel Murphy as he came trotting in to second.

Josh: I've scored an unassisted Triple Play at Chili's.

Kevin: Come again?

Josh: I can eat an entire Triple Play appetizer and still have room for my meal.

Kevin: I *thought* you'd expanded a few belt sizes since our first trip.

Although we second the prevailing opinion among Queens fans that the Mets borrowed too heavily from the Dodgers in designing their new park, the team's reverence for its National League forebears was established long before Fred Wilpon took the reins of the Metropolitans. In fact, the familiar Mets logo fuses Dodger blue and Giant orange. The bridge in the foreground represents the Mets "bridging the gap" that existed after the Dodgers and Giants headed for the West Coast. The skyline in the background depicts buildings from all five boroughs of New York City, including the Williamsburgh Savings Building, the Woolworth Building, the Empire State Building, the United Nations Building, and a church spire symbolic of Brooklyn.

As for the Mets' longtime home, Shea Stadium was named after prominent New York attorney William Shea, who worked tirelessly to bring Senior Circuit hardball back to the Big Apple after the departure of the Giants and Dodgers in 1958. In 1959, Shea announced his intention to form a third Major League, to be called the Continental League, and to place one of the charter members in New York. A year later, the league disbanded before it played a game, but not before the National League had accepted two of its prospective franchises—Houston and New York—as expansion teams. The expansion of 1962 made the NL a ten-team circuit.

The Mets played their first two seasons at the Giants' old Polo Grounds, then on April 17, 1964, christened Shea Stadium with two bottles of water—one from the Harlem River that flowed near the Polo Grounds, and the other from the Gowanus Greek Canal, which ran beside Ebbets Field. The Mets lost their first game to the Pirates, then they kept on losing. For the third straight year the Mets finished dead last in the NL, posting 53 wins and 109 losses. Nonetheless, the fans turned out at Shea to watch them play. The Mets outdrew the Yankees, who won the AL pennant that year, selling 1.7 million tickets to the Yanks' 1.3 million. A full house was on hand to witness Phillies ace Jim Bunning's perfect game against the Mets on Father's Day, and then again when Shea hosted the 1964 All-Star Game.

The team's first winning season came when the "Miracle Mets" of 1969 surpassed the previous franchise record of seventy-three wins en route to a 100–62 mark. After sweeping the Braves in the first National League Championship Series ever played, the Mets downed the Orioles in a five-game World Series.

Kevin: They'd never finished higher than ninth place in the league before that season.

Josh: A "miracle," indeed.

As the first of the so-called cookie-cutter stadiums, Shea utilized motorized underground tracks to convert its stands from baseball to football and vice versa. The horseshoe-shaped facility housed the Jets for two decades and was originally designed to be expandable up to ninety thousand seats, should management ever decide to add outfield seating on all levels.

In the years after Shea's construction, cities like Philadelphia, Pittsburgh, St. Louis, and Cincinnati followed New York's lead and built multipurpose stadiums of their own. While these highly functional and eerily similar-to-one-another facilities efficiently served two professional sports teams in each city—baseball and football—they left fans longing for the day when each ballpark was a world unto itself.

As for those Jets, they set an American Football League attendance record at Shea in 1967, selling out all seven of their games to draw 437,036 fans. But in 1973 the Jets had to play their first six games on the road because the Mets needed Shea for the postseason. Amazingly, manager Yogi Berra's Mets had won the NL East that year despite having a record of just 83-79. They then dispatched with the Reds in the NLCS before bowing to the A's in a seven-game World Series. If the Jets felt slighted by being turned out for a stretch, they didn't show it. They continued to play at Shea for another decade, before finally leaving for the Meadowlands in 1984.

Shea was home to not only the Mets, but also the Yankees during the 1974 and 1975 seasons, as The House that Ruth Built underwent a massive renovation. In 1975 the New York football Giants played their home games at Shea too, making Shea the first facility to house two MLB teams and two NFL teams in the same year.

Shea played a starring role in three of the most unusual doubleheaders in baseball history too. During the inaugural 1964 season, the Mets and San Francisco Giants played a nine-hour and fifty-minute double-dipper, the longest in baseball history. The first game must have seemed like a breeze after the second went twenty-three innings, spanning seven hours and twenty-two minutes. The Giants swept the twin bill. More than four decades later, another oddity took place at Shea. On April 15, 1998, the Yankees were forced to play a 12:05 p.m. game against the Angels at Shea after a beam fell from Yankee Stadium's upper deck. That evening, the Mets hosted the Cubs. Both New York clubs won. And finally, on July 8, 2000, the Mets hosted the Yankees for an afternoon game before the two teams traveled across town to play a night game in the Bronx. The split-venue double-header was the result of a rainout at Yankee Stadium in June. The Yankees won both games by identical 4-2 scores.

Later in the 2000 season, the Mets and Yanks met in the World Series for the first time ever. The Yanks were again victorious, as Bobby Valentine's Mets fell in five games, but not before Yankee hothead Roger Clemens threw a broken bat at Mike Piazza in Game 2 at Yankee Stadium, precipitating a benches-clearing brawl.

The Mets nearly made it back to the World Series in 2006, but the Sons of Willie Randolph fell to the underdog St. Louis Cardinals in a seven-game NLCS.

Kevin: So they've been managed by Willie Randolph and Yogi Berra.

Josh: Yeah, and Casey Stengel and Dallas Green too.

Kevin: Sounds like somebody has a bad case of Yankee-envy.

Josh: Yeah. But the Mets had Joe Torre first.

Two of the more riveting postseason games in baseball history took place at Shea. Both were extra-inning affairs won by the home team. The first occurred in 1986 when the Mets shocked the baseball world and ruined Josh's adolescence by coming back from a two-out, two-strike, no-one-on-base, 5–3, tenth-inning deficit to win Game 6 of the World Series against the Red Sox. Car horns honked jubilantly throughout New York as Ray Knight streaked home with the winning run after Mookie Wilson's groundball went through Bill Buckner's legs. Two days later, the Mets won their second World Championship.

Josh: And that's all we're gonna write about 1986.

Kevin: I thought you'd be over that incident, you know, with the World Series wins since.

Josh: A true Red Sox fan never forgets.

Kevin: You should really get some counseling or something.

The other extra-inning beaut was in 1999 when Robin Ventura hit a "grand slam single" to propel the Mets to a Game 5 NLCS win against the Braves. The hit ended a five-hour, forty-six-minute affair that took place in a steady rain. With the bases loaded in the bottom of the fifteenth, Ventura smacked a ball over the right-field fence. He made it only so far as first base, though, before being swarmed by ecstatic teammates. Because he never circled the bases, he was credited with a single and only one RBI. Had Ventura touched all four, the hit would have been the first walk-off "grannie" in postseason history. Now that's what we call "taking one for the team."

Now that they're playing at Citi Field, the Mets hope to pen a whole new chapter in their postseason history books. We'll be interested to see if such a return to glory prompts Mets fans to look a bit more kindly on a new park that made such a lackluster first impression. Perhaps then they'll start filling the Citi Field stands and maybe, too, they'll stop referring to the park by the vulgar nickname (rhymes with "city" field) by which it has come to be commonly known.

Trivia Timeout

Jumbo: Which former Met threw out the honorary first pitch at the very first game at Citi Field? And which favorite former Met caught it?

Concord: Name the only Mets player to have his uniform number retired by the team.

Delicious: Which Yankee legend was the first Mets manager?

Look for the answers in the text.

Getting a Choice Seat

Rather than experiencing an attendance bump upon opening their new yard, the Mets saw their attendance precipitously decline during Citi Field's first few years. They drew nearly fifty thousand fans per game during the final season at Shea Stadium in 2008, but attracted only thirty-eight thousand during their first year at Citi Field. By the time this book hit bookstore shelves a few years later,

> **Seating Capacity:** 41,800
> **Ticket Office:** http://newyork.mets.mlb.com/ticketing/index.jsp?c_id=nym
> **Seating Chart:** http://newyork.mets.mlb.com/nym/ticketing/seating_pricing.jsp

the Mets were struggling to attract thirty-thousand fans a game. The team's poor performance on the field during this time partly explains the fall-off. And the bad economy does too. But we suspect Citi Field's high ticket prices have also scared many working-class fans away. And we're not just talking about the posh seats on the first level. Most of the second deck/Club Level seats cost more than $100. And many of the third deck seats, which sell for about $20 or $30 at some parks, cost as much as $77 (2011 prices). Heck, a home run territory seat, some four hundred feet from home plate, is priced at $98. Now, we understand that Mets owner Fred Wilpon was one of the victims of the Bernie Madoff investment scandal, and we realize that Citi Field cost a fortune to build, but you'd think the Mets would take a good look at their one-third-empty park and recalibrate their prices.

The takeaway for road trippers is that you won't have trouble securing really good first or second deck tickets to this park. Face value isn't cheap, but on the plus side, you won't have to pay a surcharge on the secondary ticket market as you would in, say, Boston or Wrigleyville.

Field Level

The first several rows of the lower bowl incline at a gradual rate, and then as the row numbers increase, the slope of the bowl rises more dramatically. This allows for a still-close view for those standing atop the bowl on the open concourse. Another positive thing is that the overhang of the Club (200 and 300 Level) deck does little to detract from field level views.

DELTA CLUB (SECTIONS 11–20), METROPOLITAN BOX (SECTIONS 111–114 & 121–124), CHAMPIONS CLUB (SECTION 115–120), FIELD BOX PLATINUM, GOLD, SILVER, BRONZE (SECTIONS 109–110 & 125–126)

As you might expect, all of these infield seats provide premium views. They were built and priced with the thinking being that they would be owned exclusively by season-ticket holders and corporations, but we found many still available for single-game purchase via the Mets website a few days before our visit. The cost—between $126 and $440

apiece—priced us out of the market, though. We're writers, not stockbrokers.

FIELD BOX (SECTIONS 109–110 & 125–126, ROWS 21–34)

These seats located in the uppermost rows of the sections just past first base (Sections 109–110) and third base (Sections 125 and 126) may be the best you're willing to shell out for. Their cost varies, depending upon the quality of the Mets' opponent and the time of year, but they are always under $100.

BASELINE BOX (SECTIONS 104–108 & 128–132)

Note to the Mets: The baselines extend between home plate and either first base or third base. These seats are deep in the outfield corners. Calling them "Foul Line Boxes" would be more truthful. But we still wouldn't recommend them.

RIGHT FIELD RESERVED (SECTIONS 101–103), RESERVED (SECTIONS 140–143), & LEFT FIELD RESERVED (SECTIONS 133–139)

Because the right-field seats are tucked beneath the second deck, which overhangs the field, we only feel comfortable recommending these seats to people who happen to be nearing the end of their Claustrophobics Anonymous programs. This is a great opportunity for such folks to see if they're really cured. But seriously, the second deck seats upstairs in right-field homer land are much better. We do, however, recommend the low-numbered rows of Section 103, since their seats aren't smothered by the deck above like the other seats nearby.

Sections 140–143 in right-center aren't enclosed by an overhang, but they're very far from the plate. Section 143 is

SEATING TIP

We really didn't want to sit up on the third deck, but we didn't have budget to buy seats on the first or second decks. So what's a road tripper to do? We bought 500 Level seats, and then found a breezy spot on the first base side of the field level concourse. Fans can camp out in this shaded (and rain protected) part of the park and enjoy a quality view of the game. At Yankee Stadium, they sell tickets to this part of the park to folks who sit on barstools. But at Citi, these quality spots are left to the rambling masses. So, if you can't pony up for a good seat or simply want to escape the hot sun upstairs, find a spot behind Section 114 or so and you should be satisfied.

center-field view

Photo by Josh Pahigian

positioned behind the two bullpens, making it that much harder to stay involved in the game.

The home run territory seats in left aren't tucked as dramatically beneath the second deck as the ones in right are. But due to the deck's looming presence we only recommend Rows 1–8.

We'll give the Mets credit for this much: They minimized the potential obstruction posed by the foul poles by lining up wide stairways directly behind them.

The Second Deck/Excelsior Level

The Excelsior Level houses both 200 and 300 Level seats. The 200 Level extends only from third base out to the right-field foul pole, while the 300 Level spans the entire park, save for the open portion in center field where the scant view of the world beyond is obscured by billboard-sized advertising. The 200 Level seats (Sections 201–244) hang out over the lower bowl, providing amazingly low and close views. We wished they were available for single game purchase but knew that even if they were, they would be beyond our humble means.

CAESAR'S CLUB (SECTIONS 306–333), PEPSI PORCH (SECTIONS 301–305), & LEFT FIELD LANDING (334–339)

These seats sit atop the narrow 200 Level and are slightly tucked beneath the overhang of the third deck. The views

are not negatively affected by the overhang, and if anything the shade created by the upper deck is a bonus. This is the place to be on a hot day. Section 306–308 along the outfield foul line should be eschewed in favor of infield seats in Sections 311–328 or home run territory seats in right (Sections 301–305). We really liked the view from this overhanging right-field perch, where the deck extends over the field of play, a la old Tiger Stadium in Detroit. The view seems much closer than from the second level homer land seats in left (Sections 334–339). In fact, this so-called Pepsi Porch in right is probably the best value for the money at Citi Field. We highly recommend sitting out there.

The Third Deck/Promenade Level

As is also the case at the new Yankee Stadium, the upper deck seats are accessible by a semi-open concourse that allows Promenade Level strollers to either head down the stairs to their 400 Level seats or up the stairs to their 500 Level seats. If you're a ball hound, set your sights lower. You won't see too many pop-ups flying into this uppermost deck, not even fouls straight back.

PROMENADE CLUB/BOX (SECTIONS 401–437)

The views from the 400 Level are a lot better than those from the 500 Level. The 400 Level seats are much closer to field level and there are far fewer obstructions to block the view than in the 500 Level. But the difference in cost is significant.

PROMENADE RESERVED (SECTIONS 501–538)

The upper tier of the third deck rises steeply. The sunroof provides shade or rain relief to those seated in Rows 7–17. We should mention that there is a jet stream passing through the very top rows. On a hot August day, this makes Row 17 even more appealing. On a chilly April night, it makes Row 17 dreadful. Either way, the view from that part of the park is marginal at best.

Fans seated in Sections 513 and 514, high above home plate, can see the entire field of play, but if one sits even a section to either side of the batter's boxes, the nearest outfield corner begins to disappear from view. Proceeding down the baselines, the effect is magnified as the underhang of the deck conspires with railings and stretches of Plexiglas, not to mention the rise of the retaining wall at field level, to block outfield views. We were absolutely astounded by how much fair territory was lost from sight to us when we ventured into Sections 501–504 along the right-field line. We couldn't even see the right-field foul pole. The effect is similar for those seated in the upper level along the left-field line in Sections 525–528. If you really want to sit in a top-deck outfield seat (why you'd want to, we have no idea!), a better option is to aim for a straight-on view high above left field in the lower rows of Sections 534–538. But hopefully you'll have the good sense to shoot for an upper infield seat instead. Also beware that the out-of-town score-board hangs over the top rows of Sections 535–538. Rows 14–17 of these sections should be avoided.

Before/After the Game

Unfortunately for Mets fans, Citi Field was built in Shea Stadium's old neighborhood and the new park's arrival did absolutely nothing to spur the development of an entertainment district in the streets surrounding the ballpark. Aside from McFadden's sports bar, which was built right into the ballpark complex, there are no pubs or restaurants convenient to visit before or after a game. This is a sin for an urban ballpark in our book. It's one thing if a team decides to build its park outside the city at the junction of highways as in Milwaukee, or within a sports complex aside another sports stadium or two, as in Kansas City. At least then a vibrant tailgating culture may develop amidst a pastoral setting. You probably won't want to tailgate on the scalding asphalt around Citi Field, surrounded by the mechanical clanks and buzzing machinery of the auto shops across the street. But if you're still not convinced that this last resort for hungry fans in the pregame hour is unappealing, consider this policy from the Mets website:

> Tailgating will be permitted only under the following conditions:
> • No open flames of any type.
> • Only one parking stall may be used.
> • Consumption of alcohol is prohibited.
> • Inappropriate or dangerous behavior will not be allowed.

Kevin: So technically you *can* tailgate but you can't cook food or drink beer. I'm confused.

Josh: No, my friend. The Mets are confused. Clearly they don't understand what tailgating is if they think they are allowing it.

Getting to Citi Field

Citi Field is located on Roosevelt Avenue in Flushing. Parking costs $19 in the team lots, which open for business four hours before first pitch. From Grand Central Parkway East or West, take Exit 9E (Northern Boulevard East/Citi Field) and you'll practically flow right into the parking area. Even if your GPS is on the fritz (like ours was) you'll know when you're getting close, because the ballpark is clearly visible from Grand Central Parkway. This really isn't a bad park to drive to, especially compared to its Bronx counterpart. So if you're blowing in and out of New York in a single day and want to take the road trip car to Citi, don't be afraid. It's a pretty easy in and out.

If you're staying in town and planning to hit the bars or tourist attractions in Manhattan after the game, then we do suggest taking the subway to Citi. Hop on the 7 Train (Flushing Line), which takes about half an hour to travel from Midtown to the Mets/Willets Point station.

Metro Info and Maps: www.mta.info/

As for staying in New York for a reasonable rate in a (hopefully) bedbug-free environment, we recommend any of the discount chain hotels—Red Roof Inn, Comfort Inn, Best Western, Sheraton, etc.—in Flushing's Chinatown. Just a half-mile or so from the ballpark, these allow for an easy walk to the game.

Outside Attractions
CHOP SHOP CENTRAL

If you've read this book before or have poked at a couple of other chapters already, you know that this is the place in each chapter where we review the extremely seedy-looking auto shops in the ballpark neighborhood. Wait a minute. That doesn't sound right, does it? Come to think of it, we usually start off by describing the festive baseball attractions around each city's hardball cathedral, as well as the best restaurants. But the streets around Citi Field are dominated by the specter of car repair shops. We've never seen so many in such a cluster before. We observed muffler shops, body shops, transmission shops, brake shops, paint and detail centers, tire warehouses, auto glass repair shops, a scrap metal yard, and pretty much any and every other kind of car-repair, upkeep or salvage establishment we could imagine, all packed into the streets immediately around and across from the ballpark.

Josh: Do they take every broken down car in the city here for repair?

Kevin: You'd think this would be prime real estate for a trendy sports bar or two.

Josh: I think I saw a sports car shop on 126th Street?

Kevin: I said sports *bar*, not car.

Josh: Oh.

THE WORLD FAIR GLOBE

Not far from Citi Field there resides the Flushing Meadows tennis complex where the U.S. Open is played each year. And in the shadows of the tennis stands tourists find a twelve-story-high stainless steel globe commemorating the 1964 World's Fair. Kevin calls this the "Death Star" but it's actually not a half-completed inter-galactic battle station but a jumbo-sized model of planet Earth. You can see it from the 7 Train, or you can walk over for a look and to pose for a few pictures. Or, if you'd rather spend your pregame time in Manhattan, you can just visit the similar "death star" outside the Trump International Hotel and Tower at 1 Central Park West.

> *Josh:* I can't believe we just provided free ad-space for The Donald.
>
> *Kevin:* He may be a dufus but he's a rich dufus. Besides, his Death Star is pretty cool.
>
> *Josh:* I'm pretty sure it's not really called a Death Star.
>
> *Kevin:* I know. It's called a "uni-sphere."
>
> *Josh:* You're right. Death Star has a nicer ring to it.

THE MAGIC APPLE

After spending five decades behind the center-field fence at Shea Stadium, the original Mets Home Run Apple—which arose from a big black hat to celebrate Mets home runs—has found a permanent resting place outside Citi's main entrance. Adorned by a lush bed of petunias, marigolds, and lilies, the old apple now welcomes fans to the game as they vacate the Willets Point subway station and make their way toward the Jackie Robinson Rotunda. This is the perfect spot to pose for a picture with the apple and stadium in the background.

THE DE FACTO WALK OF FAME

As you trace the stadium footprint heading to, or from, the parking lot, the walkway is adorned by vertical banners portraying favorite Mets of the past. Mind you, this is a team that in its first five decades saw fit to retire just one of its playing alums' uniform numbers—Tom Seaver's No. 41—and by perusing this quasi-Walk of Fame you can kind of see why. The players represented here were all good but unspectacular in their day. We passed by banners honoring Robin Ventura, John Franco, Ray Knight, Lenny Dykstra, Bob Ojeda, Tommy Agee, Darryl Strawberry, Jerry Koosman, and Keith Hernandez, and thought it was wise that the Mets have stopped short of paying more of them the ultimate compliment. When we got to a banner for Jose Reyes we wondered first if he would stay with the Mets upon becoming

Shea Stadium's old Home Run Apple

Photo by Josh Pahigian

a free agent after the 2011 season, and then whether he would one day live to see his No. 7 hanging retired at Citi. The answer to the first question was decided in the negative before this book's arrival on bookstore shelves when Reyes signed with the Marlins. And that first answer may determine the latter one. Reyes—who hit a standup triple during our game at Citi—appears Cooperstown-bound. Unfortunately, he didn't play for the Mets long enough to become the sort of franchise icon so few players become these days.

AUTOGRAPH CORNER

For easy access to arriving and departing players, we recommend that Sharpie-carrying fanatics stake out the driveway near the right-field entrance of the park, opposite Lot G. Only a few seriously obsessed seam-heads were waiting on the day we visited, but we didn't stick around long enough to see if they had any luck. We had bigger fish to fry. We had to see if the beer at McFadden's was as cold as we hoped it would be (it was!).

Watering Holes and Outside Eats

Speaking from the standpoint of two guys traveling to baseball parks and looking for good clean fun along the way, the neighborhood surrounding Citi Field might only be described as a "black hole." Fortunately, there is one quality club attached to Citi Field. It's more a haven for swinging twenty-somethings, but it did the trick for us in a pinch. We also took the 7 Train one stop to Corona Park. We recommend going this extra mile into the Corona neighborhood only to those with time to kill. Then again, if you have free time in New York City, you can probably find something more enjoyable and culturally enlightening to do.

MCFADDEN'S RESTAURANT AND SALOON
36-2 126th St.
www.mcfaddensballparkny.com/
Built right into the ballpark complex near the Bullpen Gate and Lot A, but accessible only from the sidewalk outside, McFadden's is the only show in town when it comes to eating and drinking in the immediate vicinity of Citi Field. It offers a hopping pregame and postgame atmosphere that comes complete with blaring music, slinky waitresses, and a DJ imploring young ladies to get up on the bar and earn free shots. There is a large dining area too, where patrons can sit down and chow on reasonably priced pub food. The expected Mets decor includes a framed scorecard from the very first game at Citi Field and overhead photos of Citi Field and Shea Stadium. There is also a picture of the mythic Elysian Field. When we visited, they were offering a pregame deal: $30 for unlimited drinks before the game. If that isn't a binge-drinker's delight, we don't know what is.

BENFAREMO: THE LEMON ICE KING
52-02 108th St., Corona
http://thelemonicekingofcorona.com/
On a hot day, this Corona shop becomes a virtual "must visit." The King offers nearly one hundred flavors of Italian ice. It was a New York City scorcher when we were in town. Kevin tried the grape, which had delicious whole frozen grapes in it. And Josh ordered the lime, which was streaked with frozen lime peels.

LEO'S LATTCINI-MAMA'S
4602 104th St., Corona
This famous Italian bodega serves an array of exceptional Italian sandwiches, of both the hot and cold variety. The lunch buffet is a deal at only $6.99 per pound. We also highly recommend the Mama's location inside Citi Field, but we'll tell you more about that later.

GREEN FIELD CHURRASCARIA
108th Street and Northern Blvd., Corona
www.greenfieldchurrascaria.com/location-Corona.html
If you like skewered and seasoned Brazilian meat (Josh could eat the stuff three meals a day), then this is the place

for you. The dinner buffet goes for $28.95, there's valet parking, and the Mets game is always playing on the big screen.

SHORTY'S AUTHENTIC PHILLIES STEAKS AND SANDWICHES
576 9th Ave., Manhattan
www.shortysnyc.com/browsers/shortys/
We've included this Times Square–area Phillies bar because we know a great many phanatics from Philadelphia—finding good tickets are hard to come by at home—make the two-hour drive north to watch their boys of summer play the division rivals from New York. Not only can you watch the Phillies play at Shorty's, but they provide as tasty a steak sandwich as we've sampled in any of America's baseball cities. Yes, we've been to Pat's and Geno's, and Shorty's is every bit as tasty and a fair bit juicier for our money. Every day they import fresh-baked Italian hoagie rolls from Philadelphia. They load these up with deliciously seasoned shaved sirloin, topped with cheese whiz or mild provolone. We added peppers and onions to our steaks, along with a pair of 22-ounce drafts. It was a damned good lunch and barely cost us $12 each.

JAMESON'S PUB
975 2nd Ave., Manhattan
www.jamesonsny.com/
This East Side pub is our pick for those seeking a Mets bar in Manhattan. Hey, it doesn't hurt that it has pictures of Ireland on its walls, but we won't apologize for being a bit biased. Kevin is fully half-Irish and Josh's wife is too. The crowd skews toward the yuppie end of the spectrum and it isn't beyond the learned fans who sometimes engage in good-natured baseball arguments to invoke VORP or Zone Rating to support their theories.

Inside the Stadium

With field dimensions that measure a distant 384 feet to the fence in left-center and an eye-popping 415 feet to right-center, Citi Field is certainly conducive to a National League style of play. In other words, balls don't exactly fly out of this yard the way they do at many of the other newish parks, including the stadium in the Bronx. We like asymmetrical outfields in general, and we like the varying height of the outfield fence at Citi too. While Shea Stadium offered a continuous eight-foot fence all the way across, Citi's fence climbs at an angle from eight to eighteen feet high in right, stands at eight in center, and climbs at another angle from twelve to fifteen feet in left. This effect certainly makes deep fly balls more interesting, though it compounds the challenge that homer-seekers face in their search for the elusive Promised Land. We should mention that the foul poles are Mets orange, just as they were at Shea. Kevin, who's generally open to new things, liked this. Josh, meanwhile, thought it was sacrilege to raise non-yellow poles at a ballpark.

Josh: They might as well play with an orange ball.

Kevin: I think Charlie O. Finley tried that back in the 1970s.

Ballpark Features

THE JACKIE ROBINSON ROTUNDA

Inspired by the classy rotunda that welcomed fans to Ebbets Field decades ago, the Mets have created a similar rotunda at Citi Field and in so doing have embraced Ebbets and baseball icon Jackie Robinson—who played for the Dodgers—as their own forbears. A big blue No. 42 monument sits prominently in the rotunda, while pictures of Robinson posing with his wife, Rachel, and with Pee Wee Reese and other Dodgers hang high above. There are also quotes attributed to Robinson on the walls. Meanwhile, the virtues Robinson exhibited, such as courage, persistence, teamwork, and determination, are recalled by inspirational engravings in the marble flooring. These are taken from a children's book titled *Jackie's Nine: Jackie Robinson's Values to Live By,* which was published by Robinson's daughter Sharon Robinson in 2002. The etching about persistence reads, "Jackie and Brooklyn Dodgers general manager Branch Rickey shared a resolve to break down racial barriers and created opportunities for social change." And the others offer similar summaries of how Robinson embodied each characteristic.

We'll leave it to you to decide whether the Robinson Rotunda is out of place at the Mets home ballpark and would fit better at, say, Dodger Stadium. We will say this about it: It's a beautiful entrance, especially when it's lit up blue and orange at night. With its high ceilings and decorative light fixtures, it does much to turn what would otherwise be a functional space leading to the ballpark escalators and stairways into a grand and special part of a trip to Citi Field.

BIG TOPPS

Atop the rotunda's escalator, oversized baseball cards introduce visitors to the current members of the Mets. While we realize this is, in fact, a Topps advertisement, we have to admit it's pretty cool. How many grown-up fans *didn't* collect cards when they were kids? Practically none, right?

Mr. Met statue in museum

Photo by Josh Pahigian

And being reminded of the passion we once had for precious cardboard and stale gum put us both in the mood for a ballgame.

CELEBRATE GOOD TIMES

When Citi Field first opened, one knock on it was that its concourses were a bit drab. Another—as we've already mentioned—was that it went overboard to embrace the Mets' Long Island precursors, the Brooklyn Dodgers, but did little to celebrate Mets history. To help address both tidbits of consumer feedback, the Mets installed oversized black-and-white banners of favorite Mets celebrating great moments in team history—like the World Series wins in 1969 and 1986—on the walkways.

THE METS HALL OF FAME & MUSEUM

Located on the first base side of the Robinson Rotunda, the Mets Museum is a memento-filled emporium that also includes a classy plaque gallery and some interactive kiosks. Admission is free to ticket holders before, during, and after games. You can even take pictures inside, so long as you kindly shut your flash.

We liked seeing the 1969 World Championship trophy, but the 1986 hardware—and there's a lot of it—brought back bad memories for Josh. The endless loop video of the Mets comeback in Game Six seemed like overkill, as did the ball signed by both the Mets' Mookie Wilson and Red Sox goat Bill Buckner. There's even a bottle of Great Western Extra Dry Champagne from the Mets locker room after they beat the Red Sox. It's displayed with a letter of authenticity from a clubhouse attendant who was on the spot. There's more, too. A lot more. The only thing missing was Keith Hernandez's jockstrap and we half-expect we would have found it, too, if we hadn't turned away in disgust so soon.

We both liked the statue of Mr. Met and the plaques honoring favorite Mets like Tug McGraw, Cleon Jones, Gary Carter, Dwight Gooden, Strawberry, and others.

Another highlight is the extensive Mets timeline that consists of pictures, text, and artifacts behind glass. We learned a few things about Citi Field while studying this part of the Museum, such as that Tom Seaver threw out the first pitch before the first-ever game at Citi Field in 2009, and that Mike Piazza caught it.

In an adjoining room, game-worn jerseys (mostly from 1986) and other pieces of gear are displayed behind glass and are actually on sale, as are the pieces of an extensive (and kitschy) Mets crystal collection and autographed balls signed by the current members of the Mets.

Kevin: I can't believe anyone's going to pay $180 for a Jason Bay ball.

Josh: That's almost as preposterous as the Mets paying Bay $16 million a year.

Kevin: Hey, he's a Gonzaga alum. Lay off.

Josh: You Bulldogs are loyal, I'll give you that.

MEET THE METS, BUY A SHIRT. . . .

Citi Field offers six different gear and memorabilia shops, including Nike, New Era, Touch by Alyssa Milano Ladies' Boutique, and '47 for Men stands. But the biggest store of them all is the Majestic Mets Team Store located beside the Museum & Hall of Fame to the first base side of the rotunda.

Kevin: Aren't you coming in?

Josh: I think I'm going to wait right here.

Kevin: Still moping about the '86 Series, eh?

Josh: I was twelve years old—not quite a man, but no longer a boy. . . .

Kevin: . . . and they broke your heart.

Josh: You've heard this before?

Kevin: Yeah, when we visited Shea together in 2003 and when we saw the Mets play the Phillies at the old Vet and when we saw the Mets play the Pirates at PNC, and when we were on the 7 Train this morning.

Josh: Oh.

SHEA BRIDGE

A stroll along the first-level concourse inevitably brings visitors seeking the center-field food court across the unique and delightful Shea Bridge, which runs above the bullpens in right-center. This looks like the type of steel bridge you'd find spanning a river, only smaller. Instead of driving over it, you walk across it, keeping an eye on the game all the while. At the foot of this ballpark adornment, a plaque bearing a picture of Shea Stadium reads: "Shea Bridge. William A. Shea, a prominent New York attorney, was the driving force in the effort to bring National League Baseball back to the city after the Brooklyn Dodgers and New York Giants left for California

Shea Bridge in right field

Photo by Josh Pahigian

in 1957. Shea Stadium, home of the Mets from 1964 to 2008, was named in his honor. Shea was inducted into the Mets Hall of Fame in 1983 and the name Shea is honored alongside the Mets retired numbers on the outfield wall."

We thought this was a nice aesthetic touch. The bridge is visible from most of the park. And New York City has no shortage of famous bridges. So it seemed fitting.

Kevin: Looks kind of like the Hells Gate Bridge to me.

Josh: I'm going to defer to your knowledge of NYC bridges and take your word for it.

WALL OF HONOR

Banners painted onto the outfield wall above the "384 feet" marker in left-center commemorate the championship seasons in team history. And to the left of these hang the four numbers retired by the Mets.

Interestingly, only one of the team's retired numbers honors a Met for his playing performance—No. 41, which belonged to Seaver. No. 42 belonged to Dodgers great Jackie Robinson, of course. No. 37 belonged to Casey Stengel, who spent six seasons in right field for the Dodgers before decades later becoming the first Mets manager and guiding the team to a 175-404 record during his tenure. No. 14 belonged to Gil Hodges, who was a star with the Dodgers before spending the final two years of his playing career with the Mets. As Mets manager, Hodges then led the Miracle Mets to 1969 World Series glory.

Kevin: So why did they retire Stengel's number?

Josh: He was an all-around good guy who won seven World Series as Yankee manager.

Kevin: Well, that explains why the *Yankees* retired his number.

THE HOME RUN APPLE

Every time a Mets player hits a homer, a big apple emerges triumphantly from behind the fence in center field. Unfortunately, the Mets haven't hit too many long balls since Citi opened. And some players have complained that the ballpark's spacious outfield dimensions and high fences are to blame for this. The Mets have humored the players by reducing the height of the center-field fence from sixteen feet at the time of the ballpark's opening to its present eight feet. But that has had only a negligible effect on the number of long balls Citi surrenders. We were getting upset about the deep fences ourselves as our game at Citi played out. The seventh inning had arrived and the Mets hadn't even come close to clearing the wall. And then, magically, as "Take Me Out to the Ball Game" played, the apple rose like

a phoenix for all to see. Kevin cheered and Josh snapped pictures wildly. We'd seen what we had come to see and it didn't even matter to us that the Mets went down one-two-three in the bottoms of the eighth and ninth. For the record, the apple is four times the size of the one that sits outside the park that used to serve a similar celebratory purpose at Shea.

PERPENDICULAR PENS

The bullpens are adjacent to one another in right-center. Oddly, the pitchers throw toward the back of the outfield fence, rather than along it, as is traditionally the case with home run territory bullpens. We suppose this orientation leaves more space for the outfield seats on either side of the pens, but it looks weird. There's nothing traditional about the Astroturf in the pens either.

When Citi Field originally opened, the pitchers did throw along the fence. The Mets' pen was in front, along the wall, and the visitors' pen was behind it. Mets opponents complained that their relievers had a severely obstructed view of the game, however, prompting the Mets to reconfigure the alignment to its present perpendicular form.

Kevin: So the fans weren't the only ones to complain about the obstructed views at Citi.

Josh: It's nice to know the relievers are paying attention out there. I've often wondered. . . .

OLD GLORY

In this city where patriotism took on a deeper meaning after the events of 9/11, it seems fitting that American flags fly proudly atop the entire roof of the stadium. Josh started to count these, for the sake of providing a proper record in the book, but then decided it wasn't worth missing the events down on the field for such a trivial pursuit. Rest assured, there are a lot of flags up there. Probably somewhere between thirty-five and forty.

Kevin: You're getting lazy in your middle age.

Josh: No, just less anal about things.

Stadium Eats

Perhaps because there are so few eating and drinking establishments in the neighborhood surrounding Citi Field, the Mets have done an excellent job of providing an eclectic concession menu that reflects the culinary character of New York City. This is one of the few areas where Citi handily trumps its bigger, badder Bronx counterpart. So dig in!

We especially appreciate that in addition to providing a top-notch "Taste of the City" outfield food court on the first

While 1969 has gone down in baseball lore as the most important year in Mets history, it is unlikely the Miracle would have occurred if not for a fortuitous turn of fortune in 1966.

On April 2, 1966, the Mets acquired the rights to University of Southern California pitcher Tom Seaver, thanks to a special lottery that was conducted per orders of Commissioner Spike Eckert. "Tom Terrific" had originally signed with the Atlanta Braves in February 1966, but his contract was later voided when Eckert ruled that the USC season had already begun, signifying the end of the Braves' exclusive bargaining period. The commissioner said any team willing to match the Braves' offer should submit a bid. When the Mets, Phillies, and Indians all submitted matching offers, their names were thrown into a hat to determine Seaver's future team. Champagne bottles popped in Queens when it was announced that the Mets entry had been the first one pulled from the hat. As a rookie in 1967, Seaver won sixteen games. He won another sixteen in 1968. Then, in 1969, he won a "miraculous" twenty-seven, including a game apiece in the NLCS and October Classic. On April 22, 1970, Seaver set a record that still stands, striking out ten consecutive Padres as the Shea Stadium faithful cheered.

level, the Mets also make almost all of the premium foods available to the commoners sitting in the cheaper seats upstairs at a third-deck food court behind home plate.

As at Yankee Stadium, however, all of the concession stands post the calorie count of each item. Kevin consumed a scant one thousand, eight hundred calories during our game at Citi, while Josh stopped counting in the third inning after surpassing the three-thousand-calorie mark.

Kevin: You're gonna hate yourself in the morning.

Josh: But our readers demand that we sample every item.

Kevin: Do they really?

Josh: I don't know. But it all smells so good.

Kevin: Well, if we must, we must!

NATHAN'S HOT DOG (DOG REVIEW)

Kevin ordered a foot-long Nathan's dog from the Nathan's stand on the third deck food court and found it worth every one of the five hundred calories of stomach space it cost him. After one bite, he decided he wasn't in a very sharing mood and only allowed Josh a tiny sample. So Josh set out in search of his own Nathan's dog. Not wanting to miss the game, he settled for a regular concession stand behind Section 511 before realizing only too late that he'd ordered a pre-prepared dog that had been sitting beneath a heat lamp behind the counter. It was neither bursting with juice, nor firm and plump as Kevin's dog had been. It was a droopy disappointment. The moral of the lesson: Nathan's makes a darned good dog, but unless you get yours hot off one of the ballpark grills, you'll be doing it and yourself a disservice.

THE SHACK BURGER (TRADEMARK FOOD)

The Shake Shack stand in the center-field food court garners some of the longest lines we've ever seen at a ballpark concession counter. And for good reason. The Shack Burger is two juicy, premium patties of hand-packed beef, topped with fresh tomatoes, lettuce and onion, American cheese, and the Shack's trademark sauce. This is no ordinary burger and you'd be well advised to arrive early to Citi to stake out a space in line before the game begins.

The Shack-cago Dog is also popular. This all-beef Vienna link comes on a potato bun, topped with mustard, a special relish, onion, cucumber, pickle, tomato, pepper, and celery salt. You know, like in Chicago.

BEST OF THE REST

On the first level food court beyond deep right-center field, you'll find **Mama's Italian Specialties of Corona** within the World Fair Market beyond the fence in right-center. We ordered a hot roasted turkey and mozzarella sandwich. The sandwich consisted of approximately ten inches of freshly baked Italian bread stuffed with thin slices of fresh turkey, gooey mozzarella, brown gravy, and roasted red peppers. It was delicious. Mama's also serves an orange peel stuffed with homemade **sorbet** and **cannolis,** for those who have already sampled Citi Field's **knish** and want to embark upon a dessert tour of the park. If you don't hit Mama's inside the park, we recommend venturing into Corona where you'll find Mama's original location on 104th Street.

As for the **Kosher Grill,** it serves much more than just hot dogs and knish. There are also kosher burgers, sausages, and gyros.

There is a sushi bar in the World Fair Market, named **Daruma of Tokyo,** but it was 105 degrees Fahrenheit when we visited Citi for a 12:05 p.m. get-away game between the Mets and Cardinals, and Kevin said that was too warm even for him to eat raw fish. Josh agreed wholeheartedly.

The Catch of the Day in center field, meanwhile, offers cooked fish and chip platters, fried flounder, and shrimp "poor boy" sandwiches, among other items.

Hot and Sweet Premio Sausages cook at portable stands right on the concourse, filling the air with the savory aroma of fresh grilled meat. Although he felt it a sacrilege to say so, Josh had to admit the Sweet Italian he ordered, loaded with peppers and onions, was every bit as good as the Sausage Guy's offerings outside Fenway Park, and maybe a little better. It was juicy but not fatty, and exploded with flavor as he bit into it.

Another favorite is the **Cascarino's Pizzeria & Ristorante** (established in 1989) stand, which utilizes an actual wood-fired pizza oven on the premises. We thought our cheese slice was way better than the competing slice we sampled at Yankee Stadium and every bit as good as the ballpark 'za served at the fine ballparks in the Pizza Capital of the Midwest, Chicago. Cascarino's Vodka Sauce pie also piqued our interest, but at $6.00 a slice we decided to stand pat with the cheese slice we'd already split three ways with our friend Joe. Later in the day, a Mets fan we met heartily recommended the Meatball Parm sandwich at Cascarino's.

A **Box Frites** stand sells Belgian french fries, which come with several different dipping sauces (we recommend the Rosemary Ranch). And a **Blue Smoke** barbecue pit sells Kansas City pulled pork sandwiches, ribs, chipotle chicken wings, and barbecued beef bologna. We weren't brave enough to try the bologna, and opted for a pulled pork sandwich. The generous mound of pork was lean and tasty, but a tad on the dry side. It didn't seem to have any sauce on it, which was surprising. Nor did it come with sauce on the side, just a few pickle slices. By the time we realized this, the line was too long for us to attempt a return trip solely for sauce procurement. Don't get us wrong. It was a quality sandwich on a nicely toasted roll, but it needed some sauce. So be sure to ask for some when you order.

El Verano Taquerina has Chile-Marinated skirt steak, Carnitas, Chicken Mole Pipian, and steamed corn on the cob slathered with mayonnaise. We tasted some of our friend Joe's skirt steak and it was juicy and delicious.

In left-center on the first level, a **hot pastrami and rye** stand provides as authentic a taste of New York as you'll find in the park. Burgers and pulled pork are wonderful ballpark treats, but if you're in the Big Apple, you're in pastrami land. We couldn't find belly space to try the ballpark pastrami or knish, but the long line of salivating folks in orange T-shirts told us the offerings were to-die-for.

The Brooklyn Burger served at the **Keith Hernandez Grill** on the first level's left-field concourse is a pretty tasty choice if you don't have the patience to wait in line for a Shack Burger.

STADIUM SUDS

Here's another area in which the Mets exceed their deeper-pocketed crosstown rivals. The Beers of the Big Apple stands at Citi Field serve Stella Artois, Goose Island, Polar Garden, Kirin, Land Shark Lager, Kona Longboard Lager, Leffe Blond Lager, Hoegarden, and about twenty-five other fine brews. That's more than you find at some sports bars. Or you can be an average slob and settle for a Budweiser.

A variety of wines can also be purchased at locations throughout the park. There is also a Rum bar in the center-field food court that serves fruity frozen drinks. There are also five sit-down restaurants available to those holding Club tickets (read: not you!).

The Citi Field Experience

Ah, the ballpark. That magical place that exists in a universe all its own. That timeless fantasy land to which we escape when our mundane lives become too much to bear. In the darkest days of January, sometimes Josh will boil a half-dozen dogs, crack open a bag of nuts, water down a Bud Light, pop Game 4 of the 2004 World Series into his DVD player, and imagine he's sitting at Busch Stadium in St. Louis on the night the Red Sox won it all. He closes his eyes and meditates, ensconced by the sounds, smells, and tastes of the game. He listens for the crack of the bat, the pop of the ball hitting the catcher's mitt, the crowd rising to cheer or groan in unison, the heckling of the happy drunks, the deafening roar of the jet engines. . . . Wait a minute. Jet engines?

Welcome to Citi Field. As was the case when they played at Shea Stadium, the Mets take the field directly beneath one of LaGuardia Airport's main flight paths. The jets pass directly over the stadium all game long, and they're still pretty low to the ground. They're loud. Not a little loud. Really, really loud. So bring earplugs if you have sensitive ears and prepare yourself for the many interrupted conversations you'll have as the game plays out, as you and your buddies constantly pause to let the big birds pass before continuing whatever you were saying.

LET'S GO, METS

We found Citi Field to be a friendly place. Sure, it helped that Josh was wearing a Mets T-shirt by the third inning. He did this ironically, and told the affable season ticket holder seated next to him as much. Josh confessed to being a Red Sox fan, which prompted the man to ask whether Josh was also a New England Patriots fan. When Josh replied in the affirmative, the fellow said, "The Jets are gonna kick their butts this year," but the orange-clad gent was a fast friend. He tipped us off to the best food items at Citi and even gave us directions out of town when we confessed that our GPS had taken us to Prince Street in Little Italy instead of Prince Street in Flushing during our pregame search for our hotel. "You didn't realize you were on the wrong island?" the man asked, astounded by our lack of topographic awareness.

LET'S GO, YANKEES?

We were surprised to hear a chorus of "Let's Go, Yankees" rise from a group of twenty-somethings as they traveled en masse down the ballpark exit ramp after the game. It was soon drowned out by a resounding "Yankees Suck" from the others walking nearby.

Josh: Funny thing. We didn't see or hear from any Mets fans when we visited Yankee Stadium.

Kevin: You carry yourself with a bit more bravado once your team wins its twenty-seventh championship or so, I suppose.

Josh: Or maybe Mets fans just aren't as obnoxious as Yankee fans.

Kevin: Yeah, that explanation works for me too.

PLANE RACES, NO MORE

We miss the old jet races that used to take place on the Shea Stadium JumboTron. It was nice to know the Mets had a sense of humor, back then, about the roaring monstrosities that incessantly fly overhead. Why this Mets trademark didn't make the trip next door with the team, we have no idea, but we sure hope the Mets consider returning to their routes . . . um . . . we mean roots . . . and bring back the big birds on their bigger-than-before stadium board.

POP OPEN A CAN OF NOISE

We were a bit shocked and disappointed to hear Mets fans actually respond on cue when the JumboTron "noise meter" appeared and demanded applause and cheering at a pretty ho-hum moment in a lopsided Mets loss.

HUSTLE AND FLOW

As environmentalists we applaud the no-flow urinals in the men's room. Okay, maybe we'll wait until we finish up in the bathroom to applaud. But we think they're a great idea.

Josh: I bet the fish in Flushing Bay appreciate this ballpark nuance.

Kevin: I'm pretty sure the fish left for cleaner waters long ago.

NO BARREL OF FUN . . . AND A SPONGEBOB SIGHTING!

A big clear barrel on the first-level right-field concourse sits brimming with batting-practice balls. If you can guess how many are within, you win a prize. To submit your best guess, you text your answer to a number posted on the barrel.

Kevin: What are you doing? Stand up.

Josh: I'm counting.

Kevin: You realize this is a thinly disguised advertisement for Verizon, right?

Josh: So was that a SpongeBob mascot you just posed with?

Kevin: Hey, I already sent the picture home to Maeve and Rory. They'll love it.

Josh: If you told me during our first trip eight years ago that we'd one day do it all again *and* pose with cartoon characters, *and* wirelessly send photos home to our kids. . . .

Kevin: Life changes, but it's all good.

DUNK TANK

Out at the center-field kids play area, tikes line up with their kid siblings in tow, ready to get the little guys (and gals) wet. As parents, we think that on a hot day a ballpark dunk tank is a fun diversion. In April or May, not so much. But the kiddos will want to partake no matter what the temp is, so moms and dads should be sure to bring a change of clothes to the park.

Josh: Heather and I bring about three changes wherever we go.

Kevin: Well, that will end once Spencer is out of diapers.

Josh: Oh, not for Spencer. For me. I hate getting sweaty.

Kevin: I'll file that as Josh Pahigian eccentricity number 103.

C TRUMPS BAC IN NYC SHOWDOWN

Our friend Joe spent half an inning circling the first level concourse looking for a Bank of America ATM. But he only

---

Cyber Super-Fans

- **Mets Merized**
  http://metsmerizedonline.com/
- **213 Miles from Shea**
  http://213milesfromshea.metsblog.com/
- **Mets Are Better than Sex**
  http://metsarebetterthansex.blogspot.com/

encountered one Citibank cash dispenser after another. Finally, it dawned on him that he was at Citi Field and he resigned himself to paying the higher withdrawal charge his bank assigned to transactions on Citi machines.

COW-BELL MAN (SUPER-FAN)

Wearing a Mets jersey that bears No. 15 and the name "Cow-Bell Man" across the back, lifelong Mets fanatic Eddie Boison roams the upper levels of Citi Field with his trusty cowbell in hand, just as he used to do at Shea Stadium. Trust us, you'll hear him coming.

>*Josh:* I didn't know there were cattle farms in Queens.
>
>*Cow-Bell Man:* Ding, ding, ding.
>
>*Josh:* Do you herd *dairy* cows or *beef* cows?
>
>*Cow-Bell Man:* Ding, ding, ding.
>
>*Josh:* Because I really like steak.
>
>*Kevin:* We'll get you a Cowboy Steak in Texas, Josh. Let the poor man be.

HILDA CHESTER (SUPER-FAN HALL OF FAME)

What Cow-Bell Man is to the Mets and their fans, "Howling Hilda" Chester was to the Brooklyn Dodgers. She worked part-time filling paper bags with peanuts, then reported to the bleachers where she would sit in a flowered dress and bang on a frying pan all game with a big iron ladle. On special occasions, she would lead the Bleacher Bums through the Ebbets Field aisles in a long snake dance procession. By the 1930s, she was so well known that Dodgers players presented her with a special cow-bell that she used as a noise-maker until the team left town in the 1950s.

"THE SIGN MAN" (SUPER-FAN HALL OF FAME)

From 1964 through 1981, Mets fan Karl Ehrhardt had his own way of shouting support for and criticism of the home team. He would schlep large homemade signs to Shea Stadium and hold them up. "The Sign Man" was a fixture right behind the third base dugout. The several dozen cleverly

---

Sports in (and around) the City

Elysian Fields
11th Street and Washington Street
Hoboken, New Jersey

Baseball lore offers conflicting stories concerning the sport's origins. One nugget of folksy wisdom says Abner Doubleday invented baseball back in 1839, while another tall tale crowns Alexander Joy Cartwright the "father of baseball," pointing to a "first game" at Elysian Fields in Hoboken, New Jersey, in 1846. In actuality, neither man invented baseball. Baseball evolved out of English games like cricket and rounders during the first part of the nineteenth century. In the later 1800s, as modern transportation made Americans more mobile, the different versions of the game assimilated into one.

However, the site of Elysian Fields, where Cartwright and his friends played, is considered holy ground by many lovers of the sport. Today, the park has been reduced to a strip of lawn between two lanes of traffic. A monument reads: "On June 19, 1846 the first match game of baseball was played here on the Elysian Fields between the Knickerbockers and the New Yorks. It is generally conceded that until this time the game was not seriously regarded."

Readers will note that the inscription doesn't proclaim Hoboken the birthplace of baseball. But that doesn't mean the Elysian Fields site isn't worth a visit if you're a starry-eyed romantic for the game. The field did play a role in the development of baseball's previously unwritten rules, even if the rules employed for games there bore scant resemblance to the ones we know today.

Cartwright was a bank clerk, who spent the early 1840s playing afternoon games of "base ball" at a vacant lot in Manhattan with other professionals. Then, in 1845 the lot they used was slated for redevelopment. So Cartwright and his friends went looking for a new place to play. They found Elysian Fields, a tree-lined park just across the Hudson River. Cartwright's newly formed club of "Knickerbockers" rented the field and traveled to it regularly via ferry. And in the winter of 1845–1846, Cartwright scribbled out fourteen rules to characterize the game he and his friends had been playing for years already. He was not inventing the rules, but he was recording them. The "Cartwright rules" said that baseball should be played on a diamond, not a square, that the distance between home plate and second base should measure forty-two paces (which makes for bases approximately seventy-five feet apart), that balls struck outside the baselines should be declared foul, and that runners should be tagged out (as opposed to being struck by thrown balls).

conceived signs he brought to each game were separated by color coded tabs, so that he could hold up the most apropos ones when the events of the game dictated he ought to make his opinion known. Some of his more memorable signs included gems like "Look Ma, No Hands," which he once held up after an error by Mets shortstop Frank Taveras, "Jose, Can you See," which he displayed after strikeouts by the oft-whiffing Jose Cardenal, and "There Are No Words," which he triumphantly hoisted after the Mets got the final out of the 1969 World Series.

While We Were in New York
Josh Sold His Red-Sox-Loving Soul for a Dry Shirt

We rolled into town for a day game against the Cardinals at the height of the worst heat wave to besiege New York City in several years. Thermometers read 105 degrees Fahrenheit, and meteorologists reported the heat index had climbed to 112 degrees. We admit to having no flipping idea what the heat index is, but we can attest it was damned hot in the Baked Apple during our visit.

Appropriately, Kevin wore the thinnest Bermuda shirt in his "eclectic" wardrobe. Josh, on the other hand, wore a thick-weave "Ultimate Baseball Road Trip" golf shirt that his thoughtful mother-in-law, Judy Gurrie, had ordered for him at a specialty shirt shop.

As Josh blotted his face with a wad of wet paper towels, Kevin said, "I can't believe you're wearing that thick shirt."

"Even my fingernails are sweating," Josh replied. "And my wristwatch is all fogged up with condensation."

"You're on the fast-track to heat-stroke, my friend," Kevin quipped, then he said, "This oughta help you along," and handed Josh a lukewarm cup of Bud Light.

By the time the middle of the fourth arrived, Josh was drenched from head to toe and practically delirious. At just that time, a Citi Field pep-squad guy walked up the stairway to Section 511 where we were sitting. And Josh really let him have it. You see, the young man had an armful of bright orange T-shirts, and as the knowing fans in our section spotted him, they began to cheer. And he began to fire shirts at them. This struck

Josh as too bush league a stunt for the biggest big league city of them all. "What is this, an arena football game?" Josh heckled. "Or a New York-Penn League game?"

Everyone else, including Kevin, was standing by now, and waving their arms, in hopes that the T-shirt guy would toss some free Mets garb their way. "Like I'd *ever* wear orange even if it *didn't* have a Mets logo on front," Josh jeered. "I wouldn't wear that crappy color if it was the last shirt on earth and I was marooned at a nudist camp."

"Pipe down," Kevin said. "I think you're delirious. You're not making any sense." But practically no one else heard Josh. The others nearby were too preoccupied with trying to get a shirt. Either they were calling for one, or jumping up and down to get the shirt guy's attention, or leaning and lurching to catch a flying shirt. To his credit, the shirt guy had unleashed a barrage of a half-dozen shirts within about ten seconds of his arrival at the end of the aisle.

But he still had one more to throw, and wouldn't you know, it sailed right through the outstretched arms of the attractive, slightly inebriated woman a row in front of us, and into Josh's lap. Josh instinctively wrapped it up as if it were a coveted milestone home run ball, and started to throw his elbows around just in case anyone should try to yank it away from him.

Josh at Citi Field

Photo by Joe Bird

"Ha!" Kevin cried, lowering himself into his seat. "You didn't even want a shirt and you wound up with . . . Hey, what are you doing?"

Before Kevin could finish his thought, Josh had stripped the sweat-soaked "Ultimate Baseball Road Trip" shirt from his body, and had slipped into the bright orange Mets shirt.

"What are you doing? You hate the Mets," Kevin said.

"A dry shirt is a dry shirt," Josh replied.

"But you said you wouldn't wear a Mets shirt if it was the last one on earth."

"It was all part of my strategy," Josh replied.

"Your strategy?"

"I knew he would huck one at me if I tossed a few barbs his way," Josh explained.

"Um, I'm pretty sure he was throwing it to the cute girl in front of us," Kevin said. "You practically wrestled it away from her."

"You can believe what you want," Josh said. "But I happen to be wearing the driest shirt in Section 511."

Kevin shook his head in disbelief. "It's true what they say about a trip to the ballpark," he said. "You never know when you're gonna see something you've never seen before. And I'm taking a picture of this because I'm pretty sure I'm never gonna see it again."

NEW YORK YANKEES, YANKEE STADIUM

The House That George Built

When the original Yankee Stadium opened in 1923 at a hitherto unheard of construction cost of $2.5 million, the man credited with providing the Pinstripes with the popularity, pizzazz, and not least the bankroll, to embark upon such an ambitious venture as the world's first triple-decked baseball stadium took a good look around and commented, "Nice little yard." Babe Ruth was no doubt speaking ironically when he gave the Stadium that understated appraisal. Clearly, he understood the import of the Stadium's arrival. And the Yankees and their fans did too. Their team already boasted the game's brightest star and a steadily increasing number of rooters, and now it had the grandest facility the game had yet known. Appropriately, Ruth and his teammates capped Yankee Stadium's inaugural season by winning the club's first World Championship that fall.

Fast-forward nine decades to another grand opening in the Bronx, and this time the expectations and fanfare surrounding the latest Yankee Stadium were even greater. In the midst of America's worst economic downturn since the Great Depression, baseball's most successful team was introducing a five-level replacement for its hugely popular "House that Ruth Built." What's more, the new park carried an unimaginable price tag of $1.5 billion. That's right, *billion* with a "B." And that figure doesn't even include the land acquisition costs for the stadium site, neighborhood infrastructure improvements, the construction of community ball fields to replace the ones that had been razed to make way for the new stadium, and the demolition and removal of the old stadium. All told, the new Yankee Stadium cost more than $2.3 billion. To put this number in perspective, prior to the opening of the new Yankee palace and the concurrent opening of the Mets' Citi Field, the most expensive baseball facility ever built had been Toronto's Rogers Centre, which cost $570 million back in 1989. And Oriole Park at Camden Yards, which is often referred to as the standard bearer of the retro parks we fans love, cost only $110 million to build in 1992.

So it's fair to say that expectations were sky high for the new baseball grounds in the Bronx, where a front row seat behind the Yankees dugout would go for $2,625 per game. Nonetheless, new Yankee Stadium exceeded even the loftiest of hopes. Yankee captain Derek Jeter was one of the first to admit to being blown away by the new digs. Expressing his thoughts a bit more artfully than the starry-eyed Ruth had upon the unveiling of the previous Bronx behemoth, on the date of the home opener in 2009 Jeter admitted, "It's a lot better than I think anyone even expected. You know, I tried to come here, not ask too many questions about it, just wanted to experience it for the first time. But this is—it's pretty unbelievable."

Yankee president Randy Levine, meanwhile, explained that evoking such a jaw-dropping reaction from players and fans alike had been in the Yankees' designs from the very start because that's the way Yankee owner George Steinbrenner had wanted it. "It's always George's philosophy," Levine explained. "This is the Yankees; everything has to be done first-rate. We wanted . . . to create a stadium that, when you go in, there's a 'wow' factor."

In this regard—and countless others—the Yankees clearly succeeded. If you've gotten to know your two humble writers in the course of reading this book or its previous edition, you know that we are by no means Yankee apologists. We both root for other American League teams and through the years have come to view the Yankees about as fondly as the mildew in our bathroom grout, or the bloated wood ticks Josh yanks from the manes of his golden labs Maddie and Cooper. Heck, we co-authored a book together titled *Why I Hate the Yankees* a few years back. We want to retch every time we see a pinstriped suit, let alone a pinstriped baseball uniform. We thought the late Mr. Steinbrenner was an arrogant bully. We think most Yankee players are mercenary front-runners. And we have scrupulously shunned Derek Jeter from our fantasy teams

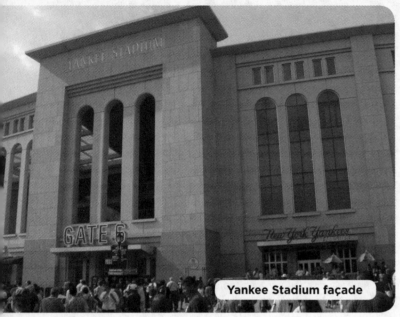

Yankee Stadium façade

Photo by Josh Pahigian

to an interior space behind the first level concourse and seats like Yankee Stadium does.

The appropriately named Great Hall is a wide and exceedingly high ceilinged (we're talking the full seven stories) room just inside the gates. It provides space for vendors, for the largest of the stadium's six apparel stores, for a bar and two restaurants, for a giant high-definition video screen, and for massive vertical banners that honor some of the Yankees' favorite players. The old players like Yogi Berra are rendered in black-and-white photographs, while more recent "greats" like Dave Winfield and Paul O'Neill appear in color. And all of this appears before fans even make their way to the ramps that lead to the first level concourse, which allows fans to walk around the entire lower bowl.

Now, rambling fans are already well acquainted with the concept of a walk-around or 360-degree concourse. Designed to provide a view of the game to strollers seeking concessions or heading to the john, these have become a staple of the ballpark experience during the retro renaissance. Usually, however, new parks unveil *first levels* that employ this design approach. At Yankee Stadium, the concept has been extended two steps further. Not only does the 100 Level have a concourse with a view, but the 200 and 300 Levels do too. This is just one of many best practices the Yankees implemented with the aid of the most renowned ballpark architects in history—the good folks at Populous (previously known as HOK Sport). Another concept the Yankees have embraced to the hilt is the in-stadium bar or restaurant. Such on-site watering holes are popular in the modern day and most parks are proud to boast one or two on their grounds. The Yankees offer no fewer than eight by our count, including the ritzy and critically acclaimed NYY Steak; the members-only Mohegan Sun Sports Bar, the tinted windows of which double as the batter's eye in center; a Hard Rock Café; the Jim Beam Suite; Tommy Bahama's cocktail bar in the Great Hall; and the Malibu Roof Deck.

Another modern innovation is the prevalence of flat-screen TVs throughout our modern parks and their concourses, so strolling fans can keep an eye on the game. And the Yankees have outfitted Yankee Stadium with an amazing 1,200 screens. The biggest one is the video board in straightaway center that is the third largest board in all of baseball. It measures 101 feet across by 59 feet high. Only the boards in Kansas City and Houston are larger.

throughout his entire career, even when he was one of the best shortstops in the game. Sorry, Derek, no Yankees welcome here.

Kevin: The Red Sox aren't much better these days.

Josh: Oh, come on. That's just sour grapes talking.

Kevin: Boston might as well be wearing red pinstripes.

And yet, we have to give the Yankees their due. We have to tip our caps to King George. We have to agree with the sentiments of Jeter and Levine. We exited the 4 train expecting to be blown away by the most expensive sports venue ever known to man. And yet we still had to admit Yankee Stadium exceeded our preconceptions in practically every regard. It's bigger, more luxurious, and more beautiful than we could have imagined. We were gaping from the moment we stepped onto the plaza outside Gate 4 and gazed up at the regal seven-story façade made of white Indiana limestone, granite, and concrete, with tall narrow arches aplenty. Truly, there's no other stadium that beams with such palatial majesty. No other stadium makes such a grand first impression. Sure, the train station at Minute Maid Park in Houston serves as a historic gateway to the baseball grounds; the rotunda at Citi Field is a crisp, clean, and beautiful structure; and the Eutaw Street entrance of Oriole Park welcomes fans to a festive place for pregame revelry. But there isn't another ballpark in baseball that welcomes fans

Kevin: Kansas City trumps New York! Who knew?

Josh: But the Royals still gave Roger Maris to the Yanks.

Yankee Stadium also offers a comprehensive team museum where all of the World Series trophies are on display, and statues of Berra and Don Larsen commemorate Larsen's perfect game in the 1956 World Series. Another prime attraction away from the field itself is Monument Park, which has been transplanted from the old yard and resurrected in center. To say it draws huge pregame crowds would be an understatement of monumental proportions. There is also a timeline spanning the entire first level concourse that pays tribute to every championship team in the Yankees' grand history. And there are two baseball collectibles stores. And there's a store just for women. And there's a special store for Monument Park memorabilia. Serious shoppers could spend an entire afternoon just eating and browsing the stores at Yankee Stadium.

As for the field, its dimensions replicate the old Yankee Stadium's as it existed in its final state after many modifications through the years. "Death Valley" in left-center is not as vast as it was in Ruth's day, but the fence still measures a deeper-than-usual 399 feet from the plate. Down the line in right, the foul pole stands 314 feet from the plate, just as it did at the old Yankee Stadium. But the right-field fence angles toward center in a straighter course than it did at the old yard, making the actual distance from home plate to the seats in right and right-center considerably less than it was previously. Perhaps this is why left-handed batters have yanked long balls with such alarming regularity since the new Yankee Stadium's opening.

The stadium's trademark feature is its decorative white filigree or frieze, which rings the entire rim of the upper deck. This slatted white steel, which looks a bit like an inverted picket fence, spanned only the outfield portion of the Yankee Stadium at which most of us remember watching games. But old-timers will recall that prior to the renovation of the old Yankee Stadium in the mid-1970s the filigree had rimmed the entire top of the upper deck, just as it does now at new Yankee Stadium. The stadium lights are mounted directly atop this white adornment. You'll notice there are no light towers at Yankee Stadium, nor are there light banks. There's just a solid ring of light atop this ornate white metalwork.

In this age when folks seem to swoon over a skyline view at the old ballgame, Yankee Stadium delivers this too . . . sort of. The skyline in right showcases several weathered brown apartment buildings on Walton and Gerard Avenue that might cynically be described as "tenements." Unfortunately, the designers of the park couldn't position the outfield toward Manhattan because then batters would have faced a setting sun. There is, however, a view of the tall, beautiful buildings of the Big Apple, for those who seek it.

interior

Photo by Josh Pahigian

A visit to the Malibu Roof Deck on the 300 Level showcases the skyscrapers of midtown out of the back of the stadium.

Kevin: Wow. There's a nice breeze here too.

Josh: And this fruity rum drink is hitting the spot.

Kevin: What have I told you about the fruity drinks?

Securing the financing for the new Yankee Stadium and building it were no small undertakings. In the early 2000s the Yankees struck a deal with then-mayor of New York City Rudolph Giuliani that would have seen taxpayers foot even more of the freight for the new park than they eventually did. At that early stage, the Yankees were talking about building a retractable roof stadium. Subsequent mayor Michael Bloomberg scaled back the public investment and the Yankees scrapped the plan to put a lid on their digs. Still, taxpayers forked over about $800 million toward the stadium's construction. Then it took nearly three years for the stadium to be built. After an official groundbreaking in August 2006, the grand opening took place on April 16, 2009. The Cleveland Indians took some of the joy out of the day by handing the Yankees a 10-2 defeat, as Cliff Lee bested former Indian C.C. Sabathia. But the Yankees had the last laugh. The Pinstripes rebounded from a sluggish April to post the best record in baseball—103-59—on their way to finishing the inaugural season at new Yankee Stadium with a champagne bath. The Yankees clinched their twenty-seventh World Championship on their home lawn, beating the Phillies 7-3 in Game 6 of the October Classic behind the pitching of Andy Pettitte and a home run by World Series MVP Hideki Matsui.

The next great memory the Yankees penned on their new field occurred on July 9, 2011, when an aging Jeter, who'd only a few games earlier come off the disabled list, went five-for-five against the Tampa Bay Rays while collecting his three thousandth hit on a home run. In an admirable gesture, the Yankee fan who caught the milestone hit—a gent named Christian Lopez, who was sitting on a bleacher bench in Section 236—gave the ball to Jeter without seeking to profit personally in the exchange.

Kevin: That guy's a hero.

Josh: He's crazy. I would have cashed in.

Kevin: The Yankees gave him Club Seats as compensation.

Josh: Well, that sounds a little better.

Kevin: Until you figure he still had to pay some hefty taxes on them.

Another early highlight for the Yankees at their new yard occurred on August 25, 2011, when they became the first team ever to hit three grand slams in one game during a 22-9 rout of the Oakland A's. The Pinstripes actually trailed 7-1 after three innings, before mounting a furious comeback fueled by bases-loaded homers from Robinson Cano, Russell Martin, and Curtis Granderson, who, true to his name, hit the record-breaking clout in the eighth inning. The twenty-two runs also went into the history books as the most by a Yankees team in a home game since 1931 when the Pinstripes of Lou Gehrig and Babe Ruth crossed the plate twenty-two times in a game against the White Sox.

As for Yankee highlights at the previous incarnation of Yankee Stadium, the home team's remarkable history of success makes it impossible for us to recount all of them in a book of this nature. We will, however, touch upon some of the most memorable moments. So, here goes: It all began inauspiciously enough for the team that would become the Bronx Bombers, with the fledgling American League franchise failing to win a pennant during its first twenty seasons.

But once the Yankees got rolling, they dominated the Major Leagues like no team before. They appeared in twenty-nine World Series between 1921 and 1962 and claimed twenty World Championships during that time. During the Steinbrenner reign, they won back-to-back World Series in 1977 and 1978, and then won five more between 1996 and 2009, including three in a row from 1998 through 2000.

The Yanks began as the American League Baltimore Orioles in 1901 before moving to the north side of Manhattan in 1903. Known as the "Highlanders," they took the field at New York American League Ballpark—aka Hilltop Park—despite protests from the New York Giants, who were afraid the Junior Circuit upstarts would erode their fan base. For a long time New York was a big enough town for both teams—as well as the Brooklyn Dodgers—but in the end those fears proved justifiable.

Hilltop Park was located on the west side of Broadway between 165th and 168th Street in the Washington Heights district, which is the most altitudinous portion of Manhattan Island. The ballpark offered bird's-eye views of the Hudson River and the Palisades in New Jersey. The center-field fence measured 502 feet from home plate. In their second season, the Highlanders, or Hilltoppers as some fans and writers dubbed them, challenged the Boston Pilgrims (who would later become the Red Sox) for the AL crown. In the end New York finished a game and a half behind their neighbors to the north. And thus, a rivalry was born. Who knew then that decades later the Red Sox and Yankees would still perennially jostle for AL bragging rights? Or that a Bambino would bless the Yankees and curse the Red Sox, until the 2004 Bostonians finally ripped the albatross from around their necks to rise from the ashes after trailing the Yankees three games to none in the ALCS? Who could have known that the two teams would stage an epic battle in 1949, punctuated by a Yankee win over the Sox on the last day of the season to clinch the pennant? Or that the two teams would finish tied for first in 1978, setting the stage for Bucky Dent's dramatic home run in a one-game playoff at Fenway Park?

Baseball certainly was a different game when the Boston/New York rivalry began. Pitcher Jack Chesbro won forty-one games for the Highlanders in 1904, tossing forty-eight complete games and logging 454 innings. Today, most front-of-the-rotation starters don't win that many games or throw that many innings over two seasons.

After regularly finishing in the AL's second division while the Red Sox racked up five World Championships in the 1900s and 1910s, the Yankees seized control of their own destiny in 1919, purchasing Babe Ruth's contract from

Boston for $125,000 and a $300,000 loan. Playing regularly in the outfield for the first time in his career after pitching for the Red Sox, Ruth hit fifty-four home runs in 1920, shattering the old record of twenty-nine he had hit the year before. While today we speculate that players are on "the juice" when they exhibit such power surges, Ruth's breakout had more to do with the advent of the juiced or "lively" ball that was introduced in 1920. By then, the Yankees were playing at the Polo Grounds, which they leased from the Giants, who needed the extra revenue. It was not uncommon for the squatting Yankees to draw more fans to their games than the Giants did to theirs. In 1921, the Yankees made it to their first World Series—losing to their landlords in an All-Polo-Grounds Series. The same two teams met again the next year, with the Giants prevailing over their tenants again.

After moving into their own digs across the Harlem River, the Yankees gained a measure of immediate revenge, by besting their former landlords in the 1923 World Series. The first triple-decked baseball facility to be built and first to be termed a "stadium," Yankee Stadium opened on April 18, 1923, with the home team defeating Boston 4–1, behind Ruth's three-run homer. Constructed in just 284 days, the stadium accommodated more than seventy-four thousand fans, more than twice the capacity of most other parks at the time. Prior to the replacement of the original wooden bleachers with seats in the 1930s and the enforcement of new fire laws, the stadium often housed crowds exceeding seventy-five thousand people.

In the post-Ruth era, new stars like Lou Gehrig, Bill Dickey, Joe DiMaggio, Mickey Mantle, Phil Rizzuto, and Berra continued to win championships for the Yankees. From 1936 to 1939, New York won four straight. The Yanks put together another string of five in a row from 1949 to 1953, and combined with the New York Giants and Brooklyn Dodgers to keep the title in New York nine times in a ten-year span (1949–58), with only Milwaukee's victory over the Yankees in 1957 bucking the trend. Prior to the departure of the Dodgers and Giants for the West Coast, New York truly was the hub of the baseball universe.

After suddenly becoming New York's lone team, the Yankees reached the October Classic five years running from 1960–1964, including a win over the San Francisco Giants in 1962 and a loss to the Los Angeles Dodgers in 1963. In the 1970s, fiery manager Billy Martin led the Yanks into battle, bolstered by a roster of larger-than-life stars like Reggie Jackson, Thurman Munson, Ron Guidry, Catfish Hunter, and Goose Gossage. The Yanks may not have been a lovable team in the dying days of disco, but they had an aura about

them that was second to none. The "Bronx Zoo" became a term that typified the team, as Steinbrenner feuded with Martin—whom he hired and fired five times. Martin and Jackson once came to blows in the dugout. Munson and Red Sox catcher Carlton Fisk brawled at home plate. But through it all the Yankees kept winning, bringing home the World Series hardware in 1977 and 1978.

The 1970s were also an important decade for Yankee Stadium. In 1974 and 1975 the Pinstripes played their "home" games at the Mets' Shea Stadium while the "House that Ruth Built" was nearly completely torn down and rebuilt. During the renovation the outfield wall was brought closer to the plate and the center-field monuments were removed from the field of play to create Monument Park. Even so, the field's most distinctive feature remained the deep gap in left-center, known as Death Valley—where long fly balls went to die. The fence originally measured five hundred feet from home plate, before the plate was moved in 1924 to eliminate the "Bloody Angle" in right, changing the distance to 490 feet. Subsequent renovations brought the fence to its final 399 feet.

Winfield, Rickey Henderson, and Don Mattingly led the Yankees of the 1980s but to no avail as New York failed to capture a World Championship in the Decade of Decadence, marking the team's first such drought since it started winning titles in the 1920s. By 1990, New York had fallen into the AL basement. Adding insult to injury, Steinbrenner was forced by the commissioner's office to temporarily relinquish control of the team when it was revealed he had attempted to gain incriminating evidence about Winfield from a reputed gambler. The Big Stein had often derided Winfield for not producing numbers to justify his lofty contract and Winfield had shot more than a few barbs back at the Boss in the *Daily News*, precipitating the incident.

When Steinbrenner returned, he meddled less, and the dynasty righted itself under the field management of Joe Torre and the steady front office hand of Brian Cashman. Gone were the days of the Bronx Zoo's tough and nasty image. Led by gritty, even likable, players like Bernie Williams, Jorge Posada, Scott Brosius, Tino Martinez, Jeter, and O'Neill, the 1998 Yanks set a new record with their 114 regular season wins and another record with their 125 total wins, counting their three Ws against the Rangers in the Division Series, four against the Indians in the ALCS, and four against the Padres, whom they swept in the World Series.

The next season the Yankees and Red Sox met in the postseason for the first time ever, with the AL East champs downing the Wild Card Sox in the ALCS en route to another

World Championship. The Yankees made it three in a row, beating the Mets in the 2000 Series. With the win, fifth-year Yankee shortstop Derek Jeter collected his fourth World Series ring. He would win yet another, of course, in 2009.

Kevin: Do you think he wears two on one hand and three on the other?

Josh: I think I'd just wear all five on the same hand.

Kevin: It must be tough deciding.

Josh: Either way, it's a nice problem to have.

Trivia Timeout

Yankee Pot Roast: Name the first two players to enter baseball's three-thousand-hit club with home runs. Hint: Both wore pinstripes at one time.

Yankee Doodle Dandies: Which trio of Yankee teammates holds the MLB record for most seasons played together as a trifecta?

Yankee Swap: Which number is twice-retired by the Yankees? Which currently retired Yankee number will surely soon be retired again?

Look for the answers in the text.

Getting a Choice Seat

Yankee Stadium is plenty big enough to accommodate even the Yankees' rabid local fan base. We had no problem getting tickets for below face value on StubHub for a July game against the A's. Games against more intriguing opponents do sometimes sell out, but tickets to Yankee Stadium are a lot easier to come by than say, tickets to Fenway Park or Wrigley Field. The good news is that even the cheap seats in the upper reaches of the 400 Level offer pretty solid views. Truly, it's hard to find a bad seat in this house, excepting the "obstructed view" bleacher seats in right- and left-center. One nice service the Yankees offer is a ticket exchange option. If you arrive at the Stadium and don't like your seat or see a lot of empties down in front, you can head to one of the interior ticket windows—in the Great Hall, or behind Section 221, or behind Section 320—and request an upgrade. If a better seat is available, the attendant will charge you the difference between your seat and the one you're moving to, and then issue a new ticket. But that's just one unique ticketing feature we uncovered. Another is the computer that lets fans retrieve their will-call tickets the way travelers get their boarding passes at the airport. Rather than waiting in a

---

Seating Capacity: 50,287
Ticket Office: http://newyork.yankees.mlb.com/ticketing/index.jsp?c_id=nyy
Seating Chart: http://newyork.yankees.mlb.com/nyy/ballpark/seating_pricing.jsp

---

long will-call line, fans visit kiosks adjacent to the ticket windows across from Parking Lot 8 and swipe whatever credit card they used to purchase their tickets. Then, their tickets instantly print and pop out of the machine.

Josh: Or you can just order from StubHub and print your tickets at home.

Kevin: When did you become a shill for second-hand ticket brokers?

Josh: When I realized I can usually score seats below face value.

As a general rule, we like the home run territory seats in right field better than the ones in left because right field is shallower and, thus, fans sitting on that side of the park are closer to the infield than those in left. However, for night games, right field is the sun field. If you're sitting in the second or third decks on a summer eve—say in Sections 205, 305, or 405—you will be squinting into the sun for a full hour while the rest of the park is in shadow. If you're fair skinned or anticipate being sunburned from a day spent goofing around at Coney Island, then you'd be smart to sit elsewhere. At the very least, be sure to bring your sunglasses. Those sitting at field level in right don't suffer nearly as much, because they're tucked almost completely beneath the overhang of the second deck, but they should still have their shades ready for the first inning.

The 100 Level

LEGENDS SUITE (SECTIONS 11–29)

The first eight rows on the infield are separated from the rest of the lower bowl by a low concrete wall. This exclusive part of the park is fiercely guarded by ushers who could probably pick up part-time shifts as Secret Service operatives to make a few extra bucks. To say they are vigilant and hell-bent on keeping out the riff raff is an understatement. As for the seats within this concrete moat, they sell for an average price of more than $500 a pop and the ones down in front cost more than $2,600. That's dollars, not pesos or rubles. And yes, that's for *one* baseball game, not a season pass. We imagine this is still a pretty sweet deal if you're Sir Paul McCartney or Keith Olbermann, since the first row of seats is only fifty-two feet from home plate. But if you're an average Joe, it's kind of an affront to reality, especially when you tune in to the YES Network and observe that these posh sections are half-empty on many nights.

FIELD/FIELD MVP (SECTIONS 103–136)

From Section 103 beside the Yankees bullpen in right-field home run territory, to Sections 120A and 120B behind the plate, and then out to 136 beside the visitors' bullpen in left-center, the Field seats offers consistently solid views. We usually don't have too much difficulty finding compromised sight lines when we visit a new park, especially down the outfield foul lines where the nearside corners often disappear from view, but at Yankee Stadium we struggled to find a seat that didn't have a clear view of the entire field. Even though there's very little foul territory down the lines, pretty much all of fair territory is visible throughout the stands. We were also highly impressed that everyone on the first level sits in a wide cushioned seat. These are easily the most comfortable ballpark seats our fannies have ever nestled into. But be advised, they ain't cheap. Even the home run territory seats cost upwards of $100. If this is beyond your capacity to spend, we recommend visiting the lower bowl right after the park opens to watch forty-five minutes of visitors' batting practice. Then, an hour and fifteen minutes before first

Yankee seating level view

Photo by Josh Pahigian

pitch, the ushers start rounding up the fans who don't have tickets to these lower sections and escorting them to the concourse.

As far as general rules go pertaining to the lower bowl, most sections have between twenty-six and thirty rows. Rows 24 and higher are under the overhang of the second deck. But the obstruction posed by the second deck is minimal. You can still see the flight of most fly balls. If you really can't tolerate any obstruction, though, shoot for Rows 26 and lower to be assured of following the flight of those big league fly balls.

The only place where the overhang is more noticeable is in right-field home run territory Sections 105–107, where the back several rows are wedged under the roof. The first row in these Sections is actually Row 10 and the last is Row 26. You'll want to be in Rows 10–20 to avoid the overhang. Or you can just sit a level higher in Sections 205–207, where you'll enjoy a pure view for half the price. We really liked the view from both of these right-field decks. It's such a shallow right field that we felt like we were right behind the second baseman.

The 200 Level

MAIN (SECTIONS 205–234)

The tucked-in Main level is called a Club Level at many other parks. These aren't the same padded seats from down below, but seat holders enjoy the benefit of the cup holders that appear generously on seat backs throughout the stadium. The slope of the deck is gradual here, as on the first level, to keep fans close to the field. And the views are excellent. The sections have twenty-two rows. If you want to be beneath the overhang of the third deck for insurance against a rainy night, aim for Row 12 or higher. There's really not much of an issue as far as the underhang or overhang detracting from the view. The architects did a great job of layering the decks so as to maximize each tier's potential. If you're worried about seeing the very tops of big league flies, then shoot for Rows 1–17 and eschew the back five rows. But this isn't too terribly necessary. If having the foul pole bisect your view of the infield is going to ruin your night, avoid Sections 207 in right and 233A in left.

BLEACHERS (SECTIONS 201–204, 235–239)

Appearing above the field level seats in home run territory, the second level Bleachers take the form of aluminum benches. These aren't the benches with backs you'll find at some parks. They're just plain metal benches. Making matters worse, nearly a quarter of them provide severely obstructed views due to the protruding presence of the Mohegan Sun Sports Bar, which juts out between the right and left-field bleachers to offer patrons a glassed-in view of the game and open view upstairs. If you're in the left-field Bleachers, avoid Sections 238 and 239 if you'd like to see right field. If you're in the right-field Bleachers, avoid Section 201 and 202 if you'd like to see left field. Heck, we couldn't even see first base from Section 239. These are some of the worst obstructed views we've encountered, all so the high rollers can enjoy the posh comfort of a private club behind Monument Park. To their credit, the Yankees mark these tickets as "obstructed view" and sell them at a steeply discounted rate but still. . . .

There are some good Bleacher seats, though. We really liked right-field Bleacher Sections 203 and 204. They're a good value, considering that most of the other tickets down low cost an arm and a leg.

The 300 Level

TERRACE (305–334)

The uppermost deck's concourse allows folks to walk down some steps to 300 level Terrace Seats or up some steps to 400 level Grandstand Seats. Unlike at some stadiums where the so-called Upper Box seats blend into the Upper Reserved ones and there is little difference between the 300 and 400 levels, there is a very big difference between the two levels at Yankee Stadium. Despite their sharing a concourse, the Terrace seats are much closer to field level. This disparity is due in part to the fact that both levels are very steep, so the Terrace really seems to hang right over the field, whereas the Grandstand quickly rises very high above the game.

If you're afraid of heights or a little unsteady on your feet, you may want to avoid the first row of the Terrace. We visited Yankee Stadium shortly after the incident in Arlington in which a fan fell to his death from the left-field seats. Maybe it was because this sad event was fresh in our minds, but we were both struck by how low the railing and Plexiglas are along the front of the Terrace. It barely came up to Josh's waist and made him feel the way he feels when driving over a high bridge. He wanted to get into the center lane—in this case Row 2—as quickly as possible.

There are seven or eight rows in the Terrace sections. And the sight lines are mostly pure. We found only a minimal loss of the left-field corner—due to the underhang of the deck below and rise of the left-field fence—from

SEATING TIP

Behind the top row of Field seats the Yankees have installed a single row of pavilion-style seats. Holders of these seats actually have high chairs to sit in and a metal shelf on which to plop their drinks or sandwiches. Unfortunately, these folks block the view of the action for Standing Room ticket holders and also for people strolling the concourse. We talked to one fan who bought a Standing Room ticket to the 2011 game in which Derek Jeter recorded his three thousandth hit. The gentleman was pretty dismayed to find that he had to stand behind these high-chair sitters. He said he couldn't see a single thing. Then he said a bunch of other negative things about the Yankees and mentioned in passing that he was a Mets fan. So, we've taken his criticism with a grain of salt and edited out most of it. But he's right, a Standing Room pass doesn't allow you to see much of the game if you camp out atop the first level seats. A better place to stand is atop the bleachers, behind Sections 235–237 in left. This open part of the concourse allows for a clear view of the entire field.

Sections 330–334. Across the diamond, the underhang claims a bit more of the right-field warning track for those sitting in Sections 305–311. But all in all, the architects did well. If you don't believe us, head to Citi Field and walk the upper level, from which vast portions of the outfield seem to disappear. In Section 307, seats marked 7 through 22 face a right-field foul-pole obstruction. In Section 333, fans in seats numbered 13 and higher will have their view bisected by the left-field foul pole.

The 400 Level

GRANDSTAND (SECTIONS 405–434B)

The top deck rises steeply and consists of fourteen rows. Even at the very top we didn't feel too far removed from the game to enjoy it. Rows 5–14 are under a sunroof that offers shade or protection from the rain. In the corners you lose more of the field to the underhang and outfield fence than on any other level. This is especially true in Sections 405 to 411 in right field. It's a tolerable loss, but noticeable on deep flies to right. In Section 407A stay in Seats 1–7 so that the right-field foul pole won't obstruct your view. In Sections 433 and 434A in deep left, the pole is not as much of a factor. We happened to be standing on the stairwell along Section 434B as the National Anthem played and realized the "Stars and Stripes" were nearly close enough for us to reach out and have a touch.

Kevin: Why is everyone looking at us?

Josh: I think they're looking at the flag.

Before/After the Game

Most folks think of the Bronx as the seedy core of the Big Apple. While the "scenery" on the Cross-Bronx Expressway hasn't done much to help this image, the "Rotten Apple Rap" is a bit overblown. We had fun checking out some of the neighborhood bars before our game. And we even headed up the hill into the heart of the South Bronx after the game. We elected to keep our wallets in our front pants pockets as a precaution (and Josh carried a virtually empty "dummy wallet" in his back pants pocket) but at no point did we feel our lives were endangered. If you stick with the pregame and postgame crowd, you'll be fine. If you stumble out of a neighborhood bar at 2:00 a.m. after the other ball fans have departed, well, you might want to carry a dummy wallet.

Getting to Yankee Stadium

Driving to the Bronx means you'll have to deal with New York City traffic. And that's a bit more stress than either of us cares to face. On the plus side, the parking situation is convenient, as spacious lots and garages operate just across 161st Street from Stadium's Gates 4 and 6. Those driving Northbound on Interstate 87 (The Major Deegan Expressway) should take Exit 3 (Grand Concourse and E. 138th Street), Exit 4 (E. 149th Street), or Exit 5 (E. 161st Street). Exit 5 deposits you closest to the park. For Southbound motorists, get off Interstate 87 at Exits 5 or 6 (E. 153rd Street and River Avenue).

A better option that allows you to avoid the traffic and $35 parking charge is to take the Metro's 4 Train to 161st Street. During our return trip to the Big Apple, we found the subway consistently cleaner and friendlier than we remembered it. We observed several attendants sweeping cars and cleaning platforms. We got directions from one of these friendly women, who seemed happy to help us along. Then later, an attendant recommended we change cars at the next stop because he said the AC was working better in the adjoining car. And he was right. The 161st Street Stop is located right in front of the stadium at the corner of River Avenue. It is serviced by not only the 4, but the B Train (weekdays only), and D Train. A trip from midtown Manhattan takes thirty minutes on a 4 local, or twenty on an express. At $2.25 per ride, it's a bargain.

Metro subway map: www.mta.info/nyct/maps/submap .htm

After the game, literally dozens of opportunists line the plaza outside Gates 4 and 6, holding signs that read "Need a taxi?" We opted to just take the train home, but if we were looking to make a speedy getaway, we imagine these folks would have set us up.

If you're heading to the game from Manhattan, consider taking the Yankees water taxi sponsored by Delta. It is a booze cruise up the East River and the cost is only a single dollar to reserve a spot on the boat. It leaves from Wall Street's Pier 11 ninety minutes before the game and makes for a great way to get to the Bronx on a steamy summer's day. It is only one way, though, so you'll have to take the subway back to your hotel afterwards. The spots are limited to 147 people, so it is best to reserve in advance.

Delta Water Taxi Info: www.nywatertaxi.com

Outside Attractions

THE GRAND FACADE

Featuring the same Indiana limestone that composed the regal white arches and towering face of the former Yankee Stadium, the even bigger façade of the Yankees' new yard is really something to behold . . . and marvel and gawk and shake one's head at. It continues nearly all the way around the yard at seven stories high, before dropping down across the outfield so that those inside may enjoy a view of the world beyond the field. With its narrow arches and pristine white glimmer, it evokes royalty.

PLAYER BANNERS

Adorning the façade at street level along River Avenue, banners celebrate the team's current members. You may not find a display for the 25th man, just called up from Trenton, but most of the Yankees are represented here. Each player is recognized with three signs in succession. One shows their number. Another provides a color photo of them. And another displays their name. If you're too cheap to buy a scorebook, this is a good way to brush up on the home team's roster before the game. And along the way you can check out the memorabilia shops beneath the elevated subway tracks along River Ave.

MACOMBS DAM PARK

Many local residents complained at the time of the new Yankee Stadium's opening that the big league park was ready on time while ground had yet to be broken on the promised youth fields that were slated to be built in the stadium neighborhood to replace the ones on which the new Stadium had been built. By the time we visited in 2011, the fields had been laid across from Gate 4 on 161st Street. And boy did they look great. These lie within the footprint of the old Yankee Stadium, bounded by 161st, River Avenue, and 157th. Surveying their lush green lawns and red infields, we recalled the dilapidated youth complex that had existed for years outside the former Yankee Stadium. That eyesore had prompted us to pan the Yankees and their players in the first edition of this book. We chastised the Pinstripes for driving past the pathetic digs on their way to work each day without ever laying out a few bucks to better the lives of the Bronx's big-league-dreaming youngsters. Well, it cost more than a few bucks. And the players didn't step up to the plate to remedy the blight (although we should mention that Curtis Granderson has done a lot to encourage inner city kids to play baseball). The Yankees front office and the City of New York allocated several million dollars to rebuild Macombs Dam Park. The fields are used by local sandlot players, youth leagues, and by the teams of All Hallows High School. As for the giant bat that once welcomed visitors to the old Yankee Stadium, it stands in its original location on the E. 157th Street side of the park.

BABE RUTH PLAZA

Along Yankee Stadium's right-field side on 161st Street, fans pose for pictures beneath the porcelain plaques of Babe Ruth Plaza. Understated placards nearby provide short narratives about the Bambino's career and import to the Yankees. We liked the idea of this plaza, but thought the Yankees could have done a bit more. The two-sided signs offering narratives are nice, but there should be more of them. There are paragraphs titled "A Career of Success," "A Legacy Remembered," and "Murderer's Row." The "Called Shot" one reads:

> *Arguably the most controversial moment in baseball history came during Game 3 of the 1932 World Series against the Chicago Cubs. In the fifth inning Ruth headed to the plate with one home run already to his name. Just before Cubs pitcher Charlie Root hurled a 2-2 pitch, Ruth allegedly pointed to centerfield. He then smashed a long home run toward the area where he had pointed.*

The validity of this story continues to be debated. The world may truly never know if Ruth was calling his shot. Regardless, the moment lives in baseball lore, and at the very least, Ruth's contributions to the Yankees during the 1932 Series helped propel the club to its third World Series sweep in six years.

Josh: How about a statue of the Bambino somewhere here?

Kevin: Then they'd be slighting Gehrig, Mantle, DiMaggio, Ford, Rizzuto . . .

Josh: No, the Bambino was in a class all his own.

Watering Holes and Outside Eats

There are a number of bars and eateries on River Avenue that are more or less interchangeable—a bit seedy and decorated with just enough memorabilia to make them worthy of a look. The several merchandise stores nearby are cleaner and more inviting. For those who don't mind venturing up 161st Street or 164th Street to Gerard Avenue, which runs parallel to River, there is more variety to be found.

Meanwhile, vendors beneath the elevated subway tracks on River sell pretzels, Italian Ice, hot dogs, pork kabobs, honey roasted nuts, and cheap water. Outside the park a bottle of H2O costs $1.00, while inside one costs $5.00. Capitalism, don't you love it? Our favorite vendor is the Fauzia's Heavenly Delights cart, which specializes in Caribbean food, but Fauzia only sets up for day games, so don't bother looking for her if you're visiting the Stadium for an evening affair.

For the record, the Yankees permit each fan to carry one unopened bottle of water into the Stadium, provided that it's thirty-two ounces or less. Isn't that kind of them? And you can carry a sandwich in too.

HARD ROCK CAFE
1 East 161st St.
www.hardrock.com/locations/cafes3/cafe.
aspx?LocationID=538&MIBEnumID=3
Built right into Yankee Stadium beside Gate 6, a Hard Rock Café stays open year-round. This is your safest pregame choice if you're skittish when it comes to exploring the Bronx Zoo.

NYY STEAK
1 East 161st St.
http://nyysteak.com/
Also built into the Stadium, NYY Steak is the place to go if you're wearing a collared shirt and don't mind shelling out $50 for a piece of meat, not counting your sides and beverages. NYY is accessible from the plaza and from inside the Stadium too. There are twenty-seven wines available, in honor of the twenty-seven Yankee championships. And we hear there is a fair amount of memorabilia inside, including a big autograph wall, signed by former and current Yankees.

They wouldn't let us inside, though, because Josh was wearing a ketchup-stained vintage Metallica T-shirt and Kevin was wearing flip-flops. It was probably just as well.

THE YANKEE TAVERN
72 E. 161st St. at Gerard Avenue

Before the Pinstripes' first summer in the Bronx came to a close in 1923, the Bastone family opened a new watering hole on the corner of Gerard Avenue and 161st. It quickly became a popular spot with Yankees fans and players alike. Nine decades later, the Yankee Tavern is still family-owned and still *the* gathering place of choice for serious Yankees rooters. While the younger crowd may prefer the drink-'em-quick bars on River, hardcore fans don't mind heading up the hill to the joint where their fathers and grandfathers used to drink before the game. And we can see why. The walls are plastered with memorabilia, there are several flat-screens tuned to the YES pregame show, and the food is very good. The menu features fried seafood, Italian dishes, and combo meals like the Triple Play (hamburger, hot dog, and french fries) and Batting Fourth (hamburger, hot dog, buffalo wings, and french fries).

CONCOURSE CARD SHOP
62 E. 161st St.

Right next to the Yankee Tavern, this baseball card shop sees steady traffic on game day. Our friend Joey "Bedbugs" Bird spent nearly an hour inside while we sampled the fare next door. We expected him to rejoin us sooner and to be toting a handful of newly acquired cards, but were surprised to see that when he did return he hadn't bought a single thing. "Just looking," he said. "Just ditching us," Kevin replied.

MOLINO ROJO
101 East 161st St.

If you like Cuban and Dominican food, Molino Rojo is a solid bet. We observed several New York City police officers chowing here a few hours before the game. The Cuban sandwich and rice and beans are excellent, especially when you wash it down with an El Presidente beer, but you can also get it to go if you'd like to eat it on the walk to the stadium. We weren't brave enough to try the octopus salad, but our friend Nathan says it's a winner too.

THE DUGOUT
880 River Ave.

This spacious drinking emporium is the best bet close to the Stadium for those wishing to eschew a chain like the Hard Rock. For a dive it ain't half-bad.

STAN'S SPORTS BAR
836 River Ave.
http://stanssportsbar.com/main.html

Many serious Yankee fans swear by Stan's. And even though it's not as close to the main entrance as it was at the old park, they still trek to Stan's for their pregame libations.

BILLY'S SPORTS BAR AND RESTAURANT
856 River Ave.

We like the murals of Billy Martin, Babe Ruth, Mickey Mantle, Joe DiMaggio, and Marilyn Monroe. The beer was ice-cold and the postgame crowd was having a good time

U.S. CHICKEN
860 Gerard Ave.

This little joint is the culinary highlight of Yankee Town as far as we're concerned. And it's dirt cheap. It costs more to get a single hot dog inside Yankee Stadium than to get four pieces of fried chicken, a jumbo order of fries, and a soda at U.S. Chicken. And this isn't any old chicken platter. The bird is tender, plump, and moist. The fries are plentiful. Aside from the scrumptious chicken, we recommend the jumbo shrimp meal. The menu also includes barbecued ribs, pizza, gyros, corn on the cob, and mashed potatoes. The only drawback is there's no seating—just a counter to stand at while you chow. But don't let that scare you off. U.S. Chicken rules!

CROWN DONUT RESTAURANT
79 E 161st St.

With a name that would make Homer Simpson salivate, the Crown is a no-frills sort of place. But the burgers are juicy, the fries come loaded with delicious gravy, and the chicken and waffles are legendary.

MICKEY MANTLE'S RESTAURANT & SPORTS BAR
42 Central Park South
www.mickeymantles.com/

Although it's not in the ballpark neighborhood, serious Yankee fans from out of town may want to visit Manhattan's Mantle tribute restaurant. The mural renderings of Yankee Stadium and Fenway Park are impressive, as are the jerseys worn by players like Mantle, Ted Williams, Jackie Robinson, and others. The in-house souvenir shop offers a diverse selection of memorabilia too. But bring your wallet. The menu isn't cheap, but the experience is a unique one, especially since the once similarly memorabilia-strewn ESPN Zone in Times Square closed its doors a few years back. In case you're wondering, the owners purchased the naming

Yankee Stadium Great Hall

Photo by Josh Pahigian

rights from The Mick in 1989. He visited frequently before his death, but he never owned the joint.

Inside the Stadium
Ballpark Features
THE GREAT HALL

Extending between Gate 4 behind home plate and Gate 6 in right field, the Great Hall runs behind the seating bowl and first level concourse. It features the highest ceilings Josh has ever seen—not just at a ballpark but anywhere. Not counting domes, where else is there a higher lid? This is essentially a concourse behind the concourse and it has seven-story-high ceilings. Kevin wouldn't concede that these were the highest ceilings he'd ever seen, insisting that he'd been to a mall once that offered just as much head room. When pressed for details, though, he couldn't name the city or even the state of said mall. Josh found his friend's reluctance to grant the Yankees highest-ceiling-ever bragging rights a bit immature, but as a fellow Yankee hater, he could see where Kevin was coming from and could quietly admire Kevin's resolve.

Despite our rooting allegiances being firmly set with the Red Sox (Josh) and Mariners (Kevin), we admit that we

looked up in wonder at not only the ceilings but the massive banners of legendary Yankees like Yogi Berra, Reggie Jackson, Lou Gehrig, Thurman Munson, and Babe Ruth. Then we paid our respects to the big color picture of Mr. October on the lower side of Tommy Bahama's bar and grudgingly stepped into the Yankee team store.

THE YANKEE TIMELINE

Once you leave the Great Hall and enter the stadium proper you step onto a concourse that runs atop the first level seats. We recommend walking this level even if you're not sitting at Field Level so you can check out the very nicely done timeline that offers a catalogue of Yankee greatness through the decades. Above the concession counters, it spans the whole first level, displaying black-and-white photos of Yankee players, coaches, fans, and front office execs (read: George Steinbrenner) celebrating the team's many championships. We liked the pictures of players like DiMaggio and Berra in the prime of their youths. Seeing the smiles of pure joy on the faces of Billy Martin and Reggie Jackson as they put their arms around one another to celebrate the 1977 title made us almost happy for them and made us almost not hate them quite so much. Almost.

Josh: If I see one more Yankee picture, shirt, or hat I'm gonna puke.

Kevin: The game starts in 45 minutes. You might see a few more then.

MONUMENT PARK

The normally bright and wide first level concourse gets dark and narrow in left-field home run territory, but there is a light at the end of the tunnel: the entrance to Monument Park. Unfortunately, there is also an insanely long line to wait in for those wishing to access the game's most famous outdoor museum. Monument Park opens each day when the ballpark gates do and closes 45 minutes prior to game time. If you want to visit, you should be waiting at Gate 8 on River Avenue right when it opens (two hours before the first pitch), then you should high-tail it out to the entrance. For those who don't follow this protocol or otherwise can't stand to wait in line, the Yankees have painted the team's retired numbers on the walls of the narrow concourse in this part of the park as a (very) small consolation prize. As for Monument Park, it features the same monuments that adorned the

Monument Park at the old Yankee Stadium, as well as a massive plaque honoring the late Mr. Steinbrenner. At five feet high and seven feet wide, the Big Stein's big bronze dwarfs the two-by-three-foot monuments that honor the Yankees' true immortals, not to mention the plaques of mere Yankee greats. The monuments belong to Ruth, Gehrig, DiMaggio, Mantle, and manager Miller Huggins. There is also a "We Remember" monument recalling the events of September 11, 2001, and the amazing strength the people of New York showed in persevering and supporting one another in a time of unthinkable hardship. We like the monuments and all of the plaques. The retired numbers are nice touches too. But the more spacious Monument Park that existed at the old Yankee Stadium was a little bit more nicely done in our humble (read: non–Yankee fan) estimation.

RETIRED NUMBERS AND STEINBRENNER TRIBUTE

While the Yankees' retired numbers can be spotted on pedestals in Monument Park, they are hard to clearly make out from most parts of the Stadium. For that reason, perhaps, the Yankees also display them on a big blue wall that rises behind the last row of left-field bleacher benches. And in the corresponding location in right field a similar blue wall rises. Only this one is dedicated entirely to George Steinbrenner. It features an artsy-looking black-and-white photo of the Boss's face, with lighting shining on his mug as if he were a saint. Beside the picture the wall reads, "George M. Steinbrenner, 1930–2010. THE BOSS." And yes, "the Boss" is in all caps. We found it curious that all of the great players in Yankee history were allocated the same amount of wall space *combined* as the one and only Mr. Steinbrenner received.

But getting back to the retired numbers, we should mention that the Yankees celebrate the careers of seventeen players with out-of-commission uniform numerals. That's more than any other team in MLB. The retired numbers are: No. 1 for Billy Martin; No. 3 for Babe Ruth; No. 4 for Lou Gehrig; No. 5 for Joe DiMaggio; No. 7 for Mickey Mantle; No. 8 for Yogi Berra; No. 8 for Bill Dickey; No. 9 for Roger Maris; No. 10 for Phil Rizzuto; No. 15 for Thurman Munson; No.16 for Whitey Ford; No. 23 for Don Mattingly; No. 32 for Elston Howard; No. 37 for Casey Stengel; No. 44 for Reggie Jackson, No. 49 for Ron Guidry, and No. 42 for the universally retired Jackie

Robinson. Even though Robinson's 42 is "retired," when we visited in 2011, Yankee reliever Mariano Rivera was still wearing the number, as the last holdout exempted by the Robinson grandfather clause. At the old Yankee Stadium the Yankees didn't, in fact, retire No. 42 when the rest of MLB did in 1997. They merely displayed the initials JR with their retired numbers. But upon opening the new Stadium in 2009, the Yanks hung No. 42 with their other numbers, even though Rivera still wore the digits. No doubt the Yankees will someday have to retire another No. 42 in honor of baseball's most successful closer. But there is precedent for this sort of redundancy. You'll notice there are two 8's already hanging at Yankee Stadium. Berra inherited fellow catcher Dickey's number in 1947 before the Yankees realized Dickey deserved retiree status. Between them, the Hall of Fame backstops hit 560 home runs and played in twenty-five of twenty-eight All-Star games between 1933 and 1962. They both later coached and managed the Yankees. In 1972 their number 8's were simultaneously taken out of commission.

Incidentally, the Yankees were the first team to ever retire a player's number. They made Gehrig's No. 4 the game's first when they paid the "Iron Horse" the ultimate credit in 1939.

Obviously Derek Jeter's No. 2 will also be retired someday. That had been firmly established long before the

Steinbrenner tribute in right field

GEORGE M. STEINBRENNER III

1930-2010

THE BOSS

Photo by Josh Pahigian

Captain became the first Yankee to collect three thousand hits while wearing pinstripes. Jeter did it in style, making number three thousand a homer against Tampa Bay's David Price on July 9, 2011. In so doing, Jeter joined Wade Boggs as the only player to enter the three thousand-hit club with a long ball. Besides Boggs, who got his three-thousandth with the Rays but did play for the Yankees for a time, the other former Yankees to eventually record three thousand safeties have been Rickey Henderson, Dave Winfield, and Paul Waner. Other than Jeter, they all got number three thousand in other uniforms, though.

Besides Jeter and Rivera, it remains to be seen if more recent Yankee heroes like Bernie Williams (No. 51), Jorge Posada (No. 20), and Andy Pettitte (No. 46) will have their Yankee jerseys hung up in perpetuity. Pettitte holds the record for most post-season wins with nineteen. That's no small feat, but it should be noted that he benefited from playing in an era of expanded playoffs. And he admitted to using performance-enhancing drugs. It would be fitting to see Jeter, Rivera, and Posada all retired, seeing as they hold the record for being the trio to play the most seasons together. They were at seventeen and counting at the conclusion of the 2011 campaign.

THE YANKEES MUSEUM

The Yankees Museum is located near Gate 6 on the Main Level. Before the game, a long line forms on the ramp that leads to the doorway. Clearly it's not possible to arrive at the Stadium early to access both Monument Park and the Museum in the pregame hours, since they both have such long lines. Visitors must choose to visit one or the other. The good news, though, is that unlike Monument Park, the Museum stays open all game long. The door attendant with whom we spoke said that the line is always ridiculous before the game but that usually most folks abandon their pursuit when game time arrives. He said the first inning is the best time to visit. Then the line begins to form again as the game wears on. Of course, we didn't want to spend our entire pregame time in line and we didn't want to miss first pitch either. So we decided to wait until later and take our chances. Since we saw a Yankee blowout on a sweltering night, by the seventh inning a lot of fans had headed for the exits. We stopped by the Museum at that late hour and found no line at all.

We waltzed in and had to admit we were impressed by the collection of more than fifteen hundred autographed baseballs of former Yankee players. The big names are represented, like Ruth, Gehrig, and manager Joe McCarthy, as well as the lesser lights, like Butch Hobson, Andy Stankiewicz, Bob

Berra statue in museum

Photo by Josh Pahigian

Wickman, and Matt Nokes. We also liked the paired statues of a squatting Berra and pitching Don Larsen, as the bronze couplet, separated by sixty feet and six inches, pays tribute to Larsen's perfect game in the 1956 World Series against the Dodgers. The home plate in front of the Berra piece serves as a marker, detailing events of the game. Another highlight is the Museum's seven World Series trophies. Why only seven, you ask? Because MLB didn't start awarding a World Series trophy until 1967.

Not surprisingly there is a large exhibit dedicated to the life and times of Steinbrenner. It includes pictures of him from his childhood at Culver Military Academy, pictures from his glory days at the Yankee helm, and all of his World Series rings. There is also an exhibit dedicated to Gehrig. Thurman Munson's locker, which sat unassigned at the old Yankee Stadium from the time of his death until the time of the ballpark's closing in 2008, is also on display. Also notable is a spinning architect's model of the new Yankee Stadium.

TEAM STORES GALORE

There are no fewer than six different merchandise stores inside Yankee Stadium. The biggest is located inside Gate 6 in the Great Hall. And it's open year-round.

The Yankees Women's Store, behind Section 114 A on the first level, hits the spot if you'd like a little pink with your pinstripes.

The Steiner Collectibles Store, also near Section 114, is a rare treat. Steiner is the biggest name going in the collectibles market and it's well-represented with its offerings at the Stadium.

There is also a collectibles stand upstairs, behind Section 211, where old Yankee gloves, autographs, programs, photos, and baseball cards are for sale. Our friend Joey "Bedbugs" Bird was very impressed by the range and relative affordability of items there. While we gaped at the triple-digit prices, he pointed out pieces—like an unused ticket stub to a 1977 World Series game at Dodger Stadium, marked at $125—that he said he could have easily bought and flipped for more money on eBay. This kind of begged the question from us: Well, why didn't he buy it? But we didn't ask.

Another popular shop is the Monument Park Store, located at field level in center field.

JETER AND OTHER "POSE-WORTHY" STATUES

Appropriately placed just outside the Women's store, a life-sized plastic statue of Derek Jeter offers a popular spot for fans to pose for the camera. You can use your own camera. You don't have to pay for a photographer to shoot you like you do if you want to pose with the big fluffy Grover mascot stationed outside the M&M store in Times Square (yeah, we found that lesson out the hard way). Also keep your eyes open when you're walking down Ramp 1, leading to the Great Hall, and you'll see a Mickey Mouse statue decked in Yankee gear and a pinstriped Statue of Liberty.

Josh: And yet, no statue of Mickey Mantle.

Kevin: Hard to believe the Yankees would pick the wrong Mick.

FADED BLUE SEATS

Behind Section 115 are two pale blue seats from the Yankees' previous home. Sitting in these, after earlier watching batting practice from the padded comfort of the seats in right-field home run territory, we were amazed at the difference.

Josh: How did people ever live like this?

Kevin: Makes you kind of want a new Fenway?

Josh: I wouldn't go that far.

GIANT BASEBALL CARDS

Behind Section 217 on a stretch of concourse that's a little darker than the rest of the second level walkway, the Yankees have added some really cool jumbo baseball cards that

reminded Josh of the old Sports Flicks he used to collect in his youth. You remember these: They were 3-D and when you tilted them to the side it would appear as though the players were swinging or delivering a pitch.

Behind Section 200 is another baseball card display. An oversized glass case spins like a slot machine, bringing a new wave of Topps cards into view with every rotation. All of the players are Yankees, of course, but they're not all stars. We observed Randy Velarde, Pat Kelly, Bernie Williams, Tony Kubek, Tommy John, David Cone, and Bucky Dent spinning past.

Jeter statue

Photo by Josh Pahigian

THE TIME AND LOCATION ARE WELL-ESTABLISHED

In a nod to the old analog clocks that appeared at our favorite parks of yesteryear, a rectangular Armitron clock appears high above the field in left, beside giant blue letters that read "Yankee Stadium," lest any visitor to the Bronx think he may have inadvertently taken the 7, instead of the 4, train, and ended up at Citi Field.

FILIGREE AND FLAGS

The ornate metalwork—called filigree or frieze—that rings Yankee Stadium's upper level has been the trademark feature of the Yankees' home park ever since the original "House that Ruth Built" opened in 1923. Pennants inscribed with the city name of each big league team wave in the breeze above this majestic finishing decor, arranged so that the teams of each MLB division appear together. The Red Sox flag in deep right field is red, while the Yankees flag is blue, the Orioles flag is orange, and so on. There are actually quite a few more Yankees flags up there than you might think. That's because the white flags appearing between each division's flags, acting as separators, bear the familiar Uncle Sam top hat and baseball bat that have composed the Yankees' logo since its creation by artist Henry Alonzo Keller in the 1940s.

WORLD CHAMPIONSHIPS REMEMBERED

On the face of the press box and luxury suite level the Yankees display the year of each championship in team history. If you missed the timeline on the first level concourse, this is an opportunity to refresh your knowledge of the Yankees' dynastic dominance right from your ballpark seat.

Josh: I bet it's intimidating to look up from the field and see all those titles.

Kevin: I think that's what they mean when they say "Yankee mystique."

Stadium Eats

Yankee Stadium offers an amazing range of dining options that includes high-end private clubs like the Mohegan Sun Sports Bar behind the batter's eye in centerfield and the Audi Yankee Club on the suite level in left, as well as casual restaurants and bars that any shorts-wearing slob can visit, like the Malibu Roof Deck. We managed to sneak into the Jim Beam Suite on the 300 Level, even though our tickets were outside the Section 317–323 range for which this licensee-only bar is reserved. Actually, we didn't sneak in. The guy working the door was really nice to us. He told us he wasn't supposed to let us in, but that since it was 100

degrees outside, he thought we deserved a little AC too. So he let us pass. We immediately took advantage of the free popcorn, free peanuts, and water, while watching the game on TV. We weren't brave enough to order drinks or food, though. We didn't want to risk getting booted out of the AC.

Aside from the many clubs, bars, and restaurants inside the park, a wide selection of offerings can be found at the concession stands. But buyers should beware: To keep the lines moving (which we observed Yankee Stadium does very well), a lot of the fare is pre-cooked, pre-wrapped, and propped under heat lamps. The effects of this pre-preparation on our Garlic Fries and pizza slice were minimal, while other items—like our hot dog plucked from an eternally spinning set of rollers—suffered more noticeably.

We were impressed by the many comfortable places to sit and eat on the concourse. On the 200 Level, near Gate E, there is an array of wicker chairs and tables that looks almost too nice to be on a ballpark concourse. On the 300 Level behind Section 310, the Malibu Roof Deck provides high bar tables where patrons can catch a breeze on a hot night while sipping a tropical drink and taking in the lights of the Manhattan skyline.

NYY STRIP STEAK (TRADEMARK FOOD)

At $15 it's one of the pricier ballpark treats we've encountered. But you know you're getting quality when you order a New York Strip Steak Sandwich from one of the several NYY stands at Yankee Stadium. This is USDA Prime Beef. It's juicy and delicious. It comes cooked medium-rare, served on a seeded weck roll, loaded with au jus. If you can't afford the ballpark restaurant (Ribeye $52, Strip Steak $50, Lamb Chops $48, Side of Mashed Potatoes $9), or don't have attire appropriate for it in your suitcase, the sandwich at the stand is a great alternative. We suggest having some Nathan's fries on the side.

NATHAN'S HOT DOGS (DOG REVIEW)

Nathan's hot dogs, corn dogs, and crinkle cut fries are served throughout the park. Unfortunately, because the dogs see such heavy sales volume, at most locations they're pre-made and packaged, then placed beneath the dreaded orange lamps. At some locations, they're "cooking" on rollers. Nathan's makes a good dog. But for our money, a dog cooked on an actual grill is a better treat. If you're a dog connoisseur, you should be selective; walk the concourse for a few hundred feet and you will eventually find a New York Grill stand where Nathan's dogs and other cased meat products are being cooked properly. A limited number of stands also serve all-beef Hebrew National dogs. We observed these being taken out of hot water and placed directly into buns as they were ordered. That's kosher as far as we're concerned.

BEST OF THE REST

Just like at Citi Field, all of the food stands show you exactly how many calories each item contains. And as at Citi, this really depressed us. If we're going to eat a bucket of popcorn we'd rather not know that it contains 2,473 calories.

We really enjoyed our stop at the Torrisi Parm Stand in the Great Hall. We rate the hand-carved **turkey sandwich** better than any other ballpark turkey we've come across, and that includes all of the roasted ballpark turkey legs out there in hardball land, including the ones they serve at Malibu Roof Deck upstairs. Torrisi's **Meatball parm** sandwich was also delicious. Don't expect a ton of cheese between your meatball and bun, but rest assured the parmesan and mozzarella is kneaded right into the supple meat.

We liked the **Carolina pulled pork** at the Brother Jimmy's. It was quality meat but a little on the dry side, which made us happy the counter attendant had provided us with two sides of barbecue sauce without our having to ask for it. They also serve **hush puppies, mac and cheese,** and **pulled chicken.**

The **Famiglia pizza** is a cut above the typical ballpark fare. Rather than getting a pre-boxed personal pizza, we opted for a $5.00 slice of hot pie. Some of the stands only have the personal ones, so be sure to rove around a bit. We found actual stands with ovens on every level. We thought the butter-glazed **garlic knots,** served with marinara for dipping, were even better than the pizza. If you're looking for something a little unique after eating knish at Citi the day before, we highly recommend them. Hey, you're in New York, you can be a little knotty!

For the East Coast, the **Garlic Fries** are really superb. They come loaded with herbs and garlic. The smell is so strong that everyone in your section will turn around to see what you're eating. Actually, they'll already know what you're eating. They'll be turning to have a look at them, though. They come in a tray with a fork for those unwilling to make a complete mess of themselves. Josh used the fork, while Kevin used his fingers.

Nathan's **crinkle cut fries** are also very good, though a bit greasier than the fries at the Garlic Fries stands. The **chicken fingers** are better than the usual ballpark chicken. They're real meat, not that preprocessed junk, and the breading is light and not too greasy.

We tried a made-to-order **shredded chicken and rice burrito** from the Latin food stand behind Section 313 and it was excellent. They also serve shredded beef. It took a few minutes for them to fill the tortilla and wrap it, but it was fresh and well worth the wait.

The **chicken kabobs** at the Malibu Roof Deck were very good, but the **jumbo turkey leg** had clearly been on the grill too long.

Hot and sweet **Premio Sausages** are available at New York Grill stands, in addition to **Brats** and **Chorizo.** These are all excellent choices. But be sure to find a stand where they're doing actual grilling, like, you know, on a grill. When it comes to the self-anointed "Roller Grills," say "no, thanks," and walk away.

SAY "NO, THANKS," AND WALK AWAY

After paying $10.75, we were disappointed to see how little steak came in our **Carl's Steak** sandwich. Then we took a bite and thought maybe it was just as well. Either our batch of steak had missed out on the seasoning shaker or they were going for a minimalist approach. Or maybe we'd just been spoiled by the "Shorty's" steak we'd had in Times Square earlier in the day. In any case, we wished we'd paid a few bucks more for a second NYY Steak sandwich instead.

Josh: That's 605 calories I already regret.

Kevin: You didn't have to eat the whole thing.

BALLPARK BREWS

We were dismayed to find that a Bud Light draft costs $11.00 at Yankee Stadium, but slightly happy to find that just about every food stand served beer, unlike at some parks where you have to get in a separate line. We also found a decent selection of better brews available for those willing to spend even more money, including Heineken, Hoegaarden, and Stella Artois.

When Josh ordered a Bud Light, the counter attendant looked at his ID and noted that he had produced a Maine driver's license. She asked if Josh was a Red Sox fan and when he replied in the affirmative, she jokingly replied that she was going to pour him a warm beer.

The roving vendors stop serving two hours after first pitch, but the concession stands keep pouring drafts and popping open bottles until the top of the eighth. The in-stadium bars keep serving long into the night too. So don't dismay when your friendly roving beer man says "last call." It just means you'll have to get off your rump and get the next round yourself.

The Yankee Stadium Experience

We're not sure if it's just a matter of the new yard being so much bigger than the old one or of its acoustics being up to modern code, but we remember the old Yankee Stadium being a lot louder than the new one. We think the new park is a friendlier place, too, than the hallowed pinstriped grounds that earned the "Bronx Zoo" rap. Granted, we were in town for a mid-summer game against the Oakland A's—who aren't exactly one of the Yankees' top rivals—but everyone we encountered was well-behaved and pretty friendly, from the ballpark staffers to our fellow fans. We even observed an attention-seeking Red Sox fan wearing a Jacoby Ellsbury jersey who was only mildly heckled by a group of twenty-somethings in our section. No profanity was used. The worst barbs the Yankee rooters tossed were ones that implied Jacoby was a juicer. Just the same, Josh didn't jump to the Bostonian's defense.

Josh: No sense picking a fight.

Kevin: Would you wear your Boston hat if the Sox were in town?

Josh: Nah, at this place it's best to fly under the radar.

NOW *THESE* ARE FRIENDLY CONFINES

Customer Service Attendants on the concourse hold signs that say, "How may I help you?" We weren't sure what they could do for us, so we asked one.

Kevin: You tell me. What can you offer?

Attendant: Directions to the nearest team store, tips on concessions, assistance if there's a rowdy fan in your section, driving directions for after the game . . .

Josh: You'd do all that for us?

Attendant: All in a day's work.

Kevin: Looks to me like you're watching the game, too.

Attendant: Like I said, all in a day's work.

BE VIGILANT

More than a decade after 9/11, New Yorkers haven't lost sight of the lessons learned on that tragic day in 2001. We think New York and its ballparks and stadiums are friendlier places in the wake of the terrorist attacks that, ironically, brought the city's diverse populations closer together than ever before. A "we're all in this together" sensibility now prevails that just wasn't present in the city before. Being a New Yorker these days also means being vigilant for anything that seems fishy. Accordingly, there are signs posted throughout Yankee Stadium that read, "If you see something, say something. To report any suspicious activity, confidentially text guest services at 69900."

GOD BLESS AMERICA

Singing "God Bless America" in the middle of the seventh inning has been a tradition at Yankee Stadium ever since 9/11 as well. You may recall that every team made the patriotic ditty a staple of its ballpark experience for the remainder of the 2001 season, but the Yankees opted to make the song a permanent part of their game-day experience. For Opening Day, playoff games, and nationally televised games, famous Irish tenor Ronan Tynan usually stops by to do the honors.

Cyber Super-Fans

Although we don't usually spend our time patrolling the web-net for more Yankee coverage than our friends at ESPN.com already provide, we do recommend these excellent fan sites.

- **The Yankee Tavern**
  www.yankeetavern.com/
- **NYY Fans**
  www.nyyfans.com/
- **Pinstripe Alley**
  www.pinstripealley.com/
- **River Ave Blues**
  http://riveraveblues.com/

ROLL CALL (SUPER-FANS)

A showman known as "Bald Vinny" Milano leads a host of happy hooligans in the right-field bleachers in performing the daily roll call. In the top of the first inning, they all stand and honor each Yankee starter by chanting his name until he turns around to acknowledge them with a wave, tip of the cap, or Nick Swisher–style salute. You don't have to sit in the bleachers to get the effect; the whole stadium reverberates with the chorus of player nicknames. Hats off to the Bleacher Creatures for creating and maintaining a special tradition that enables them to interact with the players.

HOME RUN HOOPLA

The outfield video boards combine to offer mock fireworks whenever a member of the home team hits a long ball. We got a kick out of the John Sterling "Swish-i-licious" graphic when the "Son of Steve" connected for a three-run shot into the right-field seats during our game. Then, when Mark Teixeira hit a grand slam an inning later, we chuckled along with the "Nice shooting, Tex!" graphic, even as we realized we were watching a Yankee blowout. The Pinstripes led 14-2 and would go on to win 17-7. Not a good night to be a Red Sox or Mariners fan at Yankee Stadium.

TRAINS AND PLANES

They're higher up than the jets that buzz Citi Field, but planes fly over Yankee Stadium all game long as they blast off from LaGuardia. And just like at the old Yankee Stadium, you can see the elevated subway cars rolling past the stadium through a gap in the right-field seats.

THE SUBWAY RACE

Even if the Yankees don't have a fluffy mascot like practically every team does these days, they have bought into the idea of a nightly stadium race. This takes place on the video board, featuring the orange B train, the blue D train and the green 4 train. The cartoon trains race through Times Square and then into Yankee Country. We saw the 4 win by a nose, and wondered if the 4 always triumphed, since it's the train most commonly used to access the Stadium. Then they posted the season standings and we saw that the 4 had 14 wins, the D had 15, and the B had 14. So, any train is a fair bet.

THE CAP GAME

If you're dismayed to find that most of the hot Rolex dealers and smooth-talking hucksters have been driven from Times Square, you can still get the chance to feel as though you're gambling on a street corner when the nightly cap game takes place on the video screen. Guess which Yankees hat has the ball beneath it and you just might win a few bucks from the near-sighted slob sitting next to you. We bet a beer and Kevin wound up buying for Josh and our friend Joey Bedbugs. It was about time Kevin ponied up for a round anyway!

Sports in the City

The Yogi Berra Museum and Learning Center
8 Quarry Rd., Little Falls, New Jersey
www.yogiberramuseum.org/
In 1996 longtime Montclair, New Jersey, resident Yogi Berra received an honorary doctorate from Montclair State University. Two years later, the school opened a baseball park on its campus named after Yogi, and two years after that the Yogi Berra Museum and Learning Center opened. The museum features plenty of Yankees memorabilia as well as exhibits from the Negro Leagues and interactive exhibits for the kids.

Sports in the City

Babe Ruth's Grave
Cemetery of the Gate of Heaven
Hawthorne, New York
For Bambino fans and those who simply enjoy an occasional graveyard jaunt, this burial yard twenty-five miles north of New York City makes for an interesting excursion. The massive and very scenic cemetery is where Babe Ruth (Section 25, Plot 1115, Grave 3), Billy Martin (Section 25, Plot 21, Grave 3), and MLB umpire John McSherry (Section 44, Plot 480, Grave 3) are laid to rest. You may recall that McSherry died on the field in Cincinnati on Opening Day of the 1996 season. But clearly Ruth's marker is the prime attraction. The Bambino's headstone reads, "May the divine spirit that animated Babe Ruth to win the crucial game of life inspire the youth of America." When we visited, it was adorned by empty beer bottles, pictures of the Babe, pennies, flowers, an American flag, Yankee hats, baseballs, and Yankee Stadium ticket stubs.

Martin's stone contains a quote from the four-time Yankee skipper: "I may not have been the greatest Yankee to put on the uniform, but I was the proudest."

NAME THAT BABY YANKEE

The fans get a kick out of a contest in which they show a Yankee star on the video board and then show four possible baby pictures on the screen. The fans have to guess which picture was the "Baby Bomber." They showed Jeter when we were in town and we all got it wrong. Turns out he was a cute kid.

OLD BLUE EYES IS BACK

A lot of teams have a special local song they play over the P.A. system after the home team wins. It should come as no surprise that at Yankee Stadium, the voice of Frank Sinatra (who was actually from Hoboken, New Jersey) belts out "New York, New York." The tune resonates throughout the stadium at a near eardrum-shattering decibel level as fans head for the exits.

While We Were in New York
We Had a Bedbug Scare

Our return trip to New York City took place more than a year after the well-reported bedbug outbreak of 2010. Nonetheless, the threat posed by the invasive nocturnal nibblers was still prominently placed at the front of Josh's mind as he and his friend Joe Bird rolled into the Big Apple.

Kevin would be meeting us later. A hypochondriac by nature, Josh was only partly to blame for his bedbug worries, though. This is what happened: Prior to the trip, Josh took the lead on getting tickets and booking a hotel and, since Joe was coming along, Joe partook in the decision-making. Or, rather, Joe's wife Carol did. Now, it should be mentioned that Carol is a lovely woman . . . a saint, actually, for putting up with Joe, who is not so quietly engaged in Stage Two of a five-stage plan he's concocted to turn their otherwise tasteful Bellingham, Massachusetts, home into a Red Sox autograph shrine. Joe has already "decorated" his office and their bedroom and is working his way down the stairs toward the living room. Aside from being a supportive wife, though, Carol is also a bedbug alarmist of the highest order and her fear of the critters infected Josh. You see, when Josh originally booked a room at a venerable Times Square hotel at a surprisingly discounted rate, Carol's response to Joe was, "You can go, but if you stay there I'm burning all your luggage when you get home and you're sleeping in the backyard for the rest of your life." As Carol sagely pointed out, Josh's pick had five complaints against it on an Internet bedbug registry. And a stay there would have in all likelihood been disastrous.

So, we cancelled our original booking and opted for a more recently constructed hotel—a Red Roof Inn—within walking distance of Citi Field in Flushing. Upon arriving, we were dismayed to bump into an exterminator at the front desk. He was toting a pump and hose and had evidently just finished whatever business he had at the Red Roof, because the attendant at the desk was signing his digital device to verify he'd completed a spray.

"We're definitely not mentioning this to Carol," Joe said.

"Wait till Kevin hears," Josh replied.

So, Josh and Joe checked in and proceeded to turn both of their beds inside out looking for blood-stained excrement on the mattress as Carol had advised, and/or for a nest behind the headboard. Joe disassembled the beds with a ratchet set he had brought just for the

purpose. No evidence was found, though. The Red Roof was clean.

Upon arriving that night, Kevin shrugged off the concern. "Bedbugs, schmedbugs," he scoffed. "You East Coasters are so uptight."

Fast-forward two days and two games. Despite July temperatures that surpassed 100 degrees Fahrenheit both days, we stomped all over the city. We also caught a two-hour National League game, and a four-hour-plus American League game. After the marathon in the Bronx, we returned to our rooms at 1:00 a.m., at which time Josh just happened to notice about a dozen red marks—that looked a lot like bites—on both of his ankles.

"That's heat rash," Kevin said immediately. "I've had it before. Take a cold shower and it'll be gone by the time we check out."

But Joe and Josh wouldn't hear it. In their minds, they had to be bedbug bites.

"Carol's never gonna let me come to New York again," Joe lamented.

"Help me open this window," Josh rejoined. "I'm gonna heave my luggage off the balcony. Then tomorrow I'll go to Target and buy new clothes to wear home."

"East Coasters," Kevin said dismissively. Then he went to his own room to bed.

While Joe and Josh spent two hours making use of the hotel's WiFi, researching bedbug bite pictures and decontamination protocol, Kevin snored away in the adjoining room. Then Joe and Josh caught a few fitful hours of sleep on the floor.

The next morning, Kevin was refreshed. Josh and Joe were haggard, but they were all smiles too. Overnight Josh's "bedbug bites" had pretty much disappeared. In the end, his affliction turned out to be a heat rash after all.

But just the same, you should probably check out the bedbug registry before booking your room in New York City. You can access the list of previously infected hotels at: http://bedbugregistry.com/.

TORONTO BLUE JAYS, ROGERS CENTRE

TORONTO, ONTARIO
230 MILES TO DETROIT
290 MILES TO CLEVELAND
320 MILES TO PITTSBURGH
330 MILES TO COOPERSTOWN

A Dome with a View

Back when new ballparks were opening at a clip of one or two per year in the 1990s and early 2000s, it must have seemed to each baseball owner that all they needed to do was convince their local officials to pony up a friendly financing deal for a new yard and a future of ever-increasing revenue and ravenous fan support would be assured. At the time, of course, the US economy was humming along, or at least seemed to be, as Americans plunked down credit cards to fund lavish lifestyles that included far-reaching baseball tours that brought them to cities like Baltimore, Toronto, and even Cleveland, where new parks served as the centerpieces of urban renaissances. The hapless Indians sold out 455 games in a row at Jacobs Field. The Orioles' Camden Yards was revealed as *the* display model for those seeking to bring retro-ballpark comfort and funk to their own cities. And the Toronto Blue Jays attracted more than four million fans per season (or a whopping fifty thousand per game!) while winning back-to-back World Series at the celebration of modern architecture known at the time simply as "SkyDome." While we are thankful for the new generation of stadiums this boom-time brought us, we wonder if baseball's owners ever stopped to consider how long (or short) the shelf life for some of their new yards might be. You see, somewhere along the way the owners started to take it for granted that all they needed to do was open the gates to their sparkling new digs and the fans would continue coming indefinitely. But as each one opened, the competition for travelers' dough became fiercer. Fans suddenly had *many* new yards to visit, not just a handful. And many owners lost sight of their fan bases—their home folks—and neglected the necessity of putting a winning team on the field. That's why the Pirates never parlayed beautiful PNC Park into a sustainable attendance surge and why the Orioles and Indians fell rapidly from the top of baseball's annual attendance heap to the bottom. And it's why Toronto has reverted to being a second-class baseball city once again, despite the promise it seemed to hold in the 1990s. The work-stoppage of 1994, which came when the Jays were two-time defending World Champs, and baseball's abandonment of that other Canadian outpost, in Montreal, had a lot to do with the decline in many casual Canadian baseball fans' interest in the American Game.

Today, no Major League stadium provides as great an example as Rogers Centre does of a city's flailing baseball interest. Today, the Blue Jays struggle to draw half as many fans as they did when SkyDome was still a shiny new bastion of modern technology, and more importantly, the Jays were winning AL East titles.

As for the question as to why the stadium now known as Rogers Centre has lost its luster in the eyes of traveling fans, the answer involves the inevitable, but perhaps at the time of its construction unforeseeable, evolution of our ballpark preferences as fans. When Toronto unveiled its revolutionary facility midway through the 1989 season, many observers believed it would forever change the course of ballpark construction. And for a while it looked like they were right. At a time when many multi-purpose "cookie-cutter" stadiums were still in use, Toronto proclaimed its field capable of hosting professional baseball, football, and basketball. Not only was its stadium the biggest, baddest dome on the continent, but it came complete with a retractable roof. On nice days, fans would enjoy outdoor baseball (albeit, played on a rug). And on crisp Canadian nights, they'd enjoy indoor ball. The future had arrived and for once Canada seemed to be leading the way. It must have been a pretty good feeling, especially when road trippers from around the world made SkyDome one of the hottest new tourist destinations of the early 1990s. Just how in love with SkyDome were baseball's fans? Josh recalls one popular sports-radio host in Boston calling for a "retractable roof stadium on the South Boston waterfront just like SkyDome" over and over again. Not just for days, but for years. And the guy wasn't tarred and feathered for daring to suggest Fenway should be replaced by such an ultra-modern facility. In fact, he had quite a following of like-minded thinkers.

With a successful team on the field, the Blue Jays set new American League attendance records four years running. For the first time ever, Torontonians could say their local nine played at the most popular stadium in North America. And baseball, which had seemed destined to forever play second fiddle in the Great White North to hockey and bigger-field football, seemed ready to compete for Canadians' fancy. Torontonians loved their team and perhaps loved Sky-Dome a little more. What the good folks in Ontario didn't realize, however, was that back in the States the fickle winds of change were a-blowin' and they were about to shift in a completely different direction. The ballpark designers in Baltimore had a new vision, or rather, a retro-y new vision. And it was about to set dome-lovers everywhere on their ear. Oriole Park at Camden Yards opened three years after Sky-Dome, and as word of its delights spread, other cities across the United States began planning smaller, more intimate ballparks like the ones that ruled supreme during baseball's glory years. Nosebleed seats, artificial turf, concrete construction, and symmetrical field dimensions fell out of favor as real grass, steel and brick, and quirky outfield nooks and crannies returned to their rightful places in ballparks from Seattle to Philadelphia.

"But we still have a retractable roof!" Canadians cried. "Let's see you top that." And top it the crafty Americans did. In the lower forty-eight, new ballparks sprang up offering the same safeguard against inclement weather as Sky-Dome, while also featuring full dirt infields and natural grass. In other words, these parks offered outdoor baseball, even when their lids were on. The good-hearted Canadians had been foiled by their North American allies again.

Kevin: That was after losing William Shatner to American TV, Jim Carrey to Hollywood, Shania Twain to Dollywood, the Nordiques to Denver, the Jets to Phoenix . . .

Josh: And your point is?

Kevin: They're pretty good friends to endure all the crap we put them through.

After losing a chance to three-peat when the 1994 World Series was canceled, the Blue Jays experienced a prolonged currency crisis as a weak Canadian dollar prevented them from competing for top free agents for several years. The fact that the Jays' division included the two wealthiest teams in baseball also contributed, no doubt, to the growing disillusionment of Toronto fans. And before long, many of the converts to the American Game had soured on it.

They said, "We've got hockey and curling. And three-down football! The Jays, well they can just take off, eh?" And so, sadly, the Jays now play before a 60-percent-empty Rogers Centre, struggling to draw two million fans per season.

Upon entering Rogers, fans will be impressed by the sheer size of it, even in comparison to the other retractable roof stadiums. But once the game begins, it is hard to overlook how far removed the Rogers experience is from the pleasure of enjoying a game at an idyllic American ballpark. It seems almost fitting by the time the later innings roll around that the Blue Jays kick off the seventh-inning stretch with a song other than "Take Me Out to the Ball Game." But fans should not forget the important contribution this

exterior

Photo by Kevin O'Connell

stadium did make to the evolution of ballpark design. Prior to its existence, the only retractable roof facility in big league history was Montreal's Stade Olympique, which eventually became a fixed dome due to its roof's mechanical failure, and then later, became an open-air park when the roof was removed. Fans in cities like Seattle, Phoenix, Houston, and Milwaukee who are thankful their respective roofs retract should remember Rogers Centre. And they should pay it a visit. In fact, every fan should. In archaeology, they may still be searching for the missing link. But in ballpark construction, we know right where it is: on the shores of Lake Ontario in downtown Toronto, which we might add, is one hip city.

From the outside, Rogers is too big to photograph—unless your lens is as wide as Barry Bonds' noggin. By the time you step far enough away to fit the whole structure in your frame, another building has inevitably blocked your view. Best to buy a postcard. And aren't domes usually round or at least ovular? Rogers looks like a concrete block. Leave it to the Canadians to make a square dome. We don't mean to disparage our fair friends to the north. Canada is a wonderful and peaceful nation with whom we are proud to share a border. It's just that the Jays entered the American League the same year as Kevin's beloved Mariners, and while Toronto was winning back-to-back World Series, the M's were still in search of back-to-back winning seasons. It's pure jealousy that prompts Kevin to kid. As for Josh, he's angry there hasn't been a *Strange Brew II*. On this point, Kevin agrees.

Inside Rogers the atmosphere resembles that of older-generation domes like the Metrodome and Kingdome, but on a much grander scale. The Astrodome was eighteen stories high. Rogers is thirty-one, which situates its roof nearly three hundred feet above the field. The extra space leaves room for five levels, several restaurants, and seventy hotel rooms that overlook the outfield.

Kevin: A hotel *inside* the ballpark. What would Ty Cobb say to *that*?

Josh: Umm . . . how the heck should *I* know?

Kevin: You really don't get the concept of rhetorical questions, do you?

Josh: I'm not sure. I suppose . . .

Kevin: Never mind.

As for the roof, it doesn't open all the way, but exposes about 90 percent of the seats to the sky when peeled back. Only the seats in center field remain under the hood—which consists of four panels, three movable and one stationary. When the roof retracts, the panels stack up on top of one another. Together they weigh twenty-two million pounds!

In 1995, two thirty-pound roof tiles fell during a game, injuring seven fans, but for the most part the roof has functioned well and left few injured fans in its wake. It takes about twenty minutes to open or close. If you're in town on a nice day and you want to see this phenomenon, arrive a couple hours before the game and wait for it to retract. Or better yet, time your visit to the CN Tower next door so you can look down as the roof slowly uncovers the field. It's really something to see.

The dome opened in June 1989, after Exhibition Stadium had served as the Blue Jays' roost from the time the team joined the American League as an expansion franchise in 1977. A longtime football facility, Exhibition Stadium was modified to accommodate 43,737 baseball fans. It had artificial turf and was famous for its damp and chilly conditions beside Lake Ontario. It was not laid out well for baseball. The Grandstand roof covered the seats in left-field home run territory but not the ones around home plate, and some of the seats were more than eight hundred feet from home plate. Forget about bringing binoculars to the game. Fans needed telescopes to see the action from some of the seats.

Aside from the wind gusts, snowstorms, biblical rains, and flocks of dive-bombing seagulls that often thwarted the Jays' hopes of playing ball during this era, the general shoddiness of Exhibition Stadium worked against the Jays as well. But sometimes their familiarity with the stadium's flaws and its potential pitfalls worked in their favor. In 1977, for example, Baltimore manager Earl Weaver pulled his team off the field in the fifth inning, claiming that the loose bricks holding down the tarps on the bullpen mounds in foul territory posed a hazard to his outfielders. Amazingly, the Jays were declared winners by forfeit. But the fans, no doubt, went home feeling ripped off. And the Orioles had the last laugh. While the last-place Jays won only fifty-four games that year, the second-place O's won ninety-seven.

In 1983 the Major League players, or at least one of them, struck back against this unwelcoming lakeside environment when Yankees right fielder Dave Winfield beaned a seagull with a warm-up toss that was intended for a ball boy. Canadians and environmentalists were furious but Winfield escaped the country without doing hard time. And a decade later he fully buried the hatchet with Torontonians, returning to play for the 1992 World Championship Jays.

The Ex was finally demolished at age fifty in 1998, shortly after the Blue Jays threatened to return to it if a new lease couldn't be hashed out with the dome's ownership. Later, to solidify the team's presence indoors (sort of),

Rogers Communications, which already owned the Blue Jays, bought the dome from Sportsco International. The deal went down in 2005, pricing the dome at a meager $25 million. To put that in perspective: The original cost of building the facility was $578 million.

Kevin: Well, that explains why my carved turkey sandwich cost $12.

Josh: Kevin, Kevin, Kevin . . . you still don't understand how the exchange rate works. . .

Kevin: You mind explaining it again?

Josh: Or I could just hold your wallet, like we did last time we visited Toronto.

interior

Photo by Kevin O'Connell

As for memorable dates in SkyDome/Rogers Centre history, the 1991 All-Star Game was played in Toronto, and, fittingly, for the first time ever, two Canadian pitchers went home with decisions. Toronto's Jimmy Key got the win and Montreal's Dennis Martinez took the loss, as the American League prevailed 4–2. Of course, neither was *really* a Canadian, but then again, don't we think of Neil Young as an American? So, we'll let them have those two. It's a pretty fair trade-off.

The very next year the dome hosted the first World Series games played outside the United States and the Jays claimed their first title, beating Atlanta four games to two. Key and reliever Duane Ward earned two wins apiece in the Series.

In 1993 Toronto made it back-to-back titles, beating Philadelphia in six games. Joe Carter ended that Series with a memorable walk-off homer against Mitch Williams.

The Canadian Football League's Argonauts have won four Grey Cups since moving to the dome (1991, 1996, 1997, and 2004). To facilitate an easy conversion from baseball to football, the field-level seats are on tracks, allowing them to be rolled away. And the pitcher's mound is on a hydraulic lift, allowing it to be lowered beneath the field. And there are never any of those unsightly football lines lingering on the baseball field, since the baseball turf is unzipped and replaced with football turf when conversion takes place.

Trivia Timeout

Baby Blue: Name the first player to hit a home run into Rogers' fifth level.
True Blue: Which future NBA All-Star once played for the Blue Jays?
Deep Blue: Name the five men enshrined in both the National Baseball Hall of Fame *and* the Canadian Baseball Hall of Fame. *Look for the answers in the text.*

NFL football has found a home in Toronto too, albeit through a backdoor. Since 2008, the Buffalo Bills have played two regular season "home" games at Rogers per season, in a testament to how crappy the facilities are at the Bills' Ralph Wilson Stadium. It remains to be seen whether the Bills will move to Toronto permanently, but it will not surprise us if they do when their current two-games-a-year deal with Rogers Communications expires in 2013.

The NBA's Toronto Raptors played their home games at the dome from 1995 to 1998, before moving to the Air Canada Centre.

Many musical groups have also played the dome, ranging from Kevin's beloved Three Tenors to Josh's hometown favorites, the New Kids on the Block. Other, more currently relevant acts that have packed the dome include Madonna, U2, Radiohead, Bon Jovi, the Rolling Stones, Sting, and Canada's own Avril Lavigne.

Getting a Choice Seat

Visiting the dome today, it's hard to believe the Jays set single-season attendance records four years running from 1990 through 1993. Back then they were averaging fifty thousand fans per game. But the last time they averaged even thirty thousand was 1998. So, until the Jays get good again and Torontonians suddenly rediscover their love of baseball, there's no need to order tickets in advance. Even if you're angling for primo seats, you'll be better off haggling with the scalpers than paying full price for tickets.

100 Level

The first level offers Rogers' only concourse from which fans can watch the game while waiting in line for food. There are forty-two rows of seats beneath this concourse, and the ushers check tickets rather frequently in this lower bowl to thwart seat-hoppers. The best lower-level infield seats reside in Sections 115 (at first base) through 127 (at third). If you're angling for a plate-view then shoot for Sections 119–124 of the so-called Premium Dugout Boxes. These seats are a good value. A comparably close-to-the-plate seat costs more than twice as much in Boston (and that's twice *face* value; the real price on the scalper market in Boston is much higher) and more than five times as much in New York. The Field Level Base seats are also a good deal, especially if you aim for Section 114 or 128.

Farther down the lines, we preferred the Field Level seats on the left-field side (129, 130a, 130b, 130C) to the ones in shallow right, since they offered views of the roof and CN Tower.

Be careful to avoid the back rows of Sections 119 through 121 on the first-base side, as the overhanging second deck presents an obstruction. As long as you stay in Rows 1 through 30 this is not a problem.

The first level outfield seats are quite a bit higher up than the infield ones and are plagued by their own overhang. Avoid Rows 7–13 of Sections 101–108 in right and of Sections 135–142 in left. The good news is that the foul

Seating Capacity: 49,539
Ticket Office: http://mlb.mlb.com/ticketing/index.jsp?c_id=tor
Seating Chart: http://toronto.bluejays.mlb.com/tor/ticketing/seating_pricing.jsp

poles won't block your view since they're made of see-through yellow mesh.

200 Level

If you thought the overhang was bad on the first level, wait until you get upstairs where the third deck creates a grievously low overhang and the deck beneath your feet creates an equally unpalatable obstruction. The effect is almost like watching a game on TV.

Kevin: Hey, at least it's wide-screen.

Josh: We drove seven hundred miles to sit where we can't even see the trademark roof.

Kevin: Umm . . . I think the roof's retracted.

Josh: Are you sure?

Kevin: Well, no.

Josh: My point, exactly.

From the outfield seats on this level we couldn't see the warning track on our side of the field. And from the back rows we couldn't see much of anything due to the support structures at the rear of the level. In Sections 204–206 and 242–246, especially, stay in Rows 1–6 to avoid this lousy design flaw.

Behind the plate, the 200 Level houses club seating in Sections 222–226, while along the baseline seats are available for purchase by non-VIPs or Not Very Important Persons, if you will. These seats cost just a few dollars less than ones on the first level where the views are much better. If you're going to travel all the way to Toronto to watch a ballgame, buy yourself a first level seat. You can walk upstairs before the game to check out the view, and then thank us later.

500 Level

Because the 300 and 400 Levels consist of private boxes, hotel rooms, and restaurants, the third seating level is the 500 Level. Yes, we know, this is a bit confusing. What's more, each section has a separate entrance ramp on this level, and each ramp creates an obstruction. But take heart, this level is so sparsely populated that should you choose to sit up here, simply for the sake of gaining entrance for the meager price of $11, you'll be able to relocate to a seat with a better view.

Every row in the 500 Level has its own railing in front of it. This minimizes the still-lingering feeling that you may, at any moment, stand up out of your seat to get a hot dog or visit the bathroom and suddenly lose your balance and plummet to your death from this exceptionally high and steep ballpark seating area. The personal railings allow the Blue Jays to take the concept of "stadium seating" to the extreme. Once seated, your feet will be down around the shoulders of the fans directly in front of you. The incline keeps all of the seats relatively close to the airspace above the field. But, man, are these seats high up. And the only ones that allow a full view of fair territory are in Sections 518–533. Avoid entirely Sections 504–508 in right, due to the underhang that blocks much of right field. In left, avoid all seats beyond Section 538. All the way around the upper tier, beware of seats higher than Row 22 because they may be obstructed by the light supports.

Josh: Is it me, or do the lights here seem really low?

Kevin: I think we're just up really high.

Because there were so few fans in the upper level when we visited, we found very few open concession stands on the concourse. Those that were open only offered the basics. Making matters worse, a 500 Level ticket does not allow access to the field level concourse, with its more expansive menu.

If nothing else, the fifth deck provides a landing spot for what are automatically deemed epic home runs. About

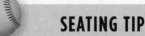

SEATING TIP

Here's a tip you can use at any stadium at which you feel entitled to a free upgrade. When you see an open seat down low, don't just go charging toward it. Instead, wait until at least the bottom of the second inning and then visit a concession stand first. Load up your arms with a cardboard tray full of food. Balance your soda precariously against your body, and clutch your ticket stub between ketchup-smeared fingers. Then, head confidently toward "your" seat, looking as though you know exactly where you're headed. At least 75 percent of the time the ushers will watch you walk right past them, assuming you're just a late-arriving fan or one who went on a food-run with a legit claim to the seat you're annexing.

ten players have reached the fifth deck as of this book's press time. Oakland's Jose Canseco was the first, doing so in Game 4 of the 1989 American League Championship Series. Later sluggers to accomplish the feat have included Shawn Green, Joe Carter, Mark McGwire, Manny Ramirez, and Jayson Werth.

The Black Market

Scalpers present a drain on revenues for the Jays since they dole out extras and leftovers below face value. Hey, when the park's two-thirds empty, what does a team expect? With just a small amount of haggling, we scored two 200 Level tickets for the price of one. Then, once inside, we seat-hopped down in the first level. The ushers were pretty sly but we were slier.

Before/After the Game

Toronto is a cosmopolitan city with a whole heck of a lot going on and many cultural influences contributing to its personality. Despite the tongue-in-cheek humor we may poke at Canada and its citizens in this chapter, the truth is we found Toronto exceptionally fun, affordable, and visitor-friendly. The people we encountered were good-humored and spoke a dialect of English similar enough to our own that we managed to avoid confusing peameal bacon with side bacon when ordering breakfast.

Rogers is not far from the Lake on the border of the Theatre District, where there are plenty of places to eat and drink. So do partake. Toronto is also home to a lively club scene. On a street corner not far from Rogers, we picked up a copy

gargoyles

Photo by Kevin O'Connell

of the free local entertainment guide known as *Eye Weekly*. Wow, was it ever an eye-opener. Not only did it list everything from alternative concerts to jazz clubs to independent films playing in the city, but it contained advertisements galore for phone sex and other adult entertainment opportunities. It was quite the little publication.

Kevin: Why didn't I visit this place back when I was in college?

Josh: Probably because the Jays were playing at a dilapidated football stadium then.

Getting to Rogers Centre

Since 2009, all US citizens traveling to Canada need a passport or NEXUS card. This is something you need to do before leaving on your trip. You may apply for a NEXUS card, which costs $50, by visiting the US Customs and Border Patrol's Global Online Enrollment System at: https://goes-app.cbp .dhs.gov/.

Now that we've made you aware of that important trip-planning detail, let us tell you how to find the dome. From the south, take the QEW/Gardiner Expressway to the Spadina Avenue Exit. Rogers is visible even before the exit, so don't worry about being taken by surprise. Follow Spadina north for a block, then turn right onto Bremner Boulevard, which leads to nearly twenty thousand underground parking spots. If you get lost, look for the CN Tower (visible from just about anywhere in Toronto) and drive toward it.

Ballgame parking costs between $15 and $30 at most lots, but one on Front Street charges just $10, as does one on Blue Jay Way (wasn't that a Beatles tune?) between Front and Wellington.

The subway is also a solid option for those staying overnight in the city. Union Station on the Yonge-University-Spadina line is only a few blocks from Rogers.

Subway Map: www3.ttc.ca/Subway/interactivemap.jsp

Outside Attractions

THE CN TOWER
www.cntower.ca/

Beside Rogers stands the tallest free-standing structure in North America, the CN Tower, which rises 553.33 meters, or 1,815 feet, from the ground. The tower, which was classified as one of the Seven Wonders of the World by the American Society of Civil Engineers in 1995, serves as both an important telecommunications center and a tourist attraction. Each year more than two million people visit to take in the stunning views from its observation deck. For the record, it's not even close to being the tallest man-made structure ever.

The Tower of Babel . . . oh, wait . . . make that the Burj Khalifa, which opened in Dubai in 2010, rises an astounding 828 meters. Still, the CN is well worth a visit. It was designed in the early 1970s to remedy the atrocious television reception local residents were experiencing as a result of a construction boom that had rendered Toronto's pre-existing TV stanchions too short to contend with the city's many altitudinous buildings. The tower was completed in 1976. Much to their chagrin, however, Torontonians soon discovered there was nothing good on Canadian TV anyway. Just hockey, bigger-field football, and occasional late-night skin flicks. Thankfully, the advent of cable was just around the corner.

Today the CN Tower serves as a communications hub for several television and radio stations. It also houses restaurants, an arcade, a movie theater, and tourist shops.

A trip to the SkyPod, 147 floors above ground level, costs just $28.

HIPPO TOURS
www.torontohippotours.com/

If you'd like to see the city by land and sea, take a Hippo Tour on one of the amphibious busses that float and drive around Toronto. We thought about it, before opting to sit this one out. There were just too many kids barking, or making whatever noise it is a hippopotamus makes. And besides, after Kevin got seasick during our short water-taxi ride in Baltimore we saw no sense courting another nautical disaster after a lunch heavy on the poutine.

LEGENDS OF THE GAME
322 King St.

Just a block from Rogers sits one of Canada's largest sports collectibles stores. With everything from trading cards and autographs to jerseys and gear, this is a great shop. We were impressed by the rich collection of hockey memorabilia (duh) and the surprising amount of Muhammad Ali artifacts.

SIGN ON THE DOTTED LINE (OR SWEET SPOT!)

After games, visiting players exit Rogers through Gate 5, where they wait for taxis or start their walk to the visiting team's hotel. On getaway days, however, the players take a bus from inside the dome straight to the airport, so don't bother waiting after the last game of a series.

THE ROGERS CENTRE TOUR
www.rogerscentre.com/about/tours.jsp

We took the Rogers tour and found it average. Our lukewarm feelings may stem in part from the fact we were unable to walk on the field because the visiting team was taking extra batting practice on the day we visited. We did get to run our greedy fingers through a small piece of turf, though. For the record, the Rogers turf currently consists of a new generation-type of Astroturf called Game Day Grass 3D. From 2005 through 2010 it had been FieldTurf, which was similar to the shag they have in Tampa Bay. And before that it had been an earlier generation Astroturf. We also enjoyed seeing the extensive collections of Exhibition Stadium and Argonauts memorabilia in the luxury boxes.

The tour began with a mildly interesting video about the construction of the dome. We wish we could provide details on this, but as soon as the tape started rolling, Josh fell asleep and Kevin struck up a conversation with a nice man named Bill from Buffalo.

THE STEAM WHISTLE BREWERY TOUR
255 Bremner Blvd.
www.steamwhistle.ca/tour/tourInfo.php
We never pass up the opportunity to take a brewery tour. And you shouldn't either. Taking this one couldn't be any easier. Steam Whistle is located in the big round building right next-door to Rogers. We recommend the Souvenir Tour, which costs just $10, and includes a Pilsner sample and a souvenir glass.

THE HOCKEY HALL OF FAME
161 Bay St.
www.hhof.com/
You're in Canada. So go to the hockey hall, you hoser! It's located just a few blocks from Rogers.

A self-proclaimed "smooth stick-handler," Kevin enjoyed sending a few wrist shots on goal in the interactive area, while Josh stared longingly for several minutes at Lord Stanley's Cup. Next, Josh checked out the full-scale replica of the Montreal Canadiens' dressing room. Then he hip-checked Kevin into the wall, just because the spirit moved him.

Kevin: What the heck'd you do that for?

Josh: I thought you wanted to get interactive.

Watering Holes and Outside Eats
Not surprisingly, the streets surrounding Rogers Centre have been developed with American tourists in mind. Familiar chain restaurants abound. But with a little extra effort, road trippers can do better. Plenty of saloons and eateries—many with patio or rooftop seating areas—reside on and around King Street, between the dome and Theatre District. Our recommendation is to sample a pregame hot dog from one of the Shopsy carts outside, eat light (read: only one or two items) at the game, and then go out for dinner afterwards.

REAL SPORTS BAR AND GRILL
15 York St.
www.realsports.ca/index.php?option=com_content&view=frontpage&Itemid=55
A festive atmosphere. A two-story high-def TV screen. A menu featuring delights like the cheeseburger spring roll. What more could you want? What's that? Hot-body waitresses? Well, Real Sports satisfies that fan need too.

GRETZKY'S
99 Blue Jays Way
www.gretzky.com/restaurant/
Wayne Gretzky's restaurant is appropriately located at 99 Blue Jays Way. "The Great One," you surely remember—unless you were born on Mars—wore uniform No. 99 during his illustrious NHL career.

A sign on the front of the trendy sports pub says, "Eat your face off." We found this rather clever, in a Canadian sort of way. With table hockey for the kids, a souvenir shop, and memorabilia chronicling Wayne's rise to greatness, this is a solid pick for a pregame or postgame meal. After all, he was and still is "the Great One."

CROCODILE ROCK
240 Adelaide St.
www.crocrock.ca/
Here's your chance to play a little air guitar and stomp around in your sneakers while chubby chicks with smoker's cough angle for drinks. When you tire of the old-school soundtrack, pay a visit to the beer garden. On Friday and Saturday nights expect to find a line outside.

LOOSE MOOSE TAP AND GRILL
146 Front St.
www.theloosemoose.ca/
Specializing in providing burgers and pints to raucous twenty-somethings, the Moose's slogan is "Eat like a King, then party like a rock star!"

Kevin: You have to appreciate a place with such bohemian aspirations.

Josh: I knew a girl in college whom everyone called a "loose moose."

Kevin: Oh no, you're not going to start telling Holy Cross stories. . . .

CRAFT BURGER
573 King St.
www.craftburger.com/
As much as we enjoyed Loose Moose (Okay, we'll be honest: We included it just because it brought back fond memories

for Josh), we enjoyed Craft Burger even more. You won't find a finer patty in Toronto than the ones at Craft. Be sure to order yours with a side of poutine (french fries topped with Ontario cheese curds and gravy). Kevin also recommends the old-fashioned milk shakes.

IRISH EMBASSY PUB AND GRILL
49 Yonge St.
www.irishembassypub.com/irish/home.html
Those looking for an elegant place to revel in Celtic pride and Irish cuisine while watching the game will find the Embassy and its Dublin Lounge quite to their liking. With a mahogany bar and leather chairs, its atmosphere is a cut above Gretzky's and the other pubby places closer to the dome. But the Embassy still has those 50-inch plasma screens fans require. We found menu items such as the Irish Stew, Kilkenney Battered Haddock, and Shepherd's Pie reasonably priced too.

PAPA CEO'S PIZZA
656 Spadina Ave.
www.papaceopizza.com/
At the other end of the fine-dining spectrum, we encourage fans to enjoy some late-night gourmet pizza after working up an appetite at the bars. If this favorite hangout of local university students doesn't live up to expectations—and we're betting it will—you can head next door and try a slice at Papa's longtime rival, Cora's.

SHOPSY HOT DOGS
Street Carts Surrounding the Dome
On game days, Shopsy carts abound. Each offers grilled beef dogs, Polish sausage, and Italian sausage, topped to the high heavens. Seriously, these carts provide an unusually large array of condiments, ranging from different kinds of relishes and mustards to pickles, onions, peppers, corn, hot sauce, barbecue sauce, and much more. So be creative. Remember, what happens in Canada stays in Canada!

Inside the Dome

Upon entering Rogers, we are always struck by the sheer size of the place. It truly is a marvel of modern technology. The field, on the other hand, is rather drab. First, the outfield is perfectly symmetrical at 400 feet to center, 375 to the alleys, and 328 down the lines. Second, the ten-foot-high outfield fence has a gutter behind it—a gap of fifteen feet—that relegates all but the most exceptionally well-struck dingers to anti-climactically fading into oblivion between the wall and

seating area. Third, we don't care for the Astroturf. The joint has a roof, so how about growing some real grass? At the very least, the Jays could install a full dirt infield, like the one in St. Petersburg. We don't think that's too much to ask. As it's currently constituted the Rogers "lawn" is the only one in the big leagues that doesn't have dirt base paths. And that's unacceptable.

Kevin: Down in the States we've left the plastic grass behind.

Josh: Yeah, make like Tim Lincecum and get yourself some natural grass.

Kevin: You want me to break out my "Let Tim Smoke" shirt?

Josh: Save it for San Fran, my man.

Ballpark Features
HOMETOWN HEROES
Before the game, check out the display cases on the concourse behind Section 102. They celebrate Canadian baseball legends and showcase all three bases from the first interleague game between the ill-fated Expos and Jays in 1997. Members of both teams signed the sacks, which have red maple leaves stenciled on them. There's also a case of balls from the Blue Jays' ten-homer game against the Orioles in 1987. Toronto established a new single-game long ball record that September day on the way to an 18-3 win at Exhibition Stadium. The signatories in the spherical dinger-diary include Ernie Whitt, who hit three long balls that day; Rance Mulliniks, who hit two; George Bell, who hit two; Lloyd Moseby; Fred McGriff, and Rob Ducey. Another interesting item is the pitching rubber from the 1993 World Series, which is signed by the wild but briefly dominant Juan Guzman.

BASEBALL IN THE GREAT WHITE NORTH
One of the Hometown Heroes displays contains a bench seat from old Maple Leaf Stadium, which was home to Toronto's International League ball team from 1926 through 1967. Also on exhibit are articles of Maple Leaf and Montreal Royals memorabilia. We found a picture of Sparky Anderson, who played for and later managed the Leafs, and another of Royals player Tommy Lasorda. Despite their roots in Toronto that dated back all the way to 1887, the Leafs left town in 1968 to become the Louisville Colonels. Five years later, they moved to Pawtucket, Rhode Island, to become the Paw Sox.

The Royals began play in 1890 but struggled to establish a fan base before being acquired by the Brooklyn Dodgers in 1939. As Branch Rickey's International League affiliate, the Royals sent Jackie Robinson afield to break organized ball's color barrier in 1946. Playing second base, Robinson batted .349 for Montreal. A year later, he crossed the MLB color line. After years of sagging attendance, though, the Royals relocated to Syracuse in 1961 to become the Chiefs.

LEVEL OF EXCELLENCE

While the Blue Jays don't retire the numbers of their former stars, they do display their names on the facade of the 400 Level. This special ring honors players like Tony Fernandez, Joe Carter, George Bell, Roberto Alomar, and Dave Stieb. In addition, manager Cito Gaston, front office executives Pat Gillick and Paul Beeston, and longtime broadcaster Tom Cheek receive their just due. The number 4,306 beside Cheek's name signifies the number of consecutive Jays games he called on the radio before his death in 2005. To put that in perspective, Cheek broadcast 1,674 more games than Cal Ripken played in during his streak of a different stripe.

One former Jay whose name doesn't appear on the Level of Excellence is Danny Ainge. The light-hitting second-sacker played for Toronto from 1979 to 1981 while also playing college hoops at Brigham Young. He quit baseball after being drafted in the first round by the Boston Celtics in 1981 and after a fine career went on to become President of Basketball Operations for the Celts. During both stints in Boston—as player and front office executive—his teams won NBA titles. Did Danny make the right choice? We think so. He hit just .220 in 211 Major League games before trading in his spikes for high-tops.

DIGITIZED PENS

The bullpens are hidden from most fans' sight behind the outfield fences in right and left. From the 200 Level outfield seats, fans can look down into the stables to see television cameras pointed at the practice mounds. These provide a feed to dugout monitors that allow both managers to watch their relievers as they warm up.

JUMBO FUN

Rogers once boasted the largest stadium video board in North America, a 101-by-33-foot behemoth that for a time seemed to be world-class. But just as that thirty-four-inch box set that once sat in the center of your living room became obsolete seemingly overnight, advances in technology have taken the luster off Jays Vision. The high-definition JumboTron at Yankee Stadium is much higher, checking in at 101-by-59, while the one at Chase Field is longer, at 136-by-46. In another sport, the Dallas Cowboys' so-called Jerry-Tron is a massive 160-by-72. Still, Toronto's is a bigger board than most and one in which the Jays and their fans take pride.

Stadium Eats

Once upon a time, McDonald's managed the concessions in Toronto, if you can believe it. Yes, *that* McDonald's. Since giving the clown the boot, Jays and their fans have seen their stadium food gradually but steadily improve, to the point where today we actually look forward to eating at Rogers. The dome scores high in the menu expansiveness department, even if many of the concession stands still look like McDonald's counters. One word of warning, though: There is a far more diverse array of foods to choose from on the lower two levels, but if you have a ticket to the fifth deck you won't be able to access these stands.

SHOPSY'S SMOKED MEAT SANDWICH (TRADEMARK FOOD)

This juicy tender sandwich may be found at the Shopsy's stand behind Section 125. If you've never had Canadian Smoked Meat before, you're in for a treat. We liken it to a moister not-so-briny version of Corned Beef. After indulging you'll understand why Shopsy's, which first opened in Toronto in 1921, is still a local favorite.

GRILLED BLUE JAY DOG (DOG REVIEW)

While the bland dog sold at the typical concession counters is nothing special, we really like the grilled jumbo dog at the specialty stands. It's on par with the Shopsy dogs outside but costs more. Slit several times and served on a poppy seed roll, this all-beef frank scores high in the areas of taste and texture. Fried onions are also available.

BEST OF THE REST

We were amazed by the wealth of new offerings at Rogers on our most recent visit. A season-ticket holder could eat something different at every game and still have a few items left to check off when Game No. 81 arrived. Highlights include "Keith's Red" **roasted sirloin sandwich** at the Roundhouse Carvery stand behind Section 122; the **Mediterranean Platter** and **Hand-Carved Turkey Sandwich** at Muddy York Market behind Section 109; the **Asian noodle boxes** available at various specialty stands; the **Halifax Burgers** and **Belgium Burgers** (you'll need silverware to eat this oddity) with kettle chips at the (uninspired) second level barbecue patio; and the **Sushi Box, Mediterranean Sausage, Sweet Potato Fries, Herb and Garlic Fries,** and colorful **Barbecue Chicken Nachos.**

SAY "NO, THANKS," AND WALK AWAY

While Pizza, Pizza may have an amazingly creative name and may be widely popular throughout Canada (though just not with any of the locals with whom we spoke), we advise you to avoid it, then after the game head to Papa Ceo's for a late-night slice.

STADIUM SUDS

LaBatt Blue is served in a twenty-ounce container, which is just big enough for the hardy fans of the northland. It's understandable that Jays rooters like their Blue. Not only does the company date back to a founding in London, Ontario, in 1847, but the brewery was the original owner of the Jays back in 1976.

Those on the prowl for mixed frozen drinks, meanwhile, will find them at stands on the first level and at the (again, we say "uninspired") second level patio.

The Rogers Centre Experience

A game at "SkyDome" must have been a rollicking good time back when the facility first opened and was packed with fans. But SkyDome is no more. There is only Rogers Centre. And Rogers feels cavernous and sterile, in large part due to all those empty blue seats. The game has a very postmodern flavor as the sound system and video board practically beg fans to stay engaged or, at the very least, awake.

BLUE JAYS DANCE TEAM

One thing these crazy Canucks have done right is incorporate cheerleaders into the American National Pastime. Actually, we can't give Canada all the credit; cheerleaders have been an important part of the Caribbean World Series for years. But the Blue Jays fly girls are impressive. They're Canadian, eh, and they're busting a move for your pleasure, so do kick back and enjoy.

FEELING LUCKY

No, we don't have a sordid tale to report regarding an interaction with a Blue Jays dancer. We're talking about the fifty-fifty raffle. For $2, fans can buy a ticket. Half the proceeds support the Jays Care charitable foundation. The other half goes to the winning ticket holder. According to the Jays, winning fans have headed home with as much as $10,000, though on a typical summer night the winner gets about $3,500, which is still a heck of a lot more than a $2 chance buys you at your local high school football field.*

POSTGAME FIREWORKS

No, we still don't have a sordid cheerleader tale. But after a Jays win the team sets off fireworks. Indoor fireworks! And you thought Neil Young was the best thing Canada had going for it!

---

* Well, maybe not if you live in Texas.

THE WORLD'S FASTEST GROUNDS CREW

Embracing the title that broadcaster Tom Cheek gave them, the men and women responsible for maintaining the four dirt patches and mound at Rogers really do race around the field in carrying out their responsibilities. Then they disappear again to their holding pen behind the Jays dugout. Fans enjoy this spectacle right before first pitch as these folks rake and mist the patches and swap out the batting practice bases for shiny white ones, then again in the middle of the fifth inning when they reappear to rapidly rake the patches while the "William Tell Overture" plays.

Certainly this nickname is meant to be tongue-in-cheek since the Jays are the only team with four little rectangles of dirt instead of a full clay infield. We couldn't help but think, though, that even the Jays were poking fun at their ballpark.

"O CANADA"

The occasion of hearing the Canadian national anthem sang before first pitch should not be too much cause for celebration for American fans, seeing as AL fans have been hearing it at their home parks whenever the Blue Jays visit for years. But Rogers is the only stadium where you'll hear the "Star Spangled Banner" performed first, as the warm-up act, before the tune that brings a tear to the locals' eyes.

For disenchanted Americans who want to "pretend" or anyone else who just likes to sing along, here are the lyrics:

O Canada!
Our home and native land!
True patriot love in all thy sons command.
With glowing hearts we see thee rise,
The true north strong and free!
From far and wide,
O Canada, we stand on guard for thee.
God keep our land glorious and free!
O Canada, we stand on guard for thee.
O Canada, we stand on guard for thee.

"OK BLUE JAYS"

Before singing "Take Me Out to the Ball Game" during the seventh-inning stretch, Torontonians sing "OK Blue Jays," the official team song, which dates back to 1983. Written by a local group called The Bat Boys, this is a kicking Canadian rock song that references key events and players in team history.

The final verse goes:

Bring on the White Sox
Bring on the BoSox
Bring on the Brewers
The Rangers and the Yankees too
We'll beat the Indians
We'll beat the Tigers
We'll beat the A's so bad it'll make
Billy blue
Waddaya want?
Let's play ball!

Cyber Super-Fans

- **Mop-Up Duty**
  http://mopupduty.com/
  This site combines a nice balance. It follows the progress of Blue Jays prospects through the Bushes, provides sabermetric analysis, and taps into Blue Jays history.
- **OK Blue Jays**
  http://home.okbluejays.com/
  We especially appreciate the Jaytabase of any and all Blue Jays records.
- **Blue Bird Banter**
  www.bluebirdbanter.com/
  This particularly interactive site provides polls and forums for fans.

Josh sent an e-mail to the Bat Boys in 2004, pointing out that Milwaukee doesn't play in the American League anymore and suggesting that they replace "Brewers" with "Angels," but they still haven't replied (he's starting to lose hope they ever will) or updated their lyrics.

Kevin: Selig's probably paying them to keep the Brewers' name in there.

Sports in the City

Exhibition Place

Don't waste your time visiting the site of old Exhibition Stadium. The ballpark is now a parking lot. Funny thing, former players say it's a better place for a game now that it's paved over.

For those who feel compelled to see the former plot of the "mistake by the lake," there are a few old stadium chairs situated at the foot of the bridge that leads to the main entrance of Ontario Place.

Josh: Why would he?

Kevin: Because he's a bad man, Josh, a very bad man.

Josh: No rush to rename the song, anyway.

Kevin: How's that?

Josh: It's been a long time since the Blue Jays were any better than *just* okay.

Kevin: True enough. Since the Joe Carter era.

AAARRR-GOS . . . AAARRR-GOS

One way to fit in with locals is to join in the familiar Aaarrr-gos chant whenever there's a lull in the game. This is about as ubiquitous as the "Yankees Suck" chant in Boston.

Also, pronounce the city's name "Tronno." If you enunciate the second "t" as Americans are wont to, everyone will know you're one of "them" and start sniffing for greenbacks. And you don't want people sniffing around you when you're trying to enjoy a baseball game.

While We Were on Our Way to Toronto
Kevin Refused to Partake in Role-Playing of Any Kind

Toronto represented the last stop on the 2002 leg of our very first road trip. We would finish the bigs for the first time in 2003 and publish the first edition of this book in 2004. And then years later we would return to Toronto together during the summer of 2011. But first . . . Kevin had to help Josh muster the courage to leave the Lower 48 for the very first time in his life. After catching a game in Cleveland the day before, we headed to Canada for a Sunday afternoon game that would bid the 2002 season adieu.

Josh was driving our rented Dodge Sebring, and was a bit antsy about the whole concept of stepping onto foreign soil.

"What if they don't let me in?" he asked.

"I'll leave you at the border and come back for you after the game," Kevin said.

"No, I mean what if they won't let me back into the States after our game?"

"Don't worry. They'll let you back in. It's Canada. They let everyone in and they let everyone out," Kevin said. Then, quite paradoxically, he launched into a lengthy story about one of his Seattle friends who had been turned away at the border on her way to Vancouver.

"I don't have my Social Security card," a post-9/11 Josh said, riffling through his wallet as he nearly veered off the road.

"Stop worrying," Kevin said. "They'll let you in."

"Maybe we could do some role-playing," Josh suggested. "You be the border guard. I'll be me."

"Come again?"

"Ask me some questions like he will. You know, just for practice."

"I really don't think this is necessary," Kevin said. "They'll ask us our names and where we're headed and that will be it. It's not like we're trying to smuggle heroin in."

"Heroin! I didn't shave this morning," Josh cried. "What if they think I look sketchy?"

"You don't look sketchy."

"I just have a feeling it's going to be an ordeal," Josh said.

And sure enough it was, no thanks to the two Wrigley Field chairs Josh had purchased in Chicago that were stashed in the Sebring's back seat.

"What are those rusty old things?" the border guard asked, pointing to the chairs.

"Wrigley Field Stadium chairs, sir," Josh stammered. "I have a certificate of authenticity for each one if you'd like to see."

"Why do you have chairs from Wrigley Field in the back seat if you're just going to Tronno for a day?" the guard asked, suspiciously.

Josh riffled through a folder of papers, looking for the two certificates of authenticity the Cubs had made up for the chairs. He handed the crumpled-up pieces of paper to the man and tried his best not to stutter. "B-b-b-because we're on a baseball road trip, sir, collecting all sorts of stuff

from ballparks and stadiums, taking pictures. You know . . . living the American, umm . . . North American . . . dream."

"Yeah," the guard said, mildly perturbed, after inspecting the documents. "Go on then. Just don't get any ideas aboot the chairs at SkyDome."

"I won't, sir," Josh said sincerely. "I swear."

"Go on!"

"For a while I didn't think they were going to let me in with the chairs," Josh said after a mile of highway lay between the Sebring and the border.

"They let everyone in," Kevin said.

"Except your friend?"

"Right, except for my friend Dana Hackett. For some reason, they thought she was sketchy."

PHILADELPHIA PHILLIES, CITIZENS BANK PARK

PHILADELPHIA, PENNSYLVANIA
100 MILES TO NEW YORK
105 MILES TO BALTIMORE
136 MILES TO WASHINGTON, D.C.
245 MILES TO PITTSBURGH

A Ballpark to Change the Phillies' Phortunes

In our baseball travels, we have learned a few things about ballparks, and the citizens that love them. One thing we've learned is that most teams that endured the "cookie-cutter/dome era" now have far superior places to enjoy the game. But we've also learned that those cities which once had intimate little green cathedrals nestled into neighborhoods prior to building their multi-use multiplex concrete abominations, have fared even better in reclaiming what they once had.

Citizens Bank Park in Philadelphia may not be located in a quaint downtown neighborhood teeming with great places to go out before and after the game, but it lacks little else. Make no mistake: A game at CBP is as good as it gets. Though it appears ginormous from the parking lot of the South Philadelphia Sports Complex, which is also the home of stadiums for the Eagles of the NFL and Flyers and 76ers of the NHL and NBA, respectively, the designers of this park went out of their way to make sure nearly every seat has a clear view of the game. Utilizing a stacked cantilever design for the upper decks, and a low-rising bowl design reminiscent of Shibe Park (aka Connie Mack Stadium), Citizens Bank Park may well offer the best views in all of baseball in a seat-by-seat comparison.

The seating capacity is just north of forty-three thousand, which isn't small, but the ballpark would fit neatly inside of its predecessor, the sixty-two-thousand-plus-seat Veterans Stadium, with room to spare.

And the South Philadelphia Sports Complex is improving as well. While the expansive parking lots do not officially allow for tailgating, it's difficult to stop the people in all twenty thousand cars (the maximum capacity of the parking lot) from eating or drinking before the game. And on the site where the old Spectrum used to be, in a parking lot between all three stadiums in the complex, is Philly Live, which provides mixed-use living, retail, and entertainment space and the sense of neighborhood that the area lacked for so long.

Upon first seeing the exterior of the ballpark, one is struck by the generous use of red brick and stone in the facade, the green copper roof, and the red steel used in the light towers and beam supports for the seating structure. At night, three smaller light towers encased in glass glow brilliantly at locations representing first base, third base, and home plate above the stadium. The four entrance plazas at the corners of the ballpark each present a unique aspect of Philadelphia's history and culture.

The park's architect was Ewing Cole Cherry Brott (ECCB) from Philadelphia, which teamed up with those giants of ballpark design fame, HOK Sport (now known as Populous). The use of classic elements from earlier Phillies ballparks gave Citizens Bank Park its distinctive and utterly Philadelphian feel. The use of red brick and brushed red steel girders combined with the blue seats ties the exterior and interior into one design. The "bowl style" seating of the lower level has an unusually low grade to it, and was inspired by similar seating at the Baker Bowl and Shibe Park/Connie Mack Stadium. The shape of the outfield fence, with its boxed-out irregular segment in left-center field, is also reminiscent of Shibe. Beyond the outfield walls, beautiful open views of the Center City skyline offer a wonderful backdrop for baseball. The batter's eye is a very attractive ivy-covered wall, which though reminiscent of Wrigley, adds a unique and distinctive touch to the ballpark. To the right of the batter's eye are banks of flower boxes that, surprisingly enough to us, we liked.

Perhaps the most distinctive aspect of the ballpark from a fan-experience point of view is Ashburn Alley, so named in honor of Hall of Famer and former broadcaster Richie "Whitey" Ashburn. Pretty clever putting an "alley" inside the ballpark, when none can be found in the sea of parking lots around the park. It's a good thing Philadelphia's ballpark was designed to offer the total game-day package, because there is still no real neighborhood surrounding the Sports Complex.

Under an agreement ratified by the City Council in December 2000, the city of Philadelphia agreed to provide $174 million toward the stadium's price tag, with $172 million coming from private financing to account for the $346 million total cost of building Citizens Bank Park. Also approved by voters was a new stadium for the Eagles. Later, the city added the Spectrum II, now known as the Wells Fargo Center. The cost of the three new facilities was well over a billion dollars. That amount of cash seems to border on the ridiculous to sports fans like us, but considering they built all three for less than the price of the new Yankee Stadium, who are we to complain? At least Philadelphia owns the new ballpark and leases it to the team. In June 2003 Citizens Bank pledged $57.5 million over twenty-five years to secure the new park's naming rights.

Phillies "phans" have been treated to a delightful gameday experience at their new home, both off the field and on it. The Phils seemed to have caught lightning in a bottle in their new home, enjoying a 103 percent capacity sellout rating. With Charlie Manuel at the helm, the Phillies became the pride of the NL East. After a disappointing playoff loss in 2007, they repeated as division champs in 2008 and won their first playoff series since 1993. Fueled by young players that the team developed from within their own farm system, such as Chase Utley, Cole Hamels, Ryan Howard, and Jimmy Rollins, the 2008 Phillies went on to capture the National League pennant when they defeated the Los Angeles Dodgers four games to one. Then, for just the second time in their 126-year history, the Phillies won the World Series, defeating the Tampa Bay Rays behind the nearly unstoppable arm of Hamels, who was the Series MVP.

A touching moment came during the pregame ceremony of Game 1, as country star Tim McGraw placed some of the ashes of his father, Tug McGraw, in the dirt of the pitcher's mound. Tug, you'll remember, recorded the last out of the Phillies' 1980 World Series victory, and died in 2004 of brain cancer. Tim McGraw then handed the ball to Steve Carlton, who delivered the ceremonial first pitch before a capacity-plus crowd of cheering Philly fans.

Though they made it to the Series again in 2009, the Phillies fell to the Yankees. In 2010 they fell in the NLCS to the eventual world champions, the San Francisco Giants.

These disappointments quickly turned to optimism, as the front office put together one of the toughest pitching lineups this side of the 1995 Atlanta Braves, when they brought Cliff Lee back to town, to go alongside Hamels, Roy Halladay, and Roy Oswalt. With Brad Lidge as their closer and the heart of their hitting and fielding crew intact, Philadelphia had plenty reason to be phanatical.

But the excitement at CBP during the 2011 season transcended mere wins and losses. On a spring night in May, ESPN was broadcasting its Sunday Night game from the Phillies' ballpark when news started to spread that Osama bin Laden had been killed by a team of US Navy SEALS in Pakistan. In a spontaneous outburst of patriotic exuberance, the Philadelphia fans broke into a chant of "U-S-A, U-S-A" that reverberated throughout the ballpark during the ninth inning of a game that eventually went fourteen frames before the Phillies finally bowed to the Mets.

The Phillies' recent success stands in stark contrast to their fortunes over the previous century and a quarter, which were nothing short of heart-wrenching during much of that period. For thirty-three seasons, the Phillies played at Veterans Stadium, which was located in the next parking lot over from where CBP now resides. They shared the facility with the Eagles, and baseball fans suffered the same fate as

third base gate exterior

Photo by Kevin O'Connell

mixed-use facility teams across the land. The stadium wasn't bad for football, but was awful for baseball.

The Vet was the largest baseball stadium in the National League (not including the year the Colorado Rockies played at Mile High Stadium), with a seating capacity in excess of sixty-two thousand, and was one of the worst places to experience a baseball game. The stadium itself looked like a gigantic air filter flung from the road trip mobile, lying alone and dejected in an empty parking lot.

With its octorad (an architect's term derived from combining "octagon" and "radius") shape, the facility was completed in 1971, four years after its groundbreaking. The Opening Day crowd of 55,352 represented the largest baseball crowd in the history of Pennsylvania. The Phils' Larry Bowa recorded the stadium's first hit.

Considering the gimmicks and odd promotions the Phillies featured throughout the Vet era, it seems likely that the team realized from the outset that the stadium was lacking when morphed from football grid into baseball diamond. Don't get us wrong, we like teams to take a proactive approach to improving their digs. But it seemed in this case that the team's marketing efforts were, at least in part, designed to keep fans from thinking too much about just how bad baseball at the Vet could be. Known for having the hardest turf in the history of the Major Leagues, the Vet had a demoralizing outline of the football gridiron always visible across the expanse of the outfield. In this city known for its cheesesteaks, the Phillies really trotted out the cheese—as in cheesy—at the start of each season. Before the inaugural baseball game on April 10, 1971, a helicopter dropped the ceremonial first pitch as it hovered high above. Though he stumbled a bit tracking the ball and bobbled it when it finally hit his glove, Phils catcher Mike Ryan ultimately held on to make the catch. But the high-flying Phillies marketing geniuses weren't through yet with their Opening Day antics. The first pitch of the 1972 season was delivered by famous tightrope walker Karl Wallenda, of the famous Flying Wallendas, from atop a high-wire suspended over the field.

Josh: What was this fascination with balls being dropped from on high?

Kevin: Maybe it was because championships weren't dropping from on high.

Josh: You think they were actually trying to make a plea to the baseball gods?

Kevin: Yeah, kind of like "seeding" a rain cloud.

In 1976, the Phillies came back to earth, as a horseman dressed as Paul Revere trotted out the season's first Rawlings in the bicentennial year.

Many of these memorable promotions came to Phils phans courtesy of team vice president Bill Giles, and we salute his ingenuity. New ballparks, with all their bells and whistles and corporate-sponsored promotions, pale in comparison to just a little good old-fashioned human ingenuity.

The Vet had plenty of quirks built in over the years—such as a center-field water fountain and a home run spectacular on the facade of the fourth level featuring Philadelphia Phil and Phyllis in Colonial garb—but these were eventually cast aside to add more seats for football. During this period, the city allowed the Vet to slip into disrepair, until finally the Phillies took over its management in 1994. New blue seats were added (similar to those found at Citizens Bank Park), as well as a new out-of-town scoreboard. Finally in 2001, to the delight of trainers throughout the National League, the worst Astroturf in the big leagues was removed, and Nexturf, a synthetic grass, was installed.

Prior to recent history, the Vet years once represented the golden era of Phillies baseball, playing host to the MLB All-Star Games of 1976 and 1996, and the World Series of 1980, 1983, and 1993. Playing half his games on the Vet's grueling rug slapped down on concrete, Mike Schmidt recorded 404 assists in 1974, the most ever by a National League third baseman. Schmidt won eight Gold Gloves in a row during one stretch, led the NL in homers eight times, and made twelve NL All-Star squads.

Fans visiting the Vet in 1981 saw history on several occasions. On April 29, Carlton struck out Tim Wallach for his three-thousandth career punch-out. Carlton was the first left-hander to cross the three-thousand-K threshold and would finish his career with 4,136, which currently ranks him fourth on the all-time list. On August 10, Pete Rose singled to break Stan Musial's NL record with his 3,631st hit while the Phils took on St. Louis at home.

It's remarkable that the Phillies survived as a franchise for nearly one hundred seasons before finally winning their first world championship in 1980. They truly put their fans through the horrors before at last delivering.

Kevin: Let that be a testament to teams that threaten to move after a losing decade or two.

Josh: You mean like the Mariners. What are they, halfway there?

Kevin: Ever since the Red Sox won the World Series, you've been a pain.

In 1883, the Worcester Ruby Legs were disbanded and the franchise moved to Philadelphia. The Cincinnati Reds may be an older franchise, but because the Reds were booted from the National League three years prior, the Phillies can claim the honor of being the oldest franchise in all of professional sports to have remained in the same city under the same name.

On May 1, 1883, Recreation Park, located at the corner of 24th Street and Ridge Avenue and with a seating capacity of sixty-five hundred, hosted the very first Phillies game, which they lost 4-3 to the Providence Grays. The field, which was occupied by Union Army cavalry during the Civil War, had been used for hardball in the 1860s. In the 1870s, it became part of a horse market, before Phillies owner Al Reach purchased the land and built grandstands. One notable player from this era, pitcher Dan Casey, claimed until his death in 1943 that he was the inspiration for the most famous baseball poem of all time, "Casey at the Bat."

Kevin: A dubious claim to fame.

Josh: Fame has always been fame.

Kevin: What the heck does that mean?

Josh: When you're famous someday you'll understand.

The Phils moved to Huntingdon Street Baseball Grounds in 1885. This ballpark was later known as National League Park and Philadelphia Park. It was also nicknamed the "Hump" because the Philadelphia and Reading Railroad tunnel ran beneath the outfield and the ground had been built up in a hump to cover it. In 1894 a fire destroyed the ballpark, and the Phils finished their home schedule at the University of Pennsylvania. Philadelphia Park was rebuilt on the spot to hold eighteen thousand and featured a cantilevered pavilion, a radical new architectural design.

When the Philadelphia A's came to town as a part of the upstart American League, they snatched away three of the senior circuit team's best hitters, Nap Lajoie, Ed Delahanty, and Elmer Flick. A cruel joke on the Phillies came later as these men won the first five AL batting titles (though none stuck it out in Philly all that long) and all were eventually elected to the Baseball Hall of Fame.

Bad times were clearly headed the Phillies' way when in 1903 Philadelphia Park collapsed, killing 12 people and injuring 232. But on the plus side, the Phils and the A's played their first "City Series" exhibition games in 1903. This interleague play precursor was a tradition that continued for fifty years and was a fitting event in the City of Brotherly Love.

In 1913, when William F. Baker bought the team, Philadelphia Park was renamed Baker Bowl. At a mere 272 feet down the line to the right-field foul pole, Baker Bowl earned the diminutive moniker of the "Cigar Box." A forty-foot wall in right made up of a scoreboard and later, advertisements, held a few balls in, but not many.

The Phils made it to their first World Series in 1915. After taking the first game from the Red Sox, they lost the next four. After this crushing defeat, dark days lay ahead for the Phils as they rarely rose from the cellar of the standings over the next three decades. Even with players like Chuck Klein and "Lefty" O'Doul on the team—Klein winning the Triple Crown for the Phils in 1933, banging out 28 home runs, 129 RBIs, and a .368 batting average, and O'Doul batting .398 and recording 254 hits in 1929—the Phillies couldn't seem to win. Three decades of disappointment took its toll on the franchise, and Baker Bowl fell into a state of disrepair that matched the flagging Phillies organization.

In 1938, the end of the Baker Bowl era had come, as the Phils left the dilapidated ballpark and took up co-residence at Shibe Park with the crosstown Athletics of the American League. Built in 1909, Shibe was designed by A's owner Ben Shibe and manager Connie Mack. It was the first concrete and steel stadium and originally seated 23,300. In 1925 a double-decked grandstand was built above the entire left-field fence, all the way out to dead center, giving the park its distinctive interior look. Before 1935, folks that lived along 20th Street could view games from their rooftops over the right-field fence without paying. Many built bleachers on their rooftops and charged admission. After Mack lost a lawsuit that attempted to prevent this, thirty-four-foot-high "spite fences" were constructed to block the encroaching view.

Josh: Sounds like what went on at Wrigley Field for a while.

Kevin: At least the Cubs finally made a deal with their neighbors.

But the real beauty of Shibe Park was its exterior. The brick facades that lined North 21st Street and West Somerset were made up of dozens of arches in two tiers. These two French Renaissance edifices came together and were capped by a glorious Beaux Arts tower with cupola and dome that formed the main entranceway. From the exterior, Shibe looked like a ballpark that belonged in Florence, Italy, next door to Il Duomo, rather than in America.

But Shibe didn't provide the mojo needed to produce the elusive championship that Phillies fans longed for. The closest they got was in 1950, when the "Whiz Kids," a group of plucky young Phils, including Robin Roberts, Del Ennis, and Willie Jones, finally made it to the World Series. But the Whiz Kids couldn't produce either, as they were beaten by the Yankees in four straight. In fairness, three of those contests were one-run games.

Josh: Perhaps "Cheez Whiz Kids" would have been more appropriate.

Kevin: Save it for Geno's, will ya?

In 1952 the Phillies hosted the All-Star Game at Shibe, then the next year the park was renamed Connie Mack Stadium, then in 1955 the A's left for Kansas City, making the Phillies sole owners of a stadium named after the manager of what was once a rival crosstown team. Doesn't quite seem right, does it? It would be a little like the Yankees moving into Shea Stadium and keeping the name. Oh well. Speaking of the Yankees, the old Yankee Stadium scoreboard, all sixty feet of it, was installed in right-center field at Connie Mack Stadium in 1956. And outside Citizens Bank Park, the home of the Phillies, stands a statue of Connie Mack himself, dressed as he always was, in a suit that made him look like an undertaker, without a smile on his face, facing the new ballpark of a team he had no affiliation with whatsoever.

The 1964 season may have been the most crushing of all for Phillies fans. With only twelve games to play, the Phils held a six-and-a-half-game lead in the NL over St. Louis. The team then lost ten straight games before winning its final two to finish in a tie for second-place with the Cincinnati Reds. The City of Brotherly Love was inconsolable, yet again.

But the 1970s brought a new stadium, the bicentennial All-Star Game, Hall of Famers Schmidt and Carlton, and a cast of great ballplayers and even greater characters that included Greg Luzinski, Bob Boone, and McGraw. But despite all this talent, the Phils' hard luck continued. The team lost three straight NLCS between 1976 to 1978—one to former Phillies second baseman Sparky Anderson's Cincinnati Reds, and two to the LA Dodgers.

Trivia Timeout

Wit Onions: A replica of the Liberty Bell hung in center field on the 500 Level of "The Vet." Name the only player to ever ding the bell with a dong of a home run.

Wit Provolone: Which three pitchers battled during the 1982 season to break the all-time strikeout record held by Walter Johnson?

Wit Wiz: Name the Phillies who have earned——and we mean earned——the honor of having their numbers retired.

Look for the answers in the text.

The signing of Pete Rose in 1978 seemed to bring the missing piece the Phillies had long been searching for, and they won their first World Series over the Kansas City Royals in 1980, after nearly a century of middling teams. Schmidt was the MVP of both the season and the Series and Carlton won the Cy Young Award and two games in the October Classic. But the heads-up play of Rose in the decisive sixth game proved critical, as Charlie Hustle snagged a pop-up with the bases loaded in the ninth after it had been bobbled by the Phillies catcher, Boone. McGraw struck out Willie Wilson for the final out in front of a crazed crowd of more than sixty-five thousand at the Vet. And the first World Series had come to Philly at long last. Cheesesteaks for everyone!

Josh: You know, I never think of Rose as a Philly. Only a Red.

Kevin: I only think of him as a bookie.

Josh: Nay, he was the guy *calling* the bookie.

The Phils returned to the Series in 1983, but after winning Game 1 in Baltimore, dropped four in a row—the last three at home. The freewheeling 1993 Phillies took Toronto to six games, led by Darren Daulton, Lenny Dykstra, and Mitch Williams, but lost the Series at SkyDome on the first-ever Series-clinching walk-off homer, struck by Joe Carter. Game 4 of the Series, played at the Vet, set new Series records for the longest nine-inning game (four hours, fourteen minutes), and the most runs scored (Toronto 15, Philadelphia 14).

But as we've said, times have changed in Philadelphia. A long history of finishing outside the winner's circle has given way to Philly Pride that now, once again, includes the Phillies. Is Citizens Bank Park partially responsible for the reincarnation of the Phillies as winners? Who's to say? But it certainly hasn't hurt anything. The Phillies once again have a world-class facility to view their (newly) world-class product on the field. Considering how passionate Philadelphia sports fans are, it will be interesting to see if the red stripes can sustain both their on-field success, and the insanely high demand for tickets at CBP; both commodities were at their highest points in the team's long history as this edition of *The Ultimate Baseball Road Trip* landed on bookstore shelves.

Getting a Choice Seat

The ballpark looks and feels small on the inside, and certainly is smaller than it appears from the parking lots. The Phillies have put in place two major design elements to protect sight lines and make the view among the best in baseball. The first is the "bowl" design of the Field Level seats, which is a low grade rise that provides for many seats with great views. The second is the stacked second and third decks, which are suspended by cantilever to put them close to the

Seating Capacity: 43,647 seats
Ticket Office: http://philadelphia.phillies.mlb.com/ticketing/index.jsp?c_id=phi
Seating Chart: http://philadelphia.phillies.mlb.com/phi/ticketing/seating_pricing.jsp

action. All of this means one thing to you: If you don't have good seats, you might wind up with no seats. So plan ahead.

Field Level (Sections 101–148)

The Phillies went to great lengths to design a ballpark that provides superb sight lines for fans. For our money, all thirty-seven rows in every one of the first-level seating "neighborhoods"—clusters of sections pointed toward the plate at their own angle—provides great views. There's no serious overhang issue on the Field Level, even at the highest rows. Flat-screen TVs hang down from the tops of these sections. The first base side is sheltered a bit from the sun, especially for an evening game, and certainly more so than the third base side or the outfield.

Most of the Field Level seats on the infield belong to season-ticket holders, but if you have the chance to pick up seats on the black market, consider the sections between home plate and first base (Sections 114–118) or home and third base (129–132). On either baseline, you might get lucky enough to score a first- or second-row seat. The sections directly behind the plate (120–128) do not offer the same opportunity, because they are behind the exclusive Diamond Club, which eats up the first several rows. And no, you're not likely to find a scalper with Diamond Club seats.

Sections 101 to 105 in right field and Sections 142 to 148 in left offer excellent chances to score batting practice homers or regulation long balls. Just be sure to steer clear of Section 106 in right field and Section 140 in left as they are screened by the foul poles.

Hall of Fame Club (Sections 212–232)

These are the second-level seats on the infield. You know, the "club" sections. As usual, we appreciate the sight lines, but not the stodgy atmosphere.

Arcade (Sections 233–237)

We don't recommend these second-level seats in foul territory in deep left field. The view is

better from the Scoreboard Porch, and costs less money, to boot.

Pavilion (Sections 201–211)

Located on the Club Level, these right-field seats offer a very respectable perch from which to watch the game. The seats don't hang out over the first level like at old Tiger Stadium or Citi Field, but they're a heck of a lot closer to the field than the outfield seats were at the Vet. We don't recommend Sections 201 to 204 in fair territory, because the loss of the corner can be significant. Sections 208 to 211 increasingly begin to lose the left-field corner down the line, while 205, 206, and 207 have foul-pole obstruction issues, especially Section 205 where seats 16 and 17 in all rows should be avoided. The first base path is blocked, as is the action at the plate. These twenty seats really should be taken out, as the Phils have worked tirelessly to protect views everywhere else in the park but here.

Kevin: Love your neighbor and lean to the left.

Josh: Hey, it's just as easy to lean right, pal.

Kevin: Don't worry, I'm not going after your cheesesteak.

Harry the K's Porch (Sections 241–245)

These home run territory second-deck seats in left field are a solid option. And if you're planning to visit Harry the K's,

view from behind home plate

Photo by Kevin O'Connell

view from right field

Photo by Kevin O'Connell

in right-field home run territory (as if a ball is ever going to be hit up here) provide a straight-on view of the field, but Sections 305, 306, and 307 have foul-pole obstructions.

Terrace Deck (Sections 412–434)

Located on the third deck, above the midlevel concourse, the Terrace Deck feels right on top of the game. Compared to the rest of the baseball universe, these sections hold up well. The roof provides more shelter from the sun than you might expect and the views into downtown Philly are great. Aim for Sections 414 to 426 to have a quality view of the infield. Don't settle for the cheap seats out in left field (Sections 430 to 434) unless you're really hard up.

Rooftop Bleachers (Section RB)

At Connie Mack Stadium folks on 20th Street enjoyed free views of the game from their own rooftops. The Phillies have attempted to duplicate the effect with two sections of bleachers atop Ashburn Alley's outfield entertainment area beneath the towering neon Liberty Bell. Although these seats are miles from the action, and suffer from serious side-hang obstruction issues from the middle deck of the upper structure that come across and block views of first base, they do embrace a feature of the old park that fans

they're even more attractive, as you will get a discount on your food. Not enough to make up for the long lines and mediocre food at Harry's, but for some people it's all about getting the discount. Sight lines lost in these sections are equivalent to about double the warning track in left field, so not too bad, because you still feel close to the action.

The seating area is named after Harry Kalas, of course, who was a Phillies broadcaster from 1971 through 2009. Mr. Kalas was a legend in his own time, and the entire city of Philadelphia wept when he collapsed in the Nationals Park press box and died in April 2009.

Terrace (Sections 312–333)

These are the upper deck seats located below the midlevel concourse. In most parks, they're called Upper Boxes. We recommend avoiding the distant sections in left field, but otherwise these are fantastic for upper level seats with very well-protected sight lines and almost no underhang issues at all until you get out to 330 and 331, which lose the left-field corner, but not too much. Sections 332 and 333 should be avoided entirely because the loss of the corner becomes more significant.

Pavilion Deck (Sections 301–310)

Sections 309 and 310 just beyond first base provide decent enough bird's-eye views of the infield. Sections 301 to 304

SEATING TIP

For thrifty readers, the tickets to get are the Standing Room Only ones, which go on sale before each game. They sell out quickly, as they are among the cheapest in the ballpark. And don't worry about finding a place to set up shop. Though seat-hopping is tough at CBP, with these tickets you can access the entire ballpark (except the club level), and by arriving early you can easily stake out your spot along the Standing Room railings lining the tops of all seating areas, the 100 level included. When we say railings, it's for lack of a better term, because these function more like bar tops, where you are encouraged to set down food and drink and stay as long as you like. The concourses are as wide as they come in the majors, so you won't feel as if you're getting edged out of your spot by the people behind you walking around. Again, these railings go fast, so get there early. If the standing room tickets are gone when you're buying your way inside, just get the cheapest 300-level ticket you can find, and do the same thing.

found special. Plus, there's something fun about sitting in the peanut gallery every once in a while, even if the light poles in Ashburn Alley block views as well. Sitting toward the center-field part of the section is more advisable, and as always, you don't have to stay if your seats aren't any good. On hot days, there's a misting fan behind the bleachers that provides a much-needed way for fans to beat the Philly heat.

Josh: Building a fan and shooting water through it?
Kevin: Brilliant!

The Black Market

Mill around in the parking lot for a few minutes and the scalpers will come to you. This is the East Coast, so expect to be locking horns with some pretty tough cookies. The town may call itself a City of Brotherly Love, but the street-hardened scalpers will rake you over the coals if you let them, so be careful. Check your ticket dates and section numbers, then double-check before finalizing any sale.

Before/After the Game

Out of necessity, the Phillies' ballpark has become a destination unto itself, complete with pregame historic attractions and drinking establishments within the gates. This makes sense, since there isn't much to do or see in the immediate vicinity of the ballpark. If you're driving to the game, we recommend arriving at the Sports Complex early to beat the traffic, get a choice parking space, and take in some of the pregame activities the Phillies have pre-planned for fans.

If you're arriving in town earlier in the day, we recommend making your way to South Street, which offers unique Philly foods, a nice choice of restaurants, and a bit of the historic feel one might expect when visiting Philadelphia. When you're ready to leave for the stadium, it's just a five-minute drive.

After the game, we recommend putting your wallet in your front pants pocket and making the daring pilgrimage into South Philly for a late-night cheesesteak. As Josh put it upon finishing his third steak, "If I've placed my life in danger, it was worth every bite."

Getting to Citizens Bank Park

The best thing about building a ballpark in a sports complex is that it's easy to get to and there's plenty of parking. And thanks to this complex's location at the intersection of two major highways, traffic isn't too bad before or after games. From Interstate 95, take Exit 17 (Broad Street), which leads right into the stadium lot. From Interstate 76, take Exit 349 (Sports Complex).

Either pay the cash to park at the complex lots or pass the complex and try to locate a free spot in South Philly. We took a left on Packer Street and followed it a block under the highway overpass to arrive at a wealth of streets on the left that led into a residential neighborhood where plenty of free street parking awaited. The neighborhood looks safe and parking there doesn't require a resident sticker. This parking was close to the Vet, but is more than a few blocks from the new park. It is, however, close to the Philadium Tavern (see below), a must-visit before the game.

For fans interested in banging around town on foot, then heading to the game, the SEPTA Broad Street Subway is accessible from the South Philly, North Philly, and Center City subway stations. Take the Broad Street train, southbound, to the last stop (Pattison Avenue).

Staying at the nearby Holiday Inn Stadium seemed like a good idea to us at first, but unless you're just looking for a convenient place to crash after the game, we don't recommend it, because there isn't much else to do in the neighborhood—have we stressed that enough now?

Outside Attractions
PHILLY LIVE

Philly Live was originally planned to be more than 300,000 square feet of entertainment space on the site of the old Spectrum, but a flagging economy has forced developers to build it in stages, the first of which was a fifty thousand-square-foot sports bar, dubbed the largest in the country. Still, if the Phils were determined to build at SPSC (South Philly Sports Complex), then Philly Live is a smart way to develop the area.

Eventually, more bars are planned, as well as restaurants, shops, a hotel, and even an outdoor music venue. All of these will improve the pregame and postgame options at the SPSC. The planners have designed the venue to bring people in year-round, but the driving factor is that there will be visitors to one of the sports venues more than three hundred days out of the year. Though it's a bit like a mall in many aspects, we applaud the effort, even if it had just started at the time of our most recent visit. Keep building, Philly Live.

HONORING THE VETS

The Phillies commissioned a bevy of new statues for their ballpark, but the old bronzes still stand at the corners, outlying the four entrances to The Vet. It's a considerable walk on a hot August day, especially if you're planning on encircling the new ballpark to view the new statues erected, but hey, some folks are true Philly phans, so who are we to dissuade them? Two of the Vet statues depict generic baseball players, while two represent athletes who played the other sport played at the venue (football). Hardcore Philly phans can seek out the Vet's old home plate, which is set in concrete.

Kevin: Pitch one to me.

Josh: Why not? The concrete isn't that much worse than the old turf used to be.

TWO OUTA THREE AIN'T BAD

Three statues adorn the outside of the new ballpark. All three pay homage to the city's baseball heritage, if not that of the Phillies themselves.

STEVE CARLTON

Though he played for six teams during an illustrious career, Philly claims this southpaw as its own, and rightfully so. The statue honoring Carlton stands outside the Left Field Gate, hurling a certain strike as he lunges forward extending toward the plate. The statue itself captures a strong likeness to Carlton's throwing style, but the face is a bit off. We're not blaming the sculptor, Zenos Frudakis, it's just that it has always been difficult to capture '70s facial hair in bronze, and the look on Carlton's face is a bit funky. Carlton's career numbers are undeniably top-notch, as he won four Cy Young Awards, was a ten-time All Star, picked 144 runners off base, and posted a lifetime ERA of 3.22 over 24 seasons. He was a first-ballot Hall of Famer in 1994.

A Three-Way Gun Fight

Toward the end of his career, Carlton battled Nolan Ryan and Gaylord Perry in a race to break Walter Johnson's all-time strikeout record. Johnson had held the mark for fifty-five years at the beginning of the 1982 season, but Carlton, Ryan, and Perry were all within striking distance. Ryan got there first, but Carlton surpassed him after Ryan landed on the DL. Perry broke Johnson's record as well, though he was closer to the tail end of his career and was not going to factor in long term. The lead for most strikeouts passed back and forth between Carlton and Ryan multiple times until 1984, when Ryan took control of the record for good, ending up with 5,714 to Carlton's 4,136. Later, Randy Johnson (4,875) and Roger Clemens (4,672) would surpass Carlton's total.

MIKE SCHMIDT

The Third Base Gate could only belong to one Philly, the incomparable Mike Schmidt. Accordingly, a statue there bears the likeness of the man many believe to be the greatest player ever at the hot corner. Schmidt's laurels include three National League MVP awards, ten Gold Gloves, twelve All-Star nods, 548 career home runs (he led the NL eight times), and a career fielding percentage of .961. The Hall of Famer played his entire career for the Phillies, and holds almost all of the team's most important offensive and defensive records.

In 2006, Schmidt wrote a book called *Clearing the Bases: Juiced Players, Monster Salaries, Sham Records, and a Hall of Famer's Search for the Soul of Baseball,* in which he candidly discusses how fans might view the Steroid Era records and Pete Rose's bid for the Hall of Fame. Though Schmidt contradicts the statement in an earlier interview with Bob Costas that he would have taken steroids in order to have remained competitive, he claims in the book that he would not have broken any rules to do so. It's a worthy road trip read from a thoughtful man.

MR. MACK—AKA CORNELIUS MCGILLICUDDY

Connie Mack's statue also adorns the outside of Citizens Bank Park, standing across from the Suite Club entrance. Though he never had any affiliation with the Phillies' franchise, other than leasing and then finally selling his ballpark to them, to not honor this quiet and distinguished gentleman of the game in this city would be a certain crime against the history of the sport. Mack managed the Philadelphia A's for the first 50 years of their existence, setting a record for the longest tenure as manager of a single team in the history of professional sports. Mack knew both success and failure, being the first manager to win three World Series and the first to win back-to-back World Series on two separate occasions. His A's also finished in dead last place in the American League seventeen times. Mack had a quiet demeanor, always wore a suit, and did not believe that managers had that much effect on the outcome of the game. He rarely substituted or pinch hit for players, didn't like positional platoons, and stuck with his lineup. He was the first man elected to baseball's Hall of Fame in 1937, and died in Philadelphia in 1956.

TAILGATE AT THE TENT

This might be one of the priciest tailgates we've ever seen! For a steep fee of more than a Benjamin Franklin, fans get access to the only officially sanctioned tailgate outside Citizens Bank

Mike Schmidt statue

The greatest third baseman of his generation.
Photo by Kevin O'Connell

Park, as well as nice seats for a "premium" game. The tailgate includes some quality food and drink options, as well as live entertainment.

Kevin: What is this, tailgating for the rich and famous?

Josh: More like First Class services for those who can't light a hibachi on their own.

Kevin: I'll take a standing room ticket and cheesesteak any day.

Josh: Well said.

"BEACONS OF LIGHT" LANTERN TOWERS

Look for the three fifty-foot-tall, glass-encased lanterns that have become the signature elements of the ballpark exterior. At night they light up like beacons, representing the

safety of first and third base, and the eternal hope of returning to home plate.

Kevin: I have to ask, "Where's the love for the second sack?"

Josh: Yeah, they used to put football goal posts on the goal line. A light tower behind second would make for a great ballpark quirk.

VIEW INTO THE PARK—NO CHARGE

While Connie Mack built his "spite fences" to keep folks from seeing into the park without paying, designers of the new ballpark welcome such peeking at a field that is twenty-three feet below street level. The designers surely realized that allowing people a glimpse of the action would do nothing but make them drool at the excitement occurring inside. These gates, accessible at street level, provide a view akin to watching a trailer for a film. They whet people's appetites.

THE ITALIAN STALLION

Sure it was only a movie and its sequels have continued a bit too long, but the first *Rocky* is still a Philadelphia classic. Rocky Balboa, you'll recall, was the hard-hitting heavyweight from South Philly who dethroned champion Apollo Creed in a 1978 rematch rumble, then later KO'd brother-in-law Paulie, the *A-Team's* "Mr. T," Cold War relic Ivan Drago, and pro fighter "Tommy Gun" Morrison.

The Rocky statue originally stood at the top of the seventy-two stone steps of the Philadelphia Museum of Art at Benjamin Franklin Parkway and 26th Street, so that fans could run up the steps and jump up and down with both fists raised the way Rocky did in the movie. But it was removed by those who understand "art" much better than we do, perhaps because they couldn't stomach the idea that a statue of Balboa held such a prominent locale in the city. For a while it stood outside the Spectrum. But now it resides at the bottom of the Art Museum's steps, which is a shame for the people who still run up them.

Watering Holes and Outside Eats

Though there aren't many places to get refreshments near the park, there are some that make a walk through the parking lots worthwhile. But Philadelphia is a great food town, and whether you're up for cheesesteaks, scrapple, soft pretzels, water ice, or Tastykakes, Philly offers lots of local flavor.

MCFADDEN'S (THIRD BASE GATE)

Though technically McFadden's is inside the park, you can access it from the outside without a ticket even on game days. It's a pretty nondescript Irish sports pub on the whole, but it has plenty of beers, an outdoor seating terrace, cute waitresses, and live music before the game. Plus, you can use your ticket to enter the ballpark proper through McFadden's own entrance, which could save time you might waste entering through the regular gates.

THE BIGGEST SPORTS BAR IN THE WORLD! (PHILLY LIVE)

Philly Live announced plans to build the largest sports bar in the world in time for the 2012 Phillies' season. Since it has two levels and more floor space than most Target stores, we just hope this bar comes with a similarly oversized number of taps and waitresses. Seriously, though, we would have settled for a dozen smaller, quality bars, but going from no bars outside to just one . . . well, it's an improvement.

THE PHILADIUM TAVERN
17th Street and Packer Avenue

There may not be many joints near the Sports Complex, but this authentic little sports bar makes up for it big-time. Look for the big "T" (as in "Tavern") on Packer Avenue. The Philadium is a great old-school joint, with cold cheap beers and delicious cheap pub food. With nothing on the menu above $8, the food has an Italian bent, but everything is available, from burgers to crab legs. This is the place that you want to go to before the game for a slice of what true Phillies phanatics are serving up. And the people inside are friendly and knowledgeable sports fans.

CHICKIE AND PETE'S
1526 Packer Ave.
www.chickiesandpetes.com/locations/
south-philadelphia

A minor chain, Chickie and Pete's is the no-frills sports bar that claims to have invented crab fries. The fries dusted in Old Bay seasoning are a good enough option, but we were excited about the "eat with your hands" menu options that allow patrons to get elbow-deep in their meals. Wings, sloppy sandwiches, cheese wiz poppers, and hot roast beef sandwiches are just a taste of the offerings. Downside? It's not cheap. Additional upside? You can pay to park at Chickie and Pete's and ride to the ballpark in Chickie and Pete's Taxi Crab, which will drop you off before the game and pick you up after.

OREGON DINER
303 W. Oregon Ave.
www.oregondinerphilly.com

If it's scrapple you're after, the Oregon Diner is the place to go near the ballpark. It comes served crispy and hot. Never had scrapple? Have no flippin' idea what it even is? It's pan-fried pork scrap meatloaf (everything but the "oink") mixed with spices and cornmeal and it's a working-class delicacy when done right. Most everything else on the menu at the Oregon is good too, but it's the scrapple that keeps 'em coming back.

BOMB BOMB BBQ GRILL AND ITALIAN RESTAURANT
1026 Wolf St.
http://bombbomb-restaurant.com

A bit farther away, but worth the trip, Bomb Bomb is *the Bomb* for baby back ribs and Italian in the vicinity of the ballpark. The first bomb explodes to the tune of authentic Italian dishes such as chicken parmesan and calamari, while the second bomb unleashes fabulous barbecued chicken and ribs, all reasonably priced. This is one explosive combination we find delightful.

L'ANGOLO RISTORANTE
1415 W. Porter St.
www.salentorestaurant.com/langolorest.html

For more high-end traditional Italian, bring your appetite to L'Angolo, but don't expect to be able to eat anything at the ballpark afterwards. The place is small, built into a former home, but the portions are big and reasonably priced (for high-end Italian), making L'Angolo a destination all its own. Try the lobster ravioli or the ricotta gnocchi for a meal you won't soon forget.

SPORTZ PAGE
10th Street and Packer Avenue

Located inside the Holiday Inn, this bar tries to cater to all four major sports played within its patrons' reach, and does a passable job, with big-screen TVs, pool tables, beer signs, and heck, even authentic Philly fans. However, we still can't get past the fact that the place is located inside a Holiday Inn. If you're passing by and need a place to stop on your way to the ballpark, Sportz Page will do the trick.

THE TURF CLUB
700 Packer Ave.

Offering off-track betting at its best (or worst, depending on your outlook), this place has lost business over the years to the offerings of the new ballpark. Let's paint the picture: If you enter the Turf Club in the middle of the day, you'll find old men drinking cheap beer, reading the racing forms, and smoking really awful-smelling cigars. Kevin likes the place, while Josh recommends driving an hour to Atlantic City instead.

CHEESESTEAKS APLENTY

Ah, the Philly cheesesteak. Boston has its chowda, Chicago its deep-dish, Milwaukee its brat. But during our road trip, few regional foods titillated our palates quite the way the cheesesteaks in Philly did.

If you've never experienced the Philly cheesesteak, here's what you need to know. First off, this is real steak, not the chopped-up grizzle your local pizza and sub shop dishes out. A Philly steak consists of slabs of rib eye—sliced just a bit thicker than deli meat—stacked on top of each other on a freshly baked roll, topped with your choice of either provolone or Cheez Whiz.

You can't drive two blocks in this town without seeing a sign for "Steaks" or "Steak Hoagies" or "Cheesesteaks." Which steak-maker is the best? It's a matter of opinion, and a new king of steaks is crowned in Philly practically every year. But that doesn't help you, so here are our favorites:

PAT'S CHEESESTEAKS AND GENO'S STEAKS
9th Street and 1237 E. Passyunk Ave.
www.patskingofsteaks.com/location.html
www.genosteaks.com/

Operating on opposite corners of the same intersection, Pat's and Geno's are the two most famous steak shops in Philly, and usually the place where most tourists head—even though they are the source of ridicule among locals. But since you're probably a tourist just like us, we think you'll find the quality good and the joints make for an interesting destination less than a mile from the ballpark. Just follow 9th or 11th away from the park and you can't miss the intersection.

Pat's has been doing business since 1930, and offers less glitz than Geno's. Pat's looks a bit seedier, but it also has more accolades to its credit. Pat's often garners "Best Cheesesteak in Philly" status from one poll or another. Of course, Geno's does too.

Geno's, which opened in 1966, features bedazzled neon signs and scores of autographed 8-by-10's of celebs on its exterior. These include pictures of Tommy Lasorda arguing with National League umpire Eric Gregg—both of whom were known to put away a few steaks in their day—Oprah, Bill Cosby, Magic Johnson, Britney Spears, Shaq, Tony Danza, pro wrestlers, and some steak-loving strippers. Geno's opened a stand inside the ballpark when CBP first opened in 2004, but that location has since closed.

Both joints stay open until 4:00 a.m. and offer outdoor service only, twelve months a year. The people-watching after the bars close is worth the price of a sandwich.

As for your choice of cheeses, true Philadelphians prefer the yellow/orange goo commonly known as Cheez Whiz, but known locally simply as "Whiz." Whatever you call it, Whiz is always simmering just a few degrees above its congealing point at any Philly steak joint. But we both prefer the provolone, which seems more like an actual dairy product and less like a synthetic one.

A quick tutorial on Philly vernacular is in order: If you want cheese on your steak, say you want one "wit." If not, say one "wit out." If you just say you want one "wit," the help will assume you want it "wit whiz." So if you want yours "wit provolone," be sure to ask for one "wit provolone." We also highly recommend getting your steak "wit" grilled onions.

TONY LUKE'S
39 East Oregon Ave.
www.originaltonylukes.com/

If you miss out on Tony Luke's in the ballpark, fear not. You can still sample the "real taste of South Philly" before leaving the area. Or you can do what we like to do, which is get the pork sandwich with broccoli rabe at the ballpark, then drive to Tony Luke's for a cheesesteak after the game.

DALESSANDRO'S STEAKS
600 Wendover St.
http://dalessandros.com/

Although it's not close to the ballpark, Dalessandro's always makes the list of top steaks in Philly. Meaty, cheesy, and with just enough juice in the roll to induce the "Philly Lean"—you know, where you lean into the sandwich so you don't lose a bite—Dalessandro's is a locals' type of place.

MAMA'S PIZZERIA
426 Belmont Ave., Bala Cynwyd
www.mamaspizzeria.com/

Mama's offers one of the biggest, most expensive, and some say best, cheesesteaks in the area. These steaks are positively ginormous, and we think you'll love every bite. Unless you can eat like Kevin and Josh, don't worry about spending the extra cash, because you're actually buying two meals in one.

RICK'S ORIGINAL PHILLY STEAKS
1625 Chestnut Ave.—The Shops at Liberty Place
www.rickssteaks.com/order-like-a-local.html

Owner and proprietor Rick Oliveri is the grandson of Pat Oliveri, the self-proclaimed originator of the Philadelphia cheesesteak sandwich. And Rick's carries on the tradition with pride. Rick's Steaks used to have a stand where Campo's now sets up at the ballpark. Of course, Rick's replaced Geno's steaks after only two years as well. We're not sure about the reasons for the turnover at the park. But we know it wasn't for lack of quality that Geno's and then Rick's left CBP.

LORENZO'S PIZZA
900 Christian St.

Located in the heart of Philadelphia's Italian Market, this joint got a nod from local son Will Smith with a mention in his song "Summertime." It has also gotten props from *Philadelphia* magazine, winning best pizza in town in the annual readers' poll. But this section (and city) is about steaks, right? And Lorenzo's delivers a mighty fine steak, too. If you're road tripping with someone who's trying to watch her cholesterol, this might be the place for you. Not only does Lorenzo's profess to serve the leanest steak in town, but it also offers grilled chicken hoagies.

LORENZO AND SONS PIZZA
305 South St.
www.lorenzoandsons.com/

The giant mural facing the street outside will draw you in, and the thinnest slice this side of the Big Apple will keep you coming back. Josh always gets a slice from Lorenzo when he's strolling South Street. Then again, he always gets a water ice, a cheesesteak, and a pretzel too. Still, you won't be disappointed by this South Street fave.

CAMPO'S DELI
214 Market St., Old Philly
www.camposdeli.com/

Yet another Philly steak joint that claims to have been voted the best, Campo's has been around since 1947 and serves up a decent steak both inside the ballpark and at their long-time location in the Old Philly tourist district. Campo's is only three blocks from the Liberty Bell, so if you're planning on waiting in line to see the dinger, we advise stopping at Campo's. You'll thank us.

JIM'S STEAKS
400 South St.
www.jimssteaks.com/

This is another tourist place for cheesesteaks. Located on festive South Street, not far from the Clara Barton House, Liberty Bell, and Rita's Water Ice, Jim's serves a decent steak and offers two levels of indoor seating. You could do a lot worse. Jim's has been in business for more than sixty years, and some famous visitors have passed through its doors, as is attested to by the many autographed 8-by-10's on its walls.

Inside the Ballpark

The Phillies did everything right with this ballpark, except maybe when it came to choosing its location. The experience is meant to be all encompassing, eliminating the need to spend your dollars outside the ballpark because everything is available inside. From a game-day-experience standpoint, it ranks among the best ballparks in all of baseball, offering everything a fan might come to expect, from natural grass to quirky field dimensions, to striking views of Center City beyond the outfield walls, to baseball-focused sports bars, to monuments and statues that pay tribute to the team's rich history. There is plenty to see and do before the game, so be sure to arrive early. And once you do get to your seat, you will more than likely be pleasantly surprised by just how good the view is.

Ballpark Features

WAVERING WALL

The dimensions and wall configuration of this park might very well be the craziest built in the modern era of retro ballparks. In their attempt to imitate the walls of Shibe Park, the architects made an outfield that is challenging for the fielders, but fair to both pitchers and hitters. A thirteen-foot-tall wall in right field runs from the foul pole out to the right-center-field power alley, some 398 feet from the plate. In left, an eight-foot-high wall runs from the pole out to the 385-feet-deep left-center-field gap. That's where things get interesting. The wall on the left side of a boxed-in area in center-field stands twelve feet, eight inches, and comes in from 385 feet to 381 feet. Then the wall runs back to almost straightaway center at 409 feet, but rises from twelve feet, eight inches to nineteen feet in the deepest part of the park.

IVY-COVERED BATTER'S EYE

A nice touch to this ballpark is the batter's eye, which is an ivy-covered wall in straightaway center. Not only does it provide for an excellent contrast on the ball for hitters, but it simply looks like a ballpark should. It makes us wonder why other teams have yet to think of this. While some would call

---

Greg Luzinski's Dinger

A replica of the Liberty Bell originally hung from the center-field roof of the Vet. Phillies slugger Greg Luzinski was the only player to ever ring the bell, dinging it with a monster shot on May 16, 1972. That dong was one of seven balls Luzinski launched into the Vet's 500 Level during his career, more than anyone else in stadium history. It seems more than just coincidental to us that a player known as "the Bull" would be the only one to ding the Bell. It's kind of like Mike Greenwell playing in front of the Green Wall for so many years in Boston. Some things are just meant to be.

it derivative of Wrigley, we like it. Our friend Thad Henninger, Philly resident and co-tour guide, said it best, "Maybe when the ivy has grown in nice and thick they'll sculpt in a bust of Charlie Manuel, like something out of *Edward Scissorhands*."

LET FREEDOM RING!

A large neon Liberty Bell above Ashburn Alley is instantly noticeable from the field. It lights up and rings every time a Philly homers. Though the effect is diminished during day games, we think efforts at ballpark uniqueness such as this are what make baseball great.

ASHBURN ALLEY

If you don't have a game-day atmosphere outside your ballpark, why not build one inside? Fans are allowed to enter this festive, history-filled, outdoor entertainment area an hour before the ballpark gates open. Named after Hall of Famer and former Phillies broadcaster Richie Ashburn, the alley extends the entire 625 feet of outfield concourse between the left- and right-field entrance gates, offering an atmosphere similar to Eutaw Street in Baltimore, only with a better view of the playing field and bullpens. Here you'll find great food, cool drinks, water ice, a statue of Ashburn, a full kids area complete with game-show style amusements, and a tribute to the history of Philly hardball. And to top it off, you can still see the game.

ASHBURN STATUE

Widely regarded as one of the top defensive center fielders of all time, Ashburn made five All-Star teams during his twelve seasons with Philadelphia, and led NL outfielders in chances per game in ten of eleven seasons from 1948 through 1958. He retired after playing the 1962 season with the Mets, having amassed 2,574 hits and batted .308 in fifteen total seasons. He then began a thirty-five-year broadcasting career, which continued until a heart attack claimed his life at age seventy in 1997. Ashburn's number 1 was retired by the Phillies in 1979. He was elected to the Hall of Fame by the Veterans Committee in 1995.

Appropriately, a ten-foot-tall bronze of Ashburn running the bases is located behind the batter's eye in center. Phillies greats whose numbers are retired by the team are honored here, too, including Robin Roberts (36), Steve Carlton (32), Jim Bunning (14), and Mike Schmidt (20).

Not far from the statue, Memory Lane provides an illustrated timeline of baseball in Philadelphia, which includes

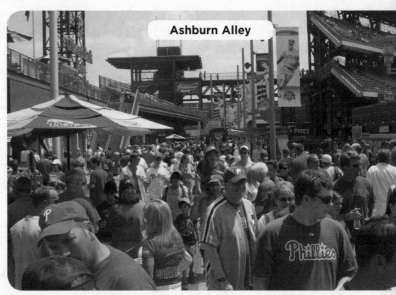
Fans enjoy a festive pregame experience inside the ballpark.
Photo by Kevin O'Connell

historic moments from the Phillies, Philadelphia A's, and Negro Leagues teams that played in the city.

GINORMOUS JUMBOTRON

Watching the big-screen, high-def JumboTron offers a clearer, better picture than your TV at home. In fact, the picture quality is so good on this mammoth TV that you can see it clearly as you drive across the Walt Whitman Bridge.

GAMECAST

A nice touch that we've also observed in other parks is the radio broadcast of the game being piped into the concourses and restrooms. It's another way to keep fans connected to the game when they have to leave their seats.

HARRY, THE STATUE

In August 2011, a seven-foot-high statue of Harry Kalas was unveiled behind Section 141, near the ballpark pub bearing the legendary broadcaster's name. The statue's $80,000 price tag was paid almost entirely by the Phillies and Kalas fans that had launched a petition to see him bronzed.

Stadium Eats

The Phillies have done an outstanding job bringing local food items of choice into the ballpark. From cheesesteaks to crab fries and back again, you can seriously get your grub on inside Citizens Bank Park.

TONY LUKE'S CHEESESTEAK (TRADEMARK FOOD)

The Tony Luke's cheesesteak in Ashburn Alley is a top-quality Philadelphia cheesesteak worthy of an exalted place within the ballpark. The Phillies must have read the earlier edition of our book because they invited one of the better cheesesteak purveyors in town into the park and the quality is evident. There's no real difference between the ballpark offering and that served in the restaurant, which dubs itself "the real taste of South Philly." The line for this place is half an hour long before the first pitch and it just keeps getting longer as the game progresses. So once again, get there early or you might spend three innings waiting for your fix of delicious grilled Philly steak.

THE SCHMITTER (TRADEMARK FOOD)

Perhaps equaling Tony Luke's cheesesteak among Philly's gastronomic delights, this monster of a sandwich can only be described as glorious in its artery-hardening prowess. Originally developed at McNally's Tavern in Chestnut Hill, the Schmitter is grilled steak, grilled onions, grilled salami, special sauce, three layers of cheese, and tomatoes (why, Lord?) piled high on a Kaiser roll. It is a sandwich that must be tasted to be understood, and we encourage you to taste away, as you can only get this baby at the ballpark, at the Philly football venue, and at the tavern where it has been served for more than forty years. We were only saddened to learn that this ultimate sandwich was not named after Mike Schmidt.

Kevin: I like the Schmitter better than the cheesesteak.

Josh: Bite your tongue.

Kevin: It's going to be hard not to. The Schmitter would pose even Dagwood a challenge!

CRAB FRIES (TRADEMARK FOOD)

Another fantastic food option that has fans lining up throughout the entire game is the Crab Fries, available from the Chickie and Pete's stand in Ashburn Alley. As our friend and tour guide Dave Hayden promised, these crinkle-cut fries dusted with Old Bay seasoning are good enough as they are, but even better with the cheese dipping sauce.

HATFIELD HOT DOG (DOG REVIEW)

The addition of a quality ballpark cheesesteak has not been paralleled by the dogs at Citizens. There are so many great options for eats inside CBP that we nearly put this limp weenie on the list of items to which you should say "no, thanks," and walk away.

BEST OF THE REST

Tony Luke's also offers a **pork sandwich,** served with broccoli rabe, that stands up well alongside the cheesesteak offering. The **BBQ at Bulls** remains at the top of our ballpark list as well, as does the Bull himself, Greg Luzinski, who hit 307 home runs in a fifteen-year career split between the Phillies and White Sox. The Bull is out grilling and meeting with fans during nearly every home game, so stop by and say hi while you're ordering your **"Bull Dog" kielbasa.** The **Hatfield Sausages** are great, served with grilled onions and peppers.

On a hot night, nothing beats a **water ice** . . . or two . . . or three. The Original Philly Water Ice has a variety of fruit-flavored deliciousness that is sure to cool you down on even the doggiest of hot and humid summer dog days.

FOR THE VEGGIE HEADS

The generic offerings at the South Philly Markets do not do service to the great food options in the city of Philly. You can do much better. Having said that, we recommend their **vegan dog, black bean burger,** and **vegan chicken sandwich** if you are indeed a vegan. Also, good vegetarian fare is the eggplant-mozzarella-roasted-red-pepper-sun-dried-tomato wrap from **Planet Hoagie.** These offerings have garnered CBP the much-coveted "best vegan food options in MLB" moniker from PETA. But we really wouldn't recommend becoming a vegan to try them, as there are so many delicious meaty options in the park.

SAY "NO, THANKS," AND WALK AWAY

Franklin Square Pizza was disappointing, as ballpark pizza almost always is. Maybe the conditions for piping hot 'za simply cannot be duplicated inside the ballpark, but you can do much better than this thick-crust option at Citizens. The other option to avoid at this ballpark is the regular cheesesteaks they serve at the Cobblestone Grill stands. It's not that they're all that bad, but the other options are simply better. If you can't bear to wait in the line at Tony Luke's, try Campo's. Both are superior to Cobblestone's steaks.

HARRY THE K'S BROADCAST BAR AND GRILLE

We loved Harry Kalas, but this ballpark restaurant should be avoided, because the service and quality of food are simply too inconsistent. If you like the restaurant-in-the-ballpark idea, you may well enjoy Harry's, as you can buy tickets to the special seating sections and get a coupon for food in the double-decked restaurant. And it is one of the two places in the park where you can get the Schmitter. But what seems to happen in all these places is that service is slow, the food is mostly mediocre and expensive, and you can always do so much better outside on the concourse.

BREWERY TOWN

The Brewery Town has the largest selection (outside of the ballpark pubs) of bottled beers, micros, and imports that they pour from bottles into cups for you.

HIGH AND INSIDE PUB

We spent more time at this air-conditioned ballpark pub than we might usually because our friend and Philly guide Dave was feeling uncharacteristically green around the gills from the previous night's exploits. It was empty when we walked in at the beginning of the game, but as the heat wore on, more and more fans sought out the air conditioning and bar service. Dave, for his part, sipped ice water and eventually felt a bit more like his old self.

The Philadelphia Experience

Folks in this town are known for being rabid sports fans. And by rabid, we mean frothing at the mouth. They cheer wildly when their team does well and boo lustily when hometown players don't meet expectations. The fans are every bit as die-hard as the Red Bird fanatics in St. Louis, only much more sardonic and short-tempered. Chalk it up as an East Coast phenomenon, as the fans in Boston and New York are just as unforgiving. In any case, the game-day atmosphere at CBP is festive and electric nearly every night. During the game we attended a fan in the second deck dropped a foul hit to her and was booed as if she'd struck out in Game 7 of the World Series. It's just that way in Philly, you're either a hero or goat, with little room for mediocrity in between.

THE PHILLIES PHANATIC

Hailing from the Galapagos Islands, this six-phoot six-inch, slightly phat, pheathery green phellow with the nose like a megaphone keeps Phills phans entertained all game long. His clowning has inspired the antics of other mascots across the nation. He's traveled the world and has appeared on many other television shows as well.

A member of the Baseball Hall of Fame, the Phanatic is the premier mascot in all of sports, rivaled only, perhaps, by the Famous Chicken. The Phanatic roams the entire park, taunting opposing players and coaches, umpires, and even fans. When not spilling popcorn, spit-shining bald heads, dancing with third-base coaches, and riding around on his ATV, the Phanatic shoots hot dogs into the crowd with his hot dog launcher.

The Phanatic debuted in 1978. Originally David Reymond wore the costume but Tom Burgoyne took the mantle in 1993. The costume, which was designed by the same company that designs the Sesame Street characters, weighs thirty-five pounds.

MONTE G (SUPER-FAN)

The large and in charge rapping Monte G is a local sports cult figure who is easily recognized by his oversized white T-shirt that's self-painted with phrases supporting the home team . . . and by his red-and-white curly wig. And by the news crews that often seek him to get his prediction before big games. And by the fact that he gets invited to dance atop the Phillies dugout with the Phanatic, where he matches the mascot move for move. Monte G first achieved fame with his YouTube Phillies' rap, which you can search.

THE IRON LUNG (SUPER-FAN HALL OF FAME)

Pete Adelis was known as "the Iron Lung of Shibe Park" due to the extraordinary volume at which he heckled the Phillies opponents back in the 1940s. He even published a list entitled "The Rules of Scientific Heckling" in an issue of the *Sporting News* in 1948. These included:

1. *No profanity.*
2. *Nothing purely personal.*
3. *Keep pouring it on.*
4. *Know your players.*
5. *Don't be shouted down.*
6. *Take it as well as give it.*
7. *Give the old-timer a chance—he was a rookie once.*

Phanatic

The Phanatic, as photographed at the old Vet.
Photo by Kevin O'Connell

While We Were in Philadelphia
We Jammed the Can, Philly-Style

We rolled into Philadelphia after midnight, road-weary and ready for some much-needed rest. No such luck. We arrived at Kevin's friend Dave Hayden's house to find the party just getting started. Sort of.

More accurately, we found the remnants of a little girl's outdoor suburban birthday party, and the dads that were keeping the party rolling into the wee hours. After grabbing a brew and feasting on the leftover crabs in the fridge, we settled in to watch Dave and his neighbors play a tailgate game we'd never seen before called Can Jam.

It was so basic it was genius. All you need are four players (two teams of two), a single Frisbee, and two plastic garbage "cans" to jam the Frisbee into.

The rules seemed a bit fluid at this late point in the evening, but we'll try to re-create them for you as best as possible.

1. *It's a horseshoes-style game played with a Frisbee and garbage cans with the tops off and a slot cut out of the front.*

2. *The major difference between horseshoes and Can Jam is that the teammate of the player that throws the Frisbee gets to slap the disc (or jam it) into the can.*
   a. *Simply hitting the can with a slapped Frisbee is worth one point*
   b. *Slapping it into the can is worth two points*
   c. *Tossing the Frisbee into the can without touching it is worth three points*
   d. *Tossing the Frisbee into the slot on the front of the can is an instant game winner*
3. *Game goes to 21—must win by two.*
4. *No matter what happens, the team that is behind gets a final set of throws.*

Pretty simple, right? Well, we wish we thought of it. We played round after round of Can Jam. We hooted and hollered into the late suburban Philly night.

"Dave," Kevin said, "Are we keeping any of your neighbors awake?"

"Nah," said Dave, "They're all here."

When in Rome.

There was drunkenness, some of the worst Frisbee throwing we've ever seen in our lives, friends that kicked the can in fits of rage at the futility of their skills, and a phone call from Dave's wife, Kate, letting him know that we were indeed keeping her awake, even though their bedroom was on the other side of the house . . . and all the doors and windows were shut tight.

Well, wanting to get to the ballpark early the next morning for a Sunday afternoon noon game, we hung up our Frisbees at 3:00 a.m. and called it a night.

The next day we loaded up the Can Jam components, all set to share our newfound love of the sport with the tailgating Philly public. The problem was, tailgating is not allowed in the parking lots of the South Philly Sports Complex!

It was frustrating, to be certain, but we knew we would have plenty of opportunities to share Can Jam with an appreciative tailgating populace, if not on this road trip, then on the next.

WASHINGTON NATIONALS, NATIONALS BALLPARK

Washington, D.C.
40 MILES TO BALTIMORE
124 MILES TO PHILADELPHIA
225 MILES TO NEW YORK CITY
244 MILES TO PITTSBURGH

The National Pastime Returns to our Nation's Capital

Washington, D.C. has a long baseball tradition, but in recent years had been without a team. When the city got back in the game in 2005, the Nationals played at Robert F. Kennedy Stadium, one of the last remaining multiuse cookie cutter stadiums, and a facility that did next to nothing to enhance the game-day experience for fans. With the 2008 opening of Nationals Ballpark in the South Capitol neighborhood known as the Navy Yard, though, the citizens of D.C. now have a ballpark they hope to call home for quite some time.

Nationals Park was designed by Populous, and its construction was funded by the city of D.C., which shelled out $611 million to lure baseball back within the city limits. To us, that amount seems like a lot to pay. Architecturally, Nationals Park's interior is its strength, while its exterior projects the image more of a generic sports stadium than of a baseball park. Perhaps the retro look has become passé, or the designers who had a hand in cranking out fifteen ballparks in the eighteen years after Camden Yards became the "game changer" decided to turn away from the past, and toward the future. This tendency can also be observed in more recent Populous-designed parks like Target Field in Minneapolis and Marlins Ballpark in Miami. Nationals Ballpark typifies this movement. Its white-and-gray stone façade are reminiscent of the Washington Monument, the Lincoln Memorial, and many of the other historical structures of our nation's capital. While this is nicely done, it doesn't cry out to the soul of the wandering baseball traveler the way the brick façade of Fenway Park does.

But inside, Nationals Park is a fan's delight. To the experienced baseball traveler, upon first glimpse, the park is sure to conjure images of ballparks past. The field and surrounding stands provide almost everything a baseball fan could want. The beautiful green grass, brown dirt, and white chalk of the field are complemented beautifully by blue and red seats all angled toward the action, several distinctive design features, a robust lineup of unique foods, and a small but growing group of fans. Together, these effects make a game in Washington a cornucopia of wondrous sights, smells, flavors, and sounds. In short, this is baseball at its finest.

To say D.C. hardball fans waited a long time for this yard is akin to saying the "goddesses" will be waiting a long time to marry Charlie Sheen. For thirty-three seasons, our National Pastime was not played at the Major League level in Washington, D.C. For true fans of the game, those were three long decades. But at long last, D.C. rooters are no longer forced to

home plate entrance

Washington Baseball History Walk leads fans into the Home Plate Gate.
Photo by Kevin O'Connell

drive to Baltimore to see a game. This happy development has transpired much to the chagrin of Orioles' owner Peter Angelos, however. For years the former-trial-lawyer-turned-owner fought to block D.C. from getting a team, claiming the city was part of the Orioles' territory. Whatever "territory" means to a migratory bird!

Not only were Beltway fans left without a team, but many hadn't even been alive long enough to remember when there had been a home team and/or quality baseball park in town. Prior to the Nationals' debut at RFK in 2005, the Senators team that eventually left the capital city to become the Texas Rangers in 1972 had been the last home team to play in D.C. The team had played its inaugural season at Griffith Stadium in 1961 before moving to the newly minted RFK in 1962.

The history of baseball in D.C., much like the histories of the many fine people who spend their lives in service to our country, working in our nation's capital, can be summed up in a single word: transient. It's a town full of people who hold dear the impressive history, stories, and culture so vital to our nation, but the transient nature of the population partly explains why our National Pastime hasn't always fared so well there. Most of the congressional staffers and K Street lobbyists arrive in D.C. with their baseball loyalties already firmly rooted in faraway cities. They still follow the game, but they're passionate for their own home team, wherever it may be, and don't quite have room in their hearts for the team that plays just down the street from where they work. And thus, baseball has a history of foundering in D.C.

Well, that isn't entirely true. For limited stretches of time, the game has flourished in this town too. And when it has, the home team has enjoyed a level of fan devotion that has bordered on the criminally insane, which we mean as a compliment, of course. From 1901 to 1960, an American League incarnation of the Washington Senators called D.C. its home, before relocating to Minnesota to become the Twins. From 1961 through 1971, the second version of the Senators played in D.C., before departing for Texas to become the Rangers. So, in essence, fully ³⁄₃₀ths of today's MLB baseball teams owe their origins to D.C.

Kevin: Oh wait. I know this one . . . that's one-tenth!

Josh: Or 10 percent.

Kevin: Is it me, or are our math skills improving?

Prior to 1900, a variety of other teams called D.C. home too, but none stayed. There were the Olympics, the Blue Legs, another incarnation of the Senators, and four different versions of the Nationals that played in the Union Association, the National Association, the American Association, and the National League. That first Senior Circuit Nats team stayed in town from 1886 through 1889. The Homestead Grays were another team that played in D.C. for a while. The famous Negro Leagues franchise played many of its home games at Griffith Stadium, even though it was always a Pittsburgh-based club.

After both the junior and senior Senators departed in the 1960s and 1970s, the fortunes of baseball fans in D.C. finally turned sunny again in 2005. For the first time in the capital city's history, a team arrived from another town instead of departing for one, when the National League Montreal Expos pulled up stakes in the Great White North and headed south. The final three name possibilities for the new team came down to Grays, Senators, and Nationals.

Surely, the fact that a National League team came had a hand in the pick ultimately being the "Nationals." The track record with the "Senators" moniker wasn't too good anyway. As for "Grays," we both think that would have been kind of blah.

While some contemporary fans may refer to the Nationals as the game's newest team, this isn't entirely accurate. The franchise carried with it a long—if less than proud—history from its days in Montreal. And we believe those years shouldn't be forgotten. During our first baseball adventure, the Nationals' franchise belonged to another nation. And our visit to the Expos' decrepit old dome took place during what we suspected were MLB's dying days in Montreal. An underhanded deal made behind closed doors had allowed the other twenty-nine Major League teams and their owners to assume control of the Expos in 2002 which, in essence, spelled their doom. Those other twenty-nine owners had ordered Expos general manager Omar Minaya to slash the team's payroll prior to the 2003 season, which forced him to deal staff ace Bartolo Colon to the White Sox. Though the final destination of the team had yet to be determined, it was clear to nearly all observers that the team's future would not be in Montreal. This was, needless to say, a sad development for the Expos' fans, who were remarkably loyal during the team's stay in Montreal until it became apparent that the team had no future there.

Believe it or not, upon entering the National League in 1969, Montreal outdrew the three other expansion teams who joined the Major Leagues that year—the Los Angeles Angels, San Diego Padres, and Seattle Pilots. The Expos were the only franchise among the trio of newbies to eclipse the one-million mark in attendance at their Jarry Park. Montreal fans brought a raucous hockey-crowd mentality to games and in fact the Expos attracted more than a million fans in each of their first six seasons at a time when the average

National League team was drawing 1.3 million. This, at a thirty-five-thousand-seat temporary stadium that was widely considered the worst ballpark in the bigs. Jarry had its clubhouses down the left-field line, which required players to walk behind the stands to get to the dugouts. And the ballpark was oriented so that the setting sun blinded first basemen as they awaited throws from the left side of the diamond. What's more, none of the seats in the one-level stadium were covered by a roof. But Jarry had at least one thing going for it. On sunny days, fans could abandon the game and make use of a public swimming pool located just outside the gates beyond the right-field fence. But most fans stayed until the last out before taking a dip.

Kevin: Take that Arizona! The folks in Montreal had a pool before you!

Josh: But did they have a retractable roof?

Kevin: Well, actually, they did . . . sort of.

While the Expos drew respectable crowds to Jarry Park, Montreal was fast at work on Olympic Stadium, which would not only host the 1976 Summer Games, but then provide the Expos with a revolutionary new ballpark. Eventually, the intention was to make "the Big O" a retractable-roof dome. Talk about being ahead of its time, eh? The facility was also to be the Major League's first fully bilingual park, providing all public address announcements in both English and French.

The City of Montreal finished constructing Olympic Stadium just in time for the 1976 Olympics. The following year, the dome became the Expos' new home. Unlike Turner Field in Atlanta, however, which was remodeled to accommodate baseball after hosting the 1996 Summer Games, Montreal did little more than throw down artificial turf and paint baselines on the plastic in preparation for the Expos' arrival. Nonetheless, the team was soon drawing more than two million fans a season.

Outside Olympic Stadium a 623-foot-high inclined tower hung above the center of the playing field like a loon's neck. A sixty-five-ton Kevlar roof, suspended by cables, hung from the tower. The roof was originally meant to open and close in forty-five minutes. But it never worked properly, so the Big O eventually became a fixed dome when management gave up on the retractable roof idea in 1989. In 1998, however, the Expos removed the umbrella at midseason, making Olympic an open-air facility. But the big top was eventually put back in place.

The Expos were poised to go deep into the playoffs in 1994. They had the best record in baseball (74-40) and had drawn 1.3 million fans to fifty-five home dates when the season ended on August 12 because of the players' strike. In their final home game, played on August 4, against the Cardinals, the Expos drew 39,044 fans. Not too shabby, eh?

As Tom Glavine led the Players Association into battle, his Atlanta Braves sat six full games behind the Expos in the NL East standings. But the season never resumed, and the next year the Expos sank to last place in their division, having lost key players like Ken Hill, Marquis Grissom, Larry Walker, and John Wetteland to the clutches of baseball's new economic realities. After the longest work-stoppage in the game's history, fans grudgingly returned to the ballparks in most big league cities, but not in Montreal. With gate revenue on the decline and the Canadian dollar plummeting faster than a Chien-Ming Wang sinkerball, Montreal was unable to retain its emerging stars in the years ahead. In addition to the players mentioned above, other key losses included Pedro Martinez, Cliff Floyd, Moises Alou, Delino DeShields, David Segui, Rondell White, and Jeff Fassero, all of whom departed via free agency or lopsided trades designed to reduce payroll. Feeling betrayed by the game, the Montreal fans stopped turning out at the ballpark. By 1999 home attendance had sagged to less than ten thousand per game.

The final death knell for the Expos came in February 2002 when Jeffrey Loria sold his controlling interest in the team to Major League Baseball's other twenty-nine owners for $120 million. In turn, Loria bought the Florida Marlins from John W. Henry, who turned around and bought the Boston Red Sox. Loria brought with him to Florida his front office staff from Montreal, leaving the Expos without personnel and even so much as scouting reports on the other NL teams. Under the ownership of MLB, the Expos finally replaced Olympic Stadium's aged green carpet. Tellingly, however, the new artificial turf was leased, not bought, by the league, with a club option for a second year, signifying quite clearly that MLB had no intention of laying down roots—even artificial ones—in Montreal.

During the final years of the Expos, San Juan, Puerto Rico's Hiram Bithorn Stadium became a sort of home away from home for the Expos as MLB sought to showcase the game to Latino fans. Before the Expos' first game at Hi Bithorn in 2003, Orlando Cepeda threw out the first pitch. Then pop star Marc Anthony sang the US and Puerto Rican National Anthems, which were followed by the Canadian anthem. Four flags flew at the stadium—those of the United States, Puerto Rico, Canada, and San Juan. When it finally came time to play ball, the Expos trounced the Mets 10-0 before 17,906 screaming fans. But most observers agreed that Hi Bithorn was not fit for Major League competition. At just 315 feet down the lines and 360 to the power alleys, the park quickly distinguished itself as a hitter's paradise. In the Expos' first sixteen games at Hi Bithorn, there were sixty-three home runs. If players "went yard" at that rate during the course of a full season, San Juan's ballpark would project to yield 319 long balls in eighty-one games, or sixteen more than Coors Field surrendered in 1999 when the Rockies and their opponents established the record for most dingers in a park. Hi Bithorn's other distinguishing feature was its bright green-colored artificial turf, which quickly had fans all across America scratching their heads during ESPN's *SportsCenter* and trying to adjust the tint on their TV sets.

But San Juan was just a stop along the way to D.C. And no one ever suspected it would be more than that. The history of baseball runs deep in Washington and for that reason we think it was a fit place to locate the Expos, even if we disapprove of the methods by which the game's overseers brought about this development. While in the first edition of this book we divided the history of the Washington Senators between the two current MLB teams the Senators spawned, the Minnesota Twins and the Texas Rangers, now we are happy to properly display D.C.'s unified baseball history in the introduction to a chapter dedicated to the city's resident team.

Nationals Park is actually the second park so-named that a Washington team has utilized. National Park was the original name of Griffith Stadium and was the home of the Washington Nationals/Senators that played baseball at its location near Florida Avenue beginning in the early 1900s. Previously, Florida Avenue was named Boundary Street, and the ballpark was called Boundary Field, home to the American Association incarnation of the Senators during the 1890s.

On the site of Griffith Stadium there had previously existed several ballparks under many names dating back as far as 1892. For a number of years the wooden ballpark was known simultaneously as National Park, League Park, and American League Park, depending on whom you asked. And we thought politics in Washington were confusing! After the park with three names burned down in 1911, it was rebuilt with concrete and steel, and was once again named National Park. Then in 1920 it was renamed Griffith Stadium in honor of Senators owner Clark Griffith.

But Griffith Stadium wasn't a stadium at all. It was a clunky old ballpark that at its peak seated only thirty-two thousand fans. Perhaps the most noticeable of the ballpark's many quirks was a huge center-field wall with an irregular indented and squared-off segment that cast two right angles protruding into an otherwise regular field of play.

Beyond this thirty-foot-high wall were five houses outside the park, whose owners had refused to sell their property to Griffith when the ballpark was being built. And so the backyards of these homes were just beyond the wall. In one backyard a huge oak tree's branches and leaves rose up over the fence and into the field of play. According to lore, Babe Ruth lodged a few home runs in that tree. A flagpole also stood atop the fence, to add to the irregularity of it all. Plus the park was simply shaped funny. Not only were its bullpens in fair play, but the left-field wall was 407 feet from the plate, while right was only 328 feet.

Walter "the Big Train" Johnson's career with the Senators was one of the franchise's great individual success stories and one of much team disappointment. In twenty-one seasons from 1907 through 1927, Johnson won 417 games, struck out 3,509 batters, and authored an amazing 2.17 ERA. But despite boasting one of the most dominant pitchers of the era, the Senators managed only two trips to the World Series, winning the October Classic only in 1924.

President John F. Kennedy threw out the first pitch for the Senators at Griffith Stadium on Opening Day 1961, before a 4-3 loss to the White Sox. The Senators' incarnation that would later become the Texas Rangers only played one season at Griffith Stadium. Newly built D.C. Stadium was ready by 1962, and the Senators won the first game at

fan embracing technology

Many fans enjoy the game with their tech devices these days.
Photo by Kevin O'Connell

the cookie-cutter, 4-1 over Detroit. The 1962 All-Star Game was also held at D.C. Stadium, resulting in a 3-1 National League victory. The park was renamed RFK Stadium in 1969, in honor of the late Robert F. Kennedy. Ted Williams managed the Senators of 1969 to a winning record—the first in their history as an expansion franchise—and won AL Manager of the Year honors in the process. And the All-Star Game was held at RFK again in 1969, resulting in another NL victory, this time by a score of 9-3.

A popular old vaudeville saying went, "The Washington Senators: first in War, first in Peace, and last in the American League," as the Senators were more often at the bottom of the standings than the top, and quite often the butt of jokes. But Griffith Stadium did manage to host three World Series: in 1924, 1925, and 1933. The 1924 set proved successful for the Senators, when in Game 7, New York Giants catcher Hank Gowdy tripped over his own mask and missed an easy pop-up. This gaffe set the stage for a come-from-behind win for the Senators when Earl McNeely chopped a grounder over the head of third baseman Fred Lindstrom to score the winning run in the bottom of the twelfth inning.

A couple of interesting traditions also began at Griffith Stadium. The first was in 1910, when President William Howard Taft threw out the first pitch of the season. During the remaining time the Senators played in Washington, D.C., the president was always on hand to toss out the first ball of the season. During Washington's long MLB hiatus, this tradition became a Baltimore Orioles' hallmark, but in recent years presidents George W. Bush and Barack Obama resumed the tradition of signaling the start of each new season by tossing a first ball at a ballpark inside the Beltway.

The seventh-inning stretch was also born at Griffith with Taft playing a starring role in the tradition's origin. According to baseball lore, the portly president stood to relieve some tightness in his back during the middle of the seventh, and the crowd, thinking he was about to leave, rose to salute him. When Taft merely rolled his shoulders a few times, the other fans did the same, then followed his lead and sat back down to watch the final two innings.

For all the fervor that was created to bring MLB back to D.C., the team's lack of success has resulted in lackluster attendance throughout their early years in town. In their first season at broken-down RFK, the Nats drew 2,731,993 fans in 2005. They narrowly surpassed two million in 2006, but that

batting practice from behind home plate

Photo by Kevin O'Connell

number dipped below two million in 2007. The team's first year at Nationals Park saw a slight increase to 2,320,400 fans in 2008. But the team couldn't maintain a place on the high side of the two million mark in the years after that. The numbers for the first three years in the new ballpark were the worst since Great American opened in Cincinnati in 2003.

Trivia Timeout

Congressman: Who hit the only fair ball out of Yankee Stadium? (Hint: He played for a while in Washington.)
Junior Senator: Who holds the record for most career home runs in a Nationals or Senators uniform?
Senior Senator: Of the four Montreal Expos who had their numbers retired at Olympic Stadium, which have their numbers now hanging at Nationals Park? (Hint: It's not all four.)
Look for the answers in the text.

Nonetheless, in its brief history, Nationals Park has seen more than its share of historical happenings. The first MLB game at Nationals Park was played on March 30, 2008, between the Nats and Atlanta Braves, and drew the largest ratings of any opening night game on ESPN. President

center-field view

Photo by Kevin O'Connell

George W. Bush threw out the first pitch as the hometown nine disposed of the Tomahawks 3-2.

Josh: I suppose you support the theory that the stylized curly "W" of the Nats is some sort of conspiracy homage to "W" himself.

Kevin: Actually, I thought they lifted it from Walgreens.

The Pope visited Nationals Park on April 17, 2008—not John Paul, but the one after him—and said a quick Mass for forty-seven thousand. Before Opening Day 2009, legendary Phillies broadcaster Harry Kalas collapsed at Nationals Park and was later pronounced dead.

Randy Johnson hurled his three hundredth win at the park on June 4, 2009, while a member of the Giants. Stephen Strasburg, perhaps the most hyped pitching prospect to yet play the game, made his debut at Nationals Park on June 8, 2010, when he went seven innings, gave up just two hits, and struck out an eye-popping fourteen Pittsburgh Pirates. Additionally, Albert Pujols knocked his four hundredth dinger over the right-field wall at Nationals Park, making him the fastest player to ever reach the mark.

Josh: Actually, he was just the fastest in terms of how many seasons it took. Name the two players who were younger.

Kevin: One of them's a Mariner. Griffey, right?

Josh: Both of them were M's, actually. Alex Rodriguez was the other, you dolt.

Kevin: Yeah, I stopped watching him when he went to Texas.

Getting a Choice Seat

As many new parks are doing, a tiered approach to pricing results in fluctuating ticket prices depending upon the relative attractiveness of the Nationals' opponent and the time of year. Thus, home dates are deemed Prime, Regular, or Value games.

Kevin: This casts no aspersions on the teams labeled as "value" game teams.

Josh: Of course not.

Kevin: So it's no coincidence the Diamondbacks are a "value" all across the league.

Josh: Capital-ism. Don't you love it?

Field Level

A low-angled, long deck without much foul territory puts plenty of seats in the lower bowl close to the action. And the stacked design of the upper levels does not contribute to any overhang issues even for the top seats in the bowl, all the way up to row UU. Sight lines are good all the way around the Field Level, and the prices match the quality accordingly. The only mistake that they made as far as we can tell on the Field Level is that the view from the concourse is blocked as you walk behind home plate. This is the case at another recently designed Populous park too—Citi Field in New York—and we don't like it.

SEATING TIP

As soon as the gates officially open, the main ticket office sells $5.00 Grandstand tickets that allow access to any part of the ballpark. The tickets do have a section and seat number attached to them, but there are plenty of places from which to view the game where you don't have to be sitting in your own seat. As is the rule with other deals like this, getting there early enough to get the tickets is key, because the line for cheap tickets gets long. The more time you spend waiting in line to buy the tickets, the more people who have tickets in hand will go through the gate to sit down in a seat that should have been rightfully yours. So plan ahead.

Seating Capacity: 41,546
Ticket Office: http://washington.nationals.
mlb.com/ticketing/index.jsp?c_id=was
Seating Chart: http://washington.nationals.
mlb.com/was/ticketing/seating_pricing.jsp

Presidents Seats and Home Plate Box (Section A–E)

The Home Plate Box seats are the upper seats in Sections A and E, while the rest of the Presidents Seats seem to be filled with the visiting dignitaries of such far off places as New Jersey and Philadelphia. Not a president of anything? Then you probably can't afford these seats either.

> *Josh:* I was president of the Chess Club in high school.
> *Kevin:* Not sure that's going to count for much.
> *Josh:* Yeah, I don't think it did on my college applications either.

Diamond and Home Plate Reserved (Sections 119–126)

These behind-the-plate beauts will cost you as well, though the Diamond Seats do offer Diamond Club access, and that means higher-end food options. Look for these bad boys on ticket broker websites and from "connected" friends only.

Home/Visitor Dugout Box /Infield Box (Sections 114–118 and 127–131)

The Infield Box seats represent the upper seats in the section, while the Home/Visitor Dugout Box Seats are the lower seats in the section. Adjust your wallet accordingly.

LF/RF Baseline Box and Reserved (Sections 111–113 and 132–134)

The Baseline Box seats are along the field while the Reserved Seats are the upper seats in the section. They're all good seats with great views and they're priced at a point where you might not need to take out a second mortgage to afford them.

LF/RF Corner (Sections 108–110 and 135–137)

Sections 136 and 137 have foul-pole blockage issues and should be avoided by those fans who find that bothersome. Some of the seats in these sections should have been left out or an aisle should have been put where the foul pole blocks the view.

Outfield Reserved (Sections 101–107 and 138–143)

Sections 101–105 are close to the action and comfortable and only lose sight of the warning track. They are much preferable to 138–143. The right-field seats are higher off the field, are in the sun, and sacrifice more of the field to sightline loss.

Avoid Section 107 as it has the foul pole running right down the middle of it, blocking the infield or outfield depending on where you sit. Avoid the left edge of Section 138 (as you face the plate) for the same foul-pole-related reason.

The lower seats in Sections 101–103 offer good access to the very open visiting team's bullpen. For gawking into the home bullpen, get a low seat in Sections 137–140.

Center Field Reserved and Lounge (Section 100)

This is Red Porch party area and most of the young urban hipsters in this section are paying more attention to getting each other's phone numbers than the game. But if they were paying attention, they'd find a decent outfield seat ... but one not really worth the price unless you plan on cashing in on the full amount of the discount at the Red Porch Restaurant.

Red Porch Seats

Photo by Kevin O'Connell

Club Level (Infield Club: 209–218) (1st and 3rd Base Clubs: 206–208 and 219–221)

These Club Level seats are meant to be enjoyed by the regular fans, or at least those who don't mind overpaying for tickets. With the price of admission, ticket holders enjoy access to all the benefits inherent to being a member of the club.

Kevin: Which is what exactly?

Josh: The opportunity to hobnob and pay more for food.

Kevin: Okay, that's what I thought.

Mezzanine Level

The sight lines are pretty good in the upper decks, but they are hot and unprotected from the sun, so bring the sunscreen or sit on the left side of the ballpark where the seating structure will protect you from the rays during the early innings of evening games. During day games, well, you're pretty much out there in the sun wherever you go.

The Pros and Cons of Seat-Hopping

Some call it seat-hopping, others refer to it as seat poaching. Either way, it's a practice you approach either with confidence, or not at all. This little guide will give you everything you need to seat-hop with the best of 'em. Here are the commandments according to Kevin and Josh:

1. *Arrive Early, Move Often.* Getting to a choice seat during batting practice is key if you want to sit very close to the action. It's the only time that ushers will allow you into the choice sections without looking over your ticket. When the ushers come through to clear the section after batting practice ends, stay one step ahead of them and never let them get near enough to you to ask for your seat. Remember, they're busy. Soon enough, they will get distracted and you'll have the chance to plop down and let them forget about you.

2. *The Usher Is Not Your Friend.* An usher may look like a kindly older man who scored a nice little retirement job earning extra cash while he enjoys the ball game, but make no mistake: Ushers are the seat-hopper's enemy. If they detect your indiscretions, they will track you down and toss you out just because some boss told them to. Avoid contact with the enemy at all costs.

3. *Don't Get Greedy.* If an empty seat looks too good to be true, it probably is. Ushers are at the park every night, and know the faces of the season-ticket holders. They know which regulars never miss a game, and which loan their tickets out. Your best bet is to try to be mistaken as one of the latter category. And you should use whatever means of deception and trickery you have at your disposal.

4. *Learn to Read Their Faces.* Like a Vegas Hold 'Em tournament champ, the experienced seat-hopper knows how to judge the situation by looking out of the corner of the eye. He can tell instantly through body language and facial expressions of the ushers who will make them move and who will let them slide to another seat because they don't like confrontation. It's a fight-or-flight moment, one that dictates your next action. Depending on your ability to forecast the future, you'll have three choices when a ticket holder approaches:

   a. *Stand pat and let them engage you.* Here you're either betting they are looking for the open seats next to you, won't bother with talking to you about being in their seats and will sit elsewhere themselves, or you feel as if you can comfortably laugh things off as an honest mistake without causing too much commotion.

   b. *The Preemptive Move.* This is used when you know by reading their body language that they seem irritable or uptight, and there are seats nearby that you can quickly and easily slide into.

   c. *The All-Out Retreat.* This move is only necessary in the most desperate of circumstances, like trying to poach seats behind home plate where free food has been offered and consumed. The all-out retreat is complete withdrawal from a section to save yourself from being booted from the area of the park altogether.

5. *Always Have Your Next Move in Mind.* Even as the innings roll past, the experienced seat hopper thinks ahead to his next move, because there is no telling for sure when the ticket holder might return. Like a chess match, the more moves you can think ahead, the better your chances for survival and victory.

6. *Don't Seat-Hop at Ballparks that Sell Out Regularly.* It simply is more trouble than it's worth. You'll have to judge for yourself whether the game will have enough empty seats for you to pluck a beauty, but a good indicator is how the ballpark looks twenty minutes before game time. If it's relatively empty, you should have a decent chance of finding a semi-permanent home.

7. *If All Else Fails—Plead Ignorance.* Tell them you got confused. Tell them you're from the backwoods and it's your first-ever trip to the big city and you're out of your element. Tell them the ink on the tickets smudged or is too small to read. Heck, tell them you had a massive head injury, but do not ever admit that you knowingly tried to sit in someone else's seat. It just isn't considered good form.

Remember, Be Bold and Happy Seat-Hopping!

LEFT AND RIGHT MEZZANINE (SECTIONS 201–205 AND 223–235)

Section 201 has a bit of a foul-pole obstruction. Section 231 has a slight underhang issue and the right-field corner disappears in this section, as well as from 229 and 227(barely). Sections 233 and 235 have foul-pole obstructions that are significant. The pick of the litter of the Mezzanine Level (other than the club seats) is Sections 223 and 225, with 223 being better.

Scoreboard Pavilion (Sections 237–243)

All of these sections have underhang issues that cause loss of sight lines of the warning track and the right-field corner. They are by no means horrible losses of sight lines, but they have not been perfectly protected either.

Terrace Level

This level, like the ones above it, is not as high up as it could be, because the Nationals made one very good decision in putting the press box and the Shirley Povich Media Center above the seating areas rather than giving them their own level, which would have pushed the upper decks farther into the stratosphere. As a result, visiting announcers often complain that Nationals Park offers them the worst vantage point of any big league park. To this we say, now you know how we upper deck fans have felt for years!

LOWER AND UPPER RIGHT FIELD TERRACE (SECTIONS 222–236)

How they get away with calling these 200-Level seats is beyond us. There are three full seating decks in this ballpark, and these seats are clearly on the third level. Seats behind the plate in the Gallery-level are far superior to these poorly named stinkers. Underhang issues don't affect 222–226, but do affect parts of section 228. Sections 230–236 should be avoided as seat holders face an underhang that will cause them to lose sight of the right fielder, foul-pole issues, and the glare of the sun. All in all, we recommend avoiding these seats altogether.

Josh: They're for the suckers who didn't buy our book.

Kevin: When will they ever learn? They could have had better seats, made up the money they blew on the tickets, and kept the book as well.

Gallery Level

The Gallery Level sections only go nine rows deep to the top of the concourse. Because of the stacked deck design, these seats feel pretty high up, but are not bad at all. Sight lines are protected throughout most of the sections, except where noted below.

INFIELD AND OUTFIELD GALLERY (SECTIONS 301–321)

These are actually great seats for the price, with good sight lines from high above the action. We'd sit here anytime, but you won't find the good food options you have down below. Sections 314–321 offer views of the Capitol but are in the sun, while 306–314 provide more shade. Sections 302–305 are the Outfield Gallery seats and are pushed a bit farther down the line, and lose a bit of left-field corner. But they're cheaper, so pick your poison. Section 301 should be avoided because the foul pole comes into play, and you can do much better one section over.

UPPER INFIELD GALLERY (SECTIONS 406–409 AND 416–420)

Even these sight lines are good. The stacked design eliminates the underhang issue and puts you right on top of the action. These seats are high and the deck is steep, but you have a completely unobstructed view of the game.

OUTFIELD GALLERY (SECTIONS 403–405)

You'll find still very nice seats in this level with good views. Just bring the good food up with you or get it before the game. Section 403 loses just the slightest bit of the left-field corner.

a view of the action

Photo by Kevin O'Connell

Grandstand (Sections 401–402)

Though you do lose the slightest bit of the left-field corner in these seats, it's less of a loss than the even numbered 200-level seats in the Upper Right Field Terrace sections. Section 401 is for the folks who want to maximize their bird's-eye view—of the ballpark, the ballgame, and the sunset going down over the Capitol.

Before/After the Game

To be quite frank, there isn't much happening outside Nationals Ballpark just yet. While the marketing folks have dubbed the area surrounding the park "Natty Town," it seems a bit like "Nothing Town" to us. In other words, it's pretty deserted. Unless you're planning on hitting one of the joints noted below, we would recommend taking advantage of the vibrancy of our nation's capital, and spending your time elsewhere. Dupont Circle, Alexandria, and Georgetown all have plenty of places to go before the game, and while they are nowhere near the ballpark, they might provide you more with the type of experience you seek (read: a fun experience!).

Getting to Nationals Park

The best way to get to the ballpark, undoubtedly, is via the Metro. With its vast transit connections, you can park at a friend's place or come in from the airport and make use of this excellent system. Simply connect with a Green Line train heading toward Navy Yard station, and you'll rise from the subway terminal just two blocks from the Centerfield Entrance to the ballpark. The bus system is also very extensive and will get you to the ballpark as well.

Metro Info: www.wmata.com/.

If you must drive, there isn't too much street parking to be found, but there are plenty of lots surrounding the ballpark, including two enormous garages that actually connect to the park. You will likely have to pay upwards of $25 to park, but you won't have trouble finding a place to do it. If you're as passionate about free parking as we are, try crossing over Capitol Street and looking behind the industrial complex near the corner of "T" and Water Streets.

Josh: Passionate about free parking!

Kevin: Yeah, by that we mean "if you're a cheapskate like us."

Outside Attractions

HOME PLATE GATE

Most people don't enter the park through the Home Plate Gate, but those who do are treated to a walk down memory lane—Washington baseball style—as they approach. Every major milestone is captured in stone, from the return of baseball to D.C. with the Nats, to the departure of the two incarnations of the Senators franchises and the garnering of their only World Series, to the Homestead/Washington Grays winning the last of their Negro League titles. The memorial is not the best monument in a city where monuments reign supreme, but it is a nice way to bring together the disparate factions of D.C. baseball history and honor them all in one location.

THE VIEW FROM CAPITOL STREET

A sneak-peek inside the ballpark from S. Capitol Street SE through the Third Base Gate provides a glimpse of a playing field that lies twenty-three feet below street level.

You Never Know Who You Might Meet

Kevin was standing in line at the ticket window, waiting for a pair of cheap $5.00 tickets, while Josh walked the exterior of the park looking for a good photo spot. While waiting, Kevin struck up a conversation with a father and son who were in line behind him. Come to find out, he was talking to Mike Russell and his son Matt from Colorado. Turns out Mike graduated from law school from Gonzaga University, Kevin's alma mater. Kevin often wears his Gonzaga Bulldogs hat for precisely this reason, but it rarely works. While Kevin and Matt discussed the "hows" and "whys" of their chance meeting and talked up the upcoming Bulldog season, Matt joked that the reason they had arrived early was to procure the Jayson Werth bobblehead that was being given out that game, and that it would be well "Werth" the wait. Nice folks, and a lesson that while out on the road, you have to be an extrovert and talk to whomever you meet. It really is a small world and it's full of friendly and interesting people.

HALF STREET

The street that runs into the Centerfield Gate is blocked off before the game to create a pregame neighborhood atmosphere. Here you'll find street vendors hawking everything from water, to chips, peanuts, sunglasses, and official Nationals jerseys and hats. One day, when Natty Town comes into its own, Half Street may well be a pregame ballpark gem akin to Eutaw Street in Baltimore. For now, it's only halfway there.

SILVER BALLS

The two large parking structures that run along N Street are fairly unsightly for a ballpark, but do have a nice little decorative element to them: silver balls. Perhaps to distract the eye from the fact that the main entrance to the ballpark in nestled between these two enormous parking structures, the designers lined the façade with silver baseballs, giving it the look of a Christmas card scene during the summer.

Watering Holes and Outside Eats

There have been other ballparks where we've warned that you'd have to walk a country mile to get to anything worth munching on or drinking. But to be quite frank, no ballpark has less going on in its immediate vicinity than Nationals Park. More than three years after the ballpark first opened, the neighborhood was still being built around it. The Navy Yard, or Capitol Waterfront, as it is now being called, was still, quite literally, under construction. High rise condos were going up fast, but sales have been slower than Pirates playoff tickets.

To illustrate how dead the neighborhood outside the ballpark really is, a national coffee chain based in Seattle was closed at 3:00 p.m. on the day of a 6:00 p.m. game. We didn't think this coffee company ever closed, at any location, for any reason. At some point in the future, people will actually be living in this part of town and they'll need places to go out, eat, and have some drinks before the game. But as of now, it's slim pickin's and slim just hung a "be back later" sign on the door.

SIZZLING EXPRESS
Corner of M and 4th Street
www.sizzlingexpress.com

This is a quick-bite kind of place, ideal for grabbing something on the go. Chinese, Italian deli and pasta, Sushi, and Mexican offerings are on the menu, as well as the steak and cheese sandwich, other sandwiches, and smoothies—and most everything is good. But it's a buffet, and like all buffets, you have to go for what looks fresh, not what you'd actually want to choose to eat. If you've just come four hundred miles and don't have time for a full sit-down meal, this place can fill the void. But beware, it can be costly.

Kevin: Worst restaurant nickname ever: SizzEx?

Josh: Sounds like hip-hop for doing the nasty.

FIVE GUYS BURGER AND FRIES
1100 New Jersey Ave. SE
www.fiveguys.com

Okay, we like Five Guys. It's as good a fast food burger as you're going to find and you get a mountain of fries. It's a tasty burger with fresh ingredients, the burger patties are packed by hand (not frozen), and the fries are made from real potatoes you can see. Though it's a regional chain, it's going

national, and though the prices are a bit high, Five Guys serves up a quality burger experience and is a great place for pregame grubbing. The only suggestions we might make: Let us order the burgers rare and serve some shakes to go with them. And oh yeah, open a Five Guys inside the park.

THE DUGOUT LOUNGE
140 L St. SE

Don't let the name fool you, this place is the bar/cafe inside a Marriott and nothing more. About the only baseball-related thing we could find was the green carpet that looked more like real grass than the turf at RFK once did.

LEVI'S PORT CAFE
1102 8th St. SE

For a taste of soul food and barbecue in D.C., check out Levi's Port Café. The cue is served North Carolina style, which means a vinegar-based sauce covers the tender bites of pulled pork. Fried chicken, mac-n-cheese, yams, peach cobbler, and sweet tea also make for a mighty fine meal. The food's all good at Levi's. This is a locals' place that can be a little sketchy after hours, but you can handle yourself, right?

THE BULLPEN
1229 Half St. SE
and
Das Bullpen
25 M St. SE
www.thebullpendc.com/www/

The Bullpen calls itself a park, but really it's a combination tailgate and beer garden located directly across the street from the Centerfield Entrance, featuring beer served in cups, live music, and tailgating games. Get under the tents if you can on hot days. It's likely your best chance for a festive good time before the game if you'd like to walk into the ballpark.

JUSTIN'S CAFE
1205 First St. SE
http://justinscafe.com/

Justin's is small café, and only partly sports bar. This place features a large variety of panini sandwiches and American-Neapolitan pizzas. Kevin had the Mutz and Sauce, which is fresh mozzarella and tomato sauce with sausage as extra. While the toppings were fairly standard, the crust was topnotch and kept him going back for another slice. Josh had the Rutledge sandwich, which is grilled chicken breast, chopped arugula, roasted red pepper pesto, with balsamic vinegar on toasted ciabatta, which he found delightful.

Kevin: Really? Delightful?

Josh: I call 'em like I see 'em.

Inside the Stadium

The outside of the ballpark is a bit uninspired in its design, with gray and white slate tiles being used, perhaps to be reminiscent in some way of the city's great monuments and memorials. It doesn't really work and the ballpark looks like it could be the home of the D.C. United MLS team, just as easily as it could be an airplane hangar. However, the ballpark's interior more than makes up for any deficiencies of the exterior. Once inside, you're treated to the sights, sounds, and smells that make a ballpark special. Nationals Park feels like a ballpark should on the inside: intimate, well apportioned, and roomy enough to get around easily, with seats that are tucked in close to the action. Sight lines have been well protected in most areas. The playing surface lies twenty-three feet below street level and the bleachers in left aren't too high, allowing for excellent views of the city. Many fans seated inside can see the Capitol building dome and the Washington Monument. This was no doubt a difficult challenge in the design, because D.C. doesn't have enormous sky-scrapers dominating its skyline. A city building ordinance keeps buildings lower than in many other cities so they do not dwarf the monuments and memorials that give D.C. its flavor.

Ballpark Features

CENTER FIELD PLAZA

Most fans enter the ballpark through the Center Field Gate, which opens into the Center Field Plaza two and a half hours before game time, and is the only area accessible at that time. This airy space gives fans access to batting practice home runs, pregame eating and drinking establishments, and a kids' area with batting and pitching cages.

THE HOLY TRINITY

Entering the Centerfield Plaza through the Centerfield Gate, one is immediately taken with the images of three statues looming overhead from Washington baseball past. . . .

JOSH GIBSON

Many experts consider Josh Gibson to be the best hitter to have ever played the game of baseball at any level. He played most of his career with the Homestead Grays, who though they were from Pittsburgh, played their home games for many seasons in D.C. Though records kept in the Negro Leagues were not always meticulously accurate, and while some competition was against barnstorming teams, The Baseball Hall of Fame credits the man often called "The Black Babe Ruth" with more than eight hundred home runs

and a lifetime batting average of .359. He led the Negro National League in dingers for ten straight years. Legend has it that Josh Gibson hit the only fair ball out of Yankee Stadium. He died just a few months before Jackie Robinson broke the color barrier and is buried in Pittsburgh.

"THE BIG TRAIN"

Walter Johnson played twenty-one seasons for the Senators between 1907 and 1927, and served as the club's manager for four more. One of the most physically dominating pitchers of any era, Johnson was said to be a long, tall drink of water with a slow windup that culminated in a sidearm thunderbolt when released. He led the big leagues in strikeouts twelve times—and eight seasons in a row—more than any other player. Johnson was the career strikeout leader for more than five decades. He remains the all-time leader in shutouts with 110.

"HONDO"

Frank Oliver Howard played outfield for the Senators from 1965 through 1971. He stood six feet eight inches tall and was nicknamed the "Washington Monument" for his height and the "Capital Punisher" for how he treated the baseball.

Walter Johnson statue

This statue of Walter Johnson in the Center Field Plaza demonstrates "Big Train's" legendary blazing speed.
Photo by Kevin O'Connell

His 237 home runs as a Washington Senator remains a Washington-based-team record. Many of Hondo's accomplishments are forgotten perhaps because the Senators teams he played for were so woefully bad.

Josh: Hey, where did you get that ball?

Kevin: Well, while you were scoping out the Build-a-Bear Workshop, I snagged it.

Josh: No way! You got a ball at our last game in San Fran on our first road trip, and now you got one on the first game on our second trip. I don't like this at all.

Kevin: Why not?

Josh: I'm afraid the mojo has changed.

MORE GREEN THAN GRASS

Nationals Park is the first stadium in the country to achieve Silver Status in Leadership in Energy and Environmental Design (LEED) by the U.S. Green Building Council, making it a truly "green" facility. Being close to the Anacostia River, the facility goes to great lengths to conserve and reuse water, as well as filtering runoff that will likely reach the river. A green roof located on the roof of the Hard Times Café in the food plaza beyond the left-field foul pole helps keep the building cool on hot days. Use of energy-efficient light fixtures reduces power usage. Recycled materials were used in much of the park's construction, and the site of the ballpark was a former brownfield that had been cleaned up. Following suit, the Marlins decided to build their new park in Miami according to LEED specs.

MACRO BEER COMPANY SCOREBOARD WALK

Three levels of standing room surrounding the bullpens culminate in the Scoreboard Walk, an open area on the second deck behind the huge-gantic scoreboard in center, which nicely provides much-needed shade. It's a club atmosphere before the game, with happy hour drink specials, several dining options, and music. Get here early to score the couch seats beneath the canopy with cold brew in hand, and to line up for the many eating options the area has to offer.

RED HAT—RED PORCH—RED LOFT

Beneath the enormous red "curly W" Nationals hat in straightaway centerfield is the Red Loft and beneath it the Red Porch. The Red Porch is a full-service sit-down restaurant that you'll likely have to get into when the ballpark opens if you don't want to wait for a seat. We're often not very approving of restaurants in ballparks, and this case is no different. If we want to go to a restaurant, we'll go to a restaurant. If we want to go to a ballpark, we'll go to a ballpark. Combining the two experiences makes a stadium feel more

like a shopping mall. However, if restaurant baseball is your thing, get tickets for the Red Porch, and your ticket will get you a discount. The Red Loft is a full bar and viewing area above the Red Porch, and slightly more our style. Except the drinks are cheaper and the views are better in other parts of the park. Again, get to the Red Loft early because this place is a popular hangout.

CHERRY BLOSSOMS

Washington is famous for its Japanese cherry trees, which blossom over a week or two sometime between late March and early April, depending on the seasonal temperatures. They were originally a gift from the country of Japan in 1912, at a time when the Japanese were looking to strengthen ties between the two countries. Look for these spring bloomers in the Center Field Plaza and on the main concourse beyond the left-field wall.

Josh: I'll bet the Nationals wish they had a few more spring bloomers in their farm system.

Kevin: Maybe Japan would be willing to part with a few more gifts, say another Ichiro or two?

RING OF FAME

At the bottom façade of the second level behind home plate appear the retired numbers from the Montreal Expos' days, and the names of favorite players from Washington's baseball past. From the Expos, find Gary Carter's No. 8 and Andre Dawson's No. 10; from the Homestead Grays, find "Cool Papa" Bell, Ray Brown, Josh Gibson, Buck Leonard, Cumberland Posey, and Jud "Boojum" Wilson; from the Washington Senators, find Joe Cronin, Rick Ferrell, Goose Goslin, owner Clark Griffith, "Bucky" Harris, Walter Johnson, Harmon Killebrew, Henry "Heinie" Manush, Sam Rice, and Early Wynn. Jackie Robinson's No. 42 is retired as well and displayed here.

Un-retired Numbers

Perhaps because this city has lost two franchises of its own, the Nationals seem conflicted about embracing their role as owners of the mantle of the Montreal Expos franchise. During their first three seasons at RFK Stadium, the four numbers retired by the Expos were not displayed. In fact, Nationals players wore numbers the Expos had retired: 8 (Gary Carter), 10 (Andre Dawson and Rusty Staub), and 30 (Tim Raines), in essence un-retiring them. However, since moving into Nationals Park, they re-retired Carter and Dawson, but not Staub or Raines. And we're not sure why.

BULLPEN ACCESS

Fans have close interactions with pitchers in the bullpens at Nationals Park, because the outfield seating sections surround the pens without a barrier. It's a great place to hang out just before the game and see if you can talk to a player or get a ball from them. We do have to wonder if the players actually like this close interaction or not. Actually, we don't wonder. We think we know the answer. But it's a treat for the fans.

THE NOTCH

The left-field power alley has a curious little notch where the bullpen wall gives way to the left-centerfield wall at the base of the Red Porch and juts forward for no apparent reason. Well, there is a reason. This peculiarity is a recreation of the notch in the same location at Griffith Stadium. However, this attempt to recreate a quirk in the old ballpark is dwarfed by the Red Porch itself, making the quirk barely noticeable.

Stadium Eats

Nationals Park offers one of the most diverse and highest quality ballpark dining experiences in the majors. There are plenty of great options, from fancy french fries and dipping sauces at Box Frites, to crab cakes, chicken and waffles, Mexican mole and Jamaican jerk meats, to more standard ballpark offerings like burgers, barbecue, hot dogs, peanuts, and shaved ice. Truly, there's something for everyone at this big eater's paradise. Unless you're a *really* big eater, though, you won't be able to try everything over the course of one game, which is a good thing.

HALF-SMOKE ALL THE WAY (TRADEMARK FOOD)

Ben's Chili Bowl gets the nod for trademark food at Nationals Park. They start simply with a bun and a grilled pork and beef dog—burned ever so perfectly at the edges. Then they smother it with chopped onions, grated cheese, cheese sauce, and slather Ben's famous "half-smoke" chili over the top. To finish it, they apply a ribbon of mustard. It smells like burnt heaven and tastes twice as good. You can also get your chili in a bowl, vegetarian, or on a turkey burger.

A TWISTED "W" (TRADEMARK FOOD)

Ever notice how if you bite the two tops off a pretzel, it makes a "W"? Probably not, right? Well, someone did at Noah's Pretzels, and another trademark food was born of these enormous soft pretzels, baked golden brown and covered in salt. Named for the owner's autistic son Noah, part of the proceeds for the gluten-free treat goes to supporting autism in the greater D.C. area.

NATS DOG (DOG REVIEW)

Grilled and with plenty of bite in its flavor, the Nats dog stacks up against any dog in the majors, which is more than you can usually say for the home team whose fans devour it. The only problem? You can't get half-smoke chili served on top without going to Ben's.

BEST OF THE REST

The **Shake Shack** will set you up with a juicy burger caked with cheese, served on a real bread bun, with lettuce and a thick slice of tomato. Don't forget the thick shake flavor of your choosing and their delicious crinkle cut fries smothered with cheese sauce. Shake Shack shakes aren't technically shakes at all because they're made with custard and not ice cream, but they are very tasty. Gotta go for the black-and-white shake. They don't come cheap, but are thick and full of cool flavor and great for a hot day.

    Blue Smoke has plenty of great options as well, even though like Box Frites and Shake Shack, it's an import from Citi Field. Pulled pork, Kansas City spare ribs, chipotle chicken wings, and a BBQ beef bologna sandwich are the order of the day. For dessert, try the salty jalapeno chocolate bar. Josh did, and then he ordered two more to take home with him. Predictably, they melted in his pockets though.

    As you rise up to the scoreboard walk on the escalator, one delicious smell wafts past you, overpowering all others: the unmistakably wonderful aromas of grilling meat covered in jerk seasonings at the **Jammin' Island BBQ** stand in centerfield. The jerk chicken and ribs combo gives you a sampling of most of their offerings and will not leave you disappointed.

    The carnitas at the **El Verano Taqueria** make for better than average Mexican eats. Try the chicken mole pipian, served with two corn tortillas, braised chicken mole, chopped onions, fresh-cut cilantro, and fresh tomato salsa and you will change your mind about avoiding ballpark Mexican food as a hard-and-fast rule to live by.

    Josh: El verano. That means "the summer," right?

    Kevin: In that case, I just ate the whole summer.

SAY "NO, THANKS," AND WALK AWAY

There are too many ballpark delicacies for you to waste stomach space on standard ballpark fare at Nationals Park. The DuPont Deli sandwiches are nasty. It might sound good, but avoid the Georgetown Grille and its more generic burgers, chicken tenders, and fries. Also avoid the Change-Up Chicken. You'll thank us, because it's truck-stop quality. Philadelphia Italian Hoagies: Don't even think about them.

You're two hours from Philly. Best to get them there when you visit town.

STADIUM SUDS

The park represents itself well in the beer selection category, but the deal of the day is the $5.00 Happy Hour before the first pitch just behind the stadium. We found High Life and Miller Lite, and Pilsner Urquell, which is a heck of a beer at that price no matter where you are.

If you want to pay more, the Red Loft in center specializes in overpriced drinks. The people are a cut younger and cooler than other areas of the park. And the drinks are that much more expensive.

Bloody Marys are big in D.C. and you won't have to go far to find a cart that will make one for you. With the heat of a day game, the good food, and the Bloody M's, it feels more like a summer Sunday brunch at the ballpark!

The Nationals Ballpark Experience

Nationals Ballpark offers a little something for all its fans. It's not as flashy as Yankee Stadium, but nowhere near bland either. If you're a corporate raider and you want to impress your clients, or a government employee hosting a visiting dignitary, there's room for rubbing elbows with other rich, famous, and powerful folks. Heck, Kevin even got mistook for the former undersecretary of the Navy by one fan. If you're a young adult, there's a scene at the park where other like-minded congressional aide and legislative assistant types congregate. If you're the head of a family that wants to take in a pro game without having to sell Daddy's organs to pay for it, Nationals Park fits that bill too. Since the franchise (dating back to the Montreal days) is one of only two to never play in a World Series, attendance naturally wavers based on how well the team is playing that season.

Josh: Remind me, which is the other team that's never played in the Series?

Kevin: Isn't it about time for you to go into "shut up" mode?

PRESIDENTS RACE

As has become a customary midgame diversion at nearly every Major League park, people dressed in large, over-stuffed depictions of city-specific iconography must run a staged race, usually in the middle of the fourth inning, to keep fans entertained. If you can't tell by our tone, we are not always big fans of goofball entertainment in the middle of a baseball game . . . at least not goofball entertainment not of our own choosing. But the Nationals have put a humorous twist on things. George, Abe, Teddy, and Tom (no, they're not the Beatles, Martha, they're former presidents direct from the face of Mount Rushmore) get to do the honors and race around the warning track. We like the ironical commentary of four dignified figures, dressed in era appropriate garb, with their bobbing oversized heads and desperately flailing arms and legs, trying to push past one another to win a completely arbitrary race. Now, that's entertainment.

A CLASS NOTE

It is difficult not to notice one rather unpleasant factor in this ballpark, and that is that most all of the people working the concessions are African American, while most all who are attending the game are not. We're not here to comment on issues of race, class, and the culture of a place that is not our home, but there is something about this fact that seems more heightened than in the other ballparks we visited. We're left to conclude that a large percentage of the working stiffs in this town are black, while the members of the pampered upper class who have enough coin to go to the ballpark for pleasure are predominantly white. And it ought not to be that way.

> ## Cyber Super-Fans
>
> - **The Curly W**
>   *http://curlyw.blogspot.com/*
> - **Capitol Punishment**
>   *http://dcbb.blogspot.com/*
>   *Great name, by the way.*
> - **Nationals Message Board**
>   *www.nationalsmessageboard.net/*
> - **Federal Baseball**
>   *www.federalbaseball.com/*

SCREECH!

No, this is not the lovable loser from *Saved by the Bell* turned angry porn star. This bald eagle mascot of the Nats started out as a nestling chick who pecked his way out of his shell while the team was still playing at RFK. But since moving his nest to Nationals Park, this little birdie has been taking wing and has really learned to fly on his own. Literally, the mascot changed from a chick to a full-grown bird, perhaps symbolizing the team's desire to do the same.

Sports in the City

Griffith Stadium
2041 Georgia Ave.

Most of the baseball history that D.C boasts belongs to the little ballpark that wanted to be a stadium, once located at Georgia Avenue. Griffith Stadium was the home of the original Washington Senators from 1911 through 1960 and the second incarnation of the Senators in 1961. It was also the home of the Negro Leagues' Homestead Grays from 1937 through 1948, Washington Elite Giants from 1936 through 1937, Washington Black Senators in 1938, Washington Potomacs in 1924, and Washington Pilots in 1932. Even the NFL's Washington Redskins called Griffith Stadium home from 1937 through 1960.

In essence, Griffith Stadium represented far more than simply a place where sporting events took place. It was a cultural touchstone for D.C., that also held concerts, lectures, and many other important events. Though its former grounds are now part of the Howard University Hospital campus, a plaque where the park once stood can be found on Georgia Avenue.

ANNOUNCER WANNABE GUY (SUPER-FAN)

With just half a set of choppers on both the top and the bottom jaws (different sides) Announcer Wannabe Guy can often be found standing on his seat located below the Shirley Povich Media Center in the upper deck, holding a frayed program in hand, and shouting out his extended and improvised starting lineups and game calls at the top of his lungs. You have your bad self a good time, Announcer Wannabe Guy!

While We Were in D.C.
We Felt Blessed to be on the Road Again

Washington, D.C., was the first stop on our second tour of all the ballparks in the bigs. Schedules had been consulted, plans had been made, and the trip had commenced. Kevin had driven from his home in Pittsburgh and picked up Josh from his flight out of Portland, Maine. And just like that, the second baseball adventure of a lifetime had begun.

"I can't believe we get to do this again," Josh said, pulling his ball cap down low.

"We were lucky to be able to do it one time," Kevin added. "Twice is ridiculous."

And while this was true, things had changed a bit since our first hardball odyssey. We were a bit older, we had jobs and families and *real* lives now. Our lives were full of people and responsibilities that we needed to pull ourselves from to make the trip happen.

We passed through the sites of the great city—Georgetown, the Pentagon, the Washington Monument, and the Capitol building—but our hearts really started pounding when we entered the Navy Yard neighborhood. With all due respect to the great buildings and sites of our nation's capital city, there is nothing like experiencing a new ballpark for the first time. The green of the grass, the brown of the dirt, the smell of the hot dogs and crack of the bat just seem to ring a little truer than usual. And we had nothing to do the next day but head to a new city and do it all again. Ah, heaven.

At that point Josh turned on the air conditioning.

"What are you doing?" Kevin asked.

"It's 95 degrees out. I'm going for some AC," Josh replied.

"Yeah, but I'm the driver," Kevin argued. "The driver decides between AC and windows."

Josh shook his head. "Didn't we go over all this on the first trip?" he said. "Driver gets to decide music and cruising speed. Passenger navigates and gets control over in-car environment."

"Yeah," said Kevin, "It's all coming back to me."

Maybe it was the heat, or maybe the traffic, but we'd already started to agitate one another. Josh was trying to hold back but his frustration could not be contained.

"Do you have to keep doing that?" he finally snapped.

"Doing what?"

"Lunging the car forward, then braking to avoid hitting the car in front of us," Josh said.

"Dude, they call it stop-and-go traffic for a reason."

"You know I hate being called dude, dude?"

"Chill out before I leave you at the side of the road like a busted tire."

We arrived at the ballpark early and after some more pleasant driving around, managed to find a place to park for a few hours without paying. We both readied our ballpark road tripping essentials: wallet, camera bag, and voice recorders for taking notes. It was then that Kevin noticed something strange.

"What the hell is that?" he asked Josh.

"My tape recorder," Josh replied. "It's the same one I used on our first trip."

"Are you really that cheap?" Kevin chuckled. "Ever hear of an MP3 recorder?"

"Cheap has nothing to do with it," Josh defended. "The quality of analog is much better."

"You're not recording the Beatles on the roof of Apple Studios, you moron. It's the sound of your own stupid voice. How good does it need to be?"

"Well, I like it," said Josh. "I have a good voice and it suits me."

"It suits you?" said Kevin. "How many tapes did you bring for the trip?"

"A dozen. Why? How many MP3s can you make?"

"As many as I want," Kevin said. "I have more than 400 hours of recording time with no need for those ridiculous little tapes. I'm surprised they even still sell those."

"Good thing," Josh laughed. "You were always losing your tapes anyway."

"Haven't lost your lame sense of humor either, I see," Kevin said.

"And I'll bet you still refuse to stop for directions when you're lost," Josh chuckled.

"As any self-respecting man would," Kevin protested. "You still listening to that God-awful Kenny G?"

"No," said Josh. "I mean, I never did."

"You did. Constantly."

"I never listened to Kenny G," said Josh.

"Whatever," chortled Kevin.

"Whatever yourself. It's just . . . sometimes I find that music soothing and when I spend time with you . . . well, I tend to *need* a little soothing."

"Starting to wonder if this trip was a good idea?" Kevin asked.

"You said it, pal."

And as we approached the outside of Nationals Park and began to take it all in, we were comforted by the thought that for everything that had changed over the years since we first hit the road together—wives (well, one each), children, mortgages, day jobs, and all the ways that we mark time moving forward in our lives—it was good to know we would still annoy the heck out of each other, just as we always had. One thing was for sure: Our second trip around the bigs was going to be just as much fun as the first.

BALTIMORE ORIOLES, ORIOLE PARK AT CAMDEN YARDS

The Ballpark That Changed Everything

When Oriole Park at Camden Yards opened in 1992, it signaled the renaissance of the American ballpark, and provided teams across the land with a blueprint for the future. A year prior, the White Sox had unveiled sterile U.S. Cellular Field, and before that the most recent additions to the big league landscape had been Rogers Centre (1989), the Metrodome (1982), the Kingdome (1977), and Olympic Stadium (1977). Notice a trend? For more than a decade, stadium designers had somehow fallen under the misimpression that fans favored arena baseball to the real thing. To put things in perspective, that's as egregious a mistake as assuming Americans like Wiffle Ball better than real baseball. Yes, Wiffle Ball may boast more adult participants each year than actual hardball, but that's a statistic born of necessity not our true preferences. The cold, hard reality is that most of us don't have seventeen able-bodied friends on hand to field the two teams needed for "real" baseball whenever the spirit moves us to take a few hacks and toss a few curveballs. So we settle for as close an approximation of the "real" experience as time, able-bodied fielders, and the confines of our backyard will allow. That's what all those fans filling the Metrodome, Kingdome, and Olympic Stadium were doing in the 1980s. What's that, you say? The fans hardly ever filled those domes? Well then, you just made our point. Baseball had strayed from its pastoral roots before Camden Yards came along just in time. When baseball needed a throwback to remind owners, fans, and players of its glory days, Camden provided one and in so doing restored the notion that the ballpark could and should be a magical place.

The park was a hit from the very start. The O's immediately boosted nightly attendance from the thirty thousand per game they had been attracting at Memorial Stadium to forty-five thousand. This led other teams and their owners to begin new stadium projects of their own or to infuse ones that were already on the drawing board with modifications meant to replicate Camden's finer points. There was

one not-so-tiny bump along the game's road to recovery, though. Two years after Camden Yards opened, the owners canceled the 1994 World Series and many fans swore they'd never come back. In some cities, like Montreal and Toronto, they were true to their word. But as new ballparks opened throughout the latter half of the 1990s and early 2000s, most fans found it in their hearts to forgive the game its imperfections and showed up in droves at the new yards. Sure, all of those steroid-propelled home runs had something to do with the game's comeback, and the fanfare surrounding Cal Ripken's amazing streak did too, but the retro ballparks—all inspired by Camden in some way—were at the heart of the reawakening.

Without Camden, we can imagine a league unable to rebound from the atrocity of 1994. We imagine team owners and cities still enthralled with their four-tiered, multifunctional, peripheral-revenue-generating, cookie-cutter stadiums and domes. Across the league we see misguided ladies and gents, each boasting of their facility's capability of hosting a bass fishing expo in the morning, a baseball game at night, a monster truck rally the next day, and a football game on Sunday. We see fans staying home, unmotivated to embark on hardball odysseys. We see an empty place on the bookshelf where *The Ultimate Baseball Road Trip* ought to be.

But thankfully Camden did come along. And today, with the benefit of hindsight, it is easy to see why it won a bevy of architectural awards upon its debut. It merges the charm of a classic old-time ballyard with the comfort and convenience made possible by modernity. That was its genius, which may not seem so revolutionary today, but was when it opened. In the shadows of the trademark B&O Warehouse, fans find a regal brick exterior that channels the quirks, eccentricities, and asymmetrical field dimensions of baseball's classic era. But fans find inside the stadium, as well, nice wide aisles, spacious concourses, and great sight lines. Not only did this park raise the bar for other MLB parks, but it did so smack dab in the middle of its city, paving the way for subsequent "urban renaissance" ballpark projects in places like Cleveland, Detroit, Pittsburgh, and Colorado.

Prior to Camden, cities built new ballparks only when their current digs started falling apart. And they built them on the outskirts of town or in the burbs where land was cheap and brand new freeway ramps could be commissioned to allow for easy-in, easy-out game-day "experiences." After Camden, owners of structurally sound, still-functional facilities began building new and improved ballparks. And they built them downtown, where fans could turn a night at the ballpark into a *full* night in the ballpark neighborhood.

Most importantly, since Camden opened, the "cookie-cutter stadium"—as a generation of nondescript facilities would be ingloriously dubbed owing to its representative members having so few unique characteristics that it seemed as though all had been created from the same symmetrical cookie cutter or mold—has gone the way of the spitball. From Queens to St. Louis, Pittsburgh to Cincinnati, and San Diego to San Francisco, teams that once played in these multi-functional stadiums now have authentic baseball parks to call their own. Each reflects its city's unique personality and celebrates the charm of the game's olden days. Only the Oakland Coliseum stands out as a holdover from an era thankfully past, continuing to host the game in a stadium better suited for football.

Somewhat surprisingly, Oriole Park was designed by the same architectural firm that drafted up the prints for U.S. Cellular Field, a park that would need—and receive—several serious rounds of renovation less than a decade after its opening to bring it up to the new post-Camden par. And it still isn't quite there. Thanks to the mulligan HOK took in Chicago and to the help it received in Baltimore from an architectural consultant named Janet Marie Smith (who would later become an HOK employee, then a Boston Red Sox employee, then an Orioles employee), HOK became the leading authority in ballpark construction. The firm, which is now known as Populous, has left its mark on yards major and minor across the country.

According to local lore, the Maryland Stadium Authority initially drafted plans for a multi-tiered stadium similar to U.S. Cellular, before Smith objected. She insisted on building

a baseball-only facility that mimicked early 1900 parks like Ebbets Field, Shibe Park, and Fenway Park. Old-style features at Camden include an ivy-covered hitter's backdrop in center field; a twenty-five-foot-high "mini-monster" in right; a low, open-aired press box; a sunroof atop the upper deck; steel-support tresses; attractive brick facades; an elegant main entranceway; and a festive plaza outside. More than that, the stadium's orientation allowed fans in the grandstand to enjoy a sweeping view of the downtown skyline across the outfield. The highlight of this stellar view was the 288-foot-high Bromo-Seltzer tower, a Baltimore landmark that bears a face clock and ornate crown. Unfortunately, though, this charming outfield view became a victim of Camden's success. Due to the urban revitalization the stadium prompted, a 757-room hotel popped up just north of the stadium footprint, as well as an apartment building. Since their completion in 2009, the sight lines beyond left-center haven't been the same.

Josh: I think I can still see the top of the tower if I stand on my seat.

Kevin: Camden brought the neighborhood back to life. Then the neighborhood grew. Now Camden is diminished because of it.

Josh: Say what?

Kevin: There's a lesson here. I just haven't found it yet.

Josh: Huh?

interior

Photo by Kevin O'Connell

Kevin: Why are you standing on your seat?

Camden was built for $110 million. In addition the land acquisition and preparation of the work site cost $100 million. This $210 million price tag seems paltry by today's standards. For example, Citi Field and the new Yankee Stadium cost $850 million and $1.5 billion, respectively. Surely that's due to two decades' inflation and the high price of, well, everything, in New York, you may say. And to that, we reply, true, but even Minnesota's Target Field cost $545 million. Camden was publically financed through a new instant lottery game that was approved by the Maryland legislature in 1987. All of the proceeds went toward the ballpark, which angered some Old Line State citizens who pointed out that the park was being funded by the poor, who typically play the lottery more often than well-to-do folks. This came after Maryland's legislature had rejected previous attempts to use money from a new lottery game to improve education. When it came down to it, Maryland didn't want to lose its baseball team the way it lost the Baltimore Colts in 1984. After the Colts left for Indianapolis in the dead of night, it took Charm City thirteen years to get back into the NFL. With the sting of that departure still festering in the local consciousness, it's no surprise the O's got a sweetheart stadium deal. And besides, there was no denying that Memorial Stadium had outlived its day. The multipurpose stadium, which had housed both the Orioles and Colts dating back to 1950, had accrued over the years such conspicuous nicknames as "The World's Largest Outdoor Insane Asylum" and "The Old Gray Lady of 33rd Street."

Kevin: Hmm . . . sounds like it was time for a change.

Josh: Can't you just see folks standing at the water cooler: "What did you do on Sunday?" "I paid a visit to the Old Gray Lady of 33rd Street." "I was at the Insane Asylum."

Kevin: Are you finished?

Josh: I think so.

Renovations to the trademark B&O Warehouse that looms over right field took just as long to complete as the stadium construction: thirty-three months. The circa 1905 building is the longest free-standing structure on the East Coast at 1,016 feet, but it had fallen into disrepair by 1988. Nearly all of its 982 windows were broken and all eight floors were rat-infested. When workers started power-washing the brick exterior, the mortar began crumbling, so they had to clean the rest by hand, brick by brick. The building once served the Baltimore and Ohio Railroad, which debuted as the first operational US rail in 1827. Today the B&O contains restaurants and shops on its lower levels and

Orioles team offices upstairs. On its roof, it houses a bank of ballpark lights.

Josh: I bet whoever built the B&O never would have guessed that one day there'd be all these glowing electric lights on its roof.

Kevin: Or that the B&O would be the cheapest square in Monopoly.

For the ballpark's rather lengthy name—Oriole Park at Camden Yards—we can thank two factions of state officials within the Maryland Stadium Authority. One group favored "Oriole Park," the name of the baseball field used by Baltimore's National League team of the 1890s, while the other preferred "Camden Yards," in recognition of the neighborhood where the ballpark resides. And thus, in this city just forty miles from Washington, D.C., and the hallowed halls of Congress, a compromise was brokered. And then, after the ribbon-cutting ceremonies were over and the politicians had had their say, the people spoke. Fans began referring to the Orioles' new digs as "Camden Yards," so in common parlance that might as well be its name, even if its "official" title is lengthier.

The O's christened Camden with a 2-0 win versus Cleveland on April 6, 1992, and went on to win ten of their first eleven contests that year, the best start in MLB history for a team opening a new park. Consider it redemption for the 1988 season when the O's set the record for the most losses to open a season with an incredible 0-23 start.

Trivia Timeout

Egg: After leaving the National League to join the fledgling American League in 1901, the early birds soon departed for what city?

Hatchling: Which two former Orioles are among the four players in big league history to amass five hundred home runs and three thousand hits?

Big Bird: Which player once hit a ball through one of the B&O Warehouse's open windows?

Look for the answers in the text.

More than forty-eight thousand fans, including President Bill Clinton and Vice President Al Gore, turned out to see Ripken break Lou Gehrig's Iron Man record when he played in his 2,131st consecutive game on September 6, 1995. As usual, Cal soaked up the spotlight, belting a dramatic home run through a sea of shimmering flashbulbs. Years later,

Ripken's record-breaker was voted the most memorable moment in Major League history by baseball fans in a promotion that concluded during the 2002 World Series.

Kevin: Wasn't it really like 2,131 moments?

Josh: That's what happens when you let fans vote.

In Camden's first playoff game, Brady Anderson homered to lead off the bottom of the first against Cleveland in Game 1 of the 1996 American League Division Series. The Orioles won 10-4 and won the series three games to one. Then they lost to the Yankees in the Championship Series. The 1997 postseason played out similarly, with the O's beating the Mariners in the first round, but losing to the Indians in the ALCS.

In 2010, the Orioles started the season playing before the largest Opening Day crowd in Camden history. But after 48,891 watched the O's blow a late-game lead to the Blue Jays, the team got off to a slow start, and by season's end average nightly attendance had dipped to an all-time Camden low of just 21,662.

As of this book's print date, the O's haven't returned to the playoffs since losing those back to back Championship Series in 1996 and 1997. In fact, they haven't even had a winning season since 1997! Considering the rigorous and deep-pocketed division in which the O's play, it seems likely these streaks will continue. Despite this, baseball has a long history in Baltimore and another renaissance is surely possible if the O's can put a winning product on the field.

Getting a Choice Seat

Camden Yards was the quickest baseball stadium ever to reach the fifty million fan plateau, accomplishing the feat in its seventeenth season in 2008. But since the Orioles drew a team-best 3.7 million spectators in 1997, tickets have become easier and easier to find. This can be attributed to the team's string of last-place finishes and to the fact that so many other parks have opened to compete for road trippers' attention. When the Yankees and Red Sox are in Baltimore, the crowds swell to forty thousand or more and the stadium sometimes sells out. But the stands are mostly filled with out-of-towners, which has got to be aggravating and depressing for O's rooters.

The O's commemorated the 20th anniversary of Camden's debut in 2011 by reseating the club level and upper deck with wider chairs, which reduced seating capacity from 48,290 to 45,971. Thus, the crowd of 49,384 that turned out at Camden for an August game against the Red Sox

Seating Capacity: 45,971
Ticket Office: http://baltimore.orioles.mlb.com/ticketing/index.jsp?c_id=bal
Seating Chart: http://baltimore.orioles.mlb.com/bal/ticketing/seating_pricing.jsp

in 2009 seems likely to stand for a while as the stadium's single-game attendance record.

100 Level Seating

FIELD BOX (EVEN NUMBERED SECTIONS 16–58)

Located between first and third base, these are great, unobstructed infield seats. The rows elevate quickly allowing fans to see over the heads of fans in front of them. Section 16 is on the outfield side of first base. Section 58 is just past the bag at third. Section 36 is directly behind the plate. If you have a chance to purchase any of these reasonably priced tickets, go ahead. Otherwise, don't plan on sitting in them. The O's ushers are pretty hell-bent on thwarting the advances of would-be seat-hoppers. We figure these once well-intentioned individuals got a taste of the power that comes from asking beer-swilling penny mongers to vacate hijacked seats back during Camden's glory days and they just can't adjust to the new reality that the team is a perennial cellar-dweller and the joint over which they once ruled with an iron fist is now half empty.

LOWER BOX (EVEN NUMBERED SECTIONS 6–14, 60–64)

We preferred the views from the Lower Boxes along the left-field foul line (60–64) to the views in right (6–14) because the seats in left angle nicely back toward the infield. From the right-field Lower Boxes, however, we found ourselves unable to see significant portions of the right-field corner. This effect is more pronounced the farther you progress into the outfield, so fans wishing to sit in the right-field Lower Boxes should favor Sections 10–14, which are closer to the infield. But if in doubt, shoot for seats in left, which also offer the looming visage of the B&O as a delightful game-long backdrop. Beware of the first four rows of Section 6 in deep right, where railings obstruct the view.

LEFT FIELD LOWER BOXES (EVEN NUMBERED SECTIONS 66–86)

This is one of the shallowest left fields in baseball so it's easy to stay engaged in the game from these seats. We suggest bringing a glove and hanging out during batting practice. We weren't crazy about Sections 66–70 in foul territory, but we liked Sections 74–86 in home run territory, which offer a straight-on view of the infield. Some seats in Section 74 are screened by the left-field foul pole but the tickets for these are clearly marked as Obstructed View seating. Those wishing to peer down into the bullpens should aim for Section 86. Unless you're hoping to spill beer on a left fielder, you might want to avoid the first row in this part of the park, where shorter folk like Josh have to sit on the edge of their seats to see over the outfield wall. Kevin, on the other hand, appreciated the extra leg room.

EUTAW STREET RESERVE (EVEN NUMBERED SECTIONS 90–98)

Baltimore's equivalent of bleachers, the Eutaw Street seats are in right-field home run territory. Section 90 is located in center field beside the dark green batter's eye, while Section 98 is in straight-away right adjacent to the out-of-town scoreboard. Because these seats are at field level, a short walk from Boog's Barbecue, and reasonably priced, we preferred them over most of the upper level seats.

TERRACE BOX (ODD NUMBERED SECTIONS 19–53)

Still on the first level, but residing above the interior concourse that bisects the seating bowl, Sections 19–53 place fans behind the infield boxes. This is the best spot to watch the game if the forecast is iffy, as the overhang of the club level provides shelter. Just don't get caught farther back than Row H, or you won't be able to see what remains visible of the city skyline across the outfield because of the overhang. Don't worry about being in Row A; the tier is elevated so that fans can see over the walkway traffic.

TERRACE RESERVE (ODD NUMBERED SECTIONS 1–17, 55–65)

Section 17, parallel with first base, provides a better view than Section 1, which is out by the right-field foul pole. On the left side, Sections 55 sits where the infield dirt meets the outfield lawn, while Section 65 sits in medium-depth left. In general, we liked the view from the left-field Terrace Reserve better than the view from in right.

LOWER RESERVE (ODD NUMBERED SECTIONS 67–87; SECTION 4)

We appreciated the open feel of the first few rows of Sections 79–87 in left-field home run territory where the overhang is not a factor, but these seats are far from the action. The crowds in Baltimore are thin enough these days that you should be able to do better.

200 Level Seating

CLUB BOX (SECTIONS 204–288)

Located on either side of the press box and extending into the outfield, the Club Boxes cater to those highfalutin types

SEATING TIP

The best seats for your dollars in the Lower Reserve are in Section 4, out near the right-field foul pole. This is the only Lower Reserve section that doesn't have another section in front of it. That's because Section 4 is below the interior concourse just like the Box sections that appear elsewhere on the first level. We liked the seats here even better than in Section 6 of the Lower Boxes because Section 4 is angled to look perfectly back at the infield.

who like to be pampered. They enjoy a special air-conditioned concourse, six full-service bars and a faux Boog's Barbecue stand. But they don't enjoy the same field level view the folks down in the lower bowl do.

300 Level Seating

UPPER BOXES (SECTIONS 306–388) AND UPPER RESERVE (SECTIONS 306–388)

We've consolidated our review of the entire upper level into one section despite the fact that there are several different pricing tiers on this deck. For reasons that are fairly obvious, the 300 Level seats around the infield cost more than the ones way out in left field. And you can probably figure out why. The bottom line is that this part of the park is usually about 90 percent empty and the ushers could not care less about seating-hopping here. For that reason, we recommend buying Upper Reserved seats and moving down to the Boxes. The good news is that it's not frighteningly steep in Oriole Park's top level like in some parks, and the sunroof keeps fans in Rows D and higher dry on rainy nights and fair skinned on sunny days. We really liked the view from Section 332 behind the plate. On the third-base side there is an underhang obstruction in Sections 374–388 that partially blocks views of left field. Across the diamond, fans seated in Sections 306–316 lose sight of just a small corner of fair territory. If you're attending a night game, consider avoiding the upper-level seats on the first-base side, unless you want to look directly into the setting sun for the first few innings. Or, if you're looking for a tan, pull off that tank top and enjoy. To each his own—that's what we say.

To see St. Mary's Industrial School for Boys—now called Cardinal Gibbons School—where native son Babe Ruth came of age, visit the top row of Section 356 and locate the long white building about a mile west of the park. Look to the right where a tall brick steeple breaks the skyline. That's St. Mary's. Is it worth visiting after the game? Only if you're an avid fan of the Babe and feel the experience could bring some greater meaning to your life. We went. But our lives have remained pretty much the same.

The Black Market

Once upon a time the Orioles had a revolutionary idea. Back in the days when they were banging out practically every game, they set up a "Scalper-Free Zone" outside the park where fans with extras could legally sell tickets at face value to other fans. Then, the team fell on hard times and suddenly facilitating the resale of tickets within a safe and non-threatening environment did not seem so appealing. Desperate to sell as many tickets themselves as possible and to limit the ease with which fans may purchase seats on the secondary market, the O's closed the SFZ in 2010. Still, it was a good idea. And it's appropriate that it's been copied in other cities across the country.

Before/After the Game

The Camden neighborhood offers a festive atmosphere. We recommend following Conway Street to the Inner Harbor. Here, visitors find plenty of places to eat and drink, and, during the summer months, outdoor music and street performers. The highlight though is the picturesque view of Chesapeake Bay.

Getting to Camden Yards

Camden is easily accessible from Route 95. Take Exit 53 onto Martin Luther King Blvd. and follow it for half a mile until it turns into a two-way street. Then turn right onto Pratt Street, which will take you to a number of metered spots or to the parking garages on South Eutaw Street. There are more than thirty thousand garage spots in the ballpark neighborhood, so prices are not too steep, especially if you don't mind walking an extra block. If you're in town on a Sunday, look for a two-hour nonresident parking spot or find an open meter. If arriving early on a weekday, find an open meter and plug it until 6:00 p.m. and stay all night. Another alternative is public transportation. The Penn Line of the Maryland Transit Authority's light rail system stops at Camden Yards, and the Charles Center Metro Subway Station is just two blocks from the ballpark.

Subway and Light Rail Maps: http://mta.maryland.gov/services/

Outside Attractions

THE "JANET MARIE SMITH HONORARY" BALLPARK TOUR
http://mlb.mlb.com/bal/ballpark/tours/index.jsp
Even when the Orioles are at home, they offer ballpark tours throughout the morning and early afternoon. We found

this to be one of the most informative and comprehensive tours in the majors. It took nearly two hours and afterward we really felt as though we'd gotten a behind-the-scenes appreciation for the ballpark. We particularly enjoyed seeing the control room and poking around in the Orioles dugout. Our friendly guide spent most of the tour singing the praises of Oriole Park architect Janet Marie Smith, which became humorous after a while. Josh counted twenty-three evocations of her name in all.

THE SPORTS LEGENDS MUSEUM AT CAMDEN YARDS
301 West Camden St.
www.baberuthmuseum.com/exhibits/slmacy/
Located inside Camden Station, this wonderfully comprehensive museum opened in 2005 to honor Maryland's rich sporting history. The Bambino is celebrated here, as well as the Orioles, whose history is traced from 1890 to the present. The 1983 World Championship trophy is a highlight, as are the exhibits remembering Memorial Stadium and Ripken's streak. Other exhibits put the focus on the state's minor league and Negro Leagues history. As for football, there are exhibits related to the Colts and Johnny Unitas, and the Ravens. The Baltimore Blast indoor soccer team, college sports heroes, and Maryland's ballparks and stadiums also receive treatment.

THE BABE RUTH BIRTHPLACE AND MUSEUM
216 Emory St.
www.baberuthmuseum.com/
Three blocks west of Oriole Park, the old Ruth house is a must-visit for touring fans. It's open seven days a week year-round. Just follow the painted baseballs on the sidewalk outside the ballpark and you'll soon find yourself standing at the museum's front door. There are sixty balls in all, one for each of the homers Ruth smacked in 1927. The Museum is situated in the very house once owned by the Babe's maternal grandfather, Pius Schamberger. It's a festive old brownstone decked with bunting, something the Babe rarely did. The highlights include the 500 Home Run Club, a celebration of Ruth's many pitching and batting records, an exhibit on Ruth's family life, an exhibit about the portrayals of Ruth in film, and, of course, the interior of the historic house itself.

Watering Holes and Outside Eats

If you only have an hour to spare before the game, you'll find plenty of chain-type restaurants at Harbor Place, including Hooters, Uno Chicago Grill, the Hard Rock Café, and the Cheesecake Factory. If you have more time, we suggest shunning the chains and going local. We paid $10 for a water taxi pass then realized the city-sponsored Harbored Connector taxi goes to the same places and is completely free. This is a fun way to explore the harbor. We enjoyed our time in Little Italy and Federal Hill, but Fells Point was our favorite nautical destination, with its cobblestone and aged feel. Oh yeah, and its plethora of pubs! One word to the wise, though: If you leave your car in many of the garages near Camden, you'll have to settle up at the bar and get back on the water by 11:00 p.m. on weeknights. Otherwise you'll be left with a long, expensive cab ride, or a cold, difficult swim, to get back to your car.

MAX'S TAPHOUSE ON BROADWAY
Fells Point, 737 S. Broadway
www.maxs.com/

Featuring hand-pumped cask ales, a rotating selection of 140 different drafts, and more than twelve hundred bottled beers, Max's is our favorite Fells Point pub. Pool tables, a lively atmosphere, a huge nacho platter, sports on the tube . . . what more could you want? Kevin tried the McHenry Lager, which had a good taste and nice finish. Josh tried the Clipper City Pale Ale, which had a light hoppy flavor. Max's could have kept us happy all day long if not for the grueling research that lay before us (i.e., sampling as many additional Fells Point pubs as possible before the game).

THE DAILY GRIND
Fells Point, 1720 Thames St.

Yeah, it sounds like a throbbing dance club, but the Grind is actually a coffeehouse. If you're in Crab City on a Sunday morning, or just in the mood for a quality cup of joe, this is the place to be.

Josh: Pretty good. But it's not quite Starbucks. . . .

Kevin: How can you even compare a place like this to a chain?

Josh: I thought you're supposed to be from Seattle.

Kevin: I *am* from Seattle, but that doesn't make me a corporate shill.

Josh: Hey, man, me either. But you can't beat the Komodo Dragon at Starbucks.

Kevin: Yes you can. And my beef with Starbucks goes back to their owner Howard Shultz selling the Sonics.

Josh: Yeah yeah. Heard it all before.

EAT BERTHA'S MUSSELS
Fells Point, 734 S. Broadway
www.berthas.com/

This is Kevin's pick for the best Baltimore seafood. He could eat Bertha's all night long. And that would be fine with Bertha, because she's got mussels in abundance.

SABATINO'S
Little Italy, 901 Fawn St.
www.sabatinos.com/

Having sampled the fare in Boston's North End and New York's Little Italy during our travels, we set a pretty high bar when it comes to Italian. Once you've had the best, it's not easy to settle for the rest. And what could hold a candle to Boston or New York, we figured? Well, Baltimore's Little Italy came pretty darned close thanks to our delicious lunch at Sabatino's. Josh recommends the meatballs and homemade rigatoni, while Kevin heartily endorses the gnocchi. The marinara was superb.

Josh (channeling Brando): Look how they massacred my boy.

Kevin: Sonny was short for Santino. Not Sabatino, you dolt.

Josh: I will seek no vengeance for my son. For I have reasons that are selfish.

Kevin: I'm trying to eat here.

PICKLES PUB
520 Washington Blvd.
www.picklespub.com/

Located right outside the ballpark, this local tavern's slogan is "Come get pickled at pickles." That seems about right. If you're looking to strap on a quick one before the game, Pickles does the trick. Locals order beer-battered pickles to go with their drafts. We didn't work up the nerve, so you'll have to let us know what you think if you try them.

GODDESS
38 S. Eutaw St.

It's rare to find a seedy strip club so close to a big league park. If you were into this sort of thing, we suppose you'd really enjoy your visit to Goddess. We didn't particularly enjoy ours, of course, but we had to make the effort to verify for our readers that the advertised nudity was appropriately, umm, nude (it was).

Josh: I find the word Goddess a bit misleading used in this context. It seems a bit too hyperbolic. Take this woman, for example: Clearly she's unfit for deification and past the age at which the Greeks and Romans would typically portray . . .

Kevin: Whoa. Hold on. You're going to get us kicked out of another strip club, aren't you?

CAMDEN STREET AND EUTAW STREET
Dozens of mom-and-pop vendors set up outside the ballpark. And the competition keeps the prices low. You'll find peanuts and all-beef dogs much cheaper than inside the

park. So if you're road tripping on a tight budget, stock up before the game.

Inside the Park

Combine shorter than usual power alleys with warm Baltimore nights. Sprinkle in Orioles rosters perennially stocked with burly sluggers and pitchers you wouldn't be caught dead owning on your fantasy team and the result is a homer-haven. When Camden first opened so many balls flew into the left-field seats and onto the landing strip between the scoreboard and Warehouse in right that management moved home plate back seven feet in 2001. But fans complained that the modified orientation of the seating bowl diminished some of the first-level views and the players complained that the relocation of home plate created a glare off the batter's eye in center field. So the O's cut their losses and restored the original field dimensions the next year.

Ballpark Features

EUTAW STREET

Eutaw Street is inside the turnstiles on game-days but outside them on off-days. Its Gate H opens two hours before first pitch, and, while the ballpark itself doesn't open for another half hour, the street provides history buffs, ball hawks, and big eaters alike with plenty to keep them occupied.

BABE'S DREAM

A nine-foot-high statue of Babe Ruth stands outside Gate H, depicting a teenaged George Herman Ruth. The future icon was born at 216 Emory St., and grew up in his father's saloon, which once existed where the centerfield seats reside at Oriole Park. This is a nice tribute, but there's one small problem with it. Well, maybe there is or maybe there isn't. It portrays Ruth holding a bat in his left hand and holding a right-handed fielding glove in his right hand even though Ruth was a lefty and should have had a left-handed fielding glove.

Shortly after Camden opened, a number of visiting sportswriters pointed out the rendering's apparent inaccuracy. Historians rebutted that due to the limited resources of St. Mary's where Ruth played his school ball and the scarcity of lefty gloves, he probably would have had to wear a right-handed one. Others claimed the flexible gloves worn back in the 1910s were suitable for use on either hand.

The truth may remain a mystery, but we found the statue a fitting tribute either way. And here's what we were able to confirm about the young Babe's upbringing. He spent his very early years in his father's rough-and-tumble saloon, learning to cuss, gamble, smoke, and drink. By age seven, he was such a menace that his parents sent him to St. Mary's, a reform school run by Xaverian Brothers. The X-Men taught Ruth to play ball. Then, in February of 1914, Jack Dunn, owner of the minor league Baltimore Orioles, signed Ruth to a contract. Because he was only nineteen, Dunn had to accept legal guardianship of him. When he arrived at spring training, his veteran teammates called him Dunn's "Baby." The nickname eventually became "the Babe." Five months later, Dunn sold Ruth to the Boston Red Sox (some guardian, eh?), and ten months after leaving reform school, he started his first big league game.

Another Maryland son, Lefty Grove, won 109 games for the International League O's before embarking on his Hall of Fame career. Though he went on to win exactly three hundred games with the Philadelphia A's and Red Sox, there's no statue of Lefty at Camden Yards. We can't help but think, though, that if there were, Lefty would probably be wearing a glove on his left hand instead of his right. And there just might be a plausible explanation for it.

NUMEROUS NUMEROS

Rather than displaying statues of their former stars, the Orioles display three-foot-high monuments shaped like the players' uniform numbers. This weird adaptation of Monument Park exists on Eutaw Street, where it honors Earl Weaver (4), Brooks Robinson (5), Cal Ripken Jr. (8), Frank Robinson (20), Jim Palmer (22), Eddie Murray (33), and Jackie Robinson (42), whose number is universally retired.

THE WALL HALL

The Orioles Hall of Fame, located on Eutaw, is actually a "Wall" of Fame. Bronze plaques honor former favorite Baltimoreans like the Cal Ripkens (Junior and Senior), Murray, the Robinson boys (Brooks and Frank), Boog Powell, Hoyt Wilhelm, Weaver, Davey Johnson, Rick Dempsey, Brady Anderson, Harold Baines, B.J. Surhoff, and Al Bumbry.

Kevin: They're not very discriminating.

Josh: What's your beef?

Kevin: There's a Gregg Olson plaque. And here's one for Chris Hoiles. Chris "Flippin'" Hoiles! These guys weren't stars.

Josh: You're just jealous the O's have more history to celebrate than your M's.

Kevin: No. Hoiles screwed my fantasy team back in '97.

Josh: And you say *I* can hold a grudge.

FLYING HIGH

A colorful flag court behind the Eutaw Street seats ranks the teams in each of the American League's three divisions from first to last. The banner of the first-place team flies closest to center field and the others follow in descending order toward right. This is similar to the system at Wrigley Field, although more elaborate. In Chicago, all of the flags are on a single pole, with the first place team's flag at the top and the others' below.

BRASS BALLS

Hang around the flag court with a glove and you might wind up with a souvenir . . . or a lump on the head. Balls frequently touch down here during batting practice. In between cracks of the bat, check out the balls emblazoned on the brickwork beneath your feet. Each commemorates the landing spot of a homer hit onto Eutaw Street during a game. The hitters' names are engraved on the balls. Through 2010, Rafael Palmeiro was the brass balls king. No, not because he lied to Congress regarding his steroid use, and not because he did all those erectile dysfunction commercials toward the end of his career, but for his five brass balls on Eutaw Street.

THE B&O

The Warehouse is only 444 feet from home plate, and though the prevailing wind blows off the water toward right field, not a single slugger has reached it during a game. This is because the wind bounces off the Warehouse and blows back into the park, knocking down flies to right. The

distance is also deceptive since the playing field is recessed sixteen feet below street level. For the record, Kevin's hero, Ken Griffey Jr., hit the Warehouse on the fly during the 1993 Home Run Derby. And Kevin Bass once bounced a ball through an open second-story window. Apparently the O's suspected balls would reach the façade more regularly: Before the stadium opened the windows on the Warehouse's first three floors were outfitted with shatter-proof glass. And then the one ball that might have made all that fancy glass worth the panes (bad pun intended) the Orioles had taken to install it just happened to find an open window. How ironic.

HIT SIGN, WIN LOTTERY

The "Hit it Here" sign on the fence in right-center features a hand pointing to an "L," in reference to the Maryland lottery, which helped finance the stadium. Before each game MASN (the local sports network that carries the O's) announces a fan of the game who wins $100,000 if an Oriole player hits the sign with a long ball.

Josh: Well, it doesn't quite have the charm of the old "Hit Sign, Win Suit" sign that once adorned the wall in Brooklyn.

Kevin: You can have the suit. I'll take the cold hard cash.

ORANGE SEATS

Most of the seats inside the ballpark are deep green but single orange seats appear in left- and right-field home run territory. The left field one commemorates the landing spot

---

Baltimore Baseball History

The O's won four straight National League pennants from 1894 to 1897 and claimed the Temple Cup in 1896 and 1897. Prior to the advent of the modern World Series, the Temple Cup pitted the National League's first- and second-place regular season finishers against each other in a best-of-seven series.

The Baltimore dynasty of the 1890s boasted six future Hall of Famers: John McGraw, Wilbert Robinson, Hughie Jennings, Dan Brouthers, Joe Kelley, and Wee Willie Keeler. The five-foot four-inch Keeler made the quote "I hit 'em where they ain't" famous and was a master of the Baltimore Chop, a batting method that saw him draw infielders toward the plate with the threat of a bunt, and then chop down on the pitch to send the ball bouncing over their heads. McGraw and Robinson became two of the game's most famous and successful managers.

As for the Baltimore team they led, it became a charter member of the American League in 1901 before moving to New York and becoming the Highlanders in 1903. Ten years later, the Highlanders would change their name to "Yankees." Baltimore, meanwhile, went more than half a century without a return to The Show, before the St. Louis Browns moved to town in 1954 and became the Orioles.

During the long wait, minor league baseball thrived in Baltimore. From 1919 through 1925 the International League Orioles won seven straight pennants, an accomplishment unmatched in professional hardball to this day.

of Cal Ripken Jr.'s 278th home run, which broke Ernie Banks's shortstop record. Ripken went on to hit a total of 345 of his 431 career homers while playing short. And his shortstop record still stands seeing as Alex Rodriguez amazingly hit just one fewer, 344, before moving from short to third base upon joining the Yankees in 2004.

The orange seat in right marks the spot where Eddie Murray's five hundredth dinger touched down. The shot made Murray just the third player to collect five hundred home runs and three thousand hits in his career, after Willie Mays and Hank Aaron had accomplished the feat. The shot also made one lucky fan very happy. The ball fetched a half-million dollars at auction. Later, in 2005, Rafael Palmeiro joined the exclusive five hundred HR/three thousand hit club when he recorded a base hit as a member of the O's. Because he got the hit in Seattle and since it wasn't a home run anyway, there is no orange seat for Palmeiro at Oriole Park or anywhere else, which given his positive steroid test, seems about right.

STYLISH AISLE SEATS

Each aisle seat in Oriole Park bears the original Baltimore Baseball Club Emblem. According to legend, Janet Marie Smith found this vintage insignia while combing through the Orioles archives. The logo, which features a baller in old-time garb holding a bat over his shoulder, flanked by ornate B's, dates back to 1890.

OLD POLES

If you're feeling nostalgic, stroll out to the outfield seats where some aged Polish fans sit. Just kidding. Every once in a while we like to make sure you're still paying attention. Actually, visit the outfield corners to check out the *foul* poles, which were brought over from Memorial Stadium when the O's moved into Camden.

ROOST, ROOST, ROOST FOR THE HOME TEAM

Flanking the analog clock atop the scoreboard in center field are two larger-than-life Orioles. These are intended to serve as weathervanes. The billowing smoke of Boog's barbecue pit is a much more accurate indicator of wind direction, though, . . . at least in our experience. We witnessed the two birds pointing in completely different directions, while the smoke was blowing a third way.

WORD TO BROOKLYN

Beneath the ornate but directionally-challenged weathervanes, a sign promotes *The Baltimore Sun*. When the official scorer rules that a play is a hit, the "H" in "The" lights up. When

clock

Photo by Kevin O'Connell

the scorer rules that a play is an error, the "E" lights up. This is reminiscent of the Schaefer beer sign that once served the very same purpose atop the Ebbets Field scoreboard.

IS A LEAKY RUBBER EVER A GOOD THING?

Baltimore takes great pride in its leaky rubber but we're not sure we like it in an old-timey park like this. The synthetic warning track is designed to be porous so that water never pools on it, even when afternoon thunder showers soak the city. The track also never needs raking, which saves the grounds crew some time before and after games. The one benefit from a fan's perspective: During BP an unusually high percentage of deep fly balls bounce into the outfield seats for fans to pocket.

Stadium Eats

While the fare at most of the concession counters inside Oriole Park is average, the yard offers a couple of specialty treats that are delicious. The team was in the process of introducing a new stadium-wide concession service provider when we most recently visited, so there is grounds to hope the general quality will soon be improving.

BOOG'S BARBECUE (TRADEMARK FOOD)

At this Eutaw Street landmark, fans find affable Boog Powell serving pit-smoked beef, pork, and turkey. The sandwiches are juicy and scrumptious, while the platter comes with baked beans and coleslaw. We both agreed that the pork was juicier than the beef, but both were superb. In 2011,

Boog introduced two new offerings, the "Big Boog" sandwich, which comes with twice the meat, and potato chips seasoned with Boog's special blend of spices. We enjoyed both innovations immensely.

Powell smacked 339 home runs in a career spanning seventeen years, the first fourteen of which were spent in Baltimore (1961–'74). We mean no disrespect to him or his exploits on the field, but his best contributions to the Orioles organization may be the ones he's making right now. The slugger usually stops by before the game to inspect the day's roast, so bring an old baseball card if you're an autograph hound. Just don't be upset if he accidentally smears a little (very tangy) barbecue sauce on your card while he's signing.

ESSKAY HOT DOG (DOG REVIEW)

This is a below-average ballpark dog. The best thing it has going for it is that it's nearly 1.5 inches in diameter. It's a stout weenie but it's not even long enough to fill a bun, which is a major league faux pas in our book. For adventurous souls, the Birdland Dog is an Esskay dog topped with smoked-pit beef, pepperoni hash, stewed tomato jam, and fried onions.

BEST OF THE REST

Crab Cakes are a Baltimore staple, and the two ballpark offerings are well worth ordering if you don't have time to visit an authentic crab shack after the game. Kevin recommends the Tabasco cake, while Josh preferred the original. We liked the Soft-shell Crabs battered in Natty Boh (National Bohemian Beer) batter. The **Boardwalk Fries,** covered with crab cake seasoning, are also a zesty treat. We found the freshly made hot and cold sandwiches at the **Third Base Deli** attractive options after eating the same old ballpark foods for two weeks before our visit to Camden. Kevin also liked the **Noah's Pretzel,** which came shaped like an O, while Josh went for a **Pretzel Dog** and found it delightful, kind of like a larger version of the crescent-roll-wrapped cocktail franks his mom used to make as an appetizer on New Year's Eve. For a taste of Little Italy, try the **Meatball Sub.**

For a more substantive snack, visit **Attman's Deli** on the first floor of the Warehouse. This Corned Beef Row landmark is famous for its . . . wait for it . . . **Corned Beef** sandwiches. So do indulge. **Polock Johnny's** sausage rates above average, to be sure.

The Bud Light Warehouse Bar is also a convenient place to get ready for the game. Sports radio 105.7 The Fan broadcasts a live pregame show. The bar also stays open an hour after the final out, for those wishing to prolong the evening without having to venture far from the field.

STADIUM SUDS

Fans find several craft beer stands at Oriole Park serving local favorites like Heavy Seas, Snake Dog IPA and Fordham Brewery's Copperhead.

The Camden Yards Experience

Back when the Orioles were vying for league championships back in the mid-90s, Oriole Park was a pretty raucous place. When the team started struggling, the crowds hung in there for a while, but after fourteen straight losing seasons (1998–2011) the atmosphere at Orioles games had come to resemble something akin to that of a Cleveland Indians game. The fans expect the worst and just seem to want to have a good time before the inevitable late-game bullpen meltdown or inexplicable fielding gaffe result in the outcome they always knew was inevitable from the start: another Orioles' "L." That said, the Orioles fans are still a proud bunch, who turn out with something of a chip on their collective shoulder when the deeper-pocketed Red Sox and Yankees are in town. Unfortunately, though, plenty of out-of-town supporters of those two teams usually turn out too and it's not uncommon for them to drown out the fans of the home team with their cheers.

Cyber Super-Fans

- **The Roar from 34**
  http://roarfrom34.blogspot.com/
  This site is named after famous super-fan Wild Bill Hagy.
- **Orioles Hangout**
  www.orioleshangout.com/
  This is the best O's site for bush league junkies and stat geeks . . . like us!
- **Camden Chat**
  www.camdenchat.com/
  This one collects any and all Orioles-related content from across the Internet and presents it in a user-friendly way. There's an open thread, so start chirping!

Sports in (and around) the City

The Ripken Museum/Ripken Stadium/Cal Sr.'s Yard
Route 40, Aberdeen, Maryland
www.cbssports.com/u/fans/celebrity/ripken/museum/museum.html

On the ride from Baltimore to Philadelphia make a pit stop in Aberdeen, Maryland, home of the Ripken sports complex. Just twenty-four miles from Oriole Park and five minutes off Exit 85 of Interstate 95, the site includes a museum, a Camden Yards replica, a minor league stadium and even a hotel. It makes for a worthwhile quickie stop or even a place to spend the night if time allows.

The Museum celebrates the careers of the three Ripkens—Cal Sr., Cal Jr., and Billy. You remember Billy, right? He played second base, posed with the obscene bat on that infamous 1989 Fleer card, and now serves as a studio host on the MLB Network's *MLB Tonight*. And Cal Senior, of course, was the O's manager in 1987 after spending thirty-six years in the organization as a minor league catcher, scout and coach. As for Cal Junior, there's plenty at the museum dedicated to his amazing streak, and to his many other accomplishments.

A nearby youth field called "Cal Sr.'s Yard" is designed to look just like Oriole Park. It comes complete with its own right-field Warehouse (which is actually a Courtyard Marriott). This mini Camden is the site of youth tournaments all summer long. A larger field, meanwhile, called "Ripken Stadium," houses the Aberdeen Ironbirds of the New York-Penn League. The team is owned and operated by Cal Ripken Jr. It is the short-season affiliate of—you guessed it—the Baltimore Orioles.

We recommend visiting the museum, catching a minor league game, and then laying over in the hotel if time allows.

JOHN DENVER SAYS "HELLO"

The locals don't just stretch in the middle of the seventh, they get up and dance around. When "Thank God I'm a Country Boy" starts pumping through the stadium speakers, the place goes bonkers. This tradition also traces its roots back to the 1970s.

SWEET ESCAPE

When the O's hit a homer, the stadium sound technician blasts Gwen Stefani's "Sweet Escape." You know, because the baseball escapes the yard.

Kevin: It's a fun song.

Josh: Not really.

Kevin: Then why are you dancing?

Josh: Because Adam Jones is on my fantasy team and he just went yard!

CRABBING

Another tradition at Oriole Park is the daily game of crab-and-seek on the video board. Three crabs appear. One hides a ball beneath its shell, making like a Times Square huckster. The crabs then frantically scramble around the screen while fans try to keep track of which one has the ball.

Josh: The one on the right. I mean the left. The middle. The middle. The middle.

Kevin: Wake me when it's over.

WILD BILL HAGY (SUPER-FAN HALL OF FAME)

A well-known fan in the 1970s and early 1980s, Orioles devotee Wild Bill Hagy was a Maryland cab driver, who would hop up on top of the home dugout at Memorial Stadium and treat fans to his trademark "Roar from Thirty-Four," so-called due to Hagy's preferred seating location in Section 34. Hagy was also the one who started the tradition of yelling "O" when the National Anthem singer gets to the "Oh, say does that Star-Spangled Banner yet wave" line in the "Star-Spangled Banner." Hagy deserves credit for inspiring a tradition that has lasted long beyond his days, a tradition that even traveled with his favorite team and its fans to their new ballpark.

While We Were in Baltimore
We Met a Legendary Super-Fan

Talk about a dream job . . . well, other than ours. After meeting one of his helpers during our water taxi ride earlier in the day, we sought out Jay Buckley in section 74 of Oriole Park's left-field boxes. Jay is the founder and director of the oldest national baseball tour business in the country, *Jay Buckley's Baseball Tours*. You've probably seen his ad in the newspaper.

Jay, who runs his company out of La Crosse, Wisconsin, told us he began traveling to ballparks in the 1970s during his vacation time. In 1982, he took his first tour groups on the road, chauffeuring forty-two people around the country. In 2011, more than twelve hundred people joined Jay on his twenty-four bus tours that departed via luxury coach from cities across the country. Jay's schedule takes him and his traveling band of fans to spring training games in Florida and Arizona each year, too, and to the National Baseball Hall of Fame.

In case you're wondering, Jay grew up a Milwaukee Braves fan. We tried to pin him down on his favorite team these days, but he wouldn't play ball. "I'm a fan of the game," he said. "I hope every division goes down to the final day of the season."

Some folks in Jay's position might have seen our book as a threat, but Jay seemed genuinely happy to make our acquaintance. He seemed to agree with our take on the matter: there's room for an ultimate baseball tour book *and* an ultimate baseball tour guide in the MLB universe. So we offer Jay our whole-hearted endorsement. If your car's in the shop, if you're waiting out a ninety-day license revocation, or if driving just isn't your thing, check out Jay's itinerary at www.jaybuckley.com/.

ATLANTA BRAVES, TURNER FIELD

ATLANTA, GEORGIA
465 MILES TO CINCINNATI
480 MILES TO ST. PETERSBURG
555 MILES TO ST. LOUIS
640 MILES TO WASHINGTON

The Tomahawk Chopping Grounds

The Braves strive to make Turner Field a game-day setting fans of all ages will find highly stimulating. And the team largely succeeds in this mission. Aside from providing a beautiful lawn for a game, the stadium also functions as something of an entertainment machine. To begin, it comes complete with two massive video boards—one for fans in the seating bowl and one for fans on the ginormous entry plaza/food court. Its nooks and crannies also house more than seven hundred flat-screen TVs throughout the park. But what would you expect in the town where cable pioneer and stadium namesake Ted Turner reinvented television and where the network he founded—CNN—still bases its world headquarters?

More than just catering to tube-heads and technophiles, though, Turner Field also meets the needs of every other stripe of fan. For hardball history buffs, it offers a plaza chock full of statues and monuments, a top-notch franchise Hall of Fame, and a portion of the left-field wall from old Fulton County Stadium, marking the spot over which Hank Aaron's record-breaking 715th home run sailed. For art aficionados, Turner features baseball sculptures and murals. For armchair managers—or perhaps we should say general managers—Scouts Alley provides vintage player evaluation reports pertaining to some of the Braves most memorable players. For big eaters and dog lovers, Turner more than satisfies. And for kids, Turner provides video games, goofy contests, fuzzy mascots, and a thirty-three-thousand-square-foot fun zone called Tooner Field. Oh, and did we mention there's a miniature field where fans can test their skills on the upper deck?

Does Turner Field try to do too much? Maybe. All of the peripheral activity can distract from the game a bit. But we enjoyed our stroll through Scouts Alley almost as much as we enjoyed watching the game. And ever since Josh left Atlanta he's been hankering for another Bison Dog. And Kevin can't stop talking about the autographs he got at Tooner Field . . . for his girls, of course, not himself.

As for its not-so-humble beginnings, Turner Field came into existence in the mid-1990s when the Braves joined forces with Atlanta's Olympic Committee to build a stadium capable of hosting the track-and-field portion of the 1996 Summer Games. From the start, the plan was to build a stadium that could afterwards be remodeled to accommodate baseball. Notice, we said, "remodeled." Unlike old Olympic Stadium in Montreal, which underwent very few modifications before being handed over to Les Expos after the 1976 Games, "The Ted" underwent a serious reconfiguring. The conversion cost the Braves $35.5 million. Clearly this was money well spent. Turner Field is a superb stadium for baseball.

Just how drastic was the remodeling, you wonder? Well, the huge limestone columns you'll notice rising on the plaza outside the main entrance once supported seats for the Olympic Games. Back then, the stadium held eighty-five thousand spectators. Now The Ted accommodates only about fifty thousand. Imagine, the expansive entrance plaza that makes the facility so distinctive today was once part of the stadium's interior. And yet, all of this work was completed between September 1996 and April 1997. That's a pretty ambitious makeover in our book.

Kevin: I got a makeover once.

Josh: Yes, I remember.

Kevin: It was back when the first edition of *The Ultimate Baseball Road Trip* came out, right before our debut appearance on ESPN's *Cold Pizza*.

Josh: Yes, our *debut* appearance, and *only* appearance.

Kevin: I still can't believe you said "bull testicles" on national TV.

Josh: Hey, Rocky Mountain Oysters deserved an honest description.

Kevin: And you sure provided one.

The Braves opened Turner Field, with a 5-4 come-from-behind win against the Cubs on April 4, 1997. Later that year, Atlanta won the first two postseason games at Turner Field,

117

interior

Photo by Kevin O'Connell

on the way to a sweep of the Astros in the National League Division Series. The Braves lost in the National League Championship Series, however, to the Marlins, who went on to win the World Series.

As for The Ted's predecessor, the city imploded multipurpose Atlanta-Fulton County Stadium in 1997. The facility had been the home of the Braves since they moved from Milwaukee to A-Town in 1966. But the stadium wasn't theirs alone. They shared Fulton with the NFL's Atlanta Falcons until the "Dirty Birds" finally migrated to the Georgia Dome in 1992.

"The Launching Pad," as Fulton County Stadium was often called, was the Coors Field of its day thanks to its altitude of more than a thousand feet above sea level, which resulted in a higher-than-usual number of home runs. Today, Turner Field sits not far from the old stadium's footprint at the very same altitude, but folks don't make as much fuss about its homer-friendliness in the wake of so many long-ball-friendly yards that have popped up in recent years. And they shouldn't. From 2001 through 2010 Turner Field only once cracked the top-ten list of parks allowing the most homers per game.

Although it was a multipurpose facility, Fulton County Stadium had some interesting features that distinguished it from the other cookie-cutters. Chief among these were some Native American features that would likely be deemed politically incorrect by today's standards. For example, when the Braves first arrived, "Big Victor" stood beyond the outfield fence. The totem pole's eyes would light up whenever a Brave homered. Then in 1967 fans welcomed Chief Noc-A-Homa to the yard. The tepee stood on a platform behind the outfield fence until it was removed in September 1982 as the Braves, expecting to make the playoffs, freed up space for extra seats. When the team began slumping, the Chief was restored to his rightful place and the Braves rediscovered their winning ways en route to claiming the National League West title by a single game over the Dodgers. Yes, you read that right. The geographically confused overseers of the American Game once had Atlanta playing in the Senior Circuit's *western* division. This madness was fortunately remedied by the realignment of 1994. As for those 1982 Braves, they were swept by the eventual World Champion Cardinals in the NLCS.

Hank Aaron made Atlanta's 1974 home opener memorable, swatting homer No. 715 against the Dodgers. The shot broke Babe Ruth's career record and has since become one of those magical baseball moments, right up there with Bobby Thomson's "Shot Heard 'Round the World" and Kirk Gibson's limp around the bases. What baseball fan worth his salt wouldn't recognize the now grainy footage of Aaron circling the bases trailed by those two goofy college kids who jumped out of the seats to accompany him?

After the 1974 season, the Braves traded "Hammering Hank" to Milwaukee, where he finished his career with two mediocre seasons in the city where it began. For the Braves, a prolonged spell of futility continued. Between 1970 and 1990 the team enjoyed just four winning seasons, despite being billed as "America's Team" for much of that time as TBS beamed their foibles into living rooms across the country. Under Turner's ownership, the team eventually recovered to post the best winning percentage in the Majors during the 1990s, though. The highlight of this resurgence was a World Series title, clinched at Fulton County Stadium against the Indians in 1995. Atlanta won the sixth and deciding game, 1-0, behind a combined one-hitter by Tom Glavine and Mark Wohlers. Dave Justice accounted for the lone run, with a sixth-inning homer.

The last game ever played at Fulton County Stadium was Game 5 of the 1996 World Series, a 1-0 loss against

Andy Pettitte and the Yankees that left the Braves down three games to one in a Series they would lose two days later. No other park closed its gates for the last time after a World Series contest.

Before moving to Hot-lanta, the Braves had called Brew City's County Stadium "home" from 1953 to 1965. To learn more about that park, refer to our chapter on Milwaukee. Going back even further, to before the Braves' stay in the Land of Brats, the team had played at Braves Field in Boston from 1915 to 1952. The franchise's history in Boston dates back to 1871 when it played as the Boston Red Stockings in the National Association, which became the National League in 1876. By 1889 the team was more commonly called the Beaneaters, and by 1909 the nickname had changed to Braves. Always second to the Red Sox in the hearts of New Englanders, the Braves struggled to draw fans in the 1930s and 1940s. In the Braves' last season in Boston, only 280,000 fans turned out to see them play. The Red Sox drew 1.12 million that year.

So the Braves moved to Milwaukee after the 1952 season as part of the NL's first realignment of the Modern Era. Initially, the move was a smashing success. The Braves set an NL attendance record, drawing 1.8 million fans in 1953. Then, in 1957 Lew Burdette blanked the Yankees in Game 7 of the World Series to bring the Braves their first title since 1914. The next year, the Braves fell to the Yankees in another seven-game October Classic. Despite the team's success on the field, attendance steadily dropped at County Stadium, though, reaching a nadir in 1965 when the Braves attracted just 550,000 fans.

interior

Photo by Kevin O'Connell

So, off to Atlanta the team headed, where in 1966 more than 1.5 million people visited Fulton County Stadium to see Aaron swat homers and Phil Niekro toss butterflies past batters. The Braves flourished in Atlanta—for a while. But by 1975 they were struggling to draw again. Having dealt Aaron to the Brewers, the Braves attracted just 530,000 fans. Turner bought the team that year and added it to his Turner Broadcasting portfolio. Soon, fans across the country were "treated" to Braves games on TBS. Fast-forward two decades and Turner shrewdly parlayed the team's revival and Atlanta's Olympics into a shiny new ballpark for his team. But Turner Broadcasting merged with Time Warner in 2001. And later, the conglomerate merged with AOL. For a while Mr. Turner played a leading role in the new company, but when he resigned his post as AOL Time Warner's vice chairman in early 2003, his reign as Braves boss officially ended. In 2007 Time Warner sold the Braves to Liberty Media Group, further distancing the team from the family of companies Ted once led.

But despite this, and despite the memories we still have of Turner and his one-time sweetheart Jane Fonda snoozing beside Jimmy Carter in the owner's box during a playoff game, fans should not forget the impact Ted Turner had on the game. He turned the Braves, perennial losers, into the most dominant team in the National League, and brought a premier ballpark to the city. And he brought about a world of new possibilities in how we enjoy the game on the tube as well.

Nonetheless, it should be noted that Atlanta had a long love affair with baseball before Mr. Turner and even the Braves arrived. The game's roots in the city run deep, even if Atlanta has only been a Major League city for five decades. From 1901 to 1965 the Atlanta Crackers were the most successful minor league team in the country. The class of the Southern Association spent most of its history competing at the Double-A level and thanks to its success was regarded as the minor leagues' version of the Yankees. The Crackers won seventeen Southern Association titles in all, playing primarily at Ponce de Leon Park and then Spiller Field, before spending their final season at Fulton County Stadium, as the city awaited the Braves' arrival.

The Negro League's Atlanta Black Crackers were nearly as successful as their white counterparts after beginning play in 1919. For more information on both teams, we recommend Tim Darnell's book *The Crackers: Early Days of Atlanta Baseball*. As the book attests, winning teams are as much a part of Atlanta culture as peanut butter and Coca-Cola. And after some down years in the 1970s and 1980s, the Braves have more than done their part to uphold this tradition.

Getting a Choice Seat

Despite their winning ways the Braves have faced a persistent challenge when it comes to filling their ballpark. Well, that may be overstating things. The team does draw a respectable two and a half million fans a year, or about thirty thousand per game. But these totals place the Braves in the middle of the pack compared to the other thirty teams. And, owing to their consistent success and the quality of Turner Field, they should be drawing larger crowds. What's more, the Braves have failed to sell out many playoff games through the years. When they were the class of the league back in the 1990s this was the case and, more recently, it has been as well. The Braves closed out the 2010 season, for example, with a Game 4 loss to the San Francisco Giants in the National League Division Series before a crowd of 44,532. More than fifty-three thousand fans had turned out the day before to watch the Braves fall 3-2 in Game 3, but with the team facing elimination Turner Field suddenly had six thousand empty seats and its standing-room areas were deserted.

Have Braves fans been spoiled by the team's success? Is Atlanta's ballpark just too big for America's thirty-third largest city? Does the fact that Atlanta is full of transplants from points elsewhere subdue enthusiasm for the home team? Is the city's steamy weather to blame? The answer is likely all of the above. In any case, we like the cheap tickets—available from scalpers outside the park or from the box office—that are the result of this lukewarm love affair between Atlanta fans and the Braves.

The North Gate opens three hours prior to game time, allowing fans the chance to watch batting practice from the outfield seats and to visit Scouts Alley and the massive food court. The concourses are wide, the seats big and sturdy, and there's ample room between rows. Even the outfield and upper-level seats are angled toward the infield. Every aisle seat showcases a swinging Hank Aaron silhouette.

On all levels of the park, odd-numbered sections appear on the first-base side, while even-numbered ones appear on the third-base side. Section 100 at Field Level is directly behind home plate. Section 200 on the Terrace Level is as well. And Section 400 is behind the plate on the Upper Level. On the Club Level, there is no Section 300 because the press box sits where it would be.

The first row of the upper level hangs over the lower bowl's back rows, thus preventing any sort of overhang obstruction for those below. This is a well-conceived seating approach.

Seating Capacity: 50,097
Ticket Office: http://atlanta.braves.mlb.com/ticketing/index.jsp?c_id=atl
Seating Chart: http://atlanta.braves.mlb.com/atl/ticketing/seating_and_pricing.jsp

Dugout (Sections 100–118)

These infield box seats extend from third base to home plate and then around the bend to first. They are sloped at a significant enough pitch to allow shorter fans to easily see over the heads of those in front of them. Really, every one of these seats is a winner, kind of like those starting pitchers the Braves used to roll out in the '90s. Fans without tickets to these sections are welcome to stop by for a peek during batting practice. But an hour before the game an announcement over the P.A. asks non-ticket holders to vacate the area. This seems fair to us. Hey, we figure that by the time this book warrants a third edition we'll be able to afford the good seats, and when that day comes, we don't want a bunch of slobs mucking up the view and leaving peanut shells on our seats.

Kevin: Who are we kidding? We'll be seat-hopping slobs till the day we die.

Josh: Umm . . . Right. I'm heading to the SunTrust Club. I'll catch you later.

Kevin: Isn't that a highly exclusive luxury club with gourmet food? They won't let you in.

Josh: Probably not. But I'll catch you later.

Kevin: Josh?

Josh: Please, don't follow me.

Kevin: You're going to the Club level. You sellout!

Josh: I said don't follow me!

Field (Sections 119–124) and Field Reserved (Sections 125–129)

The Field seats are between first base and the right-field foul pole and third base and the left-field pole. The two outfield-most sections on either side house Field Reserved seats and sell for a few dollars less. But throughout this area of the park, a first-row seat sells for the same price as one in the back row, so shoot for a lower row number. We really liked the sections in this price range closest to the infield. Section 119 just beyond first and Section 120 just beyond third are well worth the money. We weren't as impressed by the Field Reserved Sections (124–129) by the foul poles, preferring the straight-on view from the Field Pavilion in home run territory.

Field Pavilion (Sections 131–150)

Any seat in this price range will furnish its holder the hope (however remote) of snagging a souvenir. The seats in left and left-center (132–150 even-numbered sections) are especially choice for ball hawks, because the left-field power alley is ten feet shallower than the right-field alley. Odd-numbered Sections 143–151 in right-center offer the worst chance of getting a ball. Wherever you sit, don't plan on leaning over the fence to snatch a ball off the top of the wall or to dump a beer on an outfielder, as a three-foot dead zone separates the seating area from the outfield fence, eliminating opportunities for fan interference. If you're looking for a front-row seat, you'll want to remember that most Field Pavilion sections begin with Row 13. We can only assume this lucky number has something to do with the post-Olympic remodeling. Sections 131 and 133 are best to be avoided because of the right-field foul pole, while Section 132 should be avoided on account of the pole in left.

Trivia Timeout

Arrow Head: Which player appears first alphabetically among all baseball alums?
Totem Pole: Which pitching brothers recorded more wins than any other sibling duo?
Wigwam: Who wrote "Take Me Out to the Ball Game"?
Look for the answers in the text.

Kevin: The pole's really not that bad if you just lean to one side.

Josh: We came to watch a baseball game, not to stare at yellow paint.

Kevin: Where'd you get that cured-salmon sandwich?

Josh: Never mind.

Kevin: You got into the SunTrust Club, didn't you? Let me have a bite.

Josh: You wouldn't like it. It's topped with herbed crème fraiche.

Kevin: Okay. The jig is up. That's not something you'd eat either.

Josh: No. It's not. Can you believe they try to pass this stuff off as ballpark food?

Kevin: Only in the SunTrust Club!

Josh: Indeed, we'll be peanut-shelling slobs till the day we die.

Terrace (Sections 201–224) and Terrace Reserved (225–230)

Located behind the Dugout and Field seats and above a mid-level pedestrian concourse, the Terrace seats are still on the first level of the park. We really liked the view from behind home plate (Sections 201–208) but weren't crazy about Sections like 220–224 and 219–223 along the foul lines. These outfield seats sell for the same price as the seats around the infield but the view is not comparable. As for the Terrace Reserved sections, we do not recommend them. Either spend a few bucks more to sit in the Terrace sections on the infield, or spend a few bucks less and enjoy a better view from the Field Pavilion. On an architectural note, we appreciated the open concourse behind the last row of Terrace seats, which allows a view of the game to fans on the prowl for concessions.

Terrace Pavilion (Sections 231–248)

These outfield seats are elevated above the concourse that runs behind the Field Pavilion, ensuring clear, if distant, sight lines for fans in the first rows. Because these seats are in the same price range as Field Pavilion seats, while significantly farther from the field, you should avoid them if possible. If for some reason you find yourself relegated to the Terrace Pavilion, aim for the sections in left (even-numbered 232–248) that have a straight-on view of the plate, rather than the ones in right that point fans toward the third base line. On a positive note, the overhang here keeps fans dry on drizzly nights.

Club Level (Sections 307–338)

These club boxes hang down over the Terrace seats. Sure, they're good seats, but are they as good as first-level Field and Terrace seats? We don't think so.

Upper Box (400–422 even; 401–417 odd), Upper Pavilion (419–437), Skyline (424, 439)

Turner Field's upper deck keeps fans close to the field by rising at a pretty steep pitch. Sitting up here, your feet are at shoulder-level of the fan in front of you. Kevin, who gets a little bit dizzy sometimes, felt as if he needed his own railing in front of his row, similar to those found at Rogers Centre. Truly, these seats are not for the faint of heart. Unsteady older folks, drunks, and vertigo sufferers should aim for the lower levels. As for the view, it's not bad, especially in the Upper Boxes behind the plate. Tickets cost the same whether they're in Row 1 or Row 27, so shoot for the first fifteen rows or so around the infield (400–418), or Rows 1–10 of the Upper

Pavilion along the lines. The Upper Pavilion in right field feels far from the plate; it reminded us of the uppermost seats in Cleveland. A small number of seats in Section 424 in left and Section 439 in right sell for a discount price as Skyline seats. The left-field Skyline is a lot closer to the infield than the Skyline in right. We found these dirt-cheap seats much better than the Uecker Seats in Milwaukee. Here, nothing blocks your view of the field save for a very minimal underhang. These tickets go on sale three hours prior to game time and sometimes sell quickly because they are limited in quantity. We recommend showing up early and waiting in line for a ticket, then using your spare time to check out the Braves Hall of Fame and other attractions in this activity-filled park. And don't worry, you won't have to sit in your Skyline seat if you don't want to. There are usually ample Upper Box seats to accommodate seat-hoppers. Finally, for the best view of downtown Atlanta, aim for seats in odd-numbered Sections 403–421 on the first-base side.

The Black Market

Georgia law allows for buyers on the black market to be prosecuted, as well as sellers. So be very careful in your interactions with scalpers. If you purchase tickets at face value or below, you're legal. If not, you could spend the night in handcuffs. It's unlikely, but why take chances? Actually, you deserve to wear cuffs if you're waving big bills at the scalpers outside Turner Field. The ballpark never sells out, so it's a buyer's market.

Before/After the Game

Turner Field sits one mile south of downtown Atlanta, surrounded by parking lots. But don't despair. Realizing the lack of peripheral activities and seeking to capitalize on the void, the Braves provide plenty of entertainment options in and around the park. And for those wishing to truly get the full Atlanta experience, the city isn't that far away. The area around the park is safe and well maintained. Ralph David Abernathy Boulevard is blocked off before and after games, creating space for fans to revel in the streets after the home team wins.

Getting to Turner Field

Atlanta traffic tends to be horrendous no matter the hour of the day, so if you're staying in town we suggest taking advantage of a convenient public transportation option. Take the MARTA Train to Five Points Station, then hop on a free shuttle to the park. These buses begin running ninety minutes before the game and continue until an hour after. In general, however, the MARTA does not seem to cover much of the city, so we wouldn't recommend planning to spend the whole day zipping around town on it.

MARTA Shuttle Information and Map: www.itsmarta. com/shuttle-express-service.aspx

If you drive to the game, Turner Field is located near the intersection of Interstate 75, which bisects the city perpendicularly, and Interstate 20, which bisects it horizontally. Take Interstate 75 to Exit 246, Fulton Street/Stadium. From the east take Interstate 20 to Exit 58A, Capitol Avenue. From the west, take Interstate 20 to Exit 56B, Windsor Street/Stadium. The best option is to pay to park in one of the stadium lots. We saw some street spots in the residential neighborhood on the hillside about a quarter mile south of Turner Field but we weren't comfortable leaving our rental car in this part of the city. Because of the dearth of street spots surrounding the ballpark, and the monopoly the team has on the lot scene, Atlanta ranks right down there with Kansas City and Arlington as a place where you just have to bite the bullet and pay to park.

Outside Attractions

THE GREEN LOT

This parking lot resides on the hallowed ground where Fulton County Stadium once was. This spot was consecrated "baseball-holy" when Hank Aaron blasted a pitch from the Dodgers' Al Downing deep to left field for the 715th home run of his career. With the blast the man who was the first player in the MLB history books alphabetically at the time stamped his name atop the game's list of prolific swat sultans. And in our book, there his name still belongs, at least atop the dinger diary with 755 career clouts. We refuse to recognize Barry Bonds' Steroid Era total of 762. However, we do recognize that Dave Aardsma has supplanted Aaron atop the game's alphabetical alumni registry.

Aaron had finished the 1973 season one homer short of tying Babe Ruth's lifetime mark of 714. During the off-season, he suffered threats on his life from racists who didn't want him to break the record. Once the season began, however, he took care of business with a quiet grace and confidence, the same way he always had. He hit number 714 on his first swing of the 1974 season, taking the Reds' Jack Billingham deep in Cincinnati on April 4. Then a few days later, with the eyes of the nation upon him, he claimed the record as his own. In a grievous omission, though, baseball commissioner Bowie Kuhn chose not to attend the historic game.

Nonetheless, the moment was magical. The video clip of Aaron circling the bases still gives us goosebumps, even though we've seen it a zillion times and even though Kevin remembers watching it live on TV. It also gave us goosebumps to visit the spot where Aaron's historic homer left the yard, even though the "yard" is now a parking lot.

Fortunately, the Braves have marked the historic spot by leaving part of the left-field wall to honor Hammerin' Hank's feat. A plaque on the wall reads simply "715."

It is easy to visualize the footprint of the old field, because the Braves have outlined the warning track and infield dirt in brick, in lieu of the tar that covers the rest of the area. Large metal plates lie where the bases once were. So why not stand at home plate and pretend you're Aaron gunning for No. 715? Then take a trot around the bases, being careful to watch out, of course, for cars.

MONUMENT GROVE

Two brick plazas lie adjacent to one another on either side of the center-field entrance. One is inside the gates—providing a stage for the biggest food court in the big leagues and a pregame entertainment extravaganza, while the other is outside the gates—housing the ticket windows and attractions that celebrate Braves history. Build an extra half hour into your pregame itinerary to allow for perusing these interesting areas.

The plaza outside the park is known as Monument Grove. We got a kick out of the tiny home plates posted on pillars, stating how far each stands from home plate inside the park (717 feet, 682 feet, etc.). We also liked the pennants decorating the stadium façade. There is one for each of the Braves' championship years, spanning the franchise's history in Boston, Milwaukee, and Atlanta.

Thanks to a well-conceived arts project there is a string of gigantic colorful baseballs—about five feet in diameter each—on the plaza. Each team in the Majors has a ball of its own, reflecting its history or character. Kevin's favorite was the Pirates' ball, which depicts a bare-chested Buckaroo holding a baseball in his gold hooked hand. Josh wanted to like the Red Sox ball, but it was a struggle.

Next to the ticket windows plaques honor favorite sons like Aaron, Warren Spahn, Phil Niekro, Eddie Mathews, and Dale Murphy. The Braves retired numbers also appear in the form of three-dimensional red-and-blue monuments similar to the ones outside Oriole Park in Baltimore. The Braves honor Murphy (3), Spahn (21), Greg Maddux (31) Niekro (35), Mathews (41), and Aaron (44) with these four-foot-high numerals. We expect Tom Glavine, John Smoltz, Chipper Jones, and Bobby Cox to be similarly honored within the next few years.

Here, too, there are statues to honor Hall of Famers Aaron and Niekro, who played for the Atlanta Braves; Spahn, who played for the Boston and Milwaukee Braves; and Ty Cobb, a Georgia native who played for the Detroit Tigers and Philadelphia Athletics. The Aaron, Niekro, and Cobb pieces previously resided across the street outside Fulton County Stadium. The Spahn piece—which honors the winningest lefty of all time—was erected in 2003. Spahn won 363 games in a twenty-one year-career. The Aaron statue appropriately portrays the slugger watching home run No. 715 soar into eternity. Cobb is depicted sliding into a base. A quote on the base of Niekro's statue reads, "There's no better Braves fan anywhere than I."

Josh: Is that grammatically correct?

Kevin: You're the English teacher. You tell me.

Josh: Yeah. I'd say it works.

Oh Brother!

Knuckleballer Phil Niekro combined with his younger brother Joe to win more games than any other sibling duo. In twenty-four seasons, spanning 1964–1987, Phil posted 318 W's for the Milwaukee and Atlanta Braves, Yankees, Indians, and Blue Jays. Joe, who pitched twenty-two seasons (1967–1988) for the Cubs, Padres, Tigers, Braves, Astros, Yankees, and Twins, won 221 games. Phil pitched until he was forty-eight, while Joe, whose repertoire also included a knuckler, hung up his spikes at forty-four. In total the brothers posted 539 wins, ten more than Gaylord and Jim Perry.

Josh: So Jered and Jeff Weaver only need about 350 wins to break the record.

Kevin: Well, that seems optimistic.

Josh: Phil and Joe didn't light the world on fire early in their careers.

Kevin: Fair enough. Can you name the brothers who hit the most homers?

Josh: That's easy. Hank and Tommie Aaron had 768. Tommie hit thirteen in a seven-year career with the Braves, and Hank took care of the rest.

Kevin: You know your stats—I'll give you that.

Josh: Consider it the product of having no social life as a teen.

THE BRAVES MUSEUM AND HALL OF FAME

The door to this wonderful museum is beside the ticket windows. There is also an entranceway for fans already inside the park. Highlights include the 1995 World Series trophy and Aaron's 715th home run ball. We were pleasantly surprised to also find on display the knee brace lead-footed

Sid Bream was wearing when he famously slid into home to beat the Pirates in Game Seven of the 1992 National League Championship Series.

But Josh's favorite exhibit was the old B&O railroad car, just like the type the players used to ride in the 1950s. It's hard to imagine one of today's prima donnas riding in one of these for twelve hours to get to a game.

Josh: But the long rides offered time for card-playing and bonding.

Kevin: Yes, kind of like our trip across the country.

Josh: Interesting fact: The "Gas House Gang" Cardinals of the 1930s earned their nickname after a reporter joined them on a long train ride after the team participated in a celebrity chili-eating contest in Cincinnati.

Kevin: You're making that up.

Josh: Are you sure?

Kevin: Yes. That name came to be when Dizzy Dean bought a gas station one winter.

Josh: Oh.

Elsewhere in the Museum a display honors Braves who served in the armed forces, like Hank Gowdy, Bamma Rowell, Eddie Haas, Dusty Baker, Joe Torre, and Darrell Evans. Spahn's Purple Heart, which he earned after wounding his foot while on the Remagen Bridge during World War II, is displayed here.

We also liked the giant scoreboard tracking the Braves all-time leaders in a variety of offensive and pitching categories. And the "Transformation of Turner Field" video, detailing the post-Olympic reconstruction, was more interesting than we expected.

The cost of admission is $2 on game day when the Museum opens two and a half hours before the first pitch. On non-game days during the season, the Museum is open Monday through Saturday 9:00 a.m. until 3:00 p.m. and Sundays 1:00 p.m. until 3:00 p.m.

Watering Holes and Outside Eats

The only neighborhood bar near Turner Field predates the stadium's construction. For the life of us we can't figure out why other saloons haven't sprung up. But don't fret, Atlanta is a fun town with plenty of hot spots. You'll just have to drive to get to them.

THE BULLPEN BAR AND GRILL
735 Pollard Blvd.

This venerable institution has a monopoly on the just-outside-the-gates dining scene (discounting the presence of a Taco Bell). It features a hearty menu that includes fried catfish strips,

Sports in the City: Distant Replays

324 E. Paces Ferry Rd.
www.distantreplays.com/

For those exploring the city by car, Distant Replays merits a visit if time allows before the game. Selling replica uniforms, hats, and other vintage apparel it has that crap-brown Padres jersey or Popsicle-orange Astros cap your collection lacks. We had fun browsing and being reminded of the uniforms worn by the heroes of our childhood. We found a Braves cap sporting a lower case "a," a Brewers hat featuring that old Milwaukee glove, a stovepipe-striped Pirates hat, a Kansas City Monarchs jersey, a Pittsburgh Crawfords hat, and more. And that was just in the baseball section. All four major sports are represented.

Kevin: What's your pick for the worst uni' ever?

Josh: It has to be those shorts Bill Veeck made his White Sox wear in the '70s.

Kevin: If I recall, that little experiment didn't end well.

Josh: Sliding not advised, eh?

cheese steaks, red hot wings, barbecue ribs, Brunswick Stew, pulled pork and more. Games play on TVs above a long bar, while an attendant takes patrons' orders at a window then barks out the readiness of their food when it is finished. The outdoor porch provides a quality sitting area on cooler days. Prices are reasonable but seating can be limited, so arrive early.

BUCKHEAD
North of Downtown
www.buckhead.net/bars/

Atlanta's most happening nightspot offers more than one hundred clubs in the blocks surrounding the intersection of Peachtree Road and East Paces Ferry. We particularly enjoyed the hospitality shown to us at the Beer Mug (857 Collier Rd.), one of the city's oldest sports bars, and Lulu's Bait Shack (3057 Peachtree Rd.), where drinks come served in gigantic fishbowls. Like Wrigleyville in Chicago, there are just too many bars in Buckhead to do them all justice in these pages. Drive to the area, ditch your road trip car, and do some bar-hopping. You're sure to find a club that suits your fancy.

Kevin: We used to do goldfish shots in college.

Josh: Clam up. I don't want to have PETA on our case.

LITTLE FIVE POINTS
East of Downtown
http://littlefivepoints.net/

After the game we followed Moreland Avenue east to Little Five Points, which has a hippy feel to it that Kevin really appreciated. You know, coffee shops, tattoo parlors, vintage clothing stores and plenty of bars. The Vortex (438 Moreland Ave.) treated us right while we also enjoyed more upscale establishments like The Dark Horse Tavern (816 North Highland Ave.), The North Highland Pub (469 North Highland), and the classic blues hangout Blind Willie's (828 North Highland). The Junkman's Daughter (464 Moreland) is a counterculture landmark that deserves a visit between bar-hops.

MANUEL'S TAVERN
North Highland Street and North Avenue
http://manuelstavern.com/index.html

Manuel's has been pouring draughts since 1956. Though we would not define it as a "sports bar," it features a fair amount of baseball and football memorabilia on its walls. Old pictures of Atlanta Crackers players are prominently displayed. While you're at Manuel's look up at the ceiling where numerous playing cards and dollar bills are tacked some twenty-five feet above the bar. We asked the bar-keep about this and he told us a traveling magician who stopped in many years ago was to blame. The act went something like this. The magician would ask a patron for a dollar bill. Then he would hold out a deck of cards and ask the patron to think of one specific card. He would shuffle and then throw the entire deck up at the ceiling along with a dollar bill and a thumbtack. The cards would rain down, scattering on the floor. But one card would remain tacked to the ceiling along with the dollar. And according to the bartender, the hanging card would invariably be the one the patron had thought of. "It was freaky," the bartender told us.

Josh: This all sounds very hokey to me. I think this guy is screwing with us.

Kevin: Ah, my skeptical friend. Don't you believe in anything beyond that which you can see, touch and feel.

Josh: No, not really.

Kevin: I pity you.

Josh: Don't. I'm quite content.

Kevin: Are you really, though?

Josh: As long as there's a game each night at 7:10.

THE VARSITY
61 North Ave.
www.thevarsity.com/locations.php

An Atlanta institution that has a history more interesting than its menu, The Varsity sits on the edge of the Georgia Tech campus. Able to accommodate six hundred cars and

more than eight hundred people at once, this is the world's largest diner. On days when the Yellow Jackets have a home football game, it serves more than thirty thousand people. Even on typical days, it claims to serve an astounding two miles of hot dogs, two thousand pounds of onion rings, twenty-five hundred pounds of french fries, three hundred gallons of chili, and five thousand fried peach pies.

Since its founding in 1928 by a Georgia Tech alumnus, the Varsity has developed a vernacular uniquely its own. The men and women behind the counter call out to hungry patrons, "What'll ya' have? What'll ya' have?"

Ordering isn't exactly easy, though, because very few menu items are called by the names we travelers commonly know. For example: A "Glorified Steak" is a hamburger with mayonnaise, lettuce, and tomato; a "Mary Brown" is a hamburger without a bun; a "Bag of Rags" is a bag of potato chips; an order of "Strings" is an order of french fries; a "Heavy Weight" is a hot dog with extra chili; and so on. While we didn't know exactly what we were ordering, we took solace in the fact that everything was dirt cheap.

Josh ordered a chili steak with a bag of rags, and then went back for a hot-pig. Kevin chose a yellow dog with strings and a fish burger. We thought the food was okay, but nothing special. But that doesn't mean you shouldn't have lunch at the Varsity while you're in Atlanta. It's worth stopping by just to absorb the atmosphere.

FAT MATT'S RIB SHACK
1811 Piedmont Rd.
www.fatmattsribshack.com/

If you're looking for fine dining, Fat Matt's may not be the place for you. In fact, this might not be the book for you. But if you want good food, get in line. After ordering, instead of getting a number, you get a picture of a blues/jazz musician to place on your table so the wait staff can find you when delivering your order. We highly recommend the baked beans, which are made with a special rum sauce, and the country style ribs. And for local effect, you have to order a sweet tea.

ONE STAR RANCH
25 Irby Ave.
www.onestarranch.com/about.html

Featuring award-winning beef ribs, baked beans, Mexican cornbread, brisket, smoked turkey, homemade sausage, and more, the One Star is another joint that's sure to satisfy. We sat on the outdoor patio next to the stack of split hickory that fuels the brick oven. We give our highest possible marks to the brisket, beef ribs, and baked beans.

KRISPY KREME FACTORY STORE
295 Ponce De Leon Ave.
www.krispykreme.com/home

If you're a donut connoisseur, Krispy Kreme is worth a visit. This chain ranks with CNN and Coke as famous Atlanta institutions. There are stores throughout the city, but this midtown location is the one that's considered the franchise landmark. Look for the neon red "Doughnuts" sign. Krispy Kreme was actually founded in North Carolina in 1937. Now based in Georgia, the company is an international sensation, even if its stock price had plummeted from $40 a share when we first visited Atlanta in 2003 to $7 in 2011.

Kevin: Hmm. You rattled off those numbers awfully quickly.

Josh: Unfortunately so, my friend.

OUTSIDE VENDORS

We encountered a fair number of street vendors, hocking Braves gear and hot dogs outside the park. The streets around Turner don't offer the taste orgy that Baltimore and Boston do, but they're not the black hole that Kansas City is. During our recent visit we observed a new addition we hadn't seen in Atlanta before: food trucks parked outside, selling Po' Boys and other goodies.

On a tip from a friend, Kevin bought a tub of boiled peanuts. That's right, boiled. Jimmy Carter may like this Atlanta original, but we give boiled nuts four thumbs down. And if we'd eaten more than a few each, we might have had to give them two fingers down, too—down our throats! Boiled while still in the shell, these nuts become soggy and grainy, kind of like mushy lima beans.

Kevin: When Jack Norworth wrote, "Buy me some peanuts and Cracker Jack," I bet he didn't have boiled nuts in mind.

Josh: Who?

Kevin: The vaudeville entertainer who wrote "Take Me Out to the Ball Game" while riding a New York subway car in the early 1900s.

Josh: I wonder if they boil their Cracker Jacks down here too.

Inside the Stadium

Everything about Turner Field contributes to a pleasant experience. The seating areas and concourses are well maintained, while the ushers are friendly and helpful. Peripheral attractions keep fans busy before the game. The concessions are as excellent as they are diverse. And the playing field is a beautiful patch of lush green Bermuda grass, accented by the rich red clay for which Georgia is famous. Georgia's clay derives its color, in case you're wondering, from the oxidation of iron in the local soil.

The playing surface is several feet below street level so fans entering through the center-field turnstiles are already on the first-level concourse above the Field Level seats. We liked this effect. Rather than having to climb a winding ramp to get to the stands, as at many parks, fans can just walk through the gates, head through the festive inner plaza, and then head down to "batting practice seats" in the left-field Pavilion. As for us, we took some time to linger in the plaza where, in the shadows of a one-hundred-foot-wide picture of Hank Aaron's 715th home run ball, we sampled food while keeping our eyes on the interactive pregame show.

Ballpark Features

SCOUTS ALLEY

Behind the first-level left-field seats, Scouts Alley provides an insight into the inner workings of player evaluation and talent development that you just can't find at other ballparks. We found a report on Greg Maddux filed by a scout in 1986. It read, "This young man could be a good one, with a great change-up. He will not be real fast but will improve his curve ball." Dale Murphy's report, dated 1974, read, "Ideal build for catcher. Team leader. Great arm. Should get better with age and experience. Has good still bat and short stroke. More of a line drive type hitter. Would like to see him be more aggressive. Works hard." Reports are also posted for former Braves like Andruw Jones, Mike Hampton, Rafael Furcal, and Paul Byrd. There are more than two hundred in all. Displays beside them pay tribute to legendary scouts like Connie Ryan, Paul Snyder, and a bunch of other "bird dogs" you've almost surely never heard of.

Not far away, fans learn just how high an outfielder has to jump to rob a hitter of a home run at Turner Field, where the fence is eight feet high, take a few swings, test their pitching speed, and test their throwing accuracy thanks to some interactive exhibits.

Kevin particularly liked the interactive Braves trivia game, which allowed him to prove to Josh, rather definitively, that Josh does not, in fact, know everything there is to know about the game.

SKY FIELD

High above left field, a base path with real grass and the same red dirt the players run on provides a nice place for a ninety-foot dash. Josh challenged Kevin to a sprint and handily defeated his overheated, hot-dog-stuffed partner.

Kevin: Was the head-first slide necessary? You were six steps ahead of me.

Josh: I needed to be sure.

Fans looking to toe the rubber can saddle up to the slab atop a mound that also appears on the Sky Field. Just don't unleash a ball from here or it's apt to land on the field far below.

A viewing deck nearby provides mounted telescopes aimed at downtown. If you were too lazy to walk over to the Green Lot to check out the Hank Aaron Wall before the game, this might be your best chance to sneak a peek before it's too late.

COKE IS IT

While visiting the Sky Field check out the thirty-eight-foot-tall faux Coke bottle made from baseball equipment like gloves, bases, bats, balls, shoes, pitching rubbers, chest protectors, hats, batting helmets, and Braves jerseys. Coca-Cola has pledged $1 million to the first fan who catches a home run in this area. Never mind that only one-eighth of the area is in fair territory or that a statistician from Yale said there was a one-in-a-zillion chance it could happen. This area of the Sky Field is an estimated 475 feet from home plate and 80 feet above the ground.

Josh: Are you going to stay up here all game?

Kevin: I could really use the cash.

Josh: It's practically impossible.

Kevin: Oh ye of little faith.

RETIRED NUMBERS

Numbers on the face of the Sky Field honor the same players whose retired numbers appear on the plaza outside the park. Each of these is fashioned in a font distinctive from the others.

Kevin: Do you think they consulted the players first, like the Hall of Fame does before deciding which hat to put on a player's plaque?

Josh: Definitely not. If they had, Aaron's 44 would almost certainly be in Book Antiqua.

Kevin: Say what?

Josh: I recall reading that Mr. Aaron is an avid reader . . . of books . . . and that he likes antique cars.

Stadium Eats

The center-field plaza offers access to a diverse array of treats, while usual ballpark staples can also be found throughout the park. With Turner's many points of sale, the lines rarely grow deeper than a few people. Everything we tasted was fresh, hot, and fell into the "good" or "very good" category. We consider Turner one of the better eating parks and recommend that you do indulge.

COCA-COLA (TRADEMARK FOOD)

What would a trip to the Coca-Cola capital of the hemisphere be without an overpriced ballpark fountain soda? If you're going to shell out five bucks for a pop anywhere, this is the place to do it. Coke's roots in Atlanta can be traced to 1900 when the company was founded in the same building that still stands at 125 Edgewood Ave. Not long after, Ty Cobb made a fortune investing in the company's stock—much more than he ever made playing baseball. So drink up.

Josh: You can really taste the molasses in the syrup. And it seems much more carbonated than a regular Coke.

Kevin: I wouldn't know. I'm drinking Tomahawk Amber Ale.

HOT DOG HEAVEN (DOG REVIEW)

Billing itself as Hot Dog Heaven, Turner Field serves nearly two dozen different hot dogs or hot dog variations. We should mention that some of the "dogs" aren't really wieners, per se. One is a smoked sausage, another is a bratwurst, another is an Italian, another is a turkey sausage, another is a veggie dog. But don't worry, there are plenty of pedigreed options on the list, including the very tasty standard dog. The most unique dog we tried was the Bison Dog, which is also called the "heart-smart" dog, because it is lower in cholesterol than the average frank. Our buffalo wiener tasted refreshingly gamey and was much firmer than an ordinary hot dog. We liked it, but we wouldn't recommend it to older fans who don't have their original choppers. The kosher dog was also delicious, as was the Jumbo Georgia Dog, which came topped with coleslaw and sweet Vidalia onion relish. Try as many different dogs as you can. If you can't find one you like at Turner Field, here's betting you just don't like dogs. And if that's the case, shame on you.

BEST OF THE REST

The **New York–style pizza** ranks a clear cut above typical ballpark pie. Large thin slices come heaping with sauce and cheese. Fold your slice in half and pretend you're in the Big Apple.

The **Smokehouse Barbecue** serves turkey legs, ribs, a variety of pulled meats, and home-style sides.

If you like **Cuban,** we recommend the sandwich at Cubans and Reubens stand. The tasty Turner Field Cuban consists of spicy ham, sausage, and cheese served on grilled bread.

If it's Mexican you crave, **La Taqueria** serves freshly made tacos, burritos, and nacho plates.

Desperate to sneak some veggies into his diet after a week on the road but philosophically opposed to eating a veggie dog, Josh ordered an ear of **roasted corn** from a stand on the third-base side. The corn attendant removed an ear—still in its husk—from a smoking chamber, shucked the husk off, seasoned the ear with salt, pepper, and butter, and then handed it over. It wasn't the sweetest corn Josh had ever tasted (that being the butter-and-sugar corn he grows in his backyard in Maine), but it was very good.

The **Taste of the Majors** stand on the plaza offers a different treat for each Braves series, in honor of whatever team is visiting Turner Field.

The Braves also provide options for those preferring a sit-down meal. **The Chop House** and **Top of the Chop** are located in right field. The menu is less expansive up top than it is at the more formal Chop House below, but the view of the game is better upstairs. If you have the misfortune of holding an outfield upper-level ticket, visit the Top of the Chop to upgrade your view for a few innings while you sip a beer. And when you get hungry, hunker down on a turkey leg or a barbecue pork sandwich. As for the Chop House proper, it offers baby back ribs, fried popcorn shrimp, and different salads. Expect to spend more time here though, and unless you happen to get a window seat, expect to miss a good part of the game.

For kids, interactive **Tooner Field** in the east corner of the plaza serves Peanut Butter and Jelly Sandwiches and other tried-and-true faves. This colorful cartoon-character-strewn playhouse provides ample activity for young children to enjoy. So be sure to visit with little junior before the game.

BALLPARK BREW

The Braves sell twenty-four-ounce cans of macro in assorted varieties. Hey, it's not quite a forty, but it's a good gulp. Tomahawk Amber is the local specialty choice. Kevin gave it a luke-warm review, but only after he'd learned that Anheuser-Busch brews it for the Braves, so take this tepid endorsement with a grain of salt.

The Turner Field Experience

With some not-so-subtle prodding from the effects crew, Braves make a lot of noise when their team is closing in on the postseason and during the playoffs. You've surely noticed the Tomahawk Chop and its accompanying ritualistic chanting while watching a game on TV.

As for the atmosphere inside the park: well, it's a little too corporate for our tastes, considering the many nods to Coke and other companies that advertise. When we visited, a bank of TVs on the center-field plaza was showing all of the stations in the CNN family simultaneously. Meanwhile, Cartoon Network characters blend with baseball culture, which is odd, but good for the younger fans we suppose.

TOMAHAWK CHOP

Controversial? Perhaps. A rip-off of Florida State Seminole fans? Maybe. Unique in the universe of Major League Baseball? Yes. Braves fans are famous for their Tomahawk Chop and the chant that goes with it. Oh, oh-oh-oh-oh-oh, ooooh ooooh oh.

All right, maybe it doesn't translate well into text. But it does steep the ballpark in a tribal-war-is-about-to-begin vibe when fans start making the guttural sounds for which they're known. The Chop usually begins with prompting from the twenty-seven-foot-long flashing neon tomahawk above the scoreboard.

If the crowd starts chopping when you're in town, don't panic. You can do this. It takes very little coordination. Just raise your right arm, extend your hand and hold it flat and perpendicular to the ground, then bend your arm at the elbow. Then bring your forearm back up to its original position. If you're not sure about your pace, keep an eye on the guy to the left or right of you and follow his lead.

Braves neon sign

Photo by Kevin O'Connell

The Ty Cobb Museum
461 Cook St., Royston, Georgia
www.tycobbmuseum.org/

You may have heard that the Georgia Peach's bite was as bad as his bark. Well, here's your chance to do a little firsthand research. The Ty Cobb Museum houses, among other peculiarities, Cobb's dentures, which fetched $7,500 at a Sotheby's auction in 1999. Now, that's a bite. . . . we mean bit . . . of baseball trivia you weren't expecting.

We were also impressed to find Cobb's Shriner's fez and one of his original fielding gloves. As you might have guessed, Cobb's mitt was smaller than the Ken Griffey Jr. model Kevin still wears.

The museum is about one hundred miles northwest of Atlanta. From Atlanta, follow Interstate 85 to Highway 17 south to the center of Royston. The museum is inside the Joe A. Adams Professional Building of the Ty Cobb Healthcare System and is open year-round.

After our visit we followed Highway 17 South to nearby Rose Hill Cemetery, where we found Cobb's mausoleum. We peeked through the door to see his vault and those belonging to his mother, father, and sister but that's as close as we got to his corpse. Honest. In life, Tyrus was a notorious bad-ass. And his mom shot his dad to death as he sneaked through the bedroom window one night. Those are three ghosts we didn't want messing with us.

If you think the Chop disparages Native American culture, then we suggest not partaking in it. Or, you could get up and visit a concession stand or restroom. Unfortunately, however, the Chop is usually invoked at a key moment in the game, so you may miss a rally if you employ this avoidance mechanism.

THE TOMAHAWK TEAM

This cheerleading squad is composed of perky young ladies who rev up the crowd in a variety of ways. They perform on the plaza before games, provide between-innings entertainment, fire T-shirts into the crowd, lead fans in singing "Take Me Out to the Ball Game," and mingle with fans in the stands. We generally don't need cheerleaders to have a good time. In fact, they usually detract from our enjoyment of the game. But we both agreed that these ladies were a nice addition to the park. Maybe it was the Daisy Duke shorts they were wearing, or maybe the southern drawl with which one of them

called Kevin "sugar" when he asked if she'd pose for a picture with him. We're still trying to figure it out.

JUST THE GOOD OLD BOYS . . .

You're in the Deep South, so don't be surprised when the *Dukes of Hazzard* theme song plays over the Turner Field sound system, much to the pleasure of the fans in attendance.

Desperate to find a Braves super-fan, we were on the lookout for Uncle Jessie or Boss Hog, but all we spotted were the aforementioned Daisy Dukes. We're not complaining.

- **Talking Chop**
  www.talkingchop.com/
  This site's lively message board is for Brave souls only.
- **Braves Blast**
  www.bravesblast.com/
  This site bombards fans who just can't get enough Braves content.

While We Were in Atlanta
Kevin Almost Goaded One of Our Friends into Getting Arrested

During our visit to Hot-lanta we stayed with Kevin's friend Mike just outside the city. And Mike was happy to meet up with us at the game and to let us sit in his company's Field Box seats in Section 122. These were good seats, just a dozen rows from the field behind third base.

Upon arriving, Mike introduced us to one of his co-workers who had accompanied him to the game, a Southern gent by the name of Richard Cassinthatcher IV. Rich identified himself as a huge baseball fan, said that we were living his dream, and then subtly mentioned what a thrill it would be for him if we dropped his name somewhere in the Atlanta chapter, since he'd be watching the game with us and all. A few beers later, Rich began overtly pleading with us to include him in our Turner Field chapter.

"I could do something crazy if you'd like," Rich said, starting to untuck his shirt, toward what end we weren't sure. "Just tell me what it takes."

With a name like Cassinthatcher, he had us at "hello," but we didn't tell him that.

"Just tell me what it takes," he said. "Do you boys want another round of beers? How 'bout I buy you boys another round? Would that get me in the book?"

" It would be a good start," Kevin said.

"Certainly couldn't hurt," Josh agreed.

So Rich bought another round of Sweetwater 420s.

"How are those beers treating you boys?" he asked us a moment later.

"They're treating us well," Josh said.

"Thanks," Kevin added.

"So am I in?" Rich asked. "Am I in yet?"

"Well, it's going to take more than that," Kevin said, shaking his head. "If we start putting people in the book just for buying us beers . . . well . . . that sets a dangerous precedent."

"I see," Rich said, nodding his head. "I see, you're right. It's got to be more than that. I have to *do* something right?"

"Right," Kevin said. "Something . . . "

The next thing we knew, Rich had unbuttoned and removed his shirt, even though it was a chilly night by Atlanta standards.

"I'm going out there," Rich said.

"On the field?" Josh gasped.

"If that's what it takes. I want to make it into this book and that's probably my best chance."

"Probably," Kevin said. "You might as well make the most of your opportunity."

"One more beer, then I'm going."

At this, Josh shot Kevin a withering look. But Kevin leaned over and said, "Don't worry, he'd have to drag me with him. I'll take him down before he gets out of our row." And that made Josh feel a little bit better.

Rich drank his beer, then loosened his belt buckle, and started untying his shoes. "As long as I make it out there, I'm in, right?" he asked.

"Right," Kevin said, "as long as you make it out to second base."

"Second base?" Rich said, measuring with his eyes the distance between his seat and the cornerstone sack.

"Yeah," Kevin said. "You'd better slide, too, just to be sure. Now-a-days a lot of people are running on the field, but most of them don't make it to second. And barely anyone slides. If you slide into second, we'll definitely put you in."

"Wow," Rich said, processing this new information. "I'd better have another beer first. And maybe a jumbo dog. I didn't know I had to make it all the way to second."

This went on all night. Each time Rich was ready to streak his way into the pages of *The Ultimate Baseball Road Trip,* Kevin upped the ante just enough to make him reconsider.

Finally, after Kevin suggested in the top of the ninth that Rich run circles around Jason Heyward at first base, our friend gave up. "I'm starting to think I'm not going to make this book no matter what," he said.

"Probably not," Kevin agreed.

"Tarnation," Rich said. And he finally put his shirt back on.

Later, as we waited for cabs, he asked us one more time, just to be sure. "Did I make the book, boys?"

"Sorry," Josh said.

"Almost," Kevin said. "But not quite."

Well, Rich, this one's for you. As it turned out, nothing else too memorable happened to us while we were in Atlanta—Josh lost his Allegra and had a bad allergy day, and Kevin spilled boiled peanuts all over the upholstery of our rental car, but that was it. You made it!

TAMPA BAY RAYS, TROPICANA FIELD

St. Petersburg, Florida
250 MILES TO MIAMI
480 MILES TO ATLANTA
930 MILES TO WASHINGTON
940 MILES TO CINCINNATI

Catwalk Baseball in the Thunder Dome

Tropicana Field was designed to provide as close an approximation of an old-time ballpark as possible. The fact that the field exists within a domed building hampers this effort considerably, however. But it is admirable that the Rays identify their home as Tropicana Field and not Tropicana Dome, and that in some regards the facility succeeds in achieving a ballpark atmosphere, despite its artificial grass, roof, and rings of spiraling catwalks. At ground level "the Trop" looks like a bona fide baseball field, whereas all of the other domes we've visited resemble vast expanses of indoor space where for some reason born out of necessity or madness people play baseball.

This real park ethos is due in part to the dirt infield, which is a novelty, considering that before the Trop dome-makers typically painted white outlines on the plastic turf where the infield clay would meet the outfield lawn and called that meager gesture "good enough." Mixing real dirt with fake grass is not unprecedented in and of itself, but the combination's longevity in St. Petersburg makes its presence unique. The Astrodome offered just such an infield from 1966 through 1971, as did Candlestick Park (1971) and Busch Stadium (1970–1976).

Also contributing to the ballpark vibe, the Trop's outfield dimensions are asymmetrical and the outfield wall has several angles, in contrast to the older-generation domes that sported rounded, symmetrical outfield fences. The Trop's configuration—with left-center deeper than right-center—is said to resemble the dimensions of Ebbets Field. The outfield in St. Pete is much bigger than the one that once lay in Flatbush, though.

Further channeling Ebbets, the five-story rotunda at the Trop's main entrance was built from the very blueprints once used in the construction of the Superbas' old yard. The Mets, you may recall, also tip their caps to their Senior Circuit predecessors with an Ebbets-inspired rotunda at Citi Field. On the floor of the Trop's rotunda lies a giant baseball laid into the floor. Models of actual rays—which are a type of saltwater fish in the shark family—hang from the ceiling. We're pretty sure they didn't have those at Ebbets. The structure may be the same, but here's betting the rotunda in Brooklyn was classier, with its marble floor and crystal bats hanging from its ceiling.

But there is plenty else special about Tropicana Field, which has, in fact, like a slugger on steroids, gotten better with age. When the team rolled out first-generation Devil Rays—as the team was known until a rebranding in 2008—like Fred McGriff and Bubba Trammell, the Trop sported old-school Astroturf. But in 2000 the team uprooted the original plastic mat and switched to cushy FieldTurf. The Trop was a leading player in the popularization of this second-generation synthetic playing surface that combines blades of longer-than-normal plastic grass with a patented mixture of sand and ground rubber that simulates the dirt that normally exists beneath ballpark sod. The field proved more forgiving to diving players and provided truer bounces than Astroturf. Following the Rays' lead, many NFL teams, colleges, and Japanese League baseball teams have since installed FieldTurf. Its only other use in big league baseball was at Rogers Centre, but that facility switched to a new-and-improved breed of Astroturf in 2010. In 2011, the Trop switched back to a new generation of Astroturf called Astro-Turf GameDay Grass 3D60H that some claim provides the truest bounces yet. Still, it ain't real grass.

Kevin: There's gotta be a genetic engineer who can design grass that grows indoors.

Josh: That, and only that, is what our nation's best scientific minds should be devoting their labors to.

Kevin: If we don't do it, the Chinese will.

Josh: This may well be our generation's Sputnik moment.

While the roof may not appear exceptional at first, it adds a new wrinkle to the lineage of dome evolution. When the Rays win, it lights up bright orange, casting an eerie glow over fans as they head home.

Josh: My friend Joe would love this. He only wears orange.

Kevin: It looks like a giant pumpkin.

Josh: Yeah, on most days Joe does too.

Kevin: No, this looks like a *rotten* pumpkin. The backside's all caved in.

Josh: Joe's backside is nothing to brag about either.

The slope isn't due to a shortage of roofing materials but is by design. It reduces the volume of air inside, saving on air-conditioning bills and more importantly helps to make the building about as hurricane-proof as a dome can be. The roof is supported by cables and four catwalks that spiral toward the top. Unfortunately the lowest two catwalks interfere with batted balls fairly often. This is not a high dome at 225 feet above second base and just 85 feet above the centerfield wall. Tampa Bay players like Jose Canseco and Carlos Pena both learned this firsthand when they managed to hit balls (in 1999 and 2008, respectively) into the second catwalk—or "B Ring"—that never came down. Both sluggers were awarded automatic doubles, which the local ground rules allowed for at the time. In 2006 Jonny Gomes hit a ball into the B Ring that rattled and rolled around for nearly twenty seconds before dropping straight down into the glove of patient Toronto shortstop John McDonald for the longest-developing pop-out in baseball history. But Josh's favorite "catwalk moment" occurred in 2002 when Boston's Shea Hillenbrand won a game for the Red Sox with a ninth-inning grand slam that hit a catwalk in left and bounced all the way back to the infield. As for Kevin's favorite catwalk dinger, it was the very first. Edgar Martinez went deep off the D ring in 1998 to introduce a whole new sort of homer to baseball tradition. According to local ground rules, hitting the C or D rings still results in a home run but the rules have changed regarding the other two rings as we'll elaborate on later in the chapter.

Kevin: Homers were more romantic when they used to disappear into the bleachers.

Josh: Is this Wiffle Ball or baseball?

Kevin: Too late to raise the roof now.

The concourse on the first level is colorful, festive and wide enough to accommodate the meager crowds that have traditionally turned out for the Rays. An arcade keeps the kids busy and a number of drinking establishments, food courts, and shops cater to the adults. Clearly, the Trop was designed to get people into the park early and keep them late. As such, the facility has been dubbed a "mallpark" by some fans.

Tropicana Field entrance

Courtesy of Tampa Bay Rays/Skip Milos

The dome was constructed by the city of St. Petersburg at a cost of $130 million in the late 1980s specifically to lure an MLB team to town. At first, the Chicago White Sox were regarded as a potential suitor for the facility, but those talks were squashed when the Pale Hose secured a financing deal in their own back yard to construct U.S. Cellular Field. Thus, it was without a team that the Suncoast Dome opened for business in 1990. Shortly thereafter, the Seattle Mariners and San Francisco Giants kicked the tires on the dome before reaching stadium deals to remain in their current cities. Then, St. Petersburg vied for a team in the 1993 expansion but lost out to Miami and Denver. Hoping a rebranding might help, St. Pete renamed the facility the Thunder Dome in 1993 to coincide with the arrival of the NHL's Tampa Bay Lightning, an expansion team that took to the ice beneath the big top for three years while awaiting construction of the St. Pete Times Forum. For a while it looked as though the facility might never succeed in attracting a baseball team and might just be relegated to a lifetime of hosting Arena Football and auto shows, but then the hopes of Sun Coast hardball fans came true. The 1998 expansion awarded baseball's twenty-ninth and thirtieth teams to Phoenix and St. Petersburg. And shortly after, the dome underwent a $70 million makeover to make it fully big league compliant. Then, Tropicana swooped in with a $45 million, thirty-year naming rights offer.

It's a shame that in the years since, Tampa Bay residents haven't supported their baseball team better. Attendance has remained embarrassingly low since the team drew 2.5 million fans during its inaugural season. Even in the Rays first-place seasons of 2008 and 2010 they failed to average more than twenty-three thousand fans per game and finished in the bottom third among the thirty teams in overall attendance, drawing just 1.8 million a season. Some say the dome shouldn't have been built across the bridge from the larger city of Tampa. Like they say, "location, location, location." But is a twenty-mile drive really that big a deterrent to going to the ballpark, we ask?

Another popular theory to explain why the Rays lack an enthusiastic fan base points to the fact that Florida is full of transplants from up north, older residents who grew up rooting for other East Coast teams and who still follow them, instead of the Rays. Tampa Bay, in particular, is Yankee Country, owing to an on-again, off-again Grapefruit League affiliation with the Bronx Bombers that dates back to 1925.

While we were tempted to wonder whether part of the problem might be Tropicana Field and to suggest that an open-air ballpark on the waterfront might draw better, the local fans with whom we spoke did not corroborate this sentiment. They seemed to agree that in steamy Florida a dome is a necessity during the summer months.

After an inglorious beginning—as expansion teams often have—the Rays have, in fact, treated the locals who have been paying attention to a pretty good underdog story. With a smaller bankroll than their AL East counterparts, they've used a savvy draft operation and top-notch player development system to their advantage. But their success took a while to develop. On November 18, 1997, the Devil Rays and Diamondbacks held an expansion draft in Phoenix that furnished each team with a roster of thirty-five players. After having watched the cross-state Marlins become the quickest expansion team to ever claim a World Series title just a few weeks earlier, no doubt Tampa Bay fans had high

hopes for the Devil Rays that took the field in the spring of 1998. Having taken a Marlin with their first pick in the expansion draft and signed former Marlins coach Larry Rothschild to manage, the Rays hoped to follow in their neighbors' footsteps. The team drew 45,369 fans to its first game on March 31, 1998, but lost to the Tigers. That crowd still stands as the largest ever for a baseball game at the Trop. Nonetheless, the baby Rays got off to a 10-6 start, becoming the first expansion team to be as many as four games over .500 in its first season. The club came back to earth quickly, though, to finish the year 63-99. But there was no shame in that. Lots of expansion teams stink in their first season. Some manage

Tropicana Field, home view

Courtesy of Tampa Bay Rays/Skip Milos

to right the ship faster than the Rays did, though. The Rays finished in last place in the five-team AL East in nine of their first ten campaigns, climbing as high as fourth only in 2004 when they reached seventy wins for the first time.

Though their futility was certainly not by design, there was an advantage to finishing with the worst or next-to-worst record in baseball for so many consecutive years. Throughout the 2000s the Rays picked at the top of each round in the Amateur Draft, stocking their farm system with the game's very best prospects. Sure, there were misses along the way, like Josh Hamilton, whose drug problems earned him a ticket out of the Tampa Bay system before he got squared away, and Elijah Dukes, whose own personal problems derailed his once-promising career; however, there were also smart picks along the way like Carl Crawford, Delmon Young, Rocco Baldelli, B.J. Upton, Evan Longoria, Jeff Niemann, Jeremy Hellickson, Wade Davis, and David Price. Trades for budding stars like Scott Kazmir and Matt Garza also paved the way for future success.

> ### Trivia Timeout
>
> **Tangerine:** Which Ray kissed home plate after collecting his three thousandth hit?
> **Orange:** Who was the Rays' first pick in the 1997 expansion draft?
> **Grapefruit:** Name the Pittsburgh businessman who played a pivotal role in bringing Spring Training to Florida in the early 1900s.
> *Look for the answers in the text.*

When success did come to St. Petersburg, it came suddenly. In their last season as the "Devil Rays" the team went from finishing thirty games out of first place in 2007 with an MLB-worst record of 66-99 to posting a 97-65 mark the next year as the "Rays." Not only was that the franchise's first winning season, but it resulted in a first-place finish and a trip to the World Series. The Rays ultimately lost to the Phillies, but not before dispatching the White Sox in the AL Division Series and the defending champion Red Sox in the AL Championship Series. The first truly magical moment in franchise history occurred on October 19, 2008, when Garza and three relievers beat Boston, 3-1, to earn a hard-fought seven-game series victory. More than forty thousand Tampa Bay fans cheered wildly as Price, who was pitching out of the bullpen as a rookie, closed the door on the Red Sox with two strikeouts and a groundout in the

ninth. The Rays ran into a hot Phillies team, though, and fell, four games to one in the Classic. After a disappointing 2009, the Rays were right back atop the AL East in 2010, although the post-season gods did not treat them so kindly, as the World-Series-bound Rangers knocked them out of the first round of the playoffs. They made the playoffs again in 2001, but again fell to the Rangers in the first round.

Surely, the Rays will have their chance to play in October again. Making it all the way to baseball's highest seat will continue to be an uphill climb for the franchise, however, so long as the local fan support remains tepid. To compete year-in and year-out, teams need to not only run smart draft and minor league operations but also retain their very best players when they reach their primes and gain free-agent eligibility. Until the fans start filling the seats in St. Petersburg it's difficult to imagine how the Rays will afford to lock up their exciting young players. This is the same conundrum Billy Beane's A's wrestled with for years in Oakland. For a while, money-ball, smoke and mirrors proved enough to keep the A's among the game's top contenders, but the steady hemorrhage of talent eventually caught up with them. We foresee it catching up with the Rays too. Of course, it doesn't have to be that way. We challenge the Tampa Bay fans to make sure it doesn't.

As for its life outside baseball, the Trop has seen use as a NCAA basketball and football venue. It was the site of the 1999 Final Four at which the Connecticut Huskies beat the Duke Blue Devils 77-74 for college basketball's national title. And since 2008 it has been the site of the absurdly named Beef "O" Brady's Bowl, which features teams from the Big East, Conference USA, and the Sun Belt.

Kevin: This is where I'd normally make the case that there are too many bowls and that there needs to be a true championship playoff.

Josh: But . . .

Kevin: This is a baseball book, so I'll refrain.

Getting a Choice Seat

The Rays draw New Yorkers and Bostonians aplenty when the Yankees and Red Sox are in town. Otherwise, the crowds at the Trop are usually thin. When those two teams are in town, thirty-thousand or so turn out, but even then there's no urgent need to order tickets in advance. We should mention though, that the Rays charge an extremely sketchy $3 day-of-game charge for tickets purchased within five hours of the first pitch. Additionally, be advised that each game fits into one of four pricing tiers—Diamond, Platinum, Gold

Seating Capacity: 36,973
Ticket Office: http://tampabay.rays.mlb.com/ticketing/index.jsp?c_id=tb
Seating Chart: http://tampabay.rays.mlb.com/tb/ticketing/seating_pricing.jsp

or Silver—depending upon the opponent that day. This means that tickets for a match-up against the Red Sox cost about 50 percent more than tickets against a less eagerly anticipated foe like the A's.

Kevin: Until they start averaging thirty grand a night, every game should cost the same.

Josh: You're questioning the law of supply and demand?

Kevin: No, I'm questioning an unduly complicated pricing scheme.

Josh: You're just mad that the Mariners only rated "Gold."

The Trop is small by dome standards and, following the lead of the A's, the Rays cover several thousand upper level seats with tarps to give the joint a more intimate atmosphere. In general, the seats on all three levels are angled toward home plate. For those seated in the upper deck, the underhang is not as much of a factor as at most stadiums, but fans seated in the Terrace Boxes below find the trajectory of some pop-ups obscured by the deck above. On all levels the even-numbered sections are on the right-field side, while odd-numbered sections are on the left-field side.

Home Plate Club (101–108)

These seats, located right behind the plate in the foremost rows of Sections 101–108, are grossly overpriced at up to $300 (Diamond). Remember, you're at Tropicana Field, not Fenway Park or Yankee Stadium. We say, sit ten rows farther back and use the couple hundy you save to treat yourself to a night on the town in Tampa after the game.

Fieldside Box (101–124) and Lower Infield Box (101–120)

The first twelve rows of seats that don't already fall into the Home Plate Club cost more than the seats on the rest of the first level. These fall into the Fieldside Box or Lower Infield Box categories depending upon their section, row number and proximity to the field. We don't see much point in paying $100 for a marginally better view than you can get for half the money in the Lower Boxes, but if you have the cash and like to spend it, be our guest.

Lower Box (Sections 101–130)

More reasonably priced than the premium seats in front of them, the Lower Boxes provide excellent views. Shoot for Sections 101 and 102 behind the plate and you won't be disappointed. The only Sections we don't recommend are 128 and 130 behind the right-field bullpen and 127 and 129 behind the visitor's pen in left. The pens, we should note, are not boxed off from the playing field but run horizontal to the outfield foul lines. The pitchers warming up didn't bother us, but the Outfield and Press Level seats offer better views than these medium-depth outfield seats.

The Lower Boxes continue to Row Z, before starting again at Row AA and continuing until Row JJ in most sections. We recommend staying in the single letters. If you opt to sit in the double letters, which, in many sections are located above a mid-level walkway, aim for seats in Rows PP or lower, as the seats higher up subject patrons to an overhang obstruction.

Baseline Box (Sections 131–138)

Deep in the outfield foul territory, these seats aren't going to win any awards for providing good views but they earn our tongue-in-cheek nomination for the Most Nonsensically Named Seats in the big leagues. The baselines are on the infield. These seats are out by the foul poles. They should be called "Remote Foul Line" seats.

Josh: Truth in advertising is important to us.
Kevin: Where's Ralph Nader when you need him?
Josh: Actually, he's a Yankee fan.
Kevin: Seriously?
Josh: Yes. We Red Sox fans keep a detailed list.
Kevin: Anyone else I should know about on that list?
Josh: Nelson Mandela.
Kevin: You have GOT to be kidding me.

Outfield (Sections 139–150)

These home run territory seats provide excellent vantage points from which to watch the game. They aren't too far from the plate, thanks to the Trop's 370-foot power alleys. The best sections are 141–145 in left and 142–146 in right, which are aimed squarely at the infield. In most sections, the first row is Row T. After Row Z, the next row is AA. Even all the way back in YY we didn't feel too terribly removed from the game.

To gain an appreciation for the difficulty outfielders face in tracking fly balls against the off-white roof, head to the left-field seats during batting practice. Looking up from Section 141 or 143 you'll also see just how close balls often come to hitting the catwalks. During one of our visits, Boston's David Ortiz drilled a speaker that was mounted on a catwalk with a batting practice drive that would have otherwise left the yard. Josh also snagged a BP homer after it landed on the seat next to him (Section 147, Row CC, Seat 21).

Kevin: You're a human ball magnet.

Josh: That's what I used to tell Mr. Haeblar.

Kevin: Who?

Josh: My high school baseball coach.

Kevin: He wouldn't play you?

Josh: He let me keep score.

Kevin: Okay. Well. That's important, too.

Josh: That's what he kept telling me.

Press Level (Sections 203–224)

As their name suggests, the Press Level seats appear on either side of the press box on the stadium's second level. This mini-level is closer to the field than the mezzanines at many parks, and there isn't any sort of overhang to worry about. For those who like a vantage point that's raised, these are a good choice. Aim for infield Sections 203–216.

Upper Box (Sections 300–314) and Upper Reserved (Sections 300–324)

As we've said, the Trop is smaller than most domes. As such, even on the third level we didn't feel too far from the field or high above it. The first row of each section is A. Then, after Row Z, the rows start over at AA. Some sections like 310 and 319 have bleacher benches instead of seats in the top rows but unless it's playoff season or the Rays are expecting a larger-than-usual crowd, these are covered with blue tarps. Rows A through D—which comprise the Upper Boxes—are located below the concourse that circles the entire level. Above this walkway is the Upper Reserved, where fans are cautioned to avoid Rows E and F because the walking traffic can be a distraction. Rows G through M are excellent, especially in Sections 300–310. Because the upper deck is set behind the last row of Press Level seats below, there is no underhang to worry about.

Party Deck (Sections 341–355)

The second level left-field bleacher seats—which are situated a bit higher than the Press Level but lower than the Upper Level—used to be known as "the Beach." Now, they're called Party Deck seats. They begin with Section 341 in left-field foul territory and continue across the outfield before finishing with Section 355 in the left-field alley. As far as we're concerned, sitting on these uncomfortable metal bleachers

SEATING TIP

If you don't like your Upper Level seat, head down to the Batter's Eye Restaurant in center field. Grab a barstool on the outdoor patio and milk a beer while enjoying a first-rate view of the game.

is unnecessary at a park with as many good seats as Tropicana Field. As an additional drawback, the underhang hides the left-field warning track from view. This is less of a factor in the sections near the foul line, like 341 and 343, but is still an annoyance. We say leave these tickets for someone else to buy and if you're looking for a cheap night at the Trop, shoot for a seat in the Upper Reserved instead.

Before/After the Game

While the streets around the Trop aren't steeped in baseball history, they offer a few attractions worth visiting for those looking to soak up some sun before the game. Tailgating is also allowed in the lots surrounding the Trop, providing another opportunity to work on your tan. Hey, you're going to be inside all night, so why not get some fresh air while you can?

Getting to Tropicana Field

From the south or west take Interstate 75 to Interstate 275. As you cross the Bay, the dome will come into view on your right. From this vantage point, it looks something like a crushed soda can. Stay on Interstate 275 after crossing, keeping the Trop on your left, then take Exit 22 for Interstate 175 East, which leads right to the Trop. There are twelve different parking lots managed by the team, with entrances on First Avenue, Fourth Avenue and Fifth Avenue. Depending upon their proximity to the stadium, these charge $10 or $20 per game. However, if you are traveling with a large party, you should be aware that on Sundays and on days when a "Silver" game (see seating introduction above) is on the schedule, Lots 2, 6, 7, 8, and 9 are free for cars carrying four passengers or more.

The street spots on Central Avenue offer free two-hour parking until 11:00 p.m. but this isn't much help for those wishing to watch a baseball game that begins at 7:00. Follow Central away from the dome, however, until you pass under the highway, and just past the intersection of 18th Street, the street spots are two-hour parking until only 6:00 p.m. after which they become unlimited. Just a short walk from the dome, this is an easy place to score free parking for those arriving at 4:00 or later.

Outside Attractions

BASEBALL BOULEVARD

Follow the bronze home-plate markers that begin outside Tropicana Field's Gate 1 to Central Avenue and you'll soon find yourself at Al Lang Field, the former Grapefruit League home of many teams, including the Rays.

The markers compose Baseball Boulevard, a walking tour that chronicles the history of baseball in St. Petersburg. The path is well landscaped, passing over a small river, past some old railroad tracks, and along a number of aromatic perennial beds. When the path led us into a tunnel underneath a bridge near the ballpark, we encountered a lone violinist playing a sad tune.

Chronologically, the tour begins with a plaque outside of Al Lang Field celebrating Lang's efforts to lure the St. Louis Browns to the Sunshine State. On the way to the Trop, the plaques remember the contributions that some of the game's brightest stars—players like Babe Ruth, Joe DiMaggio, Tom Seaver, Cal Ripken, and Wade Boggs—have made to St. Pete over the years. They also commemorate the efforts of the civic and business leaders who helped make St. Petersburg a big league city.

TAMPA BAY WALK OF FAME

On the west side of the Trop, local men and women who have excelled in a variety of sports receive their due. Boggs is honored with a plaque here, as well as Tampa Bay Bucs star Lee Roy Selmon and dozens of others.

Josh: I've never heard of most of these folks.

Kevin: Obviously you don't follow Olympic swimming very closely.

Josh: Olympic swimming?

Kevin: Meghan got me into it.

ENTRY MOSAIC

Adding some color to the stroll from the parking lot to the Trop's entrance, a thousand-foot (Josh walked it off) mosaic walkway depicts an underwater scene. Sponsored by a local electric company, the picture is made up of nearly two thousand little tiles (Kevin counted). We especially liked the sea turtles, dolphins and rays. The sand and beach blankets at the "water's" edge are nice touches too.

Kevin: Every city should have a walkway like this outside its gates.

Josh: All they have at Fenway is a "mosaic" of fried peppers and onions that fall off people's sausages.

Kevin: That's not a mosaic. That's a health code violation.

DIRT

Always dreamed of running your fingers through the red clay on the Rays' infield? Rather than running out on the field and getting hauled away by security, visit Parking Lot

---

Al Lang, Father of the Grapefruit League

In the early 1900s teams customarily brought their players to Southern states like Georgia, Alabama, and Arkansas before the season to shed the weight they'd gained over the winter. But baseball was without a central spring training location.

In 1911, Lang, a Pittsburgh businessman, was stricken ill and told he didn't have long to live. Though he was a relatively young man—in his mid-40s—Lang accepted this sad fate and moved to Florida to spend his last few months in the sun.

After settling in St. Pete, Lang experienced a remarkable recovery and soon became mayor of the small fishing village. In 1914 he lured the St. Louis Browns to town to prepare for the season. Robert L. Hedges, president of the Browns, was attracted to St. Pete because of its great sports fishing and the fact that it was a dry town and would offer limited temptation to his rough and tumble players.

Playing under the direction of another baseball visionary, manager Branch Rickey, the Browns lost to the Cubs 3–2 in their first Florida game.

By 1929, ten of the sixteen Major League teams had spring camps in Florida, including three—the Browns, Boston Braves, and Yankees—in St. Petersburg.

When St. Pete replaced aging Coffee Pot Park with a new ballpark in 1946, the park was named in honor of Lang. Al Lang Field would house the spring Yankees (1946–'50 and 1952–'61) and Cardinals (1946–'97) before the Rays (1998–2008) eventually became its tenant. The Rays have since moved their spring camp to Port Charlotte. But Al Lang Field still sees use as a recreational field. As for Lang? He enjoyed spring ball in St. Pete until the ripe old age of 89. And you probably thought the Fountain of Youth was a myth.

6A right outside the main entrance of the park. There, a bin of surplus dirt sits waiting for the grounds crew to put it into service. On one hand, it seems kind of bush league for a Major League team to have a big bin of dirt in plain view outside. On the other hand, what a thrill it was to touch the storied infield dirt of Tropicana Field.

MAN, THEM MANNEQUINS

Mounted high above the concourse on the facade of the stadium, a larger-than-life Rays mannequin wears uniform number 98, symbolic of 1998 when the team joined the league. The plastic player reaches out to catch a fly ball with a horrified look on his face. If he hasn't pooped his pants yet, it seems as if he will very soon.

THE PIER

Second Avenue, Waterfront

Located a short walk from Al Lang Field, the Pier has been a St. Petersburg landmark since 1899. At its foot, a small beach and scenic lawns offer ideal places to play catch or take in some rays. Those with more ambitious designs, meanwhile, can rent bicycles or fishing rods. Using fiddler crabs for bait, fishermen land pompano, amberjack, snook, flounder, and sea bass on either side of the Pier. The Pier Bait House, which is encircled by pelicans looking for a handout, rents rods and reels for a small fee. The tackle shop has been a fixture of the Pier since 1926.

Inside the inverted pyramid structure at the end of the Pier, a food court offers boardwalk staples like ice cream, corn dogs, and steak sandwiches, while a restaurant provides a slightly more formal dining experience. An assortment of tourist shops operate inside, for those road trippers looking for just the right souvenir to bring home to their honey, while a small aquarium upstairs offers those too lazy to find their fish the hard way glimpses of specimens.

Watering Holes and Outside Eats

Tampa offers more in the way of nightlife than St. Petersburg and far more gentlemen's clubs for those who are into that sort of thing. Nonetheless, we found a number of fun places to eat and drink in both cities. As for watering holes near the Trop, the choices are limited, so you might consider tailgating. Perhaps one day the Rays will start drawing thirty thousand a night and bars and restaurants will spring up in the streets around the dome, but we don't foresee that happening any time soon.

TAMPA

Bern's Steak House
1208 S. Howard Ave.
www.bernssteakhouse.com

This Tampa restaurant is famous for its red meat and fine wine. The steak is aged eight weeks, and the wine cellar houses more than half a million bottles, representing some six thousand varieties. Bern's isn't cheap, but if you're looking to treat yourself, have at it. Attire is business casual to semi-formal. Otherwise they'll seat you in the lounge.

Josh: We prefer to sit at the bar anyway.

Kevin: A Mariners jersey and flip flops are business casual where I come from.

YBOR CITY

9th Avenue and surrounding streets
www.ybor.org/index.cfm?section=vs

The area of Tampa known as Ybor City is a National Historic Landmark District that was once recognized as the Cigar Capital of the World. A romp through Ybor (pronounced *ee-bore*) today brings one back to a long past era. Wrought-iron balconies combine with spherical streetlights, brick walkways, and the enchanting architecture of old cigar factories to paint a portrait of a decadent time in Tampa history. Ybor was built by immigrants from Spain, Cuba, Italy, Romania, and Germany. This heritage is still reflected in the district's cultural and culinary offerings. Don't worry: Even though today's Ybor is known predominantly as an entertainment district, it still features hand-rolled stogies. We especially recommend **The Columbia** (2117 E. Seventh Ave.), which is the oldest Spanish restaurant in the United States, and the **Green Iguana Bar & Grill** (1708 E. Seventh Ave.).

ST. PETERSBURG

Ferg's Sports Bar & Grill
1320 Central Ave.
http://fergssportsbar.com/

Across the street from a police station and right near the Trop, Ferg's is the only real option for those seeking a hopping place to eat and drink before the game. The expansive building features an upstairs nightclub with blaring DJ music as well as a covered patio with large electric fans that provide a welcome breeze. We settled onto a pair of barstools on the patio where beer bottles sat in buckets of ice waiting to be plucked, TVs showed games from around the league, and young ladies in tight pants mingled with big-bellied guys chowing on cheap wings and burgers.

BOOMER'S EXTRA INNINGS BALLPARK CAFÉ
1850 Central Ave.

If you take our tip and park for free on the corner of Central and 18th, this will be a convenient stop for a beer. Trust us, it looks better on the inside than it does from the street. Housed in an old theater, it is a solid choice for those who want a pre-game libation or who want to watch the West Coast games after the Rays call it a night. Tiered seating gives everyone a good view of the big-screen TVs above the old stage. In the lobby, a wall displays classic ballpark pictures painted on mirrors. These include Yankee Stadium, Wrigley Field, Tropicana Field, Fenway Park, and Tiger Stadium. All right, maybe they're not all classics. We found it hilarious to see the Trop arranged as the centerpiece of these hallowed yards.

LEE ROY SELMON'S
2424 Tyrone Blvd.
www.leeroyselmons.com/

This is one of six sports-themed restaurants named after the retired Tampa Bay Buccaneer who died in September of 2011 from a massive stroke. The defensive lineman became the first Buc to enter the Pro Football Hall of Fame in 1995, after being enshrined in the College Football Hall in 1988. He was much beloved in these parts, and though it's small consolation for the fans who loved him, his family-friendly restaurant lives on, serving soul food and Southern barbecue.

DERBY LANE
10490 Gandy Blvd.
www.derbylane.com/Home.aspx

St. Petersburg is home to the oldest continuously operated greyhound track in the world. The slender pooches have been running at Derby Lane since 1925, which according to our estimation equals more than six hundred dog years. During spring training the track was a favorite haunt of Babe Ruth and Lou Gehrig back in the game's glory days. In 2001, actors George Clooney and Brad Pitt spent three days at Derby Lane filming part of *Ocean's 11*.

Inside the Trop

Although the field resides beneath a roof, a bit of natural light penetrates through the lid in the hour before sunset to make the environment feel a bit less artificial. As for the AstroTurf, not only does it provide a playing surface that more closely resembles real grass in the way it affects the game, but its color is a truer shade of green than those fluorescent rugs that used to appear throughout the cookie-cutter addled game

we knew back in the 1970s and '80s. The outfield fences are attractive dark green. The seats are a pleasant light blue. The outfield dimensions are not too deep and not too shallow.

Our only major complaint regarding the field layout involves the positioning of the bullpens, which are parallel to the foul lines in right (home) and left (visitors). Really, these are not pens. They are merely practice mounds in foul territory. Now, we're willing to cut teams some slack in cities like Chicago—where the Cubs and their opponents have no choice but to warm up down the lines because of space considerations—but in St. Pete this is inexcusable. The Trop includes two separate field-view restaurant areas deeper down the lines that would seem ideally suited to house a couple of legitimate bullpens after some renovating. Relief pitchers deserve a space all their own and it's not like the Trop has any shortage of restaurants. Hopefully, the Rays will rethink their pen placement before some outfielder breaks an ankle while chasing a popup along one of the foul lines.

Ballpark Features
CATWALKS

Just how seriously should players and fans take the threat of the roof supports interfering with the game? Well, the mini foul poles that extend off the three outfield-most catwalks should give them some indication. Follow the regular foul poles up toward the ceiling and you'll see the yellow markers. This must be the only baseball field in the history of the world with eight foul poles.

Because balls frequently clang off or disappear into the catwalks, we thought we owed it to you to include the local ground rules in these pages. Thus, you'll know why the umpires are sending a batter back to the plate or are waving him around the bases when a ball strikes a catwalk during your visit.

Here are the official Catwalk Ground Rules, which were modified prior to the 2011 season. As you will see, the rules no longer allow for balls to be caught off the catwalks for outs and they no longer stipulate that ground rule doubles may result from "ring" interference:

- *A batted ball that strikes either of the upper catwalks (known as the "A-ring" and the "B-ring"), including any lights or suspended objects attached to either of those rings and including the masts that support each of those catwalks as well as any angled support rods that connect the "B-ring" to the masts that support the "C-ring," in fair territory: DEAD BALL and the PITCH DOES NOT COUNT. Any declaration of an Infield Fly after the hit shall be nullified.*

- A batted ball that strikes either of the lower two catwalks (known as the "C-ring" and the "D-ring"), including any lights or suspended objects attached to either of those rings and including the masts that support each of those catwalks as well as any angled support rods that connect the "C-ring" to the masts that support the "D-ring," in fair territory: HOME RUN.
- A batted ball that hits the catwalk, lights or suspended objects in foul territory will automatically be ruled a DEAD BALL and shall be called a STRIKE.
- A batted ball that hits the catwalk, lights or suspended objects and remains on or in the catwalk, lights or suspended objects in foul territory is a FOUL BALL and shall be called a STRIKE.

Expansion Draft

Before the 1997 expansion draft got under way, each of the pre-existing twenty-eight teams was allowed to protect fifteen players from its forty-man roster. Then, after both Tampa Bay and Arizona took fourteen players apiece, teams could pull back three of their "exposed" players before the second round, in which the new teams took an additional fourteen each. The pre-existing teams then pulled another three back, before the new teams took seven more apiece, giving each thirty-five players. The Rays didn't look far to identify their first pick. They took lefthander Tony Saunders of the Marlins, who went a disappointing 9-18 in two seasons with the Rays.

Kevin: Hah! "Exposed" players. There's a steroids joke in there somewhere.

Josh: Hey, that era's no laughing matter.

Kevin: Life was simpler when all "catwalk" meant was a strip-club runway.

Josh: I prefer O-Rings.

Kevin: How's that?

Josh: You know: onion rings. Not enough parks have 'em.

Kevin: Well, they do have a Blooming Onion here at the Trop.

Josh: Not the same.

Kevin: Pretty close.

Josh: Don't question me on deep fried delicacies.

A GOLDEN SEAT

Head to Section 144 in right field to find where Wade Boggs' three thousandth hit landed in 1999. After becoming the first player to enter the three-thousand-hit club with a homer, Boggs got down on all fours and kissed home plate. Boggs didn't maintain the distinction of being the only player to go long for his tri-millennial for too long. Derek Jeter followed suit when he recorded his three thousandth against the Rays' David Price at Yankee Stadium in 2011. Just the same, Boggs' golden seat is located amidst a sea of blue chairs in Row B of Section 144. Boggs' retired No. 12 and Jackie Robinson's universally retired No. 42 hang beside the scoreboard in center.

MURAL, MURAL ON THE WALL . . .

Wrapping around much of the first level beneath the stands, a large mural depicts an old-time ballpark with wooden bleachers where fans watch a game. Riding the escalator from the lower to upper level, we spotted Abbott and Costello in the crowd, Humphrey Bogart, Lauren Bacall, and other celebs.

Josh: Do you think Abbott and Costello really would have watched a game indoors?

Kevin: Yes. They hated humidity.

RAYS TOUCH-TANK

The thirty-five-foot long, ten-thousand-gallon tank beyond the Trop's right-center-field wall is truly a one-of-a-kind ballpark attraction. Here, fans are encouraged to reach down into the water and grope the fish, which are, as the tank's name implies, cownose rays. On some days, fans are even allowed to drop squid into the water to watch the rays feed. And should a batted ball splash down into the water, the Rays make a $2,500 donation to the Florida Aquarium and another $2,500 to a charity of the homering player's choice.

Josh: Roll up those sleeves. It's time to have some fun.

Kevin: There's no way I'm sticking my hands in there.

Josh: Didn't you once work at the zoo?

Kevin: Exactly. One of these babies took down the Crocodile Hunter.

THE TED WILLIAMS MUSEUM AND HITTERS HALL OF FAME
www.tedwilliamsmuseum.com/

In 2006 the museum that had occupied much of the Splendid Splinter's time in his later years moved from Hernando, Florida, to the Trop. Williams was born in San Diego and spent his entire playing career in Boston, but he always had a special place in his heart for the Sunshine State, which he made his home upon retirement. Not only is the museum at the Trop full of baseball memorabilia, such as Ted's first professional contract, but it also includes stuffed fish that Ted caught in the Florida Keys. Check out the 150-pound

Tropicana Field, Rays Touch Tank

Fans can actually touch the fish in the centerfield rays tank.
Courtesy of Tampa Bay Rays/Skip Milos

tarpon he once landed on fly fishing equipment, the thirty-one-pound permit he caught on live bait, and the gnarly bonefish he caught. Ted's rifle and golf clubs are on display too. The centerpiece of the museum is the Hitters Hall of Fame, which honors the best batsmen of all time (including Cooperstown ineligibles Pete Rose and Joe Jackson). The Museum is free to visit on game days and can be accessed on the right side of the entry rotunda.

Stadium Eats

The Rays offer a wide array of tasty treats. Two food courts on the first level house vendors from the community while there are three different lounge areas open to ticket holders. The Trop features an unusually high number of chain offerings too, including Outback, Checkers, Papa John's, and Carvel stands.

CUBAN SANDWICH (TRADEMARK FOOD)

Tropicana Field's signature offering lives up to the region's high expectations as far as Cuban fare is concerned. Two slices of grilled bread come stuffed with spiced ham, pork, salami, Swiss cheese, and pickles. We especially like the fact that you can order a "double" for only a few bucks more, rather than having to pay double the price.

Josh: We're splitting those, right?

Kevin: Order your own.

KAYEM HOT DOG (DOG REVIEW)

After we gave the dome dog a lukewarm review in this book's first edition, the wise folks in St. Pete took note and replaced the old dogs with all-beef Kayem franks. To this we say, "Good call." We especially recommend the foot-long dog and the "Heater," which comes loaded with chili and cheese.

BEST OF THE REST

The **Mahi-Mahi Fish Taco** is another Tampa Bay specialty, though Josh couldn't help but think it was a sacrilege to eat fish in the land of Rays.

Kevin: You ate fried chicken in Baltimore. The oriole's a bird just like the chicken is.

Josh: That's different.

Kevin: How so?

Josh: Chicken ain't fish.

Another Trop specialty is its **Po' Boy Sandwiches.** These messy creole-inspired subs trace their roots to N' Orleans, but the folks in St. Pete do a pretty good job with them. There are two varieties: one featuring grilled shrimp and another featuring

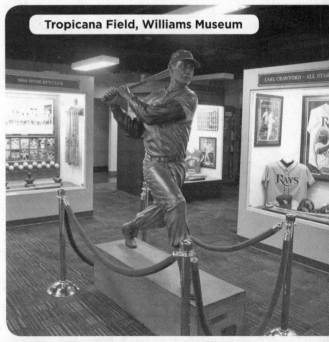

Tropicana Field, Williams Museum

This statue of Ted Williams stands at the Ted Williams Hitters Hall of Fame at the Trop.
Courtesy of Tampa Bay Rays/Skip Milos

Andouille. Both come topped with spicy slaw. We found the **Cajun Fries** were a nice complement. We also recommend the **hand-cut fries** at the first base food court. The other Trop options or "Troptions," to use a term Josh coined while we were in town, include the **Grouper Sandwiches,** the exceptional Everglades Barbecue **pulled pork** and BBQ Pork Nachos, and the **Black Beans and Rice.** At the **Wings Around The World** stand in center, patrons can order boneless wings in a variety of tasty sauces, including buffalo, Cajun, sweet red chili, and golden barbecue.

Raymond's Little Leaguers, a kiddy concession area in right field, offers junior-sized portions at reduced prices and special items like **Grilled Cheese** and **Peanut Butter and Jelly Sandwiches.**

BALLPARK BARS AND RESTAURANTS

In addition to the group party areas by the bullpens in left and right, the Trop offers three bars that anyone can visit during the game.

Everglades Barbecue in dead center has tinted windows to create the dark backdrop required by today's hitters. Seating is available on a first-come first-served basis and the menu features pulled pork that's smoked on site each day in a five-hundred-pound smoker. This is the same pulled pork that appears on sandwiches and atop BBQ nachos at concession counters throughout the park, but it's a little bit fresher inside the batter's eye. Arrive early and you can stake out a spot near the window and stay as long as you'd like. This is a smart play if you bought cheapie upper level seats.

The **Cuesta-Rey Cigar Bar** is located on the upper-level concourse behind the Batter's Eye. This is the only cigar bar in the bigs, so do spark up. While it doesn't offer a view of the game, the Cuesta-Rey provides comfy leather couches and plenty of ashtrays. The stogies range from high-end sticks to cheapies.

The **Center Field Street Brewhouse** is on the first-level concourse. Inside, it has the feel of a real sports bar, with a classy wooden counter and multiple TVs mounted overhead showing games from around the league. Unfortunately there's no view of the live action just outside (well, "inside" technically). The good news is that the House stays open until an hour after the game, and it's the site of the local pregame and postgame radio show broadcasts.

SPECIALTY BEER

Ti Dave's Po' Boy Stand sells Louisiana's Abita Beer, while the Cuban stands en el parque vende Cerveza Presidente.

Josh: Take that, Senor Bonczeck.
Kevin: Who's Senor Bonczeck?
Josh: He was my tenth grade Spanish teacher.
Kevin: En español, Josué, por favor.

The Trop Experience

Visiting the Trop, we got the distinct impression that Rays fans are slowly working their way toward establishing a collective identity. But they're not in any rush to do so. This was evident in the crowd's intermittent enthusiasm. When the Rays had men on base, the fans seemed to take notice and get involved. But when there was a lull in the action, their attention seemed to drift. The fact that there were more Red Sox fans in attendance during the series we saw than Rays fans probably didn't help. The hometown crowd was often drowned out by cheers for the visitors. That said, we should mention that whether there are thirty thousand fans inside the Trop or fifteen thousand, the joint can be quite loud as a result of a blaring P.A. system that is as tireless as it is loud. Kevin likened the experience of watching a game at the Trop to being trapped inside a giant pinball machine.

EXTREME ZONE

There is a large interactive area on the left-field concourse where fans can pose to have their picture turned into a Topps baseball card, can participate in the making of a personalized Louisville Slugger bat, can record an inning of play-by-play, and can play video games (old school Atari and Nintendo games are included along with newer ones). But our favorite part of this play area was the replica stickball alley where Josh struck out Kevin on three pitches.

Kevin: If I hadn't eaten that Double Cuban I would have taken you deep.
Josh: That'll teach you to share next time.

THE RAYS CARNIVAL

In right field, meanwhile, a family-friendly area caters to the entertainment fancies of younger fans. The boardwalk style attractions include a variety of games for rookies, including spin the wheel, skee ball, plinko and ring-the-bat.

RAYMOND

We don't pretend to be marine biologists (as George Costanza once did), but the local mascot, Raymond, looks a lot more like a bloated blue manatee than a cownose ray to us. As for the Rays, they claim he's a previously unclassified species of marine mammal that one of their scouts turned up while fishing for grouper on the Bay. We find this story highly improbable, but then again, similar scouting sojourns led to the discoveries of many of the game's Latin American stars, so we can't dismiss it entirely.

Kevin: That fellow needs to have a sit-down with Tommy Lasorda.

Josh: The famous Dodgers manager?

Kevin: The Slim-Fast pitch-man.

Josh: You realize that's just a costume, right?

Kevin: Still, I bet the guy inside is pretty portly.

Josh: Dude, Raymond is a girl. You can tell by the way he . . . I mean "she" walks.

Kevin: I thought I saw you checking out Raymond.

Cyber Super-Fans

- **D-Rays Baseball**
  www.draysbay.com/
  We especially like the Book Review sections of this lively forum. Hey, how about giving The Ultimate Baseball Road Trip 2.0 some love?
- **Rays Index**
  www.raysindex.com/
  The annual Trade Pool is a unique and popular feature of this site.
- **The Dock of the Rays**
  http://dockoftherays.com/
  "The Competition" page provides links to the best blogs related to the other AL East teams. Very clever. Very useful.

DJ KITTY

Since 2010 the fans at the Trop have been really flipping whenever DJ Kitty, aka Button the Cat, appears on the video board. Dressed in his backwards Rays cap and team jersey he spins some vinyl and bops to the beat to inspire the fans and team. In the land of cat walks, this is an appropriate shtick even if it seems a bit derivative of the Angels' Rally Monkey.

DICKY V. (SUPER-FAN)

Recognize a familiar voice emanating from the third-base boxes—high-pitched, high-strung, and bubbling with excitement? "Awesome pitch, baby! Awesome!"

That's right, college basketball guru and local resident Dick Vitale has owned season tickets since the Rays debuted in 1998. And if you think he whoops it up on ESPN, wait until you hear him at the ballpark. In 2010, he was struck in the chest by a foul ball off the bat of Toronto's Fred Lewis. The injury occurred on the first pitch of the game, but Dicky V. hung in there until the final out. Now that's what we call a "gamer."

THE HAPPY HECKLER (SUPER-FAN)

With an even louder set of pipes than Dicky V., the Happy Heckler of Tampa Bay has also done much to make his presence felt at the Trop through the years. This gentleman, who has season-tickets behind the plate, likes to pick on one opposing player each series. Whenever that player comes to bat, he really lets him have it. Then he more or less quiets down until the player appears again. For the most part his heckling is good natured but he does draw his share of angry stares.

Kevin: Clearly this guy didn't get enough attention as a child.

Josh: Heckling is part of the game. Lighten up.

Kevin: Afraid he might heckle us next time we visit the Trop?

Josh: Well . . . not if we say nice things about him.

NO HOLDS BARRED BASEBALL (SUPER-FANS)

Hulk Hogan, John Cena, Brian Knobbs, Bret Hart, and other pro wrestling personalities can often be spotted sitting in the lower boxes. In 2009, Mr. Knobbs performed a few of his trademark moves on an utterly defenseless Raymond. The "incident," as locals referred to the event during our visit a few years later, still evokes cringes at the Trop.

Sports in (and around) the City

George M. Steinbrenner Field
1 Steinbrenner Drive, Tampa
www.steinbrennerfield.com/about-george.html
Steinbrenner Field is the Grapefruit League home of the New York Yankees and the Florida State League home of the Tampa Yankees. It features outfield dimensions identical to Yankee Stadium, a facade that resembles Yankee Stadium's, and a monument park similar to "The" Monument Park in the Bronx. Its grounds also include a large Yankees gift shop.

The park was built in 1996 at a cost of $30 million. Every game is a sellout during spring training but tickets are usually available to Tampa Yankees games and Monument Park is open to visitors any time during business hours. From St. Petersburg, take Interstate 275 to Exit 41B, then follow the signs on Dale Mabry North to the ballpark.

Josh: Serves Raymond right for putting a smack-down on Wally, the Beanbag Buddy when the Sox were in town a few years ago.

Kevin: You Red Sox fans never forget a slight, do you?

Josh: Nothing real or perceived.

While We Were in Tampa Bay
We Stayed All Sixteen

During our first trip to Tampa Bay we were treated to the longest game of our road trip, a 16-inning affair between the Rays and Red Sox. The game came early in our seminal baseball adventure at a time when we were still learning the dos and don'ts of staying with long-lost friends in faraway cities. We were staying with Josh's old high school pal Aaron Fournier, who had gotten around to having kids a bit sooner than either of us had. Because we'd never had small babies at home, we couldn't understand therefore, why Aaron was looking at his wristwatch all game long. We both always hoped games would progress as slowly as possible, but he was obviously chomping at the bit for the game to end so he could get home to help his wife with the nighttime routine.

And wouldn't you know, the game was knotted 8-8 after nine innings.

Aaron also had to get up early for work at 5:00 a.m. the next morning, but as our trusty tour-guide he showed only slight signs of disappointment when the game went to extras or "freebies" as Josh likes to call them. These signs included a general scowl on Aaron's face, a ringing of his hands and a sad whimper that he took to exuding every time he glanced at his watch. For our part, we sat blissfully waiting for extra innings to begin without a care in the world.

"Look at all the people heading for the gates," Aaron said after the Rays stranded two runners in the bottom of the tenth. "They must have to get up early tomorrow too."

A bit confused by our friend's sour attitude we both opted to keep our mouths shut.

By the eleventh inning, Aaron had started mumbling things like, "I think you stop liking baseball around the tenth inning," and "My wife's not gonna let me go to another game for the rest of the season," and "I'm really tired, can't we just listen to the game on the car radio on the way home," and

"You haven't visited me in ten years, Josh, and now you come down here to ruin my life?"

But although he kept threatening to drag us out of the Trop "early," Aaron stuck it out with the true fans.

And what a thrilling game we saw. In the bottom of the thirteenth inning then-Red Sox left fielder Damian Jackson threw out a runner at the plate to preserve the tie. Then in the top of the fifteenth, Rays center fielder Rocco Baldelli returned the favor, gunning down a Red Sox runner at the plate. Talk about high drama and good times!

"If you ever ask to visit again, I'm gonna say 'no,'" Aaron said to Josh in a voice that didn't quite sound like he was joking.

The Red Sox finally took the lead at 12:30 a.m. in the top of the sixteenth inning when Kevin Millar blasted a solo homer to left.

"Good. Now can we leave?" Aaron pleaded. "The Rays aren't gonna score in the bottom of the inning."

"We don't know that for certain," Josh said.

"Yeah," Kevin added. "They could tie it up and go another sixteen innings. You never know."

Mercifully for Aaron, the Sox closed it out.

"Time spent in the ballpark," Kevin said, looking at his wristwatch as we walked down the exit ramp, "Seven full hours: from 5:45 p.m. until 12:45 a.m."

"Tough day at the office," Josh quipped.

"I hate you both," Aaron growled.

Josh patted him fondly on the back. Then Kevin did too.

"No, really. I hate you," Aaron said.

The next morning, we were both fast asleep in the family room when Aaron left for work. And when his wife left for daycare and work too. It was a long time afterwards before Aaron would reply to Josh's apologetic e-mails and even then he ended each electronic epistle, "P.S. I still hate baseball thanks to you!"

The moral of this story? We have no idea. But ever since the "Trop Incident," we've been sure to tell our gracious hosts in cities far and wide that *The Ultimate Baseball Road Trip* boys are contractually obligated to stay until the final out of each game. That way our sleepy-eyed friends can blame the Lyons Press, and not us, when games continue into the wee hours.

MIAMI MARLINS, MARLINS BALLPARK

Finally, a Tank of Their Own

It was a long time coming, but fans in South Florida finally enjoy the wonders of baseball played in a state-of-the-art facility designed specifically to showcase all that is wonderful about the Grand Old Game. The Marlins entered the Show all the way back in 1993 but were forced, along with their fans, to endure nearly two decades of play at a retrofitted football stadium before Marlins Ballpark finally arrived in 2012. Located on a portion of the old Orange Bowl site in the Little Havana neighborhood of Miami, the Marlins' shiny new park sits less than two miles west of downtown, boasting design elements and accoutrements that stamp it as distinctly Floridian.

First and foremost, the ballpark offers a comfortable, climate-controlled environment. As a summertime visit to Miami will surely convince you during your own baseball odyssey, air-conditioning is a must in these parts during the spring and summer months. The backyard swimming pool is more necessity than luxury for many Miami area locals as well, and the ballpark provides one of those beyond its outfield fences too. Sure, pools have appeared at ballparks before, most notably in similarly steamy cities like Phoenix, where the big league Diamondbacks play, and New Orleans, where the Marlins' Triple-A affiliate, the Zephyrs, play, but Marlins Ballpark boasts some other novelties we're pretty sure no one has ever seen at a ballpark before, like the live fish swimming between the dugouts. Yes, you read that right. The game's first aquatic backstop is essentially a big long fish tank, or, actually *two* big long tanks. The Marlins wisely left the area directly behind the dish water-free, so the shimmering fishies and glare off the aquarium wouldn't interfere with fielders' views of batted balls. But on either side of the plate—where fans have grown accustomed to seeing classy red brick or pale limestone during the retro ballpark renaissance—the Marlins have installed massive tanks. The aquarium between the Marlins' third base dugout and the batter's circle measures thirty-four feet in length and holds six hundred gallons of saltwater, while the one between the plate and the visitors' first base dugout stretches twenty-four feet and holds 450 gallons. The fish are clearly visible to fans sitting in the lower rows on the infield and to the players on the infield. There's no need to worry about those fouls back to the screen that make the fans seated directly behind the plate instinctively duck. The fish are protected from harm by a type of polycarbonate known as "Lexan" (aka bulletproof glass), which measures 1.5 inches thick. Still not convinced? Thin sheets of Lexan less than one-eighth of an inch thick can stop a 9 mm bullet from passing through. Sounds good enough to us.

Of course, this fact wasn't enough for the animal advocacy group PETA (People for the Ethical Treatment of Animals), which sent a letter to the Marlins shortly after the team announced its plan to build the dual aquariums, and a public dialogue ensued concerning whether the bright lights and thundering noises of a baseball park would make Marlins Ballpark a suitable habitat for living creatures. In a letter to the Marlins, PETA executive vice president Tracy Reiman wrote, "Being exposed to the loud crowds, bright lights, and reverberations of a baseball stadium would be stressful and maddening for any large animals held captive in tanks that, to them, are like bathtubs." PETA went on to request that the team "leave fish in the ocean where they belong" and suggested alternatives like an LED screen showing fish in their natural habitat, artsy blown glass fish replicas, and a tank full of swimming robotic fish. To this, Marlins president David Samson replied, "I guess that's a philosophical issue, but there are beautiful aquariums all over the world and this will be one of them. I can assure you the fish will be treated as well, or better, than any fish can be."

Kevin: So, let me get this straight. The fish have front row seats to eighty-one games a year?

Josh: Not just front row seats. Front row seats *behind the plate.*

145

Marlins Ballpark construction

The park was still a work in progress in March 2011, but the roof scaffolding was already in place.
Wikimedia Commons

While it makes good sense for the "Fish" to celebrate the marine life and water-faring culture of their home market, Miami is also famous for its visually beautiful city skyline. The tall buildings of downtown are always striking, but are even more brilliant when they're illuminated in shades of green, blue, pink and other colors on the occasion of festivals, conventions and other special events. Accordingly, the ballpark incorporates the view of the buildings into the game-day experience. Borrowing from the successes of retractable-roof stadiums in other cities that leave room for sweeping outfield views beyond their fences, the Marlins' big-top leaves space between the seats and the roof high above left field for a window view of the Miami high-rises. Even when the roof is closed, fans enjoy this gorgeous visage through glass panels that reminded us of the sliding-glass giant windows above the fields at Minute Maid Park in Houston and Miller Park in Milwaukee.

However, there will be no confusing Marlins Ballpark with a park built in the retro-renaissance era. While the ballparks of the early 2000s almost uniformly presented visitors with arching old-time brick facades at street level, the designers of Miami's later-generation park eschewed whatever muted temptation there may have been to build an old-timey brick bastion to the game's glory years, and instead crafted a facility that better fit the sharp and architecturally modern image cut by the Miami cityscape. With its abundance of white stucco, its shiny silver metal and its wealth of clear glass, the Miami field was clearly built for those looking forward, not back into the game's past. Along with Target Field in Minneapolis and Nationals Park in Washington, which similarly present more futuristic façades than the ones to which we fans came to know and love during the retro renaissance, Marlins Ballpark officially declares the end of the retro renaissance era of ballpark design, and announces a brand new era for the Grand Old Game, one that embraces the game's entrance into the 21st Century, with respect paid to technology and innovation.

The Marlins treat fans to a couple of snazzy lighting tricks and special effects at their new yard too. Through some new age fiber optics tricks we two baseball writers are ill-equipped to fully explain, the four largest columns supporting the roof appear to rhythmically sway, move and practically disappear. The effect is subtle, but noticeable and strangely hypnotic. Josh likened it to watching the Sunday night baseball game on ESPN. You already know all the scores of the day, yet for some reason you spend more time staring at the scrolling names and numbers that are ever-present at the bottom of the screen than watching the lone game that's still being played. Meanwhile, behind the center-field fence another bell and whistle of this park sits waiting to make its presence known. Equipped to rise on cue—a la the Home Run Apple at Citi Field in New York, or the lighthouse at Hadlock Field, in Portland, Maine—an ocean-themed display rises amidst a swirl of laser lights and jumping Marlins to celebrate home runs.

As the sixth and most recent retractable-roof stadium to arrive on the Major League Baseball scene, Marlins Ballpark really needs its lid. The 8,300-ton steel sunroof safeguards the game against both the famous Florida humidity and the frequent afternoon thunder showers that deterred many locals from attending games at the Marlins' former home. This is Florida we're talking about, where a higher percentage of the population exceeds sixty-five years of age than in any other state. And even if another segment of the population in Miami is a bit younger and hipper than there appears in the typical Sunshine State retirement community, it was unrealistic and unfair to expect folks to scurry down to the protection of a crowded concourse to wait out the daily monsoon, and then to sit on a wet seat, breathing clammy air for nine innings. The Marlins realized this in time. But team management and the folks at MLB headquarters didn't give up on the idea that Miami could and would one day lend robust support to the home team. With a thriving Cuban/Latin culture, a bustling finance and business district, and the usual Florida retirees and tourists, the Miami market has plenty of potential fans whose passion for the game will hopefully be reactivated now that the long-awaited ballpark has arrived.

Kevin: It's kind of pathetic that the locals didn't do more to support a team that won two World Series in its first decade of existence.

Josh: Imagine if your Mariners had turned that trick.

Kevin: Folks would have been swinging from the Kingdome rafters.

The air-conditioning keeps the game-time temp pegged at a comfy 75 degrees. Based on Miami's average daily temperature and rainfall averages, the Marlins know the roof will be closed and the AC will be pumping for approximately seventy of their eighty-one home dates each year. Anything beyond ten games beneath an open sky is a bonus. Now, to some people this might beg the question: Why spend the extra cash on a roof that's going to be closed eighty-five percent of the time? Why not just build an old-fashioned dome? The answer lies in the sad reality that though the whiz kids in our nation's bustling genetics labs have already mastered the fine arts of engineering seedless grapes and apple trees that grow McIntosh fruit on one branch, Cortland on another, and Delicious on another, they still haven't figured out how to grow natural grass indoors. And besides, even ten or eleven outdoor games a season are worth the extra effort of adding a roof that can be peeled back. Dome baseball is an abomination.

Kevin: Domed baseball is kind of like microwave pizza.

Josh: Or instant coffee.

Kevin: It will do in a pinch, but the real thing's always better.

To appreciate just how long the Marlins waited for a new park, consider this tale of two baseball cities: Miami and Denver. Both joined the National League as expansion franchises in 1993. Each had rightly been identified by the game's power brokers as possessing a growing population and a reputation as a hip and trendy city.

Both could lay claim to having a track record of supporting highly successful teams at the top level of another professional sport, namely football, where the NFL's Miami Dolphins and Denver Broncos were bona fide pigskin royalty. Both NL newbies played their inaugural seasons at longtime NFL stadiums converted for baseball, as the Marlins trotted out on the lawn at Joe Robbie Stadium and the Rockies basked in the thin mountain air of Mile High Stadium. Both arrangements were thought to be temporary, as the expectation throughout the game was that the two newcomers would settle into their own baseball yards before very long.

For the Rockies, this was true. Even as they set a home attendance record that still stands in 1993, when they drew 4,483,350 spectators through the Mile High gates, the Rockies were working to ensure the timely completion of beautiful Coors Field, which would open in 1995. For the Marlins . . . well, let's just say things didn't move quite so rapidly from a stadium development standpoint. The Fish surpassed the three million mark in home attendance in their first season and won two World Series in their first eleven years of existence, but after the excitement surrounding the team's debut wore off, it seemed they were always swimming upstream when it came to drawing fans to regular season games. They only reached the two million mark in home attendance one other time after their inaugural campaign.

Marlins Ballpark, roof construction

Wikimedia Commons

Even in their second World Championship season of 2003, when they beat the New York Yankees in the World Series, they drew just 1.3 million fans, or sixteen thousand per game, and ranked twenty-eighth out of the thirty teams in Major League Baseball in fan support.

What lessons should big league teams draw from this? First off, some cities, like Miami, Denver, and Atlanta, are filled with transplants. Growing a fan base that will outlast the novelty takes time. Second, we think it's that winning really isn't everything when it comes to drawing crowds. Fan comfort and stadium amenities are pretty darned important too. And Marlins Ballpark provides both. More than just sporting a roof and blowing cool air, it offers seats that are all perfectly angled toward the infield. And that certainly couldn't be said of the Marlins' previous home. When larger crowds turned out at the stadium for the World Series games in 1997, many fans found that the only view of the game they enjoyed was on the JumboTron, because their seats, which had been conceived for football, didn't even face the field.

Known at varying times during the Marlins' stay as "Joe Robbie Stadium," "Pro Player Park," "Pro Player Stadium," "Dolphins Stadium," "Land Shark Stadium," and "Sun Life Stadium," the orange-seated behemoth could accommodate seventy-five thousand football fans and up to sixty-eight thousand spectators for baseball. Of course, the Marlins didn't need all of those seats, so after debuting in 1993 at a stadium reconfigured to offer forty-eight thousand seats, they gradually opened fewer and fewer sections of the park to their patrons so that by the time they closed up shop there in 2011 the official baseball capacity had fallen to about thirty-eight thousand. As such, there were always more empty orange seats than people in the stadium when the Marlins played. A fit setting for baseball, it was not. Now, the Marlins welcome intimate gatherings of thirty-seven thousand people to their home. And there's never going to be the outline of a football grid on its outfield lawn. And the diamond will never be worn out between the "hash marks."

The Marlins and city and county officials talked about building a new park seemingly forever. The first serious rumblings began in the late 1990s when then-Marlins owner John W. Henry began lobbying for a new baseball-only facility. On multiple occasions a deal seemed imminent or even to have been struck, but the local politicians, who just couldn't agree on how to fund the massive undertaking, consistently dashed the Marlins' hopes. Finally, Henry gave up and sold the Marlins so that he could buy the Red Sox. All ended pretty well as far as he was concerned. His Red Sox became the first team to win two World Series in the new century. But the Marlins continued to hemorrhage fans as a cat-and-mouse game played out between the new Marlins ownership group, headed by Jeffrey Loria, and the Miami, Miami-Dade County and State of Florida politicians. At one point, it even appeared as though the Marlins might move to San Antonio, Texas.

Finally, a funding agreement was struck in 2007 that called for the construction of a $515 million baseball park in Miami. The measure called for the Marlins to foot $155 million of the tab, for Miami to chip in $13 million toward the stadium and to also make infrastructure improvements, and for Miami-Dade County to provide $347 million. Although most of the county's fare would come from the sale of bonds backed by a tourist tax, this didn't sit well with many local taxpayers who said they should have had the chance to thwart the ballpark financing plan via a voter referendum. A lawsuit to halt the ballpark plan ensued and though a circuit judge eventually ruled in favor of the ballpark proposal moving forward, the suit slowed down the effort to build the park. Finally, in March of 2009, Miami and Miami-Dade County re-approved the deal for about the twelfth time and work at the site began soon after. The first step was to demolish the Orange Bowl, which cost $10 million and was paid for by the City of Miami. Then construction began, following the blueprints drawn up by the noted ballpark architects at Populous.

We understand that the whole corporate welfare thing has gone on way too long as pertains to the construction of US sports stadiums. But at least the Marlins, who paid $120 million of their share up front, make an annual $2.3 million payment to Miami as part of their thirty-five-year lease with the city. And at least they changed their name from "Florida Marlins" to "Miami Marlins" in 2012 as part of the agreement. Comparatively, deals like this have been done in other cities where the home team has paid far less or practically nothing at all. Still, we understand where the local taxpayers were coming from in their resistance.

Josh: I'd rather hand out tax-payer dough to ball teams than Big Oil.

Kevin: Either way, public investments shouldn't lead to private profits.

After a long, arduous, and yes, controversial, struggle, the Marlins finally opened their new park just as this edition of *The Ultimate Baseball Road Trip* was landing on bookstore shelves in the spring of 2012. Thanks to our friend Marty, though, who let us borrow his plutonium-propelled DeLorean, we were able to get a sneak peek of the yard before its grand debut. Okay, we also got some help from a friend—who's coincidentally also named Marty—in the Marlins media relations office, who provided us with some great information.

The Marlins scheduled two exhibition games against the Yankees at the end of the 2012 Grapefruit League season to make sure they had all the wrinkles ironed out of their game-day presentation. Then they opened their new tank officially with a regular season series against their longtime Spring Training roomies, the Cardinals, who share a facility in Jupiter, Florida, with them during March. The new era of Marlins baseball had begun.

Kevin: We've seen the future . . .

Josh: . . . and the future is teal.

Despite the fact that their old yard was subpar, their perennially flagging attendance, and their periodic fire-sales, the Marlins' first era really wasn't that bad. The team did claim two world championships in its first eleven seasons. And the Marlins' retrofitted football field did have some quirks that the locals embraced. The thirty-three-foot-high left-field wall, known as "the Teal Monster," was the second highest outfield edifice in baseball, shorter only than the Green Monster in Boston. Meanwhile just to the left of the center-field wall was an outfield gap known as "the Bermuda Triangle" where the wall veered away from the plate at a dramatic angle, from 410 feet to 434. After struck balls disappeared into this notch they were almost certain never to return. Okay, we were just kidding; they returned but usually not until the batter was standing on third base with a triple.

Joe Robbie Stadium's conversion actually began quite a while before the Marlins debuted in 1993. The initiative to bring a team to the Miami area gained momentum in early 1990 when Blockbuster mogul H. Wayne Huizenga announced he would spearhead the city's quest for a team. For good measure, Huizenga purchased half of Joe Robbie Stadium, and 15 percent of the Dolphins. The effort to convert Joe Robbie into a facility capable of hosting baseball began in January of 1991. But it wasn't until June of that year that baseball commissioner Fay Vincent confirmed that South Florida and Denver had been selected by the expansion committee. Oh, what a feeling for South Florida. The longtime Spring Training hub and once bustling minor league hotbed would soon have a big league team of its own.

Early minor league teams that thrived in South Florida had colorful names like the Miami Magicians and Miami Beach Flamingos. The Fort Lauderdale Tarpons, meanwhile, came from the same school (bad pun intended) of thought as the Marlins, in netting a fishy moniker. While these teams played at small parks, after World War II it became apparent

that a larger facility was needed to accommodate the growing baseball culture in the region, so Miami Stadium was built in 1949 by Jose Manuel Aleman, a former minister of education in Cuba. The beautiful nine-thousand-seat ballpark housed such teams as the Miami Sun Sox, Fort Lauderdale Lions, and West Palm Beach Indians. The first incarnation of the Marlins came in 1956 when Bill Veeck brought a Triple-A franchise to Miami from Syracuse, New York. Veeck signed aging pitcher Satchel Paige, who was delivered to the mound via helicopter for his debut. The bush league Marlins lasted only three seasons in Miami, however. Other minor league teams that enjoyed success in the area were the Miami Amigos, Miami Orioles, and Miami Miracle.

Josh: I think the expansion team was smart to choose 'Marlins.'

Kevin: You're not going to launch into another bogus fishing story, are you?

Josh: My fishing stories aren't bogus.

Kevin: Well, they're not exactly true either.

To the credit of all involved, at the time of its construction the funding for Joe Robbie Stadium came entirely from private sources. Mr. Robbie, who owned the Dolphins, spent $115 million to build the stadium, which he financed mostly through the leasing of executive suites that cost high rollers $30,000 to $90,000 a year. The stadium opened for football in 1987. Unfortunately, the Dolphins' founder and stadium namesake died soon after the stadium opened in 1990. Shortly later, his estate sold the team to his onetime rival Huizenga. And Huizenga spent $10 million to retrofit the stadium for baseball.

The baseball modifications included a press box for baseball placed in the southwest corner where home plate would be. And a large, retractable out-of-town-scoreboard was built into left field with retractable baseball-only seating above it. Dugouts were dug out (as they should be) and a rubber warning track was laid. The pitcher's mound was built like those in other multiuse stadiums, on a hydraulic lift that allowed it to sink and disappear when some stadium techie threw a switch.

Major League Baseball finally arrived in Florida on April 5, 1993. The ageless Charlie Hough threw the first pitch in Marlins history against the Los Angeles Dodgers before a sellout crowd of 42,334 at Joe Robbie Stadium. They might well have been the first team in big league history whose first pitch was a knuckle-ball. The Fish went on to win 6–3. But they finished their inaugural season just 64-98. Amazingly, they finished ahead of the New York Mets in the NL East standings as the non-expansion Mets went just 59-103 that year.

Pitching proved fruitful for the young minnows of the NL as Marlins starters authored a surprising number of no-hitters in the team's early history. Al Leiter threw the team's first no-no on May 11, 1996, when he whitewashed the Rockies at Joe Robbie. A year later, Kevin Brown turned the same trick on June 10, 1997, against the Giants in San Francisco. A.J. Burnett tossed the Marlins' third no-hitter on May 12, 2001, when he walked nine batters but nonetheless beat the Padres 3-0 in San Diego. And Anibal Sanchez pitched the Marlins' fourth no-no on September 6, 2006, when he beat the Diamondbacks 2-0 at Dolphins Stadium.

The Marlins were on the receiving end of a gem, when Phillies ace Roy Halladay tossed the 20th perfect game in baseball history before a crowd of 25,086 Marlins fans on May 29, 2010. In a classy move, the Fish fans cheered for the Philadelphia righty as he continued to mow down Marlins in the later innings and inched ever closer to making history. Another noteworthy event occurred at the Marlins' home field on June 9, 2008, when Kevin's boyhood idol Ken Griffey Jr. became the sixth member of baseball's six-hundred-home-run club with a clout off the Marlins' Mark Hendrickson.

Josh: Was Junior really your "boyhood idol"? You're practically the same age as him.

Kevin: Yes, but like the Mariners, I took longer than usual to grow up.

Both times the Marlins won the World Series they joined the postseason party as the NL Wild Card. The 1997 team was led by imported talent like Bobby Bonilla, Gary Sheffield, Moises Alou, and manager Jim Leyland. The Fish swept the Giants in three stunning games to win the Division Series as clutch hits by Alou and Edgar Renteria helped win Games 1 and 2 and a grand slam by Devon White in Game 3 sent the little fish into a much bigger pond. But the pundits predicted that the upstart Marlins would be no match for the dynastic Atlanta Braves in the NL Championship Series. And the pundits were wrong. The powerful arms of rookie Livan Hernandez and Brown blew away the Sons of Ted Turner, as the two hurlers won two games apiece in the six-game set. Hernandez, who earned MVP honors, struck out a championship-series-record fifteen batters in Game 5 before a delirious home crowd of 51,982.

Next up for the Marlins came the Cleveland Indians and a World Series in which they would similarly defy the odds. Hernandez won two games, both over Orel Hershiser, becoming the first rookie to win two Series starts in more than fifty years. Memories of the climactic eleventh inning of Game 7 make Cleveland fans weep to this day. Renteria

slapped a two-out single off Chuck Nagy to score Craig Counsell and break a 2-2 tie and give the Marlins a walk-off win. The Marlins had gone from expansion team to World Champions in five seasons.

The Marlins broke many records on their march to destiny. They became the quickest expansion team to win a World Series and the first Wild Card team to win one. And they came from behind in eight of their eleven postseason wins. Game 4 in Cleveland proved to be the coldest World Series game ever played, at 15 degrees Fahrenheit with the wind chill factor. Game 6 at Pro Player Stadium was played before the largest World Series crowd since 1954: 67,498 fans. The finale was just the third World Series Game 7 to go into extras. And the Marlins became the first team to draw more than half a million fans during a postseason, thanks in part to the extra games of the NLDS, and in part to the huge capacity of Pro Player.

However, the Marlins faced tough swimming ahead, as they became caught in the current of their own finances, city, and football-flavored field. After stocking the tank . . . we mean stacking the deck . . . with talent from the free-agent pool before the 1997 season, Huizenga auctioned off the team's best players the very next year in a move that surely had legendary field manager Connie Mack smiling in his grave. Some players were lost to free agency, but most were traded away for prospects. In response, Marlins fans didn't exactly stream into the ballpark the next few years. Having won his championship, Huizenga didn't waste much time before selling the Marlins to the eccentric Henry in 1999. As mentioned above, Henry made his first priority constructing a new baseball-only park. But he couldn't get the project across the finish line and ultimately decided to move on.

The Marlins narrowly dodged the threat of contraction when an eleventh-hour work agreement was struck between the players and management in 2002. Then they went out and won another World Series in 2003. The Marlins were ten games under .500 in late May but led by 72-year-old manager Jack McKeon, who took over for Jeff Torborg at the season's quarter-pole, they rebounded. The veteran skipper (who would stay at the Marlins helm for three years, then return to manage the Marlins at age 80 in 2011) put his faith in trusted vets like Ivan Rodriguez, Jeff Conine, and Mike Lowell, and newcomers Juan Pierre, Dontrelle Willis, and Josh Beckett. The Marlins went 75-49 over the final three-quarters of the season and captured the NL Wild Card.

Once again, the Marlins dispatched with the Giants in the NLDS, and then they squared off in an epic NL Championship Series with the Cubs. In a series that will forever be

The "Grapefruit" League Gets its Name

Florida was baseball's original Spring Training hub, of course, and although fully half of the MLB teams now train in Arizona, fifteen still work out in the Sunshine State each March. Unfortunately, the most famous spring site of all—Dodgertown, north of Miami in Vero Beach—lies dormant these days as the Dodgers train in Arizona. But "dem Bums" from Brooklyn sure left their mark on Florida's spring circuit. In fact, they named it.

When they arrived at Daytona Beach to train in March 1915, the fun-loving boys from Brooklyn were commonly known as the "Robins," owing to their colorful manager, Wilbert Robinson. The players liked to prank one another, and especially their skipper. And the laidback atmosphere of training camp afforded the perfect setting for their shenanigans.

In those days, airplanes were still a novelty and when one flew over the Robins' practice field one day, twenty-four-year-old Brooklyn outfielder Casey Stengel bet Robinson that the manager couldn't catch a ball dropped from a plane. And so, after practice, Stengel set out for the nearest airport to see if he could make the arrangements, while Robinson practiced catching pop-ups.

The next day, the hum of a plane could be heard within minutes of the start of Robins practice. Robinson hurriedly got ready in the center of the diamond. Then Stengel appeared to change his mind about the deal. He told his manager that it wasn't too late to call off the bet and said he was worried that a ball plummeting from such height might rip a hole right through Robinson's glove, and maybe even his hand.

"Hogwash," the feisty manager said. But a seed of doubt, and maybe even fear, had been planted in his mind by the young Stengel, who was already quite a nuanced jokester.

Soon, a small plane was circling. And then, as Robinson looked toward the heavens, the pilot ejected a spherical object. The portly manager staggered, waited, staggered some more, and then . . . splat. He began screaming in horror when he realized that he was covered with what could only be the pulpy chunks of his own pulverized hand!

Then he realized he was only covered with the pulp of a juicy pink grapefruit.

According to some versions of the story, Stengel substituted the piece of fruit for the ball, fearing that he would kill his manager and cost himself a spot on the team. According to another version, aviator Ruth Law forgot to bring a ball and substituted an object from her lunch bag.

Whichever was the case, before long players throughout the game had heard the story and had begun calling the Florida circuit the "Grapefruit League."

---

associated with Cubs fan Steve Bartman, who interfered with the flight of a foul pop-up along the left-field line at Wrigley Field and unintentionally aided in an eight-run Marlins rally in the eighth inning of Game 6, the Marlins came back from a three-games-to-one deficit to win their second pennant. The Fish then moved on to their greatest test yet, an October Classic match against the storied New York Yankees. And they were ready for the challenge. They didn't even need seven games to dispose of the Pinstripes. McKeon decided to pitch the twenty-three-year-old Beckett on short rest in Game 6 at Yankee Stadium and the brash righty rose to the occasion. Beckett tossed a five-hit shutout to close out the Yanks 2-0. Few moments in our lives have been as satisfying as watching George Steinbrenner fume in his luxury box as his Yankees, with their payroll of more than $184 million, lost to the Marlins, who had spent a mere $54 million on players that year. It was a victory for smaller market teams everywhere.

On the heels of their second world championship, the Marlins continued to field a contending—though not quite championship—team. They had winning seasons in 2004, 2005, 2008, and 2009, even as they failed to average twenty thousand fans per game. Nonetheless, there was considerable reason for optimism as the new ballpark was being constructed concurrent to the rise of bright young Marlins stars like Hanley Ramirez, Gaby Sanchez, and Mike Stanton. Now, with a gorgeous new park in place, Marlins fans will have no excuse if they don't support the team. We expect that in the years ahead Miami, which has always been a hotbed for amateur baseball talent, will finally fulfill its promise as a bona fide baseball city that's every bit as "big league" as the other thirty towns that house teams of their own. In other words, if the Marlins are still vying with the Tampa Bay Rays and Oakland A's each year for the ignoble distinction of who will finish dead last in the game in terms of fans-through-the-gates, then Major League Baseball will have miscalculated badly in its decision to put a team in Miami and in sticking with the Marlins through some lean times. For the Marlins' sake, and baseball's sake, we hope the Miami fans rise to the occasion.

Getting a Choice Seat

Getting a ticket to the football field where the Marlins treaded water for nearly two decades was never a problem. And though tickets are harder to come by now, they're still dirt cheap, compared to tickets in practically any other big league city.

The ballpark has three levels, but the second one—which is used primarily for luxury box and club seating—is exceedingly narrow. And the third one doesn't even extend all the way to the foul poles on either side of the diamond. Nor does the upper deck rise very high. As a result, 32,300 of the park's 37,000 seats are located either on the infield or along the foul lines, leaving only 4,700 in home run territory. The ballpark feels cozy. And the views are excellent thanks to a design that angles every section toward the infield.

Promenade Level

The field level is known as the Promenade. Don't ask us why. It just is.

Kevin: Join Captain Stubing and Julie McCoy at 4 p.m. for shuffleboard on the Promenade Deck.

Josh: Who's Captain Stubing?

Kevin: Never mind.

Diamond Club (FL1–FL8), Dugout Club (Boxes 1–3) and Clubhouse Box (Boxes 4–25)

The 379 Diamond Club seats, located in the first eight rows behind home plate, sold out for the ballpark's inaugural season more than a year before the Marlins opened the park. The Dugout Club and Clubhouse Box seats, which consist of the first eight rows along the first- and third-base lines, are similarly unlikely to be available from the Marlins for single-game purchase any time soon. But you might get lucky and score these seats on StubHub if a season-ticket holder wants to sit out a game. If you can, we highly recommend it. In New York City, face value to sit down low in a posh seat like this commands a face value of nearly $3,000 per game. In Miami, the Marlins price the Dugout Club seats at $150 each and the Clubhouse Box seats at a mere $70.

Home Plate Box (Sections 9–20)

Once you get past the premium seats, the Promenade offers twenty-eight main sections that offer between twenty-six and thirty rows apiece. Section 1 is out in right field, Section 14 is directly behind the plate, and Section 28 is in deep left field. The best seats are the Home Plate Boxes, which wrap around the backstop. Section 9 is located at the mid-point of the visitors' first base dugout, while Section 20 is midway down the Marlins dugout. The seats in the lower few rows cost the most, while the price decreases in ten dollar increments every few rows higher up you climb. We like this pricing model. It ensures that you get what you pay for. The sight lines are unobstructed but the top six rows (21–26 or 24–30, depending on the section) are beneath the overhang of the second deck, so if that's apt to bother you, be sure to sit in a lower row.

Base Reserved (Sections 7, 8, 21, 22)

Appearing right at first base (Sections 7 & 8) and third base (21 & 22) these four sections might well provide the best value for the money on the first level. We were shocked by how reasonably priced they were for quality infield seats. With all other considerations being equal, we recommend sitting on the first base side, where the window view of downtown Miami in left will be in your field of sight all game long.

Baseline Reserved (Sections 1–6, 23–28)

If you want to save a few bucks over the cost of infield seats but still want to be as close to the action around the bases as possible, then aim for seats where the infield dirt meets the lip of the outfield grass in either Section 6, just beyond first base, or Section 23, just beyond third. Normally, we don't recommend the deepest foul seats in outfield foul territory because at most parks the cheaper seats beyond the home run fence in fair territory offer better straight on views. At this park, however, we really liked the view from either Section 1 in deep right or Section 28 in deep left. Because the sections are so dramatically angled toward the infield and because there's nothing in front of them to distract your view, we recommend them over most of the home run territory Bullpen Reserved seats, which place fans behind the bullpens and much farther from the field.

Seating Capacity: 37,000
Ticket Office: http://florida.marlins.mlb.
com/ticketing/singlegame.jsp?c_id=fla
Seating Chart: http://florida.marlins.mlb.
com/fla/ballpark/seat_selection_guide_
32.jsp

Bullpen Reserved (Sections 29–40)

Sections 29–32 run behind the Marlins bullpen in left-field home run territory. These sections have the window directly behind them and are not shadowed by the overhang of a looming second deck. The right-field Bullpen Reserved sections (34–40) are almost entirely overhung, however, by an upstairs Home Run Porch. Because the higher vantage point of the seats above gives them a superior view of the infield, we recommend the Porch seats over the right-field Bullpen Reserved ones. The only drawback to sitting upstairs is that you can't see the action in the bullpen below or plays right against the outfield fence.

Legends Level

This narrow second level houses luxury suites behind the plate and Club seats down the lines. We found its naming curious.

Josh: The Marlins haven't been around long enough to have any franchise legends.

Kevin: I suppose it's been a while since Devon White laced 'em up for the teal and silver.

Josh: A retiree should have to be in his sixties to be considered a legend, though.

Kevin: Yeah, and he should have a career batting average north of .270.

Josh: Excepting Reggie Jackson, of course.

LEGENDS GOLD, PLATINUM AND SILVER (BOXES 201–211, 219–228)

There are only ten rows on the second level and they are tucked neatly between the two main seating decks. There are no Legends Boxes directly behind the plate because that's where the rich and famous sit in luxury boxes. Boxes 201 to 211 run from the right-field foul pole to the first base side on-deck circle, and 219–228 run from the third-base on-deck circle to the left-field pole. You will lose some of the view of the right-field corner the closer you get to Box 201 in deep right, and will lose more and more of the left-field corner as you get closer to Box 228. We advise avoiding Boxes 211 and

219, so that you don't have to sit against the concrete walls that rise up on either side of the luxury boxes. Boxes 207–210 and 220–223 are the pick of the litter on this deck.

Home Run Porch (Sections 134–141)

We highly recommend these cheap outfield seats. They are low enough to keep fans engaged in the game, but high enough to provide a bird's eye view. Tickets cost under $15.00 whether you're sitting in Row 1 or Row 16, so aim for a seat as close to the field as possible. The right-field foul pole is not an obstruction, even for fans seated in Section 141, because it rises to the side of the Porch, rather than in front of it. We should mention that these seats are a bit narrower than the ones that appear elsewhere, so if you're a wide-body, you may want to take this into consideration. The Home Run Porch seats measure eighteen inches across, while the Vista level seats measure nineteen to twenty inches, and the Diamond Club seats on the Promenade measure twenty-one to twenty-three inches.

Josh: What sort of message does this send?

Kevin: Easy, rich people have bigger behinds and thus need the extra space.

Josh: Hence the term "fat cats."

Kevin: Precisely.

Vista Level

This upper deck offers a concourse that enables patrons to walk down some stairs to seats that overhang the Legends Level, or up some stairs to seats that overlook the entire park.

VISTA BOX (SECTIONS 306–323)

Immediately behind the plate, the Vista Boxes climb sixteen rows in a single bank of seats above the concourse level. This leaves room for the press box. On either side of the press box though, the Vista Boxes appear in two forms: as above-the-concourse seats and as seats that hang down below the concourse. The seats that hang down are preferable. They are located in Sections 306–310 and 319–323 in rows lettered B–J. The rest of the Vista Box seats (i.e., the ones that are higher up and not as desirable) appear in rows numbered 1–16. So shoot for a lettered row.

VISTA RESERVED (SECTIONS 302–305, 324–327)

The Vista Reserved seats appear deeper down the outfield lines. Although these aren't on the infield like the Vista Boxes, they begin at the same height as the lower hanging Vista Boxes (as described above), which means that the first ten rows (B–J) are actually pretty good. And you can't beat the price. It's the lowest in the ballpark.

The Marlins were pretty hell-bent on working to ensure that the railings safeguarding fans from harm obstructed views as minimally as possible. Team officials reportedly sat in every single upper level seat before the ballpark's opening and then made recommendations on any adjustments that needed to be made to keep sight lines as pure as possible.

Kevin: Wow, they sat in every seat.

Josh: Sounds like they were auditioning for our job.

Before/After the Game

The Marlins' new locale in Little Havana constitutes a major upgrade over their previous "neighborhood," especially if you like fine cigars and Cuban sandwiches like we do. Yes, we know loading up on carcinogens and cholesterol is never wise, but there are certain things you do on vacation that you wouldn't think of doing at home. And baseball road tripping counts as vacation-time for us, even if we get paid for it.

Aside from cigar and sandwich shops, Little Havana offers coffee shops, brightly colored murals and stone monuments that range from a likeness of the Virgin Mary to a Bay of Pigs memorial, and plenty of Cuban-Americans. We always get a kick out of the elder gentlemen sitting outside playing chess and especially dominoes. How you actually play dominoes, we have no idea, but if you were the patient sort and cared to learn, we bet hanging around Maximo Gomez Park for a few hours would teach you a thing or two.

Getting to Marlins Ballpark

The park is three-quarters of a mile from SR 836 Westbound via the 12th Avenue exit, or half a mile from SR 836 Eastbound via the 17th Avenue exit. For those traveling on Interstate 95 South, take the 8th Street exit and it's just about a mile to the park. For those on Interstate 95 North, take the exit for SR 836 Westbound and follow the directions above. The ballpark sits at 1501 Northwest 3rd St.

As for the parking situation, the easiest bet is to use one of the four parking garages that were built on the Orange Bowl site as part of the ballpark construction project. These have five or six levels each, and are located smartly at the four corners of the old Orange Bowl site, so that the ballpark sits in their midst. The garages cost the City of Miami about $100 million to build. As part of the new ballpark financing deal, the Marlins agreed to purchase them from the city upon their completion and to assume responsibility for their upkeep. In total, the garages have room for about 5,700 cars.

SEATING TIP

Because this recent addition to the MLB landscape is a beaut, and because Miami is a fun town, we suggest planning to catch two games when you're in town. Spend the first in a pricier infield seat on the first level, and then spend the second in the Home Run Porch. That way you'll get the full experience.

There are also plenty of private lots and garages operating within a half-mile walk of the ballpark. Keep in mind that the Orange Bowl held nearly twice as many fans as the Marlins' park now does, at a time before the four garages existed, and there was never a major problem when it came to folks finding parking in the neighborhood lots.

Another option is to take a shuttle bus from one of the nearby MetroRail stops like Culmer, Civic Center, Vizcaya, or the Miami Intermodal Center. Ideally, the MetroRail would have a stop at the ballpark, and the Marlins have expressed interest in seeing the city bring such a convenience to fruition, but at the time of this book's printing there seemed to be neither the money nor political will to make this happen. Eventually, it would seem like a no-brainer, though.

MetroRail Maps and Schedules: www.miamidade.gov/transit/rail.asp

Outside Attractions

MOTOR OIL, COOKING OIL, AND OIL KINDS OF OTHER FUN

Three of the four parking garages were designed to include restaurant and retail space as well as dank asphalt smeared with motor oil. That's right, each of these garages is a minimall unto itself, designed to keep patrons coming to the ballpark site year-round, not just when the Marlins are in season or have a game. So, if you're looking to do some window-shopping before the game, or for a bite to eat, look no further than where you've just ditched the road trip mobile.

MURAL ME, MIAMI

Miami's ballpark has been likened to a New Age sculpture. At street level though, it also offers colorful murals in the Spanish style that depict images from the vibrant Little Havana streets nearby. These are only part of an ambitious plan the Marlins will work on for years to come to pack the park to the gills with art.

ORANGE BOWL MEMORIAL

At the plaza on the east side of Marlins Ballpark, a public arts project pays tribute to the Miami Orange Bowl, which used to rise on the site.

Built in 1937, the Orange Bowl served as the original home of the Miami Dolphins, hosted five Super Bowls, hosted college football's annual "Orange Bowl," and was also home to the University of Miami Hurricanes. It was demolished in 2008 to make way for the new yard.

The tribute to the old stadium is as artsy as it is apropos. A hallmark of the facility was its gigantic sign reading "Miami Orange Bowl" in orange capital letters across its façade on Northwest 3rd Street. That distinctive sign is replicated—sort of—by ten-foot-high orange letters that can be found on the concourse outside Marlins Ballpark. But rather than merely presenting the letters in an orderly and upright manner, as you might expect, the artists commissioned to do the project decided to present them as the letters might have appeared at the very moment they came tumbling from the imploded stadium's face. As such, some are lying flat down on the plaza, others are half submerged beneath the ground, others are tilted sideways, and others stand, but at odd angles or in the wrong order.

Now, we're no art experts. But we thought this was a funky and original way to remember a classic stadium that couldn't quite have been done justice by a standard issue granite monument.

Josh: Can I have an "A," Vanna?

Kevin: You can only select consonants, moron. You have to buy the vowels.

Josh: I'm not paying extra for any vowels.

Kevin: The only thing I've ever seen you pay extra for is extra meat at that Japanese Chicken place in the mall.

Josh: You're right. I always get double meat.

CALLE OCHO WALK OF FAME

A visit to Maximo Gomez Park not only affords the opportunity to watch dominoes being played at what we can only assume is a pretty high level, but it also brings you to the foot of the Calle Ocho (Eighth Street) Walk of Fame. The path is paved with stars that comprise a veritable "who's who" of Latino stars from the arts and entertainment worlds. The more familiar names include the very first recipient of a star—Gloria Estefan, as well as boxer Roberto Duran, Julio and Enrique Iglesias, the late Selena, otherwise known as the "Mexican Madonna," and Sylvester Stallone. For the record, Stallone is Italian, not Latino, but he attended Miami Dade College.

Josh: Alex Rodriguez played at Miami's Westminster Christian High. He deserves a star.

Kevin: He's a bum now and he was a bum then.

Josh: According to Selena Roberts's book *Arod,* he did steroids in high school.

Kevin: Precisely.

Watering Holes and Outside Eats

Little Havana must be experienced for oneself to be fully appreciated. It is a place with a culture all its own. We recommend spending a full day walking around and taking it all in. We offer a few of our favorite spots along its streets, as well as some tips on other Miami restaurants we think readers will enjoy. As for the club scene in South Beach, that sort of falls outside our range of expertise, so we're going to leave you to navigate the clubs on your own if you're so inclined, which, if we know our readers, we're betting you're not.

Josh: Really, we're not clubbing? But I brought my bling.

Kevin: I was wondering why you were wearing that goofy Red Sox medallion.

Josh: Whatever. You're now officially on my frienemy list.

Kevin: You've been watching too much *CSI Miami.*

Josh: Um, *Dexter* actually.

LITTLE HAVANA CIGAR FACTORY
1501 SW 8th St.
www.littlehavanacigarfactory.com/
The lounge of this classic stogie shop features comfy leather couches, plenty of ashtrays, and two gigantic flat-screen TVs. Aside from the fact that you'll stink to the high heavens after visiting, the only other downer is that it closes at 8:00 p.m.

KING'S ICE CREAM
1831 8th St.
Cuban ice cream takes on a fruity flare, so be ready to order something besides the same old Chocolate or Vanilla you get back home. You're in Little Havana, chomping on stogies and playing dominoes, so it's time to broaden your ice cream horizons too.

EL PUB
1548 8th St.
We recommend boning up on your Spanish language skills before you visit, but even if you don't, your dinero will do the talking. We suggest the croquetas as a starter. These are a deep-fried delight you just won't find back home (unless you're from Cuba, in which case, we guess you will). Then, for an entrée, we suggest the roast pork with white rice and yucca garlic sauce.

BODEGUITA DE MARTINEZ
833 SW 29th Ave.

Looking for a place to knock back some late-night moji-tos? Or to listen to some swinging Cuban music? Then we recommend the house of Martinez, which is owned by the same family that once operated the famous Bodeguita del Medio, where the mojito was invented, and where Ernest Hemingway and his fellow bohemians used to drink when they visited Cuba.

For those who've never had a mojito, it is made by mixing spiced rum with soda water, mint, sugar, and lime juice.

SHULA'S STEAK HOUSE
5225 Collins Ave.
www.donshula.com/

If you're not just a hardball fan but a pigskin fan too, then you may want to check out the spot where legendary Dolphins coach Don Shula's restaurant chain began. Not only could he manage a gridiron squad to perfection (How does 14-0 in 1972 grab you?), but apparently Mr. Shula knows how to assemble a dynamite restaurant management team too. Who knew? As at all Shula's, the red meat and seafood are excellent, although a tad on the pricey side.

DAN MARINO'S FINE FOOD AND SPIRITS
5701 Sunset Dr.
www.danmarinosrestaurant.com/

Has the Hall of Fame Dolphins quarterback surpassed his old head coach in culinary expertise? We'll leave it to you to decide.

Kevin: Wow, they both have restaurants. I guess that means they won a bunch of Super Bowls together.

Josh: Um, I wouldn't say that too loud in these parts.

JOE'S STONE CRAB
11 Washington Ave.
www.joesstonecrab.com/

Specializing in stone crabs and key lime pie, Joe's offers the ultimate Miami experience. A landmark on the beach since 1913, Joe's isn't cheap, but it's sure to satisfy. If you are ordinarily a vegan for moral reasons or sympathize with PETA most of the time, you will be happy to know that no crabs were killed in the making of your meal. In order to ensure the continued propagation of the stone crab species, the crabs are captured and one claw is removed, then they are returned to the ocean. That way, they can keep reproducing and making more crab claws for us humans to eat.

Kevin: Somehow, I think I'd feel better if they were just killed.

Josh: I disagree. An involuntary amputation is preferable to an execution.

Kevin: If a giant crab swooped down and excised your right arm, you'd be okay with it?

Josh: How about we just shut up and eat our crabs?

Inside the Park

If the field dimensions seem quirky to you, you're right, they are. But they're not just quirky for quirks' sake. They are quirky because they offer a nod to the unusual outfield configuration that once existed at the Marlins' previous home. The converted football field quickly became known as a pitcher's park upon its arrival on the big league scene. The outfield fences used to measure the farthest from home plate in the notch called the "Bermuda Triangle" in left-center. At their new home, the Marlins moved the deep gap to right-center and made the angle of the centerfield wall not quite so dramatic. But the concept is the same. It's a place where a well-struck gap-shot might well turn into a three-bagger. And what fan of the game doesn't get a special rise out of watching a speedster leg it from home to third in the blink of an eye?

The deepest outfield point measures 420 feet from the plate just to the right of dead-centerfield, and the gaps extend 384 feet from home in left-center and 392 feet in right-center.

Ballpark Features

GONE FISHING

Unless you're sitting at field level on the infield, or even if you are, you'll want to arrive early to visit the massive saltwater aquariums between the dugouts and batter's circle. We think the colorful coral is a nice touch too, and though we're no ichthyologists we assume the fish agree.

Josh: Did I ever tell you about the time I caught a sixteen-pound flathead catfish with my bare hands in a Louisiana?

Kevin: Probably. I don't really listen when you start telling fish stories.

Josh: It was hiding under a partially submerged log and I dropped a rock on the other side to scare it toward me . . .

Kevin: Yeah, I've heard this before. This is your bogus noodling story.

GONE SWIMMING

The pool in left field is the centerpiece of the faux beach resort known as the Clevelander. This is a private part of the park, accessible to groups wishing to hold an event at the ballpark. While it's perfect for a company outing or bachelorette party, we know the real fans look down their noses at gimmicks like these, even as they crane their necks and dig out their stadium binocs to check out the females arriving at the game in bikinis.

GILLS GONE WILD

The home run extravaganzas in other cities include rising icons that emerge from beyond the outfield fences, flashing lights, explosions and even waterworks. In Miami the celebration machine that rises from behind the center-field fence incorporates all of the above . . . and then some. It's the most ambitious homer hoopla spectacle in the game, so root, root, root for a long ball.

Stadium Eats

The food at the Marlins' previous stadium ranked among the very worst in all of baseball as far as we were concerned. And apparently the Marlins weren't too impressed by what they were serving either. More than a year prior to the move to the new tank, they announced they would be inviting several stalwarts of the Miami dining scene into the park to share their expertise.

CUBAN FOOD (TRADEMARK FOOD)

Not only can you always count on getting a good Cuban sandwich at a ballgame in Miami, but you can also get arepas, which are sweet, round, deep-fried cornbread patties stuffed with cheese. They're delicious.

BEST OF THE REST

The **Taste of Miami** area in left field is your best bet to get something unique at the game. Plus, you can have a couple or three cold ones at a bar that looks out at the Miami skyline through the big glass wall that seals in the park when the roof is closed. As mentioned earlier, the ballpark officially opened just as our book was landing in early 2012, and the Marlins hadn't solidified their concession lineup at the time of our visit to Miami in 2011. By then the team had assured its fans, however, that the ballpark concessions would include such South Florida staples as **sushi, stone crabs, fresh-shucked oysters, dolphin sandwiches, Cuban coffee, medianoches, empanadas,** and **croquetas.** For the uninitiated, we can tell you that croquetas are deep-fried treats just full of savory wonder. Here's betting that they become the Marlins trademark food in the years ahead.

The Ballpark Experience

To experience a Marlins game is to immerse oneself in a more diverse gathering of seamheads than the typical big league park draws. In our experiences, we've encountered fans from all corners of the United States at Marlins games. Attending a game in Miami, you're apt to see Baltimore Orioles caps, Red Sox caps, Yankees shirts, Dodger blue, and just about anything else. We suppose that in a state of transplants and retirees, this shouldn't be surprising. Beyond that, it's tough to characterize the experience of watching a game at Marlins Ballpark, because the facility is so new and the fan base had been stuck in low gear for so many years before the park's arrival. Fish fans will surely develop their own traditions at the park, but this process will take time and must transpire organically as the characteristics of the park, the team, and the fans themselves come to the fore.

ROOF TRIVIA

The roof consists of three steel panels that, in total, weigh nineteen million pounds. The highest panel is the one over the middle of the field, which hovers two hundred feet above second base, ensuring that even the highest of pop-ups and big league flies will fail to reach it. For comparison's sake, the catwalks hanging from the roof at Tropicana Field in St. Petersburg are just fifty-nine feet above the center-field fence and 146 feet above home plate.

The roof takes about fifteen minutes to close, as the panels move at 39 feet per minute. The panels can all move at once, or they can move one at a time, so that the roof can be partially closed, if necessary, for the purpose of blocking the sun from interfering with the game. What the roof can't do is open or close under high-wind conditions. It is unsafe to operate the roof in winds exceeding 40 miles per hour. On non-windy days, however, the process of opening or closing the roof costs just $10.00 in electricity, owing to a "regenerative drive system" that we two writers lack the engineering background to explain.

Kevin: It cost more than $10.00 for that hot dog and beer I had last inning.

Josh: So you've funded one roof-closing, my friend. How about making it two . . . and close the roof again for me while you're down there?

RAIN DELAY TRIVIA

Marlins fans surely won't miss the frequent rain delays to which they were subjected at their previous stadium. But we'll miss them just a tad. After all, they provided a chance for the Marlins to broaden fans' knowledge of all-things-teal with JumboTron trivia. In honor of the rain delays that will never occur again, we provide the answers to two of the trivia questions we posed earlier in the chapter.

Livan Hernandez's two World Series victories as a rookie in 1997 represented only the second time a rookie had won two Series games. The first hurler to garner a pair of October Classic W's was Larry Sherry, who accomplished the feat for the Brooklyn Dodgers in 1959.

Before John Lynch became a Pro Bowl defensive back in the NFL, he was a pitcher for a Marlins Rookie-League team—the Erie Sailors of the New York-Penn League. After displaying a fastball that could reach ninety-five miles per hour at Stanford, Lynch was drafted in the second round of the 1992 Major League draft. A year later he was selected in the third round of the 1993 NFL Draft and gave up baseball. But first, Lynch threw the very first pitch in Marlins franchise history and recorded a no-decision as the Sailors lost 6–5 to the Jamestown Expos in thirteen innings on a June day in 1993. Today, Lynch's Marlins hat resides at the National Baseball Hall of Fame in Cooperstown. For the record, the righty's final minor league stat line included one win, three losses, and a spiffy 2.35 ERA over thirty-eight innings. In a fourteen-season NFL career, he totaled 740 tackles and twenty-six interceptions. And he made eight Pro Bowls.

Kevin: I'd say he made the right call.

Josh: Nah. Two-sport stars should always choose baseball.

Kevin: Why?

Josh: Because I like baseball better. . . .

Kevin: That's not too egocentric.

Josh: And because baseball causes fewer long-term physical problems.

Kevin: Provided we're not counting the effects of smokeless tobacco and steroid use.

Josh: True enough.

THE FUTURE IS TEAL. . . . AND GREEN

The Marlins made it their goal from the start to construct the first LEED (Leadership in Energy and Environmental Design) certified retractable roof stadium in the bigs. Washington's Nationals Ballpark is the first major sports facility to achieve LEED certification but alas, it has no roof, leaving room for the Marlins to still be first in something. And while they were still awaiting the final word on whether they had achieved this most sought-after stamp of approval in the world of environmentally friendly design, they no doubt went to great lengths in their pursuit of it. The stadium's glass façade allows much more light to filter into the stadium than the retractable roof fields in Houston or Arizona allow, for example, while the white roof reflects sunlight rather than absorbing it. Waterless urinals, like the ones they have at Citi Field in New York, are also fixtures throughout the park. There are 250 of them and they combine to save six million gallons of water a year that would otherwise be flushed down the drain. The materials used in the stadium's construction were also carefully selected to minimize their negative environmental impact. Some were recycled from other projects, while others were fabricated as close to the stadium's construction site as possible, to reduce the environmental impact of transporting them to South Florida.

Josh: If only they'd opted to power the whole yard with fuel cells.

Kevin: Let me guess, that's a stock you own?

Josh: As a matter of fact I'd like to tell you about . . .

Kevin: I'm really not interested.

BASEBALL BINGO

When the Marlins are playing a Friday night home game, they give fans a special treat: the chance to win T-shirts, caps, bobbleheads, posters and other Marlins-related prizes. On these nights, the first ten thousand fans through the gates receive Baseball Bingo cards. Some are marked for an instant prize, while the rest leave it up to their holders to keep score as the game progresses to see if they can spell Bingo and win a prize the old-fashioned way.

Cyber Super-Fans

We recommend the following excellent Marlins blogs, although we must admit that we find them all a tad fishy in terms of the information they provide. We mean that in a good way, of course.

- **Fish Stripes**
  www.fishstripes.com/
- **Fish Chunks**
  http://fishchunks.blogspot.com/
- **Fish Bytes**
  http://miamiherald.typepad.com/fish_bytes/

CASTING CALL: CELEBRITY SUPER-FANS NEEDED

The Mets have Jerry Seinfeld. The Dodgers have Alyssa Milano. The Yankees have Paul McCartney. And the Red Sox have Stephen King. All of the high-profile teams have immediately recognizable celebs associated with their home ballparks. And now that the Marlins are actually playing in

Sports in (and around) the City

The Grapefruit League
www.floridagrapefruitleague.com/
We strongly recommend planning a trip to Florida in March so that you can visit the ballparks of the Grapefruit League, before starting your regular season tour in Miami. During Spring Training, you get to see the same players in smaller ballparks, and get to sit that much closer to the field. The players are more willing to sign autographs, and less apt to punch out your camera lens. The tickets are a lot cheaper. And good beaches and championship golf courses abound at every turn. Although there are fifteen teams training in Florida, there are only fourteen Grapefruit League ballparks. That's because the Marlins and Cardinals share a home in Jupiter.

Our pick for best old-time park goes to Lakeland's Joker Marchant Stadium and Bradenton's McKechnie Field in a split decision. The spring homes of the Tigers and Pirates, respectively, these ancient yards have been extensively renovated in recent years, but continue to provide the quaint and cozy atmosphere for which the spring game is renowned.

The Yankees' Steinbrenner Field in Tampa is the most grand of the Florida practice lots, with its replica of Monument Park outside the front entrance, its massive Yankees team store, and a façade that mimics Yankee Stadium's. As for the newest park in the Sunshine State Circuit, it's the Red Sox' JetBlue Park, which opened in 2012. It has a Green Monster in left field that has seats built right into it, something like at Fenway, as well as a manually operated scoreboard on its face. And the bullpens are located in right field, just like at Fenway too. It is one of the larger Florida facilities with a seating capacity of eleven thousand. As for the smallest spring yard in Florida or Arizona? That's the Astros' Osceola County Stadium in Kissimmee, Florida, which has a capacity of just 5,300.

Here's a lowdown of who plays where:

- **Florida Marlins and St. Louis Cardinals**
  Roger Dean Stadium (Seating capacity: 7,000)
  4751 Main St.
  Jupiter, FL
- **Atlanta Braves**
  Champion Stadium (9,500)
  700 South Victory Way
  Lake Buena Vista, FL
- **Baltimore Orioles**
  Ed Smith Stadium (7,500)
  2700 12th St.
  Sarasota, FL
- **Boston Red Sox**
  JetBlue Park (11,000)
  Daniels Parkway
  Fort Myers, FL
- **Detroit Tigers**
  Joker Marchant Stadium (9,000)
  2301 Lakeland Hills Blvd.
  Lakeland, FL
- **Houston Astros**
  Osceola County Stadium (5,300)
  631 Heritage Park Way
  Kissimmee, FL
- **Minnesota Twins**
  William H. Hammond Stadium (8,100)
  14100 Six Mile Cypress Pkwy.
  Fort Myers, FL

- **New York Mets**
  Digital Domain Park (7,000)
  525 NW Peacock Blvd.
  Port St. Lucie, FL
- **New York Yankees**
  George M. Steinbrenner Field (11,076)
  One Steinbrenner Dr.
  Tampa, FL
- **Philadelphia Phillies**
  Bright House Field (10,335)
  601 Old Coachman Rd.
  Clearwater, FL
- **Pittsburgh Pirates**
  McKechnie Field (6,602)
  1611 Ninth St. West
  Bradenton, FL
- **Tampa Bay Rays**
  Charlotte Sports Park (6,823)
  2300 El Jobean Rd.
  Port Charlotte, FL
- **Toronto Blue Jays**
  Florida Auto Exchange Stadium (5,509)
  373 Douglas Ave.
  Dunedin, FL
- **Washington Nationals**
  Space Coast Stadium (8,100)
  5800 Stadium Pkwy.
  Viera, FL

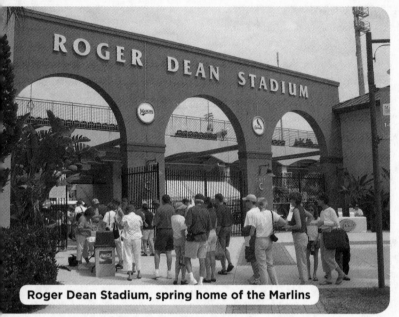

Roger Dean Stadium, spring home of the Marlins

The Marlins and Cardinals share Roger Dean Stadium in
Jupiter during Grapefruit League play.
Photo by Josh Pahigian

"Talking about it incessantly is finally paying off for you," Kevin said. "Tell me again about all the trout you and your friend Matt caught out of a storm drain."

"Um, it was a lake drain," Josh said. Then he launched into the story.

"I've been looking forward to this," Josh said upon the completion of his story. And it was true: He had been looking forward to the side tour that he still believed would include fishing for marlin in the Gulf of Mexico and a three-night stay at a resort in Cancun.

"Me, too," Kevin replied.

But as we approached the boat, Josh started to get suspicious. "This doesn't look like a fishing charter at all," he said. "It looks like a booze cruise ship."

"Have you ever been deep-sea fishing?" Kevin asked.

"Yeah, all the time," Josh said.

"But have you ever been on a marlin boat?"

"Well, no," Josh admitted.

"Then just get on the boat."

And so we boarded the large vessel along with the other tourists, none of whom, Josh noted, had fishing gear among their luggage.

"Where are all the rods and reels?" Josh asked. "And why doesn't it smell like rancid clam entrails?"

"They'll bring them out after Happy Hour," Kevin said. "Let's go to the bar and get you a daiquiri." Kevin put his arm around his friend's shoulder and guided him to the bar. He ordered himself a beer and Josh a frozen fruity drink.

After we had settled onto pub stools, Josh said, "We're not going fishing, are we?" Kevin looked at his friend for a moment, took a sip of beer, then said, "You know I don't believe in killing animals."

"But you eat meat," Josh said incredulously.

"I don't mind the killing *of* animals," Kevin said. "I just don't believe in doing it myself."

"I knew this wasn't a fishing charter."

"What tipped you off? The 'Carnival' signs?"

"So where are we going?"

"Cuba," Kevin deadpanned. "We're going to talk some baseball with the Castro brothers."

"Cuba!" Josh yelled. "Let me off this bucket of bolts."

"Hold on, hold on," Kevin laughed. "They don't just let you take a boat to Cuba. I know because I tried. We're actually

Miami, instead of out in the burbs, we expect at least a few of the beautiful people who frequent the clubs in South Beach to start turning out for games. We hear Drew Barrymore bleeds teal and silver and think she would look great on *SportsCenter*, sitting tank-side near the Marlins dugout. We hear rapper Flo Rida follows the Marlins, too, and that Gloria Estefan, who owns a small share of the Miami Dolphins, is hooked on the Fish.

While We Were in Miami
Kevin Orchestrated a (Good-Natured) Kidnapping

We walked down a long pier toward a boat that Kevin had chartered weeks in advance, both happy to stretch our legs after a long drive across the many bridges that link the Florida Keys. We were in Key West, but not for long. In a few minutes we'd be on the high waters.

"So we're finally going to do some fishing," Josh said eagerly.

"Yup, I finally got the bug," Kevin lied.

"I knew you'd come around," Josh said.

going to Puerto Rico to see the ballpark where the San Juan Senators play during the Puerto Rico Winter League."

"Is it safe?" Josh asked.

"Is it safe? It's like the 51st state."

"Yeah, but we've been through some questionable states. Like Iowa. And Oklahoma."

Space Coast Stadium, spring home of the Nationals

The Nationals play at Space Coast Stadium north of Miami in Viera during the spring.
Photo by Josh Pahigian

"True, but Puerto Rico is safe," Kevin assured his friend. "And Hi Bithorn Stadium is supposed to be a great ballpark."

"The Montreal Expos played there in 2003 and 2004," Josh remembered.

"That's right," Kevin said.

"And the Marlins and Mets played a three-game series there in 2010."

"Exactly," Kevin said.

We sat in silence for a while, sipping our drinks as other passengers made their way to the bar and ordered.

"Hiram Bithorn, eh?" Josh said at last.

"Yup," answered Kevin.

"He played for the Cubs and White Sox."

"That's right."

Then Josh launched into a lengthy story about the life and times of the first Puerto Rico–born player to make it to the big leagues. At the end of his Bithorn biography, he said, "You could have just told me where we were going."

Kevin smiled. "Yeah, that probably would have worked too," he said.

"Probably," Josh replied. "Now how about getting me another margarita?"

"It's a daiquiri," Kevin said over his shoulder, as he hurried back to the bar. "On the next road trip, we'll go fishing. And you can drink a man's drink."

ST. LOUIS CARDINALS, BUSCH STADIUM III

A Red Bird's Nest above the Rest

St. Louis baseball fans have achieved legendary status among all sports fans, as their passion for the Red Birds is boundless. And they have been lavished by the spoils of their team's excellence. In building Busch Stadium III the Cardinals have, at long last, completed the last remaining piece of their baseball puzzle: a near perfect venue in which to enjoy and celebrate the game and team this city loves so well.

Built in the retro-classic ballpark style popularized by the success of Oriole Park at Camden Yards, the third incarnation of Busch Stadium is fitting for a team with the Cardinals' history. We consider it fortunate that the park arrived just before the more recent trend of techno-modern ballpark design seen in cities like Miami and D.C. because baseball tradition runs deep in the Gateway City, both on the field, and in the hearts and minds of Cardinals fans. And nothing other than a traditional approach was going to fly in this town.

A stunning red brick exterior that is dramatic from any approaching angle greets the eye at first glance of the park. What architecturally appears to be the main entrance, at the corner of Clark and 8th Street (aka Stan Musial Drive), is actually the entrance to the team store. It features a rounded wall of high brick arches that curves outward between large square turrets adorned with the trademark St. Louis "STL" logo. The Centerfield Gate is more open, with wrought iron fencing that looks like a train stop (but isn't) and offers a sneak peek into the ballpark. The Third Base entrance might be the most dramatic, with a steel recreation of the Eads Bridge arching overtop a plaza dedicated to Cardinal great Stan Musial. The Home Plate entrance features a rotunda of arches six stories high. Capping off the many architectural adornments is rust-colored, weather-stained cornice work that surrounds the entire park, giving the building a classic finishing touch. At night, lights illuminate the arches and supports, creating a grandeur surpassed perhaps only by the Coliseum in Rome, the Bird's Nest in Beijing, the new Yankee Stadium, Notre Dame Stadium and a handful of other great venues in the history of sport. Okay, perhaps that last statement exaggerates the issue just a bit, but it is a very, very nice looking ballpark.

Throughout the park the designers went to great lengths to inspire the majesty and tradition of the Cardinals' organization. And they succeeded on nearly every level. From the inset relief images of the many red birds the team has used on its uniforms and the layered brickwork of the arches, to the generous use of steel in the exterior and light stanchions, the thought clearly in mind was that this ballpark is meant to be a very special shrine, to a very special team, in a very special baseball city.

Inside the ballpark, the same holds true. The stacked design of the upper seating decks is reminiscent of iconic ballparks of old. Tiger Stadium and Comiskey Park come to mind, as the stadium gives the definite impression that you're in a much older building. The open design of the outfield brings the Gateway Arch and the rest of downtown right in to the ballpark. And as the sun sets in the West and the lights come up under the gloaming of Midwestern dusk, the stage is set for a type of baseball magic unmatched anywhere else in MLB.

Sure, there are things that have yet to materialize or that we might have done a bit differently were it up to us. Ballpark Village—the shopping, restaurant, entertainment, and parking area overdue to open across the street from the park—remained to be built as late as 2012 due to the downturn in the economy. But make no mistake, this ballpark experience remains one of the best in the bigs. And it doesn't hurt that the city is fanatical about its team, which competes year in and year out for the NL Central Division title.

As was the case with nineteen of the thirty MLB parks currently in use, Populous played a hand in Busch Stadium's design. In fact, of the 20 ballparks built since the ballpark boom that began with Oriole Park at Camden Yards in 1992, just five MLB ballparks have been built without help from Populous: Rangers Ballpark at Arlington (1994), Turner Field (1997), Chase Field (1998), Safeco Field (1999), and Miller Park (2001). Populous' dominance over the design of the ballparks of baseball cannot be overstated. They've also contributed to many more restoration projects at the Major League level, as well as scores of Minor League and Spring Training parks. They are the big dog in the stadium design world, regardless of sport.

The cost of the "New Busch Stadium" project totaled nearly $365 million, about $20 million over the projected budget. The majority of the financing for the overall project, which was originally to include Ballpark Village, was garnered through a long-term loan from St. Louis County, bank loans and private bonds. Team ownership kicked in an undisclosed amount, with naming rights going to the Anheuser Busch Company once again.

New Busch Stadium was actually built partially on the footprint of old Busch Memorial, presenting an interesting challenge: how to play the 2005 season at Busch Memorial, then complete New Busch Stadium in time for the beginning of the 2006 season. The builders took this considerable task head on, and built New Busch right up against the right-field exterior wall of Busch Memorial. They had from the day of the last game at Busch Memorial, which happened to be a playoff loss to the Astros on October 19, 2005, until Opening Day, April 10, 2006, to complete the new yard (roughly from foul pole to foul pole) and finish demolishing Old Busch.

Despite the challenge, not even the construction workers would root against the Cards in the playoffs to buy themselves more time on the job before the winter weather set in. Up to 500 construction workers put in ten-hour days, six days a week to get the bulk of the work completed. In the final weeks about 900 workers were employed around the clock to meet the aggressive deadline. By Opening Day, enough work had been completed so that baseball could be played, but there was still much left to be done, so crews continued to work, completing construction on the seating areas in late May. Finishing touches continued to be put into New Busch throughout the 2006 season. It may not have been the most graceful opening of a new ballpark, but it was a staggering feat of architectural and construction prowess nonetheless. The

resulting ballpark remains a source of enormous pride for Red Bird fans. And rightfully so.

Josh: I had some Old Busch once.

Kevin: Yeah, me too. We visited in 2003.

Josh: No, I mean a can of old Busch that stayed in the fridge too long.

Kevin: Oh. How was it?

Josh: Let's just say it stunk about as bad as Ozzie Canseco in his brief stint with the Cards.

Perhaps it was the waiting that did the trick for the Cards. Thirty-nine years spent in Busch Memorial Stadium, a multi-use cookie-cutter if ever there was one, left fans gazing back to the glory days of Sportsman's Park, later renamed Busch Stadium (I)—one of the great ballparks of the Jewel Box Era—longing for its past glories, and the sweet memories of the team's success in a ballpark that didn't look like an air-filter on steroids.

As far as cookie-cutters go, Busch Memorial, which the Cardinals moved into in 1966, was actually one of the best, thanks in large part to renovations during the 1990s. The Cardinals made serious efforts to promote an old-time ballpark feel at Busch and for that the team deserved major kudos. Aside from the biggest renovation—the switch from Astroturf to natural grass in 1996—the Cards also removed several thousand upper-level seats in 1997 to make way for a manually operated scoreboard that was flanked by flag

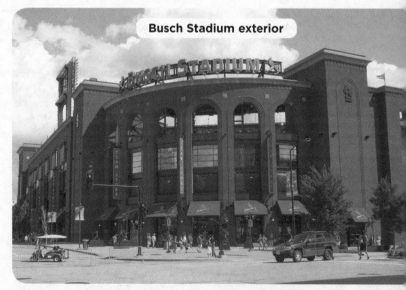

Busch Stadium exterior

The grandeur of the architecture is complemented by many fine touches.
Photo by Kevin O'Connell

courts commemorating the team's proud history. The hand-operated scoreboard in straightaway center provided the line scores of every ongoing Major League game. The flag court to the left of the scoreboard flew a pennant for each of the Cardinals' World Series championships. Meanwhile, to the right of the scoreboard, each of the Cardinals' retired numbers flew on its own pennant with the names of the players appearing on their respective flags' standards. These classy displays were done in a rich green motif that gave the super-stadium a fairly authentic old-time look.

Of course, the original inadequacies of Busch Memorial never did much to dampen the atmosphere created by the die-hard Cardinal fans who filled the seats each day. These knowledgeable fans formed a veritable sea of red regardless of the ballpark's shortcomings, bringing enthusiasm and passion to every game. When we visited Busch Memorial we were thrilled by the energy and appreciation for the game's finer points that we found in the St. Louis faithful.

Josh: Hey, that's Peyton Manning.

Kevin: Yeah, he must be in town for a pre-season game.

Redbird Fan: Is there a Rams game tonight?

Josh: Um, yeah.

Kevin: This conversation would never happen in Pittsburgh.

Ironically, before the switch to natural grass in 1996, the quick and often scalding Busch Stadium Astroturf had given the Cardinals a decided home-field advantage. In much the same way that the Red Sox perennially stock up on right-handed power hitters and the Yankees build their lineups around left-handed sluggers, the Cardinals crafted fleet-footed, smooth-fielding teams that could leg out triples and steal bases offensively and close gaps in the outfield and turn snappy double plays defensively. Players like Lou Brock, Vince Coleman, Willie McGee, and Ozzie Smith all fit the Cardinal prototype that showered the team with success.

The Cardinals boast a history as rich as any team's in the Senior Circuit. In fact, the franchise dates from 1881, when the team played in the American Association as the Browns, short for Brown Stockings. When the American Association folded in 1891, the Browns joined the National League. By 1901, a new American League team had arrived in town, transplanted from Milwaukee, and that team also called itself the Browns. So the original National League Browns took the "Cardinals" as their moniker and that's the team that still exists in St. Louis today. In the past century, the Cardinals have won eleven World Series, more than any other team except the Yankees.

redbird inset

Decorative insets of the official Cardinals used in the team's history can be found throughout Busch Stadium.
Photo by Kevin O'Connell

Perhaps no team typified the Cardinals' approach so well as the 1982 edition, which won the National League pennant despite hitting just 67 home runs during the entire season. To put that in perspective: The Brewers, who eventually lost to the Cardinals in the 1982 World Series, clubbed 216 home runs that year. St. Louis's equalizer was its speed, as the Cards swiped a league-best two hundred bases, while also leading the circuit in triples with fifty-two, and in fielding average with a .981 percentage. The same formula proved successful again in 1985 when the Cardinals hit only eighty-seven homers, but led all of baseball in steals (314), triples (59), and fielding average (.983) en route to another National League title. And it worked yet again in 1987 when the Cards finished last in homers (94) but first in steals (248) and fielding average (.982) on the way to capturing their third NL pennant in six years.

In Busch Memorial's early days the field featured a natural grass playing surface. But artificial turf was installed in

1970, except for the places where the dirt normally appears on a traditional infield, creating a diamond similar to the one that exists today in Tampa Bay. In 1977, the team switched to an all-plastic infield, however, leaving only dirt sliding pits around the bases. The Busch Stadium turf was famous for how hot it would get beneath an August sun, often reaching upward of 140 degrees Fahrenheit in the heat of summer. Finally in 1996, with the city's football team having moved to a domed stadium, the Cardinals planted real grass at Busch once again, leaving the sportscasters who'd always enjoyed frying eggs on its surface to demonstrate the degree of heat crestfallen.

It seems hard to imagine Vince Coleman, or any mortal, stealing one-hundred-plus bases per season on a dirt track, as the young Cardinal did three years consecutively (1985–1987) on plastic. The field treated Coleman rather harshly though on October 13, 1985, as the Cardinals prepared for Game Four of the NLCS against the Dodgers. With light rain falling during pregame warm-ups, the Busch Stadium grounds crew activated the electronically operated tarp used to cover the infield. No one noticed until it was too late that Coleman was standing next to first base, practicing leading off the bag. Before the fleet-footed leadoff hitter knew what had hit him, the tarp's metal cylinder had rolled over his left knee and up his leg. Screaming in pain, he was trapped under the tarp and cylinder for nearly a minute before being rescued and carried off the field on a stretcher. He suffered a bone chip in his knee and multiple bruises, which put him out of commission for the rest of the postseason. The Royals took the all-Missouri series in seven games. Who knows, if Coleman had hit leadoff for the Cards in the World Series, he might have been the difference between winning and losing.

Busch Memorial opened on May 12, 1966. The $20 million stadium, which was to also house the city's football Cardinals, was built as part of the same urban renewal project that produced the trademark St. Louis Arch. The monument was visible from inside Busch Memorial and is even more visible from inside New Busch Stadium.

Kevin: Did you know the Beatles played at Busch Memorial?

Josh: Is that right?

Kevin: Yup. August 21, 1966. It was one of the last stops on their final tour. In fact, five of the last six places they played were baseball parks. Crosley, Busch, Shea, Dodger Stadium, and Candlestick. The only one not a ballpark of the final six was the Seattle Coliseum.

Josh: You are a fountain of useless knowledge.

Kevin: Thank you.

Josh: Were you alive back then?

Kevin: Shut up.

Busch Memorial replaced ancient Sportsman's Park, which had served as home to the Cardinals since 1920 and to the American League Browns from 1902 to 1953. This joint usage represents the longest cohabitation of two Major League teams at the same park in the history of the Grand Old Game. The ballpark was of the classic ilk, featuring two seating decks around the infield and along the foul lines, and just one level of bleachers in the outfield. St. Louis baseball fans must have been in hardball heaven during the thirty-four seasons in which Sportsman's hosted a Major League game virtually every night. Plus, there was a burlesque club catering to fans, located beneath the center-field bleachers. How good can life get? Well it got even better than that for folks who liked goats. A resident billy goat used to mow Sportsman's outfield grass before and after games.

Kevin: How did the goat get the grass even?

Josh: Dual-action molars.

third base gate

Stan Musial Plaza and statue.
Photo by Kevin O'Connell

During the 1940s, a section of free seats in the far left-field stands was available for kids. The inhabitants of this section were known as the Knot Hole Gang.

Babe Ruth hit three dingers in Game 4 of the 1926 World Series at Sportsman's to set a single-game Series record. The longest of the three broke the window of an auto dealer's shop beyond the right-field fence on Grand Avenue. Ruth duplicated the feat in Game 4 of the 1928 Series, also at Sportsman's. The Yankees won both Series.

On a regrettable note, Sportsman's was the last Major League facility to integrate its stands. Until 1944 African American patrons were restricted to the seats on the right-field pavilion. On the positive side, the St. Louis Stars won three Negro National League pennants: in 1928, 1930, and 1931.

The tenant Cardinals enjoyed considerably more success at Sportsman's than the landlord Browns, highlighted by the Cards' win against the Browns in the 1944 All-St. Louis "Streetcar Series." While 1944 represented the Browns' only trip to the October classic, the Cardinals racked up nine World Series appearances in the 1920s, '30s, and '40s. The most famous of these teams was the "Gas House Gang" edition of the mid-1930s, known for its rowdy players and zany personalities. Brother hurlers Dizzy and Daffy Dean stifled opposing teams, while shortstop Leo Durocher, first baseman Rip Collins, and left fielder Ducky Medwick slugged their way to glory.

As the Cardinals thrived, attendance waned at Browns games. But the Browns did contribute a few lasting memories to baseball lore during their final days in St. Louis. In 1945 one-armed outfielder Pete Gray debuted for the Browns at Sportsman's. Gray, who made it to the Majors when many of the regular ballplayers were away at war, batted .218 in 234 at bats in his only big league season. After losing his right arm in a childhood accident, he taught himself to catch the ball and in the same motion, tuck his glove under the stub of his right arm. He would then grab the ball as it rolled out of the glove and unleash his throw. At the plate, he batted from the left side.

In 1951 Bill Veeck purchased the Browns and hired a hypnotist to convince the team's players they could hit. And the players responded, batting a combined .264, good for second best in the league. Veeck also sent Eddie Gaedel up to pinch-hit against the Tigers that year. Wearing the uniform number 1/8, the three-foot seven-inch Gaedel walked on four pitches. Later that season, Veeck let the fans seated behind the Browns' dugout manage a game against the Kansas City Athletics. The fans would hold up "Yes" or "No" signs in response to questions posed on signs held up above the Browns' dugout like: "Bunt?" or "Steal?" or "New Pitcher?" Believe it or not, the Browns won the game.

When the Browns left for Baltimore to become the Orioles, they sold Sportsman's Park to the Cardinals. August Busch, owner of the Cards, renamed the ballpark "Busch Stadium," but only after Major League Baseball told him he couldn't call it "Budweiser Stadium." So, you see, the idea of using a ballpark's name as a marketing device isn't all that new. Busch also installed a mechanical eagle (yes, an eagle, not a cardinal) above the scoreboard in left field that would flap its wings whenever a Cardinal player hit a home run. And he drove a team of Clydesdales onto the field on a number of occasions, much to the fans' delight.

In the days since the opening of Busch Stadium III, fans have enjoyed a number of significant accomplishments, the greatest of which have been the celebration of the Cardinals' World Series championships during the 2006 and 2011 seasons. While the Cardinals' epic comeback in Game 6 of the 2011 October Classic will forever warm the hearts of Red Bird fans, the 2006 title over the Tigers was, perhaps, even more surprising and delightful. After managing just eighty-three

interior

Photo By Kevin O'Connell

wins during the regular season and slumping their way into the playoffs, the 2006 Cards became the team with the lowest win total to ever win a World Series. As for the 2011 team, it twice battled back from being two runs behind and a strike away from defeat in Game 6, before posting an eleven-inning 10-9 win. Then the Cardinals vanquished the Rangers in Game 7, winning 6-2 on the Busch Stadium lawn.

Trivia Timeout

Red Egg: The Cardinals have won the second most World Series next to the Yankees. But what is the record of these two teams in head-to-head World Series competition?

Red Hatchling: Of all the Cardinal symbols that the team has worn on its uniforms that you find adorning the ballpark, what is the distinction of the current red bird?

Free Bird: We all know that Jackie Robinson broke the color barrier in baseball during the 1947 season. But before Robinson, who was the first African-American to play in a Major League exhibition game after the "so-called" *gentlemen's agreement* (and we use this term very grudgingly) banned African-Americans? *Look for answers in the text.*

The first game ever played at New Busch, on April 10, 2006, treated fans to a bit of a reversal when the ceremonial first pitches were tossed out by current players Albert Pujols and Chris Carpenter, and thrown to retired greats Bob Gibson and Willie McGee, instead of the other way around. Also honored on that day were the living legends enshrined in bronze in front of the ballpark: Stan Musial, Lou Brock, Ozzie Smith, and Red Schoendienst. Bruce Sutter, a legend who has yet to be honored with a statue outside Busch, was also on the field that day. Mark Mulder came away with the win, as the Cards defeated another team whose park is named after a brewery, posting a 6-4 win over Milwaukee.

The 2009 All-Star game returned to a stadium named Busch for the first time since the inaugural season of Busch Memorial back in 1966. Sadly for the hometown National League fans, the 2009 affair continued the AL streak of victories, as the Junior Circuit notched a 4-3 win. President Barack Obama threw out the first pitch, donning a White Sox jacket, while Musial hoisted across another ceremonial pitch. The Rays' Carl Crawford garnered MVP accolades with his dramatic catch that robbed Brad Hawpe of a certain home run.

Other than all that, we suppose it was a pretty uneventful first few years at the new yard! Although the P.A. system has rattled and hummed with a little extra special vibe on nights when stadium acts like U2, the Dixie Chicks, the Eagles, and the Dave Mathews Band have visited.

Getting a Choice Seat

Tickets to New Busch can be difficult to come by, or not so much, depending on a number of factors. If the team is not in playoff contention after the All-Star break, tickets to games not against the archrival Chicago Cubs and other top-drawing teams are relatively easy to come by. Red Bird fans are loyal, but they expect to see a winning product on the field. When they don't, tickets to all sections start to drop. On the other hand, when the Cards are in contention, tickets are hotter than passes to a Taylor Swift show at an all-girls junior high.

Remember, walking this ballpark and trying to keep in touch with the game is a difficult endeavor. Not only are you forced behind the exterior walls, but there is no interior concourse to walk the park. It's really the worst of both worlds. Perhaps it's because Cardinals fans remain in their seats that the designers made this odd choice. We can't think of any other reason for it.

Field Level

By and large, these seats are going to treat you nicely. There is no overhang issue for any seat on the field level except for in a handful of places mentioned below. But beware and consult the Seating Tip sidebar for these sections, as it can be very confusing the way the stadium's viewing areas are numbered. All seats in each section are not created equal.

Cardinals' Club (Sections 1–8)

These are the Green Seats, as in for people with lots of "green." Holders are either wealthy, lucky, or smart. Wealth will buy a ticket. Luck will allow them a friend to pass them a ticket. And the smart ones know how to buy them cheap on StubHub. Average games go for about two or three bills. Cubs, Yankees, Red Sox go for much more. Ticket holders are treated to valet parking at the Home Plate entrance. A gourmet dinner awaits. If you sit here, at the end of every inning, an attendant will take your food and beverage order. There is a healthy waiting list to purchase these season tickets.

The Commissioner's Box

Located just to the right of the home team's first-base-line dugout, we suppose this is where Bud sits when he comes to town. We have no idea who sits here when Bud is not in town.

Kevin: His minions?

Josh: Probably. I just wonder if Bud orders a Bud at Busch Stadium, or does he have Miller flown in?

Kevin: Judging by his dour demeanor, I'm going to say that he doesn't drink.

Diamond Boxes (Lower Sections 140–145 & 155–160)

Diamonds on the soles of your shoes, as Paul Simon once sang, might be the prerequisite for nabbing these babies.

Infield Field Boxes (Sections 141–160)

If you're sitting in these sections, you're sitting pretty. These are the best seats we mere mortals can get. The ends of the sections run from the lip of where the outfield grass meets the infield dirt on the first base side (141) to the same on the third base side (160). Sections 148 through 154 constitute the sweet spot.

Dugout Boxes (Lower Sections 132–139 & 161–166)

Getting to be a bit far from the action around the plate, but great for people who prefer their sight lines close to the field, and for those eager to catch a foul, these are more than passable in our book.

third baseline view

Photo by Kevin O'Connell

SEATING TIP

Be sure to consult your seating map when choosing your section, especially for the First and Third Base Field Boxes, and the nearby Infield Boxes, Diamond Boxes, and even the Left and Right Field Boxes and Dugout Boxes, so you know which seats you're getting for your buck. No other ballpark is quite this confusing, as the people that laid out the seating sections put the same number on a variety of sections. This is especially important when buying on StubHub or the Black Market, where you might not have a friendly ticket sales person there who cares to take the time to explain the quirks of the seating numbers to you.

First and Third Base Field Boxes (Middle and Upper Sections of 135–140 & 160–165)

These sections have nice views of the action but are organized very oddly. For instance, there are three sections marked 140: a Diamond Box, a middle Field Box, and an upper Field Box, all offering a variety of viewing experiences and prices. The same is true of Section 160 on the right-field side: The lower section is Diamond, the Middle Section is Infield Field Box, and the Upper Section is Third Base Field Box—all labeled Section 160. Ay carumba! Josh skipped his high school geometry class more often than he attended. And Kevin took Advanced Woodworking instead. Couldn't they have made it a little easier?

Right and Left Field Boxes (Lower and Upper Sections 127–134 & 166–172)

These are the "tweener" seats that wrap around the foul poles. They're "tweeners" because they aren't quite outfield bleachers and they aren't quite baseline seats. As usual, we're not big fans of them. If you like distant corner views, however, they might be for you. For our money, though, we'd rather head for upper decks behind the plate. Sections 127–131 and 168–172 are glorified bleacher seats, and you'll probably like your seats much better if you simply buy bleacher tickets. You will have paid less for them. Sections 170–172 have overhang issues, and also lose a bit of the warning track, and 170 also has the left-field foul pole blocking views throughout the section, especially down rows 8 and 9. The foul pole remains a concern in Sections 168 and 169, while 167 is clear of obstruction. The Upper Sections of 163–167 feel a bit removed from the action, but aren't too bad.

Avoid seats 4 and 5 in all rows of Section 129, as the right-field pole blocks your view of the plate. The rest of 129 and Sections 130 and 131 have foul-pole obstructions, too, but you can actually see the action areas where 95 percent of the game takes place. By the time you reach Section 132, the foul-pole obstruction is essentially gone. The only loss of sightline is the extreme right-field corner. The upper seating sections that have foul-pole issues are Sections 130–133. Avoid Upper Sections of 129 for foul-pole obstructions, especially seats 12 and 13 in all rows.

Kevin: Why don't they just put aisles here like they used to?

Josh: Or a big brick warehouse like in San Diego?

The choice sections on the right-field side are in Section 134, both Upper and Lower, as these seats cost less than the next section over but get you nearly as good a view.

Party Suites and Club Level

Unless you buy seats to one of the many clubs on this level, the standard seating sections are in the Loge sections. If you are heading for the club seats, by all means take the stairs. You know, to work off all those brats you've been eating lately. If you're heading up to the Pavilion or Terrace Levels, head for the ramps where you'll have to walk ten times as far, because you will be shooed away from the stairs as we were.

For the fancy-pants among you, these are the super exclusive clubs:

Home Redbird Club (Sections 247–253)
Infield Redbird Club (Sections 241–246 & 254–257)
BOA Club (Sections 258–260)
Champions Club, Party Suites, and Legends Club

Left Field Porch (Sections LP1–LP3)

These are the only seats in the Club Level not reserved for the rich and famous of the Midwest. They are nice and close to the action in left-field home run territory. However, there is significant loss of outfield sight lines from all three sections.

First and Third Base Loge (Sections 235–240 & 261–265)

Sections 261–265 lose the left-field corner. We really think it's better to get a choice seat behind home plate on the Terrace or Pavilion levels. There are simply better seats for less money.

Right and Left Field Loge (Sections 228–234 and 267–272)

If you don't like foul pole and underhang issues, don't sit in Sections 269–271. Especially avoid seats 1–5 in all rows of Section 271. Sections 267 and 268 are preferred, though they have underhang issues, as well, and lose a bit of the left-field corner.

Big Mac Land Is 272

Donning the other arches of a famous burger joint, Big Mac Land is the section where Mark McGwire's homers once went to become EBay postings in the sky. The seats are fine, but we find the tribute of a seating section named for McGwire to be an interesting expression of the dual dance that Red Bird fans have with their former slugger and current hitting coach.

Pavilion Level

Pavilion: a fancier way of saying "third" deck. It sounds much better, doesn't it? Thank you, marketing department!

Mark McGwire's Legacy

Mark McGwire represents an interesting phenomenon for St. Louis fans, since he admitted to Bob Costas in a tearful 2010 interview that he used steroids for more than a decade. By all accounts, McGwire's a caring, thoughtful man. Heck, we even saw him throwing pitches to his sons before the game. However, he will forever suffer from the taint of the Steroid Era. When Tony La Russa brought him back to St. Louis as his hitting coach, the skipper had to sell the idea at a press conference to the no-nonsense-minded Midwesterners. Unlike others of the era, though, McGwire is no longer lying through his teeth to protect his records and ego. And that makes him somewhat endearing to a fan base that would just as soon forget about the homer-happy days of PED (performance-enhancing drugs) use. If history has shown us anything, it is that America will forgive most all sins except the sin of arrogance. Look at the other players who have admitted what they've done: A-Rod, Andy Pettitte, Manny Ramirez, David Ortiz, and Jason Giambi; PEDs are not the first thing that comes to mind when we think of these players, even though they've all admitted to using them. Now think of Barry Bonds, Roger Clemens, and Rafael Palmeiro. Steroids and human growth hormone *are* among the *very first things* you think about when it comes to these players. And they've all denied using them all along.

left centerfield view

Photo by Kevin O'Connell

Terrace Level

Level 4, anyone? Once again, we prefer walking up the ramps to the upper decks and sitting behind home plate to being lied to about how great lower-level views are from behind the right-field foul pole.

INFIELD TERRACE (SECTIONS 446–454)

Sections 453 and 454 are better than any seats on the 200 level. You are higher up, but you can see the entire field. The view of the game is better and the view of downtown is better. Sections 451 and 452 also hold up to scrutiny just fine.

FIRST BASE TERRACE (SECTIONS 435–445)

These seats are all nicely shaded and preferable to the 200-level seats below them.

RIGHT FIELD TERRACE (SECTIONS 428–434)

Section 433 begins to feel a bit far away. You lose the right-field corner from view increasingly as you head toward Section 428 in deep right. You won't have the stunning downtown view to enjoy from here either. Section 432 has a foul-pole obstruction across the outfield. Sections 431 and 430 have an infield foul-pole obstruction. Section 429 should be avoided because the foul pole blocks the view of home plate.

Bleachers (Sections 501–511 & 589–597)

This is the most honestly named seating section in the park. Whether you're in Left, Center, or Right, they're actual bleachers. You know it, you love it, you bought it. Don't expect individual seat backs, you're in the bleachers.

Sections 598–591 are above the visiting bullpen. Sections 593–597 in left center don't feel far away, but are unprotected from the sun, so avoid those if you turn lobster . . . er . . . Red-Bird red when the rays hit your skin.

Sections 501–504 are good bleacher seats in front of the area known as Homer's Landing. There's no standing at the tops of these sections, because there are paid areas that get ticket holders into the family fun plaza in centerfield. Here you can keep one eye on the kiddos playing the games, and another eye on the ballgame. Okay, you can't. You'd have to have your head on a constant swivel. But that's our story and we're sticking to it. Actually, there are attendants inside Homer's Landing to assist you in your child rearing and retrieving endeavors.

However, it's still the third deck, so get used to it. At least you'll get a nice view of the Arch from up here and the upper seats are under the rooftop. Actually, the sight lines from up here are fairly protected, given the provisions noted below.

INFIELD PAVILION (SECTIONS 341–360)

There is really nothing wrong with any of the seats in these sections. Lower than their Terrace counterparts, these seats are among the best in the ballpark for the price.

FIRST BASE PAVILION (SECTIONS 335–340)

The seats in these sections are still quite nice, but we recommend popping the extra few bucks and going for an Infield Pavilion ticket. For not that much more money, you can shift your seat from beyond third base, all the way to behind home plate. It's a worthwhile upgrade.

RIGHT AND LEFT FIELD PAVILION (SECTIONS 328–334 & 361–372)

Sections 361 and 363 lose a bit of the left-field corner, and the loss increases in Sections 365 and 367. Section 368 suffers from underhang issues from the lower deck that juts out beneath it. Section 371 is another to avoid due to foul-pole obstructions, especially seats 16, 17, and 18 in all rows. Plus there are underhang issues.

Sections 507–511 really aren't that good, as you deal with railings, aisles, and people getting up and down in the lower and nicer Sections 127 and 128. You'll be much happier in 501–504.

The Black Market

Along Stan Musial Drive (8th Street) opposite the ballpark and directly above the Metrolink Stadium Station is the perch of most all of the Red Bird ticket scalpers. And they are a boisterous flock, chirping loudly and aggressively at passing cars, shouting, "Hey! I've got your ticket right here!" Sounded a bit too much like a come-on to us, but we digress. If the Cards aren't hosting the Cubs or another top-drawing team, plan on paying a little above face value from these guys. They're kinda like Ticketmaster, in that you can whine all you want, but you can't deny them their markup.

Before/After the Game

One downside to the area is that until the Ballpark Village is built, the streets around Busch Stadium don't offer much in the way of restaurants and bars. You'll find plenty of touristy things to do in this city, though. Pregame and postgame activities might include visits to the Gateway Arch and Museum of Westward Expansion on the banks of the Mississippi River, the Riverboat rides, casinos on the Mississippi, or the nearby Anheuser-Busch Brewery. If you're interested in having a more traditional night out at the bars, take the Metro a few stops down, or walk if you're game, to the historic Laclede's Landing district, where you'll find a host of pubs, restaurants, and nightclubs, and a whole lot of fun people to enjoy them with.

Getting to Busch Stadium

Busch is easy to reach by a number of highways that all provide ample signage for the ballpark. But if you somehow get lost, just look for the Gateway Arch and drive toward it. If you're coming into town from the west, take Route 40/I-64, which passes right by the ballpark. From the south, take I-55 to I-70, which also leads right to the park. From the north, take I-70. From the east, I-70, I-64, and I-55 all merge on the way into town, leading right to the park. Busch is located at 250 Stadium Plaza, right off 8th Street.

The large parking garages that once serviced Busch Memorial are still open and operational at New Busch Stadium. There are also plenty of other garages and lots surrounding the ballpark, and none of them are too expensive. You'll pay more for a couple of dogs inside the park. Beware:

The city garage closes one hour after the last out is recorded. We almost learned this lesson the hard way. After watching the Cardinals bullpen surrender two runs in the ninth to lose 2–1 against the Astros on our first road trip, we headed to the Bowling Hall of Fame to roll a few frames (yes frames, not strings). Then we visited the Arch to snap a few pictures. By the time we returned to the garage, our car was the only one left, along with one less-than-thrilled city employee who was pacing at the front gate, trying to decide whether to wait another five minutes or to lock us in for the night. Not only had this kindly gentleman waited for us, but he also gave us directions out of town. Gotta love the friendly Midwest.

For night games and Sundays, the streets around the ballpark offer plenty of free meter spots. Just remember that street parking is prohibited between the hours of 3:00 a.m. and 6:00 a.m., so don't plan on staying out all night and getting your car the next morning. Chances are it will have been ticketed, booted, or towed.

For those staying around town, the Metrolink provides a convenient way to get to the game. Buy your ticket beforehand and head for the Stadium stop. You'll wind up right across the street from the ballpark. On our second trip we bought full-day Metro tickets but nobody bothered to check them, either coming or going. But again beware: Sneaking on the train without buying a ticket could get you a healthy fine.

Outside Attractions

The activity level outside the park before the game is very high, much higher than outside most ballparks. Folks have come from near and far to attend this blessed event, and they tend to want to maximize their experience. From walking the surrounding park snapping photos, taking the tour, and following the history built into the surrounding sidewalk, to posing for pictures among the many statues that honor the greatest of the great to don Cardinal red, to lining up outside all the gates to get in early and watch batting practice, Red Bird fans take full advantage of the experience. It just makes us wish there were a few more watering holes at which to enjoy the pregame atmosphere even more.

CARDINALS HALL OF FAME

Once upon a time, the Cardinals Hall of Fame was proudly located inside the International Bowling Hall of Fame. Both facilities closed down after the opening of New Busch, though. While the Bowling Hall reopened in Arlington, Texas, the Cardinals Hall is not scheduled to reopen until Ballpark Village gets off its feet, across the street from New Busch. When it does put its exhibits on display once again, you'll find plenty of neat things to pique your baseball interest. The Museum will honor not only Cardinal greats but members of the St. Louis Browns who made lasting contributions to the Gateway City's hardball memory bank. The Cards' most recent World Series trophies will be on display too, along with a number of the MVP trophies won by Cardinal players. Whether or not the 1962 Cardinal-Red Corvette that once belonged to Mark McGwire will still be on display, though, is anyone's guess.

THE PLAZA OF CHAMPIONS

The Plaza of Champions that once offered "smaller than life" statues of St. Louis baseball greats outside Busch Memorial now resides at the corner of Clark and 8th Streets. It includes renderings of former Cardinals Stan Musial, "Red" Schoendienst, Bob Gibson, Lou Brock, Ozzie Smith, George Sisler, Enos Slaughter, Rogers Hornsby, and Dizzy Dean. Negro League star Cool Papa Bell, who played for the St. Louis Stars, is also honored with a statue.

The statues portray the players in action—diving to make catches, sliding into bases, throwing, and swinging—making them very lifelike. The plaza is a very nice tribute, and fans before the game are constantly having their photos taken with the greats.

statues of three great redbirds

Stan Musial hitting, Ozzie Smith catching, Dizzy Dean throwing.
Photo by Kevin O'Connell

STAN MUSIAL PLAZA

A larger statue of Musial that also once stood outside Busch Memorial now stands at the Third Base entrance to the ballpark, in a Plaza named for the greatest Cardinal ever who's name doesn't rhyme with "blue rolls." A replica of a baseball bearing Musial's signature is embedded into the concrete of the plaza, while overhead the arching Eads Bridge replica looms.

The large statue of "The Man" depicts him with shoulders that seem too broad for the rest of his body, a waist smaller than a ten-year-old girl's, and a batting stance that looks like Timmy Lupus from *The Bad News Bears*. His oversized eyes seem rather ghoulish too, with long horizontal slits that resemble a cock-eyed owl. Cardinals fans don't seem to mind a bit, as they climb up onto the likeness (and we use this word loosely) to get a photo with the iconic figure. We think the likeness is awful. See what you think.

Josh: This statue still creeps me out.

Kevin: Try not to think about it too much.

Josh: Don't you think it's weird?

Kevin: Most certainly. But unlike you, it won't give me nightmares.

Josh: The only nightmare I'll get is if any guy tells me Musial was a better hitter than Ted Williams.

The quintessential Cardinal, Musial collected 3,630 hits, including 475 homers, in a twenty-two-year career spent entirely in St. Louis between 1941 and 1963. A winner of seven batting crowns, Musial finished with a .331 career average and three MVP awards. He was a National League All-Star in each of his final twenty seasons. What many folks don't know is that Musial actually began his minor league career as a pitcher before an arm injury moved him to the outfield. At the plate he used an unorthodox stance that saw him coil his body in the left-handed batter's box, as if he were looking around a corner. He would hold the bat straight up, then uncork a mighty cut.

Though he didn't have quite as much power as his American League contemporary, Ted Williams, many considered Stan the Senior Circuit's equivalent of the Splendid Splinter. Both players could hit for power and average but when they faced each other in the 1946 October Classic—which St. Louis won in seven games to capture its third and final World Series title of

Stan Musial statue

The iconic, yet grotesquely misshapen statue of Stan Musial.
Photo by Kevin O'Connell

posted a 15–15 record during the regular season for a team that won ninety-eight games.

CARDINALS WALK OF FAME

Embedded into the sidewalk around the park, the Cardinals have put their own twist on the Hollywood Star Walk of Fame. Starting at the Home Plate entrance, fans can follow the course of great moments in the history of the franchise from its beginnings in 1892, with each square highlighting an important milestone. Players, pennants, significant achievements, events, and World Series victories: everything you wanted to know about the Cardinals but were too afraid to ask, appear at your feet, memorialized in granite. Surrounding many of these, Cardinal fans purchased bricks to place their names in stone alongside their heroes'.

TAKE THE TOUR

Want to sit in the dugout where the manager sits, brooding over how to execute his next double-switch? We did, and it was worth it. Our tour guide was a delightful gentleman who proved very knowledgeable. Warning: Tours are capped at forty tickets. We arrived at the ballpark hours early and snagged the last two tickets for the last tour of the day. We almost missed it. Cards fans span the entire region, and will drive hours for a game and a tour, so if you want to be certain of getting your tickets, reserve them online ahead of time.

THE ARCH

It wouldn't be a trip to St. Louis without paying an obligatory visit to the Gateway Arch. It's silver, shiny, and enormous, and Kevin likened it to a giant croquet wicket. From the ballpark, walk in the general direction of the river and soon enough you will encounter a pleasant tree-lined path leading to the Arch. The walk is quite scenic, with classy globe lights illuminating the way. If you hear church bells tolling, look to the old cathedral, also known as the Basilica of St. Louis, a short distance from the Arch. Originally blessed in June 1770, the cathedral became a basilica in 1914.

Walk up to the Arch and give it a few raps with your knuckles. Josh did. It may look like it's made of aluminum, but it's not hollow. Next, check out the underground visitor center that contains the Museum of Westward Expansion, which celebrates the opening of the West. Here, theaters show movies about the discovery and development of the American West and about the Arch's construction.

The thing we liked best about the complex was the Arch Tram, which for just a few bucks takes visitors on the ride of

the decade—neither fared particularly well. Musial batted .222 with 0 homers and four RBIs in what would be the final World Series appearance of his career, while Williams hit .200 with 0 homers and one RBI in the only World Series appearance of his storied career.

The difference in the 1946 Series was Cardinals southpaw Harry Brecheen, who threw complete game victories in Games 2 and 6, and then came out of the bullpen to quell a Boston rally and win Game 7. Brecheen was 3–0 with a 0.45 ERA in twenty innings in the Series. That, from a pitcher who a lifetime. Okay, that may be overstating things. But the Tram does take folks on a very impressive ten-minute sojourn to the top, sixty-three stories above the ground. Josh gaped in awe at the view of the expansive west, while Kevin discussed the catenary equation with an architect from Belleville, Illinois, named Butch.

Watering Holes and Outside Eats

With the delay of the Ballpark Village project, the area surrounding the ballpark remains on the meager side when it comes to providing great dining and drinking options nearby. We trust that the Cardinals will remedy this in the same manner as they have approached everything else: slowly, methodically, and getting it pretty near perfect when they finally get around to it. Until then, we'll give you some of the joints worth hitting up, but you may have to search the greater St. Louis downtown area for an establishment more to your liking, because things are not happening outside the ballpark.

Kevin: Look, the drug company that makes Tums is right across the street.

Josh: And in a beautiful old building. It would be great if a few pubs opened up there.

Kevin: It would. But as a man who's had more than his share of stomach issues, I'm comforted that Tums has a good home.

Josh: You need Tums because you've been to more than your share of pubs.

Kevin: I never really made the connection before.

PATTY O'S
618 S. 7th St.

Still rockin' since our first ballpark tour, Patty O's remains one of the few places close to the ballpark—it's actually just under the highway overpass from the Home Plate entrance. Since New Busch is now a block closer, Patty O's has gone all in, doing a tremendous job remodeling the place to look like it's part of the park. A younger bar crowd packs the place before and after games. College kids were lining up to get choice seats in the new rooftop deck at high noon for a six o'clock start on the day we were in town. Inside, big-screen TVs show games from around the league, a full-scale airplane hangs suspended from the ceiling, and baseball memorabilia appears sporadically on the walls. We were particularly fond of the Babe Ruth "Pinch Hit Chewing Tobacco" sign located in the foyer. Patty's is definitely the best bet for younger fans looking for a happening spot near the ballpark.

J. BUCK'S BBQ
1000 Clark Ave.
jbucks.com/downtown/

Though named for both Joe and Jack Buck, J. Buck's BBQ is a bit like Joe's announcing: kinda bland. You're either a fan, or you're not. Put us in the latter category. About the best things we can say for the place is that it's only two blocks from the park, has outdoor and rooftop seating, and is air-conditioned. Also, you don't have to listen to Tim McCarver blather on and on about his playing days, if you eat there. Other than that, it's an expensive Applebee's with nicer interior decorating. If you can't find better BBQ for less cash in St. Louis, you just aren't looking. Sorry, Joe, this one is a not a winner. Speaking of bland, we did see milk-toast Peyton Manning there.

MIKE SHANNON'S STEAK AND SEAFOOD
620 Market St.
www.shannonsteak.com

This steakhouse changed its location and name, but is essentially the same upscale place owned by former Cardinals player and radio broadcaster Mike Shannon, who hit .255 with the Red Birds between 1962 and 1970. This is a family place with great steaks. Mind you, the grub will not come cheap. When we say upscale, that's secret code for expensive.

OZZIE'S RESTAURANT AND SPORTS BAR
www.ozziesrestaurantandsportsbar.com

Is everything related to Cardinals baseball on the move in St. Louis? Ozzie's was changing locations at the time of this edition's publishing. We hope it's moving closer to the ballpark, as the first location was excellent, but more than a mile walk from the ballpark.

Named after Cardinals Hall of Famer and fifteen-time All-Star Ozzie Smith, this reasonably priced restaurant and excellent sports bar has a huge menu that ranges from All-Star steaks, to Hall of Fame pastas, to Grand Slam ribs, to Shortstop of the Border Mexican food. The decor is not surprisingly composed entirely of Cardinals memorabilia, with plenty of pictures of "the Wizard" featured throughout, as well as all of his Gold Gloves.

JOHN D. MCGURK'S IRISH PUB
1200 Russell Blvd.
www.mcgurks.com/

With more than sixty beers, live Irish music seven nights a week, and a menu that includes such items as lamb stew, potato soup, and homemade chips, McGurk's offers the quintessential Irish pub experience. On hot days, take advantage of their eight-thousand-square-foot outdoor garden. Arrive early on weekends to get a seat near the band.

CHARLIE GITTO'S ON THE HILL
5226 Shaw Ave.
http://charliegittos.com/
Located in southwest St. Louis on "The Hill" where Yogi Berra and Joe Garagiola spent their childhoods in the late 1920s and early 1930s, Charlie Gitto's offers the authentic Italian dining experience—Tommy Lasorda reportedly comes to St. Louis just to eat there. The specialties range from homemade pastas and breads to fine wines and delicious Sicilian beef, pork, chicken, and seafood. Expect to pay a few dollars extra, but to go home feeling more than satisfied. And be sure to order the cannelloni for an appetizer.

AMIGHETTI'S
5141 Wilson Ave.
www.amighettis.com/
For a sandwich you'll not soon forget, visit Amighetti's in Rock Hill. They have pasta and salads, but the specialty is their sandwich. They start with freshly baked Italian bread, toss on a mélange of meats—genoa salami, ham, and roast beef—cover it with cheese, pickles, onions, and pepperoncini, and pour on a house dressing that ties all the flavors together. If you find your way up The Hill and want to eat well on the cheap, Amighetti's is your place. A cannoli for dessert tops things off just right!

As for the neighborhood known as "the Hill," it is still largely populated by descendants of Italian immigrants who began settling in St. Louis in the 1850s. The lawns are well manicured, the community is close-knit, and the many restaurants are top-notch. Even the fire hydrants in this part of town are painted with the red, green, and white of the Italian flag.

TED DREWES FROZEN CUSTARD
6726 Chippewa St.
www.teddrewes.com
Don't miss out on this local dessert if you can help it. The frozen custard is incredible and nearly as famous as the St. Louis Arch. Remember Bill Cosby shilling for pudding pops? Well, this stuff's even better than the stuff the Coz was peddling. Articles have been written in the *Wall Street Journal* and other national publications about Ted's, the city's favorite custard joint since 1929.

LACLEDE'S LANDING
One area that we can recommend is Laclede's Landing, which is a decent walk or a two-stop Metrolink ride from the park. This historic district, with cobblestone streets and warehouses, boasts a large selection of pubs, restaurants, micro-breweries, comedy clubs, and live music venues. We wished the ballpark had been built across the street. But at least you can park at the Landing, have something decent to eat and drink, and then take advantage of the shuttle service to the ballpark.

Kevin: You know the band Wilco mentions "the Landing" in its song "Heavy Metal Drummer."

Josh: Whatever. I'm hitting the Wax Museum.

WASHINGTON AVENUE—DOWNTOWN WEST
Beginning at about 8th Avenue and continuing down Washington Avenue down to 17th or so, you'll find plenty of bars and restaurants. This loft district offers higher-end clubs, pubs, and places to grub.

ANHEUSER-BUSCH BREWERY
12th Street and Lynch Street
www.budweisertours.com/toursSTL.htm
Two miles south of the ballpark, the Anheuser-Busch Brewery offers free tours Monday through Saturday from 9:00 a.m. until 4:00 p.m. and Sunday 11:30 a.m. until 4:00 p.m. Tours of the one-hundred-acre facility are free, and include visits to the Clydesdale stables, as well as to the beech-wood aging cellars, brew house, and Hospitality Room. From the ballpark, follow I-55 south to the Arsenal Street exit and then follow the signs to the Brewery.

BALLPARK VENDORS
We encountered a few vendors selling peanuts, Cracker Jack, and pretzels on 8th Street. Their prices were much more affordable than the cost of the same items inside the ballpark. This is also a good spot to pick up a scorecard and game-program for cheap bucks. The "Red Bird Review" costs just $1.00 outside the park, while inside the official program published by the team costs nearly five times as much.

Inside the Stadium
The designers of New Busch Stadium gave the interior of the ballpark a feel that is distinctively St. Louis. The seating decks are neatly stacked atop one another to protect sight lines. The steel roof is prominent, along with decorative elements practically everywhere you look. And many of the folks inside enjoy sweeping views of the Arch and downtown beyond the open outfield.

While the design elements of Busch Memorial were dedicated to the Arch, the overriding theme at New Busch is The Eads Bridge, an iconic bridge that carries people, cars and trains across the Mississippi River. You find architectural nods to the Eads Bridge primarily in the steelwork of the ballpark, but most especially in the lighting stanchions and the bridge that spans Stan Musial Plaza at the Third Base Entrance.

As we've stated before, it's really the little touches that add so much to the classic feel of the ballpark. Little baseballs top the fences and are set into decorative pieces, little bats adorn seats, and of course there are all the many cardinals that the team has used on its uniform appearing throughout the ballpark. The significance of the cardinal the team currently dons on player uniforms (which can be found throughout the ballpark) is that it is the first of all the birds that is ornithologically correct. In other words, it looks more like a real cardinal than a cartoon one.

And hey, the Cards even took our advice and painted the exposed concrete at the base of the seating decks green, which really adds to the park's classic look.

Kevin: Hey, someone out there is listening to us!

Josh: Don't bank on it.

One fairly serious miss with this ballpark: Why, in this day and age, did they not allow for open viewing of the field as you walk the concourses? Or at least allow fans to walk the park from inside concourses that circle the field. You can't do either at New Busch. This really is the biggest flaw with the ballpark, and a fairly inexcusable one in our modern times. Compared to Citizens Bank Park or New Yankee Stadium, where the concourses are open to view the game from nearly every level, the fact that you can't see the game from behind home plate brings Busch Stadium back a few decades in its design.

Ballpark Features

DUGOUT BANNERS

The top of the home dugout is painted with banners that commemorate the years in which the Cards won the World Series. Meanwhile the top of the visitors' dugout lists the years in which St. Louis won the National League pennant but lost in the World Series.

Being the second winningest franchise ever in terms of World Series titles is a strong point of pride for the Cards and their fans. And they are quick to point out that of the five times the Red Birds have faced the Yankees in the Fall Classic, the Cards have won three.

Kevin: Does that mean they're throwing their NL brethren under the bus for not doing their part?

Josh: All I know is I've heard the same stat four times since we've been in town.

WHERE'S THE WHIP?

Electronic display boards mounted above the bullpens—the Cardinals' in right field and visitors' in left—show up-to-the-minute statistics for the two pitchers currently in the game. Fantasy baseball buffs will love this, as it spares them the mental undulations of multiplying their pitchers' earned runs allowed times nine, then dividing by the number of innings pitched while the game is ongoing. On these display boards, pitchers' season-long ERAs fluctuate to reflect each out recorded or run allowed.

THE BOB GIBSON MOUND

Notice that New Busch's pitching rubber is exactly ten inches higher than the rest of the playing field. It should come as no surprise. That's the height of all regulation MLB mounds ever since it was lowered from fifteen inches after a 1968 season in which Cardinal icon Bob Gibson posted a modern-era-record 1.12 ERA in 304 innings pitched. Gibson completed twenty-eight of his thirty-four starts, including thirteen shutouts.

After Gibson and Denny McLain took home the Cy Young Awards in their respective leagues and league MVP honors to boot, MLB decided to lower the mound by 33 percent to encourage more offense. With less of a height advantage, pitchers would get less leverage, and pitch planes would be more level. In another adjustment, the top boundary of the strike zone, which had been raised in 1963 from the batter's armpits to the top of his shoulders, was lowered to its previous level.

These modifications, in tandem with the arrival of four expansion teams in 1969—the Kansas City Royals, Montreal Expos, San Diego Padres, and Seattle Pilots—tipped the scales back a bit in the hitters' favor. In 1969, the overall batting average climbed to .250 in the NL and .246 in the AL. During the height of the Steroid Era, we suggested raising the mound back up to fifteen inches to level the playing field once again, but as testing for PEDs took hold in MLB, baseball became a pitcher's game once again.

Having said all this, and as against steroid use as we are, we know there are other factors that went into MLB's home run binge during the late 1990s and early years of 2000s, the lower mound being only one of them. Ballparks are much smaller these days than they were a generation ago. Outfield fences have been moving toward the plate faster than Josh moves upon hearing the dinner bell ring. Were PEDs bad for the game? Of course. But remember, pitchers were using them as well, which one might think would even things out a bit. There have been other factors that have also contributed to the increase in the overall number of dingers players hit during the Steroid Era, including the shrinking of the strike zone. Let's face it, all of the homers were great for TV ratings and the fans filled the seats better than they ever had before.

Now, we aren't crazy idiots who want to see everything in baseball return to the way it was back before Bob Gibson decimated NL hitters. As if that era was any better than this one. Baseball is a game of eras, each with its own positives and negatives. We're just tired of seeing MLB turn its back on players, letting them take the fall for an entire era known as the Steroid Era, after MLB itself did more than any single player to disrupt the natural order of how the record books read. Were the steroid players wrong? Yes. Every single one of them. But there's blood on MLB's hands as well. That's all we're saying.

CHAMPIONSHIP BANNERS

Atop the scoreboard fly the flags honoring the World Championships won by the mighty Cardinals. At the time of this printing there were eleven: 1926, 1931, 1934, 1942, 1944, 1946, 1964, 1967, 1982, 2006, and 2011. The Dodgers and the Giants have been to the Series as many times (eighteen each), but the Cards have come away with more wins. Nipping at their heels are the A's with nine world titles, and the recently resurgent Red Sox with seven.

Josh: Seven and counting!

Kevin: Give it a rest.

Josh: I'm gonna shout it from the hilltops!

Kevin: My next book might be titled: *Confessions of a Former Friend to a Red Sox Fan.*

CARDINALS TIME

The Budweiser/Cardinal-logo clock is a nice element of the ballpark. With the beer logo and the Cardinal birds built into the design, it is equal parts both, and telling about how tied together these two brands are. This beer company has had naming rights for three consecutive stadiums! In any case, the clock is non-digital, and continues to project the old-time feel that is present throughout the rest of the ballpark.

RIGHT FIELD FOUL LINE OF OLD BUSCH MEMORIAL

Most people will miss this unless they are looking for it, but painted in white on the concrete floor of the first level, beyond the left-field foul pole where the outfield plaza

transitions into the exterior concourse, you can find the foul line from Busch Memorial. They've recreated it, but when you stand on the line and walk toward the center-field plaza, you're walking from what was once right field into right-center of the old ballpark. Look on the wall near the foul line for a rendering in bronze of the overlap of the two ballparks.

RETIRED NUMBERS

Listing the retired numbers for the Cardinals is like listing all of the XXX clubs in Amsterdam. Looking out to centerfield, above seating Sections 501–505 and to the right of the batter's eye, you'll see those so honored: number 1 for Ozzie Smith, 2 for Red Schoendienst, 6 for Stan Musial, 9 for Enos Slaughter, 14 for Ken Boyer, 17 for Dizzy Dean, 20 for Lou Brock, 24 for Whitey Herzog, 42 for Bruce Sutter and Jackie Robinson, and 45 for Bob Gibson. The number 85 is also retired for former owner August (Gussie) Busch Jr., and longtime Cardinals broadcaster Jack Buck is honored with a microphone symbol. Hall of Famer Rogers Hornsby, who played in the days before players wore numbers on their uniforms, is honored by the "SL" symbol. All these tributes can also be found along the outfield fence in the left-field corner of the ballpark.

Kevin: If once is good, twice is better, right?

Josh: Wrong. Once is sufficient.

Kevin: You're not still sore I made you eat that second plate of El Birdo nachos?

Josh: I told you I was stuffed before you got in line.

Kevin: But I paid for it, so you had to eat it.

REMEMBERING THE FALLEN

Two pitchers who passed away during past seasons are also honored by the Cardinals. In the back of the Cardinals bullpen, "DK" and "JH" hang in remembrance. The DK is for Darryl Kile, who passed away during the 2002 season due to coronary disease. The JH is for Josh Hancock, who died in a car crash early in the 2007 season.

PERSONALIZED BAT

At Busch, fans can fashion their own handmade bats on the first-level center-field concourse. While Rawlings employees look on, fans use lathes to make their hitting sticks.

Josh: I'm calling mine Wonder Boy.

Kevin: How about "Savoy Special"?

Josh: Annie Savoy?

FAMILY PAVILION

The amusement area in centerfield fills up with families whose kids have short attention spans. The area is nicely done, for what it is. It just looks like a mall out there, not a ballpark.

CENTER-FIELD BIZARRE, UM, WE MEAN BAZAAR

The mall feeling gets worse as you head out to the "Big Auto Company" Plaza. There are cars on display (we assume for purchase) as well as tractors. Meanwhile, sales agents set up in tents, peddling insurance, fan photos, cell phones, and Cardinals' game-worn apparel.

Josh: I never expected this. It is so sales-y.

Kevin: It really feels like they're out to make a buck, doesn't it?

Josh: Takes you right out of the game and puts you on the showroom floor.

FRED BIRD, THE RED BIRD

Okay, the Cardinals' mascot doesn't have quite the cachet of the Famous Chicken, but in our book he's more legit than Wally the Green Monster and Billy the Marlin. At least his species is recognizable upon examination. And he's got a following of children, men, and women who emulate him. Some St. Louis fans—young and old—wear foam Cardinal-heads that come complete with feathers that flow down to their shoulders. They're pretty hilarious and not in the least bit ridiculous.

MAKE YOUR OWN (BIZARRO) MASCOT

Inside the main team store you can stuff your own Red Bird mascot. While this may not be high on your list of things to do at the game, Josh got a kick out of making a ridiculously obese Red Bird to bring home for his son Spencer. You know, there's just something hilarious about a really fat Red Bird.

Stadium Eats

The food at New Busch Stadium was a big disappointment for us, especially after we so enjoyed the eats at Busch Memorial our first time around the bigs. The Super Smokers, Pork Chop Sandwiches, and toasted raviolis we'd enjoyed at the old park were no longer on the menu. Note to management: Bring back the toasted ravioli, at the very least. No, sadly, the food selection in the common seating areas to which we were granted access has gone down considerably in quality, while nearly everything else about the ballpark has gotten better. You know things are pretty bad when we actually considered putting the Hardee's Burger as a Trademark Food!

BROADWAY BBQ (TRADEMARK FOOD)

Luckily, Broadway BBQ is there to save the day. If you only eat one thing at Busch Stadium, make it the beef brisket. It's a deliciously rendered brisket, juicy and bounding with flavor. The turkey leg is also a solid choice, as is the pulled pork

sandwich. The sides were good as well. We liked the smokey beans and fries we could dip in all the sauces.

BACON-WRAPPED BBQ HOT DOG (DOG REVIEW)

The first hot dog we tried was mealy, the same way a mealy apple turns to mush in your mouth. The Hebrew National dogs from the carts are grilled and as good as always. But then, when we were trying to think up incredibly average things to say about the average dog, we discovered the St. Louis-style, grilled, bacon-wrapped barbeque hot dog. And we thought they only had these lovelies outside Dodger Stadium! You can get these with any combination of beans, pickles, barbecue sauce, spicy mayo, pico de gallo, and grilled onions. You don't have to put all that on there, but we think you should for a wonderful mélange of flavors competing to burst through. There, we used "mélange" twice in this chapter. That's got to be a new record for baseball writers!

BEST OF THE REST

The **foot-long brat** is about the only other worthwhile thing you're going to find on this meager menu. They're grilled up nice and the folks packing them know how to put together a nice brat in these parts. Again Josh went for the ketchup, which Kevin finds to be wrong on multiple levels. The **pulled pork potato skins** are awfully nice little slices of heart attack waiting to happen, too. But what a way to go. The pork is cooked separately and then drizzled over the crispy skins. Another treat to sample is the **Waffle Supreme,** which is a thick waffle doused in chocolate sauce, and topped with fresh strawberries, blueberries, and whipped cream. We don't care if it's dessert, it's good.

If you're interested in healthy options, you should choose a different sport to watch. Seriously, though, there are some decent options at the **Farmer's Market** stand. If it's 100 degrees Fahrenheit and you just can't bear the thought of eating anything fried, greasy, or hot, why not try some fresh fruit, yogurt, a smoothie, or even a delicious wrap sandwich. Yeah, we're not buying it either. Ben and Jerry's ice cream will do the trick twice as nicely.

SAY "NO, THANKS," AND WALK AWAY

Don't let the Mexican blankets and the red Chile pepper on the logo fool you into thinking that El Birdo's gourmet nachos are anything other than el regular 7-Eleven nachos, and rank as some of the worst ballpark food we've ever tried . . . and this is after they let us build our own. We get that these Midwesterners want to deep-fry everything then dip it in cheese. We do too, but we've had much better nachos at a truck stop. At least there you expect them to be awful.

Since the toasted ravioli isn't offered any longer, we again sampled the deep-fried beef cannelloni, a St. Louis original. Talk about going from first to worst. For some reason, the cannelloni wasn't as good as we remembered from our first trip. The casing was nice and crispy, but the beef filling was putrid. And the marinara that we so enjoyed last time came in a plastic cup with a peel-off lid, sort of like you'd serve applesauce to a three-year-old. Severely disappointing, as we were really looking forward to this ballpark treat.

Josh: Hardee's Burgers? Really?

Kevin: I thought you like Hardees.

Josh: No, that's Arby's.

STADIUM SUDS

Bud, Bud Light, and Bud Select are the dominant beers available, as you might expect at a stadium named Busch. And there is something very good about draining a cold brew that's watered down when it's dang hot outside. But strangely enough, you can't get a Busch Beer at Busch Stadium. It's odd the way the world works.

Anheuser Busch was bought by InBev to become AB InBev, which makes it a bit easier to find quality microbrews as well, if that's your thing. Schlafly Brewery products are readily available, such as their Pale Ale, Hefeweizen, and Summer Lager. Where Busch Memorial only had two locations for this local microbrew, the new Busch Stadium even advertises the brew. Also available for the avid drinker is the Back Stop Bar behind home plate, and the Casino Queen Party Porch, which feature beers by Schlafly, Fat Tire, and O'Fallon, as well as a fully stocked bar.

The Busch Stadium Experience

Cardinal fans are among the best in any sport. Sure they may not wear hilariously self-deprecating and irreverent T-shirts like Giants fans do (they save their snarky T's for tooling on Cubs fans), and they may not act like jerks like fans in Philly and Boston when their team loses, but they are fiercely loyal to their Red Birds, and we admire them for it. Because nearly everyone at the park wears some kind of Cardinal red, the red seats don't seem to change much in appearance before, during, or after the game. The seats merely appear to grow faces, as the red crowd takes its place as part of the game-day backdrop. Fans expect to win, and will begin to voice their displeasure only when the team is not doing exactly that. But they never turn hostile.

Here you have baseball tradition, a rabid fan base, and now—finally—a ballpark setting worthy of it all. From the Clydesdales that trot out for special occasions, to the knowledgeable and friendly Midwestern fans who stay until the last out is recorded, Busch Stadium offers one of the best experiences in baseball, and is a must stop on any road trip.

CLYDESDALES

In homage to the Budweiser culture that dominated Busch Memorial for years and in memory of the late Gussie Busch, they still drive a team of Clydesdales around the warning track every Opening Day and before playoff games. The "Budweiser Horses," as they are commonly known, trot to the tune of polka music.

MARY JANE THAMAN AND JACKIE NIEKAMP (SUPER-FANS)

Ms. Thaman and Ms. Niekamp are our kind of super-fans. Ms. Thaman has been coming to the ballpark since 1926, the year the Cards won their first World Series. Her daughter Jackie started joining her in 1951. Now they never miss a game together, rain or shine, winning season or losing. Every ballpark should be so lucky to have fans as true as these two wonderful ladies.

Cyber Super-Fans

Here is a selection of some of the better Red Bird bloggers and message-board junkies.

- **Red Bird Central**
  http://redbirdcentral.com/
- **Cards Diaspora**
  http://cardsdiaspora.com/
- **Viva El Birdos**
  www.vivaelbirdos.com/
- **The Pitchers Hit Eighth**
  www.pitchershiteighth.com/
- **Die Hard**
  https://diehardcardsfan.com/Home.php

THE HAT MAN (SUPER-FAN)

Hat Man Thomas Lange designs his own elaborate hats that he wears to the ballpark, each one paying tribute to a special player or moment in Cardinals history. One hat commemorates the Cards winning eleven World Series, another honors Stan Musial, and one even honors Fred Bird.

Josh: Those are some fancy lids.

Kevin: Honorable Mention for super-fan—the person in the seat behind the Hat Man.

CARDS' DIE-HARD (SUPER-FAN)

Don't be alarmed if you're sitting in Section 501 and a big-bellied fan sits down next to you without a shirt. And oh yeah, his belly, back, and entire torso will be painted white so as to better create a background on which to write hilarious messages like: "Cubs, Cursed Since 1908." His name is Kirk Pound and he is happy to pose for pictures with like-minded Red Bird rooters.

FATHER TIME (SUPER-FAN HALL OF FAME)

From 1985 to 2007, Paul Pagano showed up at Cardinals games to spread good cheer. A St. Louis icon, Paul also attended local fairs and carnivals, traveled as far away as Milwaukee for the Italian Festival, and marched in Chicago's Columbus Day Parade. At Cardinals games, fans recognized him as the older fellow decked out in the colors of the American flag, walking around with a "No. 1 Fan" sign.

Known locally as "Father Time," Pagano, a retired produce merchant, lived in St. Louis his entire life. Before games, he patrolled the plaza outside the park and offered every fan he saw a boisterous "Welcome," and hearty handshake. He played fifty tunes on his harmonica, ranging from "God Bless America" to "Take Me Out to the Ball Game." As game time approached, Paul passed through the stadium turnstiles free of charge, courtesy of the Cardinals.

SPORTSMAN'S PARK / BUSCH STADIUM I
Intersection of N. Grand Boulevard and Dodier Street

There's not much to see in the now rundown neighborhood that was once the center of the St. Louis baseball universe. Dating all the way back to 1866 and continuing until Busch Memorial opened in 1966, the ballparks that stood on these grounds reflected the times in which their fans lived. Through the years the facilities were remodeled and adapted to suit the changing needs of the times. This evolution saw the intersection of North Grand and Dodier begin with a humble grass park on its grounds, then a wooden ballpark, then a multi-decked concrete and steel Jewel Box ballpark. Remember, not just Cardinals' history is tied to this plot, but also the history of the original American League Milwaukee Brewers, who came to St. Louis to become the Brown Stockings, then flew the coup to Baltimore to become the current Orioles. A white sign on the side of a building standing at the location is all you'll find commemorating the place where St. Louis baseball once reigned supreme.

There were many great moments in the history of Sportsman's Park, but none greater perhaps than when in 1941 Satchel Paige was asked to play in an All-Star style

The Walk of Fame
6504 Delmar Blvd.

"The Loop" on Delmar Boulevard features the St. Louis Walk of Fame, which honors famous St. Louis natives and residents with stars on the sidewalk and plaques that summarize their accomplishments. Among the folks honored are poets Maya Angelou and T. S. Eliot, cabaret starlet Josephine Baker, musician Miles Davis, and poet Tennessee Williams. And, oh yeah, an assortment of baseball players and broadcasters also have stars, including Yogi Berra, Bob Gibson, Lou Brock, Cool Papa Bell, Stan Musial, Harry Caray, and Jack Buck.

game there. He agreed and did play, essentially breaking baseball's color barrier six years prior to Jackie Robinson. Of course, it was only for a single game, and it was only an exhibition. But Paige agreed to play, assuming he was granted one consideration: that any fan would be allowed to buy a ticket, regardless of the color of their skin.

While We Were in St. Louis
We Looked West and Liked What We Saw

With some time to kill in St. Louis before our next game, Josh wanted to go up to the top of the Arch, just as he'd done the first time we visited the Gateway City. Kevin wanted to do anything else but that.

"Come on," Josh said. "It'll give you something to tell your girls about when you get home."

"How about we just watch the documentary in the visitor center?" Kevin said, approaching the towering structure with a glint of skepticism in his eye.

"It's the Gateway to the West," Josh persisted. "It's time for you to look West, young man."

"I'm *from* the West," Kevin said. "Besides, now I live in Pittsburgh, which was the Gateway to the West back when St. Louis was considered the Far West."

"I'm not going to force you," Josh snapped.

"Thank you. I won't be forced," Kevin said coolly.

We continued walking until the 630-foot-tall, 630-foot-wide structure arched over the top of us.

"It's a once in a lifetime experience, though," Josh persisted.

"Yeah, and you did it *last* time we were in St. Louis," Kevin said uneasily.

"But *you* didn't," Josh said.

"Nope," said Kevin elusively.

"I know what your problem is," Josh said, walking toward the ticket seller.

"I don't have a problem," Kevin replied.

"Yes, you do," Josh insisted, still walking. "You're afraid of heights."

"I am not afraid of heights," Kevin yelled. "I just don't want to go up, that's all."

"Then why do you cross yourself whenever we drive over a high bridge?"

"I do not. I just don't like . . . tight spaces."

"You're claustrophobic?" Josh asked dubiously.

"I feel like I can't breathe . . . up high . . . sometimes," Kevin whimpered. "There. I said it."

"Cripes. And you call me uptight."

"You *are* uptight."

"Maybe. But at least I'm not afraid to go up in the Arch tram. And you're not either. Come on, man."

In the end, we both ascended in a tram that took us to the highest point in any of our baseball travels (except for the upper deck at Rogers Centre!). Kevin turned a pale hue of green about halfway to the top, but then slowly returned to his normal pasty-white tone as the amazing view overwhelmed his simmering fear. When we got down, he was all smiles (after kissing the ground, just for effect).

"What a ride!" he said. "You must have been able to see for twenty miles."

"Thirty, actually," Josh said. "And to think, you were afraid."

"I wasn't . . . afraid," said Kevin.

"You weren't afraid, huh?" said Josh.

"No. We've been in a car together for two weeks. Did you ever think I just didn't want to get into a cramped little elevator with you?"

"Okay," Josh said. "You weren't afraid. You just pined for a little time alone."

The moral of the story: Sometimes being a good road trip partner means ceding the point to your fellow traveler, like Josh did at the *very* end. But it's important that you *only* do this *after* thoroughly harassing them and insisting that they face their worst fears. Only this way will you expand each other's horizons.

KANSAS CITY ROYALS, KAUFFMAN STADIUM

KANSAS CITY, MISSOURI
250 MILES TO ST. LOUIS
408 MILES TO MINNEAPOLIS
554 MILES TO DENVER
646 MILES TO HOUSTON

A Ballpark in the American Pastoral

As game time approaches and the sun sets, Kansas City's little ballpark lights up the Heartland night. While Kauffman Stadium may not be full on most nights, the experience of witnessing a game within its bounds is sure to fill any fan with the same warm feelings our forbearers must have felt when they visited the village square to watch early practitioners of America's Game show off their talents. A visit to Kansas City not only reminds us that small-market baseball can be a delight, but hearkens us back to those pastoral times when the game first took root in the American psyche.

Built in the middle of the cookie-cutter era, Kauffman Stadium somehow escaped the conventional thinking of its time and through the years has continued to shine. From the start, Kauffman was conceived as a baseball-only facility. "The K" as it is sometimes called, was originally known as "Royals Stadium" when it debuted in 1973.

It sits southeast of downtown within the Truman Sports Complex, which it shares with the NFL Chiefs' Arrowhead Stadium. As is often the case when a sports complex is involved, an interstate runs just beyond the stadium footprint and in lieu of a neighborhood there is open space aplenty. Some might consider this a drawback, but to us it seemed to be the point. Before migrating to the city, baseball was a barnstorming game played in green pastures in small towns. And Kauffman is the nearest big league equivalent to that earliest of links in the game's evolution. From its horseshoe design to its signature fountain bubbling across the outfield, Kauffman Stadium is one of those parks that must be visited in person to be fully appreciated.

When the park opened it was symmetrical in nearly every way and sported artificial turf. For our thinking these two less-than-appetizing ingredients usually spell disaster. But Kauffman bucked the right trends at the right times and has been renovated through the years to keep up with changes in fan expectations. The first-level concourse is wide open and provides views of the action for those on the prowl for concessions. That's right, an open first-level concourse at a park that was built all the way back in the 1970s. See, we weren't kidding when we said Kauffman wasn't like the other parks of its era. The switch to real grass occurred not a moment too soon in 1995. Then, most importantly of all in its efforts to keep up with the times, Kauffman underwent a $250 million renovation between 2007 and 2009. The price tag dwarfed the stadium's original cost of $70 million. This new work was funded by an 0.375 sales tax increase that Jackson County voters approved in 2006. While we normally roll our eyes a bit when the public gets hit with a bill that's going to put extra money in a private business interest's pockets, we've come to accept that this is the way pro sports works these days. And we have to respect the Royals fans for caring enough about their team to turn out at the ballot box and at the cash register. And there's no arguing with the fact that the ballpark makeover was done right.

The centerpiece of the work was the addition of a festive outfield plaza that not only makes the first level concourse a 360-degree walking experience but leads to new home run territory seats, an expansive play area for kids, a right-field sports bar with barstools overlooking the field, and a Royals Hall of Fame. The work also added a high-def video screen where the old low-def one used to be in center, and updated the exterior façade, entrances, restrooms and concourses. As far as renovations go, this was a major one.

Kevin: The Royals were immediately rewarded for their efforts.

Josh: You mean the fans returned?

Kevin: No. The Royals still only draw twenty thousand a night, but they were awarded the 2012 All-Star Game.

On television, the water display may look like it belongs within an oversized mini-golf course. Although "The K" does in fact have a baseball-themed regulation-sized mini golf course in the outfield kids' zone, this is not the case. From the ballpark seats, the fountains look like they are in absolutely the right place atop the outfield fence. Not only are they pleasing to the eye but sitting near the running waterfalls calms the soul.

The massive LED scoreboard in dead-center is also distinct, bearing at its top an enormous crown that lets all who visit know that baseball, Midwestern style, is king. Unlike most ballpark video boards, which have tended to stretch out horizontally in recent years to tap into the wide-screen TV "phase" (as Kevin calls it), the centerpiece of Royals vision rises vertically. On the backside of the new crown, the familiar KC logo is visible to folks driving past the park on I-70.

The story of how the Royals have come to bear the hardball mantle in history-rich Kansas City began in 1968 when the Kansas City Athletics decided to move from Kansas City to Oakland. The next year, KC was awarded one of the four expansion franchises that would debut in 1969. The other newbies were the San Diego Padres and the ill-fated Seattle Pilots and Montreal Expos. By the time Charlie O. Finley decided to move his A's to the West Coast, Jackson County voters had already approved a bond issue to build the stadium that would eventually come to be known as Kauffman Stadium. So that piece of the puzzle was already in place for the fledgling Junior Circuit team to be named later in KC. The next piece was finding a committed owner, which the team did in the person of Ewing M. Kauffman who named his new club "the Royals" as a tribute to the old Kansas City Monarchs who were one of the best-known and most successful franchises of the Negro Leagues.

Josh: A competing theory of causation says Mr. Kauffman named the Royals after the American Royal livestock show, which has been held in Kansas City since 1899.

Kevin: The Monarchs' and Royals' names are too close to be a coincidence. Besides, that story is far more romantic.

Josh: Let's agree to disagree and say the Royals were named after the monarchs *and* the American Royal livestock show.

Kevin: Considering I never agree to disagree, I refuse.

Josh: So that means you agree with me?

Kevin: Horse-lover!

Josh: Are you accusing me or Mr. Kauffman? If it's the latter, I agree.

Kevin: I'm going to let you have the final word, but only because we have a lot more to cover in this chapter.

One thing we both agree on is that Mr. Kauffman made his fortune as founder of Marion Laboratories, a pharmaceutical company that brought to market products like the anti-smoking gum Nicorette, Cepacol mouthwash, and the antihistamine Seldane.

Kevin: If you've used all three of the products in the past month this means you have a smoking addiction, bad breath, and a bad case of the sniffles. . . .

Josh: . . . and maybe you should get your health situation squared away before hitting the road.

The ballpark was designed before Kauffman bought a controlling stake in the local team but completed a few

Even from the outside, Kauffman strikes a regal pose.
Courtesy of Don Schmidt/Kansas City Royals

years afterward. It took the shape of a cookie-cutter but eliminated the worst two-thirds of the standard seating bowl. If the cookie-cutters looked like concrete hockey pucks, Kauffman looked like a hockey puck slashed in half diagonally, with the vital seats behind home plate remaining, as well as the lower-level seats down the baselines. As for the customary upper-level seats down the outfield lines that offer the worst views? The stadium planners in KC simply didn't build any.

These new digs were constructed while the Royals played their first four seasons at old Municipal Stadium. The first game at Royals Stadium was on April 10, 1973. In it, the Royals crushed the Rangers 12–1. More than thirty-nine thousand fans cheered as Amos Otis recorded the first hit for the Royals. On May 15 of that year, California's Nolan Ryan struck out twelve Royals, en route to treating the KC fans to the first of his seven no-hitters. The All-Star Game also came to town during that inaugural season. It would be the last of Willie Mays's long career. Although Johnny Bench led the National League to a 7–1 victory, three of the five hits for the American League came from Otis and fellow-Royal John Mayberry.

Before the Royals' brief residency, Municipal Stadium had served as the home of the Athletics during their layover in Kansas City on their journey from Philadelphia to Oakland. Built in 1923, the stadium was originally named Muehlebach Field after George Muehlebach, the local beer baron who owned the Double-A Kansas City Blues. The single-decked ballpark was also home to the Kansas City Monarchs from 1923 until 1950.

It is difficult to overstate how important the Monarchs were to Kansas City. As charter members of the Negro National League, they won ten pennants and played in the first two Negro League World Series—both against the Hilldale Daisies. The Monarchs won the first, but dropped the second. In their history they only suffered one losing season, and that was when rosters were heavily depleted due to players serving in World War II. The Homestead Grays were the only other Negro League team to claim ten pennants, and in the only meeting of the two dynasties the Monarchs swept the Grays in the 1942 Negro Leagues World Series. Ernie Banks, Satchel Paige, Buck O'Neil, and Jackie Robinson rank among the Monarchs' most famed alums. They helped establish a tradition of championship baseball in the small Midwestern city and fueled a desire in local residents to bring Major League ball to town.

When the New York Yankees acquired the minor league Blues in 1937, Yankees owner Jacob Ruppert renamed the ballpark Ruppert Stadium. After Ruppert passed away, the ballpark officially became known as Blues Stadium. Then it was completely rebuilt and renamed Municipal Stadium in 1955 in anticipation of the A's arrival. At a cost of $2.5 million, a partially covered second deck was added to nearly double capacity to thirty thousand.

The innovative and controversial Finley bought the A's in 1960. By then KC's trouble attracting fans had begun to show. After the A's had posted the second best attendance in the American League in 1955, when 1.4 million fans turned out at Municipal Stadium, they quickly plummeted to the bottom of the league, averaging fewer than a million a year. It didn't help that during their thirteen years in town they never won more than seventy-four games and only once finished higher than seventh place, when they finished sixth in their first season. Finley tried to lure fans to the park, even if the teams he fielded left something to be desired. He introduced a mule to serve as the mascot and named it "Charlie O" after himself. It lived in the children's petting zoo behind the left-field bleachers. The zoo also contained rabbits, monkeys, sheep and pheasants. "Little Blowhard" was another Finley inspiration. The device blew air across home plate so the big-bellied umpires of the era wouldn't have to bend over to dust it off. Another Municipal Stadium trademark during the Finley days was a mechanical rabbit named Harvey that would spring out of the ground to deliver baseballs to the home plate ump.

Josh: Finley was buttering up the umps.

Kevin: The way the A's played, they needed every advantage they could get.

But Finley didn't stop at these gimmicks. He also constructed a fence that reduced Municipal Stadium's right-field home run porch to 296 feet, the same as right field at old Yankee Stadium. Dubbing the protrusion "Pennant Porch," Finley was convinced the Yankees' success arose from their short home run porch, and felt his team deserved the same advantage. Unfortunately the American League only allowed Pennant Porch to stand for two exhibition games before passing a rule that all newer parks needed to have fences at least 325 feet from home plate.

Kevin: Just another case of East Coast bias.

Josh: Either the rules are the same for everyone or they're not really rules.

Kevin: That's what I've been saying about the DH rule since the '70s.

Although the A's didn't win too many games, local fans were treated to some special moments during their time in town. Early Wynn got a win late in his career, as the Indians hurler notched victory number three hundred at Municipal Stadium on July 13, 1963. With the W, Wynn became the second pitcher to finish his career with exactly 300 wins, joining Lefty Grove. The Municipal Stadium fans witnessed another rarity on September 8, 1965, when shortstop Bert Campaneris played all nine positions in a game against the Angels.

Kevin: Hey, nine positions, nine innings.

Josh: Think that was a marketing ploy?

Kevin: I guess Finley got desperate toward the end.

Later that September, fifty-nine-year-old Satchel Paige pitched three shutout innings for the Royals against the Red Sox. The appearance, which came twelve years after the former Negro Leagues star had retired from Major League Baseball, made Paige the oldest player to ever appear in an official game. It also made him eligible to receive a big league pension.

When the Royals arrived in 1969, they won their first game at Municipal in extra innings over the eventual AL West division champion Twins. The Royals finished in fourth place in the six-team AL West that year, besting the White Sox and their fellow expansion brothers, the Pilots. Left fielder Lou Piniella won Rookie of the Year honors to cap that first campaign, batting .282 with eleven HRs and sixty-eight RBIs.

Kevin: I guess it wasn't a great year for rookies.

Josh: Don't forget, it was a pitcher's game back then.

The real celebrations for the Royals would come at Kauffman Stadium, which opened in time for the 1973 season. Who can forget Cookie Rojas and Fred Patek jumping into the water fountain after clinching the 1976 AL West title? But it's difficult to think of the Royals' success without thinking of their teams of the 1980s that were led by third baseman George Brett. After losing three straight AL Championship Series to the Yankees in 1976, 1977, and 1978, the Royals faced their arch nemeses again in 1980. That season Brett pursued the mythical .400 mark with a vigor few had exhibited since 1941 when Ted Williams hit .406. Though he would finish with a batting average of .390, Brett kept fans across the country checking the box scores at the breakfast table through September. And Brett gave folks something to talk about in October. His seventh inning homer off Goose Gossage at Yankee Stadium capped a three game sweep to lift the Royals into the World Series. After dropping the first two games against the Phillies, the Royals won the next two at home, before bowing in six.

The Royals returned to the October Classic in 1985 and this time would not be denied, not even by the neighboring St. Louis Cardinals. The Royals had won 91 regular season games that year, while their in-state peers had racked up 101. But aided by a blown call by the men in blue the Royals overcame a brush with mortality in Game Six to stave off elimination. First base umpire Don Denkinger ruled Jorge Orta safe at first, when replays showed he was clearly out. Then the Royals rallied to score two runs and tie the series at three games apiece. Bret Saberhagen tossed a five-hit shutout in Game 7 to lead the Royals to an 11–0 win. Afterwards, the twenty-year-old pitcher was named Series MVP. Then, a few weeks later, he was named the AL Cy Young.

Were the Royals cursed after winning a Series they probably would have lost if fate hadn't intervened on their behalf? We can't say for sure. But it's noteworthy that as of this book's publication date they hadn't returned to baseball's post-season in three decades since the series Denkinger helped deliver.

On July 2, 1993, Royals Stadium was renamed Kauffman Stadium, in honor of the only owner in franchise history. A month later Ewing Kauffman lost his bout with cancer at age seventy-six. Kauffman had provided the club with a vision and a winning attitude and had helped guide the Royals from an expansion team to a World Series winner. His mark on Kauffman Stadium goes much deeper than

The Royals installed a massive new centerfield video board in 2011.
Courtesy of Don Schmidt/Kansas City Royals

merely his name though. He etched out a beautiful ballpark in countrified Kansas City at a time when bland cookie-cutters were being built elsewhere. Unlike all of its contemporary stadiums, Kauffman Stadium still stands, some forty years after its opening, following no trends, and showcasing small market baseball at its very best.

Trivia Timeout

Duke: How did George Brett show his appreciation for Kauffman Stadium in his final game?
Earl: How many feet long is Kauffman Stadium's right-field water display?
Monarch: Which Royal hit the longest home run in Kauffman Stadium history?
Look for the answers in the text.

Getting a Choice Seat

After attendance peaked in the late 1980s when the Royals were drawing 2.5 million fans per season, the club has struggled to sell savvy Midwestern fans on the imperative of turning out to watch a losing team. Throughout the entire first decade of the 2000s, the Royals failed to top the 1.8 million mark in a single season, which wouldn't be bad if this were forty years ago but isn't good enough to support a winning team in the twenty-first century. More than half of the seats in the park are on the first level. Practically, this means that getting a decent seat won't be a problem even if you wait until game day. But the Royals offer a considerable discount to those who buy advanced tickets rather than walk-ups. So we advise buying your tickets ahead of time to save a few dollars.

There are three different decks. The lower bowl includes 100 Level seats below an interior walkway and 200 Level seats above it. The second deck, which includes 300 Level seats and luxury suites, is called the Loge. The third deck, which houses the 400 Level seats, is called the Hy-Vee. While you might think this stands for "High View," it is actually a tip of the cap to a Midwestern retail chain. The team and store have had a partnership since 2001. Well, we suppose most other cities have sold the name to their *entire* stadium to corporate interests by now, so a mere level isn't that bad.

Josh: "Special K Stadium" has a nice ring to it.
Kevin: It would give Coco Crisp a place to play.
Josh: Or Zach Wheat.

Seating Capacity: 38,177
Ticket Office: http://kansascity.royals.mlb.com/ticketing/index.jsp?c_id=kc
Seating Chart: http://kansascity.royals.mlb.com/kc/ticketing/season.jsp#seatingpricing

---

Kevin: Yeah, especially if Sean Berry and Darryl Strawberry could join him.

Rather than numbering the sections so that Sections 100, 200 and 300 appear directly behind the plate, as some teams do, the Royals start the lower three levels with the lowest numbered section in deep left field. Then each level wraps around the infield before heading out to the highest numbered section in deep right field.

Lower Level

CROWN SEATS (1–6), DIAMOND CLUB BOX (126–129), DIAMOND CLUB SEATS (A-F)

It seems excessive for a team like the Royals to have three different categories of luxury seating behind the plate, but we guess the small market teams have to make their money where they can. These are great seats but for a heck of a lot less money you can do pretty well sitting on either side of them.

DUGOUT BOX (SECTIONS 116–139)

Perhaps the best deal in Major League Baseball, these seats are highly affordable for road trippers. They're located below the midlevel concourse, and the views are superb. Sections 116 to 125 run behind the visitors' dugout along the third-base line. Sections 130 to 139 run behind the Royals dugout on the first-base line. These are comfortable, padded seats and we can think of very few other places where we'd rather rest our weary behinds after weeks on the road.

DUGOUT PLAZA (SECTIONS 216–225 AND 230–239)

We mentioned it above, but just to remind you, the Plaza/200 Level seats appear above the midlevel walkway. While still decent infield seats and a good deal for the money, we can't help but think that if you've got seven extra dollars you'll be happier in the Dugout Boxes.

FIELD BOX (SECTIONS 107–115 AND 140–148)

These boxes run from the corner bases down to the foul poles. They offer solid views from below the midlevel concourse. The gentle curvature of the ballpark keeps them pointed toward the action. For this reason and because we especially liked the atmosphere on the third-base side (107–115), we prefer these seats over the Dugout Plaza, which actually cost a few bucks more. Those fans who like having the chance of snagging a home run ball looming as a remote possibility should head for Sections 107–109, which are on the fair side of the pole in left, or Sections 146–148 in right. Otherwise, you'd be wise to aim for Sections 113, 114, 140 or 141, which are the cream of the crop in this tier.

FIELD PLAZA (SECTIONS 206–215 AND 240–249)

The same that is true for the Dugout Plaza is true for the Field Plaza, only the seats are that much worse because they're farther from the field. Don't get us wrong, these are still decent seats, it's just that only a few bucks more will situate you on the other side of the mid-level walkway. So why not make that small investment in a majorly enhanced view?

OUTFIELD SEATS (SECTIONS 101–106, 150–152, 201–203, AND 250–252)

During the last renovation the Royals added outfield seats to "The K." In right field, high above the field, Sections 250–253 are situated between Rivals—the stadium sports pub—and the Royals bullpen. These are nice seats from which to appreciate the fountain. In left, Sections 104–106 sit perched above the visitors' bullpen and Sections 101–103 are beside the bullpen in the left-center power alley. Behind these seats are Sections 201–203.

If you've been to Kauffman before and for the sake of trying something new would like to take in a game from an outfield vantage point, we recommend Sections 101–103. Otherwise, we say shoot for an infield seat instead.

Loge Level

LOGE BOX (SECTIONS 301–325)

The very best real estate on this narrow second deck houses the Triple Crown Suites. Unless you have a connection within the Kansas City business community or your last name is Buffett (Warren, not Jimmy), expect these luxury suites to be off-limits. But on either side of this behind-the-plate high-end district are some seats that are open for you to enjoy. Sections 301 to 311 run from just past third base to the visitor's on-deck circle, while Sections 312–325 run from the home on-deck circle out to medium depth right field. Since the seats extend farther on the right-field side, the worst seats in this range are in Sections 323 to 325. We preferred the first level seats (don't we always?) but the Loge is a nice option on a rainy night when you'd like an overhang to keep you dry.

Hy-Vee Level

HY-VEE RESERVED BOX (SECTIONS 408–432)

These seats are the best the upper deck has to offer, located along the railing. Because the Loge Level is a small one the seats aren't as high as in many other parks. Section 400 is right behind the plate and offers a nice view of the field and outfield view. The upper deck is a bit steep and with all of its concourse ramps it's not too easy to navigate for seat-hoppers or guidebook writers.

Josh: How come I always have to be the one who scopes out the upper level?

Kevin: You're like a mountain goat. You thrive at high altitudes.

Josh: Back at the hotel you said I thrived with spiders too . . . then it bit me when I tried to get it out of your shaving case.

Kevin: We've got to play to our strengths. Now get up there and finish that Hy-Vee. I've got food to sample down here.

VIEW LEVEL INFIELD (SECTIONS 409–431)

Though there are almost no underhang issues, these seats are not recommended. As intimate as Kauffman is throughout most of the park, these seats will not provide that type of desired effect, especially in the upper rows. The park takes on a decided cookie-cutter upper-level feel in the top rows. Josh was sorry he'd ventured into this part of the park as it almost started to remind him of the upper level at old Shea Stadium.

HY-VEE BOX/VIEW (SECTIONS 401–407 AND 433–439)

The only way we can recommend these seats is if budget is your only concern. Use them to get into the park on the cheap, if you must. They reminded us of sitting out on the wings of an airplane. At the extreme ends the lighting is rather dim. It feels like watching a concert in the dark, so if you seek a private place to roll a fatty or to do some serious necking with your gal, this might be the place for you. Otherwise, we can't imagine why it would be.

Before/After the Game

Being that Kauffman Stadium is the premier example of baseball in America's rustic Midwest, it is fitting that the park is surrounded primarily by pasture. Or the modern form of pasture—parking lots. Kauffman Stadium is part of the Truman Sports Complex and shares its lots with Arrowhead Stadium. But there is some grass out beyond left field too. One major downfall of this park is that there are no restaurants or bars nearby. Some would say that this is a plus since a strong tailgating culture has developed in response. Pregame parties take on the local flavor: ribs, steaks, and bratwursts.

Getting to Kauffman Stadium

Unless you like walking long distances in highway breakdown lanes—which we don't advise and which we're pretty sure is illegal—you'll be driving to "The K." There is no public transportation servicing Kauffman Stadium. But don't worry, this is probably the easiest "driving park" in the bigs. From the north or south, take Interstate 435 to Exit 63B, the Sports Complex exit. From the east or west, take Interstate 70 to Exit 9, the Blue-Ridge Cutoff/Sports Complex exit. Passersby on Interstate 70 are treated to a quick view into the ballpark. We found the parking scene well managed and affordable at $10.

Outside Attractions

THE MAIN ENTRANCE

As part of the last renovation the aesthetic appeal of the main entrance was greatly enhanced. Where once there was concrete, concrete, and . . . (wait for it) . . . more concrete, now there is an attractive brick plaza outside Gate A. Looking down, visitors find messages that local fans have contributed through the Legacy Brick charitable program. Looking up, they are met by an architecturally unique façade that lights up Royals blue at night. We found this delightful.

ARROWHEAD STADIUM

Unless you're a football traveler too, this might be the closest you ever get to the home of the Chiefs, which opened in 1972. Hey, it's worth at least snapping a photo or two, isn't it?

THE NEGRO LEAGUES BASEBALL MUSEUM
1616 East 18th St.
www.nlbm.com/

There may be no other baseball-related attraction as worthy of a visit during your road trip as the Negro Leagues Baseball Museum. It began as a labor of love in the 1990s as the great Buck O'Neil and other former Kansas City Monarchs began assembling mementos from their careers. Until permanent funding was secured, these trailblazing men paid the monthly rent for the building that since 1997 has held the Museum and the Jazz Hall of Fame. Here, visitors celebrate a league that was as ripe with talent as the Major Leagues.

The self-guided tour traces the history of the game and of American race relations. The photograph- and artifact-laden chronology begins with an exhibit devoted to baseball's earliest years, immediately following the Civil War. Then it examines the experiences of a largely unknown cast of African American pioneers that integrated baseball at the semi-pro, college, and professional levels in the 1880s and 1890s. Next, an exhibit explores the "gentlemen's agreement" that unofficially banned blacks from the Majors at the turn of the century, and to the barnstorming teams of black stars that formed as a result.

The next section of the Museum, devoted to the founding and 40-year history of the Negro Leagues, is the largest. It tells the stories of how the Negro National League was founded, of how night baseball debuted in the Negro Leagues in the 1930s, of how the Negro Leagues experienced a renaissance during the Great Depression, of how Satchel Paige became the most famous Negro League star of them all, of how black baseball spread to Mexico, and more. Next, are exhibits related to the integration of the major leagues and to the eventual dissolution of the Negro Leagues.

Visitors end their tour by walking onto a replica baseball diamond. The Field of Legends is home to life-sized statues that portray some of the best Negro Leaguers ever to play the game. The bronzes include Rube Foster, O'Neil, Paige, Josh Gibson, Buck Leonard, Pop Lloyd, Judy Johnson, Ray Dandridge, Cool Papa Bell, Oscar Charleston, Leon Day and Martin Dihigo. Among this group, O'Neil is the only player not also honored with a plaque at the National Baseball Hall of Fame at Cooperstown. Many within the baseball establishment consider this oversight a travesty, but O'Neil never shed any tears on his own behalf. He was happy to keep telling stories about the great Negro Leagues players

Negro League Museum

Photo by Kevin O'Connell

and the teams he competed against, and he turned out at the Negro Leagues Baseball Museum regularly in his later years to share his love of the game with others.

Watering Holes and Outside Eats

Unless Denny's or the sports bar in the Howard Johnson's lobby sound good to you, you'll need to get in your car and drive to one of the many great places to eat and drink in Kansas City. Prior to the game, we recommend enjoying one of the best tailgating scenes in baseball, then after the game head for a steakhouse or saloon.

CHAPPELL'S SPORTS BAR AND MUSEUM
323 Armour Rd., North Kansas City
www.chappellsrestaurant.com/chappells/
Just fifteen minutes north of Kaufman Stadium, fans find the largest collection of sports memorabilia in any bar in America. Since opening in 1986, Chappell's has steadily expanded so that it now boasts more than ten thousand items. Back in the day, owner Jim Chappell was a friend of Charlie Finley. Today, Mr. Chappell leads visitors from wall to wall, providing information on his treasures. These include the 1974 World Series trophy, which was a keepsake from Finley, who apparently had trophies to spare after his Oakland A's won their third in a row. There are baseballs autographed by Babe Ruth, Ty Cobb, Dizzy Dean and dozens more, vintage uniforms, a beautiful Leroy Nieman painting of George Brett, and Chesterfield cigarette posters of Ted Williams and Stan Musial. You should arrive early, order a beer or soda, and walk around for a while before settling at a table for dinner. Tell Jim that his friends Josh and Kevin sent you, and you'll get the extra-special treatment and maybe even a guided tour.

FUZZY'S SOUTH
1227 W. 103rd St.
This popular bar boasts a slew of TVs. Aside from watching about a dozen games at once when we visited, we also enjoyed putting on a show for the locals in the National Trivia Network game. Then when the music started up at about ten o'clock, we sat back and watched the joint turn into a meat-market for middle-aged suburbanites.

MIKE'S TAVERN
5424 Troost Ave.
www.mikestavern1964.com
By day Mike's is a fairly average local bar, but at night it turns into a hangout for the college kids from the University of Missouri at Kansas City. If you fit into this demographic, Mike's might be the place for you.

STROUD'S
1015 E. 85th
www.stroudsrestaurant.com/
If fried chicken is your thing, then Stroud's may be the best you'll find on the American road. Pan fried to golden brown, and then baked the rest of the way, we found this fowl deliciously crisp and juicy. Serving family-style, Stroud's provides heaping portions of chicken, potatoes, green beans, and cinnamon rolls to fill you up. Though not the cheapest place we visited in our travels, it was one of the best.

STEAKS IN KC
There are numerous places to get a prime cut in Kansas City. The two we sampled and can personally recommend are **The Golden Ox** (1600 Genessee) and **The Hereford House** (8661 N. Stoddard Ave.). We loved the names almost as much as the beef and although we drove out of town with spiking cholesterol levels, it was well worth it.

BARBECUE IN KC
The best "Q" we sampled on our trip was in Kansas City. Sorry, Atlanta. Sorry, St. Louis. But KC has you beat. Local landmark **Arthur Bryant's** (1727 Brooklyn St.) is a must-visit. The ribs come piping hot and with a side of bread—nearly a whole loaf—to soak up the juice, plus beans and fries. Located just four blocks from the location of old Municipal Stadium, Bryant's is also right near the Negro Leagues Museum.

With its several locations, **Gates Bar-B-Q** (1026 State Ave.; 1325 East Emanuel Cleaver Blvd.; 1221 Brooklyn St.; 3205 Main St.) is another local fave that even sells bottles of its own sauce for tailgating use later on your trip.

And finally, there's **Oklahoma Joe's** (3002 W. 47th Ave.), which dishes 'cue out of an old gas station.

BLUES AND JAZZ IN KC
The neighborhood of 18th and Vine was once among the most vibrant in the city and was a jewel of African American culture. With a ballgame going on at Municipal Stadium (22nd and Brooklyn) and all that jazz, the excitement was palpable. Jesse Fisher once said, "If you came to Kansas City on a Saturday night it was like trying to walk through Harlem when there was a parade. It was really something to see. Everybody that was everybody was at 18th and Vine."

Today, blues and jazz are still on the menu in this part of town. We recommend **The Blue Room** (1600 E. 18th) and **The Gem Theatre** (1615 E. 18th), which both are easily spotted from the Negro Leagues Museum. In addition, **The Grand Emporium** (3832 Main St.) is considered by many to be the best blues bar in America.

Inside the Stadium
Ballpark Features
THE WATERFALL SPECTACULAR

While they've been imitated at other parks, the idyllic fountains and waterfall in Kansas City have never been duplicated. But what would you expect in the City of Fountains? Designed by Ewing Kauffman himself, the fountain runs behind the right-field fence and into center for an incredible 322 feet, making it the largest publicly funded fountain in the world. A ten-foot-high waterfall flows from an upper pool down to two lower pools that feed the fountains. At night, colored lights shine on the water between innings, providing a backdrop for the game that is as tranquil as it is in daylight. Now, thanks to the renovation, fans once left to admire the waterworks from afar can walk up close to enjoy them.

A ROYALLY HIGH SCOREBOARD

Above the water spectacular beyond the center-field fence, the twelve-story scoreboard tower stands in the shape of the Royals Crest, topped with a crown. Adorned with lights that illuminate the night like crowned jewels, this scoreboard perfectly caps the design of the outfield, and makes for one of the most recognizable and beautiful backdrops in baseball. Bo Jackson's first Major League home run, hit off Seattle's Mike Moore, was the longest dinger in Kauffman Stadium history. The 475-foot shot clanked off the scoreboard on September 14, 1986.

RETIRED NUMBERS

Appearing on the face of the Royals Hall of Fame in left field are the Royals' retired numbers. From left to right these read 42, 20, 10 and 5. Jackie Robinson's universally retired No. 42 appears in blue, set off from the others behind the foul pole. In Kansas City No. 42 has an even more special significance than in most baseball cities because Robinson once played for the Kansas City Monarchs. Appearing in off-white on the fair side of the foul pole, No. 20 honors Frank White, No. 10 honors Dick Howser and No. 5 honors George Brett.

THE LEGACY SEAT

Robinson's old friend Buck O'Neil was a Kansas City icon from his playing/managing days until his death in 2006. He became a household name throughout the country, of course, thanks to his stage-stealing role in Ken Burns' wonderful PBS documentary *Baseball*. The Royals honor the old Kansas City Monarch with one red seat among a sea of blue ones in Section 127 behind the plate.

STATUES

Fans will find statues of Brett, White and Howser on the outfield plaza. Howser was the Royals manager when they won their only World Championship. His likeness kneels down on one knee. White was a defensive whiz at second base for the Royals. His statue makes a throw to turn a double play. And Brett crouches in his familiar batting stance.

The story of George Brett's career is the story of the Kansas City Royals. Few players in the modern era have

Kauffman Stadium from the fountains

The Royals' fountains compose the game's best water display.
Courtesy of Don Schmidt/Kansas City Royals

George Brett statue

Photo by Kevin O'Connell

shown more loyalty to a city or made their name more synonymous with its team. You think of Ted Williams, you think Boston. You think of Stan Musial, you think St. Louis. You think George Brett, you think KC.

In twenty-one seasons—1973–1993—Brett amassed a .305 average and led the American League in hitting three times. His 317 career home runs and 1,595 RBI are tops in Royals history, as are his 137 triples. Brett, who had just slightly above average speed, could thank the expansive Kauffman Stadium outfield and its quick turf for helping him rack up many of those three-baggers. He was an All-Star every season between 1976 and 1988, and garnered the MVP in 1980.

Brett showed his appreciation for how good Kauffman Stadium and its fans were to him by dropping to his knees and kissing home plate after his last game.

Kevin: Didn't Wade Boggs do that too?

Josh: Must be a third baseman thing.

Kevin: Yeah, they're always close to home, but not quite there.

ROYALS HALL OF FAME
http://mlb.mlb.com/kc/ballpark/hall_of_fame.jsp
Located behind Sections 104–106 in left field, the Royals Hall of Fame is a must-visit for any fan. You should plan on

spending nearly an hour in the Museum if you're a serious geek like us. This means you should enter the park right when it opens, an hour and a half before first pitch, and head out there, so you won't have to miss any of the game later. Or, you can visit the Museum on an off-day. Entering the Museum, fans encounter a tunnel like the one that runs from the Royals clubhouse to dugout, lockers set up to honor Brett, White and Howser, the 1985 World Series trophy, giant newspaper headlines from great moments in Royals history, a giant No. 5 made up of 3,154 baseballs (one for each of Brett's career hits), a display of White's Gold Glove Awards, an exhibit honoring O'Neil, a celebration of the minor league Blues and Negro Leagues Monarchs, and more.

THE OUTFIELD EXPERIENCE
Any local parent will attest that the festive play area on the left-field concourse was the best money the local voters spent during "The K's" 2009 facelift. There's more than enough here to tucker out the little guys so they'll snooze peacefully during the crucial later innings. The kids' paradise features a massive playground, a carousel, a baseball-themed mini-golf course, a miniature field with 100-foot home run fences, batting cages, video games, a stage where children's acts perform on the weekends, and more.

Stadium Eats
On the whole, the food at Kauffman Stadium rates better than at most ballparks. While you can still find grub that is bland, tasteless, and odorless, following the guide below will get you into eats that taste more like treats.

STROUD'S CHICKEN (TRADEMARK FOOD)
In left field, fans find the best fried chicken in the big leagues. With an interest in sampling as many different treats as we could, we ordered a two-piece meal to share, and then wound up going back for another order a few innings later. Then, the next day, we visited the restaurant where Stroud's has been serving fried fowl since 1933. The cinnamon buns are also delicious.

SCHWEIGERT HOT DOG (DOG REVIEW)
A tradition in the Midwest, Schweigert dogs can be found deliciously grilled inside the stadium at many stands. We thought the one we got from a cart just inside the ballpark entrance on the first level was the freshest and best.

BEST OF THE REST
There used to be a Gates BBQ stand inside Kauffman Stadium but today the **Royals All-Star Barbecue** operates in

walk-off win

The Royals celebrate a walk-off win.
Courtesy of Don Schmidt/Kansas City Royals

its stead. Don't worry, all of the meat is hickory-smoked on site and it's delicious.

In the later innings, **Sheridan's Frozen Custard** is a much-appreciated dessert. Where else can you eat frozen custard while watching a big league game? Not anywhere we can think of. And it's made fresh daily, so don't worry about any of that freezer-burn that used to put a damper on your enjoyment of those Bill Cosby endorsed pudding pops back in the 1980s. The several Hot Corner Grills serve **rib-eye** steak sandwiches that are juicy and delicious. **Sluggerrrr's Training Table** in the outfield offers a menu for kids.

SAY "NO, THANKS," AND WALK AWAY

The KC Cantina Mexican stands serve margaritas. We liked these, but recommend staying away from the culinary offerings, especially the tamales. These had Kevin doing his best Fernando Valenzuela as he looked to the heavens for relief.

STADIUM RESTAURANT

With its floor-to-ceiling windows and patio seats, Rivals Sports Bar looms over the field in right. The menu features cheesesteak sandwiches, pulled pork and banana splits. A local fan told us the fare is pretty quality stuff but we opted to spend the day roving the different seating areas and eating on the move instead of settling down. That's kind of our M.O. when we visit a park, whether it's for the first time or

the fifteenth. After you've been doing the book research thing for a few games, it gets oddly addictive. You learn to experience the old ballpark in a whole new way.

Josh: I can eat two different foods, take pictures, and talk into my micro-cassette recorder without missing a single pitch.

Kevin: You know the game's been in a rain delay for the past fifteen minutes, right?

Josh: Like I said, without missing a pitch.

The Kauffman Stadium Experience

Kauffman Stadium doesn't look like an older ballpark in Boston or Chicago, and the fans don't appear as actively involved in the game as at those parks either. However, at Kauffman, baseball is to be enjoyed the way these folks enjoy the rest of life: at a calmer, more laid-back pace. The park is mellow, and so are the fans. And while visitors from the East may consider the experience less emotionally charged than at the hardball palace back home, rest assured that the passion for baseball runs deep in these pleasant Midwesterners, even if they express it less vocally. So sit back, enjoy the fountain, and root for the boys in blue.

SLUGGERRRR

A lion with a mane that dips and rises like a golden crown, Sluggerrrr wears number 00 on his back. Among his most useful ballpark functions is shooting hot dogs into the stands with a cannon. We were slightly disturbed later, though, to observe Slugger walking into a first-level ladies' room. Slugger has a mane. That means he's a "he" lion. So what gives?

Josh: He should meet up with Raymond the next time he's in Tampa Bay.

Kevin: I don't think they take Sluggerrrr on the road.

Josh: Probably not in their budget, eh?

"BASEBALL IN KC"

Remember the tune from the early 1980s "Talkin' Baseball, Luzinski and Piniella?" Well, the song that has become popularly known as "Talkin' Baseball," was originally titled "Willie, Mickey and the Duke." It was penned by Terry Cashman as a tribute to baseball's golden era of the 1950s. The Royals have their own version with lyrics modified to highlight Kansas City's baseball past, and they play it over the P.A. system before the game. We both liked the jingle.

Cyber Super-Fans

Prior to our trip we enjoyed the musing of several Royals bloggers. In fact, we were surprised by just how many top-notch Royals pages there were to choose from. Here are our three favorites:

- **One Royal Way**
  http://oneroyalway.com/
- **Royals Review**
  www.royalsreview.com/
- **Kings of Kauffman**
  http://kingsofkauffman.com/

While We Were in Kansas City
Josh's Wildest Fantasy Almost Came True

We re-visited Kauffman Stadium for a Thursday night game in August, needing to check out all of the new outfield features, the new Hall of Fame, and the new seats by the water display. In other words, although there was a game going on, we had work to do. Nonetheless, Josh remained preoccupied all night by the darling of his fantasy team, Alex Gordon, who had finally bloomed into the player the Royals had always hoped he'd be, just after Josh had picked him up off the waiver wire earlier in the year. "I bet Gordon gets me four hits tonight," Josh said, as we chatted with Sluggerrr out by the baseball themed mini golf course at the kiddie area.

Sports in (and around) the City

The College World Series
TD Ameritrade Park, Omaha, Nebraska
Why not plan to be in Kansas City just before the last two weeks of June, so you can head to the sparkling new park that opened in 2011 to serve as college baseball's highest stage? Although it's 185 miles north, Omaha is closer to KC than any other Major League city. And attending the CWS at least once is a must for any serious fan. Sure they use aluminum bats that make that annoying "dink," and sure it may seem like Florida State, LSU, and Texas are always in it, but it's a fun trip and not too expensive.

"Impossible," Kevin said.

"He's one-for-one," Josh noted.

Later, we were standing on the concourse behind the plate, taking a dog break, when Gordon came up to bat again. "I'm telling you, four-for-four," Josh said. And wouldn't you know it, right on cue, Gordon knocked a double off Orioles starter Zach Britton.

"Hmm, you might be on to something," Kevin said. Then he started thumbing away on his smart-phone (while still juggling his hot dog and beer), before noting, "Actually, he's never had a four-hit-game before."

"Well, he's getting four tonight," Josh said confidently.

"Right, just for you," Kevin said.

We were watching the game from the Fountain Bar in left field when Gordon came up again two innings later. And sure enough, he notched another safety. That made three.

Now, Kevin was a believer. "You're right, he's doing it for *you*," he said.

"Really?" Josh replied, "You think he knows I'm in town?"

"No," Kevin laughed. "But you must be bringing him luck."

Gordon fell a bit short of Josh's perfect four-for-four prophesy, but he did wind up four-for-five, with the most hits he'd ever gotten in a game before.

"Where are we heading next?" Josh asked as we searched for the road trip mobile in the parking lot after a 9-4 Royals' win.

"Texas," Kevin said.

Josh nodded. "Well then," he said, "I guess that means Michael Young's going four-for-four tomorrow.

Young didn't fulfill the prediction perfectly, either. But he did get two hits, one of which was a long ball, in an 8-7 Rangers' win.

CINCINNATI REDS, GREAT AMERICAN BALL PARK

CINCINNATI, OHIO
250 MILES TO CLEVELAND
290 MILES TO PITTSBURGH
295 MILES TO CHICAGO
350 MILES TO ST. LOUIS

A Queen City Jewel

The Cincinnati Reds are the oldest professional baseball team, dating all the way back to 1869 when they debuted as a member of the American Association. They waited more than a century for it, but in 2003 they opened Great American Ball Park, which is as gorgeous a yard as you'll find in the bigs today. It is, in many ways, a fusion of Cincinnati ballparks past, providing the natural playing surface, charm, and the intimacy of Crosley Field at the same riverside location where Riverfront Stadium (aka Cinergy Field) once resided. The Ohio River meanders just beyond the center and right-field fences providing a rustic backdrop for baseball. Embracing a riverboat theme, two smokestacks rise prominently beyond the fence in right-center. They flash lights, blow smoke and launch fireworks at various times during the game. The batter's eye in dead-center, meanwhile, takes the form of a riverboat. The deck appears high above the field, while the hull is painted black to provide an ideal backdrop for hitting. Between home plate and third base, another distinctive ballpark feature, known as "the Gap," provides a view of the downtown skyline. It's as if they cut a thirty-five foot wide notch into the upper deck. It separates the upper deck into two sections and opens the interior of the park to the city, providing lucky folks who work in the buildings along Sycamore Street a peek in at the game from their offices and those within the park a view of the skyline.

There's plenty more that's distinctive about Great American too, starting with the fact that it is an incomparably better place to see a game than its predecessor. The first row of seats has been tucked slightly below the level of the playing surface. With innovations like this, it's easy to see that the architects designed the ballpark with the fans in mind. HOK of Kansas City (now known as Populous) put its stamp on Reds country, serving as the primary architect, while receiving local assistance from GBBN architects of Cincinnati. The designers also drew up prints for a double-decked

bleacher section in left field that evokes memories of Crosley, as well as other parks built in the classic era. The exterior of Great American is somewhat similar to that of the other big league park in Ohio. As in Cleveland, the main structure of the seating bowl is supported by huge steel girders, while the façade is made of brick and cast stone.

Most fans enter the yard through a sculpted plaza that features statues of Reds greats from the Crosley era. Inspired by the old park, Crosley Terrace recreates in miniature many of the eccentricities that made Crosley Field unique, but could not be incorporated into the new park. But this impressive entrance is just one of several nods to the Reds' rich history fans will encounter during a visit to Great American. We'll fill you in on the others as the chapter progresses.

Making the new park a reality sure wasn't easy. Financing negotiations dragged on for years and years, largely because the Reds were wary of laying out wads of cash for the project while other teams were cashing their respective cities' and states' corporate welfare checks to build parks, or sticking local taxpayers with the bill. Finally in March of 1996 Hamilton County taxpayers approved a one-half percent sales tax increase to fund separate facilities for the National Football League's Bengals and National League's Reds. The original price for both stadiums was expected to total $544 million, but the football field alone ended up exceeding that. Great American came in at $297 million. As romantic as the ballpark's name is, it was actually coined as the result of a naming-rights deal the Reds struck with Great American Insurance Group, which paid $75 million for the honors.

Great American was built on land directly adjacent to Riverfront Stadium. Though the property acquisition costs were relatively low, an enormous section of Riverfront—from the left-field foul pole to right-center field—had to be removed while the Reds were still playing there to make room for the new park's construction. For two full seasons the Reds played with a huge tarp, known as the Black

Monster, in right-center. It's ironic that in order to make way for a new yard, the destruction of this huge segment opened the old cookie-cutter to the Ohio River, and with the addition of natural turf, Riverfront finally took on the look of a ballpark itself. Cutting the stadium open was akin to the time Kevin cut the roof off his Corvair to make a convertible.

Josh: Really, you used to rock a Corvair?

Kevin: A convertible one at that.

Josh: I seem to remember Ralph Nader saying the Corvair inspired his book *Unsafe at Any Speed*?

Kevin: That seems about right.

Sad as it was, the Senior Circuit's senior member had to play in one of the worst cookie-cutter stadiums ever conceived. And the Reds played there for more than three decades. With four tiers of seating, Riverfront was as sterile a structure as any of its cloned brethren. But the architects managed to find ways to make it even worse. Not only was it built on the edge of the beautiful Ohio River with no view of the water or downtown, but it had artificial turf for nearly all of its life. Worse still, the entire structure was surrounded by parking lots and was even built on top of an enormous underground garage. That's right, cars were parked beneath the infield while each game was being played. Convenient, yes. Romantic, no. Perhaps all of these black marks combined to prompt Cubs pitcher Jon Lieber to state after pitching the 2002 season opener at the concrete behemoth, "Cincinnati is a great town. But that stadium . . . it's just like a

big ashtray." And we must agree. In all of our travels, we have yet to encounter a multipurpose stadium that works—not in Montreal, South Florida, Philadelphia, Pittsburgh, Minneapolis, San Diego, Toronto, or any of the other places that embraced or still embrace the cost-effective approach to hosting multiple sports in a single venue. Baseball requires a diamond and football requires a long grid. And baseball always loses when architects try to accommodate both. It's that plain and simple. Yet, for some reason, it took MLB years of foibles to learn this lesson. If only the baseball owners and city planners had spent a few more games in the cheap seats through the years, maybe they would have gotten smart sooner.

In any case, there was mass applause in the Queen City when the Reds finally imploded Riverfront on December 29, 2002. It took 1,275 pounds of dynamite and nitroglycerine, detonated in successive blasts in a counterclockwise motion, before the structure came crashing down with a final angry groan. The dust cloud from the exploding "ashtray" plumed high into the sky, and winds carried the smoke along the banks of the Ohio for miles.

Despite its many unbecoming characteristics, Riverfront was often packed during its thirty-two seasons, and was the site of the most exciting era of Reds history—the glory days of the "Big Red Machine." It saw its share of unforgettable events too, like the day of its opening in June of 1970. No lesser a baseball light than the great Hank Aaron knocked the first homer in stadium history in an 8–2 Braves win. That inaugural season would also witness the unforgettable moment when Pete Rose barreled over AL catcher Ray Fosse for the decisive run in the All-Star Game. Later that year, the stadium hosted two World Series games, as the Reds fell to Baltimore in five games. But the Big Red Machine was just getting revved up.

Many sportswriters and fans point to the 1975 October Classic—between those Reds of Rose, Tony Perez, Joe Morgan, George Foster, Johnny Bench, and Ken Griffey, and the Boston Red Sox—as the greatest World Series ever played. Bernie Carbo and Carlton Fisk lifted Josh's Red Sox to victory in Game 6, only to have the Reds rally from a 3–0 deficit in Game 7 on a two-run homer by Perez and a winning ninth inning single by Morgan to win the Series. The Big Red Machine repeated in 1976, when the Sons of Sparky (Anderson) went

home plate

Photo by Meghan Coughlin

102-60 in the regular season, and then won all seven of their post-season games, culminating with a sweep of the Yankees in the World Series. Those 1976 Reds led the Majors in an incredible ten major statistical categories, including batting average, stolen bases, doubles, triples, home runs, runs, slugging percentage, fewest errors, fielding percentage, and saves. Without a doubt, the 1976 team was the best Cincinnati ever produced.

Over the years, Riverfront also witnessed the shattering of two of baseball's most impressive records. On April 4, 1974, Aaron hit his 714th home run there to tie Babe Ruth's all-time mark. And then, on a kinder September 11th in 1985, Pete Rose broke the all-time hits record when he singled in the first inning off the Padres' Eric Show. It was the 4,192nd hit of Rose's stellar career, and Ty Cobb was rumored to have rolled over in his grave. Perhaps Cobb cursed Rose, because four years later "Charlie Hustle" was handed a lifetime ban from baseball for gambling.

Kevin: I guess the 'Charlie Hustle' nickname wasn't for Rose's on-field heroics alone.

Josh: I'd keep the cracks to myself. In these parts the guy is still adored.

In 1988 Reds lefty Tom Browning pitched a perfect game against the Dodgers at Riverfront. Then, in 1990 the Reds won the World Series over the heavily favored Oakland A's behind their "Nasty Boys." No, the Reds didn't invite a boy band to sing the National Anthem; the Nasties were relievers Norm Charlton, Randy Myers, and Rob Dibble. Their combined ERA in the Series was 0.00 in 8.2 innings. It doesn't get much nastier than that.

Rose was banned from baseball for life in 1989, after admitting that he consorted with gamblers and sometimes made wagers. He denied at the time that he bet on baseball. Then, in his 2004 autobiography he admitted that he sometimes bet on the Reds during his time as manager. Still later, he tweaked his story further, stating in an ESPN Radio interview, "I bet on my team to win every night because I loved my team, I believed in my team. I did everything in my power every night to win that game."

For the record, we both think Rose's ban should be lifted. While we don't necessarily want to see him in the dugout filling out a lineup card ever again, we think some leniency is in order in this age when Tiger Woods' carousing is considered symptomatic of a disease, just as Josh Hamilton's substance abuse was. Anyone who's ever stood next to Kevin at a Craps table in Vegas will attest that gambling is every bit as addictive as any other vice. Heck, even Alex Rodriguez has been investigated by MLB for allegedly

playing in high-stakes illegal poker games at a Beverly Hills hotel with Hollywood darlings like Ben Affleck, Matt Damon, Tobey Maguire and Leonardo DiCaprio. Sure, betting on baseball games is different and a whole lot worse. But gambling is a national obsession that runs almost as deep as our passion for the Grand Old Game. Or maybe it runs a little deeper. Rose exercised terrible judgment and got caught up in a pattern of self-destructive behavior. And for that, he paid a hefty price. Now it's time to let him partake in the periodic ceremonies that honor the game's greatest living legends. And oh yeah, a plaque in Cooperstown is in order too. They should put right on it that he was banned for gambling. But they should mention too, his otherworldly 4,256 lifetime hits.

Josh: Both of the game's most notorious betting scandals involved the Reds: the Black Sox lost to the Reds in 1919, then the ultimate Red bet on games.

Kevin: Are we hitting the Riverboats after the game?

Josh: For some reason I'm not in the mood.

Unfortunately, Rose's banishment doesn't even rank as the saddest single memory in recent Reds history. In 1996 tragedy struck when home plate ump John McSherry collapsed and died of a heart attack in the first inning of the season opener against the Montreal Expos. The players and remaining umpires opted not to continue the game. But that somber moment notwithstanding, the Reds' years at Riverfront were wildly successful and mostly joyous ones.

Riverfront was built at the behest of city officials who backed a publicly funded stadium on the banks of the Ohio that would also house the football franchise they were courting. When the NFL awarded Cincinnati the Bengals in 1966, plans went ahead for a multipurpose facility, the kind that was being built in so many cities across the land. Then owner of the team, Bill DeWitt, wanted instead to build a baseball only facility in the suburbs. A man of convictions, DeWitt sold the club rather than approve the Reds' lease at the new stadium. Riverfront would draw two million fans in eight consecutive seasons during the heart of the Big Red dynasty (1973–1980). To put that in perspective, its predecessor Crosley Field drew a million fans only four times in eighty-six seasons.

But Crosley wasn't the only previous lot the Reds called "home." Previously, they played at a variety of ballparks, built and rebuilt at a few different locations. The undefeated Red Stockings of 1869 (57-0) played at Union Grounds, currently the site of Union Terminal. The Reds wouldn't lose a game until 1870, going an amazing 130 contests in a row without a loss. Though some of those games weren't exactly against elite competition, the achievement is noteworthy nonetheless.

The Red Legs remained at Union Grounds until moving to Avenue Grounds on Spring Grove Avenue in 1876, the inaugural year of the National League. But in 1884 when the Queen City franchise of the upstart Player's League snatched up the lease on Avenue Grounds, the Reds had to move to an old brickyard at the corner of Western Avenue and Findlay Street. The plot was cleared and made ready for baseball. A grandstand was erected, and the brickyard was renamed League Park. The deepest part of the outfield in left had an incline that rose four feet to the outfield wall. An underground stream caused the ballpark's signature deformity that eventually took on the nickname "the Terrace" when players began to hit the ball far enough for it to become a factor. The Terrace, as crazy and wonderful an outfield quirk as ever there was, remained until the park (by then named Crosley Field) closed in 1970. When Babe Ruth switched over to the National League at the end of his career, he fell flat on his face, confounded by his first encounter with the Terrace.

Josh: The Babe wasn't exactly in prime shape by that point.

Kevin: He was about as bloated as you were after our Midwest tour.

Josh: Ouch. What did I do to deserve that zinger?

Kevin: You ate all of my peanuts when I went for a beer.

While it was still called League Park the primary grandstands burned down on May 28, 1900. The Reds responded by moving home plate to where right field had been, thereby making use of the grandstand that hadn't burned down. In 1902, perhaps because Cincinnati is named after the Roman dictator Cincinnatus (458 B.C.) the team erected a grandstand incorporating Roman and Greek architectural elements, including columns, cornices, and arches. The new structure, dubbed "Palace of the Fans," presented a façade that was unique in the long history of America's Game. Inside, nineteen "fashion boxes" adorned the Palace and each could hold fifteen well-to-do fans. This was the genesis of the luxury box. Directly beneath these, a standing room section called "Rooter's Row" offered a place where less affluent fans could watch. Surely, your humble authors would have spent their time in Cincinnati down there, sloshing beer and yucking it up with the odorous penny-mongers if our road trip had taken place in the early 1900s.

Josh: Hey Hollywood, you readin' this?

Kevin: Yeah, great premise for a movie: *The Ultimate Baseball Road Trip* meets *Bill and Ted's Excellent Adventure*.

Josh: It's a sci-fi buddy flick. The boys take a roadie through the Dead Ball Era, liberating female fans and telling everyone they meet to put their life-savings under the mattress before the banks crash.

After the 1911 season, Reds owner Garry Hermann came to the conclusion that the Palace of the Fans was too small for the team's rapidly growing fan base, and the structure was demolished. Yet another grandstand was built on the same spot, and this incarnation of the park was called Redland Field. The Reds opened Redland Field a month after Fenway Park opened in Boston on May 18, 1912, with a 10-6 win over the Cubs. The terrace still rose up to the outfield wall, but now there were bleachers in the outfield. Very much like Fenway, the bleachers in right-center began with just a single seat, with rows added angling back toward a full-square bleacher section in right. This angled point in right-center was known as the "Sun Deck" (and later the "Moon Deck" during night games) and is a feature replicated at Great American in left-center.

The infamous World Series of 1919 is a sticking point for many baseball buffs in Queen City. Reds fans feel that the blemish of the Black Sox scandal tainted their very first World Series victory and feel the Reds would have won the best-of-nine championship regardless of the supposed "fix." Of course, what would you expect them to say? "We really should have been crushed and our World Series title is bogus"? Not likely, but the black mark on the Sox also had a flip side: a tainted title for the Cincinnati nine through no fault of their own.

In 1934 Powel Crosley bought the Reds and renamed the ballpark after himself. In order to attract more fans, the first night game in Major League Baseball history was played at Crosley Field on May 24, 1935. More than twenty thousand rooters gathered to watch baseball beneath a glowing, incandescent canopy provided by 632 bulbs. While day games had been averaging just over forty-five hundred fans, the new night games averaged more than eighteen thousand for the remainder of the season. The experiment had worked.

On January 26, 1937, a local creek overflowed its banks and handed Cincinnati the worst flood in its history. Twenty-one feet of water stood across the Crosley infield when the creek finally crested. But two Reds pitchers, Lee Grissom and Gene Schott, used the opportunity to stage perhaps the most memorable stunt in Reds history when they paddled a rowboat along Western Avenue and over the waterfall pouring over the outfield wall.

Over the years several Negro League franchises made attempts in Cincinnati, none with more than a few seasons of success. From 1934 to 1937 Cincinnati was home to the Tigers, who enjoyed moderate success as an independent team. The Tigers' most famous player was Ted "Double Duty" Radcliffe, who got his name because he would pitch the first game of a doubleheader, then serve as catcher in the second. In 1942 the Cincinnati Buckeyes departed after only one season for Cleveland. The Cincinnati Clowns played in 1943, then the Cincinnati-Indianapolis Clowns (no relation) played in the Negro American League from 1944 to 1945, calling both towns home. Indianapolis became the Clowns' sole home in 1946.

Crosley Field would continue to be expanded and renovated through the years. Double-decked outfield bleachers were constructed in anticipation of a 1938 World Series appearance that did not materialize. But this feature of the park was so beloved that it has also been included in the left-field bleachers of Great American. In 1957 a new fifty-eight-foot-tall scoreboard, topped with the iconic Longines Clock, replaced the existing board at Crosley and became the ballpark's signature feature.

Trivia Timeout

Big: Which Red ranks second to Pete Rose in the team record book in career hits?
Red: Which Reds hurler is the only Major Leaguer to toss back-to-back no-hitters?
Machine: Which Reds catcher was known as "The Schnozz" due to his prominent nose?
Look for the answers in the text.

After moving into Great American, the Reds struggled through seven straight losing seasons. That is not the type of start teams imagine when opening new digs. And as a result of all that floundering, attendance suffered. By 2009, the Reds were barely drawing twenty thousand fans per game. But the team rebounded to finish first in the NL Central in 2010. That exciting Reds edition—led by National League MVP Joey Votto, Jay Bruce and Drew Stubbs—won 91 regular season games before suffering a first-round play-off sweep at the hands of the Phillies. The squad did manage to breathe some fresh life into the fan base though, as the crowds at Great American swelled as the summer wore on. The Reds have as rich a history as any team in the National

League, and as scenic a ballpark. Great American is a jewel that those in Queen City ought to wear (and fill) proudly in the years ahead.

Getting a Choice Seat

Even in the years immediately after it opened, sellouts were a rarity at Great American. And they remain so. Various reasons have been cited, but the bottom line is it's not too difficult to get a good seat at Great American. Upon our most recent visit, we waited to get tickets until two days before the date, in July—on Aroldis Chapman action figure night, no less—and had no problem scoring Field Box seats.

Diamond (Sections 1–5), Scout Box (Sections 22–25), Scout (Sections 122–126), Club Home (Sections 220–228), and Club Box (Sections 301–307)

We have grouped together all of the seats that are likely beyond your budget and means of procurement. Why anyone would shell out between $100 and $250 to sit in one of these sections behind the plate is beyond us. Seats in the Infield Boxes on either side of them are almost as good and cost a fraction of the price. This is Cincinnati, not New York City. Why they incorporated so many primo seats is a mystery. Actually, we know why: to make money. We suppose all the high rollers pay so much so cheapies like us don't have to.

Infield Box/Dugout Box (Sections 113–121, 127–133)

The lower bowl has a medium grade, steep enough to see over the guy in front of you, but not too steep. The first four rows around the infield sell as Dugout Boxes while the rest of the seats are labeled Infield Boxes. Sections 120 and 121 offer a home plate view nearly as good as the one from the primo seats that cost three times as much. Besides those, the best seats in this category, for our money, are the ones in Sections 118 and 119 behind the visitors' third base side on-deck circle, and 127 and 128 behind the Reds' first-base line on-deck circle. Those seated in the first row of the Dugout Boxes in Sections 114 and 132 and of the Infield Boxes in Sections 113 and 133 enjoy the unique experience of having their feet below field level. We're not sure what this does to enhance the game. All seats in the ballpark are red, which makes for a great visual when the ballpark is not sold out. The overhang is not much of a factor on the first level, but we still recommend avoiding the back few rows of the Infield Boxes. In general, seats along the third-base line are

Seating Capacity: 42,271
Ticket Office: http://cincinnati.reds.mlb.
com/ticketing/singlegame.jsp?c_id=cin
Seating Chart: http://cincinnati.reds.mlb.
com/cin/ticketing/seating_pricing.jsp

preferable because they position spectators so as to best appreciate the river view in right.

Field Box (Sections 107–112 and 134–139)

Sections 108 to 112 run from the lip of the outfield grass to the left-field foul pole, while Section 107 is right behind the pole. Sections 134 to 139 begin a bit deeper into the outfield on the right-field side and rap around the right-field pole. Because it's behind the pole, Section 139 really ought to be avoided. The same goes for Section 107 across the field. Those in Sections 138 and 108 have foul-pole obstructions of the outfield, which isn't as bad.

One unfortunate thing about the lower bowl is that the gradually rising walls along the foul lines create minimal foul territory but block the views of the corner for those seated on the nearest side. The seats in left rise a bit more steeply than the ones across the diamond and thus the view doesn't suffer quite as much. The right-field bullpen has been well placed near the foul pole to eliminate much of the obstruction that it often causes.

Sun Deck/Moon Deck (Sections 140–146)

These right-field home run territory seats are the reincarnation of the Sun Deck at Crosley Field. The steepness of this uncovered section and the low right-field wall ensure that fans sitting here have a great view of the action. We're not sure if we've seen any outfield seats as well done as these, even at the top of the section. Section 140 offers a view of the Reds bullpen down below. However, avoid seats in Row L and higher in Section 144, as they are severely blocked by the smokestack and paddle wheel feature in center. Otherwise, a seat in these sections is a solid choice.

Terrace Outfield (Sections 101–106) and Bleachers (401–406)

The Terrace Outfield Seats are the left-field home run territory seats. Not only do they feel farther from the plate than their right-field counterparts, but they face other problems as well. The left-field wall is an electronic out-of-town scoreboard and thus the seating begins significantly higher up. The pitch of the rows is not as steep, and there is an overhang

for seats in the back three rows (N, O, and P). Section 106 also has foul-pole issues and should be avoided. The right-field Outfield Seats are much better, and cost only $3 more. The second tier in left is composed of actual bleacher benches with backs (Sections 401–406). Apparently the whiz kids who put together the seating chart in Cincy never studied marketing because labeling these seats as 400 Level seats, instead of 200 Level, makes them sound that much higher up. Though Crosley Field had double-decked bleachers, we doubt if they were as bad as these Great American replicas. Not only is even more of the outfield lost to the underhang, the glass barriers that are used to mark and protect the tunnels also block views. It's far better to pay a few extra bucks to sit in unobstructed seats high above home plate in the upper deck.

Mezzanine (Sections 408–419)

This seating section consists of the lower half of the double-decked seats running above the lower seating bowl along the left-field line. While in theory we like the idea of creating a replica of Crosley Field's double deck, some of these seats simply have poor sight lines.

The infield seats (Sections 415–419) are much preferred, though only Sections 417–419 are free from underhang obstructions. If you cannot get into these three sections, and an underhang bothers you, you might do better to sit along the right-field side of the park. The outfield-most seats (Sections 408–414) have a variety of problems. Sections 408, 409, and part of 410 are obstructed by the lower seats of the Machine Room Grille. In the rest of Section 410 through Section 414 the left-field corner is lost to the underhang of the 400 level. To make them more appealing, the Reds have designated Sections 408, 409 and 410 "All You Can Eat" seats, offering unlimited hot dogs, popcorn, peanuts and soda to those who accede to sit where they'll have a lousy view of the game.

View Level Box (Sections 420–437), View Level (Sections 511–535) and Outer View Level (Sections 509, 510, 536, 537)

From the Gap to around the plate and out to right field are three different pricing tiers, the best being the View Level Boxes in Sections 420 through 430 on the infield. These seats are a bit farther from the field than their counterparts on the left-field side (Mezzanine Infield Seats) but sight lines are perfectly unobstructed. We prefer these seats to the ones in the Mezzanine level, except those in Sections 417 through 419, which are a bit closer for the same price.

View Level Boxes 431–437 all present ticketholders with a partially blocked view of the right-field corner, but less so than their left-field counterparts. Plus there is the added bonus while sitting on the right-field side of enjoying the breeze off the Ohio River on hot summer days.

Above these are the 500 Level View seats. Sections 515 through 531 are on the infield and thus, preferable to the rest, and we recommend them, except for Sections 515–516, and 531, which suffer from a bit of an underhang. Sections 511 through 514 and 532 through 535 on the View Level offer the second worst views in ballpark. They're distant from the action, and the underhang issues increase in severity the farther out you sit.

Lastly and definitely least, are the Outer View Level seats in Sections 509, 510, 536, and 537. By the time you get to these seats deep in the outfield corners it will likely be about the 5th inning. They're cheap, but bad, so you know the drill. Buy them for cheap bucks and sit somewhere else. Seat-hopping, especially on the third level, is fairly easy.

The Black Market

Plenty of scalpers hang out along Third Street and are easy to spot by the signage they wear. They must shop at the same place because all of the signs were the same: white with red text that read, "I need tickets." Clearly they were both buying and selling. Scalped tickets for Great American aren't exactly selling like U2 tickets, so do take advantage if you're looking for a primo seat at a cheapo price. Patience is the best weapon in a ticket-buyer's bag of tricks. Hang around and wait for a while. As the first pitch approaches, scalpers know their commodity cools off drastically, and you should reap the benefits of rapidly dropping ticket prices. There are also several slightly more legitimate ticket brokers operating out of offices on Third and Fourth Streets.

Before/After the Game

In the days of parking-lot-ensconced Riverfront there was no neighborhood around the park. There wasn't room for one. In the years since the new park opened, the restaurant and bar scene in the immediate vicinity of the park hasn't improved as immensely as in other cities where new parks have sprouted because, like its cookie-cutter predecessor, Great American is bordered by a freeway, the Ohio River, parking lots, and U.S. Bank Arena. But a quick venture either into downtown or across the river into Covington, Kentucky, can increase your prospects.

SEATING TIP

The best seats for the price in our estimation are in Mezzanine Section 419, right next to "the Gap." One of the features of the notch is that along with providing views of the city behind the stadium, it allows the smaller left-field grandstand to be self-supported, and hung in closer. So take advantage of having a close view of the game, an elevated view across the river, and a view of the city through "the Gap." There's even a nice breeze up there on hot days. The seats directly across "the Gap" in Section 420 of the View Level are the same price, but the section is smaller and doesn't offer as much of that "hanging out in space" feel. But if Section 419 is sold out, 420 is a good option, as are the upper Sections 519 and 520.

Getting to Great American

From US Route 50 eastbound, take Interstate 75 northbound or southbound or Interstate 71 northbound to the Second Street exit. Turn onto Main Street or Vine Street for downtown garages. From Interstate 71 southbound or US Route 50 westbound take the Third Street exit, then take a left onto Walnut and a left again onto Second for the team garage. Or take the Third Street exit, then turn right onto Main, Broadway, or Vine for downtown garages. There is a team parking lot underneath the stands of the ballpark at the corner of Second Street and Pete Rose Way. Well, at least it's not under the infield like it used to be. The financial district of Cincinnati, like most financial districts, provides plenty of parking spaces. Garages offer game-day specials once all the suits start heading home. But here's one better: At the edge of town near the park are meters which, after three o'clock, can be loaded so you can stay all night for just a few dollars. After 5:00 p.m. street parking is free and you're in the clear until 8:00 a.m. the next morning.

The Metro, Cincinnati's bus system, is a viable way to get to the park if you're staying in town. Also referred to as SORTA, the Southwestern Ohio Regional Transportation Authority offers many different routes that eventually make their way near the park.

SORTA Info and Maps: www.sorta.com/

Outside the Park
CROSLEY TERRACE

No new park has done so well to memorialize one of its city's old yards as Great American has. Crosley Terrace sits at the corner of Second and Main, welcoming fans to the game. And boy does it shine. Landscaped grass inclines at the same grade as the terrace that once rose to the outfield wall at Crosley. Inscribed bricks scattered about the plaza reflect messages from adoring fans. A mound rises, built to the specifications of the bump at Crosley Field and four favorite Reds from the Crosley era participate in a game as if they've been frozen in time. The first of these exceptionally well done bronzes that are the work of sculptor Tom Tsuchiya is of Joe Nuxhall, who won 135 games—all but five for the Reds—in a sixteen-year career. Sixty feet, six inches away, in the right-handed batter's box, Frank Robinson is captured in mid-swing, while behind him catcher Ernie Lombardi squats, waiting to receive. Lombardi was nicknamed "The Schnozz," and "Cyrano of the Iron Mask" due to his prominent nose, and the statue does well to replicate that facial feature. Meanwhile, Ted Kluszewski waits in the on-deck circle. Somehow we think it's going to be a while before Big Klu takes his hacks.

We really appreciate the fine job the sculptor did in making these true to life. We love that the statues are interacting with one another. And we love that the four players so honored were chosen in a ballot by Reds fans who were asked to pick a pitcher, catcher and two hitters from the Crosley days to be immortalized in bronze.

As for the players themselves, only Robinson was alive and healthy enough to participate in the unveiling ceremony and to take stock of just what it meant to be bronzed outside the Reds home. When his statue was unveiled in 2003 he choked up in appreciation. "The statue probably means more to me than my number being retired," he said. "How many people—I don't care what they've done for a ball club—have a statue in their honor at the ballpark? That is very special, very warm."

We can only hope that after the Reds have played fifty seasons or so at Great American and have amassed a memory bank full of favorite players from the "Great American Era" there will be a similar tribute to Great American and its stars outside the new park's gates. We hope Joey Votto gets every bit as emotional as Mr. Robinson did. We figure that will be in the year 2065 or so, when this book will be in its fifteenth edition, written by our heirs, of course.

REDS HALL OF FAME AND MUSEUM
100 Joe Nuxhall Way
http://mlb.mlb.com/cin/hof/index.jsp

The Cincinnati Reds Hall of Fame and Museum is located at the east end of the ballpark. The hall connects with the park via a bridge and is open year-round. Adult tickets cost $10. With the recent closing of the Legends of the Game Museum at Rangers Ballpark in Arlington, the Reds Museum now ranks with the Braves Museum in Atlanta as one of the best ballpark museums in the bigs. Fans find traveling and permanent exhibits to honor great moments and players in the long history of baseball's most historic team. Carved figures honor the members of the Big Red Machine, a wall-sized panoramic photo of the first game ever played at Crosley Field serves as the backdrop of a plaque gallery, and a fifty-foot-high wall of balls incorporates one shiny white Rawlings for every one of Rose's record 4,256 hits. "The Ultimate Reds Room," meanwhile, looks a lot like the bedroom Josh had until he was twenty-five years old and his parents finally kicked him out of the house, only instead of Reds paraphernalia wallpapering every inch of free space, Josh's not-so-swingin' pad was adorned with Red Sox collectibles.

RIVER BOAT LANDING

Beyond the center-field fence is a dock where riverboats drop off passengers headed to the game. There's even a gate beyond center to let them into the park. The dock is highlighted by a sculpture that features a riverboat paddle-wheel with a dozen smokestacks that emit blasts of steam. The sculpture is a gathering place for children who play in it as if it were a fountain.

This is a nice tribute to the river-boating heritage of Cincinnati. But even if you don't get a chance to visit the landing, you'll still feel the presence of the river and the subculture that developed around and upon it through the generations. While sitting inside Great American, you'll observe riverboats continuously passing by, giving the park an atmosphere utterly its own.

Kevin: I half expect to see Huck Finn go floating past.
Josh: I'm pretty sure Huck was a *Mississippi* River rat.
Kevin: It doesn't matter which river. It's a metaphor.
Josh: Whatever.

ACTUALLY, WE DID PROMISE PETE A ROSE GARDEN

A rose garden marks the exact spot where Pete Rose's 4,192nd hit landed in Riverfront's left-center field, as Rose broke Cobb's record. A single white rose—symbolizing the ball—blooms amidst a sea of otherwise red flowers. Does this town ever love Charlie Hustle! They also renamed a road nearby "Pete Rose Way," and they held a bunch of events, at the park and across the city in 2010, to celebrate the twenty-fifth anniversary of Rose's ascension to Hit King.

Kevin: What are you doing down there?
Josh: Picking a flower for Heather.
Kevin: Dude. Not cool.
Josh: There's no sign saying you can't.
Kevin: I think it's assumed.

Watering Holes and Outside Eats

A freeway separates the ballpark from downtown Cincinnati, leaving little of that classic urban ballpark feel. Though there are places worthy of a visit, we recommend taking the short walk across the river into Kentucky. But first we'll list a few watering holes and eateries worth visiting for those determined to stay in The Buckeye State.

SKYLINE CHILI
254 East Fourth St.
www.skylinechili.com/

Skyline Chili is a minor phenomenon in Cincinnati, as this popular local chain prepares its chili in some unique "ways." Unlike the familiar Texas-style chili, the classic three-way Cincinnati-style is served over spaghetti and covered with shredded cheese. Four-way adds onions or red beans to the mix. Five-way adds red beans, onions and cheese. According to local lore, the original recipe was brought to America by a Greek immigrant named Nicholas Lambrinides.

Josh: The Greeks make great chili! This is surely their greatest achievement!

Kevin: Yes, right before inventing democracy.

IN-BETWEEN TAVERN
307 Sycamore St.

Directly across the freeway from Great American, at the corner of Third and Sycamore, fans find an outdoor patio that's the perfect setting for a pregame beverage. The In-Between is a no-frills kind of place that draws good crowds. Pictures of old Reds players adorn the walls. The food is typical pub-grub along the lines of burgers and chicken sandwiches.

HEAD FIRST SPORTS CAFÉ
218 Third St.

This sports bar is small inside but does have pool tables and dartboards. Eclectic sports memorabilia hangs on the walls: everything from baseball to the Kentucky Derby to golf to college football. Catering much more to the Bengals crowd, this is the kind of place you go to if you want to see a lingerie show with your beer. But we're not promising anything. We can verify that they offer fans free peanuts and popcorn on game days. Hey, that counts for something. And Head First has actor/director George Clooney's stamp of approval, for what it's worth. In 2011, Clooney shot scenes for his movie *The Ides of March* at the bar.

TINA'S BAR AND GRILL
350 W. Fourth St.

Tina's caters more to football and racing fans than seamheads, likely because it's closer to the Bengals' Paul Brown Stadium than to Great American. But it's a decent little joint.

GAME DAY SPORTS CAFÉ
537 East Pete Rose Way

This good sized club often features live bands after games and the local sports radio shows broadcast on-location too.

MONTGOMERY INN
Boathouse, 925 Riverside Dr.
www.montgomeryinn.com/index.php

If the barbecue pork and chicken sandwiches at Great American have you hankering for some ribs, why not head for the source? With three locations in the area, this long-standing Cincinnati institution has been Q-ing it up since the 1950s. Though it's on the pricey side, the lunch menu is reasonable, and all entrées are sure to tingle the taste buds. Upstairs, the Boathouse showcases a room full of Cincinnati sports memorabilia.

FOR THOSE WILLING TO GO THE EXTRA MILE

For a better selection of bars and restaurants, we recommend taking the short walk across the bridge into Covington Landing, Kentucky, or parking there and then crossing the bridge to get to the game. Either way, this is the hot spot in the area. It may look a tad seedy with check-cashing places, pawn shops, liquor stores, tattoo parlors, and strip clubs, but we managed just fine.

WILLIE'S SPORTS CAFE
401 Crescent Ave., Covington, KY
www.williescovington.com/

Not only do they have a top-notch Stadium Nacho plate and $12 buckets of domestic beer, but there's a Golden Tee for hackers like Josh and free Wi-Fi for hackers like Kevin.

KEYSTONE BAR AND GRILL
313 Greenup St., Covington, KY
www.keystonebar.com/

With its craft beers, small-batch bourbon, and delicious burgers, Keystone is a solid choice. There's a jukebox and outdoor patio too. Kevin recommends the Fuller's London Pride, which he described as "malty" before ordering another. Josh recommends the homemade nacho chips.

TICKETS SPORTS CAFE
100 West Sixth St., Covington, KY
www.ticketssportscafe.com/

This popular local hangout inhabits a fire station that was built in the late 1800s. It is comfortable and homey inside. After games it offers a nice laid back atmosphere, though we hear it can get pretty packed on fall Sundays when the Bengals are playing. The Shoe String Catch fry plate is a solid appetizer choice, while the Sinker (ham, pepperoni, Mozzarella) is one heck of a hoagie. We love places that name foods after baseball slang.

BEHLE STREET CAFE
50 East Rivercenter Blvd.
www.behlestreetcafe.com/

If you're looking for a more upscale meal at prices that still won't break your bank, Behle Street is an excellent option. But we recommend going after the game for Martinis and dessert. Just kidding, but if we were into that sort of refined postgame scene, this would be our pick for it.

Inside Great American Ball Park

We're both suckers for parks that offer city skyline views or views of water-bodies. For some reason, they just get our juices flowing. And Great American offers both. Beyond the outfield fence, the Ohio River drifts lazily past, with its riverboats and bridges in full view. Looming over the infield, meanwhile, the Gap showcases the city skyline to those inside the park.

Ballpark Features
ANALOG AND LOVIN' IT
Though not the original Longines clock that sat upon the scoreboard at Crosley, the rectangular clock at Great American is a good re-creation. In this digital age, there is something very fitting about having an old-time analog clock looming above a baseball park, keeping our minds set to all the history and richness of the National Pastime. Well done, Cincinnati.

GRASS, GLASS, AND HIGH CLASS?
The batter's eye at Great American is also a nice nod to Crosley Field. The lower section is comprised of sloped grass, recalling the Crosley Terrace. Above the grass rises the black hull of the

faux riverboat that serves as a private party venue in dead-center. The hull is attractive, but there's more than meets the eye. It's made of tinted glass and behind it sits a party room that can accommodate more than one hundred and fifty people, who enjoy a window-view of the game.

THE BIG RED PARTY MACHINE
To the right of the riverboat, two sixty-four-foot-high smokestacks rise into the air, accompanied by a riverboat paddlewheel, and misting machine. The power stacks go off whenever something good happens for the Reds, shooting fireworks, making noise, and spewing mist all over the place. Sounds a little bit like how Kevin "goes off" after he's had a few too many beers. While we are rarely fans of these attractions, the "Big Red Party Machine" (as we have dubbed it) definitely makes the game more fun for the kids. Plus it doubles as a misting station, cooling down folks on hot days. So, we give it our stamp of approval.

WIDE-OPEN CONCOURSES
Modern ballparks need wide concourses because, to be blunt, we Americans keep getting wider. And there are a lot more of us these days than there used to be. At Great American Ball Park most concourses are forty feet across, as compared to the concourses that measured twenty feet wide at Riverfront. In addition to their width these concourses provide excellent opportunities to keep an eye on the game

Big Red Machine mural

Photo by Kevin O'Connell

to those walking around the park. To top it all off, the upper deck has its own concourse that offers views of the field. This feature makes the upper deck feel more open and should be copied at ballparks everywhere.

IMMORTAL HUES OF RED

Just inside the main entrance two tiled murals honor the two most significant moments in Reds history. The first, titled "The First Nine," represents the 1869 Red Stockings, the first professional baseball team. The second, titled "The Great Eight," honors the 1975 Reds. The Big Red Machine, who won 108 games that year, fielded an assortment of players widely regarded the best starting eight of all time.

Kevin: The ninth guy on the team must feel "not so great."

Josh: The ninth guy was a different pitcher every night.

Kevin: Right. I knew that.

FRAMED AND NOT FORGOTTEN

Encircling the concourse's interior are photographs rendered in glass of great Reds moments, year by year. The second-level concourse features a quote band with entries from players from across the league. One of our favorites was from former Dodger Roy Campanella, who said, "You gotta be a man to play baseball for a living, but you gotta have a lot of little boy in you too."

RETIRED IN GLORY

The Reds retired numbers hang below the press box. In addition to Jackie Robinson's universally retired No. 42, fans will find No. 1, which belonged to Fred Hutchinson, the manager who led the Reds to ninety-plus wins three times during his career, which was cut short, as his life was, by cancer. Hutchinson's number was the first ever to be retired by the Reds. See the Seattle chapter for more information on "Hutch."

No. 5 was on Johnny Bench's back when he won his ten Gold Gloves, made fourteen All-Star appearances and collected two NL MVP awards. Bench is perhaps the most recognizable name of a catcher even to this day, as he led the Big Red Machine to consecutive World Series titles in 1975 and 1976. And he was a regular on Josh's second-favorite TV show of all time—*The Baseball Bunch*—to boot. Josh still hums, "We have a hunch you'll love the baseball bunch," every Saturday morning as he pours over the previous night's West Coast box scores.

No. 8 was second baseman Joe Morgan's number. Morgan, who won the NL MVP in both 1975 and 1976, collected

689 stolen bases, 1,133 RBI, and 268 homers during his twenty-two-year career.

No. 10 belonged to manager Sparky Anderson, who piloted the Big Red Machine and won three Manager of the Year awards while at the Reds helm.

No. 13 belonged to David Concepcion, who was the starting shortstop on the Big Red Machine. He ranks second to only Rose with his 8,723 at bats as a Red and 2,488 games, and he ranks third in team history with his 2,326 hits. For the record, Barry Larkin ranks second in team history in hits with his 2,340 lifetime safeties.

Reds fans recognize No. 18 Ted Kluszewski as their greatest left-handed first baseman. On defense Big Klu led the NL in fielding percentage for five straight seasons, 1951–55. Surely he would have won the Gold Glove Award those years had it existed. He hit 1,028 RBI and 279 home runs, including a whopping 49 in 1954. He finished with a batting average of .298.

No. 20 belonged to Frank Robinson, a twelve-time All-Star. Robinson hit 586 home runs in his career. He hit 38 bombs during his rookie season to easily win the ROY award. In 1961 he won the NL MVP Award hitting for a .323 average, 37 HR, and 124 RBI.

No. 24 belonged to the heart and soul of the Big Red Machine, Tony Perez. Playing for an amazing twenty-three seasons, Perez was a seven-time All-Star and MVP of the 1967 Midsummer Classic.

The Reds got into the retiring-of-numbers game a bit late, putting up the display for the first time in 1996. Perhaps this explains why most of the players retired are from the more recent era, despite the team's long history. We wonder why Johnny Vander Meer's jersey hasn't been hung up. After all, he threw back-to-back no-hitters for the Reds on June 11 and June 15, 1938.

Kevin: Back-to-back no hitters: what does a guy have to do?

Josh: Well, it seems like a .500 record should be a prerequisite for having one's number retired. Even with his two no-no's the "Dutch Master" was only 119–121 in his career.

Kevin: You looked that up on your smartphone, didn't you?

Stadium Eats

In addition to its robust selection of foods at the concession stands, Great American offers three different restaurants. We found plenty of folks in The Machine Room Grill and Microbrewery before the game. Located on the 200 Level in the left-field corner, the Machine Room is a better sports bar than you'll find in the area surrounding the ballpark and it's air-conditioned. It offers plenty of memorabilia honoring Cincinnati's Big Red Machine, and is open before, during, and after the game to fans with tickets. In the right-field corner, meanwhile, the Riverfront Club is more upscale, with tiered seating and white tablecloths. Not our scene. Another area for club members only is Club 4192, located on the first-base side. All they have to say is "club" and we want no part of it even if the joint is named after Rose's record breaking hit.

MONTGOMERY INN BBQ AND MR. RED'S SMOKEHOUSE (TRADEMARK FOODS)

Barbecue pork and pulled chicken sandwiches can be found at the **Montgomery Inn** stand behind Section 127 run by this longtime Cincinnati institution. This was some of the best barbecue we had on the entire trip. Tangy, with just a hint of spiciness, these sandwiches are served with a fork so you can eat the meat piling over the bun without making too big of a mess. Josh got a cup of extra sauce on the side, and drizzled it over his french fries.

Mr. Red's Smokehouse, at the end of the first base concourse, overlooking the Ohio River, is also a must-visit for barbecue lovers. It is an actual wooden shack with a smoker inside. Serving beef ribs, turkey legs, chicken wings and pulled pork sandwiches along with baked beans, corn on the cob, mac and cheese and coleslaw, it "brings a little bit of Louisiana" as one fan told us, "to Reds games." They were also serving "Smoked Cardinal" when we visited. Josh wasn't brave enough to try it, but Kevin said it tasted a lot like chicken.

So, which ballpark Q is superior? A traditionalist, Josh favored Monty's, while Kevin, who is generally more open to new experiences, gave the nod to Mr. Red's. You'll have to conduct a ballpark taste-test of your own to break the tie.

KAHN'S HOT DOG (DOG REVIEW)

While we're not big fans of the standard Kahn's dog, there are plenty of other dog choices at Great American that are more than respectable. Kevin sampled a very tasty all-beef grilled kosher dog. The Skyline Cheese Coney Dogs are popular too, piled with chili and shredded cheddar. Josh could hardly control himself while waiting in line at one of their several stands.

BEST OF THE REST

Another processed meat wonder that could very well have been our pick for Cincinnati's trademark ballpark treat is the **Big Red Smokey.** Made by Kahn's and sold in supermarkets throughout Ohio, this skinless sausage, true to its name, is big, red and plenty smokey enough. We split one, then went back and got another. The **Queen City Bratwurst, Cheddarwurst** and **Brat Burger** served at the several Frank's Franks stands are also worth more than just a sniff.

The Penn Station stands at Sections 130 and 515 have a decent **Philly Cheesesteak** and even better **Hand-Cut Fries.**

The Reds kindly offer two **Kids Zone Stands,** behind Sections 132 and 533, where you can buy hot dogs, popcorn, peanuts, sodas and ice cream cups for $1.00 each. Hand these small-sized items to your youngsters or eat them yourself. No one checks to make sure you're actually toting kiddies. The lines sometimes get long as the game wears on, so do take advantage of this good deal before first pitch.

The **Cheese Fries** are a nice option for those who like their deep-fried foods. Fried on the spot but not overly greasy, they're warm all the way to the bottom. And the cheese sauce has a nice spice to it.

STADIUM SUDS

Great American Ball Park features much the same beers available everywhere else in the Western world except for Redlegg Ale. This microbrew specialty is brewed by Barrel House Brewing Company, located at 22 E. 12th St. in Cincinnati. The neighborhood is a bit dicey if you're planning to visit. But this brew is not too shabby, and we like the name.

Speaking of suds, the Redlegs were expelled from the National League in 1880, in part for selling beer at the ballpark. This outrage kept the Reds out of the NL for ten seasons. They were reinstated in 1890, and thus far they have stuck.

The Great American Ballpark Experience

Reds fans are a serious breed, a veritable army of devotees donning red. Their team accomplished big things in the 1970s and is looking to repeat that magical decade with another dynasty. The field itself is known to favor hitters, as Great American usually ranks among the top five easiest big league parks in which to homer each season. This is particularly so when left-handed pull-hitters—like former Reds slugger Adam Dunn—are at the plate, seeing as the right-field fence is closer to the plate than the one in left and the breeze tends to carry balls toward the river. This tendency has earned the stadium the nickname "The Great American Small Park."

GAPPER AND MR. RED

Most every Reds fan is as rabid as heck and willing to talk your ear off about the time Tony Perez signed their baseball on his way out of the Riverfront parking lot, or the time they were at Great American to witness a walk-off homer by Brandon Phillips or some other recent Red. However, some Reds fans are just a little more rabid than the rest.

Mr. Red, for example, is a seam-head if ever we saw one. He's a mascot whose actual head is an oversized baseball. We're not sure if he's related to Mr. Met but we think it's a pretty good bet. Maybe we'll ask Tom Seaver—who pitched for both teams—the next time we see him. In any case, Mr. Red cheers for the Reds during games, and attends functions all over Cincinnati while they're on the road. He has represented the Reds very well over the years and is

sometimes joined by his crush Rosie Red and his handlebar-mustachioed uncle Mr. RedLegs.

For kids who are a little freaked out by ball-heads—let's be honest, aren't we all a tad spooked by them?—Gapper is a whole different breed of fanatic. With a furry red face and pointy blue nose, Gapper looks like a prankster and plays the part to perfection. So beware.

FREE AGENT FRIDAYS

If you're unattached and hoping to make a new friend or two during your trip, you'll be happy to learn that every Friday night game at Great American is designated a "Free Agent Friday."

Josh: Free Agent Friday? I don't like the sound of that.
Kevin: Sounds like trouble.

All this really means is that before Friday night games the Reds encourage single men and women to congregate at the Fan Zone in left-field home run territory for mixers that feature drink specials, a DJ spinning tunes, and the lovely Mynt Martini girls making the rounds. The fun begins at 5:40 p.m., allowing smooth operators just enough time to get to first base by game time.

On special Free Agent Fridays the Reds play up the dating theme all night. They've held "Battle of the Sexes" trivia nights, "Speed Dating" nights, dancing contests, and even a "Win a Girl" contest that was sort of like the TV show *The Bachelorette,* only instead of getting married at the end, the two winners watched a game together in an improved seating location. We should also mention that

Sports in the City

The Three Incarnations of Crosley Field

The first tribute to Crosley Field in these parts is Crosley Terrace, located outside the ballpark. That one's easy to check off your list.

The second site is the corner of Findlay and Western Streets where a plaque marks the former location of Crosley. A janitorial supply company operates on the corner now, but six seats from Crosley sit outside the front door.

The third and most comprehensive site is located in Blue Ash, Ohio, where the Crosley Sports Complex features replica baseball fields of Riverfront and Crosley. Just like at the original Crosley, a banked outfield rises to the home run fence and a Longines sits atop a replica of the scoreboard. The lineups posted on the board are from the final game at Crosley, June 24, 1970, against the Giants. Ticket booths and a section of seats from the old park are on display in Blue Ash as well. And along the dugouts, plaques honor visitors to the field like Dave Concepcion, Dave Parker, Johnny Bench, Cesar Geronimo, George Foster, Blue Moon Odom, Danny Ozark, Ken Griffey Sr., Walt Terrell, Pete Rose, and others. Many are autographed. Some players have written their uniform numbers as well as their names on their plaques, and some have drawn smiley faces. Josh tried unsuccessfully to trace several autographs onto a ball. To get to the Crosley Sports Complex take Route 71 to the Blue Ash exit. Follow Glendale Milford Road toward Blue Ash. Turn right onto Kenwood Road, another right on Cornell Road, then take a left onto Grooms Road. The complex address is 11540 Grooms Rd.

Sports in (and around) the City

The Louisville Slugger Museum and Bat Factory
800 West Main St.
www.sluggermuseum.org/

Whether on your way to St. Louis or Kansas City, a trip to Louisville offers the chance to marvel at the biggest baseball bat in the world. The 120-foot-tall, 68,000-pound whopper is made of steel, but painted to resemble the wood grain of a real bat. It rises higher than the five-story brick building it leans against, serving as a beacon for those in search of the Louisville Slugger Museum.

Inside, exhibits trace the evolution of the bat, offering examples of the sticks that famous sluggers like Ty Cobb, Babe Ruth, and Ted Williams wielded, as well as models that modern players like Derek Jeter, Ken Griffey Jr., and David Ortiz swing. Another popular attraction is a twelve-foot-long baseball glove made of 450-year-old Kentucky limestone, in which children can sit and play. The glove weighs seventeen tons and could only be installed after the Museum's front doors were removed to allow for its entrance.

The twenty-minute tour of the Hillerich and Bradsby factory demonstrates how planks of white ash and maple harvested from the company's 6,500 acres of forest in Pennsylvania and New York are lathed into the best baseball bats in the business. Hillerich and Bradsby sells more than one million bats a year, thanks largely to the more than 60 percent of current major leaguers who swing its popular Louisville Slugger. The typical big leaguer goes through about one hundred per season.

The woodworking shop that grew to one day become the most prolific bat-maker in the industry was founded in Louisville in 1856 by German immigrant Fred Hillerich. In those early days, the shop made balusters, bedposts, bowling pins, and butter churns, not baseball bats. Then in 1880, according to local legend, Bud Hillerich began work as an apprentice in his father's shop. When Fred wasn't looking, his son made baseball bats for himself and for his friends. Then one day young Bud made a special bat to help his favorite player out of a horrific slump. Pete "The Old Gladiator" Browning was the star of the American Association's Louisville Eclipse, but he was really struggling in the early part of the 1884 season. He couldn't buy a hit and was willing to try anything to change his mojo. So on a warm spring day he stepped into the batter's box with one of Bud's handmade bats on his shoulder. Before long Browning was knocking balls all over the yard. He went on to bat .336 that season and never swung another type of bat until his retirement from the game ten years later. By then word had spread. Many other major leaguers were swinging Louisville Sluggers too, including Pittsburgh Pirates star Honus Wagner, who helped cement Hillerich and Bradsby's place in the game when he signed an endorsement deal with the company in 1905. Then Ty Cobb signed a similar contract in 1908.

Today, the Museum that tells the story of this unique American enterprise is open Monday through Saturday from 9:00 a.m. until 5:00 p.m. and Sunday from noon until 5:00 p.m. Factory tours run every day but Sunday, and every fan who takes the tour receives a miniature souvenir bat.

the Reds have fireworks at the ballpark after every Friday game all summer long. And what's more romantic than fireworks?

Now, you may be wondering how the Reds would get any available ladies to turn out for one of these pregame mixers. After all, we statistic-citing, sausage-slobbering baseball fanatics have not exactly excelled on the dating scene historically. So how do the Reds do it? Very simply: with chocolate and Cyndi Lauper. When we visited during 2011, a Free Agent Friday had drawn a fair number of females to the Fan Zone before the game where they were enjoying not only a chocolate-dipping fountain but free massages from a local parlor, and other beauty enhancement booths. Then, the fireworks exploded after the game to the crooning of Ms. Lauper and other female singers.

Josh: I have a feeling Reds fans are gonna hate us for including this section.

Kevin: Yeah, but the Pink Hats will love us.

Josh: Do they have Pink Hats in Cincinnati?

Kevin: More like light-red hats, I suppose.

MORGANNA, "THE KISSING BANDIT" (SUPER-FAN HALL OF FAME)

One of the game's most recognizable super-fans of all time got her start in Cincinnati in 1971. Morganna was an exotic dancer whose "baseball stats," as she called them, measured a mythic sixty by twenty-three by thirty-nine inches. She used her considerable bust and bubbly personality to make her presence known throughout the game in the 1970s and 1980s as her "victims" came to include Frank Howard, Johnny Bench, Nolan Ryan, Cal Ripken Jr., George Brett,

Don Mattingly, Steve Garvey, and many other stars. But Morganna's very first ballpark smooch occurred at Riverfront Stadium, when at the age of seventeen, she bounded out to Pete Rose and planted a big wet one on him. Rose reacted angrily and chewed her out, but then the next day he turned up at the lounge club where she was performing and apologized with a dozen roses.

While We Were in Cincinnati
We Played "Schott for Brains"

We put our heads together to assemble a list of the five most deplorable things Marge Schott said and did while running the Reds from 1984 until 1999. So, with apologies to the late George Steinbrenner, whom we may have erroneously called the most arrogant moron to ever own a big league team, here goes:

- *Schott instituted a St. Bernard named Schottzie as the Reds mascot, named after herself rather than anything to do with the team. Schottzie, who smeared the Astroturf at Riverfront with his leavings, eventually became the first mascot banned from his home park. You know what they say about pets taking on the personalities of their owners? Well,*

the players, fans, and pretty much everyone else associated with the Reds other than Marge eventually came to hate the obnoxious mutt. And Schottzie II was even worse.

- *Schott once said she didn't like her players wearing earrings, because "only fruits wear earrings." She later apologized for her remarks, saying that she was "not prejudiced against any group, regardless of their lifestyle preference." Later, pitcher Roger McDowell bought earrings for the entire team to wear.*

- *When umpire John McSherry collapsed on the field and died, Schott's comment was: "Snow this morning and now this? I don't believe it. I feel cheated. This isn't supposed to happen to us, not in Cincinnati. This is our history, our tradition, our team. No one feels worse than I do." Once again, Schott later apologized for the insensitivity of her comments.*

- *When questioned in an interview about owning a swastika armband, Schott responded, "Hitler was good for Germany in the beginning, but he went too far." She was again fined by the league and suspended for a full year.*

- *Schott used highly offensive racial slurs in referring to two of her own players—Eric Davis and Dave Parker. She later apologized but was fined $25,000 by MLB and suspended from the Reds' day-to-day operations for nine months.*

PITTSBURGH PIRATES, PNC PARK AT NORTH SHORE

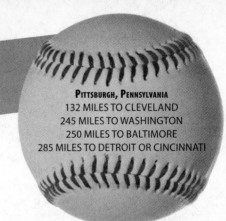

PITTSBURGH, PENNSYLVANIA
132 MILES TO CLEVELAND
245 MILES TO WASHINGTON
250 MILES TO BALTIMORE
285 MILES TO DETROIT OR CINCINNATI

Raise the Jolly Roger along the Allegheny

The plan to build PNC Park, bring about a return to Pirate dominance, and appease the Pittsburgh fan base seemed simple enough. It was certainly efficient. And it seemed well thought out. The details went something like this: Step One: Build the finest new ballpark in America, one centered in a region where its citizenry is all but addicted to sports. Step Two: Reap massive increase in ticket sales and use accompanying profits to build a championship-caliber team. Step Three: Wallpaper the bathroom with pennants and build a new case for all the trophies sure to follow. And oh yeah, and don't forget about making some space in the basement for all of the victory champagne that would surely be needed.

Ah, but what is that famous saying about "the best laid plans of pirates and men?" Who besides John Steinbeck himself could have known things would go so horribly wrong for the Pirates? Team management knocked off Step One with relative ease. They built a very fine ballpark. PNC is beautifully crafted with local steel and brick. It has nary a bad seat. With a backdrop of the city's panoramic downtown, the view across the Allegheny River is surpassed by no ballpark in America. And PNC remains within spitting distance of where part of the first-ever World Series was played, on Pittsburgh's North Shore. All should have been right with the Bucs' world.

Allegheny River

Photo by Kevin O'Connell

However, steps Two and Three have proved trickier to realize. Let's see if we can figure out where things went awry.

Prior to the opening of PNC Park in 2001, the Pirates played their home games at the much loved Three Rivers Stadium. Located between where PNC now resides and the Steelers' Heinz Field on a site that now houses a parking lot and outdoor amphitheater, Three Rivers was the site of the greatest era in the history of Pittsburgh sports: the 1970s. That memorable decade earned Pittsburgh its familiar "City of Champions" moniker. The Pirates nabbed two of their five World Series crowns at Three Rivers, in 1971 and 1979, while the Steelers tallied four Super Bowl rings between 1975 and 1980. It was, as they say, a glorious time to be a fan in "Da Burgh," and gave the city a much-needed shot in the arm and ego, as the decline of the region's famed steel industry had Pittsburghers feeling mighty low about themselves and their future prospects.

Few Pittsburghers complained that Three Rivers was a multisport stadium that could have easily been swapped out for "The Vet" in rival Philadelphia (God forbid) or for Busch Stadium in St. Louis without too many people noticing. There weren't many letters to the editor being written by fans demanding the delights of baseball played on natural grass or before open views of the city rather than a wall of orange and yellow seats so high it blocked the sun and rested on concrete decks so steep that a Sherpa would have been more useful than an usher. Few even seemed to mind when the concrete began to brown with age. No. Pittsburghers liked Three Rivers Stadium quite a lot, thank you very much.

Josh: Is it true you can buy pictures of the implosion suitable for framing?

Kevin: You can still buy snow globes with Three Rivers inside.

Josh: They probably don't sell many snow globes of the Kingdome in Seattle, do they?

Kevin: No. Because it rarely snows there.

Why such undying devotion to an ugly relic from a suspect era of stadium design? The sweet memory of victory, of course. Winning heals all wounds. And Pittsburghers enjoyed some pretty incredible moments during the life of that big ugly ship at the confluence of the town's three trademark rivers.

The last game Roberto Clemente ever played was at Three Rivers. Willie Stargell led crowds in singing "We Are Family" all the way to the 1979 championship. Franco Harris made the Immaculate Reception on the Three Rivers turf in the 1972 NFL playoffs. "Mean" Joe Greene gave a kid his jersey in the Three Rivers tunnel in a famous Coke commercial.

Mega-rockers and J.R.R. Tolkien enthusiasts Led Zeppelin played there, as memorialized in the documentary film *The Song Remains the Same*. And who could forget Pete Rose, one of the celebrity endorsers of "Hands Across America," locking hands at Three Rivers with his Reds teammates and Little Leaguers alike in 1986? Ah, sweet memories. Despite its relatively short life—it opened on July 16, 1970, and was imploded on February 11, 2001—the field sure hosted some amazing moments.

More than fifty-five thousand fans turned out on October 1, 2000, to watch the Pirates play their final game at Three Rivers, a loss to the Cubs. It was the largest crowd ever to see a regular season baseball game in Pittsburgh. Three Rivers had served the Pirates since July 16, 1970, when they also lost to the Cubs. Baseball, like history and Josh when he's telling fishing stories on long road trips, tends to repeat itself.

Josh: Did I ever tell you about the time I caught an eel in a quarry pit?

Kevin: Yes, you told me when we were in Cleveland last week.

Considering all this warmth for Three Rivers that Pittsburghers held in their hearts, the question arises: Where did the need arise to build a new ballpark? In essence, the sun was setting on the era of the multi-purpose monster stadium, and the era for each sport to build its own ballpark was dawning. The Pirates were simply smart enough to figure this out and capitalize on the phenomenon—though not completely without trouble. With the Pirates struggling in the mid-1990s and some of the team's corporate owners wanting out, management threatened to sell the team to another city if a local buyer couldn't be found. Finally in 1996, a group led by Kevin McClatchy purchased the Pirates with MLB's condition that the city would build a new baseball-only facility within five years. As is the case in most cities, though, wanting a new park was the easy part. Figuring out who should pay for it turned out to be more difficult. A sales tax increase was brought before voters to finance a new baseball park, a new football stadium, and a new convention center that city officials had long discussed. Taxpayers twice rejected this hike in all eleven counties in which it was proposed.

Pittsburgh Mayor Thomas Murphy viewed the Pirates as a brand name of the city and drove the metaphorical stake in the ground to keep the stadium project moving forward. Even though taxpayers voted a resounding "no," Plan B was put into effect. We're not kidding, the plan was actually called "Plan B." According to the plan, the Regional Asset District Board, which administers the funds raised by 1 percent

Roberto Clemente statue and Clemente Bridge

Photo by Josh Pahigian/Kevin O'Connell

Josh: Now that we have the Tea Party do you think pols will spend as liberally on new stadiums?

Kevin: I think we'd better leave the politics to George Will and Arianna Huffington.

The total cost of PNC was to be $262 million, with the construction timeline scheduled to span an ambitious twenty-four month schedule. On April 7, 1999, a groundbreaking ceremony was held for PNC Park, and the Sixth Avenue Bridge was officially renamed "The Roberto Clemente Bridge." A very classy move by Pittsburgh, which had not always treated Clemente with the respect he deserved.

Ever since the Pirates had left Forbes Field, some Pittsburgh baseball purists had remained haunted by the ghost of a beautiful ballpark they'd once enjoyed: their own steel green cathedral. The brown dirt, the green grass, the blue seats, the brick walls, and the cozy confines Forbes had provided for so many years howled and moaned in the memories of old-timers seated in cavernous Three Rivers. And the Pirates wanted the glory and the memory of Forbes back. They wanted the luxury boxes, club seating, and wide concourses and concession areas of modern parks too, and they wanted it on the North Shore.

Kevin McClatchy has been much maligned for his captainship of Pirate Nation. And while it is true that during the years McClatchy was majority owner (1996–2007) the Pirates never posted a winning season, his legacy will always be PNC Park. McClatchy oversaw every detail of the design and building of PNC. And let us say for the record that in this regard McClatchy's work was exemplary. PNC is the most intimate, and perhaps most beautiful, ballyard of the recent ballpark renaissance. On April 9, 2001, the Bucs opened PNC Park at North Shore, which not only brought back natural grass to the Burgh, but synthesized many elements of the old-time ballparks with the best elements of the new. PNC is the Pirates' fifth home and is very much an alloy of Pittsburgh's storied baseball past, combining features of the other parks the Pirates have called home.

PNC was built with unique local materials. Steel has been used in every ballpark and stadium since the construction of Forbes Field, but more than just providing structural support, it is a featured part of the beauty and strength of PNC. There is more exposed structural steel and decorative brushed steel at PNC than at any other park, and nowhere is it more fitting than in Pittsburgh, the city that made U.S. Steel King. A yellow limestone called Kasota stone replaced the red brick that has nearly become a retro cliché among ballparks built over the last two decades. In 2010, this same Kasota lime would debut on the façade of the Twins' new

of the sales taxes already in place, guaranteed the ballpark project $13.4 million dollars per year for thirty years, giving the new ballpark the anchor it needed to continue. The Pirates chipped in $44 million more, $30 million of which came from PNC Bank for the naming rights. And while we would have liked to see the funding come totally from private sources, at least taxes weren't raised to finance the ballpark when people had clearly voted against that measure. Then Pennsylvania Governor Tom Ridge granted the remaining $75 million in a deal that brought new football stadiums and ballparks to both Pittsburgh and Philadelphia. As we've seen elsewhere, none of the politicians felt their careers could suffer the blame for the home team leaving because of finances.

Target Field in Minneapolis. This distinctive stone is also used prominently in other buildings in Pittsburgh. Throughout the city and at the park, it suggests a certain warmth and friendliness that seems to invite would-be visitors inside. PNC was designed with the visitor in mind—specifically fans who like to watch baseball games. This might sound more obvious than it actually is, but there are few extras at PNC to detract from fan focus.

Kevin: With the way the Pirates have played the last two decades, a little off-the-field distraction might not be such a bad idea.

Josh: There's a pirogue race going on, quiet down.

PNC is not an amusement park or entertainment venue. Its sole purpose is to get fans close to the ballgame so they can enjoy it. This single minded devotion has made PNC a no-frills shrine to the game itself. You will find no carousel here, no roller-coaster, no circus clowns. Heck, it took us twenty minutes to find the kiddie area—which, by the way, was tastefully done in a tiny baseball park within the ballpark theme. What does all this add up to? A ballpark, built in the old style, the way it should be, with distinctive local materials and all the modern amenities required for the new era, PNC is a thoughtful return to all that was good about the small and glorious ballparks of yesteryear. It accomplishes this without sacrificing the wide concourses, comfortable seating, and cup-holders that enhance the experience of new ballparks. So as it was in the beginning, so shall it ever be, a world without end. Amen.

Josh: You're praying? Is this a church or a baseball park?
Kevin: Both.

Beautiful as PNC is, we would be remiss not to mention that the experience of visiting this gem of a park has indeed been more than a bit hampered by the Pirates' lack of success on its field. After going 96-66 in 1992 and playing the Braves for the National League championship, the Pirates went the rest of the 1990s and the entire first decade of the 2000s without posting a winning record. This gave them the dubious distinction of having the most consecutive losing seasons of any pro sports team in North America.

There are those who would claim that Pittsburgh is, and always has been, a football town, and that baseball will always play second fiddle behind the Steelers, or third fiddle behind Pitt Panther football, or even fourth fiddle behind any random high school football team that might happen to play nearby. And a cursory view of the sporting section of the *Pittsburgh Post-Gazette* might support this theory. But it is a mistaken notion—and one that we ourselves made in

the first edition of this book. The fact is, Pittsburgh is a town that loves winners, and especially those that have "Pittsburgh" emblazoned on their chests and carry the trademark black and gold. It's a town that loves sports so much that it will support nearly any local team that does not tarnish its reputation as "City of Champions."

Sadly, the current Pirates owners have been accused by their own fans, perhaps rightfully so, of not really truly trying to compete. Pirates' fans have accused the owners of selling off every decent player that comes up, right before he is due to earn a competitive paycheck. They have accused the owners of putting teams on the field that simply are not equipped to be competitive, and they support their argument by pointing to the Pirates' dismally low payroll. They have accused the owners of milking the corporate welfare system in place—MLB's revenue sharing (known as the Luxury Tax)—to deliver profits to their investors, without putting proper monies back into the franchise to be competitive via payroll. And perhaps worst of all, they have accused owners of simply not caring, of taking a once glorious franchise and shamelessly flushing its reputation down the drain and into the Allegheny River like a goldfish grown too big for its bowl.

The current ownership group, which is led by Bob Nutting, claims small market inequities dictate the necessity of the Pirates' personnel moves. But this doesn't fly with the general Pittsburgh sports fan—especially not when they continue to win Stanley Cups and Lombardi trophies just down the street. Nutting and the rest of the Pirates owners have made it difficult to refute any of the fans' complaints. And their public relations effort is often so horrific that they seem to vacillate between not understanding what they are doing and not caring. Owing to this ownership continuum that has gone from mediocrity to ineptitude, many potential fans have simply written off the Pirates as losers. Meanwhile, a generation of potential new fans has been born, grown up, and graduated from high school having never known the Pirates to have a winning season.

In this dysfunctional world of Pirates family dynamics, the fans have even turned against one another. The boycotters claim the only way to send a message to the owners is to steer clear of the ballpark. The loyalists, who continue to go to the games, claim a variety of reasons for still going, but mostly because they simply love the game too much and can't stay away. To this, boycotters say loyalists are part of the problem. The loyalists claim that boycotters are fair-weather fans, and that they themselves are the true fans, having stuck by the team through high tide and low. Sadly, both sides simply want a team they can be proud of, but without management's cooperation, they're powerless to produce one. It's criminal that the Pirates have been mismanaged into such a state of ineptitude and fan disaffection, given the great success the franchise has enjoyed over its long history. As bad as the Pirates have been recently, only six franchises can claim more World Series victories than the Buccos, and only four can claim more inductees to baseball's Hall of Fame. Think of Clemente, Stargell, Honus Wagner. Quite simply, those are some of the best players to ever play this game and they were Pirates.

Josh: How many World Series rings does Seattle have again?

Kevin: Hey bud, your Sox haven't won since 19—, um. Oh, never mind!

Most Pittsburghers point to the 1992 NLCS loss to the Atlanta Braves in Game 7 as the exact point in time when the Good Ship Pirate began to submerge. Starter Doug Drabek pitched eight masterful innings only to see a catastrophic turn of events. When submarine-armed closer Stan Belinda took the mound in the bottom of the ninth, the Pirates still led 2-0. With the bases loaded and two outs, Francisco Cabrera lined a single to left field to bring in the go-ahead run, Sid Bream, a former Pirate who couldn't have lumbered in from third more slowly if he'd been named Forrest Gump. Some Pirates fans took heart. With a roster that included Barry Bonds, Bobby Bonilla, Jay Bell, Denny Neagle, Tim Wakefield, and Drabek, fans felt the next championship would come their way soon. But it didn't. One by one, the Pirates' top players departed via free agency, and the team sank in the standings year after year.

Josh: I remember watching that game my freshman year of college. Since then I've completed college and grad school, worked for fifteen years, gotten married, bought a house, had a child, written some books . . . and the Pirates still haven't had so much as a winning season.

Kevin: When you put it that way it seems even worse.

Despite their recent hard times, the franchise has enjoyed many shining moments:

- *The Pirates fielded what is generally regarded as the Major League's first all-minority lineup on September 1, 1971.*
- *The Pirates won a World Series the year after moving into Forbes Field by beating Detroit in 1909, and a little more than a year after moving into Three Rivers, they*

won their fourth October Classic, beating Baltimore in 1971. Clemente batted .414 in the Series, and hit a Game 7 homer while Steve Blass tossed a four-hitter. The Series also featured the first night game in World Series play.
- *When the Pirates won the World Series again in 1979, they did so with the catchy disco number "We Are Family" as their anthem and with the big bats of Dave Parker and Stargell leading the way.*
- *In 1994 Three Rivers played host to its second All-Star Game (the first was in 1974). It was the largest crowd to see the Midsummer Classic, as 59,568 fans witnessed an 8–7 NL victory that took ten innings to complete.*

As mentioned, Pittsburgh's hardball history ranks among the richest in the Majors. Back in 1887, the Pittsburgh Alleghenies played at Recreation Park, a facility that seated fewer people than Wheeler Field, in Centralia, Washington, where Kevin played his Babe Ruth ball. Not really, but it was small. It was there that the team garnered the name "Pirates," when a Philadelphia newspaper claimed the team had hijacked slugging second baseman Louis Bierbauer away from the Athletics. There was no wrongdoing, but the name stuck.

In October 1903 the Pirates played the Boston Pilgrims in the first World Series, but lost five games to three in the best-of-nine set. The Pirates did manage to win the first-ever World Series game, which was played in Boston, before returning to Pittsburgh—spelled "Pittsburg" at the time—to host the early Red Sox at Exposition Park. The small wooden facility sat on the north shore of the Allegheny, spitting distance from where PNC Park would open a century later. A historical marker of the first Series has been erected on the site, just a short walk from PNC.

Even before that, way back in 1882, the old American Association Alleghenies played baseball in the open fields of Exposition Park. But the park flooded often and the league folded. There were no outfield fences at "The Ex" and crowds respectfully lined up behind rope boundaries. Clearly this was another era for baseball fans. It may not have had outfield fences, but an interesting innovation debuted there when the Pirates used a tarp to cover the infield during a rainstorm. Other cities quickly followed suit.

In 1909 Pittsburgh opened gorgeous Forbes Field, named after British General John Forbes, who in 1758 captured Fort Duquesne from the French and renamed it Fort Pitt. It was the first ballpark in the country built completely of steel and poured concrete. A beautiful structure with a stone facade and arched windows along its exterior, its most important feature was its seats close to the action. Forbes was a park of the grand design, a rival to Wrigley and Fenway. The outfield was enormous and the park itself had a clunky shape. The flagpole in left field was actually in play. To commemorate their love for the old park, the Pirates designed PNC to imitate Forbes' blue steel, tall "toothbrush style" light standards, and blue seats.

In the first season at Forbes, Wagner led the Pirates to their first World Series title, downing Ty Cobb and the Tigers in a Series that went seven games. Wagner—whose tobacco card fetched a record $2.35 million in a 2007 auction—had help in the Series from rookie hurler Babe Adams, who won three games, including a Game 7 shutout in Detroit.

There were many firsts and lasts at Forbes Field. The last tripleheader in MLB history, for example, was played there on October 2, 1920, between the Pirates and Reds. The first radio broadcast of a baseball game emanated from Forbes in 1921. The first elevator in the Majors was built to shuttle fans up to the "crow's nest" bleacher seats. And Forbes was the first stadium to install foam crash pads on its outfield walls.

In 1925 the Pirates claimed another championship, sealing the deal at home in storybook fashion. In the eighth inning of Game 7 with two outs and the bases loaded and fire-baller Walter Johnson on the mound for the Senators, Kiki Cuyler laced a three-run double to propel the Pirates to a 9-7 win.

Another amazing Forbes moment occurred on May 25, 1935, when Babe Ruth—playing for the Boston Braves—hit the last three home runs of his career. Ruth's final blast, number 714, cleared the right-field roof to mark the first time a shot had ever left the Forbes yard.

In 1955 Forbes witnessed the debut of a twenty-year-old rookie from Puerto Rico by the name of Roberto Clemente. No. 21 would prove to be the last right fielder to play at Forbes for the Bucs, patrolling the post until the ballpark closed in 1970.

In 1960 Bill Mazeroski hit a shot in the bottom of the ninth to break a 9-9 deadlock and carry the home team past the Yankees in Game 7 of the 1960 World Series. The legendary swat, which cleared the left-field fence, gave the Bucs their third World Series title and first in thirty-five years.

interior

Photo by Kevin O'Connell

Even if the Pirates' glory years seem a distant memory, PNC provides Pittsburghers a premium environment in which to see a ballgame. Just as steel is an alloy that derives its strength by the fusion of two or more other metals, PNC Park has taken the best of Forbes, Three Rivers, Exposition Park—as well as Wrigley, Fenway and other more contemporary ballparks—and fused them into a single structure. The city and the team should be proud of PNC.

Trivia Timeout

Schooner: Which Pirates pitcher authored the first no-hitter ever thrown in Pittsburgh? Hint: He did it in 1976.
Frigate: Of the four players honored with statues outside PNC, which has a museum in his honor?
Man-O-War: Which Pirates player passed away the day PNC Park opened?
Look for the answers in the text.

All that remains for the plan to come together is for the owners of the Pirates to field a championship team—or at least one with a reasonable shot at achieving a .500 record. When they do, the fans will stop their bickering and return to arguably the best new ballpark in the country. Then we'll see if Pittsburgh is really a football town or not.

A partial answer came during June 2011 when a red hot Red Sox team came to town for interleague play. Odd as it was, the Pirates had been flirting with .500 well into June, a feat that had been so long in coming that nary a Bucco fan could remember the last time it occurred. A PNC Park attendance record was broken for the Saturday night game, June 25th, when 39,441 fans turned out, then broken again the next day when 39,511 fans attended. The Pirates took the series 2-1 from that much-ballyhooed Sox team, and the three-game series broke the PNC Park series attendance record as well, drawing 118,324 fans.

Josh: We travel well, don't we?

Kevin: You might as well be wearing red pin stripes.

Getting a Choice Seat

PNC is the most intimate new park when it comes to seating, as is evident by the fact that the press box is up above all of the fans, even those who pay the least money. Only Nationals Park in Washington has a more altitudinous press box than the one in Pittsburgh. Luxury boxes hang from the upper deck rather than garnering their own level. There is very little foul territory, getting fans even closer to the action. And the seats all angle toward the infield, with aisles that are lowered to prevent views from being blocked. The only problem with this feature is if you've gone to the game to gab with your buddies, the angled seats will have you talking over your shoulder. But who cares? You can yuck it up afterward over a few pints.

Lexus Club (Sections 14–19)

We don't know anyone who can afford these seats. Sure they're better than outstanding, but why spend $160–$200 in this park for a better than outstanding view, when you can spend $27 for outstanding? Move down to these in the eighth inning, once the rich duffers tucker out and the ushers lose interest.

Dugout Box (Sections 9–13, 20–24)

These seats will cost you at least double as much at almost every other park in the country. As Ferris Bueller said, "We recommend them highly if you have the means . . . they are so choice." Money seems to go farther at PNC. With so little foul territory these seats are only forty-five feet from the corner bases.

Seating Capacity: 38,127
Ticket Office: http://pittsburgh.pirates.mlb.com/ticketing/index.jsp?c_id=pit
Seating Chart: http://pittsburgh.pirates.mlb.com/pit/ticketing/seating_pricing.jsp

Baseline Box (Sections 1–8, 25–32)

Again this is a "can't-go-wrong" situation. These seats are right at the hot corners of the diamond, so keep your eyes on the ball. At only $2 more than the seats in the sections behind them, you can't afford not to get these seats.

Infield Box (Sections 109–124)

Usually we'd say purchase elsewhere and move down, but these are only a few bucks more than the outfield boxes, making this price too good to pass up. Now is the time to put out a little dough, sit back, and have a dog and a few barley pops, without worrying about who might come along to claim your seat. Perhaps for the first time on your road trip you can enjoy a primo seat that you paid for. Feel free to ask others if they're in the correct seats, because for once, you are.

Left/Right Field Box (Sections 105–108, 125–128)

Sections 128, 127, and 125 face the plate and are located just a bit off the third-base line for a beautiful view. Even in the back rows of these sections the overhang is not a factor. Right Field Sections 101–108 get much less direct sun than the right-field bleachers (142–147), so keep that in mind if it's an extremely hot day and you're an extremely fair-skinned individual. On a cold spring day, on the other hand, you might appreciate the sun.

Outfield Box (101–103 and 129–132)

In Sections 132, 131, and 130, try to sit as close to the infield side of the sections as possible. These seats feel right on top of the third-base line and are well worth the money. As you get closer to the field, you're right at the corner. There are comparable seats at Fenway, but here they cost a fraction of what they do on the secondary ticket market in Boston. The seats in Section 129 angle slightly toward home plate, giving a nice view of the action.

Outfield (RF) Reserve (Sections 139–145)

These are great seats, which we generally recommend, with two caveats. Seats in the center of Section 145 are blocked by the right-field foul pole. On a cool dry day, try instead for Sections 139–144, which are clear of any obstruction. These seats are exposed to the elements, but they are elevated and nice for those looking to snag home run balls or long fouls

All You Can Eat Seats (Sections 146–147)

Same view as the Outfield Reserve sections for twice as much money. Why? Because in these seats you get the added "benefit" of stuffing your face with all you can eat hot dogs, hamburgers, nachos, salads, popcorn, peanuts, peanut butter filled pretzels, and ice cream.

Josh: These seats have their own dedicated food lines. I didn't have to wait for fourths in the fourth.

Kevin: Fourths in the fourth?

Josh: Yeah, you know, right after thirds in the third?

Kevin: Good Lord, do you plan on watching this game?

Josh: Before you judge me, I brought you some more peanut butter filled pretzels.

We should also mention that some seats in Sections 146 and 147 have a slight blockage looking across at left field.

Bleacher Reserved (Sections 133–138, 235–238)

These left-field bleacher seats are a good place to stand during batting practice and a solid choice for the game. They offer a great view, facing home plate, and the very low wall is a great place to snag a dinger or BP ball. Just remember, the 200 Level seats cost the same as those on the 100 Level so try to get down close. Section 138 offers a mixed bag. While some seats are perfect, on the left side of the section the bullpen blocks part of the view of the outfield. We recommend Section 137 for the same price because it has completely clear sight lines.

Sections 235–238 are in straightaway left field. Here, the seats aren't up as high as the second level and they're well below the Club seats. They are about the same elevation as the uppermost seats of the first tier. Not too shabby. All of these left-field bleacher seats face the sun as it sets.

Pittsburgh Baseball Club (Sections 207–228)

This is where the "party suits," uh, we mean where the party *suites* are located. There is no significant loss of sight lines on the 200 Club level, the party suites, or in the 200 Level restaurants like Keystone Korner and Bierbauer's. The only thing to envy about having 200 Level access is that there are some nice restaurants inside and several nice displays of uniforms, memorabilia, and photos on this level. The best of these is the collection of bats and gloves, one from each Pirates batting champ and Gold Glove Award winner.

For more "party suits" check out longtime Pirates announcer Bob Prince's collection of colorful sport coats

SEATING TIP

The Right Field Reserve sections are more elevated than the left field-bleachers (though they are the same price) giving a more downward sightline, which some prefer. But there is an underhang and you will lose a bit of the warning track from the seats in right. Plus the scoreboard is difficult to see from these seats. Also sitting in right, your back is to the skyline, which at this park is a bit like going to the Grand Canyon and facing the minivan the whole time. Advantages to the right-field seats are that they have seat backs (making them not technically bleachers) and are closer: 320 feet from the plate, versus 389 for most sections in left.

Though the left-field bleachers start 325 feet from home plate and the wall quickly runs out to 389, we like them better than the right-field bleachers because of the extremely low wall—just six feet—the lowest in any new park. When a home run comes to the left-field section it's exciting being down near the left fielder who may have to fight it out with a fan for the ball.

that made him famous. The man had style, both in word and dress.

Josh: Is that why Craig Sager always wears those goofy jackets on TBS? He's trying to make a Prince of himself?

Kevin: I'm not sure. We'll have to ask him if he ever interviews us.

Pirates Cove (Sections 205–210)

These seats are an extension of the Club level and are available only for group purchase. So unless you're road tripping with your fraternity, or in a very crowded Volkswagen microbus, forget it. Fear not, you can do better.

Deck Seating (Sections 335–338)

Those who purchase a table seat at the Hall of Fame Club located on the second level have the option of sitting in the Deck Seating Sections. Tables can be reserved for parties of four, five, and six. The seating charges include a food credit.

Grandstands (Sections 308–325)

These are perhaps the best second level seats of any new ballpark in the country. That's right, we said second level. Don't let the 300-something on the ticket fool you. There is no true third level at this ballpark, making PNC the first two-tiered ballpark to be built in the Majors since Milwaukee's County Stadium opened in 1953. The highest row of seats is only eighty-eight feet above the field—that's closer to the plate than first base. We recommend sitting in the second level and taking in the game from above—but not too far above. And keep in mind that there are some seats to avoid. Supporting the press box are seven small beams, which obstruct the views of those seated behind them. These are in Sections 315–317.

As you enter the grandstands, the standards that support the stairwells have glass windows, so if you're seated behind those you'll have a minor obstructed view as well. It's best to sit up higher than Row 7 so you won't be bothered at all. But until the Pirates become contenders again, you should be able to move back or forward with ease.

Left/Right Field Grandstands (Sections 301–307, 327–329)

The entire upper deck is close to the field and offers great views of the game and the city. With the Roberto Clemente Bridge stretching across the Allegheny and the sun going down over the river and buildings downtown, we suggest sitting at least one game in the upper deck (something we thought we'd never say) or at least taking a walk up there to see the view. With the three steel bridges lyrically repeating their spans across the river, it's quite lovely, and perhaps the best city view in all of baseball.

Sections 301 and 302 have the slightest underhang obstruction in the right-field corner due to a little terrace that juts out. But all in all, PNC has done a nearly perfect job of managing the overhang/underhang issue. As for rainy nights, head for rows Q and higher to get under the small sunroof. Row Y catches a nice breeze off the river.

Left Field Terrace (Sections 330–333)

In these sections you can't see a bit of the left-field corner. Avoid Section 333, as its seats are further obstructed by the steelwork of the Rotunda, which is beautiful, but blocks the view of the scoreboard. Better to spend an extra $2 to sit in the Right Field/Left Field Grandstands. Or better yet, buy these seats, move over to the third-base line or behind home plate and use the extra cash to reward your cleverness with a beer.

Standing Room

Though there has yet to be much need for it, the Rotunda not only allows fans to traverse from one level to another, but it also acts as a standing-room area, as people pause for extended periods to take in the magnificent view from all four circling ramps. It's a wonderful arched-roofed steel structure, painted blue and decorated with blue lights, standing as a beautiful tribute to Pittsburgh's steel-working heritage. There is also a very good standing area with a few seats (it didn't make any sense to us either) above the "out-of-town" scoreboard and underneath the Right Field Reserved sections. You have to look through a screen, but it is a pretty cool view.

The Black Market

Finding cheap tickets from scalpers outside PNC is a bit like finding D-listers on *Dancing with the Stars*. But as our friend Lyle Applbaum tells us, the best scalpers offering the best prices can be found across the Allegheny River along 6th Avenue. Simply cross over the Clemente Bridge and on the other side you'll find scalpers with stacks of cheap tickets, unless there are fireworks or a bobblehead giveaway on the schedule. Remember, prices skyrocket the closer you get to the park, so if you need tickets, park in one of the garages on the other side, have your ticket-scalping adventure and then walk across the Bridge. The corner of Fort Duquesne Boulevard and 6th Street is your best bet.

Before/After the Game

Getting to PNC Park

PNC Park is located on the north side of Pittsburgh's Allegheny River, surrounded by General Robinson Street, Federal Street, and Mazeroski Way. If you have a map that predates 2001, Mazeroski Way may not appear, as it was created during construction of the ballpark. Though PNC lies just off of Interstate 279, that's not all you'll need to know. Nearly every option for getting to the park was created with some walking in mind to preserve an urban atmosphere. How unlike Three Rivers can you get?

Pittsburgh is a city of rivers and thus a city of bridges, so a wrong turn driving can be costly. Some of the bridges aren't accessible from certain freeways, while others enter tunnels without letting you off where you'd like. Don't simply look at the map and expect that a bridge or highway will get you where you need to be, because there's no guaranteeing it. As a rule of thumb, if you're coming in from and returning to the north, then park north of the park. If you're coming in and returning to the east, south, or west, then you should park downtown, south of the ballpark, and walk across the Clemente Bridge. The downtown lots vary in price, but the best bet is the Ft. Duquesne and 6th Street Garage at 126 Sixth St. That will give you an after 4:00 p.m. rate between $2 and $5. Steer clear of garages near Theater Square, especially between 7th and 9th Streets on Penn Avenue, because there are theater shows going on most nights of the week that drive the event price up. Be wary of parking at any city meters. In 2011, the city moved the time that they would charge for parking meters past the standard 6:00 p.m. and they decreased the amount of minutes you get for each quarter you plug, so the old standard of finding a meter at 5 p.m. and plugging it for an hour won't always work any longer. You may get booted or ticketed for not reading the meter closely enough. There are still a few free parking spaces on the North Side of the city, specifically north of West Park, but losing the meters makes the walk to PNC quite a bit longer. If you're staying in town, you might be able to get to the game by bus or the light-rail/subway system, known as the "T." The Wood Street stop is only three blocks from the Clemente Bridge. A tunnel known as the North Shore Connector now brings a "T" stop to this side of the Allegheny River, but the closest stop is the North Shore Station, which is two blocks from PNC's Home Plate Gate. By contrast, the Allegheny Station stop a few blocks away lets off directly in front of Heinz Field. Maybe the city does love its Steelers more.

Light Rail Info: www.portauthority.org/PAAC/Customer Info/BuswaysandT/LightRailTransitSystem/tabid/186/Default.aspx

If you're on the south side and you have an extra $10 burning a hole in your pocket, a great way to get to the game is by taking the Gateway Clipper, a passenger ferry system that departs from Station Square. You can park or take the "T" there, then ride a ferry across all three of "the Burgh's" famous rivers: the Monongahela, the Ohio, and the Allegheny. The line gets pretty crowded at the Station Square dock before the game and at the dock along the Riverwalk afterward, so plan ahead. But then again, there are plenty of places to go out in Station Square, and someone else is driving the ferryboat, so relax and have a brew or two during or after the game.

Ballpark Tours

PNC offers tours beginning in mid-April. You can schedule a tour by calling the tour hotline at (412) 325-4700, or by e-mailing pncparktours@pirates.com.

Outside Attractions

THE CLEMENTE BRIDGE

Whether or not you park downtown, walking across the Roberto Clemente Bridge is an essential part of the ballpark experience when visiting PNC. Formerly known as the Sixth Street Bridge, this steel cable-suspension bridge is one of three similar bridges that cross the Allegheny and date from the mid-1920s. They are collectively known as the Three Sisters and are an essential part of the beauty of the skyline, all painted yellow.

Before, during, and after each game, the city closes the Clemente Bridge and connecting Federal Street that runs in front of PNC to car traffic, making them pedestrian-only areas that truly become part of the ballpark. You'll find street musicians and people hawking tickets, peanuts, Pirates banners, shirts, and memorabilia. We'll be honest, we saw quite a bit of Steelers paraphernalia on sale as we crossed, too. As you cross the Allegheny you're treated to a wonderful view of the park, the river, and the city. The bridge ends at the ballpark where there stands an impressive statue of Clemente.

RIVER WALKING

Equally important as crossing the bridge is walking under it along the Riverwalk. This long stretch of developed embankment along the Allegheny will make you further appreciate the urban renaissance that the north side has undergone in the past few years. The bulkhead that embanks the ballpark was built during the construction of the park and is made of the same Minnesota limestone as PNC. The archways that decorate the embankments were designed to recall those that surrounded Forbes Field. And don't forget, the Riverwalk is just beyond the right-field wall and is the place players are trying to hit with long fly balls during batting practice. Boating ball fans will travel up the rivers of the Burgh to moor their crafts along the Riverwalk prior to games, with the hope of catching one on the bounce, or one delivered right to their craft. But in order to hit the water, a ball must travel at least 443 feet from home plate. And only a few have managed this feat. Daryl Ward of Houston remains the only player to ever hit a ball into the Allegheny on the fly during an official game. Ward did it on July 6, 2002, while playing for Houston. Kip Wells was the pitcher who gave up the blast.

The only players to have sort of matched the feat did it during the Home Run Derby when the 2006 All Star Game was held at PNC. It was the fifth time Pittsburgh hosted the Mid-Summer Classic (twice at Forbes Field and twice at Three Rivers) and the five blasts that sailed over the right-field wall and into the Allegheny rang out like cannon fire that evening, but still paled in comparison to Ward having accomplished it during an actual game.

STATUES TO THE FOUR

A walk around the entirety of the ballpark footprint reveals four statues honoring the greatest Pirates to ever don the gold and black.

THE GREAT ONE

Clemente's statue is the first you'll encounter crossing the Bridge and originally was erected at Three Rivers. Engravings beneath his figure list important dates spanning his outstanding life and career, right up until the date of his tragic death in a plane crash. He was bringing relief supplies to earthquake-torn Nicaragua. Clemente was more than one of the greatest ballplayers to play the game. He was a humanitarian and a graceful man who never forgot his roots—a citizen of the world, and one of those people who make you proud to be a human being. The Pirates have done well to honor him thusly.

"POPS"

Along Federal Street is the statue of Wilver "Willie" Stargell. Loved by the city first, and then by the nation, Pops is shown ready to put his ample frame fully into his mighty cut, as he did for a career mark of 475 home runs. Sadly, on April 1, 2001, PNC's Grand Opening and the day of the statue's premiere, Stargell passed away at sixty-one years of age from longterm health complications. "Pops" will never be forgotten as long as PNC stands.

Beneath Pop's feet are the "Bucco Bricks" that fans purchased for minimum donations of one dollar, that now bear their engraved names. All money gathered by the project went toward construction of the ballpark.

"MAZ"

The third statue, a fourteen-and-a-half-foot depiction of Bill Mazeroski, was erected in September 2010 to commemorate perhaps the greatest moment in Pirates history—Game 7 of the 1960 World Series against the Yankees. With the Bronx Bombers favored to win, the game was tied 9-9 heading to the bottom of the ninth inning. Leading off against Ralph Terry, Maz knocked the second pitch over the ivy-covered wall to bring the title home to Pittsburgh. The statue depicts Maz as he rounded second base after hitting his dinger, leaping into the air and waving his hat around in circles as he navigated his way through the fans who littered the field. Many people, even outside Pittsburgh, still consider this one of the greatest World Series ever played. Maz, always the gentleman and humble as can be, became very emotional at the unveiling of the statue, stating he always knew that his team would have won that game even if he

Honus Wagner statue

Photo by Josh Pahigian/Kevin O'Connell

didn't hit that home run. Well, he did. And Pittsburgh cannot forget it. For more on that fateful "Shot heard round the Burgh," check out the segment below on visiting the location of Forbes Field.

THE FLYING DUTCHMAN

The final statue stands near the west entrance. Honus Wagner was perhaps the greatest Pirate of them all. Wagner won eight batting titles and was a member of the first class of inductees to the Baseball Hall of Fame, along with Babe Ruth, Ty Cobb, Walter Johnson, and Christy Mathewson. Not bad company. This statue stood in Schenley Park near Forbes Field, and at Three Rivers previously.

BANNER PLAYERS

To honor the remaining Pirate greats, banners extend around the entire exterior block, emblazoned with names like Ralph Kiner, Arky Vaughan, Vern Law, Chuck Tanner, and Tony Pena. John Candelaria has his own banner, too. The "Candy Man" threw the first no-hitter in front of a Pittsburgh crowd on August 9, 1976, blanking the Dodgers 2–0. It was the five hundredth game for the Pirates at Three Rivers. Also honored on the banner walk are Francisco Cordova (nine innings) and Ricardo Rincon (one inning), who combined to hurl the first multi-pitcher extra-inning no-hitter, on July 12, 1997, against the Astros, before a capacity crowd at Three Rivers.

WORTH GOING THE EXTRA MILE
The Clemente Museum
3339 Penn Ave.
www.clementemuseum.com

No baseball trip to Pittsburgh would be complete without a stop at the Roberto Clemente museum. This museum is open by appointment only, so visit the website or call ahead. The proprietor is Duane Rieder, who besides being a highly accomplished photographer and baseball super-fan has, with the help of the Clemente family, put together the world's finest collection of photographs, uniforms, Gold Glove awards, letters, baseball cards, and everything else under the sun that you could imagine relating to Clemente. If you have any love of baseball or humanity in general, you will seek out this museum. As it says on the website: "All will leave inspired."

WESTERN PENNSYLVANIA SPORTS MUSEUM
Heinz History Center
1212 Smallman St.

A surprisingly short walk from the ballpark (a mile or so) is a comprehensive museum of sports in Western PA, a region fairly well obsessed with its residents' sporting lives.

UNDER THE BRIDGE DOWNTOWN
Also worth seeking out in the city is the intersection of Ross Street, Court Place, and Second Avenue under a bridge overpass. A wonderful mural has been painted here honoring all of Pittsburgh's baseball players from the Pirates to the Crawfords and Grays. The Art Institute of Pittsburgh presented the mural to the city in 2000. It features Honus Wagner, Willie Stargell, Roberto Clemente, Josh Gibson, and many others all standing together on the same field of dreams.

Watering Holes and Outside Eats
PNC Park has managed to deliver what so many other parks have promised and failed to bring about: an economic boon to the surrounding area in the form of good places to eat and drink that have risen out of a vast sea of parking lots. A dozen restaurant/pubs, three hotels, a couple of sports stores, and even an outdoor music venue have popped up since the opening of PNC. Okay, some of the development is the result of Heinz Field (home of the NFL Steelers) as well, but you get the point. Besides that, there is no shortage of places to get a drink in this town.

DIAMOND PIZZA
101 Federal St.

Not the best slice you'll ever have, but not too shabby, either. Diamond offers a nice selection of pregame grub for those who want to get into the ballpark quickly so they can snag a batting practice ball. We recommend the four cheese.

ATRIA'S RESTAURANT & TAVERN
103 Federal St.
www.atrias.com

This is part of a local chain of moderately expensive restaurants, but with a twist. Local Rock-n-Roll legend Johnny Angel (Jerry Lee Lewis era, that is) is the owner. Johnny is usually in the place. You'll recognize him by the platinum blonde pompadour and colorful jacket. He and his band, The Halos, operate this Atrias as their own personal Hard Rock Café, with guitars and trademark jackets on the walls. The band often plays in the restaurant and hosts other bands as well. The food? It's good enough, but not cheap. Like Johnny Angel himself, your parents would like this place a lot.

HALL OF FAME CLUB
115 Federal St.

This space used to be an Outback Steakhouse. They've converted it into club seating for all ticket holders. Unlike the actual Club Level, it's out in left field. But hey, what do you want for nothing? This would be a great place to host a party or a Little League sports banquet. The food is unremarkable, but if you do go, try the crab fries appetizer.

DOMINIC'S FAMOUS DELI AND BOTTLE SHOP
115 Federal St.

Of all the choices of places to go out on this strip attached to the ballpark, we recommend Dominic's. It's a delicatessen that might not be as famous as the name suggests, but it should be. Meat and cheese are piled high on sandwiches made of soft and fresh breads. The hot dogs are good too. And don't forget the bottle shop, which sells more than grape soda.

MULLEN'S BAR & GRILL
200 Federal St.
http://mullensbarandgrill.com/pittsburgh/

This pseudo-Irish pub imported from Wrigleyville now occupies prime real estate outside the ballpark on the corner of Federal and General Robinson Streets. A selection of pizza, burgers, and other pub grub will feed the pregame munchies and is relatively inexpensive, but not distinctive. The specialty of the house has to be the Italian beef, which is recommended. The offerings may be more Chicago than Pittsburgh, but Pittsburghers have room for another sandwich in their hearts.

SOHO (KITCHEN – COCKTAILS – CLUB)
203 Federal St.
www.sohopittsburgh.com

From the outside, this looks like it might be a yuppie hell-hole. But it's not. One part sports bar, one part hotel restaurant, it suffers from a bit of a dual-personality. But there are plenty of beers on the list and the menu has some decent food. It is however a bit on the frilly end of pregame options.

NORTH SHORE SALOON
208 Federal St.
www.northshoresaloon.com

This looks like the kind of place mindless frat boys go before the game, and it is. One of the cheaper places to get a beer near the ballpark, you had better get a seat at the bar early if you plan on drinking before a game.

FINNEGAN'S WAKE IRISH PUB
20 E. General Robinson St.
www.finniganspittsburgh.com

Finnegan's Wake has come a long way since we published our first ballpark guide. It's grown into a decent little (read: BIG) Irish pub, with traditional Irish music and a staff that has learned to pour a nice pint of Guinness. The food is good, as Irish food goes, but we recommend doing what the Irish do—drink your meal and eat later at the ballpark.

BRÜ LOUNGE
20 E. General Robinson St.

We try to avoid places with umlauts in the title on basic principle alone. This is your place if you wear a tie to bed and need to have cocktails while you network before completely missing out on the baseball road trip experience. If you're like us the Brü is too frou-frou for you.

CLARK BAR AND GRILL
503 Martindale St.
www.thepipagroup.com/clarkbar/

Now here's a gem of a place that could have coined the term "hole in the wall" as it is more than a bit difficult to find if you're from out of town. Just two blocks from the Home Plate entrance of PNC, the Clark Bar is hidden away in the D.L. Clark building, where they used to make the actual Clark Bars. Don't remember those? Think Butterfinger and you've got it.

The Clark is a sports bar with a bit of history (it opened in 1989) and is decorated as such. The food is delicious and well-prepared without being pretentious. Seafood options, such as salmon and mussels, are among the high-end options. But we recommend the Boomer Burger, which is served as you like it and topped with tomato, onion, egg, and cheese.

MCFADDEN'S SALOON
211 North Shore Dr.
www.mcfaddenspitt.com

This may now be Pittsburgh's biggest Irish bar, taking the title away from Finnegan's Wake. Except for the fact that McFadden's is about as authentically Irish as Josh is. It's a chain, there is one in every major city in America, and so we have to say "avoid it" like overcooked cabbage. On the positive side of the ledger, it is close to the right-field entrance to the ballpark, the food isn't that expensive, and it is the place where you are most likely to see waitresses or other random women dancing on the bar top. If you're looking for a frat party, this is your place.

HYDE PARK PRIME STEAK HOUSE
247 North Shore Dr.
www.hydeparkrestaurants.com

Though it's a high-end chain throughout the Great Lakes region, this is a nice place, with a dress code, valet parking, quality steaks, chops, fish, fine wines, scotches, and cigars. Yeah, we can't afford it either.

RIVERTOWNE NORTH SHORE
337 North Shore Dr.
www.myrivertowne.com

A local chain with a fine reputation, this location has yet to deliver on the promise of the franchise. We recommend going to the Clark Bar instead, for the same done better.

THE TILTED KILT
353 North Shore Dr.
www.tiltedkilt.com

Busting out of Las Vegas and onto the local pub scene is this breastaurant. Think Hooters girls in micro-kilts and push-up bras. We can't say any more about this place than they say about themselves in a clever little limerick:

"Come men, have no fear" (because no self-respecting woman would go into this place)

"Good food, (meh) pretty girls," (um, okay) "and cold frothy beer" (one out of three ain't too shabby).

"Where the girls wear their kilts" (so do the male wait-staff, btw)

"The Pints always tilt" (when you can get one)

"And there's no place friendlier than here." (If by friendly, you mean half-dressed, hair sprayed big, and full of attitude.)

DAMON'S NORTH SHORE
300 Block, North Shore Dr.
www.damons.com/

You are sure to get a few things when you enter a Damon's: plenty of big-screen TVs, a decent sound system, and ribs,

ribs, ribs. Not the best ribs you'll ever have, but not the worst.

JEROME BETTIS GRILLE 36
375 North Shore Dr.
www.jeromebettisgrille36.com

Jerome "The Bus" Bettis was a likable player and a Pittsburgh favorite. This is a nice place to sit outside and have a few drinks and some apps before the game. Higher-end food options are available alongside more standard fare, but the dish to try is the Black and Gold Lobster Raviolis. It's a bit pricey, but so delicious. One really weird feature of the place is its two way mirrors in the men's room that allow urinal users to see restaurant-goers while taking care of their duties. Just don't get stage fright like Josh. Trust us, they can't see you.

THE RIVERS CASINO
777 Casino Dr.
www.theriverscasino.com

Keep walking along the Riverwalk or past Heinz Field and eventually you'll make it to the Rivers Casino. After a game, this place is always open to take your money, um, we mean to offer you a gaming experience. It's a full service casino with spectacular views of the three rivers and downtown, complete with table games, dance clubs, and places to eat, ranging from a decent buffet to steaks and chops.

Josh recommends saving on parking or cab fare to the game by jumping the hotel shuttle at your hotel and walking to the ballpark from the casino.

Kevin: The casino bars have cheap drink and wings during happy hour, which runs from 6 to 8 p.m., making for a nice pregame.

Josh: Why not? You know we're going to wind up there afterwards anyway.

Other Cool Spots to Visit in Pittsburgh

For a bit more traditional pregame experience, East Carson Street in the South Side Flats offers blocks and blocks of bars and clubs that are worth visiting. There are a bevy of great spots to have a beer or hear some music on this street including Fatheads for a sandwich as big as your head, Club Café to catch some cool tunes, Smokin' Joe's Saloon for an excellent beer selection, and Piper's Pub.

Station Square is another place to park and get something to eat before the game or to go out for some nightlife afterward. Station Square is the place to head if you're interested in finding the local Hard Rock Café and places such as that. You can even take the "Monongahela Incline," sort of a

cross between a ski lift and steep streetcar, up to the top of Mount Washington for a truly spectacular view of the city.

Another neighborhood with great late-night action is the Strip District, though Josh was disappointed to find its name misleading. At least he had plenty of one-dollar bills handy during the rest of the road trip whenever he wanted to buy a soda. This is a club-heavy, dance and music scene for those who want to drop some cash to see bands or meet members of the opposite gender. On Penn Avenue, visit Mullaney's Harp and Fiddle, one of Pittsburgh's best Irish bars.

PRIMANTI BROTHERS
Multiple Locations
www.primantibros.com

Though a limited selection of Primanti Brothers sandwiches is available inside PNC Park, you should make some time to stop into the original sandwich shop in the Strip District while you visit Pittsburgh. The specialty of the house has always been "working-man sandwiches," for the men who plied the mills and had no time to fuss with side dishes. With fries and coleslaw piled high right into the sandwich, along with your choice of meat and cheese, these sandwiches will disappoint no one, except Josh. When he ordered the number two bestseller, "steak and cheese," he was expecting Philly style. The Pittsburgh-style Salisbury steak did not "agree" with his delicate palate. But Kevin's Capicola was delicious. And they're open late.

Josh: The first time we ate here the woman making our sandwich was smoking a cigarette.

Kevin: Yeah, you were pretty freaked out.

Josh: Now Pittsburgh has an ordinance against smoking.

Kevin: That's only in restaurants, pal. This place is technically a bar that serves food.

Josh: Splendid.

THE ORIGINAL HOT DOG SHOP
3901 Forbes Ave.

The "O" is another place not to be missed. It is located in Oakland near the University of Pittsburgh and is a quick detour if you're headed to visit the remnants of Forbes Field. "O" dogs are legendary in Pittsburgh and Kevin recommends the big kosher. Perhaps these delicious dogs are only outdone by the "O" fries. Pittsburghers adore french fries, even as a main course, and these are served nice and greasy with salt and cups of cheese, vinegar, and Heinz ketchup. Each heaping order spills out of its paper container. Don't get the large unless you can eat like Willie Stargell used to.

Pittsburgh Crawfords versus Homestead Grays

Both of these clubs can make a strong argument for having been the most successful Negro League team in history. Interestingly, they do so claiming many of the same players as alumni.

The Homestead Grays were founded in 1910 and played their games at West Field in Homestead, Pennsylvania, and later in Pittsburgh at Gus Greenlee field and at Forbes. They won the Eastern Championship defeating the New York Lincoln Giants in 1930. Then they won it again the next year as Josh Gibson hit for a .367 average and belted seventy-five home runs. But the onset of the Depression brought hard times to the Negro Leagues and it would take the Grays years to reestablish their dominance. And by then, the franchise had moved to Washington, D.C.

When Gibson jumped ship to the crosstown Pittsburgh Crawfords in 1932, so did the championships. But this time he had the help of the great Satchel Paige. The Crawfords played home games at Ammon Field and Greenlee Field in the Hill District, and finished a single game behind the Chicago American Giants in the first half of the 1933 Negro National League's split season. The second half was never completed and Greenlee, who was also the league manager, awarded the Crawfords the disputed Negro National League championship. The Crawfords went on to defeat the New York Cubans in 1935 for their first undisputed pennant in one of the greatest series the Negro Leagues ever played. They also claimed another confused pennant in 1936. During the '30s Gibson routinely hit better than .400 while also banging in home runs at a staggering pace, and with Paige winning twenty-five to thirty games per year, it's no wonder the Crawfords are widely regarded as the most successful team in the history of the Negro Leagues. For a bit of this history, a marker stands at 2217 Bedford Avenue designating Ammon Field and some of Gibson's accomplishments. A ball field has been built on the site, keeping the spirit of the Crawfords and Greenlee Field alive in the Hill District. You can also visit the gravesite of Josh Gibson, the man many called "the black Babe Ruth," by heading to Allegheny Cemetery at 4734 Butler St.

PIEROGIES PLUS
342 Island Ave., McKees Rocks, PA
www.pierogiesplus.com

In Pittsburgh you can get these tasty little Eastern European treats just about anywhere. Though they're great inside the park, our favorite spot for them is Pierogies Plus. It's an old gas station where you can get your drive-through pierogies in a Styrofoam container. Now Josh just needs to convince Heather to wear a babushka.

Inside the Park

As we have stated, PNC Park endeavors to excel at one thing and one thing only: ensuring fans enjoy the game of baseball. That's it. Its class comes from the fact that there are not too many frills. PNC has the design and feel of an old park, with all that you want in a brand new facility. You'll find no merry-go-rounds for the kids, no gigantic corporate promotions that masquerade as entertainment. Other than a fizzing sound made in the right-field bleachers by a cola company that we refuse to name, there are few distractions at PNC. Rather you'll find good old-fashioned baseball in its most natural environment. In making the park a two-level facility, keeping a very limited amount of foul territory (seats behind home plate are only fifty-one feet from the batter's box), and by putting the press level above all the others, they have clearly set the priority on the fans, and the action of the game.

At PNC they've also done a good job prioritizing modern amenities—wide concourses, lots of different places to eat, and a lot of good food set on the outside of the concourse, again to not get in the way of the game for those taking a stroll.

Kevin: Apparently, if you build it, they still may or may not come.

Josh: Still waiting for a legit contender here in the Burgh.

As we stated previously, what we like best about the park is its use of local and unique materials. Steel, limestone, and yellow brick on the outside facade and in decorative places inside add beauty and local flavor. The steel is prominent on the Rotunda concourse that takes you up and around, but also in the lighting fixtures and the steps on the stairs. In order to hang the luxury boxes under the second deck, thicker steel I-beams were necessary and can be found fastened with huge exposed bolts, adding beauty along with support.

Ballpark Features
LEGACY SQUARE
If you come into the park through the Left-field entrance you'll be impressed to find a fitting tribute to the town's

Negro League players and teams. The team has hung over-sized fiberglass bats above the entrance, bearing player and team names. There are also life-sized bronzes of Cool Papa Bell, Oscar Charleston, Josh Gibson, Judy Johnson, Buck Leonard, Satchel Paige and Smokey Joe Williams. Kiosks give information about each player who's earned a statue, making Legacy Square a fun and informative way to spend some pregame time.

RETIRED NUMBERS

Retired numbers for the Pirates hang at the bottom of the second deck and above the boxes and light up in neon. Down the right-field line are: Jackie Robinson's No. 42; Roberto Clemente's No. 21; Bill Mazeroski's No. 9; Pie Traynor's No. 20; and Ralph Kiner's No. 4. Down the left-field line are Billy Meyer's No. 1; Honus Wagner's No. 33; Willie Stargell's No. 8; and Danny Murtaugh's No. 40.

STRAIGHT OUT OF FORBES FIELD

Though the hanging luxury boxes and the press box attached to the roof clearly draw from the beauty of Wrigley Field, the influence of Forbes Field on the design of PNC cannot be overstated. Fans of the old park will quickly recognize the seven vertical steel light towers of blue painted steel surrounding the park, and the choice of blue seats, all heavily influenced by Forbes. But there are a few others we'd like to point out that might not be so obvious, unless you visited Forbes back in its glory day. (We didn't.)

RIVERWALK ARCHES

Along the Riverwalk on PNC Park's exterior, stone arches are reminiscent of those at street level along old Forbes Field's exterior.

"21"

The right-field wall is twenty-one feet high. Why? If you can't guess this one you haven't been paying attention. Number 21 patrolled right field for the Pirates for more than eighteen seasons. Fans loved him, his teammates and the world respected him. It seems fitting that the Pirates honor him in this wonderfully understated, but ever-present fashion.

OUT-OF-TOWN SCOREBOARD

Not only does the old-fashioned electric scoreboard on the right-field wall provide the scores of all the games, it also tells what inning the game is in, how many outs there are, and how many runners are on base, with a cool retro-lighted diamond system, just like they used to have at Forbes Field.

Our only suggestion for improvement: Give us the number of who is pitching for each team so we'll know how our fantasy teams are doing.

When a ball hits this scoreboard a tinny clanking sound rings out, so we're not too sure what it's made of, but it's one of several surfaces that a ball could hit, including chain-link and exposed concrete. Right fielders have to deal with the ball bouncing differently depending on where it hits this scoreboard. In case you're wondering, the team slates are manual, but the rest is updated electronically over the wire.

THE NOOK

The nook in left-center is reminiscent of the deep left-center of Forbes, which was 457 feet from the plate and helped Owen "Chief" Wilson set the Major League record for triples with thirty-six in 1912. The bullpens extend out to the right of the nook at PNC, which gives the field's odd protrusion a bit more of a naturally occurring feel than the similar oddities at other ballparks recently built.

THE DREYFUSS MEMORIAL

This memorial that used to be in play in center field at Forbes was moved first to Three Rivers and now sits inside the home plate entrance to PNC. It honors Barney Dreyfuss, the Pirates owner who built Forbes Field. At the time, the public sentiment was that Dreyfuss was building the park too far from downtown. Thus, many people referred to Forbes as Dreyfuss's Folly in its early days. But the ballpark survived to outlive many of its detractors.

THE KIDS ARE ALL RIGHT

Behind left field is a nice little picnic area, a place to scarf down some food, and a kids' play area, complete with a small jungle gym. There is also a tiny replica of the ballpark—complete with the limestone that adorns PNC's exterior.

Josh: So, there was a jungle gym at Forbes Field too, I take it.

Kevin: Um, no.

HEY, NICE VIEW

We noticed that the Pirates dugout is on the third-base line, visitors on the first. Perhaps even the team wants to take in the beautiful view of downtown while its players wait to take the field. If you're interested in ambience, sitting along the left-field bend is best, because in right you lose the view of downtown a bit with the outfield bleachers above the high right-field wall. And the downtown view is one of the best in baseball: the skyline, Clemente Bridge, and the boats sailing past. There is no ballpark view better in all of Major League Baseball, except perhaps the view over the Bay at AT&T Park in San Francisco.

In straightaway center is the batter's eye—a large green blockade of the river and downtown area that prevents the distraction of the hitters. At the base of the batter's eye, sculpted into the grassy knoll 399 feet away, beyond the center-field fence, are low shrubs that spell out "Pirates" in surprisingly distinctive script.

Kevin: If only they took care of their infield this well.

Josh: Do you mean the field, or the players?

TECHNOLOGICALLY SPEAKING

While Three Rivers had a sound system located in center field that often was inaudible, PNC has a top-notch system that can be heard everywhere in the park. The JumboTron at PNC cost $2.1 million, more than the entire cost to build Forbes Field. It includes a full entertainment package that features the Pirate Parrot, a scurvy-ridden pirate, and an opening sequence of Pirate ships sailing into the Three Rivers that is worthy of a Johnny Depp movie. Beneath the scoreboard is a small closed-captioned scoreboard for the hearing impaired that provides a print version of everything the public address announcer says. Also, beneath the scoreboards that run along the baselines, is another scoreboard that gives the speed of each pitch.

Kevin: Pretty easy to tell the curve balls from the fastballs judging by the pitch speed alone.

Josh: Not for the home town team.

Kevin: "Ouch."

IN CASE OF ENCROACHING BOREDOM . . .

If the game is dull and you've already bought and read the newspaper, look across the river into the city and you should be able to make out what looks like a movie screen mounted atop one of the buildings. It's actually a plasma screen courtesy of the Art Institute of Pittsburgh. The screen projects different colored shapes and designs for your own interpretation.

WHAT YOU WON'T SEE

The Pirates clubhouse inside PNC is eighteen thousand square feet, as opposed to the four-thousand-square-foot room the team used at Three Rivers. It too has much steel in the design, as well as old-style wooden lockers. Next to the clubhouse is a warm-up mound and batting cages so players can stay loose during rain delays. The floor of the cages is covered with artificial turf from Three Rivers.

Inside Eats

There's a lot to try in Pittsburgh, and much of it is tough to find in other cities' ballparks, so dig in. We found some of the best and most unique food in baseball in this park.

KAHN'S HOT DOG (DOG REVIEW)

This is a pretty good dog and it's affordably priced. We've had Kahn's franks in other parks, and this dog is fairly typical of Kahn's. We recommend instead getting the Hebrew National dog at the Federal Street Grille (inside the park).

PIEROGIES (TRADEMARK FOOD)

These little Eastern European pasta ravioli are stuffed with potatoes, cheese, onions or garlic. You sure as heck aren't going to find them anywhere else, so eat up. We suggest butter, salt, and pepper to top them off, and watch out, they're steaming hot!

> ### Chicken on the Hill
>
> Team announcer Bob Prince is primarily responsible for coining this phrase. Once when Willie belted a homerun, Prince began shouting "Chicken on the Hill!" having claimed earlier that the chicken restaurant Stargell owned in the Hill District was going to give out free chicken if he homered. Of course they weren't, but the phrase "Chicken on the Hill" became a trademark Prince used whenever Pops went deep.

PRIMANTI BROTHERS SANDWICHES (TRADEMARK FOOD)

While Josh was partial to the pierogies, Kevin fell in love with this Pittsburgh treat so we decided to award two trademark foods. Primanti Brothers is located behind Section 310. These sandwiches are served piled with your choice of meat and with french fries and coleslaw tossed right on. There are no special orders at the Primanti Brothers stand until after the sixth inning. The sandwiches are good if you get them early, being that they're premade. But they fade in quality as the game goes on and they cost a buck and a quarter more inside the park than at the shops in town. So if you're heading toward one of their locations, we recommend getting your sandwich from the source. Or wait until after the sixth inning and ask for a sandwich sans the slaw, which will be made fresh for you on the spot.

BEST OF THE REST

Super Fries stands offer cheese fries, garlic fries, and chili fries. They're tasty and greasy and deep-fat fried—just how

Pittsburgh's Old Ballparks

Since the Pirates have had so many ballparks, why not visit them all? Or what's left of them. The closest, Exposition Park, was located in the parking lots in between PNC Park and Heinz Field. Look for the historic marker because that's all that's left.

Recreation Park was located in the historic Allegheny West District, near Allegheny and Pennsylvania Avenues. There is nothing left to even indicate that a ballpark stood there.

The remains of Forbes Field on the University of Pittsburgh campus offer the most to see of the former Pirates homes. The outfield wall still has ivy growing over the brick, and the flagpole that was "in play" is perhaps the most fitting remnant of an old park we've found yet. The numbers marking the distances are still painted on the brick in white (457 feet to the flagpole in left-center, 436 to right-center). Follow the brick outline of the ballpark wall that runs across the street, marking the location of the left-field fence, until you reach the plaque dedicated to Bill Mazeroski. Die-hard fans gather here once a year on October 14th to listen to the radio broadcast of the 1960 World Series when "Maz's" shot sailed over these very walls and brought another championship to the Pirates.

Inside the lobby of the Joseph M. Katz Graduate School of Business building across from the wall you will find Forbes' home plate. Walk around looking at the ground and you'll see it resting peacefully under Plexiglas in its original location. The skyscraper across the street is Pitt University's Cathedral of Learning. While an impressive blend of Gothic and modern architecture, the cathedral also provided a view right down into Forbes Field, and during the World Series (and other crowded games) held the honor of being the highest bleacher seats in baseball history.

For fans of the Negro Leagues, Pittsburgh is a veritable Mecca. Though the historical marker at 2217 Bedford Ave. is all that remains of Ammon Field, it is a nice tribute to Josh Gibson. There is a field still on the location, in Ammon Park, behind the Macedonia Baptist Church. Greenlee Field was just a few blocks down Bedford, along the 2500 block. There is very little remaining of the ballpark that was once the pride of the Negro Leagues, but a ball field has been built on the site to remind folks of the proud heritage of the Negro Leagues.

The Crawford Grill at 2141 Wylie Ave. was closed down and moved to the Station Square area of the city. It was an enormous loss to the Hill District community when the Grill closed, a veritable Mecca for the area, so Franco Harris has led a group of investors to buy the Crawford Grill and restore it. We wish the group well, because the place has such a wonderful baseball and jazz history that it should be preserved just as it was, a place where all could come and enjoy a great atmosphere and great food. Plus, John Coltrane, Mary Lou Williams, and Pittsburgh's own Art Blakey and Earl "Fatha" Hines once performed there.

A drive across the Homestead Grays Bridge (formerly the Hi-Level Bridge) will take you across the "Mon" River from Pittsburgh and into Homestead, opening up a plethora of sights to fans of the Negro Leagues. The bridge itself has been adorned with large metal placards depicting heroes of the Grays and Crawfords. Fittingly, there are nine for each team, facing off against one another just as the teams did so many years ago. Heading toward Homestead, the Grays are depicted on these large metal signs shaped a bit like elongated home plates, accented in Prussian blue, and bearing photographs. Heading back over the bridge into Pittsburgh, the Crawford greats are honored, accented in cranberry Crawford red. Dino Gaurino, a local sports painter, got the commission on these, and he did a fine job.

Once you're in Homestead, look for the marker dedicated to the Grays that stands on Amity Street, near Fifth Avenue, detailing just a slice of the team's accomplishments. Very close by, at the corner of 6th and Amity once stood the Sky Rocket Lounge, the owner of which owned the Grays for a time.

But the crown jewel of the Negro League historic nostalgia has got to be West Field, located in the town of Munhall, along Main Street between 19th and Orchard and behind the Munhall Borough Building. Huge rusted metal light stanchions and ornate masonry surround this decaying ballpark, letting visitors know what a grand baseball palace once stood on the grounds. The seating bowl is still in use, and the field, though a tad shabby, gives the feeling that great deeds were accomplished there. We sat in the ragged dugouts where Josh Gibson and Cool Papa Bell used to sit, and it gave us shivers.

Unlike Ammon Field and Greenlee Park, West Field remains in use, though now it is primarily a place where high school teams practice. Though it is in disrepair, it's not too far gone to be saved. Behind the park, the old entrance is used as a storage and salvage grounds.

Any account of the mighty Homestead Grays will tell you that this ballpark was once a jewel. With as much of the ballpark still intact as there is we could not figure out why it is not registered as a National Historical Site, as it should be. With a bit of effort, money, and political will, the surrounding cities of Munhall, Homestead, and West Homestead (or one of our readers) could put forth the effort to restore this hallowed ground and return it to its former glory.

Why should this ballpark be restored? Because of the nine players immortalized in bronze on the miniature field at the Negro League Museum (considered the greatest nine to have played in the Negro Leagues) five played a majority of their career with Pittsburgh teams, and four were Homestead Grays: Gibson, Judy Johnson, Buck Leonard, and Bell. Three more players who played a while with the Homestead Grays (Smokey Joe Williams, Bill Foster, and Martin Dihigo) are immortalized in the Baseball Hall of Fame in Cooperstown. If you include two more Hall of Famers, Pittsburgh Crawford Oscar Charleston and the great Satchel Paige who spent time in a Crawford uniform, it's clear that this area of the country has fielded some of the greatest talents in the history of the game. Surely, the legacy of these great players is worthy of the restoration of West Field. We implore interested parties to invest some money in this piece of living history.

we like 'em. Since there's no Major League ballpark in Buffalo, we also recommend getting some hot wings from Quaker Steak and Lube. Their large bucket isn't cheap, but "dere's like forty wings in dere."

Pops' Plaza is an area of Willie Stargell–themed stands off the main concourse on the first level. Head for the blue neon near the Rotunda in left field and see if you can guess all the Pops' references. Pub 475 serves Penn draft and Premium draft as well as pub grub. Familee BBQ is better than Manny's BBQ in the outfield. Pop's Potato Patch has freshly cut fries with toppings that include chili, nacho cheese, garlic, chives, and sour cream. Chicken on the Hill has two-, three- or four-piece dinners. Willie's Hit offers New York kosher style hot dogs, sauerkraut, chili, nachos supreme, and hand-rolled pretzels topped with salt, cinnamon and sugar, or garlic.

As for Manny's Barbecue, former Pirates catcher Manny Sanguillen operates this barbecue in center field and serves up sandwiches and platters of pit beef and smoked pork. We tried the pork, which was very tasty, healthy on the barbecue sauce but perhaps a bit too salty. It was also pricey for our liking, but good nonetheless.

Rita's Italian Ice is a cool and sweet treat on a hot day.

SAY "NO, THANKS," AND WALK AWAY

Most of the food offerings at PNC are good. In fact, one of their marketing campaigns was "Come Hungry!" We can only assume that people have not been coming merely for the baseball experience for the past two decades. However, there are items to avoid. The pizza is downright dreadful. Follow our "avoid pizza at the ballpark rule" here and thank us later.

BEERS OF THE BURGH

Pittsburgh has more than a few of its own breweries that offer beers at PNC. Penn Brewery has a nice selection that includes Penn Lager and Augustiner, a dark bock-style beer. The brewery is on the North Side and is worth a visit. But

for the old-time Pittsburgh beer drinkers, Yuengling is still what it's all about. This very tasty beer originates from the oldest brewery in America, dating from 1872. Iron City is yet another macro-brewery for which the Burgh is famous. Try an IC Light if you're counting calories.

The PNC Experience

The same limestone and yellow bricks used on the exterior of the park also line the openings of the tunnels leading to the seats and are visible along the low wall behind home plate. This ties the entire park together in a unified theme. But behind home plate it can actually affect play. If a wild pitch gets past the catcher, the uneven angles of the limestone can send the ball in crazy directions and lead to extra bases, or even runs. Here's hoping the hometown Bucs figure out these nuances and play them to their advantage . . . or file the edges off their fancy rocks.

TAILGATING HEAVEN

Since PNC opened, scores of pregame pubs and restaurants have opened near the ballpark. One might think this would signal the death knell of the more traditional tailgating that Pittsburghers have perfected on cold fall football days in support of their gridiron glories. Not so. Tailgates are alive and well in the Burgh, regardless of the sport or weather forecast. So why not break out the Hibachi, crack open a 40, pull up on a stretch of concrete, and enjoy the good life wandering among parking lots full of friends who are doing the same? There aren't many cities that can do it as well as Pittsburgh. Plus, it's within the road trip budget.

PIEROGIE RACES

Practically every ballpark has some kind of racing entertainment during one of the breaks between innings these days. We're not sure why. In Pittsburgh it's a pierogie race. Jalapeño Hanna, Cheese Chester, Sauerkraut Saul, and the highly sarcastic Oliver Onion are the pierogies in the running. First they compete on the scoreboard, then they finish as actual characters racing out onto the field. By the way, in a competition between the pierogies of "The Burgh" and the sausages of Milwaukee, the pierogies won out. See the Milwaukee chapter for more details on "Sausage Gate."

STILL HUNGRY? STRAPPED FOR CASH?

Watch for hot dogs being fired out of an air-gun by the Pirate Parrot. The Pirate Parrot is the team's mascot and is usually patrolling the park between innings, offering promotions that you might find in a minor league park. During play, look for him to roost atop the Pirates dugout.

LEFT FIELD LOONIES (SUPER-FANS)

The Left Field Loonies sit in Bleacher Reserved seats (Sections 133–138) and are easily the greatest super-fans still attending games at PNC. The short porch in left (325 feet) and the low wall just six feet above the field allow the Loonies to get into the ears of the opposing left fielder. Check out their website at www.leftfieldloonies.com and maybe they'll invite you to one of their tailgates. Trust us, it's worth it.

Cyber Super-Fans

- **Pittsburgh Sports**
  www.pittsburghsports.net
- **Bucs Dugout**
  www.bucsdugout.com/
- **Rum Bunter**
  http://rumbunter.com/
- **Pirates Home Plate**
  www.pirateshomeplate.com/

THE LEMONADE MAN (SUPER-FAN HALL OF FAME)

Kenny "The Lemonade Man" Geidel passed away in May of 2011, and the city lost one of its greatest super-fans. For decades Geidel could be heard at Pirates, Penguins, and Steelers games shouting "Limon-aaaaaaade" in his distinctive squealing style. He also sold cotton candy and soft drinks. This town will likely not see another vendor who worked harder, had more charm, and embodied the teams he loved. Rest in peace, Kenny.

"SCREECH OWL" MCALLISTER (SUPER-FAN HALL OF FAME)

Back in the 1930s, Bruce "Screech Owl" McAllister rose to prominence at Forbes Field as the most famous Pirates

---

The Local Bushers

The Altoona Curve, Erie Seawolves, and Buffalo Bison are minor league teams that won't take you too far out of your way. But also check out the Washington Wildthings who have introduced perhaps the funniest minor league team name since the Toledo Mudhens. An independent member of the Frontier League, the Wildthings just opened a new park, Falconi Field, twenty minutes away, in the town of Washington, Pennsylvania.

---

rooter yet. His screech, which some compared to the sound a train-whistle made, prompted Pirates management to bribe him to put a sock in it with the promise of free season-tickets for life. He took the deal, but continued to screech, just not as frequently, and only at key moments in the game.

On Our Way Out of Pittsburgh
We Got Lost . . . Very Lost

As we've already mentioned, if you don't know where you're headed in this city of bridges and tunnels, you can get really lost, really quickly. Here's a story from our first baseball road trip that was too good not to retell.

After an enjoyable game at PNC where we witnessed a Pirates loss, we walked back across the Clemente Bridge to the car. We had an early game the next day in Cincinnati and needed to get a head start. We were on the right road for a while, but something happened. Something bad. Yeah, we got lost. Josh attributed it to Kevin not paying attention to his driving. Kevin blamed Josh for being a bad navigator. Josh blamed the stereo, which had been "acting up" and distracting him. It turned out, it was just one of Kevin's many Bob Dylan CDs and it was working fine. But before we knew it, we were in a town called Beaver, Pennsylvania. We're not making this up.

Finally Josh realized he had the map upside down and set us on a course along the Ohio River in search of Interstate 70 South. What we found were the remaining steel mills, coalmines, and nuclear facilities that once made this region famous. At night, however, it was eerie as hell, the steam glowing orange from the fires in the kilns.

To make matters worse, Kevin had let the gas gauge drop down near empty and we were going to have to stop in one of these little towns for petrol.

"How could you let it get down so low?" Josh cried, doubtlessly envisioning his demise.

"I thought we'd get gas off the Interstate," huffed Kevin. "How was I to know you'd lose the entire freeway."

"I didn't lose the freeway!"

"Well, the freeway certainly didn't lose us!"

In any case, neither of us was looking forward to stopping for gas in one of these little shanty work towns, at night, and in a fancy rental car (we always travel in style) with out-of-state plates.

Eventually the main highway turned into a minor highway, and then into a country road. Then a funny thing happened somewhere south of East Liverpool. The road we were traveling on, that once was a highway, ended. It turned into a dirt road, then made a hard right turn. Then it was gone.

"What happened to the highway?" asked Kevin.

"I dunno," said Josh.

We slowed the car to see rickety wooden houses with dark shadowy figures sitting on the porches. Just then Kevin starting humming "Dueling Banjos" from the film *Deliverance*.

"Ba-da-da, dee-da-da-dee-dee-da."

"Cut that out!"

"Sorry," said Kevin. "Ba-da-da De-da."

"Stop!" cried Josh. Kevin laughed, but realized he was getting scared too.

And along this road we traveled, the porch sitters watching our every move. Then the dirt road made a hard left, and the car lunged, and the road was suddenly paved once again. A little town with an old gas station that still had its lights on became visible and we pulled in and got gas from a very normal-looking man with a very normal pattern of speech and a fair number of teeth.

About twenty miles down the road, however, as we recounted the details of our adventure, laughing and joking, Kevin was pulled over for speeding and was issued a ticket, which made Josh bust out laughing, until he remembered that we had previously agreed to split the cost of any moving violations.

CLEVELAND INDIANS, PROGRESSIVE FIELD

A Gateway Yard in the Forest City

Every fan worth his or her proverbial salt has seen the 1989 baseball film *Major League,* in which a failing Indians team in a failing ballpark in a failing city decides to shock the world and make a run at the pennant. The movie ends with those fictional Indians beating the dreaded Yankees in a one-game playoff to decide the AL East. What happens beyond that is anyone's guess. The future, as they say, is yet to be written.

In an instance of life imitating art, the real life Cleveland Indians moved into a new ballpark in 1994 and seemingly enjoyed the type of overnight success portrayed in the movie. The new park accomplished what every big league town hopes a new yard will do. It breathed fresh life and energy into the local nine, the fan base, and the city streets, to the tune of six playoff appearances between 1995 and 2001, 455 straight sellouts, and a thriving Gateway District restaurant and entertainment district.

The Indians staked their claim as one of the best teams of the 1990s and their ballpark became one of the best attended. Cleveland appeared likely to remain an AL force for a good long time. What moviegoers didn't learn until the second *Major League* movie, however, also came to pass in Cleveland. The fictional Indians team from the first movie didn't win it all. In the second movie we learn that the Tribe of Willie Mays Hayes and Ricky Vaughn, fresh off their defeat of the Yanks, promptly lost to the White Sox in the ALCS. Sure, they made a good run at baseball's ultimate prize, but in the end they fell short, just like the real Indians who came close, but were defeated in both the 1995 and 1997 World Series. We have to think that if there were a *Major League V,* set two decades after the magical run that reinvigorated the franchise, the silver screen would show the team floundering once again, before a discouraged fan base.

It seems hard to believe now that once upon a time, "Jacobs Field," as Cleveland's jewel of a park was originally known, was a lock to draw forty thousand fans per night and ranked at or near the top of the MLB attendance ledger. And the Indians finished each season at or near the top of the AL Central. But by 2010 the Indians' since-renamed ballpark sat more than half empty as the team stagnated in the AL's lower division. Even when the 2011 Indians stood in first place heading into the All-Star break, they did so having played the first half of their home slate before barely twenty thousand fans per game at Progressive Field. But even that was an improvement after they played two April games that season before announced crowds of 8,726 and 9,853 fans. Commentators and pundits thought those crowds actually numbered more like three thousand. In any event, they were the two smallest crowds in ballpark history and they weren't good signs. We're not sure if this ennui—which has been symptomatic of the Indians' fan base since the team's last title in 1948—is a product of not winning the "big one," or if the bad economy hit Cleveland's working class fans harder than the rooters in other cities, or if it's LeBron's fault. But we do know that the Indians veered off the template that's supposed to read: New Ballpark + Good Young Players = Success. And teams that build new yards in the future would be wise to study the situation in Cleveland and to learn from it. What happens once the novelty of a new park wears off? What happens if the home team has two or three ninety loss seasons in a row? What happens when the first wave of trendy new bars and restaurants to open around the park starts to disappear? Do things go back to the way they were before, or can a franchise regain its footing without sinking to the depths it once inhabited? We can't answer these questions. The future is yet to be written. But Cleveland, better than any other city that built a park during the retro renaissance, enjoyed instant success, and then fell on hard times, is the place where the first glimpse of an answer will be penned.

We're hoping the Indians return to their former glory sooner rather than later. When they do, no doubt Progressive Field will play a leading role. It's a great ballpark. Though it seats more than forty-three thousand people, most areas of the park feel quite intimate, with only a few sections being too far from the action for our taste. The field is eighteen feet below street level, which helps give the exterior more the look of a ballpark, rather than a towering stadium. From street level, the ballpark only rises 120 feet in the air, not including the light towers.

"The Prog," as it is often called, was designed with grandeur in mind, as well as baseball. Therefore, it is unashamedly larger than some of the other retro parks such as the ones in Pittsburgh and Miami. The Prog's exterior reflects the look of Cleveland itself, with light towers reminiscent of the town's smokestacks, and steel girders that recall the many bridges that cross the Cuyahoga River. The ballpark's pale yellow brick combines with the exposed steel to invoke the visage of classic ballparks past, as well as postindustrial stadiums.

Asymmetrical field dimensions are always nice, but since most all of the retro parks include them, what we really like to see in a field is distinctiveness, and Progressive Field is brimming with local flavor. Rising above the left-field scoreboard is the city of Cleveland, a wonderful backdrop that ensconces the yard in Cleveland-ness from the left-field corner to the home bullpen in right-center. Few cities can boast this kind of skyline view and it's a definite improvement over the backdrop at the team's old digs. A bit closer to the field than the Terminal Tower and other looming edifices, the "mini monster" in left field provides an added dimension for pitchers, hitters, and especially outfielders to consider. This nineteen-foot-high home run wall used to feature a manual scoreboard but now houses a lengthy LED board. The times they are a-changing even in places where retro-funk is celebrated.

Looking at the beauty of the field and skyline, it's hard to believe the original ballpark proposal called for a dome. Voters turned down a ballot measure that would have raised their property taxes to fund the ill-conceived notion. In turn, team owner Richard E. Jacobs turned to HOK for some open-air blueprints. The sticker price checked in at $175 million, which seems like a steal compared to subsequent ballparks that would open. Jacobs himself claimed naming rights—for a time—by funding 52 percent of the new park's construction. The remainder was publicly funded through a so-called "sin tax," a fifteen-year increase in alcohol and tobacco sales tax in Cuyahoga County. Hey, we can understand taxing smokers—but why alcohol? No fair, especially when doctors say drinking a beer or two a day promotes good health. But anyway, at least it's a voluntary tax—for most people. The Indians also presold all of the park's luxury boxes, and sold tax-exempt bonds to cover the remaining costs.

Previously, the Indians played at Municipal Stadium, an enormous structure that seated more than seventy thousand people. The ballpark felt empty and cavernous, even when a respectable crowd of, say, thirty thousand turned out. Municipal Stadium was meant to be the Yankee Stadium of Cleveland, built with high hopes that crowds would fill the place. In our baseball journeys we have found other cities like Toronto that have pejoratively nicknamed their stadiums the "Mistake by the Lake," but clearly the one in Cleveland, which was exposed to the brutal winds off Lake Erie, was the originator of this infamous moniker.

There are conflicting reports about why Cleveland built Municipal in the first place. Known as "Lakefront Stadium" when it opened in 1931, the park, some say, was

exterior

Photo by Kevin O'Connell

built in an effort to draw the 1932 Olympics to town. That theory would further the "Mistake by the Lake" mythos, but we found the claim to be unsubstantiated. As far as we can tell Los Angeles had already been chosen to host the 1932 Games when ground was broken on Cleveland's super-stadium. Lakefront—a cookie-cutter prototype—was built to house baseball, football, and other functions under one roof, or in this case, beside one chilly lake. Optimistically, the city thought it might draw eighty thousand people to a baseball game, and publicly funded the $2.5 million mon-strosity—making Cleveland's the first publicly funded big league stadium ever built, and during the Great Depression no less.

Municipal was declared ready for play on July 1, 1931. But the Indians had yet to agree with the city on the terms of a lease, so their first game at the park didn't occur until July 31, 1932. We're thinking this probably wasn't the grand debut the city had imagined. Once the Tribe took roost though, they made the park their home for the remainder of the 1932 season and for the 1933 season. But the ball-park was frequently deserted, and so, beginning in 1934, the Indians played there only on Sundays and holidays when larger crowds than usual were expected. The high cost of operating the huge facility made it preferable for the Indians to play most of their games at League Park, their former and much more intimate home.

League Park, the first home of the Indians, sat on the corner of 66th and Lexington, in the heart of what was once Cleveland's most prosperous area. Though the team underwent several name changes, Cleveland was one of the original members of the American League when it was founded in 1901. The "Cleveland Blues," as they were first known, became the "Broncos," then the "Naps" in honor of star player Napoleon Lajoie. The Indians moniker gained popularity when Louis "Chief" Sockalexis, the first Native American known to play professional baseball, rose to fame in Cleveland. Sockalexis had great talent but his years in Cleveland (1897–1899) were marred by personal problems, and his performance slipped dramatically after a promising rookie campaign in which he batted .341. Before his Major League career Sockalexis played for the College of the Holy Cross in Worcester, Massachusetts, Josh's alma mater.

On October 2, 1908, Cleveland's Addie Joss tossed a perfect game against Chicago. Tragically Joss would die three years later of spinal meningitis. A benefit game for the Joss family was held at League Park in 1911, featuring many of the greatest players of the day, including Ty Cobb, Walter Johnson, Tris Speaker, Cy Young, and Lajoie. The game, which raised nearly $13,000, would be a forerunner of today's All-Star Game.

Baseball had a convoluted history in Cleveland even before League Park. The city played host to a National Asso-ciation team called Forest City in 1871 and 1872. From 1876 until 1884, Cleveland placed an entrant in the National League, and in 1886 and 1887 a Cleveland team played in the American Association. The year 1890 saw two Cleve-land outfits in action, one in the NL and one in the ill-fated Player's League.

On May 1, 1891, the Cleveland Spiders, led by the great Young, played their first game at League Park. Though the Spiders never led the NL in wins, the "arachnids" did find their way to the Temple Cup, the equivalent of today's World Series, three times—in 1892, 1895, and 1896, winning the 1895 series with a victory over Baltimore. But the team made the record book in another way in 1899 when owner Frank Robinson transferred all of its best players to the St. Louis Browns, which he also owned. After the departure of players like Young, Jesse Burkett, and first baseman/manager Patsy Tebeau, the Spiders posted an all-time-worst 20-134 record, finishing eighty-four games behind first-place Brooklyn. After the season, the Spiders were eliminated, as the NL shrunk from twelve to eight teams. There are now rules against owners holding controlling interest in more than one Major League team at a time.

Kevin: The Yankees might as well own half the teams in the league.

Josh: Yeah, they wind up with all the best players.

Kevin: Well not all of them. Your Red Sox take the other half.

League Park had an odd square-shaped field, with its deepest corner just left of center field stretching to 505 feet from home plate. The right-field corner, meanwhile, was a very shallow 290 feet from the plate, so a forty-foot-high wall was constructed. Atop the wall rose twenty feet of chicken wire that kept balls in play. A sixty-foot wall? Now that's what we call distinctive. Why such weird field dimen-sions, you wonder? Well, prior to the park's construction, the owners of surrounding properties had refused to sell their land and buildings to the city.

The Indians won the World Series over the Dodgers in 1920, in a battle of two teams that had never won it all. Under Speaker, the Tribe disposed of the boys in blue five games to two in a best-of-nine series. Game 5, which the

home plate

Photo by Kevin O'Connell

Indians won 8-1, saw Elmer Smith hit the first grand salami in October Classic lore. Also in the game, Jim Bagby, who led the Junior Circuit with thirty-one wins that year, hit the first homer by a pitcher in World Series play. And perhaps most remarkably, Indians second baseman Bill Wambsganss pulled off the first unassisted triple play in Series history in the fifth inning. With runners on first and second, Wambsganss snagged a line drive for one out, stepped on second to double off one runner, and tagged another runner coming from first to second. All this on October 10, 1920, at League Park.

Several Negro Leagues teams tried to make a go of it in the Forest City, with the Buckeyes being the one to last the longest. Some of the others were the Bears, Browns, Buckeyes, Cubs, Elites, Giants, Hornets, Red Sox, Stars, Tate Stars, and Tigers. The Buckeyes played at League Park from 1943 to 1948, winning the Negro League World Series in 1945 when they swept the Homestead Grays.

As for the Indians, they finally moved to Municipal Stadium full-time in 1947 under the ownership of Bill Veeck. Yes, that Bill Veeck. Veeck had been at the helm for less than two years when he brought the World Championship back to Cleveland in 1948, as the Tribe beat both Boston teams in the playoffs. That's right, even before the days when there were multiple divisions in each league and Championship Series. Behind the hitting of Larry Doby—the AL's first African-American player—and the pitching of Bob Feller and Satchel Paige, Cleveland was tied at the end of the regular season with the Red Sox. Both teams had 96–59 records. The Indians prevailed in a one-game playoff at Fenway Park, thus robbing Boston of its chance for an all-Beantown Series. Then the Indians defeated the Boston Braves, four games to two. After that great moment, Veeck left for St. Louis where he attempted to resurrect the Browns. Nonetheless, the Indians returned to the World Series in 1954 to face the New York Giants. But the Tribe lost in a four-game sweep. They would not return to the Big Dance until 1995.

Kevin: A four-decade wait? Big whoop.

Josh: Spoken like a never-been-kissed Mariners fan.

Kevin: Yeah, the Tribe beat my M's in 1995. But I'm not bitter.

Josh: Sure, you're not.

Originally 470 feet to center, the fences at Municipal were brought closer to the plate through the years, eventually reducing the distance to center to 404 feet. This and other ballpark tinkering occurred while the Indians became one of the worst franchises in baseball. But at least there were plenty of hijinks to keep the locals entertained. When the Indians were eliminated from the pennant race in 1949, Veeck ceremoniously buried the 1948 pennant in center field before a game. Then, during the seventh inning of a doubleheader dubbed "Nickel Beer Night," Indians fans threw bottles at the umps, and the home team ended up forfeiting both games. And you wondered why the beverage attendant always insists on pouring your bottle into a plastic cup these days!

There were some highlights too. On May 15, 1981, Len Barker tossed a perfect game against the Blue Jays that is still replayed in local taverns on the anniversary. And it's a good thing because only 7,290 fans were on hand to see it live. Municipal Stadium was also the site of the famous play on which Jose Canseco drifted back to the wall in pursuit of a deep fly ball only to witness it bouncing off his noggin and over the wall for a "ground rule" home run. Then there was Boston pitcher "Oil Can" Boyd's much-publicized quote about the stadium. When a game was called off because of fog in 1986, the Can quipped, "That's what you get for building a ballpark next to the ocean." Oh, the humanity. In Oil Can's defense, John Kruk made a similar statement and then got a gig as a talking head on the MLB Network, and there was once a movement to rename the Great Lakes "the great north salt-free ocean."

Municipal Stadium's life as an MLB facility ended in 1993 and its life as a National Football League grid ended in 1995 after the Browns left town to become the Baltimore Ravens. The city wasted no time in demolishing it. Eager to put the "Mistake by the Lake" in its rearview, Cleveland imploded the monstrosity the very next November.

Trivia Timeout

Scout: How old was Bob Feller when he debuted with the Indians?
Warrior: Name the only player to die as the result of injuries sustained during an MLB game.
Chief: In what year did big league players first wear uniform numbers?
Look for the answers in the text.

After playing an abbreviated first season at Jacobs Field due to the work stoppage that cancelled the second half of the 1994 baseball season, Cleveland quickly turned around its baseball fortunes in its new yard. Veterans like Eddie Murray, Dennis Martinez, Omar Vizquel, and Jose Mesa combined with a young core of up-and-comers like Kenny Lofton, Carlos Baerga, and Albert Belle to propel the Tribe to the World Series in both 1995 and 1997. In the 1995 Classic the Indians met an unstoppable Atlanta Braves team. In 1997, their loss to the Marlins was much more heartbreaking, because the team came so close to winning it all. It was, dare we say, Bill Buckner-esque. Cleveland was within two outs of victory in Game 7 when Craig Counsell hit a sacrifice fly against Mesa to tie the game at 2–2 and send it into extra innings. In the bottom of the eleventh, Florida's Edgar Renteria singled over Chuck Nagy's head with the bases loaded to plate Counsell with the winning run.

But the Indians bounced back, just not all the way back. They kept winning the AL Central. By 2001, they had won the division six out of seven seasons. Their management, farm system, and fan base had all improved by leaps and bounds, from mediocre to top notch. But in 2002 things fell apart when the front office surrendered to the pressures that face a smaller market team, trading ace Bartolo Colon and losing Jim Thome to free agency. Not surprisingly, the team's 2003 edition won just sixty-eight

games. But the Indians rebuilt and by 2007 were showing championship form once again. Led by the hard-hitting Travis Hafner, the multi-dimensional Grady Sizemore, and the eminently personable Victor Martinez, they won ninety-six regular season games to top the AL Central. Next, the Tribe vanquished the Yankees in a Division Series best remembered for the biting midges that swarmed flustered Yankees reliever Joba Chamberlain in the second game played in Cleveland. In the AL Championship Series, the Indians held a three-games-to-one lead over the Red Sox, before the wheels came off their wagon and they lost three straight to fall short, once again, in their bid for a first world title since 1948. When the team traded ace C.C. Sabathia to Milwaukee the next season rather than risk losing him to free agency, the fans understood that another rebuilding phase was underway. And they stopped turning out at Progressive Field. When the return to glory does come for the Indians, and we believe it will, let's not forget the role Cleveland's beautiful ballpark has played in the team's return to respectability. For many years, this team was the laughing-stock of the American League, until the park gave it, and its fans, new life. The baseball tides in Cleveland may ebb and wane more often than in most big league cities, but they will never fall so low again as they did during the desolate days of Municipal Stadium.

Getting a Choice Seat

By 2012 it was hard to believe that a seat in Cleveland once ranked harder to come by than a seat at any other big league stadium. The Indians sold out 455 straight games at one point to set a record that would later be broken by the Red Sox in Boston. Still, selling out five-and-a-half seasons worth of games was an impressive feat. Luckily for road tripping fans, but sadly too, getting a good seat in Cleveland is no longer a challenge. You can show up on game day and do fine at the box office.

The Indians are one of many teams to charge different prices for the same seats depending upon the quality of the day's opponent. There are three such game designations, Super-Value, Value and Prime. This means a ticket to watch a summer game against the Yankees or Reds will cost more than twice as much as an early season tilt against the A's or Royals for those hoping to sit in the lower boxes around the infield. If you're going to sit in the upper deck or bleachers, on the other hand, you'll only pay a couple of dollars more on a Prime night. That said, even when the calendar says "Prime," Progressive

> **Seating Capacity:** 43,441
> **Ticket Office:** http://cleveland.indians.mlb.com/ticketing/index.jsp?c_id=cle
> **Seating Chart:** http://mlb.mlb.com/cle/ticketing/seating_pricing.jsp

Field's seats are affordably priced compared to those at other ballparks. And it's a good thing because this is a park where we sincerely recommend sitting in the lower bowl.

First Deck

FIELD BOX (SECTIONS 136–167)

The entire lower bowl offers a fairly gradual pitch, which can make the back rows of these sections farther from the action than expected. The lowest rows of nearly all sections are called the Diamond Box seats and are occupied mainly by season-ticket holders. However, in sections 136 and 138 at first base and 165 and 167 at third, the first few rows are sold as regular Field Boxes while the rows behind them are labeled Lower Boxes. These are a good value for those who wish to sit as close to the infield as possible for the lowest price. Though there is ample foul ground behind home plate, it decreases down the lines, making the seats in Sections 136, 138, 165, and 167 very close to the action.

In Sections 136–149 avoid the double-letter rows (i.e., AA, BB, etc.) if you mind an overhang. Behind home plate and on the left side (Sections 150–167) the overhang is not an issue.

LOWER BOX (SECTIONS 128–138, 165–174)

These are almost all good. They're nice and wide, and angled toward the action. On the right-field side, fans in the back rows of Sections 128–134 face an overhang obstruction, so stick to Rows A-Z, and avoid the double letters, to be safe. That goes for Sections 122–126 in the next seating designation too.

On the left-field side, Section 168 is the only "pure" section as far as sight lines are concerned. Seats in Section 170 lose the tiniest bit of the left-field corner beneath the foul pole. In Sections 171, 172, and 173 this loss of sight lines is not too noticeable, but the loss of the corner increases until Section 176, from which the left-field wall and corner are obscured.

LOWER RESERVE (SECTIONS 101–125, 175–179)

This outfield seating category actually houses seats from three different parts of the park. One is really good and the other two are pretty bad. The seats we like are the ones in Sections 101 through 113, in right-field home run territory. From here, only the tiniest bit of the field is blocked by the low wall, but it's nothing compared with the bleachers in left field. These seats get a lot of sun, and angle nicely toward the plate. Section 101 is a good section, but do avoid the top four rows (Y, Z, AA, and BB) as the view is obstructed by trees growing in the batter's eye.

The other two seating areas grouped into this pricing tier are the seats in deep right field (117–125) and left-field (175–179) foul territory. These are perhaps the worst value in the park. They are 300 feet from the plate and at a vastly inferior angle than the seats in home run territory. Compounding matters, Sections 115, 116, and parts of 117 are behind the right-field foul pole. Section 119 is oddly detached from the rest of the bowl in the right-field corner and feels removed from the field. Across the diamond, Sections 177 and 178 are blocked fairly significantly by the left-field pole. The seats in the back rows of Section 178—W through Z and AA through GG—have a significant blockage of sight lines and should be avoided.

INFIELD LOWER BOX (SECTIONS 250–267)

Rather than being their own level (as the 200 labeling suggests) these are really just the top rows of the Field Boxes. Section 250 is aligned with the visitor's on-deck circle on the first base side and Section 267 is just past third. There is only an overhang in the back few rows, and even then only a slight one. When we were sitting in our seats, it was barely noticeable. These are a much better value than the Lower Reserved seats in deep foul territory.

BLEACHERS (SECTION 180–185)

For ten bucks the left-field bleachers are the right price, but in a park this nice that often has a great many open seats, you should aim to do better. Then again, if you want to sit near the "drum guy" the bleachers may be your choice.

SEATING TIP

The first-level seats on the left-field line are vastly superior to their right-field counterparts for the same price. The right-field seats are obstructed by an overhanging Club deck while the left-field seats are not. The left-field seats also get afternoon sun, while the right-field seats are more often in the shade.

Second Deck

CLUB SEATING (SECTIONS 326–348)

The three-story Club level bumps the upper deck that much higher than it should be. Worse still, the Club houses almost entirely luxury boxes behind its triangular windows that run down the third-base line into the left-field corner. But there is one stretch of Club seats on the first base side. These hover nicely over the real fans sitting down below.

MEZZANINE SEATING (SECTIONS 303–311, 316, 317)

Located in straightaway right field, these second deck home run territory seats are much better than the 400 and 500 Level seats above them. And some sections are not too bad compared with the bleacher seats down below. As was the case for the seats below, the low outfield fence blocks only the tiniest bit of the field. Section 303 in deep right is pretty far away and should be avoided, while Sections 316 and 317 are in foul territory but are angled toward the infield.

Third Deck

VIEW BOX (SECTIONS 436–468)

We're not quite sure what the Indians are thinking with the pricing structure of these. They're decent enough 400 Level seats, but for just a few dollars more you can buy yourself a Lower Box seat at one of the corners instead. These seats ring the top deck around the infield. You might consider avoiding Sections 436 and 437, though, because of underhang issues that hide from view the right-field corner.

UPPER BOX (SECTIONS 403–434, 469–478, 529–572)

These seats are high above the field for "boxes." The best of them are in Sections 537–567. In these sections you'll be sitting behind the folks in the View Boxes but your view will be better than the folks holding lower row tickets farther down the line in the right-field corner. In general, shoot for the lower rows. Once you get above Row S, you start to feel a long way away from the action, even when seated high above home plate.

When you sit in Section 477, the corner near the left-field foul pole is lost from view. Sections 420–429 all have some portion of the field blocked by the right-field foul pole. Section 567 is obstructed by the scoreboard, which shaves from view the foul line.

UPPER RESERVE (SECTIONS 504–577)

We recommend the first-base side of the Upper Reserve over the third-base side, as opposed to the lower level where the left-field side is preferable. The seats in Sections 528–525 angle more toward the plate, and the whole right-field side offers a sweet view of downtown. But once you get to the outfield—forget about it. The Upper Reserve seats in deep right field are pretty terrible. Better to sit closer to the infield and higher up than way out there in the Upper Reserve.

Like most upper decks, the sections have spots of blockage—with the railings, the extended corners of the tunnels, the glass safety structures above the tunnels, and other stadium infrastructure components coming into play. There are also underhang issues, as the deck below blocks the left-field corner in Sections 564–572, although the view improves farther from the plate in Sections 575–577.

In Section 533, the right-field corner disappears almost totally from view because of the underhang. The foul pole is nearly completely blocked, and all of right-field foul territory and most of the right-field corner are blocked.

Josh: I didn't want to see that part of the field anyway.

Kevin: Sure you did. Shin-Soo Choo is on your fantasy team.

Josh: No, I just traded him.

Kevin: It was so much easier to keep up before you got a smartphone.

Black Market

Scalpers lurk on the streets surrounding the park. It's not like they're selling Taylor Swift or Beyonce tickets. They're hawking seats to a half-empty baseball park. So be smart.

Before/After the Game

Progressive Field is the cornerstone of the "Gateway District," and is part of the downtown sports complex that also includes Quicken Loans Arena, where the NBA's Cavaliers and AHL's Lake Erie Monsters play. We don't traditionally like sports complexes, but the Prog is also nestled in a historic downtown neighborhood full of restaurants, giving it the feel of an urban ballpark. Strange as it is to say, it's a mixture of both ideas. Keeping the ballpark close to city streets has allowed the surrounding bars and restaurants to flourish, while building it into a quasi-sports complex has made for easy access and ample parking. It's the best of both worlds. As distinctive as the exterior facade of the Prog is, it fits well into its surroundings. Eschewing the red-brick of many retro parks, the park showcases huge white trusses connected by Atlantic

Bob Feller statue

Photo by Kevin O'Connell

green granite, Kasota limestone—like the kind used in the construction of the parks in Minneapolis and Pittsburgh, and a nearly-white brick. It's distinctive, and looks like Cleveland.

Getting to Progressive Field

Most folks drive to the Prog, as it sits in the confluence of Interstates 90, 77, and 71. Finding the ballpark from whichever direction on these three Interstates is fairly hassle free, as Progressive Field has its own exits and signs guide cars into the parking lots. If you're not taking the freeway, head for the area between East 9th Street, Carnegie Avenue, Ontario Street, and Eagle Avenue. Most of the parking lots around the Prog charge about $10, but keep looking. You'll find discount lots on Ontario and Huron. We were happy to find that the Cleveland Tower City Center parking garage on Huron—a five minute walk away—still charged only $6. Take the elevator up to the Tower Center Mall and it will put you on Prospect Street. When coming in off of Huron, aim for the large guitar of the Hard Rock Hotel and you'll run into the parking lot. If you're like us,

and you want to find any way possible to get to the park without driving, try taking the Rapid Transit Authority or the bus from your hotel.

RTA info and maps: www.riderta.com

Outside Attractions

FELLER PLAZA

Located just outside Gate C is a plaza named after the greatest Indian pitcher of them all (no offense intended, John Farrell and Greg Swindell). A statue of "Rapid Robert" stands here, honoring a man who pitched three no-hitters for the Indians, including one on Opening Day of the 1940 season, and led the team to two World Series, one of which they won. Feller, who broke in with the Indians when he was just seventeen years old in 1936, went on to make eight All-Star teams and win twenty games in a season six times. Many folks—mostly Indians fans—consider him the best pitcher in history. We think that is overstating things. But there's no denying that the man who finished with 266 career wins and a 3.25 ERA was one of the best of his era.

WHO'S ON FIRST?

A closer look at the marble benches scattered about Feller Plaza reveals that when taken together they form letters to spell out "Who's on First." For this, fans can thank local artist Nancy Dwyer, who stamped the unique nod to baseball pop on the landscape as part of a public arts project.

Kevin: So Abbott and Costello walk into a bar. Abbott says . . .

Josh: Do you ever shut up?

SNEAK A PEEK

Between Gates A and B on Eagle Avenue is a tall iron gate from behind which passersby can actually look down into the ballpark and see the field. It's a great place to catch a glimpse, or watch for a while longer if no one hassles you.

THE ROCK AND ROLL HALL OF FAME
1100 Rock and Roll Blvd.
http://rockhall.com/

If you have time to kill before a night game, the R&R HOF isn't a bad way to blow some time in Cleveland. Kevin thinks it pales in comparison to the Experience Music Project in Seattle, but you're in Cleveland with time to kill. What else are you going to do? Kevin's favorite exhibit during our visit was Johnny Cash's old tour bus, though he kept singing "I've Been Everywhere" until the attendant urged us along. Josh thoroughly enjoyed the 3-D U2 concert film. It made him feel, he said, as if Bono was right there singing a private show for him (and Kevin).

Kevin: Why didn't they put the R&R Hall of Fame in Detroit?

Josh: Why Detroit?

Kevin: I can name fifty bands from Detroit. The Stooges, all the Motown acts, Ted Nugent and Alice Cooper, The MC5, The White Stripes, Madonna.

Josh: Stop. Stop.

Kevin: Well, who can you name from Cleveland?

Josh: Dean Martin.

Kevin: My point exactly.

Watering Holes and Outside Eats

The Gateway neighborhood offers everything from dance and blues clubs, to country-and-western joints, to fine dining and comfortable pubs. With the nearby arena hosting NBA hoops, minor league hockey, and arena football, these places see steady business during not only the baseball months but all year round.

PANINI'S BAR AND GRILL
840 Huron Rd.
www.paninisgrill.com/

Panini's is our favorite place in Cleveland for great food and cheap beer. It features a variety of delicious sandwiches, loaded with meat, cheese, tomato, and with the french fries and coleslaw piled right in there, similar to Primanti Brothers in Pittsburgh. While there are twenty locations in Greater Cleveland, the Gateway franchise offers outdoor seating, as well as two large bars.

THE WINKING LIZARD TAVERN
811 Huron Rd.
http://winkinglizard.com/

The Winking Lizard advertises "Great American Food" and we agree: It is a great place for cheap food and drinks. The joint doesn't overextend itself with too many offerings: just sandwiches, burgers, salads, wings, steaks and barbecue. Nearly every menu item is under $10. Be sure to arrive early, because the Lizard is usually packed before games.

Josh: Did I ever tell you about the time a lizard tried to wink at me?

Kevin: Please, no more fish stories.

THE CLEVELANDER BAR AND GRILL
834 Huron Rd.
www.clevelanderbar.com/

A favorite of our friend Dave Hayden, this place is much like the man himself: no frills and a tad hokey. The name may

sound upscale, but there is always country music on the jukebox, and happy hour runs from 4:00 to 7:00 p.m. The menu is inexpensive, and the back alley leads right to the Prog. This joint was only starting to rock as we headed out to catch first pitch. We didn't take it personally.

THIRSTY PARROT
Bolivar Avenue/812 Huron Rd.
http://hrcleveland.com/tparrot.php

Tucked behind two parking lots in a back alley close to the park, the Thirsty Parrot features loud music, outdoor seating, and a Caribbean vibe. This is definitely the place where Jimmy Buffett and his parrot-headed friends go when they congregate in Cleveland. It's a place to drink fruity drinks and cruise for women wearing leis and grass skirts. But those are just the waitresses. The cantina seats many and does a good job of blasting its tunes toward the Prog. If you're looking for an outdoor deck on a sunny day, this is your best bet in the Gateway District.

FERRIS STEAK HOUSE
2120 E. 4th St.
www.ferrissteakhouse.com/

Since 1940 this Cleveland chophouse has been the place red-meat-loving locals go when they're hankering for a steakering . . . and someone else is footing the bill. In other words: They serve really good meat but at high prices. Now mind you, this is Cleveland "high," not New York City high, which means you can still order a quality entrée in the $40 range. The restaurant has roll-up windows that gives it an open-air feel on warm days, plus a few TVs behind the bar showing the game.

FAT FISH BLUES
21 Prospect St.
www.fatfishblue.com/about.html

Now, here's a place where you'll fit in just fine in blue jeans and a T-shirt. And you won't have to shell out $40 to fill your gullet. Like the establishment's name suggests, the Fat Fish is a great place to get a hunk of Creole-cooked fish, or to groove to some Cajun tunes. Burgers and sandwiches also abound. But we recommend getting some jambalaya and making like you're in the French Quarter.

LITTLE BAR AND GRILL
614 Franklin Ave.

If you're looking for a less crowded place that's still only a short walk from the park, the Little Bar and Grill may be your best bet. The atmosphere is a tad darker and less exciting than the trendier places but the beer is cold and they serve a very respectable hamburger. This is the kind of neighborhood joint Kevin loves.

VENDORS

After downing a few pints, you'll find plenty of vendors hawking their wares outside the Prog, from guys selling peanuts to gals selling sports apparel. A funny thing we noticed: The plethora of orange and brown banners and T-shirts that read "Pittsburgh Sucks." Now since the color scheme was way off for the Indians and since the two teams don't play in the same league, we knew these were playing off the Browns-Steelers rivalry.

Kevin: For hating each other so much, the two towns have an awful lot in common.

Josh: I suppose you could say the same thing about New York and Boston.

Kevin: Yeah, they both have arts and cultural landscapes that . . .

Josh: I was talking about the food.

Kevin: I should have known.

Inside the Prog

Although it seats nearly as many people as Oriole Park, the Prog feels considerably larger. Perhaps this may be attributed to the three levels of luxury boxes that push the upper deck so high. If you stay on the first level, this isn't a problem, though. The most distinctive feature of the field is the left-field wall. Directly below the left-field bleachers—down the line at 325 feet in the corner and 370 feet in left-center—the nineteen-foot-high "mini monster" invokes comparisons to the nearly twice as altitudinous Wall in Boston. In straightaway center, the wall abruptly drops down to a more conventional eight feet, at which it remains for the rest of its path around the outfield. Behind it in deep center, the batter's eye takes the form of some decorative trees that blend in with the rest of the park. While a similar living backdrop drew the ire of batters in Minneapolis and had to be replaced before Target Field's second season, there have been no such complaints about the trees in Cleveland. Tucked behind them, where there once existed a picnic area for fans, sits a classy tribute to past Indians who have left their mark on the franchise. This is Cleveland's version of Monument Park and it's very well done. In right-center, nearly 400 feet from the plate, the Indians relievers warm up in an elevated bullpen that allows fans to easily spot who's warming up. The visiting pen is situated in the right-field corner at 325 feet from the batter's box. In both pens, the relievers throw toward the outfield

Ray Chapman

The twenty-nine-year-old Chapman was just entering his prime when he stepped into the right-handed batter's box at the Polo Grounds to face the Yankees' Carl Mays on August 16, 1920. A submarine-style right-hander whose ball ran back in on righties, Mays was known as a headhunter but had no reason to be throwing at Chapman given the game situation; the score was tight and Chapman was leading off an inning. Whether it was intended to or not, however, Mays unleashed one of his trademark deliveries that from the start appeared to be heading up and in. Battling the late afternoon sun, Chapman never moved. The ball crashed into his skull, making a thud so loud that Mays thought the ball had hit the bat. The pitcher picked up the ball, which had rolled nearly all the way back to him, and threw to first. But Chapman lay writhing on the ground. He was eventually able to stand and walk halfway to the Indians clubhouse with teammates supporting him. But then his legs gave out and he collapsed. He was rushed to a New York City hospital but by the next morning had slipped away. Today, Chapman's plaque at Progressive Field reads: "Shortstop of the Cleveland baseball club from September seventeenth nineteen hundred and twelve until his death on August sixteenth nineteen hundred and twenty."

fence, rather than parallel to it. This orientation allowed the Indians room to place more seats along the top of the home run wall than a more conventional bullpen approach would have allowed.

Josh: It just looks weird.

Kevin: At least they're not in foul territory like in Tampa Bay.

Josh: Or half under the stands like in Houston.

Ballpark Features

HERITAGE PARK

In 2007 the Indians officially opened an expanded version of Heritage Park in the area beyond the centerfield batter's eye. We liked the picnic tables that used to reside here. But we appreciate this classy tribute to the team's history even more. Favorite Indians from every era are honored by monuments and bronze plaques. Recent honorees include popular Indians like Sandy Alomar Jr. and Charles Nagy, while team legends like Feller and Boudreau are represented too. The Andre Thorntons and Al Rosens of the world are honored too, as is "Shoeless" Joe Jackson, who played for the Indians from 1910 to 1915, just before his infamous turn with the White Sox. The plaques sport player busts above a few words to memorialize each man. The saddest belongs to the ill-fated Ray Chapman, who remains the only big league player to die as the result of a game-related injury.

A PRETTY BIG SCOREBOARD

When it was originally installed in 2004 the video board in left field was the largest such screen at any sports facility in the world. It has since been surpassed, of course, several times over by the ever-expanding boards at other stadiums. We're not sure if these newer cheaper boards have been made in China, like the three progressively larger widescreen TVs Josh has bought during that time, but we wouldn't be surprised. Being so large however, we wonder if it wouldn't have been better to have a smaller scoreboard elsewhere at the Prog so the view of downtown could loom above the field to a greater degree. Then again, you have to keep up with the Joneses.

TOOTHBRUSH LIGHTS

The distinctive ballpark light towers are shaped like tooth-brushes. No, not like the electric Oral-B you use today to clean your pearly whites. They look like the old-fashioned handle and brush devices we used back in the 1990s when we thought nothing would ever replace the CD as the most space-efficient recording device ever invented and we thought Grunge was here to stay. We like these lights. They project a nice clean image above a city that sometimes feels like it could use a little scrubbing.

DON'T MESS WITH THE TINT

A distinctive feature of the field is the gray dirt. On the mound, around the bases and on the warning track, it is a lot less red than the Georgia clay or crushed brick used at most parks. The first time Kevin saw this on television, he futzed with the color-control knob on his set, but once seen in person, the gray dirt is wonderfully unique. Dredged from the Ohio River, this playing surface is considered a local trea-sure. We'd like to point out that we're not advocating that every ballpark in America comes up with its own color of dirt—orange dirt for Baltimore, teal for Miami, and so on. This isn't the NBA.

RETIRED NUMBERS

Above the right-field seats appear the names and num-bers of the Indians who have reached the Happy Hunting Grounds. While most of the retirees are standard, there is one that's pretty cool. Number 455 has been retired to honor the fans who sold out the first 455 games at "The Jake" as the park was then nicknamed. Now our memories of twenty-five hundred people watching a day game at Municipal are officially erased. Oh wait, the Indians drew about that many for a pair of April games in 2011. Maybe those memories will never die. But the memory of "the streak" lives on too. And that's worth something in a city where the sports psyche has often oscillated between despondent and despairing. The other retired numbers belong to Bob Feller (19), Bob Lemon (21), Earl Averill (3), Larry Doby (14), the shifty Lou Boudreau (5), Mel Harder (18), and Jackie Robinson (42).

Incidentally, the Indians were one of the first two teams to play a game in which both squads wore uniform numbers. After the Indians experimented with numbers on their sleeves during the 1916 season before abandoning the practice after just a handful of games, they squared off against the Yankees on May 13, 1929, at League Park with both teams sporting digits. No. 3, Babe Ruth, and No. 4, Lou Gehrig, led the Bronx Bombers to a 4-3 win.

Stadium Eats

We found the food inside the Prog improved upon our return, but this is still a park where you'll want to visit the first level to get your meal, even if your seats are upstairs. Just about all of the good stuff is down below.

SUGARDALE HOT DOG (DOG REVIEW)

The Indians sell approximately 400,000 hot dogs per season, or, to put that in perspective, about a quarter as many as the Dodgers sell at Dodger Stadium. Cleveland's isn't the best dog in the world, but it isn't the worst. The taste is big league material, but the texture is Triple-A. Topped with the right mustard, though, it does the trick.

The Indians also serve a massive half-pound all-beef dog at the "Sausages and Dogs" carts. We were tempted but wanted to save room for other treats. Eight ounces is a lot of hot dog.

STADIUM MUSTARD VERSUS BALLPARK MUSTARD (TRADEMARK FOOD)

As far as great sports rivalries go our favorites will always be Red Sox v. Yankees, Cardinals v. Cubs, Lakers v. Celtics, Army v. Navy and Ohio State v. Michigan. In the world of stadium condiments, though, there is no rivalry more fero-cious and contemptuous than that between Authentic Sta-dium Mustard and Bertman's Ballpark Mustard in Cleveland. Both of these brand names are widely available at Cleve-land grocery stores, but only Stadium Mustard is available at the Prog's standard concession counters. Thus, it garners our vote as Cleveland's trademark food. Yes, we are aware that it's "only" a condiment. But whether you put it on your dog, an Italian, or a brat, nothing will make you feel more like you're in the land of Cleve than biting down into something (anything) slathered in Stadium Mustard. It's brown and spicy to the point of even being a little hot. Now while it would be our preference to have both mustards available at all of the park's concession stands (as was the case at Municipal Stadium), such is life. Why not pick up a container of both on your way out of town and conduct a taste-test at your next tailgate? Did we mention Milwaukee's only 430 miles away?

BEST OF THE REST

The **Loaded Burgers** stand behind Section 107 also serves a grilled chicken sandwich, fried fish sandwich and veggie sandwich. We were impressed by the plethora of toppings that range from banana peppers to pizza sauce, buffalo sauce, chili, and blue cheese crumbles.

The Cleats stand, at Section 164, serves **chicken wings** in BBQ, Buffalo, and Kentucky Bourbon sauces.

The Cleveland Pops stands serve a delicious **Triple Pop** of Caramel Corn, Cheese Corn, and regular buttered Popcorn.

We managed to find some **Bertman's Ballpark Mustard** at the Food Network Cart behind Section 172. They were slathering it on a tasty **Cleveland Steak Sandwich** that came on a rustic roll with a bed of potato sticks. The sauerkraut was a bit much for our taste, but the rest of the sandwich was a winner.

The **half-pound brats** and **third-pound Italians** at the "Sausages and Dogs" carts are solid options but almost too filling.

The Fresh Cut french fries and Potato Wedges **at Spuds and Suds** (Section 163) are worth the extra buck if you're a potato lover.

STADIUM SUDS

Kevin found a number of craft beers—including Great Lakes Dortmunder and Great Lakes Burning River—at a bar behind Sections 102 and 103, where they were also pouring Guinness, Blue Moon, Labatt's, Leinenkugel Summer Shandy, and Leinenkugel Sunset Wheat.

What says baseball like a bag of Pork Rinds and one of your dad's favorite old-time beers? If you say "nothing," then visit "Your Dad's Beer Stand" behind Section 119. Blatz, Pabst Blue Ribbon, Schaeffer, Genesee, Rolling Rock, Stroh's, and Iron City are available. And they have old-fogey munchies like Pork Rinds and Andy Capp Fries too!

Josh: I think I'll stick with the fresh cut fries at Spuds and Suds.

Kevin: I like pork rinds.

The Progressive Field Experience

There is a prevalent feeling among Indians fans that the Supreme Being will not allow any team from Cleveland to win a sports championship ever again because "God hates Cleveland," for some unspecified reason. Upon first visiting Cleveland and rubbing elbows with the locals, Josh took umbrage at this attitude, claiming the Tribe had won two World Series since his beloved Red Sox had last triumphed. After the BoSox became the first team to win two World Championships in the new century and the ChiSox won one too, Josh thinks the Cleveland fans just have to hang in there a little longer. Either they're going to see their boys of summer win the big one soon, or the Cubs fans will finally have reason to throw a postgame party and Cleveland will have to wait another fifty years or so for its turn.

Josh: At least the fans will stop whining in one of those cities.

Kevin: I'm surprised you're not more empathetic after all those years rooting for the Sox.

Josh: There's no crying in baseball.

Kevin: You cried for three weeks after Boone's homer against Wakefield.

Josh: I have no memory of that.

YAHOO FOR WAHOO!

Despite the expectation that things will eventually go wrong for the Indians, there is an endearing sense of fraternity among Tribe fans. After all, Indians apparel has never reached critical mass in "coolness" across the country, and you'll rarely see the latest hip-hop star donning Chief Wahoo on a cap the way he might wear a Yankees or White Sox lid. Rather, if you see someone brandishing Chief Wahoo, dirtied and road-weary, you know that person has a Cleveland connection. He has either lived in Cleveland, has relatives there, went to school there, or recently saw his first game in the land that boasts Bob Feller, Halle Berry, and Jesse Owens as its own.

This sense of camaraderie all comes together at the Prog to create a great game-day atmosphere. Wahoo Nation is an excited and friendly faction. Fans are crazy, mostly about their Indians. The atmosphere is infectious, so don't be surprised to find yourself rooting for the home team.

SLIDER

The shaggy purple fellow imploring Tribe fans to get involved in enthusiastic fan behavior is one of the hardest working mascots in the game, even if we're not sure exactly what type of animal he is. Back during the 1995 playoff run he got a little overzealous and fell off the outfield wall, doing permanent damage to his knee.

> *Josh:* He's a bird, obviously. He thought he could fly.
> *Kevin:* Looks more like a hippo.
> *Josh:* He sure dropped to the field like a hippo.

FIREWORKS ON THE ROOF

If you're like us, you haven't enjoyed fireworks on top of the garage since prom night. But at the Prog fireworks are shot from the top of the parking structure across Eagle Avenue that is attached to the ballpark. We saw the kind that shoot flaming colored rockets into the air and the cannon-fire-with-big-boom kind. The team fires them off after the end of the National Anthem, when the Indians hit a home run, and when the Indians win.

A SWEET SOCIAL SUITE

In 2011, the Indians introduced a new hospitality room for any fan who is blogging, tweeting or otherwise using social media to comment on the game. Fans can go to this comfy luxury box and have some quiet space to fire off their ideas into Cyber Space. For a blogger, we have to think this would be about as good as it could get. After all, they spend most of their time sitting in their bathrobes working out of home offices, right?

> *Josh:* It's a brave new world, my friend.
> *Kevin:* Burgers with cheese on the inside in Minneapolis, and now this.
> *Josh:* Everything's changing so fast.
> *Kevin:* We're just getting old.

THE DRUM GUY (SUPER-FAN)

Major League made this guy one of the most famous super-fans in the bigs. Sitting atop the left-field bleachers, he beats the drum to inspire Indians rallies. He has an arrangement with the team that dictates when he is free to bang away. He only hits the drum when the Tribe has runners in scoring position and he always quits well before the pitcher delivers the ball. He sits in a nice shaded spot underneath the scoreboard with his wife. His name is John Adams and he began banging away at Municipal Stadium back in August 1973. He played his three thousandth straight game in 2011.

> *Josh:* Take that, Cal Ripken!

> *Kevin:* Yeah, this Iron Man never had to move to third base!

CHARLEY LUPICA (SUPER-FAN HALL OF FAME)

The 1949 season saw Indians fan Charley Lupica gain national fame. With the World Champion Tribe in lowly seventh place, Lupica climbed sixty feet in the air to a perch atop the flagpole above his Cleveland deli, vowing to remain there until the Indians either clinched the AL title or were eliminated from the pennant race. His vigil saw him atop the pole for 117 days, where he missed the birth of a child but garnered national newspaper and magazine coverage. Never missing a marketing opportunity, owner Bill Veeck sent a truck to transport Lupica—still sitting atop his flagpole—to Municipal Stadium on September 25, the day the Indians were officially eliminated from the pennant race. As Lupica finally descended, a crowd of thirty-four thousand was on hand to cheer him on. Don't ask us how he went to the bathroom during his time in the clouds. You don't want to know.

> *Kevin:* I don't suppose either of those guys gives a hoot one way or the other today.
> *Josh:* Yeah, they're probably pretty much decayed by now.
> *Kevin:* Um, I was thinking of them playing catch together in the afterlife.
> *Josh:* That's a bit more romantic, I guess.

Cyber Super-Fans

- **Let's Go Tribe**
  www.letsgotribe.com/
  We love the fan-confidence meter.
- **Wahoo Blues**
  www.wahooblues.com/
  A good source for trade rumors.
- *www.indiansconfidential.com/*
  A good site for game recaps and series previews.

While We Were in Cleveland
We Ate "Dirty Water" Dogs

Finding ourselves unable to score any tickets to a playoff game while in Cleveland several years ago, we watched the game between the Indians and Mariners with our friend and Cleveland tour guide, Mr. Dave Hayden, Esq. As soon as we walked in the door of Dave's apartment, he had a pot of hot

Sports in the City

League Park Site
666 Lexington Ave.
www.leaguepark.org/

We recommend that visitors to Cleveland pay a visit to the grounds where Nap Lajoie played. League Park Center sits at the corner of Lexington and 66th, offering youth fields and a portion of old League Park's facade. The actual ticket booths are intact in addition to a large stretch of the left-field exterior brick wall. The old ballpark almost takes shape as you look at these structures. There are efforts under way to restore the site, but the city should get on this one fast. It would be a shame to let it deteriorate any further. League Park is definitely worth a visit and a photo for anyone who is a fan of old ballparks.

Visiting League Park reminded us that it was the setting for one of the most disputed batting titles in history. In 1910 the Chalmers Automobile Company pledged to give one of its cars to the AL batting champ, and as the season wound down, it became clear that either Ty Cobb or Nap Lajoie would be driving home in style. Cobb skipped the last two games to protect the lead he enjoyed. Nap's last two games came in a doubleheader against the St. Louis Browns, and he took full advantage, bunting six times for hits, and ending up going eight for nine on the day, his lone blemish being an error charged on a throw to first. The bunt hits proved enough to give him the lead over Cobb.

There was a problem, however. The reason Nap bunted so often was that a rookie named Red Corriden was playing a deep third for St. Louis. After the game, Corriden said his manager Jack O'Connor told him to play back, because one of Nap's line drives might otherwise take his head off. O'Connor was a former Cleveland Spider and teammate of Lajoie. Also, it was reported that Browns coach Harry Howell tried to bribe the official scorer with a new suit, if he were to change the error to a hit, but the scorekeeper declined.

Cobb fans and Tiger president Frank Navin were furious when the next day's papers declared Lajoie the winner. But not everyone in Detroit was upset. Eight of Cobb's friendly Detroit teammates sent a telegram to Lajoie congratulating him on his victory. AL president Ban Johnson conducted an investigation into the events and determined that O'Connor and Howell had done nothing wrong, but soon after they were both removed from their positions, and were never involved with baseball again.

The Sporting News settled the dispute when it listed the official averages as Cobb .3850687 to Lajoie's .3840947. Cobb had won anyway. But Chalmers gave cars to both players.

But wait, there's more. In the 1980s baseball historian Paul McFarlane discovered two hits with which Cobb had been incorrectly credited during the season, giving the posthumous title to Lajoie. But Baseball Commissioner Bowie Kuhn did not revoke Cobb's 1910 title, thus preserving his streak of nine consecutive AL crowns.

And hold on, there's still a little more. Today's definitive source for baseball stats——Baseball-reference.com——lists Lajoie as the winner at .384 and Cobb as the runner-up at .383.

---

dogs boiling and we settled in for what would prove to be a great series.

First Dave brought out a few beers. What a great host. Next came the salted peanuts. We all shelled away and then noticed Dave do something odd. He just threw the shells down on the hardwood floor of his own apartment.

"What are you doing?" Josh asked.

"Oh, I like a *real* ballpark atmosphere here," came Dave's response, not taking his eyes off the television set. So with that, we dropped our handfuls of shells onto the ground, and tee-heed, looking at one another. We still weren't sure if Dave was kidding.

Then Dave left the room to get the dogs, which smelled just about ready to us.

A moment later, Josh was applying ketchup and onions to his, while Kevin slathered on a healthy dose of Stadium Mustard. We all bit down into the dogs at the same moment. Ah, the joys of baseball.

But we both tasted something peculiar. Not wanting to appear ungrateful, neither of us commented at first. But there was an odd flavor, not quite in the dogs, but on them. We exchanged a confused look. After ingesting so many dogs in our years of baseball travels together we were pretty expert in the ways of the hot dog. But here was something new and not altogether pleasant we were encountering.

"Dave," Kevin finally said, "What's with these dogs? They taste . . . funky."

"That's because they're 'dirty water dogs,'" said Dave, smiling from ear to ear.

"Dirty water!" shrieked Josh. "The horror!" He spit a mouthful of hot dog, bun, and ketchup onto the floor.

Even Kevin was disconcerted by this revelation. His mind raced with all kinds of definitions of dirt: disease, pesticides, nuclear waste, scurvy.

"Of course," said Dave calmly. "The Tribe won yesterday, so I couldn't very well change the water. It would kill the mojo."

"Is it sanitary?" asked Josh, a bit relieved his dog hadn't been soaking in scurvy.

"Who gives a crap? You don't mess with a streak," said Dave. "The real question is, how do they taste."

Kevin looked at Josh, who was looking somewhat regretfully at his discarded dog on the floor.

"How did you come up with this little, uh, tradition?" Kevin queried.

"I used to work the concession stand at Municipal," said Dave, "and when it came to boiling dogs, we used the same water over and over until it couldn't be used any more. Stalagmites of grease steam collected on the ceiling above the pots, dripping back down. Now whenever the Indians win a playoff game, I use the same water to keep the wins coming."

Dave's interesting superstition did bring the Indians luck when we visited, as the Tribe took a two-games-to-none lead over the Mariners in the series. However, the M's came back to win. We're not sure if Dave's girlfriend made him change the dirty water, or if the dirty water trick only works when the Indians are playing at home. We do know that ever since then, we don't eat boiled hot dogs handed to us from strangers or even friends without first asking how recently their water was changed.

DETROIT TIGERS, COMERICA PARK

DETROIT, MICHIGAN
170 MILES TO CLEVELAND
230 MILES (370 KILOMETERS) TO TORONTO
265 MILES TO CINCINNATI
285 MILES TO CHICAGO

A Motor City Miracle

A once-proud and highly successful franchise, Detroit hit rock bottom in the 1990s. The Tigers were perpetual cellar dwellers, their once-glorious Tiger Stadium had fallen into disrepair, and even many loyal fans cringed at the thought of visiting the crime-addled streets of Tiger Town. Something had to be done.

Now, you know we're normally purists and urge the restoration of the classic era ballparks whenever possible. And you may have noticed that we usually praise those teams that have revitalized their dilapidated urban neighborhoods with new ballpark projects. But in this case, we think Tigers ownership made the right call. While it may have been feasible to renovate the old yard or build a new one somewhere in its desolate vicinity, our visits to Tiger Stadium had convinced even us that it was time for Major League Baseball to pull up stakes and head for greener pastures elsewhere in the city. The team wisely opted to make the new ballpark part of a downtown entertainment district, with the other pro sports venues and theatres and restaurants right nearby.

Beautiful Comerica Park opened on April 11, 2000, with the Tigers beating the Mariners 5-2 on a balmy April day. Actually, it was 34 degrees. But it could have been worse; the day before it had snowed in Detroit.

At first Comerica did little to improve the team's performance, but as a renewed interest in the Tigers mounted, attendance surged, and the men and women in the front office put their noses to the proverbial grindstone. It all culminated, of course, in 2006 when the Tigers snapped a string of twelve straight losing campaigns by going 95-67. That record was good enough for a second-place finish in the AL Central and a claim to the AL Wild Card. The Tigers went on to shock the heavily favored Yankees in the AL Division Series and then swept the A's in the ALCS before succumbing to the Cardinals in the World Series. It was a pretty impressive run from a team that had won just seventy-one games the year before and had set the AL record for most losses in a season just a few years earlier when it went 43-119 in 2003.

Little Caesar's pizza maven Mike Ilitch, who has owned the Tigers since 1992 and the NHL's Red Wings since 1982, played a leading role in Comerica's design. And though amusement park rides, liquid fireworks, and other novelties sometimes make the stadium seem more like an ideal setting for a carnival than for a baseball game, Comerica presents a warm, festive environment for true fans too. Once you get past the kiddie rides and reach your seats, it feels almost as if you're at an old-time park. The dirt path from the pitcher's mound to home plate is a very nice touch as is the steel and brick construction, the center-field ivy, and the outfield view of downtown.

The 50-percent-privately-funded stadium project cost $350 million to complete, or to put it another way, Comerica cost more than a thousand times what it took to build Tiger Stadium. That venerable yard debuted as Navin Field in 1912 after having been erected for $300,000. Now that's what we call stadium inflation!

Kevin: But did they have a Ferris Wheel at the corner of Michigan and Trumbull?

Josh: Well, no.

Kevin: That must explain the difference.

Comerica's main entrance is one of the most distinctive in baseball. For our money, it ranks right up there with the colorful plaza in Atlanta and old-timey rotunda in Queens. In Motown eighty-foot-high baseball bats flank the front gate and a massive sculpture of a tiger lurks in the courtyard. On the front of the ballpark itself, drain spouts sculpted to look like enormous tiger heads chomp down on oversized baseballs. Clearly, these are not the happy-go-lucky cartoon Tigers you knew and loved in the 1980s. These angry cats announce to all comers that their bite is as bad as their growl and they're ready to tear the opposition to pieces.

fountain

Photo by Kevin O'Connell

Inside the park, the batters' eye in center is made of mesh and covered with ivy, in an obvious tip of the cap to Wrigley Field. Up on top there's a Chrysler logo. While usually we don't like Corporate America making itself too prominent inside the park, in Detroit, this struck us as a nice touch. After all, this is Motown.

Kevin: But there's also a Toyota sign on the right-field fence.

Josh: A sign of the times, my friend.

A walkway behind the ivy doubles as a misting tent on hot days, connecting right field and left, and allowing fans a peek—but just a peek—of the action between the vines. When a Detroit player hits a home run, liquid fireworks explode out of the vines in celebration. The water show is no match for Kauffman Stadium's fountain, but it's still a spectacle. If the Tigers don't homer, don't despair, we were treated to a postgame water show after the last out, even though the Tigers lost. But root for a hometown homer, because that way you'll also get to see the eyes of the colorful tigers atop the scoreboard light up too.

Realism collides with art on the left-field pavilion where statues depict several Tiger heroes. These include Charlie Gehringer, Hank Greenberg, Ty Cobb, Willie Horton, Al Kaline, and Hal Newhouser. A sculpture of Hall-of-Fame Tigers broadcaster Ernie Harwell, meanwhile, appears just outside the entrance to the park. The latter gentleman was so beloved in Detroit that upon his death in 2010 his body

was laid in repose at Comerica Park. More than ten thousand mourners turned out to pay their last respects to the man who was the Voice of the Tigers for more than four decades.

As for the large metallic statues of the players, they are not meant to appear entirely true to life. The movement of one player's bat whipping through the strike zone is simulated by a long blur of batlike steel. Another depicts three balls coming off a bat, and another shows turf flying in the air as a player runs. These fine works were sculpted by the husband-wife team of Omri Amrany and Julie Rotblatt-Amrany, the same Illinois artists who created the Michael Jordan statue outside Chicago's United Center.

Kevin: It's always been a dream of mine to be statue-ized outside Safeco Field.

Josh: That's a little disturbing.

Kevin: Just sayin', it would be pretty cool.

Josh: I don't think they do that for guide-book writers.

The Detroit Tigers joined the American League as a founding member in 1901. But the franchise actually existed before the Junior Circuit did. The early Tigers were in Ban Johnson's Western League, which evolved into the AL, and played on "the Corner," a Detroit hardball hotbed since the early 1890s. Bennett Park stood at the intersection of Michigan and Trumbull, with elm and oak trees in-play in the outfield. The trees, which predated the American Revolution, were removed in 1900 as the Tigers prepared to join the Majors.

Tiger Stadium was originally called Navin Field to honor team president Frank Navin. It opened on April 20, 1912, the same day as Fenway Park in Boston. The Tigers capped the historic day by downing the Indians, 6-5. Like many other parks of its era, Tiger Stadium was constructed to fit into an actual city block, giving the field its quirks organically, and not as a matter of design. The distance to straightaway center field originally measured 467 feet. While the 125-foot-high center-field flagpole was technically on the field, it didn't come into play often. In 1938 the center-field fence was brought in to 440 feet, where it would remain.

Milestone moments at Tiger Stadium included Ty Cobb's three thousandth hit in 1921, Eddie Collins's three thousandth in 1925, and Babe Ruth's seven hundredth homer in 1934. Ruth's blast cleared the right-field roof and left the yard entirely. The only All-Star Game won by the AL between 1962 and 1983 was played at Tiger Stadium in 1971. A mammoth third-inning clout by Reggie Jackson struck a light tower above the right-center-field roof, propelling the Juniors to a 6-4 victory.

While twenty-three home runs cleared Tiger Stadium's right-field roof, only four carried over the more distant left-field roof. The culprits: Harmon Killebrew (1962), Frank Howard (1968), Cecil Fielder (1990), and Mark McGwire (1997).

Kevin: No light weights in that group.

Josh: A pretty fair list of sluggers, indeed.

On September 27, 1999, Harwell delivered a touching eulogy for the ballpark before a sellout crowd shortly after the Tigers beat the Royals 8-2 in the finale. Then, with the assistance of a police motorcade and several Tigers players, home plate was driven one mile to Comerica's construction site.

From the start, the new park "played big," yielding homers sparingly and offering a great many triples. In 2005, the Tigers tinkered with the outfield configuration to bring in the fence in left-center from 395 feet to 370, and in center from 435 feet to 420. The move facilitated a relocation of the bullpens from right field to left-field home run territory. Even in the years since, Comerica has maintained its reputation as a pitcher's park. But it's not the hitter's graveyard it once was.

The highlights of the ballpark's first decade included playing host to the 2005 All-Star Game. On that July day, Al Kaline and Willie Horton threw out the ceremonial first pitches, and then the AL jumped out to a 7-0 lead thanks to homers by Miguel Tejada and Mark Teixeira, and a two-run

single by Ichiro. The AL held on for a 7-5 win. Six years later, Comerica was the site of Jim Thome's 599th and 600th home runs, which he hit on the night of August 15, 2011. Both long balls were of the opposite field variety, flying over the left-field fence, and they came in successive innings. In the sixth inning, the Twins' designated hitter took Tigers' starter Rick Porcello deep. Then, in the seventh, he became the eighth Major Leaguer to join the six-hundred-homer club with a three-run clout against reliever Daniel Schlereth.

Trivia Timeout

Chrysler: Which Tiger holds the record for being the youngest batting champ in Major League history?

Chevy: The famous headline "We Win!" appeared in the *Detroit Free Press* in what year?

Ford: Name the three Tiger pitchers who have won the AL MVP award. (Hint: One won it more than once. Another won it after eclipsing the thirty-win mark. And one was a reliever.)

Look for the answers in the text.

Speaking of the Twins, they finished ahead of the Tigers in the AL Central standings by just a single game in 2006. But that didn't stop the Tigers from advancing all the way to the World Series. As the AL Wild Card team, Detroit beat the Yankees three games to one in the Division Series and even got the chance to celebrate the clincher on the Comerica lawn. Then they moved on to face the A's in the AL Championship Series. And not only did the Tigers win, but they registered a decisive series sweep, which they completed in the most dramatic fashion imaginable. Magglio Ordonez sealed the deal with a three-run walk-off homer in the bottom of the ninth to send the 42,967 fans at Comerica into a frenzy of delight. But in the October Classic the Tigers came up a little bit short. They and the NL champion Cardinals split the first two games, which were played in Detroit. Then the Tigers' bats went dormant and their pitchers, oddly enough, started committing errors left and right. Tiger hurlers were charged with five miscues in the five-game series that sent them home to ruminate over what might have been. That 2006 season was an important one for Detroit, though, as it reestablished the Tigers as

Tiger greats statues

Photo by Kevin O'Connell

a perennial force in the AL Central. The Tigers returned to the playoffs in 2011, but lost to the Rangers in a six-game ALCS. We suspect the Tigers will have plenty more opportunities to taste October champagne in the years ahead and when they do, no doubt beautiful Comerica Park will shine for the entire baseball world to see.

> **Seating Capacity:** 40,950
> **Tickets:** http://detroit.tigers.mlb.com/ticketing/index.jsp?c_id=det
> **Seating Chart:** http://detroit.tigers.mlb.com/det/ticketing/seating_pricing.jsp

Getting a Choice Seat

The Tigers perennially rank in the upper third of the baseball pack, averaging more than thirty thousand fans per game, or nearly three million a year. Nonetheless, with more than twenty-three thousand seats in the lower bowl, this is a ballpark that offers ample opportunity for you to treat yourself to an excellent view for relatively cheap bucks. And we advise doing so, because many of the upper seats at Comerica aren't terribly good.

Instead of stacking two steep decks on top of one another to keep upper fans close to the field, Comerica's designers strove to keep fans as low to the field as possible. As a result, both the lower- and upper-seating decks extend from the playing field very gradually, leaving fans in the back rows far from the action. We're not proponents of treacherously steep upper decks, like the one at Rogers Centre, but there must be some sort of happy medium, like the upper deck in Kansas City, that the modelers of Comerica might have been better off aspiring to duplicate.

On-Deck Circle/Tiger Den (Sections 120–135)

The On-Deck Circle seats are in the first few rows between the dugouts. At under $100, even on weekend dates during the summer, which the Tigers designate as "premium" days and for which they charge a surplus, these are much more affordable than comparable seats at most other stadiums.

The Tiger Den seats, meanwhile, are moveable wooden chairs. These are wide and padded, and their holders order off a fancy menu and get wait-service. But the Tiger Den is located behind the Infield Box and On-Deck Circle seats at the very back of the lower bowl. We appreciate that they're padded, but found them a tad far from the action.

Infield Box (Sections 118–137)

These are all good seats for the money. Pay attention to what row number you're purchasing, however, as the boxes go all the way up to Row 35, and the gradual incline of the lower bowl leaves fans in back far from the field. The opportunity to sit right behind home plate for $50 is appealing. And sight lines throughout the section rate above average.

Because of the gradual slope and larger-than-average foul territory, only small portions of the outfield corners are out of view from any seat. The wide and open concourse behind these sections allows for glimpses of the field to those waiting in line or walking about between the many concession carts.

Terrace (Sections 116–118 and 136–141)

The seats in the back rows of the Field Boxes and first few Outfield Boxes along the right field (116–118) and left-field (136–141) lines sell for less than the Infield Boxes. Still, they're pricier than the Outfield Boxes, many of which offer closer views. We don't recommend these unless the pickings in the rest of the first level are slim.

Outfield Box (Sections 115–117 and 138–140)

The Outfield Boxes are located between the Infield Boxes and Lower Baseline Boxes, which are deep in foul territory. If the Infield Boxes are sold out, consider Outfield Boxes in Sections 138, 139, 117, 116, and 114. These are angled nicely toward the infield. If these sections are unavailable, we recommend passing on the remaining Outfield Boxes and opting for a straightaway view from home run territory for less money.

Section 115 is probably the worst section in the lower bowl as its position makes it impossible to see much of the right-field corner. So avoid it like Kevin avoids yuppie bars. Row 37 of these sections is behind a walkway, so try for seats in Rows 36 or lower to avoid the traffic. Any row higher than Row 40 is under the overhang of the upper deck, which, if nothing else, provides a nice umbrella on rainy nights.

Lower Baseline Box (Sections 112–114 and 141–143)

These seats deep in the outfield corners were our least favorite in the lower level. You can and should do better.

Pavilion (Sections 144–151)

Located in home run territory beyond the left-field bullpens, the Pavilion is lower to the field than the right-field bleachers. It is also a bit farther from home plate owing to the ballpark's asymmetrical dimensions and the presence of the pens, which run along the wall, adjacent to one another.

As the result of these two factors, the view from the Pavilion is not as good as from the seats in right. If you're hell-bent on sitting in the Pavilion (say, to heckle a certain Yankees out-fielder), try for the single-letter rows, as Rows AA and higher are behind an aisle and farther from the field. Parts of Section 144 are screened by the foul pole.

Right Field Grandstand (Sections 104–106)

Tiger fans now find three sections of comfortable seats where the bullpens once resided in straight-away right. We think these exist just to make the bleacher-bound fans sit-ting behind (in the double-lettered rows) and beside these seats jealous. Nonetheless, these are the best home-run-territory seats in Comerica, so if hawking is your thing, you should rest your tired rump here.

Bleachers (Sections 101–106)

Kevin liked the view from the bleachers and applauded the Tigers for offering these at such a low price. Most of the seats in Section 101 are partially obstructed by the center-field wall, as fans can't see part of the center-field pasture. But otherwise the views check out fine. They are bleacher benches though, not seats, so we'll leave it to you to decide whether this is the three-hour ballpark experience you seek. Stadium security swarmed upon the only beach ball that fans (okay, it was Kevin) tried to send aloft one time when we visited. Even a simple bit of ball bopping was apparently too rowdy for management's taste, which led us to wonder if too much family atmosphere at a ballpark might be a bad thing. If you've ever seen the look on a six-year-old's face when an usher tears an inflatable ball from his hands and rips it to shreds, you know what we mean. Should secu-rity be focused on keeping people safe rather than being the fun police? We think so, as through all our research we found nary a single beach-ball-related accident at a sporting event of any kind.

Kaline's Corner (Sections 107–111)

Tucked behind the right-field foul pole these cheapie seats are best to be avoided, unless you're just looking for a way into the park in order to spend a game seat-hopping.

Upper Club/Upper Box (Sections 321–333)

The first row of the upper deck hovers in the airspace directly above the last row of Infield Boxes. The deck extends very gradually away from the field. If you are afraid of heights and shudder to recall your recent trip to the upper reaches of Rogers Centre (have we panned that place enough?) or U.S. Cellular Field, you might like the effect in Detroit. Otherwise,

you probably won't care much for it. The seats may be low, but they are distant from the field.

The Tigers call the first few rows the Upper Club and charge an extra $6 for them. The seats and aisles are a bit wider than elsewhere but that's it. No slinky waitresses or special concessions. We think there should be uniform rules governing what can and cannot be called a "Club" seat. We also think the pitcher's mound should be raised, the DH abolished, and the amateur draft expanded to include the Latin American and Asian countries. But those are all issues we're currently negotiating with Bud Selig. He's a tough nut to crack, but we think he's coming around. Either that or he thinks he might be able to sell us a used car somewhere down the line and he's trying to keep things simpatico just in case.

But back to Comerica's upper deck. The Upper Boxes represent the seats on the infield (321–337) behind the "Club" rows. These are decent but we recommend buying lower-level Infield Boxes instead, even though they're twice the price.

Upper Box Left Field (Sections 338–346) and Upper Box Right Field (Sections 210–219)

The Tigers call the first five rows of the left and right-field upper levels "Box Seats" and charge extra for them. Avoid these seats, especially the so-called Box Seats in Section 345 and 346, where ticket holders pay $24 to sit one row in front of Skyline ticket holders who paid $5. This is the biggest rip-off in the park and quite possibly in the whole world! Across the diamond, meanwhile, the Upper Boxes in right field are lower than their counterparts in left, owing to the fact that the right-field mezzanine is set closer to the first level than the upper deck in left.

Upper Reserved (Sections 338–344)

Similar to many new parks, railings and glass plates appear above all upper entranceways, obstructing the views of fans in a number of seats behind them. In Rows 6–8 throughout the upper level, avoid aisle seats numbered 19–24 or 1–5 for this reason.

Because of the underhang, the left-field corner starts to disappear at Section 336. This becomes worse as you con-tinue toward the outfield. The sunroof above the upper level will keep you in the shade if you're in Row 17 or higher.

Mezzanine (Sections 210–219)

Because the suite level does not extend past first base, the Tigers opted to construct an intermediary level at a height between the lower and upper decks. This was done in lieu of a right-field upper level. Fifteen feet lower than the 300 Level, the 200 Level consists of four thousand seats. However, this deck is sloped even more gradually than the 300 Level and as a result we felt exceptionally far from the action here. Hey, there's a reason all of the movie theaters are adopting "stadium seating," you know.

At the very least, avoid the first row of the Mezzanine seats (Row 5, since the first four rows of the deck constitute Upper Box Right-field seats) since the railings and glass plates obstruct sight lines. Also beware: Fans sitting in Sections 210–213 will not be able to see the right-field corner.

Skyline (Section 345)

Kudos to the Tigers for continuing to let fans in for a five-spot. Just remember you don't want to actually sit in these seats unless you have binoculars, Superman vision, or only a passing interest in the game. So here's your plan. Score a $5 seat in 345 and hop into the Upper Boxes behind the plate. There are usually plenty of empties and ballpark staff doesn't seem to mind folks moving around within the upper altitudes. Follow general seat-hopping protocol and you should be fine: Wait until the bottom of the second inning, load your arms with food and drink, then stumble toward an open seat while pretending to study your ticket stub to make sure you're in the "right" place. And don't get greedy. If you're going to head for a front-row seat down on the first level, you might as well just tell the usher on your way past that you don't have a ticket.

The Black Market

Reselling tickets at any price is illegal in Michigan. We doubt this law has anything to do with it, but there is a noticeable dearth of scalpers as you approach the park. Tickets are reasonably priced from the team, we suppose, and Detroit's bad boys have bigger fish to fry on the mean streets of Motown or at the nearby casinos.

Before/After the Game

As long as you stay within a few blocks of the ballpark in the area known as Foxtown, you should feel comfortable and safe. However, getting to the ballpark does require driving through some of Detroit's poverty-stricken streets. Detroit was once one of the most prominent of America's great manufacturing cities. Although we understand that the forces of globalization and free trade have already severely limited the boundaries of just how far back it can bounce in

the years after the Great Recession, we sincerely hope that it finds a way to recapture some of its lost glory. Whether the path to prosperity is lined with autos, as in the past, or with some new consumer product to manufacture, or with a whole new industry, we don't know. But there's no doubting that the industrious, hardworking people of the city will flourish if big business only gives them more of a chance than they've had in recent decades. And here's hoping baseball does its part, too, to bring better times to the Motor City.

Getting to Comerica

Comerica is located just south of Interstate 75 on Woodward Avenue. Its main entrance is across the street from the Fox Theatre. Follow Interstate 75 to the Grand River Avenue exit. Off the ramp, cross Grand River and take a right onto Woodward Avenue. Follow Woodward to the ballpark. Most of the private parking lots in the immediate area charge $10, while the official team lot charges $25. Keep your eyes open on the streets a few blocks away from Comerica and you'll likely spot an $8 lot or two. The People Mover monorail deposits passengers at the Broadway and Grand Circus Park stations, which are both near the park. At only fifty cents per ride, this elevated loop is a highly affordable option for those staying overnight in town.

Monorail Information: www.thepeoplemover.com/Overview.id.26.htm

Outside Attractions

WHEN CATS FLY

Perched atop the marquee of the Fox Theatre at 2211 Woodward is a pair of winged lions that predate by seventy years construction of Comerica. William Fox, founder of Twentieth Century Fox Pictures, built the theatre in 1928. In 1987 the Ilitch family purchased the building and restored it to its elegant present condition.

Josh: This represents an opportunity to fuse high culture and hardball.

Kevin: I wonder if they've ever staged *Damn Yankees*.

WITH GOD ON OUR SIDE

A few blocks away, at 2326 Woodward, stands St. John's Episcopal Church, a beautiful example of neo-Gothic architecture. The church was constructed in 1927. On one of the occasions we visited, a large banner hung outside reading, "Pray here for the Tigers and Lions." We found this a unique appeal, to say the least. And who knows, maybe one of these days it'll work and the Tigers will win their first World Series since 1984.

Josh: Take heart, Tigers fans. Whenever we write something like that, it happens, immediately making our book seem outdated.

Kevin: To wit, the 2004 Red Sox and 2005 White Sox, who broke their long droughts right after the first edition of this book came out.

Josh: I can't believe you just said, "to wit." Are you trying to sound like George Will?

FORD FIELD

Both an easy place to visit and an easy place to walk past without noticing, the new home of the National Football League's Detroit Lions resides beyond Comerica's left-field seats on the corner of Adams Street and Brush Street. The sixty-four-thousand-seat domed stadium is remarkable for blending in so well with the urban landscape. Because its playing field is forty feet below street level, fully 45 percent of its seats are actually underground. Thus, the building does not rise excessively high into the sky. Though we didn't make it inside, we were impressed. Football stadiums don't usually look this innocuous. Way to go Detroit! Now, if Lions fans pray real hard, maybe their team will put together a winning team.

DETROIT CASINOS

There are no less than five casinos in Detroit, all located right near each other, on the waterfront. We visited MGM Grand Detroit (1777 Third St.). Kevin quickly lost all of his food and ticket money, while Josh got on a nice little run at the roulette table. This prompted Kevin to call Josh a "piker," and some hard feelings developed on both sides. After an "uncomfortable" hour or two, we kissed and made up in the bleachers, metaphorically speaking, of course.

TIGER STADIUM SITE
Intersection of Trumbull and Michigan

After the Tigers' relocation to Comerica there was considerable debate as to what should become of Tiger Stadium. At one point, efforts were made to find a developer who would renovate the facility and convert it into a mixed-use residential and entertainment center, with lofts, shops, ice rinks and a community swimming pool. But that failed to materialize. Then the Old Tiger Stadium Conservancy and US Senator Carl Levin endeavored to raise money to preserve the infield portion of the stadium structure, to build a baseball museum on the site, and to avail the remaining field to the community. That effort, though, fell short or ran out of time, depending upon whom you talk to.

In September 2009 the stadium's demolition was completed. Ah, the march of progress. . . .

As of early 2012, competing local groups were still debating the merits of several proposals, including one to put a charter school on the old stadium site, one to make it a home for local non-profit agencies, and one to revisit the original idea of building a commercial/residential development. Meanwhile, the field still lay in place, growing dandelions. We will leave it to you to scope out the area during your visit and to see if Detroit has finally sorted out the best use for this potentially valuable urban space.

Kevin: They should build a state-of-the-art youth field and rec center here.

Josh: Money talks. When this part of town rebounds, it's prime real estate.

Kevin: Give the community something to take pride in and it will rebuild around the best youth field in America.

Josh: Paid for by . . . ?

Kevin: Some wealthy Michigander should step to the plate.

Josh: Michael Moore?

Kevin: Or the big three auto builders . . .

Josh: Or a few of the Tigers could pony up a million apiece.

Kevin: Now we're talking.

Josh: How 'bout it, Tigers? Do the right thing and your city will always remember you.

FREE STANDING ROOM

Because Comerica's field is sunken below street level, the view of the action is surprisingly good from Adams Street behind the left-field Pavilion where a number of gates allow a peek for those on the extremely low budget, like Kevin after he lost his ticket-money at the casino.

Kevin: Hey, buddy. You're not really going to leave me out here, are you?

Josh: If I don't, you'll never learn your lesson.

Kevin: If you do, the road trip car's gonna roll out of Motown without you.

Josh: Well-played. Here's a sawbuck. Sit in the Skyline.

Watering Holes and Outside Eats

Foxtown offers a decent bar and restaurant scene. And for folks who care to look beyond the sanitized view of Detroit the ballpark neighborhood offers, we recommend venturing a bit deeper into Detroit. Hey, we did and came out of the experience just fine. (Disclaimer: Joshua R. Pahigian,

Kevin T. O'Connell, and The Lyons Press shall bear no legal responsibility for any misfortune that befalls any reader in any part of Detroit, or anywhere else in the continental United States, for that matter.)

ELWOOD GRILL
300 Adams St.
www.elwoodgrill.com/

With indoor and outdoor seating, the Elwood looks like a diner from the 1950s. Buy a beer on the patio. Shoes and shirt not required! Well, shoes may be, but we saw a topless patron (unfortunately male) seated on the patio one time when we visited. It was a hot September day. Inside, the atmosphere is more civilized with a full bar and wait service. Best of all, the foods are named after great Tigers. Kevin's Ty Cobb Salad didn't have any corn in it. Rather it featured a generous portion of grilled chicken atop romaine lettuce.

HOCKEY TOWN CAFE
2300 Woodward Ave.
www.hockeytowncafe.com/

Located beside the Fox Theatre, Hockey Town offers your best bet for a quality pregame or postgame meal. Entrées range from $15 to $25. The three-story bar and restaurant is all hockey, all the time. Busts of famous Detroit Red Wings like Gordie Howe, Ted Lindsay, and Sid Abel are displayed, along with plenty of cups and trophies. Kevin tried his hand at some of the interactive hockey games and was happy to win back some of the money he had lost earlier in the day. The parents of the kids were none too pleased.

CHELI'S CHILI BAR
47 East Adams St.
www.chelischilibar.com/

Owned by former Red Wing Chris Chelios, this is actually one of two eateries the great defenseman owns in Michigan. The other is in Dearborn. The conveniently-located Foxtown restaurant offers a gift-shop replete with #24 souvenirs and the requisite memorabilia as decor. It also boasts 36 TVs and a Detroit-themed menu. Three types of chili—original, veggie, and chicken—are served in cup, crock or bread-bowl sized portions. Our favorite was the original. It was meaty, spicy, and just the right call before a long car ride together.

NEMO'S
1384 Michigan Ave.
www.nemosdetroit.com/

Those visiting the old Tiger Stadium neighborhood will find this iconic Motown bar, which has often turned up in articles attempting to quantify the best sports bars in America.

Despite the team's move, it still sees steady traffic on game day, thanks in part to the shuttle buses it runs to and from Comerica for patrons. We suggest stopping in for a few pints and a burger and then perusing the collection of framed newspaper pages hanging on the tin walls to honor great moments like Kirk Gibson celebrating the 1984 World Series victory or Cecil Fielder rounding the bases after hitting his fiftieth homer in 1990. When you're done with this unique stroll through memory lane, you can hop on one of the refurbished green-and-white school buses and ride to the game.

THE TOWN PUMP TAVERN
100 W. Montcalm Way
www.thetownpumptavern.com/TownPump/Welcome.html

On the fringes of Foxtown but still only a short walk from the park, The Town Pump Tavern resides on the ground floor of what must have been a pretty nice hotel at one time. Really, we can't overstate the eloquence of the ivy-covered stone exterior. Inside, the rectangular bar has a nice old-time feel to it. Local brews include Motor City Ale, Oberon, and Belles Amber, and the menu features cheap appetizers, hand-tossed pizzas, burgers, sandwiches, and salads. Kevin dug the atmosphere and Josh dug the prices. A road tripper's delight.

Josh: When I was a teenager in Charlton, Massachusetts, there was a girl we all called "the town pump."

Kevin: I'm not touching that one.

Josh: That's what I said!

Inside the Park

In this era of homer-friendly parks, Comerica initially offered a variation of the game more akin to the one our fathers knew back in the 1960s. Yet long-ball-loving rooters and stat-consumed sluggers complained the field was too spacious. The last straw came when Detroit's right-handed batters combined to hit only sixteen home runs in 1,288 Comerica at-bats in 2002. So the Tigers did some remodeling to bring the dimensions more in line with the typical ballpark specs these days. Even still, Comerica's outfield is larger than average and its gaps make it a doubles- and triples-hitter's paradise. We hope it doesn't shrink any more in the years ahead.

Ballpark Features
ONE DECADE AT A TIME
The walking museum on the first-level concourse features monuments dedicated to each decade in Tigers

The 1950s monument salutes Al Kaline, the youngest batting champ ever, who hit .340 in 1955 as a twenty-year-old. Incidentally, fellow-Tiger alum Ty Cobb won a crown as a twenty-year-old himself in 1907. But Cobb was 12 days older than Kaline when his winning season concluded. Thus, he was relegated to second-youngest batting champ ever when Kaline won his crown.

The 1960s pillar displays the famous *Detroit Free Press* headline, "We Win!" celebrating the 1968 World Series triumph over the Cardinals.

THE CARNY COMES TO TIGER TOWN

Behind the home plate concourse, Major League Baseball's most elaborate kiddie area offers chances for children and adults to ride on the fifty-foot-high Fly Ball Ferris Wheel and on the colorful painted tigers that comprise the Tiger Carousel.

If you're scrounging for loose change, check out the Wishing Well at the mouth of the Big Cat Food Court. Roll up those sleeves and dive in like Kevin did. Or join with local fans in wishing for a hometown win and cast a coin into the water.

CASTING CALL: PREDATOR III

Remember the monster in the *Predator* movies that could blend in with its surroundings? There was an *X-Files* episode devoted to a similar creature back in "the day," as well. Yes, we know we're dating ourselves with these references, but please bear with us, because the camouflaged cameramen who stand on a platform amid the center-field ivy do a pretty good imitation. Well, they do when water isn't cascading onto their equipment when the liquid fireworks erupt. We were intrigued, as well, by the puddles that formed on the center-field warning track whenever the fountain squirted. Shouldn't the Players Association put a stop to that sort of thing?

GEOMETRY

The dirt path from the pitcher's mound to home plate leads to a pentagon—or home-plate-shaped—patch of dirt that surrounds the batter's box. This, opposed to the dirt circle found at most parks. It's a nice touch, but it's also a really big plate. As for the path itself, which is similar to the one at Chase Field in Phoenix, we like it. It is a nod, of course, to the ball fields of yore that sprouted little grass on that part of the infield due to the primitive ground keeping practices of the era, which were no match for the wear and tear of the catchers' and pitchers' repeated footsteps.

Tiger Ball

Photo by Kevin O'Connell

history, beginning with the 1900s and continuing through the 2000s. The display cases are on wheels with big tires, embracing the car culture that, like baseball, is as American as it gets. The 1930s exhibit was Josh's favorite. Not only does it feature memorabilia from the 1935 World Series but also a number of cartoons from the Series, including one of a tiger killing a cardinal with a baseball bat. Okay, perhaps that's a bit violent, and Josh should get into some anger management sessions.

A history buff, Kevin liked the 1940s monument and its "Baseball Answers America's Call" exhibit, featuring Tigers players who served in the armed services during times of war. Hank Greenberg, Virgil Trucks, and Dick Wakefield all appear in their military uniforms.

SPACIOUS

The dugouts at old Tiger Stadium were loathed throughout the bigs due to their cramped quarters. So when the Tigers built Comerica, they sought to remedy this affront to player comfort. But perhaps they over-corrected a bit. Comerica's dugouts are known as the widest in the game. They're so wide in fact that most players stand along the screen, rather than sit on the bench, so as to have a better view of the game.

Josh: Well, at least they allowed plenty of room for Jim Leyland to hide while smoking his cigarettes.

Kevin: When it comes to setting a bad example for today's youth, smokeless tobacco is baseball's real scourge.

Josh: More than steroids?

Kevin: Look at how many more people die of tobacco than steroids.

Josh: This is the type of conversation we just didn't have on our first trip.

Kevin: Parenthood changes your perspective a bit, doesn't it?

POLE POSITION

The flagpole in left-center field is huge. Until Comerica's remodeling, it was on the field of play, just as it had been at Tiger Stadium. Using his compass, a protractor, a slide ruler, the backside of a hot dog wrapper, and a blue Sharpie, Josh calculated its height to be 123.5 feet. During the entire three-inning ordeal, Kevin kept shaking his head and muttering, "We can look up the height on the Internet when we get home."

THE SCULPTURES

In the introduction to this chapter we already discussed the amazing statues that stand behind the left-center-field wall at Comerica, so we won't take up too much space rehashing them here, other than to say make sure you take a stroll to pay them homage. They're really superbly done. Additionally, check out from other vantage points in the park how the Tigers have likewise honored these individuals by printing their names and uniform numbers on the brick wall facing home plate that stands in front of each distinctive monument. Similarly, the names of other legendary but not quite statue-worthy Tigers like Sparky Anderson appear on the wall in right-center.

SCOREBOARD

We don't usually do flips or summersaults or acrobatics of any kind over scoreboards, but this one caught our eye and struck our fancy. Let's just say we did a few jumping-jacks upon seeing it, which, given our present conditioning, is about as close to acrobatics as we can safely get. Two tigers prowl at the top, while a face clock with the Detroit logo appears in the center. These effects, we liked. Of course, the board also leaves ample room for advertising, which, as you know, we absolutely love being bombarded with at the ballpark. You never know when you're going to glance up—say to see how many outs there are, or who's batting—and discover a whole new kind of beer that just might change your life. But seriously, we liked those glowing-eyed tigers atop the board.

SEA LEVEL

The upper-deck seats behind the plate offer the best view of the downtown skyline. The most prominent building is the Broderick Tower, which looms over right field displaying a 65-by-180-foot undersea/above-sea mural. This was crafted by internationally renowned marine life artist Wyland, a Detroit-born guy who just goes by one name, kind of like Ichiro, Bono or Oprah.

Josh: What Ichiro does with a bat in his hand is equivalent to what Wyland does with a paintbrush.

Kevin: I'm not sure he uses a brush way up there.

Josh: What, then?

Kevin: Rollers? Actually, I'll be damned if I know. But he's no Ichiro.

Josh: (Sigh) You Mariners fans sure are sensitive when it comes to Mr. Suzuki.

Kevin: We're sensitive about a lot of things.

CANADIAN, EH?

During one of our September visits to Comerica we were slightly horrified to find many of the TVs on the concourse tuned to a Canadian Football League game between Saskatchewan and Edmonton.

Josh: Sweet fancy Butkus. Those hosers just punted on third down!

Kevin: Welcome to the Great White North.

Stadium Eats

As mentioned above, fast-food magnate Mike Ilitch owns the Tigers. Despite this, or perhaps because of it, the offerings at Comerica are rather unexceptional. This, despite a diverse food court that always gives us hope before leaving us a tad disappointed. Sorry, Mike, we'll keep cramming as much as we can eat in three hours, if you keep trying.

LITTLE CAESAR'S PIZZA (TRADEMARK FOOD)

We generally try to avoid ballpark pies unless we're in Chicago. But since the Tigers and Little Caesars share a common

---

When Tigers Reigned

The Tigers won the AL pennant in 1934 with a record of 101–53. That .656 winning percentage still stands as best in franchise history. Hank Greenberg hit .339 during that season with 139 RBIs, Charlie Gehringer hit .356 with 127 RBIs, and player-manager Mickey Cochrane won the AL MVP with a .320 average and 76 RBIs.

The Tigers' bid for their first World Series title proved unsuccessful, however, when they fell to the Gas House Gang Cardinals in seven games. If you think Yankee Stadium is rowdy today, you should have been at Tiger Stadium for Game 7. After the Cardinals hung a seven-spot on the board to break a scoreless tie in the third inning, fans began throwing debris on the field. Then, after Cardinal Joe Medwick slid spikes-up into third baseman Marv Owen in the sixth, all hell broke loose. As Medwick headed out to his position in left field for the bottom of the frame, frustrated Detroit fans threw bottles, partially eaten frankfurters, and other trash at him. The game was delayed for nearly half an hour before Commissioner Kenesaw Mountain Landis (previously of Black Sox fame) ordered Medwick to leave the game.

The Cardinals went on to win 11–0 behind the pitching of Dizzy Dean. Ole Diz combined with brother Daf to go 4–1 with a 1.43 ERA in the Series. Remarkably, the Deans pitched forty-four of a possible forty-five innings in their five starts.

The loss represented the fourth time the Tigers had come up empty in October. But the very next year, they redeemed themselves, winning the AL behind the play of league MVP Greenberg and beating the Cubs in a six-game Series. They beat the Cubs again ten years later to win the October Classic in 1945, a year in which pitcher Hal Newhouser won his second straight AL MVP award. They won their third title, against the Cardinals, in 1968, the year Denny McLain won thirty-one games en route to claiming an MVP of his own.

Detroit's fourth and most recent title came in 1984 when the Tigers beat the Padres. That club got out of the gates 9–0, finished April with a mark of 18-2, and eventually amassed a 35-5 record over the first quarter of the season. Closer Willie Hernandez won the Cy Young and MVP Award.

In every one of their championship seasons, a Tigers player has won the MVP.

---

owner, we figured we ought to split a slice. It was decent and freshly-made, but it was still just Little Caesar's. That said, if you happen to be a finicky eater or have a child who happens to be one, this may be one of the safer bets at the park. Like the Little Caesars back home, it's consistently good but something less than life-altering.

TIGER DOG (DOG REVIEW)

Comerica's standard stadium dog always lets us down. On more than one occasion, our dog has seemed less than fresh, limp, and lifeless. That said, it's worth visiting the Singing Hot Dog Vendor, just for the experience. This operatic fellow works the Section 100 beat. You'll know him when you hear him. Trust us. From our observation, he does the steadiest business among all of the wiener-schleppers and, consequently, his dogs are most frequently replenished. Although this basic dog is a disappointment, ultimately, there are several opportunities to score specialty dogs within Comerica. These are sold at mobile stands on the concourse and at a special dog stand in the food court. We recommend opting for one of those two methods of dog procurement if you're hankering for a frankering. We tried the **Chicago Style Hot Dogs Stand** in the food court. The stand specializes in Chicago Style or Coney Island dogs,

which cost a dollar more than the regular ballpark offering. It's worth it. This natural-casing Kowalski dog is grilled and tasty. They got the Chicago dog toppings just right, but the Coney sauce wasn't what we were expecting. In Detroit, the Coney sauce has quite a bit of chili powder and cumin in it. It tasted good, but took a few bites for us to get used to. The fact that it comes smothered in cheese too, certainly helped in winning over our palates.

BEST OF THE REST

There's something to be said for arriving early and visiting the **Beer Hall,** a reasonably priced sports bar located within the Brushfire Grill. This becomes a much less appealing option once game time arrives, because with wait service and no view of the field, a trip to the hall will keep real fans away for too long. We found the entrees reasonably priced and of higher quality than most of the food we sampled elsewhere. Hard lemonade and wine are available, while the bottled beers include Labatt Blue, Molson Canadian, Heineken, Corona, Sam Adams, Killian's Red, and Guinness Stout. Yes, that's right folks, honest-to-goodness Guinness at the ballpark—Kevin was MIA from innings two through seven. With its pictures of Tiger greats, we found this an inviting place.

As for our favorite selections from the Big Cat Food Court, they included the **Hand Rolled Pretzel,** which we seasoned with cinnamon and sugar. Clearly, this hand-rolled pretzel is one of the best in the big leagues.

The orange chicken stir fry at the **Asian Tiger** was better than we expected. We don't usually look for Chinese at the old ballgame, but it more than held its own.

Josh tried a **turkey leg** at the Brushfire grill and gave it a solid eight out of ten (belches, that is).

Kevin liked the **Kielbasa** sandwich he got at a mobile stand on the Mezzanine. Then again, Kevin's never met a piece of Kielbasa he didn't like.

For dessert, we split an Elephant Ear from the **Lemons and Ears** stand in the food court. We were tempted to try the **Italian Beef** at a portable stand behind Section 131 but decided not to push our luck. If any of our readers would like to try it and shoot us an e-mail with the thumbs up or thumbs down, please feel free. Similarly, if anyone wants to take a stab at calculating how many calories we consumed at Comerica, based on our review of the items mentioned above, you also have our blessing.

BALLPARK SUDS

During our most recent visit, we were pleasantly surprised to find a local microbrew had been allowed to set up a stand inside Comerica. The **Atwater Block Brewery** cart resides out behind the left-field foul pole. The taps were pouring Michigan Lager and Dirty Blonde when we visited. As we're both married to brunettes, naturally we immediately gravitated toward the Dirty Blonde and both found it tasty and light.

The **Labatt Jungle,** behind Section 104 in deep right, offers a distant window-view of the field.

The **Tiger Den Beer Stand** on the first base concourse is a find. They have several varieties—Amstel Light, Corona, Guinness, Heineken, etc.—in twelve-ounce bottles.

Yard-sized **Frozen Daiquiris** are available at several stands. Typical flavors include Blue Sky, Strawberry, and Piña Colada. Kevin tried the strawberry and found it a refreshing choice—effeminate, but refreshing. As Kevin repeatedly reminded Josh, he is secure enough in his masculinity to indulge in a frozen drink at the ballpark now and again. To this, Josh replied, "Methinks me lady doth protest too much!"

The Comerica Park Experience

Detroit's baseball resurgence has helped put the growl back into the Tigers fans. We observed a ballpark intensity during a recent visit that had been decidedly lacking when we visited Comerica in 2003. To this, we say "hoorah." Still, this is a ballpark that goes out of its way to cater to families. It is a friendly place for all.

FRIDAY NIGHT FIREWORKS

All summer long the Tigers put on a free postgame fireworks show after Friday and Saturday night games. That must make the Fourth of July seem anticlimactic but we're sure the local kiddies appreciate it . . . and their fathers too, who suddenly have some leverage to make sure the whole family stays until the last out and then a little longer.

SUNDAY IS FOR KIDS

Children under the age of fourteen are invited to run the bases for free after Sunday games. On the day we visited, one gangly thirty-something (who shall remain nameless) tried to take the field to touch all four along with them, but was turned away by ushers.

Kevin: Such is life. It's all downhill after the innocence of childhood passes us by.

Josh: I'll be by to bail you out after I finish this beer. You've really had a banner day in Detroit, incidentally.

LADY JANE'S HAIRCUTS FOR MEN

Maybe Kevin had imbibed in one too many daiquiris, or maybe the Lady Jane's commercial they played on the video board really was hilarious. Josh was visiting a bathroom and missed the spectacle. According to Kevin, the between-inning ad portrayed Lady Jane's as a haircutting chain that specializes in its sexy stylists, making it sort of akin to the Hooters of the barber shop world. Apparently, one of the stylists severely nicked a patron's ear during the course of a fictitious haircut in the ad but the dumb bloke didn't even mind, so smitten was he with her feminine form.

So there you have it, being ridiculous enough to crack up Kevin on one of his "tipsy" days just earned Lady Jane's Haircuts a free plug (pun intended!) in *The Ultimate Baseball Road Trip* 2.0, for whatever that's worth. Legal disclaimer: Josh and Kevin assume no responsible for any haircut or facial injury you may sustain at Lady Jane's.

MOTOWN MUSIC MACHINE

Comerica has hosted several concerts during its short life. Usually these occur during the summer when the Tigers are out of town. Chief among the acts to play the park have been local sons Eminem and Ted Nugent. Other acts to play Comerica have included the Rolling Stones, the Dave Matthews Band, Bruce Springsteen and the E Street Band, Kid Rock, Kiss, and Aerosmith.

Cyber Super-Fans

- **Detroit Tigers Web Log**
  www.detroittigersweblog.com/
  This was the very first Tigers site to hit the blogosphere. It traces its roots all the way to 2001. We really like the user-friendly front page and when we were in town we even heard its host yucking it up on 101.9 WDET.
- **Motor City Bengals**
  http://motorcitybengals.com/
  You can really tell that the four guys who run this site love their Tigers. This is a great place to get a sense for the morale of the local fan base before swinging into town.
- **Bless You Boys**
  www.blessyouboys.com/
  Another long-time Tigers voice, Bless You Boys is ready to ordain the Tigers best in the kingdom. Now all the team has to do is win the big one.

PATSY O. (SUPER-FAN HALL OF FAME)

Famous Tigers fan Patsy O'Toole made such a ruckus at the ballpark that when he traveled to Washington, D.C., for a World Series game between the Yankees and Senators at Griffith Stadium in 1933, President Franklin D. Roosevelt found him too obnoxious to bear and requested that O'Toole be relocated to another part of the ballpark. If that's not one of the most egregious abuses of executive power in US presidential history, then we don't know what is.

While We Were in Detroit
Josh Beat the House

The MGM Grand Detroit Casino is just a ten-minute walk from Comerica. Follow Michigan Avenue across Woodward, then take a left on Third Street and a right onto Abbott and you'll soon be there. Just be sure to drive if visiting after dark. Actually, driving is a good option anytime, since we had a difficult time finding a walk-up entrance. Like everything in downtown Motown, they're expecting that you'll come by car.

We visited The MGM after watching the Yankees beat the Tigers. Though Josh figured the Yankee victory would surely bring him bad karma and resolved to stay away from the roulette table, as soon as he caught a breath of the cold casino air and caught a peek of the cocktail waitresses in bikinis, he perked up.

Kevin went first, bellying up to a table and losing his modest bankroll pretty much immediately. Then Josh picked a table and asked for his trademark purple chips. He employed a system that had served him well in the halcyon days of his gambling youth when he and his college friends would visit Connecticut's Foxwoods. P.S. Josh has a system for nearly everything.

The system revolves around hedging one's bets. At a $15 minimum table, the player puts $15 outside on red, then 15 dollar chips inside on 15 different black numbers, thus covering 30 of the 38 possible numbers. Any red number means the player breaks even, 15 black numbers yield a net gain of $6. And the eight remaining black/green numbers result in a loss of $30. And it only takes two hours to make any real money. But conversely, it also takes a great deal of time to lose any money. The system was designed by Josh and Holy Cross pal Rich Hoffman to keep them at the table long enough to consume at least four free drinks, before cashing out.

"You know, Josh," Kevin said, "if you bet equal number of chips on red and black, or odd and even, you could play this game all night long."

Josh humbly reminded Kevin that he was still at the table playing while Kevin was broke, watching like a lap dog.

In Detroit, Josh's system broke down when a cocktail waitress informed him that his rum-and-coke cost $3. Never before had he been asked to pay for a drink while playing. Nonetheless, he played for more than an hour and actually made a few bucks before Kevin reminded him that the road trip car needed to hit the road soon if they were to make it to Cleveland in time for the next day's game. So he started taking chances. First, he loaded up on Kevin's lucky numbers, playing 17 and 00, then he took Kevin's suggestion and played his birthday, twenty-two. A few rolls later, he was up more than $100. After giving half his winnings back, he cashed out up $50. Not a bad hour's work.

"So this means you're buying dinner, right?" Kevin asked.

"You betcha," Josh replied almost too quickly.

"Really?" Kevin gushed.

"No," Josh laughed.

CHICAGO CUBS, WRIGLEY FIELD

CHICAGO, ILLINOIS
7 MILES TO U.S. CELLULAR FIELD
90 MILES TO MILWAUKEE
285 MILES TO DETROIT
300 MILES TO ST. LOUIS

The Friendly Confines

For any student of the game and its history, Wrigley Field is as good as it gets. The weathered green steel of the ballpark's exterior may not present quite the regal edifice that Yankee Stadium projects to the world, but inside the essence of class abounds—not in a retro, overly done, twenty-first-century way, but subtly, genuinely. Wrigley Field is authentic. And while it may be the *second* oldest ballpark in the Majors, it feels much older than any other existent park—and not just because male fans (and quite possibly female ones too, for all we know) still have to pee in troughs. Unlike its only remaining contemporary, Fenway Park, which has been significantly updated in recent years, Wrigley still offers a strikingly similar environment to the one it provided at its debut in 1914. Sure, it has been renovated to add more seats and there are lights now, but the fact remains that a JumboTron remains conspicuously absent. Also left out are the electronic advertisements, overpowering sound bites, and modern amenities that allegedly make the new parks "fan friendly." The only sounds inside Wrigley are those emanating from an old-fashioned organ, the crowd, and the unobtrusive PA announcer.

Upon entering "the Friendly Confines," our attention was drawn to the green grass and red dirt of the field. The focus is where it should be. And watching the game, we felt as though we were sitting in the 1920s. We felt a kinship with our fellow man as we sat elbow-to-elbow celebrating the game we love. If this ain't heaven, it's pretty close.

More than just being ancient and reeking with history, Wrigley also exemplifies the vital role a ballpark can play in the American city. Nestled in festive Wrigleyville, this gem of a yard is the cornerstone of a hopping entertainment district. Even when the Cubs are on the road, tourists come to see the ballpark and sample the neighborhood restaurants and saloons. And that is true during wintertime too.

Wrigley was built on the site of a former seminary for the meager cost of $250,000. When it opened it was called Weeghman Park and served as home not to the Cubs, but to the Chicago Whales of the Federal League. The "Fed" folded a year later—no small wonder given the league's uncanny knack for accepting teams with completely inappropriate nicknames. Whaling in the windy city? What a gas! Or perhaps local history ignores the reality that the humpback once frolicked in Lake Michigan?

In 1915 Charles Weeghman, former owner of the Whales, purchased the National League Cubs and moved them to Weeghman Park. The new digs represented the Cubs' sixth home since going pro in 1870. Immediately prior to their final move, they'd been at West Side Park on the corner of Polk and Lincoln. Then, on April 20, 1916, the Cubs played their first game at Weeghman, posting a 7–6 win over the Reds. Ten years later, the park was renamed Wrigley Field in honor of new team owner William Wrigley Jr., a chewing-gum magnate who had purchased the team in 1921. The Cubs would remain in the family for sixty years before being sold to the Tribune Company in 1981.

Today, the team is owned by J. Joseph Ricketts, the founder of TD Ameritrade. His son Tom Ricketts is in charge of the team's day-to-day operations. The deep-pocketed Ricketts have suggested they'd like to work out a deal with the State of Illinois and the City of Chicago to orchestrate a multi-hundred-million-dollar renovation of Wrigley to ensure its longevity. It remains to be seen how much funding will come from the Ricketts' bankroll and how much will come from taxpayers. Also, still being debated is what exactly the work might entail, and when it might begin.

Kevin: It would be nice to know this place will be around forever.

Josh: But if the renovation too drastically changes things . . .

Kevin: There's the rub.

Josh: Hopefully, they'll strike the right balance.

Just how old-school are the Cubs? Well, they're older even than the National League. In 1870 they were founding members of the National Association. Known as the White Stockings, they had to drop out of that league in 1872 and in 1873 because the Great Chicago Fire destroyed their park, uniforms, and equipment. In 1875 team president William Hulbert led the charge to form a new league, and the National League was born.

Chicago won the first NL championship in 1876, out-scoring opponents by more than five runs per game. In the late 1890s and early 1900s the franchise tried on a number of nicknames reflective of the team's youth, including the "Colts" and "Orphans," before settling on the Cubs.

In 1906, the early Cubs clashed with the crosstown White Sox in the World Series, which was won by the "Hit-less Wonder" Sox in six games. The Cubs rebounded to win the Series in 1907 and 1908, both times against the Tigers. They have not won a World Series since, despite having had seven October opportunities. Their last Series appearance was a little while ago now, though. It played out amidst some controversy in 1945 but we'll discuss that Series later in the chapter.

For a while the Cubs' long drought wasn't quite so ignominious, since two other venerable franchises were working on epic stretches of futility of their own. The White Sox had gone since 1917 without an October Classic victory and, in fact, hadn't even appeared in a World Series since 1919 when the Black Sox purposely lost. Meanwhile, the Red Sox had gone without October glory since winning the whole ball of wax in 1918. But then all that changed in a span of two years when those teams posted matching clean sweeps of their National League foes in the 2004 (Red Sox over Cardinals) and 2005 (White Sox over Astros) World Series. Now the Cubs are baseball's lone poster-child for being "long overdue," "star-crossed," and all those other adjectives that pundits reserve for seriously hapless losers. The 2003 "Bartman Incident" in the National League Championship Series against the Marlins only perpetuated the notion that the Cubs are plagued by a curse.

Amidst this perpetual disappointment, Cubs fans seem more impatient than they were a decade ago. But they are still a relatively content bunch, considering their lot in life. For now, they are left to harken back to glory days several generations removed from modern times. At least they can take pride in the fact that during the first two decades of the twentieth century, the Cubs fielded the most prolific trio of defensive infielders ever seen. The second baseman was Johnny Evers; the shortstop, Joe Tinker; and the first baseman, Frank Chance. Third-sacker Harry Steinfeldt was no slouch either, leading the league in fielding percentage three times. But "Tinker to Evers to Chance," became a familiar refrain among Chicago fans, who delighted in watching the boys zip the ball around the infield to complete one double play after another.

Two of the most dramatic home runs in history were struck at Wrigley. Unfortunately for Cubs fans, though, only one was hit by the home team. During Game 3 of the 1932 World Series, the Yankees' Babe Ruth stepped to the plate in the fifth inning with the score tied 4–4. After yelling something at Cubs pitcher Charlie Root, Ruth pointed his bat toward center field, and on the next pitch smacked a titanic clout into the bleachers, right where he had pointed. The "Called Shot" propelled New York to a four-game sweep.

exterior

Photo by Kevin O'Connell

Kevin: The big fella was probably swatting away a mosquito and the colorful writers of the day amped it into something it wasn't.

Josh: Speak for yourself. I'm a believer. Anyone who can eat thirty-eight hot dogs in a sitting can call homers and maybe even walk on water as far as I'm concerned.

Kevin: Dude, you just compared Kobayashi to Jesus. Not cool.

Josh: I thought we were talking about the Bambino.

Kevin: Lennon did the same thing and it was all downhill for the Beatles afterwards.

scoreboard

Photo by Kevin O'Connell

Sox, Indians, and St. Louis Browns got his start in the game managing a hot dog stand at Wrigley while his father served as Cubs general manager. The original vines consisted of 350 Japanese bittersweet plants and 200 Boston ivy plants. When the ivy originally sprouted, eight Chinese elms accompanied it, growing out of large pots in the bleachers. But leaves started falling on the field and the trees had to be removed.

The hand-operated scoreboard also dates to 1937. Due to its historic landmark designation, the board appears almost exactly as it did in the 1970s, offering room for just twelve out-of-town scores. This means that on days when all thirty MLB teams are playing, three scores cannot be posted. In its day, the board must have seemed like a colossus, rising eighty-five feet above the field. It appears drab and small by today's standards, but charming. Listen for the rhythmic clicking it makes when the numbers change. No one has ever hit the board with a batted ball, though a shot by Roberto Clemente once came close.

What better place to fly a flag than the Windy City? After each game, the Cubs raise a banner bearing either the letter "W" or the letter "L" to let commuters on the "L" know how the home team fared.

Josh: What the hell are you talking about?

As for the other really famous homer in Wrigley lore, it was struck on the penultimate day of the season in 1938. Cubs player-manager Gabby Hartnett hit the "homer in the gloaming," to break a 5-5 tie against the Pirates. The walk-off, which put Chicago a game ahead of Pittsburgh in the standings, came with two outs and no one on base in the bottom of the ninth when, because of the encroaching darkness, the umpires had already announced they would rule the game a tie after Hartnett's at-bat. But it never came to that. As the shot sailed into the early autumn night, the screams of euphoria rang up and down Waveland Avenue. The next day, the Cubs won the pennant.

One of the best-pitched games ever was spun at Wrigley. On May 2, 1917, the Cubs' "Hippo" Vaughn and the Reds' Fred Toney posted matching goose-eggs for nine full. That's zeroes as in no-hits. Then, after Vaughn gave up a clean single to Larry Kopf and saw him score on a bunt single by Olympic hero Jim Thorpe in the top of the tenth, Toney finished his no-no, retiring the Cubs in order.

No less a baseball visionary than the great Bill Veeck is credited with planting the trademark ivy that grows on Wrigley's brick outfield walls. He patted the vines into the soil in 1937. The man who would go on to own the White

Wrigley was the last ballpark in the Majors to welcome night baseball, adding lights in 1988. But it wasn't always meant to be that way. The Cubs were set to install lights in 1942, but owner Philip K. Wrigley donated the steel light towers to the World War II effort after the Japanese bombed Pearl Harbor. In the decades following, Wrigley Field would wait and wait for night baseball, then it would wait one more day. The first scheduled night game was rained out, making the team's first official evening affair an August 9, 1988, Cubs' win over the Mets. The day before, the Cubs and Phillies had played three innings before the heavens opened.

Wrigley has always been a home run hitter's paradise thanks to several factors. First, there is the steady breeze that blows out toward left in the summertime. Second, Chicago is a hot city and the ball travels farther when it's warm. Third, the park is more than six hundred feet above sea level. Lower air pressure allows the ball to fly longer (See the chapter on Coors Field for the physics-in-baseball lesson). And fourth, the greater-than-usual number of day games gives hitters an edge. Batters from the low minors to the Majors always hit for a higher average before sunset. Even on bright and sunny days, they see the ball better out of the pitcher's hand than they do under the lights.

As for some of the more interesting "other uses" Wrigley has seen through the years, we are always impressed by the long list of movies that have been filmed, at least in part, at the old park. Its appearances on the silver screen include cameos in *The Blues Brothers, Ferris Bueller's Day Off, The Break-Up, Rookie of the Year,* and *It Happens Every Spring.* And who can forget Punky Brewster's trip to Wrigley Field for a National League Championship Series game in 1984?

Kevin: Seriously, if even *one* of our readers remembers that, I'd be shocked.

Josh: Wherever my old gang is today, those founding members of the Jenning's Drive Punky Club, they remember.

Kevin: What have I told you about the Charlton, Massachusetts, coming-of-age stories?

Josh: Keep them to myself?

Kevin: There you go.

There has been one other unusual Wrigley event we'd be remiss not to mention. On New Year's Day 2009 the Chicago Blackhawks hosted the Detroit Red Wings for the NHL's Winter Classic at Wrigley. Unfortunately for locals, Detroit won 6-4, but the 40,818 who turned out on a chilly day still got to experience the ballpark in a whole new way.

Getting a Choice Seat

This is one park for which you'd be wise to order tickets well in advance, unless you don't mind paying a mark-up on the secondary market. Many games sell out before the season even begins. This is easy to understand when you consider that more than 115,000 fans are currently on the waiting list for season tickets. Counterintuitively, the bleachers, which accommodate about five thousand fans per game, sell out first. That's because the quintessential "Wrigley experience" is to be had in the narrow rim of general admission lining the sun-soaked outfield.

Seating Capacity: 41,160
Ticket Office: http://chicago.cubs.mlb.com/ticketing/index.jsp?c_id=chc
Seating Chart: http://chicago.cubs.mlb.com/chc/ticketing/seating.jsp

Don't ask us why they call the sections "Aisles" throughout the park; they just do.

The hardest tickets to get are usually ones for series against the archrival Cardinals and crosstown White Sox. But any summer afternoon game presents a high probability of being sold out. Depending upon the opponent and time of year, the Cubs slot each home game into one of five ticket pricing tiers. From highest to lowest, they are: Marquee, Platinum, Gold, Silver, and Bronze.

Josh: Which one of the five doesn't fit the theme?

Kevin: Marquee.

Josh: All the rest are precious metals.

Kevin: So what's more "precious" than Platinum?

Josh: Maybe we should visit the Chicago Commodity Exchange to find out.

Kevin: You can do that while I finish sampling the Chicago dog stands.

Bleachers

Be sure to spend at least one game in the bleachers. We speculate that the frat-house atmosphere may have something to do with the many graduates of Big Ten schools who settle in Chicago. So arrive early to stake out a spot, treat yourself to a few Old Styles, roll up your sleeve to catch some rays and embrace the madness and pleasure of it all.

As stated, the bleacher sections are general admission, with the exception of three small sections (316–318) out by the right-field foul pole. These Bleacher Boxes are comfortable green chairs, unlike the rest of the Bleachers, which are green benches. The park opens two hours before first pitch and usually there is a line outside the left-field entrance for those hoping to get in early to claim a spot. The first row isn't necessarily the best, as the rather high retaining wall blocks the view and front-row fans aren't allowed to stand once the game starts. So, aim for a spot in the third or fourth row in left-center and you'll have one of the best seats in the house.

A downside to the bleachers is that Wrigley policy prohibits bleacher patrons from entering other sections of the park. Also, when the bleachers are full, it is difficult to find your way to the exit ramps to buy a brew or visit the latrine because of the narrow walkways. On the other hand, if you're looking to get lucky, start in the bleachers and work your way to the bars. Ballpark scoring has never been easier.

Club Box (Boxes 3–39)

The Infield Club Boxes (8–34) are available almost exclusively to season-ticket holders. They're great seats, but the atmosphere is a tad tame for our liking. Nothing against the gray hairs and corporate types, but if this is your once-in-a-lifetime trip to Wrigley, you might find yourself looking to rub elbows with the rank-and-file. You'll have a better chance of finding them farther down the lines in the Outfield Club Boxes. In left field (3–8) or right (35–39), these are still excellent choices.

Field Box Infield (Boxes 110–132) and Outfield (101–109 and 133–143)

Located directly behind the Club Boxes these are also prime seats that offer great views of the field, skyline, and rooftop bleachers across Waveland Avenue. They are hard tickets to come by, though.

If given the choice to pay a bit more to sit in the Infield Boxes, instead of the Outfield ones, we trust you'll do the right thing. If you sit in Boxes 101–105 in left or 139–142 in right, you won't be able to see a parcel of fair territory in the nearest outfield corner because of the rising brick wall. Even so, we recommend 101, 102, 141, and 142, which are angled nicely toward the infield.

Terrace Boxes (Boxes 205–237)

The Terrace Boxes are the first few rows of the 200 Level. These seats are still in the lower bowl, tucked beneath the overhang of the upper deck. But the view of fly balls is not obstructed. These are a good choice on a rainy night.

Terrace Reserved (Sections 201–244)

The Terrace Reserved seats are directly behind the Terrace Boxes and account for the largest portion of seating in the ballpark, offering more than twelve thousand seats. The good news is that many of these seats are close to the action. The bad news is that unless two sinker-ballers are matched-up, you might feel as though you miss much of the game. More than just a few of these seats are obstructed by the overhang. This is more of an issue for fans sitting in the higher-numbered rows and is worst behind home plate (215–219) where a ramp leading to the luxury boxes comes into play. As a rule, try for seats no higher than Row 15. We liked the right-field seats (235–238) where there are

SEATING TIP

Family Section (Aisle 101A)

If you're only in town for one day and want to check out Wrigley from all the angles, we recommend buying a Family Section seat in Section 101A. This catwalk section was added in 1985 and is the only section in the park that allows you to access the main seating area and the bleachers. Technically, these ticket holders are not supposed to enter the bleachers, but it's more of a one-way restriction. Bleacher fans can't get in, but you should be able to pass into bumsville then safely back when you show your stub.

no overhanging luxury boxes. In addition, many seats in the Terrace are obstructed by support poles. We counted twenty-six in all. Kevin wasn't sure why Josh felt the need to count them, but Josh said it was necessary, kind of like counting the TVs in a sports bar. Unfortunately there is no hard-and-fast rule as to what row or seat number will be safe. For example, any row lower than Row 22 is pole-free in left field's Aisle 202. But you need to be in front of Row 5 to be "safe" behind the plate in Aisle 222. Another thing to keep in mind is that with most games being sellouts, you'll have few opportunities to seat hop if you don't like your view.

Upper Deck Box (400 Level)

The press box is not housed between the lower and upper decks as you might expect. Rather, it hangs down from the ballpark roof atop the 500 Level behind home plate. In addition, there is no distinct luxury suite level at Wrigley because the private boxes cling to the underbelly of the upper deck. Consequently, Wrigley's upper deck keeps fans in both its 400 and 500 Levels relatively low and close to the field. At the same time, there is no underhang to block the view. Beware, however, that if you buy seats in the upper deck you may wind up going home with a stiff neck. These seats are not angled toward the plate. If, for example, you sit in Section 434 in right field, you'll be looking over your left shoulder all day to see the infield. The best of these sections are 410 to 430 on the infield. Section 420 is right behind the plate.

Upper Deck Reserved (500 Level)

As with the Terrace downstairs, all you can do is hope you don't wind up behind one of the support poles that, on this level, brace the roof over the 500 Level. On the plus side, there is no underhang to worry about and the first row is not obstructed by concourse traffic thanks to a steep grade between the 400 and 500 Levels. And its proximity to the field and field level makes this one of the best upper decks in the bigs. If given the choice, we would rather sit in the Upper Reserved than in any seat behind Row 15 of the Terrace. You can follow the whole flight of the ball, catch a bird's-eye view of the interesting rooftop parties, and even enjoy a breeze on a hot summer day.

Standing Room

SRO tickets are sold only after all other seats have sold out and only on the day of the game. Because of the overhang, there isn't much of a view from the standing area, which is located above the Terrace. We don't recommend this option if it can be in any way avoided.

The Black Market

Be prepared to pay at least double face to sit with the bleacher bums, and a bit less of a markup for most other sections. You shouldn't have trouble finding a scalper on the streets around the park. Just take a stroll down Waveland and they'll come to you. Somehow, like Santa Claus, they always seem to know.

Before/After the Game

While Wrigleyville may not offer much in the way of parking places, there are scores of unique restaurants and bars in the neighborhood. That's a trade-off we'll gladly accept. This is easily the most festive ballpark setting in baseball, so plan on spending a few hours sampling the saloons before and/or after the game.

Getting to Wrigley

Wrigley is bounded by Sheffield Avenue, Waveland Avenue, Clark Street, and Addison Street. Take Interstate 90 to the Addison Street exit and follow Addison east to Wrigleyville. Or take Interstate 290 east to Route 55 north, to Lake Shore Drive, to Irving Park Road, to Clark Street.

Unless you're attending a Sunday game, don't bother looking for a street parking spot nearby. Most spots are marked residential parking, while others have two-hour meters. Chicago parking authorities aggressively monitor these and tow violators, so don't take chances. On Sunday, though, you can avail yourself of the meter spots on Sheffield or Clark. We also observed some residents on Sheffield selling spots in their driveways, which seemed like a safe and easy option for those willing to pay. If you are arriving early, you may be able to find your way into one of the small parking lots on the corners of Waveland and Sheffield and on North Clark. These charge less for a "full game" spot, which means your car will get boxed-in by other cars and

you won't be able to leave until the guy whose car is in your way is finished with the Wrigley bars. For more money, you can get an "easy-in, easy-out" spot, which means your car won't get boxed-in. There is also a lot on the corner of Cornelia Avenue and Clark a ten-minute walk away.

If you've gotten the drift that parking in Wrigley is a challenge, you're right. For this reason, we strongly suggest taking the "L" train to the game. Get off at Addison Station, right across from the park. Because of the large postgame crowds on the platform, be sure to buy a token in advance for your return trip, or if you forget, follow the tracks to either the Belmont or Irving Park stops, which are short walks away in either direction.

CTA Map: http://chicago.cubs.mlb.com/chc/images/ballpark/480x480_CTA_map_2004.gif

Another public option is the Cubs remote parking program, which offers lot spaces at the DeVry University near Addison and Western for $6. Once you pay to park, a free shuttle bus takes you to the game. For more information, call (773) 836-7000.

DeVry Shuttle Map: http://chicago.cubs.mlb.com/chc/images/ballpark/525x410_devry_map_07.gif

Outside Attractions

ROOFTOP BLEACHERS

Walking along Waveland or Sheffield behind the left-field bleachers, you may look up to see more bleachers atop the many private apartment buildings. One rooftop has a foul pole aligned with Wrigley's left-field line and a 460-foot marker. Another has a funny Harry Caray Face. Others sport Latin phrases praising the home team. These rooftops are home to private clubs composed of members who pay annual dues for roof-view privileges. Many are also available to be rented out for corporate flings on a nightly basis.

The rooftops were at the center of a neighborhood-versus-Cubs controversy in the early 2000s and at one point the Cubs even built spite-fences around the field. Eventually the warring sides negotiated, however, and today the Cubs receive a portion of all revenues derived from these unusual "ballpark" seats.

As for the tradition of watching games from outside the park, it dates all the way back to the 1929 World Series when the Cubs themselves erected temporary bleachers on Waveland and Sheffield to accommodate overflow crowds. They did the same again for the World Series games in 1932 and 1935. Over the years, local residents would sometimes catch some sun and watch the games from atop their buildings. Then organized rooftop viewing swept through the neighborhood in response to the Cubs' magical 1984 season. And it's been growing ever since.

BATTING PRACTICE BLISS

Is the wind blowing in or out? That's the most important question swirling around Wrigleyville as game time approaches. Okay, it's not the most important question to everyone. But to the dorky guys carrying their baseball gloves around everywhere they go, it is.

A few hours before first pitch, a legion of ball hawks assembles at the corner of Kenmore and Waveland behind the bleachers. Wearing gloves and toting ball bags, they wait for BP dingers to come bouncing into the street. Then they scramble like fire ants overwhelming a wounded antelope to claim their prize.

A few years back, Josh spent an afternoon jostling among the regulars and was impressed by their enthusiasm and glove-work. A guy named Kenny claimed to have more than eight hundred balls at home. Ray claimed to be the best at catching balls on the fly. Because the wind was blowing in, however, the regulars predicted few if any balls would escape the confines. And they were right.

HAVE CHAIRS WILL TRAVEL

Though he didn't get a ball while waiting on the sidewalk beyond the bleachers Josh did meet an avid Cubs fan named Doug who made him an offer he couldn't refuse.

A longtime ball hawk, Doug explained that the team was selling used Wrigley Field stadium chairs for $25 a pop or four for $75. And he reasoned that if Josh and he pooled their money, they could each walk away with a pair of chairs for only $37.50 apiece.

"What do you say?" Doug asked. "Are you in?"

"You had me at 'hello,'" Josh replied, already trying to think of the words he would use to convince his wife the chairs would look great in their living room and to convince Kevin they would be no bother to have in the backseat of the car during the remaining 1,400 miles of the road trip.

Josh and Doug met after the game to complete the deal. Kevin allowed the chairs into our rented Dodge Sebring.

But Josh's wife Heather banished the chairs to the Pahigian Family Basement shortly after he brought them in the house. And it's not even a finished basement!

THE KING IS GONE . . . LONG GONE

The Mets' Dave Kingman hit the longest homer in Wrigley history on April 14, 1976. The 550-footer smashed a porch railing on Kenmore. Kingman, who would join the Cubs in 1978 and a year later hit forty-eight dingers for them, became the answer to an interesting trivia question in 1977 when he played in every Major League division during a single season. There were only four divisions at the time, of course. Kingman began the season with the Mets in the National League East, before being traded to the Padres in the National League West, then to the Angels in the American League West, and finally to the Yankees in the American League East. Keeping things in perspective, he may have played in four divisions, but only two states. And how did all that packing and unpacking affect his play? In 132 games he batted .221 with twenty-six HRs and seventy-eight RBIs, compared to the .236 average he posted over a sixteen-year career in which he averaged thirty-seven HRs for every 162 games played.

HUNG LIKE A HORSE

On the corner of Sheridan and Belmont stands a statue of Civil War General Philip Henry Sheridan on his horse. The horse has very large testicles and it is a National League tradition for visiting teams to haze rookies by making them paint the horse's testicles in the team's colors on their first trip to Chicago each year. You think that's bad? Imagine being the guy whose job it is to clean off those horse balls in the morning?

"Mommy, what's that man doing to that horse?"

CUBS STATUES

On the corner of Sheffield and Waveland, a statue memorializes one of baseball's greatest broadcasters. Harry Caray, posed in his trademark Cubs jacket, points his microphone at an unseen crowd as an imaginary chorus of "Take Me Out to the Ball Game" fills the afternoon air. Caray's career began in St. Louis in 1945. After twenty-five years in the Red Birds' booth, he moved to Oakland for the 1970 season, then became the White Sox play-by-play man in 1971. In 1982, he moved across town, where he would remain until his passing in 1998.

On the corner of Sheffield and Addison, meanwhile, stands a statue of Billy Williams. "Sweet Swingin' Billy" spent fifty-two years with the Cubs as a player, coach, and member of the front office. With a .290 average, 2,711 hits, and 426 home runs, his place in the Hall of Fame was well deserved.

On the corner of Addison and Clark, Ernie Banks is emblazoned in bronze. "Mr. Cub" played nineteen seasons at shortstop and first base at Wrigley, belting 512 homers along the way. He coined the phrase, "It's a beautiful day for a game. Let's play two!"

Shortly after his passing in December of 2010, the Cubs announced that Ron Santo would become the fourth Cub honored with a statue. The statue was erected in 2011, then later that year the baseball Hall of Fame's Veteran's Committee chose Santo for long-overdue enshrinement in 2012. Playing in a pitchers era, Santo spent all fifteen of his big league seasons with the Cubs, amassing a .277 average and 342 HRs. He made nine All-Star teams and won five consecutive Gold Gloves at third base in the 1960s.

Watering Holes and Outside Eats

Wrigleyville offers scores of great places to hang out before or after the game. Whether you consider yourself a yuppie, slacker, bohemian, or karaoke queen, there's something in this distinctive neighborhood for you. So do enjoy.

MERKLE'S BAR & GRILLE
3516 N. Clark St.
www.merkleschicago.com/
This joint is named after the New York Giants' Fred Merkle whose infamous base-running blunder helped the Cubs win the 1908 pennant. Because this is a family publication we'll try to refrain from using the word "boner," as baseball lore officially does, to refer to Merkle's mistake.

It is fitting that this joint be named after one of the game's most famous goats seeing as it resides in the same storefront where the Billy Goat Tavern once welcomed fans. We'll get to the story of the Billy Goat's Curse a little bit later.

GIORDANO'S FAMOUS STUFFED PIZZA
140 West Belmont Ave.
www.giordanos.com/index.html
Gooey cheese. Thick, rich tomato sauce. And loads and loads of toppings. More toppings than you've ever seen on a pizza. Chicago is famous for its deep-dish pies and Giordano's makes one of the best in town. The pizzas are served with marinara on top of the cheese, an interesting and not in the least bit regrettable culinary innovation. Eat up!

THE WIENER CIRCLE
2622 North Clark St.
This place is a bit of a walk from Wrigleyville, but it has exceptional Chicago-style hot dogs. In case you don't know, a Chicago dog is a char-grilled all-beef natural-casing

---

Merkle's Boner

The 1908 season was winding down when the Cubs visited New York for a crucial September affair against the Giants. With a week to play, the teams were tied atop the National League standings. No one imagined they'd still be tied at the end of the day. The skies offered no threat of rain, so the game would certainly be played to its conclusion and the winner would assume sole possession of first.

As the afternoon wore on, the game entered the later innings as a pitcher's duel.

After eight and a half the score was tied 1-1. Finally, with two outs in the bottom of the ninth, the Giants advanced Moose McCormick to third base on a long single to right by nineteen-year-old first baseman Fred Merkle, who was starting his very first game of the season in place of an injured teammate. The Polo Grounds crowd rose to its feet, as the roused grandstand fans joined the army of onlookers who had been standing all game long behind roped off areas in the deepest reaches of the outfield. The Giants crowd anticipated a victory that would propel their team into first place. And the next batter, Al Bridwell, delivered. He lined a clean single to right-center. Bridwell sprinted toward first base. McCormick trotted home from third. And the game was over. Or so it seemed.

There was one problem: Merkle never ran to second base. He took several steps toward the keystone sack, but then, as the jubilant crowd spilled onto the field, he took a right turn and ran toward the Giants clubhouse, which was located beyond the centerfield fence.

However understandable Merkle's panicked flight may have been, the play was still technically live as long as there was a potential force-out for the Cubs to record at second base, and Merkle was still a live runner. Savvy Chicago second baseman Johnny Evers braved the stampeding masses to retrieve a ball—whether it was the actual one Bridwell hit was later debated—and then stepped on second to end the inning and negate the apparent winning run. The umpires huddled and then ruled Merkle out.

The game was still tied. But with the crowd on the field it was impossible to resume play, so the umps ruled the contest a tie. The two teams played out the remainder of their schedules and finished the season with identical 98-55-1 records.

To determine the NL champion, the teams made up the controversial tie by starting a new game on October 8. The Cubs prevailed 4-2. Simply because Merkle had failed to run from first to second on a single . . . well, actually a fielder's choice . . . his team was denied a trip to the World Series. He would be derided as a "Bonehead" for the rest of his life. As for the Cubs, they would go on to beat the Tigers in a five-game October Classic. And they haven't won a World Series since.

Vienna served on a poppy-seed roll and topped with mint, green relish, chopped onion, red tomato, a spear of dill pickle, hot peppers, celery salt, and mustard. Just remember, folks don't call their dogs "dogs" in these parts. They call 'em "red hots."

We should warn you. Be prepared to be treated viciously by the foul-mouthed staff. This place is famous for after-dark shouting matches between drunken patrons and the counter help.

Also, think twice about doing a Google search for "the wiener circle." You might be surprised by what pops up on your computer screen. Now that we think of it, be careful searching for "Merkle's Boner" too.

CLARK STREET DOG
3040 North Clark St.
www.clarkstdog.com/

We found this a convenient place to grab a pregame wienie or Italian dipped-beef sandwich. A dipped beef is a hot roast beef sandwich, loaded with sautéed green peppers and onions, then doused, and we do mean doused, with au jus. This soaking bread and beef makes one delicious mess.

THE CUBBY BEAR LOUNGE
1059 West Addison St.
www.cubbybear.com/

A Wrigleyville classic, the Cubby Bear offers a spacious bar area, pub grub, a roof deck, and live bands. If you like to run with the yuppie crowd, this might be the best place for you in the immediate vicinity of the park.

MURPHY'S BLEACHERS
3655 North Sheffield Ave.
www.murphysbleachers.com/

The favorite hangout of bleacher bums is located right outside Gate N. With outdoor seating and a limited menu centered around cased-meat, it's one of those places worth stopping into just to say you've been there. Order an Old Style and drink it out of a plastic cup, then hurry across the street in time for first pitch. If you're looking to get lucky after the game, stick around.

SLUGGERS
3540 North Clark St.
www.sluggersbar.com/

This spacious bar features the best sports decor in Wrigleyville and an upstairs game room with real live batting cages. When we visited, Ronnie Woo Woo was cutting the rug with an attractive blonde.

After a few frosties, we headed to the batting cages where, for just $1 for twelve balls, fans line up to see if they're cockeyed yet. Native son John Cusack was allegedly once a regular in the "Major League" (eighty to eighty-five mile-per-hour) cage.

We tried the "Triple A" (seventy- to seventy-five-mile-per-hour) cage. After stretching and strapping on a helmet, Josh stepped up to the plate and slapped a few weak liners to right field. Then Kevin took his turn, which turned out to be much less a "turn" than an exercise in futility and ever-lasting embarrassment. He foul-tipped two pitches, but couldn't put a ball in play. Afterward, he whined that the strike zone was calibrated for someone much shorter than him.

GOOSE ISLAND
3535 North Clark St.
www.gooseisland.com/pages/wrigleyville_brewpub/66.php

Located directly across from Sluggers, this local microbrewery abides by the slogan "Get Goosed!"

The Island is worth a visit if for no other reason than to check out the first-floor mural that depicts a number of all-time statistical leaders standing side by side: Hank Aaron, Joe Jackson, Babe Ruth, and many others.

GINGER MAN TAVERN
3740 Clark St.

For bohemian Cubs fans or simply those tired of drinking out of plastic cups, we recommend the Ginger Man Tavern. While not a sports bar, this is a cool place for those wishing to avoid the ball game crowd, and a favorite hangout of Kevin's friend Paul who served as our tour guide during one of our Windy City stays.

TRADER TODD'S ADVENTURE CLUB
3216 North Sheffield Ave.
www.tradertodd.com/

Check out this friendly place, just try not to get lost in the side stories.

First, everything inside the bar is for sale, from the assorted neon beer signs, to the mirrors, to the arcade games. Second, the owner personally mobilized fans in the days leading up to the near strike of 2002 and continues to forward fan-mail to the commissioner as he receives it. Third, this is one of Chicago's premier karaoke clubs. And finally, this is your best bet in Wrigleyville to trade barbs with a bona fide Chicago-based movie star. Don Gibb, who played Ogre in *Revenge of the Nerds*, is part of the management team. He has his own brew, Ogre Beer, on tap for patrons to try.

WILD HARE
3530 North Clark St.
www.wildharemusic.com/
The Hare's a swinging reggae bar. You dig, mon?

Inside the Park

Sure, it's a bit cramped on the concourses beneath the stands. And parts of it look a bit dingy. And the seats at many newer parks all face in the direction of home plate and are not obstructed by support poles. But if they ever tear this place down, they'll be making a huge mistake and we'll be among those who chain ourselves to the marquee in the hours before the wrecking ball is set to descend. It really is perfect, not despite these imperfections, but because of them. It's an old-time ballyard. So sit back and enjoy.

Ballpark Features

WRINKLED LINES

You know you're at a ballpark with limited foul territory when the bullpen mounds, along the right and left-field lines, actually spill into fair territory. Take a look at the white chalk and you'll see that a sizable portion of fair territory rises to accommodate the bumps. Curved foul lines—those will definitely will be a determining factor in a life-or-death Cubs game someday. Here's hoping the ball bounces the home team's way.

DISTANT POLES

Though its power alleys are rather shallow, Wrigley plays rather deep down the lines, at 355 feet to the left-field pole and 353 feet to the poll in right. Flags honoring the retired numbers of Ernie Banks (No. 14), Ron Santo (No. 10), and Ferguson Jenkins (No. 31) fly atop the left-field pole and flags for Billy Williams (No. 26), Ryne Sandberg (No. 23), and Greg Maddux (No. 31) fly on the pole in right.

Kevin: Have I had one too many Old Styles or am I seeing double?

Josh: Your vision is unimpaired my only slightly inebriated friend.

Kevin: But there's a 31 on both poles.

Josh: I guess the Cubs were a bit late when it came to honoring Fergie.

FROM TOP TO BOTTOM

Flagpoles stand atop the scoreboard ranking the Major League teams in the six divisions according to place in the standings. Variations of this feature have since appeared at other stadiums but to our knowledge, this is where the practice began.

Josh: Looks like the Mariners are still at the bottom of the AL West.

Kevin: You already told me that this morning when you logged onto ESPN.com.

The Billy Goat's Gruff

The Legend of the Billy Goat dates to 1945. It explains how the Cubs were cursed and why they've gone longer than any other team since winning a World Series.

The story goes something like this. A gentleman named Bill Sianas owned a goat named Murphy that he tried to take into a 1945 World Series game at Wrigley. Apparently Bill was a big fan. And Murphy was, too. But when the goat was denied entrance to the park, an irate Sianas appealed to Pete Wrigley himself, who upheld the ban on the grounds that the goat would stink up the joint. When the Cubs lost the series to Detroit in seven games, Sianas sent a telegram to Wrigley asking, "Who smells now?" Sianas then put a hex on the Cubs. "Goatless, they will remain winless," he said. The Cubs have not even won a National League pennant since.

Bill's nephew, Sam Sianas, now owns several Billy Goat Taverns in Chicago. In 1984 he tried to lift his uncle's curse, parading a goat onto the field on Opening Day. The Cubs responded by winning the NL East, but fell to the Padres in the NLCS.

When the ill-fated 2003 Cubs lost in the NLCS to the Marlins, after a fan interfered with what might have been a foul pop-out, the perception that the Cubs really were cursed grew. We'll discuss that play in greater detail later.

Josh: I believe they really are cursed.

Kevin: That's what you used to say about the Red Sox.

Josh: What else would you call it?

Kevin: Somebody's gotta lose.

Double Your Pleasure, Double Your Fun

In 1925, before Weeghman Park changed its name to Wrigley, the Cubs' minor league affiliate in Los Angeles dedicated its own "Wrigley Field" on Avalon Boulevard. Mimicking Weeghman Park, the original Wrigley sported deep outfield foul lines and power alleys only five feet deeper at 345 feet to left- and right-center.

The expansion Los Angeles Angels played their inaugural season at that Wrigley in 1961, and combined with their American League opponents to set a new big league record with 248 dingers in their eighty-one home games.

Look in the Los Angeles Dodgers chapter for info on still one more ballpark named Wrigley Field.

THE BARTMAN SEAT

Let us begin by saying that our hearts go out to Cubs fan Steve Bartman, who somehow became the unintentional "goat" of the 2003 NLCS when he did what just about 99 percent of red-blooded American males would do when a pop-up came his way at a ballgame. Rather than letting it fall on his head or hoping a fielder would come along to reach into the stands and catch it before it did, he tried to catch it.

Unfortunately, Chicago left fielder Moises Alou probably would have caught the foul pop to bring the Cubs, who were nursing a 3-0 lead against the Marlins at the time, within four outs of a trip to the World Series. Instead, the Marlins' Luis Castillo was allowed to return to the plate and he walked. Then the Marlins scored eight runs and won Game 6 going away. They won Game 7 too.

A lot happened after the Bartman play to thwart the Cubs' hopes—a lot that was not his fault. We don't think he should be viewed as the anti-Christ or even the anti-Maier (Jeffrey, that is). The Cubs organization spoke up in his defense and several of the Cubs players did too. But a certain percentage of fans made him a lightning rod for their frustration. And some still hold a grudge.

Today, Wrigley pilgrims often visit the fateful seat in which Mr. Bartman was sitting when the fateful incident occurred. It's Seat 113 in Row 4 of Aisle 4.

Kevin: Looks just like any other seat.

Josh: I would *not* want to sit there. Not for a single inning.

Kevin: Why not?

Josh: Some of that bad mojo might rub off.

IVY

Concerning the green growth on the outfield wall, the house rules are simple enough. If a ball goes into it and comes out, it's in play. If it goes in and disappears it's a ground-rule double.

Stadium Eats

The Wrigley food is unexceptional. But you're visiting for the amazing old-time experience, and the neighborhood around the park is teeming with places to eat and drink, so this is nothing to get upset about.

VIENNA BEEF DOGS (DOG REVIEW)

Vienna Beef has been churning out tube steak in Chicago since 1894. And Gonnella Baking Company, which makes the poppy seed rolls the dogs come on, has been around even longer. We found our dogs superb in just about every way and applaud the Cubs for switching back to Vienna in 2011 after a thirty-year baseball hiatus for the iconic Chicago company during which time the rather bland Sara Lee Ballpark Frank was the official wiener of Wrigley Field.

We should mention that there are also Hebrew National dogs and bison dogs available at most stands for those concerned about keeping it Kosher or low in cholesterol. Your best bet at Wrigley, really, is to have a dog or three and to eschew the temptation to be much more adventurous than that.

BEST OF THE REST

The **Big Slugger Nachos,** which weigh two pounds and come served in a souvenir helmet, are a cut above the usual ballpark chips. We also liked the offerings at the Italian Hot Spots stand behind Aisle 112. Here, fans find an **Italian Beef and Sausage Combo** sandwich that just might take a few years off your life and is messy as hell but is pretty tasty. If that sounds like too much to handle, the dripping Italian Beef sandwich might be more your speed.

The **Foot-long Brat** at Big Dawgs also more than holds its own.

Kevin: At this point, my arteries are just begging me to stop.

Josh: Then why are you still eating it?

Kevin: I owe it to our readers.

Josh: You owe them a bite. You don't have to finish.

Kevin: Buy your own brat, I'm not sharing.

The **Chicken Wings** from the 50/Fifty Restaurant of Chicago are better than the usual ballpark chicken. The **pizza,** which we recommend, comes courtesy of D'Agostino's, which opened its first Chicago location not far from the park in 1968. In 2011, it replaced Connie's Pizza as the official slice of Wrigley Field. But don't worry ye Connie disciples, you can still get a slice of Connie's at U.S. Cellular Field while you're in town.

When you're finally ready to wash down all the grease and calories, we suggest a **Frosty Malt,** a frozen treat that you eat with a wooden spoon.

STADIUM SUDS

Two words: Old Style. We found people of all ages, shapes, and sizes drinking this stuff. So reach for the beer your grandfather loved—or perhaps your grandmother—and enjoy!

The Wrigley Field Experience

As mentioned above, for the optimum Wrigley experience, bleacher seats are in order. It's all about having a good time. Whether the home team wins or loses, fans enjoy the afternoon sun and have entirely too much to drink. Maybe the reason the outcome doesn't seem so important is that Wrigley is usually full of folks who skipped work to spend an afternoon at the game. And like they say, a bad day at the ballpark beats a good day in the office.

Josh: I'm a ballpark writer. This *is* my office.

Kevin: You lucky son of a bitch. Oh wait, it's my office too!

THROW IT BACK

Wrigley is where "throwing back" home run balls by the opposing team began. And though we love the tradition, this is where we feel it should remain. If you're sitting in the bleachers and catch a dinger hit by the visitors, you have only two options. One: Throw it onto the field before the crowd turns violent. Or two: Tuck it into your pants and run for the ballpark gates. P.S.: You won't make it to the ballpark gates, at least not with your pants.

Josh: If I catch a ball, I'm keepin' it.

Kevin: And I don't know you.

CALLING ALL TENORS

In a tradition started by Harry Caray in 1982 after having similarly led the South Side crowds during his stint at Comiskey Park, a different guest leads fans in singing "Take Me Out to the Ball Game" during the seventh-inning stretch each day. Cubs Hall of Famers have played the role of maestro as have celebrities from all walks of American pop culture.

Kevin: My pick for worst-ever is Mr. T.

Josh: I think Nancy Kerrigan did a pretty sad job of it.

Kevin: Ozzy Osbourne didn't even know what song he was supposed to sing.

Josh: When they ask us, we'll know we've *arrived*.

Kevin: Yeah, someday.

Josh: How 'bout it, Cubbies?

Kevin: We've had practice harmonizing along with the Pogues on our long rides together.

Josh: Yeah, we'll sing it MacGowan-style.

Kevin: Most of the world can sing better than Shane.

RONNIE WOO WOO (SUPER-FAN)

Wrigley Field is home to one of the most famous super-fans in baseball, the fully uniformed Ronnie "Woo Woo" Wickers. Ronnie is so well known and well regarded that when Cubs rookies get called up to the bigs, they ask for autographs. Spend five seconds with Ronnie and you'll understand where he got his nickname. His distinctive high-pitched "woo" can be heard eighty-one games a year, resonating in the bleachers and in the streets surrounding the ballpark. The subject of documentary films and magazine articles, Ronnie gets into Wrigley for free. People shake his hand, ask him to pose for pictures, and ask him to "woo" into smartphones for friends to hear back home.

Cyber Super-Fans

- **Bleed Cubbie Blue**
  www.bleedcubbieblue.com/
- **Chicago Cubs Blog**
  www.chicagocubsblog.net/
- **Another Cubs Blog**
  www.anothercubsblog.net/
- **Chicago Cubs Online**
  http://chicagocubsonline.com/
- **View from the Bleachers**
  http://viewfromthebleachers.com/

CELEBRITY SUPER-FANS

In much the way that it is trendy to root for the Red Sox, Yankees and Dodgers in richity-rich circles, the Cubs garner a celebrity following of their own. Among the faithful are household names like Hillary Clinton, Pat Sajak, Bill Murray, Jim Belushi, Vince Vaughn, Billy Corgan, Eddie Vedder, and even Tony Romo.

Crypt Creeping in the Windy City

Within the Chicago city limits, you have the chance to visit the gravesites of no less than four Hall of Famers. Red Faber, who won 254 games in a twenty-year career for the White Sox, is buried in Acacia Park Cemetery (7800 W. Irving Park Rd.). He rests in the Rose Section, Block 5, Lot SE2, Grave 2. William Hulbert, the White Stockings president who played an instrumental role in founding the National League, is buried in Graceland Cemetery (4001 N. Clark St.). Cap Anson, who recorded 2,995 hits in a twenty-two-year career spent mostly with the Cubs, and Judge Kenesaw Mountain Landis, the commissioner who banned Joe Jackson and seven of Joe's Black Sox teammates, are buried in Oak Woods Cemetery (1035 E. 67th St.). Anson rests in Section E, Lot 4, Grave 10, and Landis in Section J, Lot 1, Grave 123. Happy haunting!

While We Were in Chicago
Ronnie Woo Woo Introduced Us to a Baseball Legend

During one of our trips to Chicago, we bumped into Ronnie Woo Woo at Sluggers after a game.

"Stick around," he said. "I'll introduce you to some players." He then escorted the latest in a long line of surprisingly attractive dance partners to the floor.

By players, we were not sure what Ronnie meant.

"I think he means, like, cool cats," Josh said.

"No, he means baseball players, and I'll bet he delivers," Kevin reassured his friend.

When Ronnie finally relinquished the dance floor, he led us to the bar and introduced us to the ageless Minnie Minoso, who had been sitting in our midst all along.

In case you need a memory jog, Minnie tied Nick Altrock's Major League record by playing in parts of five decades with the White Sox, Indians, Senators, and Cardinals. He shook our hands, posed for a few pictures, and wished us well on the rest of our trip. He said his favorite ballpark was Tiger Stadium. Josh looked up Minnie on Baseball Reference upon returning home and was shocked to discover that he was more than eighty years old at the time of our encounter. He didn't look a day over sixty.

A native of Havana, Mr. Minoso began his career in 1949 and initially retired in 1964, before returning to the White Sox for Bill Veeck's end-of-the-season cameos in 1976 and 1980. He made it six decades in pro ball when he stepped to the plate for Mike Veeck's St. Paul Saints of the Northern League in 1993. Minnie has hit .298 in his Major League career to date (we're not ruling out another at-bat or two), and actually recorded a base hit in 1976 at age fifty-four.

But getting back to Mr. Woo Woo. Before we parted, Ronnie summed up his evolution as a super-fan and his philosophy on life: "I didn't know fifty years ago that I was going to be Ronnie Woo Woo. It just kind of happened. I try to make people happy. It's great to be healthy and to be outside in the sun for the games. The most important thing, as far as I can tell, is to just be yourself and let life come to you."

CHICAGO WHITE SOX, U.S. CELLULAR FIELD

CHICAGO, ILLINOIS
7 MILES TO WRIGLEY FIELD
90 MILES TO MILWAUKEE
280 MILES TO DETROIT
300 MILES TO ST. LOUIS

Finally, Occasion to "Cell"-A-Brate

When we last checked in with the good people on the South Side during our first tour of major league ballparks, there was a profound feeling of disappointment, and sadness at what might have been. The ballpark that was to replace the great Comiskey Park, Comiskey Park II many were calling it, had opened its doors to great, um—what's the opposite of fanfare? The new Comiskey, it turned out, had opened its gates just a bit too soon. You see, what happened to the new yard, built directly across the street from the cozy old one the team had called home for eight decades, was that—nearly overnight—it had become a relic, a monument to large multi-tiered suburban stadiums with little charm, set among a vast sea of parking lots.

In hindsight, the choices that park's designers made don't seem to make much sense: concrete over brick; enclosed design rather than open views of the city; five steep decks in lieu of a more intimate design; parking lots in favor of a ballpark neighborhood. But of course, this represents the changes in ballpark aesthetics that the entire country underwent shortly after Comiskey II opened for business. Now we take such ballpark features for granted, thanks to the revolution Camden Yards started that swept across the nation.

And there standing alone, in stark contrast to the little green gem that once stood across the street and having missed the glorious revolution by just a few short years, was Comiskey II. The White Sox and their fans faced a baseball future from which fate seemed to dictate they would be excluded. Their massive stadium was representative of a baseball past that no one was recalling with much fondness. And to make matters worse, the team hadn't won a World Series since 1917.

And so the good people of Chicago, the fans and management of the Pale Hose, were hit smack in the face with a dilemma: either to hang their heads and bemoan their unfortunate timing, or to put on their hard hats and work boots, and get busy improving things. If you've ever been to Chicago, you need not ask which direction the residents of the City of Broad Shoulders chose. They got to work, and through seven phases of renovations have turned their massive monolith back into the ballpark that most Sox fans always dreamed it could be. Now don't get us wrong, few would place "The Cell" in their list of top five ballparks.

Josh: Would we put it in our top ten?

Kevin: No.

But thanks to much thought, renovation and hard work, the White Sox have a home they can be proud of. And though The Cell still has the bones of a Stadium, oftentimes it really is the little things that make all the difference. The nuances are now there, at least on the 100 level, to give The Cell a great game-day feel.

The new Comiskey Park was initially constructed for $167 million, nearly all of which came from a 2 percent sales tax on hotels in the city. In 1986 a bill was passed by the Illinois General Assembly to fund a new ballpark to be built across the street from the old Comiskey. This bill came in response to White Sox owner Jerry Reinsdorf's threat to move the team to Tampa Bay. The pressure created a hurried environment and the rush was on to build a new South Side park as soon as possible. In 1989 Chicago Mayor Richard M. Daley—son of former Mayor Richard J. Daley and a die-hard Sox fan—helped break ground on the new Comiskey.

On April 18, 1991, more than forty-two thousand fans poured through the gates with high hopes for the first game at the new park. Comiskey II opened and received favorable, but not gushing, reviews. Remember, this was before Camden so people didn't have much to compare it to. Sox fans seemed to like it, as the Pale Hose set a new team attendance record in that inaugural year when nearly three million fans visited the new ballpark.

While many of old Comiskey's attractions and idiosyncrasies were imitated or duplicated in the new park, such as the exploding scoreboard, the only thing brought directly over from the old park was the infield dirt. What was to be the first baseball-only facility built in the American League since 1973, turned out to be overly huge, unfriendly to fans, and sterile. The main complaint was that the upper deck left a lot of concrete showing, was far too steep, and was miles away from the action. It is true that the first row in the upper deck is farther from the field than the last row of upper-level at the old Comiskey was.

Fast-forward a few years, post-Camden, and, rolling up the sleeves of their blue-collared shirts, to work they went on the South Side. The number of renovations is detailed later in the chapter, because as we've said, there have been many, but the major improvements to the ballpark include the following: replacing the original blue seats with green seats; establishing an overall color scheme of green and black; resetting the outfield fence to make the field dimensions less symmetrical; the addition of murals to the interior concourses; a tiered concourse beyond the center-field wall; the addition of a black-and-white screen around the top of the upper deck; the addition of statues throughout the park; and the removal of six thousand seats to make room for the addition of a canopy roof supported by trusses. The roof, and its supportive posts and decorative trusses, more than anything create the feel of an older ballpark, one where the elements of architectural theory might actually have been

exterior

Photo by Kevin O'Connell

consulted. And while the poles block the view from some of these top seats, in reality, you couldn't see anything from these seats anyway, so we approve. Architecturally, Chicago has been a world leader for more than a century. So should it be with its ballparks.

Speaking of beautiful architectural touches, there are those who feel the former Comiskey Park was among the best baseball parks ever. It was certainly a quirky little yard, with its own timeless beauty and full of memories destined to fade more quickly if the team would have moved. Could Comiskey have been saved? Should the monies spent to build the new stadium have been spent to remodel the old? Perhaps. One independent study said that it could be accomplished. Another, conducted by the team, said it would not be economically feasible. The stark reality of the economics of the game, as it has become, that enter into discussions such as these are troubling. Fans are left with the impression all the owners care about are luxury boxes and revenue streams from sources other than ticket sales, such as restaurants and retail shops. As rooters, we're left with a bad taste in our mouths.

Kevin: As though the public is supposed to help fund a glorified shopping mall.

Josh: One where there just happens to be a game going on if you're interested.

Kevin: But if you're not, don't worry. There are plenty of other ways for you to spend your money.

Eventually, whether we like the idea or not, the game leaves our favorite parks in its past. We're told we can only care for and preserve the old parks for so long. Then we must turn out the lights. And if we don't agree to pay the price at the box office and concession stands, ownership threatens to move to some place like St. Petersburg, Florida, where the locals don't even care if there's a team or not.

Josh: I hate owners.

Kevin: Don't talk to me about it; my city has lost two professional franchises now.

Josh: Really? The Pilots were a professional franchise?

Kevin: Well, sort of.

That fateful day of reckoning came to the South Side. When the White Sox told their fans that beloved Comiskey Park, a jewel of the American League, could be expanded, refurbished, and polished no longer, it was time to act. Its era had come and gone, they said, and as painful as the idea was to all, a new Comiskey would have to be constructed, one that would accommodate the Sox and their fans in the twenty-first century. Most White Sox faithful accepted the painful truth with the optimism and forward-thinking vision that has made Chicago one of the greatest cities in the world. And after all, this was to be a new and improved Comiskey: one that would bear the old-school look of its predecessor along with the conveniences of modernization.

Josh: That makes it sound pretty good.

Kevin: It's called clever marketing.

Josh: I wish we could get someone to spin our book as well as that.

Before the two World Series wins in their four-game sweep of the Houston Astros in 2005, which we'll discuss in further detail shortly, one of the sweetest moments early in The Cell's history came on Opening Day 1993, when Bo Jackson, coming off hip-replacement surgery, crushed the first pitch he saw into the right-field bleachers. Jackson had previously dedicated the game to his mother, who had recently passed away. The Sox went on to win the American League West that year, their first divisional title in ten seasons. The next year, Chicago led Cleveland by a single game in the AL Central standings when the strike ended its playoff hopes. In 1997 interleague play began and the new Comiskey hosted the Sox and Cubs for the first regular season "L Series," so named for the "el"-evated rail that connects the two ballparks, and oh, yeah, the rest of the city as well. The Cubs nabbed the opener 8–3, but the Sox won the final two games to claim bragging rights to the city.

This is a city rich in tradition and mindful of its history. And for that reason the initial stab at the new South Side ballpark—which most rated as subpar—was tough for locals to stomach. White Sox history and Chicago history are deeply intertwined. The American League was formed in Chicago in 1899, then officially in 1901 when the Junior Circuit expanded to a 140-game schedule and declared itself a second Major League. In 1900 Charles Comiskey had bought the St. Paul Saints and moved them to the South Side Grounds at 39th and Princeton, where they played their games in a small wooden stadium and captured the pennant by defeating the Cleveland Blues. This park, which doubled as home of the American Giants, Chicago's Negro League team, was torn down in 1940 to make way for housing projects. The White Stockings kicked off the 1901 season by playing the first "official" game of the new American League, winning again against Cleveland 8–2. They went on to win the pennant that

inaugural season. Nixey Callahan tossed Chicago's first no-hitter against the Detroit Tigers on September 20, 1902. On October 14, 1906, the Sox won the only "All-Chicago" World Series, downing the Cubs in six games.

A green cornerstone for a new White Sox park was laid at 35th and Shields Avenue on Saint Patrick's Day in 1910, thanks in no small part to the Irish who lived in the South Side neighborhood of Bridgeport. White Sox Park opened its "palatial" gates just three-and-a-half months later on July 1, 1910. It didn't take long for the new park to become known as "Comiskey." And it wasn't just owner's pride from which the park drew its name. Mr. Comiskey had financed the entire structure and helped in its design, along with architect Zachary Taylor Davis and pitcher Ed Walsh. Perhaps the fact that a pitcher had a hand in the layout explains why the field was 362 feet down each foul line and 420 to straightaway center. The Sox lost 2–0 to the St. Louis Browns in their Comiskey debut on July 1, 1910.

The fans who turned out at old Comiskey witnessed the rise and fall of a sweet-swinging hick named Joe Jackson. "Shoeless" Joe signed his name with an X and sometimes shagged balls barefooted, just like he used to growing up in South Carolina. But he could sure punish a baseball. In 1915 he joined the White Sox via Cleveland, signing a contract for $31,000 a year—huge money in those days. Two years later, the Sox picked up their second World Series title, downing the New York Giants four games to two.

Tragedy struck a few years later when eight White Sox were suspended by Comiskey for allegedly conspiring to fix the 1919 World Series, which Chicago had lost to the Cincinnati Reds five games to three. The players were later found not guilty in the "Black Sox" trial, which nonetheless stained the reputation of the National Pastime and shook the confidence of American values to their very core. Despite the verdict, after the 1920 season Baseball Commissioner Kenesaw Mountain Landis banned all eight players from baseball for life, including Shoeless Joe, though his numbers in the Series were outstanding. The debate over his guilt or innocence carries forth to this day, and the scandal is well documented in the movie *Eight Men Out,* directed by John Sayles. In any case, it was the Steroid Scandal of its day, being likely far more insidious than ever came forth in the press, and a moment of crisis for the game that shook fan confidence for a generation.

In 1927 a double-decked outfield grandstand was constructed at Comiskey, completely enclosing the park while accommodating more than twenty-three thousand new seats. Though it seated many, the enclosure gave Comiskey an intimate feel that most folks from the South Side remember fondly. The first ever All-Star Game was played at Comiskey on July 6, 1933. See what renovation and modernization, done well, can accomplish? But the Sox weren't done improving the grounds yet. Lights were added in 1939 to facilitate night games. Then on July 5, 1947, lights of a different kind went on in Comiskey when Cleveland's Larry Doby broke the American League color barrier pinch-hitting against the White Sox. Doby struck out in his first at-bat but got a hit the next day, starting at first base.

The Midsummer Classic returned to the grand old park in 1950 in the form of a thirteen-inning marathon that saw the National League win 4–3. White Sox shortstop Luke Appling would retire later that year after playing 2,422 games in a Chicago uniform. In 1951 Minnie Minoso became the first African-American player to take the field for the Sox, and he did so in grand style, homering off Vic Raschi of the Yankees in his first game. Who knew then that fifty years later Minnie would meet Josh and Kevin in Wrigleyville when their seminal road trip brought them to Chicago?

In 1958 the first Bill Veeck era began, one that would bring the White Sox many of their current traditions and many enhancements to the old ballpark. Veeck would become a baseball marketing legend, to the extent that South Shields Street is today known as Bill Veeck Drive. There are too many interesting stories about Veeck's wacky promotions to list them all, but we'll do our best in the pages

ahead to hit some of the highs and lows. If Veeck's style catches your fancy, we suggest reading his autobiography *Veeck, as in Wreck,* or the simply titled biography *Bill Veeck,* by Gerald Eskenazi.

The Sox quickly flourished under Veeck's inspired leadership, winning the pennant in 1959 to end a forty-year drought. Unfortunately for the Sox, Veeck was forced by ill health to sell his interest in the team in 1961. He would later reemerge as owner in 1975. In between the Veeck years some even crazier things happened on the South Side, but none held any comedic value to Sox fans. The low point came when the Sox, in an effort to bolster flagging attendance, played one "home" game against each of their AL opponents in Milwaukee at County Stadium. They had losing records both years, and fears that the team might permanently make Milwaukee its home made Chicago fans mighty nervous. Also, in 1969 Astroturf was laid at Comiskey. The team responded to the plastic grass by having its worst season ever in 1970, losing 106 games. Ouch.

But by 1973 the Sox were on the rebound. A May 20th doubleheader against the Minnesota Twins drew a Comiskey record 55,555 fans. And by 1975 Veeck was back at the helm, and the hijinks and fun picked up where they had left off, even if the Sox still couldn't bring home a World Series title. In 1976 natural grass returned to Comiskey. "Thank you, Lord." Perhaps the secret to success for an owner comes in knowing what features not to mess with in order to preserve the history of the game alongside being adventurous enough to try something new. Veeck tried morning baseball, scheduling the first pitch for 10:30 a.m. to accommodate third-shift factory workers. This was another innovation that didn't catch on. In 1978 Larry Doby replaced Bob Lemon as manager, becoming the second African-American manager in AL history and the first for the Sox. On July 12, 1979, in a move way ahead of its time, Veeck sponsored "Disco Demolition Night," during which fans were encouraged to bring disco records to the ballpark for their destruction between games of a doubleheader. Good idea, Bill—at least on paper. We hate disco, too, but after fans sent thousands of records Frisbeeing onto the field and a riot started in the stands complete with small fires, the nightcap against the Tigers was forfeited. Ouch again.

Perhaps Disco Demolition Night was the beginning of the end, because Veeck sold the

interior

Photo by Kevin O'Connell

team to Jerry Reinsdorf in 1981. In 1982 a new exploding scoreboard, with improvements such as a color video board, appeared, as did new dugouts and luxury suites. In 1983 Comiskey hosted the All-Star Game, played on July 6. Fifty years earlier to the day, on the same field, the first All-Star Game had taken place. In the Golden Anniversary game, the AL won 13–3, paced by a Fred Lynn grand slam. Lynn's blast was the first grand salami in the history of the Midsummer Classic. The Sox would go on to clinch the AL West title that year and win the division by twenty games—an MLB record that stood until 1998 when the Yankees finished twenty-two ahead of the Red Sox. But the White Sox fell to Baltimore three games to one in the 1983 ALCS. In 1984, the longest game in AL history was played at Comiskey between the White Sox and Brewers. The game lasted twenty-five innings and spanned two days before Harold Baines ended it with a walk-off homer to give the Sox a 7-6 win.

It took thirteen years after moving into their new ball-park, but in 2005 the White Sox at last put together all the ingredients necessary for a World Series run. Sox fans had endured decades, eras, and generations of disappointment that spanned the Black Sox years, the era of the Go-Go Sox, and the South Side Hit-men's day. They'd witnessed playing greats such as Luis Aparicio, Carlton Fisk, and Frank Thomas fail to deliver a championship. They'd survived an attempt by Bud Selig to buy and relocate the team to Milwaukee and even threats from the White Sox owner to move the team. And they'd survived the move from Old Comiskey to "The Cell." They'd endured all of it, and in the end, through an improbable run, they came out on top.

After leading the AL Central for most of the summer of 2005, a late-season slump saw the Sox slip behind the Cleveland Indians. Where earlier White Sox editions might have folded, the 2005 Sox were different. Their manager, the fiery, contentious, and hilariously difficult to understand Ozzie Guillen had infused the club with his tough, never-say-die personality. Playing what became known as "Ozzie-Ball," or "Grinderball," which took the focus off power hitting, and put it on winning through a gritty style of play, the White Sox dispensed with the other Sox, those of the Red variety, in three straight games in the AL Division Series.

Josh: We know who the true Sox are.

Kevin: You know that Chicago is a far bigger city than Boston, right?

Josh: Yeah, but we have better chowder.

The Los Angeles Angels of Anaheim, of Orange County, of Southern California, of Los Angeles, of the United States,

handed the Sox their only playoff loss during 2005, in Game 1 of the AL Championship Series. It was a march of destiny for the Sox from then on, as four straight Sox pitchers—Mark Buehrle, Jon Garland, Freddy Garcia, and Jose Contreras—threw four straight complete-game victories to dispose of the Angels. For Sox fans, Game 2 of the World Series against the Astros will be the one to remember, because it was at home, and it ended in such dramatic fashion. In the bottom of the seventh inning, with two outs and down 4-2, White Sox slugger Jermaine Dye was at the plate with two runners on base. Dye was hit by a pitch and awarded first, though replays confirmed that the ball hit his bat. Paul Konerko stepped up and rocketed one of two epic Game 2 home runs, a grand slam to give the Sox a 6-4 lead. The other epic shot came from an unlikely source, Scott Podsednik. After the Astros tied the game at six in the top of the ninth, the light-hitting lefty came to the plate in the bottom of the inning having not hit a single home run during the regular season. Scotty Pods' blast to right-center lifted the Sox to a 7-6 victory. As Sox fans celebrated, listening to Journey's "Don't Stop Believing," they came to believe theirs was a team of destiny, and they were right. Though there was much great action in the rest of the series, it became apparent throughout the four games that the Sox were not going to lose. It was their year. The two epic home run blasts that gave the Sox the win in Game 2 are marked where they landed by blue seats in the outfield.

Trivia Timeout

Strong Breeze: Which two White Sox hit homers that are commemorated with specially colored outfield seats at The Cell?

Gale Force: Name five Grinder Rules from the Ozzie Era.

Hurricane: Name five (of the many) players honored with statues at The Cell.

Look for the answers in the text.

Kevin: It's interesting that the Red Sox and White Sox droughts ended a year apart.

Josh: Who's next? The Indians or the Cubs?

Kevin: How about the Mariners?

The Sox' World Series victory was truly one for the fans. The parade route began at The Cell and wound through all the neighborhoods of the South Side on its way downtown. It was one of the better tributes to a fan base hanging in there with their team, always showing their support and love, and never losing the faith, if you will pardon cliché. All teams claim to love their fans for their support, especially after a playoff run, but what do they actually do for their fans? When the time came to "Cell-a-brate" the White Sox brought the party to their fans' historic neighborhoods and very doorsteps. It was as true an act of mutual devotion and respect as we have seen from an organization.

Another sweet moment was Buehrle's perfect game against the Tampa Bay Rays in 2009, a game saved in the ninth inning when defensive replacement DeWayne Wise made a ridiculous catch in center field to rob Gabe Kapler of a home run. Wise had the ball in his glove but it popped out and he had to snare it with his bare hand before he (and it) fell to the ground. A poem titled "The Catch" can be found printed at the location where Wise saved the game. Look for the spot above Frank Thomas's retired number.

Getting a Choice Seat

Even with the recent success of the team, White Sox tickets aren't as tough to come by as they are expensive. But there's no ballpark in the league where we recommend ponying up the extra change more than at The Cell, because the difference in the experience can be dramatic. If you buy an upper deck seat, you will have a fairly lousy experience. If you get into the 100 level, the atmosphere is infinitely better, and so is the food.

Unless the hated North Side Nine are in town, getting a ticket on game day shouldn't be any hassle. Unless the Sox are making a playoff run, they don't sell out too many of their games.

Infield Box and Club Level (Sections 121–143, 312–357)

Forget about these seats unless you have a Chi-town connection. They're available for season ticket plans only. But if you can find them from a broker or on the streets they are quite good. Sections 131–133 are the sections directly behind home plate, in case there's any discrepancy with the scalper who's trying to make a deal with you. A crooked scalper in Chicago? Get outta here!

Lower Deck Box (Sections 109–120, 144–155)

These are the best seats we plebes are allowed to buy, and they are pretty good. It feels spacious on the first level at U.S. Cellular Field, likely because the upper deck is pushed back away from the lower level. The design of the park ensures that there's no overhang problem at all, which is

Seating Capacity: 40,615
Ticket Office: http://chicago.whitesox.mlb.com/ticketing/index.jsp?c_id=cws
Seating Chart: http://chicago.whitesox.mlb.com/cws/ballpark/cws_ballpark_seating.jsp

good for the lower level, but pushes the upper deck into the stratosphere.

A very low retaining wall separates the field level seats from the field, which is great for autograph hounds or for those wishing to lean over to snag a ball along the third-base side during batting practice. Josh got a ball during infield warm-ups after only five innings of pestering.

The lower bowl has more rows than most parks, twenty-eight by Josh's count. Again, good if you can get them. You may have to take a rather lengthy hike to find the men's room or get another beer, but find a seat in these sections. There are times on a baseball road trip to open up the wallet and let some of the road flies out. U.S. Cellular Field is one of them as the good seats are pretty good, but the bad seats are horrible. Another thing about the rows on the first level: They rarely go more than seventeen seats across without an aisle break, and the aisles are nice and wide. So with only eight or fewer seats to either side of you, it's almost like everyone has a box seat.

Lower Deck Reserved (Sections 100–108, 156–159)

If you buy your tickets from the window on game day, these will most likely be the best seats available. So make the most of the situation. Avoid Sections 156 and 108 as they have foul-pole obstructions. Also steer clear of Sections 100 and 101, as the batter's eye and the massive concrete patio in center field wreak havoc on the sight lines. In Section 101 sit only in Row 15 or lower, and in Section 100 don't get caught behind Row 10. Other than that, the advantage of building a field with fairly symmetrical dimensions is that the sight lines are largely preserved. And remember, old Comiskey had symmetrical dimensions, too, so we're not arguing with that decision. That's not the problem here. Candidly, we feel one of the main problems with U.S. Cellular Field is old Comiskey Park. People who don't remember how intimate the old park was (or who grew up watching the Mariners play in the Kingdome) don't have nearly as much to say about how large and sterile the new park is.

If you plan on sitting in the outfield, the seats in right field are farther away than in left because the patio area in right

SEATING TIP NO. 1

We'll state this again, because it is the key factor of this ballpark: Do not buy an upper deck seat unless you don't mind being relegated to the upper deck only. Unlike other parks, there is no access to the main concourse if you hold 500-level tickets, and there is no way to enjoy the many patio areas that have been added, which is a great way for people to upgrade their seats. All the cool stuff that we talk about in this book will be unavailable to you, and your seats will likely be very disappointing.

SEATING TIP NO. 2

Tickets are half-price on Monday nights. Since tickets to The Cell are relatively expensive, try to shoot for getting to town on a Monday and watch your ballpark buck go twice as far.

pushes the seats back about twenty feet. We recommend left-field Sections 157–159 over any in right field. Section 159 is prime, as it is lower to the field and closer to the action. The bullpen in left field is elevated and a see-through outfield fence allows the pitchers and fans seated near ground level to see through the mesh. Though initially against the idea, it did add to the experience for Josh. The benefit of chain-link is that it diminishes what would be an obstructed view.

Bullpen Sports Bar and Patio Seating

Situated just beyond the right-field fence, the Bullpen Sports Bar is located behind the visiting pen and separated by a glass wall that also offers a view of the rest of the field. You can have an Old Style and watch the relievers warm up. We found it amazing to hear how much snap is on the ball from this close. But honestly, the setup smacks a bit of the monkey cage at the zoo. The players know you're there but won't look at you. It's awkward for both sides and probably should be altered a bit.

Inside, a wooden bar sits in a cinderblock locker room. There are plenty of tables and places to sit, but not all of them offer views of the field. They should. And the place lacks the warmth that a bar should offer. Picture putting the bar from *Cheers* inside your high school locker room and you've got the idea. Now this may have seemed like a great idea when you were sixteen, but when Kevin was sixteen he also thought it would be cool to cut the roof off his car to make it a convertible—unfortunately, he was living in rainy Seattle at the time and his upholstery got ruined.

Both the Bullpen Sports Bar and the Patio in right field have been dubbed "the Party Area" by the signage. If you

have crappy seats, by all means head on down. Even if you don't pop the $10 extra to get from the Bullpen Sports Bar to the Patio area up above (which provides much better access to the players to snag autographs) you'll be upgrading your seats. But beware. The Patio has only eighteen tables with seats at each that cannot be seen from inside the Pub, so if seating is a priority for you like it is for us, scope it out from up above before you pull out the green down below.

Bleachers (Sections 160–164)

The seats in left-field home run territory are actual bleachers benches, but on the plus side they have contoured seat backs and there is enough space in between the numbered sitting spots to give your rump some room to breathe. All in all, these are pretty comfortable for bleachers, so we're not sure why they're two bucks cheaper than their right-field counterparts (Sections 100–103) that are the same distance from the plate. Just don't expect the shenanigans of the cross-town team's bleachers. That kind of funny business doesn't fly on the South Side, except when Josh is using the public shower on the concourse.

Section 164 in left field has serious visual obstructions caused by the concrete of the batter's eye, unless you're in Rows 1–12, which are okay.

Upper Deck Box and Reserved (Sections 506–558)

We learned a great deal about ballparks visiting U.S. Cellular Field. For the most part, the first levels of nearly all ballparks offer pretty good seats. It's what the architects do with the challenges of the upper deck that makes a ballpark distinctive and makes up the criteria of how the park will inevitably be judged. If the upper deck hangs out a great distance above the lower, thus providing a steep but close upper level, it will then be compared to Yankee Stadium. If the upper deck is small, not terribly steep, and tucked close to the field, as on the North Side, a "Wrigley-like" quality will be observed. If neither strategy is employed and the upper deck is high up, not hung close to the field, and still very steep, the park will unfortunately be dubbed "U.S. Cellular-esque." We cannot stress this enough: If at all possible, stay away from the upper deck at U.S. Cellular Field. The first row of these seats is farther from the field than the last row was at old Comiskey. Not only is there a level of luxury boxes and a Club Level, but also a level for the press in between the lower and upper decks. We do not recommend sitting in the upper deck at all. Between the decks is almost sixty feet of sterile cement. What the architects were thinking building an upper deck like this, we have no idea, except perhaps to

35th and Shields: Construction Junction

Our friend and tour guide of the South Side on our first road trip was John Murphy. After the ballpark opened, to the fanfare of dozens, John took part in a neighborhood focus committee investigating what could be done about the upper deck at U.S. Cellular Field, and improving the ballpark in general. Apparently, the Sox got the memo, either from the focus groups or our book, because several phases of construction have vastly improved the ballpark since its opening. Good work, John, and all the citizens and fans who encouraged ownership to get busy fixing the mess they'd made. Here's a list of what has been accomplished thus far:

In 2001

- *Changed the distances to the outfield wall, de-unifying the field dimensions.*
- *Added restaurant in the outfield and a tier to the patio plaza.*
- *Moved the bullpens to give fans a view of pitchers warming up.*
- *Added bleachers where the old pens were.*
- *Added three rows of seats at field level between the dugouts and the foul poles.*

In 2002

- *Built multi-tiered batter's eye in center field and added the Party Deck.*
- *Replaced poorly designed backstop, removing netted roof to allow more balls to drop through for souvenirs.*
- *Beautified the Main Level concourse, adding brick and lighting fixtures.*
- *Made Club level improvements.*

In 2003

- *Added 28 x 53-foot-high-resolution video screen to center-field scoreboard and two 300-foot-long "ribbon" LED boards to the upper deck façade.*
- *Spiffed up the Outfield and Upper Deck concourses to match main concourse.*
- *Built Fan Deck patio in center field.*
- *Painted outfield steelwork gray and stained the concrete in seating areas and pedestrian ramps.*

In 2004

- *Removed 6,600 seats from the upper deck.*
- *Constructed a flat roof, elevated twenty feet and supported by pillars.*
- *Built the translucent wall, partially enclosing the Upper Deck Concourse.*
- *Upgraded Fan Deck to feature tiered and standing room seating.*
- *Added Lower Terrace balcony.*

In 2005

- *Began seat replacement project to switch out the dreadful blue seats with Comiskey green. Project was completed in 2008.*
- *Added 314 "Scout" seats behind home plate.*
- *Built FUNdamentals Deck, kids area on the left-field concourse.*

In 2006

- *Completed restaurant for Scout Seating.*
- *Hung World Series and AL Pennant and Division banners on light towers in the outfield.*
- *The flags for these titles, now on the banners, were replaced with flags of all the Sox logos in club history.*

In 2007

- *Built a new press box on the first base side on the 400 Level.*
- *Added the restaurant (named Gold Coast Tickets Club in 2011) at the locale of the former press box.*
- *Began construction of White Sox Champions brick plaza outside Gate 4.*

Believe it or not, we haven't listed all the upgrades to this park because there have been so many. Phases VIII–X include the completion of Champions Plaza, a beer garden and a restaurant outside Gate 5, a new Metra Station, and the first ecofriendly permeable paving parking lot in Major League baseball.

Josh: So, Mr. Environmental, what's a permeable paving parking lot, anyway?

Kevin: It's a specially developed type of concrete that retains water, which actually saves money by keeping waste water out of the city's storm water system and greatly reducing the Urban Heat Island Effect.

Josh: Sorry I asked.

keep it back and eliminate all overhang for the lower levels. Spend the extra two bucks and sit in the bleachers.

Scalper Scene

A sign outside the park reads, "Resale of tickets at any price is prohibited." That said, we did see a few folks walking around, and we don't think they were selling Girl Scout cookies. By now you should know the drill, but beware, it is against the rules. StubHub is always a good option, especially if you're cruising toward town in your road trip mobile, the North Side nine are visiting, and you have access to a smartphone.

Before/After the Game

Way back when your dad was a lad, there used to be a neighborhood surrounding Comiskey, but it was torn down when the Dan Ryan Expressway was built and before the project buildings arrived. The South Side had an inner-city ball-yard neighborhood much like the one the cross-town team now enjoys. It seems urban renewal is not always a good thing. So, in an effort to recapture what they once had, the team has begun to develop the parking lot behind the left-field wall, making it inhabitable for a restaurant and bar scene.

Getting to U.S. Cellular Field

There really isn't any street parking during ball games in the residential neighborhoods. Don't waste your time looking like we did. Folks have been scoping out the neighborhood for secret spots for more than eighty years. There aren't any left. If you're driving, U.S. Cellular Field is one of those places where drivers need to bite the bullet and park in the team lot, though it is very expensive. Because of the high cost, we recommend parking your car anywhere other than The Cell, and taking public transportation. But if you must drive, U.S. Cellular Field is located just off the Dan Ryan Expressway at 35th Street. You'll see it from the freeway.

We took the "L" Red Line train to the game. Get off at the Sox/35th stop and U.S. Cellular Field will be on your right as you come up to street level above the Dan Ryan. If you're leaving by way of the "L," use the same protocol that you'd use in the Bronx. Get on the train soon after the game ends, before the crowd disperses.

L Train Info: www.transitchicago.com/

Tailgating, Uh, Yeah

The White Sox website claims that tailgating is encouraged in White Sox Parking Lots A–F. We don't know if we hit it on a bad day the first time around or what, but we saw a lot more tailgating during our second tour of the ballparks. Maybe that's because our first trip was in September when folks weren't in a grilling frame of mind. But again, you're going to spend some serious coin to set up that game of cornhole. Then again, if a lengthy pregame walk to and from a pub isn't your thing, then tailgating might be the right option for you. Get those grilles fired up and expect to drop a couple more bills than seems reasonable to park close.

Outside Attractions

CHAMPIONS PLAZA

This sculpture/buy-a-brick tribute to the 2005 World Series is actually very nicely done. Look closely to follow great moments in White Sox history. And in case you might not be aware, the statues represent some of the heroes of 2005: Paul Konerko, Joe Crede, Orlando Hernández, Geoff Blum, and Juan Uribe. But we all know it was a team effort, right? But we'll talk more about the players immortalized in bronze at The Cell a little later.

OLD COMISKEY PARKING LOT

Rather than tailgate, why not seek out some of the history of the old park that used to be right across the street? In the parking lot just to the north of the new park resides old Comiskey's home plate. White lines mark the location of the batter's box and where the baselines once ran, whereas yellow lines tell you where to park your car. Imagine the players that walked the grass of that once glorious park. Imagine the home run that Al Smith hit to set off the exploding scoreboard for the first time. Imagine the five glorious All-Star Games that were played here. No, you say? Your count is different? Well, there was the inaugural game played in 1933, the 1950 All-Star Game, the Negro League All-Star Game in 1933, the fiftieth anniversary All-Star Game played in 1983, and the seventieth anniversary game held across the street in 2003. If you want to imagine White Sox pitcher Ed Walsh winning forty games in 1908—a feat no one has matched since—it might be more inspiring to visit 39th and Princeton, the site of old Schorling's Park, five blocks to the south.

THE SHOT HEARD 'CROSS THE BLOCK

Armour Square Park to the north of the old ballpark was the supposed landing site of a ball Jimmie Foxx knocked completely out of old Comiskey in 1932. Today, the park is a good place to have a catch before the game as it sits right next to Lot B. The park was established in 1904 and the Sox are working with the city to spruce up the grounds.

THE BABE'S BOTTLE

Just to the left of the Gate 4 ticket window, vines of ivy grow on the side of U.S. Cellular Field. This location used to be just across the street from old Comiskey, and there used to be a bar here called McCuddy's, an infamous joint where legend had it Babe Ruth used to go between innings to toss back beers when the Yankees were in Chicago. It's a romantic image, isn't it? Imagine how well "the Sultan" could have swatted if he'd played the game sober. Then again, perhaps he hit better after a few belts. Kevin plays pool better, as long as he's well within the "beer window," a sliding scale of beers where improvement is noticeable within its confines. Before or after, well, that's another story.

American Giants

Schorling's Park was also the home of Rube Foster's American Giants—Negro League World Series champs in 1926 and 1927. Andrew "Rube" Foster was the father of the Negro Leagues who as a pitcher won fifty-one games himself during the 1902 season with the Chicago Union Giants. He posted an unimaginable 54–1 record in 1903 with the Cuban X-Giants. Prior to forming the Negro National League, his American Giants won every championship from 1910 to 1920. He excelled as player, manager, and league administrator before suffering a nervous breakdown and dying in 1930. He was named to the Baseball Hall of Fame in 1981.

Chicago was also home to many other Negro League teams, including the Columbia Giants, Leland Giants, Unions, Union Giants, Lelands, and, of course, the Chicago Giants. For complete information on the teams of the Negro Leagues, we recommend *The Biographical Encyclopedia of the Negro Baseball Leagues,* by James A. Riley.

GRANDSTAND, LTD
600 W. 35th St.

This memorabilia shop features more White Sox gear than we found anywhere else, including inside the park. They have street signs bearing players' names (Frank Thomas Way, Paul Konerko Boulevard) as well as autographed balls and shirts, old packs of baseball cards to fill out your collection, and more. Kevin was excited to find a Ken Griffey Jr. uniform, from his days as a Mariner.

Watering Holes and Outside Eats

BEER GARDEN TBD

Outside Gate 5 there now stands a wonderful Beer Garden called, curiously enough TBD's. No really, that's the name. You don't need a game ticket to get in, and they serve beer, wine, and soft drinks. Plus, the place is open well before and after the game. It's all part of the effort to improve the ballpark neighborhood and adds a much needed point of interest outside the park and place to meet up with people before the game.

BACARDI AT THE PARK

Continuing their efforts to offer some kind of experience outside the ballpark, the Sox have opened up a full restaurant outside Gate 5 to go along with their beer garden that never really got a name.

Josh: Unfortunately, the restaurant never got a real name either.

Kevin: They could have called it "Cuervo at the Yard."

Josh: Or how about "Jack Daniel's at the Dium"?

Kevin: What's the Dium?

Josh: Hello? Stadium.

Despite the name, Bacardi At The Park is operated by the Gibson restaurant group, and offers a very nice selection of burgers, brisket and pulled pork. They've kept prices reasonable and are by far the best close option outside the ballpark. There's great Chicago sports décor in the joint. We recommend getting a mojito or rum drink of your choice and diving into the smokehouse maple chicken wings and smoked corn on the cob with barbecue butter. Then head for the meat of your choice. You really can't go wrong.

Josh: Mmm. Barbecue butter.

Kevin: No, Joe. This ain't heaven, it's Chicago.

MORRIE O'MALLEY'S HOT DOGS
3501 South Union Ave.
www.morrieomalleys35.com

After almost a decade of trying, we still have yet to figure out the Irish hot dog connection that is famous in Chicago. But you still gotta hit O'Malley's before the game for a charred Vienna beef dog that is as good as it sounds. Also the joint has four green seats from the old Comiskey out front that patrons can use while they eat. In this town, dogs come loaded with pickles, tomato, relish, kraut, and more if you ask for it, but never ketchup. O'Malley's also serves Italian beef, and an assortment of other treats sure to raise your cholesterol.

Josh: I'm putting ketchup on. Convention be damned.

Kevin: Dare to dream, Josh. Dare to dream.

SCHALLER'S PUMP
3714 S. Halsted St.

Schaller's is a great place to "get pumped" before the game. It's the pub with the longest history of supporting the Sox, dating from 1881. It's also a great place for cheap pregame grubbing. The name stems from prohibition, where a local brewery pumped their beer to the speakeasy located on the site. Access was given only to those approved through a keyhole. Inside today you'll find friendly people, a smoky atmosphere, and cheap beers served in the can. The bar feels like an American Legion bar, with aged regulars downing Old Style. Schaller's was a favored haunt of Mayor Daley the elder, a famous fan of Bridgeport and the White Sox. Remember to bring cash, because no credit cards are accepted.

THE CORK AND KERRY AT THE PARK
3258 S. Princeton Ave.
www.corkandkerrychicago.com/

A short walk across Armour Park will land you in the vicinity of the Cork and Kerry, in the spot where Jimbo's used to be. The menu is broken down into "home" and "away" team offerings. On the *home* side you'll find reasonably priced standard pub fare, burgers and sandwiches. But the *away* side features offerings themed toward the team visiting the South Side nine. If Seattle's in town, you might see grilled salmon; when Boston visits, you might find a lobster roll.

COBBLESTONE'S BAR AND GRILL
514 W. Pershing Rd.

If you're in the mood for a nice meal, Cobblestone's is a pregame option. Along with a diverse menu that includes muffulettas (New Orleans style sandwiches), pasta and sauces, steaks, and seafood, this place offers free Sox game parking for parties who spend at least $20 on dinner. It's a mile or so walk to the ballpark, but Cobblestone's food, drink, and parking make it worth the effort.

MITCHELL'S TAP
www.mitchellstap.net/Homepage.html
3356 S. Halsted St.

What was once Puffer's neighborhood bar is now Mitchell's Tap. It still has the open-air windows and a long wooden bar. While we were disappointed that they wouldn't let Kevin in with his baseball hat around backwards, we approve and can recommend this place.

Kevin: We mistakenly called this place Huffer's the first time around. It was Puffer's.

Josh: You think that had anything to do with its demise?

Kevin: I do believe that would be overstating our influence.

FIRST BASE
3201 S. Normal Ave.

Look for the baseball diamond on the awning. Inside, a square bar offers limited seating. This is a "drink 'em while you stand and don't talk to anyone" kind of place. Plan on spending about as much time here as Aparicio or Podsednik used to spend at first base.

MAXWELL STREET DEPOT
411 West 31st St.

While you can expect good dogs from this longtime Chicago vendor, their specialty is the pork chop sandwich. Loaded with grilled onions, mustard, and served dripping with grease, this sandwich is a Chicago original, though Kevin claims he's sampled them in Butte, Montana, as well.

LA PASADITA
1140 N. Ashland
www.pasadita.com/

After the game why not try a burrito that is as big as your head, and tasty too? La Pasadita is open until 3 a.m., so after the bars close this is a solid choice.

Kevin: We were told these burritos would help allay the inevitable next-day hangover.

Josh: How's that working for you?

Kevin: Can't tell if it's working, or if I'm in the middle of a burrito hangover.

Josh: You're still well within your "burrito window" my friend.

For Those Willing to Go the Extra Mile
TUFANO'S VERNON PARK TAP
1073 W. Vernon Park Place
www.tufanosrestaurant.com

A good Italian restaurant with a liquor license to boot! It's not really a White Sox place but it is a quality Italian place to eat close by the park.

Josh: This place was featured on that show, you know with the guy with the spiky white hair who drives around to all those diners and drive-ins?

Kevin: Yeah, we thought of that first.

Josh: We should have a ballpark road trip reality show.

Kevin: Hey E! Are you reading this?

GENO'S EAST PIZZA
633 N. Wells
www.ginoseast.com

Not only is this town divided over its baseball loyalties, there's also a pizza war between deep dish and stuffed, both Chicago originals. Though the battle lines are a bit less clear, we suggest you try them both. Geno's East is a great place for deep dish. But only go to the original location. For stuffed, head to the North Side and the North Side team's chapter of the book.

GARRETT POPCORN SHOPS
670 N. Michigan Ave., Other Locations
www.garrettpopcorn.com

Sure it's a touristy thing to do and you're going to be standing in line with a bunch of blue hairs with cameras hanging from their necks and with short pants exposing their aged spotted legs. But this here is some good corn.

HAROLD'S CHICKEN SHACK
518 W. Harrison
http://haroldschickenshack45.com/

Why not have some chicken where President Obama and Dwyane Wade used to eat? The fried chicken at Harold's is something else, and the people-watching, especially after dark, is even better than the eats.

AL'S ITALIAN BEEF
1079 W. Taylor
www.alsbeef.com/

"You gotta' try Al's Italian beef over dere by Taylor Street," our friend Jim told us. Italian dipped-beef sandwiches are something to see. Italian beef is a hot steak sandwich drowned in au jus. The bread soaks up the juice turning the whole thing into one big sloppy delicious mess.

Inside the Park

As stated, U.S. Cellular Field started out as no small disappointment to White Sox fans, despite attempts to bring over much of the character of the old park. But the Sox have been diligently working on the situation. The addition of the new roof and the glass windows to cover the concrete seating bowl make the place look almost, dare we say it?, Yankee Stadium-esque. This place has improved greatly and there is more going on here than at most parks, so take some time to walk around and see the many sights.

Ballpark Features

A GRAND ENTRANCE

Upon entering the park on the first level, you will notice that the ballpark designers attempted to recreate the facade at old Comiskey with elegant glass windows. While the old park was done in brick, these windows are about as regal as you can get when a precast colored concrete frontage is

---

Grinder (Ball) Rules!

There are hundreds of official, or maybe we should say "unofficial" Grinder Rules posted at The Cell. This vestige of the Ozzie Guillen Era makes for a great ballpark experience even if Ozzie has since taken his act to Miami, where he took over as manager in 2012. Some of our favorites are:

- *Win, or die trying.*
- *Every pitch is full count. Every inning, the ninth. Every game, game seven.*
- *Be a man. Play like a boy.*
- *Ixnay on talkin' about the ayoffsplay.*
- *When attending a Chicago White Sox game, don't blink.*
- *Pitch. Hit. Win. Repeat.*
- *Crying in baseball is acceptable only if champagne burns your eyes.*
- *Taste victory and be hungry forever.*

- *Respect the past, people that are shoeless, and anyone named Joe.*
- *In the unlikely event an opposing player turns a lucky swing into a home run here at U.S. Cellular Field—home of the White Sox—and an unsuspecting fan catches said ball, he or she should NOT throw the ball back onto the field of play.*

But perhaps our favorite is:

- *Hoist the city up on your shoulders. It'll return the favor.*

There are hundreds of Grinder Rules that can be found on Facebook and other Internet sources, but looking for them at The Cell is more fun.

used in imitation. Banners commemorate great White Sox players as well as other star players from baseball's glory days, providing some of the game's more famous quotes.

Entering at street level we had to use an escalator to get to the first concourse. Talk about instantly dismissing the mystique of the old park. Why couldn't they have dug down below street level so fans could enter at the same level as the first concourse?

FUNDAMENTALS

Here's something special worth arriving early to take your kids to see. During every home game White Sox training center coaches conduct a baseball clinic for kids—and it's free! After their lessons, kids hone their skills in batting cages and on practice pitcher's mounds. Why-oh-why didn't they have this when we were young? Josh tried to convince the attendant he was thirteen, and the guy almost bought it, until Josh went into a rant about "kids today" throwing too many curveballs in Little League. He was subsequently ejected from FUNdamentals. Anyway, to get to FUNdamentals, enter U.S. Cellular Field at Gate 3, or ask a Guest Services Representative for directions if you're already inside the park.

RETIRED HEROES

The Sox used to use the concrete between decks as a place to honor players whose numbers they had retired. But after installing the now somewhat obligatory "ribbon LED screens" in that location, ownership moved the retired numbers to the outfield wall. The team has also erected statues on the outfield concourse to honor most all of its greats, but for some reason not Ted Lyons. In the order they were retired, the numbers are 4 for Luke Appling, the Sox all-time leader in hits, runs, walks, at bats and games; 2 for Nellie Fox, a twelve-time All-Star; 9 for Minnie Minoso, the only Major Leaguer to play in five different decades; 11 for Luis Aparicio, a ten-time All-Star and nine-time Gold Glove winner; 16 for Ted Lyons, a 260-game winner; 19 for Billy Pierce, a seven-time All-Star; 3 for Harold Baines, who played for the Sox on three separate tours and had to have his number taken down upon returning the third time; 42 for Jackie Robinson, whose number is universally retired; 72 for Carlton Fisk, who spent thirteen seasons behind the plate for the White Sox and held the record for games caught by a catcher until Ivan Rodriguez passed him in 2009; and 35 for "the Big Hurt," Frank Thomas, perhaps the greatest steroid-free hitter of his generation.

IT'S A HALL OF FAME/GIFT SHOP

The White Sox Hall of Fame is located behind home plate on the first level. Actually, it's located inside the ballpark gift shop. The hall is small but impressive. We enjoyed the pictures of old Comiskey and Schorling's Park and the auto-graphed team balls going back all the way to the 1940s. There's a great memorial to the first All-Star Game, dubbed the "Game of the Century." There's something for every Sox fan, old and new here, including baseball cards featuring such White Sox as Fisk, Eddie Farmer, Jorge Orta, and Baines.

Inside the gift shop portion of the area you'll find the actual lockers from the old park, from such players as Robin Ventura, Thomas, Fisk, Guillen, and others, with bats and other equipment inside them. Also in the shop you'll find the original showerhead that Bill Veeck installed on the center-field concourse of the old park.

THE PATIO AND BATTER'S EYE

The batter's eye in center field was renovated and trans-formed into a multi-tiered, ivy-covered terrace to give hit-ters a green background. The top level now features a semi-transparent screen. The patio behind the batter's eye has picnic tables and chairs and is a large area where fans can sit and enjoy their meals while they watch the game through the mesh.

NEVER TO RETURN

Originally there was a ball-return screen behind home plate that ran back to the press box and blocked much of the view for fans in Sections 130–134. A new vertical screen has been installed that is much less distracting to fans and allows for more souvenirs.

A BIT OF THE OLD COMISKEY FLAVOR

Behind Section 158, murals honor famous White Sox players. We found it odd that there is a portrait of the infamous 1919 team here. Really odd. A picture of Eddie Cicotte and Joe Jackson highlights the display, and there is a team picture in the center. These are very cool photos, but didn't these guys throw the World Series for cash? On the other hand, let's not forget Grinder Rule #46: "Respect the past, people that are shoeless, and anyone named Joe."

HOW DOES IT KEEP ON EXPLODING?

The idea for an exploding scoreboard was one of Bill Veeck's most commendable strokes of genius. Fortunately, the White Sox brought over the full effect from the old park. Though today's scoreboard is in fact a new one, its festive rolling pinwheels and fireworks are similar to those that lit up the Chicago night for years whenever a Sox player homered. We watched an Alex Rios dinger set the scoreboard ablaze, and though we're not usually ones to wax rhapsodic about a bunch of lights (we think scoreboards are for keeping score) we thought the exploding board was really something to see. It adds a spectacular and heroic, Roy Hobbs–type aspect to the show.

GOING OLD SCHOOL WITH THE SCOREBOARDS

Perhaps to offset the scoreboard in center that explodes, Sox management added an old-time out-of-town scoreboard in right field. This LED board offers continually updated information on games, including diamonds for base-runners, as well as numbers that inform who is currently pitching and hitting. The left-field scoreboard offers information in a more traditional fashion, listing score, balls, strikes, and outs. But we suppose it's not too old-school if it uses LED technology.

STATUES OF THE GREATS

Behind sections 100, 105, and 164 on the center-field concourse, the team has erected life-sized statues of great White Sox. Stroll out here and take in bronzed Mr. Comiskey, Minnie Minoso, Carlton Fisk, Luis Aparicio, Nellie Fox, Harold Baines, Billy Pierce, and Frank Thomas. We're not usually big fans of putting up a legion of heroes in bronze or stone, simply because with each one you erect, you somewhat diminish those already bronzed. The Romans reserved this honor only for the elite. However, looking over these statues and their stats, we couldn't think of a compelling reason not to include all of these greats. For the record, if you count Geoff Blum, Joe Crede, Orlando Hernandez, Paul Konerko, and Juan Uribe, who are honored in bronze on the 2005

Champions sculpture, there are thirteen individuals honored in bronze at The Cell.

THE BLUE TWO

Although The Cell has since undergone a reseating, two seats were kept from the original batch of blue chairs that filled the new park. They mark the landing spots of Konerko's left-field homer and Podsednik's right-center-field dinger, which both came in Game 2 of the 2005 World Series.

THE RAINMAKERS

Sure enough, there is an outdoor shower on the left-field concourse behind Section 158. The showerhead is sponsored by the plumbing council of Chicago and is a replica of the one installed at Comiskey under Veeck. If a cold shower isn't enough to cool you off on those Dog Days of August, there is also a Rain Room behind Sections 107 and 537. It's a misting station that provides for those poor souls whose sweat glands can't kick into overdrive.

DOGS AND CATS LIVING TOGETHER

Also brought over from the old park is the Pet Check area behind Section 157, in case Buster can't bear to be left home alone. Remember, only bring your pet on special pet days. Sweet Fancy (John) Moses, what has happened to this game we love?

Stadium Eats

The food offerings at U.S. Cellular Field have gone from good to great, and because many of the places to go out in the

---

"Barnum Bill" Veeck

We've mentioned some of the memorable promotions and traditions that Bill Veeck brought to Comiskey. Now we thought we'd mention some that were less successful. Sox fans may find these a bit embarrassing. But we love Bill, and after all, no one bats a thousand, right?

1. The famous little people. Veeck would routinely send onto the field a trio of small folks dressed up in carnival garb. One time they came out as tiny Martians in silver space suits complete with baseball bats and equipment.
2. In the 1970s Veeck had ex-Bears quarterback Bobby Douglass suit up and take a tryout for the Sox pitching staff. A sportswriter suggested that opposing batters could protect themselves from ever being hit by Douglass simply by donning number 88, because clearly Douglass couldn't hit anyone wearing a wide receiver's number.
3. Perhaps the most embarrassing moment of all came on August 8, 1976, when the White Sox came out for the first game of a doubleheader wearing shorts. Yes, Martha, shorts for a baseball game. After Kansas City's John Mabry quipped, "You guys are the sweetest team we've seen yet," the Sox put on long pants for the second game.

We fully appreciate the efforts of Bill Veeck and everyone else who over the years has tried to improve the ballpark experience without disrupting the game too much. Rather than corporate-sponsored crap, why don't teams take a few thousand pages outta Bill's book and bring back some of the promotions, stunts, and gags that made baseball fun?

neighborhood are quite a walk, finding quality eats inside is important. Here you'll find Chinese, Mexican, German, and Cuban food offerings that you will enjoy. Oh, and this being a very special pizza city, you'll find some top-notch ballpark pie too.

SOX DOG (DOG REVIEW)
We refuse to eat a dog in any ballpark or stadium that has a pet-check area! Just kidding, U.S. Cellular features a very tasty Vienna Beef dog. But like most other ballpark dogs, it's just too expensive. Why not try Morrie O'Malley's, which offers way more toppings and sells its dogs at half the price of the ones inside the ballpark. So if you're going for value, this might be one ballpark treat you'll want to pick up on the way to the ballpark, rather than once you arrive. If you need to have a frank in your stadium seat, you'll find the Sox Dog will hit the spot too, though.

DIGIORNO PIZZA (TRADEMARK FOOD)
In 2011 the White Sox bid adieu to longtime ballpark staple Connie's pizza and replaced it with DiGiorno. It's still one of the best things going inside the park, but it ain't quite what it used to be.

BEST OF THE REST
The **Cuban sandwich** is worth sampling. The one we tasted had freshly grilled ham, Barbacoa, melted Swiss and pickles. It was delicious. Speaking of Barbacoa, the **nachos** that come topped with the spicy meat are pretty darned good too.

Chico Carrasquel's dogs and Polish sausages remain a tasty option. We like how all these stands are named for players. One of our big discoveries the first time around was the **chicken dinner.** Good chicken at the ballpark is a pleasant surprise. Another strong choice are the **bao** from the Wow Bow stand on the left side of the main concourse. Bao are hot buns filled with meat and vegetables that you can carry around and eat easily.

We also must mention the surprisingly tasty **corn off the cob.** It may sound odd, but a woman slices the corn off the cob right in front of you, then mixes it with whatever you'd like—butter, sour cream, mayonnaise, garlic, cheese, lime, or chili. Perhaps it tasted so delicious because we had been eating processed meat exclusively for ten straight days. Or perhaps it was really sweet corn. But in any case, we rate the corn as delicious as it is distinctive.

We also liked the **Brats** and **steak sandwiches** at Lollar's "Guard the Plate" Grill behind Section 524. Hey, if you're going to endure a game upstairs, you might as well pig out.

If you have kids or immature eating habits, head for Kids Korner, behind Section 100. Alongside the play area and kid-size gift shop, you'll find the sure-fire, always-a-hit-with-every-kid-in America meal, good old-fashioned **PBJs** (if you were born in Russia, these are peanut butter and jelly sandwiches). If you have peanut allergies, well then, we really don't think you're a Russian. Actually, you have our sympathies.

SAY "NO, THANKS," AND WALK AWAY
The enchiladas may have been better than we expected, but our expectations were awfully low. Best to save your appetite for these for when you're in the Southwest.

STADIUM SUDS
The Beers of the Midwest stand is one disappointment we can point to in the gastro offerings at The Cell. First, all those great Midwestern beer brands like Pabst Blue Ribbon and Schlitz went national a long time ago, right? So what are we left with, overpriced microbrews that really aren't that great. When in Chicago, Old Style is our drink of choice. Sure, it tastes like the dog's breakfast, but after you down a couple, you hardly even wince any more. Or if it's a hot and sticky Chicago night, why not try a cool margarita? José Cuervo himself will come by with a barrel of tequila strapped to his back and a hose in his hand that will deliver you a margarita. Okay, it's not really Mr. Cuervo, but the margaritas are cold and delicious.

The U.S. Cellular Experience
Games on the South Side have become quite intense since the Sox have been winning ballgames. There's a level of energy at the game now that puts a focus on the importance of each play. Sox fans attending games these days want to win. Everything else is nice, but secondary. In many ways, it seems the opposite of cross-town Wrigley, where the emphasis is on the experience of being there. Make no mistake, Sox fans are intensely on edge until their team wins. Only then do they return to their "normal" non-Sox obsessed selves, if only for a few hours until they start thinking about the next game.

Just like every other team, White Sox fans come in all varieties. What we found on the South Side was something rather special: good old-fashioned working-class folks who are there to see the game. They're knowledgeable about their team and the sport in general, and like the team that represents them, they're gritty and tough-minded, but with a Midwestern friendliness and civility that we appreciate. Sox fans are straight shooters. They're full of humor and jokes without coming off

The K&J Guide to Fan Etiquette

After spending good portions of this book telling players, owners, and management what they can do to make the game better for fans, we thought this would be a good opportunity to list what fans need to do to keep baseball from turning into something ugly.

1. Do not go on the field for any reason. Sure, it was funny back in the day when some lunatic would run around on the field at Yankee Stadium, eluding inept security for as long as possible. But those days are now officially over. If you go on the field now, not only are you risking your own neck, but also those of everyone involved.

2. Do not interfere with a batted ball. If you reach down out of your first-row outfield seat to scoop a rolling ball off the ground, you run the risk of depriving the entire crowd of seeing the batter go for a triple. If the catcher throws aside his mask and runs toward the front row of seats to catch a foul pop-up, get out of his way. If you reach out your hand to snatch it before he does, chances are you'll only deflect it, and it will wind up hitting you, the player, or another fan in the face. Remember what happened on the North Side during the Cubs' 2003 playoff run.

3. After getting treats or using the can, wait until there is a break in the action before you move through the aisle to your seat. People seated on the aisle have to deal not only with you, but hundreds of other people in your section streaming past them, and it's rude. With all the standing room at these new ballparks, watch the action from the top of the concourse and wait until an out is made, then head to your seat. You'll thank others for their courtesy when you have seats on the aisle.

4. For folks with seats behind the plate: STOP WAVING and stay off of your cell phones. The "miracle" of television has been with us for years now, so don't distract the pitcher, or the fans seated near you, or the home-viewing audience, by acting like a fool. If you want to wave to the camera and act like a baboon, go stand outside The Today Show.

5. Do not, after drinking ten or twelve beers, get it into your head that you're going to start the Wave. While you're running back and forth on the concourse yelling "one . . . two . . . three . . . wave!" everyone else is trying to see around you and wishing you'd drop dead, because—get this—they're trying to watch the game. Besides, the Wave is for football.

6. When you see a player outside the ballpark, be respectful. Don't do rude things, like interrupt a player while he's eating dinner and grovel for an autograph or snap a picture with your phone. How would you feel if people were always bugging you while your mouth was half full of linguine? Bugging players at inappropriate times does nothing but widen the gap between them and us. If you really want an autograph that badly, wait until the player is done eating, then ask nicely. Who knows, he might even take a picture with you. Or better yet, send him a thoughtful, handwritten letter addressed to his team's ballpark.

---

as too cocky. They'll tell you to your face that they're going to beat you 10-0, then they'll buy you a beer once they do.

The Sox seem to have arrived at a place of perfect symmetry between the product they are putting on the field, and how their fan base completely represents who they are. There are plenty of Sox fans that used to watch the games only at home, perhaps because they lived in the suburbs or couldn't afford a ticket. But in U.S. Cellular Field, with all its many and continued improvements, the White Sox have created a compelling place that their fans truly want to visit, and one that they can afford.

CLASSY DR. FAUST

Though no longer with the organization, it's worth remembering Nancy Faust, who was the White Sox organist beginning in the early 1970s until her retirement in 2010. Nancy was a hip tickler of the ivories who was very clever about what she played. She was credited with playing songs that were copied across the nation and have become required stadium anthems. One such tune was when she played "Kiss Him Goodbye" when an opposing pitcher gave up a home run to the Sox. We can't imagine a world without Nancy Faust, and she will be missed at the ballpark, and in the hearts of Sox fans, and baseball fans everywhere. The good news is, the White Sox have hired a new organist in the wake of Nancy's departure. So keep an ear out for the melodies of keyboardist Lori Moreland when you're at The Cell.

ANDY THE CLOWN (SUPER-FAN HALL OF FAME)

Though never an employee of the White Sox, Andy the Clown went to games at old Comiskey for years dressed in full funny man regalia and brought people joy, we think. You see we're not sure because when the new park opened Andy wasn't invited to return. Perhaps some traditions ought to "go gently into the good night." But we thought we'd mention Andy for his many efforts.

CROSS-CHI RIVALRY

We learned a lot about Sox history during our visit, and this seems as good a place as any to talk some more history, as the Pale Hose have history coming out their ears. The rivalry is still fierce between the North Side Nine and the South Side Hit Men. At one time back in the 1990s a billboard above the L train outside Wrigley Field portrayed "the Big Hurt" pointing his formidable bat back toward U.S. Cellular Field. It read "Real Baseball, only 7 miles back."

But our pal and tour guide Douglas Hammer takes issue with the false notion that because the Cubs routinely sell out their games, they have more loyal fans than the Sox. According to Hammer, team loyalty is split fifty-fifty in Chicago, and the attendance disparity is more due to tourists and college kids looking for a good time in the Wrigley bleachers.

The South Side was once populated heavily with Irish and African-American residents, who jointly supported the Sox. But when many of the Irish left for the suburbs during the so-called "white flight" of the 1970s, Sox support suffered, resulting in a situation that saw many people in the fan base choose to stay at home to watch the team on TV. Now we are left with two notions that further divide the baseball fans of Chi—that Sox fans are urban blacks and Cubs fans are white, yuppie, Big-Ten fraternity punks. Neither of these stereotypes is true.

Cyber Super-Fans

Check out these bloggers and message board moguls who have dedicated their lives to Sox fame and glory over the Internet.

- **South Side Sox**
  www.southsidesox.com
- **White Sox Interactive**
  www.whitesoxinteractive.com
- **White Sox Mix**
  www.whitesoxmix.com/
- **White Sox Locker**
  www.whitesoxlocker.com/

BLACK SOX TRIAL LOCATION

An office building at 54 West Hubbard St. was at one time the Chicago Criminal Courts Building where the infamous Chicago eight were found not guilty of all charges by a jury. A plaque outside marks the court's role in the Black Sox Trial, as well as other famous trials in the history of Chicago.

Sports in the City

Monsters of the Midway

The South Side is a short distance by car from the Midway. What's the Midway you ask? Ever heard the term "Monsters of the Midway" used to describe the Chicago Bears? Sure, you have. Well, though it's only a field, check out the Midway where the World's Fair was once held and where those Bears were once mighty and victorious and may one day be again.

While We Were in Chicago
We Passed a Crucial Test as Travel Partners, Sort Of

Chicago is the kind of a city where you want to be shown around by someone familiar with the turf. We went to the game in a large group of Kevin's friends that included Jim, Hammer, Paul and Rebecca, Trisha, and of course the two of us. We were earlier treated to a tour of the city by Paul Schmitz and Rebecca Murphy, two of Chi-town's most avid enthusiasts. We did as much as we could that day. We rode the "L" loop through town, checking out Cabrini Green and Old Town. We saw the great modern architecture of the Monadnock Building, the Rookery Building, and Marshall Field's department store (now a Macy's). We went to Navy Pier and saw the fountain that appeared during the opening credits of *Married with Children*. We saw public sculptures and art by the likes of Chagall and Picasso. We walked past the Tribune Building, the original Playboy Mansion—oh la la—and Oprah's Harpo Studios. We saw the Magnificent Mile and Lincoln Park. We felt a bit like Cameron in *Ferris Bueller's Day Off*.

But when the game ended, Josh called his friends Kristen and Kevin on the North Side of the city to see what they were doing that night. Kevin's friends Hammer and Rebecca suggested going to Harold's Chicken Shack, and then out to the Checkerboard Lounge for drinks and blues. Everyone agreed that it would be a great idea.

Josh wasn't keen on going to a blues bar, plus his friends had whet his appetite with tales of the famous Chicago stuffed pizza near their house in Wrigleyville. And when Josh gets a hankerin' there's nothing in the known universe that can hold him back from his quest. So after the game the lingering group stood in a standoff outside the ballpark.

"You already had pizza twice today," reasoned Kevin.

"So what?" Josh said. "I can't have pizza three times in the same day?"

"Sure you can, but everyone here wants to stay on the South Side," said Kevin.

"Yeah, you and Moby," Josh said. "I'm heading North with my friends."

"South Side!" Kevin shouted.

"North Side!" Josh shouted back.

"South Side!" Kevin screamed. Clearly, we had reached an impasse.

"Yeah," said Josh, "Well the White Sox stink. I hate the South Side."

"And the North Side is full of yuppies," Kevin replied.

"North Side!" shouted Josh again.

"Why are you being so stubborn?" Kevin asked.

"Why did you root for the White Sox, over my Red Sox?" said Josh.

"I always root for the home team," shouted Kevin.

"I rooted for the Mariners when we were in Seattle," yelled Josh.

"South Side!" Kevin yelled back.

Things had been tense between us many times on the road, but never quite like this. Neither of us would budge an inch.

"Will you listen to yourselves?" Kevin's diplomatic friend Paul said. "You sound like you've lived in Chicago your entire lives."

We're not sure if it was the city of Chicago that had gotten into our blood so quickly, or if we had simply spent too much time on the road together. And while an amicable solution might have been reached together, we decided that Josh should go out on the North Side with his friends, and Kevin should stay on the South Side with his. We both went our separate ways and spent some much needed time apart. The next day it was as if nothing had happened. We went to the game together on the North Side, and out together afterwards (starting in the South Side and finishing in the North Side) as close as ever. Perhaps during every road trip there should be some time built in for doing your own thing. We recommend it.

MILWAUKEE BREWERS, MILLER PARK

MILWAUKEE, WISCONSIN
90 MILES TO CHICAGO
340 MILES TO MINNEAPOLIS
375 TO DETROIT
380 MILES TO ST. LOUIS

A Brew City Flip-Top

Since migrating from Seattle to Milwaukee in 1970 and changing their label from "Pilots" to "Brewers," the team that Bud Selig built has enjoyed some memorable seasons and has presented fans with many talented players to cheer. But through the years the Milwaukee nine has also asked a lot of their fans in the way of patience. The Brew Crew has asked Milwaukeeans to endure seemingly one prolonged rebuilding phase after another. And for the most part, the beer- and brat-loving locals have patiently hung in there, waiting for the day when the Brewers would win their first world championship. It hasn't always been easy, though, considering that prior to their division-winning 2011 season the Brewers had enjoyed only eleven winning campaigns over the previous four decades.

For years, of course, the Brew Crew's fortunes rose and fell at County Stadium, which despite its colorful history was not really up to big league snuff by the end of its baseball life. But the fans hung on. Additionally, the Brewers asked their fans to accept the awkward ascent of team owner Bud Selig to the commissioner's chair, even as he continued to maintain his involvement with the Brewers. And then the Brewers switched from the American League to National League, asking fans to disregard two-generation-old rivalries. These indignities, combined with all of the losing, might sound like a recipe for fan disengagement and franchise implosion. And yet, the loyal fans rolled with the proverbial punches and kept providing steady support of the local nine, making Brew City not just "viable" for big league ball in the twenty-first century but a candidate for a shiny new ballpark. And in 2001 that gleaming new yard became a reality. After some initial fits and starts, during which the team suffered through some lean years after Miller Park's opening, baseball in the land of brats has flourished. The Brewers closed out the first decade of the 2000s by perennially finishing among the top third of teams in attendance, attracting upwards of three million fans per season. Not bad for the smallest city (by population) in MLB. Just how "small market" is Milwaukee? It has a metro population of 1.5 million. At the other end of the spectrum, the Mets and Yankees draw from a city of nineteen million. Even teams in the middle of the population pack, like the Tigers and Diamondbacks, draw from metros of 4.4 million people.

And that brings us back to Miller Park, a post-modern facility, huge in almost every way, which boasts a space-age roof that opens and closes in a fanlike motion and takes just ten minutes to do so. The roof dominates both the interior and exterior of the park. To Kevin, it looks like the gills of a huge space fish. To Josh, who lacks quite the same imagination but likes to make up new terms, it merely looks "techno-classy." It weighs twelve thousand tons, covers 10.5 acres, and is capable of withstanding twelve feet of snow, or roughly 170 pounds of powder per square foot. When it's open the park has a remarkable open-air feel. When it's closed, the building can be warmed 30 degrees Fahrenheit above the temperature outside.

We like this roof a lot. But it does have one dark side that we'd be remiss not to mention. When fully opened and stacked in foul territory the roof's orientation allows for a large swatch of sunshine to soak the infield during afternoon games. This effect also creates some very dark shadows, though, which has prompted more than a few hitters to complain after 0-for-4 performances. Some fielders have claimed that the dual lighting has made it hard to follow the flight of fly balls too. In 2010 the Brewers began partially closing the roof during day games so that two panels hover over left field and three over right to create a more consistent shadow over the entire infield. That way the pitcher and batter are in the same light environment. But the sun is kept out, and the park doesn't feel as open to the outside world.

We said earlier that this felt like a big stadium to us. And that's because it is rather big. The park rises 330 feet, making it roughly three times the height of old County Stadium. But despite this magnitude parts of the park feel very open to the outside world, thanks to the gigantic windows spanning the outfield. These appear on either side of the hitter's backdrop and video board in center field and continue almost all the way to foul territory on either side of the outfield. Additionally, there are massive arched windows between the top of the upper deck and the roof along the foul lines. These colossal windows are actually composed of many smaller panes of glass all framed together. In total, they allow for light to enter the stadium, even when the roof is closed, for the grass to grow, and for that open-air feel we really appreciate.

Kevin: I pity the guy who has to squeegee all that glass once a month.

Josh: Yeah, you have that fear of heights thing.

Kevin: I was speaking from a housekeeping point of view.

Josh: I guess that means Meghan cleans the windows back home?

Kevin: No, they flip around from the inside.

Josh: Well, la de da, Mr. Fancy Glass.

Outside, the red brick facade is nearly the only nod to the classical ball era. Clearly, the designers at HKS were going for a grand stadium design, rather than an intimate old-time one. Intimate is not ever going to be a word used to describe this place. Not with its abundance of escalators and elevators, its four seating levels, and its multiple underhangs obstructing views. The upper deck seats are pretty poor, but the folks in the lower two decks are treated to a pleasant enough experience.

Upon our first entering Miller, with brats in hand, we found the field as beautiful as it seemed spacious. It sure felt like a ballpark, not a quasi-dome. If you try to measure a second-generation retractable roof job like this to an earlier generation facility like Rogers Centre, you're not even comparing apples and oranges. More like apples and pineapples. They might sound similar. But the aesthetics of the two are really nothing like one another. And here's something you won't find in Toronto, or at any other retractable roof field that we know of: a drainage system beneath the immaculately groomed Kentucky bluegrass that can handle twenty-five inches of rain an hour just in case the roof ever malfunctions.

Josh: Twenty-five inches per hour? That sounds like Noah's Ark territory.

Kevin: If a tsunami ever rips across the East Coast, sweeps over the Lakes and cascades across Milwaukee, the safest place in the city will be the pitcher's mound.

More than just looking ultra-super-modern from the outside, with its glass "bug eyes," Miller Park has tried to include many of the features that have become staples of the modern ballpark experience. The concourses are nice and wide, there are patios, restaurants and luxury seats aplenty, and the place is kept nice and clean. But of all the new parks we've visited only U.S. Cellular Field does a poorer job at maintaining an intimate feel in the upper reaches. When we were in the lower two decks, we felt involved in the game and sufficiently ensconced in the sort of baseball atmosphere we like. But up in the fourth deck, we felt like we were in a whole different baseball stadium.

Kevin: Hmm. I can't believe people willingly pay to sit up here.

Josh: Now I understand why Bob Uecker is a Milwaukee icon.

Kevin: Did the second baseman just miss the tag?

Josh: I'm pretty sure they're still just throwing the ball around the infield.

Kevin: You mean the inning hasn't started yet?

Miller's journey into being was arduous. When attendance was dropping and the team struggling, funding for the project was slow in coming and then just barely secured. It took State Senator George Petak changing his vote on a proposed funding package late at night on the third ballot to officially set the stadium ball in motion in 1995. Shortly thereafter, the Republican lawmaker was recalled from office. But eventually Wisconsin Governor Tommy Thompson signed the Stadium Bill into law at a ceremony in the County Stadium parking lot. The law guaranteed taxpayer funding of the new park and stipulated that the Brewers would stick around for at least thirty years.

There were still hurdles to clear though as the funding plan had to be restructured when it became apparent the Brewers didn't have the collateral to insure a loan. When all that got sorted out, controlling interest in Miller Park belonged to the State Stadium Board because the taxpayers of five Wisconsin counties had paid $310 million of the $400 million price. How did they pay this, you ask? With a 0.1 percent sales-tax hike that raises about $20 million a year. The Brewers, meanwhile, own 23 percent of the park, having chipped in $90 million. Miller Brewing Company paid $40 million for the naming rights, which run through 2020.

roof

Photo by Kevin O'Connell

The construction contractors broke ground on the project in November of 1996 and it took a longer-than-usual five years to build the stadium. The outfield dimensions were designed with help from Brewers Hall of Famer Robin Yount and former general manager Sal Bando. Yount's intention in deepening the outfield wall between the power alleys was to increase the frequency of what he considers the most exciting play in baseball: the triple.

The building of Miller was fraught with peril. Three construction workers were killed in July of 1999 when a 567-foot-high crane collapsed while lifting a four-hundred-ton roof panel that bent in half and crashed to the ground. The accident also caused $100 million in damages to the construction site. Some blamed the deaths of Jerome Starr, Jeff Wischer and William DeGrave on high winds at the time of this delicate construction procedure and questioned whether the rush to finish the stadium had prompted unwise decisions at the work site. Mitsubishi, which was contracted to construct the $47 million roof and oversee the project, faced penalties if the stadium was not ready in time for Opening Day 2000 and some pointed to it in the rush to apportion blame. In the aftermath of the horrific accident, a court ruling found Mitsubishi 97 percent negligent and another company 3 percent negligent and awarded $99,250,000 in damages. Ultimately the case wound up

being appealed to the Wisconsin Supreme Court, which in 2005 upheld that decision.

The final game at County Stadium took place on September 28, 2000, and was attended by Yount, Hank Aaron, Rollie Fingers, Warren Spahn, and other Milwaukee luminaries. Finally, the next spring, the day Milwaukeeans had been waiting for arrived. On April 6, 2001, the Brewers defeated the Reds 5-4 on an eighth-inning blast by Richie Sexson in Miller Park's inaugural game.

During that first year, the Brewers drew more than 2.8 million fans to their new digs, setting a new franchise record. In 2002 Miller Park played host to the All-Star Game, a moment in baseball history that will forever be tarnished because it disappointingly ended in a tie when Selig declared the game finished rather than let it continue past the tenth inning. In 2008, the Brewers passed the three million mark in attendance for the first time, averaging nearly thirty-eight thousand fans. They won the NL Wild Card that year too, and made their first playoff appearance since falling to the Cardinals in the 1982 World Series when they were still an American League franchise. This time, the Brewers fell to the Phillies in a four-game NL Division Series.

Interestingly, two Major League teams besides the Brewers have called Miller Park "home" during its short life. In 2007, the Indians hosted the Angels at Miller for an April series when an unusually snowy spring in Cleveland made a mess of the Indians' first two weeks schedule. The Brewers were on the road and Miller was available, so MLB moved the series, and announced that all tickets would sell for $10. Only fifty-two thousand fans turned out for the three games, but at least the Indians' weren't home shoveling like the rest of Cleveland. In September of 2008, an even more historic home-away-from-home moment occurred at Miller, when the Astros moved two games to Milwaukee to escape the path of Hurricane Ike. Carlos Zambrano started one of the two games for the visiting Cubs and pitched the first neutral site no-hitter in baseball history. It was also the first no-no in Miller Park history. It was a shame, though, that only twenty-three thousand fans were on hand to see Big Z's masterpiece.

Long before Miller Park or even the modern Brewers' arrival, professional baseball had enjoyed a vibrant life in

Milwaukee. The first incarnation of the American League Brewers took the field in 1901 when Milwaukee was one of the Junior Circuit's founding members. The team played at Athletic Park, a site now covered by Interstate 43. Those Brewers lasted only one season before leaving to become the St. Louis Browns. The "Brewers" nickname would return from 1902–1952 as a minor league club that played in the Double-A American Association. In 1919 a Milwaukeean named Otto Borchert bought the team and Athletic Park was renamed Borchert Field. Borchert was an oddly shaped park. It was like a square with the power alleys on the corners. Its dimensions were 266 feet down the lines, 395 feet to straightaway center, and considerably deeper in the alleys.

In 1941 the "Suds" were purchased by a young Bill Veeck—yes, that Bill Veeck—as the baseball visionary got his first stab at management. Veeck wasted no time in experimenting with the sort of promotions that would garner his nickname, "Barnum Bill." Some of the more memorable gimmicks were giveaways of livestock, ladders, and vegetables, and the institution of morning games for the enjoyment of third-shift workers. Veeck also installed a right-field retaining fence that could be used to keep balls in the park. The only problem was that Bill retracted it when the home team came to bat. The fence was banned after only one day.

In 1923 the Milwaukee Bears—the city's entrant in the Negro National League—also played at Borchert Field. But the Bears didn't draw well enough and couldn't finish the season. Another high point for baseball in Beertown involved the beloved Milwaukee Chicks of the All-American Girls Professional Baseball League, who enjoyed much success during the war years. But sadly the league declined once the men returned and eventually folded. The Chicks called Borchert Field "home" for twelve seasons.

Major League Baseball returned to Milwaukee in 1953 when Boston Braves owner Lou Perini decided to stop trying to compete with his more successful cross-town rivals, and moved west. The Braves were the first franchise to change cities since 1903 when Baltimore moved to New York. Many baseball historians point to the Braves' move as the beginning of a new era in baseball migration. In 1953 the Milwaukee Braves broke the National League record for attendance, drawing more than 1.8 million fans to County Stadium. Surely the Brooklyn Dodgers, New York Giants, and Philadelphia Athletics, who would all head West in the subsequent years, were aware of this when they made their own decisions to seek greener (as in dollar-bill-green) baseball pastures. Brooklyn, you can blame Boston for showing your team the way out the door.

Josh: Ah, they're New Yorkers, they got what they deserved.

Kevin: The Milwaukee Braves won a World Series four years after leaving Boston.

Josh: So?

Kevin: I bet your forefathers felt ripped off.

Josh: Nah. There was never more than one team in Beantown as far as my forefathers were concerned.

The Braves' attendance record was no small feat, considering County Stadium seated only thirty-six thousand back then. Built on the site of a stone quarry, the park resembled Tiger Stadium in its exterior, its eventual size, and its roof, which was supported by steel pillars that obstructed many a view. It had deep, rounded outfield dimensions that ran from 320 feet in left and right to 404 in dead-center. Year by year, seats were added in the bleachers, the fences were altered, and the park was spruced up, literally. Spruce trees were planted in 1954 behind the center-field fence and became known as Perini's Woods.

Led by a young Aaron, the Braves won the 1957 World Series, defeating the Yankees in seven games. The Braves also won the NL pennant in 1958, but lost a heartbreaking World Series to the Yanks. No one really knows why attendance began to sag so rapidly after that. Perhaps because Milwaukeeans had been to the heights so quickly and couldn't cope with the eventual leveling off? For whatever reason, folks stopped turning out at the ballpark in record numbers.

Our best seats EVER!

Photo by Kevin O'Connell

292

A year after purchasing the team from the Perini Corporation in 1962, John McHale and six former White Sox stockholders offered 115,000 shares of the Milwaukee Braves to the public. The IPO was withdrawn, however, after only thirteen thousand shares were sold. Rock bottom came in 1966 when the Braves left for Atlanta, only twelve years after moving from Boston.

Well documented in the Seattle chapter are Kevin's feelings about the relocation of the Seattle Pilots to Milwaukee after only one season. But he doesn't want his bitterness to poison Milwaukee fans, whom he considers among the best in baseball. Kevin was only three years old at the time of the Pilots' desertion, and the Mariners are his team now, so he is willing to let bygones be bygones. This is how it went down, though: A few days before Opening Day 1970 was scheduled in Seattle, Bud Selig and Edmund Fitzgerald acquired the Pilots. The Pilots were renamed "the Brewers" and they headed to Milwaukee. Today, Kevin enjoys drinking a fine Milwaukee-brewed beverage very much while he watches his Mariners, so all's well that ends well.

Josh: The song "The Wreck of the Edmund Fitzgerald" has suddenly taken on a whole new meaning to me.

Kevin: Dawn breaks on Marblehead.

Trivia Timeout

Yeast: What popular baseball movie was filmed at County Stadium in the 1980s?
Barley: Who was the only player to hit a home run clean out of County Stadium?
Hops: We all know the 2002 All-Star Game at Miller Park ended in a tie. Name the only other Mid-Summer Classic to end in a deadlock.
Look for the answers in the text.

After debuting in the American League West, the Brewers were shifted to the AL East in 1972 to make room for the brand new Texas Rangers. After a snowstorm buried Milwaukee, the 1973 Opener had to be delayed four days. In 1975 County Stadium was expanded to seat 53,192. In 1976, Aaron—who had been acquired in a trade with the Braves—hit his 755th and final home run against the Indians at County Stadium. After much rebuilding and a few years of playoff flirtation, the Brewers met the St. Louis Cardinals in the 1982 World Series, which was dubbed "the Suds Series."

Seating Capacity: 41,900
Ticket Office: http://milwaukee.brewers.mlb.com/ticketing/index.jsp?c_id=mil
Seating Map: http://milwaukee.brewers.mlb.com/mil/ticketing/seating_pricing.jsp

Manager Harvey Kuenn's "Wallbangers" lost in seven games. But 1983 was another blue-ribbon year as the Brew Crew broke the two-million mark in attendance.

Big changes came to Milwaukee and all of MLB in 1994, when "interim" commissioner Selig realigned the divisions from two per league into three per league, reformed the post-season to include eight teams instead of four, and introduced Wild Card playoff berths for the first time. That year the Brewers switched from the AL East to the NL Central. Milwaukee fans bid adieu to traditional rivals like Cleveland and Boston and welcomed the Cubs and Cardinals as new adversaries. Some skeptical fans said Selig was positioning his team to better succeed. Where previously the Brewers had competed in the deep-pocketed AL East, they moved to a not-quite-so-competitive division. And they have flourished in many ways since the move. They've got their new yard. And they've got an enthusiastic fan base. Now all they need is a World Series win.

Getting a Choice Seat

Miller Park is four decks worth of enormous, and the Brewers have been nearly filling the joint in recent years. During the summer months, sell-outs have become more and more common, to the point where the Brewers have strung together several double-digit sell-out streaks in recent years. This is reason enough to order your tickets in advance. And when you factor in the reality that the bad seats can be awfully distant at Miller, there's even more reason to lock in a good seat or two before you leave home. As a last resort, the Brewers sell three thousand standing room tickets.

Field Infield Box (Sections 110–125)

Why use the word "field" twice? Though screaming to be renamed (we'll just call them Infield Boxes), these are good seats. And they're not outrageously priced. In this park, where the upper deck is really up there, you should spend the extra cash to sit down low. Sections 117 and 118 are right behind the plate, while 110 is at first base, and 125 is at third. The first few rows are designated Field Diamond Boxes and are available to season-ticket holders only, but the rest of the seats are ripe for the picking.

The pitch of the lower bowl is fairly gradual, putting fans a little farther from the action than if it were steeper. But, conversely, fans aren't as high up as at some parks. It's a trade-off, but a low grade means there will be overhang issues to discuss later, as the upper decks must hang over the lower bowl.

Field Outfield Box (Sections 106–109, 126–131)

Again, bad name. But the seats are pretty good. Section 126 on the left-field side is the best place to sit, as its inclusion in this pricing tier means it's cheaper than but just as close to the infield as Section 110 (an Infield Box) across the diamond. There is little foul territory, which positions fans close to the action. The way the park angles from Section 126 out to the foul pole in left, combined with the high outfield wall, causes a sight-line blockage of fair territory in the left-field corner. But these are still good seats.

The seats in Sections 127–129 do not angle toward home plate, but Sections 128 and 129 remain parallel to the arching of the concourse, which does set fans up looking toward the action. This oddly seems to make 128 a better section than 127.

In Sections 131 and 106 along the walls, rather than a low wall, the Brewers have opted for a slatted fence. If you are sitting in the seats next to this fence it will be a factor. Fans seated here are forced to look through the slats, whereas a few seats farther back from the fence fans don't face any obstruction.

Field Bleachers (Sections 101–104)

Most of these right-field bleachers are decent, somewhat comfortable (they're benches with backs), and offer a good view. We should mention, though, that some are blocked by the pillars supporting the loge bleachers above. We thought the days of pillars at the park were over, but Miller Park has them. Also, there is a loss of the tiniest bit of the warning track from these seats. Sections 101, 102, and parts of 103 provide views right down into the bullpen, with no obstructions. Remember, Loge Bleachers cost the same and are up a level higher, so these first level bleachers are the better deal.

Loge Diamond Box (Section 210–227) and Loge Infield Box (Section 210–227)

The Loge Diamond Boxes are the first five rows of the low-to-the-field second deck. These sections are numbered to

SEATING TIP

Wait in line at the ticket office on game day when a few hundred of these obstructed-view upper-level one-dollar seats go on sale, then hop over to some better seats, or at the very least sit on the patio and play a few hands of euchre, and thus Uecker the Brewers in the way they tried to Uke you. Or sit in your Uecker seats and get Uke'd, spending the money you saved on tickets on Miller Lite.

Kevin: Euchre has to be the closest card game to baseball. I mean, if you can cheat and get away with it, it's kind of legal.

Josh: I would never play cards during a game.

Kevin: How about between innings?

Josh: Well, maybe if we were playing tegwar.

Kevin: Tegwar? Never heard of it. Is it easy to learn?

Josh: I'll teach you sometime when you have some spare cash in your wallet.

appear more or less directly above/behind their 100-level counterparts on the first deck, with Sections 218 and 219 behind the plate.

For folks sitting farther back in the Loge Infield Boxes, the low overhang of the third deck does not obstruct the view of the field. The overhang does sometimes block the flight of high fly balls for those in Rows 18 and higher, though.

Loge Outfield Box (Section 206–209, 228–232)

Beginning in Section 209 and continuing to 206 in deep right-field foul territory, you will lose sight of a certain amount of the right-field corner to the underhang. In Section 208 it is moderately annoying but if you sit beyond Section 207 any ball hit into the corner is blocked. We had to watch on the big screen. Even in the front-row, huge patches of the outfield lawn were missing. We recommend the bleachers instead.

Loge Bleachers (Sections 201–205, 233–238)

The Loge Bleachers provide almost as good a view as Section 206, but go for half the price. Sections 204–205 are not as affected by the underhang; really only the wall is blocked from view. At the bottom of the aisles all along the Loge grates rise to obstruct the view slightly. Basically anything higher than Row 16 or lower than Row 3 is poor.

Club Infield Box (Sections 320–339)/Club Outfield Box (Sections 306–319, 340–345)

All of the seats on the Club level have a slightly obstructed view. These seats are almost as expensive as the Infield

Boxes but don't offer half the view. So sit downstairs if you can. The Infield Clubs come with wait service, while the Outfield Clubs require folks to run their own errands.

Terrace Box (Sections 404–440)

These seats are in the first few rows of the fourth level. But we don't recommend the Terrace Boxes. In fact, if you consider yourself a baseball purist (like we do) and must see every blade of grass, every inch of dirt, do yourself a favor and do not sit anywhere in the Terrace Level. Even directly behind home plate the view is not completely clean, as the bottom parts of the foul poles on either side are not within view. Many seats in the upper deck only have a small amount of field blocked, but who knows, an important play might take place out there. Rather, head for the Loge bleachers or, better still, the Field bleachers, which are far superior for less cash.

Terrace Reserved (Sections 404–440)

We had trouble grappling with the phenomenon of an upper deck without any pure fan sight lines. Now, we realize that in building a ballpark, trade-offs have to be made. Not every seat can be perfect. In the case of Miller Park the Brewers clearly decided to build a multilevel stadium with stacked decks that hang over one another. Fine, but this is a four-level stadium that feels like a six-level stadium. The upstairs seats are affected by not one, but two underhangs. This, it seems to us, could have been avoided by eliminating a few hundred (or thousand) seats, making the Terrace level smaller, and tucking it in closer to preserve sight lines.

Also some Terrace seats are stuck in the place that would (should) normally be the aisle, making it difficult to walk all the way around the park and seat-hop. Crossing over someone's legs and suffering those annoyed looks add additional barriers to wandering the upper level at Miller Park.

The only piece of positive advice we can offer about this level is that if you prefer the shade, sit down the right-field line. The sun favors the left side. All sections beyond the outfield walls are in the shade, even when the sun is shining. Beyond Section 437, the foul pole becomes a blockage. In Sections 438 and 439 it cuts the view in half.

Bernie's Terrace (Sections 441–442)

Even though the kids may want to sit here deep in the left-field corner to catch a glimpse of beloved mascot Bernie, the Bernie's Terrace seats are terrible. Many in Section 442 are actually behind Bernie's Dugout, which is no small obstacle, and are worse than Uecker seats. Furthermore, the concourse up here is desolate, looking like a corridor out of *28 Weeks* or some other sci-fi movie. There are no close concession stands or bathrooms. Worst of all, the seats feel about 100 miles from the game.

> ### Bernie's Chalet and Beer Stein
>
> In time for Opening Day 2003 the Brewers upgraded Bernie Brewer's digs to include an air-conditioned enclosure. Score one for the drunk guy!
>
> But in the old days of County Stadium, Bernie Brewer spent each game in a wooden chalet. Whenever a home player homered, Bernie would slide into a giant stein of beer. Some things are better when they're less-politically correct. If you're interested in seeing the old Chalet and slide, head for Lakefront Brewery (details below).

Uecker Seats (Only a Dollar)

The old adage, "You get what you pay for," clearly applies. The $1 Uecker seats are just plain bad. Not only do fans fight multiple underhang obstructions from these seats, but the right-field foul pole is in the way too. Still, the seats have a certain comedic appeal. They were named after the always-entertaining Bob Uecker, whose Miller Lite commercials gave us such memorable lines as, "I must be in the front row," and, "He missed the tag!" that Bob shouted from his seat in the very top row.

Josh: From the Uecker seats, right field is a myth and center field is a rumor.

Black Market

Local rules prohibit scalping within eight hundred feet of the ballpark, so we followed the bridge over the river and into the far parking lot, where we found scalpers operating in plain view roughly 801 feet from the park.

Scalping 101: Know the exact bills in your wallet and have the amount you intend to spend at your fingertips. In Milwaukee Josh talked a scalper down from $20 to $15 per ticket, but only had two twenties. The seasoned ticket-trader wouldn't make change for him, so we wound up paying the higher price. Learn from our mistake.

A more legitimate, but slightly less exciting, option is to merely visit the Ticket Resale Zone that the Brewers oversee between Helfaer Field and the Aaron Parking Lot. Here, reselling tickets at or below face value is allowed.

Before/After the Game

Before we left on our first road trip, we never thought we'd change our minds in the way we did while visiting Milwaukee. We thought every park that wasn't in the middle of a festive downtown neighborhood was third-rate. But we learned in Brew City that this assumption was faulty. We (gulp) recommend driving to Miller Park and parking in one of the team-run lots (gulp, again). These open three hours before first pitch. Game day is all about the tailgating in Wisconsin, and what we experienced during our Brewers series beat any college football tailgate we'd ever attended. Little kids played catch with their dads, college guys threw the pigskin around, and tailgaters participated in such nontraditional sports as a ring-toss game that was much like horseshoes and parking-lot-bowling using real bowling balls, ten pins, and one drunk guy named Lenny who kept getting knocked down only to stand back up and resume his spot as the seven pin. Many of these folks had brought their kids along to shag beers and reset the pins. Very clever. We also saw parking lot volleyball, hopscotch, and people playing games with food used as balls and/or goal posts. All of this, of course, was brought on by copious amounts of alcohol. The people in Wisconsin are among the nicest in the world. Walk around and talk to folks and don't be surprised if someone hands you a brat or offers you some of grannie's pickled dilly beans. Tailgating etiquette states that you, too, should bring something to the party. We suggest picking up some cased meat to throw on the hibachi. Then sit back and talk to your neighbors. It won't take long to make friends. As for the preferred brand of brats? Local sausages like Klement's, Sheboygan, and Johnsonville are king.

Getting to Miller Park

From the east or west, take Interstate 94 to Miller Park Way and take the Miller Park Exit.

From the north, take Highway 41 south to the Miller Park Exit, or take Bluemound Road and access Miller from Story Parkway or Mitchell Boulevard. From the south, take 43rd Street/Miller Park Way north and take the Miller Park exit.

Friendly men with fluorescent clothing will guide you to a tailgating spot in one of the many lots surrounding the park. The general parking price is $8 and the lots are named after former Brewer stars. Professional tailgaters know where and when to enter to get where they need to be. If you want to look like one, rent an RV and bring it to the game. Just beware that you'll have to buy two parking spaces for an eighteen-to-thirty-six-foot vehicle.

The Milwaukee County Transit System bus stops right outside the park. Riding the bus allows you to set up your mobile tailgate unit anywhere you'd like, but it also means you have to schlep everything with you on the bus, then leave it in the parking lot, unattended, during the game. Routes 10, 18 and 90 service the park.

Milwaukee County Transit Info: www.ridemcts.com/seasonal_services/index.asp?id=802

Outside Attractions

HAVE A CATCH

Beautiful Helfaer Field was built in the connecting lot to Miller Park, roughly on the grounds where County Stadium once stood. Local youth league teams play at this wonderful diamond in the rough, as well as softball teams. The outfield fences are only two hundred feet from the plate and the same grounds crew that works on the big league diamond cares for Helfaer. Informative murals surround the little field, offering facts and trivia about baseball in Milwaukee. Reading them, we learned that "Bud the Wonder Dog" used to chase seagulls out of right field at County Stadium.

COUNTY STADIUM MEMORIALS

Behind Helfaer you'll find a memorial to County Stadium as well as one for the World Series Champion Braves of 1957. It's not hard to picture County Stadium standing on this very spot. But it is hard to visualize the fateful game when Detroit's Cecil Fielder became the only player to ever hit a fair ball completely out of the expansive yard.

Josh: It should have landed right about where that guy is choking on that brat.

Kevin: Nah, over there where that drunk woman just knocked down every pin but Lenny.

The day we visited, a tour group from Japan was listening to a guide reverently talk about the great "Hammerin' Hank Aaron." We found it funny to hear a Japanese guide say "Hammerin' Hank Aaron" amidst a string of words we didn't know. How about translating *The Ultimate Baseball Road Trip* into Japanese and letting these folks in on our secrets?

Kevin: Anyone want to volunteer for that job?

Josh: Or to invent a smartphone app that will do it?

PLAYER, PLAYER, USED CAR SALESMAN

Outside the Miller Park gates stand statues of Aaron, Yount and Selig. The Selig statue was erected in 2010 to honor the former team owner's commitment to bringing baseball to Milwaukee and his championing of the new ballpark. It was *not* built, we've been assured, to honor his work as commissioner.

We were more impressed by the statue of Yount, who played his entire career in Brewer blue, a feat rarely seen in the free-agent era. "Rockin' Robin" played 242 games as a teenager. He won the MVP at two positions—shortstop and center field—and was an instrumental member of the 1982 World Series team. Yount banged out 3,142 career hits and was a first-ballot Hall of Famer.

The Aaron statue stands not far away. While there is nothing about Mr. Aaron that we could say that hasn't been said before, we'll try. The player who broke Babe Ruth's homer record was understated, humble and graceful in practically every way. Aaron began and ended his career in Milwaukee, hitting his first big-league home run as a Brave and his last as a Brewer. Elected to the All-Star team in twenty-one of his twenty-three seasons, many people forget that he also won two batting titles and four Gold Gloves in right field. Averaging thirty-three homers a year and never hitting more than forty-four, Aaron has been remembered for his durability and consistency. He broke the Braves' color barrier in 1954, then two decades later weathered hate-mail and death threats on the way to breaking Ruth's longstanding record of 714 career dingers.

THE WALK OF FAME

Starting near the Yount statue, granite home plates form a "walk of fame" that fans can traverse to honor the greatest Brewers of year's past. In addition to the previously discussed statue-worthy team icons, these members also include Rollie Fingers, Paul Molitor, Cecil Cooper, Uecker, Gorman Thomas, Jim Gantner, Eddie Mathews, Warren Spahn, and a handful of former managers and front office executives.

Watering Holes and Outside Eats

The best way to enjoy Miller Park is to tailgate. No doubt about it. Why drink in a bar when you have to drive to the parking lot anyway? But if you're inclined to go to a brew pub before or after the game, you'll find no shortage of joints from which to choose. You don't have to look far to find a watering hole in Milwaukee. Be it an old brewery-sponsored bar, a new microbrewery, a traditional bar, or a corner hole in the wall, the beer is always flowing. The Water Street area has a wealth of pubs within walking distance of one another and is a nice area for dining and nightlife. Additionally, crossing the bridge over the Milwaukee River offers the opportunity to identify one of the "Seven Smells of Milwaukee." Also try the East Side neighborhood for some great joints, dives, and local hangouts.

Josh: I think I smell brats. Is that one of the famous smells?

Kevin: That might be a burp backing up on you.

KLEMENT'S SAUSAGE HAUS

If you're like Josh and you're too timid to mooch from fellow tailgaters like Kevin happily did, the sausage barn that stands between the Gantner and Yount lots is the best bet in walking distance of your parking space. We got a kick out of the electronic sausage races and found the Italian a delightfully spicy variation. The brat was also a winner. We should mention, however, that by the time the busy summer months roll around, the Haus is often reserved for private parties,

Robin Yount statue

Photo by Kevin O'Connell

so you'd be wise to bring your own meat for your primary course and to stop by the Haus just to check out its decor on the way into the game.

WATER STREET BREWERY
1101 N. Water St.
www.waterstreetbrewery.com/home.htm
This is your standard microbrewery, with reasonably priced food. The Honey Light Lager and Old World Oktoberfest have won medals at the Great American Beer Festival. But what we really liked was the huge collection of suds-related memorabilia. Some of this stuff would fetch quite a price on Antique Road Show.

BUCK BRADLEY'S
1019 Third St.
www.buckbradleys.com/
Buck Bradley's dates back to the 1800s. It offers a decently priced lunch menu, but by dinnertime the prices were a bit rich for our blood.

> *Josh:* This is the longest bar I've ever seen.
> *Kevin:* Same here, my wide-eyed friend.

LAKEFRONT BREWERY
1872 N. Commerce St.
www.lakefrontbrewery.com/lakefront-brewery-home-page.html
This off-the-beaten-track micro-haus offers a terrific selection of homemade beers. They have about any flavor you can think of. We tried the Big Easy, Cream City, and Golden Mapleroot. The Milwaukee Brewer ambiance is enhanced by Bernie's old Chalet and Slide from County Stadium. The only thing we suggest: Let patrons slide down into a huge stein of beer.

THURMAN'S 15
1731 N. Arlington Place
www.thebeyondlevel.com/thurmans15/
If you're tired of all the yuppies at the microbreweries why not hang out with hippies? This is the kind of joint where you might find yourself talking to a beautiful local hippie chick, or to some old booze-hound. Probably the latter. But how can you go wrong at a joint named after Thurman Munson.

> *Kevin:* What was Munson's Yankee uniform number?
> *Josh:* Do you really have to ask?

WOLSKI'S
1836 N. Pulaski
www.wolskis.com/
This is a place to drink a PBR in true Milwaukee fashion. Stick around until closing and the bartender will hand you an "I

Closed Wolski's" bumper sticker for your road trip car. After we got ours we started seeing them everywhere. Unfortunately, when we turned the car back in to Hertz, they were not happy. And we lost the sticker forever.

LANDMARK LANES
2200 N. Farwell Ave.
www.landmarklanes.com/
This pool hall, brew pub, and bowling alley is an East Side landmark that we fondly describe as disgustingly fabulous. Incidentally, Miller Park weighs 500,000 tons, which is roughly equivalent to 62.5 million bowling balls (sixteen-pounders, not those little candlestick balls that Josh and other lightweights used to roll beneath Fenway Park).

VON TRIER TAVERN
2235 N. Farwell Ave.
www.vontriers.com/
Just down the road from Landmark you'll find a true German beer garden, and a hell of a place to sing "Beer Barrel Polka." There was no music when we visited, but Kevin sang anyway, while Josh slowly inched away from him and scanned the crowd for "new friends." The beer-garden owners are still waiting for the Brewers to get back to the World Series so they can hold the biggest Oktoberfest since 1982.

HOOLIGAN'S
2017 E. North
www.hooligansuperbar.com/
Head to historic Hooligan's for tasty grub, or great Bloody Marys. If you're lucky, you just might get booted.

RYAN BRAUN'S GRAFFITO
102 North Water St.
www.ryanbraungraffito.com/
Not only does Brewers slugger Ryan Braun have his own line of bats, his own clothing line, and his own energy drink, but he's part-owner of a trendy restaurant in Milwaukee's Third Ward that specializes in Italian cuisine with a baseball twist. The menu is a tad pricey, and there isn't much in the way of the baseball décor you might expect, but according to a few locals with whom we spoke, the food is very good.

Inside the Stadium

When we entered Miller Park on the first level and walked around the concourse we thought we might have found Baseball Heaven. When the roof is open, the park really feels like an open-air ballpark. The glass wall beyond the outfield

---

A League of Their Own

In order to keep baseball alive during World War II, fast-pitch softball evolved into overhand hardball. The movie *A League of Their Own* pays tribute to this version of the game, which lasted from 1943 to 1954. Ten teams played in the AAGPBL, which drew 910,000 patrons at its height in 1948. The local gals were called the Milwaukee Chicks, and starred Thelma Eisen and Connie Wisniewski. The 1992 cinematic treatment of the league starred Tom Hanks and Madonna, among others.

Another movie filmed in Milwaukee was the 1989 comedy *Major League.* Even though the ballpark in the film is supposed to be Cleveland's Municipal Stadium, all the stadium interiors were shot at County Stadium. Brewers' announcer Bob Uecker, who had previously starred as "George" on television's *Mr. Belvedere,* has much more than a cameo in the story of the underdog Indians.

Josh: I always thought that Wesley was a rascal.

Kevin: You mean Wesley Snipes who played Willie Mays Hayes in *Major League?*

Josh: No, mischievous son Wesley, who was played by Brice Beckham on *Mr. Belvedere.*

Kevin: You really had your finger on the pulse of pop culture back in the 1980s, didn't you?

Josh: Mr. Belvedere's nickname was "Brocktoon," in case you're interested.

Kevin: Trust me, I'm not.

---

remains bright and cheery at all times, and when the roof is open, from some angles it's like there's no roof at all. As you sit in different seats around the park you do begin to notice the fanned-out segments and design of the roof, which is a featured part of the ballpark. Sitting behind home plate it looks all wedged up like the gills of some beast from *20,000 Leagues Under the Sea* and is clearly the most interesting of all the retractable roofs built to date. The roof is also quite functional on those snowy April days when the wind whips off Lake Michigan. Though we had a fantastic experience at Miller, we began to notice many of the flaws and inadequacies that make a book like ours useful when we left the first level for higher ground. The first level is the only level where you can walk around the entire park, but even on this ground floor much of the concourse is stuck behind the seating, offering no view of the field. This dismantles the outdoor feel and leaves one feeling as though walking in a domed stadium or cookie-cutter. Kevin even had a flashback that he was in the Kingdome during his grunge days. This was bad on many levels.

Josh: Did you just rip a hole in the knee of your jeans?

Kevin: Umm . . . maybe.

Ballpark Features

THE HOT CORNER

The concourse down the third-base line offers a collection of shops, restaurants and memorials. While we like the historic nods, the shops made us feel like we were in a mall. There were even a few preppy teens blocking the walkway as they frantically thumbed out messages on their smartphones.

Friday's Front Grille in the Hot Corner features darts, billiards, bowling, soccer, and lacrosse. You can sit in the restaurant with a window-view of the action. But there are many more seats with no view of the field, so be careful what you get yourself into. The placement of the restaurant forces the concourse to run behind it so fans walking on the concourse can't see a thing. Not impressive at all, as far as design goes. We would have liked the ballpark designers to prioritize the fans walking around ahead of a chain restaurant.

Autograph Alley is one cool area in the Hot Corner. Fans can find zillions of autographs here of current and former players, as well as notable Brew Crew fans. These aren't just famous Brewer signatures. You'll find the penmanship of such immortals as Babe Ruth and Ty Cobb, Satchel Paige and Joe DiMaggio on display too.

The Walls of Honor pay homage to Wisconsin's MLB alums, Negro Leaguers, and members of the All American Girls' Professional Baseball League. Display cases offer a nice collection of balls, caps, uniforms, and bats, as well as photographs and stats. The Negro Leagues display honors all players of the Negro Leagues nationwide, not just the Wisconsin Bears.

RETIRED NUMBERS

The retired numbers hang high above the field on either side of the massive video board in center. They are mounted on baseball placards to honor: Aaron (44), Molitor (4), Fingers (34), Yount (19), Uecker (50), and Jackie Robinson (42).

As for that oversized video board: At the time of its debut in 2011 it ranked third-largest among baseball's stadium screens. It offers 1080p high-def resolution, which means it could play any Blu-Ray in Kevin's collection and look pretty damn good.

A BRADY BUNCH BULLPEN?

The bullpens do not have grass in them. Rather they are covered with artificial turf with a little grate in the middle for drainage. How cheesy is this? We suggest, respectfully, that the Brewers fix this in future years. We hear geneticists are working on some great shade-loving grass.

SPEAKING OF BULLPEN DEBACLES . . .

Miller Park hosted the 2002 All-Star Game. While the extravaganza was a success on some levels, it will go down in history as one of the biggest flops of Bud Selig's reign as baseball commish because he allowed the game to end in a 7–7 tie. In order to ensure every player got into the game, there were no pitchers left when the game went into extra innings. So Selig decided not to penalize teams in playoff contention whose hurlers would have to remain on the mound indefinitely. Strangely, Kevin sides with Bud on this one. Well, perhaps not so strangely, as the last remaining AL pitcher was Freddy Garcia, of his beloved Mariners.

Not long after the game that never ended, the St. Paul Saints rose to the comedic challenge and sponsored "Tie one on for Bud" night. On July 10, 2002, the independent league team gave away Allan H. Selig memorial neckties, complete with a picture of "Bud" himself in the center. We suppose this promotion was in better taste than one sponsored by the Saints later that year that presented fans seat cushions featuring pictures of the faces of Selig and then players association chief Donald Fehr.

Incidentally the only previous All-Star Game to end in a deadlock was the 1961 affair at Fenway Park. Because of heavy rains, that game was called after nine innings with the score tied 1-1.

"BREWING" AARON AND "PAPERMAKING" YOUNT

"Home to Heroes" murals can be found all over the park. These intertwine the region's heritage of brewing, manufacturing, tourism, papermaking, and agriculture with baseball players from all eras. They are very well done.

Stadium Eats

If you haven't had your fill of brats, Italians and Polish sausages in the parking lot, fear not. This is the land of spicy encased meats, and the offerings inside Miller Park do not disappoint. The remaining fare is just that, fair. So enjoy the brat and sausage Mecca that is Milwaukee.

BRATS WITH SECRET SAUCE (TRADEMARK FOOD)

Leave the chicken, pizza, and nachos to other parks, and enjoy the best brats baseball has to offer. While it's true that there is no substitute for a home (or parking lot) grilled brat of your own design, these ballpark beauties come awfully close. And whether you get your brat inside the park or out, they come with the trademark Secret Sauce, which we thought was a lot like Arby's Sauce. It tasted ketchupy and vinegary, with perhaps a dash of horseradish for good measure. According to local legend the Sauce was invented in the 1970s when a bulk-order ketchup delivery delivered to County Stadium accidentally arrived as a mismarked bulk-order of barbecue sauce. The industrious food-service workers at County mixed the small quantity of ketchup on hand with the freshly delivered barbecue and passed it off to fans as a new top-secret culinary creation. They served "dipped" brats all homestand and the fans just ate them up. Now they sell jars of the stuff by the dozen at every game.

Just be sure to bite down all the way through the natural casing of your brat, or you might get Secret Sauce all over your brand new Ryan Braun jersey like poor Kevin did.

We also loved the Italian, Polish and Chorizo. Kevin recommends getting a 24-ounce cup of suds to wash down all of the cased meat you can eat.

KLEMENT'S HOT DOG (DOG REVIEW)

The Klement's dog was squishy, rather than firm. This dog isn't worth a whistle—especially when so many other great cased-meats are grilling nearby.

BEST OF THE REST

After you try the brats, Italians, and beef brisket, your tummy might need a little cooling. Ours did and we used some **Home Sweet Home** ice-cream to cool us down. The Home features soft serve in a dish or waffle cone, in a root beer float, or in a chocolate or strawberry sundae. We're not sure if after weeks on the road we were simply in need of some dairy or what, but it hit the spot.

We also tried the **Toasted Ravioli,** which is a real treat, and the **Beer-Battered Mozzarella Sticks** (more dairy!), and they were good as well. But if you have to choose between them, go for the Toasted Ravioli. You just can't get that at many places.

The **Grab and Go** stands offer an assortment of fresh salads and fruit cups as well as **Cheese Curds.** We didn't try the curds. Our trip to Toronto had taught us to be wary. But they do have **Poutine** at Miller Park if you like curds and fries.

Josh: Ha! "Grab and Go" would be a great name for a serial groper.

Kevin: For some reason I found your comments much funnier on our first baseball trip.

Josh: That's because you grew up, while I'm still working on it.

STADIUM SUDS

Well, you're at Miller Park, so you might as well embrace Miller or MGD, because that's the house brew. On the plus side, the 24-ounce cup is a fistful. Buy two and you should be all set for at least a couple of innings. Specialty stands, meanwhile, serve regional favorite **Leinie's Draft** (courtesy of Leinenkugel Brewing Company in Chippewa Falls). By the way, Leinenkugel offers a variety of other great beers, if you get the chance to sample them anywhere else in the city.

The Miller Park Experience

HAVE A BARREL OF FUN

Now here is a Brew City tradition that has survived from the County Stadium era. During the Seventh Inning Stretch, fans enjoy a rousing rendition of "Roll out the Barrel." Ushers get into the spirit, dancing a two-step while the crowd cheers. Unfortunately the barrel isn't being rolled out, it's being rolled up. Shortly after the music ends, all beer sales cease for the day.

Kevin: We still have a cold six-pack in the parking lot.

Josh: Yes, but we're not leaving until the final out.

Kevin: I know. I know. Just thought I'd remind you.

SAUSAGE RACES

Miller Park stages daily Sausage Races in the middle of the sixth inning, featuring a Brat, Polish, Italian, Chorizo and Hot Dog. Sometimes, on Kids Days, child-sized Wienie Links take part too. The assorted meat mascots make their way from the video screen to the field. Both times we've visited Miller

Sausage Racers

Photo by Kevin O'Connell

the Brat won, which made a lot of sense to us. It's the best of the packed meats the stadium offers. During a game in 2003, Pirates first baseman Randall Simon knocked over one of the sausages with his bat. While the YouTube video of this looks as if Simon was trying to behead the sausage racer, this was really a case of a joke that went bad. But nevertheless, Sausage Gate was born, causing strife between Pittsburgh and Milwaukee for years to come.

BERNIE BREWER'S DUGOUT

Hey, what gives? Bernie Brewer, the team's infamous drunk from the old days, used to live in a chalet and slide into a vat of beer. Now Bernie lives in an air-conditioned pad on the third level and slides down to . . . (wait for it) . . . a home-plate-shaped platform on a lower level.

Bernie still casts hexes on opposing players and hangs Ks when Brewer pitchers strike out opponents. But what happened to the old sud-soaked drunk we used to love?

Josh: He cleaned up his act. It was time.

Kevin: You East Coasters always have to be so politically correct.

Josh: It was time for Bernie to grow up.

Kevin: Exactly. He used to throw up all the time!

Josh: I said 'grow,' not 'throw.'

Kevin: Oh.

HOG CROSSING

Harley Davidson motorcycles are made in Milwaukee and a biker dude takes the game balls onto the field with a Harley before each game. The motorcycle manufacturer has been headquartered in Milwaukee since its founding in 1903.

TAXI ANYONE?

The "Safe Ride Home" program seems like a necessity for a number of reasons. The park is isolated by its own off-ramps from the highway, and other than the bus, there is no way in or out except by car. The team name is the Brewers and the park is named after a major beer label. Tailgating is encouraged (in true Wisconsin fashion) and the team mascot is a reformed brewmeister still struggling to get his life on track. The team plays "Roll Out the Barrel" in the middle of the seventh. The beer culture that pervades Milwaukee is celebrated at the park, so the team offers fans free rides home if they get sufficiently tanked. The rules state that a cab will be called for you at the discretion of management. Head to the Guest Relations Office on the Field Level behind home plate for the staffers there to see if they think you're inebriated enough to qualify.

Josh: If you're turned down, can you have a few more beers and try again?

Kevin: I don't see why not.

Josh: Well then, this is kind of like a *Mr. Belvedere* episode when Kevin abused Bob Uecker's offer to drive him home if he ever called drunk at a party.

Kevin: Will you please stop with the *Belvedere* stuff.

BOB "THE VOICE" UECKER (SUPER-FAN)

There is no greater athletic supporter (just kidding, Bob) in Milwaukee than "Mr. Baseball," who has been the voice of the Brewers since 1971. A Milwaukeean who made good (to the tune of a .200 lifetime batting average!), Uke turned a very mediocre catching career and larger-than-life personality into great celebrity. Because Uke is the radio announcer for the Brewers you won't be able to hear him from your seats, so cruise into the bathroom where he can be heard all game long. How appropriate (just kidding again). But seriously, aside from being an actor, entertainer, and fabulous storyteller, Uke is a very solid radio man. In July of 2003 he was honored with the Ford C. Frick Award and entered the broadcaster's wing of the Baseball Hall of Fame. When a member of the home team hits a home run, Uecker's trademark homer call flashes in lights above Bernie Brewer's left-field dugout. "Get up! Get up! Get out of here! Gone!" it says, then Bernie hops on his slide to begin his celebratory descent to the home plate shaped platform below.

While We Were in Milwaukee
We out "Ueckered" the "Uecker Seats"

After buying $1.00 "Uecker" tickets, we met Glenn Dickert, who proved to be our guardian angel.

Kevin was at Helfaer Field, taking pictures and talking to strangers as he usually does on road trips. "One of the best ways to learn about a ballpark," he has said on countless occasions "is to talk to ushers and season-ticket holders. After all, they're here every day, the lucky bastards." Yeah, yeah, yeah. Heard it all before.

Glenn, a particularly kindly usher and former math teacher, was working at the little ballpark outside the big one when Kevin stopped by, and he fed Kevin all kinds of factoids about Miller Park. While gabbing, Kevin got around to handing Glenn our cheesy homemade business card, and telling him about the book. Glenn was genuinely excited.

"Where are your seats?" he asked.

"We had to buy Uecker seats," Kevin said, "We didn't plan ahead, and the other cheap seats were sold out."

"Ah, that's a shame," Glenn said. "You won't get any good pictures from up in the rafters."

"Probably not," Kevin lamented. "But we thought we'd walk around early and take some shots."

"Well, I'll tell you what," Glenn said, with a fatherly glint in his bright Wisconsin eyes, "I'm the usher behind home plate. Come on down after the third and we'll see if we can put you in some good seats."

We thanked our prospective benefactor and promised to meet him later in the day. After doing our legwork for the book—i.e., eating a half-dozen sausages each—we settled briefly into our Uecker Seats.

"I must be in the front row," Josh yelled.

"He missed the tag!" Kevin cried.

"Wesley, did you steal Mr. Belvedere's girdle," Josh hollered.

When we met up with our new friend Glenn, he walked us down to the seats we had always dreamt of. Seats 1 and 2 of Row 1 right behind the plate!

"We *are* in the front row!" said Josh.

"We out Ueckered the Uecker seats!" Kevin chortled.

"We pulled a reverse-Uecker."

Take it from us, the folks in Milwaukee are the nicest people you're likely to meet on your trip. Thanks, Glenn!

MINNESOTA TWINS, TARGET FIELD

MINNEAPOLIS, MINNESOTA
290 MILES TO FIELD OF DREAMS
340 MILES TO MILWAUKEE
410 MILES TO CHICAGO
440 MILES TO KANSAS CITY

Outdoor Ball in the Land o' Lakes

It took the Twin Cities longer than just about every other big league market to embrace the turn-of-the-century stadium construction wave, but with the opening of gorgeous Target Field in 2010 the Twins finally got on board. And did they ever! With the eagerly anticipated opening of Target Field, the dome-bound fans who were forced to suffer through the Metrodome's three-decade reign finally breathed a big deep breath of fresh air. It was a long wait, but it was worth it. After observing the successes and foibles of new stadium projects in other cities, the Twins got Target Field almost exactly right. Besides offering a natural playing surface, sweeping views of downtown, and an open-air experience, the park delivers a focus on the field so the game—which was sometimes obscured by the acoustic and aesthetic realities of the facility at the Twins' previous home—can stand front and center.

The fact that this sparkling yard ever came to be is a credit not only to the baseball cunning of a shrewd front office that thrived competitively for a decade despite its antiquated facility, disaffected owner, and payroll measuring a fraction of larger market clubs', but also to a local fan base that consistently turned out en masse at the Dome. There was a time, and it wasn't that long ago, when the Twins were on baseball's endangered species list. Contraction of the team loomed as a real—even likely—possibility in the early 2000s. And if Bud Selig and then-Twins owner Carl Pohlad had had their way, it would have come to pass. But a court ruling in 2001 staved off the dissolution of the Twins, and by extension, Expos, just as the Twins were to begin a ten-year run of excellence during which they finished first or second in the AL Central eight times, while racking up six division titles. Thanks to a bevy of homegrown players that arrived just in time to resurrect the franchise, the team emerged from the doldrums of the waning years of Tom Kelly's leadership to thrive under new manager Ron Gardenhire. Products of the farm system like Johan Santana, Justin Morneau, Joe

Mauer, and Michael Cuddyer helped the Twins assert themselves as a perennial division heavyweight. And the fans turned out to watch, making the team a middle-of-the-pack attendance finisher each year. In short, the team's success and fans' enthusiasm made the notion of contracting the team seem ridiculous. And so, the guardians of baseball's gates called off the dogs, opting instead to leave the Twins alone and move the Expos to Washington.

Ironically, though, just as the Twins' successes afield and at the gates kept the franchise viable, those factors conspired to prolong the wait for a new stadium. With the fans turning out in solid numbers at the Metrodome throughout the 2000s, there was no screaming imperative to build a new park.

The Twins, in proper Midwestern fashion, did things their own way. In the wake of Camden Yards' glorious opening in Baltimore, the path to new ballpark bliss in other municipalities usually began with a team letting its aging facility slip into disrepair. When fans stopped turning out at the decrepit yard, they started spending less on talent and losing games and began floating rumors that they might just have to move away to greener baseball pastures. This prompted taxpayers to approve emergency funding measures to keep their beloved boys of summer in town. All of this played out, of course, during the boom-time late 1990s and early 2000s. The Twins were struggling during these years, but the call to build a new yard fell on deaf ears. So the Twins just skipped all the intermediary steps and with some keen drafting and smart trades, general manager Terry Ryan's front office rebuilt the team without a new stadium. And Gardenhire and his young players took care of the rest.

Meanwhile, a funding plan for a stadium meandered through the Minnesota state legislature at a pace reminiscent of the glaciers that gouged out the ten thousand odd lakes in the Gopher State some ten centuries ago. Finally, the bankroll for a new yard was approved in 2006. Then, Hennepin County surmounted several rolls of red tape to acquire by eminent domain a just-big-enough-for-a-park parcel of land in Minneapolis's Warehouse District, west of downtown. In May 2007, work began to demolish and cart off the buildings on the site, and then in August local luminaries took part in an official groundbreaking ceremony. The Twins contributed about $170 million of the $420 million stadium price. Factoring in the cost of the land, site preparation, necessary infrastructure improvements, and financing, however, the true cost of Target Field checked in at more like $520 million. That's no small investment in the local nine but still represents much less than it would have cost to build the retractable-roof facility some pundits and fans expected. As it turned out, even without a lid, we think the Twins did just fine. They did fine when it came to negotiating a naming-rights deal too. It's easy these days for writers like us to dress down teams that give in to the corporate powers that continue to infiltrate our game, but how can you blame the Twins for selling out when the sweetheart deal they signed with Target will yield a reported $125 million between 2010 and 2033?

Kevin: That's fine, but I for one won't be shopping at Target anymore.

Josh: But you drink Miller, Coors, and Busch and they all have parks named after them.

Kevin: Only reluctantly do I drink those macros when nothing better's available.

Josh: You drank Minute Maid orange juice at breakfast today too.

Kevin: Juice is another exception.

Josh: Correct me if I'm wrong, but didn't you just buy that Pork Chop on a Stick with a Citibank debit card?

Kevin: Let's just watch the game.

Target Field occupies a smaller than typical stadium plot in a location just a stone's throw from the Minnesota Timberwolves' Target Center and a commuter rail station, within a Warehouse District full of restaurants and bars. The park's most unique design aspect is its generous interior and exterior use of a tan-colored limestone from Minnesota's Kasota Quarry. This is the same stone that was used in the construction of PNC Park in Pittsburgh, but it's featured much more prominently at Target, which is a fancy way of saying "slabs of the stuff are everywhere, here." In fact, the ballpark incorporates more than one hundred thousand square feet of it. From the street outside the smooth lime is complemented by glass panes and plenty of steel. We found the façade, while unique and modern, a bit cold.

Josh: We just redid our bathroom with these exact tiles.

Kevin: I wouldn't say that too loud here.

Inside, the limestone appears behind the plate at field level and on the Club level, on the dugout roofs, in deep foul territory, and atop the right-field fence. It presents a nice contrast to the forest green seats. Here, we liked the effect better. Truly, in the seating bowl and on the field this park shines. The relatively small confines offer room for just a shade over forty thousand spectators, including those holding standing passes, making for a cozy, if slightly cramped, atmosphere that offers good views of the action all the way around the diamond. There are three decks of seats, but none extends too far back or rises too sharply to leave fans feeling removed from the game.

A grove of twelve six-foot-tall black spruce trees originally stood beyond the fence in center to serve as the batter's eye but the trees were uprooted after the 2010 season because batters complained about the shadows they cast. In their place, the Twins installed a honeycomb-like material that supposedly provides an ideal backdrop for ball-spotting batters. We just hope it doesn't attract bees! Or bears! The evergreen batter's eye was actually only a small facet of a larger complaint several Twins hitters voiced during the first season at Target. The main

home view

The downtown skyline is on display in right field.
Courtesy of the Minnesota Twins

side view with interior limestone

The limestone above the right-field fence is one of Target Field's signature features.
Courtesy of Shilad Sen

criticism was that Target—which had been billed as a neutral setting that favored neither hitters nor pitchers—was a pitcher's paradise. While it's tempting to say sluggers like Justin Morneau and Joe Mauer were merely spoiled by playing so many games at the "Homer Dome," the stats do back up their contention. In Target's first season, the Twins—whose lineup remained practically identical to the year before—saw their long balls in home games dip from ninety-six in 2009 to just fifty-two in 2010. Mauer and Michael Cuddyer especially suffered, as the All-Star catcher hit just nine HRs compared to twenty-eight the year before, and Cuddyer saw his homers drop from thirty-two to fourteen.

Josh: Some "neutral" park.

Kevin: Yeah, but those guys both had career years in '09.

Josh: I'm just bitter because I had Mauer on my fantasy team.

Instead of spending their money on an overblown frill like the riverboat in Cincinnati, the choo-choo train in Houston, the swimming pool in Arizona, or the fish tank in St. Petersburg, the Twins eschewed what must have been an obvious temptation to add a few lakes or at least a walleye pond inside Target Field and sank their money instead into more practical ballpark accessories. Amidst concern

that cold April showers would subject fans to a degree of misery unbefitting paying customers, the Twins saw to it that Target Field include a more-expansive-than-usual sunroof over the upper deck to provide shelter on rainy nights. And realizing that the average nightly low in April in Minneapolis is 36 degrees Fahrenheit, they installed 250 overhead heating units on the main concourse in time for Target's opening. Then, after the first season, they installed 130 more heaters on the main concourse and terrace. Additionally, they outfitted the upper deck with radiant heating. And from the start, they've kindled a bonfire on cold nights out on the left-field party deck. The fire burns in a big rectangular pit around which fans huddle on frigid eves.

Kevin: You read that right: a freaking bonfire inside the park.

Josh: You won't see that anywhere else in the bigs.

Kevin: Well, there's an outdoor fireplace at Safeco.

Josh: That's not the same thing.

It's nice of the Twins to go to such lengths to ensure their fans won't freeze to death, but probably unnecessary. After all, the fans survived for years at heater-less Metropolitan Stadium before the opening of the Dome in 1982. The Twins of Harmon Killebrew, Tony Oliva, and Rod Carew had played at that Bloomington, Minnesota, yard dating back to the franchise's arrival via Washington in 1961. Prior to the erstwhile Senators' migration, the minor league Minneapolis Millers had called the "Met" their home since its opening in 1956.

The Metrodome supplanted the old park on April 6, 1982, following the Astrodome and Kingdome to become baseball's third dome. (We're not counting Olympic Stadium in Montreal, because it was technically a retractable-roof facility, even though the roof usually refused to cooperate.) Today, the NFL's Minnesota Vikings still play at the Metrodome, although a movement is afoot to build a new stadium in town too. For the time being, traveling fans can still pay the Dome a visit while in town, though. It is something to see. The ten-acre roof measures just ⅟₃₂nd of an inch thick. It is made of Teflon-coated fiberglass and kept aloft by two hundred and fifty thousand cubic feet of air pressure per minute, supplied by electric fans. It was named after Hubert Horatio Humphrey, the thirtieth vice president of the United States. After serving as second in command to Lyndon Johnson,

Humphrey received the Democratic nomination for president in 1968, but lost to Richard Nixon. During his tenure as VP, the liberal champion served as chairman of the National Aeronautics and Space Council, so perhaps Minnesotans thought it fitting that their "space-age" ballpark should bear his name. Or maybe they just wanted to honor a local pol, who after graduating from the University of Minnesota, served as mayor of Minneapolis and then represented Minnesota in the Senate.

Through the years the Homer Dome earned a reputation of being not only hitter-friendly but difficult for visiting teams to navigate. Perhaps trickiest of all was the off-white roof, which caused many a visiting outfielder to lose sight of the ball. Fair balls sometimes bounced off the public address speakers suspended 180 feet above the field as well. Fly balls to right would swish off the Hefty Bag—a twenty-three-foot-high plastic curtain that served as the outfield wall—and barely carom, dropping down to the warning track. A hockey-rink style stretch of Plexiglas ran atop the left-field wall, and homers to right clanked somewhat less than idyllically into a bank of folded-up football seats.

Due in part to these eccentricities, the Twins posted an 8-0 record at home in the 1987 and 1991 World Series against the Cardinals and Braves. In both October Classics they went 4-0 at home and 0-3 on the road. In 1991, the Twins won Game 6 on an eleventh-inning walk-off homer by Kirby Puckett, then won Game 7 on a tenth-inning walk-off single by Gene Larkin as native son Jack Morris, who was born across the river in Saint Paul, went ten innings for the 1-0 victory. These were some great stories spun by the hardball gods.

As for less glorious moments at the Dome, one occurred in April 1983 when the roof collapsed under the weight of heavy snow, forcing the Twins to postpone a game against the California Angels, the only postponement in the stadium's baseball history. Three years later, a game also against the Angels, was delayed for nine minutes when high winds tore a hole in the roof. And most catastrophically of all, in December 2010, after the Twins had moved to their new yard, heavy snow collapsed and deflated the roof, allowing tons of white powder to pour down onto the fake green turf. The footage of the collapse made national news and went viral on YouTube, while the damage forced the Vikings to move their Monday Night Football game against the Giants to Detroit's Ford Field. Now, with the opening of a real, honest-to-goodness baseball field, the Twins will have no such calamities with which to concern themselves. Sure, there will be an April blizzard or two to contend with, but that's small potatoes compared to the drama and hijinks of playing in the Dome.

The first baseball game at Target Field took place on March 27, 2010. It was played between the University of Minnesota and Louisville. Next, the Twins played two exhibition games against the Cardinals at the end of spring training. Then, finally, they hosted the Red Sox on April 12 for the first regular season big league game in stadium history. Beneath cloudy skies on a comfortable 65-degree day, the Twins prevailed 5-2 behind six innings of one-run ball by Carl Pavano and three-hit days from Mauer and Jason Kubel. The Twins then went the rest of April without suffering a single opening-month rainout at home. Take that, you retractable-roof fanatics!

All in all, the first campaign at Target was a smashing success. Despite the team's power-outage and the pallor cast by a season-ending concussion suffered by Morneau in July, the Twins added another Central Division pennant

upper-deck sunroof

The larger-than-usual sunroof over the top deck provides shelter from the sun, but also protection on those rainy April nights.
Photo courtesy of Shilad Sen

to their resume before falling to the Yankees in the American League Division Series. They had the best home record in baseball, going 53-28, and finished sixth in attendance, drawing more than 3.2 million fans, or an average of nearly forty thousand per game. Comparatively, the Twins had spun the turnstiles to the tune of about 2.3 million fans per season or twenty-eight thousand per game during the final several seasons at the Metrodome. We can see why the locals are eating up their new digs. Target Field is a stellar addition to the Major League landscape and rates as a destination any serious baseball wanderer should make a point to visit.

Getting a Choice Seat

Amidst the excitement of Target Field's grand opening, the Twins sold out seventy-nine of their eighty-one home games in 2010, setting a new franchise attendance record along the way. While it was impressive to see the Twins outdraw such large-market clubs as the Cubs, Red Sox, Giants, Mets, and Braves, that sort of support is to be expected during the first season of a new yard's existence. But the Twins fans carried their rabid enthusiasm into the next season, or preseason to be precise. More than 129,000 loyalists filed through the gates of William Hammond Stadium during the team's sixteen-game home Grapefruit League schedule in Fort Myers, Florida, to set a new Twins spring training record. During the 2011 regular season to follow, the fans kept turning out at Target, even as the Twins struggled mightily during an injury-riddled campaign. For the time being, at least, Target Field is a tough ticket.

What this means to you, the traveling fan, is that you'd be wise to purchase your Twins tickets well in advance, preferably when seats go on sale during the winter. For those of you like Kevin, though, who prefer to wait until the last minute, fear not . . . as long as you don't mind standing. Because Target Field offers probably the best experience in the bigs for those holding Standing Room passes. The whole first level concourse is wide open, which allows standers to camp out right behind the big wigs sitting in the boffo seats behind the plate. Or fans can stand alongside the fellow slackers on the plaza in right, or along the specially provided standing bars in center and left field. These standing rails provide something to lean on, and even room for a sandwich or drink to rest. The view from the main concourse around the infield was our first choice, but we also liked the view from the standing bars out near the foul pole. Only in straight-away center did we feel as though we were standing just a bit too far from the action to soak in the full Target Field experience. Finally, it should be noted that on a cold night some fans might be happier standing on the main concourse, beneath the overhang of the Club Level, than sitting in an Upper Level seat. The view is great and the heaters keep pumping out warm air!

In composing a seating map for their new yard, the Twins broke Target Field's thirty-nine-thousand-plus seats into twenty-three different pricing categories. Then they broke the regular season schedule into three different tiers, depending upon the quality of each opponent. That means your ticket to Target could cost any one of sixty-nine different prices if our math is right. But wait, it gets worse. Just before the start of the 2011 season the Twins tossed this little curveball fans' way, issuing a presser that read:

New for 2011, the Minnesota Twins have chosen leading demand-based pricing provider, Digonex Technologies, Inc., to provide demand-based pricing for some sections of Target Field. . . . Seats in the Home Plate Box and Home Plate View seating sections of Target Field will be priced according to fan demand.

Kevin: So, if there's no regular price for those primo seats, how can we tell fans whether they're a good value?

Josh: I remember when I used to go to Fenway as a kid. There were three options: Bleacher, Grandstand, or Field Box.

Kevin: And?

Josh: Life was a whole lot simpler.

Anyway, describing all of Target Field's seating categories individually—including the ones subject to an eBay-like pricing scam—would present a lot of redundancy and confusion for you, the reader, and would very likely make Kevin's head explode. So, to keep things reasonably easy to understand and assimilate into your ticket-buying plan, we will

Seating Capacity: 39,504
Ticket Office: http://minnesota.twins.
mlb.com/ticketing/index.jsp?c_id=min
Seating Chart: http://minnesota.twins.
mlb.com/min/ticketing/singlegame_
pricing.jsp

take a level-by-level approach to rating the views instead of a price-category-by-price-category approach. There are three main decks at Target, although the top one might as well count as two mini-decks, since the 200 Level Terrace and the 300 Level Terrace are separated by a big height difference. In general, the view from the third-base line is preferred, as it places the city skyline directly in one's line of sight and also offers a good view of the Minnie and Paul sign in center. The massive hi-def video board in left, though, is a bit easier to see for those sitting on the right-field side.

The Lower Bowl (100 Level)
Approximately half of Target's seats are at field level in the lower bowl. The first twelve rows around the infield lie below an interior walkway, behind which appear another 25 rows. The seats in the lower twelve are owned almost exclusively by season-ticket holders and run between $72 and $295 per game. Chances are you won't be sitting in them. But you might well have the opportunity to purchase nearly-as-good seats in the "demand-base-priced" Home Plate Boxes directly above them. Section 115 is behind the plate, 108 is at first base and 120 is at third. Take your pick; you really can't go wrong here.

Farther down the lines in outfield territory, four sections of Diamond Boxes pick up where the Home Plate Boxes leave off. Sections 104–107 in shallow right and 121–124 in shallow left offer great seats, particularly 104 and 121 from which the views are practically indistinguishable from the higher-priced Home Plate Boxes. As we said above, if all things are equal, you'll probably be happier on the third-base line than on the first.

Still farther down the lines, three sections of Field Boxes fill out the spaces that remain before the foul poles. Here the seats are not bisected by a midlevel walkway and the vertical aisles that lead all the way from the concourse down to the front row seats by the field are the only means of entry or egress for fans. For the price, these are

good seats but once we got into the outfield corners (101 in right; 127 in left) we felt as if we'd have been better served sitting in the field level home run territory seats.

Throughout the lower bowl, we found the seats and rows plenty wide and thought the grade of the rise was just right. Sure, the stadium is squeezed into too small a parcel of land, but this minor defect shows up on the crowded concourses, not in the seats around the field. The overhang of the Club Level around the infield does not interrupt views for those seated in the Home Plate Boxes or first sections of Diamond Boxes. Those seeking shelter from the elements should aim for (Rows 19–28) of the Home Plate Boxes.

The Club Level (Second Deck)
Of the twenty Sections on the Club Level, only four are accessible to ordinary fans. The rest are reserved for the special fannies who sit in the broad wooden seats that mark, apparently, one's placement a few notches above the Average Joe on the Twin Cities food-chain. But wait: It gets worse, as these Club sections usually do. There are also three bars that are open to season-ticket holders only—The Sky 36 Legends Club, the Champions Club, and the Metropolitan Club. These establishments combine to showcase two-story-high laser-burned murals of Kirby Puckett and Rod Carew, as well as some other really neat memorabilia that ordinary fans just can't access during the game. In any case, Sections A through R on the infield are the domain of these corporate

third-base-seat view

With the opening of Target Field, the Twins' dugout has rightly been restored to its proper place on the first-base side.
Courtesy of the Minnesota Twins

mucks and high-rollers. The other four sections are in left field, above the Field Boxes. These aren't really "Club" seats, but are a solid midlevel option. Appearing in Rows 1–14 in banks that begin with Section S in shallow left and end with Section V closer to the left-field foul pole, these so-called Skyline Deck seats offer a nice raised view of the field and downtown, but we preferred the sight lines in the comparably priced Field Boxes where we didn't feel like wannabes.

Home Run Territory Seats

There are four distinct options for fans seeking just-beyond-the-wall seating in long-ball land. Then, higher up, there are three more seating tiers available.

The Bleachers (Sections 139–141) in the right-field corner are actual aluminum benches with flat aluminum backs. Appearing in Rows 1–15, they are perched above the twenty-three-foot-high right-field wall, and provide an excellent vantage point. There is a three-foot wide railed off dead space between the first row and the top of the wall, which prevents fans from "accidentally" interfering with the flight of balls destined to smack against the fence top.

Adjacent to the Bleachers in right-center, three narrow sections of Overlook seats (Sections 136 to 138) provide seven rows of more comfortable sweet-seats for homer-hounds. The first row actually overhangs the warning track by quite a bit. To the center-field side of the Overlook, four sections of Powerball Pavilion seating (Sections 132–135) offer three rows apiece tucked below the overhang of the 200 Level Right Field Grandstand (237–240). Finally, after the batter's eye and tiered bullpens, four sections of Field Terrace (Sections 128–131) bleachers appear in straight-away left to comprise a second swath of benches with backs. The first rows of the Field Terrace offer the lowest to the field outfield viewing locale because the fence in left is only eight feet high, or, a third of what the fence in right is. We liked the Field Terrace but were lukewarm on the 200 Level and 300 Level US Bank Home Run Porch seats above it. Surely, the back rows of this left-field seating deck house some of the worst seats in the house. On the plus side, this left-field grandstand reminded us more than just a bit of the similar outfield seating bank at old Metropolitan Stadium. So on the nostalgia scale, it rates high but you should probably get yourself a closer view if you're only going to be visiting Target once or twice in your lifetime.

The Terrace (Third Deck, 200 Level)

Above the Club deck, the lower third of the upper deck contains the Terrace seats. These begin with Section 201 in deep

SEATING TIP

We suggest that if you wish to spend most of your time inside Target Field wandering around to check out the game from all of its angles, that you purchase a Skyline View seat in deep left field instead of Standing Room, since the cost for the two tickets is nearly identical (between $14 and $19 depending on the quality of opponent, time of year, alignment of Mars and Jupiter, and other factors that factor into the Twins' pricing formula). That way, if your wary knees give out in the later innings, you'll have a seat with your name on it just in case.

left field, continue to Section 209 at first base, make the turn at Sections 215 and 216 behind the plate, and head down the other line with Section 221 at third, before concluding with 228 in deep left-field foul territory. These sections hang below the upper deck's covered but open concourse. There are between four and eight rows in each Terrace Section so even a "back" row seat is just fine. For upper level seats, they are a solid value for the money. From any section on the infield we liked the view a lot. We were impressed by the fact that the underhanging deck didn't affect the quality of the view as is sometimes the case.

The View (Third Deck, 300 Level)

Ringing the top of the stadium, the View sections offer fourteen rows, almost all of which receive some shelter from the expansive sunroof. For the best view of the trademark Minnie and Paul sign as well as of the city skyline, aim for seats in Sections 316–322 on the left-field side of the diamond. The buildings that rise behind the outfield seats in right are chic and modern and combine to form a crisp, aesthetically pleasing backdrop for a game. The ingloriously named 33 South Sixth building is among the most prominent of the high-rises, while other monoliths like the well-rounded Capella Tower and the IDS Center are also on display.

Before/After the Game

Following in the learned footsteps of the Seattle Mariners and Colorado Rockies, who took up residency in their cities' club- and studio-laden warehouse districts to excellent effect, the Twins welcome fans to a vibrant Warehouse District of their own where a lively club and restaurant scene abounds amidst ample studio and gallery space. We suggest arriving in the neighborhood early to take a stroll along First Avenue. Speaking realistically, you'll need at least a few hours to sample the food, drink, and culture.

Getting to Target Field

There are four large parking garages on the outfield side of Target Field—known as the A, B, C, and Hawthorne municipal ramps. These are accessible via 2nd and 3rd Avenues and their bisecting roads. Another just-outside-the-gates option is the Rapid Park lot on the corner of 3rd and 5th Street, which sprawls under the highway overpass. There are also surface lots and smaller garages throughout downtown on the first-base side of the park. Typically these charge between $4 and $15. Supply is high, it seems, so prices are relatively low.

For those staying overnight in Minneapolis, we recommend taking public transportation to the game. This will allow you to maximize your time in the Warehouse District before and after. The Northstar Commuter Rail and Hiawatha Light Rail Line both drop fans off outside the ballpark gates at Target Field Station. Or, those looking to do some bar-hopping before the game, can get off the Light Rail three blocks farther into the Warehouse District, at Hennepin Avenue Station.

Northstar Info: www.northstartrain.org/station_mpls.html

Hiawatha Light Rail Map: www.metrotransit.org/hiawatha-line-route-55.aspx

Outside Attractions

STAR GATING

Before we get you too totally confused by referring to the landmarks surrounding the park in relation to their proximity to the nearest stadium entry gate, we should mention that rather than numbering Target Field's ramps in the traditional (Gate 1, Gate 2, Gate 3) manner, the Twins opted to fly atop each gate the old uniform number of one of the legendary players whose numbers have been retired by the team. This was a clever touch that we really appreciated . . . after, that is, Kevin spent about twenty minutes circling the park, scratching his head in search of Gate 1. In any event, Harmon Killebrew's Gate 3 sits in center field, Tony Oliva's Gate 6 sits in left by the train station, Puckett's Gate 34 and Carew's Gate 29 are in right at Target Plaza, and Kent Hrbek's Gate 14 is behind the plate.

Kevin: Hey, isn't Bert Blyleven a Hall of Famer? Why doesn't he have a gate?

Josh: He joined the Hall in 2011, and his No. 28 was retired by the Twins in 2011, but . . .

Kevin: . . .Target Field opened in 2010.

Josh: Exactly.

GOLDEN OLDIES

Among the many points of interest on Target Plaza is a large sculpture of a Gold Glove. This, to honor standout Twin City fielders like Jim Kaat, who won eleven Gold Glove Awards for the Twins between 1962 and 1972 amidst a streak of sixteen consecutive Rawlings trophies he won overall, including his years with the White Sox and Phillies. While Kaat's sixteen in a row is a record for pitchers and ranks Kaat tied for second in total Gold Gloves in a career with Brooks Robinson, Kaat places second among pitchers in total Goldies to Greg Maddux, who won eighteen over his distinguished career. Other terrific Twins leather-men have included Puckett, who won six Gold Gloves, Torii Hunter, who won seven while with the Twins, and third baseman Gary Gaetti, who won four back in the 1980s.

As for the statue, its placement on the plaza is no random thing. It sits 520 feet from home plate, which is the distance the longest home run in Twins history traveled. It was struck by Killebrew at Met Stadium. If you keep reading, you'll learn a bit more about that famous clout, because we'll revisit it when we discuss the Mall of America.

LARGER THAN LIFE

The Plaza also offers an unusual degree of personal access to oversized statues of Puckett, Carew, Killebrew, and Oliva. The first three debuted in March 2010, while the Oliva one was unveiled on Opening Day 2011. And in 2011 the Twins added statues of former owners Calvin Griffith and Carl and Eloise Pohlad. Yes, that's right, the same Carl Pohlad who offered to sell the Twins to a group fixing to move the team to North Carolina in the 1990s and offered to sell them to MLB so they could be contracted in the early 2000s.

Josh: These friendly Midwesterners are more forgiving than folks back East.

Kevin: You guys still booing Bill Buckner?

Josh: No, he's been forgiven. But we spit on John McNamara's grave for leaving Billy Buck at first instead of inserting defensive whiz Dave Stapleton.

Kevin: Classy.

Josh: Especially considering Johnny Mac ain't dead yet!

The Twins bronzes are plopped in patches of infield clay right at ground level, allowing fans to walk up and pose for pictures. You can wrap your hand around "Killer's" extended bat as he completes a home run swing, or give Kirby a fist-bump as he celebrates his walk-off homer against the Braves in Game 6 of the 1991 World Series.

The statues were crafted by Minneapolis sculptor Bill Mack. When Josh caught up with Mr. Mack, the sculptor emphasized the uniqueness of the street-level placement of his work. "I have to hand it to the Twins," Mack said. "They really wanted these to be interactive. If you create a monument and put it high in the air or on a pedestal, it's more of a decoration. With these, people can touch them, pose with them, and even hang from them if they want, although I don't necessarily encourage that. This type of presentation allows for a much more personal interaction."

For the record, the nearly horizontal bat that extends from Killebrew's hands is fortified by a steel rod and was stress-tested before leaving the California foundry where the statues were produced.

Mack isn't worried about the Carew statue either, even though it stands near a busy intersection. "It seems only a matter of time before a car jumps the curb and runs into it," Mack said, chuckling, "We'll see who wins. My money's on the statue."

Such permanence seems fitting for Carew, a class act, who won the AL MVP with the Twins in 1977 when he batted a franchise-record .388 with 239 hits. He also crossed the plate 128 times while racking up sixteen triples, fourteen homers, one hundred RBIs and twenty-three steals. And his 1.019 OPS led the league. With his .388 BA he claimed the sixth of seven batting crowns he would win during twelve seasons in Minnesota. And that season he played in his eleventh straight All-Star Game, continuing a streak that would eventually extend to Mid-Summer Classic appearances in his first eighteen seasons from his Rookie of the Year campaign of 1967 to his penultimate 1984 season with the Angels.

KINETIC WIND ART

Fans on the plaza are also treated to a whole new kind of art. At least it was new to Josh, who wasn't even sure it *was* art. He had to admit it was pretty cool, though. Each small panel of the façade is hinged so as to shift slightly in the breeze, making the patterns of the wind visible. It's really an amazing effect that you have to see in person to fully appreciate, especially when it's lighted at night. Or you can do a YouTube search and watch it on your computer, but it's not quite the same.

TWINS TRADITION WALL

Located between the Carew and Puckett gates, this unique monument takes an all-inclusive approach to honoring current and former Twins. Rather than just celebrate the franchise's greats—a la Monument Park at Yankee Stadium—the Twins inscribe the name of every player to don

a Twins uniform on hanging metal pennants. There are also quotes from the franchises' icons and from fans who have added their messages to the wall for a cost. We also found on the wall the lyrics to "Take Me Out to the Ball Game" and "We're Gonna Win, Twins."

Kevin: This is a really nice touch. . . .

Josh: But?

Kevin: . . . it seems more like a fence than a wall.

Josh: "Tradition Fence" doesn't have the same ring.

Watering Holes and Outside Eats

Because there's something to be said for nostalgia, we thought that after first offering our take on the best bars and eateries in the new ballpark neighborhood, we'd include a few golden oldies from the days when the Twins played at the Dome. In all likelihood, you'll spend most of your pregame and postgame time in the Warehouse District, but downtown isn't far away at all, so don't be afraid to explore this clean and exceptionally friendly city.

THE LOON CAFE
500 First Ave. North
http://looncafe.com/

If you're looking to watch an out-of-town West Coast game, like Kevin was, this just-outside-the-gates saloon is a solid bet. Not only does the Loon offer the MLB package but its chili is pretty good too. If you're an early riser like Josh, they offer a Sportsman's Breakfast before Twins day games.

SMALLEY'S 87 CLUB
100 North 6th St.
www.smalleys87club.com/

Owned by switch-hitting former Twins infielder Roy Smalley, who was a member of the 1987 Twins, this place is worth visiting to check out the impressive championship murals that celebrate the '87 and '91 teams.

Josh: At the end of a thirteen-year career Roy's last action came in the '87 Series. And he reached base in all four of his plate appearances. How cool is that?

Kevin: I bet he even got a hit in his last at-bat.

Josh: Well, no. In his last official AB he reached on an error. But he walked twice after that.

Kevin: Still, talk about going out on top!

DARBY O'RAGEN'S
315 North 5th Ave.
www.darbyoragens.com/

If the sun is shining and you're looking for an outdoor patio, Darby's fits the bill. You'll even be able to see Target Field from your picnic table . . . on the other side of the highway overpass. The Frickles (fried pickles) and Beer-Battered Sunfish are local favorites but we played it safe and ordered the Wimpy Burger and Pulled Pork. Both were just what we were looking for.

THE UGLY MUG
106 North 3rd St.
www.uglymugminneapolis.com/

Don't let the name fool you, the head-banging "Roc Bar" upstairs offers the cutest barhops you'll find in the Twin Cities and your best chance of getting lucky after the game. Indeed, if we were doing the trip fifteen years ago we would have been all over this place. As it is, we'll leave it to our younger readers to carry the torch. Have at it boys!

CUZZY'S BAR AND GRILL
507 Washington Ave. North
www.cuzzys.com/dntn/dntn_index.html

Now here's a bar that's more Kevin's speed. Sure it's a dive, but the patrons are friendly, the food is tasty, and the beer is cold. Oh yeah, and there's a ghost named Betsy that haunts the place. Stop by after you've had a few and you'll see what we mean. Trust us.

MACKENZIE PUB
918 Hennepin Ave.
www.mackenziepub.com/

With cheap eats, twenty-four beers on tap, and five jumbo TVs, Mackenzie's offers a friendly atmosphere to get warmed up for the game.

KIERAN'S IRISH PUB
600 Hennepin Ave.
www.kierans.com/

Josh liked the Corned Beef Reuben and Kevin liked the Guinness. And we both liked the fact that they open at 10:00 a.m. when there's a day game.

SNEAKY PETE'S
14 North 5th St.
http://ultimatefunbar.com/

If you're into this whole bar-hopping thing because you seek primarily hot waitresses in skimpy clothes, then Sneaky Pete's may be your choice. If you're looking for a really sneaky experience, you can also check out Dream Girls next door. We have opted not to include a web link because this is a family publication, but rest assured this is a place where sufficiently naughty women attend to the pleasure of "gentleman" patrons.

Downtown/Dome Era Favorites
HUBERT'S BAR AND GRILL
601 Chicago Ave.
www.hubertsmpls.com/

Even though it's a bit out of the way for today's road-warriors, those looking to soak up the full Twins experience should make the short trek to Hubert's, which from 1984 to 2009 was *the* place to be on game day. The Dome classic now also operates a satellite location inside the Target Center but it was always more of a baseball fan's joint than a basketball or even football fan's. Spacious, with a square bar, the joint is decorated with a wealth of local sports memorabilia. We enjoyed especially the pictures from the 1965 World Series between the Twins and Dodgers, the University of Minnesota football relics, and the Big Ten Standings board.

MURRAY'S
26 South Sixth St.
www.murraysrestaurant.com/home.html

This upscale steak house is as famous for its gaudy orange sign as for its twenty-eight-ounce sirloin strip. Murray's priced us out of an extended evening visit but if you're a business traveler with an expense account, you should make a point to settle in at Murray's for a full-course meal. For our part, we enjoyed the "Twins Special," which consists of a half-pound burger and bottle of beer for $9.95. Then we went to Target Field and ordered a Murray's Steak Sandwich at the Murray's concession stand.

LYONS PUB
16 South St.
www.lyonspub.com/

We enjoyed the Twins Special, which consists of mini-brat-sliders at a fair price. Josh ate nine, and that was after devouring a burger at Murray's. Did we mention the name of our pub (short for publisher)? That's right. Lyons. Here's to our next edition of *The Ultimate Baseball Road Trip*, perhaps sometime in the 2020s!

Inside Target Field

Target Field has been criticized for being a tad cramped. Perhaps that's because the park was squeezed into a smaller-than-normal geographic footprint due to the constrictive realities of downtown land acquisition. But perhaps the criticism is also the result of misguided fan expectations. Since the concourses at the old Dome were "cozy" when the house was full, fans logically expected more room to roam on the new yard's walkways. Instead, they've encountered elbow-to-elbow . . . umm . . . *camaraderie* with fellow fans on the concourses and many escalators inside a new park that's been filled to capacity since opening.

Kevin: Nothing a few seventy-win seasons won't fix.

Josh: I seem to remember them having this same problem in Cleveland back in the 1990s.

Ballpark Features

THE RIGHT-FIELD OVERHANG

At the Twins' previous home, a blue plastic tarp, known as the "Hefty Bag," served as the right-field fence, turning balls hit off the wall into adventures for visiting outfielders and doing little to make the experience of playing or watching a game in Minneapolis magical. Today, balls hit to deep right are still cause for fans to hold their breath but for a different, much more romantic, reason. In a nod to the right-field upper deck at old Tiger Stadium, perhaps, the protrusion of the Overlook extends over the warning track by a whopping eight and a half feet. If you don't think that's a big deal, head out to Section 101 for a look from the side.

Kevin: Mark my words: at some point an important game will be decided by a lofted fly ball that settles into the Overlook as an outfielder waits to make the catch.

Josh: How do you know?

Kevin: Baseball just has a way of shining a spotlight on its own idiosyncrasies.

MINNIE AND PAUL

High above the field in center a giant neon version of the Twins logo lights up in red, white and blue to celebrate Twins' home runs and other game-events. As far as logos go, this one is more creative than most and a bit more cryptic. On the surface it looks like two pear-shaped middle-aged fellas in baseball garb shaking hands over a flowing brook. But upon closer inspection the "M" on the sleeve of one gent and the "S," "T," and "P" on the chest of the other come into focus. This is the embodiment of Minneapolis and St. Paul joining hands to become "The Twin Cities." And the bridge-spanned stream? That's the Mighty Mississippi.

The logo was created in 1961 by a freelance illustrator from St. Paul named Ray Barton. Mr. Barton received $15 for his effort, thinking the logo would be used in a Twins ad campaign and on Metropolitan Stadium cups. He had no idea it would become the official team insignia. It just sort of happened.

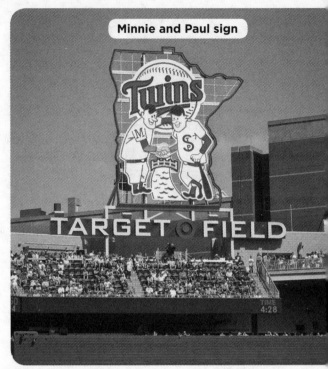

Minnie and Paul sign

The Twins logo appears in the form of a giant blinking sign above the centerfield batter's eye.
Courtesy of Shilad Sen

Kevin: Fifteen bucks? That dude got hosed.

Josh: But he's immortalized in team lore. That type of honor is priceless.

Kevin: I suppose . . . but fifteen bucks?

Josh: The Twins had just arrived. They were on a tight budget.

Kevin: I still say he got jobbed.

THE FLAGPOLE

The tall black pole on the right-field concourse is the very one that once flew the Stars and Stripes at Metropolitan Stadium. A small plaque at its base marks its historic significance.

DUGOUT

You'll notice that the Twins dugout has been restored to its proper place along the first-base line. That's where it resided at Metropolitan Stadium before the Twins moved across the diamond during their three decades in the Dome.

Kevin: Isn't the home team always on the first-base line?

Josh: Yeah, that way the home manager knows whether to argue calls at first.

Kevin: And that's important because in all the years baseball's been played first base umpires have overturned exactly zero calls due to managers protesting.

Josh: Just ask Armando Galarraga.

Kevin: Or Jim Joyce.

RETIRED (BUT NOT NECESSARILY IMMORTAL)

The Twins' retired numbers hang in left-field foul territory on the glass tower that houses the team's executive offices. Killebrew's No. 3 is closest to the foul pole while Jackie Robinson's 42 is farthest from it. Hrbek is the only member of the Twins to have his number retired despite his status as a non-member of the National Baseball Hall of Fame. Were the Twins premature in honoring the hulking first baseman or is his inclusion among the short-list of Twins' greats just dessert for a guy who played on both Minnesota championship teams? We'll let you decide. He played his entire fourteen-year career with the Twins, racking up 1,749 hits, 293 homers, 1086 RBIs and a .282 average. He made his only All-Star team as a rookie in 1982 but was sort of represented at the Mid-Summer Classic in 1988 when teammate Gary Gaetti famously wrote "Hi Rex" on his batting glove and held it up for the cameras during pregame introductions. More than that, Herbie was a hometown hero who was born in Minneapolis in 1960.

Kevin: Even Joe Mauer wasn't born in Minneapolis.

Josh: I have no problem with teams retiring iconic players' numbers even if they were something less than baseball royalty.

Kevin: But if Herbie gets his number retired, there ought to be a plaque with Tom Kelly's No. 10 on it, too.

Josh: Did you know Kelly's career winning percentage was below .500?

Kevin: Umm . . . I do now.

MORE WALL ART

Killebrew's distinctive handwriting appears in jumbo form on the right-field fence. Penned in yellow paint, against the wall's green backdrop, the legend's signature appears along with the familiar "HOF '84" that he always added to his scribble after he joined the Hall of Fame in 1984.

PLANTERS

We love that the Twins have red flowers growing atop the left- and right-field walls in wall-top planters. This idea may have originated at Busch Stadium in St. Louis, but it's been executed to perfection in Minneapolis.

LOOK MA, I'M ON TV!

Visiting fans interested in learning what the local chattering class is yammering about should seek out the Fox Sports North pregame and postgame studio, which sits on the left-field concourse. This is where Blyleven does his pregame interview with the Twins manager each day. The big righty has been calling games beside Dick Bremer in the Twins booth since 1995.

GAMERS OF THE WORLD UNITE

Not only does Joe Mauer put in an All-Star performance on the field, but he's reportedly one of the best players at the center-field Gaming Zone. That's right, Target Field has an area inside Gate 3 where patrons can play all of the latest baseball video games.

Kevin: I'd kill my kids if I took them to a game and they spent it playing video games.

Josh: Umm . . . I stopped by in the fourth inning and it's not just kids down there.

BUDWEISER DECK

They call the first inning the "thirst inning" in these parts and they have a whole roof deck named in honor of Budweiser. Aside from the corporate moniker, it's a unique part of the park that fans should find time to visit. This left-field perch is a great place to view downtown if your seat below faces away from the skyline. The bird's eye view of the field and the long rectangular fire pit are also attractions.

Josh: The fire pit, I like. But I'm lukewarm on those concourse heaters.

Kevin: Lukewarm. Very clever, my man.

Josh: Minneapolis's average April low is 36 degrees. In Detroit, it's 38. In Boston, 41.

Kevin: Yeah, but 36 degrees is plenty warm enough to thaw out from all that ice-fishing.

Stadium Eats

While the Metrodome menu did little to enhance the gameday experience, Target Field very quickly established a well-deserved reputation as one of the better eating parks. There are plenty of regional favorites on the menu. Where else in MLB can you find Walleye on a Stick? There are also all of the ballpark classics fans expect, done right. So don't fill your belly while tooling around the Warehouse District. Save room for the worthwhile treats awaiting your pallet inside.

SCHWEIGERT'S JUMBO DOG (DOG REVIEW)

During our first trip around the bigs, we were both duly impressed by the all-beef Hormel Dog that reigned supreme at the Metrodome for a generation. Therefore, we were a bit skeptical when we heard that perhaps the lone saving grace of the Dome concession stands had been replaced by a different brand of oversized frank. We kept open minds, open mouths, open stomachs and ultimately open hearts, however. And by the time we'd finished our quarter-pound all-beef Twins Dog, courtesy of Schweigert's, we were converts. This sucker is as juicy and tasty as it is long and plump. Even notoriously fast-eating Kevin needed a few minutes to put it down. And we both agreed that the accompanying Barrel O' Fun Potato Chips were a nice complement.

Think a quarter pound of processed beef is more than you can handle? You might be right. And if that's the case, you'll be happy to hear there are several other hot dogs at Target Field. The Original Twins Dog is a pork and beef mix specially commissioned by the Twins who requested that Schweigert use the same exact recipe fans once enjoyed at Metropolitan Stadium. The roving vendors, meanwhile, pack cases full of steamed Dugout Dogs. These are natural casing franks that have a nice crisp bite to them. We appreciated the fact that they aren't pre-wrapped but get placed in the bun upon being served to patrons. The extra-long Dinger Dog may be found at select Hennepin Grille stands. Finally, there are Hebrew National Dogs for Kosher fans and anyone else who likes to keep-it-Kosher once in a while just in case our Kosher friends are right.

WALLEYE ON A SPIKE (TRADEMARK FOOD)

The Minnesota State Fair is kind of a big deal in these parts. If you're from either Coast, you may not appreciate just how big, but trust us, the state fair is an Upper Midwest phenomenon that really is, well, phenomenal. The Minnesota version, which traces its roots all the way back to 1859 when Minnesota wasn't even a US State yet, is held at the 320-acre State Fairgrounds in Falcon Heights over twelve days at the end of summer. Attracting nearly two million visitors per year, it is the third largest state fair in the country. Surely, all of those Gopher State fairgoers enjoy gawking at the animals on display and the massive pumpkins, but they also love the unique fair foods, many of which come deep-fried on a skewer. Among these, Walleye on a Spike is a tried and true favorite that the Twins wisely adopted to be one of Target Field's signature offerings. It appears at the State Fair Classics stand on the first level concourse. Here, fans also find **Corn Dogs, Turkey Legs, A Giant Juicy Turkey Sandwich, Shish Kabob, Pork Chop On-a-Stick, Deep-fried Cheese Curds, Roasted Corn on the Cob,** and **Minneapple Pie.** We found the filleted fish stick crispy on the outside

and nice and moist inside. Be warned, it is a bit greasy. But if you're not going to be in Minnesota during the last week of August and you'd like to see what the fair-food to-do is about, this is a must-try. But that could be said about nearly all of the State Fair Classic items listed above.

BEST OF THE REST

The sausages at the carts on the concourse come courtesy of Kramarczuk's Market, which makes them just a mile from the park at its shop on Hennepin Avenue. Naturally, we started with the **brat.** You just can't find brats this good at most parks, so we really savored this one. Next, we moved on to the **Polish,** which was surprisingly garlicky but in a good way, before we finished up with the paprika-infused **Hungarian,** which was good but not as amazing as the first two. Honestly, we may have been sausaged-out by the time we got to the Hungarian.

The Twins tap into the Minneapolis dining scene to include several offerings with a local connection. The **Steak Sandwich on Garlic Toast** is served at the Murray's Restaurant stand. There may be a long line for this one once the game begins, so hit the Murray's stand early if you're interested. The **Chili** is provided by Warehouse District fave The Loon Café, and we already mentioned the Pork Chop on a Stick, courtesy of J.D. Hoyt's.

Famous players are the inspiration for foods at Target, too. In honor of Tony Oliva comes the **Cuban Sandwich,** which included all the right ingredients except for the Cuban bread, much to Kevin's dismay. In honor of curve-balling lefty Frankie "Sweet Music" Viola, the Frankie V's stand offers **Calzones, Meatball Subs,** and **Italian Salads.** And in honor of former reliever Juan Berenguer is the Señor Smoke stand where **Nachos, Burritos,** and other "Mexican" offerings are served beneath the banner of the Panamanian set-up man who played for four seasons in Minnesota.

At the Town Ball Tavern near Section 202 fans will find the **Juicy Lucy** burger. A St. Paul original, this patty is packed with cheese before cooking. That's right, it's a cheeseburger with the cheese on the inside. It was a gooey mess that Kevin enjoyed immensely, while Josh, who's a purist when it comes to cheeseburgers, kept muttering, "It ain't right, I tell ya," and refused to taste it. He instead opted for a Rex Burger at Hrbek's Restaurant near Gate 14. Little did he know that this burger comes stuffed with caramelized onions and jack cheese!

Neither of us tried the **Vincent Burger,** which is stuffed with smoked gouda and braised short ribs. This heart-attack-on-a-bun isn't cheap but the patrons to whom we spoke said it was pretty darned good. We were just too full, though.

CARRY-IN WELCOME

In this age when so many teams require fans to turn out their back-packs and pockets at the gate and to dispose of any consumables they might be trying to smuggle into the park, we thought we'd pass along this refreshing (pun intended) policy from the Twins website:

The Minnesota Twins permit guests to bring food into Target Field as long as items are consumed in the general seating areas. Outside food cannot be brought into any restaurant, club lounge or suite. Food containers must be soft-sided and fit under a guest's seat. Food that could be thrown as a projectile should be sliced or sectioned (e.g., apples). Additionally, any food purchased from the concession areas on Target Plaza is allowed into Target Field.

Now, that's the sort of Midwestern hospitality we really appreciate. It's obnoxious when pimple-faced ticket scanners in other cities act like food Gestapos just so their team's concession stands can make a few extra bucks. With that said, we found plenty to like about the food at Target, so we don't necessarily recommend that you make a ham and cheese sandwich to carry in. But if you have special dietary needs, it's nice to know you can see to them without facing an argument at the turnstiles.

STADIUM SUDS

When we saw that looming Budweiser Deck in left, we got worried, but pleasantly enough, we found ample micro options at Target. St. Paul's Summit Extra Pale is a popular draft, while many fans go for the bottled New Ulm Grain Belt Premium. Farm Girl Saison from the Lift Bridge Brewery in Stillwater, Minnesota, is a beer you won't find anywhere else in the bigs. Kevin described the golden ale as "well-rounded," which Josh noted just so happened to be the same thing he said about the St. Pauli Girls we'd enjoyed a few days before.

Kevin: I mean this in a different context.

Josh: Well-rounded how?

Kevin: Just write it down. Our readers will know what I mean.

The Target Field Experience

When we researched the first edition of this book in 2003, we found reason to liken the experience of attending a game at the Metrodome to that of visiting a Monster Truck Rally or Arena Circus Show. Now, in truth, it had been years since either of us had attended a Ringling Brothers three-ringer and neither of us had ever witnessed a Bigfoot mashing competition. But the comparison seemed about right. The Dome was loud and obnoxious. Now, don't mistake that to

mean we found the Twins fans obnoxious. We didn't. We're talking about the facility and how its personality impacted the game. The P.A. system was blaring. The artificial turf was a gaudy green. There was a plastic bag serving as an outfield wall. When visiting outfielders weren't losing balls in the roof they were watching them bounce over their heads. Like the experience at most of the old-fashioned domes, baseball was not quite baseball when played in this environment. And yet, we found in Twins fans a delightful mix of older folks who'd grown up watching games at Metropolitan Stadium and younger folks who'd come of age in the era of indoor baseball. To a person, they all expressed a longing for a day when outdoor ball would return to the Twin Cities. At the time, that seemed like a pipe-dream. Now, it's their reality and these knowledgeable fans love it. They bring enthusiasm and energy to Target Field and seem to care more about whether the home team wins than the fans at some of the other Midwest parks appear to. We're thinking of the Cubs and Brewers fans, in particular, many of whom just seem to enjoy the game-day experience without putting too much emphasis on the outcome.

LOGO-RHYTHMS

Don't be deceived by the old-time Minneapolis Millers and St. Paul Saints uniforms Minnie and Paul are wearing on the gigantic neon rendition of the Twins logo in center. This is a pretty high-tech ballpark effect and a pretty cool one, especially at night. Here's a cheat sheet that explains when the logo will alight and what all that flashing has to do with the game:

- *Twins Score: A strobe light traces the edges of the sign to suggest a runner rounding the bases.*
- *Twins Homer: Minnie and Paul shake hands over the flowing river.*
- *Twins Pitcher Gets a Strikeout: The corners of the sign flash.*
- *Twins Pitcher Throws a Scoreless Frame: The strobe lights flash.*
- *Twins Win: Minnie and Paul shake, the river flows, and the T and S in "Twins" flash.*

CIRCLE ME, BERT

Want to beam your ugly mug out on the Twins TV broadcast? Then bring a "Circle Me, Bert" sign to the game or paint those letters on your chest, or shave them into your hair, or find some other way to attract the attention of Bert Blyleven up in the Twins television booth. When Blyleven spots someone who fits the bill, he gives them props on his

"Circle Machine," which to Twins fans is an elusive and much-cherished honor. More ironically predisposed fans, meanwhile, who realize Bert's circle gag has gone on a bit too long, may be seen sporting "Triangle Me, Dick," signs as a nod to Blyleven's partner Dick Bremer, who hardly ever gets to use the Circle Machine.

TC THE BEAR

Like everyone we encountered in the Twin Cities, we found the Twins mascot, TC the Bear, to be congenial and generous with his time in answering our questions. However, as soon as one of his handlers put a super-soaker in his paws, he turned into a whole different breed of animal. If you see that oversized squirt gun, be prepared to hand over your Walleye on a Spike or at the very least run for cover on the concourse.

Cyber Super-Fans

- **Twins Dugout**
  www.twinsdugout.net/
  This long-running blog offers daily commentary, as well as an updated Twins "magic number" to clinch the AL Central, baseball jokes, a Twins fact of the day, baseball card of the day, and more.
- **Puckett's Pond**
  http://puckettspond.com/
  This site does a solid job previewing each series, commenting on the games, and keeping track of the latest trade rumors. We like the space to reflect back on team history too.
- **Aaron Gleeman Dot-Com**
  www.aarongleeman.com/
  It may be a little unorthodox to name your blog after yourself, but for this guy the formula worked. Aaron does a superb job shining a humorous light on not only Twins baseball but pop culture and politics as well. How superb? Well, he's attracted nearly eight million visitors to his site over the past decade. Hey, AG, how about a shout-out for The Ultimate Baseball Road Trip?

MINNESOTA MUSIC MACHINE

In 2010 the Twins started a tradition of beginning each game with a few songs by bands like Atmosphere or Hold Steady from the lively local music scene. As the final preparations were made to the infield before the Twins took the field, the songs would play through the P.A. while the band's name appeared on the big screen. When we visited in 2011,

though, it appeared that this cool tradition had been discontinued, and replaced by Top 40 fare.

Kevin: At least they still play "Highway to Hell" when Morneau steps to the plate.

Josh: Aren't those Canadians always head-bangers?

AN ORGAN-IC EXPERIENCE

Twins players and fans aren't the only ones who finally got the chance to breathe some fresh air when the team moved to Target Field. Longtime Metrodome organist Sue Nelson moved to the new yard too. Nelson can be found tickling the keys of her Yamaha on a raised platform behind home plate on the Terrace level. And her music and accent notes can be heard throughout the park.

A CREATIVE LURE FOR FANS

When they were a small market team playing in a lousy facility, the Twins smartly embraced a robust promotions policy that saw them give away a greater than usual number of door prizes to fans. Now that they're a small market team playing in a top-notch facility, they've fortunately (for fans) continued the tradition. While the fare at the gates consists mostly of the usual ballpark swag—bobbleheads, posters, mini-bats and the like—some of the items can be pretty creative. The most outside the (tackle) box item in recent years has been an annual Twins Fishing Lure courtesy of Rapala. Each one features a different player and bears the Twins logo. Among the players to be so honored have been Mauer, Morneau, and Matt Capps.

SUNDAY = FUN DAY

After the game on Sundays the Twins let kids fourteen and under onto the field to run around the bases. When the game ends, just head to the North Ramp area on the Main Concourse, near Section 130, and an attendant will direct your youngster onto the field.

Kevin: Now, this is the important part, so listen up.

Josh: If you have a very young child, the Twins allow an adult onto the field to accompany him or her around the bases.

Kevin: I never knew having a kid would be so rewarding!

While We Were Driving to Minnesota
We Visited the *Field of Dreams* Movie Site
www.fieldofdreamsmoviesite.com/distance.html
On the way from Milwaukee to Minneapolis we passed up a scintillating opportunity to visit the Spam Museum in

---

Sports in the City

The Mall of America
Killebrew Drive, Bloomington
www.mallofamerica.com/home/
No visit to the Twin Cities would be complete without a trip to the Mall of America, the world's largest covered shopping center, in nearby Bloomington.

Yeah, we know, malls are to shopping what domes were to baseball: covered, sterile, and all similar. But this jumbo emporium has a legit ballpark landmark beneath its roof. Head for the Mall's seven-acre indoor amusement park and after a bit of a scavenger hunt you'll find a unique tribute to Metropolitan Stadium, which stood on this site from 1956 until 1984. The ballpark attracted twenty-two million people in twenty-one Major League seasons. The mall attracts nearly twice that many in a typical year.

Inside the amusement park, look for the red stadium chair mounted above the water ride some 520 feet from where the Met's home plate resided. The seat commemorates the landing spot of Killebrew's longest homer in team history, which he smacked against the California Angels' Lew Burdette in 1967.

Before departing in search of an Orange Julius or plate of Bubba Gump's shrimp, pace off 520 feet and find the marker commemorating home plate.

Austin, Minnesota, and opted instead to hit Dyersville, Iowa, where the field that was created for the 1989 film *Field of Dreams* can still be found. It is about 185 miles from Milwaukee, 210 from Chicago and 290 from Minneapolis.

The field exists on two abutting plots that are owned by two different families. Parking is free, fans are encouraged to bring their gloves and have a catch, and there are two small souvenir stands on site. In a typical summer, baseball pilgrims hailing from all fifty states and from several foreign countries stop by for a catch and to sit in the same bleachers where Ray and Annie sat.

The Ameskamp family owns the left and center-field portions of the diamond, while the infield and right-field portion of the diamond belonged to the Lansing family until October

---

Sports in the City

Midway Stadium, Home of the St. Paul Saints
1771 Energy Park Drive, St. Paul
www.saintsbaseball.com/home/
Across the Mississippi in St. Paul, Kevin wanted to see the birthplace of F. Scott Fitzgerald. Josh, meanwhile, wanted to visit Cretin-Derham Hall, where Joe Mauer played his high school ball, and Mauer Chevrolet in Inver Grove Heights, which is owned by Joe's brother Billy, who played minor league ball in the Twins system before an injury forced him to retire.

We compromised and set a course for one of the most successful minor league operations in the country. We visited Midway Stadium, home of the St. Paul Saints.

The American Association Saints have been filling 6,329-seat Midway Stadium since the early 1990s. The team is owned by Mike Veeck—the son of baseball promotions guru Bill Veeck—and comedian Bill Murray, who sometimes coaches third base. Management, players, and fans all embrace a "fun is good" motto. A pot-bellied pig waddles around the field delivering fresh balls to the home plate ump, fans get haircuts and massages while watching the game, and the Saints stage one goofy promotional night after another. In 2011, after the Metrodome roof collapsed during the previous football season, prompting the NFL's Vikings to move a home game to Detroit, the Saints staged "Deflation Night," during which a park full of fans sat on Whoopee Cushions. Another recent draw was "Life Before Toilet Paper Night," when the Saints paid tribute to the history of butt-cleansing toiletries while collecting rolls of TP at the gates for the benefit of a local food pantry. Our all-time favorite Saints theme night remains, however, Bud Selig "tie" night, which occurred shortly after the ill-fated 2002 game that ended in a deadlock. On that night, the Saints gave out neckties bearing Selig's face.

2011. The field and house appear exactly as they did in the film, except for the power lines that bisect the field, running from behind third base out through centerfield, which were apparently there all along but deleted from scenes by the technical whiz kids working the mixer board at Universal Studios.

Upon our visits to the field, Don Lansing, the elderly gentleman who lived in the farmhouse from his childhood until his senior years, was happy to recount for us his initial reaction on being approached by a Universal Studios executive proposing to turn under his soybean and tobacco plants, build a baseball field, and plant cornstalks across the "outfield" portion of Don's land. "You want to build a ball field here?" Don recalled asking incredulously. If that sounds like the response Ray Kinsella got from his friends and family members in the movie, you're right.

In any case, Don stopped asking questions when Universal cut him a check, and then he watched in amazement as his land was leveled, sod was laid, and light towers were erected, all in a span of a few days. After the movie was shot—including the dramatic final scene that included some 1,500 local residents and their cars making their way up Don's driveway—Don decided to maintain the field for local residents and visitors to use. Never did he imagine it would become a site of national tourist interest.

When we visited the Field of Dreams for a second time in 2011, the larger portion of the field was for sale. In fact, the whole 193-acre Lansing plot was, along with the farmhouse and several barns and garages. Later, in October of 2011, the Lansings found a buyer. The plot sold to Mike and Denise Stillman of Go the Distance Baseball LLC. Upon closing the multi-million-dollar real estate transaction, the Chicago-based couple announced their intention of turning the Field of Dreams into a massive youth baseball complex that should be completed by 2014.

HOUSTON ASTROS, MINUTE MAID PARK

HOUSTON, TEXAS
255 MILES TO ARLINGTON
750 MILES TO KANSAS CITY
800 MILES TO ATLANTA
870 MILES TO ST. LOUIS

Juice Box Baseball in Space City

When Houston unveiled baseball's first domed stadium in 1965, many billed the Astrodome the Eighth Wonder of the World. And when Minute Maid Park replaced the aging dome in 2000, many Houstonians dubbed the new retractable-roof facility the Ninth Wonder of the World. Certainly, that is overstating the significance of Minute Maid Park on the Major League Baseball landscape. Minute Maid was not the first ballpark to be built with a retractable roof, nor does it make use of technology that is noticeably superior to the retractable-lid parks in Phoenix, Milwaukee, and Seattle. Nonetheless, it is understandable that folks in the humidity capital of the world are proud of their downtown ballpark. While we could write something along the lines of "For a retractable-roof stadium it acquits itself rather nicely," we will go a step further and say, "Without qualification, Minute Maid is a gem."

Smaller than its retractable sister stadiums, Minute Maid provides a great environment for a game, whether the roof is closed or opened. Old-time brick arches rise up beyond the outfield fence, a massive window above left field allows an abundance of sunshine to soak the field as well as a glimpse of the stars at night, and quirky field dimensions keep outfielders and fans on their toes. Best still, the playing surface is natural grass. Even in the land where Astroturf was invented, it has been forsaken. Are you reading this Toronto?

It will come as no surprise to those who have visited a number of the current MLB parks that Minute Maid was designed by the architectural firm once known as HOK that has since changed its name to Populous. The park oozes retro charm. Concrete and steel are featured prominently in the interior and exterior design along with brick, brick and more brick—behind the plate and even on the upper levels' interior concourses where ordinarily mere concrete would appear. The facade is made of limestone, while the top two stories are nicely done in brick with arched windows. The facade juts out every one hundred feet or so with a building-type edifice, giving the ballpark more the look of an office building than a typical ballpark. The roof is a color significantly paler than traditional ballpark green, channeling a corroded copper look.

The main entrance—located at the corner of Texas Avenue and Crawford Street—is one of the most distinctive in all of baseball. This gateway to cooler air and good times to follow makes use of Houston's pre-existing Union Station, which the new structure was built around. The classy marble pillars and regal arches inside the main entrance were originally envisioned by Whitney Warren, the same architect who designed Grand Central Station in New York City. Built in

roof

Photo by Kevin O'Connell

1911, Union Station was once the hub of Houston's bustling railroad industry. Today, along with providing an entrance to the ballpark, it houses an Astros souvenir store, a café, and the Astros' executive offices.

Complementing the old-time motif anchored by Union Station is a tall tower that rises up from the ballpark's edifice. From atop this perch emanates the sound of chiming bells (not real bells, but a good-sounding imitation) playing "Take Me Out to the Ball Game," as if calling baseball worshippers to mass. Large windows beside the Union Station entrance to the ballpark furnish fans with a street-level peek at the sunken playing field inside. From inside the park, meanwhile, fans can look through the arches that rise behind the left-field seats and see clear through the station to the world outside the park. High above it all, for the viewing delight of those inside and outside the park, a replica nineteenth century locomotive chugs along an eight-hundred-foot track that traces the arches running from center field to left field. The train weighs more than fifty thousand pounds and comes complete with a linked coal-tender's car that is loaded with faux oranges that are in fact big enough to be pumpkins. While we usually don't go for such bells and whistles, we are happy to make an exception in this case seeing as the ballpark is built at and makes such classy use of an old train depot.

In another thoughtful nod to the local ethos, an oversized vintage gas pump resides on the left-field concourse, between two of the arches, perpetually updating the number of home runs the Astros have hit at Minute Maid since its opening. Oil is king in Texas and will remain so no matter how many windmills T. Boone Pickens manages to sell.

Kevin: Hey look, there's a Citgo sign high above left field too, just like at Fenway.

Josh: Um, the one at Fenway isn't mounted on a big retractable window.

Another neat feature at Minute Maid is its in-play embankment in center field, which recalls the similar outfield knolls that once appeared at Crosley Field in Cincinnati and Fenway Park in Boston just to name a couple. Houston's embankment, named Tal's Hill after longtime team president Tal Smith, rises at a twenty-degree angle, measures ninety feet at its widest point, and spans one hundred feet of outfield fence. You don't realize just how big it is when watching a game on TV. While we think this is an interesting and unique touch, we dread the day when a hard-charging visitor like Carlos

Gonzalez or Shane Victorino tears an ACL stumbling after a long fly ball, or worse, runs into the flagpole that is in-play atop the hill. We're thinking Tal's Hill wouldn't be very popular after that. And if an Astros player got hurt, Tal Smith might not be either. But maybe we're just worry-warts. The flagpole is some 436 feet away after all. And the hill rises gradually.

The roof, which is similar in its three-panel design to the one in Seattle, allows for the largest open area of any of the sliding-roof parks. It weighs eighteen million pounds and covers more than six acres. Unlike the umbrella in Seattle, however, the Minute Maid roof seals up airtight to keep the heat and humidity out and the air-conditioned air in. The aforementioned window in left—which is actually a fifty-thousand-square-foot sliding wall of glass—offers fans a view of downtown Houston when the roof is closed. When the roof is open, the window is retracted into the bowels of center field. This design element, combined with the ballpark's relatively cozy confines compared to the other roofed yards, makes Minute Maid a vast improvement over Chase Field and Miller Park, which also seal up airtight. While Safeco in Seattle may be larger than Minute Maid, it maintains an outside feel even when the roof is closed. And that's worth major points in our book.

Besides the roof and sliding glass door, the grass on the field is also especially designed to mitigate Houston's sweltering summer days. Known as Platinum TE Paspalum, the grass

interior

Photo by Kevin O'Connell

was developed to thrive near salt water and in high temps, making it a popular choice for golf courses overlooking the ocean waves. All of these weather-related modifications are necessities in Houston, where the average high temps remain above 90 degrees Fahrenheit throughout June, July, and August, before it cools all the way down to 88 in September. But to co-opt an old and annoying cliché, it's not the heat—it's the humidity. With summer dew points perpetually hovering in the "you'll sweat your butt off zone," Houston would be a sticky place to watch, much less play, outdoor baseball.

After several years of mounting dissatisfaction with the Astrodome on the part of fans, players, and Astros management, rumors began swirling in 1995 that the team was pondering a move to northern Virginia. Fearful of losing the home team, the City of Houston got to work exploring new ballpark possibilities, and in November 1996 voters approved a referendum to construct a new downtown ballpark. Financing was provided through a combined effort by the private and public sectors with a partnership of fourteen Houston-area businesses contributing $35 million in the form of an interest-free loan to the city. The entire project cost $250 million, comparatively little considering the price tags of the retractables in Seattle ($500 million), Phoenix ($350 million), and Miami ($515 million). We're not sure if the Astros cut corners, used non-union labor, or propped up their roof with discount steel from China. However they did it, we say, "Well done!" The savings are reflected in the ballpark's reasonable ticket prices. And if a few unattractive HVAC ducts—exposed on the ceiling of the first-level concourse—are the price to pay for cheap tickets, we say that's a trade we'll make any day, especially considering that those ducts are working hard to keep the joint cool.

Construction began on October 30, 1997, and was completed in time for Opening Day 2000. After a preseason tilt between the Astros and Yankees, the ballpark made its regular season debut before a full house on April 7, 2000, with the Phillies downing the home team 4-1.

In its first two years of existence the new ballpark sported three different names. It was originally called Enron Field, thanks to a thirty-year, $100 million naming-rights deal with Enron. But when the "Infamous E" filed for bankruptcy in 2002 amidst a swirl of scandal, the Astros did everything they could to disassociate themselves from the notorious energy company. The team paid $2.1 million to buy back rights to its own ballpark's name and temporarily renamed the park Astros Field. Just a few months later, the Astros announced a deal with local orange juice company Minute Maid, and renamed the yard Minute Maid Park.

In effect the Astros swapped one juice company on their marquee for another. And you probably thought only the players and balls were juiced back in the early 2000s! Kidding aside, Enron's collapse actually benefited the Astros. The new deal with Minute Maid was more lucrative, paying $170 million over twenty-eight years, or $6.07 million per season. Of course, these days a team's lucky if it can sign a fifth starter for $6 million a year, but hey, every little bit helps. The ballpark's unofficial nickname, "The Juice Box," is also kind of cool.

While the Astros and their fans are ecstatic to have a new ballpark to call their home, they are still proud of their former digs—and perhaps that is why the Astrodome still stands beside the Houston Texans' Reliant Stadium. At the time of this printing, there were three plans being considered for the venerable granddaddy of the domes. The first would demolish the dome and replace it with a public green space. The second would preserve its outer shell, while demolishing the stands and concourses to create an expansive ground-level capable of hosting conventions, weddings and other events. The third would make the changes described in option two, but rather than making the ground level into a function space would make it into a science and technology learning center, complete with a planetarium.

Kevin: Boy, I sure hope they don't rush into anything they'll later regret.

Josh: It's been sitting empty for more than a decade.

Kevin: That was a joke.

While allowing that its era passed it by, we should not forget the Astrodome and the defining moment its opening represented in the life of our National Game and in the life of American sport. While looking back on it we now see the dawning of a regrettable era of artificial playing fields and sterile, oversized facilities. But in its day the dome was a marvel, an example of a team reaching for the stars and forever upping the ante in the field of stadium architecture. The Astrodome originally symbolized American decadence. From the cushioned seats and comfortable air-conditioned environment, to the shoeshine stands behind home plate, to the ballpark lighting system that required more electricity than a city of nine thousand homes, the Astrodome represented American opulence. Elvis played the Astrodome. And the Rolling Stones. And Billy Graham led huge Bible-thumping crusades there. For a number of years, the Astrodome was the world's ultimate entertainment venue. It stood for something bigger than just Houston. It was a monument to American industrialism, workmanship, and vision. And most importantly to local ball fans, the Astrodome brought Major League hardball to Texas. When Houston was awarded an expansion team in 1960, the dome was already in the works. Had Houston not had specific plans for a weatherproof ballpark, it would have never been granted a franchise. The Colt .45s—as the Astros were originally called—joined the National League with the Mets in 1962. While the Mets would go on to capture a World Series title before the end of the decade, Houston continues to seek its first World Series championship. The Astros are currently the longest existent Major League team to have never won one. In fact, they'd never even appeared in the World Series until 2005 when they were swept by the White Sox.

Originally the big leaguers played outdoors in Houston. For three seasons, the Colt .45s hosted NL opponents in a thirty-two-thousand-seat temporary facility called Colt Stadium, which was dubbed "Mosquito Heaven" by locals. With its hummingbird sized mosquitoes and oppressive heat, the ballpark didn't draw well. The Houston expansion team averaged just 789,000 fans per season from 1962 to 1964 while the dome was being constructed.

Kevin: That old guy was kidding about the hummingbird sized mosquitos, right?

Josh: I don't know. I've heard the bass grow larger down here so it stands to reason the bugs would too. A smallmouth in Maine is lucky to reach four pounds whereas a largemouth in Mississippi or Texas can . . .

Kevin: The only time I want to hear you use the word "Bass" is if you're getting me a Black and Tan.

When the Harris County Domed Stadium was completed in 1964 and promptly renamed the Astrodome in recognition of Houston's contribution to the US space program, the team too was renamed. And fans started turning out to see the local nine. More than 2.15 million fans visited the Astrodome in its initial season. That seems impressive at first, but not when you consider that the dome seated 54,370, which means it was more than half empty each night as the Astros drew about 26,500 per game. As for Colt Stadium, it was disassembled in the early 1970s and shipped to Torreon, Mexico, for use in the Mexican League. Its old footprint is now buried beneath asphalt in the Astrodome parking lot.

Many have mistakenly called the Astrodome the first weatherproof American ballpark, which is not exactly correct. It was indeed the first dome, but the New York Cubans of the Negro National League played at a ballpark beneath the 59th Street Bridge in Queens during the 1930s. The field was entirely covered by the bridge.

Kevin: I bet the ushers didn't wear funky silver space suits like at the Astrodome either.

Josh: I'm thinking you're right.

Another thing many people may not remember is that initially the Astrodome had a real grass infield that featured special Bermuda grass engineered for indoor play. The grass field necessitated a see-through roof that allowed some sunlight to reach the field. When the glare from the sunroof gave infielders fits on pop-ups, the roof was painted white, and as a result the grass died. And the trademark plastic grass dubbed "Astroturf" was laid in 1966. At first, the team left the normal amount of dirt on the infield, but in 1970 the switch was made to virtually maintenance-free dirt sliding pits, a model that would become the norm at domed stadiums and multipurpose stadiums across the nation.

The Astrodome hosted its fair share of memorable moments—including several no-hitters, Willie Mays's five hundredth round-tripper, and Nolan Ryan's four thousandth strikeout. On April 15, 1968, the Astros beat the Mets in twenty-four innings at the Astrodome in the longest 1-0 game in history. Later that year the National League beat the American League 1-0 at the Astrodome in the first one-run All-Star Game. On May 4, 1969, the Astros turned seven double plays against the Giants on the slick turf to set a big league record. On September 25, 1986, Houston's Mike Scott clinched the AL West title at the Astrodome with a no-hitter against the Giants.

Josh: Talk about getting it done in style.

Kevin: That's as good as it gets.

Scott then shut out Dwight Gooden and the Mets 1-0 in the opening game of the National League Championship Series at the Astrodome, and pitched a complete game three-hitter in Game 4 at New York to even the Series at two games apiece. But Houston lost gut-wrenching twelve- and sixteen-inning affairs in Games 5 and 6, and Scott never got a chance to start a potential Game 7.

The Astrodome also had its share of wacky moments, like the time in 1965 when Mets announcer Lindsey Nelson broadcast a game from a gondola suspended from the apex of the dome; or the time in 1965 when the Mets accused the Astrodome groundskeepers of manipulating the air-conditioning to blow toward the outfield when the Astros were batting and then reversing the currents when the visitors were at the plate, thereby helping fly balls travel farther for the home team. In 1974, a fly ball by Philadelphia's Mike Schmidt struck a P.A. speaker in center field. The slugger was awarded only a single, even though the speaker was 330 feet from home plate and 117 feet above the field and the blast would have surely cleared the outfield fence. In 1976, a game was rained out, or "rained-in" as some said, when flooding in the streets prevented players and fans from reaching the dome.

By the 1990s just about everyone agreed that the Astrodome had outlived its day. Cavernous, dark, and sterile, it wasn't conducive to festive ballpark revelry. Though conceived with the future in mind, its time had passed. Minute Maid Park—a real jewel—arrived just in time to give Houston fans the breath of fresh air they craved and inject new energy into the Astros franchise. That was the plan. And it actually worked. Minute Maid arrived amidst the most successful run in franchise history. After reaching the post-season just three times in their first thirty-five years, the Astros qualified for October play six times in a nine-year run, spanning 1997 to 2005. They closed the Astrodome and opened Minute Maid right in the middle of this era of excellence and rode a wave of fan enthusiasm all the way to the 2005 World Series.

Trivia Timeout

Big Dipper: Which former Houston slugger was nicknamed "The Toy Cannon"?

Orion: Which player once dented the flagpole that stands in fair territory in centerfield with a long fly ball?

Milky Way: Which former Astro whose number is retired by the team later saw his son play for the 'Stros?

Look for the answers in the text.

After losing a heartbreaking seven-game National League Championship Series against the Cardinals in 2004, that 2005 team may not have been the best in team history but it was surely the most exciting. Despite winning just eighty-nine regular season games, the Astros claimed the NL Wild Card and made the most of the opportunity. In a short series, their top three starters could shine. Roy Oswalt, who went 20-12 with a 2.97 ERA, was joined by a pair of former Yankee stable-mates who had decided to return to their home state to pitch for the team they'd grown up loving. Andy Pettitte (17-9, 2.39) and Roger Clemens (13-8, 1.87) combined with Oswalt to give Houston as dominant a top three as any in the National League. But it was an unheralded hitter that used the postseason platform to author what would come to be the most memorable moment in Minute Maid Park's early history. Chris Burke connected for a walk-off homer in the bottom of the eighteenth inning of the Astros' first-round matchup against the Braves' Joey Devine to deliver a three-games-to-one series win. Because that game took an excruciating five hours and fifty minutes to play, making it the longest in post-season history, and

because it ended so dramatically, Burke's shot immediately became the stuff of legend. And it gave the Astros momentum heading into the NLCS where this time they beat the Cardinals in a six-game match. The Astros ran out of gas against the White Sox in the World Series, though. And so, a World Championship remains the only thing lacking on the resume of this half-century-old franchise that already boasts some great players, colorful moments, and two stadiums both deemed revolutionary in their day.

Getting a Choice Seat

A small ballpark by today's standards, Minute Maid contains plenty of excellent seats. Most of the field-level sections provide solid views of the action. The upper-level seats are also decent since the deck only extends back seventeen rows and doesn't extend all the way across the outfield. As for pricing, the box seats around the infield seem underpriced compared to similar seats at other MLB parks. We should mention that there is a sun-effect here. If you are visiting for a late-afternoon game on a Saturday or even for a night-game during the summer and the sun is shining, a seat on the first base side of the park—whether along the first-base line or even out in the right-field home run seats—you had better keep your sunglasses handy. Otherwise you'll spend the first couple innings squinting. The setting sun shines through the massive panels in left field, soaking a large swath of outfield, infield and stands. You think you have it tough? Because the full stadium is not open, only the portion exposed by the window, there are some pretty severe shadows on the field too—around home plate and deep in the outfield—and the contrast makes it difficult for batters to pick up the ball.

The First Level
DUGOUT BOXES (SECTIONS 112–126)
The architects were no doubt going for an old-time feel when they designed Minute Maid's lower bowl. The seats begin low to the field and close to fair territory, and extend back in rows that rise at a very low pitch. The stadium-seating effect is minimal, putting Row 2 only about six inches higher than Row 1 and so on. This won't be an issue for tall guys like Kevin, but fans under six feet, like Josh, will find themselves having to sit on the edge of their seats all game long to see over the head of the person directly in front of them. Keep in mind that the seats extend back thirty-nine rows on the first level. And seats are the same price in Row 1 as Row 39, so don't take it for granted that a Field Box seat is going to be

right on the field. And if you sit in Rows 34–39 you won't be able to see the full flight of fly balls because of the overhang of the Club deck and the HVAC pipes.

One flaw in the ballpark's design is that fans seated directly behind home plate on the first level can't see the entirety of fair territory. From the dugout seats, the left-field corner is partially blocked due to the Field Boxes, which jut out midway down the left-field line—reminiscent of the left-field stands at Fenway Park in Boston. The left-field grandstand at Minute Maid rises much higher than the grandstand in right field as it straddles the foul line. Thus the left-field corner is only fully visible from Sections 122 to 134 on the right-field side of the diamond, but by then the view of the right-field corner has begun to wane. We do applaud the Astros for adding three-foot-high screens instead of a solid wall to separate the seats from the field of play, but we still think it best to shoot for seats on the first-base side, rather than third, considering that fans seated in right field also enjoy a view of the setting sun and then later of the stars through the window above left field. Just be sure to bring those sunglasses!

FIELD BOXES (SECTIONS 105–11, 127–134)

These begin just past the first- and third-base bags and extend out to the foul poles. The sections nearest the infield provide good views, while the ones out near the poles are rather fowl. As with the Dugout Seats, try for tickets in Row 33 or lower to minimize the effects of the overhanging Club deck. We especially recommend Sections 127 to 129 on the first-base side. Sections 110 and 111 on the third-base side are also good. Be sure to avoid Section 108, which is tucked behind Sections 107 and 109 and doesn't contain any seats close to the field. Before buying tickets in Section 134 deep in the right-field corner, consider that a seat in Section 152 of the Bullpen Boxes is 33 percent cheaper while providing a superior view of the field. A fairly significant obstruction affects Section 105 in left field, where you'll want to stay in Row 28 or lower to avoid losing much of center field from view because of the Crawford Boxes that jut out in home run territory.

CRAWFORD BOXES (SECTIONS 100–124)

Named after Crawford Street, which runs along the ballpark's left-field perimeter, these home run territory seats are close to the action to begin with, because the left-field foul pole is just 315 feet from the plate. The twenty-five hundred seats in this price range are elevated. And they project right out into left field. The view of deep center isn't very good because fans have to look over their left shoulders to see plays there. And fans can't see plays up against the left-field

Seating Capacity: 40,950
Ticket Office: http://houston.astros.mlb.com/ticketing/singlegame.jsp?c_id=hou
Seating Chart: http://houston.astros.mlb.com/hou/ticketing/seating_pricing.jsp

wall or the left-field scoreboard. They're good seats for home run territory—don't get us wrong—but they may be a bit over-hyped. The worst of the lot is Section 104 where the foul pole blocks much of the view.

BULLPEN BOXES (SECTIONS 150–156)

The bad news is that the so-called boxes in right field are no better than the "boxes" in left. In fact, they're not as good. These seats are very far from the plate and they're lower to the field, which makes it more difficult to see balls on the infield. Making matters worse, the Mezzanine deck casts a significant overhang above a large portion of these sections. Unless your seat is in Row 10 or lower don't plan on seeing the tops of any fly balls. So take your pick, would you rather contend with the overhang that afflicts these first-level right-field seats, or the underhang that hampers the left-field Crawford Boxes? We prefer sitting in the Crawford Boxes.

Sections 150 and 151 are tucked way behind the foul pole and are the worst in this price range. Sections 155 and 156 provide a nice look into the Astros bullpen. But for the most part, we take a pass on these seats that angle fans more toward the left-field line rather than toward home plate. One other thing to keep in mind: because of the space the home bullpen takes up, the first row of Section 155 is numbered Row 8. Yet the first row of Section 156—parallel to Section 155's Row 8—is numbered Row 1. Go figure. In any case, it's better to sit in Rows 1–8 of Sections 153 or 154 where Row 1 really is the first row and Row 8 really is the eighth row. At least then you'll be able to find your seat if you misplace your ticket stub.

The Second Level

CLUB (SECTIONS 205–236)

These second-level seats provide a clear view of the action, with the only significant obstruction being the protrusion of the Field Boxes in left that cost fans in Sections 205–209 a sizable chunk of the left-field corner. The food up here may be a cut above the concession offerings in the rest of the park, and the ushers may call you "sir," but ask yourself: Is it ever worth sitting in the second level when first-level seats are available for less money?

SEATING TIP

Free Upgrades—For Those Who Don't Mind Standing

If you don't like the view from your upper-level seats, head on down to the home run porch located to the right of the Crawford Boxes in center field. The porch furnishes standing space beneath the brick arches that support the train tracks above. The view is actually better from this center-field location—where more of the field is visible—than in the Crawford Boxes in left. If it feels like you're hanging out over the field while standing on the porch—it's because you are. Enjoy this unique location to watch a game.

MEZZANINE (SECTIONS 250–258)

The Mezzanine seats in right-field home run territory are located on the same second deck that houses the Club seats. Extending from the right-field foul pole to deep right-center, not only are these cheaper than the Bullpen Boxes below, but they provide a clearer view of the action. The Mezzanine's slight underhang effect is far preferable to the overhang that obstructs views from many of the seats below. We recommend Sections 252 or 253 in straightaway right, which are much closer to the plate than the seats farther out in Sections 257 and 258.

The Third Level

TERRACE DECK (SECTIONS 305–338)

Both the 300 Level Terrace Deck seats and 400 Level View Deck seats are on the upper deck. The difference between them is that the Terrace Deck seats hang down below the concourse, like the seats called "upper boxes" in some stadiums, while the View Deck seats are above the concourse. Here it's definitely worth spending a few extra bucks to sit closer to the field in the Terrace Deck.

The Terrace Deck seats are all the same price, whether they're located in the outfield or behind the plate, so be smart and shoot for Sections 311–329 for the best view. Avoid Sections 305 to 307 in left field where the underhang blocks a good portion of left field from view.

View Deck (Sections 409–431)

Beginning about fifteen feet higher than the Terrace Level, the View Deck in Houston still isn't all that bad. Encompassing only seventeen rows, it is half as expansive and towering as some upper decks in the bigs. Unlike the ungodly heavens in Toronto and Arizona, which seem to keep going and going, Houston's upper reaches top out at just the right spot.

Sections 413–425 behind the plate are best, while the quality quickly diminishes in the sections leading to the Outfield View Deck sections. The underhang isn't much of a factor in any of these infield sections. We recommend Rows 3–8, which are high enough to allow a view unobstructed by the grate that runs along the first row over the concourse, and low enough to keep fans in the flow of the game.

In some of the level's upper reaches a number of seats are situated behind the lighting banks. Thus, it can get rather dark in these back rows. And it can get loud too, as P.A. speakers hover above many of the back rows.

Kevin: Hmm. Sounds like a great place to see a show.

Josh: Taylor Swift will be here in November if you're interested.

Kevin: Not exactly what I had in mind.

Outfield View Deck (Sections 405–408, 432–438)

Located in the outfield before the foul poles, these upper-level seats are to be avoided, unless you're just trying to get into the park for less than ten bucks a ticket so you can move down to one of the standing areas. The underhang obstructs the view from all of these sections to varying degrees. Here again, the jutting out of the first level's grandstand in left blocks the view of the left-field corner for those sitting on the third-base side of the Outfield View Deck. This effect is most noticeable in Sections 405–408, which house the worst seats in the ballpark. In right field, Sections 432–438 contend with a less dramatic obstruction of the right-field corner. We do applaud the Astros for charging just $1.00 for these seats for children 14 and under.

Standing Room

The Astros put a limited number of standing-room tickets on sale if all of the seats are sold. In a pinch, these are worth the expense as there is ample standing room on the Home Run Porch that serves as the left-field concourse. During the Astros' playoff runs, they typically put three thousand standing passes on sale, bringing the park's total capacity to about 43,800.

The Black Market

Scalping is illegal in Houston but we observed a fellow waving people into one of the parking lots near the ballpark while holding a sign that read, "I have tickets."

Before/After the Game

Despite the half-dozen bail-bond businesses within a few blocks of the ballpark—owing to the nearby courthouse—the neighborhood around Minute Maid feels both safe and festive on game days. By constructing Minute Maid in a once-forgotten corner of Houston, doubtless the city was hoping to use the ballpark as an impetus for the revitalization of the area. And by all accounts, the plan has worked.

Getting to Minute Maid Park

From the north, take Interstate 45 south to the Scott Street exit, then take either Pease Street or St. Joseph's Parkway and follow the signs to the ballpark. From the east or west take Interstate 10 to the US Route 59 South exit, then take the Hamilton Street exit to downtown.

Private parking lots near Minute Maid charge in the $10 range. We saw a lot on the corner of Crawford and Congress Streets charging a bit less, so be sure to shop around. Or better yet, find a spot on the street. Almost all of the streets near the ballpark offer two-hour meters that can be plugged until 6:00 p.m. and then become free for the night. Congress, Fannin, and Carolina Streets are all worth a look. We should mention that we saw two tow trucks patrolling the perimeter of the ballpark, tire-booting cars in front of expired meters. So be smart.

The local Metro Bus is another option for those staying in town. It stops at the ballpark's main ticket window on Texas Avenue.

Outside Attractions

THE PLAZA

A brick courtyard outside the Crawford Street entrance flies pennants to remember Astros teams that were National League Central and previously National League West division winners. And, of course, a pennant flies for the 2005 National League Champion squad. Rest assured, Astros rooters, there is plenty of room too for additional pennants.

Plaques, meanwhile, honor memorable Houston players like Jose Cruz, Mike Scott, Doug Jones, Don Wilson, Jim Umbricht, Nolan Ryan, and Larry Dierker, and pitcher Darryl Kile, who died during the 2002 season of congenital heart failure at age thirty-three. Additionally, plaques acknowledge a team MVP for each of Houston's seasons. The Colt .45's logo—a pistol with the word "Colt" written parallel to its shaft—appears on a number of the team's early plaques. If the NBA had to rename the Washington Bullets to satisfy the new rules of political correctness, we're guessing the Colt .45's wouldn't have lasted for the long term either. Then again, they played deep in the heart of Texas, so maybe the Colt .45's would have held onto their guns a little longer than the hoopsters did.

The plaza also showcases two slightly larger-than-life-sized statues of former Astros Jeff Bagwell and Craig Biggio. Customarily, players aren't so honored outside ballparks until after their playing days have ended, but these two bronzes were erected while both players were still active. Stretching off first base, the Bagwell reaches to take a throw from the Biggio, which steps across second base as if turning a double play. These are well done. Biggio, a member of baseball's exclusive three-thousand-hit club, went into the record books as the first Astros player to record a hit at Minute Maid Park, in 2000, and a year later Bagwell, who smacked 449 lifetime homers, became the first Astros player to hit for the cycle at Minute Maid.

CLOCK TOWER

Reminiscent of Ebbets Field, a tall clock tower is built into the ballpark facade on the right side of the home plate gate. Unlike the tower in Brooklyn, however, the face of this clock is designed to resemble an orange-colored baseball and comes complete with a green stem at its top. This orange-work turns what could be a classy element of the ballpark's design into a cheesy marketing device for Minute Maid. We still kind of liked it, though.

MAN OF STEEL

As a tribute to the Houston blacksmith shop that was founded on the ballpark site in 1902 and grew into a global corporation known as Stewart and Stevenson, a statue of a steelworker forging a horseshoe resides on the sidewalk not far from the plaza. Dedicated in 2002 on the hundredth anniversary of the company's founding, the statue is called "Forging the Future."

BALLS OF CONCRETE

On the sidewalks surrounding the park appear large baseball designs done in brick, with each red brick serving as a stitch in the lacing of the ball. There is also faux baseball stitching stamped into concrete to break up the brickwork every ten feet or so. This subtle touch makes the sidewalks around the ballpark unique.

Watering Holes and Outside Eats

Contributing to the festive ballpark neighborhood is a row of bars located across the street from the main ticket window on Texas Avenue. It ain't Wrigleyville, but it gets the job done. And for those wanting to score some higher quality eats, we found a few gems not far from the ballpark.

IRMA'S SOUTHWEST GRILL
22 North Chenevert St.

If you're looking for an authentic Mexican meal served with a side of atmosphere, we highly recommend Irma's. This

Houston institution is famous for attracting visitors from around the world. You may recognize owner Monica Galvan from her appearances on the Food Network, and from her appearances on many other cooking shows. While she is a familiar face nationally, in these parts she is more than that—she is also a respected voice in the community. When the Astros were lobbying to build the new downtown ballpark, Galvan flew to Austin on one of Enron's private jets to testify before the state legislature on how she believed the project would benefit the local community. Despite Enron's collapse, Irma's continues to be a popular hangout among city and state politicians.

Nestled among some old warehouses, the New Orleans–style building offers a porch and outdoor patio overflowing with lush green plants. Inside, Irma's is no less quirky—a collage of collectibles adorn the walls, and the men's room urinals brim with crushed ice and fresh-smelling lemon peels. Chances are Irma's john will be nicer than the hotel room you stay at while in Houston. But the best part of all is the menu, which offers a full range of homemade Mexican entrées, including an award winning enchilada and amazing lemonade.

IRMA'S SOUTHWEST GRILL
1314 Texas Ave.
www.irmassouthwest.com/ho.htm

Closer to the ballpark we found another Irma's—this one owned by Monica Galvan's son, Louis. We really can't say enough in the way of praise for Irma's Southwest Grill. When we reached Houston on our first road trip, it was the seventh city we'd visited in ten days and we were tired. Believe it or not, we were both getting sick of eating hot dogs and bratwurst at the ballparks and fast food along the road. Like finding an oasis in a hot desert, we stumbled into Irma's.

Everything we tasted was superb, from the homemade fresh fruit lemonade (Kevin had five glasses) that came complete with floating strawberries, grapes, and melon, to the chile con queso and chips and two homemade salsas we tried, to Josh's beef enchiladas and Kevin's Chilean sea bass and shrimp.

THE B.U.S.
1800 Texas Ave.

With a wide-open window front on nice days, the B.U.S. is a good spot to grab a quick one before heading into the game. The music is loud, seating is limited, and the crowd is on the younger side.

HOME PLATE BAR AND GRILL
1800 Texas Ave.
http://homeplatehouston.com/

Home Plate is a convenient place to have a quick burger, hot dog, or chicken sandwich before the game. The appetizer menu is anchored by wings, pretzels, chili, and jalapeño peppers. The upstairs patio, called The Drink, is a nice place to catch a breeze on a warm day. Mind you, it may be a humid breeze that blows through these streets.

TEXAS BAR-B-QUE HOUSE
2401 Texas Ave.

Though a bit farther away from the park than the other Texas Avenue watering holes, this is a solid choice for those craving saucy meat and fixings before the game. Josh recommends the chopped barbecued beef. Normally they're more of a lunch spot, but they stay open until 8:00 p.m. on game days.

JAMES' CONEY ISLAND HOT DOGS
Sixteen Houston Locations
www.jamesconeyisland.com/

A Houston institution since 1923, James' Coney Island has expanded to the point where its wiener shops are a ubiquitous part of the Houston landscape. From the ballpark, head north on Interstate 45 and within a mile you'll see a large neon sign for one of James' locations on the left. We thought the Vienna franks were of excellent quality but the chili was a bit watery. And of all the places in the world where we might have expected to find watery chili, Houston wasn't one of them.

Inside the Ballpark

The playing field at Minute Maid is top-notch. We like its quirky angles and dimensions. Tal's Hill in center field—a knoll of grass, appearing on the "other side" of the dirt warning track—gives the field a batter's eye that is entirely unique in the modern game. The left-field home run porch is shallow, while the center-field fence resides a distant 436 feet from the plate at its deepest point. The American flag in center-field flies on a pole that rises up from the field of play, while the Texas state flag and Houston flag fly atop masts that rise from just behind the outfield fence. The home bullpen in right field is well done, featuring real grass and an old-style wooden bench for the pitchers to sit on while they watch the game through a chain-link portion of the outfield fence that creates something of a fishbowl effect for fans looking to see who's warming up. The visitors' pen is another story. It exists tucked halfway underneath the left-field stands, partially illuminated by fluorescent lights and sporting artificial turf. It seems like the ballpark designers could have done a better job with this. On the plus side, the warning track is real dirt, not rubber as we've observed at some of the other semi-domes. And the longer than usual dugouts are classily done with their Astros auburn tops.

The Union Station arches that extend from center field to left, above the playing field, are a classy touch that looks great on TV, but we were slightly disturbed by the asymmetry created by the one double-sized arch in left field. This especially offended Kevin's sense of aesthetics.

Some parts of the interior—mostly those hidden from the TV cameras' lenses—could be made more attractive, such as the overhead wires, tubing, and HVAC, but for the most part the ballpark is a clean and comfortable place to watch a game.

Ballpark Features

TAL'S HILL AND FLAGPOLE

Amazingly, the flagpole that stands on Tal's Hill is in the field of play and balls that strike it aren't ground-rule doubles. They're live balls. In 2003, the Brewers' Richie Sexson hit a long fly ball that would have been a sure home run if the pole hadn't gotten in the way. After denting the pole, three quarters of the way up, the ball zipped past center fielder Craig Biggio and wound up going as one of the seventeen triples Sexson would hit in his 1,367-game career. Nonetheless, Sexson was disappointed that a ball he'd hit 430 feet hadn't left the yard for a home run. And he said so after the game. But that wasn't the only day the unusual center-field landscaping drew criticism from players. Longtime Astros star Lance Berkman also once spoke out in disapproval of the field feature, saying it was a hazard to outfielders.

JUST PLAIN LOCO

To say the Minute Maid locomotive "runs" along its track—from center field to left field—may be overstating things a bit. The train crawls along like the Little Train That Could—but just barely—then stops, and drives in reverse back to its normal resting point in center. It travels about 800 feet to complete its sojourn. An actual conductor drives the train, which chugs along as the final notes of the National Anthem fade into the night.

When the roof closes and the left-field window slides into place, the support beams for the window actually slide past the train on either side of the track, briefly encasing it,

before reaching their destination in left field. The conductor, for his part, sits in the train looking slightly uncomfortable while all of this is going on around him.

About ten or twelve home run balls per season wind up on the track, some four hundred feet above the field. We considered ourselves among a lucky few (thousand) therefore when Boston's Darnell McDonald put one on the tracks when we attended an interleague game at Minute Maid in 2011.

EL GRANDE

High above center field resides the second largest HD video screen in baseball. Installed in 2011, it measures 54-by-124 feet and is surpassed only by the extra jumbo JumboTron in Kansas City. Take that, you moneybags in New York!

BAD CHICKEN

We consider it a foul that the Astros have sold the naming rights to their foul poles to a chicken restaurant and rebranded them "Fowl Poles" complete with a corporate logo down the bottom of each one. This got us wondering how many other parts of the field might be conducive to double-entendre ads.

Josh: I'm gonna visit the left-field fence after the game.
Kevin: You mean the scoreboard on the left-field wall?
Josh: No, the guy selling hot watches in left field.
Kevin: Ha, ha. Okay, no more of those.
Josh: But I want to visit the press box too.
Kevin: Fine, last one. Why?
Josh: My pants are a little wrinkled.

HOME RUN ALLEY

The first-level concourse behind the seats in center—called Home Run Alley—offers a couple of interesting displays. One exhibit holds bolted-down baseball bats that belonged to former and present Astros players. The thickest handle of all was on a bat that had belonged to Cesar Cedeno, while the thinnest was on the stick swung by Jose Cruz. The other exhibit we especially liked consisted of bronze casts of the gloves worn by former and current Astros players.

HOME RUN PUMP

A replica of an old-fashioned gas pump sits on the Home Run Porch in center, keeping track of the homers the Astros have hit at Minute Maid since the park's opening in 2000. Hey, this is the oil capital of the country, what did you expect? While fans can see the pump from anywhere in the ballpark, it's impossible to read the very small numbers that reflect the current homer tally from anywhere but right beside the pump.

Kevin: The numbers should be big and bold for all to see.

Josh: It's a gas pump, not a billboard.

Kevin: Actually, if you want to get technical, it's got a corporate logo on it.

Josh: Point taken.

PAINTED PENNANTS

Above the Crawford Boxes in left field appear the outlines of pennants painted on the masonry, commemorating years in which the Astros have made the playoffs. Why painted pennants and not real flags? Well, there isn't much of a breeze inside Minute Maid, especially when the roof is closed. A painted white baseball appears inscribed with the initials DK in memory of Darryl Kile. It seems odd to us that Kile is remembered this way, while the premature deaths of two other Astros hurlers resulted in their numbers being retired by the team.

RETIRED NUMBERS

Mounted just below the roof in right field are the franchise's retired numbers: No. 5 for Jeff Bagwell, 7 for Craig Biggio, 24 for Jimmy Wynn, 25 for Jose Cruz, 32 for Jim Umbricht, 33 for Mike Scott, 34 for Nolan Ryan, 40 for Don Wilson, 49 for Larry Dierker, and 42 for Jackie Robinson. Statistically, this is not a remarkable group of Colts and Astros once you get past Bagwell and Biggio, who played during the inflated days of the Steroid Era. We should mention that neither of those guys was ever implicated in the PED scandal, but nonetheless Bagwell received just 41.7 percent of the writers' vote when he became eligible for induction into the National Baseball Hall of Fame in 2011. It will be interesting to see how history judges statistically impressive players like these two who may well wind up having their reputations tarnished by the era in which they played.

Nicknamed "The Toy Cannon," the five-foot ten-inch Wynn surpassed twenty homers for the Astros eight times between 1965 and 1973 on his way to hitting 291 home runs in a fifteen-year career. As for Cruz, he played thirteen seasons in Houston on the way to finishing with 2,251 hits and a .284 batting average in nineteen total seasons. His son Jose Cruz would later play briefly with the Astros in 2008 at the end of his own twelve-year career. Umbricht's number was retired posthumously after he died of cancer in 1964. The right-hander won eight games for the Colts in two seasons. Scott registered 110 of his 124 career wins in nine seasons with the 'Stros.

Ryan won 106 games (of his 324 total) in nine seasons with Houston. Wilson won 104 games for Houston before dying in 1975 at age twenty-nine of carbon monoxide poisoning. Dierker earned all but two of his 139 career wins with Houston before going on to manage the team in the 1990s.

SCORES, HOWEVER FLEETING

Below the Crawford Boxes on the left-field wall, a hand-operated scoreboard provides the full line score of every Major League game in progress. But for some reason, once a game ends, they take down the inning-by-inning numbers, leaving up only the final score. This is no good if you're a fantasy baseball owner wondering how one of your pitchers did in a game that started earlier in the day. Sometimes knowing that a team won 6-5 is not enough. You want to know if the victor scored five runs in the bottom of the ninth to steal a win for one of its relievers, or if the team staked its starter to an early lead that he carried all game long.

Kevin: Maybe they need the zeroes to use elsewhere on the board?

Josh: Maybe they need to invest in some more zeros then.

Slinging Heat

While Ryan may hold the MLB record for career strikeouts, the most he ever notched in his seasons with the Astros came in 1987 when he led the NL with 270 Ks to go with a circuit-best 2.76 ERA and a hard luck 8–16 record.

J. R. Richard actually holds the team record for most whiffs in a season with the 313 he recorded in 1979. Scott also registered more punchouts than Ryan ever did with Houston when he fanned 306 in 1986.

THE THIN YELLOW LINE

You know the outfield fence is an irregular one when the home team has to install a bright yellow line across the entire expanse of the outfield to demark its top from home run territory. We were amazed by the different heights and angles this line follows, especially by its presence on the slanted railing that faces the infield as it runs along the edge of the Crawford Boxes in straight-away left to determine whether a deep fly will be a long ball or merely a long double.

Stadium Eats

We were pleasantly surprised to find the Minute Maid concession offerings vastly improved upon our return visit to the park. There were many more freshly made offerings than when we had visited in 2003 and it seemed as though the Astros had really made an effort to improve the quality of the regional specialties—i.e., the Mexican fare and Texas barbecue—at the park.

BARBECUE STUFFED POTATO (TRADEMARK FOOD)

Available at the Spuds Crossing stand behind Section 106, this Texas-sized potato is a meal unto itself. It comes loaded with shredded cheddar, pulled pork, barbecue sauce, sautéed onions and jalapenos. Yes, believe it or not there's a jumbo potato underneath all that mess. And it's nice and creamy just the way it should be.

ASTROS DOG (DOG REVIEW)

The saving grace of the dogs at Minute Maid lies in the number of different toppings available. The trademark Texas Dog comes loaded with chili, grated cheddar, and jalapeños. For a few bucks more, the Super Dog is easily twice the size of a regular dog and comes similarly loaded with toppings. The New York dog, Diablo dog, Chicago dog, and Cincinnati Cheese Coney are also popular sellers. Or you can create a dog of your own design.

BEST OF THE REST

Little Bigs concession stand behind Section 111 serves the same burgers and pork sliders that Houstonians enjoy at the city's Little Bigs restaurant owned by Astros head chef Bryan Caswell. These tasty sandwiches come served with chips.

The jalapeño sausage ranks as one of the spiciest in the big leagues. **The Big League Macaroni Company** behind Section 106 serves four types of Mac and Cheese: Taco Mac, Chili Mac, Rustic Mac, and Enchilada Mac.

Kevin: What says baseball better than Mac and Cheese?

Josh: I don't know. Beer and peanuts?

For Mexican, **El Real** behind Section 132 serves fresh beef and chicken fajitas that are made to order. For Texas BBQ, **Mavericks Smokehouse** has stands behind Sections 125 and 409. The chopped BBQ beef sandwich we shared was good but the all-beef sausage was even better. The best spot to head with the kids is the **Minute Maid Juice Stand** behind Section 133 which has junior sized/priced options. For healthier eaters, Sam's Bistro behind Section 224 and the Signature Carvery behind Section 156 are the best bet. The Carver's **Texas Tom Turkey Sandwich** was a popular seller when we visited. For dessert, the **Grand Slam Sundae** at the Dreyer's stand behind home plate is served in a bigger-than-usual plastic replica helmet. With four scoops of cream, chocolate sauce, or hot caramel, this is a good value.

There are two restaurants worth checking out at Minute Maid. One is **Larry's Big Bamboo,** located behind home plate on the first level, and named after former Astros manager Larry Dierker who used to frequent a spring training watering hole in Kissimmee, Florida, named "The Big Bamboo." Like the original, Larry's BB resembles a Florida beach hut, complete with surfboards adorning the walls. There are also TVs above the bar. The fish tacos and hot wings are the house specials. **The FiveSeven Grille,** in centerfield, meanwhile is named after Bagwell and Biggio, who wore numbers 5 and 7, respectively, while playing their entire careers in Houston. Here, fans find some of the better desserts and salads at Minute Maid as well as TVs showing games from around the league.

Kevin: When did it become hip to smash together two words like FiveSeven?

Josh: Probably around the time folks stopped using the word "hip."

STADIUM SUDS (AND SPIRITS)

Glasses of wine are available at a stand on the level left-field concourse. Daiquiris, frozen and fruity, are also available throughout the park. As for beer, twenty-four-ounce bottles of Corona and Dos Equis are unique to Houston. On tap, Shiner Bock and Shiner Blonde are the local choices. Kevin tried the Bock and called it "microbrew for beginners."

The Minute Maid Experience

Like the food at Minute Maid, we found the Astros fans we encountered had vastly upped their game upon our return. A higher percentage of fans wore the team colors than when we previously visited—Kevin speculated that they stocked up during the 2005 World Series run—and they made a lot more noise. We couldn't help but feel that the city, which has been in the bigs for a long time now, had finally come into its own.

STRETCH TIME

After singing "Take Me Out to the Ball Game," the Astros play "Deep in the Heart of Texas" over the P.A. system and a handful of fans join in. So be prepared to carry your section.

It starts like this:

The stars at night—are big and bright
Deep in the heart of Texas.

The prairie sky—is wide and high
Deep in the heart of Texas.

The Sage in bloom—is like perfume
Deep in the heart of Texas.

BOOM GOES THE DYNAMITE

Don't sketch out when the person performing the National Anthem gets to "the rockets' red glare," and fireworks come shooting out of left field—even when the roof is closed. Indoor fireworks are legal in Texas.

BIRDS OF A FEATHER

Bring your binoculars if you fancy yourself a bird-watcher because we observed plenty of feathered friends flying inside Minute Maid, even though the roof was closed.

Kevin: Hey, birds are better than flying bats, right?

Josh: The folks in Port St. Lucie, Florida might not agree.

Kevin: Say what?

Josh: The Mets' spring training park there has a bat house on site. And the little critters help maintain the mosquito population.

Kevin: Oh. I thought we were talking about baseball bats.

> ### Cyber Super-Fans
>
> We recommend these excellent Astros fan sites, which are both as cleverly named as they are informative.
>
> - **Crawfish Boxes**
>   *www.crawfishboxes.com/*
> - **Climbing Tal's Hill**
>   *http://climbingtalshill.com/*

SPORTS CLIPS

If you find yourself getting a little shaggy after so many weeks on the road, you can get a haircut while watching the game courtesy of Sport Clips, which operates several chairs overlooking the field on the left-field concourse. These seats reminded us of Midway Stadium in St. Paul, Minnesota, where fans of the American Association Saints were treated for years to haircuts courtesy of an aged nun. Fear not: In Houston, perky young stylists more along the lines of the ones you'd find at Super Cuts do the shearing while you don't miss a single pitch.

CLOSED CAPTIONS

A board in right field displays the text of everything the stadium P.A. announcer says.

WI-FI

Available for free throughout the ballpark, Wi-Fi enables fans to search the web while (sort of) watching the game.

> ### Sports in the City
>
> #### The Houston Astrodome
>
> We took a drive to check out the Eighth Wonder of the World, which stands across the street from a Six Flags Over Texas amusement park, southwest of the Interstate 610 loop that circles Houston.
>
> Expecting to be blown away by the size of the legendary dome, we were disappointed to find it currently dwarfed by Reliant Stadium, which is right beside it. Reliant, home of the NFL Texans, sits in a larger footprint than the dome and rises quite a bit higher. The football field, which opened in 2002, was the NFL's first retractable-roof gridiron.

Josh: Hey, why not buy the Kindle version of our book while you're trying to decide what to order for ballpark food?

Kevin: That's some shameless self-promotion right there.

Josh: When did I ever admit to having an ounce of shame?

While We Were in Houston
We Witnessed the Birth of the Third Inning Stretch

Unbeknownst to us, when we plopped down in Row 25 of the Dugout Seats, we were just 24 rows behind former President George H.W. Bush and his lovely mother, um, we mean wife, Barbara, as well as aviation legend Chuck Yeager, and a whole gaggle of Secret Service agents.

Once the game began, Kevin headed upstairs to snap some pictures from the upper deck. He hadn't been in Section 419 for two minutes when a ballpark security guard approached and began brusquely interrogating him.

"Excuse me, sir," the uniformed officer said from the concourse below. "I need you to come down here so I can have a word with you."

Kevin, a wannabe hippie at heart, is not always the most eager person in the world to readily comply with law enforcement, but went along. When he reached the lower level, the eager young officer looked him over from behind mirrored sunglasses as he worked a toothpick back and forth from one side of his mouth to the other.

"How do you feel about our former president?" the man finally asked.

"Excuse me?" Kevin replied.

"Oh, you heard me," the man snapped. Now, Kevin had heard the man just fine. It's just that he didn't think the officer would very much enjoy hearing the truth about his feelings about the former president, and he feared how the officer might react to such feelings.

He then looked Kevin over again, as the toothpick ping-ponged from side to side. He asked Kevin why he was taking pictures and was occasionally speaking into a micro-cassette recorder.

Kevin explained that the pictures were for a wonderful new ballpark book he and his friend Josh were writing and that he often used a microcassette recorder to take notes for his photo-log because it was so much easier than writing things down.

"I see," the officer kept saying. "I see." Then he said, "How about you let me hear some of these notes?" When the man said "notes," he raised his hands and encompassed the imaginary words with quotation marks made of flesh and bone. All of this was greatly disturbing to Kevin, who observed to his left and right men and women clad in cowboy boots and dirty jeans, talking into cell phones as they slowly converged on him. But he played along and let the man have a listen. "Shot one—exterior façade on Texas Avenue . . . Shot two—exterior roof . . . Shot three—exterior train . . . Shot four—Irma's Southwest Grill . . . Shot five—Biggio statue in Plaza."

Apparently convinced that Kevin was no assassin, the guard looked him up and down one last time, then handed back the recorder. "Stay out of trouble," he said, then walked away.

Baffled, Kevin resumed taking pictures. Then in the middle of the third inning, suddenly everything made sense when the ballpark announcer said, "Ladies and Gentlemen, we have two special guests in attendance tonight. Seated behind home plate are Chuck Yeager and former President George Bush." Yeager and Bush stood, as did a reluctant Barbara who looked a bit miffed that her presence hadn't been deemed worthy of acknowledgment over the P.A.

The many cowboy-hat-wearing Republicans in the crowd stood up and cheered, while the Democrats politely clapped. George and Chuck waved, and Barbara smiled. Soon everyone was standing regardless of party preference.

"And so, a new tradition is born," Josh said, "the third-inning stretch."

"What?" Kevin asked.

"This is just how the seventh-inning stretch started," Josh said, and he went on to explain that the first US President to throw out a ceremonial first pitch at a baseball game was William Howard Taft on Opening Day in 1910. According to legend, before the season opener between the Washington Senators and Philadelphia Athletics at Griffith Stadium in D.C., on a whim umpire Bill Evans handed Taft the game ball and asked him to toss it to the plate. The president happily obliged and every chief executive since Taft except for Jimmy Carter has kicked off at least one season during his tenure by tossing out a first pitch in D.C. or Baltimore.

"But what does that have to do with the seventh inning?" Kevin asked, when Josh appeared finished with his story.

"Oh, yeah," Josh said. "I nearly forgot my point." He then explained how Taft, the most obese president ever, once stood up to stretch his legs in the middle of the seventh inning. Everyone else in the stadium rose to show respect to the chief executive, thinking the president was about to leave. A few minutes later Taft nonchalantly sat back down after cutting to the front of the concession line and getting a half-dozen hot dogs. Afterwards he was quoted as saying, "What, me leave a game early? Are you kidding? [Walter] Johnson had a shutout going."

The next night, the Washington fans stood to stretch their legs in the seventh inning just as the president had, and soon the practice spread throughout baseball. People all across America were getting plumper and the ballpark seats weren't getting any bigger, so the stretch came along just in time.

"Good story," Kevin said when Josh had finished. "You know your baseball trivia. But here's one for you. Where did Taft go to college?"

"I have no idea," Josh said.

"Yale University," Kevin replied. "Same as George H.W. Bush."

TEXAS RANGERS, RANGERS BALLPARK IN ARLINGTON

A Texas-Sized Ballpark

The saying "Everything is bigger in Texas," could have been coined exclusively in reference to Rangers Ballpark in Arlington. If this is a ballpark, it's the biggest one we've ever seen. But Texans have a reputation for being fiercely independent in their thinking and for doing things their own way. Rangers Ballpark is in reality a stadium masquerading as a ballpark, an impressive structure with an exterior facade that gives the impression of being a baseball fortress complete with turrets at its beveled corners. The walls do not attempt to mask the seating bowl or minimize it, but rather corral the structure, giving fans inside plenty of room to spare. There is no pretense of intimacy from the exterior, though within, Rangers Ballpark has more than its share of good seats, personality, and charm.

Rangers Ballpark is reminiscent of several stadiums built during the game's classic era. A roof-topped, double-decked outfield porch in right field is quickly recognizable to fans of Tiger Stadium. The white steel filigree ringing the upper deck would please any fan of old Yankee Stadium. And the many irregularities of the outfield fence are clearly patterned after the nooks and crannies created by the old wall at Ebbets Field. As for the granite façade, it combines the red brick and retro turrets of Camden Yards with the arches of Comiskey Park. When Rangers Ballpark first opened, it had a manually operated out-of-town scoreboard built into the sixteen-and-a-half-foot-high left-field wall too. That edifice and its scoreboard were reminiscent, of course, of Fenway Park's left-field Monster and slate board. The old-timey score-tracker was replaced by a modern electronic board in 2009, though. And then that board was updated to an ever better high-definition one in 2011. Who knows, perhaps by the time the next version of this book comes out fans in Arlington will be wearing 3-D goggles so as to best appreciate the latest scoreboard techno-upgrade.

Despite these nods to other yards, Rangers Ballpark projects a distinctly Texan flair. Lone Stars and longhorn steer-heads adorn the exterior walls and are visible throughout the ballpark inside. While many of the facilities built during the retro renaissance opened their outfields to allow for city skyline views, the Rangers enclosed the ballpark with a four-story office building in center that provides the ballpark with a signature look. Consisting primarily of glass, the building has a white steel multilevel facade, which provides porches for the offices and a unique backdrop for baseball. This white steel also traces the roofline of the ballpark, both inside and out, providing a nicely unified theme. The office building and the two-story-high billboards on its roof temper the strong Texas winds that would otherwise wreak havoc on fly balls. The playing surface is also sunk twenty-two feet below street level to minimize the effects of the wind.

In the shadows of the office building resides a grassy berm. Appearing between right and left-field bleachers, this sloped lawn serves as a unique center-field batter's eye. It provides an ideal backdrop for hitting and is the frequent landing site of home run balls in this hitter-friendly park. Behind the berm and bleachers is a picnic area for fans to enjoy. And clearly fan enjoyment was paramount in the minds of the Rangers brass when they conceived their new digs. Residing next to a two-hundred-acre amusement park, Rangers Ballpark offers as complete a game-day experience as you'll find in the American Southwest. As well as the restaurants and shopping facilities that have become standard fare in today's parks, and concession stands that offer a wealth of options, there is plenty else to do and see inside on game day. Unfortunately, though, the expansive baseball museum that once resided in right field—the Legends of the Game Museum and Learning Center—has shuttered its doors and packed up.

Josh: An usher told me they wanted to make more room for corporate events.

Kevin: Why do you tell me things you know will upset me?

335

exterior

Photo by Kevin O'Connell

Rangers Ballpark resides adjacent to the Dallas Cowboys' massive retractable-roof stadium amidst a more-attractive-than-usual sports complex that features well-manicured lawns, tree-lined trails along the shores of manmade ponds, a youth ballpark, and an outdoor amphitheater. With seats to accommodate more than eighty thousand football aficionados, Cowboy Stadium, or "The Jerry Jones Dome" as it is sometimes called, rates as the largest domed stadium in the world. It was built far enough from the baseball park, though, so as not to dwarf it too much.

The park rises from these environs beckoning fans to come inside where a lush green diamond awaits. "Sunset Red" granite mined at Marble Falls, Texas, is the most distinctive local material on display in the park's structure. Meanwhile, decidedly Texan scenes that range from settling, to ranching, to space exploration, appear etched into white murals between the two levels of exterior arches. This classy sculpture work—which is called bas-relief, in case you were wondering—makes it well worth your tracing the perimeter of the stadium footprint outside for a look-see.

The funding for the ballpark came primarily from public sources, as the citizens of Arlington voted on January 19, 1991, for a one-half-cent sales tax increase to finance up to $135 million of the $191 million needed to complete the project. The remaining $56 million was provided by the Ranger ownership group, which included a Texan named George W. Bush. "Dubya" would go on to become governor

of the Lone Star State and would eventually travel to Washington, D.C., to become president of the United States, retracing the path of the Rangers franchise, which in 1972 had made the reverse trip after starting out as the Washington Senators.

This is just one of many connections the Rangers share with the nation's capital city. David M. Schwartz Architectural Services of Washington, D.C., was chosen to design the ballpark, while Dallas firm HKS, Inc., was the local architect of record.

Construction began in the spring of 1992 and took twenty-three months. When the facility opened in 1994 it was known officially as The Ballpark in Arlington. It kept that moniker for a decade before being rechristened as Ameriquest Field in Arlington courtesy of a naming-rights deal with Ameriquest Mortgage Company. It bore that corporate tag from May 2004 until March 2007 before being reintroduced, yet again, as Rangers Ballpark in Arlington. The Rangers lost the first game played in their yet-to-be-renamed new yard, an exhibition tilt against the Mets on April 1, 1994. Then they lost the regular-season opener ten days later against the then-American-League Brewers. Though their start was rough, the first season in the new park signified a time of great optimism for a team that had never before reached the postseason. Kenny Rogers highlighted the good fortune a new ballpark can bring to a franchise when he threw the first perfect game in Rangers' history, a 4–0 blanking of the Angels at the Ballpark on July 28, 1994. With the gem, Rogers became the first left-hander in American League history to achieve perfection. He has since been joined on this short list of flawless Junior Circuit southpaws by David Wells (1998), Mark Buehrle (2009), and Dallas Braden (2010).

Speaking of history, Texas is one of two current American League teams that originated as the Washington Senators. The Minnesota Twins are the other. But the Rangers, perhaps, best exemplified the hapless Senator spirit. When the longtime Senators left Washington in 1960 to become the Minnesota Twins, the city was awarded an expansion franchise the very next year. And that expansion Senators team became the Rangers in 1972 when baseball struck out for a second time in the nation's capital.

It's hard to imagine that D.C. lost two baseball clubs in twelve years or that the members of the D.C. political establishment had such anemic pull they didn't keep them in town. Maybe lawmakers, who hailed from home districts spread across the country and arrived in the Beltway with rooting interests already wed to teams back home, just didn't care. But fans in the D.C. area cared. And in the final Senators game on September 30, 1971, with two outs in the bottom of the ninth, they made like Jimmy Stewart in *Mr. Smith Goes to Washington* and took a stand. Or rather, they created a stampede. They poured onto the field at RFK Stadium and refused to leave. Though the Senators were leading 7-5, the game had to be called and forfeited to the Yankees. That sort of eleventh-hour activism notwithstanding, fan support in D.C. really wasn't sufficient to keep a

façade

Photo by Kevin O'Connell

franchise. The Senators drew just 824,000 fans in 1970 and only 655,000 in 1971. With that final home forfeit, the 1971 club finished 63-96, below .500 for the tenth time in the franchise's eleven seasons.

Meanwhile Arlington was more than happy to open its doors to the American League's perennial whipping horse. The Dallas/Fort Worth/Arlington Metroplex had been attempting to attract a Major League team for years with Arlington being the logical base to put the newcomers owing to its geographic location twelve miles east of Fort Worth and twenty miles west of Dallas. Two years after an attempt by Kansas City A's owner Charlie O. Finley to move his team to Arlington failed, construction began on Turnpike Stadium in 1964. The ten-thousand-seat facility opened in 1965 and became the home of the minor league Dallas/Fort Worth Spurs of the Texas League. But Arlington would fall short of making the Show again in 1968 when the National League approved Montreal and San Diego as expansion sites.

Not long after, though, the push to bring baseball to Arlington gained new momentum when Robert E. Short, the Democratic National Committee treasurer, bought controlling interest in the Senators at the winter meetings in San Francisco in 1968. Turnpike Stadium was expanded to twenty thousand seats in 1970 and then in the latter half of the 1971 season Short received permission to move the Senators to Arlington for the beginning of 1972.

Turnpike Stadium was again expanded, this time to accommodate more than thirty-five thousand fans, and was renamed Arlington Stadium, because Arlingtonians felt Turnpike Stadium sounded too "bush league." They were right. Then, after a long struggle to bring Major League Baseball to the area, local fans prepared for the arrival of big-league ball. And a player's strike delayed the first game. Instead of starting in early April, the 1972 Rangers didn't play their first home game until April 21 when they returned from a one-and-three road trip to beat the California Angels 7-6 in their first home game. They went on to post a four-game sweep of the Halos in a series that attracted a disappointing total of forty-two thousand fans. They went on to finish the year 54-100 and ranked tenth in the twelve-team AL in attendance, drawing just 662,000 fans to seventy-seven home dates. Neither the Rangers, their fans, nor their ballpark seemed ready for the big time quite yet.

Arlington Stadium had been reconstructed several times before its opening, and the resulting patchwork of misfit sections and bleachers shared more than a passing similarity to the woebegone Washington Senators' old Griffith Stadium. Arlington also had the reputation for being the hottest place to play in the Major Leagues, as temperatures rarely dipped below ninety degrees during the summer months. Making matters worse, the seats in Arlington were completely uncovered, so fans were exposed to the unforgiving Texas sunrays during day games. For this reason, most games were played at night, even on Sundays, and the Rangers were the first team to forego the use of flannel uniforms. Like they say, necessity is the mother of invention.

The field at Arlington Stadium was forty feet below street level, and before yet another set of bleachers in the upper deck was constructed, fans entered the stadium at the highest level. The Stadium had the most expansive bleachers in baseball, which gave it a symmetrical and very bowl-like outfield look. Aesthetically, it was nothing too impressive. The most distinctive ballpark feature was its massive scoreboard, a large section of which featured a cut-out of the state of Texas. But the many billboards gave the park a minor league feel that it never really overcame. Much like Rangers Ballpark in Arlington, the signs at Arlington Stadium served as windscreens. At the old yard these spanned from foul pole to foul pole. One advertisement of note was an enormous Marlboro Man, leaning, smoking, standing watch like a sentinel, and seemingly caring about very little other than his smooth-as-smoke Cancer Stick. In the land where football rules supreme, neither the Marlboro Man nor the Texas fans seemed too concerned about the local nine. Of course, the Rangers didn't help their cause by going twenty-four seasons before their first postseason appearance. What's more, Arlington Stadium was never chosen as the site of an All-Star Game, a fan-building tool often used by MLB to showcase new facilities.

But the true seam-heads in Arlington were treated to plenty of great players and wonderful baseball moments, under such colorful managers as Ted Williams, Whitey Herzog, Billy Martin, Don Zimmer, and Bobby Valentine. One such moment came when eighteen-year-old pitching phenom David Clyde made his Major League debut, beating the Twins 4-3, just twenty days after graduating from Houston's Westchester High School in 1973. Another was the time Dave Nelson stole second base, third base, and then home—all in one inning—on August 30, 1974. And who could forget August 4, 1993, when forty-six-year-old Nolan Ryan beat the stuffing out of Chicago's Robin Ventura, who had charged the mound after Ryan beaned him.

But Ryan did much more damage to batters while they were still in the batter's box. Ryan holds a special place in the hearts of Texas sports fans, even football fans. Ryan is a Texan and the most overpowering pitcher of his generation and arguably of all time. When Ryan pitched, fans packed Arlington Stadium. The hard-throwing right-hander treated the home crowd to his seventh and final no-hitter, as well as his five thousandth strikeout. In 2008 Ryan became team president, then in 2010 he and his business partner Chuck Greenberg scored the winning bid to purchase the Rangers from Tom Hicks after the much-maligned Rangers owner had nearly run the franchise into the ground by tossing Texas-sized contracts at players like Chan Ho Park and Alex Rodriguez without the local gate or television revenue to really make the investments worth the Rangers' while. As part-owner and team president, Ryan has a hands-on approach. He has worked with pitching coach Mike Maddux to implement a new pitching program whereby Rangers prospects and big leaguers do a lot more throwing than most teams' hurlers to build arm strength. The plan is designed to not only help pitchers last deeper into games with higher pitch counts but to help them withstand the summer heat in Arlington. The throwback approach to managing mounds-men paid off big-time in 2010 when a cadre of power arms—belonging to the likes of C.J. Wilson, Colby Lewis, Alexi Ogando, and Neftali Feliz—combined with crafty port-sider Cliff Lee and other veteran arms to lead the Rangers to their first World Series appearance.

Josh: In addition to all that, Ryan has been an ardent supporter of Texas Republicans.

Kevin: Please toss info like that in the "Kevin Doesn't Need to Know" file.

Before the upstart Rangers of the new century, there were some pretty good teams back in the 1990s when Johnny Oates was the manager. Two years after moving to Rangers Ballpark in Arlington, the Rangers and their fans got to taste post-season champagne for the first time when the team posted its first-ever division title in 1996. Led by players like Rafael Palmeiro, Ivan Rodriguez, Juan Gonzalez, Will Clark, and Rusty Greer, the big-swinging Rangers defeated the Yankees at home in their first-ever postseason game, a 6-2 win on October 1, 1996. But the Yanks took the next three games to win the series. The Rangers got another shot at the Yankees in the 1998 Division Series, but were swept, with the final insult coming at home in the form of a 4-0 blanking. In 1999, the Rangers and Yanks squared off in the first round of the playoffs again, and New York made it another clean sweep, handing the Rangers their ninth straight playoff loss.

Josh: That's almost three sweeps in a row.

Kevin: Nearly.

Josh: Three-Sweep. I like that. Maybe I can get a trademark on it.

After the ill-fated A-Rod experience, which lasted just three years during which the juiced Rodriguez led the AL in homers three times while the Rangers finished dead last in the AL West, and a middling first decade of the new century that was capped by the revelation of the Rangers precarious balance sheet, a new potential dynasty seemed on the cusp of emerging as the Rangers enjoyed a glorious 2010 season. After failing to make the October Classic in their first fifty seasons as a franchise (counting the first eleven years in Washington) the Rangers relegated the Seattle Mariners, who debuted in 1977, to the status as longest-running franchise that's never made a trip to the Big Dance. Those 2010 heroes of Arlington were led by the amazing Josh Hamilton, who got himself clean, resurrected his career, bashed his way to Mid-Summer glory in the 2009 Home Run Derby at Yankee Stadium, and wrote a best-selling book along the way to winning the 2010 AL MVP and 2010 ALCS MVP.

Joined by longtime Rangers hit-machine Michael Young, the multi-dimensional Ian Kinsler, and the flashy Elvis Andrus, Hamilton led an offense that batted .276 to rank first in the big leagues. In the first round of the playoffs, Texas dispatched Tampa Bay in a grueling five-game tilt in which the road-team won every game. That first post-season series victory in franchise history left just the dreaded Yankees standing between the Rangers and the World Series. This time, the Rangers delivered on their home turf, winning all three of the games played at Rangers Ballpark, including the Game 6 clincher in which Lewis and Feliz combined to hold the Yankees to three hits in a 6-1 win. Fifty-one thousand and four hundred fans turned out to watch the Rangers finish off the Yanks and raise the AL Pennant. But that Rangers Ballpark attendance record didn't last for long. Some 52,419 claw- and antler-bearing fanatics jammed the Ballpark to watch the Rangers win Game 3 of the World Series against the Giants. But that 4-2 victory would turn out to be the only highlight for the Texas nine which fell in five games to a pitching-rich San Francisco squad that held the Rangers' big bats in check.

Still, the excitement of the 2010 season lingers. On the heels of that success, applications for 2011 season tickets spiked and Arlington was officially stamped on the baseball map as a bona-fide big league city. Led by Ryan's management, the Rangers returned to the World Series in 2011, only to twice come within a strike of a series victory before losing an extra-inning heartbreaker to the Cardinals in Game 6, and then also falling in Game 7. Sad as it is to do so, we would be remiss not to mention that one of the worst ballpark tragedies in recent memory occurred at Rangers Ballpark in 2011. Shortly before the All-Star break Hamilton tossed a ball toward a fan in the outfield seats and, attempting to make the catch, the gentleman fell over the thirty-four-inch-high railing and suffered head wounds that caused him to die later that night. The man had only been trying to procure a keepsake for his six-year-old son. Hamilton had been trying to do the right thing by being a sport and making a child happy. This should be a lesson to us all not to go too overboard trying to get our hands on a ball. After all, it's only a ball. It should be a lesson to the big league teams too. They need to do a better job of making sure their stadiums are safe for fans. We're guilty in this, too, we know. When we find our view of the game blocked by retaining walls or railings, we complain about it in our book. From now on we'll try to be more understanding. And all MLB teams, we suspect, will be more vigilant in their safety inspections of their facilities. As for the Rangers, within two weeks of the horrific accident, they raised all of the railings at Rangers Ballpark to forty-two inches high.

Trivia Timeout

Longhorn: Name the only Major League player to have his number retired by three teams.

Side of Beef: Prior to the ninety-five-win Rangers team of 1999, which Rangers edition had won the most games in a season?

Filet Mignon: How did the term "Texas Leaguer" come to signify a bloop hit?

Look for the answers in the text.

Getting a Choice Seat

This is a park where you want to shoot for the first level. The upper seats in the top deck are some of the farthest away in all of baseball. So don't skimp. Wait until you get to Colorado or San Francisco—where a top-shelf seat at least comes with a primo outfield view—to start pinching pennies. The park offers a reasonable average ticket price, but don't let that fool you into thinking the average seat is well priced. The average ticket price is lowered by the fact that there are a great number of bad seats in the upper tank.

The First Level
VIP INFIELD/HOME PLATE BOX
So pricey they don't even have section numbers, the first two rows behind and beside the two dugouts are reserved for

Seating Capacity: 49,170
Ticket Office: http://texas.rangers.mlb.com/ticketing/index.jsp?c_id=tex
Seating Chart: http://texas.rangers.mlb.com/tex/ballpark/tex_ballpark_seating.jsp

the likes of the Bush sisters and those rascally Ryan grand-kids. Unless you're Texas royalty or baseball royalty, don't get your hopes up. The same goes for the first two rows between the dugouts—the 88 Home Plate Seats, which were added down on the field in 2009.

Josh: I've got to be honest, I kind of thought you and I would be baseball royalty by now.

Kevin: Because the first edition of our book did so well?

Josh: No, because I collected souvenir ice cream helmets from all thirty parks.

Kevin: And you didn't even clean them out before stashing them in the trunk of the road trip mobile.

PREMIUM INFIELD (SECTIONS 18–34)

The incline of the seats on the first level is steeper than at most parks, and all of these seats between the bases feel like they're right on top of the action. Section 18 is at third base, Section 25 is directly behind the plate, and Section 34 is at first base.

LOWER INFIELD (SECTIONS 18–34)

Appearing in the middle of the lower bowl, behind the Premium Infield seats and in front of the raised lower boxes, the Lower Infield seats are nicely angled toward the action. This is probably where you'll wind up sitting if you're a bit too thrifty to shell out big bucks for a primo seat but fan-enough to want a very good seat at Rangers Ballpark. If you're a moderate spender, you really can't beat Sections 26 or 27 behind the plate.

LOWER BOX (SECTIONS 14–17, 35–38, 115–136)

This hodgepodge of pricing represents two kinds of seats, those infield seats just beyond the bases, and the seats just behind all the infield seats on what appears to be the first level. We say this because the seats in Sections 115–136 are actually on the first level, but can only be accessed by an upper concourse. They are located immediately behind the section in front of them, and thus the illusion is created that they are part of the same section, yet there is no access to them from the first-level concourse. There are only nine rows of seats in these upper Lower Box sections. And they

are covered by the overhang of the Club Level. They're not a bad option, but we like the Lower Box seats along the base-lines a bit better because they are closer to the field.

We should mention, though, that the seats in right field (Sections 35–38) begin to angle away from the plate, forcing fans to look over their left shoulder a bit. The effect is not as dramatic on the left side.

CORNER BOX (SECTIONS 10–13, 39–42, 112–114, 137–139)

Here is another hodgepodge of sections thrown together more by pricing level than by the fact that they're in a similar location. These are probably the best value for the money on the first level. Getting seats in the lower rows of Sections 13 or 39 will not disappoint you. The other important factor with these seats is that (except for Sections 41 and 42) they are all clear of any foul-pole obstructions, while the lower-reserved sections nearby have obstruction issues. If this is important to you, spend the extra ten bucks to stay in the clear.

LOWER RESERVED (SECTIONS 3–9, 44–49)

These are the home run territory seats, where you'll want to bring your glove. Compared to other parks, they're a bit on the pricey side at more than $30 a pop. A distinctive and kitschy section to sit in is the lower deck of the grandstand in right field. If you want a unique experience, remember not to sit in Section 44, which is not under the roof. The aisles are built around the pillars, and the pillars themselves

SEATING TIP

On a per game basis, the Premium Infield seats sell for between $80 and $90, depending on the quality of the Rangers' opponent. For us, that's bumping into the upper range of our feasibility range. However, season-ticket holders purchase tickets at a steeply discounted rate in Texas. For example, Premium Infield seats only cost $50 apiece for those ten-gallon hat wearing Texans willing to sign up for all eighty-one games. As a result, if you can find a season-ticket holder selling his seat on eBay or Craigslist, chances are he'll be asking considerably less than the box office's price for a comparable seat.

Josh: I don't care if he's a season-ticket holder or not, if some clown sits in front of me wearing a ten-gallon hat, I'm asking him to take it off.

Kevin: Because you wouldn't be able to see the game?

Josh: No, because this is a *baseball game*, not a rodeo. And because I wouldn't be able to see.

are narrow, so the inevitable blockage of view is not terrible in this delightfully "old-timey" part of the park. Sit in the center of the sections and down low if you want to avoid the "experience" of sitting behind a pole, regardless of the kitsch factor. Sections 3 to 7 in left are elevated above the high-tech scoreboard. These sections obscure just a tad of the warning track, but all in all they're not bad. A small gully separates the first row of seats from the outfield wall. Sections 8 and 9 down the left-field line are the poorest in this range. The back rows are under a significant overhang, and the field view is cut in half by the foul pole. The lower seats in Section 8 are not as bad, but most of the seats in Section 9 have some type of obstruction.

BLEACHERS (SECTIONS 50–54)

The full bench bleachers were brought over from Arlington Stadium (they had plenty) and put to use at Rangers Ballpark. If you can get into the lower rows you may be mildly satisfied as upper seats don't allow a view of the outfield corners.

Club Level

CLUB INFIELD (SECTIONS 222–230)

Sure these are great just-above-the-plate seats. But do you really need to be pampered, coddled, and have your hand held? We've said it before and we'll say it again: real fans sit down near the field, not up where people have one eye on the game and the other on the price of oil futures.

CLUB BOX (SECTIONS 217–221, 231–235)

Overheard in this section: "The firm who 'comped' me these seats can't afford the Club Infield." Also overheard in Sections 217 and 235: "Did anyone else notice the seats one section over are half the price?"

Josh: You made that up about the guy in the suit complaining.

Kevin: Maybe, but if I was a corporate shmuck and they stuck me out here, that's what I'd say.

Josh: Trust me, you'll never be a corporate shmuck.

Kevin: Hey, thanks!

CLUB TERRACE (SECTIONS 201–216, 236–245)

The seats in the Club Terrace are closer to the field of play than the Club Infield seats, even if they're down the lines, while the Club Infield seats are, well, on the infield. This can be attributed to the design of the decks. But that still doesn't make these great seats. Sections 213–216 on the left side are the pick of this somewhat attractive litter. Sections 201–209 in deep left-field home run territory are the worst.

ALL-YOU-CAN-EAT PORCH (SECTIONS 246–252)

Almost every seat will have some kind of obstruction from the poles, which support the roof. But then again, you get to shout "incoming" when Josh Hamilton launches his latest torpedo. And, really, the support poles are relatively narrow. If you lean a little you can see any play. These seats are far better than anything on the Upper Level even if a large part of the right-field wall is lost to the underhang. As an added attraction, and so they can charge more for these seats than they used to, the Rangers have made this part of the park an all-you-can-eat section. Here's the menu, direct from the Rangers' website:

"Each ticket includes all you can eat grilled chicken sandwiches, hot dogs, nachos, peanuts, popcorn, and soft drinks, served in the air-conditioned grill behind Upper HomeRun Porch. Food service begins when the ballpark gates open and ends two hours after the scheduled game time."

The Upper Level

UPPER BOX (SECTIONS 316–335) AND UPPER RESERVED (SECTIONS 301–338)

The lower seats in Sections 316 to 335 are the Upper Boxes. These are okay, but not great. As for the Upper Reserved, we don't know who they would be reserved for, as they are fairly horrible. These seats are distant and windblown. The Rangers have done a few crazy things with the upper deck to make it one of the farthest from the action in baseball. The Club deck is hung a bit over the first-level bowl, but the third deck is pushed back behind the second deck. And with the Press level also in between, these seats are in the upper stratosphere. The sky at night sure is big and bright (deep in the heart of Texas) from this level. We found the nearest outfield corner obscured from view by the faulty design in many of these sections too. In Section 301 you can't see the left-field wall or corner at all, and a huge chunk of center field is blocked by the white steel facade of the building. Sitting in Sections 302 to 305 (unless you're in the first three rows) will also prevent you from seeing the wall and corner. In Sections 306 to 312 the wall becomes visible but the corner is still blocked. Sit in the lower seats of Sections 316 and 317 for the best value in the upper deck.

GRANDSTAND RESERVED (SECTIONS 339–345)

There's no way around it: These seats stink. To qualify the level of sucky-ness, we would only pay Confederate money for these seats. Only Section 339 is clear of the underhang issues that plague this deep-right-field portion of the upper deck.

Before/After the Game

Rangers Ballpark is surrounded by plenty of parking in the stadium lots. Whether your pregame ritual includes a picnic by a man-made lake, or a ride on a roller coaster at Six Flags, the baseball game still takes center stage to anything you might do beforehand. This isn't Wrigleyville or even a tailgate-friendly scene, but at least it isn't a giant field of concrete and asphalt deep in the heart of Texas. The Rangers obviously made a priority of creating around their park a lush green oasis and the effort they went to should be applauded.

Getting to Rangers Ballpark

Most Rangers fans drive to the game owing to the lack of a centralized mass transit system in Arlington. That said, the no-fare trolley, which stops at many of the hotels in town, does service Rangers Ballpark. And did we mention it's free? If you're staying at the Days Inn Six Flags, you'll be within walking distance of the ballpark, but otherwise look for a hotel that boasts a trolley stop on its grounds. For those swooping into Arlington and then swooping out—perhaps staying overnight in the livelier hub of Dallas—driving is pretty easy owing to the park's placement right off Interstate 30. From Fort Worth take Interstate 30 east to the Nolan Ryan Expressway exit. Follow the Ryan Express to Randol Mill Road and turn left. From Dallas take Interstate 30 west and exit at Ballpark Way south. The different parking areas are lettered, with each letter representing a famous Texan. For example, the "A" lot is called the "Stephen F. Austin" lot, while the "H" lot belongs to Sam Houston. A parking spot in these team lots cost $10.

Arlington Trolley: www.arlingtontrolley.com/ATTRACTIONS/tabid/56/Default.aspx

Outside Attractions

RANGERS WALK OF FAME

Along the north and west sides of Rangers Ballpark brick panels are laid into the walkway featuring the rosters of each Rangers club since 1972, the year the Senators moved to Texas. There are special markers for Gold Glove Award winners like Ivan Rodriguez and MVPs like Juan Gonzalez, and for other various award winners. We were amazed to learn that the second-winningest Rangers edition ever didn't even make the playoffs. That's right, the 1977 team overcame a slow start to finish a franchise-best 94-68 but finished in second place. They missed the playoffs by eight games, owing to the Kansas City Royals' stellar 102-60 campaign. That Texas team caught lightning in a bottle after

skipper Frank Lucchesi was supplanted by Billy Hunter. Under Hunter, the team went 60-33 but it wasn't enough to catch the Royals. By way of comparison, the World Series Rangers of 2010 only won ninety regular season games and the World Series team of 2011 only won ninety-six.

For a price, fans can have their names etched in brick too, beside the year of their choosing. Each panel is made of 2,600 bricks. Josh counted, while Kevin fibbed to passersby, asking them to steer clear of the walkway so Josh could find his "contact lens."

Kevin: Why don't you just multiply the number of bricks in the length by the width?

Josh: Trust me, my method is *way* more accurate.

A MINI RANGER'S DELIGHT

A kid-sized ballpark resides north of the big league stadium, on the far side of a little lake. A replica of Rangers Ballpark, this little yard is available for rental. Complete with a P.A. system, lights, decorative steel, and a scoreboard, it is also used for Rangers instructional camps and baseball clinics. The little guys' yard closes an hour prior to each home game. Not far away, the North Lawn provides a great spot for a picnic.

> ## Baseball Vernacular
>
> One thing we learned while visiting Arlington was the origin of the term "Texas Leaguer." A Texas Leaguer, of course, is baseball-speak for a blooper that lands out of reach of the infielders, but too shallow for the outfielders to catch. Because the sun-baked fields of the Texas League were very fast (to borrow a golf term), outfielders would play deeper than normal throughout the minor league circuit so as to prevent balls from shooting up the gaps. As a result, many lightly-struck balls fell in for singles. Today the idiosyncratic term has become common baseball lingo, as familiar as "Baltimore Chop" or "Can of Corn."

COWBOYS STADIUM

Follow Randol Mill Road two Texas-sized blocks west of the park and before you know it you'll be standing in the shadows of the most immense dome known to North American sports fans, or fans on any continent, for that matter.

Josh: It kind of looks like a giant football.

Kevin: I think that's by design.

Josh: You see it too?

Kevin: Well, now that you mention it.

The Cowboys offer fans the opportunity to partake in a variety of different tour options, ranging from a self-guided tour to an audio-device directed tour to a tour focused on the facility's rich collection of art (and you probably thought Jerry Jones didn't have much interest in art!). To learn more, visit: http://stadium.dallascowboys.com/tours/tourInfo.cfm.

SIX FLAGS OVER TEXAS
www.sixflags.com/overTexas/index.aspx
What can we say about this expansive amusement park that hasn't been said before. Really, what can we say? We have no idea. We're ballpark buffs, not roller coaster experts. Given the proximity of the amusement park to the ballpark, though, it would seem like a good side-destination for those road tripping with the kiddoes in tow.

Watering Holes and Outside Eats
While the pregame eating and drinking options offer little in the way of local character, on the plus side there are several chain restaurants within a mile or so of the baseball and football complex. So at least you know what you're getting. If you do a loop around the ballpark and Cowboys Stadium you will likely find an acceptable but not-too-exciting spot for a pregame lunch or beverage. We will stop short of "reviewing" all of these familiar chains, but we will list them here so you won't settle for your fourth-least favorite chain, when you might have enjoyed a burger at your third-least favorite instead if you'd driven a block farther.

CHAIN RESTAURANTS ON NORTH COLLINS STREET
Just west of the park, a drive down North Collins will reveal Chili's, Hooters, TGI Fridays, Chik-fil-A, Country Kitchen, Panera, Buffalo Wild Wings, Arby's, Taco Bell, Panda Express, Subway, Popeye's Chicken, and plenty of other quickie spots. For our money, Buffalo Wild Wings is the pick of this litter.

Josh: "Chains on North Collins Street" would be an apropos name for a bike shop.

Kevin: Yeah, or a kinky sex club.

HUMPERDINKS RESTAURANT
700 Six Flags Dr.
www.humperdinks.com/locations/arlington/
This local chain tries to be all things to all people. A sports bar with many TVs, a brew pub with its own handcrafted brews on tap, and a family restaurant. In a land where chain restaurants are king, we think Humperdinks succeeds. Being only eight blocks from the park, this may be your one-stop-shopping place for pregame and postgame entertainment. The menu features everything from burgers to calzones to seafood and steak to Tex-Mex and Cajun. A full list of national beer and wines is available, plus a selection of home brewed

micros. Josh sampled a Texas Blonde, while Kevin enjoyed a Total Disorder Porter. Humperdinks boasts the tallest barroom ceiling in Texas, which we guess is worth something.

THIRD BASE SPORTS BAR AND GRILL
812 Six Flags Drive
www.3rdbasesportsbarandgrill.com/index.html
This sports bar boasts good food and a roster of attractive young ladies who like to dress up in kinky little outfits for the pleasure of their male guests. Kevin likened it to Hooters without the corporate consideration that requires some semblance of political correctness and decorum. Check out the PG-13 rated photo gallery on their website and you'll see what we mean.

BOBBY VALENTINE'S SPORTS GALLERY CAFÉ
4301 S. Bowen
www.bobbyvsports.com/
This restaurant owned by former Texas Rangers manager Bobby Valentine is distinguishable from any other restaurant in Arlington by the raised boxing ring in the middle of the dining room that allows a few select parties to eat inside the ropes. The exceptional chili comes served in a bread bowl while the Major League Burgers feature the trademark flavors of different big league cities. All of the memorabilia is a nice touch too: from the Troy Aikman and Roger Staubach mementos to the Ivan Rodriguez and A-Rod stuff.

Josh: I sure hope Bobby V. opens a joint like this in Boston.

Kevin: Well, if history is any indication, he soon will.

MESQUITE CHAMPIONSHIP RODEO
1818 Rodeo Dr., Mesquite
www.mesquiteprorodeo.com/
For a real Texas experience, drive about half an hour to Mesquite. This popular stop on the ProRodeo circuit has it all, including bull riding, bronc riding, tie-down roping, and of course, lovable rodeo clowns. But most of all, Kevin enjoyed the unique Texas music, and Josh enjoyed the hickory smoked brisket from the barbecue wagon. During baseball season the ranch is open Friday and Saturday nights. We were tempted to conduct our usual seating survey, but decided against it.

Rodeo Seating Chart: www.mesquiteprorodeo.com/group-sales/rodeo-group-seating-chart

Inside the Stadium
Inside the main entrance, the square shape of the vast entry level makes the concourse feel more like a plaza. The gated arches cast shadows across the concrete floor and give the

plaza a charming baseball feel. But the real personality of this park is down near the field. Rangers Ballpark in Arlington is instantly recognizable thanks to that looming building in center and the well-manicured grass batter's eye.

Ballpark Features

CENTER-FIELD OFFICE BUILDING

The first floor of the white-porched office building in center houses some retail shops and the Rangers box office. And the fourth floor houses the team's executive brain trust. But floor two and three are leased to regular old companies. Each floor offers thirty-four thousand square feet of office space that leases for between $22 and $26 per square foot. Among the tenants are a custom jewelry shop named Baseball Diamonds that does a lot of business with the Rangers players, a real estate firm, and a mortgage company. Many of the office suites come with their own ballpark views, yet when the Rangers made the playoffs in 2010, MLB made those tenants wishing to stand on their office balconies to watch the games purchase standing-room tickets.

GREENE'S HILL

The sloped lawn batter's eye is named after former Arlington Mayor Richard Greene. Fans gather in the bleachers on both sides during batting practice, while the players attempt to launch pregame blasts toward the knoll. When a ball strikes Greene's Hill, a mad scramble ensues for the souvenir. Then fans politely return to the bleachers and await the next bomb. Yes, Josh scrambled onto the hill, but he was beaten out by a gangly thirteen-year-old bully.

At various times the trademark Rangers "T" has been painted onto the lawn. And flag-waving young ladies have taken to the Hill after home runs to lead the crowd in a college-football-style celebration.

Even once the game begins, fans are allowed to leave the seating area and take to the hill whenever a homerun ball plops down. The Texas scramble is one of the most unique homer traditions in baseball and we love it.

VANDERGRIFF PLAZA

Named after former Arlington Mayor Tom Vandergriff, who was integral to bringing the Rangers to Texas in the first place, then to seeing to it that they got a shiny new ballpark, the plaza between the office building and the center-field berm is a festive spot to visit before or during the game. It is an interactive sports area, where kids can play Wiffle Ball, toss a few at the speed-pitch meter, or take a few hacks in the tee-ball cages. History minded chaps can also pay tribute to a regal statue of the local car salesman, turned politician, turned big-league recruiter. There is also a statue of a business-suit–attired Vandergriff at Arlington City Hall and during the 2010 post-season it was dressed up in a red Rangers jersey and cap.

THE RYAN STATUE AND RETIRED NUMBER

A statue honoring Nolan Ryan also stands in Vandergriff Plaza. It depicts Ryan raising his cap in salute to the Texas fans after whiffing Roberto Alomar to complete his record seventh no-hitter with a 3-0 whitewashing of the Blue Jays on May 1, 1991. Ryan's No. 34 hangs on the façade of the left-field upper deck, along with Jackie Robinson's universally retired No. 42 and manager Johnny Oates's No. 26.

Ryan is the answer to an interesting trivia question, by the way. Besides Robinson, he is the only player to have his number retired by three different teams. Well, we should say his numbers. The first team to honor Ryan was the Angels, who retired his No. 30 in 1992. Then, the Rangers retired the No. 34 he wore for them in September 1996, and just two weeks later, the Astros retired No. 34. Ryan's plaque in Cooperstown, by the way, depicts him in a Rangers cap, even though he only notched 51 of his 324 career wins with them.

batting practice

Photo by Kevin O'Connell

HOME RUN PORCH

The double-decked grandstand section in right field is one of the signature features of this ballpark. The pillars that support the upper deck and roof give the outfield the distinctive look of a classic park. This may make the ballpark look old-timey, but in reality the seats aren't anything to write home about. Even if you're sitting elsewhere, though, it's worth visiting the porch during your pregame stroll, just to take in the old-time effect before returning to your unobstructed field-level seat.

BEST "FANS" IN BASEBALL

Overhead electric fans hang from the roof of the Home Run Porch, cooling folks seated in these sections on hot days.

Josh: These remind me of the heaters in Minneapolis.

Kevin: What a difference a thousand miles can make, eh?

Josh: It's too cold. It's too hot. Baseball fans are a finicky bunch.

Kevin: Not just baseball. Here in the football capital of the south the Cowboys used to have a partial dome that covered the fans but not the playing field.

Josh: Given the blustery winters in East Texas, that seems forgivable.

Kevin: I know some Packers fans who wouldn't agree.

SAVE THE POLES

Perhaps the only things from old Arlington Stadium worth saving were the foul poles. Other than the bleachers in center field, all of the other features that resemble the old Stadium were re-created, such as the State of Texas cutout between the American and Texas flags in center. But they transported the big yellow poles.

FOR WHOM THE BELL TOLLS

From 2004 to 2006 there was a giant bell situated in Section 201 and whenever a member of the Rangers homered it would toll. This neat effect was actually a tribute to then-stadium-namesake Ameriquest. It had a big company logo smack dab on its base. When the mortgage behemoth was broken into different companies and dissolved, the naming-rights deal ended and the Rangers discreetly removed the bell. As it turned out, in the end the bell tolled for thee, Ameriquest.

BULLPEN CONFIGURATION

The home bullpen is located in right-center field and causes the outfield wall to jut back toward the infield, creating difficult angles for center fielders. We like this design. Not so well done is the visiting bullpen. With the seats for the pitchers located underneath the outfield grandstands in left-center, hurlers must walk behind the scoreboard to get to the throwing area. The visitors warm up, throwing perpendicular to the outfield wall, rather than parallel to it as is the case in the home pen. While this asymmetry might be acceptable, the pen itself is oddly shaped, such that it gives the impression of being an afterthought. While we realize that dissing the opposing team is part of the game, this just looks shoddy.

TEXAS RANGERS HALL OF FAME

In a small portion of the space previously occupied by the Legends of the Game Baseball Museum, the Rangers honor their franchise icons like Ryan, Ferguson Jenkins, Charlie Hough, Jim Sundberg, Buddy Bell, and Tom Grieve with plaques and mementos from their careers. This right-field gallery is open to ticket holders on game day.

Stadium Eats

Rangers Ballpark offers the basics, with a few delightful Southwestern twists. Upon our return to Arlington, we observed a far beefier menu than we encountered during our first visit, which was a pleasant development as far as our taste buds were concerned, but maybe less so for our arteries.

CHOPPED BRISKET SANDWICH (TRADEMARK FOOD)

Introduced midway through the 2010 season, this steaming slop of juicy meat comes courtesy of Rick's Barbecue, which can be found behind Section 327 where an actual hickory wood smoker is set on the concourse. This is Texas barbecue, so it's beef not pork, but the brisket is pretty much shredded (technically chopped) so the consistency is nice and soft. Rick also offers bacon-wrapped hot dogs topped with sautéed onions.

NOLAN RYAN ALL BEEF HOT DOG (DOG REVIEW)

When we visited in 2003, we were disappointed by the limp and lifeless Decker Dog and we let the Rangers know it. As a direct result of our criticism, no doubt, one of Nolan Ryan's first priorities upon taking the Rangers' reins was to replace those Decker Dogs with his own brand of bursting-with-flavor all-beef franks. And he got around to it right after he revamped the team's pitching philosophy. So now Rangers fans get to enjoy a nice firm ballpark dog while they watch their Texas starters throw 130 pitches before walking off the mound limp-armed. Seriously, though, it's a much better dog.

BEST OF THE REST

We also were impressed by the **Texas Steak Sandwich.** It came on a nice fresh roll, topped with salsa. The **Nachos**

Supreme at the TexMex Express come loaded with jalapeño peppers, taco meat, shredded cheese, lettuce, salsa, and black olives. Not too shabby. The **Taco Salad** is also a big seller, and the lines for these stands are the longest in the park.

The smoked **Turkey Leg** at the Red River Stand on the first level concourse is quite good. We enjoyed our **Jalapeño Sausage** but it could have had even more pepper in it as far as we were concerned. It was close to a toss-up but in the end we decided that we liked **Nolan Ryan's All-Beef Hickory Sausage** just a little bit more. The last bite convinced us.

We didn't weigh the **Three-Pound Pretzel** to check its authenticity in labeling but we can verify that it is a hefty twisted loaf of dough that comes served in a pizza box. It comes with three different dipping sauces: nacho cheese, marinara, and honey mustard, and is said to check in at 3,700 calories! If you can handle that many carbs, go for it. The **Cajun Fries** and **Garlic Fries** came in portions more our size and were a tick better than decent.

On a hot day (gee, do you think?) try the **Big Kahuna Giant Chocolate Chip Cookie Sandwich.**

STADIUM SUDS

Most beer stands have Bud, Miller, and Coors products while there are also Beers of the World stands on all three levels that serve a range of familiar brews for the more refined palate. In addition there are two Beers of Texas stands—behind Sections 121 and 209—that serve some Lone Star State favorites. Kevin tried the Saint Arnold Lawnmower, a golden beer, and liked it a lot. The Shiner Bock is also a popular local choice. Another big seller in Texas, where it's always scorching, is the foot-long **Frozen Margarita.** It may seem like a girlie-drink but if you can find a guy or two in your section with one—preferably a macho-looking dude with a cowboy hat on his head—then you can probably pull it off too.

The Rangers Ballpark Experience

Texans are a vocal bunch. We came to this conclusion after observing folks yelling like East Coasters during our first visit, sparing no one, not the players, umps, or batboys. So we thought we'd found another baseball mecca, an oasis in the desert of football and NASCAR. But we were wrong. With the game tied and going into the top of the seventh inning, fans began to leave. And not just a few, in droves.

Kevin: The game was tied before you got here!

Josh: Yeah, why bother coming out? The food was not *that* good.

We expected this dynamic to have changed upon our return trip in 2011. After the team's amazing run in 2010, we assumed the fan base would have solidified into one that took the game just a bit more seriously. And yet, as is often the case, we were proven wrong again. In a one-run game a third of the place had cleared out by the top of the eighth inning.

Kevin: If the traffic gives you so much worry, why not just stay home?

Josh: You're gonna miss Neftali!

THE DOT RACE

In the middle of the sixth inning the Rangers video board lights up with red, blue, and green dots that race one another. This is nothing new. The nightly dot race has been part of the Rangers experience since debuting at Arlington Stadium in 1986. But in 2010 the dots took a page out of the Brewers' book and began extending their race down onto the field. They begin on the video board, and then emerge down the left-field line to race to third base.

THE LEGENDS RACE

In 2011, the Legends Race took the place of the Dot Race on select nights. This innovation features prominent Texans like Sam Houston, Davy Crockett, Jim Bowie, and Nolan Ryan portrayed with giant bobbing heads that appear above period-specific costumes. To say these figures are a bit goofy is an understatement.

Josh: Wow, Nolan must have taken his Advil today. He's really booking it.

Kevin: I'm pretty sure that's not really him.

Josh: Well, he's always kind of had a big head . . .

Kevin: Dude, the real Nolan Ryan is sitting right by the Rangers dugout.

Josh: Oh yeah. I forgot.

THE TEXAS TWO-STEP

After "Take Me Out to the Ball Game" in the middle of the seventh, "Cotton-Eyed Joe" blares through the P.A. system. And boy, do the locals ever eat it up.

Josh: Have you heard the contemporary version by Michelle Shocked?

Kevin: Umm. No.

Josh: Well, you oughta.

Kevin: Do you want to be a music reviewer or a baseball author?

Josh: Umm, the latter.

Kevin: Then you'd better keep the musical asides to a minimum.

THE CLAW AND ANTLER CLUB

Despite this late-inning petering out, 2010 did mark the dawning of a new era for not just the Rangers' team but their fans as well. During the playoff run the whole country became familiar with the local rooters' "Claws" and "Antlers." Don't worry, in the event that you've forgotten, we'll explain.

That Rangers lineup possessed a nice balance of speed and power. On the base paths shortstop Elvis Andrus registered thirty-two swipes while four other Texas starters totaled fourteen or more. And at the bat, Hamilton hit thirty-two dingers to pace a lineup that cranked 162 long balls. To celebrate this multi-dimensionality, as game events dictated, Rangers fans took to flashing a Claw hand-signal, symbolizing force and power, whenever a local son homered, and dual Antler hand-signals above their ears, symbolizing speed.

The unique fan tradition actually began with the players. According to local lore, Esteban German started the Claw when he was playing for the Rangers' Pacific Coast League affiliate in Oklahoma City in 2009. After he introduced it to the big league team in early 2010, Nelson Cruz and Hamilton started the Antlers. The fans picked up on it and the rest is history.

If you can't quite figure out how to hold your hands, look for the Deer Cam and Claw Cam on the JumboTron during the eighth inning and the locals will show you how.

Ryan, Texas Ranger

No, Cordell Walker was not the most kickass Texas Ranger of all time. Nor was C.D. Parker. Nolan Ryan was. Yeah, we know this pop-culture reference is a bit dated, but *Walker, Texas Ranger* is still on in syndication, so we say it still works. After all, comparing a baller to a real (well, sort of) ranger as dominant as Walker, is about as high a compliment as we can pay a gun-slinging Texan. Two of Ryan's most memorable feats came in a Rangers uniform at the end of his career. When the old man threw his final no-no on May 1, 1991, against the Blue Jays, he was forty-four, making him the oldest player ever to turn the trick. His other Texas-sized accomplishment had come two years earlier when he whiffed Oakland's Rickey Henderson for career strikeout number five thousand on August 22, 1989. The Ryan Express went on to rack up 714 more K's. His 5,714 is the all-time record and the next-best guy——Randy Johnson, who had 4,875——isn't even close.

COWBOY WAYNE (SUPER-FAN)

Scan the front row of box seats on the third-base side and you're apt to spot Cowboy Wayne—a veritable Kenny Rogers look-alike—just beyond the visitors' dugout. He'll be wearing a big old cowboy hat, sporting a baseball glove on his left hand, and holding a colossal green fishing net in his right hand. This guy wants a ball.

A season-ticket holder, Wayne has been getting plenty of foul balls in recent years. He started bringing the net to games in 1995 and claims to have scooped up hundreds of balls since then. Don't worry, as soon as Wayne sees lightning in the sky, he puts the aluminum-framed net under his seat.

Cyber Super-Fans

- **Lone Star Ball**
  www.lonestarball.com/
  Lone Star not only covers the Texas scene but the rest of the Majors as well.
- **Nolan Writin'**
  http://nolanwritin.com/about/
  Great name for a blog and the content gets a Silver Boot too.
- **Dallas News Rangers Blog**
  http://rangersblog.dallasnews.com/
  If you want the inside-the-clubhouse scoop, the Dallas News *site is the best place to go.*

TEXAS RANGER

The Lone Ranger theme song, or "William Tell Overture" as people with class call it, revs up the crowd when the Rangers are trying to mount a late-inning rally.

While We Were in Arlington
We Acted Like Star-Struck Kids

When we wrote to the Texas Rangers telling them of our seminal baseball road trip and plans to write a book, we hoped they might send us a pair of tickets to a future game. But the Rangers did us even better. They gave us field-access press credentials for batting practice. Of course, we didn't know how we were supposed to get onto the field or where we'd be allowed to stand once we got there. So we milled around in the stands for five minutes before Kevin mustered the nerve to ask a security guard how the whole deal worked.

Sports in (and around) the City

Mickey Mantle Boulevard

If you're on the way from Arlington to Kansas City or Denver, why not drive a few hundred miles out of your way to visit Commerce, Oklahoma, where Mickey Mantle grew up. The Mick was born on October 20, 1931, in Spavinaw, Oklahoma, but his family moved to a modest home in Commerce, a lead and zinc mining outpost, when he was three. His boyhood home is still standing at 319 South Quincy St., but of even greater interest is the statue of Mantle (batting right-handed) that can be found beyond the outfield fence of the youth baseball field on Mickey Mantle Boulevard/Highway 69.

"Not a bad detail to pull," Kevin said.

"I've had worse," the guard smiled, and with that we were off and running. The guard told us which gate to use and where we were allowed to go. Basically, as long as we stayed in foul territory on the infield, we'd be okay.

The Rangers had already taken their swings and the Oakland A's were hitting. So we scampered onto the field, trying to look cool, like we'd done this a thousand times before. We stood behind the cage and rubbed elbows with Jermaine Dye and Terrence Long, while Miguel Tejada raked.

We stared in amazement at each hitter, like we'd never watched anyone hit a baseball before. Man, did the ball jump off those bats. And standing that close, the pitches, considered "meat" to the big leaguers, looked pretty fast to us.

Josh spent most of his time trying to pilfer a ball.

"Will you knock it off?" said Kevin.

"What?" Josh asked.

"It's pretty obvious you have a ball in each pocket. And do you think it looks professional to be resting your foot on a ball?"

"Well," Josh said, "those cut-off shorts you're wearing don't exactly make us look professional either."

"True enough," Kevin admitted.

"So I'm getting myself another ball."

Just as Josh was bending over to pocket another Rawlings, the Rangers manager at the time, Buck Showalter, came bounding up the dugout steps and gave him a look of consternation. Nervous and attempting to recover his dignity, Josh tossed the ball toward the mound and snapped into reporter mode, asking Buck if he could have a few minutes.

"Sure," Buck said.

"What are your favorite ballparks?" Josh asked.

"Yankee Stadium's at the top of the list," Buck said. "I also like Baltimore a lot." He paused, then said, smiling, "And I like the ballpark here in Texas. Wrigley Field . . . Fenway . . . I coached at the old Comiskey. I'll tell you the one I really like—I've broadcast from the new ballpark in Pittsburgh, and I think that's a new park that will really stand the test of time."

The dubious start aside, the interview was a real thrill for Josh, as was being down on the field for both of us. And for the record, Josh's final till was four balls, which he called "a fair day's work."

COLORADO ROCKIES, COORS FIELD

DENVER, COLORADO
605 MILES TO KANSAS CITY
820 MILES TO PHOENIX
850 MILES TO ST. LOUIS
915 MILES TO MINNEAPOLIS

A Rocky Mountain High

The Rocky Mountains, which rise beyond Coors Field's left and center-field walls, provide as spectacular a backdrop for a ballgame as travelers will find in this great wide land of ours. As the sun sinks behind the snow-capped peaks, an orange glow illuminates baseball's magical twilight hour. There may be no more beautiful setting in American sports. With this breathtaking view well worth the cost of admission on its own, fans at Coors Field receive the additional treat of getting to watch a baseball game. And not just any game. At Coors, fans are practically guaranteed a highly entertaining game, full of offense. Sure, the once gaudy homer totals for which the park was originally known have declined somewhat thanks to the introduction of a ball-soaking humidor hidden within the bowels of the stadium, but rest assured, runs will be scored, often and in bunches, when you're in town. And no lead will be safe until the final out. This is mile-high baseball we're talking about, where long flies morph into home runs, where the curve ball flattens out, and where the deeper than usual outfield fences result in gaps that leave enough room for a skilled pilot to land a 727 between the outfielders. For the record, the ballpark measures 424 feet to right-center, 415 to straightaway center, and 390 to left-center. Even the foul poles—350 feet away in right and 347 in left—are distant.

Despite its enormity, Coors feels like a ballpark, and not a stadium. And it's a good thing, because Coors represents an important link in ballpark evolution. At the time of its debut in 1995, it was the first new National League ballpark to open since Montreal's Olympic Stadium in 1977, and the first baseball-only facility to be unveiled in the Senior Circuit since Dodger Stadium in 1962. Coors appeared on the MLB landscape a year after the Indians and Rangers opened their new yards in the American League, and two years before the Braves would open Turner Field. From the very start, Coors has fit well in its retro-classic lineage, blending into its warehouse district neighborhood with an attractive facade made of Colorado limestone at street level and red brick upstairs. If any ballpark has the right to feature red rock in its construction, it's this fine field in Colorado, which is flush with red rock formations. Colorado, you may recall, was once part of Mexico and its name, in Spanish, means "colored red."

Kevin: So you aced high school Spanish and you're still showing off?

Josh: Actually Mr. Bonczeck gave me a C+.

Kevin: The bastard!

Josh: Yeah. ¿Who's laughing now, Señor Bonczeck?

As fans soon discovered upon Coors' opening, the altitude at which the park is set not only gives road trippers

exterior

Photo by Kevin O'Connell

349

who may be unaccustomed to the thin air "wicked bad" ice cream headaches, only without the ice cream, but also turns ordinary-appearing fly balls into home runs and ordinary-appearing home runs into massive feats of earth-shattering strength. It didn't take long for the Rockies' fans and players to realize this and to develop a liking (well, the hitters anyway) for this special breed of hardball. After the expansion Rockies spent their first two seasons at Mile High Stadium, the first game at Coors took place on April 26, 1995. Appropriately, the Rockies and Mets combined to hang twenty runs on the scoreboard, with the home team prevailing 11–9 in fourteen innings. And that was just the beginning. In 1996, the Rockies and their opponents set a new Major League record, smacking 271 dingers in eighty-one games at Coors. The previous record of 248 had been established at Wrigley Field of Los Angeles, where the expansion Angels played in 1961 before moving temporarily to Dodger Stadium, and then, ultimately, to Anaheim Stadium. But the Rockies and their opponents weren't done yet. With the Steroid Era in full swing and the air oh so thin in Denver, the new record fell in 1999. That year, Coors rooters witnessed a whopping 303 home runs or, to put that in perspective, 3.79 long balls per game. In comparison, the Rockies and their opponents hit just 157 home runs in the Rockies' eighty-one road games that season, or 1.92 per game.

It came as no surprise then, when the 1998 All-Star Game took place at Coors—during the so-called "Year of the Home Run"—and the two teams combined for a Midsummer Classic record of 21 runs. The American League prevailed, posting a 13-8 W behind an MVP performance from Roberto Alomar, after Robby's older brother, Sandy, had won the trophy the previous summer.

Josh: For the record, the game featured about fifty guys we suspect of PED use.

Kevin: But our publisher won't let us print their names.

Josh: Probably a wise call. The last thing we need is for Roger Clemens or Barry Bonds to sue us for character defamation.

Kevin: Agreed. That would be bad.

As the nightly installments of home run derby continued, it didn't take long for people to realize Coors was a launching pad. Hence, the park's "Coors Canaveral" nickname in its early years. Remarkably, though, before big league ball arrived in Denver, no one had worried much about the effects of the city's elevation on the game. No one, that is, but original Rockies manager Don Baylor. When the hulking skipper suggested that special high-altitude balls might be needed for games in Denver, his words of wisdom were

fluffed off. After seven years of double-figure run totals, the doubters were finally ready to listen in 2002, though, and the league approved the Rockies' request to bend the rules a bit. That year, the equipment staff started storing its boxes of official game balls in a humidor at 40 percent humidity in the hopes that the soggy balls (which are imperceptibly heavier and drier on the exterior) wouldn't fly as far. There was only a slight drop-off in homers, but according to our sources several members of the home team smoked exceptionally dank stogies all season long. The fact is, they could soak the Rockies' game balls in tar and vinegar and they'd still be flying out of Coors. In 2010, for example, the Rockies and their opponents combined for 1.496 home runs per game, which was second only to the dingers surrendered at U.S. Cellular Field to the White Sox and their opponents. The "Cell" gave it up to the tune of 1.545 long balls per game, but keep in mind, it is an American League park and faced a season-long assault by designated hitters unlike Coors. So even if it's not off-the-charts homer-happy anymore, it's still safe to say Coors is a homer haven.

But it isn't just the prevalence of home runs that makes Coors a graveyard to once promising pitching careers. Yes, a batted ball that travels four hundred feet at sea level will carry 5 to 10 percent farther (420 or 440 feet) a mile above sea level. But more than just that, breaking balls don't break as sharply in the lower-density air, enabling Coors batters to tee off on curveballs and sliders that might otherwise elude the fat part of their bat. To make matters worse, line drives shoot up those wide Coors outfield gaps, forcing outfielders to play a step deeper at Coors than they ordinarily would. This means even poorly struck bloopers are more apt to fall in for hits between the infielders and distant outfielders.

As a result, the Colorado club perennially ranks near the top of the NL in runs scored and near the bottom in runs prevented. These trends affect the Rockies' ability to compete financially with other teams in two ways. First, the Rockies must overpay to lure qualified free-agent pitchers to Colorado. Second, they must overpay their own offensive stars who expect big contracts after putting up inflated stats that are the product of playing eighty-one games per season in Denver.

The thin air has also affected the way fantasy baseball owners across the country manage their squads. Savvy owners (read: super-nerdy like Josh) never draft Rockies pitchers, but load up on Rockies hitters. Once the season begins, the objective is to bench any pitcher on your roster whose team is heading into a series at Coors, and activate any batter whose team is playing in Denver. Even when Tim

Lincecum—the staff ace of Josh's Ultimate Baseballers—is scheduled to pitch at Coors, Josh gives him a night off. It's just too much of a ratio stat risk to let even "the Freak" pitch in Lando Calrissian's "Cloud City."

Kevin: Nice old-school *Star Wars* reference.

Josh: I always liked Lando. He's one of the few Armenians who have been to outer space.

Kevin: What about NASA's James Philip Bagian?

Josh: Good Lord you can be infuriating.

But never mind the fantasy baseball and *Star Wars* banter. Besides sogging their balls, we challenged ourselves to wonder, how else could the Rockies compensate for the thin air? A natural reaction at first blush might be to move back the fences still farther from the plate, but that would force outfielders to play even deeper, which would result in even more dying quail singles and stretch doubles. Home run stats would decline, but batting averages and runs per game would not.

Josh suggests growing the infield grass four inches high to turn potential ground ball singles into ground outs. Another brilliant Josh idea is to add ten feet in height to the outfield fences by installing see-through Homer-Dome-style Plexiglas extensions to the wall tops. These shields would turn some of those fly ball homers into long doubles.

Kevin thinks the Rockies should take away the first few rows of seats down at field level to enlarge the already expansive foul territory and increase the number of foul pops. He also thinks batters should have to put their noses on their bat handles and spin around three times before stepping into the batter's box to hit.

No doubt, balls would still fly out of Coors, but with these modifications we think pitchers would have more of a fighting chance. In the meantime, the Rockies should teach every pitcher in their player development system how to throw a forkball/splitter before they reach "the Show." After all, the first pitcher to throw a no-hitter at Coors was Hideo Nomo, master of the splitter, who turned the trick September 17, 1996, pitching for the Dodgers.

To put in perspective how altitudinous Coors Field is, consider that prior to the arrival of Major League Baseball in Denver, Atlanta-Fulton County Stadium held the distinction of being the loftiest yard in the bigs at one thousand feet above sea level. Coors is 5,259 feet above the waves, and that's after you subtract twenty-one feet because the playing field is below the street outside. A row of purple seats amid the otherwise green seats of the upper deck—Row 20—marks the mile-high plateau. We know what you're thinking, and the answer is "no." The ballpark is too well populated to ever consider joining the "mile-high club" in its stands, no matter how cute and/or adventurous your partner may be.

Speaking of big crowds, Coors welcomed 49,983 fans through its gates for the first World Series game ever played in Denver on October 27, 2007. And the ballpark lived up to its billing as an ERA killer. The Red Sox and Rockies banged out twenty-six hits and combined for fifteen runs. After that 10-5 Red Sox win, however, the Red Sox posted a more modest 4-3 victory in Game 4 to sweep the upstart Rockies, who had won twenty-one of twenty-two games down the stretch, including a one-game playoff with the Padres to decide the NL Wild Card.

Despite bowing in the October Classic, that magical summer of 2007 represented a glorious coming of age moment for Denver as a baseball city. It had been a long time, and a lot of hard work, in coming. After Major League Baseball announced Denver was one of six cities being considered for an expansion franchise, city voters passed a .1 percent sales tax increase in 1990 to finance construction of a new ballpark, in the event MLB awarded the city a team. The other expansion sites under consideration were Buffalo, Orlando, Washington, D.C., Tampa/St. Petersburg, and Miami.

The next year, Denver and Miami were chosen to become the first NL expansion teams since the Expos and Padres joined the Senior Circuit in 1969. The Rockies commissioned architectural firm HOK, fresh off its success in Baltimore, to design a ballpark befitting Denver's downtown warehouse setting. In the interim, the team played at Mile High Stadium, the former home of the NFL's Denver Broncos and Triple-A Denver Zephyrs, who were a Milwaukee affiliate for years. Denver was awarded a team largely due to its history of supporting the Zephyrs (1985–1992) and the Denver Bears before them (1955–1962, 1969–1984). After Denver broke ground on Coors Field in October 1992, the Zephyrs moved to New Orleans where they remain.

In 1993, the Rockies set a new record for most wins by a first-year team, going 67 and 95. But the big news wasn't the team's sixth-place finish in the seven-team National League West (the Padres were 61-101 that year). Instead, the Rockies made headlines for finishing atop the game's attendance ledger. Playing at Mile High Stadium, they drew more than eighty thousand fans to the season opener—an 11-4 victory over the Expos—and the crowds kept coming. By season's end, nearly four and a half million people had visited the converted football field to watch Major League Baseball in the Rocky Mountain air. In two seasons at Mile High, the Rockies averaged an astounding fifty-seven thousand fans per game. For its efforts, Mile High was tapped for a date with the wrecking ball shortly after the Rockies moved next door and the Broncos moved to brand new Invesco Field.

But due to the remarkable fan support at Mile High, the construction of Coors Field was modified to increase capacity from the originally planned forty-three thousand seats to more than fifty thousand, bringing the total cost of building the yard to $215 million. Despite the work stoppage of 1994, which adversely affected attendance in many cities after baseball resumed, the extra seats in Colorado were filled night in and night out in 1995. The Colorado team went on to attract more than three million fans in each of its first nine seasons. The club had never played before a home crowd of less than thirty thousand, in fact, before doing so in 2002. Nowadays, the Rockies typically finish among the top ten teams in baseball in terms of average nightly attendance, attracting about thirty-five thousand per game, which puts them pretty close to the three-million mark by each season's end.

More than just being a beautiful park that introduces spectators to a version of the game that is a little bit different than the breed of ball we enjoy practically everywhere else, Coors Field also sits amidst a lower downtown Denver neighborhood that adds quite a bit of excitement and flavor to the game-day experience. Just as LoDo's impact on a baseball excursion to Coors cannot be overstated, Coors's impact on LoDo must be acknowledged. What was a rundown part of the city before big league ball's arrival, has become a trendy hangout for visitors and locals who appreciate the fine restaurants and brew pubs that operate

in the renovated warehouse buildings. The centerpiece of the whole neighborhood, of course, is a ballpark that looks almost like an old warehouse itself from the exterior. The park offers the total game-day experience: a hip urban entertainment district, a festive pregame plaza, seats with great sight lines, and a ballpark rife with unique local flavor. So enjoy your visit.

Trivia Timeout

Tree-line: Who scored the winning run for the Rockies in their 2007 one-game playoff against the Padres?
Snow-line: In how many series sweeps were the Rockies involved during the 2007 playoffs?
Summit: What are Rocky Mountain oysters?
Look for the answers in the text.

Getting a Choice Seat

What was once a difficult ticket to find has become readily more available. Although the typical summer crowds of thirty-five thousand to forty thousand may be the equivalents of sellouts at the smaller parks in Boston or Pittsburgh, at spacious Coors such respectable gatherings still leave abundant open seats. So picking out a seat that suits your tastes and fits your budget should be easy, right? Think again. Not only do the Rockies divide the Coors stands into seventeen different pricing tiers, but they price these categories differently depending upon which opposing team is in town and what time of year the game is taking place. There are four different pricing tiers, as listed here in ascending (cheapest to priciest) order: Value, Premium, Classic, and Opening Day. We'd need Ph.D.s in statistics to explain exactly what this means to you, the average American ticket-buyer. And between us, all we have are two Masters of Fine Arts degrees in Creative Writing and Kevin's welding certificate. However, you should be able to use your smarts to assess whether the game you've chosen is going to rate on the higher or lower end of the pricing scale. You can assume that if it's summer and a quality opponent is in town, you'll be paying top dollar. If you're heading to Denver for an April matchup between the Rockies and the Pirates, on the other hand, you'll likely be paying the discount price. In a sense, we suppose this is equitable. But it can get confusing. At least the outfield Rockpile seats are always $4.00—the same as when Coors opened. The hottest tickets are for games against the Cardinals and Cubs, owing to the larger number

Rockpile seats

Photo by Kevin O'Connell

Seating Capacity: 50,445
Ticket Office: http://colorado.rockies.mlb.
com/ticketing/index.jsp?c_id=col
Seating Chart: http://colorado.rockies.mlb.
com/col/ballpark/seating_pricing.jsp

of transplanted Illinoisans and Missourians in Denver. Inter-league games also draw well, especially those infrequent matchups the Rockies have with the Red Sox, Yankees and White Sox.

As a rule, the sight lines at Coors are superb. The Club Level is set far enough behind the lower bowl so as to avoid the type of overhang complications that often afflict the back rows of first-level seats at other parks. Likewise, the Upper Level is set far enough from the field to prevent the underhang from being a factor in most upstairs sections, with the exception being those composing the Upper Right Field Reserved.

Field Level

INFIELD BOX (SECTIONS 120–141)

Upon visiting Coors Field we are always struck by how wide the seats are and how much room there is in the aisles leading to the seats. This is true in the lower bowl and throughout the park. You really can't go wrong with a seat in these primo sections around the infield. Shoot for Section 131 or 132 if you want to sit right behind the catcher, or for 120 to call the bang-bang plays at first, or 140 or 141 to see if you can crack the third base coach's code.

Thanks to a low retaining wall between the first row and the field, there are hardly any blighted views on the first level.

If you're haggling with a scalper on a rainy night, shoot for a seat under the overhang of the Club Level in Rows 29–38. As far as overhangs go, this is not an obtrusive one, but if you're the type of fan who likes to see the whole flight of the ball on those Major League pop-ups around the plate, we recommend avoiding Rows 34–38.

MIDFIELD BOX (SECTIONS 118, 119, 142, 143)

What is this, a soccer pitch? In one of the few gaffes committed in building and labeling their beautiful baseball park, the Rocky Mountain baseball neophytes chose to categorize the seating sections along the foul lines in medium-depth right and left field as Midfield Boxes. But don't fret. As long as you don't have your hopes set on seeing a header or bicycle

kick, you'll enjoy a first-rate view of the action from these field-level seats. A minor drawback is that the seats along the left-field line point fans toward right field, and the seats along the right-field line point fans toward left. The seats are angled to a degree, in an effort to provide fans a better view of the infield, but Kevin still had a stiff neck after sitting in Section 116.

As is the case in the Infield Boxes, the rows range from 1–38, with the first row in each section costing the same as the 38th. So shoot for seats down near the field.

OUTFIELD BOX (SECTIONS 110–117, 144–150)

Out past the Midfield Boxes, the Outfield Boxes are still quality first level seats. But in our opinion they're priced a bit too high, given their proximity to the Pavilion seats in left-field home run territory and the Right Field Boxes in long-ball land in right. Both of these straight-on seating locales provide equally solid views for less money than the Outfield Boxes. As a rule, the left-field seats (144–150) offer a better view of the left-field corner and entire field than the right-field seats (110–117) do of the right-field corner and field, because of the higher retaining wall between the field and seats in right.

RIGHT FIELD BOX (SECTIONS 105–109)

Located above the out-of-town scoreboard in home run territory, these seats provide an excellent view of the game. Seats in Rows 10 and back are beneath the overhang of the Club deck. This is worth remembering on a rainy night. The obstruction from the overhang is negligible. We suggest avoiding Section 109 where the right-field foul pole interferes with some views. Seats 1–5 in all rows of the section provide a particularly poor view of home plate, while the pole blocks other portions of the field for those sitting elsewhere in the higher-numbered seats. Section 105, beside the bullpens in straight-away right, is ideal for ball hawks. So bring your glove. The ball carries well here, you know.

PAVILION (SECTIONS 151–160)

If you don't mind sitting on a bleacher bench (with a back), then the Pavilion is a legit option. It is not only lower to the field than the Right Field Boxes but offers a view of the out-of-town scores. Wisely, the ballpark designers did not place seats behind the left-field foul pole, where instead there is a runway used for field equipment. As a result, the pole doesn't interfere with the views for fans in left. We especially liked the Pavilion seats near the left-field line in Sections 151–153, which are much closer to the infield than Sections 156–160 in deep left-center.

Leave the (Unsliced) Watermelon at Home

The Rockies' website lists a number of items that fans are prohibited from bringing into Coors Field. Among these are such no-brainers as illegal drugs, fireworks, weapons, animals and beach balls. But there are some weird ones too. To wit, any fruit or vegetable larger than a grapefruit must be sliced! And confetti and wineskins are strictly prohibited. Wineskins? Are people really using boda bags to transport alcohol to baseball games these days? We had no idea! We also had to laugh at some of the items that *are* permitted at Coors. Brooms of six feet or less are permitted so that fans can celebrate those series sweeps. But could you bring one to the first game of a series, we wonder? Motorcycle helmets are also allowed. To their credit, the Rockies allow fans to bring individually portioned food items to the park, which many other clubs disallow these days to in effect force fans to buy the overpriced ballpark food. If you'd like to learn more about what you can and cannot bring into Coors Field, review the full list at: http://colorado.rockies.mlb.com/col/ballpark/information/index .jsp?content=security.

Second Level

CLUB LEVEL (SECTIONS 214–227, 234–247)

The Club Level shares the same deck that the press box is on. The deck is set a bit farther from the field than the Club decks at most three-level stadiums, but on the plus side is relatively low, which keeps fans in the flow of the game. Sections 221–227 on the first-base line and 234–241 on the third-base line are the pick of the litter and sell as Club Infield tickets. The Club sections that run from the corner sacks into deep foul territory sell as Club Outfield tickets.

RIGHT FIELD MEZZANINE (SECTIONS 201–209)

Beginning in right field where the Club seats end, the Right Field Mezzanine offers solid views for the cost. We recommend aiming for the first or second row, perched above the right fielder. Even in the back row—Row 12—the overhang of the upper deck is not a factor. In Rows 6 and higher a minimal underhang blocks the view of the right-field warning track, but it's not too bothersome. Sections 201–204 are above the bullpens in straight-away right, while 205–209 are above the Outfield Boxes and Right Field Boxes.

ROCKPILE (SECTIONS 401–403)

These $4.00 center-field bleachers aren't a bad deal when you consider that a comparable bleacher ticket at Fenway

Park costs about $30. Then again, at Fenway the bleachers are composed of individual chair back seats. But the view really isn't bad from this distance perch at Coors. Because the sections are well elevated and set back from the center-field fence, the field is not at all obstructed by an underhang or by the outfield fence itself. Though these seats bear the 400 Level stigma, they are actually located a full level below the 300 Level seats in right field. The downside is that unlike the first-level Pavilion sections in left, the Rockpile seats are plain old metal benches without backrests. But Rockpile ticket holders are free to roam the rest of the park and to settle where they may.

A limited number of Rockpile tickets are always available on game day. They go on sale two-and-a-half hours before the game at Gate A. If the game is otherwise sold out, be sure to arrive early to wait in line.

UPPER LEVEL (301–346)

If you're in Colorado primarily to gaze at the snow-capped Rockies and baseball is your second priority, consider sitting in the Upper Level. The mountains are visible from all upper

Kevin and Josh

Photo by Josh Pahigian/Kevin O'Connell

seats, and particularly from those on the first-base and right-field side of the park. Ironically, the worst seats in the house—those in Upper Right Field Reserved Sections 301–304—offer the most panoramic and breathtaking views of the mountain range.

Generally speaking, the Upper Level at Coors is steep and expansive. Rows 1–9 hang below the midlevel concourse and are called Lower Reserved seats—even though they're in the Upper Level. We found this a tad confusing. Most ballparks call the seats in this area "Upper Boxes" or "View Boxes." There's nothing "lower" about these seats.

The Upper Reserved seats begin behind the Lower Reserved seats and span Rows 10–25. Rows 19 and higher are beneath the sunroof for those in search of a shady or dry spot—depending on the weather.

Even all the way out in Section 347 in left field, the Upper Reserved seats are free of underhang obstructions. It's another story entirely, however, in right field, where Sections 301–315 are tarnished by the extension of the deck below. The right-field warning track is hidden from view for those in Sections 311–315, while even more of right field and center field disappear for those in 301–310. These seats are to be avoided like Rocky Mountain Oysters—but more on that so-called delicacy in our food review.

No alcohol is allowed in Section 342 on the third base side, so teetotalers had best aim for tickets in this Family Section.

Scalpers Abound

Scalpers can be found peddling their wares on the corner of Blake and 20th Streets. They usually have wads of tickets, so don't overpay. Remember, if the game isn't sold out, you can usually do better than face value on the street.

Before/After the Game

Denver is a decidedly Western town. Though Los Angeles is farther west and is often billed as the center of the *Urban* West, Denver epitomizes the *Old* West. Josh likens it to the Cactus League hotbed of Scottsdale, which projects a similar gun-slinger's vibe. In Denver, you'll find stores to buy grain for your cattle, a saddle for your horse, and chaps for your rugged ridin' legs. The atmosphere still exists in LoDo, whereas deeper into downtown the city becomes more generically metro-stuffy. So be sure to wear your Stetson and cowboy boots to LoDo and spit some "tobbaccy" juice if the spirit moves you. No one will think any less of you for your eccentricities.

The Race to the Plate

With the passage of time, every MLB franchise creates its share of magical moments that contemporary fans witness and immediately swear they'll one day tell their grandkids about in intricate detail. Josh will one day tell the heirs to his Topps, Donruss and Fleer 1983–1998 baseball card collection of the incredible ALCS of 2004 when the Red Sox came back from a deficit of three games to none to shock the archrival Yankees and forever put to rest the ghost of Babe Ruth that had been haunting the BoSox for generations. Kevin's seminal Mariners moment occurred in 1995 when the "Refuse to Lose" M's beat the Angels in a one-game playoff to claim the AL West title. For Colorado seam-heads, the moment when time stood still in Denver was the occasion of the one-game playoff to decide the NL Wild Card winner at Coors in 2007. Not only did the game last five hours and thirty-seven minutes, and span thirteen innings, but it forced Colorado fans to confront the agony of defeat before suddenly delivering unto them and their team a reprieve in the most dramatic fashion imaginable. The Rockies' hard work down the stretch in 2007 seemed about to be rendered moot as the Padres scored two runs in the top of the thirteenth to take an 8-6 lead, then sent all-everything closer Trevor Hoffman to the mound for the bottom of the frame. But the game's all-time saves leader surrendered doubles to Kaz Matsui and Troy Tulowitzki, then a game-tying triple to Matt Holliday. After an intentional walk, the game ended amidst controversy, when Holliday was ruled safe at home on a sacrifice fly to right field by Jamey Carroll. Holliday dove into the dish head-first and collided so violently with Padres catcher Michael Barrett that he appeared to be temporarily knocked unconscious. While home plate umpire Tim McClelland ruled "safe," Holliday lay motionless near the plate while the Padres scrambled to retrieve the throw from right fielder Brian Giles and persisted that Holliday had never touched the plate. After the men in black conferred, it was decided that McClelland had made the correct call.

The Padres went home and the Rockies went on to sweep the Phillies and Diamondbacks in the National League playoffs. They ran into an equally hot Red Sox club in the World Series, though, and the rest, as they say, is history. The Red Sox swept the Rockies, leaving Colorado with an 8-4 post-season record. That was good for the best post-season winning percentage (.667) ever for a team that didn't win the World Series.

Coors Field is located at the corner of 20th and Blake Street amongst a bevy of renovated brick warehouses. The hood was reportedly a bit grimy before the ballpark was built, as it had been decades since original road trippers Jack Kerouac and Neal Cassidy roamed the streets, hooting and hollering into the mountain air. But Denver's beauty of a ballpark has had a delightful impact on its surroundings. If the yards in Baltimore and Cleveland were the prototypes for the ballpark as a catalyst for urban revitalization, Coors is the master example. What were once abandoned warehouses and pawn shops have reopened as hip yuppie bars and have been converted into trendy loft apartments within a lively entertainment district.

Getting to Coors Field

The ballpark is accessible from Interstate 25 via Exit 213 (Park Avenue). From the east or west, take Interstate 70 to Interstate 25 first. Street parking is not an option on most days because the metered spots on 19th and 20th allow only two-hour parking and remain active until 10:00 p.m. However, on Sundays these meters are free all day. The team run parking lots charge $13 (Lot B) or $15 (Lot A). Lot A is a bit closer to the main entrance, hence the extra cost. But there are also several private lots in the neighborhood that charge less than the team does. The cheapest one we found was the bus station lot on the corner of 19th and Curtis Street. There was also a discount lot at the corner of 18th and Market Street.

The Regional Transportation Department (RTD) offers bus service to the game from points throughout Denver, while the Light Rail drops fans at 20th and Welton Street as part of the RockiesRide program.

RockiesRide Map: www.rtd-denver.com/PDF_Files/RockiesRide_map_and_fares.pdf

Outside Attractions

BALLS APLENTY

LoDo boasts more than ninety restaurants and bars and is also the home of more than thirty art galleries. Josh counted them to be sure, while Kevin just took the local chamber of commerce at its word. In any case, it makes good sense that travelers find plenty of examples of urban art within LoDo, including an especially apropos piece at the pedestrian bridge that spans Wynkoop Street. A colorful arch rises over the walkway celebrating the evolution of the ball. It offers representations of baseballs, tetherballs, meatballs, mothballs, matzo balls, cheese balls, masquerade balls, crystal balls, beach balls, dust balls, snowballs, rubber-band balls, lacrosse balls, jai alai balls, soccer balls, pearl balls, screwballs, typewriter balls, Christmas tree balls, foosballs, volleyballs, snooker balls, bowling balls, punch balls, skittle balls, kick balls, fireballs, racket balls, tennis balls, basketballs, softballs, roulette balls, wrecking balls, laurel balls, eyeballs, ball-point pens, spitballs, billiard balls, skeet balls, and more. The sculpture was produced by local artist Lonnie Hanzon, whose work can be found throughout LoDo. It was commissioned in 1995 by the Denver Metropolitan Major League Baseball Stadium District.

Josh: I hate to be a ball-buster, but where are the Rocky Mountain Oysters?

Kevin: It's a celebration of balls, not seafood. You should smarten up.

Josh: Okay, wise guy. I'll show you who's smart.

Kevin: C'mon, I want to try a pint of that Railyard Ale before the game.

TIME CHECK

A brick clock tower rises above the home plate entrance on 20th Street. The numbers on the face appear in Rockies Purple, while a purple sunshield provides a small roof over the face. This wonderfully understated finishing touch reminded Kevin of Ebbets Field, and Josh that it was almost game time.

UNION STATION
1701 Wynkoop St.

Just a short walk from the park, fans find glorious Union Station, which dates back all the way to 1881. It too, features an old-time clock beneath its arching orange sign. Inside, visitors find Amtrak trains, public restrooms, long wooden benches and a throwback concession stand. There is also a large model train set downstairs courtesy of the Denver Society for Model Railroaders. To be clear, we are not model railroaders ourselves, but we found the train set well worth the time it took to seek it out in the basement.

Kevin: There's something about a train that puts me in the mood for baseball.

Josh: Must be a West Coast thing.

Kevin: True, we Seattle fans like our train, but the folks in Houston dig theirs too.

Josh: Like I said—a West Coast thing.

Kevin: To you New Englanders anything west of Pittsfield, Mass. counts as "West Coast," huh?

Josh: The only Choo Choo that puts me in the mood for a game is Shin-Soo Choo.

THE PLAYER

Some players are synonymous with their city: Ted Williams and Boston; Babe Ruth and New York; Sandy Koufax and L.A. The Rockies, however, haven't been around long enough to ordain any statue-worthy icons of their own. In fact, as of press time the team's only retired number was that belonging to Jackie Robinson, whose No. 42 is universally retired throughout MLB (or will be when Mariano Rivera finally retires). In the absence of a statue or two outside dedicated to a particular player, the Rockies offer a statue named "The Player." This attractive nine-footer portrays a baby-faced player with a bat over his right shoulder. It was commissioned by the Denver Rotary Club and is dedicated to the memory of groundbreaking baseball executive Branch Rickey, who championed Robinson's integration of the game. Each year since 1992, the Rotary Club has crowned a Branch Rickey Award Winner to acknowledge the big league player, coach or executive whose contributions to society reflect the courage and generosity of spirit Mr. Rickey so nobly embodied. Past winners include Dave Winfield (1992), Ozzie Smith (1994), Tony Gwynn (1995), Paul Molitor (1998), Jamie Moyer (2004), Tommy Lasorda (2006), and Vernon Wells (2010). Their names, along with all of the other winners', are etched onto the base of the bronze statue.

ROCK GARDENS

Huge flower pots reside on the plaza outside the main entrance beneath the clock tower. These hold small spruce trees as well as piles of baseball-sized boulders that add a distinctive touch to the area.

Kevin: Check it out. They're growing rocks.

Josh: Well, they are the Rockies.

BALLPARK TOURS

The Rockies offer a seventy-five-minute tour of Coors Field that takes fans into the Club Level, Suite Level, press box, clubhouses and dugouts. The Tour departs from Gate D at the corner of 20th and Blake Street and costs a reasonable price of $7.00. While on the clubhouse level, we recommend checking out the bronze stars between the two locker rooms that honor each Rockies player who has made the National League All-Star squad. You'll observe multiple stars for such repeat All-Stars as Dante Bichette, Brian Fuentes, Andres Galarraga, Todd Helton, Matt Holliday, and Larry Walker.

For more information or to buy tickets for the Tour, visit: http://colorado.rockies.mlb.com/col/ballpark/tours/index.jsp.

SPORTS FAN
1962 Blake St.
www.sportsteams.com/bColoradob-W6C143.aspx
This memorabilia and apparel store features old-time jerseys and hats for all four major sports. If you've been looking for that heinous old-school Denver Nuggets jersey with the rainbow-band over the city skyline, this might be your chance to pick it up. Negro League and college teams are also well represented. Our favorite items were the Colorado Rockies salt and pepper shakers shaped like beer bottles.

Watering Holes and Outside Eats

Second among Major League neighborhoods only to Wrigleyville, LoDo houses scores of bars and restaurants. Some predate Coors Field, while others have sprung up as part of the urban renaissance the ballyard incited. Offering open warehouse settings, a range of foods in the Southwestern tradition, and local microbrews, the eating and drinking establishments of Lower Downtown compose a baseball fanatic's paradise. Arrive early and stay late. Cruise down 20th, Blake and Wynkoop and see what strikes you. Hop from bar to bar, and eat hearty! The Mexican fare is damned good, at least by our standards.

As was also the case in Cubbie Land, there are too many fine LoDo watering holes for us to do them all justice in this format. But here are a few of our favorites.

JACKSON'S
1520 20th St.
http://jacksonsdenver.com/
This enormous warehouse hangout offers three first-level barrooms as well as an outdoor patio at street level and another on the roof. The bar predates the ballpark by nearly twenty years and has long been a favorite of Denver sports fans. Jackson's may be your best bet to catch an out-of-town game on the big screen via satellite. It is also a fine place to check out tipsy hard-bodied females, to score All You Can Drink specials on Thursday and Friday nights and to have a pregame brunch on Saturdays and Sundays.

EL CHAPULTEPEC
1962 Market St.
This is the first place we visit whenever we're in LoDo. Pre-existing the ballpark by many decades, El Chapultepec (literally, "the hill of the grasshopper," according to Kevin, who otherwise can't speak a lick of Spanish) combines dirt-cheap Mexican with live jazz in the wee hours. Josh favors the beef burrito and green chili, while Kevin goes for a smothered burrito and bottle of Fat Tire. You'll get a kick out of the autographed pictures hanging in the barroom of famous visitors like Branford Marsalis and Bill Clinton.

Kevin: Seems time they put our picture on the wall. We plug this place enough.

Josh: Yeah, that will always be the dream.

THE LAUGHING DOG DELI
1925 Blake St.

This is our second-favorite place to grab a bite before a game at Coors. For our money, the comic canine's best offerings are the delicious Chicken Parm sandwich, the Ellis Island (prosciutto, roasted red peppers, fresh mozzarella, basil, and pesto parmesan), and the Staten Island (smoked turkey, fresh mozzarella, basil, and pesto). As for the hilarious hyena's motto: "Eat well, play ball, take naps"? We say, what else is there in life? Oh yeah, "watch ball." How could we forget?

LODO'S BAR & GRILL
1946 Market St.
www.lodosbarandgrill.com/denver_home.php

This warehouse hangout offers cheap eats and a rooftop patio with a view of the ballpark. But we have time to talk about the park later. Let's get back to the food. From steaks and seafood, to barbecue platters, to burgers and hoagies and Mexican, there's a great variety here. Josh recommends the Buffalo Fries, while Kevin gives two thumbs up to the Denver Burger—a half-pounder that comes topped with avocado, fried onions, roasted red peppers, Jack cheese and Ranch dressing.

BRECKENRIDGE BREWERY & PUB
2220 Blake St.
www.breckbrew.com/food/pubdenver.html

The Breck Brew serves an authentic taste of the Rockies. Kevin enjoyed the Avalanche Ale, an amber with a clean-as-Colorado finish, while Josh preferred the Oatmeal Stout, which tasted like a blend of dark-roasted coffee and semi-sweet chocolate. The menu features a variety of burgers and chicken sandwiches, and Southwestern specials like burritos, and tamales. They don't sell tamales at the Coors Field concession stands anymore, so this might be your last best chance to get one while you're in town.

WYNKOOP BREWING COMPANY
1634 18th St.
www.wynkoop.com/

Aside from being Denver's oldest brewery, Wynkoop also bakes its own bread daily. How earthy-crunchy is that? The "big-mouth burgers" and "two-fisted sandwiches" are trademarks. Meanwhile, billiards, darts, and the on-site comedy club keep patrons in good spirits. According to Kevin's fine palate, the Railyard Ale and Union Hub Light Ale are engineered for perfection. Josh waited until Kevin had drunk more than a few of each and had progressed past his "beer window" before challenging him to a game of darts.

Josh: So tell me about your "beer window" theory again.

Kevin: There is a very narrow span of time, when you are a better dart player, pool player, trivia player, writer, lover—you name it—after a few brews.

Josh: And then what happens?

Kevin: Never anything good.

THE BLAKE STREET TAVERN
2301 Blake St.
www.blakestreettavern.com/

When Josh is feeling homesick and in need of fellow Red Sox fans with whom to watch the East Coast games, he heads to The Blake. Just a block north of Coors, it provides a fun, open atmosphere for pregame and postgame revelry. And the games from around the league are always on. The Green Chili Fries and Barbeque Pulled Pork Sliders are winners too.

Inside the Stadium
Ballpark Features
THE MOUNTAINSIDE

Something usually goes wrong when the designers of new ballparks opt to install local landscape displays beyond the outfield fences. These either end up looking really artificial (See: Anaheim, Styrofoam Monstrosity) or really corporate (See: Detroit, Auto Maker Batter's Eye). But at Coors, the center-field fountain and rock garden provide a classy organic touch to the park. The display includes not only the spring, but Navajo sandstones, granite-marbled river boulders, spruces, piñon pines, mahogany trees, and gamble oaks. To appreciate this unique ballpark oasis, we recommend taking a stroll out to center field on the first-level concourse, which allows fans to look down into the area and abutting bullpens. We thought it was pretty neat that there's no wall separating the visiting bullpen from the rock area.

Kevin: All they need now are a few rattlesnakes.

Josh: Some mule deer might be nice too.

Kevin: No, that would be going too far.

RETIRE LARRY WALKER NOW

The Rockies had not yet retired a single one of their former stars' uniform numbers as of this book's printing. We would like to suggest that after two decades of National League play, it's time for the franchise to honor a few of its finest.

Iconic "Blake Street Bombers" like Larry Walker (No. 33) and Todd Helton (No. 17) would seem to be great players around which to build an all-time alumni roster.

Josh: They should probably wait for "The Toddfather" to retire first.

Kevin: The Astros built statues of Bagwell and Biggio while they were playing.

Josh: Yeah, but those are the Astros.

Kevin: Meaning?

Josh: Never mind. The last thing I need is hate mail coming my way via Houston.

SMOKING GRASS

No, we're not talking about the type of grass former and current big leaguers like Bill Lee, Dmitri Young, Tim Lincecum, and Elijah Dukes have all admitted to smoking at one point or another. We're talking about the type that grows in the outfield. In Denver, it can be warmed up by an elaborate system of underground wires. The system is capable of melting away any snow that accumulates on the Coors lawn during the late-arriving spring. The lawn is also equipped with a drainage system that can handle up to five inches of rain per hour . . . or five feet of freshly melted snow.

LAVA

The gray warning track—as opposed to the red infield dirt—consists of 90 percent crushed lava and 10 percent red clay. We applaud the Rockies for not taking the easy way out and installing a porous rubber warning track, such as the kind that appears at too many big league parks these days.

THE WILD, WILD WEST

Behind the batter's eye on the first-level concourse, a long mural depicts a landscape that is uniquely representative of Colorado. The mural includes images of red rock formations, like the ones at Pike's Peak in nearby Colorado Springs, and the kind you probably remember from the old Road Runner cartoons. Also pictured on the mural are Navajo tepees, buffalo, railroad cars, miners at work, brick buildings under construction, and Mile High Stadium. This is a well-done tribute to the state and its history, and we suggest taking a pregame stroll to check it out. For those who need a nutritional incentive, plan on picking up a bag of Kettle Corn when you get there.

THE PURPLE ROW

The exact point in the Upper Deck where the elevation reaches 5,280-feet above sea level contains purple seats. All of the other seats in the top deck are forest green. To sit exactly a mile high, then, aim for any seat in Row 20. If you'd like to be *more* than a mile above the ocean waves, then aim for Row 21 and higher.

Stadium Eats

Coors Field offers traditional ballpark grub, local fare like Mexican, and Rocky Mountain Oysters. The items we tried were consistently good.

ROCKY MOUNTAIN OYSTERS (TRADEMARK FOOD)

These deep-fried balls of horror may be a Denver trademark and featured item at the stand behind Section 144, but we don't recommend them. You see, Rocky Mountain Oysters are Colorado's cruel joke on the rest of the world. Rocky Mountain Oysters are one of the reasons a book like ours is a road trip necessity. But we'll explain . . .

After making a bathroom run, Josh returned to the seats with a cardboard tray loaded with food.

Kevin: Did you get me some of those oysters?

Josh: I sure did.

Kevin: Wow, they're deep fried and they come with cocktail sauce! I just love deep fried oysters. They're huge. These are the biggest oysters I've ever seen!

Josh: And to think, they're available so far from the ocean.

Kevin: They sure are meaty. And tasty. Mmm . . . these are great. Are you sure you don't want one?

At this point, Josh burst into a fit of hysterical laughter, a fit so severe that he nearly wet himself. Actually, he did wet himself a little.

Kevin: What? What's so funny?

Josh: You'd be unbeatable on *Fear Factor.*

Finally, Kevin started to put two and two together. He examined what he was eating, then retraced Josh's steps and found his way to the stand behind Section 144. After waiting in line for a moment, he leaned forward to ask the girl behind the counter what exactly Rocky Mountain Oysters are.

Blushing, the girl replied, "Bull nuts."

Kevin: Do you mean "bull" as in a male cow and "nuts" as in testicles?

The girl nodded.

If you can get drunk enough to try these, God bless you. Otherwise, steer clear of them. And for the record, the only way Josh could earn Kevin's grudging forgiveness was by buying him four pints of Fat Tire Ale after the game. And even then, it wasn't until the road trip car rolled into Phoenix a few days later that Kevin let go of his grudge.

According to the vendor with whom we spoke, the Rockies sell about twenty-five orders of Oysters per night.

ROCKY DOG (DOG REVIEW)

The foot-long Rocky Dog comes topped with sautéed peppers, sauerkraut and onions. We were very satisfied with it, but what would you expect? It's a Hebrew National.

There are also several other types of hot dog available at the Top Dogs stands throughout the park. These include the Denver Dog (green chili, shredded cheese, jalapeño peppers), Tucson Dog (red chili, shredded cheese, sour cream), New York Dog (sauerkraut, peppers, onions, spicy mustard), Rockies Bacon Blue Dog (blue cheese crumbles, bacon bits, chopped red onion, blue cheese dressing) and Chicago Dog (tomatoes, cucumbers, peppers, celery salt, relish).

BEST OF THE REST

We bought a bag of sweet and salty **Kettle Corn** from a stand in right-center and were glad we did. Josh nearly splurged and bought the three-foot-long bag. But the smaller one, for half the price, turned out to be more than enough for the two of us.

Coors Field may not be home to the spiciest **bratwurst** in the big leagues, but it's surely home to the biggest. This grilled behemoth is a meal in and of itself.

The **Mesquite grilled chicken** from the Fanfare stand is tenderized in a subtle but unique marinade. It ranks right with the best ballpark poultry sandwiches in the Majors.

Blake Street Burrito offers a chicken burrito that rates pretty high on our big league burrito barometer, but nowhere near as good as the burrito at El Chapultepec (Note to management: Did we mention we're still waiting for you to put that autographed 8-by-10 of us on the El Chapultepec wall?).

The **Roundin' Third** stand serves a tasty homemade meatball sub and made-to-order pizzas.

And here's something we haven't seen at too many parks: a stand on the third base side offers a full range of **gluten-free options.** They serve a burger on a gluten-free bun, a chicken sandwich, brownies, and even gluten-free beer.

The **Famous Dave's** stand on the outfield concourse serves not only barbecue but **chocolate covered bacon.** We weren't brave enough to try it, though. Another stand, behind Section 223 on the Club Level, serves chocolate-covered bananas, strawberries, and marshmallows.

STADIUM SUDS

Predictably, Coors and Coors Light are the featured beers at Coors Field. But don't despair. A brewery at Coors Field actually produces an award-winning craft beer right on site. The Blue Moon Brewery at the Sandlot, behind the right-field stands, is accessible from within and outside the stadium. This is where Blue Moon was invented and is where they still mass-produce the stuff. Blue Moon, in case you haven't guessed, is owned by Coors. But don't hold that against it.

The Coors Experience

Denver is home to many transplants from other parts of the country. It took us nearly three innings to find someone in the crowd who was born and raised in Colorado—and it turned out to be the fluffy team-mascot Dinger, the triceratops. Owing to the low percentage of truly "local" locals in town, the fans don't bleed Rockies Purple quite the same way the fans in St. Louis bleed Cardinals Red or the fans in L.A. bleed Dodger Blue. We got the impression that most folks leave Coors happy as long as the Rockies and their opponents hang a few crooked numbers on the board. Great baseball may not always be on the agenda, but games at Coors are hardly ever boring. So sit back and enjoy the barrage of homers. It's the Rocky Mountain Way.

DIZZY YET?

If you travel to Denver via road or rail, chances are your body will gradually acclimate itself to the altitude as you weave your way through the mountains. But those arriving by plane should beware: Sudden immersion in the thin air can cause dizziness, nausea and extreme ass fatigue. This is no joke. We repeat, pay attention before setting out to run a pregame 5 K. The air in this town contains less oxygen than the air back home. As a result, you'll find yourself panting like a schoolboy on prom night if you break into anything more than a slow saunter on your way into the ballpark. And all of that respiration can lead to a case of dehydration. Drinking alcohol only compounds the effect, as beer consumed at high altitude affects you more than usual.

Josh: We won't even try to tell you how to adjust any baking recipes you may attempt while in town. But trust us, your times and temps will be all messed up.

Kevin: Are you serious? Do you really think our readers are going to make Toll House Cookies at their hotels?

Josh: You were the first to complain when my bundt cake didn't rise.

Kevin: Fair enough.

To counteract these effects, be sure to drink plenty of water before and after arriving in Denver. If, like Josh, you fly into town two hours before first pitch with already low H2O levels, drive straight to the ballpark, and then spend an hour dragging your butt up and down the aisles of the upper deck to scope out the sight lines for your readers, don't be surprised if you wind up retching in the Coors Field men's room.

Kevin: That's a nice image. I'm sure our readers will appreciate it.

Josh: Want some more oysters, funny man?

PLAY ME OR SPRAY ME

On hot days, ballpark staffers dressed in purple wander the lower level stands equipped with water tanks on their backs. As fans cheer, these men and women hydrate the masses with wide streams of cold water. It's not quite the outdoor shower fans enjoy on Chicago's South Side, but it's not bad. And when you consider that most of the young women in Denver keep in excellent shape by hiking, rock climbing, and mountain biking, well, it's even better. We say, soak 'em good!

ROCKY MOUNTAIN WAY

When the Rockies are one inning from victory, the ballpark tune-meister cues up Joe Walsh's "Rocky Mountain Way" on the PA and plays the first few power chords to rev up the crowd. Another chord plays to celebrate each subsequent out, then, when the final out is recorded, the song begins in full force.

Stick around for a minute and listen for the baseball reference in the later verses, when the crooner sings, "the bases are loaded and Casey's at bat . . ."

FROM SOUTH PARK TO THE SHOW

Coors Field has appeared in two episodes of the hit Comedy Central cartoon *South Park*. The show is set, of course, in the fictional town of South Park, Colorado, which is reportedly based on the real-life town of Fairplay, Colorado, a community of approximately 600 people, located 85 miles southwest of Denver. Coors Field's first appearance was in a 2002 episode entitled "Professor Chaos." In that episode, the boys take one of their new friends to a Rockies game and he commits the rather large faux pas of ordering tea and crumpets.

Cyber Super-Fans

- **The Purple Row**
  www.purplerow.com/
- **The Rockies Review**
  www.rockiesreview.com/
- **Heaven and Helton**
  http://heavenandhelton.blogspot.com/

Sports in the City

Colorado Silver Bullets

In 1994 an all-female professional baseball team called the Colorado Silver Bullets took the field for the first time. Led by Hall of Fame skipper Phil Niekro, the team was formed to expand hardball opportunities for women of all ages by demonstrating that ladies could more than hold their own on a regulation diamond with a little white ball, and not just on a little diamond with an oversized white ball.

The Bullets originated in Knoxville, Tennessee, but when the Coors Brewing Company agreed to sponsor them on behalf of the Coors Light brand, they moved to Colorado.

Barnstorming across the country, the Bullet Girls made national headlines playing minor league, semipro, and collegiate men's teams. They went 6–38 in their inaugural campaign, playing in Major League facilities like San Francisco's Candlestick Park, the Oakland Coliseum, the Seattle Kingdome, and Mile High Stadium.

Kevin: An argument could be made that none of those were actual "Major League" stadiums, at least not according to how that term is currently defined.

Josh: Harsh words. And from a Mariners' fan no less.

The Bullets improved steadily over the ensuing four seasons before disbanding in 1998 when Coors, which had spent more than $3 million to back them, opted not to extend its sponsorship. There's no denying, however, that the Bullets pried the door open just a little wider for women who wanted to play hardball at a high level. Two of their alumnae, Lee Anne Ketcham and Julie Croteau, went on to play for the Maui Stingrays of the Hawaiian Winter Baseball League, and in 1997, Ila Borders, a left-handed pitcher who had posted a 4–5 record at Whittier College, became the first woman to pitch in a men's professional game when she appeared for the independent league St. Paul Saints.

Kevin: One of these days a female knuckle-baller is going to come along and blaze a path to the big leagues.

Josh: It could happen sooner than you think.

Kevin: I've got two little girls at home I could teach to throw the knuckler. Maeve and Rory, dad has a new plan for a college scholarship!

Three years later, the gang returned to Coors in "The Losing Edge," which portrayed their *Bad-News-Bears*-style Little League squad advancing to the regional tournament in Denver. The boys were overjoyed when they lost, because that meant they wouldn't have to waste their entire summer vacation playing in the national Little League tournament. Unfortunately, though, Kenny was killed during the filming of the latter episode.

GET INTERACTIVE . . .

Behind the bullpens on the first level is the Coors Field Interactive Area. Whether tee-ball is your thing, video batting cages, or speed pitch, this is a great place to work out some of that excess energy you've accumulated during all those hours riding in the car. Just remember what we said about the thin air, though, and don't overdo it.

The Interactive Area also houses a Fantasy Broadcast Booth where fans can record themselves doing play-by-play for a half-inning while the game is in progress.

Josh: This is easy enough to do at home. Just turn down the volume on the tube, press the little red button on your microcassette recorder, and start yapping.

Kevin: Actually, I'm pretty sure there's a smartphone app for that nowadays. You're the only person I know who still uses a microcassette recorder.

Josh: I was wondering why I can't find fresh tapes at Staples anymore.

Kevin: I think they file them with the 8-tracks in back.

CLEAN CATCH

Whenever a fan catches a foul ball or home run, a ballpark staffer presents them with a special Rockies pin commemorating the accomplishment. Batting practice grabs don't count, nor do catches made after the ball bounces off another fan, an umbrella, railing or seat.

While We Were in Colorado
We Committed an Embarrassing Breach of Clubhouse Etiquette

Prior to visiting Coors Field for the first time in 2003, the greatest thrill of our seminal trip had been watching batting practice in Arlington while standing on the field, donning press passes. The Rangers had granted us field access, something none of the other teams had been willing to do, and we responded by respectfully watching the A's and Rangers take BP, while being careful not to create any scenes.

A few weeks later, the Rockies did us one better. Not only did Colorado grant us pregame field access, but the team (foolishly?) granted us clubhouse access as well. And boy, did we ever drop the ball.

Giddy as Shriners at a Fredericks of Hollywood convention, we wandered wide-eyed down the Club House Level corridors beneath the stands before the game. We were about to set foot into a big league clubhouse for the first time and we had no idea what to expect.

"Who was that who just walked past?" Kevin asked Josh in a whisper.

"Art Howe," Josh responded.

"The Rockies are playing the Mets?" Kevin asked.

"Yes," Josh said tersely. Eager to have the limelight all to himself, Josh was a bit peeved to have to share this special moment in his life with anyone—even his good friend Kevin. His good friend Kevin who had arrived at the ballpark wearing blue jeans and a three-day-old five-o'clock shadow.

"Just be cool," Josh muttered.

"I am cool. I'm always cool," Kevin said. "If anything . . . I'm cool."

"Right," Josh said. "Just follow my lead."

"Whatever, boss."

The next thing we knew we were standing inside the Mets clubhouse. A reporter talked to Roberto Alomar in a far corner of the room. A TV hanging in the center of the room was showing the Yankees game. Half-empty pizza boxes littered a buffet table at the front of the room—demystifying the clubhouse in our eyes to some degree.

Other than Alomar and Mo Vaughn, all of the other players were out on the field taking batting practice. We looked around for a moment, fingering the "Working Press" credentials hanging from our necks and pretending we belonged there. Then we exchanged glances and headed for the door. And then it happened. Into the room walked Tom Glavine. He breezed past the two of us without a word. Kevin continued toward the door, but Josh froze and then did an about-face. He watched as the ace pitcher took off his practice jersey and rolled his shoulders a few times. It occurred to Josh that for a Cy Young Award winner, Glavine had a bit of a pot-belly and somewhat flabby lats. In any case—emboldened by the successful interview he had conducted with Buck Showalter in Texas—Josh moved in for the kill. Questions percolated in his mind. First he would ask Tom to talk about his favorite ballparks, then he would ask him to explain his role as the Players Union Representative during the work stoppage of 1994. Then he would ask the lefty if he regretted leaving the Braves.

"Um . . . Mr. Glavine . . . er . . . Tom," Josh said. "Umm . . . can my friend . . . er . . . colleague Kevin and I have a word with you?"

Half naked, Tom turned and looked at Josh somewhat disparagingly. "Not now, dude," he said. "I'm pitching today." With that, he turned back to face his locker.

We high-tailed it out of the clubhouse with our tails between our legs and found our way to the cheap seats in left field as quickly as possible. That was where we belonged, sitting among the riff-raff far from the field and even farther from the players.

"How could I have known he was pitching today?" Josh lamented later as the game was about to begin.

"He was the only pitcher in the clubhouse," Kevin said. "That might have tipped you off. He was also changing out of his practice jersey and putting on his game jersey while all the other pitchers were in the field shagging batting practice flies. Or you could have bought a newspaper before the game and checked to see who was pitching. Or you could have watched *SportsCenter* or logged onto ESPN.com."

"But what were the odds?" Josh continued.

"Oh, given the prevalence of the five-man rotation, I'd say about one in five," Kevin said, chuckling.

"I know I was out of line," Josh said, "but I still hope he gets waxed by the Rockies tonight. I'd like to see him really get his clock cleaned."

"What?" asked Kevin. "We were the ones at fault here, not him."

"Doesn't matter," said Josh wryly. "I still hope he gets shelled."

Predictably, Glavine did fine. The Mets jumped out to a 7-0 lead and appeared to be cruising toward a win. The lefthander departed after allowing just one runner to cross the plate in six-plus innings. But the Rockies hammered the New York bullpen for four runs in the seventh inning and five more in the eighth to claim a pretty exciting 9-8 victory in a typical twenty-eight-hit Coors Field slugfest.

"A tough-luck no-decision for flabby-Glavvy is good enough for me," Josh chuckled on his way out of Coors Field afterwards.

"Yeah, me too," Kevin said. Then after a pause he added, "Hey, here's an idea. How about tomorrow you follow my lead instead of the other way around like we worked it today?"

"Will your lead take us anywhere near the clubhouse?" Josh asked.

"No way," Kevin said. "I was thinking we'd spend a day up in the Rockpile."

"Sounds good," Josh said.

And that was the last time either of us set foot inside a big league clubhouse.

ARIZONA DIAMONDBACKS, CHASE FIELD

A Baseball Oasis in the Valley of the Sun

The climate in Phoenix is just right for baseball in March. And it's not too bad in November. But from May through October, the players would sweat like pigs, the fans would get heatstroke, and the grass would burn down to its roots by the completion of the third inning if they ever tried to play then. But after years of having their baseball appetites whetted by the Spring Training games their state hosts, Arizonans wanted a regular season team. One solution would have been to build a dome. But by the time the bug to plant a regular season baseball flag in Phoenix had taken hold of the Phoenix area fans, politicians and business leaders, the American people had clearly soured on watching their National Pastime be played on a plastic rug. For a time, though, it must have seemed as if the good people of Arizona had a choice to make between three alternatives, none of which was perfect. Either they could build an outdoor stadium and set up a triage center on the premises for the purpose of diagnosing all of the heat-related maladies the players and fans would suffer, they could build a shiny new dome complete with a fluorescent green carpet, or they could just content themselves to get their baseball fix in the spring, during Cactus League play, and in the autumn, when the Arizona Fall League brought the game's best prospects to the area. That was the conventional wisdom. But "cooler" heads eventually prevailed, and the so-called experts were proven wrong by Chase Field. Thanks to the stadium's retractable roof and massive air conditioners summer baseball is not just possible but quite enjoyable in Phoenix. And the natural grass, which gets all the sunshine it needs when the roof is open in the hours before game time, is as plush and thick as any in the league.

From the exterior, Chase Field does not appear to be a baseball haven. It looks more like an oversized aircraft hangar. The roof, whether open or closed, dominates the design. The two ends of the open roof move toward the middle to close as each side consists of three telescoping panels that can be operated independently or in unison. That's nine million pounds of steel up there, enough to cover nearly twenty-two acres. At ground level the brick and steel attempt to capture the retro-warehouse look of other new ballparks, but because the roof rises so very high—two hundred feet—the supportive structure above the brick kind of overshadows the intended effect. These huge panels of white and green give the park its hangar look. Chase Field conjures not baseball's antique parks of yore, but rather makes a bold statement about man's—or, rather fans'—ingenuity and determination in rising up to meet the challenges posed by the blistering desert sun. Closer to ground-level, both baseball fans and the local power grid benefit from a visually appealing expanse of solar panels. This unique awning shades the entry plaza and ticket booths while harnessing the sun's rays into useable clean energy.

When the roof is closed Chase Field presents the controlled environment of a dome despite its natural grass surface. Having grown up watching baseball in the Kingdome, Kevin swears indoor ball has a certain smell to it that he detected a whiff of at Chase. The closed roof creates darkness where there should be light and ensconces those inside with a staleness that so many of the other retractable roof stadiums—such as the ones in Seattle, Milwaukee, and Houston—have overcome. The outfield windows common at other "convertible parks" are present in Phoenix, but they are smaller than the bays at other such facilities. Instead, Chase has large advertising billboards across the outfield where there should have been more glass. When the roof is on and the billboards are in closed position, it feels more like a domed stadium than it would have if these billboards were windows instead. When the roof is opened, however, the atmosphere improves considerably. Late-day sun tickles the grass and reveals the patterns of the grounds crew's last sweep across the infield dirt. We don't say this all as mere criticism, though. We allow that serious alteration of the environment is a necessity in these parts during the late spring and summer months. At the time Phoenix built its giant transformer the only pre-existent retractable roof stadium was SkyDome (soon to be renamed Rogers Centre) and by that measure, the crafty desert folk certainly excelled with their Bank One Ballpark (soon to be renamed Chase Field). We also applaud the Diamondbacks for opening the roof each day to keep the grass alive and to let some fresh air in, and for making a priority of opening it whenever possible at game time. Unlike in Toronto, where fans sometimes sit beneath the big-top while it's sunny but, perhaps, a wee cool outside, the Phoenicians make every effort to play beneath the stars.

Chase is the most spacious of the retractable-roof yards and it feels that way. As far as manufactured character goes, there's a swimming pool in right-center, which is an apropos trademark in this land where keeping cool is imperative to one's survival. Most of the seats are between the foul poles, but they tend to feel far from the action. A "close" seat at Chase, between the bases on the first level, for example, does not feel right in the game. Perhaps this is due to the wealth of foul territory. But there are many innovations in this bold park to celebrate. Before Chase, it was considered impossible to grow grass within a "domed" facility. Now, it's a common practice. Without Chase, the game may have never seen the construction of even more successful retractable roof parks in Seattle, Houston and Milwaukee

where the boys of summer play on natural grass while the respective lids safeguard the field and stands from intemperate weather of another kind.

The folks who designed Chase didn't listen to naysayers telling them what could and could not be done. They went ahead and did what was necessary. But how? One secret to their success is that the retractable roof is kept open as long as possible each day to let as much sunlight as possible hit the lawn. After some experimentation with Anza, Kentucky bluegrass, and some shade-loving mixes ordinarily unfamiliar to Arizona, where the state flag is a big burning sun, the Diamondbacks settled on Bull's Eye Bermuda. The turf gets as much sunlight as possible without overheating the stadium. The dual-action panels of the roof can be opened in a variety of manners to put the most direct sunlight on the grass without raising the temperature of the concrete and steel around the field.

Three hours before fans arrive, the roof can be closed and the AC cranked so that by the time the rooters settle into their seats it's 30 degrees cooler inside. In a city where the average daytime high is 93 degrees in May, 103 in June, 105 in July, 103 in August, and 99 in September, AC is not a luxury, it's a necessity. Contrary to popular belief, the entire ballpark doesn't fill with cool air. Because hot air rises and gets trapped up near the roof, it is only necessary to cool the air at the lower levels. An eight-thousand-ton cooling system makes use of an enormous cooling tower located on the south side of the ballpark. Then air handlers push 1.2 million cubic feet per minute of cool air past air coils containing water chilled to 48 degrees. The cool air is forced down where it is needed by the layers of progressively warmer air trapped under the roof.

aerial view

Courtesy of the Arizona Diamondbacks

Kevin: Warm on top, cool on bottom? Sounds like the recipe for a tornado to me.

Josh: Sounds like an upside down Brownie Sundae dessert to me.

While sometimes "new" baseball cities must wait for the locals to warm up to the ways of the big league game, this was not the case in Arizona. The game had an avid following in these parts long before the debut of the expansion Diamondbacks in 1998. Since the 1940s big league teams—particularly those from the West Coast—had made their Spring Training camps in the Valley of the Sun. Through the years, Phoenix failed to draw much more than a sniff of interest from the other owners when talk turned to possible regular season expansion sites, though, due to the summer heat. But with the advent of the moveable roof, it became clear that a sustainable facility could be built in Phoenix. To design an indoor structure, perhaps it is best to go with someone who is familiar with such facilities. The architectural firm chosen for this massive undertaking was Ellerbe Becket from Minneapolis, best known for Boston's TD Banknorth Garden, Portland's Rose Garden, and New York's famous Madison Square Garden. The official cost of the Phoenix ballpark was $349 million, though some estimates that account for cost overruns tack on an additional $55 to $60 million. The residents of Maricopa County funded $238 million of the project with a quarter-cent sales tax increase, and are thus the owners of the building, which is leased to the Diamondbacks. The remaining $111 million came from the Diamondback ownership, with $2.2 million per season coming originally from Bank One for the naming rights. When the ballpark opened its official name—Bank One Ballpark—lent itself to the acronym "The BOB." With the merger of Bank One and Chase, however, it was renamed Chase Field on September 23, 2005.

In anticipation of the Diamondbacks' arrival, construction on the ambitious facility had begun in 1995. With the official Grand Opening scheduled to take place on March 31, 1998, the field enjoyed the benefit of a dress rehearsal on March 29, when 49,198 fans turned out to watch the White Sox defeat the Diamondbacks 3-0 in the final Cactus League game of the spring season. After losing that trial run, the Diamondbacks lost the official opener to the Rockies 9-2. The Diamondbacks lost their next four home games too before finally posting a W. Andy Benes, the same pitcher who had lost the franchise opener a week earlier, registered the first win in team history when Arizona beat San Francisco 3-2 on April 5, 1998.

To say that the Diamondbacks enjoyed more than their fair share of success as a still-fledgling franchise would be an understatement. After their first expansion season resulted in a typical 65-97 record, they remarkably won 100 games and the NL West crown in just their second year of existence. After falling to the Mets in the NL Division Series, they were right back in the playoffs two years later, beating the Yankees, of all teams, in a dramatic seven-game World Series. Fans in these parts will never forget the early contributions that veteran players like Randy Johnson, Curt Schilling, Matt Williams, Steve Finley, Jay Bell, and Luis Gonzalez made to the city's baseball fortunes.

Josh: How many years did it take your Mariners to have a hundred-win season?

Kevin: Last I checked your Red Sox haven't had one since 1946.

Josh: But we've won two world championships since then.

Before Schilling would play a role in the Red Sox' 2004 World Series run, he was integral to the Diamondbacks amazing 2001 season and post-season. He joined the team that spring and, paired with Johnson, gave Arizona a devastating "one-two punch." Schilling became the first twenty-game winner in D-Backs history, while Johnson kept striking out batters and maintaining an ERA lower than a snake in a wagon rut.

The 2001 NLDS matched Arizona against the St. Louis Cardinals, and the series went the full five. Next, the Diamondbacks dispatched the perennially "post-season challenged" Braves of Bobby Cox in a five-game NLCS. The young upstarts, only in their fourth season, were now ready to take on the dreaded Yanks, who just happened to be gunning for their fourth consecutive World Championship. The D-Backs took the first two games at home, the second in a masterful three-hit complete game by Johnson that saw eleven Yankees go down swinging. When the Series returned to New York, the Yanks rallied (as they always seem to) winning three in a row to take a 3–2 Series lead. A New York Four-Peat appeared imminent.

As so often turns out to be the case, Game 6 of the World Series was the pivotal game. Returning home gave the Rattlers back their venom, and they bit hard, pounding the Yankees 15-2. But instead of rolling over and dying, as many losers of Game 6 do, the Yanks took charge early in the finale. They carried a 2-1 lead into the bottom of the ninth, in fact, and then sent nearly unhittable closer Mariano Rivera to the mound to put the final nail in the Diamondbacks' proverbial coffin. The brash New Yorkers thought—strike that—they *knew* the Series was in the bag. Everyone in America seemed to know. After all, wasn't that the way it always went for the Yankees?

Everyone knew, that is, except for the Arizona Diamondbacks and their loyal fans. And a strange thing happened. The untouchable Rivera became mortal, if just for that one inning, and the Diamondbacks tagged him with a loss. In as dramatic a finish to a season as any the game has seen, with two outs Gonzalez blooped a single into left field that scored Bell and put the finishing touches on a two-run ninth that gave Arizona the Championship. Chase Field proved to be central to the home team's feat, as the D-Backs notched all four of their wins at home. Johnson shook off any concerns regarding his ability to deliver in the postseason, as he and Schilling earned co-MVP honors. For the season Johnson won his second straight Cy Young Award, while Schilling finished second among NL vote-getters.

Though the D-Backs were swept in the 2002 NLDS by the World Series–bound San Francisco Giants and then swept again in the 2007 NLCS by the World Series–bound Rockies, those seasons were also full of magical moments that the local fans turned out to cheer.

Chase Field also drew crowds during the spring of 2006 when it served as one of the first-round sites for the World Baseball Classic. The United States downed Mexico 2-0 before more than thirty-two thousand fans in the first game, while two subsequent games featuring teams other than the US squad averaged about seventeen thousand fans apiece. A more recent showcase event at Chase was the 2011 All-Star Game, in which the NL prevailed 5-1 behind MVP Prince Fielder's three-run homer. The day before Robinson Cano had won the annual Home Run Derby, narrowly edging Boston's Adrian Gonzalez in the final round.

Kevin: The boys at ESPN must have loved that one.

Josh: Because it pitted two great players in the final round?

Kevin: No, because it pitted a Yankee against a Red Sox player.

Trivia Timeout

Sun Soaked: Name the first player to drop one in the drink (splash down in the pool for a home run).

Scorched: Which visiting slugger once hit a batting practice homer through one of the open outfield windows?

Burnt to a Crisp: Cooperstown, a sports bar near Chase Field, serves a jumbo hot dog that gets its name from which famous Diamondbacks pitcher?

Look for the answers in the text.

Chase Field has also been used for college football, college basketball, super-cross events, professional bull-riding, monster truck rallies and international soccer matches. And in 2004 it even served as one of President George W. Bush's rallying sites during his reelection campaign. At its heart, though, Chase Field is a baseball diamond. Imperfect though it may be, it presents a vast improvement over the previous generation's domes and even over its immediate predecessor in Toronto. While the ever-expanding reach of technology upon our already ultra-modern lives can be at times daunting and at times a bit much for the purists among us to swallow, the advent of a field fit for the Grand Old Game in the inferno of Phoenix is something for which all fans—and Phoenicians especially—should be grateful.

Getting a Choice Seat

Getting a ticket to Chase Field is not the problem. It's getting a seat that won't make you feel as though you're watching from atop one of the Camelback Mountains. If you're after that "every seat is intimate" ballpark feel, we can only suggest driving to Dodger Stadium. Joking aside, the closest you can get to achieving intimacy within the Arizona stadium is by getting a seat on the lower levels between the bases . . . next to your special someone. Bada-bing. That's the last intimacy joke, we promise. The good news, as far as the plight of the traveling fan goes, is that the Diamondbacks only average about twenty-five thousand fans per game, so there are usually some pretty good (just not intimate) seats on the first level available to those who plan in advance.

Lower Level (Sections 100–145)

The lower bowl has a medium grade that's just steep enough so that you can see over the guy in front of you, unless he plays for the Suns. And those guys are up in the luxury boxes. Seeing as there are nine price tiers within the lower sections, we'll try to simplify things a bit.

By the time you read this, the lower rows of Sections 113–131 will already be sold to season-ticket holders and other high-level schmucks in monkey-suits. Those are the most expensive seats in the ballpark, so there are really only five lower level ticket options with which we need to concern ourselves. See, we're making it easier for you already.

The seats in Sections 115–128 are between the bases. They sell as Infield Boxes at a price that we consider pretty reasonable compared to comparable chairs at other parks. So snatch these up if the opportunity presents itself. Low retaining walls down the lines provide clear sight lines for nearly all of the first level, so that is not a concern as it is at some ballparks. In the upper reaches of each section a good rule for the entire first level is to avoid any row higher than thirty-nine. It's not that the overhang is much of an issue, but the industrial piping that clings to the bottom of the second deck. This heavy duty venting can block the view.

The Baseline Box seats in Sections 112–114 and 130–132 are still very good, appearing just beyond the corner bags. Shoot for 114 and 130 over the other sections in this tier.

Seating Capacity: 49,033
Ticket Office: http://arizona.diamondbacks.
mlb.com/ticketing/singlegame.jsp?c_id=ari
Seating Chart: http://arizona.diamond-
backs.mlb.com/ari/ballpark/seating_
pricing.jsp

A bit farther down the lines, in shallow outfield territory, a Baseline Reserve ticket grants visitors access to Sections 109–111 in right field or 133–135 in left field. Although these are preferable to the deeper-still Bullpen Reserve (106–108 and 136–138) seats, we don't recommend any of these sections as a whole. But there are four sections where some of the seats are worth considering. The lowest rows of Sections 109 and 108 in right and 135 and 136 in left place fans right down near the field, with the added advantage of having the bullpens nearby. If you can get into the first ten rows, we say go for it. If not, you'll be happier paying more and sitting much closer, or paying significantly less and sitting in the bleachers.

The Bleachers in Sections 101–105 in right and 139–144 in left offer the best seat for the money at Chase. That's right: They're real seats, not uncomfortable benches. From these home-run territory sections there is a sight-line loss of the warning track, but nearly none of the grass is obscured from view. Also a tad unfortunate but not devastating is the gully between the bleachers and fence. While the D-Backs use this gully well for handicapped seating—which we applaud, and which the Chase has in spades—we're never really fans of space between us and our chance to interfere with the game.

Though not really a seating area, parties of up to thirty-five people can rent the pool/hot tub patio for a mere $6,500 per game. That king's ransom covers the price of admission, pool maintenance, lifeguard, twenty stadium chairs, 16 lounge chairs, five parking passes, complimentary caps and towels and $750 in food and beverage vouchers. If that sounds like a good deal to you and you have thirty-four friends who aren't really that interested in the ballgame, then go for it.

Insight Diamond Level (Sections 200–224)

At the home of the Diamondbacks, it makes some sense that the Club level is called the "Diamond Level." Some, but not a whole heck of a lot. While the seats are mostly good the boxes themselves are tucked beneath the third deck. This decision goes a long way toward protecting the sight lines of the folks upstairs, but would most likely anger us if we were corporate big wigs who'd paid extra for the luxury accommodations. We say kudos to the Diamondbacks. Thanks for putting the little guys first! That said, the Diamond boxes hang down nice and low over the first level, so the view from most of them is still quite good. As a general rule, we suggest that you seriously consider any seat in Sections 203–217, though it's best to avoid the back row (Row 11) or two so as to minimize the overhang. As for the remaining Diamond boxes—those in the outfield corners—you can do better.

Upper Level (Sections 300–332)

We applaud the Diamondbacks for making things simple by only breaking the Upper Level into three pricing tiers. And we give them credit for offering all of the top-shelf seats at affordable prices. In addition, the views are unobstructed by the underhang that plagues many of the triple-deck stadiums. However, the deck climbs and climbs seemingly forever, rising more steeply and to a greater height than many of the cliffs in the surrounding mountains. We do not recommend any of the Upper Level seats higher than Row 20. In the sections behind home plate—Sections 310–322—you could probably get away with sitting as high as Row 32,

Courtesy of Arizona Diamondbacks

SEATING TIP

While the bleacher seats are better than the first level seats in the corners, the bleachers on the left-field side are lower than those in right, and don't have that annoying space separating them from the outfield wall. Sitting down low in bleacher Sections 140–143 offers the best view of the outfield and corner sections, and at the cheapest price. But be wary: Seat-hopping into this section can be a bit of a problem as the ushers check tickets fairly diligently.

which is the highest row. The view is a tad eagle-eyed, so, appropriately, there are plenty of birds living in the rafters, snacking on french fries.

As mentioned previously, Chase Field's system does not cool the entire air mass inside. The higher you go, the hotter it gets. Seats in rows higher than twenty-five remain pretty warm on a typical Arizona day—and the money you save on tickets by sitting up here will be spent on extra sodas, beers, ice waters, slushies, and the like. Then again, if you're trying to lose a few and sweating off a few pounds sounds appealing, then these uppermost seats might be the way to go.

Sections 300 and 301 in right do have underhang issues, severe ones. But when you're sitting this far away, who cares if the right-field corner is missing? You're so far from the action you might as well bring a portable TV.

The Black Market

Being a scalper in Phoenix (when the Suns aren't playing) is akin to being a snow-cone salesman at the North Pole. Nonetheless, there are determined folks who make a living plying hot passes to this large ballpark that practically never sells out. Whatever you do, don't pay a penny more than face value for a ticket to Chase.

Before/After the Game

Chase Field is located in Copper Square (aka the Downtown Phoenix Business Improvement District), a historic part of town bounded by Fillmore Street, Jackson Street, 7th Street and 3rd Avenue. This is a culturally rich area filled with more than 200 shops, restaurants, and bars. It's a very solid setting for a ballpark that keeps getting better.

Kevin: Arizona was once known as the Copper State and produced more precious metal than the other forty-nine states combined.

Josh: Makes you wonder why they didn't call the local nine the Copperheads.

Getting to Chase Field

Accessing Chase from the freeway involves getting off at the Seventh Street exit from Interstate 10 or Interstate 17.

Parking studies have shown that there are more than twenty thousand spaces within a fifteen-minute walk of the ballpark. Lot spots start at as low as $5 per game and rise as high as $20. For a night game we found a nearly unlimited number of two-hour meter spots within a few blocks walk of the ballpark that could be plugged with quarters until 5 p.m. when they become free for the night. There are also free spots north of Van Buren on streets like McKinley and Garfield for those who don't mind a half-mile walk and like to show off their knowledge of US presidents.

Josh: Did you know Martin Van Buren was the first US president who spoke English as a second language?

Kevin: Are you setting me up for a George W. joke?

Josh: Van Buren grew up speaking Dutch. He was also the second-shortest prez at five-foot-six-inches. Can you tell me which head honcho was shorter?

Kevin: I really don't care.

Josh: James Madison. Five-foot-four.

Kevin: That's half the size of Randy Johnson.

Josh: Or something like that.

Phoenix offers public transportation to the ballpark area through several bus lines that disembark at Central Station.

Valley Metro Maps and Info: www.valleymetro.org/

Another way to get to the game, or back to your car, is by bike taxi—or as we like to call it—the modern rickshaw or "bike-shaw." That's right, some poor slob on a twelve-speed will pedal and sweat in temperatures exceeding 110 degrees Fahrenheit while you and your pals recline in comfort, waiting for your frozen water to melt. Phoenix is a nice flat city for this type of thing, but man were those guys sweating when we visited. We tipped our guy well. Josh suggested that he buy himself a Gatorade, while Kevin suggested that he find a new line of work. We thought those were two tips that would serve him better than any extra monetary dispensation would have. And yet, he didn't seem too appreciative.

Outside Attractions

THE ENTRY PLAZA

Phoenix has more than its fair share of street vendors and pregame hawkers. All this activity comes to a head in the plaza just outside the Chase Field gate. Radio stations broadcast live, there are street games, and of course, more vendors. All in all, the atmosphere is very lively.

GIANT BAT SCULPTURE SIGN

The official sign welcoming fans to Chase Field, which comes complete with the blue interlocking Chase logo, is supported by three twenty-foot-high faux baseball bats. This is a popular place for road trippers to pose for a picture, with the ballpark in the background. Thus, people turn their road trip memories into subtle advertisements for Chase, which their friends and relatives will observe and subconsciously be affected by. This is kind of like when an actress in a movie not-so-discreetly reaches for a can of Coca-Cola at an opportune time for the camera to zoom in. Only this time, the person doing the product placement is you, the fan, and you're not being paid anything for your efforts.

Josh: I'm cutting out the Chase logo with a pair of scissors as soon as I get this roll developed.

Kevin: Isn't that a digital camera?

Josh: Yeah, so?

Kevin: There's this new thing called Photoshop.

DESERT WINDOW ART

The large outfield bays that sometimes open to allow fresh air into Chase and to expose a modest view of the world beyond its walls are decorated on the inside by advertising, but on the outside they expose delightful baseball images. Done in sunburnt hues that suggest the desert in the twilight hour, these portray baseball players running, swinging, pitching and going through a range of other motions fans will recognize. It's worth walking around the stadium footprint to check them out.

MISSION STATEMENT

One thing outside the ballpark that we've never noticed at any other ballpark is the team mission statement that appears in bronze beneath a statue of a generic Diamondback near Gate K. The plaque reads:

The Arizona Diamondbacks mission is to establish a winning tradition that embodies the genuine spirit of baseball; an organization to which all Arizonans will point with pride, which conducts its business with integrity and community responsibility; so that Arizona's children will grow up knowing the rich tradition that has made baseball America's National Pastime.

Watering Holes and Outside Eats

The Chase Field neighborhood offers a game-day atmosphere that rates firmly above average as far as big league settings go. Though Phoenix's city blocks are long—like Las Vegas long—there are no massive parking lots surrounding Chase, which makes the just-outside-the-gates eating and drinking establishments that much closer. And while many of the places are chains (such as Hooters at 445 N. 3rd St. and the Hard Rock Café at 3 S. 2nd St.), there are a number of unique spots to have a beer or meal. Phoenix offers some of the best Mexican eats in the bigs too, so do partake.

COOPERSTOWN
101 E. Jackson St.
www.alicecooperstown.com/

I'm eighteen and I like it! But you've got to be twenty-one to get into this joint, owned by 1970s rocker Alice Cooper. Cooperstown describes itself as a place "where jocks and rock meet." It's kind of like the Hard Rock Café and ESPN Zone rolled into one. Barbecue food is their specialty, and it's surprisingly good, though not terribly cheap. "The Big Unit" is a twenty-two-inch-long one-pound hot dog named after The Big Unit, Randy Johnson. It was inspired in part by Johnson, and in part by the giant python Alice used to brandish on stage. We were impressed that it comes with a baguette bun to match its considerable length. There are also menu items named after Charles Barkley, Shaq, Magic Johnson, Tony La Russa, Tommy Lasorda, Ty Cobb, Kurt Warner, Megadeth, Sammy Hagar, and Marge Simpson.

Big Unit Photo: www.alicecooperstown.com/Alice-Big Unit.html

JACKSON'S ON 3RD
245 East Jackson St.

Jackson's is close to the park and should be a lead player when it comes to beer-drinking and pregame partying. And yet, it's had trouble staying open consistently through the years. In 2011 it reopened under new management. Here's hoping it sticks. With air-conditioning, TVs everywhere, multiple bars inside and out, and a vast selection of beers on tap, the only thing missing is a bit more baseball memorabilia. After the game, expect loud music and drunken twenty-somethings looking to hook up with a new friend or two.

MAJERLE'S SPORTS GRILL
24 North 2nd St.
www.majerles.com/

Fans of the Phoenix Suns will want to visit Dynamite Dan's sports bar. Long before Majerle's 2002 retirement from the NBA, he had thrown himself into the restaurant business. His friendly downtown pub, which opened in 1992, is still going strong two decades later. And he recently opened a satellite location in Scottsdale. The menu is not as interesting as the photos and memorabilia on the wall that feature Dan and his famous friends.

COACH AND WILLIE'S
412 South 3rd St.
www.coachandwillies.com/

For those willing to spend a few bucks more on dinner, Coach and Willie's is a sound choice. From wood-fired pizza to filet mignon, this wonderfully Arizona-decorated restaurant is sure to please. The patio and the balcony are nearly worth the price of admission in themselves. This is the kind of place where players are more likely to hang out than ordinary slobs.

SEAMUS MCCAFFREY'S IRISH PUB
18 West Monroe St.
www.seamusmccaffreys.com/

This place is an authentic Irish pub and is worth a mention because Kevin seems to derive some special thrill from pointing out every Irish pub in America. It's a great sports pub if you're into football: not our kind of football. When they say "football," they mean soccer. When they say "American football," they mean football. But more often than not, they only talk about football.

SOLD ON THE STREET
Vendors line the sidewalks hawking goodies, giving this ultramodern ballpark an old-time baseball vibe. We found everything from souvenir programs to Cajun nuts, which by the way are delicious. The Vienna beef dog stands are great for a pregame snack, and the kettle corn is always fresh. But what we couldn't understand were the vendors selling bottles of frozen water. We had both always called frozen water "ice," but the vendors outside Chase call it "frozen water" for some reason. This is a solid choice if you'll be walking around in the heat for a while, but if you're thirsty *now* it's kind of a tease.

Inside Chase Field

Chase Field might have the most refreshing main entrance of any park in baseball. To enter, fans pass through a gauntlet of misting stations that gingerly spray them with refreshing drops of water. But sadly, that's where the misting ends. When you get inside your body acclimates very quickly to the air-conditioning, and because it's 115 degrees outside, that means it's only 85 degrees Fahrenheit inside on the lower level, and hotter as you climb up to your seats in the Upper Level.

statues

Courtesy of the Arizona Diamondbacks

Clearly seeing a game in the AC isn't the same as going to a movie in the summer and coming out chilled. With very wide and open concourses that keep fans close to the game, there is plenty to do while on the prowl. A variety of restaurants and vendors inhabit the concourses. And the upper reaches provide the same quality concession offerings that the lower-level concourses do, which we appreciate very much. Though Chase does not like to be called a dome, when the arched roof is closed, it truly stretches the definition of a retractable-roof stadium. Nonetheless, even in its domed condition Chase presents a better atmosphere than, say, Tropicana Field, where the artificial turf further detracts from the game.

Ballpark Features
ROTUNDA
The first level of the entry rotunda is adorned with a mural depicting the history of sports, with pictures ranging from medieval jousting to games of Native Americans to Ancient Greece and Rome. Of course, the display concludes with the formation of the Diamondbacks in 1998, the crowning achievement in the history of game-playing, from an Arizonan's perspective. On the upper levels, there appear scenes chronicling the history of Arizona.

Kevin: Can you name the five Cs of early Arizona's economic prosperity?

Josh: Cattle, Climate, Copper, Citrus, and Cotton. I read the historical marker, too.

WORLD SERIES TROPHY CASE

Be sure to have yourself an up-close look at the 2001 World Series trophy just inside Gate E.

Kevin: Big deal. All these World Series trophies look exactly the same.

Josh: Spoken like a fan whose team has never won one.

THE BIG TOP

Of all the ballparks with retractable roofs, only Rogers Centre feels domier—to coin a new term—than Chase Field. The roof does not open parallel to the base paths as in Seattle and Houston. It opens from the middle, following an imaginary line that runs from foul pole to foul pole. When it's retracted the outfield feels more exposed than at the other retractable-roof yards (excepting the one in Seattle). But the downside is that seats at both ends of the park are still covered when the roof is open, making parts of the stadium always feel indoors. Both Seattle and Houston have huge areas outside where their roofs can telescope when opened. This allows those ballparks to open a bit wider.

SIGNS, SIGNS, EVERYWHERE A SIGN

Huge billboards above the outfield seats reside on panels that open when the weather allows. These measure about sixty-by-sixty feet by our estimation. When closed, they help seal Chase for maximum cooling and add to the notion that the park is in fact one big ad machine. When popped open, they provide window views of downtown.

Josh: Do you think the sponsors pray for sun?

Kevin: I don't think corporate America prays.

While visiting Phoenix with the Cardinals, Mark McGwire once hit a batting practice homer that bounced out of the window just to the left of the video board. The shot was estimated to carry some 510 feet, which we figure would have been about 410 if "Big Mac" hadn't been juicing.

START POOLING YOUR MONEY NOW

The pool is as mandatory to the everyday survival of folks in Phoenix as the subway is in New York City. Life is simply more feasible because of it. But for the price they charge at Chase, you could have a pool installed in your backyard and still have some coin left over for a bleacher seat to the ballgame. That said, this would be a great setting for a bachelor's party. For that sort of thing, it's not a bad venue.

Future Arizona first baseman Mark Grace became the first player to hit a homer into the swimming pool while playing for the Cubs on May 12, 1998. Less than a week later, the Diamondbacks' Devon White became the first player to hit two homers into the drink. White "went swimming" on May 16 and May 18. Keep your eye on the water, because whenever a D-Backs' player homers fountains above the pool spray water into the air. For the record, the pool is 415 feet from home plate, or 60 feet farther than a home run down the right-field line in San Francisco must travel to reach McCovey Cove.

Kevin: You want to take a swim, don't you?

Josh: No, I was just checking out a woman in a bikini.

Kevin: Don't worry, I won't tell Heather.

ALL PENNED IN

The bullpens sit behind the outfield wall down the lines in right and left, bisected by the big yellow foul poles. This means shots that wind up in the relievers' realm are either home runs, or long strikes.

Kevin: Looks a little Mickey Mouse to me.

Josh: At least they're not parallel to the foul lines like at Wrigley.

THE THIN YELLOW LINE

The outfield picnic pavilion is an ill-conceived area of the ballpark. The tables are too far from the field to make attractive sitting places, and they protrude over the field on either side of the batter's eye to tarnish the ballpark's aesthetic with a cluttered look. The batter's eye itself is little more than a black wall that rises from the field all the way up to the scoreboard, with a yellow home run line drawn across it midway up that continues across to the picnic protrusions on either side. So all that separates a home run from any other ball hit off the wall in dead-center is a painted yellow line?

Josh: I'd call that unromantic.

Kevin: I'd call it un-American.

THE LANDING STRIP

At the time of its opening, Chase Field was the only ballpark with a dirt track running from the pitcher's mound to home plate. A short while later, Comerica Park in Detroit opened and mimicked the old-time effect. This feature was common to ballparks of yesteryear, of course, as catchers wore a path on their trips to the mound in an era when grounds crews lacked the sophisticated field management techniques to combat all that wear and tear.

Kevin: What do you think that adds to the game?

Josh: Who do I look like, Ty Cobb?

FUTURES FIELD

The left-field concourse houses an expansive kiddie land complete with a miniature sandlot field and other facilities designed to let the youngsters burn off some steam.

Needless to say, Kevin demanded that the little guys let him pitch, then proceeded to spin a shutout. The moms in attendance were not impressed.

Stadium Eats

The food at Chase Field will not rock your world. But this is not one of those parks where you should endeavor to sneak in food from the outside either. A decent meal can be had at Chase if you're a little bit selective. The team boasts of its concession space totaling nearly a quarter of a mile, and we believe it. The Diamondbacks have done well to make space on the concourses for stands representing local establishments as well as chains like Fatburger, Mrs. Fields, Cold Stone Creamery, Subway and Panda Express.

HUNGRY HILL SANDWICHES (TRADEMARK FOOD)

With five different types of sandwiches made fresh before your eyes, Hungry Hill is the best thing going at Chase. The meatball with marinara and Parmesan is a wonder. The homemade sausage with peppers and onions puts the other ballpark links to shame. Also available are Polish sausage, bratwurst, and Italian beef that made us feel like we were back in Chicago. And to top it off, these delicious sandwiches are reasonably priced.

OSCAR MAYER DIAMOND DOG (DOG REVIEW)

Pre-wrapping this all-beef wiener detracts from what would otherwise be a respectable house dog. Diamond Dogs are pretty tasty, as Arizonans know, and can be purchased across the state at grocery stores. The dog weighs a quarter-pound. But dogs need to be yanked off the grill before our

eyes to really wow us. Sorry, Oscar, it's a tough market out there in MLB that leaves no room for lukewarm meat and crumbly buns. Better options inside the park include the Arizona Dog, which is actually a foot-long chorizo topped with nacho cheese and tortilla strips, and the freshly-made grilled dogs at the Big Dawgs stands.

BEST OF THE REST

The **Fruit Medley** is a refreshing treat. Fresh melon, grapes, and berries form a zesty mix. Meats and cheeses are available to complement your fruit, as are strawberries and cream.

Kevin: What is this? Wimbledon?

The **Cactus Corn** stands on the first and third levels offer different types of fresh popped corn like Jalapeño, Cajun, Parmesan, and Chili. We were highly impressed. **Tamales** come courtesy of a Rey Gloria's stand near Section 138, while there are two **margarita** stands on the first level and one on the third.

The several **Big Dawgs** stands offer foot-long all-beef dogs topped with untraditional items like french fries and Cole Slaw.

The stands on the Diamond Level really do go above and beyond to make the Club Level patrons feel special. They include a fresh **steak sandwich stand,** a Tex-Mex **A-Zona Grill,** a **Burger Burger** stand, and an **Extreme Loaded Dog** counter where fans can top their hot dogs with even funkier toppings than at Big Dawgs. Ever want to try mac and cheese or taco meat on a hot dog? Well, then, this is your chance. The Big Kid Dog is topped with mac and cheese and Fritos. And the Taco Dog is loaded with spicy

---

The Arizona Fall League

http://mlb.mlb.com/mlb/events/winterleagues/league.jsp?league=afl

The Arizona Fall League, or AFL, is a developmental league run by Major League Baseball. It exists for the purpose of providing the game's brightest prospects a Winter Ball experience in which their parent organizations can keep a closer eye on them than they are able to with players participating in the Caribbean leagues. The AFL allows MLB coaches and front office types to micromanage pitch counts and innings caps better than they can for players in the Puerto Rican or Venezuelan Leagues. The league also ensures that these rising stars are testing their mettle against top-notch competition. Each big league organization sends seven minor leaguers to the league, six of whom must be at the Double or Triple-A level and one of whom may have played at Single-A during the past season. Each big league organization's septet joins one of the AFL's six teams——the Mesa Solar Sox, Phoenix Desert Dogs, Scottsdale Scorpions, Peoria Javelinas, Peoria Saguaros, and Surprise Rafters——to play alongside the prospects from four other big league clubs. The games take place at Spring Training ballparks in the Phoenix metro area, beginning in early October and ending around November 21.

Notable AFL alums include Ryan Braun, Roy Halladay, Josh Hamilton, Ryan Howard, Derek Jeter, Evan Longoria, Joe Mauer, Dustin Pedroia, Albert Pujols, Jimmy Rollins, Mark Teixeira, David Wright, and Kevin Youkilis. With names like that, it's easy to see how the AFL has produced ten future Rookies of the Year since its founding in 1992.

ground beef, lettuce, pico de gallo, cheese, sour cream and jalapeños.

SAY "NO, THANKS," AND WALK AWAY

The most obvious place to steer clear of at Chase Field is Subway. This is a baseball game. You can do better than the same deli sandwich you eat on your lunch break.

STADIUM SUDS

While there are some nice beers (Sam Adams, Corona, Fat Tire, Beck's, Heineken, Foster's) throughout Chase, the true fan of good hoppy frost will want to head to one of the two Beer Gardens on the Upper Deck. On Friday and Saturday nights don't be surprised to find a hip, swinging atmosphere at these locations, with a DJ spinning discs and young women downing beers and grooving. Need we say more? Some serious ball fans may shake their heads disapprovingly at a party patio at a baseball game, but Kevin didn't mind.

The Chase Field Experience

From folks wearing strings of purple and turquoise beads, to those shaking Diamondback rattles during rallies, the Arizona fans support their D-Backs enthusiastically if not in record numbers. They may not be the most knowledgeable fans in the circuit, but they understand winning, something their team has done plenty of since entering the league, and they understand how to make noise to spark a rally.

LATINOS BEWARE

Usually we leave politics out of these chapters, but when a local sheriff hell-bent on making a political statement starts parading illegal immigrants on a chain-gang outside a city's pro sports stadiums and other public gathering places, well, we're kind of left with no choice but to mention it. In the wake of Arizona's controversial 2010 law that gave local law enforcement the right to detain any suspicious looking Latino person unless they could produce papers guaranteeing their citizenship on the spot, Joseph M. Arpaio, the sheriff of Maricopa County, has become a hero of the anti-immigration crusade. And one technique he uses to rally support for his cause is by making an example of his latest batch of criminals by showing them off at pretty much any sports or civic event apt to attract a large crowd of out-of-towners. We won't wade too deeply into the politics of this, other than to say we felt less than great about visiting Phoenix in 2011. And we understand why many Latino fans are staying away.

SECOND HIGHEST ELEVATION

At more than one thousand feet above sea level, Chase Field is the second highest ballpark in the Majors. Other than making the nosebleed sections actually give people bloody noses, expect the ball to carry approximately seven feet farther than it would at other parks.

Josh: Seven feet, that's about the length of Randy Johnson.

Kevin: It doesn't seem so far when you put it that way.

THE LEGENDS RACE

In 2010 the Diamondbacks jumped on the ballpark race bandwagon, introducing their very own Legends Race. Unlike the humorous midgame races that take place in other cities, though, the Phoenix version features caricatures of former Diamondbacks players. After the fifth inning, mascots portraying Johnson, Luis Gonzalez, Matt Williams and Mark Grace take to the field. And only one thing is ever really certain: The Grace mascot will lose the race. According to our sources he's never won one!

OLD-TIME ORGAN

This space-aged ballpark features an old-time pipe organ. Tickling the keyboard since Chase opened has been a fellow named Bobby Freeman, who previously played for the Phoenix Firebirds of the Pacific Coast League.

> ### Cyber Super-Fans
>
> We know that the old saying "You can't judge a book by its cover" really is true in most cases. However, the three Diamondbacks blogs we came across with the most badass names also turned out to be our favorites. See what you think.
>
> - **AZ Snake Pit**
>   www.azsnakepit.com/
> - **Venom Strikes**
>   http://venomstrikes.com/
> - **The D-Blog**
>   http://dblog.mlblogs.com/

D. BAXTER

Named by young Brantley Bell, the son of Jay Bell, the mountain lion mascot of the D-Backs has been patrolling Chase since 2000. Josh wishes the team had chosen a snake as its mascot. Kevin couldn't care two hoots one way or the other.

Sports in (and around) the City

The Cactus League
www.cactusleague.com/
Why not begin your road trip in March when the Cactus League brings fifteen teams to the Phoenix area for Spring Training? You can see the little parks at the beginning of your sojourn before venturing on to the regular season yards.

Here's an overview of who plays where:

- **Arizona Diamondbacks and Colorado Rockies**
  Salt River Fields at Talking Stick (Seating Capacity: 11,000)
  7555 North Pima Rd.
  Scottsdale, AZ
- **Chicago Cubs**
  HoHoKam Stadium (13,074)
  1235 North Center St.
  Mesa, AZ
- **Chicago White Sox and Los Angeles Dodgers**
  Camelback Ranch (13,000)
  10712 West Camelback Rd.
  Glendale/Phoenix, AZ
- **Cincinnati Reds and Cleveland Indians**
  Goodyear Ballpark (10,311)
  1933 S. Ballpark Way
  Goodyear, AZ
- **Kansas City Royals and Texas Rangers**
  Surprise Stadium (10,500)
  15960 North Bullard Ave.
  Surprise, AZ
- **Los Angeles Angels of Anaheim**
  Tempe Diablo Stadium (9,315)
  2200 West Alameda Dr.
  Tempe, AZ
- **Milwaukee Brewers**
  Maryvale Baseball Park (8,000)
  3600 North 51st Ave.
  Phoenix, AZ

- **Oakland Athletics**
  Phoenix Municipal Stadium (7,881)
  5999 East Van Buren St.
  Phoenix, AZ
- **San Diego Padres and Seattle Mariners**
  Peoria Sports Complex (11,333)
  16101 North 83rd Ave.
  Peoria, AZ
- **San Francisco Giants**
  Scottsdale Stadium (10,500)
  7408 East Osborn Rd.
  Scottsdale, AZ

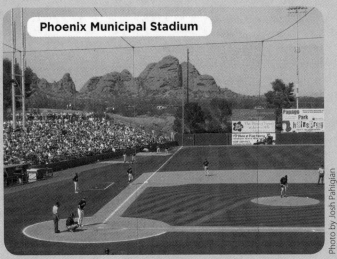

Phoenix Municipal Stadium

Photo by Josh Pahigian

AUTOGRAPH HOUNDS

Autographs can be sought on the infield side of the D-Backs' dugout prior to the start of the game. It's a very organized autograph session that only features a handful of players and begins promptly at 5:20 p.m. for a 7:05 start and runs precisely ten minutes. The JumboTron counts down the time so players don't have to be the bad guys when they sign their last hat, then turn to leave.

GNOME

A popular item at the D-Backs merchandise stands and on their giveaway nights, the Diamondbacks Garden Gnome is practically the unofficial mascot of the club.

Kevin: The gnome brings good luck.

Josh: Put it in your garden and your flowers will bloom.

Kevin: Put it near your pool and no one will pee.

Josh: But what does it have to do with baseball?

COVER UP

It takes only four minutes for the roof to close, and the Diamondbacks have a special song that plays as it does. According to the team, it costs just $2.00 for it to close or open, which is hard for us to believe considering moving the nine-million-pound structure requires two 200-horse-power engines and miles and miles of steel cable.

On Our Way Out of Phoenix
We Made an Ill-Advised Pit-Stop

While heading out of Phoenix, we found ourselves traveling through the desert. Mountains rose in the distance in mighty beauty that held us both awestruck. Unfortunately Kevin was driving, and Josh had to keep reminding him to keep his eyes on the road, and not the scenery as we wound our way along the narrow canyon roads.

The other problem was that the air conditioning in the road trip car was on the blink (Thanks for nothing Budget Rental!). It worked, but sporadically. The inside of the car was hotter than the surface of the sun.

"Hot enough for you?" Josh joked.

"Yeah, but it's a dry heat," Kevin replied.

"Why do people say that stuff?" Josh asked.

"Got me," said Kevin. He was not trying to cut the conversation short, he never did anything of the sort. Rather, the infernal heat and many days of eating Mexican food morning, noon, and night were beginning to catch up with him.

"I need a pit stop," he said.

After driving for another 20 miles without the hint of a rest stop, or even a road sign, things began to get urgent. We were passing through a particularly beautiful canyon, with the road hugging cliffs that dropped 200 feet or more. There was no place to stop, but the alternative seemed worse, so Kevin pulled off at a scenic vista that offered the most majestic span of the canyon yet.

"Drastic times call for drastic measures," Kevin said, the sweat pouring off the brim of his ballcap. Then he put the car in park, opened the door, and climbed over the guardrail.

"Watch out for rattlers," Josh yelled. "I read on the plane that it's nesting season."

Kevin just raised his hand in the air in recognition, descended about ten feet below road-level, and got about his business. When he returned a few moments later he was a new man. It may not have been the most comfortable bathroom experience—hanging off the side of a cliff—but it was satisfying. And the view was breathtaking. He was ready to drive another 500 miles if necessary.

Kevin climbed back up to the asphalt slab, and found Josh on the other edge of the cliff, sitting on the guard rail. "Quite a view, eh?" he said.

But Josh didn't respond.

"I say it's quite an impressive view," Kevin repeated.

"There's a diamondback, right there." Josh whispered through clenched teeth.

"Which one?" said Kevin, noticing that a few other cars had pulled into the scenic lookout. "Is it Justin Upton? He's on my fantasy team."

Kevin began looking around when Josh grabbed him.

"Not a ballplayer, you idiot, a snake," he said. "It's right in front of me."

Sure enough, a real diamondback lay coiled 15 feet away, which seemed like a safe enough distance. But then again, you never could be sure with snakes. This one was fat with diamonds all along its back. It wasn't rattling, but it looked mean. And it kept sticking its tongue out at Josh, which didn't seem like a good sign.

We backed away slowly, the snake eyeballing us like we were the last morsel of food on earth. The slower we backed away, the more the snake watched our every step.

Finally, we managed to escape unharmed and lived to write the second edition of the book. And as an added bonus, Kevin's bladder didn't explode.

SAN DIEGO PADRES, PETCO PARK

An All-American Ballpark in Sunny San Diego

The good people of San Diego certainly enjoy spending time outdoors. And why shouldn't they? We would too if it was 72 degrees and sunny every day of the year. Whether it's surfing the perfect waves of the Pacific, hiking in the cool mountains that surround the city, or simply kicking back wherever and soaking in some sunshine, spending most of one's day outside is integral to the life of San Diegans. And with the outdoor themes of sky, sunshine, ocean, and earth in mind, they built the Padres their first exclusive home.

When Petco Park opened in 2004, the Padres, their fans, and all of baseball exhaled a collective sigh of relief. The Pads were able to finally play their home games in a facility that was designed exclusively for baseball. No longer would Qualcomm's decidedly football aesthetics impose themselves on the game. And no longer would the game being played there feel as if it had been retrofitted and remodeled into a facility designed for something else. From its beautiful interior that incorporates the Western Metal Supply Company building into its design, to the "Park at the Park" beyond the center-field wall, to its uniquely lush exterior, Petco is a tremendous place to see a ballgame. San Diego and its home team have plenty to be proud of with this wonderful ballpark. And they will tell you so, as they routinely call Petco "The Greatest Ballpark in Baseball."

Petco Park opened to glorious reviews. The newly built park had quirkiness designed right in, as have so many of the newer ballparks. And the designers went to great lengths to give the park a sense of place and location—succeeding on many levels to reflect elements that are strictly San Diego in nature. In our earlier edition of this book we said that the exterior had a Mission-style design, but that's not quite right. More accurately, Petco combines many elements that are native to the region that serve to bring about the unique outdoor feeling.

Petco will never be described as an intimate ballpark. It's vast on the inside, with a reputation as a pitcher's park matched only by Busch Stadium in St. Louis. As for the exterior footprint, the stadium resides on seventeen acres—which by comparison is eight acres larger than Fenway Park and 4.5 acres larger than AT&T Park in San Francisco.

The design team consisted of the ballpark architectural firm HOK Sport and Southwest architect Antoine Predock. As we said previously, the designers attempted to capture elements native to the region. And on most accounts, they succeeded. From the outside the ballpark doesn't exactly scream "ballpark" at passersby. There's no red brick and green seats and rising walls. There's no crowded little turnstile gates people must jam through to get to the expansive field within. Rather, Petco feels wide open to the outdoors and beautiful weather the city has to offer. The exposed white steel trusses of the exterior are more reminiscent of the city's maritime military heritage than anything baseball-related. The outer buildings that surround the seating bowl look vaguely Aztec in style, sloping like pyramids and covered in sandstone and stucco and all the lush greenery one would expect in a place that doesn't really have winter. Two of the buildings are actually called "garden buildings" and from them hang flowering gardens as beautiful as any you'll find. At street level, the grounds are exquisitely manicured, featuring jacaranda trees, bubbling waterfalls, and a courtyard full of airy palms. The outer buildings only appear close to the seating bowl from a distance, but as you approach you see they are actually quite distant, echoing the distant mesas common to the Southwest and adding to the vast open outdoor vibe of the park. It's all very beautiful, and if there is any knock on the design of the ballpark itself, it's that it doesn't truly feel like a ballpark until you're actually sitting in your seat.

Petco Park also fits into its surrounding environment remarkably well. Though not directly on the water, the park offers striking views of sailboats, navy vessels, cruise ships and the Coronado Bridge, spanning San Diego Bay from both its inner and outer grounds. Red trolleys dart past as the Orange Line of the San Diego Trolley system reaches its terminus a block away. And the park was nestled into the existing Gaslight District, an area teeming with restaurants, bars, and hotels. When Petco was being built, the Gaslight District was several shades seedier than it appears today. As a measure of good faith for the generous public funds used to build the ballpark, the Padres and their development partners agreed to spend $311 million on new construction surrounding the ballpark. Everyone seems to be a winner with this ballpark development, as a better location could scarcely be imagined.

Inside the ballpark, the most distinguishing feature that viewers on television rarely get to see is the "Park at the Park," an elevated grassy knoll beyond the center-field fence that can accommodate as many as twenty-five hundred fans, most of whom seem to want to keep one eye on the game and the other on their children, or singles in swimsuits playing Frisbee. At first we weren't too sure about the "Park at the Park," but then it occurred to us that for years Cactus League fans have been sunbathing during Spring Training on the grassy embankments beyond the outfield fences of the ballparks in Arizona. Perhaps regular-season sunbathers

view from Park at the Park

Fans enjoying two parks in one.
Photo by Jordan Parhad

were long overdue in the Major Leagues. And what better place for them than in laid-back and always sunny Southern California?

For those who want to keep both eyes on the game, Petco offers protected sight lines from nearly every section. A revolutionary "fractured" approach to the ballpark seating configuration creates clusters of independently angled sections that all point toward the batter's box at slightly different angles. This makes it impossible to walk the full circumference of the park on the upper levels, but having good sight lines will always be more important than being seat-hopper friendly in our book. And Petco Park offers quality views from all levels.

A few days after the Padres were swept by the Yankees in the 1998 World Series, the voters of San Diego approved a proposition to provide partial public funding for a new downtown ballpark. Under the plan, the city kicked in $304 million toward the project's $457 million budget and the Padres contributed the rest. The ballpark cost $285 million to build, with the remaining portion of the price tag attributed to land acquisition and infrastructure. Most of the city's financial support came from newly issued municipal bonds to be paid back with the revenue generated by a new hotel tax. This makes good sense for the city and its residents. Let the tourists pay a little more when they're in town, and let the locals reap the benefits. We inconvenienced friends and relatives for places to stay during our road trip (and you should too), so the hotel tax didn't bother us one bit.

Josh: My Aunt Jane didn't charge me a dime to sleep on her couch, so my tax was zero!

Kevin: And she did your laundry and cooked your breakfast too.

HOK has surfed atop the leading edge of the recent ballpark construction wave. The company, which since Petco's opening has changed its name to Populous, made its mark with Oriole Park at Camden Yards and its success just snowballed from there. Fans who have been to Baltimore will note the similarities between the use of its trademark B&O Warehouse and San Diego's use of the landmark Western Metal Building in the two ballpark complexes. But unlike the B&O, part of the Western Metal Building actually juts out into the field of play at Petco. The building's southwest corner forms the left-field foul pole. That's right—the ballpark was constructed, literally, around this old masonry building. If the ball hits the face of the building to the left of the pole, it's a long foul; if it hits to the right, it's a home run. The building also houses restaurants and observation suites for high rollers, as well as a rooftop standing-room area. What a unique trademark feature to build a ballpark around. And to think, we were starting to feel like we'd seen it all.

Petco Park was originally slated to open in April 2002, but several lawsuits brought against the city by citizens opposed to the hotel tax led to a construction halt in 2000. Since San Diego couldn't sell municipal bonds backed by the tax hike until the disputes were resolved, there was no money to continue the project. After construction resumed, the Friars struck a naming-rights deal with Petco, the familiar pet-supplies retailer. Just a few days after announcing the twenty-two-year, $60 million agreement in January 2003, the Padres again faced resistance from the local community when PETA called for the Padres to cancel the agreement. PETA was boycotting Petco (the store, not the yet-to-be-completed ballpark), claiming that an unacceptable number of animals died from diseases and overcrowding while in Petco stores.

Josh: PETA! Are those the same soy-huggers who petitioned the Brewers to add a tofu-dog to their Sausage Race?

Kevin: Yup.

Josh: Ridiculous.

Kevin: You talk tough, but I saw you reach for your wallet when that Sarah McLachlan commercial came on TV last night.

After joining the National League in 1969 as an expansion team along with the Montreal Expos, the Padres played their first thirty-five seasons in the multipurpose, multi-named stadium that has also served as home to the National Football League's Chargers. At the time of this book's print date, the footballers were lobbying for a new stadium in or around San Diego but had not yet broken through the political red tape. There may have been decorative palms beyond the old outfield fences, but make no mistake about it, the stadium currently known as Qualcomm was one of the cookie-cutters. It wasn't the worst cookie-cutter to ever come down the pike, and it served the Padres well for many years, but in the end, it was wearing out its welcome for baseball. The stadium's main problem was that it was too gigantic to provide an authentic ballpark

The view from right field.
Photo by Jordan Parhad

experience, especially after it was remodeled in 1983 to add ten thousand extra seats in right and center field for football. This expansion increased the stadium's seating capacity to more than sixty-seven thousand. Perfect for hosting bowl games, lousy for baseball. And lousy for regular season football too. The Chargers have had trouble selling out the four-level stadium, which has meant the city (as per an agreement with the team) has had to buy the unsold tickets from the Chargers to avoid the NFL's television blackout rule. This has really eaten local residents whose tax money has been spent to subsidize the NFL.

From 1967 until 1980 the Chargers' present facility and the Padres' longtime facility was called San Diego Stadium, then from 1981 until 1996 it was called Jack Murphy Stadium in honor of the local sports editor who campaigned to bring Major League ball to San Diego. After Murphy championed the movement to garner support for a big league team, a 1965 voter referendum approved construction of the $28 million stadium in Mission Valley. This suburban neighborhood had previously housed Westgate Park, which belonged to the Triple-A Pacific Coast League Padres. Like many of the PCL cities, baseball fans in San Diego still carry tremendous reverence for the original incarnation of the Padres, as is evidenced by the many references to the club, the league, and the era inside Petco.

If ever a city paid its dues before earning a place in the Show, that city is San Diego. The PCL Padres migrated to town from Salt Lake City, Utah, in 1936. In just their second season in Southern California, the PCL Padres captured the league championship, buoyed by the play of slugging native son Ted Williams, who was just nineteen years old at the time. Theodore Samuel Williams was born in San Diego on August 30, 1918. He would fight in two foreign theaters of war and put the finishing touches on a Hall of Fame career with the Red Sox, before groundbreaking would take place for a new stadium in San Diego on Christmas Eve, 1965. A year and a half later, the Chargers dedicated the facility on August 20, 1967, with a preseason loss to the Detroit Lions. With a stadium in place, Major League Baseball awarded San Diego a National League franchise in May of 1968. Less than a year later, the Padres fielded their first starting nine.

Big league ball was not an immediate hit in San Diego. And while some might argue that hardball still hasn't captured the hearts of sports fans in this town to the degree that it has in other West Coast cities, the baseball culture and interest in the team have grown considerably since the team's early days. The Padres didn't surpass the one million mark in home attendance in any of their first five campaigns and nearly jumped town for Washington, D.C., following the 1973 season. By early 1974, team owner C. Arnholt Smith had found a prospective buyer who planned to move the franchise to the nation's capital. New uniforms were being manufactured, and the team's front office employees were packing for the move. But at the last minute Ray Kroc, a San Diego native who had made his fortune building McDonald's fast-food franchises, jumped in and purchased the team. Kroc vowed to make the Padres viable in his hometown.

The team was atrocious before Kroc took the helm. In their first five seasons, the Padres never finished closer than twenty-eight and a half games out of first place in the National League's newly formed West Division. The team averaged just 600,000 fans per season during that time, or seventy-four hundred per home game. Ouch! By comparison, the Montreal Expos, who entered the National League at the same time, attracted a million fans in each of their first six seasons. And they were playing in the barren snowbelt known as the Great White North. It is important to note, however, that California baseball in general was not flourishing when the Padres entered the league. The Oakland A's, California Angels, and San Francisco Giants did poorly at the gate in the late 1960s and early 1970s as well, attracting less than a million fans per year themselves. Only the Dodgers thrived, routinely welcoming two million per season to Dodger Stadium.

In any case, the Padres finished last again under Kroc in 1974, forty-two games behind the first-place Dodgers, but attendance jumped from 611,000 the year before to just north of one million, thanks to the ray of hope Kroc had provided. In the years ahead, the emergence of exciting rookies like Dave Winfield and Ozzie Smith, and the acquisition of veteran stars like Rollie Fingers, Gaylord Perry, Steve Garvey, and Goose Gossage, gave the Padres a foothold in San Diego.

Josh: Didn't San Francisco's Willie McCovey play his final season with the Pads?

Kevin: "Stretch" became "Big Mac" at the McDonald's owner's insistence.

In 1984 a San Diego team led by Tony Gwynn, Kevin McReynolds, Graig Nettles, and the tireless Garvey won three straight games in the National League Championship Series to post a come-from-behind three-games-to-two win against the Cubs and advance to the World Series. But Detroit proved too powerful for the Friars in the Series. Jack Morris tossed two complete games, leading the Tigers to a four-games-to-one victory.

In 1998 the Padres tasted postseason champagne again after beating the Braves four games to two in the National League Championship Series. But the Yankees swept the Padres in the October Classic. Although the Padres lost both of their home games in the Series, including the clincher, the 1998 World Series would represent one of Qualcomm's greatest baseball moments. More than sixty-five thousand fans were on hand the night the Yankees closed out the series with a 3-0 shutout behind Andy Pettitte, Jeff Nelson, and Mariano Rivera in Game 4.

Concrete and massive, Qualcomm offered few features to tug at the heartstrings of romantic baseball fans. Large parcels of foul territory in the right-field and left-field corners were not visible from the infield due to the configuration of the seating bowl. The JumboTron would get so hot that fans in the back rows would feel the heat burning through their shirts. The foul poles were actually two feet behind the outfield fences. But the stadium did play host to some memorable moments, like Willie Mays's six hundredth career home run in 1969, and the ten innings of shutout ball pitched by the Dodgers' Orel Hershiser in 1988, which extended his consecutive scoreless innings streak to fifty-nine frames, breaking Don Drysdale's Major League record. Hershiser didn't pick up the win, though, as the Padres prevailed 2-1 in sixteen innings. In 1995 another game went into extra innings tied at 0-0, as Pedro Martinez, then of the Montreal Expos, pitched nine perfect innings against the Padres before losing his perfect game and no-no in the bottom of the tenth. Martinez still got a 1-0 victory with help from his bullpen.

Perhaps Qualcomm's most ignominious moment came in 1990 when Padres management made the ill-fated decision to let controversial actress Roseanne Barr sing the "Star Spangled Banner" before a game. After a purposely off-key rendition of the national anthem, Roseanne theatrically grabbed her crotch and spit. Though the comedian claimed she was parodying the antics of ballplayers, her joke was lost on the crowd, which booed lustily as she was escorted from the field by then-hubby Tom Arnold.

Kevin: Didn't she realize that San Diego is a town surrounded by Naval, Marine, and Coast Guard military bases?

Josh: Yeah, it's the home port of the Navy's Pacific Fleet.

Kevin: Talk about not knowing your audience.

The clip replayed on TV stations across the country for months, rarely alongside favorable commentary. At least Tom eventually moved on to bigger and better things with *The Best Damn Sports Show, Period,* which he has parlayed into an acting career.

Since its opening, The Pet has hosted its fair share of noteworthy baseball moments. The Pads lost the longest game in their history, a twenty-two-inning affair with the Colorado Rockies, by a score of 2-1 on April 17, 2008. A year earlier, Barry Bonds had hit his 755th home run at Petco on August 4, 2007.

Josh: Some wouldn't call that a shining moment.

Kevin: True, but it's a historical fact.

Josh: It's a part of baseball history that should be expunged. I mean, if they put an asterisk beside Roger Maris' 61st, what are they going to do with this?

Kevin: You're going to write another letter to the commissioner, aren't you?

Josh: I've already sent several.

Petco hasn't just served as a pitcher-friendly baseball yard since its opening in 2004. Some other funky events have played out on its lawn as well. During the Februarys of 2007–2009, it hosted the USA Sevens rugby tournament. And the stadium's first-ever concert was a pretty sweet gig. The Rolling Stones played Petco in November 2005 as part of their "A Bigger Bang" world tour. Madonna also played The Pet on her "Sticky and Sweet" tour.

Kevin: When are you going to remove that "music" from your iPod, by the way?

Josh: When you acknowledge that Madonna is *the* visionary genius of our generation.

Whether hosting musical acts, rugby, or National

Trivia Timeout

Beach Break: Who are the only two Cy Young Award winners to post losing records over their entire careers?

Point Break: Which native San Diegan was the first African American to play in the Pacific Coast League? Hint: He was a Padre.

Reef Break: Who were the first baseball teams to play a game at Petco Park?

Look for the answers in the text.

League baseball games, Petco is a fine facility both inside and out. If there is any knock on it from the exterior, it's that it doesn't look much like a ballpark. It's open, and appears obviously to be a stadium, but the sandstone walls and hanging gardens of the exterior buildings look like they could be adorning a mall in the city. There's no dead giveaway whether Petco is a baseball park, a football stadium, or a soccer pitch. In avoiding some of the classic elements, such as red brick and green seats, the designers made the park more regionally appropriate, but left it fairly well disguised to those who may stop short of stepping inside to take in the fine field it surrounds. But this is a small knock if it is a knock at all. Who knows? Maybe Petco will set the new standard for ballpark aesthetics.

Getting a Choice Seat

We missed the full Petco experience on the first road trip because the park wasn't finished yet. Blame it on those silly lawsuits. We did, however, manage a game there on our second hardball odyssey, and we can tell you that in our first attempt at characterizing the park we were right about some things, and others, well, let's just say we may have relied too heavily on the advance billing provided by the Padres' press packet.

For instance, Petco is no "small-park." The field dimensions are deep. And while its capacity of forty-six thousand (counting standing room) made it relatively small

Seating Capacity: 46,000
Ticket Office: http://sandiego.padres.mlb.
com/ticketing/singlegame.jsp?c_id=sd
Seating Chart: http://sandiego.padres.
mlb.com/sd/ticketing/seating_pricing.jsp

compared to the several cookie-cutter parks that were still in operation in 2004, it's not one of the smaller ballparks out there today, now that the cookie-cutters have gone the way of the spitball. In fact, it's just about exactly in the middle of the pack as far as seating capacity goes. However, its wide open design gives most seats a clear view of the action, even if some feel a bit farther from the action than those at some parks.

As with many of the newer parks, nearly every seat in the lower bowl is a winner. Upstairs, meanwhile, an extended cantilever truss supporting the upper deck brings fans closer than usual to the playing field, and the unique design of the seating bowl offers fragmented "seating neighborhoods" that all point toward the plate at their own angle. Only a few of these sections suffer from underhang or blockage issues.

Padres management is committed to leaving a number of Field Level seats available for day-of-game purchase. We think this is a great idea and hope it catches on in other cities. So don't rule out the possibility of nabbing decent last-minute seats. But do arrive at the box office early if you hope to score some of these tickets.

Field Level (Sections 101–135)

The Field Level extends thirty-nine rows on the infield and forty-four rows in the outfield. Yes, this is a deep first level. There are nearly fifteen thousand seats on the first level between the foul poles at Petco. Sections 101 and 102 are directly behind the plate, with even-numbered sections continuing down the left-field line and odd-numbered sections on the right. The first five rows of seats on the infield are reserved for members of the Padres Premier Club. The next best seats are in Rows 6–22 below the mid-level concourse in Sections 100–110, and these belong exclusively to season-ticket holders. These seats are very nice and have wait service. Farther back, the Field Reserved seats (Rows

36–44) are tucked underneath the Club Level. These should be avoided if possible because the overhang does block views of fly balls.

The best seats likely to be available to the average member of the ticket-buying public (read: you) are in Rows 26–35 of the Field Reserved sections just beyond the first- and third-base bags. Row 26 is the first row behind the walkway, which is set down low enough to not ruin the view for "front-row" seat holders. We recommend Sections 111 and 112, just beyond the corner bags. If you want to get closer to the field with a lower row number and are willing to sacrifice your proximity to the plate to do so, shoot for Field Box Sections 116 to 124 in the outfield.

The first row of seats in Section 124 near the Western Metal Building is Row 14. So if you want to sit down near the field, pass up that fifth-row seat in Section 120 or that third-row seat in Section 122, and aim for Section 114, Row 14. Just be advised that the large brick building immediately to your left may block your view of the left-field fence.

Sections 125 to 137 are located in right-field home run territory—with two levels of seating above them. The foul pole obstructs the view of the batter's box for those in Section 127, and bisects the outfield for those in Section 125, especially seats 6–10 and on up. We recommend

interior

The view down the first baseline.
Photo by Jordan Parhad

avoiding 125 and 127 altogether. Section 131 also has foul-pole obstructions and should be avoided.

Sections 126 to 134 in left field not only offer fans the hope of catching a home run ball, but the chance to sit near legendary superfan Harry "the Heckler" Maker, and Josh's wife's cousin Michael Hernandez, a certified bleacher bum and Heckling Harry's protégé. If you see Michael at a game, buy him a hot dog and a beer and he'll be your friend for life.

Just past Section 134 and above the Padres' bullpen is a section known as the Picnic Terrace. This is a specialty ticket section for private parties only, with unprecedented access to the bullpens (which aren't really pens at all, but simply a place for the relievers on a bench at ground level). Fans in this section sit behind long tables and well-manicured garden boxes. These seats are okay (they're still outfield bleachers) but they're reserved for groups.

The Sand Lot

If your kids wish you'd taken them to the beach instead of the ballpark, there is a large sandy area below the Bleachers to the right of the batter's eye in right-center called "The Beach" where kids can build sand castles while mom and dad watch them and the game beyond. These seats are cheap, have well-formed seat backs and have a decent view. They represent more of what Petco does well, which is provide cheap seating options. Beware, though: The Beach section offers about as much protection from the sun as the actual beach. So bring the sunscreen—especially for afternoon games. For a few dollars more, you can sit in your own beach chair in the "Beach Club" section of the Bleachers.

Club Level (Sections 201–235)

At fifteen rows deep, the Club Level contains more than five thousand seats, many of which come complete with wait service. The level also houses four lounges. In our book, though, an afternoon spent in the outfield bleachers easily trumps any Club experience. Although, we must admit this is a low Club level that offers excellent views. And peeking in through the glass of the outer concourse, the food looked pretty good too.

Sections 225 to 235 are located in the second deck in home run territory in right field, while Sections 226 to 230 are in homer territory in left. Although these sections are on the Club Level, they do not come with Club privileges. The seats in right field seemed far from the action to us. And the foul pole blocks the view of the plate for many of the seats in Section 225, 227 and 231.

Standing Room and General Admission Bleachers atop the Western Metal Building

The ballpark designers went to great lengths to ensure that fans have room to linger and lounge at Petco, whether by choice or necessity in the event of a sellout. Petco can accommodate fifteen hundred standing-room ticket holders in designated standing areas on all three levels. Our favorite general admission area is the bank of bleachers on the roof of the Western Metal Building, some eighty feet above the field. Most of the seats inside the historic Western Metal Supply Company building belong to the suites on the second and third floors, and the Hall of Fame Restaurant on the fourth. On the roof is a pricey bleacher area for large groups and then a bleacher space for some commoners like you. Your only shot of getting on that roof is by waiting in the often long line that forms on the left-field side to access this area. Expect to stay only a short while, three innings at most, as they keep the line moving so that as many people as possible may have a chance to experience the signature element of the ballpark in all its glory.

Upper Level (Sections 300–328)

Since the ballpark is a full three levels, the upper deck is pushed pretty high into the stratosphere. The seats directly behind home plate in Sections 300–306 are definitely the best. If you'd like to call balls and strikes, stake out a spot in Section 300, directly behind (and above) home plate.

SEATING TIP NO. 1

The best seats aren't always the cheapest. In fact, most often the old adage "you get what you pay for" rings true. But at Petco, this adage and a little advice from your friends can save you dollars and get you into a better seat than you deserve (or at least can afford).

At Petco, the cheapest seats are the best seats. For a mere sawbuck, you should buy a "Park Pass." Not only can you take advantage of all the amenities of the "Park at the Park" but the ticket also grants you access to the entire first level of the ballpark, which as you might guess, is great for hanging around in a standing room area until the third inning or so, then hopping down into the best unused seats Petco has to offer.

The problem is that because of the access, these tightwad hill specials are the hottest tickets in the park and are often sold out before the game actually starts. So our best sitting tip is to get to the ballpark early and secure these tickets well before first pitch because they do go fast.

Sections 307–312 are okay, but we would avoid anything beyond the light towers (315–328), as there are underhang issues that will compromise your view of the game. The worst seats in the house are in Section 328 where the Western Metal Building blocks most of left field and you have underhang issues as well.

The most unique seating in the upper decks are the Tower Lofts (Sections 313 and 314). These sections are built right into the large light towers that give the ballpark part of its distinctive look. These seats are a bit gimmicky and don't feel as close as those in either section directly beside them, but if you want to tell your friends you climbed the light pole to get a better view, then have at these seats.

The first several rows of Petco Park's upper deck are called the Upper Boxes. These sell for a bit more money than seats in the Upper Reserved (Rows 7–27) located behind the concourse. We suggest throwing down the extra couple bills to sit in one of the deck's first rows. You won't even be able to get a Friar Dog with the difference in price if you disregard our advice and the seats down low offer much closer views.

The midlevel concourse is sunken adequately to allow fans in the first few rows of the Upper Reserved to see over the walkway traffic. The railings of the stairways leading to the Upper Reserved, however, present something of an obstruction for fans seated in Rows 9 through 11.

The "Beachers"

The bleacher section in right-center field is actually called the Beachers, and provides benches in one of the deepest parts of the outfield. These are also behind "the Beach" party area. Situated as they are, these are exceptionally far from the infield. Heck, they're not even that close to the outfield. While usually we counsel fans to get as low to the action as possible, in this park we recommend upper-level seats on the infield rather than the Beachers.

Park at the Park

The grassy park beyond the outfield fence has room for twenty-five hundred fans. This is a great area for families, especially those with younger kids who can't sit still for the full nine innings. A very nice miniature baseball field for the little ones, complete with real dirt and chalk-lined base paths, is a nice touch to get kids more actively involved. Adults are encouraged to watch the action from outside the little fences. Josh refrained from running the base paths, or should we say he was held back by Kevin, his brother Sean,

SEATING TIP NO. 2

Fireworks Fridays Park Passes

Fans attending Friday games have the added treat of seeing fireworks after the last out. Why does this information belong in the seating section? Well, those fans with Park Passes are invited onto the field to view the fireworks show. That's right, you can stand or sit on the field. This tip comes courtesy of Kevin's cousin Erin.

SEATING TIP NO. 3

Catering to the Fat Cats

There are so many restaurants and special group areas built into Petco Park, it's difficult to keep track of them all. Some are only accessible at the Club level, while others are for private parties. However, you can sneak into the Mercado area if your seats are as bad as ours were. For the full breakdown or if you want to host a corporate event or have your wedding reception at Petco Park, we suggest visiting the Padres' private event website at: http://PETCOparkconcerts.com.

Otherwise, simply remember this: If you're a regular ticket holder, you can't get into many of the restaurants. The Baja Bistro, Club 19, Coronados, the Hall of Fame Bar and Grill, and the Wind and Sea Lounge are not accessible unless you have a Terrace-Level ticket. You can peer inside the Omni Hotel Club restaurant, but you can only access it via the footbridge that leads to and from the hotel itself.

Kevin's cousin Erin, and our friend Jordan—all of whom had joined us for the day.

Fans can spread out the picnic blanket or throw a Frisbee, let the kids play on the playground equipment, and see a bit of the game. There was even a stage set up with a live band playing for this section. However, we wouldn't call the views from this part of the park "great." But there is a grassy knoll that improves the view a bit—it looks like it's made of Astroturf, yet it's actually real grass. We also appreciate the see-through outfield fences that maximize fans' views of outfielders chasing deep fly balls, as well as the mini JumboTron on the back of the batter's eye for fans who actually care about what is happening on the field. Fans can visit the ballpark to watch away games on this screen as well.

The Black Market

The city's strictly enforced anti-scalping laws keep the ticket hustlers at bay. But don't worry, the laws of capitalism apply, and where there is demand, there is supply. Fans and scalpers just have to be a bit sneakier than usual. Don't look for the ticket hawkers within a one-block radius of the ballpark;

rather, head two blocks away—where you can't see the park itself—and you'll find them. The corner of L Street and 5th Avenue and the corner of J Street and 7th Avenue are good places to start.

Before/After the Game

The city of San Diego and its voters agreed to finance the lion's share of the new ballpark in the hope that it would anchor a massive urban revitalization effort. The newly minted Ballpark District consists of twenty-six blocks that just a few years ago represented one of San Diego's seediest neighborhoods. Keep in mind, however, that a "seedy" neighborhood in America's Finest City is still nicer than 75 percent of the urban hoods in the country.

We're happy to report that Petco Park, its legions of fans, and the money contracted to the development of the area have indeed paid dividends, and the revitalization of the neighborhood has occurred in full force. The Ballpark District and the Gaslamp Quarter represent the second best pregame neighborhood environment we've come across—second only, of course, to Wrigleyville.

Josh: Fenway? It's better than Fenway?

Kevin: Sorry, my friend. Objectively, San Diego gets the nod.

Josh: Oh, right. You West Coasters are always objective.

Getting to Petco Park

The ballpark is accessible from five major freeways: Interstate 5, Interstate 805, Interstate 15, Highway 163, and Route 94. The intersection of Route 5 (which runs north and south) and Route 94 (east and west) is about a mile northeast of the ballpark. As part of the new ballpark initiative, San Diego marked all of these roads with signs pointing fans in the direction of Petco. The ballpark is adjacent to the San Diego Convention Center, bordered by 7th Avenue, K Street, Harbor Drive, and 10th Avenue. L Street serves as a game-day pedestrian mall between 7th and 10th Avenues.

PARKING

On-site parking is limited to five thousand spaces, which seems like a low number. Chalk it up as the price fans pay to have their ballpark located in an actual city neighborhood. Private lots provide another eleven thousand spots within the Ballpark District. The cheapest lot we found was on Imperial Street between 13th and 14th Streets. The lot is on a triangular plot and it's much smaller than the two bigger and more expensive lots across the street, so get

there early. The larger lots do have better tailgating going on, however.

PUBLIC TRANSPORTATION

Fans wishing to avoid the parking scene and traffic may take advantage of one of the several MTS light-rail trolley stations within walking distance of the ballpark. The Orange Line's Seaport Village, Convention Center, and Gaslamp Quarter stations all service the ballpark and are within a few blocks of Petco. The closest station is the Gaslamp stop. The trolley is a very affordable and easy way to get to the ballpark. MTS Info: www.sdcommute.com/

Watering Holes and Outside Eats

TAILGATING LIVES ON AT PETCO!

We were pleasantly surprised to find that not only are there parking lots at Petco for motorists, but that the tailgating culture that was so vibrant at the Padres' old stadium has traveled with the grilling fan base to Petco. With so many restaurants to choose from, and with Petco not being surrounded by parking lots, this was in question. But find them you will, tailgaters. We observed brats grilling, solo cup jockeys, and parking lot games in particular abundance in the lots off Imperial at the intersection of 13th directly outside the park.

GASLAMP QUARTER

The Gaslamp Quarter is an old warehouse and historical area. This was already an established entertainment destination before the ballpark opened, but it has grown greatly in the years since the Padres moved in. The Gaslamp Quarter now features practically every discernable type of bar and restaurant you could imagine. You'll know you're there by the gas lamps that serve as streetlights, as well as by the large welcome sign. The Gaslamp District has a Bourbon Street kind of feel to it. It's comfortable, friendly, and has a lot going on. You almost feel as though you might be able to walk around with a drink in your hand—though we're not recommending that. When we visited we noticed a man making his way up and down the streets wearing a Hawaiian shirt, swimming trunks, and Crocs. He had a dusty cowboy hat on his head, was smoking a cigar, and was holding a guitar with a live macaw perched on it. We provide this interesting image just so you know what kind of neighborhood you're stepping into.

Truly, there is a bar, restaurant, and nightclub for every fan's desire and budget. A stroll down Fourth, Fifth, or Sixth Avenues offers scores of bars and restaurants from which to choose. Whether you want sushi, Mexican, Chinese, Italian, Irish, burgers, pizza, pub food, coastal seafood, wine bars, whiskey bars, they're all present. There are far too many options to list, which is a great problem to have, so we'll highlight some of the more interesting ones.

DICK'S LAST RESORT—THE SHAME OF THE GASLAMP
345 4th Ave.
www.dickslastresort.com/domains/sandiego

This franchise of Dick's Last Resort from Boston's Back Bay has outside seating complete with an outside bar. There are picnic tables, umbrellas, and a lifeguard chair with an attractive young lady working it. Dick's is a great place to drink and sightsee, and an okay place to eat. Expect plenty of off-color jokes on the menu and from the wait staff. All in all, it's not a bad place to be before a game and it's definitely our choice of all the loud and rowdy-themed restaurants.

JOLTIN' JOE'S
379 4th Ave.
www.joltinjoes.com

Great food and great times await courtesy of Mr. Coffee himself, Joltin' Joe DiMaggio. Actually, the food is average and we have no idea if this place has any relation to the Yankee Clipper, but with a name like that, we had to at least mention it.

GASLAMP PIZZA
505 5th Ave.
http://gaslamppizza.com

Finally, we found a place on the West Coast where we could get a thin crust slice before the game! If you're still wandering around the neighborhood late at night and have the munchies, this is your spot. Try the BBQ chicken topping and you won't regret it.

LA PUERTA
560 4th Ave.
www.lapuertasd.com/

This is the spot for Mexican in the Gaslamp. Skip the other places and dig in to their cheap and delicious menu. We recommend the guacamole, carne asada fries, three street tacos, and the TJ dogs. With plenty of happy hour specials, you may want to hit this place before *and* after the game.

BUB'S @ THE BALLPARK
715 J St.
http://bubssandiego.com

This is a big, open place with outdoor seating, big crowds, and lots of TVs. And there are Christmas lights to boot! It's not unlike a frat party: full bar, cheap beer, peanut shells all over the floor, shuffle board and pool tables, and a fairly warm atmosphere if you're a cute girl. Here's a tip—check in online at FourSquare, show your server your Check-In pass on your smart phone, and get a free order of tater tots. You can't beat free tots. And the rest of the menu is better than you might expect. Try the patty melt. If it's a Wednesday, head straight for the 25-cent wing special.

THE FIELD
544 5th Ave.
www.thefield.com

We had lunch at this authentic Irish pub. Josh had the beef stew, which was nice and peppery, with the vegetables still firm and tasty. Kevin had the rasher (Irish bacon) and cheese boxty with a nice cream sauce across the top. Kevin's brother Sean ordered the shepherd's pie, which was also very good. Our friend Jordan ordered the fish and chips, which came moist and flavorful on the inside and crispy on the outside. With good Guinness and solid Irish music, this was certainly Kevin's favorite place in the Gaslamp.

TIVOLI'S BAR AND GRILLE
505 6th Ave.
www.tivolibargrill.com

Around since 1885, this place claims to be the Gaslamp's oldest bar. In an area with far too many high-end eating and drinking choices, it's certainly the district's oldest dive-bar, which makes it okay in our book. A beer won't cost you half a week's wages here. Use your ticket stub for $1 off your first beer. For a Canadian favorite, try the poutine, which is fries soaked with gravy and smothered with cheese curds and Montreal steak seasoning. It's the house special. But if you tried the poutine at Miller Park in Milwaukee and didn't like it, the burgers here are good too.

ROCKIN' BAJA COSTAL CANTINA
310 5th Ave.
http://rockinbaja.com

This regional chain is famous for its baja buckets, which are really exactly as you're probably picturing them: buckets of fish that include everything from shrimp to lobster to mahi mahi. Some of this is fried, some not. With plenty of drink specials, this place is like other theme restaurants you've been to—grass hut roofs and mojitos made by an amateur.

CINE CAFÉ
K Street and 4th Avenue

This is a cheap deli, liquor store, bakery, grocery store, ATM location, and lottery-ticket seller all rolled into one. It's the kind of place you'd expect to find in the Bronx outside

Yankee Stadium. It's seedy, but we liked it. We cannot vouch for the baked goods, however.

THE GASLAMP STRIP CLUB
340 5th St.
www.cohnrestaurants.com

Don't let the name or the scantily clad woman on the logo fool you: This isn't a "girls get naked" strip club but rather a place to order strip steaks and martinis—unless there was a back room they weren't telling us about. They actually let you grill your own steak at this place, which is kinda cool.

> *Josh:* Do they still expect a tip?
> *Kevin:* Yes, as a matter of fact, they do.
> *Josh:* Can I pay in singles?
> *Kevin:* Don't you always?

LOLITA'S AT THE PARK
202 Park Blvd.
http://lolitasmexicanfood.com

Now, this is our kind of Mexican food—simple, fresh, cheap, and de-scrumptious. Order anything off the menu, because this is the kind of place where you cannot go wrong. The carne asada fries are the bomb. Josh recommends the carnitas, because you know, you have to go with pork when you're having Mexican. And while Kevin agrees, he's got a thing for chile rellenos, and he recommends the chile rellenos specialty plate highly. And remember the Lolita's motto: Patience is the essence of fine Mexican food.

THE TILTED KILT PUB AND EATERY
310 10th Ave.
http://sandiego.tiltedkilt.com

Detailed in the Pittsburgh chapter, this chain tries to combine kitschy Scotch-Irish kilts with Hooters-type serving girls, and rolls it all into a pub that serves American food and beers from all over the world. We'd like to pan it, but the reality is . . . it's close to the ballpark. The food is average, but there are kilts aplenty. So we'll let you visit the website and go to the photo gallery to make the call if this is your kind of place or not. Sure, they're popping up all over the place, but is that such a bad thing?

THE CORNER BAR—BURGERS AND COCKTAILS
10th and J Street
www.thecornersd.com

Hipsters will migrate to this joint, and will find here some tasty burgers and cool drinks upon their arrival. The building itself is very appealing—two stories with a very open feel. The menu is simple, sticking to what they do best, which is burgers and pub fare. P.S.: Sandos is hipster-speak for

sandwiches. Josh recommends the Jalapeno Burger, which is hot. Kevin prefers to build his own burger with a side of fried pickles. Add the draft of your choice to wash it down.

> *Josh:* We should do the three-pound Burger Challenge. If we eat all six patties, the toppings, and the cheesy tater tots in under an hour, it's free!
> *Kevin:* We just came from Lolita's.
> *Josh:* You really have gone soft.
> *Kevin:* I prefer to think of it as going "smart."

BASIC
410 10th Ave.
www.barbasic.com

We didn't make it into this popular pizza joint. We were too stuffed to eat another bite. But the line after the game was long—and that's usually a good sign. A quick review of the menu did let us know that this is a build-your-own-pie kind of joint. There are four "basic" pies, and you add the toppings you like. Judging by the line around the block, they seem to be doing something right.

RANDY JONES' ALL AMERICAN SPORTS BAR AND GRILL
7510 Hazard Center Dr., Ste. 215
http://aagrill.com

If you just can't get enough of the fuzzy-topped pitcher from SD, or if you only feel comfortable in a sports bar, then you might want to make the journey by car to Jones's place. The food and atmosphere are precisely as described: All-American, so choose from burgers, barbecue, wraps, sandwiches, chili and more. The menu's actually quite extensive and we just had to mention the place, because Randy's a heck of a guy who was also a pretty good pitcher in his day.

Inside the Park

Petco features an asymmetrical outfield that offers a bevy of angles, nooks, and crannies. In left field, the corner of the Western Metal Building is 334 feet from home plate. The gap in left-center is 367 feet away, dead center is 390 feet, and the deepest part of the park in right-center is 409 feet. A spacious right-center-field gap measures 387 feet away before tapering to just 322 feet down the right-field line. How does this measure up to Qualcomm? The Q was 330 feet down both lines, 375 feet to the power alleys and 405 feet to center field, with its outfield wall taking one long and unwavering trip along the outer perimeter of the field: Boring!

Petco's front row seats along the first- and third-base lines are just thirty-three feet from fair territory, as opposed to the forty-four feet it measured from the front-row seats at the Q to the white lines. The first row of the Club deck is thirty-four feet above the field, as opposed to the forty-four feet above the field it was at the Q. And the first row of the upper deck is sixty-six feet high, as opposed to seventy-nine feet at the old park.

Does The Pet offer some quirks just for the sake of quirks? Perhaps. And we are well aware that these things can be overdone. But we were glad we weren't seeing a game at nondescript Qualcomm. We liked the unique dimensions and quality views of this interesting ballpark. We do have one suggestion for management, though: There's too much exposed concrete inside Petco, and it takes away from the feeling the Padres are no doubt trying to create. Please continue the Indian sandstone tiled theme you did so well outside Petco, and cover up some of the concrete on the deck supports. It will truly enhance the interior look of your park. You might refer to Target Field in Minnesota or Minute Maid Park in Houston, where such efforts to dress up the facing of the upper levels have contributed to aesthetically warm and appealing parks.

Ballpark Features

THE WESTERN METAL SUPPLY COMPANY BUILDING

Building the ballpark around this building and then making it physically part of the field of play was the true stroke of genius in Petco's design. The left-field foul pole runs along the corner of the building such that balls that hit the wall on the left of it are foul, and those that hit the right face are home runs. On the HR side, supporting decks house luxury seats, and while perhaps not among the best in baseball as far as views are concerned, they certainly are among the coolest. On the building's roof are standing-room bleacher seats that fans with any seats at all can sit at for a maximum of three innings—eighty feet above field level. The building is decorative, functional, and simply a very distinctive part of the ballpark.

The ninety-five-year-old building had to be seismically retrofitted in order to comply with the new earthquake-proof standards of the day before it could be incorporated into the ballpark. Concrete was poured in all levels, including the roof, to accomplish this in early 2003. Then openings were created on each level to serve as ramps to the seating decks.

The Padres team store is on the first floor, as is a doorway leading to the general admission area. The second and third floors house luxury suites, and the fourth floor houses a restaurant. The first level concourse passes through the building and it is worth checking out both the Padres Hall of Fame and the exhibit dedicated to the history of the Pacific Coast League and baseball in the San Diego area. Also worthy of a stop is the Hall of Fame restaurant.

PADRES HALL OF FAME

The San Diego Padres Hall of Fame honors players, coaches, and executives who have left their mark in the Padres' history books. At the time of this printing, six men had been inducted into the hall since it was created to honor the club's thirtieth anniversary in 1999. The group includes four players, two executives, and one broadcaster/manager.

The inaugural class included pitcher Randy Jones, who won ninety-two games in eight seasons with San Diego (1973–1980), outfielder Nate Colbert, who averaged twenty-seven home runs per year in six seasons with the Padres (1969–1974), and former owner Ray Kroc (1974–1984).

In 2000, outfielder Dave Winfield, the first player to be enshrined in Cooperstown wearing a Padres hat on his plaque, was inducted into the Padres Hall. Winfield jumped right from the University of Minnesota campus into the Padres lineup in 1973, without playing a single game in the minors. He played eight seasons with San Diego, before joining the Yankees in 1981. Though his prime years were spent in the Big

The Western Metal Supply Company building

Photo by Jordan Parhad

Apple, the slugger's distaste for George Steinbrenner and fondness for America's Finest City were taken into account when it came time for the Baseball Hall of Fame to make his plaque, which portrayed him in a Padres hat.

The team's first president, Buzzie Bavasi, and longtime radio broadcaster, Jerry Coleman, were inducted in 2001. Coleman, who has been calling Padres games since 1972, actually stepped out of the broadcast booth to manage the team to a 73–89 record in 1980, paving the way for broadcaster Larry Dierker to pull the same trick in Houston several years later with considerably better results. Coleman, you may also remember, won the 1949 American League Rookie of the Year Award playing second base for the Yankees.

Tony Gwynn, who holds nearly every Padres batting record, assumed his place in the Padres Hall in 2002 and joined the Baseball Hall of Fame on his first ballot attempt in 2007.

FRIAR TONY

Atop the grassy knoll in Petco's "Park at the Park" is a statue of "Mr. Padre" himself, Tony Gwynn. "Mr. Padre" won a National League record-tying eight batting titles and was selected to fifteen All-Star teams. His .338 lifetime average is the highest by any Major Leaguer since Ted Williams. In a career that spanned 1982 to 2001, Gwynn recorded 3,141 hits. He also notched 1,138 RBI and 319 stolen bases. Today Gwynn is the head baseball coach at his alma mater, San Diego State University. The statue is a nice likeness of Gwynn, who is portrayed with his distinctive swing dashing yet another pitcher's hopes. The statue was unveiled as part of "Tony Gwynn Weekend" during July 2007.

THE GREATEST OF THEM ALL—6, 19, 31, 35, 42, 51

Atop the batter's eye are the numbers of retired Padres greats. Steve Garvey wore No. 6 for the Friars for five seasons. Though he was not with the team long, Garvey helped the Padres make it to their first World Series by hitting a clutch two-run homer against the Cubs' Lee Smith during Game 4 of the 1984 NLDS. No. 19 belongs to Gwynn, who, aside from the aforementioned statue, also has a street named for him. Petco Park, in fact, is located at 19 Tony Gwynn Dr. No. 31 honors Winfield, whose remarkable twenty-two-year career began in San Diego. No. 35 was worn by Randy Jones, perhaps the most popular Padre to ever play other than Gwynn. We met Randy at his barbecue stand on the first road trip, and it's easy to see why this very affable man remains a great ambassador for Padre baseball. No. 42 belongs, of course, to Jackie Robinson. No. 51—which was retired late in the 2011

Mr. Padre, Tony Gwynn statue

TONY GWYNN
"MR. PADRE"

Photo by Jordan Parhad

season—belongs to Trevor Hoffman, whose 601 career saves made him one of the best relievers ever.

What many who visit Petco may not notice is that beneath the batter's eye are mounted replicas of the bronze plaques of those Padres who have entered Cooperstown. You'll need to bribe an usher to get down here, but it might be worth it to you.

THE PACIFIC COAST LEAGUE BAR AND GRILL

Serving as the home for the Padres players who have been inducted into the PCL Hall of Fame, the Pacific Coast League Bar and Grill is a great place to get something to eat while soaking up the seven decades of Padres' baseball in San Diego. Look for the statue of Johnny Ritchey inside the grill. A native San Diegan, Ritchey was the first African American player in the PCL and played for the Padres in 1948 (just a year after Jackie Robinson broke the color barrier at the Major League level). Ritchey hit .323 during his rookie season and his grace and dignity in assuming the role he did to break down barriers garners him the respect he deserves.

> ## Inaugural Game
>
> The Padres played their first game at Petco Park on April 8, 2004, posting a ten-inning win over the San Francisco Giants. But that wasn't the first baseball game played at the Pet. A month earlier, Tony Gwynn had coached his San Diego State Aztecs to a win over the University of Houston Cougars on March 11, 2004, as part of a four-team NCAA baseball tournament. This is an interesting fact, to be sure, and we wonder whether the Padres would have allowed another team to play the first game at their new yard if anyone other than Gwynn had been coaching at SDSU. Hey, we told you this town can't get enough Tony.

MILITARY HONORS

In the Kidzone section on the outer concourse, near the standard pitching and batting cages, stands a miniature replica of the USS *Midway*, encased in Plexiglas to honor the military heritage of the region. A mural honoring all MLB players who have served in the military is on the wall nearby and contains the San Diego Padre logo set within the U.S. Military red, white, and blue stars and stripes emblem. Also, on the third level flag plaza near the right-field foul pole, you'll find the flags of every National League team interspersed with the flags of all the branches of the US Military.

Stadium Eats

A tradition we hoped would be left at the old ballpark and not brought to Petco was the mediocrity of the ballpark food. Sadly, we are still left to hope that one day this city, with the freshest ingredients known to man, will offer more consistently delicious ballpark fare. But as of today we must warn you that the food at Petco is perhaps suitable for pets, but most of it is not for humans. There are a few notable exceptions, but by and large, the tailgaters and the folks chowing down at restaurants in the Gaslamp Quarter have it correct. Eat before you get to the game.

RUBIO'S SHRIMP BURRITO (TRADEMARK FOOD)

This dish is comparable to what you would get in the restaurant, a big old burrito that you can hold in two hands, and stuffed with beans, rice, cheese, freshly diced tomatoes, jalapeños, salsa fresco, and slathered in a nice chipotle sauce that's not too overbearing. Ralph Rubio opened the first Rubio's stand in Mission California in 1983 after bringing the recipe for his fish tacos to the States from San Felipe in Baja, Mexico.

THE FRIAR DOG (HOT DOG REVIEW)

Though an improvement over the Wienerschnitzel dogs we tried at Qualcomm, the Friar Dog still only garners our most average rating. But hey, much like the Friars themselves, a C is a massive improvement over the failing grade earned in the past. The Friar dog was boiled, not grilled, had little snap, and average flavor. You can still get the Wienerschnitzel dog too; we can only guess this is for nostalgia purposes other than culinary ones.

BEST OF THE REST

The **carne asada fries** available at the Bayview Grille stands are not cheap, but they are delicious. Maybe more than even the shrimp burrito, these fries, dripping in carne asada and smothered with cheese and jalapeno peppers, taste like what you might expect in the Southwest. And it's all served up in a bowl over deliciously crispy fries. You can get better carne asada fries at Lolita's just across the street from Petco, but then again, those might be the best on the planet.

Anthony's Fish Grotto has a **Cajun crispy fish sandwich** that is quite tasty, as is the **New England clam chowder** served in a breadbowl. Inside the Western Metal Building you'll find a couple of offerings you'll enjoy: The **beef brisket sandwich** from the Carvery is a solid choice, as you can hardly ever go wrong with brisket; the **Sonora sausage** from the Sausage stand is wrapped in bacon and has a nice spicy flavor to it. Of course, you can always get **nachos** with so many different options for toppings you'll have trouble deciding.

Another favorite place for us at Petco is **Randy Jones' Barbecue** where we not only sampled a tasty plate of Brush Back Ribs, but we also met the former Cy Young Award winner. Jones was friendly and personable and took time out from running the stand to talk to us about our travels. Aside from the ribs, we also recommend the Fowl Territory plate, which consists of half a barbecued chicken with a choice of two side dishes. Jones sells the barbecue sauce that carries his name, and has since 1994. Jones has two locations in the ballpark—in the Mercado area alongside other restaurants and in the outfield.

A southpaw, Jones became the first Padre to win the Cy Young Award in 1976 when he posted a 22–14 record to go with a 2.76 ERA and twenty-five complete games. He remains the team's all-time leader in innings pitched (1,765), starts (253), complete games (71), and shutouts (18), and is a member of the Padres Hall of Fame. For his career, however, Jones was an unremarkable 100–123. He and another former Padre, Mark Davis, are the only two pitchers to finish their careers with losing records after winning the Cy Young Award. Davis, who posted forty-four saves and a 1.85 ERA to claim the 1989 Cy, hung up his spikes in 1997 with a career record of 51–84.

SAY "NO, THANKS," AND WALK AWAY

The Padres' Mexican Café carries what we once called the ballpark's trademark food, Rubio's Baja shrimp tacos and fish tacos. Last time we gave the nod to the crispy fried fish tacos, but this time we tried the shrimp and fish tacos and they were pretty awful. We'd like to see this offering come back to its former stature, but the fact was, when we tried it, the shrimp was rubbery, the tacos were too soupy to hold onto, it was over-spiced, and had little of the delicate flavor we remembered from our first trip. Just to prove we weren't imagining things, we went to a Rubio's restaurant and ordered both the shrimp and the fish tacos, and they were just as good as before. So this is not a case

of, it's just better at the restaurant. In this case, say no thanks and get the carne asada fries or the shrimp burrito instead.

BALLPARK BREWS

Outside Section 105 you will find Ballpark Brews which has an extensive selection of beers from all over. Whether you fancy a Shinerbock, a Widmer, a New Castle, or an Alaskan Amber, there is a bottle of beer here to suit you. Though the beers come in bottles, the attendant pours them into plastic cups for patrons.

Josh: A beer always tastes better out of a plastic cup.
Kevin: You're kidding, right?
Josh: Obviously.

La Cantina Bar outside section 102 serves top-shelf liquors (and others) as well as ice-cold premium drafts. If you want it, they pretty much have it here, whatever your beverage needs might be.

"WE WILL SELL NO TEQUILA BEFORE ITS TIME"

The Family Carmarena Tequila stands offer tequila margarita and straight shots for $9. We are always pleased to see hard liquor at the ballpark, and the Family Carmarena brand, which is made by the Ernest and Julio Gallo Company of winemaking fame, is often considered to be a decent tequila for the price. The problem is, for this price you could get a really good shot of tequila at a nearby bar, which we would recommend you do.

Baseball Says "Hola" and "Aloha"

On August 16, 1996, the Padres and Mets played the first regular season MLB game ever played in Mexico when a series between the two teams was moved out of San Diego to accommodate the Republican National Convention. Monterrey's Estadio Monterrey hosted La Primera Serie. Mexican native Fernando Valenzuela made the first game memorable, starting on the mound for the Padres, who earned a 15-10 win. Fans chanted "Toro, Toro," Valenzuela's nickname in Spanish, throughout the game.

The next April the Padres hosted the Cardinals for a regular season series at the University of Hawaii's Aloha Stadium in Honolulu in an effort to re-establish a local following in Hawaii. From 1971–1983, the Padres' top farm team had been the Pacific Coast League Hawaii Islanders, who played first at Honolulu Stadium, and then, beginning in 1975 at the brand new fifty-thousand-seat Aloha Stadium (currently the site of the NFL Pro Bowl each February). But despite the historic connection, the Padres lost two out of three to the Cards in the Paradise Series. And *Magnum PI* star Tom Selleck wasn't spotted at any of the games.

The Friars weren't finished traveling to home games. In 1999 they returned to Monterrey to host the Rockies in a Sunday night season opener. Played a day before the rest of the 1999 season began and broadcast nationally, the Padres' return trip to Mexico was less successful than their first visit. The presence of Mexican slugger Vinny Castilla on the Rockies made Colorado a decided fan favorite. The 27,104 people who jammed tiny Estadio Monterrey cheered wildly for Castilla, who responded with four hits, leading the Rockies to an 8-2 victory. The game marked the first season opener ever played outside of the United States or Canada.

The Petco Experience

Petco Park has reinvigorated the Padres fan base, the area surrounding the park, and everything else except for the team, which has struggled to score runs on a consistent basis since Petco opened. Kevin's cousin Jeremy, who lives in San Diego, says, "Being a Padres fan can become a chore." But we've heard similar sentiments expressed by fans in other cities who later changed their tunes. Josh felt that way until his Red Sox won two World Series in the first decade of the new century. Much like the surrounding area, however, San Diego fans remain a laid back bunch (Harry the Heckler aside).

While the team fades in and out of competitiveness, the Padres have yet to truly rise to an acceptable level of relevance since surging toward the World Series in 1984 and 1998—both of which they lost. Sure, things aren't as bad as when owner Ray Kroc took over the PA microphone and said of his new purchase: "I've never seen such stupid ball playing in my life," but they aren't that good either. When you live in a place where the weather is often perfect, going out to the ballpark seems like a great idea. But so does going to the beach, or hang-gliding, or rock climbing. Like many West Coast cities, San Diego has a lot of summer activities competing against each other for patrons' attention.

So the question becomes whether the experience of playing at Petco adds or detracts from the quality of team the Padres' front office is putting on the field. The sad reality is, Petco doesn't offer much to lure free agent bats to town. It's a pitcher's haven.

And as we've said before, Petco doesn't much look like a ballpark from the outside, so the anticipation of walking through the turnstiles amidst the absence of red brick often synonymous with going to the ballpark is lost at Petco. With its white steel girders and sandstone, the Pet feels a bit like a suburban shopping mall, until you get inside and see the green grass and brown infield dirt.

But once inside, the ballpark experience is a pretty darned good one. The fans are decked out in uniforms old and new (though we prefer the brown and yellow of old), even if they're not all as intense and die-hard as your average Phillies or Yankees fan. And a game at the Pet is sure to be played amidst beautiful weather even if the team is playing ugly. But it seems that it will take a team capable of a playoff run to get bandwagon fans off the beach and into the ballpark where they belong.

THREE GREAT F-WORDS

Fireblasts, Foghorn, and Fireworks. What words were you thinking of? Whenever a Friar belts one out to the beach, a foghorn blows, fireworks explode, and flames blast (visually reminiscent of the *Wizard of Oz* and smelling like a burger joint) near the center-field JumboTron. Sadly, there isn't a guy blowing, or is it cranking (?), a real live foghorn. The sound is a canned recording of the horn on the USS *Ronald Reagan*, a nuclear aircraft carrier that once resided nearby.

THE SWINGING FRIAR

This mascot is one of the most original in all of sports. The balding, robe- and sandal-wearing man of the cloth who symbolizes the Padres can't get enough baseball. Picture Friar Tuck carrying a baseball bat instead of a staff and with the thick face of, say, Fred Flintstone. The Friar actually predates the big league club, having served as mascot to the Pacific Coast League incarnation of the Padres.

One interesting twist comes in the middle of the 5th inning when the Swinging Friar turns into a gun-slinging Friar, shooting red hot bullets of meaty hot dogs from his baseball gun out into the crowd.

Kevin: I never expected to see that.
Josh: What can we say but, "Amen"?

MEN AND WOMEN IN UNIFORM

San Diego is a town that takes great pride in its servicemen and servicewomen. And the members of the Navy and Marines who are stationed in San Diego return this affection by going above and beyond the ordinary call of duty in their interactions with the greater community. Oftentimes on Sundays, a large number of Marines march into the ballpark to present the color guard, then they spend the afternoon watching the game in uniform from the outfield seats. And sometimes on Sundays the Padres wear special camouflage jerseys.

HARRY THE HECKLER (SUPER-FAN)

Harry Maker has spent more than a decade making life miserable for visiting left fielders in San Diego. When we spent a few innings sitting with Harry on our visit to Qualcomm years ago, he told us the Padres had already promised him front-row seats at Petco. When we returned to San Diego to visit Petco, we found that the Padres had delivered on their promise. With his handlebar mustache, ponytail, yellow and brown Padres hat, and throwback Tony Gwynn jersey, Harry is perhaps the most hated fan in all of baseball among visiting players. The man was born with a healthy set of lungs and over the years he's learned how to use them to his team's best advantage. Visiting left fielders cringe each time they trot to their position, because they know they're going to hear an earful.

Heckling Harry Superfan (at Qualcomm)

Photo by Kevin O'Connell

The great thing about Harry is that he keeps it clean and never gets personal. He doesn't have to resort to low-brow heckling, because he does his homework. "I spend each off-season researching all of the left fielders in the league," he told us. "I look for their weaknesses as players—deficiencies in their games—and I write myself notes for when the season begins."

Harry's not a drinker either—at least not when he's at "work" inside the ballpark. He told us he drinks lemonade instead of beer because it's better for his vocal cords, which he needs to keep well hydrated if he's going to last nine innings. Did we mention this man is loud, very loud?

When we were in town on our first baseball trip, Harry was riding "Larry" (aka Chipper) Jones. Before the game, Chipper had sent a clubhouse attendant out to the left-field seats to offer Harry an autographed bat as a bribe. Wow, that's respect. But Harry gave Chipper the business just the same, complaining that the Braves star didn't hand-deliver the bat to him. "How do I know it's really your autograph, Larry?" Harry called to Chipper, knowing full well that Chipper Jones simply hated being called by his given name.

Bribing Harry is something many players do. He's gotten scores of autographed bats over the years. And he also gets more than his share of balls. As each inning begins, the Padres' left fielder tosses a warm-up ball to Harry. He keeps the ball in the first inning, then gives the remaining eight to the youngsters seated nearest him.

As for the player who got most upset at Harry's act—hands down, Harry said, it was Barry Bonds. "Bonds swore he

[would] kill me if he [could] ever get his hands on me," Harry said. "But I eventually wear on them all. Some players give me a lot of feedback, while others hardly give any indication that I'm bothering them at all. But I know I'm getting to them."

The only visiting players Harry doesn't harass are out-of-town left fielders who previously played for the Padres. Harry gives them a break. Whether you love him or hate him, Harry is a San Diego institution. As a kid in the 1960s he used to ride his bike to Westgate Park to watch San Diego's Pacific Coast League team play. Now as an adult, he's not just a spectator but a player of sorts himself.

"It's one game between nine players and nine players, but it's another game between me and the one player in front of me," Harry said. "The grass in left field is my grass, and I let them know it."

You can find Harry the Heckler on Facebook if you want to be his "friend."

THE FAMOUS CHICKEN

If any mascot has transcended his role as kiddie entertainer and become a veritable folk icon, it is the Famous Chicken (aka the San Diego Chicken). The *Sporting News* even named him one of the hundred most powerful people in sports for the twentieth century, along with Muhammad Ali, Babe Ruth, Jesse Owens, and other great athletes. The chicken has appeared on baseball cards, shown up at rock concerts (Elvis, the Doobie Brothers, Jimmy Buffett, Cheap Trick, the Ramones, Chuck Berry, Jerry Lee Lewis), and performed in all fifty states and numerous foreign countries. But most of all, he is associated with the San Diego Padres.

Cyber Super-Fans

- **Padres Nation**
  www.padresnation.com/
- **Padres Talk**
  www.padrestalk.com/
- **Duck Snorts**
  http://ducksnorts-igd.blogspot.com
- **RJ's Fro**
  www.rjsfro.com/
- **A Padres Blog**
  www.apadresblog.blogspot.com/

The San Diego Chicken was born as part of a radio promotion in 1974 when Ted Giannoulas signed on to wear a silly chicken suit—one his mother had made—for $2 a day at the

San Diego Zoo. Giannoulas was told to set up a nest at the zoo and hand out candy to kids as they passed through the turnstiles during the week before Easter. But this was not to be a one-week gig. The man inside the suit had a vision. He was more than just a mercenary. He was an actor at heart, a showman with unparalleled flair. The crazy bird became famous.

The Chicken debuted at San Diego Stadium on Opening Day 1974 during a game against the Astros and quickly became a mainstay at the ballpark, delighting crowds with his antics. *The Baseball Bunch* called looking for an interview, then the *Tonight Show*, and so the legend grew. Soon other teams started hatching their own mascots, but none—save perhaps the Philly Phanatic—won the hearts of fans in quite the way the Chicken did.

Then in the late 1970s the Chicken almost lost his feathers when Giannoulas and KGB—the radio station that had originally hired him to wear the suit—had a contractual dispute regarding when and where he could perform. Eventually KGB fired the Chicken. Later the California Supreme Court declared Giannoulas a free agent and he returned, wearing a brand-new chicken costume in June 1979. The return was memorable, to say the least. Flanked by a California Highway Patrol motorcade, he rode into San Diego Stadium inside a gigantic egg atop an armored truck. After the egg was lowered to the field by Padres players, the Chicken hatched out, to the roaring approval of the forty-seven thousand fans in attendance.

Sports in (and around) the City

Lake Elsinore Storm

Strange Brew jokes aside, the Diamond—home of the California League Lake Elsinore Storm—is worth visiting on your ride out of San Diego. Try to catch a game at this terrific minor league park if the schedule works out. Just an hour north of Petco, the Padres' Class A affiliate plays in a beautiful eight-thousand-seat facility. The Diamond features a grass berm sitting area beyond the right-field fence similar to the "Park at the Park" at Petco, only a whole lot closer to the action. From San Diego follow Highway 15 north to the Diamond Drive exit and follow Diamond Drive to the ballpark.

While We Were in San Diego
We Visited Ted Williams's Boyhood Home

"Well, what do you want to do today?" Kevin asked. Our research at Petco had gone beautifully the evening before and the next game on our schedule, in Anaheim, wasn't until the following day. We had before us an off-day in San Diego with time aplenty to kill.

Josh didn't say anything. He just looked down into his Grand Slam breakfast longingly.

"We could hit Sea World or the San Diego Zoo. We've got the beach. We could go to the Air and Space Museum," Kevin said, relishing the break in our hectic road trip schedule. "So Josh, what's it going to be?"

"Ballgame," muttered Josh, his head slung down toward his breakfast plate.

"We don't have any ballgames today, buddy. We checked the schedules, remember?" Kevin said. "There's not even a decent minor league game nearby to hit. Besides, we're in the vacation capital of the world!"

"Ballgame!" Josh spat, and this was where Kevin became worried for his friend. It had been a long trip. We were road-weary and a long way from home. Kevin was afraid it might have become too much for Josh.

"You okay, man? Can I have the waitress get you another orange juice?"

Then Josh looked Kevin dead in the eye and said, "Teddy Ballgame." And it was then that Kevin understood. The beaches, the amusement rides,

Petco Park, after the game

Photo by Jordan Parhad

the wildlife parks, none of it meant anything to Josh compared to visiting the boyhood home of one of his idols, Ted Williams.

"Okay," said Kevin. "That sounds great."

It was then that Josh began to perk up. In fact, he became positively giddy with excitement. "Do you think we'll get to see his room?" he said. "I hope they have a gift shop."

Thanks to the marvels of modern technology, we quickly looked up the address.

"We take the Ted Williams Expressway, right?" Josh asked as we headed back to the road trip mobile.

"Actually, it says we should take the Cabrillo Parkway through Balboa Park," Kevin replied.

A confused look came over Josh's face, but he resigned himself to trusting the Internet. We made the short drive past the zoo and into the North Park neighborhood, and the road trip mobile turned onto Utah Street.

"What a name for a street for a boy to grow up on," Josh said looking out the window. "Utah Street. It's almost mythical." Kevin nodded and kept driving.

"I don't see any signs," Josh said. "Are we getting close? How could there not be any signs?"

"According to the GPS, we're here," Kevin said, slowing down the car. "It's gotta be one of these right along here." It was then that Josh saw the address—4121—on a modest bungalow-style house.

"Where's the museum? Where's the gift shop?" Josh shouted. His world was crashing down around him.

"I think it's a private residence," said Kevin as gently as he could.

"But how could they not turn this house—the house that the greatest hitter who ever lived grew up in—into a museum," Josh cried. "It doesn't make . . . It's not right . . . It's . . . It's. . . It's a crime!"

Josh bolted from the still moving road trip mobile and stumbled across the grass toward the house. And before Kevin could park the car and get out to stop him, Josh had knocked on the door. By the grace of God, there was no one home—or at least no one who answered the door. When Kevin reached the doorstep, Josh's head was hanging low again.

"You wanted to see his room, didn't you?" Kevin said, putting a hand on Josh's shoulder.

Ted Williams's boyhood home

Photo by Matthew Schmitdz

"Yes. And I wanted to buy something at the gift shop for my son, Spencer," said Josh.

"Think of how much better it will be when you take him to a game at Fenway, and you can tell him the stories your dad told you about watching him play."

"It's okay. I'm over it. Let's go to Sea World," Josh said. "I heard they have a whale that can do long division. Maybe he can figure out batting averages too. I'm gonna start him off with 456 divided by 185."

"Umm, do I want to know why?" Kevin asked skeptically.

"Because those were Teddy Ballgame's at-bat and hit totals in 1941 when he hit .406," Josh answered. "I figure if he's a dividing whale from San Diego, he ought to be able to get that one in a blink of the eye."

"Okay," Kevin said, becoming a bit concerned for his friend once again. "I just hope you're not setting yourself up for disappointment with unrealistically high expectations."

"Don't worry, I'm not," Josh said. "It's just like Ted said in *The Science of Hitting*: If you're content to hit .300, that's the best you'll ever do. If you're never content, you'll keep surprising yourself."

And so we headed to Sea World in search of the calculating whale.

LOS ANGELES ANGELS OF ANAHEIM,
ANGEL STADIUM OF ANAHEIM

ANAHEIM, CALIFORNIA
31 MILES TO LOS ANGELES
95 MILES TO SAN DIEGO
335 MILES TO PHOENIX
365 MILES TO OAKLAND

Baseball in the O.C.

Upon our first-ever venture to Angel Stadium of Anaheim we were unsure of exactly what to expect and, frankly, any expectations we did have were not high. We knew the facility had undergone extensive renovations in the late 1990s and that then-owner Disney had played a leading role in those efforts. And that wasn't the only thing that gave us cause for concern. We also knew that the "Big A" had served as the home of the NFL's LA Rams from 1980 to 1994, which left us with the impression the facility was one of the few remaining cookie-cutter stadiums, despite any sprucing up Disney might have done. What's more, we rolled into La La Land believing the old rap about Angel fans that portrays them and their nearby National League brethren as tardy arrivers and early departers more concerned with making an appearance at the ballgame than actually cheering on the home team to victory.

In the end, just about every negative expectation we had proved unfounded. Indeed, many of the fans were an inning or two late in arriving. But beyond that, everything else we expected to find disagreeable about the "Big A" failed to materialize. Angel Stadium is indeed a stadium, not a ballpark. There's no denying that. But it is one of the better ones. Of course, it doesn't measure up to Yankee Stadium, but it sure beats the heck out of the Oakland Coliseum. Not only are the views superb from all three seating decks, but the earth-tone decor and ballpark accents promote an old-time flair. As for the fans, once they got settled into their seats they were loud and involved in the game. Yes, they are a little bit too sunnily disposed toward that silly Rally Monkey, but most of them know their baseball and stay until the final out. And the game-day presentation the Angels and their ballpark staffers make is so much fan-friendlier than at Dodger Stadium. We can see why Angels' attendance has been increasing every year while the Dodgers have been steadily slipping from the once lofty perch they inhabited near the top of the game's attendance ledger.

With the San Bernardino Mountains rising in the distance beyond the left-field fence, Angel Stadium provides some sweet views when the smog isn't too thick, as well. Inside, the Angels embrace the mountain theme with an outfield rock-and-water display in left-center that—while less impressive than the similar feature at Coors Field in Denver—provides a trademark accent that meshes nicely with the distant mountain view.

Josh: The rocks look fake to me.

Kevin: Use your imagination.

Josh: I'm trying. But all I can picture is a fake mountain.

Kevin: I forgot. You're from back East. Never mind.

Other than the outfield scenery and a gaudy but strangely pleasant main entrance, Angel Stadium is not too overdone. We like that. Baseball is the main attraction, the way it should be and the way it was back in 2002 when the Angels went 8-1 at home in the three playoff rounds en route to their first World Series. Ever since, the Angels have been perennial contenders for the AL West title and the team has continued to gain followers.

By claiming that 2002 Championship, the Angels officially stamped Anaheim on the MLB map as a bona fide big league town. Previously, the team had played second fiddle in the hearts and minds of many fans who'd grown up vowing allegiance to the Dodgers. But that was before the fourth-ever all-California World Series pitted the Angels against the Giants. Today's Angels not only have a World Series trophy to go with their resilient stadium, but a strong following. They also have a committed owner who isn't afraid to spend his money on premium talent. Arte Moreno acquired the club from Disney back in 2003 for $185 million and launched an aggressive rebranding campaign that has increased the team's presence in the LA market and brought new revenue streams flowing into the coffers.

Getting back to that 2002 season and just how significant a moment it was for this franchise: Consider that in 2001

exterior

The main entrance still reflects the Disney Era extravagances.
Courtesy of the Los Angeles Angels of Anaheim

the Angels had finished forty-one games behind the first-place Mariners in the AL West. That's right, forty-one back! And the Angels hadn't been a factor in the division since blowing a thirteen and a half game lead in 1995 and then losing a one-game playoff to the Mariners for the division title. In the years between the Angels' 1986 implosion against the Red Sox, in their only previous American League Championship Series, and 2002, the team went through six managers, four general managers, three logo changes, a ballpark make-over, and a geographic identity crisis that saw them change their name from the California Angels to the Anaheim Angels. Never mind the World Series, the Angels' 2002 AL Championship represented the team's first league title in its 42-year history. The Angels came on strong in the second half of that season to finish with a 99-63 record—the best in team history. But they still finished four games behind Billy Beane's money-balling Oakland A's in the AL West. Fortunately, they earned the AL Wild Card berth. And after running through the Yankees and Twins, they overcame a three-games-to-two deficit in the October Classic and 5–0 deficit in Game 6, to win the whole ball of wax. In the decade to follow they finished among the top six teams in baseball in average nightly attendance every single year. Usually the Yankees, Dodgers, Phillies, and Cardinals finish ahead of the Angels and they vie with a handful of other clubs for the fifth best attendance mark. They consistently average more than forty thousand fans per game and more than 3.2 million per season.

Kevin: And you said West Coast teams weren't serious about their baseball.

Josh: When did I say *that*?

Kevin: Trust me, if I've said it, which I have, you've said it.

Angel Stadium was originally known as Anaheim Stadium. It opened for baseball in 1966 and was expanded in 1979 to accommodate the Rams. It was remodeled again between 1997 and 1999 to undo much of what the 1979 renovation had wrought. Ballpark architectural firm HOK Sport played a leading role as the Big A was retro-fitted from cookie-cutter back to baseball stadium in the wake of the Rams' departure for greener—though more artificial—pastures in St. Louis. With some help from Disney, which footed most of the $118-million price tag, HOK eliminated nearly twenty thousand outfield seats, added a video board and out-of-town scoreboard, and created the fake mountainside in left. During this time, the ballpark shed the name Anaheim Stadium and became "Edison International Field of Anaheim" after a hefty payout from the local energy company. In 2003, Moreno opted to return to a geographic and team focus and renamed the facility "Angel Stadium of Anaheim." Though Moreno would have liked to have changed the name of the team itself to the Los Angeles Angels, contractual obligations with the city of Anaheim mandated that the city name be in the team title, so the team was given the rather clunky and redundant moniker "The Los Angeles Angels of Anaheim."

Prior to opening "Anaheim Stadium" in 1966, the Angels had spent their first five seasons as vagabonds, crashing wherever they could find an open field. Well, maybe that's a slight exaggeration. But it's true that the team founded

397

interior

The Angels perform the national anthem in style.
Courtesy of the Los Angeles Angels of Anaheim

by movie star Gene Autry and former football player Bob Reynolds in 1960 played its inaugural 1961 season at Los Angeles's Wrigley Field, an expanded minor league park that once belonged to the Cubs. How cozy was little Wrigley? The seating capacity was 20,500. And the Angels and their opponents combined to hit a record 248 home runs in eighty-one games at the park that season. The next year, the Angels moved to Dodger Stadium, where they played until Anaheim Stadium was constructed. With the move to Anaheim, the team changed its name to the California Angels.

After the 1979 remodeling to accommodate the Rams, folks took to calling the facility the Bigger A as the once-open skyline across the outfield was shuttered by all of the new seats. Now that these seats have been removed, Angel Stadium resembles the original Anaheim Stadium once more.

From the start, Angel ownership attempted to fuse baseball with the area's reputation as an entertainment hub, as the team passed from the estate of the "Singing Cowboy" to the Walt Disney Company in 1996. Shortly thereafter the team changed its name to the Anaheim Angels. After the team won the 2002 World Series, both the old and new ownership groups took part in the celebration. Gene Autry's widow, Jackie, stood beside Disney boss Michael Eisner on the field, and together they accepted the World Series trophy, along with Troy Glaus, the Series MVP. While Jackie Autry reached for the championship trophy with one hand,

she held up her late husband's cowboy hat with the other. It was a touching moment.

Autry was more like legendary Red Sox owner Tom Yawkey than he was like George Steinbrenner. He was an aged father figure who loved his team and its players, maybe too much for his own good. As for Disney's short reign? Well, not only did Eisner and Co. fix up the set but they significantly hiked the studio … er … ticket prices. They even had the gall to charge admission to the Victory Parade in October 2002. Perhaps because Anaheim didn't have any buildings tall enough to have a true ticker-tape procession, or because Disney was out to make a buck, the celebration was held at Disneyland. In any case, Disney sold the Angels in the middle of the next season, bringing an end to its short tenure as team steward.

As for historic moments, this ballpark has seen a few. In 1967 it was the setting of the first All-Star Game played during prime-time evening hours on TV. The NL prevailed 2-1 in fifteen innings. Tony Perez homered off Catfish Hunter—working his fifth inning in relief—in the top of the fifteenth for the deciding margin.

Josh: How the game has changed!

Kevin: Hard to imagine a "short man" going that long today.

On September 23, 1973, Nolan Ryan struck out sixteen Twins in his final start of the season to break Sandy Koufax's single-season strikeout record. The Ryan Express racked up 383 punch-outs to best Koufax by a single K. Afterward it was revealed that Ryan had pitched the eleven-inning game with a torn thigh muscle.

In his final start of the next season, Ryan pitched his third career no-hitter and his first in Anaheim—again baffling the Twins—on September 28, 1974. But the Big Texan was just getting started. The next season Ryan authored his record-tying fourth no-no, beating the Orioles 1-0 in Anaheim. He would pitch three more no-hitters before retiring after the 1993 season with 324 wins, 5,714 strikeouts, and a 3.19 career ERA. The Angels retired Ryan's number 30 in 1992. In 291 games for the Angels, he posted a 138–121 record to go with a 3.06 ERA. The 138 Angel Ws were the most Ryan earned with any one team during a career that also saw him pitch for the Mets (29 wins), Astros (106), and Rangers (51).

Josh: Funny, but he's more commonly remembered as an Astro or Ranger.

Kevin: Not in these parts.

When the Big A hosted its second All-Star Game in 1989, Bo Jackson and Wade Boggs made the first inning memorable, hitting back-to-back jacks to lead off the bottom of the first inning against forty-year-old NL starter Rick Reuschel. The AL went on to win 5-3. Appropriately, Ryan, wearing a Rangers uni', earned the W in relief, making him the oldest pitcher to win the Midsummer Classic at the age of forty-two.

The most recent Mid-Summer Classic to take place in Anaheim occurred in 2010, when the NL prevailed 3-1, a day after Boston's David Ortiz won the Home Run Derby.

In the spring of 2006 Angel Stadium was one of the sites used by the World Baseball Classic. It hosted several second-round games that drew big crowds.

As for milestone moments, Reggie Jackson hit his five hundredth homer at the Big A in 1984, while Vladimir Guerrero hit his four hundredth at the park in 2009. Don Sutton recorded his three hundredth win in Anaheim in 1986. And two Hall of Famers joined the three-thousand-hit club in Anaheim—the Angels' Rod Carew (1985) and the Royals' George Brett (1992). The latter was summarily picked off first by Angel pitcher Tim Fortugno.

Kevin: How embarrassing.

Josh: Oops!

Trivia Timeout

Michael: What two members of the Angels family are honored with statues inside the park? (Hint: Neither played for the team.)

Gabriel: Who was the first player selected by the Angels in the 1961 expansion draft?

Goofy: We've told you about the Wrigley Fields in Chicago and Los Angeles. Where was the third Wrigley Field located?

Look for the answers in the text.

Getting a Choice Seat

Despite the fact that there is plenty else to do in their neck of the woods, the Angels perennially rank among the top teams when it comes to putting fannies in the seats. Casual baseball fans in the O.C. seem to prefer the more family-friendly and more affordable experience at the Big A to the corporate and pricy experience at stodgy Dodger Stadium. That said, the Dodgers have never had trouble enticing fans to turn out at Chavez Ravine, so they simply don't have to work as hard as the Angels have in recent years to make the game-day experience fun and to ensure that it offers something for everyone.

Seating Capacity: 45,050
Ticket Office: http://losangeles.angels.mlb.com/ticketing/index.jsp?c_id=ana
Seating Chart: http://losangeles.angels.mlb.com/ana/ticketing/seating.jsp

Be advised that Angel Stadium is a difficult place for seat-hoppers to navigate. Usually the top of the second is when we start looking for a free upgrade, but here, due to the typically laggard crowd, seat-hopping prior to the end of the third is an exercise in futility. Just as soon as you start to feel secure in your sly new vantage spot, folks holding legit tickets for your liberated seats show up to give you the boot. Yes, we know the local traffic situation is horrendous, and we know the good folks of Orange County lead important lives—what with the daily movie shoots, premiere parties, tofu tastings, and power yoga sessions to attend.

Diamond (Sections 115–122)

The seats right behind home plate sell as Diamond MVP, Diamond Hall of Fame or Diamond Club seats, depending on their row number. If you have the cash and opportunity to snag Diamond Clubs, by all means do. More than likely the top two tiers will be unavailable to you. But there are plenty of other fine seats on the first level.

Dugout/Field Seats (Sections 123–126, 110–113)

The first level consists of Dugout and Field Boxes (100 Level seats) below the midlevel concourse and Terrace Boxes (200 Level seats) behind the concourse and beneath the overhang of the Club deck. As near as we can tell, all of the first-level seats on the infield belong to season-ticket holders and local businesses.

Adventures in Seat-Hopping

Josh had spent almost three innings in a primo seat in Section 124 when a preppy-boy fan showed up and started waving a ticket stub in his face.

"Umm, you're outie," the waiter/aspiring actor/director/producer said.

"Haven't you ever heard of squatter's rights?" Josh asked playfully, as he gathered his glove, binoculars, baseball card case, ball bag and other accoutrements, preparing to re-join Kevin in the cheap seats.

"What?"

"Squatter's rights."

"If that means what I think it does," the pretty boy said, scanning the crowd for an usher, "you'd better find some paper towels and clean it before you leave."

Just then, the pretty boy's smartphone started ringing, and in a whirl he was gone. So Josh sat back down and kept the seat warm for his new friend for the rest of the game. He never came back.

The moral of the story: You're the real fan in this situation and if you see an open seat, do your best to get your butt in it and keep it there.

Field All Star (Sections 108–109, 127–128) and Field Preferred (Sections 106–107, 129–130)

The closest to the plate average fans can get on the first level is just beyond the first- and third-base bags in Sections 108 (left side) and 127 (right side). The first row is Row A and the last is Row Z. The low retaining walls separating the stands from the field allow excellent views all the way into the outfield corners.

Field Box (Sections 101–105 and 131–135)

The Field Boxes are the lower-level seats in outfield foul territory. They run from medium-depth foul territory out to the poles and just a little beyond. Avoid Sections 134 and 135 in deep right field, where the right-field Terrace juts out to block the view of center field. Plus, there is a pole obstruction. If you're dying to relive Scott Spiezio's dramatic Game 6 homer from the 2002 Series from the point of view of the fan in the first row of Section 135 who caught the ball, however, then this would be the place for you. Sections 101 and 102 in deep left field are slightly obstructed by the protrusion of the Angel bullpen, but are much better than their counterparts in deep right. The left-field foul pole blocks a portion of the field for those seated anywhere in Section 102 and for those in Seats 13 through 21 in Rows N through Z of Section 101.

Closer to the infield (105, 106, 131, 132) the views are better but the seats angle fans slightly toward the outfield rather than toward home plate, reminding us that this park was once meant to be easily converted for football.

Left Field Pavilion (Sections 257–260)

The first-level seats in left field are lower to the field than the outfield seats in right, but are farther from the action because they are behind the bullpens, which run parallel to one another horizontally behind the left-field wall. As such, the first row of Left Field Pavilion seats begins some forty feet from the field. Not good. The outfield fence in left-center is also about fifteen feet farther from the plate than the fence in right-center, which makes these even worse.

Section 260 should be avoided because the visitors' pen screens the view, and the first row of all sections should be avoided because of the railing that blocks sight lines. Section 258, in the middle portion of the bullpens, provides the clearest view of the field.

Terrace MVP (210–213, 221–224) and Terrace All Star (Sections 207–209, 225–227)

As mentioned above, the Terrace seats are behind the lower bowl's interior walkway. For the most part, these are good seats along the baselines. The Terrace MVPs are closest to the plate, while the All Stars are out near the corner bags. To take the overhang out of the equation, stay in Rows A–D. Those fans in Row A have to contend with the aisle traffic early in the game. On the whole, these are good seats that have the benefit of a roof overhead on sunny days.

Terrace Preferred (Sections 204–206, 228–230) and Terrace Box (Sections 201–203, 231–233)

We suggest avoiding Sections 231, 232, and 233 in deep right field. The sight lines aren't pure and there is a significant overhang. As for the rest of these seats above the mid-level walkway in outfield foul territory, the Terrace Preferred offerings are definitely a cut above the ordinary Boxes.

Right Field MVP (Sections 236–240) and Right Field Pavilion (Sections 241–249)

The Right Field MVP is in front of the Right Field Pavilion, providing a breezy porch from which to watch the game. We highly recommend these for any fan traveling on a limited budget. The first row is Row A and there's no aisle to block the view. Tickets to the Pavilion are just a bit cheaper but are much farther from the field.

Club Level (Sections 301–351)

A sizeable portion of these second-level seats sell as Club MVP seats and fetch nearly $100 per game. For our money, we'd rather be in outfield foul territory. As for the more reasonably priced Club-level seats, they're out near the foul poles and we'd rather sit in the Right Field MVP for less money.

Lower View MVP (Sections 411–426)

These are the first nine rows of third-level seats behind the plate and extending to the first- and third-base bags. These are below the walkway. As far as upper box sections go, this is a rather deep one. At most parks, the upper boxes extend

SEATING TIP

Do your best to locate the beautiful people and then seat-hop as close to their box seats as possible. This is your chance to casually tell your pals back home in Buxton, Maine, "Yeah, I caught a game with Celebrity X when I was in Hollywood."

Kevin: Wow. You've been on the West Coast too long.

Josh: You're just jealous I spent two innings next to Matt Damon.

back about five rows, but all of these seats provide solid, if unexceptional, views of the field.

Lower View All Star (Sections 407–410, 427–430) and View All Star (Sections 401–406, 431–436)

We don't recommend these seats. Not that they're awful, but the View MVP seats (500 Level) on the infield provide better views than these outfield seats. On the right-field side, avoid Section 435 where the foul pole blocks the view of the mound, and Section 436 where the pole blocks the plate. In left, avoid Sections 401 and 402 for the same reasons.

View MVP (Sections 512–529) and View (Sections 501–511, 530–540)

This is one of the best-designed upper decks in MLB. The underhang does not block the view as at most multi-level stadiums and the upper deck does not extend up too high, continuing only until Row S. That's only nineteen rows, for non-math majors. And Row A is raised above the concourse to take the aisle traffic out of play. In all regards, the Angels hit a home run when they built this deck. Angle for seats in Sections 513–529 and enjoy an Angel's-eye view of the infield. Sections 523–529 also provide the best view of the San Bernardino Mountains beyond the left-field wall. If it's a smoggy day, you may not see the peaks, but trust us, they're there.

Before/After the Game

The area immediately surrounding Angel Stadium will never be confused with a festive downtown neighborhood. Urban sprawl surrounds the complex housing the ballpark and Honda Center, where the NHL's Mighty Ducks play. On the plus side, several highways provide easy access to the area and magical Disneyland is not far away. This is not a terribly pedestrian-friendly part of town, so once you park at the stadium plan on staying the rest of the night. Although the stadium is surrounded by tar, a number of palm trees and perennial beds create a visually appealing oasis for baseball.

And the subtle beige and green of Angel Stadium's exterior make it warm and inviting. Other teams like the Blue Jays and A's would be wise to take a page out of the Angels' playbook and dress up their similarly generic stadiums in the way the Angels have done.

Getting to Angel Stadium

If you're driving up the coast after catching a game in San Diego or Lake Elsinore, follow Interstate 5 to State Route 57 north, then take the Orangewood Avenue exit, which lets off right near the park. If you're coming from downtown Los Angeles, take Interstate 5 south to the Katella Avenue exit. Follow Katella east for a mile, then turn right onto State College Boulevard and take a left onto Gene Autry Way. From the east, follow Interstate 10 west to State Route 60 west, to State Route 91 west, to State Route 57 south, to the exit for Katella.

There are entrances to the three Angel Stadium lots on Douglass Road, State College Boulevard, and Orangewood Avenue. The lots charge $8 per car. We found a private lot on the corner of Katella and Howell Street that charged $5. Considering that Kevin ripped a hole in his new shorts hopping the fence to get to the park, though, it probably would have been better for all involved (Kevin, Josh, and Kevin's brother Sean) if we'd each shelled out an extra buck each. Or Kevin could have walked the extra block to get around the fence like Josh and Sean did.

A Pacific Surfliner Amtrak/Metrolink station is located a short walk from the ballpark. For just $7 patrons may purchase round-trip fare from LA's Union Station to the ballpark.

Metrolink Maps and Information: www.metrolinktrains .com/spevents/?id=76.

Outside Attractions

THE BIG A

Shortly after the stadium opened in 1966, fans took to calling it the Big A. The 230-foot-tall scoreboard looming over the field shaped like a giant "A" probably had something to do with that. Originally it stood right behind the centerfield wall with its trademark halo around its top. But in 1980 it was transplanted to the parking lot beyond the stadium in right field to allow football fans clearer sight lines from the newly added upper-level seats. Management also explained the break from tradition as a move to ensure greater safety should an earthquake ever send the massive capital letter plummeting to the ground. But the unfortunate reality is that rather than being visible from every seat in the park, like it used to be, today the big A can only be spotted by those seated on the left-field side of the diamond. Its peak can be found to the right of the centerfield scoreboard for those sideways-peering fans.

Josh: We'd better not park under it. You know, just in case.

Kevin: It's withstood Mother Nature for nearly 50 years.

Josh: Still, earthquakes can be pretty bad, I hear. We should play it safe.

Kevin: Relax, Boston boy. I don't think "The Big One" is going to hit today.

BIG HATS

The main entrance is adorned by some super-jumbo-colossal baseball bats holding up the Angel Stadium sign. There are also colorful pictures of current Angel stars posterized on the façade above the gates. And on either side of the entrance, fans find giant red Angels hats. The oversized lids are remnants of the Disney Era. They are so big that fans can walk beneath them and inspect their scaffolding. We found ourselves unexpectedly taken by these, despite their gaudiness.

Josh: What do Juan Rivera, Luis Polonia, and Chad Curtis all have in common?

Kevin: They all played outfield for the Angels.

Josh: Wrong. They all hit for a higher lifetime average than Angels Hall of Famer Reggie Jackson, who batted just .262.

Kevin: But they also played outfield for the Halos, right?

Josh: Well, yes.

Kevin: So my answer was essentially correct.

Josh: Keep fanning that ego. You've still got a way to go to catch that notoriously big-headed Reggie.

Kevin: Let me guess. He refused you an autograph when you were twelve and you still can't let it go?

Josh: Wrong. The *Jackson Incident* occurred when I was twenty-three.

Whether or not you agree that Mr. Jackson's head was a few sizes too big for his hat, you'll marvel at these gigantic caps on display outside the park. If they were fitted caps, Kevin calculated that they'd be Size 649.5. No, not really. Kevin's not very good at math. In fact, that's what the faux tags on the inside rims say. They also say 100 percent wool, though, which is clearly not the case.

BALLPARK BRICKS

Also outside the home plate entrance is a regulation size infield made of brick. The grass portion of the diamond is represented by gray bricks, while the clay portion is represented by red bricks. The bases and pitcher's rubber light up fluorescent colors at night. We found this kitschy but also kind of cool. If you trot out to one of the infield positions, you will find the name and year of each Opening Day Angels' starter at that position inscribed on a brick. Again, very cool.

Both the right-handed and left-handed batter's boxes contain bricks inscribed with the team's Opening Day designated hitters for each season. And not to be left out, the fans have left their mark as well, in the form of personalized bricks between the pitcher's mound and home plate. We found a few inscribed with verses from the Bible. These seemed particularly goofy when they abutted other bricks advertising website addresses and other commercial goods. Several read like tombstones, noting the dates of birth and death for Angel fans.

If you want to leave something behind so that the Angels and their fans always remember your trip to Anaheim, consider shelling out $99 for a brick of your own. Or to save a little coin, leave a wad of Big League Chew on the bottom of your seat like Kevin did.

CLASS "A" CITY

At eye level beside the main gate, a bronze plaque is attached to the face of the stadium. It reads, "City of Anaheim, California, founded in 1857," and features a depiction of orange trees and rolling hills. Unless there's a part of Anaheim we missed somehow, the image on the plaque is a whole lot woodsier than Anaheim today. But we assume there are places in Orange County that still retain some pastoral charm.

Watering Holes and Outside Eats

Chain restaurants abound on State College Boulevard and Katella Avenue. But there are a number of local establishments for visitors to enjoy as well.

J. T. SCHMID'S BREWERY AND RESTAURANT
2610 Katella Ave.
http://jtschmidsrestaurants.com/
Maybe it's a California thing, but we found this fine brewery oddly placed within a strip mall. It's worth a visit, though. From the appetizer menu, we recommend the sweet potato fries. At meal time, order a Mexico City Burger (Jack cheese, guacamole, cilantro, roasted salsa, lettuce, and tomato) or an eighteen-ounce Rib Eye and you won't be disappointed. From the bar, we suggest the house-brewed Hefeweizen or Grandpa's own Emil's Amber. There is outdoor seating on a lush patio.

FRITZ: THAT'S TOO
701 Katella Ave.

We're still trying to figure out what's meant by the name of this gentlemen's club. Did they mean "two" instead of "too"? We're also trying to figure out what a seedy topless place is doing so close to Disneyland. And we're wondering whether *Wally World* adventurer Clark W. Griswold would have visited after his wife and kids fell asleep.

PANDA EXPRESS
2055 Katella Ave.
www.pandaexpress.com/

This is a popular chain in these parts. There is also a Panda Express stand inside the stadium but it is much more expensive than the one outside the park. So if you're in the mood for Chinese, why not enjoy some before the game?

Kevin: And the best part is, by the third inning you'll be hungry again.

Josh: Hey, we're traveling on a limited budget.

OC SPORTS BAR & GRILL
450 East State College Blvd.
http://ocsportsgrill.com/

The highlight of this otherwise straightforward sports bar is the array of misters out on the patio. No, not gentlemen. We mean *water* misters. We found these a welcome touch on a hot afternoon.

THROWBACKS BAR & GRILL
1759 Claudina Way
www.throwbackssportsbar.com/Home

A mile from the park, the Angels and Dodgers are always on the tube at this popular watering hole. As an added attraction, the bar ferries fans to and from Angel Stadium on its own shuttle buses.

DISNEYLAND BARS AND RESTAURANTS
Downtown Dr.
http://disneyworld.disney.go.com/destinations/downtown-disney/

Downtown Disney—a land of colorful make-believe houses and storefronts—is only a mile or so from the ballpark, so why not stop by for an overpriced cocktail and a bite to eat? At least the help is always smiling. Don't worry, you don't have to pay the amusement park admission fee to get into Downtown Disney. Heck, you don't even have to pay to park. A large lot on Downtown Drive offers free three-hour parking. If you manage your time wisely, this is a good way to get a taste of the Disney experience without having to hand your entire wallet over to that money-grubbing mouse.

Follow Katella to Disney Drive and take a right. After you pass the theme park proper, take a left onto Downtown Drive and you'll head right into the parking lot.

We stopped by the **Disney ESPN Zone** to watch the Red Sox play the Yankees on satellite. Kevin's brother Sean rated the "pour" on his Guinness better than the average tap job in L.A. Sean also enjoyed a Bloody Mary. As for the two of us? Well, wary of these chain-type places, we played it safe and ordered Bud Lights the size of vats. We found the most interesting item of décor the American flag made of 383 red-white-and-blue baseballs—one for each strikeout Nolan Ryan had for the Angels in 1973. Each ball bears the name of one of Ryan's victims, beginning with No. 1, Fred Patek, and ending with No. 383, Rich Reese. We don't know what's more remarkable, the fact that Ryan struck out 383 batters in 1973, or the fact that he completed twenty-six games and still wound up three behind league leader Gaylord Perry in that category.

Other eateries in Downtown Disney include the **House of Blues, Rain Forest Café, Ralph Brennan's Jazz Kitchen, Tortilla Jo's, Uva Bar,** and **Naples Ristorante e Pizzeria.**

Inside the Stadium

The open view of the mountains beyond the left-field fence goes a long way to improve the atmosphere and character Angel Stadium was lacking during its NFL days. The park does not have the Hollywood cachet of Dodger Stadium but is still an attractive place. Even a decade after the Disney era, the stadium retains a Disneyland-type feel, with ushers who are very courteous, and exceptionally clean concourses, bathrooms, and seating areas.

Ballpark Features
EXTRAVAGANT INDEED

The fake-rock formation beyond the outfield fence in left-center was created in the late 1990s to give Angel Stadium a trademark feature. Of course, signature stadium features that come about organically—like the Wall in Boston or the ivy in Chicago—are more meaningful, but we can't blame the Angels for trying something to dress up a once-uninspired part of the park. With its hundred-foot-high geyser, fireworks, and assortment of rocks, the "Outfield Extravaganza" is meant to resemble the rocky California coast. Or maybe it's the geyser at Yosemite National Park that's being replicated? We found it hard to tell for sure. What we do know is that the rocks at the top of the waterfall form the shape of a capital letter "A," while down below, the center-field cameramen hide in a cave. Perhaps the display would look better had real rocks been used instead of Styrofoam. As actor/comedian/all-around-good-guy Robin Williams stated, "It looks like a miniature golf course on steroids." And as writer/comedian/all-around-good-guy Kevin O'Connell remarked, "It looks and feels a lot like Disney's Country Bear Jamboree. All that's left is to install animatronic bears to play banjos when the Angels homer."

In case you're wondering, Walt Disney Imagineering served as manager of the project, while HOK Sport drew up the actual blueprints. So, as far as we can tell, blame Disney for the Styrofoam and thank HOK for the tiered bullpens to the left of the display.

Also to the left of the rocks, fans find red-and-white flags honoring Angels teams of yore that made the playoffs. These are a nice touch.

BRADY BUNCH BATTER'S EYE

The uppermost portion of the batter's eye in centerfield consists of artificial turf between the rock display and seats. While hitters have given this rave reviews as an effective backdrop for slugging, we must say that aesthetically it's pretty revolting. Fortunately, closer to the field the backdrop is much more appealing thanks to the presence of a green hedge that rises above the home run wall.

Kevin: Wonder if Torii Hunter ever had to fight it out with the hedge to snag one of the many homers he robbed.

Josh: Torii never met a shrub who wanted it as badly as he did.

STATUES

A number of ballparks display likenesses of great players in team history. In Anaheim, the team founder and a player's daughter are memorialized in this way. Heartfelt though this may be, we found it odd.

Inside the main gate on the third-base side stands a bronze of Gene Autry smiling, as if for the cameras, and holding out his trademark cowboy hat.

On the first-base side stands a statue of Michelle Carew, holding a puppy dog in her arms. A beautiful bed of flowers surrounds the piece, which depicts Ms. Carew from the waist up. Rod Carew—who poked and bunted his way to 3,053 hits in a nineteen-year career with the Twins and Angels—had a daughter named Michelle who died of leukemia, but not before inspiring others to fight back against the disease. The base of her statue reads, "Her spirited battle

against leukemia raised awareness for the national marrow donor program throughout this country and in the process her legacy has saved countless lives. When she went to sleep, she woke up the world."

RETIRED NUMBERS

High above the seats in right field appear the Angels' retired numbers. These include: No. 11 for Jim Fregosi, who played for the Angels from 1961 to 1971 and managed the Angels in 1978; No. 26 for Autry, the team's metaphorical twenty-sixth man; No. 29 for Carew, who not only played for the Halos but served as their batting coach from 1992 to 1999; No. 30 for Ryan; No. 42 for Jackie Robinson; and No. 50 for coach Jimmie Reese, who began his seven-decade professional career as a batboy for the Pacific Coast League Los Angeles Stars in 1917, went on to play for the Yankees and Cardinals, and finished hitting fungos at the Big A from 1972 to 1994.

Josh: Let me get this straight: Autry wasn't on his death bed or even sick when they retired his number in 1982?

Kevin: He lived something like another fifteen years. What's your point?

Josh: Seems self-aggrandizing to me. Even the Yankees waited until Big Stein had headed to that big baseball field in the sky before unveiling a monument in his honor at the Stadium.

Kevin: Point taken.

CHAMPIONS ON DISPLAY

The team store is located on the 100 Level. Outside it a classy exhibit displays the 2002 World Series trophy and other mementos from the Angels' championship, such as a Rally Monkey, a "Yes We Can" Halo Stick, and a World Series ring. Not far from the display, a huge American flag is mounted on the concourse wall. The flag was flown over the US Capitol at the request of congresswoman Loretta Sanchez in commemoration of the opening of the remodeled stadium on April 1, 1998.

Kevin: Seriously?

Josh: I guess Congress didn't have anything more important to do that day.

TIME KEEPS ON SLIPPING INTO THE FUTURE

On the 200 Level behind home plate a timeline reflects in words and pictures the story of the Angels. The history begins all the way back in 1960 when Gene Autry went to the MLB winter meetings looking for a team to broadcast on his radio station and left as owner and chairman of the expansion Los Angeles Angels.

To Angel fans their team's curse is much more frightening than the supposed Curse of the Billy Goat hovering over the Cubs. In Chicago, the players have a history of losing. In Anaheim, they have a history of dying. This caused Gene Autry to publicly consider rumors (which were never substantiated) that the stadium resided on the site of a former Indian burial ground and that angry Native American spirits were to blame for the Angels' awful luck. The most recent example of this terrible phenomenon was the death of rookie pitcher Nick Adenhart in a car crash. On his way home from Angel Stadium in 2009, after hurling six scoreless innings against the Oakland A's, the car Adenhart was travelling in with two others was broadsided by a van that had run a red light. The driver of the van fled on foot, but was apprehended and charged with drunk driving. Adenhart was taken to the University of California, Irvine Medical Center, where he died in surgery. The driver of the car, Courtney Francis Stewart, and the other passenger, Henry Nigel Person, were pronounced dead at the scene. While older cases like the untimely deaths of Donnie Moore, Lyman Bostock, Chico Ruiz, Mike Miley, and Bruce Heinbechner are painful memories to a fan base that has watched its idols endure more than their fair share of tragedies, the loss of Adenhart still causes many Angel fans to tear up and ask that most unanswerable question: Why?

While most years get only one or two blurbs of text, no less than nineteen magical moments from 2002 are remembered on the timeline.

While perusing this well-done display, we learned that Yankees pitcher Eli Grba was the first player selected by the Angels in the 1961 expansion draft. The right-hander, who had won eight games in two seasons with New York, went 11-13 with a 4.25 ERA for the Angels in their inaugural season.

Kevin: Eli Grba. I'd like to sell you a vowel.

Stadium Eats

Between our first visit to Angel Stadium in 2002 and our most recent trip to Anaheim, we were delighted to find that the Angels took some of the advice we offered in this book's first edition and seriously upgraded the concession offerings. Well done!

CLYDE WRIGHT'S BBQ (TRADEMARK FOOD)

Former Angel pitcher Clyde "Skeeter" Wright may have had a lackluster 100-111 record in his ten-season career, but the Tennessee native serves up a mean Pulled Pork sandwich. Fans can find the affable Wright manning the stand that bears his name just inside Gate 1. Josh also recommends the Brisket and sweet and spicy Franks and Beans.

WIENERSCHNITZEL HOT DOG (DOG REVIEW)

While we don't necessarily consider this breed of dog among our very favorites, we did find much to like about the hot dog experience in Anaheim. Rather than getting the basic stadium dog, though, be sure to head to one of the Major League Dog stands (behind Sections 259 and 424), where you can order a freshly made wiener bearing the regional condiments popular in points elsewhere in the big leagues.

The Halo Dog is a foot-long frank, wrapped in bacon and topped with jack cheese, beans, and Anaheim peppers.

BEST OF THE REST

The **Ruby's Diner** stand behind the waterfall and rock display in center field has trademark Ruby's burgers as well as zesty **Parmesan Garlic Fries** and **Milk Shakes** that Kevin gives four stars out of a possible three . . . in other words, the shakes are off-the-charts good.

For Specialty Sausages, head to the **Home Plate Grill** behind Gate 3. For fresh Mexican, visit **Angelino's Grill** inside Gate 2. For a grilled sandwich, visit **Panini's Café** behind Section 112. For a range of healthy chicken menu items, see what's clucking . . . er . . . we mean cooking at **CHIX** behind Section 103.

Josh chickened out when it came to trying the sushi at **Toro** (Section 124) but we did note that sake and several Japanese beers were also available.

STADIUM SUDS

Josh: Where else in the bigs can you get a Sapporo?

Kevin: That's an easy one: Safeco Field.

Josh: Well, beside that?

Kevin: Are we counting the Nippon Pro League?

Josh: Never mind.

The Angel Stadium Experience

One nice thing about sunny Southern California is that you can always count on there being a game when the Angels are scheduled to play. As of press time in 2012, the last rainout in Anaheim was 1995.

When the home team is in contention—especially late in the season—Angel Stadium can be a raucous place to watch a game, with the fans opting not to sit back as simple spectators but to play a part in the action. All it takes, really, is a 3-2 count when the Angels are at bat and the fans start stirring and stand up out of their seats. For the ordinarily laid-back West Coast, we found this impressive.

Josh: But they were still late getting to the park.

Kevin: Lighten up, man. You'll live longer.

CALLING ALL ANGELS

Before each game the Angels pump up their fans with a blaring rendition of Train's "Calling All Angels" while a montage of great moments in team history plays on the big video board. The song doesn't have anything to do with baseball, but, then again, "Sweet Caroline" doesn't either, and Red Sox fans seem to never tire of it.

Kevin: So who are you to criticize Angel fans?

Josh: I purposely didn't criticize them.

Kevin: But you did criticize "Thank God I'm a Country Boy" in Baltimore.

Josh: I don't remember that.

Kevin: As I recall, you said it was an affront to both Abner Doubleday and John Denver.

Josh: Wow. I must have been having a bad day.

PRIMATES APLENTY

Leave it to a movie hub like L.A. to borrow its team's mascot from such a high-quality flick as *Ace Ventura, Pet Detective*. But if it works—who are we to judge?

The Rally Monkey may look like nothing more than fun and games on TV, but there's actually a method to the madness that first began in Anaheim during the 2000 season. First, the Rally Monkey cannot make his first official appearance until the seventh inning. Second, the Angels must be trailing in the game when the monkey squeaks his first shrill cry of encouragement on the video board. Third, the Angels must have at least one runner on base for the monkey's spirit to be properly invoked. Fourth, once he does appear, fans are free to whip out whatever monkeys of their own they may have brought with them, or to start monkeying around if the spirit moves them (you know: picking bugs out of each other's hair, swinging from the rafters, and making general baboons of themselves).

Now just so we're clear, when we talk about the Rally Monkey we're not talking about that ridiculous twelve-year-old in the orange orangutan suit who kept running up and down the aisle behind home plate during the 2002 postseason. He was a poor excuse for a monkey and a little too old to be dressed like that in public as far as we're concerned.

We're talking about the real Rally Monkey. The one from the Angels TV commercials who lights up the stadium with his effervescence and enthusiasm, kind of the way Kevin lights up a barroom when he stumbles in singing "Irish Eyes are Smilin'." You'll know him when you see him: a crazy little bugger with a long tail and beady eyes.

It may be hard to understand how or why Angels fans get so excited over this moronic monkey, but they do. Whenever he appears on the screen, they hold up their own mini-monkeys and wave them back and forth frantically. Whether you laugh at this ritual as we did, or buy into it, you have to admit that the power of the monkey often proves legitimate.

NUTTY

Hey, as long as you're embracing the circus theme, you might as well have some peanuts. The Angel Stadium ushers wear straw hats and old-style vests. During the seventh-inning stretch they stand on the field facing the crowd and with varying degrees of enthusiasm lead fans in the singing of "Take Me Out to the Ball Game." When it gets to the part in the song that goes, "Buy me some peanuts and Cracker Jack," they throw bags of peanuts into the crowd. When the song finishes, they take a bow. So weasel your way down to the front row by the middle of the seventh, and you might be in for a treat.

Kevin: Almost as much fun as the square-dance in Milwaukee.

Josh: I still prefer Toronto's "OK Blue Jays."

Kevin: Don't forget about those cheerleaders, too.

Josh: Oh, I haven't.

Cyber Super-Fans

We tip our caps to a couple of excellent Angels bloggers:

- **Halos Heaven**
  www.halosheaven.com/
- **True Grich**
  http://truegrich.blogspot.com/

FIREWORKS

The Angels really do it up with fireworks when one of their players goes yard. And they offer a weekly fireworks show after Friday night games. Maybe the team is still working its way through Disney's leftover rockets or maybe Arte Moreno owns stock in a pyrotechnics company. Most parks

> ### Sports in (and around) the City
>
> **Catalina Island**
>
> From 1921 to 1951 the Chicago Cubs spent their pre-seasons on Catalina Island, a seventy-six-square-mile paradise twenty-five miles off the coast of Los Angeles. Cubs owner William Wrigley acquired a majority interest in the largely undeveloped terrain in 1919, hoping to turn it into a resort. The chewing gum millionaire installed streetlights and sewers, erected hotels, and built the world's largest dance hall—the Avalon Grand Casino. But with the Great Depression looming, the island failed to catch on.
>
> Catalina did, however, provide the Cubs with an exotic Spring Training base for the better part of three decades. The island featured a practice field—named Wrigley Field—that matched the exact field dimensions of Chicago's regular season Wrigley. Even the famous Waveland Avenue rooftop-viewing decks of Chicago's North Side were mimicked by clubhouse patios built into the mountainside overlooking the field.
>
> Cubs players would get in shape by running along the island's many goat trails. Then afterward they would soothe their burning feet with fresh eucalyptus, which grows on the island. A few weeks before the regular season, they would head to the mainland to scrimmage other teams.
>
> But after several rainy springs, the Cubs left Catalina in 1952 in favor of Mesa, Arizona. Today, the beautiful island has finally become the beach resort Wrigley envisioned, offering visitors a glimpse of what California looked like two centuries ago: a wilderness of oaks, cactus, and sage surrounded by the sea. The island is just a fifteen-minute helicopter ride from Los Angeles and makes for an enjoyable day trip or longer excursion—especially if you're road tripping with your significant other and want to give her a treat after so many days spent in the smelly road-trip car.
>
> As for the ballpark? It was razed years ago, but the Wrigley Memorial remains—featuring a botanical garden and the Wrigley Mausoleum.

that use fireworks send two or three colorful rockets into the air when the home team has something to celebrate. But at Angel Stadium more like a dozen rockets launch from the rock display.

Josh: As if there isn't enough smog out here already!

Kevin: Go back to Maine, country boy.

DAYS OF THUNDER

If you can hear them over the most unholy din baseball has to offer, Angel fans will happily tell you that Thunder Sticks debuted during the playoffs that led up to the fourth-ever all-California October Classic in 2002. We say these things—which always seem to rear their head come playoff time—should be banned. This ain't NASCAR. It's baseball.

While We Were in Anaheim
We Went Back to LA

No, we didn't go to Disney. While we were in Anaheim, we went in search of the Angels' roots, a quest that inevitably landed us back in Los Angeles.

With Kevin's brother, Sean, leading the way, we fearlessly ventured into South Central Los Angeles to find the site of old Wrigley Field, which had housed the expansion Angels in 1961 and the Pacific Coast League Hollywood Stars before them.

Arriving at the Gilbert Lindsay Recreation Center on Central Avenue, we were happy to find several youth ball fields and a skater's park on the eighteen-acre site, but no remnants of the old ballpark. After stomping around for about fifteen minutes with our eyes on the ground—looking for an historical marker or old home plate laid in the ground—we were ready to abandon our quest.

But then, just in the nick of time, James Lee III popped his head out of the park's modest Rec Center and asked if he could help us find anything. "Are you looking for a contact lens?" James asked jokingly. And when we saw that he was wearing a Dodger hat and Dodger jersey, we figured we had found the right person to talk to about the old park.

And we were right. Before becoming an assistant on the Lindsay Recreation Center staff, James grew up in the shadows of Wrigley in the 1960s. Now he helps manage the Wrigley Little League program and other programs at the Lindsay Center.

James led us about twenty feet to the left of the Rec Center building and showed us where the old home plate used to be. There was no marker on the ground, just grass. James knew the spot.

While others in the South Central community may prefer to forget all about the Angels' history in LA, and focus on the hometown Dodgers, James and a handful of other baseball fans still remember. He said the old home plate is currently stored under lock and key inside the large metal storage bin next to the Rec Center building.

"Wrigley was a part of this neighborhood that a lot of people took a lot of pride in," James said, "and it would be a shame for that to be forgotten."

We agreed with him and wished him luck.

Then, with our "work" for the morning completed, we moved on to our ulterior motive for visiting the site. With a five-gallon bucket of balls and a thirty-three-inch wooden Louisville Slugger, we headed for the Little League field.

Kevin batted first, while Josh took to the mound and Sean played roving outfielder. Then Josh batted while Sean pitched and Kevin played the field. And then Sean batted while Kevin pitched and Josh shagged.

Then we picked up all of the balls and did it again, rotating the pitching and batting alignment for a variation.

So, you might be wondering: Did we answer the questions raised in the Sluggers' batting cages in Chicago? Could Josh's moderately quick bat catch up to Kevin's moderately quick fastball? Could Kevin's embarrassingly slow bat connect with Josh's embarrassingly slow fastball?

Well, after Sean showed us both up, we decided neither of us should be bragging about anything when it comes to playing the game. We'll stick to baseball writing and backyard Wiffle Ball tournaments, thank you. But just the same, one day we'll be able to tell our grandkids we took BP at Wrigley Field. We won't mention, of course, that it was the Wrigley Little League Field in Los Angeles.

LOS ANGELES DODGERS, DODGER STADIUM

LOS ANGELES, CALIFORNIA
32 MILES TO ANAHEIM
126 MILES TO SAN DIEGO
380 MILES TO SAN FRANCISCO
385 MILES TO PHOENIX

Dodgertown USA, 90090

It's a difficult concept for us to wrap our heads around, but Dodger Stadium is one of the oldest ballparks still standing. It is a piece of ballpark perfection that staved off the new ballpark wave that swept away many of the old yards. Only Fenway Park and Wrigley Field are older than Dodger Stadium, and Dodger Stadium remains one of the few to have avoided the blight of corporate naming that has overtaken the modern era. We now live in a baseball reality where Dodger Stadium, set in a West Coast city that prides itself on being on the cutting edge of entertainment culture and ahead of every conceivable trend that courses through the country, is one of the grand old ballparks in the game of baseball.

Dodger Stadium is as much a part of Los Angeles as the in-ground swimming pool and the movie studio. In L.A., image is everything. And Dodger Stadium provides the local nine with that perfect image of baseball in paradise. Carved into the Elysian Hills in an area known as Chavez Ravine, the stadium stands like a shining beacon on the gloried hill of baseball success. And while no other baseball park in the Majors is built on a hill, the Elysian Hills of L.A. bring to mind that dreamlike ideal of an ethereal ball field in the heavens.

A more ideal setting would be difficult to imagine. The stunningly consistent weather has accounted for less than twenty rainouts in the stadium's fifty-plus years. The San Gabriel Mountains loom above, snowcapped in the spring and fall, purple under the setting summer sun—and ringing the outfield in an ever-glorious backdrop for the game of baseball. Meanwhile, out in the back of the stadium, a breathtaking view of the downtown L.A. skyline rises from the valley below.

Dodger Stadium is no small and quaint ballpark. It's a big old pitcher's park, a ballyard with expansive foul territory and five decks for seating. But still it manages to maintain a feeling of intimacy. The cliché "not a bad seat in the house" is almost applicable, as sight lines are outstanding for nearly every seat. And though it's completely symmetrical in every way, Dodger Stadium's wavy-topped Pavilion roof and wonderful views of the action, scenery, and Hollywood stars make attending a game at Chavez Ravine an experience unlike any other in sports.

Like all other teams, Dodger fans come in every conceivable variation and type. Much press has been given to the "gang" element in parts of the stadium, and much blame has been laid at the feet of the owners for cutting security. We did not experience this drop in security. Sure, there are pockets of fans willing to fight anyone not wearing the local blue and white. There's a rough element that shows up seemingly every night in the Pavilion seats to do little more than pick fights with opposing fans—especially when the Giants are in town. Make no mistake: It can be quite a dangerous situation in these seats, as well as in various sections of the upper deck. You might think you're watching the movie *Colors,* and there's a strong debate as to whether the team has actually marketed to the gang element the way the L.A. Raiders did in the 1980s. One thing's for sure: Security has been beefed up and trained in anti-gang tactics to keep the peace once again in the wake of a near-deadly incident on Opening Day 2011 when a Giants fan was nearly beaten to death in the parking lot after the game. Meanwhile, the Angels draw more and more fans in Anaheim, while attendance at Dodger Stadium has lagged.

But most of the ballpark gives off the kind of vibe one might expect: easy-going and fairly lukewarm in the expression of fanaticism. Most Dodger fans don't yell much, with the exception of "that guy" who came to the park by himself and is drunk by the third inning. But you're going to find "that guy" in any ballpark. Most fans wait in traffic for three hours to get to the park, and by the time they do arrive, all they want to do is relax, enjoy the game under the stars and chill out.

Josh: My students say "Chill-ax" . . . you know, "chill and relax combined."

Kevin: Why? Why do you even try?

Josh: What'd I say?

Dodger Stadium is rarely full when the first pitch is thrown, or when the last out is made. Many fans arrive "fashionably late" and leave early—blaming traffic for both breaches of fan decorum. Aside for their lack of punctuality, there is no shortage of other reminders that this ballpark is pure Hollywood. You'll see fans arriving with dress shirts and sunglasses (even during night games) and trophy wives on their arms who could care less about the game. These fans spend all game long gabbing on their cell phones (probably to their agents). Seeing and being seen are important parts of the experience—just as is the case in all other parts of L.A.

Still, Dodger Stadium is well maintained. It is repainted every season to keep any blight from fans' eyes. During the game, the ballpark is kept more immaculate than Josh's bathroom. There is no cleaner or better maintained facility in all of sports.

The grounds outside the park are immaculate as well. In addition to a grounds crew that tends the field, the Dodgers keep on the payroll a full-time crew of gardeners who care for the three-hundred-acre site, which comprises ubiquitous palm trees, lush bushes, and flower beds that surround the twenty-one landscaped and terraced parking lots. This obsessive attention to the sparkling image of the ballpark is a very L.A. phenomenon, and is as important to the team as Vin Scully's velvet voice.

Winning quickly became the norm after the Dodgers moved west in 1958. Dodger Stadium transformed the team's attitude from "Wait Till Next Year" to pennants and world championships accumulated at a rate exceeded only by the New York Yankees. The Dodgers have hosted nine World Series since moving to Los Angeles, and the Blue Crew has won five of them. Team owner Walter O'Malley was the man responsible for moving the club out of Brooklyn. After a four-year wait for new digs following the move, during which time the Dodgers played at the Los Angeles Memorial Coliseum, Dodger Stadium opened on April 10, 1962, with the home team falling to the Cincinnati Reds, 6-3. The huge stadium seated fifty-six thousand, but was built to be expandable to eighty-five thousand should the team ever decide to continue the decks all the way around the outfield.

Plenty of misinformation surrounds the Dodgers' move to Chavez Ravine. Rumors that the police evicted poor Mexican-American families that were living in the area at the behest of the Dodgers organization are simply not true. The L.A. police did forcibly drag people out of their homes, but these heinous acts were committed with the city's intention to build housing at Chavez Ravine, and occurred long before the land was sold to O'Malley. This is not to say that the land was obtained from the primarily Spanish-speaking owners by purely altruistic means. Dirty pool was played during the *Battle of Chavez Ravine*—the decade-long struggle for O'Malley to acquire the land from resistant homeowners. We

exterior

Photo by Kevin O'Connell

interior

suggest reading *City of Quartz,* by Mike Davis, for an excellent account of the times, but in essence, the real estate purchasers used Spanish-speaking agents to offer cash to the local homeowners, then continually lowered their pricing offers to drive fear up and the price of property down.

Captain Emil Praeger, an esteemed sea captain from New York, was the man chosen as the architect and engineer of the stadium. His original designs of the ballpark consisted of translucent tubes for visitors to walk through, but the tubes never saw the light of day. It was the first multi-level tiered stadium built without support columns, so every seat had a clear view of the field. The Vinell Construction Company of Los Angeles built the structure at a cost of $23 million. O'Malley and his partners paid for all of it, making Dodger Stadium only the second ballpark to be entirely privately funded during the twentieth century. Yankee Stadium was the first (1923) and AT&T Park in San Francisco was the only other (2000).

Early on, Dodger Stadium was dubbed by some the "Taj Mahal of baseball," but some critics pejoratively called the stadium the "Taj O'Malley." One obvious Opening Day gaffe was that the foul poles were installed completely in foul territory instead of lined up with the foul line (we're left to wonder why they don't call them fair poles if they belong in fair territory). For the first season, special dispensation from the league had to be granted for the unorthodox placement until they could be moved. Another early blunder: In

a city where drinking water can be as precious as gold, no water fountains were installed at the park for fans that first season.

The Dodgers shared their new digs with the expansion Los Angeles Angels during the 1962–1965 seasons. Dodger Stadium was quietly called "Chavez Ravine" when the Angels played, so they did not have to continually publicize the name of their landlord and in-town NL rival. Despite the fact that they had to share their stadium with an expansion team, 1962 was a glorious year for the Dodgers, as they won 102 games and finished in a tie for the National League lead with their archrivals, the San Francisco Giants. On October 3, 1962, the two teams squared off in a one-game playoff at Dodger Stadium to decide who would represent the NL in the World Series. Unfortunately for the Dodgers, the Giants rallied with four runs in the ninth to post a 6-4 win, but the crowd of 45,693 gave the Dodgers an MLB record-setting attendance total of 2,755,184 for the year. Earlier in 1962, Jackie Robinson was inducted into the National Baseball Hall of Fame.

Aptly, since Dodger Stadium has always been a pitcher's park, overpowering hurlers have led the boys in blue to their success. In 1963, left-hander Sandy Koufax posted a 25-5 record alongside an ERA of 1.88 en route to winning the MVP, Cy Young, and MVP of the World Series after the Dodgers swept the Yankees in four straight games. In the final game the Dodgers managed only two hits, but Koufax pitched a complete game to beat the Yanks 2-1.

During the 1960s the Dodgers also had Don Drysdale and Johnny Podres in their rotation, as well as a fearless closer in Ron Perranoski. Koufax was the ace, however, and proved it in 1965 when the Dodgers captured another World Series as residents of Dodger Stadium. After a tough battle with the Minnesota Twins, the Dodgers prevailed in seven games, behind two complete-game shutouts by Koufax. In the finale he tossed a masterful 2-0 gem. Then almost mythically, after leading the NL in wins again the next season with twenty-seven, in 1966 Koufax, seemingly in the prime of his career, and with two World Series rings and MVPs to his credit, bowed out of baseball, exiting the game at the top of his form. His early retirement confounded many critics and fans at the time. Though he cited worsening arthritis and pain in his pitching elbow, he was still better than anyone else in the game. Five years after retiring, Koufax became the youngest man to be elected to the Hall of Fame, at the age of thirty-six in 1972. And yet, there's no statue of Sandy outside Dodger Stadium. Many Dodgers fans think there should be; the sentiment is so strong that one fan has started an online petition. If you agree, you can sign your name as a backer of the cause at www.baseballsavvy.com/index.html.

The 1970s were also kind to the Blue Crew, as no Dodgers team in the decade posted a divisional finish lower than third place. Though the Dodgers would lose in the World Series three times (to Oakland in '74, and to the Yankees in '77 and '78), those teams had some of the most memorable players to ever wear the Blue. Tommy Lasorda took over as manager in 1976, a post he would remain at as a fixture until moving up to the front office in 1997. Lasorda's lifetime record in twenty-one seasons as manager was 1,599 wins and 1,439 losses, for a .526 winning percentage. Outfielder Dusty Baker wore Dodger Blue in the 1970s and would later square off against 1980s Dodger catcher Mike Scioscia as opposing managers in the 2002 World Series that pitted two other California teams—Baker's Giants and Scioscia's Angels—against one another.

Four dynamic infielders were the heart and soul of the next Dodgers championship team. Consisting of Ron Cey at third base, second bagger Davey Lopes, shortstop Bill Russell, and Steve Garvey at first, this infield stayed intact until 1981 when the team won the World Series. Fans responded well to these exciting players by showing up at Chavez Ravine in huge numbers, and Dodger Stadium became the first ballpark to surpass the three-million mark in attendance, in 1978, then did it again in 1980.

While the infield was stellar, dominant pitching also played a hand in bringing a championship back to L.A. On Opening Day of the 1981 season "Fernandomania" began to sweep across Dodgerland when Mexican rookie Fernando Valenzuela shut out the Astros 2-0. The twenty-year-old sensation pitched four shutouts in his first five starts that April. Not only did he begin the season 5-0 with a 0.20 ERA, but he batted .438 in the month. Fernando's famous windup, where he would look to the heavens, perhaps for help from above from the angelic namesakes of the city, in addition to his sparkling smile and personality, helped Fernandomania go nationwide. Valenzuela went on to capture not only Rookie of the Year honors, but also the Cy Young Award in that strike-shortened season. After the Dodgers dropped the first two games to the Yankees in the 1981 World Series, Valenzuela took the hill in Game 3. Though the rookie gave up nine hits and seven walks, he hung on for a 5-4 win, fueled by a three-run dinger by Cey in the first. The win gave the Dodgers the new life that Lasorda wanted, and the Blue Crew never looked back. Game 5 at Dodger Stadium would prove critical as the Series was deadlocked at two games apiece. The game was tied 1-1 heading into the bottom of the fourth when Yankee manager Bob Lemon decided to pinch-hit for his ace, Tommy John (a former Dodger)—a decision that proved catastrophic. The Yankees failed to score in the inning, and John, who had been brilliant as the Game 2 winner, was suddenly on the bench. His replacement on the mound was George Frazier, and the Dodgers' Pedro Guerrero treated him the same way Muhammad Ali treated Joe Frazier, by clobbering him for five RBIs. The Dodgers went on to win the series four games to two, after having dropped the first two games. Coincidentally, this was the same trick the Yankees had pulled on the Dodgers the last time the teams met in the World Series, in 1978.

Valenzuela was still with the Dodgers in 1988 when they returned to the World Series, but by this time he was the "old shoe" of the rotation, something that every pitching staff needs. A young Orel Hershiser had assumed the mantle of ace, and pitched fifty-nine scoreless innings during the regular season on his way to the Cy Young before being named MVP of the World Series. Tommy Lasorda dubbed him "the Bulldog" in an effort to make him appear more intimidating than his mild-mannered personality projected.

With Dodger history being so rich, the moment voted by L.A. fans as the greatest in Los Angeles sports history came in Game 1 of the World Series, on October 15, 1988. Pinch-hitter Kirk Gibson hobbled up to the plate looking aged and injured, yet still somehow got enough meat on a Dennis Eckersley pitch to lift it into the Pavilion seats in right field and propel the Dodgers over the Oakland A's. Gibson's only at-bat of the Series gave the Dodgers the momentum they needed and they won the Series in five games.

In 2004, Frank McCourt (no, not the guy who wrote *Angela's Ashes,* the Boston real estate developer who tried first to buy the Red Sox) bought the Dodgers from Rupert Murdoch's NewsCorp for $430 million. The McCourt ownership of Dodger Stadium resulted in nothing but tumult and appeared to be coming to an end as we wrote this new edition to the book in 2011. At the time, the Dodgers had just filed for bankruptcy and MLB Commissioner Bud Selig and Co. appeared to have the upper hand in the effort to oust the financially ruinous McCourt from the game. Nonetheless, Dodger Stadium saw many changes during the McCourt era and not all of them were bad ones. A year before his arrival, 2003 brought DodgerVision—a new video screen and scoreboard that was once the largest in all of baseball at twenty-six feet six inches high and forty-six feet six inches wide, but has since been surpassed by the boards in Houston, Kansas City, and the Bronx.

Josh: Nice to see Kansas City lead the big leagues in something other than barbecue.

Kevin: Ouch.

Next, the Dodgers replaced every seat in the primary seating bowl in the original, now iconic, Dodger Stadium color palette: yellow for level one, orange for level two, turquoise green for level three, and, sky blue for level four. This phase of renovation also included repair work on the concrete structure supporting the seating bowl area and the introduction of Baseline Box seats complete with little tables. In 2008, a multi-million-dollar Field Level restoration project was completed that widened the concourses, added concession stands and restrooms, and installed two new clubs for Baseline Box seat season-ticket holders only. Thinking not blue but green, the Dodgers made additional improvements to Dodger Stadium to make the ballpark more environmentally friendly. A stadium-wide cooling system keeps the temperature in all the concession areas comfortable. Hand dryers and waterless urinals stand in the restrooms to save water and energy. And the team installed a new energy-efficient lighting system, designed to eliminate unnecessary light outside of the stadium and keep unnecessary light out of the eyes of the players and fans. We say a little extra light on the parking lot outside also wouldn't be such a bad thing.

In 2008, McCourt announced a $500 million renovation of Dodger Stadium to make the location a year-round destination that would include a Dodger History Museum, a landscaped plaza behind centerfield complete with restaurants and shops, and of course, plenty of parking. The City Council of L.A. gave the area its own zip code, 90090, and the official new name of Dodgertown.

Kevin: We like to call it Dodgertown, USA, 90090.

Josh: Will Tori Spelling and Shannen Doherty be coming?

Kevin: Um. Maybe.

We joke, but the need to bring Dodger Stadium up to par with the ballparks recently built and into the twenty-first century was a priority for McCourt. But the bitter divorce of McCourt and his wife, Jamie, who was vice chairman, CEO, and president of the Dodgers organization, combined with a sluggish economy, put this round of renovations on hold. When it came to light that McCourt was using Dodger Stadium as collateral to borrow more and more money, Bud Selig seized control of the Dodgers on April 20, 2011, and appointed a representative to oversee day-to-day operations

of the club. This event occurred shortly after a *Los Angeles Times* article revealed McCourt had taken a personal loan from Fox News Corp. to make payroll for April and May 2011.

Josh: See, I told you they shouldn't have given Manny Ramirez all that money.

Kevin: I believe your exact words were, "Manny will ruin that team."

So, as you might suspect, this is all a pretty far departure from the days of Dodger yore, down on Flatbush Avenue in Brooklyn. If we all remember, those Dodgers were a hard luck bunch, who could never seem to beat the Yankees. There is, perhaps, no more profound turning point in the history of baseball in New York than 1958, when the Brooklyn Dodgers, along with the New York Giants, decided to pull up stakes and head west. For the cities of Los Angeles and San Francisco it was a dream come true: Two of the most successful and storied franchises in baseball were coming to play in their towns. And a fierce baseball rivalry continued, further fueled by the Southern versus Northern California feud already in place.

Back East, the Dodgers leaving Brooklyn completely crushed the city. Brooklyners have always had a proud, separate identity from other New Yorkers. And whether it was the fact that the move coincided with the economic downturn in the city at the time, or because the Dodgers were such a symbol of that separate and proud identity, two things were certain: The Dodgers were gone forever and Brooklyn would never be the same.

New York Mets fans, whose ranks were initially supposed to consist of ex-Dodgers and ex-Giants faithful, to this day despise both these teams for abandoning New York. It's odd, because most living Mets fans saw neither the Dodgers nor Giants play in Brooklyn or Manhattan, respectively. Ah, well, baseball loyalties run very deep, especially in a town as rich in baseball history as New York.

Baseball had been played professionally in Brooklyn since 1849. The team that began playing in the early 1890s eventually emerged as the most prominent team in the area. The official name of the club was originally the "Brooklyn Baseball Club." But that name was lengthy, and didn't have much pizzazz. The club played under such nicknames as the Brooklyn Bridegrooms (because seven players got married at nearly the same time) as well as Hanlon's Superbas, Ward's Wonders, Fout's Fillies, and the Robins, all after successful managers.

Though the original home of the ballclub had been Washington Park, it was at Eastern Park where the name "Trolley Dodgers" came about because fans had to cross over a maze of trolley lines to reach the field. Though the Brooklyn club continued to be called a variety of names, the Dodgers name slowly gained popularity and eventually won out.

A small wooden facility had been constructed at Washington Park and so the team returned in 1898. Washington Park, located at 3rd Avenue, between 1st and 3rd Streets in Red Hook, was built on the approximate location of George Washington's headquarters while the Continental Army fought the Battle of Long Island. The Dodgers won a few national battles of their own, securing NL titles in 1899 and 1900 behind such stars as "Wee" Willie Keeler and "Brickyard" Kennedy.

In 1912 team owner Charles Ebbets started buying up property in the Flatbush area of Brooklyn where he would build his team a new ballpark. The area was known less than affectionately as "Pigtown" because swine roamed freely through the nearby dumps looking for food. It was a nicely poetic expression that symbolized the Brooklyn Dodgers who would eventually reside there. The Dodgers' reputation as the working man's team would remain with them as long as they stayed in Brooklyn.

Ebbets bought many parcels of property and eventually had to sell off half his interest in the team to raise funds to build the new park. But it was worth it. Ebbets Field opened in 1913 and closed in 1947—only thirty-four short years—but no other ballpark has had as great an impact on our National Pastime and its new stadiums to follow. At least one aspect of the mythical ballpark has shown up in practically every new park built during the recent retro renaissance. Ebbets Field still floats ethereally in the minds of baseball fans, like the ancient walled city of Troy—a place where many great battles were fought, some won and some lost. A place that is no more.

The clearest image etched in the minds of folks who never attended a game at Ebbets Field is of the majestic front rotunda. Located at 55 Sullivan Place, the rounded front entranceway featured grand arches and square windows and fit seamlessly into the landscape of Brooklyn, a borough with more than its share of churches. Inside, the rotunda was decorated in Italian marble, with a floor tiled with baseball stitching as decoration. Hanging from the twenty-seven-foot-high domed ceiling was a chandelier made of baseball globes and bat arms. Ball fans came to worship at Ebbets and plopped down their money at beautifully gilded ticket windows.

Although Ebbets Field had these high-class elements, what made it special was that it was bursting with the local personality of Brooklyn. Brooklynites were not Giants fans. They didn't socialize in the finer places that Manhattan had

to offer. Brooklyn was working-class. Dodger fans drank in the beer halls and went to the game to blow off steam and root for "dem bums." They weren't the highfalutin fans of the pinstriped teams across the rivers. Ebbets Field reflected the fans' personality. Ebbets was a crazy place, where the feeling that just about anything was liable to happen was justified almost nightly. The right-field wall was concaved, accounting for an estimated 289 different angles that sent shots bouncing off in thousands of different directions. To make matters more difficult for outfielders, a giant scoreboard jutted out of the stands at a forty-five-degree angle in center field.

The ballpark opened without a press box but one was added in 1929, hanging from the roof. Added in 1931 was a double-decked outfield grandstand, which effectively turned the ballpark from a pitcher's park into a hitter's park, enclosing all but the right-field wall and increasing the seating capacity to thirty-two thousand. The roof above the upper deck actually hung over the field of play. But the ballpark's quirks were beloved at the time and made the park feel all the more homey to fans.

Ebbets Field was a magical place to watch a game, a cozy little ballpark where fans were right on top of the action. This closeness endeared the Dodgers to their fans, and made life miserable for opposing teams. One remarkable fan was Hilda Chester, who incessantly clanged her cowbell from the second deck of the left-field bleachers, often to the dismay of even Dodger fans. "Shorty's Symphony Band" kept spirits lively with a cacophonous barrage of tunes, though many folks felt they couldn't find the tune they were playing to save their lives. And there were many other super-fans who frequented Ebbets—home to the notoriously rowdiest fans in all of baseball.

The ballpark hosted four All-Star Games. The first televised game in baseball history was played at Ebbets on April 26, 1939, between the Dodgers and Cincinnati Reds. And the Dodgers and Reds played a nineteen-inning scoreless tie there on September 11, 1946.

During the 1940s and 1950s, baseball in New York blossomed into its halcyon years, as the Yankees seemed to be forever playing either the Dodgers or the Giants for the world championship. During the twenty-year span of the two decades, a New York team played in fourteen World Series, and in eight of those years both teams competing in the Series were from New York. During this time, the Dodgers thrived, advancing to the World Series seven times. But despite all the Dodgers' NL pennants, the Yankees were always at the World Series waiting for them, to snatch away the final glory.

In 1941 Dodgers catcher Mickey Owen dropped a third strike that would have ended Game 4 of the World Series; instead, his blunder set the stage for a Yankee comeback win. Had Owen held onto the ball the Dodgers would have evened the series at two games apiece, but instead the Yankees took a three-games-to-one lead. The pitcher who threw that dropped ball, Hugh Casey, admitted years later that he had thrown a spitball, taking some of the heat off Owen.

Brooklyn owner Branch Rickey had the guts in 1947 to undo what never should have been done in the first place. He searched the country for a player—a very special player—who would have the physical skills, as well as the mental strength and fortitude of character, to cross the hatred of the color line and integrate baseball for the first time since the unofficial owners' agreement had barred African Americans from playing in the Major Leagues in 1898. The player he found was Jack Roosevelt Robinson.

Behind the clutch hitting of shortstop Pee Wee Reese, the power of Duke Snider, and the excellent all-around play of Robinson, "Dem Bums" from Brooklyn reached the World Series in 1947, 1949, 1952, and 1953, but lost to the Yankees in every one of those years.

The year 1952 ended particularly cruelly for Brooklyn as a quick second baseman named Billy Martin saved Game 7 of the World Series for the Yanks. Down 4-2 with two outs in the seventh and the bases loaded, Robinson hit a pop-up behind the mound. Reliever Bob Kuzuva and infielder Joe Collins couldn't locate the bloop as Dodgers runners came rushing around the bases. At the last second Martin made a spectacular diving catch, just inches from the ground.

Dodgers fans could do nothing but shout back their mantra "Wait till Next Year!" But even the most die-hard fans of the beloved losers must have started to suspect that "next year" might never come. For a city that seemed to have less and less going for it, the Dodgers and their losses became symptomatic of its troubles. The Dodgers were doomed, born losers. Even their name "Dodger" seemed a bit on the shady side.

But "next year" finally came for Brooklyn in 1955. Snider knocked a three-run shot into the second-level grandstands of center field to win Game 4 of the Series against the Yanks. Sandy Amoros caught a well-hit Yogi Berra drive to the left-field corner in Game 7 to preserve a 2-0 lead. The blue-collar losers from Brooklyn went on to beat the perennially winning Yanks, and people all over Brooklyn, the city that couldn't buy a break, celebrated wildly and drank themselves silly in the madness of the Flatbush night. There is a famous

photograph in which a bartender holds up a newspaper that reads "WE WIN" in bold and brazen ink on the front page of the *Brooklyn Eagle*. But perhaps more importantly, the toasting Dodgers fans all have glasses of beer raised in celebration. This photo symbolizes what it meant to a city of three million people, the fourth largest in America, for their bums, their lovable losers whose ballpark was built on a dump, to at last slay the mighty dragon and defeat the team that boasted all the talent that money could buy.

But even in victory, the Dodgers found a way to lose. When they failed to repeat as World Series champs, losing to the Yankees in seven games in 1956, the end was near. The long-standing Dodger mantra "Wait till Next Year" was changed by Brooklyn writer Roger Kahn to "Wait till Last Year." Brooklyn would forever look backward at their Dodgers. Kahn's 1972 best-seller *Boys of Summer* is a classic text of the era that chronicles the Brooklyn Dodger teams of the 1950s.

O'Malley, after failing in his attempts to obtain funding for a new ballpark from city officials, made arrangements to move the Dodgers out of Brooklyn. The move of the Braves to Milwaukee had preceded the Dodgers' migration west and had proved that it was financially lucrative to do so. O'Malley saw little chance of remaining competitive in Brooklyn without the new ballpark he deemed necessary to increase revenue for the team. There were massive protests and scathing articles written. But the last game was played at Ebbets Field on September 24, 1957, witnessed by just 6,702 fans. So hurtful was the team's impending departure that the rowdiest and most loyal fans in baseball couldn't bear to show up. When asked to list the three most notorious villains of the twentieth century, Brooklyners chose Adolf Hitler, Joseph Stalin, and Walter O'Malley.

In moving to L.A., O'Malley transformed that old Brooklyn soul from one of bums and perennial losers to clean-cut winning boys of summer. These new Dodgers were no longer allowed to be called "Dem Bums" by the newspapers. That moniker died in Brooklyn alongside Ebbets Field. An all-American image in Dodger Blue was crafted, one more suitable to Los Angeles, and along with it, a tradition of winning World Series.

L.A.'s Memorial Coliseum, as horrible a spot to view a baseball game as ever was retrofitted, was where the Dodgers awaited the building of their Elysian ballpark on the hill. The Dodgers played at the Coliseum from 1958 to 1962, and though it was fairly awful, it seated plenty. The farthest seats were more than seven hundred feet from home plate. In 1958 the L.A. Dodgers drew 1.85 million fans, some 600,000 more than the Brooklyn Dodgers had drawn the year before.

415

The Coliseum seated well over ninety thousand per game, as opposed to only thirty-two thousand at Ebbets.

Fifty years after the Dodgers moved to L.A., a promotional stunt reopened the Coliseum for baseball during the spring of 2008 so that the Dodgers could host the Red Sox for a Saturday night spring training game in late March. The game drew 115,300 fans, making for the largest crowd ever to watch a baseball game. The distance from home plate to the left-field foul pole was just 201 feet, and a sixty-foot-high screen ran across left field toward center to keep liners in the yard. Clearly, this was never imagined to be more than a one-time thing, just a stunt.

In its proper day, the Coliseum set World Series attendance records in 1959 when the Dodgers defeated the Chicago White Sox in six games. In the 1963 World Series the Dodgers swept the Yankees in four games. Clearly, the face-lift of the old Dodger Bums was complete.

Since claiming their fifth World Series title in 1988, the Los Angeles Dodgers have seen some of the greatest players of the game play at Dodger Stadium. Hideo Nomo, the first Japanese-born star to join the big leagues, came to America first as a Dodger, then after leaving, returned to the team. Pitching phenom Pedro Martinez and perennial All-Star Mike Piazza also came up through the legendary Dodgers farm system. More recently, Matt Kemp, Andre Ethier and Clayton Kershaw have showcased the good work being done in the Dodgers outposts from Albuquerque to Rancho Cucamonga.

Trivia Timeout

People's Choice: How is it possible that the seating capacity of Dodger Stadium has never changed although the Dodgers have added seats?

Golden Globe: How many ballparks remain in MLB with completely symmetrical outfields?

Oscar: Name the three players who have hit balls out of Dodger Stadium.

Look for the answers in the text.

Kevin: You just like saying Cucamonga, don't you?

Josh: Guilty as charged.

The McCourt years proceeded to turn many fans off. While the Angels offered a super-friendly fan environment a short drive away, Dodger fans feel, and rightfully so, that McCourt, out of sheer ineptitude, took a team that should be considered the Yankees of the West Coast (market size, television revenue, etc.) and squandered those advantages. The fans have let their feet do their talking. In 2009 the Dodgers ranked first in all of baseball in attendance, averaging 46,440 per game. In 2010, they dropped only slightly to third, averaging 43,900. And then, in 2011, the McCourt ousting, the Dodgers dropped all the way to, averaging just coinciding with eleventh north of thirty-six thousand per game. Certainly McCourt made some interesting decisions, culminating in MLB taking the Dodgers into receivership in 2011. We can only hope that brighter days lie ahead for this once-proud franchise and fan base.

Getting a Choice Seat

Despite having the most seats of any ballpark in baseball, Dodger Stadium nonetheless boasts some of the best sight lines. Because the Stadium is completely symmetrical in every way, it's not hard to figure out where the good seats are. But there are a few caveats at Dodger Stadium, so follow the guide below to maximize your visit.

Interestingly, Dodger Stadium has always held exactly fifty-six thousand due to a conditional use permit that limits its capacity. For every seat upgrade that has placed new seats at field level, an equal number of seats have been removed to keep the total at fifty-six thousand.

The first point to remember is that nowhere in baseball is it more imperative to purchase a seat on the level in which you intend to sit. Ushers at Dodger Stadium are very kindly and polite, but they will only allow you to access the level of the stadium for which you have a ticket. Kevin tried his smooth-talking techniques on more than a few, but to these ushers it was like he was trying to talk his way into an exclusive Hollywood club. This means that unless you are skilled at the very dangerous practice of stadium-level hopping (please do not try this), you'll do yourself a favor by purchasing a ticket for the tier in which you intend to sit. You can then perhaps do some seat hopping on that particular level.

Dodgers fans may arrive fashionably late, but they traditionally show up for games whether the Dodgers win or lose. Finishing in third place is considered a poor year for the Boys in Blue, so they are usually at least competitive. This means that seat hopping in the early innings is likely to get you pinched. So wait until the relative safety of the fourth inning, unless traffic on the 101 is particularly heavy.

Also beware of calling the ticket line by phone, as the ticket office charges a $2.25 per ticket handling charge.

> **Seating Capacity:** 56,000
> **Ticket Office:** http://losangeles.dodgers.
> mlb.com/ticketing/singlegame.jsp?c_id=la
> **Seating Chart:** http://losangeles.dodgers.
> mlb.com/la/ballpark/seating_pricing.jsp

Josh: There are more than thirty different price points for seats at Dodger Stadium.

Kevin: Yeah, it's damn confusing. So what's your point?

Club Seating

The seats in the Dugout Club, a section between the dugouts added in 2000, are undoubtedly better than their Stadium Club counterparts. Both have access to their own clubhouse, where if you can afford it you can talk to other members of the club, and basically *be* in the club. Sounds like a real good time to us. The only way to get these seats is to contact Premium Seating at (323) 224–1320.

Kevin: Hello, premium seating. Yes, *Brangelina* and *Bennifer* and I were looking to go to a game.

Josh: Wha'd they say? Wha'd they say?

Kevin: They hung up.

Field Level

Apparently you have to be dating a high-level Hollywood exec or your last name has to be Lasorda or Garvey to sit in the Inner Field Box Seats (Field Aisles 1–41), because we couldn't even find pricing for them. When we asked about them we were taken to a special room and strip searched. Not really, but purchasing these seats is out of the question. Middle Field Box Seats (Field Aisles 42–49) are pricey, but excellent. Outer Field Boxes (Field Aisles 50–57) are less pricey (but still too much in our opinion) and less excellent. Much less excellent are Aisles 54–57, which all have foul-pole obstructions to some degree. When you're paying this much for seats, foul poles should not block anything.

Loge Level

Inner Loge Box Seats (Loge Aisles 101–147) were also unavailable to us, unless we were willing to rent wheelchairs and angle for handicapped seating. While Josh toyed with the idea for a moment, we decided that it would be better not to spend the hefty sum of cash required. Middle Loge Box Seats (Loge Aisles 148–157) are worth the three dollars more than they charge for Outer Field Boxes. But the Outer Loge Box Seats (Loge Aisles 158–167) don't seem worth the price. If you can get into Aisles 158–159, then these seats are a better bargain than the Inner Reserved Seats, which are two more levels up. Aisles 164–167 have foul-pole obstructions and should be avoided.

Reserved Level

The Inner Reserved Seats (Reserved Aisles 1–20) are also too pricey considering how high up they are. Better to sit in a low row of the Top Deck and pay almost a third of the price. Outer Reserved Seats (Reserved Aisles 13–60) are probably the best for the money if you can get them in Aisles 23–40. Inner Reserved Seats in aisles lower than 20 share the middle concourse with Outer Reserved Seats that are above the concourse. These Outer Reserved seats are therefore that much worse, but they are also significantly cheaper seats, so it's a bit of a trade-off.

We don't recommend sitting in the Outer Reserved Seats, Aisles 41 and higher. You'll be much happier with seats in the Top Deck or the Pavilion. Any aisle higher than 54 will have some type of foul-pole obstruction.

Top Deck

In an odd, but wonderful pricing move, the Dodgers offer Top Deck Seats (Aisles 1–14) at cheaper prices than are available on the lower level. These beauties are cheap and right behind the plate, a combination that we love. If you like sitting on top of the action, these seats are better than any of the Outer Reserved seats.

Pavilion (Pavilion Aisles 301–314)

The wavy topped roof that gives the stadium its distinctive look shades the upper sections of these seats. The orange seats up above the middle concourse are the same price as the blue seats down near the fence. So why not head down for the good seats? Often the ticket office will sell out the left-field section before even opening up the right-field Pavilion seats. So

SEATING TIP

Notice that there is an overlap between Inner Reserved and Outer Reserved Seats in Aisles 13–20. That is because these aisles service both sections and price ranges. So beware: Some aisles only head up from the concourse toward the worse seats, while others go up toward the poorer seats, but also head down toward the better seats. Ask for seats in the lower rows of Aisles 23–24, 27–28, 31–32, 35–36, and 39–40 (as these rows also head upward), and your seats will be vastly improved within the same price range.

if all they have available are the top rows, we suggest waiting them out a few minutes until those crummy seats sell and getting into the newly opened section as soon as it opens.

After a number of instances where Pavilion fans dumped cups of beer, bottles, and trash on Cincinnati Reds left fielder Pete Rose, selling beer was banned in the Left Field Pavilion seats until 2009, when it resumed. That's a good thing, right? Wrong. The lack of security in these seats makes them some of the most dangerous in baseball, especially if you're a fan of an opposing NL West team.

Fan Danger Alert

No matter what you do, realize this: If you wear the opposing team colors—especially Giants' orange and black—you are taking your life into your own hands. We wish we were joking about this but, sadly, we are not. There have been many incidents of fights in these sections, often caused by Dodger "fans" taunting opposing players and fans. On a few of these occasions, the fights have turned ugly. On a particularly gruesome Opening Day in 2011, a number of Dodger fans were arrested in an incident where three Giants fans were attacked near the end of the game. One Giants fan, Bryan Stow, was beaten unconscious and subsequently went into a coma following the attack.

Once again, until this situation changes, we recommend avoiding these sections and wearing only neutral colors. Or blue.

Bleacher Beach

At the top of the Pavilion Level is a new area known as Bleacher Beach. Essentially, these are the same old seats as they used to be, only with a bit of marketing spin. Fans in the Lower Reserve sections 55 and 59, along the third-base line, enjoy deejay music, cooling off with misters, and decorations of tiki huts and lifeguard towers. There's also the benefit of all-you-can eat barbecued chicken and hamburgers, as well as the standard Dodger Dogs, nachos, peanuts, popcorn, watermelon slices, and soft drinks. And weekend games net you a complimentary T-shirt.

The Black Market

Seeing as the Dodgers keep such a tight watch on everything not directly related to fan safety, there isn't much of a scalper scene directly around Chavez Ravine. You will find a smattering of ticket sellers at the corner of Academy and Stadium way. If a game is sold out and you like your tickets in hand before heading to town, online ticket brokers are your best bet.

Before/After the Game

The folks in Southern California sure know how to build parking lots. The twenty-one terraced levels surrounding Dodger Stadium are landscaped to perfection. The only problem is that tailgating is strictly prohibited. Since there is absolutely nothing else to do in these lots, we wonder if the Dodgers know what kind of opportunity they're wasting here. Think of the possibilities of inebriated entertainment: beer golf, downhill bowling, skateboarding.

Traditionally a ballpark's exterior is not its most attractive feature. But with all the money spent on landscaping, the Dodgers challenge conventional wisdom. Walking up the hills will bring you alongside all sorts of California foliage, flora, bushes, and desert trees. And the blue and teal exterior paint of the ballpark itself is very soothing. A walk around the exterior is a must, with expansive views in all directions.

Getting to Dodger Stadium

Freeways, freeways everywhere. This is Super-freeway-land, so navigating difficult. But if you can find your way to the 101 freeway, shoot on over to the Alvarado exit. Then spin right on Sunset and shoot left onto Elysian Park, which spits you out into the parking lots. From the 110 freeway, take the Dodger Stadium exit and the off-ramp will dump you right out into the parking lots. From Interstate 5 north, exit at Stadium Way. Make a left onto Riverside Drive and then turn left again onto Stadium Way. Follow the blue baseball signs until you enter Dodger Stadium off of Academy Road. From Interstate 5 South simply take the Stadium Way exit and turn left, then follow the blue signs and enter Dodger Stadium off Academy Road.

PARKING

As you might expect, the parking section of the L.A. chapter will be quite extensive. The first tip is that if you are parking in the lots, get there early. It is possible, as the cars rush to get to the ballpark at some point before the fourth inning, that you will get caught in traffic and indeed arrive with the rest of the throng in the fourth! Earlier is definitely better.

The team lots are all marked by numbered baseballs, twenty-one in all, and are the only ones remotely close. If you intend on parking in the team lots, we suggest parking close to the "Think Blue" sign, near Gate C. The walk to the game will be a bit longer—much longer if you're not sitting in the outfield. But you'll thank us when it comes time to leave. While all the other nearby lots feed into the same lane to exit, and thus are backed up for hours, people parking in these lots are treated to their own exit lane, exclusively marked by cones. You'll stroll past all the folks who left early and are stuck in the chaos of cars, get into your own vehicle, and be back on the freeway in no time.

For the more daring, there are free parking spaces on Academy Street, just beyond the outermost lots. A word to the wise: Park on the side of the street that faces downhill, otherwise you'll spend half your life trying to execute a three-point turn after the game. Another word to the wise, if you plan on tailgating in these free parking spaces on Academy Street, please realize that Academy Street gets its name from the Los Angeles Police Academy, which is on the street directly across from where we parked and set up our hibachi.

Parking lots are also available closer to downtown and are fairly cheap for ballgames. But the walk up the hill is a killer.

Speaking of a killer walk, you might be tempted to enjoy some pregame time at Elysian Park, which surrounds Dodger Stadium, before the game. After all, it seems close, parking is free, you can take your shoes off and toss the Frisbee around before the game. What's not to like, right? Well, first, there are no open containers of alcohol allowed in L.A. city parks. And second, the walk is another thing that's what not to like. It is a long walk uphill and across the parking lots to get to the game. And even if you do it early enough, after the game you'll be walking on the street (there are no sidewalks) alongside traffic that would rather run you down than share the road. If you want to hit the park before the game, do it early, then drive up and park nearer to the ballpark. You'll thank us.

MASS TRANSIT OPTIONS

While we were busy laughing, L.A. has been busy building subways. Still, none of them go to Dodger Stadium . . . yet. We're still holding out hope.

For folks who still prefer the bus, its best to contact Metro Bus via the Web at www.mta.net.

If you can find your way to the Union Station/Gateway Transit Center, shuttle service on the Dodger Stadium Express runs from Union Station to Dodger Stadium every ten minutes, beginning ninety minutes before the game and ending forty-five minutes after. Plus, it's free if you can produce your game ticket.

Outside Attractions

"THINK BLUE"

Reminiscent of the "Hollywood" sign and sitting atop a small hill just beyond the parking lots is a sign in Dodger Blue that reads only "Think Blue." Well, we thought "blue" for about as long as we could bear to, but being that we're not Dodgers fans, we didn't come up with much. Perhaps this is some new brand of philosophy, a particularly Dodger-esque form of existentialist thought. Or it could be just a gimmick cooked up by Tommy Lasorda and the gang. We're not sure. But we do like the fact that the sign lights up at night.

COULD YOU CHECK MY BRAKE FLUID TOO?

There is a gas station beyond the center-field fence in the parking lot at Dodger Stadium. We are not kidding. Could something this perfect be made up? Now while we could make a cheap joke here about how the lines to get out of Dodger Stadium are so long that you will inevitably run out of gas and require a fill-up, we won't. Let's just call this a particularly Californian convenience, and leave it at that.

YOU CANNOT BE OVER "THIS" TALL

Shorter fans (or Josh sitting on a footstool) can catch a view of a sellout game through small fences beyond the outfield walls. Only four times have these West Coast "knotholers" been lucky enough to chase balls hit completely out of the stadium and into the parking lot. Mark McGwire did it most recently in 1999. Before Big Mac, a Mike Piazza shot left the yard in 1997. And before either of them, Willie "Pops" Stargell sent two shots out, the first in 1969, the second in 1973.

VISITING TEAM AUTOGRAPHS

If you're an autograph hound like Josh, hang just outside the lower level gates in right field after the game. The visiting players walk right past this gate on their way to their cars, and there are usually only a few people waiting so the players don't seem to mind. It's a little-known fact but a very easy way to get autographs.

Watering Holes and Outside Eats

With the maze of parking lots that cover Chavez Ravine, and with tailgating strictly prohibited, there is no place to have a pregame meal or drink in the area without getting back into your car. But of course this is L.A., and no one ever expects to go anywhere without a car, so it all has a strange sense of normalcy to it. And as L.A. is far too huge a city to try to list any number of cool places to go out, we're sticking to places close by the ballpark and places we like.

ECHO PARK NEIGHBORHOOD

The Echo Park neighborhood is overloaded with places to eat, drink, and have a coffee.

Drive down Sunset Boulevard and you can find great Mexican food, Cambodian, Chinese, Vietnamese, French places, and more.

THE SHORT STOP
1455 Sunset Blvd.

This Echo Park dive is tough to find. There's no sign posted any-where on the darkly painted building. Look for the sandwich board sign out front that lets you know what the drink spe-cials are each day. The Short Stop used to be an LAPD hang-out where officers hung up their guns to knock down a few. Now it is the quintessential Dodger bar and a great place to go before or after the game. Why? How about this: longest happy hour in L.A.! We also like the drink specials. Free pool. Cheap beer on game days. And if that's not enough, how about a DJ? *And* it's owned by a former member of the Afghan Whigs.

MEAT WRAPPED IN MORE MEAT!
A culinary attraction found in L.A. and one that you might not want to miss as you drive toward the ballpark are the bacon wrapped hot dogs you may (or may not) find available from street vendors. There are usually a couple of these ven-dors outside the Short Stop. These are the "guerilla warriors" of the hot dog world, as selling grilled hot dogs on the street, by a non-approved vendor, is strictly illegal. Apparently, only boiled hot dogs are allowed in the city. Just like L.A., these dogs are part Mexican, part American, and all delicious. Get yours with onions, tomatoes, ketchup, mustard, mayonnaise, and on occasion, a poblano chile. Now you see them, now you don't; don't be surprised if one of these purveyors of dog deliciousness picks up his makeshift sterno grill and bolts upon seeing one of L.A.'s finest arrive on the scene.

Kevin: Bacon wrapped dogs are so good, it's no won-der they're illegal.

Josh: Shut up and eat. We need to get four more before this guy gets busted.

BURRITO KING
Sunset Boulevard and Alvarado

Though its reputation has slipped lately, the Burrito King still offers cheap "drunk food." It sure hit the spot when we visited, though we can't recall for certain exactly what we ordered.

THE GOOD MICROBREW AND GRILL
www.goodmicrobrew.com
3725 Sunset Blvd.

Farther down Sunset, in the Silver Lake neighborhood, is a place worth the extra drive, especially for those who appreciate a nice craft-brew. The Good Microbrew and Grill is a hipster's paradise, with more than one hundred beers avail-able and plenty of them on special. If you're coming to the ballpark from Hollywood, up Sunset Drive, or heading there after the game, this brew house makes the perfect stopover.

EL PRADO
www.elpradobar.com
1805 W. Sunset Blvd.

This hipster hangout is another beer bar, as it appears that L.A. has (finally) discovered the snobby beer bar craze known as the microbrew revolution. El Prado bills itself as featuring: beer, snacks, and records. If you're stuck in the '70s this is your place. The sound system is a record player . . . that's right, vinyl rules! The walls are covered in dark wood and the tables and brass fixtures are like the ones you might expect at the Regal Beagle (the bar the gang from *Three's Company* frequented). El Prado has a nice selection of beer and wine—they carry drafts from the Eagle Rock Brewery, one of the few brewer-ies in L.A. It is small and can get very crowded, but it's a solid choice if you manage to snag a table.

THE DRESDEN
www.thedresden.com
1760 Vermont Ave.

Remember that scene in the movie *Swingers* where Mikey, played by a thin Jon Favreau, finally stops whining over his girlfriend back in New Jersey, goes out swing dancing, meets Heather Graham, and gets her phone number? That scene was shot at the Dresden, which has since become a place where hipsters drink with their "beautiful baby" friends.

Kevin: Is this where the Dresden Dolls got their start?

Josh: Um, I'm pretty sure they're a Boston band.

Kevin: Really?

Josh: Trust me.

YE RUSTIC INN
1831 Hillhurst Ave.

Near Silver Lake in Los Feliz, this small, dark quasi-sports joint caters to hipsters and locals. Waitresses heavily adorned with tattoos and piercings serve beer and mixed drinks. Like many of the folks in Silver Lake, the gals want to look like Bettie Page and the guys are aiming for a Beck-like quality of cleanliness.

THE DRAWING ROOM
1800 Hillhurst Ave.

The Los Feliz/Silver Lake area has become one of the cool-est neighborhoods in town in recent years, and another of its many cool spots is the Drawing Room. This bar is cool in

Kevin's sense of the word. In other words, it's a dive. You'll find would-be actors, bikers, and local hipsters drinking it up in happy spirits.

THE RED LION TAVERN, GERMAN GASTHAUS AND BEER GARDEN
www.redliontavern.net
2366 Glendale Ave.
With German beers on tap in the authentic outdoor beer garden on the second floor, and the waitresses bringing them wearing their traditional German dirndl serving outfits (think the girl on the St. Pauli Girl label), this place is a must for any self-respecting German. So bring your lederhosen. Go for the knockwurst, liverwurst, and bratwurst. Check out the wall of fame on the stairs, dedicated to famous Germans and German-Americans.

Places Worth the Drive

PINK'S HOT DOGS
www.pinkshollywood.com
Corner of Melrose and La Brea
Kevin's brother, Sean, who lives in L.A., took us to this place, known as "Hot Dogs to the Stars." Since 1939 Pink's has been doling out dogs, and no visit to Hollywood would be complete without a stop. Options range in price and Pink's has found as many dog variations as any place we've visited. Sean had the Huell (Howser) dog, named after the host of California's Gold travel show. The order had two hot dogs stuffed into one bun if you can believe it. Kevin had the Brooklyn pastrami dog and it was delicious. Josh sampled the chili-cheese dog and was very pleased as well. Hoffy is the brand name for these dogs that are made especially for Pink's and they were some of the best cased meat we ate on the entire trip. The word is out on this place, so expect to stand in line for at least twenty minutes, regardless of the time of day.

OLVERA STREET
For great Mexican restaurants and Mexican culture, head down to Olvera Street, located in the pueblo at the heart of downtown. Olvera is a cobblestone street that boasts many places to eat, shop, and even listen to roaming mariachi bands. Try **La Luz Del Dia Mexican Restaurant,** or if you're like Kevin, simply pick a restaurant at random.

THE TIKI-TI
www.tiki-ti.com
4427 Sunset Blvd.
There's just something wonderful about a top-notch tiki bar, and if that's what you're hankering for, the Tiki-ti will not disappoint. When you're surrounded by wooden tiki masks, the fruity tropical drinks from the South Pacific go down fast. The fishbowl drinks may cost $12 and up, but one'll do ya.

PHILIPPE'S FRENCH DIP SANDWICHES
www.philippes.com
1001 N. Alameda St.
Now this is the kind of place you're not likely to see again. Philippe's is an old-style L.A. lunch counter that's been in this location since 1952 and in business since 1908. Offerings from behind the huge stainless steel warming counter include pork sandwiches a full breakfast, pies, potato salad, and much more. Regular coffee is just nine cents. But the specialty of the house is the French dip sandwich, which they claim to have invented. It's a piling of roast beef served on a fresh baguette and dipped in *au jus*. While most places will serve the *jus* in a cup on the side, these originators submerge the bread completely before it's assembled, for a deliciously wet meal. Near the front door, an old wooden and glass drugstore counter contains candy and cigarettes for sale. The back room is dedicated to train memorabilia, and there are even a handful of early Dodgers photographs and signed baseballs displayed, with signatures rapidly fading.

Don't miss the lunch counter waitresses. With traditional uniforms and hair piled high, these women give the place its aura. The system of payment is unique, as the waitresses aren't allowed to actually touch the money. You place your bills down on a plate, then a nice lady hands the plate back to the cashier who makes your change, which is brought back to you on the same plate.

IT'S CHINATOWN, JAKE.
Ocean Seafood Restaurant (747 N. Broadway St.) is one place we can recommend in Chinatown, and **Yang Chow** (819 N. Broadway) is another. But there are literally hundreds of restaurants to explore, if you're game. Old Chinatown is a great tourist spot where many movies have been shot.

Inside Dodger Stadium

At fifty-six thousand seats, this stadium is now the biggest ballpark in terms of seating capacity, but does not suffer intimacy issues when compared to the smaller ballparks in the league. Dodger Stadium offers some of the best seats in the game. If you're looking for a ballpark filled with quirks, you should move on. Completely symmetrical in every way, Dodger Stadium has never been described as a quirky ballpark. In fact, it's the only completely symmetrical outfield left in the National League, and one of only four left in baseball.

Jackie Robinson

Born on January 19, 1919, Jackie Robinson first put on a Dodgers uniform and stepped onto Ebbets Field on April 15, 1947—a moment in the history of baseball, the importance of which cannot be overstated. A brilliant second baseman for the Kansas City Monarchs as well as the Montreal Royals—a Dodgers minor league team—Robinson was hand-chosen by Branch Rickey in 1945 not because he was the best player from the Negro Leagues, but because Rickey was, in his words, "looking for someone with the guts not to fight back."

Jackie Robinson had a history of exceptional success as an athlete. He was an All-American at UCLA, breaking school records in football, basketball, baseball, and track and field. He was the school's first four-letter man, and as such had achieved a certain degree of national fame. The fact that he was allowed to compete on the same field as white athletes in these other sports and that he excelled was a powerful argument for the integration of baseball.

Another important factor on the résumé of Jackie Robinson was the fact that he had been a soldier in the US Army from 1942 through 1944. Robinson had served his country during World War II, and was a decorated platoon leader. Also significant during his career in the military was an incident that was to set Robinson ever further apart from the field in terms of character. He fought a court-martial leveled against him over an incident in which he refused to give up his seat on a bus. Jackie Robinson was not court-martialed, but rather discharged from the Army honorably after the trial. His strength of character had already been proven, as he had fought racial injustice and won a significant if small victory.

But even Rickey—who expected Robinson to succeed—must have been impressed by the inner strength of character Robinson displayed on the baseball diamond. Robinson was called ugly names, was intentionally spiked by players, was ignored by teammates as if he wasn't even there, and had his own life and the lives of his family members threatened constantly. The St. Louis Cardinals threatened to strike rather than play Robinson's Dodgers. But on May 9, 1947, Ford Frick, the National League president, stopped them, stating: "If you do this, you will be suspended from the league. . . . I do not care if half the league strikes. . . . I don't care if it wrecks the National League for five years. This is the United States of America, and one citizen has as much right to play as another. The National League will go down the line with Robinson, whatever the consequence."

While many have stated that Rickey's interests in breaking the color barrier had financial undertones—the Dodgers instantly became black America's favorite team—the fact is that Rickey and Robinson needed one another to accomplish what they did. And though it may have been true that Robinson could not have accomplished all he did without Rickey and Frick, it is also true that these accomplishments would have not been possible for lesser men than Jackie Robinson. Imagine, being kicked and punched, and not taking any action to defend yourself, when you'd be very morally correct to do so. After all, which is easier? Giving in to your emotions, your natural feelings of rage and anger, or fighting anger and hatred with an air of indifference? Robinson taught us all (again) that the strength needed not to fight is far greater, surely.

After his career in baseball, Jackie Robinson continued to fight injustice. He marched in Birmingham, Alabama, with the Reverend Dr. Martin Luther King Jr. He testified before Congress on the unequal treatment of African Americans, and he worked for his people's causes in the political arena as well.

On October 23, 1972, Robinson died of a heart attack in Stamford, Connecticut.

People like Jackie Robinson make us all proud to be fans of the game of baseball. And perhaps the most laudable act of Commissioner Bud Selig was retiring Robinson's number 42 throughout all of baseball, never to be worn again.

The other three are the O.co Coliseum, Rogers Centre, and Kauffman Stadium in Kansas City. But inside this house of symmetry, there is plenty of charm to keep fans happy.

Ballpark Features

TRADITIONALLY A PITCHER'S PARK

Since its beginnings, Dodger Stadium has always favored pitchers. Even after lowering the mound and adding Field Level seating that has all but removed the expanse of foul territory that once gave Dodger Stadium its distinctive design, this yard still makes things easier on the hurlers. Its deep power alleys (385 ft.) certainly help, but the symmetrical shape also works to contain extra base hits. There are two signs that look to be in dead center which read 395 feet, but in fact these are to the right and left of true center field, which is 400 feet.

WAVY-TOPPED PAVILION ROOF

Other than the multi-colored seats, perhaps the most distinctive feature of the ballpark is the roof that covers the outfield Pavilion. Slanted up and down, it's a wavelike design that looks like a row of cabana huts lined up. This architectural design element can be seen surrounding the upper deck of the park as well, though television cameras rarely show this.

NUMBERS, NUMBERS, NUMBERS

Nearly hidden in the very blue outfield wall between the ads are the numbers most significant to Dodger history: 104 was the number of wins for the Dodgers in 1942 when they finished second to the Cardinals, who won 106 games, and is the number of bases stolen by Maury Wills in 1962; 382 was the number of strikeouts Koufax had in 1965; 153 is the total of RBIs in 1962 by Tommy Davis; 6 is the number of Dodgers World Series titles; 233 is the number of Don Sutton's victories as a Dodger; 81 was the magical season of 1981 for Valenzuela and Co.; 59 was the year the L.A. Dodgers first won the World Series, as well as the number of consecutive innings pitched by Hershiser without giving up an earned run; 49 is the team-record number of home runs hit by Shawn Green in 2001; and 52 is the record number of saves in a season by Eric Gagne in 2002.

RETIRED NUMBERS

The Dodgers also boast their share of retired numbers, which hang below the pavilion roofs in the outfield. They are No. 1 for Pee Wee Reese; No. 2 for Tommy Lasorda; No. 4 for Duke Snider; No. 19 for Jim Gilliam; No. 20 for Don Sutton; No. 24 for Walter Alston; No. 32 for Sandy Koufax; No. 39 for Roy Campanella; No. 42 for Jackie Robinson; and No. 53 for Don Drysdale.

Josh: What is the significance of the numbers 1, 71, 11, and 9?

Kevin: You know I'm not good with numbers.

Josh: They belong to today's umpires. Look, they're listed on the scoreboard all game.

ROOKS

One number not listed that should be is the number 16. This is the number of Dodgers rookies who've earned the Rookie of the Year honor. From 1992 to 1996 the Dodgers boasted a streak of five players in a row to win the award: Eric Karros, Mike Piazza, Raul Mondesi, Hideo Nomo, and Todd Hollandsworth. But the Dodgers also had another string of four ROYs in a row from 1979 to 1982. They were Rick Sutcliffe, Steve Howe, Valenzuela, and Steve Sax, in that order.

Stadium Eats

The food at Dodger Stadium used to be like the food at a movie theater: expensive and worse than a Keanu Reeves movie (*The Matrix* and *Bill and Ted's Excellent Adventure* excluded). But it looks like the Dodger brass got the memo and read our first edition, because the eats at the Stadium (at least on the Field Level) have improved. With the remodel, new vendors have been added to some of the old favorites. Eating options more closely reflect nearby Chinatown and Mexican East L.A.—or at least as much as the

---

The McCourt Family Legacy

Here's a list of some of the more hilarious (or sad) things by which a generation of fans will remember Frank McCourt's ownership of the Dodgers:

1. Bought the Dodgers from Fox with money loaned by Fox.
2. Divided the Dodgers empire (the team, the stadium, the parking lots, etc.) into different companies and then took a personal salary for himself and his wife of more than $100 million over six years out of those companies to fund a lifestyle of opulence.
3. Took out a $30 million loan from Fox to keep the Dodgers afloat—because he couldn't make the team's payroll—then threatened to sue MLB for trying to block the deal. What did he think MLB was going to do?
4. Hired a spiritual guru to watch Dodgers games on TV (from upstate New York) and send "good vibes" to the ballclub via the airwaves.
5. Got caught up in a Hollywood champagne lifestyle on a Boston beer budget.
6. Cut security at the Stadium, sold beer inside, while banning tailgating in the parking lot so that the Dodgers would be the only ones profiting from drunken fans, and allowed rowdy drunken fans to throw hot dogs at other fans. The result: A Giant fan was beaten so severely in 2011 that he slipped into a coma. Days later, the Dodgers announced a "zero-tolerance policy" concerning violence at the ballpark.

corporate ethnic variety that Panda Express, California Pizza Kitchen, and Comacho's Cantina can offer. And while none of the new offerings are truly delectable, the entirety of the fare is better.

Josh: Is that what you call a backhanded compliment?

Kevin: I don't know. Try my backhand.

Josh: Ouch!

THE FAIRFAX SANDWICH (TRADEMARK FOOD)

If you have the scratch to afford first level seats, head to Canter's Deli and pick up the one truly delectable thing at Dodger Stadium—the Fairfax. Corned beef and pastrami are piled high on rye, the meat is nicely grilled and goes down well with a beer. If you don't have a Field Level ticket, getting to the ballpark early to view batting practice while you take a Fairfax to the house is a nice way to get warmed up for the game.

COMACHO'S NACHOS (TRADEMARK FOOD)

We know what you're thinking: Chalky tortilla chips topped with sludgy orange cheese goo does not a tasty meal make. And you're right. But the nachos at Comacho's Cantina are a diamond in the rough at Dodger Stadium. They start with real restaurant chips—fresh and lightly oiled. Then they add to the cheesey goo, real pico de gallo, sour cream, and a guacamole-like substance. They top the whole mess with chicken or carne asada, and the result is a delicious, if sloppy, ballpark snack.

Kevin: There's no way you would order them without the jalapeños, is there?

Josh: There's no way you would order them without a beer, is there?

DODGER DOG (DOG REVIEW)

We actually received a lot of mail regarding our review of The Dodger Dog in the first edition of this book, and most of it was not kind. One reader actually suggested that he would find us at a ballpark one day and force-feed us Dodger Dogs until we conceded that they were pretty darned good. Another said plainly that if we didn't agree with him that Dodgers Dogs ruled the baseball world, then we were both idiots and nothing else we had to say in the book was worth his reading. Angelenos seem to want to will the Dodger Dog to greatness. But the reality remains, if you're not getting it grilled, it's actually a very bland dog. The Farmer John–brand dog itself is longer than the bun (which is good) but is also on the thin and skimpy side. We like to call it the "Not too this, not too that" dog. Not too spicy, not too bland, not too salty, not too bursting with flavor. It's the most average dog we have ever tasted, designed seemingly to offend no one. We therefore rate it mediocre once again.

There was a controversy a few years back when Dodger fans—who rarely get worked up over anything—protested that their Dodger Dogs were no longer being grilled. The protests won out, and now all Dodger Dog stands advertise that the dogs are grilled. But beware. Most of the stands read "Dodger Dogs—Grilled." These were grilled at some point earlier in the day, then pre-wrapped. Look for the stands that read "Grilled Dodger Dogs" and get one hot off the griddle for the best results.

BEST OF THE REST

Gordon Biersch's **Garlic Fries** are a San Francisco thing and expensive, but they remain one of the most edible things at Dodger Stadium. Krispy Kreme is a chain, but the **doughnuts** are always good, and aren't any worse inside the ballpark than they are outside. The **picante dog** is a spiced up version of the bland Dodger Dog, and much tastier. **Chips and salsa** are difficult to screw up, so we can recommend that with confidence.

SAY "NO, THANKS," AND WALK AWAY

The Cheese Pizza at the **California Pizza Kitchen** might be the blandest we've ever encountered. Tasted like glue on cardboard.

We know it sounds like it might be good, but the **Louisiana hot sausage** tasted like a Jimmy Dean breakfast sausage.

Our **Wetzel's Pretzel** was old and stale, or new and fresh but just not very good. We couldn't be sure which, and certainly didn't want to try another one.

STADIUM SUDS

The Beers of the World stand offers beers from across Europe at steeply inflated prices. Gordon Biersch is the California regional microbrew that is worth the money.

The Dodger Stadium Experience

Dodger Stadium has one of the best scenic environments of any ballpark in the Majors. The view of the game and of the mountain background is unrivaled. Weather is so rarely an issue at Dodger Stadium, the threat of rain is almost a joke. The ballpark is clean and well maintained. The Dodgers have done a great job keeping advertisements from being too obtrusive, and they've essentially maintained the feel of the ballpark from the era in which it opened.

NO STANDING . . . NO SITTING . . . NO WALKING . . . NO TALKING

The ushers and food servers at Dodger Stadium are polite and very well dressed. But there are more do's and don'ts at Dodger Stadium than at any other ballpark in the country. These polite ushers will ask you to leave the area behind the last row of seats within seconds if you so much as slow down

Dodger Days in Ebbets Field

When the Dodgers were still in Brooklyn, they played in the carnival-like atmosphere of Ebbets Field. Huge, colorful, and gaudy advertising signs hung wherever there was space to fill. Perhaps the most famous signs were those above and below the huge scoreboard. The upper sign was for Schaefer beer, where the "h" in Schaefer would glow in neon when there was a hit, and the first "e" would light up to indicate that the official scorer had ruled an error. Below the scoreboard was mounted a long low sign for a clothier named Abe Stark. "Hit sign, win suit," the famous marker read.

A singing newsboy patrolled the grandstands, selling papers and singing songs of Dodgers victories and woes. And for many years the hapless Dodgers provided much sad material for the young town crier. The Phillies defeated the Superbas 1–0 in the first game at Ebbets on April 9, 1913. Casey Stengel had recorded the first unofficial hit at Ebbets a few days earlier during an exhibition game. Stengel was traded to the Pirates in 1918, but later returned in 1918 to perform a gesture that would become a part of Ebbets Field folklore. Anticipating the raucous and crazed Dodger fans, Stengel came out to stand near the batter's box to boos and jeers. He calmly turned toward the stands, and tipped his hat to the crowd. When his hat came up, a bird flew out from under it, and away to the freedom of the Flatbush skies.

Though the early Dodgers didn't win many games, there was plenty to keep folks entertained at Ebbets Field. The hated Giants, or "Gints" as they were called by Brooklyn rooters, always played sellout games at Ebbets. On one occasion in 1924, tickets were so scarce that misguided fans used an old telephone pole as a battering ram to pound down the door of the banged-out park. Ebbets was also where yellow baseballs were introduced——and then quickly shelved——where a milkman threw batting practice, and where an umpire was once pummeled by an overexcited Dodgers fan after a questionable call.

there to look at your ticket. It's as if they'd prefer you stand in the middle of the concourse and block traffic there. The mission of these friendly fascists seems to be whisking folks like sheep from their seats to the concession lines or bathrooms, and then corralling them back again to their seats as quickly as possible before they start to cause trouble. Josh half expected an usher to visit his seat and re-fold his napkin for him when he got up to use the bathroom, like at a fancy restaurant. Why would the Dodgers have such inane policies while, at the same time, they neglect the real security issues in some of the seating sections? They're not fan friendly, and they're an anomaly throughout all of baseball.

THE RETURN OF THE REAL BASEBALL ORGAN

Now this feature is a bit more like it. Nancy Bea Hefley is the Dodgers' organist and she fills the stadium with the classic sounds that your grandparents remember hearing in their childhood. It's a classy thing for the organization and a feature you just don't find at many ballparks anymore. Newer parks seem to prefer hearing the opening riff to "Paranoid" by Black Sabbath four times a night, as players get their own theme music when they approach the plate. We prefer Nancy's happy fingers.

INFO-TAINMENT

The Dodgers have teamed up with Hollywood to provide trivia questions that come off feeling like commercials for summer blockbusters. It's cheesy, but it's very L.A.

CENTURY BOULEVARD—WE LOVE IT

When the Dodgers win, the meager sound system plays "I Love L.A." by Randy Newman.

RADAR GUN GUY (SUPER-FAN)

Mike Brito can always be found behind home plate clocking pitches and people speeding by on the 101 freeway as well. If Mike could only find a Dodger pitcher doing 101.

PEANUT MAN (SUPER-FAN)

Ultra-accurate peanut vendor Roger Owens has been patrolling Dodger Stadium for more than fifty years, selling his nuts and giving away the entertainment for free.

> *Josh:* Is he any match for the peanut guy in Seattle?
> *Kevin:* No.

BALLPLAYERS ON THE HOLLYWOOD WALK OF FAME

There are two former players who later went into acting and earned stars on the Hollywood Walk of Fame. Johnny Beradino hit .249 in eleven seasons with the Pirates, Indians, and Browns before turning his career aspirations toward Hollywood. His most memorable role was a thirty-three-year stint as Dr. Steve Hardy on *General Hospital*. Of course, when Johnny went Hollywood he changed his name slightly to John Beradino. Another former Major Leaguer on the Walk is Chuck Connors, star of TV's *The Rifleman*. He batted .238 in sixty-seven games, one for his hometown Brooklyn Dodgers in 1949, and sixty-six for the Cubs in 1951. Did the Rifleman have a rifle of an arm? We're guessing no, since he saw the majority of his action at first base. Of course, former Angels owner Gene Autry can also be found on the Walk of Fame. We're not sure if it's some kind of blasphemy to include "The Singing Cowboy" here, but we're sure fans of the crosstown rivals will love that we did. Autry owned the Angels for thirty-seven years. Vin Scully also has his own star, as does Danny Kaye, a former owner of the Seattle Mariners.

JACKIE ROBINSON SIGHTS AND LOCALES

Though born in Cairo, Georgia, in 1919, most of Jackie Robinson's young life was lived in and around Los Angeles. The baseball field on the UCLA campus was renamed for Robinson on February 7, 1981, three years before his induction into the UCLA sports hall of fame. Both are worthy of a visit. His boyhood home is located at 121 Pepper St. in Pasadena, California. Look for the marker placed in the sidewalk as a dedication. Unfortunately, you're on the wrong coast to visit Robinson's grave, which is at the Cypress Hills cemetery in Brooklyn, New York.

World Series plaque

Photo by Kevin O'Connell

Cyber Super-Fans

The Dodgers have their fair share of hopelessly devoted followers of the Boys in Blue, and thus have their fair share of hopelessly devoted cyber fans blogging every detail of their on- and off-field endeavors. The following are the best of the best.

- **Baseball Savvy**
  www.baseballsavvy.com/index.html
  Our friend Howard Cole—who was at Dodger Stadium for Koufax's perfect game in 1965—manages this long-running site.
- **Dodgers Blue Heaven**
  http://dodgersblueheaven.blogspot.com/
  Isn't this the title of a Pogues song?
- **Sons of Steve Garvey**
  www.sonsofstevegarvey.com/
  No need for a paternity test on this one. They have the true spirit, if not the actual bloodline.

While We Were in Los Angeles
We Had Security Issues

After picking up Kevin's brother, Sean, who lives downtown, and driving for what seemed like four hours to find a grocery store to stock up on tailgate brats and beers for the pregame celebration, we drove into the lots at Chavez Ravine, paid nearly half a year's salary to park the road trip mobile, and licked our chops at the tailgating nirvana that certainly lay before us.

"With all this parking, there must be every kind of tailgate sport imaginable," Josh predicted.

"Roller-skiing," Kevin shouted.

"Pool diving!" Sean answered back.

"Naked mud wrestling!" Josh shouted, prompting Kevin and Sean to exchange a confused glance.

After we parked, Josh pulled the hibachi out of the trunk. Kevin laid open the cooler, which was filled to the brim with beers and ice, and we set up our chairs. It was 11 a.m. and the game didn't begin until 1:35 p.m. We had more than two and a half hours of blue tailgating heaven before us.

Or so we thought.

Not three minutes after cracking our first beer, a police officer pulled up behind us, pinning the road trip car into its spot with its heavy bumper. Two officers stepped out of the cruiser who bore a striking resemblance to Judge Reinhold and the bald cop from the movie *Beverly Hills Cop*.

"Gentlemen, how are we this morning?" said Reinhold.

"All right, Hamilton," said Kevin.

"What do you think you're doing with the beer?"

"Drinking it," said Sean. "You want us to throw a couple of brats on for you?"

"No, sir," said Bald Cop.

"Ah, a ribs man," said Josh, dumping briquettes into the hibachi. "I'll put you each down for a couple."

"Gentlemen," said Reinhold sternly, "I'm afraid we have ourselves a situation here."

"A situation," said Josh trembling, dropping the bag of briquettes. "What kind of situation? Kevin, what does he mean by *situation?*"

"I mean there's no tailgating at Dodger Stadium," said bald cop.

"Really?" said Sean.

"Really," said Reinhold.

"But that's such a waste of all this great parking," said Kevin.

"Be that as it may," said Bald Cop, "You all need to come with us to the police holding facility inside the stadium."

"But we didn't know," said Sean. "These guys are from out of town."

"I'm sorry about that gentlemen, but rules are rules."

"Shoot," said Josh. "We're going to jail." And he began to put the bricks back into the bag one-by-one as quickly as his hands would move.

"Listen officer," said Sean, working some of his best LA charm. "It was an innocent mistake. Could we pay some sort of fine, or something?"

"We haven't had more than a sip," said Kevin.

Reinhold looked us over carefully. There were no empty beer cans anywhere around the car. "I suppose if you dumped the open containers, we could let you off with a citation."

"A citation!" Josh said, raising his voice.

"That sounds perfect," said Kevin, dumping his own beer onto the black top and dumping Josh's out as well. When the cans were empty, Kevin said, "By the way, officer. Where could we set up our tailgate?"

"Anywhere but here," said Bald Cop, looking up from his writing of a very steep ticket and pointing to the fence.

Once the cop ripped the ticket from his pad, Kevin looked it over and said, "I guess we'll be sitting in the bleachers when we get to Petco."

As the cops left, we continued packing everything back into the road trip mobile.

"Well," said Josh, "what do we do now? Waste all this beautiful tailgating sun, or waste our money parking?"

"Don't worry gentlemen," said Sean. "I think I have a way to preserve both." We finished packing up the car and pulled it to the very last spot in the lot, but still inside the gates. Then we carried our hibachi, cooler, and lawn chairs directly outside the gate and set up on the sidewalk. Across the street from us, in plain view, stood the LA Police Academy.

When the hibachi heated up, Kevin tossed some cased meat on and said, "I love the smell of brats, especially in front of the Police Academy . . . smells like . . . Victory."

Josh was flummoxed. "You mean we can tailgate here, in front of the LA Police Academy,* but not inside the stadium parking lot?" Josh asked. "I'll never understand the West Coast."

* Please note: Tailgating on city streets in LA, or in any other public place, especially directly in front of an establishment teeming with freshly minted and overeager members of the law enforcement community, is a strictly "swim at your own risk" activity. We don't recommend it. But we did it and lived to tell the tale.

SEATTLE MARINERS, SAFECO FIELD

A Shining Jewel in the Emerald City

Growing up in Western Washington, Kevin, along with the rest of the region's fans, had no hometown hardball team to call his own. After losing the Seattle Pilots after a single season to some used car dealer from Milwaukee by the name of Bud Selig, all hope for a regional franchise appeared lost. Then, magically, in 1977 his prayers were answered when Major League Baseball added Seattle and Toronto to the American League. Like all baseball fans in the Pacific Northwest, Kevin was elated. Seattle would have its own team, and it was an expansion team, which meant it wouldn't be breaking the hearts of countless fans of another city, the way Bud Selig had done to so many when he stole the Pilots. But there was a catch. Along with the Seattle Seahawks of the NFL, the Mariners intended to play their home games at the Kingdome. Indoor baseball? Though it wasn't ideal, Kevin tried his best to embrace it, since it was certainly a far superior alternative to having no baseball to watch at all.

The Mariners truly were awful from the start. It took them fifteen seasons to post a winning record, and their uniforms rivaled the Astros and Padres for worst in baseball. Perhaps the funniest thing of all about the hapless M's—who couldn't seem to get much of anything right—was their home stadium, the Kingdome, named after King County, in which Seattle resides. While the venue was enjoyed as a place to escape the rainy fall and winter weather during football season, and while Kevin saw the Monsters of Rock tour there in 1988 and, perhaps, most importantly the Seattle SuperSonics (formerly of the NBA) win the city's only major championship there, the game of baseball suffered in the dome.

Grass, as we all should know, doesn't grow well without sunlight, so the Kingdome sported artificial turf that looked about as real as the grass in the Brady Bunch's backyard, covered by a concrete roof that looked like a gigantic orange juicer. Still, Kevin stuck by his hometown team. Like millions of other Seattleites, he never gave up hope that outdoor baseball might return to the Pacific Northwest, even as Mariners ownership threatened to move the team out of the city during the early 1990s.

Many point to the Mariners' playoff run of 1995—now commonly referred to as "the season that saved baseball in Seattle," as having played a major role in bringing about the baseball renaissance in the city. The M's inspired playoff run also did well by hardball fans all around the Majors who were frustrated by the strike-shortened seasons of 1994 and 1995. Some would say that the Mark McGwire and Sammy Sosa battle for home run supremacy was what brought fans back. But the fact is that both of those men, rightly or wrongly, have the taint of performance-enhancing drugs on their records, and when people remember that battle that seemed so epic at the time, in truth, it leaves them feeling ripped off.

Not so with the Mariners and their inspiring playoff run of 1995. In the afterglow of that magical year, plans were made to leave the Kingdome to football and monster truck rallies, and for the Mariners to build a new future for themselves. A future where the team would continue its recently found competitive ways. A future with uniforms that didn't look like they should be worn on Halloween. And, perhaps most exciting of all to hardball fans in the Northwest, a future where the game would be played in a baseball-only park that the team's growing fan base could be proud of. A park that would combine the charm of the classic older parks with all of the latest amenities—beneath a ginormous retractable roof big enough to land the space shuttle under.

By all counts, "the Safe" has delivered this promised future in spades. When Kevin first laid eyes on Safeco's green grass and rust-colored dirt, and looked up to see the Seattle skyline set against a perfect blue horizon, he wept with joy. Literally, he cried.

Josh: But you cried at the end of *Toy Story 3*, too.

Kevin: Every toy had a purpose again. It was beautiful and symbolic.

Making Safeco a reality was no small task given the local economic climate in the mid-1990s and voters of the Pacific Northwest routinely voicing their displeasure with the idea of using public money to support private industry. A bill to increase the sales tax by .01 percent was voted down by King County voters in September 1995. However, city and county officials recognized that the small margin of defeat of the proposition meant a good number of folks would likely vote against them in upcoming elections. If the Mariners left town under these officials' collective watch because a new ballpark could not be secured, well, proverbial political hay could be made of it. Or maybe all these elected officials quickly became loyal Mariner fans overnight. We're not sure which. At any rate, not long after, a financing package for Safeco Field was adopted that included hotel, rental car, and restaurant tax increases, ballpark admissions taxes, the selling of Mariner license plates, and scratch-ticket lottery games. One lottery game was called "My-Oh-My," named for a catchphrase of the late Dave Niehaus, the Mariners' colorful commentator. After this financial stake was driven into the ground, the Safeco Insurance Company shelled out $40 million for the naming rights to the park.

Josh: I bet you bought a zillion of those Niehaus scratch-offs.

Kevin: Sure, I did. I had to support the team.

More than thirty thousand fans came out to cheer on Ken Griffey Jr. as he slapped on a pair of work gloves and partook in Safeco's ceremonial groundbreaking on March 8, 1997. From groundbreaking until the ballpark officially opened for play more than two years later, a webcam provided fans with continuous coverage of Safeco's construction site.

Safeco's most distinctive feature is without doubt its remarkable retractable roof. It provides, in our opinion, the penultimate example of a how a retractable roofed stadium should be built. From the street behind Safeco, the roof of the building looks postindustrial. While from the street out front, the Safe's brick facade provides a classic ballpark feel. But unlike other retractable roofs that have been built in baseball, Safeco's roof covers but does not enclose the field, which allows wind to whip through, and preserves an open-air playing environment. The massive roof sections are supported by trusses on wheels, and actually rest on elevated tracks that were built much higher than they needed to be. The reason for all this is that it gives the feeling that baseball is being played beneath an enormous umbrella, rather than indoors. Whether the roof is open or closed, baseball at Safeco always feels as if it's being played outside, which enhances the game-day experience over the Kingdome tremendously.

The roof's three independently moving panels span nine acres, weigh twenty-two million pounds, and contain enough steel to build a fifty-five-story skyscraper. The lid is capable of withstanding seven feet of snow and seventy-mile-per-hour winds. During Safeco's first few weeks there were frequently reported mechanical errors that caused the roof to open and close unexpectedly. These early kinks have since been ironed out. The roof's arching support trusses are "in play," provided the ball hits a truss in fair territory and comes down in fair territory. To date, this has yet to occur, but there have been two occasions where the trusses were hit by balls in foul territory, which makes some sense because they are much closer to the playing surface as they arch down toward the ground.

The roof is certainly an engineering marvel. In many ways it set the standard for what a retractable roof at a ballpark should be. But there were other technological implementations innovative to Safeco that have since been copied by other ballparks, too. The playing field

exterior

Photo by Kevin O'Connell

itself is capable of absorbing twenty-five inches of rain in twenty-four hours, thanks to a layering of sand, pea gravel, and genetically engineered grass, combined with underground heating and drainage systems.

Josh: Kind of overkill, considering Safeco has a roof, don't you think?

Kevin: Perception is reality. And the perception that the game will never be cancelled, ever, rules at Safeco.

Interestingly enough for meteorologists and baseball geeks like us, even though Safeco's umbrella protects its fans from the legendary rains, it does little to protect them from the cool winds that can come off Puget Sound. The left-field bleachers are particularly exposed on cold and windy days—which, let's face it, in Seattle is about three-quarters of the summer. And the center-field bleachers only fare a bit better, getting a bit of wind blockage from the centerfield scoreboard.

A bit of irony for Seattle ball fans . . . Safeco opened not to too much rain, but too much sun. The open-air feel also allowed for the rays of the setting sun in the west over the Olympic Mountains (which are a beautiful backdrop from much of the park) to stream in and cause problems for hitters as it reflected off the batter's eye. The Mariners were able to solve the problem early on by constructing a series of screens that protected the batter's eye and the eyes of the corresponding batters. However, rosy fingered sunsets still tickle at the eyes of fans, in the orange and purple gloaming.

Most parks make their debut on Opening Day. But did we mention that this city and franchise don't usually care much for convention? The Safe opened on July 15th, midway through the 1999 season, with a 3–2 Mariners loss to their supposed interleague rivals, the San Diego Padres. Once fully established in their new home, the Mariners captured consecutive American League West titles in 2000 and 2001 and tied the MLB record for the most wins in a season with a blistering 116 in 2001. Unfortunately, though, the M's lost to the Yankees in the American League playoffs both years. The fact that the Mariners have never even been to the World Series—even while newer baseball arrivals like the Florida Marlins, Tampa Bay Rays, Arizona Diamondbacks, and Colorado Rockies have—actually staggers the mind.

Kevin: Not even when we had A-Rod, Junior, Jay Buhner, Edgar Martinez, and Randy Johnson. Not to mention Lou Piniella managing. Sheesh.

Josh: Your guys blew it!

Though it did little to enhance a ballgame, the Kingdome still holds more than its share of Mariners history, both for the good, and what has passed as standard operating procedure in Seattle baseball, the hapless. One part they got right was

when they blew the place up. The demolition, on March 26, 2000, was streamed live on the Internet, allowing multitudes worldwide to watch the implosion of the "Concrete Goiter," as it was not-so-affectionately called by some locals. The structure that was "built to last a thousand years" came down after twenty-three, and in just 16.8 seconds. Up until the time of its demolition, the Kingdome boasted the largest thin-shell concrete-domed roof in the world. No ball ever hit the roof, though players in batting practice constantly tried. On two occasions balls went up and never came down—in 1979 a ball hit by the Mariners' Ruppert Jones, and in 1983 a ball hit by Milwaukee's Ricky Nelson. Both got stuck in the sound system speakers and were ruled foul.

While the Jones and Nelson balls never fell to earth, fifteen-pound tiles from the roof did in 1994, necessitating repairs that sent the M's on an extended road trip for the last month of the strike-shortened season.

Before achieving their first winning season in 1991, the Mariners had posted a sub-.500 record in each of their first fourteen campaigns. They were often considered a laughingstock around the league and the butt of jokes on late-night TV. During their many lean years, the Mariners, not unlike the Triple A team they acted like, had to be creative to get people to come to their stadium. In 1983 the USS *Mariner* was launched behind the left-field fence. The sloop was a gold-colored boat that would rise up and fire a cannon blast for Mariner wins and every time an M's batter hit a home run. Another gimmick was the Bullpen Tug, which ferried relievers to the mound from the bullpens the Kingdome never had. Fence distances were measured in fathoms alongside the more traditional feet. And for home runs and wins, another Mariner innovation, indoor fireworks, exploded near the roof of the Dome.

Josh: Indoor fireworks?

Kevin: My wife liked them.

Josh: You think the constant booming contributed to the ceiling tiles falling?

Kevin: Unfortunately, it wasn't that constant.

Another fan favorite was the annual Buhner Buzz-cut Night, when the team would offer free admission to fans who shaved their heads to resemble Mariner right fielder and living chrome-domed legend, Jay Buhner. Hundreds took part in the promotion every year.

Josh: Too bad they don't have that promo now. You could get in without having to do much actual shaving.

Kevin: Too bad they don't offer free Red Sox tickets to geeks like you who know the batting averages of the Salem Red Sox.

Josh: You say that like it's a bad thing.

A low-water mark for the Mariners came in the early 1990s when Dave Valle, a defensive catcher if ever there was one, was squatting for the M's. Calling attention to Dave's futility at the plate, nearby Swannie's Bar offered well-drinks at the daily price of the weak-hitting backstop's current batting average, before having to cancel the promotion when Dave's average dipped below .175. They simply couldn't afford to keep the promo going.

There's no way to sugarcoat it; the early Mariners were tough to love. Their slow start and legendarily poor attendance belied a long tradition of support for baseball in the Northwest, however, though Seattle teams always seemed to be either coming or going. The city's earliest hardball championship came with the Seattle Reds, who won the Pacific Northwest League in 1892 playing in Madison Park. Unfortunately financial woes caused the PNL to fold soon thereafter. Professional baseball returned to the region when D. E. Dugdale started up the Seattle Indians as part of the Northwestern League in 1896. That team played in a ballpark known as YMCA park. The league included teams from regional cities such as Portland, Spokane, and Tacoma. By 1902 the Seattle and Portland teams had merged with teams from California to form the Pacific Coast League. For a brief while a second Seattle team, the Siwashes, were members of the PCL, and played in Recreation Park along with the Braves. But Seattle proved too small a town to support two teams, and the Braves were the team to close up shop. Another Seattle ballclub was the Seattle Giants, who played at Yesler Way Field from 1907 to 1913. But again, no one seemed to be able to stick around for the long term.

After leaving the city, Seattle baseball greats showed a tendency for later displaying their talents on the national stage. In 1903 Harry Lumley batted .387 and was sold to Brooklyn where he led the Majors in home runs and triples as a rookie in 1904. The next year Emil Frisk went to St. Louis to become a Brown. The Siwashes continued to play in the PCL, though losing their best players hurt attendance. They departed the league for the Class-B Northwestern League in 1907. Dugdale became the chief operator for the club, which played its home games at a ballpark named for him. Dugdale Park seated fifteen thousand and was located at the corner of McLennan Street and Rainier Avenue South.

The Siwashes made it back up into the PCL by 1919, though they were now called the Indians once again. They won the PCL title in 1924 but fell on hard times after that and dabbled in mediocrity. Dugdale Park burned down on July 5, 1932; the reason was never discovered. The Fourth of July fireworks had gone off without a hitch and were blameless in the blaze. The team finished its season at Civic Stadium.

By 1937 the team was bought by Emil Sick, owner of the Rainier Brewery. Sick renamed his team the Seattle Rainiers, and they were commonly called the "Suds." Sick built a new ballpark in 1938 on the very site of old Dugdale Park and called it Sick's Stadium. The ballpark was very small, seating only twelve thousand fans, but featured a grassy knoll beyond the left-field fence. The hill was dubbed "tightwad hill" because cheaper fans could watch the games while picnicking on the hill without paying a dime. A modern version of tightwad hill can be found at the big league ballpark in San Diego.

Josh: I don't understand why thrifty people are always called tightwads.

Kevin: We know where we'd be sitting.

Rookie pitcher Fred Hutchinson won twenty-five games in 1938 for the Suds, before he was traded to the Detroit Tigers for cash and players. The Rainiers went on to win the PCL in 1940, 1941, and 1942, led by George Archie and Jo Jo White, players from that trade. When the PCL changed from being an independent professional entity to being essentially a league of AAA affiliates for the Majors, Seattle Rainier attendance steadily declined.

Big league ball returned to Seattle for one season only, when the expansion Seattle Pilots of the American League played their 1969 home games at Sick's Stadium. The Pilots were never really given the chance to succeed. Sick's Stadium had been built in 1938 and was too tiny and cramped of a ballpark for a Major League team to call home. Poor management and city officials who were inflexible caused the relationship to sour quickly.

Since 1969, Allan H. "Bud" Selig has been known to Seattle sports fans as the Milwaukee auto dealer who sneaked the Seattle Pilots out of town in the middle of the night. After trying to move the White Sox from Chicago to Milwaukee, he found a team that was less well entrenched in its city, and in essence, took it out of the area before it could gain much of a footing.

Josh: Not too many "Bud" fans in these parts.

Kevin: Maybe that's why the microbrews do so well.

If you can't tell, we're not fans of moving ball teams without very good reasons. And though the Pilots only drew 678,000 fans in their only season in Seattle, they did outdraw the AL teams in Chicago and Cleveland that year. The Pilots remain the only professional franchise to be given only one year in their city. Their record was 64–98. The Brewers, in their first season in Milwaukee, by the way, only managed a record of 65–97, but their ballpark, County Stadium, helped increase attendance by a third.

There are, however, some interesting coincidences concerning the Seattle team's and the Seattle Mariners. For example, the starting pitcher in the Mariners' inaugural game in 1977 was Diego Segui, who also pitched for the Pilots. Another Pilot, Lou Piniella, was the team's fourteenth pick in the expansion draft. Piniella was not that highly regarded by the Pilots and was traded to the Kansas City Royals, for whom he went on to become Rookie of the Year. Later Piniella became the most successful manager in Mariners history, leading the M's to most of their winning seasons. Fans interested in learning more about the ill-fated Pilots should pick up a copy of pitcher Jim Bouton's classic book, *Ball Four*, which dishes more dirt than Pig Pen from the *Peanuts* comic strip. At the time, some baseball insiders said Bouton did a disservice to baseball in writing this book. But in retrospect, even though it did reveal the darker underbelly of the supposedly "All American" boys of summer, the book is considered a classic.

Though the Kingdome was an inhospitable kingdom for Seattle baseball, there were many moments and memories that could only have occurred in that dimly lit concrete tomb. Why they never painted the outside at least with a bright coat of Mariner blue, we'll never know. But it's part of the history of the team and the city. To quote Hall of Famer and the voice of the Mariners, Dave Niehaus, "That first opening night, I thought the Kingdome was the most beautiful place I'd ever seen. I thought the team would probably be a .500 team within three years."

Kevin: I remember asking my dad if they could win the World Series their first year.

Josh: Hope truly springs eternal, doesn't it?

The 1979 All-Star Game was held at the Kingdome. The only Mariner on the roster was Bruce Bochte, and that was probably because they had to have at least one. Gaylord Perry slung his three hundredth career win at the Kingdome, as the Mariners beat the Yankees 7-3, on May 6, 1982. "Mr. Mariner" Alvin Davis won the Rookie of the Year Award in 1984. The second-place finisher was Mariners pitcher Mark Langston. And Harold Reynolds played outstanding second base for the M's from 1983 to 1992 before going on to be an even bigger star on ESPN and the MLB Network. But none of these exceptional players or moments led the Mariners to sustained success in the win-loss column.

That would come after a nineteen-year-old phenom named Ken Griffey Jr. took the town by storm. "The Kid" clobbered the first pitch he saw at the Kingdome, knocking it over the fence as he would go on to do more than any other player in team history. Griffey finished hitting dingers at the Kingdome when he belted the 377th of his career on its closing day, June 27, 1999. Junior also played Gold Glove–caliber defense in center field, alongside his father Ken Griffey Sr., who came out

West to play left field for the first time on August 31, 1990. The Griffeys became the first father-son duo to play on the same team. To further this great accomplishment, the Junior/Senior combination connected for back-to-back home runs at the Kingdome on September 14, 1990, against the Angels.

Kevin: Obviously he was juicing!

Josh: There's no proof of that.

Kevin: You'd say anything to protect a Boston player.

Josh: As you would with Edgar.

Kevin: Fair enough.

Edgar Martinez won his two batting titles in the Dome, hitting .343 in 1992 and .356 in 1995. Martinez was the first AL right-hander since Joe DiMaggio to win more than one batting title. Later, Boston's Nomar Garciaparra would join the exclusive club with his back-to-back titles in 1999 and 2000.

The Mariners gave birth to the phrase "Refuse to Lose" in 1995, as they came back in dramatic fashion to catch the faltering Angels—coming from eleven games behind in August to end in a tie for the AL West title, which resulted in a one-game playoff on October 2, 1995. The playoff game at the Kingdome was winner-take-all, as a loss by either team would put it one-half game behind the New York Yankees in the wild-card race. It was baseball's first one-game playoff in fifteen seasons. Cy Young Award winner Randy Johnson came into the game as a relief pitcher for the Mariners and defeated the Angels' Mark Langston, the man the Mariners had traded to Montreal to obtain Johnson. With the Mariners leading 1-0 in the seventh and the bases loaded, bad ball slapper Luis Sojo hooked a ball inside first base that rolled along the right-field wall. A cruel bounce for the Angels and a throwing error by Langston allowed four runs to score on the play. There was no turning back for the Mariners. With destiny on their side, they prevailed 9-1.

The 1995 M's went on to sweep the Yankees at home in the Dome, after losing the first two games in the Bronx. Griffey tied the postseason home run record with five—all in the first round. In the final game, with the M's down 5-4 in the bottom of the eleventh inning, Edgar Martinez hit "the Double" down the first baseline to score two runs. The come-from-behind win was for many folks in Seattle the greatest moment in Mariners history. And though they lost a hard-fought series against the Cleveland Indians for the American League Championship, fans stayed after the final game ended and gave the Mariners a standing ovation—for nearly half an hour—for the great ride that was the 1995 season.

We don't know if it was fate or fortune, but Seattle voters were asked to decide on a ballot measure for building a new ballpark during the very same week that the Mariners were entering postseason play for the first time. There is little doubt that if the 1995 playoff run hadn't occurred, baseball in Seattle would have sailed on for greener pastures. That fortuitous season had been only Seattle's third with a winning record.

Since 1995 the Mariners have had their share of successes and failures. Randy Johnson struck out nineteen hitters in a game not once, but twice in one season—1997. But with free agency looming, he left in a trade to Houston midway through the 1998 season. The next Seattle superstar to debut was Alex Rodriguez. A-Rod became the first shortstop to hit forty home runs and steal forty bases in 1998 and went on to become the highest-paid player in sports history, signing mega-deals with the Texas Rangers and then the Yankees.

After the Mariners' move to their new ballpark was set firmly in motion by the exciting play of these superstars and others, the team couldn't stop the hemorrhage of future Hall of Famers. In four consecutive years the M's lost Johnson, Griffey, Rodriguez, and manager Piniella. While the losses should have been devastating, the M's rebuilt their team with players whose egos didn't get in the way. The entire team was worthy of mention, no one player more than another, as it broke records in 2001. Along with their Major League record-tying 116 victories came a record twenty-nine road series won and Ichiro Suzuki's most hits by a rookie at 242. Other AL records broken during that year included the team's most road wins (59) and Ichiro's most singles (192).

And Ichiro, himself, having become the face of the franchise since the departure of all the other stars, went on to take up the mantle of quiet superstar in the understated manner akin to his newly adopted home. In his first ten seasons as a Mariner, Ichiro had more than two hundred hits every year, batted over .300 every year, and won ten straight Gold Glove Awards. He also made ten straight All-Star teams. In 2004 Ichiro broke George Sisler's eighty-four-year-old record of most hits in a single season with 262. The record-breaking game was broadcast live on television across Japan, where Ichiro spent the first seven seasons of his career. The quiet bad-ball hitter is certainly one of the most underrated superstars in the history of the game.

To say that it was disappointing that the Mariners never made it to a World Series during their brief flirtation with success between 1995 and 2002 would be an understatement. They remain the only team in the American League and one of only two teams in all of baseball to have never made it to a World Series. The Montreal Expos/Washington Nationals are the other. Between the 1997 and 2004 seasons, ballpark attendance routinely topped three million in Seattle, peaking at 3,542,938 in 2002. By 2011 it had dwindled to just less than two million.

Josh: That's a net loss of 1.5 million fans—per year!

Kevin: I believe the proper term is hemorrhaging.

Josh: That's more fans lost than the Marlins, Pirates, or Athletics drew last year.

Kevin: Thanks for putting that in perspective for me.

The M's nosedive after their glory years is on par with that of Britney Spears and Charlie Sheen. When GM Bill Bavasi took control of the team in 2003, a steady decline in the team's on-field performance began and persisted until the end of his tenure in 2008. Though it may not have been entirely his fault, the Bavasi years for the Mariners were dark, characterized by high payrolls (above $100 million) and high loss totals.

Josh: That's not a good combination.

Kevin: Sure as heck ain't ketchup and mustard.

Seattle fans did what techie hipsters always do and circulated Internet flyers crying for Bavasi's removal from his post. After a while, the signing of overpriced and under-performing free agents (Carlos Silva, anyone?) began to boggle the mind, along with the trading away of young talent (Adam Jones, anyone?). Upper management had to let Bavasi go.

But the damage was done and the team will no doubt be reeling from the impact of the Bavasi years for some time. As a result fan attendance and season tickets are down again, with even the area surrounding the ballpark feeling the negative impact. Woefully, Seattle seems to have sailed the USS *Mariner* back into the doldrums once again.

Trivia Timeout

Tug: Who is the undisputed greatest designated hitter of all time? (hint: The DH Award is named after him.)
Schooner: Which local bar used to sell a beer at a price to match Seattle catcher Dave Valle's current batting average?
Man-o-War: Which rock band caused the Mariners to play a "road" game at Safeco Field in 2011?
Look for the answers in the text.

The M's are currently owned by Hiroshi Yamauchi, a Japanese businessman who is also president of Nintendo. Though he's owned the team since 1996, Yamauchi has never seen a Mariners game in person. He was hoping to catch one on March 25, 2003, when Seattle and Oakland were supposed to travel to Tokyo to kick off the big league season in Japan. But because of the outbreak of war with Iraq, MLB canceled the games.

And yet there is still a glimmer of hope on the horizon in Seattle. GM Jack Zduriencik has seemingly righted the ship. The M's have stopped making boneheaded trades (this is not a reference to Jay Buhner) and have begun to restock the cupboards of their farm system. Time will tell if they can bring back the fans lost during the Bavasi years, and if the team will ever fulfill the promise of the 1995 season, and finally get to its first World Series.

Getting a Choice Seat

"If it ain't broke, don't fix it" said a *New York Times* article about Safeco a while back. Well, maybe the *Times* didn't use the word "ain't," but you get the idea. This ballpark, though not tiny, continues be among the league's best. Tickets are difficult to come by when Seattle is competitive—which hasn't been a consistent threat. When the team is not making a run, the ballpark has enough empty seats in it to rival a Bangles reunion tour. Most all the seats have clear sight lines, but some are much preferable to others.

Diamond Club (Sections 127–133)

We still call these the "screw you" seats, because if you can afford the Diamond Club, which is made up of the 370 box seats located directly behind home plate, you have enough dough to say "screw you" to just about anybody. Not only do these $100-plus seats provide their elite holders with Safeco's sweetest views but they also furnish complimentary food and beverage refills all game long. Ticket holders are allowed access to both the Diamond Club Lounge and a special parking lot that comes complete with its own private entrance to the park.

Lower Box (Sections 119–141)

Without exception, these seats provide great views of the action, and we recommend them highly if you have the means. As an added attraction, the vendors are very attentive in the Lower Boxes. They're no fools; they know where the money's at.

Field Box (Sections 110–118, 142–150)

Located between where the infield dirt meets the outfield grass and extending to the foul poles on either side of the diamond, this seating section offers a number of quality viewing points. The first few sections (116–118, 142–144) are a good deal but beyond these, we recommend saving your money and sitting in the Lower Outfield Reserved. The foul poles have been designed to run down the aisles, thus eliminating much of the blockage of views, but there

Seating Capacity: 47,116
Ticket Office: http://seattle.mariners.mlb.com/ticketing/singlegame.jsp?c_id=sea
Seating Chart: http://seattle.mariners.mlb.com/sea/ticketing/seating_pricing.jsp

are still some seats that suffer infield obstructions. Section 150 is one to avoid, but if you must, be sure to get close to the Section 149 side for the better view. On the right-field side, avoid Section 110 if a foul-pole obstruction bothers you. Or, Section 109 provides cheaper seats without the obstruction.

We should mention that the Mariners unveiled a pretty neat promotion during the 2011 season. On days when reigning Cy Young Award winner Felix Hernandez was scheduled to pitch they dubbed Section 150 the "King's Court," and sold tickets to sit in it at a steep discount. Not only did purchasers of Section 150 seats get cheaper than usual tickets, but they also got complimentary Felix Hernandez T-shirts, and yellow and blue "K" placards to hold up en masse after each strikeout recorded by the Mariners' ace. They also received the rare privilege of sitting in a seating section alongside one fellow fan who showed up to the park in full court jester regalia for each and every one of the discounted games. Yes, the discount attracted a slightly motley crew. But in a good way. The reduced-price King's Court tickets generally went on sale about five days before each of Hernandez's home starts.

Lower Outfield Reserved (Sections 102–109, 151, 152)

For a great view at a decent price, we highly recommend Sections 105–109. These sections are in home run territory along the right-field wall, and get better as you approach the wall. Plus, you'll increase your chances of catching a homerun and winding up on Sports Center—that is provided you actually catch it. Section 103 is an alcohol-free family section. Sections 151 and 152 beside the bullpens in left field are much better than Section 150, which is pricier. Sections 151 and 152 are close in price to the View Boxes on the 300 Level and they're much closer to field level.

Terrace Club (Boxes 211–249)

These second-level boxes are pricey and exclusive. They're not bad seats, but we've noticed that high fly balls disappear because of the overhang of the View Level.

All Star Club

In order to draw interest from groups, and by "draw interest" we mean make things less expensive, the club has taken a few suites along the first-base line and combined them into one "new" larger seating area. They dub the area a 140-member luxury lounge, but don't be fooled. Unless you're taking your entire graduating class out to the ballpark for ten games in a row to show them how you've "made the big time," these seats will remain exactly what they are—big corporate luxury boxes for people who want to seem more important than everyone else.

View Boxes/View Reserved (Sections 306–347)

At this altitude we don't see much reason to shell out the extra money for View Box seats, which are just a few feet closer to the action than the first row of the View Reserved. Of course, if you're left with a choice between the first row of the View Boxes and the very last row of the View Reserved, then that's a different story.

This upper deck is called the View level for a reason. Its exterior walkway extends from foul pole to foul pole, offering sweeping views of Puget Sound, the Olympic Mountains, and downtown Seattle. Above the highest seats are windowed panels offering more impressive views and also protection from the wind. Fans seated on the third-base side (Sections 337–347) are treated to a view of downtown and of the football stadium, while on the first-base side (Sections 315–323) the Cascade Mountains in the east form the backdrop.

Steer clear of Sections 306–314 in right field, if possible, as there is significant underhang in these sections. If you're relegated to the upper deck, the cheaper bleacher seats in straightaway center are preferable. If the roof is open, Sections 306–310 face directly into sunlight for the first half of evening games, or for the full game during afternoon affairs—which can be a good thing or a bad thing, depending on how warm it is outside. Luckily, it's usually not too oppressive in Seattle.

Josh: Do I see shirtless men, tanning at the ballpark?

Kevin: Any excuse for a few rays in this town.

You'll find the best View seats in Sections 318–342, which provide a nice overview of the infield. The architects did an excellent job of protecting sight lines in these sections, and they are not significantly diminished as the row numbers increase. Beware of Section 342, as it is a "family" section. That means no beer is allowed, not even for dad.

Sections 346–349 in the upper left-field corner also suffer a bit of a loss of the left-field corner from the dreaded underhang, so avoid them if possible.

Center-Field Bleachers (Sections 390–395)

If you're getting your tickets on game day, we highly recommend these. Despite their dirt-cheap price, they offer a surprisingly decent second-deck view of the action directly facing the plate. These seats are highly preferable to the 300 Level seats in the right-field corner, and they're cheaper.

Left Field Bleachers (Sections 380–387)

The warning track is missing from view in these high bleacher seats, but that is the only loss. All the grass is in full view, and there shouldn't be much of the actual game missed from these sections—except dramatic catches at the wall (which are kinda nice to see in person, we admit). Be sure to sit in the lower rows of these sections, as the lighting stanchions block views in the top rows. These aren't bad for cheap seats, but we prefer the view from the center-field bleachers.

The Beer Garden

Just outside the centerfield fence and across from The 'Pen eating area, is *the* location to be for singles, people who want to get closer to the action than their seats allow, or anyone else wanting a break from the experience of walking around the ballpark. Since Safeco opened, this area across from the high-end foodie restaurants has always been a singles party. When the restaurants were called "The Bullpen Market," we affectionately dubbed the area the "Meet Market."

An important change to note in recent years is that the Beer Garden is usually re-purposed during premium games and converted into bleacher seating in order to sell more

SEATING TIP

Like other teams, the Mariners have added new "flexible" pricing options, which is corporate-speak for charging higher prices for games against more appealing opponents, on weekends and during the summer months. That means if you want to see the Red Sox on a Saturday in July, you'd better be prepared to pay more than for a Royals game on a Tuesday night in April. Unfortunately for those who are pursuing the absolute cheapest deal, Monday games when the Mariners play the lowly Mariners are not available!

Josh: Not even M's fans would pay to see this team scrimmage itself.

Kevin: Would the beer stands be open?

Josh: I don't see why not.

Kevin: Well, I'd pay a few bucks then.

tickets. If you're visiting when tickets are a tough draw and/or the team is playing a playoff game, there is no guarantee that this area will be open to the public.

The Black Market

When the M's are not competitive, you don't need to find the scalpers, they'll find you. And when business isn't good for scalpers, it's likely good for you. We observed a regional peculiarity on the scalper scene. Maybe it's a Northwest thing, or perhaps it's the general courtesy of folks who refuse to even jaywalk, but fans seeking tickets say nothing. They simply raise their arms extending fingers displaying the number of tickets they need. Then the scalpers approach them. Quietly and without much posturing, tickets and money change hands. Leave it to Seattle to find a civilized way to navigate the illicit (and illegal) ticket black market.

If you're like Josh and want to go the more traditional, (legal) route, try the season ticket trade-in plan, where season-ticket holders trade in tickets for games they won't use for future games. Take a chance on game day and hit the box office asking for "best available," and you may well get a top-notch seat that a season-ticket holder has traded in. But know this: Season-ticket holders get a discount at concession stands by having the bar code scanned on their tickets—but not tickets purchased through the trade-in program. You have to get your tickets straight from a season-ticket holder for the discount. If you do the math here, and you can get an actual season ticket for a weekend game, the concession credit cancels out the premium cost.

Josh: I want that discount. How do we find a season-ticket holder?

Kevin: Look for someone who looks like they work for Microsoft.

Before/After the Game

The Safe resides in Seattle's SODO District. SODO used to stand for South of the Dome, but since the Kingdome was imploded the term SODO has come to mean South of Downtown. The industrial SODO district has given rise to plenty of "SODO-Mojo" banners and a number of new loft-style warehouse spaces. Even now, most of the bars that are worth attending near the ballpark are holdovers from the days when the Kingdome was still around. The woes of the M's during the Bavasi years have caused a tremendous dent in season ticket and individual game sales, and this loss has put a serious strain on the eating and drinking establishments in SODO. Again, we'll

make the call to Seattle publicans and restaurateurs: If you built a good enough pub, they will still come.

Getting to Safeco

There are public parking lots both north and south of the park. These fill up early, are not cheap, and the streets around them are always clogged with traffic. In fact, traffic has become a major issue in Seattle over recent years. We strongly recommend that you spare yourself the aggravation and take advantage of the Metro Bus system. But if driving into the city is your only option, be sure to stay away from the freeways, especially coming across Lake Washington from the east on either of the floating bridges—they're murder during game-day rush hours.

The Metro has been voted one of the top bus services in the country. It's clean, comfortable, and efficient, but you're still stuck in rush-hour traffic, so allow extra time. For fare information, visit: http://metro.kingcounty.gov.

Here are a couple of tips to avoid the crowd in the immediate vicinity of the ballpark: From the north, park near the Seattle Center, then take the monorail to Westlake Center, about halfway to the ballpark. From there you can switch to the Link light-rail system that will take you directly to Safeco. Plus, how often do you get the chance to ride a monorail?

Josh: Mon-O-rail! Mon-O-rail!

Kevin: Cheap Simpson's reference.

Josh: Say it with me: Mon-O-rail! Mon-O-rail!

Kevin: Do shut up.

The Link light rail transit system is your best bet if coming from SeaTac Airport. You'll reach the Stadium stop in quick time, and it's especially handy if you have someplace to ditch your luggage. And remember, the last trains leave between midnight and 1:00 a.m.

If you're coming from farther away, say Tacoma or Bellingham, take The Sounder commuter rail line to King Street Station. It's a short walk to the ballpark, and you won't have to drive on any of the freeways. Have we mentioned that they're murder?

If you must drive and you must park close, you should go see a game in Kansas City. We jest, but finding a parking spot in Pioneer Square or the International District can be a challenge. If you are lucky enough to find a space, plug the meter with enough quarters to get you until 6:00 p.m.—after which time street spots are free—then walk or take the Metro Bus to the park. If your spot's within the ride-free zone, you can take the bus at no charge to Jackson Street at the edge of Pioneer Square, then walk the last six blocks, or keep riding and pay from Jackson to Royal Brougham, which doesn't cost much.

Outside Attractions
EDGAR MARTINEZ DRIVE

Check out the street named after the greatest DH of all time. We must admit, Bud Selig did get this one right. Edgar Martinez was honored in September of 2004 at Safeco Field as the greatest DH of all time, when the award formerly known as the Outstanding Designated Hitter Award was renamed the Edgar Martinez Award. Martinez won the award that would later be named after him a total of five times. The other player to win the award five times: David Ortiz.

We would be remiss in our duties—actually, Kevin would never let us get away without mentioning it—if we didn't discuss the importance of Edgar Martinez to the city of Seattle. There are only six players in the history of the game of baseball who have demonstrated ability to be considered superior all-around hitters. By this, we mean hitters who have more than two thousand hits, more than five hundred doubles, more than three hundred home runs, more than one thousand walks, a lifetime batting average above .300 and an on-base percentage of .400 or higher. Those six men are Stan Musial, Rogers Hornsby, Babe Ruth, Lou Gehrig, Ted Williams, and Edgar Martinez

And Edgar did all of this after languishing for seven years in the minors while the Mariners thought the third baseman of their future was going to be Jim Presley. The big knock against Martinez being a Hall of Famer seems to be that he didn't play in the field, and spent too much time as a DH. Kevin supposes this is true for Hall of Famers Frank Thomas and Paul Molitor, too. But the fact is that Number 11 played 564 games at third base, and only left the position because he never recovered from a serious hamstring injury. He did play more games at DH than any player in history, 1,412, which is just 101 games more at the position than Frank Thomas. The fact remains that with his bat, any NL team would have found a place to play him. And last time we checked, DH was still part of the team.

Mariano Rivera called him the toughest hitter he ever faced. And Edgar accomplished all this without the suspicion of performance enhancing drugs ever being cast over him. Baseball writers, please do your job and research and vote Edgar into the Hall of Fame. He deserves it.

Josh: You have a real man-crush on Edgar Martinez, don't you?

Kevin: Facts are facts. But I *love* me some Edgar.

EBBETS FIELD FLANNELS
408 Occidental Ave. South
www.ebbets.com/

Ebbets Field Flannels Factory Outlet is a must-visit for true baseball fans. The store specializes in high-quality woolen hats, jerseys, and jackets bearing the emblems of lost teams, ranging from the Pacific Coast League to the Negro Leagues, to the Caribbean Leagues, and dozens of other leagues as well. Whether you're a fan of the Xalapa Chileros of the Mexican League, Josh Gibson's mighty Homestead Grays, or the Seattle Rainiers, this store has something for you. The hats and flannel jerseys do not come cheap, but they are made to last. In recent years the store has expanded to include soccer, football, and hockey gear as well, but baseball jerseys and hats remain their hallmark. A few years back the Ebbets Field Flannels acquired longtime sporting goods manufacturer Stall & Dean of Massachusetts. Stall & Dean has been in business since the 1890s and manufactured some of the original baseball uniforms that the joint company now produces as replicas.

WE SCORE THIS ONE: E-5

Outside the left-field entrance to the park (where an Edgar Martinez statue should be) you'll find a big bronze baseball mitt. Josh calls this "the Swiss Cheese Glove," while Kevin calls it "the Russ Davis Memorial." Davis, who hit the first home run in Safeco history, played third base like he had a hole in his glove for the Mariners from 1996 to 1999. Now, we understand that good art is often nonrepresentational and that the hole is supposed to symbolize a ball. But come on! It's a hole and it's inside the mitt—a clear disconnect between art and subject. The glove was part of a $1.3 million investment by Seattle's Public Art Program to fill the park and surrounding area with works by prominent Northwest artists.

DAVE NIEHAUS STATUE

In June 2011, the Mariners unveiled the statue of their most devoted employee and fan, Dave Niehaus. Niehaus, who broadcasted the play-by-play of every single game for the Mariners from their inception through the 2010 season, died of a massive heart attack on November 10, 2010. The statue is the first the Mariners have commissioned, and is fitting. It does well to honor the man who was the voice of the franchise for thirty-three years. He will never be replaced. So, rather than fail in our attempt to honor Mr. Niehaus, we'll let Dave tell it in his own words. His catch-phrases were, "Swung on and belted!" and "Get out the rye bread and mustard, grandma, 'cause it's GRAND SALAMI time!" and "My-Oh-My!" Niehaus is also credited with being the first person to dub Ken Griffey Jr. "The Kid," and to call Alex Rodriguez "A-Rod."

The statue, which features Niehaus seated and in front of his microphone, has become a popular place for fans to have their pictures taken.

SNEAK A PEEK

As you walk along Royal Brougham you'll notice that you can see right into the park from street level. On our first visit to the ballpark, on a rainy August day, we peeked in before the game. The roof was closed tight while the grounds crew was busy at work inside hosing hundreds of gallons of water onto the field. Don't ask us why. We're just reporting what we saw.

LITERARY GATES

As authors, we think it's pretty cool that the Mariners have adorned the ballpark gates with placards bearing baseball quotations. We both really liked the one from Donald Hall's lyrical book *Fathers Playing Catch with Sons,* which reads, "I need to enter the intense, artificial, pastoral universe of the game, where conflict never conceals itself, where the issues are clear and the outcome uncertain. I enter an alien place, or the child in me does, and the child plays for a little while."

Watering Holes and Outside Eats

OCCIDENTAL AVENUE STREET VENDORS

After lengthy public battles with health inspectors, restaurants blocking competition, and general ignorance regarding how drastically street vendors improve society, portable food purveyors are finally taking back the streets of Seattle. Occidental Avenue, which runs along the west side of Qwest Field, is the epicenter of a growing revolution. On busy game days you'll find hot dog carts, peanut vendors, and kettle corn being popped in enormous vats. We say "Here, here!" and "It's about time." We'd still like to see more of them and a bit closer to the ballpark, please. Late-night carts cater to the post-bar crowd in Pioneer Square. Josh wonders why they don't wheel their carts into SODO to peddle to hungry baseball fans.

JIMMY'S ON FIRST

1046 First Ave. South
www.jimmysonfirst.com

This place is about what you'd expect from a martini and cocktail bar located inside a high-end hotel: kind of expensive; kind of long lines; and kind of mediocre. This really isn't our kind of joint, except for maybe having Bloody Marys at brunch before a Sunday afternoon game.

PYRAMID BREWERY AND ALEHOUSE

1201 First Ave. S
www.pyramidbrew.com

Pyramid remains one of the best places to go before or after a game (and during if the M's are stinking up the joint). Remember, at Pyramid, the food is okay, but it's the microbrews that keep people coming back. Seems like since our first book came out, microbreweries have been popping up in every town from coast to coast. Well, while you're in Seattle, be sure to sample one of the originals (and by that we mean they go all the way back to the 1980s). Here's what you need to know: The Hefeweizen (German for "wheat beer") with a wedge of lemon is for a warm summer day (if there were such a thing in Seattle). Try the Curve Ball Ale—it's a hit before any game. Or, just get a sampler, which provides a number of different beers in small glasses. The goal is to taste as many as you can and still be standing when the clock strikes game time or midnight. So get into a West Coast groove, kick off your shoes (figuratively speaking), and let the good times roll.

BEER GARDENING

Germany may have invented the beer garden, but Seattle has perfected it, at least in America. If you can't get a table at Pyramid, head for the spacious beer garden located in its parking lot.

Here's a primer on the scene: (1) There are fewer selections on tap; (2) the cups are plastic; (3) the girls think they're in college again and are much flirtier; (4) spilling on the ground, or on each other, is fair play; and oh yeah, (5) occasionally there's food. Think of beer gardening as tailgating without the hassle of parking the Winnebago, tapping the keg, and fumbling with the hibachi.

IVAR'S ACRES OF CLAMS

On the Waterfront at Pier 54
www.ivars.com

If your pleasure is a sit-down dinner with all the delights of the seven seas, then Ivar's Acres of Clams is the place for you. It will cost you, but if you've travelled from Nebraska and have a hankering to down some of the finest seafood available this is your place. Salmon, local oysters and clams, and Alaskan king crab are favorites.

For the late-night crowd, the place to chow down is Ivar's Fish Bar, which is vastly cheaper than Acres, but just as good in its own way. A Seattle waterfront institution, the Fish Bar features deep-fried foods until 3:00 a.m. There's usually a line, but the salmon and chips are well worth the wait. The chowder is delicious too.

Josh: Why did they stop serving the salmon and chips at the ballpark?

Kevin: Let me consult my Magic 8 Ball.

Josh: You have a Magic 8 Ball app on your smartphone?

Kevin: It still says "answer unclear."

F. X. MCRORY'S WHISKEY BAR AND CHOP HOUSE
419 Occidental Ave. South
www.fxmcrorys.com

A favorite of Seattle sports fans, F.X. is a vintage Irish sports bar—though it leans more towards the sports than the Irish. Pacific oysters on the half-shell are a house favorite. Kevin devoured two dozen in twelve minutes while Josh didn't like the combination of gooey oysters and dark microbrew.

If old Kentucky moonshine is your thing, F.X. also boasts the largest selection of bourbon in the country. Daily specials are written on chalkboards along the wall. A few of our favorites are: Himan Walker's Ten High, Pappy VanWinkle, and Old Kentucky Senator.

Also featured at F.X. is the artwork of famous sports artist and *Playboy* magazine contributor Leroy Neiman. Mr. Neiman's painting of the F. X. McRory's bar hangs on the wall as you head toward the restrooms.

Josh: I wonder if Jeff Niemann's related to him.

Kevin: Seeing as their names are spelled differently, I'd say it's a fair bet not.

SLUGGERS
538 1st Ave. South

True to our prediction in the first edition of this book, Sluggers is still here, and it remains a popular place to meet up before the game. With lots of microbrews and Seattle sports memorabilia mounted on the walls, this would seem to be just what the fans ordered. Trivia buffs will enjoy playing the computerized nationwide satellite trivia game.

Josh: Are you crying?

Kevin: I have something in my eye.

Josh: What are you looking at? That old school Sonics banner?

Kevin: No. Definitely not that.

Josh: But you said the NBA was dead to you.

Kevin: They were our only championship team, man.

TRIANGLE PUB
533 1st Ave. South
http://trianglepub.com

The beers are cheap at this historic Seattle pub, and hey, the building's shaped like a triangle. Peanuts are free and shells must be thrown on the floor. It's a house rule, kind of like at our friend Dave Hayden's apartment back in Cleveland, only they sweep up the Triangle at the end of the night unlike at Dave's place where the floor gets cleaned about once every lunar cycle. We highly recommend this pub for the off-the-beaten-path types. Arrive early, though, because the joint is tiny. One other rule: no squares allowed.

ARMANDO'S SALUMI
309 3rd Ave. South
www.salumicuredmeats.com

And by Salumi, they mean salami, which they make themselves. This is a high-end place, opened by famed restaurateur Armando Batali, and it shows by calling itself a purveyor of "artisan cured meats." But you can still sneak in here before the game (check the website on the hours) and for not too much money, to get yourself a delicious pregame sandwich that will be the best thing you've eaten all day. Josh likes the hot sopressata, while Kevin remains a fan of the coppa.

PIONEER SQUARE NIGHTLIFE

One reason that the SODO district has been slow to develop its own Safeco scene is that the pub scene in the Pioneer Square district has been *the* happening spot in town for many years. While the area can be a bit on the touristy side, there are plenty of places to get a cold one, a great meal, and even play a hand of cards . . . for money. That's right, card rooms have been legal in Seattle since the days of the pioneers, so grab a space at a table if you're game and get in on some serious poker playing. The J & M Café & Card Room, located at 201 1st Ave. S, is a popular spot, but like most places in Pioneer Square, the serious action is over well before game time, as these bars turn into little more than frat parties in the later hours.

If you're the type who likes to shake your booty after a full day of baseball, we recommend getting in on the Pioneer Square joint-cover. A bunch of bars have banded together to offer a single cover charge to patrons who get a hand stamp allowing them to access any of the member clubs. It's a good deal and it's a hopping part of town seven nights a week. While just about all of these places are good, our favorites are Larry's Blues Cafe, Doc Maynard's, and the Central Tavern. In any of these establishments, you can find a map to, and list of, the other participating bars.

THE CENTRAL SALOON
207 1st Ave. South
http://centralsaloon.com

Around since the Yukon gold rush days, the Central is Seattle's oldest saloon. A true Seattle delicacy and a must-taste for any adventurous baseball road tripper is the Central's alligator on a stick. Tastes like chicken to us. For grunge fans, seminal Seattle rock band Soundgarden was the house band here for years. Kevin saw them often back in his glory days.

NEW ORLEANS CAFÉ
114 1st Ave. South
www.neworleanscreolerestaurant.com/
Sample the gumbo or have a brew in this pub named for another great city. Cajun and Creole are the specialties, while jazz, zydeco, and Dixieland are the most common musical offerings.

SWANNIE'S SPORTS BAR AND RESTAURANT
222 S. Main St.
Once the famed locale of well drinks that cost the same as Dave Valle's batting average, now Swannie's is a dive sports bar with cheap beer during the day and a comedy club in the basement at night. On occasion, you may find Mariner players kicking back here after games.

MAC'S SMOKEHOUSE
1006 1st Ave. South
This is the place to go if you like good old-fashioned barbecue. The brisket was a big winner with Josh. Though it used to be located closer to the park, Mac's is still only a short walk. It is closed, however, on Sundays.

Josh: Wha? No BBQ on Sunday?

Kevin: What are they, religious?

Josh: You see how we are divided when we should be united?

Kevin: What the hell are you talking about?

Inside the Park

Seattle is a city infamous for making ill-advised public works decisions, but they finally did something right with Safeco Field. Old-timers and baseball purists will thoroughly enjoy the Safeco atmosphere. And "newbies" will too. The purposely asymmetrical playing field features an unusual gap built into the 405-foot-deep left-center field. This is where late September home runs go to die in this notoriously pitcher-friendly yard.

Josh: I like to load my fantasy roster with M's pitchers.

Kevin: Yeah, M's and A's deliver solid WHIPs and ERAs due to their parks.

Josh: If only their lineups could score a few runs and get them some Ws.

Ballpark Features

ON THE ROOF
We are still not sure why Seattle built a retractable roof for baseball, even though studies indicated an open-air stadium in Seattle would have fewer rainouts than Boston, New York, or Baltimore. Then the city turned around and built an open-air football stadium, even though it rains every day during the winter in Seattle.

Josh: Their last mistake was to let the NBA and David Stern bully them, sending the Sonics to Oklahoma City.

Kevin: Yeah, all so that his buddy Clayton Bennett could have a team.

Josh: Add another commissioner to the list of Kevin's least favorite people.

With that said, the retractable roof is impressive and we give Seattle the edge as best ballpark with a flip-top. Whether viewed from inside or out, the arching steel supports are reminiscent of a postindustrial homage to labor. It's worth sticking around until after the game is over, to hear Wagner's "The Ride of the Valkyries" playing over the P.A. system as the roof closes. You know this tune. Think of a cowboy-hat-wearing Robert Duvall in the helicopter scene from *Apocalypse Now*. Ringing any bells? If not, maybe it's time to rent the movie.

Major League Baseball Rule 6.10 Broken

To make way for a 2011 U2 concert at Sun Life Stadium in Miami, the oddest of occurrences happened at Safeco Field. The Mariners agreed to host the Florida Marlins at Safeco—which is not odd at all. What is strange, is that the Mariners agreed to be the away team at their home park—and during interleague play. Which means that the congenial M's wore their away uniforms, hit first, and played by the rules of the National League—which means that the pitchers hit in an American League ballpark for the first time since the Designated Hitter Rule was instituted in 1973.

Kevin: A pitcher hits in an AL park!! Blasphemy!!

Josh: Do not underestimate the magnificence of Bono.

Kevin: You sound like my wife.

If you're only in town for one game and the always iffy Northwest weather has you fretting, fear not. The game doesn't suffer much when the roof is closed because Safeco doesn't lock up airtight. Though a closed roof may give the illusion that baseball is being played under the "big top," it also preserves an outdoor atmosphere by leaving open the north and west sides of the park. So dress as you would for any other outdoor destination in Seattle—in layers, but leave the umbrella at home.

HOW DO YOU STOP A SPEEDING LOCOMOTIVE?
Safeco's trademark feature was the procession of booming horns from the locomotives that rumble right through the

bleachers in right field. This may sound like an exaggeration, but it isn't. The tracks of the Portland-Seattle Railroad line actually run directly beneath the ballpark's retracted roof on the inside of its huge supports. However, when they built the extension that takes cars from I-90 to Edgar Martinez Drive, they built a bridge over the tracks, so the trains are no longer required by law to blow their horns. It's a loss, to be sure, because that wonderful sound that used to blast from the outfield really meant something to Mariner fans. Some of the train engineers still lay down the horn to honor tradition, but it's far less frequent than it used to be.

IRON MAN

When Safeco played host to the 2001 All-Star Game, it served as a glorious stage for Cal Ripken's last Midsummer Classic hurrah. The venerable Oriole walked away with the game's MVP honors after blasting a dramatic home run that still gives us shivers when we watch the replay on YouTube. See if you can spot the plaque in the Seattle bullpen that commemorates the spot where Cal's All-Star dinger landed.

I DIDN'T REALIZE THEY'D ACTUALLY BE PENS!

While close access to pitchers warming up has become common at many parks, Safeco takes the idea a step further. Fans can close in on relievers from almost every imaginable angle—at eye-level on the first level, above from the second deck, through the portholes in the Bullpen Pub, or from the Center Field Terrace.

While we appreciated such rare access to the pop of a ninety-five-mile-per-hour fastball, we wondered if the fans might be a bit too close to the players here. Surely, we thought, relievers must resent being gawked at like zoo animals through the chain-link screen. That was our initial impression. But we have to admit the fans were exceptionally well behaved during the games we spent sitting along the visitor's pen. Here's our theory: The very proximity of players and fans is what keeps the drunken hecklers at bay. At other parks where fans aren't so close, they don't mind yelling "Hey, Rivera, you SUCK!" But at Safeco fans are close enough to see the effect of their words on the players' faces, so they don't get really nasty. That's our theory anyway.

KIDS CLUBHOUSE

Like many of the new parks, Safeco features a romper room for rambunctious kids and stressed parents. The KC is located toward the back of the center-field plaza. It offers a playground, interactive baseball activities, a kiddy store, and

center field plaza

Photo by Paul Lukinich

even a chance to pose for pictures with the Mariner Moose in the Moose Den. Again, this feature was a fairly new concept when it was first put into Safeco, but has become a very common feature of ballparks built since.

HOME PLATE GATE

By far the most impressive of the several entrances to the park, the Home Plate Gate is really something to see. The rounded rotunda design was directly influenced by the rotunda of Ebbets Field. Though Safeco's rotunda is unique, comparing the two side by side reveals the obvious influences of mythical Ebbets. After passing through the gate, you'll ride up an escalator, below a chandelier made of one thousand translucent glass resin baseball bats. This is one of the many pieces of art integrated into the Safe's design. You'll see another as you reach the main concourse. It's easy to be distracted by your first sweeping view of the field, but take a moment to look down. Tiled into the floor is the Nautical Compass Rose—the Mariner emblem—as well as the signature of each Mariner who played in the inaugural game at Safeco.

SAFECO ART

Baseball inspired artwork abounds at Safeco Field. Along with the chandelier, look for plenty more art inside Safeco, beginning with a mural by Thom Ross entitled "The Defining Moment" which depicts the double that Edgar Martinez belted down the left-field line against the Yankees in Game 5 to clinch the 1995 ALDS. Look to the main concourse level for baseball themed "quilts" of stitched metal, pop cans, and old license plates, by Ross Palmer Beecher, and metal sculptures located throughout the park depicting large hands gripping baseballs and showing how to grip common pitches, created by Donald Fels. There are many other examples of fine art throughout Safeco—nearly all worthy of your time.

Josh: When I grew up dreaming of being a baseball writer I never would have guessed I'd wind up writing about quilts.

Kevin: Shut up and appreciate the art!

THE BASEBALL MUSEUM OF THE PACIFIC NORTHWEST

Located on the main concourse level of Safeco, the BMPN honors the developments of the game and the teams that have graced the fields of the region—including Washington, Idaho, Oregon, Montana, and British Columbia. It's a neat little exhibit full of history and pride, and there are plenty of interactive exhibits to convey the touch and feel of Northwest baseball, past and present. Perhaps the most unique exhibit is the "You Make the Call" booth, dedicated to Dave Niehaus and the fan experience of the game. Old and young fans will get a kick out of adding their own personal descriptions of the game as it plays out before them on video monitors.

THE MARINER HALL OF FAME

Located inside the Baseball Museum of the Pacific Northwest, the Mariner Hall of Fame opened its doors for the first time during the 2002 season. The M's announced just two charter inductees: Alvin Davis, the 1984 AL Rookie of the Year, and Niehaus. Since then, Jay Buhner and Edgar Martinez have been added. Can Ken Griffey Jr. be far behind?

Stadium Eats

The delicious aroma of coffee wafts around the ballpark in combination with the seafood smells and the wonderful saltwater scent coming off Elliott Bay. The eating experience at Safeco will not disappoint. While there are foods to avoid, there is plenty of local fare to enjoy. Another Safeco first, 411-ing yourself some eats. That's right, you can use your cell phone, computer, iPad, or any other device fit for the task to request that anything on the menu be delivered right to your seat. Several other ballparks have since picked up on this innovation.

IVAR'S FISH BAR (TRADEMARK FOOD)

Local seafood establishment Ivar's features two stands inside the stadium. This is not only a great trademark food of the ballpark, but also of Seattle. You have to try the Fish Dog, which is exactly what it sounds like, and all we hoped it would

be. A deep fried link of cod, smothered in tartar and coleslaw. The deep-fried fish and chips is a staple of the Seattle dining experience. The fish is lightly fried to perfection and will warm your soul on those sea-breezy evenings of spring or fall. The homemade chowder and salmon sandwich are also exceptional. Deep-fried salmon and chips used to be our favorite, but they took it off the menu at the stadium stands. Bummer.

Kevin: Last time we pleaded that they bring back the salmon! Isn't anyone listening?

Josh: Ivar, hear our prayer.

SAFECO DOGS (DOG REVIEW)

Several great dog options abound at Safeco. The Superdog is an oversized red hot with a respectable amount of snap to it. The aforementioned Ivar's Fish Dog takes the top ranking of all dogs not made of pork. For a special treat outside the park, try the Ichi-dog.

BEST OF THE REST

Many fans have been lauding Safeco's **garlic fries** as the ballpark's trademark food. We agree that chopped garlic and herbs unabashedly spread over crispy french fries makes for a delicious ballgame treat. But the problem is, they've been serving garlic fries in San Francisco for years—first at Candlestick and now at AT&T Park. Seattle ain't San Fran, nor is anywhere else for that matter. It has its own personality that should be reflected in its most cherished munchies. To this day the aptly named **Ichi-roll** remains our favorite Best of the Rest selection. This is a sushi roll made of spicy tuna and rice, wrapped in delicious seaweed. It has become so popular at the ballpark in recent years that restaurants around town have started serving the Ichi-roll. Now to us, that is how ballpark food should be, leading the epicurean charge rather than lagging behind.

FOR SERIOUS FOODIES ONLY

Yes, Martha, they do offer authentic **Parisian crêpes** at the ballpark in Seattle. Now, we know what you're thinking. Crêpes? Aren't they a bit messy for ballpark food? Sure they are, but then again so are nachos, and we're not seeing anybody getting rid of those anytime soon. And the crêpes are good. Perhaps not the best ever, but definitely worth a try.

Seattle continues to up the ante for ballpark food. We look at it this way: Seattle hipsters led the way with sushi at the ballpark, so maybe they're on to the next big thing. They remodeled the old "Bullpen Market," out in centerfield, now calling it simply "The Pen," and it features food from prominent chefs. There's **grass-fed beef burgers** and

A Tale From Our First Road Trip

"What?" Kevin asked incredulously as Josh shied away from an Ichi-roll.

"Raw fish and weed don't do it for me," Josh hissed.

"Come on," Kevin goaded. "You love to watch Ichiro playing right field Japanese style, and you bow down when Kaz Sasaki unleashes that forkball from the land of the rising sun."

As Kevin dipped the roll into wasabi and soy then took a hellacious bite that made his nose run, Josh backed away from him like he was a leper on fire. "I will not be sampling that . . . that . . . that . . . that thing!" he cried. "Stop pointing it at me!"

"We need to experience each park's unique flavors, colors, smells, and noises, so you've gotta take a bite," Kevin said. "You owe it to our readers."

Josh considered this for a long time as Kevin continued to aim the fragrant end of his half-eaten Ichi-roll squarely at him. He looked at the sushi, then at his feet, then at the sushi again, then up at the roof. It seemed like he almost wanted to take a bite, but when it came down to it, he just couldn't shake his inhibitions. "Those garlic fries really filled me up," he said. "I'll try the Ichi-roll tomorrow."

When the next day came, Josh predictably forgot his vow and bought two Kid Valley burgers and a double order of garlic fries to fill up on.

Kid Valley burgers are another solid "Best of the Rest" selection. These delicious handfuls of grease and meat are neither your standard issue ballpark burgers, nor are they the mega-chain fast-food variety. This is more like a greasy delicious mom-and-pop-style burger, cooked fresh and topped with onions, lettuce, tomatoes, and cheese. If you like burgers, Kid Valley is for you.

sausages made in beer by chef Ethan Stowell at the Hamburg & Frites stand; and **Mexican tortas** by chef Roberto Santibanez at Tortugas Volandoras that are surprisingly fresh and delicious. There is also the **New Haven–style thin crust pizza** made with local ingredients and fired in a real brick oven by chef Bill Pustari at Apizza.

Kevin: It's a bit yupp-ity, isn't it?

Josh: I have tasted the future of ballpark food, and I like it!

Kevin: You're eating a crêpe at the ballpark. I mean, it's more like a dessert than a meal, right?

Josh: What can I tell you? I like sweet as much as savory.

Kevin: Turn off the food channel, Emeril.

SAY "NO, THANKS," AND WALK AWAY

We still give our most mediocre rating to the Hit It Here Café, which is located on the second deck. While ideas like this often seem great when stadiums are being designed, they usually turn out pretty average. This is no exception. The food is nothing special and it's hard to see the game from all but a few tables. Save your money and eat at one of the Terraces instead.

Also beware of High Cheese Pizza, available at several stadium locations. We rank this a half-step above freezer pizza.

STADIUM SUDS: THE MICROBREW REVOLUTION WILL NOT BE TELEVISED

On our first trip across baseball America, we tried to alert our readers to the joys of microbrews at the ballpark. It seems as if someone out there was listening, because nearly every stadium in the land now offers microbrewed goodness in some form or another. But some of the best remain in Seattle.

Our favorites at Safeco are Alaskan Amber, Mirror Pond, Widmere Hefeweizen (pronounce the Ws as Vs, lest ye sound like a tourist), Mac & Jack's African Amber, and of course, Red Hook.

Josh: What are you doing drinking a Pabst? I thought you were Mr. Microbrew?

Kevin: It's the counter-revolution, my friend.

Josh: No, you're just getting old.

The Safeco Experience

Seattle fans have been through it all. The good times, the bad times, and the ugly times when their franchises have picked up and left town. But through it all, they've developed a true love for their hometown ballclub that is certain not to fade. And their love of team infuses their attitude and behavior at the park.

An example of this civil behavior was told to us by Kevin's friend Jim Sander, who accompanied us to a game. As Jim tells the story, the M's were leading their divisional rivals, the Oakland A's, late in a game. David Justice was in right field when a few loud and drunken men began yelling "Hal-le Ber-ry! Hal-le Ber-ry!" in reference to the fact that Justice and the actress were once married. This offended one Seattle woman, who stood up and shouted back at the men, "Stop saying that! You could really hurt his feelings!" And that was it. The men shut up.

Though taunting a rival player occurs often, it rarely gets as vicious as it does in cities like New York and Boston. Seattle fans seem to prefer cheering on their favorite Mariners stars.

While some might misread this as a lack of passion among Seattle fans, we don't see it that way. We see Seattle fans as folks who embrace the power of positive thinking.

GRIFFEY'S RETURN

We all dream of the glory days returning again. But alas, it never comes to be. And so Seattle fans longed for the return of their departed heroes, Ken Griffey Jr., first among them.

That dream first began to take shape in 2007, when the aging star returned to Seattle while his Reds visited during an interleague matchup. Over the three-game series, every time Griffey came to the plate or a ball came near him, the Seattle crowds rose to their feet and roared their approval for the superstar who'd left town so many years before. Griffey, obviously overwhelmed by the outpouring of love from the city where his best (and least injury-plagued) years took place, joked that he wouldn't mind winding up his career in a Mariner uniform. Edgar Martinez and Jay Buhner were on hand to greet him, and as the fans cheered at the sight of Junior's sweet swing, it all seemed as much a pipe dream for Mariner fans that Griffey might actually return.

Well for Mariner fans the dream did come true. Though it took a playoff stopover with the Chicago White Sox in 2008 to break Junior free of Cincinnati, the 2009 season brought Griffey back to Seattle. "The Kid" was a kid no longer, and he retired with the Mariners midseason 2010. His "Victory Tour" lasted a little more than a season, but brought few victories. He was a shell of his former self, of course, batting just .214 and .184 in his two final seasons with the M's, but it was still nice to see him finish in the city where his illustrious career began.

OUTDOOR FIREPLACE

Many ballparks have signature outdoor seating areas: picnic spots, outfield hot tubs, etc. Since this is Seattle, the signature outdoor seating area is a small outdoor fireplace, located behind the centerfield batter's eye with no view of the field. On a positive note, it provides the one area in the entire ballpark where you can be warm prior to the Fourth of July.

LOUIE, LOUIE

During the seventh-inning stretch, after the obligatory singing of "Take Me Out to the Ball Game," Safeco fans sing along to "Louie, Louie," popularized by the 1960s Northwest rockers, The Kingsmen. When the tune first became a national sensation, J. Edgar Hoover had a team of FBI special agents dedicate hundreds of taxpayer-financed hours trying to crack "the code" hidden within its cryptic lyrics. Why? We haven't a clue. Might as well ask why Hoover went parading around in ladies underwear. Makes you wonder, doesn't it?

In the 1970s "Louie, Louie" was featured in the Northwest film classic *Animal House*, which was filmed on the University of Oregon campus. In the 1980s a recurring ballot measure was voted on in the Washington State Legislature to make "Louie, Louie" the official state anthem. None of these measures passed, but the Mariners still play the song religiously.

BASEBALL GEEKS UNITE! THE EMBRACING OF SABERMETRICS

GM Jack Zduriencik came to Seattle from Milwaukee, where he was known as a general manager who embraced sabermetrics as a form of talent evaluation. Coincidentally (or perhaps not), with his arrival to the Jet City, that knowledge is being passed on to the Mariner fan base. Scoreboards throughout the ballpark have been tweaked to show not only the standard pitch count and MPH, but the first pitch strike ratio and summary ball/strike breakdowns for pitchers, as well as on-base and OPS percentages for hitters. In addition, the scoreboard not only records when a player is out, but also displays the proper scoring syntax for those interested in keeping score at the park.

Josh: Well, this guy's record is 3-7 but he has a sweet WHIP.

Kevin: I guess that means Zduriencik is doing a good job.

THE CODE OF CONDUCT – WE GOT RED CARDED

There is an official Code of Conduct at Safeco Field, and breaking that code will warrant receipt of a red ticket. On the ticket is printed Safeco's code of conduct and unacceptable behaviors:

1. *Foul/abusive language or obscene gestures*
2. *Intoxication or other signs of impairment related to alcohol consumption*
3. *Displays of affection not appropriate in a public, family setting*
4. *Obscene or indecent clothing*
5. *Any disruption of a game or event, including throwing of objects or trespassing on the playing field or other restricted areas*
6. *Sitting in a location other than the guest's ticketed seat*
7. *Fighting, taunting or making threatening remarks or gestures*
8. *Smoking or the use of tobacco products, in any form*

Josh: I told you no real baseball fans would behave this civilly of their own volition.

Kevin: Start working on your excuses for infractions 1, 2, 5, 6 and 7.

THE MOOSE MAN (SUPER-FAN)

If you see a guy with more than 200 Mariner Moose plush toys strung around his neck, you've found The Moose Man. Yeah, he's not too hard to find. The Moose Man has been adding to his soft collection ever since he attended his first game at Safeco, and thinks that each time he buys one, he's buying the M's a bit of good luck. The Moose Man is very approachable and loves being asked to have his picture taken.

"BIG LO" (SUPER-FAN)

Lorin "Big Lo" Sandretzky gets our nod for the super-est of the super-fans in town, not only for his support of the Mariners, but of all Seattle sports teams. This crazy gent is famous for greeting Seattle's pro teams at the airport when they return from the road. "Big Lo" is tough to miss, at six feet eight inches tall and more than 450 pounds. He's even received his own action figure. Look for "Big Lo" in section 142, along the third-base line.

Cyber Super-Fans

- **USS Mariner**
  www.ussmariner.com/
- **Jason Churchill at Prospect Insider**
  http://prospectinsider.com/
- **Lookout Landing**
  www.lookoutlanding.com/

THE ORIGINAL CRAZY PEANUT GUY (SUPER-FAN HALL OF FAME)

Rick "The Peanut Man" Kaminsky was still tossing peanuts to Mariners fans well into his 70s. But, sadly, he passed away in 2011 and will be missed as an essential part of the Seattle baseball experience. Ever since the Kingdome opened in 1977, Crazy Peanut Guy had made an art form out of his profession. Though he looked like a brown-haired Harpo Marx, Crazy Peanut Guy was still an ace who rarely, if ever, missed in his tosses of bags of hot salted nuts. Before he passed away, he became a YouTube sensation and he even had a Facebook page.

DAVE NIEHAUS (SUPER-FAN HALL OF FAME)

There is, and forever will be, only one voice in the ears of Mariner fans. And that golden throat belongs to Mr. Dave Niehaus, the Mariners' number one fan. Dave Niehaus's voice, his passion, his sheer and unwavering love for the Mariners, and the unique and wonderful way he expressed that love in

---

Sports in the City

Sick's Stadium
2700 Rainier Ave. South
We don't necessarily recommend it, but fanatics of bygone Seattle sports might consider visiting the site of old Sick's Stadium (and Dougdale Park prior), which was home to the American League's short-lived Seattle Pilots. The Pacific Coast League's Rainiers played at Sick's, too, as did the West Coast Baseball Association's Seattle Steelheads, a well-named Negro League team that—like the Pilots—played just one season (1946) in Seattle. It was a beautifully clunky little park that hosted outdoor baseball in Seattle for more than eighty years. But it was woefully small and inadequate for big league play.

Those who embark upon this somber pilgrimage will find a large chain hardware store where Sick's Stadium once stood. It's enough to break your heart. Inside the store there is a glass display featuring Pilots' and Rainiers' memorabilia.

---

clever phrasings, is the very reason many Seattleites became Mariner fans. He is honored in the Mariner Hall of Fame inside the ballpark, and outside as well, with his own statue. The city and the sport of baseball owe a debt of gratitude to Dave Niehaus that simply can never be repaid. He was one of a kind—and he loved the Mariners with his entire heart.

THE TUBA MAN (SUPER-FAN HALL OF FAME)

Edward Scott McMichael was the Tuba Man, and we want to honor him. In more than three decades, Tuba Man rarely missed a major sporting event in the greater Seattle area, puffing away on his instrument like the professional he was. He was an odd-looking man, a gentle giant, rather hairy, and decked out from head to toe in Seattle sports paraphernalia. And boy, oh boy, could Tuba Man blow his horn. Any song you want, he'd play it. All with a cheerful smile and warm thumbs-up.

A visit to the ballpark in Seattle simply was not complete unless you heard Tuba Man's low tones rumbling as you hurried toward the gates. Unfortunately, Tuba Man was assaulted by some street toughs, badly beaten, and later died from the injuries he incurred. The outpouring of grief from the city was tremendous. Few people in life have such a wonderful effect on so many. Tuba Man was well loved and will be missed.

BILL, THE BEER MAN (SUPER-FAN HALL OF FAME)

Bill "The Beer Man" Scott used to be an actual beer man at the Kingdome who took breaks from peddling foam to lead

Tuba Guy Superfan

Photo by Kevin O'Connell

the crowd in cheers. He quickly became a minor celebrity and quit sloshing suds to lead the crowd in cheers full time for the M's, Seahawks, Sonics, and Huskies, but passed away in 2007.

While We Were in Seattle
We Almost Won the Whole Damned Thing

After a beautiful day of outdoor baseball, highlighted by a 16-4 Mariners win over Detroit, we decided to look for some "action." Because we're both married, we decided against a singles bar and instead headed for Sluggers, where we logged onto the daily nationwide satellite trivia game. After lengthy debate, we settled on "The Baseball Boys" as our

team name. If you were online that August night, chances are you'll remember our legendary run.

After fumbling with the controller for a round, we were damned near "unconscious," nailing question after question, as other patrons began to take note and marvel at our cumulative wealth of obscure—and for the most part, useless—knowledge.

Josh carried the team early thanks to his remarkable knowledge of the atlas. Who knows where Timbuktu is, specifically? Josh does. He's also great with numbers. Did we mention that? And Kevin's knowledge of all-things-nautical scored major points during a prolonged string of submarine queries. Just when it looked like things couldn't get any better, the waitress brought over a free round of brews, compliments of the house. Buoyed by a fresh lager, Kevin ran the table on an *Ancient World History* category as the growing crowd around our table cheered him on. The way he carefully enunciated each answer—"Hieronymus of Cardia, historian and statesman of ancient Greece who chronicled the life of Alexander the Great"—made Josh wonder if his friend was channeling the spirit of living trivia deity Alex Trebek.

The crowd roared. Josh beamed. And Kevin channeled.

But then tragically, a full day's worth of hot dogs, microbrews, Ichi-rolls, and garlic fries, came crashing down around us. After building a lead of 2,500 points—nationwide, mind you—we flailed miserably (picture Gorman Thomas trying to hit a curveball) at the next eleven questions. A *Cheeses of the World* category brought us to our knees. Kevin kept saying "Munster," and Josh kept keying it in. From havarti to gorgonzola, neufchatel, brie, and cheddar, all other cheeses came up on the screen, but never Muenster.

"Damn," Kevin said. "I could have sworn that last one was Munster."

"You're blowing it," Josh barked. "If we don't nail the next question, I swear to God, you're walking to San Francisco to eat garlic and cheese fries by yourself."

"Whatever," Kevin chortled. "The rental car's in *my* name."

The next category, *Famous Confederate Horses of the Civil War*, focused not surprisingly on the equines who reached rock star status in the day of our forefathers. When the question came, we were ready for it. *What was the name of the battle steed killed at Perryville while being ridden by Major General Patrick Cleburne?*

After a long and thoughtful pause, Kevin answered the anxious stares of Josh and others with an uncertain, "Munster?"

The answer turned out to be *Dixie*. Our huge lead having evaporated, we entered the last round tied for first with a team of Cleveland yahoos who called themselves "A Tribe Called Jest."

Fate was in our corner as the last question came, coincidentally enough, straight out of the Seattle Mariners archives.

"Which Mariners player kneeled down on the carpeted Kingdome floor on May 27, 1981, and tried to blow a dribbler down the third-base line foul?"

The relieved smile on Kevin's face made it clear that he knew the answer. Josh pumped his fist in the air and made a "raise-the-roof" gesture to the crowd, which had more or less lost interest by this point since the barman had just announced "last call."

"Come on, people," Josh yelled. "We're about to claim our rightful place as the most knowledgeable drunken trivia team in all of America." Then, as he turned to Kevin for the winning answer—(D) Lenny Randle—in his excitement he knocked over Kevin's pint of beer, spilling it on the control pad. Kevin kept hitting the D button, but it was no use. A Tribe Called Jest had already answered.

Kevin blamed Josh for the goof, and Josh blamed Kevin for leaving his beer so close to the controller. For a few minutes, tensions ran high. But when the waitress sauntered over with another free round, and the crowd burst into a mixture of applause and jeering laughter, we buried the hatchet and stumbled out the door as best of friends again.

OAKLAND ATHLETICS, O.CO COLISEUM

OAKLAND, CALIFORNIA
17 MILES TO SAN FRANCISCO
365 MILES TO LOS ANGELES
739 MILES TO PHOENIX
810 MILES TO SEATTLE

Overdue for Replacement in Oak-Town

If we were betting men, and if the bookies took wagers on things like which ballparks would be replaced and how soon, then after our first baseball road trip back in 2003, we would have bet the farm that by the time a second edition of this book became necessary, the Grand Old Game would have deserted the cavernous football stadium to be re-named later in Oakland for cozier, more baseball-friendly pastures. Either that, or they would have left Oak-Town altogether. See, back then the money-balling A's were the talk of the game as they continued to compete for the American League pennant each year despite possessing a payroll a fraction the size of their peers'. In fact, when *The Ultimate Baseball Road Trip* hit bookstore shelves in early 2004, the A's were riding a four-year playoff run. Despite the team's success, though, there were ominous signs that this franchise that had long played second fiddle to the San Francisco Giants would soon be venturing into troubled waters if it didn't resolve its stadium situation. And indeed, while the Giants have flourished on and off the field in a beautiful waterfront park, attendance at the concrete behemoth in Oakland has tailed off precipitously.

When A's general manager Billy Beane's boys ran out of magic, the A's plummeted to the bottom of MLB's attendance barrel. And hey, let's face it: Their games really weren't that well attended even when they were winning. By the time of this revision's print date, the A's had been struggling to draw twenty thousand fans per game for several years. Everyone seems to agree a new ballpark is necessary for the storied Athletics franchise, but they can't agree on where to put it. For more than a decade the topic has been debated. Various plans involving various sites have been explored and then abandoned, shattering fans' hopes. As a final insult to the green-and-gold-clad rooters still following the A's, the football stadium in which they play has embarrassingly been named and renamed and renamed again, ad nauseam, to the tune of six name changes since 1998. In April 2011 it adopted the handle Overstock.com Coliseum, then two months later, when Overstock.com announced it would be changing its corporate name to O.co, it adopted the abbreviated company name as its own. Before that it was the Oakland-Alameda County Coliseum (2008–2011), McAfee Coliseum (2004–2008), Network Associates Coliseum (1998–2004) and the Oakland-Alameda County Coliseum (1966–1998). It was also briefly called UMAX Technologies Coliseum back in 1997, but that naming rights deal dissolved amidst a legal dispute before the field could see any action for baseball.

One thing is certain: The A's need a new *baseball* park if they're going to compete in the modern game. Preferably for locals that park would sit somewhere inside the Oakland limits or close by, but among the ideas to reinvigorate the A's have been serious proposals to move them to San Jose, Fremont and even Las Vegas. At the time of this writing, the most likely destination for the A's appeared to be San Jose, where a deal to build a thirty-two-thousand-seat, $400 million park and name it Cisco Field was coming closer to fruition. The proposal, which called for the new baseball-only facility to be completed in time for the 2015 season, still faced many hurdles, though. At the top of the list, the A's and their owner Lew Wolff still needed the Giants to rescind their exclusive territorial rights to Santa Clara County. Whether this is the new home for the A's or whether it's just the latest in a series of possibilities that eventually fall apart, we can't say. But let us repeat: The A's need a new park.

Kevin: Three words: Jack. London. Square.

Josh: Succinct. To the point. Great location. Authorly. I like it.

With an exterior consisting of lots and lots of cement and some grassy slopes, the O.co makes an awkward impression right from the start. Plopped down in the middle of a sports complex, surrounded by asphalt and industrial warehouses, we suppose it didn't have much of a chance.

There is little of the awe here that Yankee Stadium inspires, the charm that Oriole Park projects, or the intimacy that Wrigley Field holds. Completely round when it was originally constructed, this ballfield twenty-one feet below sea level, has become a paradise for pitchers. The circular shape of the seating bowl best accommodates a football gridiron, not baseball diamond, and results in the most expansive foul territory in the majors. The cool night air combines with the large field to stifle the prospects of the homers today's fans so love. Indeed, everything about the O.co is large. The stadium accommodates more than sixty-three thousand Raiders fans during football season, but when the A's are playing the stadium staff unrolls large green tarps to cover massive swaths of the upper deck. As a result, instead of playing home games before twenty thousand fans and forty thousand empty seats, the A's play before twenty thousand fans, fifteen thousand empty seats, and a shiny plastic sheet. If this is an improvement, it is only a slight one.

Kevin: Green tarps cost a heck of a lot less than new ballparks.

Josh: They were on sale at Lowe's last week.

Kevin: They might be calling this dump the Lowe's Coliseum by the time we leave.

Despite the A's success during the Billy Beane years in building rosters around solid pitching and defense, with just a enough hitting to edge the opposition, during their earlier days the A's better teams were characterized by rough-and-ready hitters, guys like Reggie Jackson, Rickey Henderson, Jose Canseco, Mark McGwire, Eric Chavez, and Jason Giambi. Perhaps this is because the club plays in Oak-Town, a rough-and-ready city that's full of blue-collar—perhaps we should say "green-collar"—folks. While the dot-com boom of the 1990s gentrified sections of the East Bay, Oakland remained at its core a no-nonsense place. In this regard, we suppose, the O.co is a reflection of the city in which it resides. It does very little to please the eye, nor does it project the impression it is trying very hard. As visitors cross the chain-link fence lined pedestrian bridge from the BART station to the stadium, the landscape below is industrial, showcasing wooden shipping pallets, lumber, railroad tracks, and a backwater slough. Though it may not be the most attractive ballpark entrance, it is perhaps the most congruent with the stadium it presages. The O.co is an ode to cement and green plastic.

Built to serve the Oakland Raiders, as well as to potentially lure the A's from Kansas City, Oakland-Alameda County Coliseum, as it was originally known, opened for football in 1966. The City of Oakland and Alameda County have remained its owners ever since. Charlie O. Finley, who had failed in his bid to move the Kansas City A's to Arlington, Texas, in 1962, took his club to Oakland in 1968. Seattle was also considered by Finley as a possible destination for his A's, but Oakland got the nod since it already had the Coliseum ready and waiting. The O.co had been designed by architectural firm Skidmore, Owings & Merrill and built at an original cost of $25.5 million. The multi-use stadium anchored a complex that would include an exhibition hall and the basketball gym once known as Oakland Arena—now Oracle Arena—that has served the NBA's Golden State Warriors since 1966.

During their five decades in Oakland, the A's have been a colorful, hard-scrabble bunch. Think of the "Mustache Gang" of the early 1970s that won five straight AL West titles (1971–1975) and three straight World Series (1972–1974). Those guys fit the attitude of the city well. You couldn't picture them eating caviar at a trendy downtown restaurant or sitting down for a snifter of brandy in an elegant hotel ballroom. Guys like Catfish Hunter, Vida Blue, Rollie Fingers, Sal Bando, and Joe Rudi played hard-nosed ball that made them heroes to the working class who rooted them on.

interior

Photo by Kevin O'Connell

Sure, Jackson was on the team too, but he was a lone star-let and that was long before his head really swelled as he arrived in New York and pronounced he owned the place. Mr. October notwithstanding, those guys were dirt-dogs who played like their lives depended on it. They went to the park and got to work as if baseball was their job. Come to think of it, it *was* their job. And they attacked other teams the way a mechanic dismantles a manifold.

Before that glorious run for the fighting A's of the '70s, fans in the Bay Area hadn't taken much interest in the team. Afterwards, they were hooked. It took six seasons before the A's cracked the one-million mark in attendance, and that was with Finley at the helm, one of the most promotion-happy head honchos in big league history. But Finley wasn't always the most popular guy in Oakland. He could be a penny-pincher and when he sold off the "Swinging A's" of the '70s, some local rooters vowed never to forgive him. Today, the A's, who won three straight World Series, are rarely mentioned in discussions of greatest dynasties. We're not sure why.

Josh: Name the other franchise that's three-peated.

Kevin: You mean there's only one other?

Josh: But they've done it three times.

Kevin: Oh, right, the Yankees.

Josh: They won between 1998 and 2000, 1949 and 1953, and 1936 and 1939.

Kevin: Whoop-de-do for them. Do we owe Pat Riley money for saying three-peat?

By the late 1970s the A's were again less than competi-tive as they finished in last place in 1977, next to last in 1978, and then last again in 1979. The Green and Gold failed to win seventy games in any of those seasons. When the score-board went black one day, the nearly empty concrete Coli-seum took on the nickname "the Mausoleum." The Bay Area's own Billy Martin, who had grown up in Berkeley, took over the managerial reins in 1980 and brought to town a brand of play dubbed "Billy Ball" that would characterize the next era. "Billy Ball" was an NL style of play. Aggressive base-run-ners and strong pitchers who could go all nine became the trademarks of Martin's pugilistic squad. But the toll taken on sore-armed pitchers had its downside, as numerous pros-pects blew out their arms.

The return to glory for the A's was enabled by a strong farm system and some chemical help. The renaissance began in 1986 when the admittedly juicing Canseco hit thirty-three home runs on the way to claiming AL Rookie of the Year honors. The next season, fellow user McGwire kept the ROY in Oakland, bashing forty-nine long balls. In 1988 an A's player won the ROY for the third straight year

when shortstop Walt Weiss took the trophy. McGwire and Canseco became "the Bash Brothers," and along with team-mates Rickey Henderson and Dave Henderson, led the A's back to postseason play.

While these sluggers paced the offense, A's manager Tony La Russa was hard at work redefining how to utilize a pitching staff in the modern day. He introduced the one-inning closer in 1988 when he used Dennis Eckersley for the ninth inning and the ninth inning only. Each setup man knew his role—his inning—and La Russa rarely deviated from the script. Now it's common for each team to have a closer, an eighth-inning guy, a seventh-inning guy, a lefty-specialist and so on, thanks to La Russa's vision and the success it enabled.

As the A's evolved, so too did their stadium. And no discussion of that evolution would be complete without acknowledging the role the Raiders played in reshaping the contours of the Coliseum. After Raiders owner Al Davis dev-astated the city when he moved the Silver and Black out of Oakland in 1981, heading for the Los Angeles Coliseum, the Raiders' twelve-year southern hiatus left an enormous hole in the hearts of Oakland's costumed fans. And so, in an effort to lure their Raiders back, Oakland began a reconstruction of the Coliseum in 1995. The baseball-friendly outfield bleach-ers were replaced with a massive four-tier seating and luxury box structure that has come to be known derogatorily as "Mount Davis." A total of ten thousand upper-deck seats were added, all of which are tarped over during baseball season. Also added were two giant clubhouses, 125 luxury suites, a nine-thousand-square-foot kitchen, two new color video boards, and two matrix scoreboards in the end zones. The price of the undertaking was supposed to check in at $100 million, but swelled to double that.

Kevin: They could have built a nice little park on the Bay for less.

Josh: But then they wouldn't have 125 luxury boxes in deep center field where corporate types are just clamoring to sit . . . during football season.

Kevin: And they'd have nowhere to put their pretty green tarp.

We think the whole Davis saga left the City of Oakland and Alameda County gun-shy when it comes to providing funding for a new ballpark. Folks here just don't believe the local sports owners will live up to their word, and it's easy to see why, given their history with Davis. To say that Al Davis is to the NFL what George Steinbrenner was once to MLB may be an insult to the memory of Mr. Steinbrenner. Al Davis passed away in 2001, and leaves a legacy behind that is glo-rious to some and infamous to others.

What the new construction did, in essence, was transform the Oakland Coliseum from a relatively nice pitcher's park into an oversized stadium that really shouldn't be used for anything other than football and maybe soccer. While once fans could watch games for free from the concourse behind the field-level seats by peeking between slats in the fence and could sit in the left- or right-field bleachers with a grassy hill at their backs, or enjoy a view of the Oakland Hills, these aesthetically appealing ballpark accents gave way to Mount Davis, or the Death Star, as our friend Matthew calls the megalith. The price tag of Mount Davis also made it more difficult for the A's to convince Oakland to build a new ballpark for them.

Though the A's organization has traveled across the country in its history, casting off cities and ballparks the way most of us change batting gloves, it has been one of the most successful franchises in the game's history when it comes to winning World Series. The A's of Philadelphia collected nine American League pennants and five World Series trophies. The twelve years in Kansas City were not as productive, but since arriving in Oakland the A's have won four World Series in six trips to the big dance. That's fifteen trips to the October Classic and nine victories. Only the Yankees and Cardinals have more World Championships to their credit.

The Athletics were formed by a lanky Irishman named Cornelius McGillicuddy—better known in baseball lore as "Connie Mack"—whose Philadelphia A's joined the American League in its inaugural season of 1901. When the A's won the American League in 1902 and challenged the Senior Circuit to a "World Series," another Irishman, John McGraw, the hot-blooded manager of the National League's New York Giants, dismissed the American League's best team, calling the A's "white elephants." While McGraw's jab meant to imply that Mack should not be allowed to spend indiscriminately on players as coveted as albino pachyderms, the dual meaning of the metaphor is interesting. Calling something a "white elephant" is also a way of saying it's more trouble than it is worth. And that's pretty much the way McGraw felt about the American League. In any case, Mack decided to wear the insult as a badge of honor and adopted a white elephant as the team's insignia. Posters and paraphernalia related to the team came to bear the white elephant with its raised trunk. Check out the left sleeve of today's A's uniform, and you'll find an elephant there still. The A's won the American League in 1902, but the NL winners wouldn't play them. In 1905 the A's won the Junior Circuit again and fell to McGraw's Giants four games to one in the second World Series ever played. Christy Mathewson shut out the A's in Games 1, 3, and 5, allowing only fourteen hits in the three

contests. Mathewson and Joe McGinnity combined to pitch forty-four of the forty-five innings in the Series. But Mack would not be denied, nor would his Athletics. The man who managed the A's for fifty seasons (1901–50) proceeded to assemble his legendary $100,000 infield of 1909.

Josh: With today's league minimum at $400,000, a rookie shortstop makes that in forty games.

Kevin: Wow, that's almost as much as we'll make on the book.

Josh: Umm, right.

For the record, Mack's legendary infield had Stuffy McInnis at first, Eddie Collins at second, Jack Barry at short, and Frank "Home Run" Baker at third. Justifying the owner/manager's investment, the quartet led the A's to World Series wins in 1910, 1911, and 1913. Sweeter still, two of those October triumphs came against McGraw and the Giants. Baker earned his nickname by hitting an incredible eleven dingers during the 1911 season and two more in the World Series. Remember, this was before Babe Ruth. Freak pitches like the spitball had not yet been banned and the ball had not yet been made lively and white. It's been said of Mack that he fielded two kinds of teams: either unbeatable or horrible. After assembling his first dynasty, he just as quickly disbanded it, selling the best players off to other teams. The A's of the late 1910s and early 1920s wallowed in the cellar. Then Mack did it again, fielding what many argue was the greatest team ever in 1929. Led by Jimmie Foxx, known as the right-handed Babe Ruth or "Double X," the A's went 104-46 to win the pennant, and then defeated the Cubs in a five-game World Series. They repeated in 1930, downing the Cardinals in six. What was perhaps most impressive about that A's edition was how deftly it handled the Yankees: Ruth, Gehrig, and all. While the 1931 team won 107 games, led by Foxx, Al Simmons, and Lefty Grove—who posted an incredible 31–4 record—this time the A's were downed in the Series by the Cardinals.

The slide began for Mack's club again as he auctioned off his stars. The players he had developed went on to win pennants in other cities. The distinguished old man, who wore a suit and tie in the dugout to the very end, was getting old and his teams suffered. In 1943 the Athletics lost twenty games in a row, tying the AL record set by the 1906 Red Sox. The mark stood until 1988, when the Baltimore Orioles lost their first twenty-one. But it was not until 1950 that Mack left the dugout. The A's were eventually sold to Arnold Johnson in 1954 and moved to Kansas City the next year. Mack was the very soul of the Philadelphia A's, and perhaps things had changed for Philadelphians with Mack no longer at the helm. Finley, the team's second great owner, bought the A's while they were in KC, and tried to move them all over North America, but not before putting on a pretty good show in Kansas City.

In the A's first season in Oakland, Catfish Hunter hurled a perfect game against the Minnesota Twins on May 9, 1968. Not only was it the first perfect game in the American League in forty-six years, but Hunter drove in all three runs for the A's that day. Not a bad effort for the twenty-two-year-old right-hander who would one day see a plaque bearing his likeness raised in Cooperstown. As the A's became competitive again, Finley kept the ballpark atmosphere lively with promotions galore at the Coliseum. To kick off the 1970 season, the A's introduced gold-colored bases for their home games. Oh, that incorrigible Charlie O. Needless to say, bases colored anything but white were banned soon thereafter by the Rules Committee.

"Charlie O., the Mule" reappeared at the Coliseum, after first garnering fame in Kansas City. And video dot racing, where dots race around the scoreboard, debuted in Oakland under Finley. World-class sprinter Herb Washington served as Finley's "designated runner" during the 1974 and 1975 seasons. Washington played in 105 games without recording a single at-bat or ever appearing in the field. On the base paths he stole thirty-one bases in forty-eight attempts, while scoring thirty-three runs. It seems that Finley was awaiting Rickey Henderson, who would burst onto the scene in 1979, stealing bases quicker than Josh pockets coupons to Arby's. Rickey (we call him "Rickey" not out of disrespect, but because that is what he always called himself) went on to break the single-season steals mark in 1982 when he swiped 130 bags. Then he broke Ty Cobb's AL career record, stealing his 893rd base in 1990, and Lou Brock's all-time record by stealing his 939th in 1991. Then Rickey broke the only swipes record left, the world record of 1,065, held by Yutaka Fukumoto of Japan. There might have been a base stealer on Mars who stole more bases, but for our money Rickey is the greatest base stealer our universe has ever known. Rickey also holds the record for most homers to lead off a game with his eighty-one. His rare combination of power, speed, and charisma made him a first-ballot Hall of Famer in 2009.

After falling to Kirk Gibson and Orel Hershiser's Dodgers in the 1988 World Series, La Russa's A's won the "Bay Bridge Series" of 1989, but not before Game 3 at Candlestick Park was postponed by a massive earthquake that rocked the entire region. When the Series resumed twelve days later, the A's picked up where they left off, taking the final two games to complete the sweep. Staff ace Dave Stewart took home the MVP honors, pitching a five-hit shutout in the first game

and a three-run, five-hitter in the third. Stewart became the first pitcher in history to notch two wins in both the World Series and the ALCS. The next season the A's lost the 1990 Series in a four-game sweep against the underdog Reds.

After the departure of La Russa, Canseco, and McGwire, Oakland's solid player-development system continued to bring All-Star caliber talent to the bigs under Beane, whose economical approach to the game was chronicled in the book *Moneyball: The Art of Winning an Unfair Game,* by Michael Lewis and the subsequent movie starring Brad Pitt. But the A's haven't won a World Series since 1989. And with their fan support trailing off each and every year, and even middle-tier free agents eschewing their entreaties due to the poor condition of their facility, the franchise's days in Oakland appear numbered. It's like Kevin's friend Tim says, "It's easy to be an A's fan, but pretty difficult too." We know what he means. Without a new park, it becomes more difficult every year.

Trivia Timeout

Acorn: Which California Governor threw out the first pitch at Oakland-Alameda Coliseum's inaugural game in 1968?
Sapling: Which famous rapper was discovered by Charlie O. Finley dancing outside the Coliseum for ticket money?
Mighty Oak: Name the A's pitcher who appeared in all seven games of the 1973 World Series.
Look for the answers in the text.

Getting a Choice Seat

Getting a ticket to the O.co is not a problem. The stadium is big enough for you plus every other A's fan who decides to go to the game on the day you visit. The only time you might have difficulty getting inside is when the Giants are visiting for an interleague series or U2 is playing a stadium show. Why they don't take the green tarp off the upper level and sell more seats when the Giants visit is beyond us. They could. Those games sell out. Whereas you can get serious discounts for Giants tickets on StubHub (especially on weeknights), you can't really get lower than face value for A's tickets. Our working theory is that since there are so few A's season-ticket holders, no one has tickets to dump.

The design of the seating bowl provides a very gradual incline, which is something less than ideal for shorter fans like Josh who don't like it when they have to peer through a sea of heads. In fact, even Kevin found the effect annoying on the first level behind the plate.

Seating Capacity: 34,077
Ticket Office: http://oakland.athletics.mlb.com/ticketing/index.jsp?c_id=oak
Seating Chart: http://oakland.athletics.mlb.com/oak/ballpark/seating_chart_printable.jsp

More than that, the bowl is rounded, which positions the seats behind the plate fairly close to the action, but leaves the seats down the lines—as the circle extends outward—farther and farther away. This especially becomes a factor on the third level, where the tarp permanently covers the seats, preventing anyone from viewing the game from up here anyway.

Field Level

MVP BOX (FIRST TWENTY ROWS OF SECTIONS 109–125) & FIELD INFIELD (ROWS 21–38 OF SECTIONS 109–125)

The first twenty rows around the plate and extending out to the corner bases are the MVP Box seats and are the best your game-day dollar will buy. The O.co boasts the cheapest sweet seats in the bigs, so take advantage. Rows 21 and higher—where the gradual incline is less annoying—are even cheaper. Just be sure to avoid Rows 33 and above. It's not the overhang of the seating deck above that's the problem, but the supporting concrete structures that detract from sight lines. There's more trouble in Sections 122–123 and 111–113 where camera platforms hang down, further blocking views. Avoid all seats in these sections above Row 25.

LOWER BOX (FIRST TWENTY ROWS OF SECTIONS 103–108 AND 126–130) & FIELD LEVEL (ROWS 21–38 OF SECTIONS 101–108 AND 126–133)

Sections 101 and 102 have right-field foul-pole obstructions, but are otherwise decent. Sections 131 and 132 have left-field foul-pole obstructions and sit behind the BBQ Terrace so they're a little worse. Sections 101 and 133 are beside the terraced steps that give the ballpark its "coliseum feel." You can do better in this price tier, though, by aiming for Sections 107, 108, 126, and 127, which are practically on the infield.

BLEACHERS (SECTIONS 132–150)

While these are individual chairs, which is a good thing, they are raised pretty high up and feel far from the field. They're not nearly as good as the old bleachers before Mount Davis was built. Nonetheless, this is where many of the more rabid rooters sit, especially in left field. Drums beat and green-and-gold flags fly freely in Sections 134–139. Unfortunately, these folks can't see the warning track and many of the sections don't provide a straight-on view of the field.

Second Level

PLAZA CLUB (SECTIONS 212–214)

These Club Level seats hover over the visitors' on-deck circle on the first-base side. That's right, in a departure from tradition the A's dugout is on the third-base line instead of the first.

Josh: Do you suppose they put the ritzy seats here so fans can peer into the A's dugout?

Kevin: Is there anyone that exciting in there to see?

Josh: (peering inside) Not really. No.

PLAZA LEVEL INFIELD (SECTIONS 210–211 AND 215–224)

The second deck is hung close to the action, but doesn't give that awkward feeling of being right on top of the field, looking down. As a result of the curve of the circle, the Plaza Level Infield seats are much closer to the action than the other seats on the deck, and are well worth the extra coin.

PLAZA LEVEL (SECTIONS 205–209 AND 225–229)

These are significantly worse seats than their infield counterparts, not only because of the shape of the bowl, but because of the direction they face, which positions support structures between fans and the field in the back most rows.

PLAZA OUTFIELD (SECTIONS 200–204 AND 230–234)

These should really be avoided. Unless you're heading to the O.co for a World Series game (or that U2 concert), better tickets will be available on the first and second levels. These may be good football seats, but for baseball they're a swing and a miss.

PLAZA RESERVED (SECTIONS 235–249)

These second-tier bleacher seats span the outfield. They're a good choice if you're looking for a way inside the O.co for under ten bucks and don't mind seat-hopping once inside.

SEATING TIP

One way for autograph hounds to maximize their experience is to sit along the aisle in the first few rows of Section 115. Players walk past as they emerge from the tunnel leading from the clubhouse. Sitting here will put you in close contact with the players. Josh got Terrence Long and Chris Singleton to sign during our first visit to the Coliseum—two autographs that today, much to his chagrin, are valueless.

Loge Level

Most of the Loge Level is occupied by the Loge Suites, which are the O.co's luxury boxes. But Sections 1–3 and 65–66 at both ends of the field are available for single-game purchase. The problem is they're not good seats. It would be better to sit in one of the three Upper Deck sections they still open behind the plate. They are much cheaper and offer better sight lines.

Third Level

VALUE DECK (SECTIONS 316–318)

As mentioned, most of the upper deck is covered with big green tarps. But the A's do open three sections right behind the plate. The view is actually pretty good and the seats are dirt cheap.

Before/After the Game

Outside the sports complex, fans will find a downtrodden strip of unappealing run-down joints between the Coliseum and airport. Even the fast-food places are few and distant. We were heartened, though, to find a **Starbucks** on Edgewater Drive that was as clean and shiny as Starbucks joints always are. So maybe there's hope. Seriously, though, this is not a destination most fans will need too much time to explore. So what do folks do when there's no place to go out near the ballpark? They tailgate, of course. The tailgating scene in the team lots is modest but clearly the best option for those arriving at the stadium early. The parking lots are a bit too vast for any real camaraderie between grilling brethren, such as you'll find in Milwaukee. Plus, this is Oakland, bub, not the friendly Midwest. If you want free tailgating grub, you'd better be a hilarious drunk decked from head to toe in green and gold, or the AAA guy coming to offer someone a jump.

2 Legit 2 Quit

Hanging around outside the Coliseum in the 1970s, a kid from the neighborhood named Stanley Burrell got his first break in showbiz. He could be found dancing for ticket money on game days. Finley finally hired him because of his obvious talent and his ability to entertain. Burrell worked in a variety of capacities for the team, starting as batboy, and then one day Stanley Burrell blossomed and became better known to the world as MC Hammer. Think they've forgotten about Hammer in these parts? Think again. During the 2011 season the A's staged an MC Hammer Bobblehead giveaway that drew a pretty nice crowd.

> *Josh:* Hey, Kev, bet you can't touch this.
>
> *Kevin:* Are you really break dancing? No, I don't think that I would call that dancing.

Getting to the O.co

Take Interstate 880 from either direction to the 66th Avenue exit and follow the signs toward the Coliseum lots. These open two and a half hours before first pitch. If you're planning on tailgating, this is the way to go. In 2011, the A's instituted "Free Parking Tuesdays." Does that mean it's worth planning a trip to Oakland on a Tuesday just to save $17? Probably not. But if you're staying in San Fran and you happen to be going to a Tuesday game at the O.co, it might make driving to the game a more appealing option than taking the BART.

There are free parking spots available on the street near the BART station and in the BART parking lots, as well as on the other side of the stadium beyond Interstate 880. The BART spots get nabbed pretty quickly, so arrive early to park on the cheap. The spots near Interstate 880 are usually available. Our friend Anne, an Oakland resident, tells us the area can get pretty sketchy at night, so cheapskates beware.

Public Transportation is an excellent option in the Bay Area. Take the Fremont/ Richmond line of the BART to the Coliseum-Airport Station, and walk across the bridge to the stadium.

The BART, or simply "BART" as locals call it—omitting the definite article—stops at stations on either side of San Francisco Bay, including the aforementioned one right beside the Coliseum.

BART Map: www.bart.gov/stations/index.aspx

Outside Attractions

There couldn't be less to do outside the O.co. In contrast to the beautifully landscaped and fancifully adorned ballpark across the Bay, no statues rise outside as tributes to the great players of the A's glory years.

> *Kevin:* A Catfish Hunter statue would look great here.
>
> *Josh:* I'd settle for Terry Steinbach at this point.
>
> *Kevin:* Hey, Terry was an All-Star Game MVP. Don't knock him.

THEY CONSIDER THIS BANNER DECOR?

Green-and-gold A's banners decorate the exterior ramps and facade. At the end of the hurricane-fence-lined entrance bridge from the BART to the stadium (which is topped by some very attractive barbed wire), one such banner lists the four World Championship years in Oakland: 1972, 1973, 1974, and 1989.

Watering Holes and Outside Eats

Oak-Town has great sports bars and plenty of places to get a meal on the cheap. And if you don't mind the overall seediness of International Boulevard, you can make your way to a strip of good taquerias on the drive to the stadium. These include **El Huarache Azteca** (3842 International Blvd.), **Taqueria Del Oro** (5801 International Blvd.), **Taqueria San Jose** (3433 International Blvd.), **La Costa** (3625 International Blvd.), and **Tacos Guadalajara** (4400 International Blvd.). You'll also find taco trucks like the **Casa Jimenez** food truck at 4345 International Blvd., which had as tasty a bean-and-cheese pupusa as either of us had eaten in a while. If you're hankering for a burger, though, unfortunately the once-famous Coliseum Burger has closed. But there is an **In & Out Burger** at 8300 Oakport St.

HEINOLD'S FIRST AND LAST CHANCE SALOON
56 Jack London Sq.
http://firstandlastchance.com/

While most of the joints in Jack London Square are a tad too trendy and pricey for our tastes, Johnny Heinold's is a noteworthy exception. Jack London actually drank and wrote in this iconic saloon, and that gives it all the street cred it needs with us. Called "first and last" because it was the closest watering hole to the docks, it served passengers heading in or out of town. London listened to tales of drunken sailors who had traveled the world and then tweaked their stories slightly. Okay, we made that last part up. But London did drink, chat, and write here.

LUKA'S TAP ROOM
2221 Broadway
www.lukasoakland.com

A bit more upscale than your average sports bar, Luka's is still a good place to watch a game. The beer selection is amazing. We especially love the Belgians. The burger, macaroni and cheese, and sweet potato fries are all excellent.

LOIS THE PIE QUEEN
851 60th St.

This famous North Oakland establishment is famous not only for its many delicious pie selections, but also for its Reggie Jackson breakfast. Two fried pork chops, eggs, and

grits kept "Mr. October" swinging all day long, and we bet you'll belt a few over the wall after eating here as well. They also have fried chicken, beef sausage, fried rib-eye steaks, biscuits, and a range of other stick-to-your-ribs breakfast treats.

ROCKRIDGE/COLLEGE AVENUE AREA

Rockridge will tickle your fancy if you dig hitting multiple pubs within a short walk of one another. College Avenue runs toward Berkeley and is loaded with coffeehouses, burrito shacks, restaurants, and trendy shops. **George and Walt's** (5445 College Ave.) is a dive favored by Raiders' fans, with cheap beer and stiff drinks. **Ben & Nick's** (5612 College Ave.), right next to the Rockridge BART station, makes a yummy half-pound burger as well as a sliced beef and Swiss sandwich named after President Obama, and if you wear the kitschy T-shirt from the bar and its sister joint, **Cato's Ale House** (3891 Piedmont Ave.), you get a discount. Bright green **McNally's Irish Pub** (5352 College Ave.) boasts that it's the premier Irish Bar in the East Bay, and we can't disagree. Off the beaten path is **Kingfish Pub and Café** (5227 Claremont), which resides in an old bait shop. Tickets from sporting events from all around the Bay Area adorn the walls. Kevin could hardly resist a dive bar with live music and sports memorabilia that also serves a great pint of Guinness.

Inside the Coliseum

Like any stadium its size, the O.co can be a rocking place when it's full. When empty, though, it has all the charm of a rock quarry. Oak-Town loves a winner and hates a loser. So if the A's are in the thick of the AL West race, expect fans to be crazier than Milton Bradley after spending two hours on a plane beside Carl Everett. If the A's are struggling, you can at least enjoy the ease of getting a choice seat and the spectacle of the few crazies who have dedicated their lives—or at least their summers—to the A's. While we've stated many times before that facilities attempting to accommodate two sports always short-change baseball, this is not entirely the case in Oakland. Though the dimensions are symmetrical and Mount Davis is a huge intrusion, the Coliseum still feels something like a baseball field. A real dirt warning track and a grass field contribute much to the atmosphere. Plus, the traditional green wall with yellow foul poles and home run lines gives the park an authentic look while reflecting the team colors.

Kevin: There's nothing worse than a ballpark with orange foul poles.

Josh: I still have nightmares about the foul nets they used to hang in Montreal.

Kevin: I still have nightmares about the poutine.

Ballpark Features

STEAL A HOMER, WIN NIGHT IN JAIL

Fans unlucky enough to be sitting near the foul poles have one opportunity for revenge. Due to the curve of the wall and positioning of the poles, they can lean out and catch a fair home run ball. Just be careful. It is strictly prohibited. A ballpark usher told us so. And Alameda County Jail is no place to spend the night. Then again, neither was the discount hotel near the airport that Josh booked for our stay in Oakland.

THE DEATH STAR

Our friend Matthew calls Mount Davis "the Death Star," and we can see why. The memory of its singing construction workers notwithstanding, the structure has permanently compromised the atmosphere of the park. Where once there were real bleachers, a walking terrace, and baseball pennants flying from flags, now stands nothing but gray cement and green seats and plastic sheeting as high as the eye can see. All views of the Oakland Hills are blocked by this "monster of rock" designed to maximize football luxury boxes. Even during the A's most recent trips to the playoffs they couldn't sell the seats atop the structure. For baseball, the altitudinous grandstand serves no useful purpose but to house yet another giant green tarp.

BULLPENS BEWARE!

Josh: Hey, there are no bullpens.

Kevin: The relievers warm up in foul territory like at Wrigley. You said it was "quaint and old-timey" when you saw it there.

Josh: Are you comparing the O.co to Wrigley Field?

FLY YOUR FLAG

The A's world championship banners fly proudly above the power alleys, behind the 367-foot markers on both the left- and right-field sides.

Kevin: What I wouldn't give for just one of those flying in Seattle.

Josh: Keep dreaming, pal.

Kevin: You know, I'm starting to understand why people are hating on the Red Sox and their fans these days.

TARP TRIVIA

Rather than just smothering the upper level with a basic Lowe's-style green tarp, the A's have gone to some small effort to make better use of all that space. White-and-blue ovals appear on the tarps to celebrate special years when the A's won the World Series. These date back to the team's years in Philadelphia. The first such marker remembers 1910, while the last recalls 1989.

GOLDEN AND MASSIVE

Gold-colored retired numbers are painted onto the tarp across Mount Davis to honor A's greats since their arrival in Oakland. These include No. 34 for Rollie Fingers, who was a four-time All-Star with the A's, from 1973 to 1976, and was the MVP of the 1974 World Series; No. 27 for Hunter, who began his career with the Kansas City A's in 1965 and won a Cy Young Award in Oakland in 1974; No. 24 for Henderson, who stole every base he saw; No. 43 for Eckersley, who saved fifty-one games and won a Cy Young and AL MVP Award with the A's in 1992; and No. 9 for Jackson, who was the 1973 MVP.

HOF

Down the right-field line on the 300 Level, the Oakland Sports Hall of Fame honors local sons and daughters who excelled in a variety of sports. Among those in bronze are Jackson, Martin, Curt Flood, and Willie Stargell.

Game Time for Bonzo

Back when the Coliseum first opened and looked more like a baseball park, California governor Ronald Reagan threw out the first pitch of the inaugural game on April 17, 1968. The A's lost 4-1 to the Baltimore Orioles.

LOW-TECH

In light of all the massive high-def boards popping up at other ballparks, we were struck by how small the video screens are. They're too small to allow a view of replays and the scoreboard is too small to list the players of both lineups. Instead, they only list the lineup of the team at bat (player numbers only, so you better have a media guide). They have flat-screen TVs in some of the concession areas, but the picture is not high-def and it's a little bit fuzzy. The TV monitors for fans in obstructed seats are old monitors, not flat-screen and certainly not high-def.

The Birth of Free Agency

Baseball before 1974 was a very different game, at least as far as the owners were concerned. MLB had the "reserve clause" in place, which bound players to their teams and gave them no say in where they could be traded. That is, until former St. Louis Cardinals outfielder (and Oakland-raised) Curt Flood wrote a letter to baseball Commissioner Bowie Kuhn in 1969, objecting to a transaction. The trade would have sent Flood, along with catcher Tim McCarver, pitcher Joe Hoerner, and outfielder Byron Browne to Philadelphia, for first baseman Dick Allen, infielder Cookie Rojas, and pitcher Jerry Johnson. Flood's refusal to report to Philadelphia resulted in a lawsuit against MLB, challenging the legality of the system that gave players no say in where they worked or for whom.

Flood lost his lawsuit, which went to the Supreme Court, and was traded to the Phillies anyway. The reserve clause survived, at least temporarily. Flood sat out the 1970 season, played a bit in 1971 with the Washington Senators, then retired after only a few games. He spent the 1978 season with the A's in the broadcasting booth. But the defiance he showed had started a quiet revolution that would not be put down. The first free agent would depart Oakland in 1974, after an arbitrator ruled that a breach of Catfish Hunter's contract by Finley invalidated the entire contract, including the reserve clause. With his contract invalidated, Hunter could pursue a contract with any team he chose. Free agency as we know it was born. Steinbrenner & Co. bought the rights to Hunter, signing him to a deal worth $3.75 million. Mind you, Steinbrenner had purchased the entire Yankees franchise for only $10 million. Incidentally, a 2010 Forbes report valued the Yankees at $1.6 billion today, which means Steinbrenner's investment appreciated at 16,000 percent. But we digress.

After Hunter's deal, free agency became a part of the game. And though the reserve clause was unfair, we can't help but think that what has resulted from free agency—paying a middling starter $12 million a year to finish a few games under .500—is not good for the game. In their quest to win, owners now compete with one another to pay even mediocre free agents ridiculous sums. Under other circumstances, the unbridled inflation of salaries wouldn't bother us so much. But these costs have been passed on to the fans at a time when many of us don't exactly have piles of cash to spend at the ballpark. In other words, we pay more because the players make so much, and we don't like it.

Is it any surprise that before free agency only Busch Stadium was named after a corporation, but since then, in order to remain competitive and keep up with skyrocketing payrolls, teams have had to pimp themselves out like two-bit street corner hussies? So as a matter of helping baseball keep the common folk like us interested in the game, we offer a not-so-simple solution: How about getting real and striking a compromise at the next bargaining session? Free agency has not had a completely positive impact on the game from the fans' perspective. Nor do we believe that going back to the rigid reserve clause is the answer either. The luxury tax on big-spending teams' payrolls currently in place is a good idea that channels some funds from big market teams to smaller ones, but the "tax" rate should be higher on teams like the Red Sox and Yankees, while teams like the Royals and Pirates should be forced to invest that found money in players or their player development system, or their ballpark, instead of just pocketing the cash to puff up their balance sheets. Tweaking the system will go a long way to repairing how fans feel about the players, owners, and the game. Remember, baseball is a game that we fans try our best to love. And it's easier to love the game when money, greed, and politics remain as far from the field as possible.

Stadium Eats

While the restaurant scene in the neighborhood outside is poor at best, the food inside is pretty good.

LINGUISA SANDWICH (TRADEMARK FOOD)

Oakland specialty meat-maker Saag's operates two stands at the O.co—behind Sections 118 and 223. At these locations fans scoop up several varieties of freshly made and freshly grilled sausages that come topped with onions and fried peppers. The options include Atomic Hot Links, Louisiana Hot Links, Polish, Italian, Bratwurst, and, most delightfully of all, Linguisa.

This Portuguese sausage is both smoky and spicy. Josh used to eat the stuff in great abundance during his college years whenever he'd visit his friend Matt Guilbeault in New Bedford, Massachusetts, where they even put linguisa on their pizza.

Kevin: So how does this compare to the linguisa of your glory years?

Josh: Float me six bucks, I need to get another.

MILLER'S DOGS (DOG REVIEW)

Thicker than nearly every other dog in the Majors and certainly juicier, the all-beef Miller's dogs are grilled to perfection. Prepared the same way since 1910, these delicious dogs made us want to skip all of the other ballpark treats and have another. And if we didn't have to sample all the rest of the offerings for the purposes of this book, that's exactly what we would have done. For big eaters who do want to skip the rest, we recommend the one-third-of-a-pound "big dog."

BEST OF THE REST

Red's All-Star Smoke House (Section 104) serves ribs and pulled meat sandwiches, while **Rosa's Fresh Mexican** (Section 115) is not greasy and is, well, fresh. Score one for truth in advertising. We also recommend the **Burrito Bowl. The Burger Shack** (Section 132) offers cheeseburgers, fast-food-style french fries and Texas Grilled Cheese. It may not be Coliseum Burger—a joint that used to cater to fans just outside—but it's pretty good. The **Monster Chicken Nachos** come loaded with chicken and will keep you busy for a couple of innings anyway. Although you may be all-garlicked-out if you caught a game across the Bay the night before, the **Garlic Fries** at the O.co are awfully good too. As our friend Anne says, "Beware of the garlic hangover," or in other words, have a bottle of Scope on hand for the morning. We tried the **Bacon and Meatloaf Sandwich** (Section 113), which comes with hand-cut bacon, jalapeno meatloaf, sharp cheddar cheese, and crispy fried onions on a brioche bun, and were impressed. Josh put ketchup on his half while Kevin ate his dry.

STADIUM SUDS

Shock Top, Corona, Dos Equis, Blue Moon, Sierra Nevada, Trumer Pils, Lagunitas, Widmer, Heineken, Kona, Fat Tire, Gordon Biersch, Sierra Nevada, and Pyramid Ale top the surprisingly impressive ballpark brew list. For ladies and gents who live by the adage "liquor is quicker," the mixed drinks at the O.co are stiff and will treat you right.

THE FIELD—IRISH PUB

The very idea of an Irish Pub might seem at odds with the O.co ethos, especially considering that most of the Irish in these parts settled across the Bay. Though not the authentic Irish pub experience offered at, say, The Plow and Stars in San Fran, we commend the A's for their attempt. And Jameson's tastes the same no matter where it's served. The Guinness came in a plastic cup, and even so, it was not the worst pint Kevin had ever sampled.

Kevin: Here's to Connie Mack! And Charlie O. Finley!

Josh: And to Charlie O., the Mule!

THE WEST IS THE BEST

The huge East Club buried inside Mount Davis and the equally enormous West Club behind home plate on the 200 Level open their doors to plebeians such as us during the game. Full meals are served at the tables, complete with white tablecloths and views of the action. And the bar is open as well.

Josh: I still would rather be down near the field.

Kevin: Me too. Let's get outta here.

The O.co Experience

Oakland is a city with an East Coast mentality stuck out West. It's a hard-nosed town that loves its sports teams, so expect a rabid fan base to reemerge if and when the A's finally get their new ballpark and a winning team to go with it. The game-day tradition of donning green and gold is carried on to an extreme, as you'll notice even the average fan with his hair dyed or his face painted as you settle into your ballpark seat. He may be wearing yellow socks too! Any jersey with the right tint of green will do, regardless of what it says. Green Bay Packers fans may want to wear their cheese-head garb and call it "close enough." Kevin tried wearing one of his old Seattle SuperSonics basketball jerseys, which the locals seemed to perceive more as an ironic gesture than any kind of political statement, though one guy yelled, "This is Oak-Town, not Oklahoma City."

Oakland fans care deeply about their team and will boo even the greenest of their club's rookies when they fail to deliver. In fact we saw a kid with a mitt drop a batting-practice line drive out near the foul pole that was hit pretty hard. He was harassed unmercifully by two ushers for the drop. "You shoulda brung two mitts wit ya," one of them yelled derisively. And that brings us to the topic of the ushers. They weren't particularly friendly to us. Not that they owed us anything, but we like to strike up conversations or at least say friendly hellos to the people we meet along the way and when we were at the O.co, neither the ushers nor the attendant at the ticket window were particularly pleasant. In this era when there's plenty of competition for customers' entertainment dollars, user-friendliness is one area in which the A's might care to invest a little more effort. Like we said, the O.co has more of an East Coast vibe.

THE A'S DRUM AND FLAG CORPS (SUPER-FANS)

The left-field bleachers house the most famous A's fans, though the Drum and Flag Corps can be seen and heard anywhere in the Coliseum. On most summer nights, an entire row of mad flag-waving fans hoist their green and gold banners into the air over the railing, blowing horns and chanting obscenities, while behind them sit the A's drummers, banging away at their broken down tom-toms with reckless abandon. They drum nothing special, a simple three-beat "Let's Go, A's." But their enthusiasm and sheer volume are infectious. So popular did the drummers get at one point, that the team gave them all season tickets and used them in a series of TV ads. During the 2001 playoffs, Steinbrenner so feared the A's that he tried to steal their mojo by having the drummers removed. He said that since they didn't pay for their season tickets they were actually "employees of the team" bent on distracting his hitters. Though their season tickets may have been taken away because of this, the drummers remain, beating their skins. Though now they can only drum while the A's are hitting.

Josh: Is that the same guy who was banging a drum for dollars on the bridge outside?

Kevin: Trust me when I say "No."

When we visited in 2011 we observed these guys waving plenty of signs critical of management and of the notion the A's might relocate to greener pastures. But no one from the A's staff tried to remove them from the game. For example, one read, "Wolff Lied, He Never Tried" and another said, "Don't Take Our A's Away!"

Cyber Super-Fans

- **New A's Ballpark**
  http://newballpark.org/
  This amazingly comprehensive website has been providing daily updates about the A's new ballpark quest since 2005. It lists each new game's paltry attendance at the Coliseum and updates how many days it's been since the A's began exploring the idea of a new park. We applaud the effort and hope it eventually pays off in the form of a beautiful new park somewhere on the Bay.

GIVE ME A "Y"! GIVE ME AN "M"!

The nationwide ballpark phenomenon that has seen fans spell out "YMCA" with their bodies as they sing along with The Village People began in Oakland when construction workers were building Mount Davis. One day the working men started dressing like the Village People and using their bodies to spell out letters and the fans followed their lead.

Josh: So not only do we have those workers to thank for Mount Davis but for that annoying song too?

Kevin: At least they didn't start the wave.

Sports in the City

The Oakland Public League

Oakland attracted much of its African American population during and after World War II because of the jobs available in the shipyards. And because baseball was king back then, the Oakland Public League became a hotbed of talent. Future ballplayers who weren't necessarily born within the Oakland city limits but came of age there during their high school years form an impressive list that includes Rickey Henderson, Joe Morgan, Dennis Eckersley, Dave Stewart, Ruppert Jones, Gary Pettis, Willie McGee, Lloyd Moseby, Kenny Williams, Claudell Washington, Frank Robinson, Curt Flood, Vada Pinson, Jimmy Rollins, and Dontrelle Willis.

The decline of baseball in the inner city has given way to basketball being the new pastime of choice on the urban scene. Oakland has adopted this tradition too, sending such locals as Bill Russell, Gary Payton, and Jason Kidd to the Association.

IT ALL "ADS" UP

If you look into the dugouts you'll see advertising wallpapered all over the place. And you'll see company logos smothering the outfield walls and facades too. The ads are everywhere.

Kevin: At least they bring some color to all this concrete.

Josh: And ballpark ads are as ancient as the game itself. Back in the 1940s Fenway's Green Monster was covered.

Kevin: Not with ads for virus protection software.

Josh: C'mon. Virus protection and baseball go together like hotdogs and ketchup.

Kevin: You mean mustard.

Josh: Whatever.

While We Were in Oakland
Josh Went Native

Our seats were on the second deck, and not in the good part. So we decided to walk around and see if we could do a little creative upgrading. We wound up down the left-field line quite a ways, but with an improved view over where we started.

"Those drums are really distracting," Josh said.

"But I kinda wish Seattle had a tradition like that," Kevin said.

"Well that kind of thing would never fly in Boston, I'll tell ya that."

"You're right. Way too uptight in Beantown."

"It's not that we're uptight," replied Josh, "we just have better taste."

"All uptight people always claim they are acting uptight in the name of good taste," said Kevin.

We continued watching the game, which turned "out to be quite a pitchers" battle. Gio Gonzalez was on the mound against the Royals, and he was spinning a beauty. He had only given up one hit through four, but the score remained tied at zero. But Josh was distracted by the drummers, fidgeting in his seat. And because Josh was distracted, Kevin was distracted.

"Don't those guys know anything besides Let's Go A's? Bap-Bap-Bap?"

"Who are you, a long lost Steinbrenner? Let the kids drum if it makes 'em happy."

But Josh's head kept turning from the game and over to the drumming.

"Hold my binocs. I'm going to get something to drink," he said at last. "This pretzel's making me thirsty."

"Bring me a beer," Kevin shouted after Josh as he walked up the aisle.

After half an hour, Kevin started to wonder about his friend. "Probably never get my beer," he muttered.

By the time the seventh inning stretch rolled around, Kevin, who is not one prone to worry about much of anything, began to get concerned about Josh. As the locals sat back down after a rousing rendition of YMCA, Kevin stood up, raised Josh's binoculars, and had a look around the Coliseum. He searched the ballpark over, but he couldn't locate Josh. Eventually, he sat back down.

Finally Kevin decided to get himself a beer before last call, and at the end of the inning he headed to the top of the concourse. The beer stand behind the section didn't sell Pyramid, so Kevin moved on until he found one that did. He wound up near the foul pole where he stopped to watch the game as he sipped the foam off his beverage. The A's had begun to pull away, opening a four run lead.

Though his eyes were on the game, Kevin caught a glimpse of Josh in his periphery. Josh had not only found a way down into the left-field bleachers, but he was pounding away on a drum like a madman. He stood shirtless above the tom-tom, beating the skins as if his life depended on it. Kevin tried to get down to the section to meet up with his friend. But a security guard stopped him. He could only stand there at the top of the concourse and watch in shock.

After the game Josh met up with Kevin at the original seats, the bad ones on the second level, wearing his Red Sox shirt once again.

"Have fun?" Kevin asked.

"Sure," Josh said. "I sampled a couple more sausages at Saag's and checked out the view from the third deck."

"That's it?" Kevin asked, knowingly.

"Oh yeah, I tried the macaroni and cheese hotdog too."

"You didn't do anything else?"

"I peed twice," Josh said, growing suspicious.

To his credit, Kevin let the matter drop. He had spied the Mr. Hyde buried somewhere deep within his ordinarily uptight friend but didn't reveal his new knowledge . . . until right now!

SAN FRANCISCO GIANTS, AT&T PARK

Restoration of a Winning Tradition

San Francisco's baseball fans seem to have access to their own private genie lately. Not only did they build one of the grandest stadiums in the Grand Old Game, but they managed to break their fifty-six-year drought and win their first World Series since the franchise left New York. Though it was an unlikely band of rag-tags and journeymen that pulled off the seemingly impossible in 2010, that win and playing in a ballpark as majestic and beautiful as AT&T Park have restored the team and its fans to their rightful place in the game—as winners. After all, the franchise has more wins to its name than any team in North American professional sports history. Yes, that includes the Yankees, but the Giants, who formed in 1883, had a bit of a head-start on them, since the Pinstripes didn't start playing until 1901 and thus rank only eighth on baseball's all-time wins list. As for the Giants' recent winning ways . . . if you didn't believe in feng shui— the Chinese belief that living somewhere that's in harmony with heaven and earth improves your fortune—then AT&T Park and the return of the Giants' winning tradition just might convince you.

First off, AT&T Park could scarcely be in a better location. Few ballparks in history can boast better views both inside and out than AT&T Park does. Built at the water's edge on glimmering San Francisco Bay, and part of the formerly aging warehouse district called China Basin, AT&T Park fulfills Giants fans' vision of a downtown ballpark on the Bay. And better still, this yard is shielded from the bitter evening winds that tormented the Giants and their fans when the team played at Candlestick Park. The ballpark is nearly perfect, and is truly the culmination of Bay Area fans' most fantastic and idyllic dreams.

AT&T was designed to fit on a thirteen-acre parcel of industrially zoned land owned by the San Francisco Port Commission, to whom the Giants still pay an annual lease. With the water of the bay just beyond the right-field wall, this ballpark comes by its eccentric short porch in right field (309 feet to the corner) very naturally. There are no quirks for quirks' sake at AT&T, as have been engineered and manufactured at so many other ballparks of the retro renaissance. Rather, this ballyard was designed—oddities and all—in the same manner as Fenway Park, the Polo Grounds, and all of the clunky but endearing ballparks of old: by building it into the space available. And the result is a gem of a field, with distinctions and idiosyncrasies that are honest, unforced, and far more beautiful than had the quirks been added simply because of some regrettable notion conceived during the post-dome and cookie-cutter eras that they were missing.

Also as a result of the limited available space, the upper-seating structure rises very steeply, getting in as many seats as is reasonably possible. The structure extends down the right-field line to the foul pole on the lowest level, but only three quarters of that distance in the upper deck, angling back obliquely to where it, too, meets the waters of McCovey Cove (so named after Hall of Famer and Giants fan favorite Willie McCovey). The entire seating structure on the left-field side extends to the foul pole and wraps around the outfield as one might expect. The overall impression is that the park would have been built symmetrically if that had been possible, but that things were cut short down the right-field line out of necessity. But the quirks that the space limitations have created in the ballpark have resulted in its distinctive design and local flavor. And who can argue that this park is something special, something unique, something so very San Franciscan?

The story of how the "Miracle on 3rd Street" came to be is as heartwarming to us as the Christmas tale of a similar title. With the Giants faltering throughout the 1970s and 1980s, and playing their games in the cold and clammy Candlestick Park, talk of moving the team to another city would arise every few years. Real estate mogul Bob Lurie bought the team in 1976 specifically to save it from being sold to

exterior view from McCovey Cove

Photo by Kevin O'Connell

a Canadian brewery that intended to move the Giants to Toronto. During his ownership, which lasted until 1993, Lurie would make countless unsuccessful attempts to get a ballpark built downtown, but there was little political will. Finally and reluctantly, Lurie agreed to sell the Giants to a group of investors who planned to move the team to Tampa Bay, the often publicized Holy Grail of baseball relocation destinations. The transaction was nearly complete, but in an eleventh-hour deal a local investment group headed by grocery store magnate Peter Magowan kept the team in San Francisco.

Magowan and his partners knew that the long-term security of the franchise in the city rested on building a downtown ballpark. And so "Proposition B" came before the voting public, which proposed building a ballpark in the China Basin district of downtown San Francisco, which would be the first completely privately funded ballpark in baseball since Dodger Stadium opened in 1962.

Over the next several years, sponsorship agreements were secured with companies that ranged from Anheuser-Busch to Visa and Old Navy, and many others that would eventually help finance the ballpark. Naming rights were purchased by Pacific Bell Telephone and Telegraph Company for $50 million over ten years. Then, Pac Bell was bought by SBC Communications, and so the ballpark was renamed SBC Ballpark in 2004. Just when the ink on the new signage was dry, it all had to come down again, as SBC (Southwestern Bell Company) Communications bought out its parent company AT&T, and changed its name to AT&T, Inc. The newly re-conglomerated AT&T took on the corporate logo of the old, and the ballpark got a new name.

Kevin: Any of this ringing a bell?

Josh: Stop phoning in the jokes, please.

In addition, fifteen thousand prime seats were sold on a lifetime basis to thick-walleted fat cats for big money.

Kevin: It's a good thing all these corporate sponsorships and seats sold to wealthy dot-com-ers in the nineties. If it were today, the park might not have been built.

Josh: Yeah, Enron was one of those sponsors.

With the noted firm HOK signed as the architects, San Franciscans felt they were going to get something special in the design of AT&T Park. They had no idea how special. Ground was broken on December 11, 1997. In August 1998 the official address of the ballpark changed from One Willie Mays Plaza to 24 Willie Mays Plaza, in reference to the number worn by the "Say Hey Kid" as a Giant. By the time construction had finished, the ballpark cost $318 million to build.

The first game at the new park pitted the Giants against their archrivals, the Dodgers, on April 11, 2000. Unfortunately for the Giants, the Dodgers won 6–5, but it was an exciting game as the teams combined for six home runs, setting a record for a ballpark inaugural. Another record, though rather dubious, came when the Giants lost their first six games at their new home. But fan support never faltered, as Giants rooters kept turning out to see the superb new ballpark that sold out every single game of its first season. More than 3.3 million fans visited the park in 2000, and they were rewarded when the Giants captured the National League West title.

Though reviews of the new park's beauty and setting were glowing from the start, perhaps the most significant improvement fans noticed over Candlestick Park was the weather. AT&T, though located on the very same bay as "the Stick," is affected far less severely by the notoriously chilly evening winds that besieged fans at the Giants' former home. Prior to construction, an environmental review process showed that if the ballpark orientation was turned at a certain angle, the wind off the water would be minimized by a staggering degree. Plus the location of China Basin simply has milder weather than Candlestick Point.

These revelations have made all the difference in a city known for its "outdoor air conditioning." As Mark Twain once commented, "The coldest winter I ever spent, was a summer in San Francisco." Thankfully technology and environmental awareness have lessened the effects of the wind, cold, and fog that plagued Candlestick. However, after a nice San Francisco summer's day, it can still be awfully chilly standing on the exterior concourse of AT&T, but inside the ballpark a comfortable environment for baseball awaits. Who says you can't control the weather? See what we mean when we say genie?

Despite these pleasant developments, since moving into AT&T, the Giants have seen their share of heartbreak as well. In 2002, in a World Series that pitted the Giants of northern California against their cultural and geographic rivals, the Anaheim Angels in the southern part of the state, the Giants were leading the series three games to two entering Game 6. The Giants had just crushed the Angels 16-4 in Game 5, and all was looking up in San Fran. Taking a 5-0 lead into the bottom of the 7th inning, manager Dusty Baker inexplicably took the ball out of pitcher Russ Ortiz's hands, though Ortiz had been masterful on the mound. Reliever Felix Rodriguez gave up a three-run shot to Scott Spiezio that not only propelled the Angels to a 6-5 victory in Game 6, but also a Game 7 victory to win the World Series

the following night. It also propelled Scott Spiezio to an ill-advised musical career with his band Sandfrog.

It was an epic collapse, and one that cost Dusty Baker and many other Giants their jobs.

Kevin: I watched that game with my good buddy and long-suffering Giants' fan, Paul Schmitz. After being up by five in the seventh, I think he finally started to believe it was the Giants' year.

Josh: You think I don't know how he feels? Bill Buckner, my friend.

Kevin: Yeah, well the Sox and the Giants have both since got their World Series. What have the Mariners got, except the two worst seasons of Scott Spiezio's career?

But there was still more tragedy to be snatched from the jaws of victory for the City by the Bay. Hometown hero Barry Bonds went on to break Hank Aaron's all-time home run record, posting 762 dingers by 2007. It was a record that nary anyone outside of San Francisco wanted Bonds to break, but break it he did. Bonds hit number 756 to surpass Aaron before an adoring AT&T fan base that didn't want to believe the rumors of his alleged steroid and HGH use. San Franciscans wanted the moment to be theirs. They wanted their native son to make good. And they wanted it to happen in the ballpark with the short right-field porch that had been built specifically with Bonds' left handed bat in mind.

Action from the left-field line.
Photo by Matthew Schmitz

And while San Franciscans got what they wanted in the short term, the public opinion on Bonds and his record would continue to sour, until finally, not one team would offer the newly minted HR king a contract. Not one American League team in need of a designated slugger who could surely hit twenty-five HRs and put butts in the seats could find a space on its roster for Bonds. Not even the Tampa Bay Rays, who welcomed admitted juicers Jose Canseco and Manny Ramirez to their roster, would take Bonds.

After blowing up the party in Bonds's honor, the hangover hit San Francisco pretty hard. Though many clung to the fact that Bonds was never convicted of steroid use, he was convicted of obstructing justice. And in the court of public opinion, he remains guilty as sin. The Giants responded by quietly taking down the tributes to Bonds and the accomplishments they once lauded so enthusiastically at AT&T Park. After the 2008 season, no longer could Bonds's image be seen without evoking a wince. No longer was the number 756 as mythical, magical, and visible as it had been just a season before. In fact, the quiet was deafening.

As for the Giants' longtime owner Mr. Magowan, though he tried to deliver a championship before his tenure at the helm ended, he could not. Upon his retirement, a new ownership group led by William Horlick "Bill" Neukom, a former president of the American Bar Association and longtime legal counsel for the Microsoft Corporation, took over.

Kevin: There's no joke here.

Josh: You're telling me a middle name like Horlick is no joke?

After the Barry Bonds/Peter Magowan era ended in San Francisco, it wasn't long before the Giants returned to their winning ways. Their 2010 march to the World Series was as unlikely as it was captivating to watch. A team filled with has-beens and castoffs, names such as Aubrey Huff, Juan Uribe, Cody Ross, and Edgar Renteria, joined forces with young talents like Buster Posey and Tim Lincecum, and a few oddballs such as Brian Wilson (not the Beach Boy, the bearded one) and (again) Lincecum, to win one of the most improbable World Series matchups in recent memory.

At the onset of the 2010 season, more experts picked Charlie Sheen to give up drinking than picked the Giants to make the playoffs. However, when the baseball gods smile on a team, it can seem as if no matter what that team does, it marches on toward destiny. That smile from above became visibly apparent through the foggy skies of San Francisco during August 2010. Examples of the preordination of the 2010 Giants included:

- *The Padres lost ten straight games beginning in late August, while the Giants won eighteen out of twenty-six during September. As the teams battled back and forth for first place, they entered their final series of the year pitted against one another, with the Giants needing only a single win during the three-game set to clinch the division. After losing the first two games, they won the third, in a winner-take-all match that would send the Padres home for the off-season.*

- *Paired against the Braves in the NLDS, late-season pickup Cody Ross, who'd had an uneventful regular season, spoiled Derek Lowe's Game 3 no-hit bid in the top of the sixth with a first-pitch home run to tie the game 1-1. It seemed to be the fuel the Giants needed, because after they lost the lead in the bottom of the inning, Juan Uribe notched a bases-loaded fielder's choice to score one run, which was followed by a Cody Ross single to score two more and lock down the win.*

- *Up next came the NLCS against a Phillies team practically everyone had picked to win it all before the season began. However, the unlikely Giants somewhere along the line had found their swagger, and their playoff train was rolling downhill and picking up speed. Game 4 was pivotal, and all tied up going into the bottom of the ninth, when the Phillies brought in Roy Oswalt for a rare relief appearance. A Posey single sent Huff to third with only one out. Up to the plate came Uribe to pinch-hit, and he hit a long fly to left that scored Huff for the win as the Giants took a 3-1 series lead they would not relinquish.*

- *Entering Game 1 of the World Series, the Giants had to face Cliff Lee. The Rangers lefty carried a record of post-season perfection to the mound not seen since the reign of Sandy Koufax. Fueled by a three-run dinger by (you guessed it) Uribe, the Giants managed to do what the Yankees, Rays— and let's face it, every other team in baseball—could not do: make Cliff Lee stumble. Lee gave up seven runs to the Giants, and that set the tone for the Series.*

- *To finish the Series off with a poetic touch, we give you "the Barranquilla Baby," Renteria, whose $18-million-plus deal had been maligned for two seasons because of his advanced age and low production. Down in the Series 3-1 at home, and with Lincecum and Lee back on the mound, the Rangers were against the ropes. After joking with former teammate Andres Torres, Renteria crushed a seventh inning shot off Lee to deep center field that cleared the fence and put the Giants up 3-0. Lincecum combined with the bearded one, Brian Wilson, to secure the World Championship for San Francisco.*

Though there were exciting moments in the 2010 World Series, the Giants never made their fans sweat all that much. Somehow, they always showed up with the pitching performance or hit they needed at just the time they needed it most. Renteria, who hit .412 with two home runs in the Series, won the Series MVP award. He also became only the fourth player in MLB history to get the winning hit in two different World Series. Remember, it was a younger and spryer Barranquilla Baby who got the walk-off single for the Florida Marlins way back in 1997. Renteria's efforts and those of his teammates in 2010 managed to accomplish what Willie Mays, Bobby Bonds, Juan Marichal, Willie McCovey, Will Clark, Matt Williams, Barry Bonds, and countless other San Francisco Giant heroes never could: Bring the world title to San Fran. The 2010 players won the big one and in so doing cemented their names as Giants royalty. Of course, most of those great Giants of the past didn't have the luxury of playing at AT&T Park.

The Giants' prior home, Candlestick Park, was built onto Candlestick Point, in a more suburban section of the city. The Stick offered sweeping views of San Francisco Bay and provided as picturesque a setting for a game as anyplace in the big leagues at the time. Often warm and sunny when games began, the Stick was anything but warm later in the day. The wind, nicknamed "the Hawk" by Giants fans, would begin to blow, picking up a chill off the waters of the Pacific at an average speed of fifteen miles per hour. As the evening progressed, the Hawk picked up, and would often gust up to fifty miles per hour or higher. Swirling around Bayview Hill and into the ballpark with alarming force, the Hawk had an unpredictable effect on the flight of batted balls. To make matters worse, in the evening the fog would roll in, cutting down visibility and cooling things off even further. Temperatures would often drop twenty degrees in a few hours. Stories about the effects of wind, cold, and fog on games at Candlestick have become the stuff of legend.

The Stick was joked about, maligned, and even feared. It was clearly a disappointment from the beginning, even if true Giant fans harbored a great love for the place, as true fans will. It was easy to spot the diehards, bundled in scarves and winter coats on warm days. They knew what was coming and they would ridicule unsuspecting and underdressed visitors, especially from rival Los Angeles, who would scoff at their attire in the early innings, then suffer the bone-chilling freeze that could only occur in San Francisco during August and September. The cold was so bad that Giants management supplied "Croix de Candlestick" pins to all fans who braved the elements through extra-inning games. And the diehards still wear the pins as badges of honor, a distinction of true fans who have lived through the horrors and survived.

In 1972 the Stick was renovated to accommodate the 49ers of the National Football League. The addition of seats in the outfield served to close in what was once open. Giant fans hoped, perhaps wishfully thought, that their sacrifice of the open outfield view might be an exchange that would block the dreaded winds. Afterward, some claimed the effects of the wind were diminished, while others felt the renovations caused the wind to swirl around inside the park in new and unpredictable patterns. Whichever the case may have been, the seating capacity was increased from 42,500 to 58,000. The natural grass that the ballpark sprouted at the time of its opening was replaced by artificial turf in 1971, but then returned in 1979. Heavy red clay was mixed with the infield dirt to prevent the winds from turning the ballpark into a reenactment of the dust-bowl scenes of the *Grapes of Wrath*. The fences were brought in eventually to give right-handers some chance against the wind, but nothing really helped that much.

In its day, Candlestick was no joke, though. Its designers set out to create the finest, most state-of-the-art baseball park in the country. And on many levels, they succeeded. Candlestick was the first ballpark built entirely of reinforced concrete, which eliminated the need for pillars and poles, and resulted in the best sight lines in baseball at the time. They installed radiant heating in the concrete to warm the upper deck on cold San Francisco nights. However, they buried the hot-water pipes too deep in the concrete, and the warming effects could not be felt. Candlestick was also the first Major League park built in the suburbs, foreshadowing a trend that followed soon after, as many Americans left the inner-cities.

Candlestick Park hosted two All-Star Games and two World Series. The first Fall Classic was in 1962 when a McCovey line drive snagged by Yankees second baseman Bobby Richardson ended San Francisco's quest for a championship. But the structure really proved its mettle during the earthquake that rocked San Francisco during the Bay Bridge World Series of 1989. The A's held a 2–0 series lead heading into the start of Game 3, when at 5:00 p.m. on October 17, 1989, an earthquake measuring 7.1 on the Richter Scale walloped the region, collapsing the Embarcadero Freeway and causing Millions of dollars of damage to homes, freeways and buildings, and causing bodily harm to many people. Though Candlestick Park was packed with people, the concrete held, and not one person inside was injured. After brief repairs to the ballpark, the Bay Bridge World Series continued, unfortunately enough for Giant fans, as their East Bay counterparts in the American League, the dreaded Oakland A's, swept the remaining two games.

For all the abuse Candlestick Park took over the years, the ballpark performed well under duress. Though it held in time of crisis, the earthquake finally did in the structure. The toppling of the Embarcadero Freeway was one of the events that opened up the China Basin district of the city to redevelopment, offering new views of the Bay and newly created space on which the new downtown ballpark could be built. Actually, the '89 Earthquake was the second quake to aid in the construction of AT&T Park. The famous earthquake of 1906, which destroyed much of San Fran, played a part too. After it reduced much of the city to rubble, the crumbled buildings were carted off and used as the landfill that created the area that became China Basin. So in essence, it took two earthquakes and a whole lot of political tumult to get this ballpark built where there was once only water.

During its history, Candlestick played host to more than its share of special moments. The Alou brothers, Felipe, Matty, and Jesus, made up the first all-brother outfield while playing for the Giants in 1963. Willie Mays broke Mel Ott's National League home run record on May 4, 1966, when he smacked his 512th dinger. Back-to-back no-hitters were thrown at Candlestick Park on September 17 and 18, 1968, the first by Giant pitcher Gaylord Perry, and the second by St. Louis Cardinal hurler Ray Washburn. Baseball's one-millionth run was scored at the Stick by Houston's Bob Watson, on May 4, 1975. And of course, the Beatles played their last concert (not including the jam session on the roof of Apple Records in London) at Candlestick Park on August 29, 1966.

Josh: And where did the Beatles play their first US stadium show?

Kevin: That's easy: Shea Stadium.

Ask any Giants die-hard today and he or she will tell you that no ticket is hotter than when the hated Dodgers visit the Bay. This rivalry has spanned two coasts, as the teams despised each other in New York and still do. Former Dodgers manager Tommy Lasorda would anger Giants fans by blowing kisses at the screamers and hecklers on his way back to the dugout. Years of extra watering by the grounds crew near first base created "Lake Maury," a home field trick designed to slow down Dodger speedster Maury Wills. Ah, we love a good rivalry, even if it was exported from the East Coast.

After departing New York after the 1957 season along with the rival Dodgers, the Giants played two seasons at Seals Stadium, the home of the Pacific Coast League San

Francisco Seals and San Francisco Missions, while they awaited construction of their new baseball park by the Bay.

Three famous former Seals were Joe DiMaggio along with his brothers Dom and Vince. Joltin' Joe, famous for many baseball feats, still holds the record for most consecutive big league games with a hit, at fifty-six. But few may recall that Mr. Coffee notched his first extended hitting streak of sixty-one games as a rookie Seal in 1933. As great as DiMaggio was, the most popular Seals player was Lefty O'Doul, who also managed the team during the 1935–1951 seasons, when he would occasionally pinch-hit.

With the Giants arriving in town, however, the Seals were forced to find new digs, and the eventual collapse of the PCL's independence in 1958 caused great sadness among the Seals' old followers. Many great players came up through the PCL, including Ted Williams, Lefty Grove, and the aforementioned DiMaggio and O'Doul.

The Giants organization dates back, of course, to New York, where the club won championships and World Series for years, while the upstart Yankees of the Junior Circuit were mere fledglings. Such was the Giants' early dominance that baseball teams from around the world—from as far away as Japan and Central America—named themselves "Giants" to honor the classiest team in the big leagues. The Negro Leagues had scores of teams named after the Giants, too, from Rube Foster's Chicago American Giants to the Brooklyn Royal Giants and the Cuban X-Giants and the Washington Elite Giants.

The original New York Giants of the National League came to call the Polo Grounds their home. The horseshoe-shaped but oddly attractive ballpark sat just across the Harlem River from Yankee Stadium in the Coogan's Bluff area of Manhattan. Because of the long and narrow shape of the ballpark, along with the fact that it was named the Polo Grounds, a common assumption was that polo was once played on the site. But in actuality, the ballpark was built for baseball only. The narrowness of available space in Coogan's Hollow dictated the park's unusual shape.

Polo was played at the original Polo Grounds during the 1870s. That first park also served as home of the New York Gothams, who would later come to call themselves the Giants. By 1883 baseball emerged victorious at the field located at 110th Street and Sixth Avenue on the northern end of Central Park. The Giants' first World Championship came in 1888, when they defeated the St. Louis Browns of the American Association. The next year, they left the original Polo Grounds for a parcel of land in the southern half of Coogan's Hollow, where they built Manhattan Field at 155th

Street and Eighth Avenue. This ballpark became known as the Polo Grounds, too. The upstart Players Association had first dibs on the choice land in the northern half of the hollow, where it erected Brotherhood Park. Located at 157th Street and Eighth Avenue, Brotherhood's elongated shape was the result of needing to squeeze in between the second Polo Grounds and Coogan's Bluff, which arose next to it. Though the double-decked outfield bleachers had not yet been built, the trademark rounded double-deck grandstand behind home plate was in place from the beginning.

After just a single season, the Players Association folded, and the Giants benefited by moving into the larger facility in 1891. Again they named their ballpark the Polo Grounds. The outfield was open to the Harlem River, and many folks would stand or park their carriages along the river to watch the game.

The Giants' second title came in 1894, when they bested the National League incarnation of the Baltimore Orioles (the American Association version of the team had met its end two years earlier). Christy Mathewson, the team's ace during the era, threw his first no-hitter and what many experts consider to be the first no-hitter of the modern era on July 15, 1901. Though the Giants finished the 1901 season in seventh place, a new reign of excellence began for them in 1902 led by one of baseball's greatest legends, the iconoclastic and famously aggressive manager John McGraw. In a move that today boggles the imagination, McGraw declined the opportunity to participate in the newly created World Series in 1904, arrogantly insisting that the recently minted American League was only a "minor" league.

Kevin: McGraw was right.

Josh: Yeah, but the American League team from Boston won the first World Series ever played the year before.

Kevin: I know, against Pittsburgh!

McGraw lessened his stance by 1905 and agreed to play the Philadelphia Athletics in the World Series that year, after his team once again dominated the NL. Behind Mathewson, who threw three shutouts in the Series, the Giants added World Series champs to their already impressive list of accomplishments.

A play at the Polo Grounds near the end of the 1908 season became one of the most famous blunders in the history of baseball. It is known mythically to this day as the "Merkle Boner." The score was tied in the bottom of the ninth when Al Birdwell's single appeared to bring home Harry McCormick with the winning run. But rookie Fred Merkle, who was on first base at the time of the hit, never touched second base. Instead, he headed for the Giants' clubhouse as

fans flooded the field. Cubs second baseman Johnny Evers retrieved the ball, though, and touched second, prompting umpire Hank O'Day to rule Merkle out. Later, the NL president upheld O'Day's ruling and declared the game a tie. Since the two clubs had identical records at the end of the season a few weeks later, a one-game playoff took place on October 8, which the Cubs won 4-2. The Cubs went on to win the 1908 World Series, while the Giants read about the October Classic in the newspapers.

Kevin: What are you giggling at?

Josh: The Cubs owe their last World Series appearance to Merkle's Boner.

Kevin: Good Lord, you can be juvenile.

In 1911 tragedy struck the Polo Grounds as a fire destroyed the grandstands. Afterwards, the Giants shared the Yankees' Hilltop Park until June, before the Polo Grounds was rebuilt and deemed suitable for play again. Despite all the season's adversity, the Giants won the NL pennant, but lost in the World Series against the Philadelphia A's. The team John McGraw had callously dubbed "White Elephants" six years earlier had become a force. Who knew that one day these two rival teams would be located a few miles from one another on either side of San Francisco Bay?

A full renovation of the Polo Grounds was completed before the 1912 season, and this time the ballpark reflected the team's championship status. Decorated with Roman Coliseum frescoes on the facade, the new structure was regal. The coats of arms of all the National League franchises were displayed above the grandstand facade and gargoyles perched on the roof near flags and banners that flapped in the wind. This park fit for champions also became home to the Yankees, as McGraw leased space to the Junior Circuit upstarts. While the younger franchise struggled to survive, the Giants struggled in their success, making it to three successive World Series (1911–1913) without garnering another title. It wouldn't be until 1921 that the Giants would reclaim the championship, defeating the Yankees. It was the first time in World Series history that all seven games were played at the same ballpark. The next year the Giants repeated the accomplishment, downing the Yankees 4–0–1 in the 1922 Fall Classic. That Series couldn't be called a true sweep because Game 2 ended in a tie, when it became too dark to finish.

But the fortunes of the Giants had begun to change by that time. The Yanks had begun to outdraw their landlords, due to an exciting young hero named Babe Ruth. McGraw's reaction to losing the attendance race in his own park was to evict the Yankees. And the Pinstripers responded by building a ballpark that better suited the talents of their home run king. The home-field advantage the Yankees enjoyed at The House that Ruth Built proved too much for the Giants to overcome in 1923. Though they faced the Yankees in the World Series as two-time defending champs, the Giants lost to the upstarts in six games.

After the Yankees' departure, the Polo Grounds was renovated again. It was at this time that it took on the shape most people associate with it. The double-decked grandstands were extended all the way down the lines so that only the outfield bleachers remained single-decked, divided by a sixty-foot-high building in center that housed the team offices, clubhouses, and, later, the famous Longines Clock.

But the Polo Grounds was awkward for baseball. The narrowness and length of the horseshoe made for very short porches at both the right and left corners, which offered pull hitters an enormous advantage. A poke of 257 feet would clear the right-field wall, and an even shorter shot could reach the second deck in left. Yet it took a tremendous blast to reach the fence in either power alley, as right-center stood 449 feet away and left-center was 455 feet from home. In fact, only four balls ever reached the center-field bleachers at the Polo Grounds; the first was hit by Luke Easter of the Homestead Grays in 1948, the second by Milwaukee's Joe Adcock, and the next two came in 1962 by Milwaukee's Hank Aaron and Chicago's Lou Brock. No ball ever hit the clubhouse building in straightaway center.

An example of knowing your ballpark well and pitching accordingly came in the first game of the 1954 World Series, when the Giants' Don Liddle threw a meatball across the center of the plate that was tattooed by Cleveland's Vic Wertz. The 460-foot shot would have sailed out of any ballpark today, but to Cleveland's dismay, a fantastic catch by center fielder Willie Mays turned the blast into a long out. Surely the expansive center field of the Polo Grounds was a perfect spot to display the talents of Mays. In the 10th inning of the same game, Indians starter Bob Lemon allowed Dusty Rhodes to hit what should have been a routine fly out into the upper-level seats for a game-winning dinger. The tale of the tape: 261 feet.

A hitter who took full advantage of the Polo Grounds' dimensions was Mel Ott, who hit 323 home runs at the park. He clubbed his first, five-hundredth, and final dinger—his 511th—at the yard, spending twenty-two seasons in a Giants uniform.

Kevin: I'm a tremendous pull hitter. I wonder if—

Josh: You'd have to make contact first, slugger.

Plenty of other quirks could be found at the Polo Grounds as well. The outfields were sloped and so crowned that managers in the dugout depths could only see the tops of their outfielders' heads. The bullpens were in fair territory in the power alleys. A five-foot statue was erected in center field of Captain Eddie Grant, who was killed in World War II. And fans sitting atop the rocks of Coogan's Bluff could look into the park and watch games for free.

Bobby Thomson's famous "Shot Heard 'Round The World" was hit at the Polo Grounds, of course. The moment is considered one of the most exciting in baseball history. After being thirteen and a half games out of first on August 11, the Giants went on a sixteen-game winning streak and wound up tied for first with their archrivals, the Brooklyn Dodgers. In a one-game playoff the Dodgers carried a 4–1 lead into the bottom of the ninth. The Giants got one run across before Thomson came to the plate with one out and two men on base. Dodgers manager Charlie Dressen brought in Ralph Branca to face Thomson, who took a strike, then made history.

We can still hear Russ Hodges with the call: "Branca throws . . . there's a long drive. It's going to be . . . I believe . . . the Giants win the pennant! The Giants win the pennant! The Giants win the pennant!" Though the Giants lost the World Series to the Yankees in six games, nothing could tarnish their comeback. For a superb and interesting rendering of the events of that game, read the first chapter of *Underworld* by Don DeLillo. Despite this and other great moments, though, the same wrecking ball that brought down Ebbets Field leveled the Polo Grounds on April 10, 1964.

Trivia Timeout

They Might Be Giants: How many Giants are in the 500 Home Run Club?

My Giant: How many complete games did Juan Marichal throw in his career?

Andre, The Giant: What is the prize for hitting the oversized glove in left field at AT&T Park with a home run ball?

Look for the answers in the text.

While the move to the Left Coast transformed the "bums" of Brooklyn into a clean-cut, winning franchise, the reverse was true of the Giants. Finally, in 2010, though, they returned to championship form, and lived up to their reputation as the first franchise to reach ten thousand wins. Will this rekindled glory blaze brightly for years to come in the new century? No one knows for sure, other than the baseball gods themselves. But two things are certain—whether they win or lose, the Giants possess an amazing ballpark and a devoted fan base to support them.

Getting a Choice Seat

It would probably be easier to get a pair of scissors through Tim Lincecum's hair than it is to get your hands on a good ticket to AT&T Park. San Francisco's love affair with baseball means tickets to AT&T will cost you, but the experience is one you'll never forget. This park is one of the very best in the Major Leagues, so don't be a cheapskate. About the only thing they didn't get right was the name, so please forgive us as we continue to refer to this ballpark as AT&T Park, because no suitable nickname seems to stick.

Josh: How about Ma Bell Park?

Kevin: No.

Josh: Big Phone Park

Kevin: No.

Josh: Phone Field?

Kevin: No.

Josh: Worst Corporately Named Ballpark Ever?

Kevin: No, that belongs to the O.co Coliseum, across the Bay.

Field Club (Sections 107–124)

We love these Club seats, mostly because AT&T Park also offers far more desirable Premium Club seats. This further division of the good seats into more elite and premium-seating choices makes these lesser club folks feel second class.

Kevin: Now you know how we usually feel!

Josh: No, we can only aspire to be second class.

Premium Lower Box Seats and Lower Box Seats (Sections 101–135)

The grade of the lower bowl is fairly gradual and all seats angle toward the action. It's best to avoid rows 37 and higher, as the overhang will affect views of fly balls. But the only seats that have perfect sight lines are in Sections 113–115. All others on the first level lose one of the outfield corners to a slight obstruction.

Sections 105–106, 125–126, and the middle rows of 107–124, make up the Premium Lower Boxes and go for a bit more. Sections 105–106 and 125–126 extend all the way down to the field and are the best for the buck in this price range.

Sections 101–104, the uppermost sections of 107–112 and 119–124, and Sections 127–135 make up the Lower Box Seats. The seats down near the field in Sections

Seating Capacity: 41,503
Ticket Office: http://sanfrancisco.giants. mlb.com/ticketing/singlegame.jsp?c_id=sf
Seating Chart: http://sanfrancisco.giants. mlb.com/sf/ballpark/seats_3d.jsp

127–135 are preferable to any of the upper seats in Sections 105–126. The vantage point is closer to the field, plus they are cheaper. Seats above Row 31 in Sections 123–125 and 107–108 are blocked by a photographer's perch that hangs down from the second level. These seats cost far too much to be obstructed.

The uppermost seats in Sections 130–135 are called the Left Field Lower Boxes and are fairly poor. You can do better.

Club Infield (Sections 202–234)

Our friend Matthew Schmitdz, who provided wonderful insights into this ballpark during both of our visits, recommends these sections, if you can get the tickets via StubHub. Matty thinks the views are good and the food is better than in other parts of the park. An additional advantage: With Club seating, you have a place to head if the temp drops in the later innings, which, though it may sound a bit weenie, is a plus during early or late season games.

Josh: I can't believe you just recommended watching the game from inside.

Kevin: I'm not twenty-five anymore and neither are you. There's something to be said for a few innings in a climate-controlled environment.

Josh: Yikes, I can't wait to see what the tenth edition of the book will look like when we're both in our seventies.

View Level (Sections 302–336)

Though the close seats on the first level give the park an intimate feel, the seats on the View Level make the park seem huge. The best seats in all of these sections are the View Level Boxes, but we don't recommend spending the extra money. If you want better seats for fewer bucks, head for the bleachers. If you want to take in the sweeping views of the Bay, then perhaps the View Level is a good choice, but make certain to get the first ten rows in Sections 311–321. And beware, this upper level is among the steepest in baseball, so if it's your turn to make the beer and dog runs, think about making two trips. Even a mild fear of heights is cause to sit elsewhere.

The first-base side is preferable to the third-base side, because less of the corner is lost and the views are better.

From the seats on the left-field side, the Bay Bridge and Treasure Island are in full view, while the right-field side offers views of mostly industrial areas and parking lots.

The ballpark designers did a good job of protecting sight lines in the View Level, but by Section 326 the corner of the field is shaved off and it gets worse as the section numbers increase. Section 332 feels very removed from the action, and we cannot recommend sitting anywhere past it. Sections 333–335 suffer a severe loss of the corner and of the left-field wall, as well as foul-pole obstruction. Section 336 is just plain terrible. These seats are bad enough that management took our previous advice and lowered the prices—or so we like to tell ourselves.

Bleachers (Sections 136–144)

We love these bleacher sections and prefer them to the many more expensive seating options throughout the park. The low wall along the left-field line blocks only the warning track, so most plays against the wall remain in view.

Bleacher seats to avoid, however, are the high seats near the batter's eye. The seats right next to the batter's eye may not have views of the opposite portion of the infield, and should be removed. In Section 143 steer clear of Seats 1–10 in Row 33, and then angling down to Row 30, while in Section 142, avoid any seat numbered 25 or higher in Rows 30–33.

Arcade (Sections 145–152)

The Arcade-level seats are completely unique to AT&T Park. The sections are only two seats wide and run along the high oblique fence out in right field. The seats face the action, but the wall is angled, giving these sections a very distinctive feel. Section 149 has a few seats to avoid, because they have been poorly placed right behind the foul pole. Don't sit in Row 2 Seat 20, or Row 3 Seats 19–21.

The Black Market

It's not a problem finding ticket hawkers outside AT&T. But buying a scalped ticket can be as cutthroat as a sellout game in Boston. Scalpers may not be as aggressive as they are in the Fenway, but they've got paper gold in those orange and black tickets in their hands and they don't let them go on the cheap.

BEWARE: There have been incidences of counterfeit tickets being sold outside AT&T Park. They look fine, but the barcode readers won't scan them. And by then, the scalpers are long gone. This means that for sellouts you have four options: (1) Bite the bullet, dig down into your wallet, pay scalper prices and pray they're real, (2) get tickets from

SEATING TIP

The left-field Bleachers (Sections 136–138) are far better and cheaper than any Lower Box seat in the left-field corner (Sections 132–135). Some seats in Sections 135 are obstructed by the foul pole, while the bleachers are free from obstruction. The downside is that the bleachers have no seatbacks, but they're half the price and offer better sight lines, especially if you can get right along the left-field wall.

StubHub, or another online ticket broker, (3) wait until the second inning until the prices outside come crashing down, and pray they're real, or (4) visit the Dynamic Deals section on the Giants website. In essence, the Giants are scalping their own tickets here, so expect to get a seat and pay a little more, but at least you know it isn't a counterfeit. Remember that the Giants introduced the idea of "dynamic pricing" a few years back. What this means is that the team charges less for games against the bad teams (low demand games) than the good teams (high-demand games). As long as you're not trying to score tickets to see the Dodgers, you'll probably make out okay, but we recommend StubHub out of all these options.

Before/After the Game

Two large clock towers that adorn the brick exterior of AT&T Park along King Street are the most prominent features of the ballpark's facade. The towers are capped by pyramid-shaped roofs, and flagpoles, and stand outside the Willie Mays Plaza and near the Second Street Plaza entrance. Along with the smaller clock towers located at the Seals Plaza and Marina Gate entrance that honors the San Francisco Seals, and at the Lefty O'Doul Plaza and Bridge honoring the local son and baseball great, these featured architectural elements tie the ballpark to the neighborhood and the similarly sculpted King Street Railroad station a few blocks away.

Getting to AT&T Park

There are far too many ways to get to AT&T for us to list them all. But here are the major routes. Coming from the west on Interstate 80 or north on Highway 101, take the exits marked for the ballpark and follow the signs. Otherwise aim your road trip mobile for the corner of Third and King Streets, though the official address is 24 Willie Mays Plaza for those using a GPS.

Unless you're arriving on a motorcycle, don't even think about finding that elusive secret parking spot in this

SEATING TIP

On a nice day Section 302 offers one of the most spectacular 180-degree views in all of baseball. The game is in full view below, without obstruction, and from these seats it is easy to track the entire flight of any ball headed toward McCovey Cove. The tops of the downtown buildings can also be seen, as well as the marina, the harbor, the Bay Bridge, Treasure Island, Oakland across the Bay, and the Lefty O'Doul Bridge. These are some of the coolest seats in baseball and they won't cost you nearly what the seats down below in the supposedly "better" sections will.

town. Trust us when we say it doesn't exist. We looked. Of the seven parking places actually in the city limits of San Francisco that are available, none of them are down by the ballpark. Rather, look for a cheap parking lot within the acceptable five-block walking radius. We found one at Fourth and Brannan. The team lot, located just across the Lefty O'Doul Bridge, will cost you quite a bit more than you'll find a bit farther away.

AT&T Park is also convenient for folks using public transportation. The Embarcadero BART Station is a fifteen-minute walk from the ballpark, or you can get a transfer to the MUNI train that runs right out front and is only half-price if you're going to the game. MUNI trains can also get you to AT&T from all other points of service as well. Yet another train option is the CAL-TRAIN: The downtown station is just three blocks away. For those still unsatisfied with the amount of public transportation, ferries service the ballpark from Oakland and other points of departure, but the ferries are generally booze-cruises, rather than quick rides for folks who'd like to get to the ballpark efficiently. If you don't mind getting to the game right as it's beginning and leaving a half hour after it ends, take the ferries that operate right in McCovey Cove. They're cheaper than parking or taking BART, and you can enjoy a nice boat cruise (one hour each way). If you can't get direct specialty service, there is always the option of taking the regular ferry to the Ferry Building, then transferring to the Muni. Eating at the ferry terminal once you arrive is also a great way to go. To learn more, visit: http://goldengateferry.org/schedules.

Finally, if you bike to the game (which a surprising number of people do) just wheel around to the promenade and drop off your two-wheeler at the check stand where folks will watch it for you all game. Pretty nifty.

For a full rundown of these and other transit options, check out this wiki dedicated to the subject: http://www.transitunlimited.org/Main_Page.

Outside Attractions

WILLIE MAYS STATUE AND PLAZA

The main entrance to AT&T Park draws visitors through Willie Mays Plaza, a cozy palm-tree-lined pregame landmark where folks meet up with friends.

The centerpiece of the plaza is a statue of the Say Hey Kid. Mays' swing is unmistakable for any other, and the sculpture captures perfectly the power he once uncorked. Mays' lower right leg drags parallel to the ground and on first glance makes him appear off-balance. But the distant look in the eyes of the statue make it clear that the imaginary ball is headed for the fences.

Mays hit the fourth most home runs in Major League history (behind his godson, Barry Bonds; Hank Aaron; and Babe Ruth) playing half of his games at Candlestick, though fewer than a third (203) of his 660 dingers came at home. Had Mays played elsewhere, or had he been a left-hander so the wind gusts of Candlestick could help his fly balls rather than harm them, many experts say his career home run total would have been closer to eight hundred. Fellow Giants joining Mays in the 500 Home Run Club are Mel Ott (511), Willie McCovey (521), and Barry Bonds (762).

Willie Mays statue

Photo by Kevin O'Connell

Kevin: I told you in the first edition of the book that Bonds would break the record.

Josh: Don't even go there. He was juicing and I knew it.

Kevin: He was never convicted. Besides, everyone was cheating.

Josh: Even Edgar Martinez?

Kevin: Bite your tongue.

THE DOMINICAN DANDY

A statue of high-kicking Juan Marichal stands in Lefty O'Doul Plaza, just outside the 3rd Street entrance. Marichal had a delivery unlike any other, and the statue depicts his left foot high over his head and his right arm gripping the ball and slung low.

Orlando Cepeda statue

Photo by Matthew Schmitz

Marichal threw 244 complete games during his career, including the most impressive two during 1963. On June 15, he no-hit the Colt-45s at Candlestick Park. Then, eighteen days later, he threw a complete game shutout against the Milwaukee Brewers and Warren Spahn. Did we forget to mention that that game lasted 16 innings before Willie Mays clubbed a home run against Spahn to end the marathon, 1-0? The day the statue was erected the Giants wore jerseys that read "Gigantes" across the chest to honor Marichal, a native of the Dominican Republic.

THE BABY BULL

There's a statue of Orlando Cepeda outside the 2nd Avenue entrance. After playing his first season the year the Giants moved to San Francisco, Cepeda had a memorable career. He won the Rookie of the Year in 1958 and the MVP in 1967. He was a career .297 hitter who clubbed 379 home runs and drove in 1,364 runs over 17 seasons. The statue is impressive, standing nine feet tall atop a five-foot-high pedestal. The day it was erected the Giants also donned their "Gigantes" jerseys.

WALK THE WALK

Strolling the promenade that runs behind AT&T Park and along the marina constitutes a "must-do" for any first-time visitor to the ballpark. To truly appreciate the beauty of this setting, get to the ballpark early and watch folks in rafts and kayaks battling for batting practice homers that fly over the wall and into the drink.

KNOTHOLE GANG REDUX

You can watch batting practice from out on the promenade as well, through screened-in viewing areas. These free peek areas, reminiscent of the "knotholes" of ballparks past, remain open all game, and are the best free viewing locations in all of baseball. Courtesy dictates that if others are waiting, three innings is the maximum stay. Josh likened this to fly fishing etiquette to which Kevin put both of his fingers in his ears and started humming "San Francisco (Be Sure to Wear Some Flowers in Your Hair)." Josh took this to mean Kevin didn't want to hear any more about fishing during the trip. But getting back to the knotholes, our friends in the Bay report that during the 2002 and 2010 World Series runs, ticketless San Franciscans took full advantage, crowding the promenade for a chance to catch at least a few innings of history in the making.

free seats

Photo by Kevin O'Connell

WILLIE MCCOVEY POINT AND STATUE

Cross over the Lefty O'Doul Bridge to get to McCovey Point. Honoring perhaps the most beloved Giant of all, the great number 44, a walkway features tiles that fans purchased to help fund the ballpark. Between each section of these are plaques that comprise the Giants History Walk, one for each season the team has played in San Francisco. The stats emblazoned in bronze record batting and pitcher leaders, Opening Day lineups, and team attendance figures.

At the end of the walkway, standing guard over the cove, is a larger-than-life sculpture of "Stretch" himself. McCovey played baseball with dignity. His quiet manner and humble style earned him the admiration of the press, the fans, and of his fellow players. Today, the Giants' annual Willie Mac Award is the highest honor a Giant can receive. Each recipient is honored with a bronze plaque, laid in the stone plaza around the sculpture's feet.

JUNIOR GIANTS FIELD

Keep walking to check out the Junior Giants Field, a T-ball park across McCovey Cove from AT&T. There's just something very cool about a field that kids can play real games on in the shadow of a big league ballpark.

Watering Holes and Outside Eats

China Basin has been one of the ballpark neighborhoods that has benefited from the building of a new facility. The neighborhood was already under development, in a place where real estate costs roughly one arm and one leg, so it's a bit of a chicken-or-egg argument as to which came first: the ballpark or the cool hood. But one thing is for certain, the neighborhood surrounding AT&T continues to improve and offers great places to grab a pregame or postgame drink and meal.

THE PUBLIC HOUSE/MIJITAS
24 Willie Mays Plaza
www.publichousesf.com/

This place used to be Acme Chop House. Now, it's a combination restaurant that isn't cheap, but the food is good and they have an excellent beer selection. We recommend the sausage and the pulled pork sliders, but advise staying clear of the potato salad. At Mijitas, try the huevos rancheros. Plus, a primary benefit of eating at a restaurant connected to the ballpark is that you can enter AT&T with your ticket through the back door—and thereby avoid the lines. And if that's not enough, you can bring your food and beer inside the park with you.

PETE'S TAVERN
128 King St.
www.petestavernsf.com

The horseshoe shaped bar, close location, great beer selection, and reasonably priced food make Pete's one of our favorite pregame sports bars in town. They have a diverse menu, ranging from snapper to chili, with daily blue-plate specials—and nothing costs all that much. Try the house-smoked pastrami.

ZEKE'S SPORTS BAR
600 3rd St.

Though small, this traditional place gets packed near game time and remains one of the most authentic sports bars in the area. Burgers and sandwiches are rather un-San Franciscan; in other words, they're not fancy and they are cheap. Entrées run $6 to $9. We sampled a local microbrew called Humpback Wheat Ale, which was refreshing.

RED'S JAVA HUT
Pier 30/Embarcadero Street at Bryant

If you want to hang out with longshoremen and the occasional Giant player getting a cup of joe, Red's is the spot. This long-standing dive on the pier is one of the few yet to cash in and sell out during the recent real estate boom in China Basin. The special, a burger and beer, is a solid choice for $5 before the game. This is a blue-collar burger, well done, topped with pickles, onions, and ketchup on a sourdough roll. Steer clear of the hot dog, though.

Another place on Embarcadero is simply called The Java House and is not to be confused with Red's. The Java House special is a hot dog and a beer for $5, but we recommend walking the extra three blocks to Red's.

21ST AMENDMENT BREWERY, CAFÉ & BAR
563 Second St.
http://21st-amendment.com/restaurant

This joint jumps before the game, perhaps because of its delicious home brewed micro-beer, but more likely because it caters to the yuppie crowd. The sandwiches and pizza are a tad fancy, while items like arugula, Andouille sausage, and roast cumin-marinated pork among other options. An impressive list of beer brewed on the premises includes Watermelon Wheat Summer Brew and Oyster Point Oyster Stout, made with real oyster shells.

CHICKEN AND DONUTS
761 3rd St.
www.chickenanddonuts.com

Though the dismantling of Happy Donuts made us anything but, we once again feel happy with Chicken and Donuts in its place. This place serves some of the best chicken and donut combinations this side of, well, anywhere. They've got the more common chicken and waffle combinations too, as well as delicious Angus beef cheeseburgers with waffles serving as buns. (Try it, you'll like it.) The chicken is Louisiana style, and comes with great sides like dirty Cajun rice and mac-n-cheese. The donuts are fine as wine, too. The shop is open 24 hours a day, 365 days a year.

TRES TEQUILA LOUNGE AND MEXICAN KITCHEN
130 Townsend St.
http://rocksnosalt.com/san-francisco

This joint is a higher-end Mexican Restaurant, but worth the money if you are so inclined. We usually think of Mexican food as needing to be cheap to even be considered, but Tres breaks a few rules because it's close to the ballpark, has Happy Hour specials, and features a large variety of tequilas.

AMICI'S EAST COAST PIZZA
216 King St.
www.amicis.com/locations.asp

While this chain is not one of our favorites, it's very close to the ballpark and you might find an occasion to stop in. For instance, you might be from New York and need a slice or else you're going to break out in a rant of "fougettaboutits." Or, you might be leaving town after the game and need some thin crust to eat while you're driving.

MOMO'S AMERICAN BISTRO
760 Second St.

With a menu on the pricier side, MoMo's strengths are its location and outdoor seating. Getting a table on the patio is a key to enjoying the experience. The beer and drinks aren't cheap, but the people-watching is worthwhile. Entrées run from $15 to $30.

GORDON BIERSCH
2 Harrison St.
www.gordonbiersch.com/locations/san-francisco-ca

Located on the Embarcadero along the waterfront, this brewpub gone mini-chain is a great spot to get authentic garlic fries before the game from the folks who invented them. The menu is vast and a tad on the pricey side, but the food is very good. The biers, uh, we mean beers, on tap are Gordon Biersch's own, and range from Pilsner to Dunkels and every color and flavor in between. Look for unique seasonal beers. Our friend Kate recommends the delicious cocktails on the patio.

KATE O'BRIEN'S
579 Howard St.
www.kateobriens.com

Kate O'Brien's is best defined as "California Irish." Laid back with standard Irish pub grub, this is a great spot to stop and have a few, and is especially convenient to those traveling on foot from the Embarcadero BART Station. A meal will run right around $10, be it fish-n-chips, pizza, or a burger. The beer and wine selection make the place a winner.

PARAGON
701 Second St.
www.paragonrestaurant.com/san-francisco.html

Paragon is more typically San Franciscan than many other places you'll find near the ballpark. What do we mean by that? It will cost you a decent chunk of change to eat here, they have an extensive wine collection, and it's probably not the type of joint you and your friends envision visiting before or after a ballgame.

THE SLANTED DOOR
1 Ferry Building, #3
www.slanteddoor.com

Perennially voted one of the top restaurants in the city, see our review of Paragon and double it. Great high-end restaurant. Eat here if you can afford to eat anywhere you'd like.

THE RAMP
855 China Basin St.
www.theramprestaurant.com/

For those Giants fans wanting to kick it, old style, the Ramp has been a Giants hangout since the team's days at the Stick. There's plenty of deck seating on the water, even if the view is of a dilapidated pier. With tropical drink specials and barbecue, the Ramp is half tiki lounge, half Margaritaville. You'll miss this bar if you're not looking for it. Cross the Lefty O'Doul Bridge, make a left onto 18th, and look for the sign at the intersection of Illinois.

SOUVENIRS IN MCDONALD'S PARKING LOT
Corner of Third & Townshend

The souvenir dealer that sets up in the parking lot of McDonald's offers great deals on official Giants gear, but he also has loads of more interesting stuff that you can't find in the team store.

McCOVEY'S
1444 North California Blvd., Walnut Creek
www.mccoveys.com

This Walnut Creek sports bar is not close to the ballpark, but it's a Bay Area instant classic, and well worth the trip if you have the extra time. From the outside, the place looks like AT&T Park, and inside the seating area is laid out on a faux baseball diamond, surrounded by an overwhelming display of memorabilia. There's standard pub fare at McCovey's if that's what you're after, but the catfish po'boy is a favorite and we recommend it along with the baked and fried chicken and the barbecue.

ON A MISSION

If you're willing to go the distance or have an extra day to spend in the city, the Mission District, which is accessible by BART at either the 16th Street or 24th Street stations, is a food lover's paradise. Courtesy of our pal Matthew Schmitdz, we list some of the choice locations:

- *Tartine Bakery (600 Guerrero St.): A great French pastry shop with bread and good cappuccino.*
- *Bi Rite Creamery (3692 18th St.): The ice cream is the best in San Francisco, in both the soft-serve and hard-packed variety. Try the salted caramel. If you're hungry, the market has good sandwiches.*
- *Pizzeria Delfina (3611 18th St.): Many consider Delfina the best pizza in San Francisco; expect long lines, and it won't be cheap, but it's worth it.*
- *Taquerias: If you're hankering for a big burrito or a meaty taco, here are a number of great taquerias in the Mission District to try:*
  - *La Taqueria (2889 Mission St.)*
  - *La Corneta (2731 Mission St.)*
  - *El Metate (2406 Bryant St.)*
  - *Taqueria Los Coyotes (3036 16th St.)*

The Outfield Glove

Photo by Matthew Schmitz

Inside the Stadium

The view and amenities aside, AT&T Park is a terrific place to see a game. But the bells and whistles are everywhere you look. From the authentic cable car near the Arcade seats in center field that dings its bell for home runs, to the many advertisements that have been incorporated into the fabric of the park, AT&T is designed to entertain. Most of these gizmos must be experienced in person or they lose some of their effect. For example, anyone who's seen a game televised from San Fran knows there is a giant mitt, fashioned after the old four-fingered ones from the 1920s, in left-center. But do those same TV viewers know that the mitt was created by scanning a 1927 mitt into a computer file—every bump and wrinkle—then rendering a computer router to be exactly thirty-six times the size of the original? This ballpark is full of such surprises. Incidentally, for a player to hit this old-style mitt with a batted ball it would take a poke of well over five hundred feet. Though the Giants have offered to donate one million dollars to a lucky fan if any player hits the glove on the fly, no one has hit the target yet.

Though this park is no Candlestick, the winds are still very much a factor. The gales off the Bay hold up fly balls that would float out of warmer, more humid ballparks. AT&T routinely yields fewer than one home run per game on average, making it an ideal park for fly-ball pitchers.

Barry Bonds and the Steroid Era

In the first edition of this book, we were fairly effusive about the dominance of one Barry Bonds. Today, there has been far too much press on Bonds and the issue of whether or not he knowingly took performance-enhancing steroids and/or human growth hormone for us to be able to add much to the commentary. If Bonds knowingly took steroids, it will eventually come out. And even if it never does, the public will make a decision about Bonds and Roger Clemens, and all the others who already have the stain of the era hanging over their careers, statistics, and personal character that is far worse than any asterisk that could be placed next to their names in the record books. And this is as it should be. Players that cheat deserve to be punished for cheating. Even if practically everyone else is doing it.

But there is a bit more to consider here. The American baseball public seems willing to forgive. All evidence points to the fact that as long as a rule-breaker apologizes in a contrite manner, his sins will be forgiven. Look at Alex Rodriguez as an example, or Andy Pettitte as another. Both admitted to using steroids and now no one seems to care.

What baseball fans don't seem able to forgive is not the use of steroids—but being lied to about it. Bonds and Clemens stand out as the most egregious examples of players incapable of admitting to what they have been accused of. And who are we to say? We have no more knowledge of whether or not Bonds or Clemens knowingly took PEDs than anyone else. But there is one thing we know: America will not forgive anyone who doesn't admit doing wrong.

Bonds and Clemens have higher hurdles to overcome than other proven users, precisely because their names stand among the giants of the game in the record books. Bonds broke Hank Aaron's all-time home run record that many felt was unbreakable. He bested the single-season record McGwire took from Roger Maris. Similarly, if the claims about his using PEDs are true, Clemens seemed to have been unsatisfied with merely being the greatest pitcher of his own generation—he wanted to be the greatest of the next two decades too.

If the Baseball Writers of America choose not to honor these men and those others of the so-called "Steroid Era," it will be because of their arrogance, plain and simple.

Ballpark Features

DROP ONE IN THE DRINK

Fenway has its Monster Shots and AT&T Park has its Splash Landings. With arches built into the brick wall and an out-of-town scoreboard built into the arches, the right-field boundary of the field is impressive enough. But more than this, home runs that clear the wall can sail over standing-room fans, square pillars, and into the waters of McCovey Cove. As if this spectacle weren't enough, the pillars shoot mist into the air to enhance the celebration. Though splash home runs were primarily a Bonds phenomenon, it's even more exciting when other players reach the drink because it happens less frequently these days than back when Barry was popping balls over the fence.

BALLPARK QUIRKS

Okay, so they could have built the ballpark somewhere else and avoided the quirks. But at least AT&T comes by its quirks naturally. For instance, there are no bullpens, simply warm-up mounds alongside the fences. Wrigley Field has a similar quirk, and the argument seems to rage among critics of this ballpark as to whether or not the team put these in by choice or necessity. But we don't much care. We don't find

the bullpen location nearly as odd as the color of the warning track, which is dirt in the infield but rubberized in the outfield between the foul poles. Also odd to us is the fact that the dirt of the pitcher's mound is decidedly lighter than the traditional rust-colored infield. Either that or they water it less.

AN OLD-TIME FEEL

AT&T is a beautiful ballpark that makes us nostalgic for the game. Perhaps we're saps, but we like ballparks that feel like ballparks, not shopping malls, and in this regard AT&T delivers. One nice touch is the orange-and-black clock above the JumboTron that simply reads "San Francisco Giants." Four pennants fly in right field, one for each year the San Francisco Giants have topped the National League. Also adding to the classic feel of the ballpark are the many other flags— flags go a long way in our book. Attached to the small roof, flags flap fiercely in the considerable wind, one for each team in the majors.

EVEN LARGER THAN THE OTHER GIANTS

Between the decks in the left-field corner constitutes a poor place for the retired numbers, especially for a team that has a history as rich as the Giants. There are two "NYs" that have been retired, one for John McGraw and the other for Christy

Mathewson, both of whom played before players wore numbers. Number 3 belonged to Bill Terry, who hit .401 in 1930, marking the last time a National League player topped .400. Number 4 was worn by Mel Ott when he led the league in homers six times between 1932 and 1942. Number 11 was worn by Carl Hubbell, a nine-time All-Star who stitched together five twenty-win seasons from 1933 to 1937. Number 24, of course, belonged to the great Willie Mays. Though his accomplishments are too numerous to detail fully, Mays was an All-Star for twenty straight seasons, a Gold Glove Award winner for twelve straight seasons, a two-time MVP, ranks fourth (until A-Rod passes him) on the all-time home run list, and is considered by many to be the greatest player ever. Number 27 belonged to Juan Marichal, the nine-time All-Star who averaged twenty wins a season for ten years and posted a career ERA of 2.89. Number 30 was worn by Orlando Cepeda, a six-time All-Star who smacked 379 dingers and won the MVP in 1967. Number 44 was worn by Willie McCovey, who tied Ted Williams with his 521 home runs and drove in 1,555 runs. Number 20 belonged to Monte Irvin, whose greatness was recognized in both the Negro and Major Leagues, and who was one of the first players called up after the color barrier was broken. And, finally, Number 36 belonged to Gaylord Perry, whose lifetime ERA was 3.11 over nineteen seasons, during which he won 314 games and recorded 3,534 strikeouts. Perry was also the first pitcher to win the Cy Young Award in both leagues.

ADVERTISEMENTS DISGUISED AS BALLPARK FEATURES

A gasoline company has its advertising built into the wall in the left-field corner. The rounded roofs of three cars actually form the wall down near the foul pole. Meanwhile, a cola company has a huge slide built into its signature bottle, located in the Kids Plaza above the bleachers in left, but large enough to be visible to everyone in the park. Advertising in baseball parks has always been part of the game. In the case of AT&T Park, we suppose this is the price we pay for a privately funded ballpark that did not increase the taxes of the citizenry. But the ads do little to enhance the charm of the park.

KIDS PLAZA

Above the bleachers in left field resides one of the most expansive kiddie areas in all of baseball. Whether little Giants prefer sliding down the slide that runs through the enormous neon cola bottle, pitching, or running the bases at the tykes' park, this is the place for fans of any age who have an attention span that doesn't last the full nine innings.

Stadium Eats

When AT&T opened for business (it was called Pac Bell then) it offered a rather disappointing spread. Management read our book, though, and subsequently changed the park's ways so as not to be further embarrassed by our reviews. Or so we like to tell ourselves. Either way, the fare at AT&T is far better than it was back when the park opened. And for this, we applaud the Giants' efforts.

GARLIC FRIES (TRADEMARK FOOD)

This delicacy, began by Gordon Biersch back at Candlestick Park, has sprouted many imitators throughout America's ballpark landscape. While back in the day, you'd spend a few innings waiting for the servers to grind fresh garlic and Parmesan onto your fries, the process has become much more streamlined. Minced garlic is used now to speed things up, and as such, the garlic fries are not as good as they used to be. But still, they are pretty tasty. Just take our friend Anne's advice and beware of the "garlic hangover" that results from consuming too much.

Josh: And beware if your travel partner has too much garlic if you'll be trapped in a road trip mobile with him.

Kevin: What are you trying to say?

HOT DOG (DOG REVIEW)

With nothing snappy about it, the Giants Dog sagged in the bun and then on our taste buds. Though they advertise that these dogs are made in Stockton, California in the Swiss tradition (we weren't even aware the Swiss made dogs!), we recommend avoiding them. You can find a much wiser dog option at the Hebrew National carts.

BEST OF THE REST

While the stadium sausage is a pass, the **"Say Hey" Sausages** are a hit. Though the Italian was boiled rather than grilled, a big disappointment, the spicy Louisiana Hot Link was one of the better items in the park. Another good option in the sausage department is the Sheboygan available at the **California Cookout** stands.

The **King Street Carvery** station is a solid option. The trio plate of slider sandwiches (corned beef, beef brisket, and turkey) was quite tasty. The **Crazy Crab** stands have a crab sandwich that Kevin thought was quite good. On cold nights, head for the **Pete's Coffee** stand or for the hot chocolate at **Ghirardelli.**

SAY "NO, THANKS," AND WALK AWAY

Avoid the Baby Bull at Orlando's BBQ. This beef sandwich with barbecue sauce (applied afterward) and garlic-caramelized onions may sound good, but believe us, it's not. The meat is steamed and cut along the grain instead of against it. What does this mean to you? Two foot-long pieces of meat that are impossible to bite through that cause a sloppy mess of onions and sauce on your pants. Our friend Paul described eating the Baby Bull as "exactly like eating a whole raw octopus."

STADIUM SUDS

All of the usual beers are available, though like at most ballparks they offer one beer at each station. We guess they don't want you to waste too much of their time deciding if you're getting a Miller Light or Michelob.

Luckily the selection of microbrews throughout the park is extensive. Aside from the standard offerings, look for **Firestone** Double Barrel, **Gordon Biersch** Hefeweizen & Marzen, **Lagunitas** IPA, **New Belgium** Fat Tire Amber, **Pyramid** Hefeweizen, **Red Hook** E.S.B., **Mendocino** Red Tail Ale, **Speakeasy** Prohibition Ale, and **Widmer** Drop Top Amber and Hefeweizen.

Hard liquor is cheaper than beer at AT&T Park and we recommend the Irish Coffee on cold summer nights. It's good, warming, and liquoring.

A good selection of California wines are available from the California Wine Carts.

Josh: This red wine has really nice legs.
Kevin: What are you talking about?
Josh: The legs, you know.
Kevin: Did you watch *Sideways* again before the trip?

The San Francisco Experience

In this city by the Bay, baseball is a treat. Don't miss AT&T Park on any road trip where you have the chance to get close. You will hear stories from other fans and you will regret missing this gem with the shimmering and twinkling lights coming in from across the water. You shouldn't expect San Franciscans to behave the way their Southern California statesmen do. Especially since the World Series win, Giants fans bring as much passion and heart in rooting for their team as the fans in Boston, New York, or Chicago.

Like the city of San Francisco itself, AT&T boasts a younger and hipper crowd than many cities, which comes off a bit more Rock-n-Roll than one might expect for a franchise this old and time-honored. No matter what happens, there seems to be a soundtrack provided. Hipster fans wear attention-grabbing T-shirts that read "Fear the Beard" and "Let Tim Smoke." Other fans, meanwhile, still wear their old-school off-white flannel (looking) uniforms without names across the back.

Giant Tunes History

For years the Giants have penned theme songs that honor each year's team in an attempt (we assume) to boost morale and attendance. On occasion fans in groups large and small will burst out into song, ironically recalling one of these nearly forgotten jingles. Okay, it doesn't happen all that often, but the lyrics to these tunes are just too funny not to reprint. One choice title was "I'm a Believer in Giants Fever," a dance number from the disco era. Our friend Paul recalls some of the lyrics from the Giants' 1984 song "Giants, Giants, Hang in There," perhaps the most defeatist of them all:

> Sometimes you win, sometimes you lose
> But winning's not a thing you can always choose,
> So Giants, Giants, Hang in There.

Does that convince fans it's going to be a long season or what? Another favorite of ours pointed to the fans' acknowledgment of the drawbacks of Candlestick Park, and came out when the Giants were trying to draw folks to the ballpark for day games. The music was inspired by the Beach Boys:

> When the night winds blow and the fog rolls in
> You know Candlestick's no fun
> So we play real old-fashioned baseball
> In the California Sun
> Catch some rays, scream and shout
> Giants, Giants, air it out.

The Pacific Coast League Trail

The first stop for those folks interested in the PCL would have to be the site of former Seals Stadium, located at the corner of 16th and Bryant Streets. While today it's nothing more than a Safeway Grocery Store it's rumored that ghosts of Seals players walk the aisles at night. The light stanchions and some of the seats from Seals Stadium are still in use today at Cheney Stadium, home of the Tacoma Rainiers of the current incarnation of the PCL.

The second stop on the PCL trail will take you to 333 Geary St. This has been the location of Lefty O'Doul's Restaurant since 1958. While this Union Square haunt is a terrific sports bar, complete with a lunch counter as well as a Hoffbrau for fans of circular meats, there are also dozens of pictures on the walls of PCL players and Seals teams. Newspaper articles from the *San Francisco Chronicle* and other papers adorn the walls and tell the tales of great Seals moments when the PCL was the king of West Coast baseball.

Francis Joseph "Lefty" O'Doul is something of a local baseball legend. Having pitched early in his career for the Seals, O'Doul left to play for the New York Giants from 1919 to 1923. O'Doul hit .398 in 1929 for the Philadelphia Phillies to win the batting crown. O'Doul also set the National League single-season record for hits that year at 254. That mark ranks third on the all-time single-season hits list, tied with Bill Terry and behind Ichiro Suzuki (262) and George Sisler (257). With a lifetime batting average of .349 in eleven seasons, Lefty belongs in the Hall of Fame as far as we're concerned, but he has been shut out because of the relatively short duration of his batting career.

When O'Doul returned to San Francisco to manage the Seals, he led them to PCL championships in 1931 and 1935. Lefty was the Seals manager who sent Joe DiMaggio to the big leagues. And he was also known for putting himself into games as a relief pitcher and pinch-hitter. He collected his last hit at age fifty-nine while managing the Vancouver Mounties of the PCL. O'Doul went on to become a spokesman for the PCL, as well as an ambassador of the game of baseball in his many trips to Japan.

Kevin: You gotta love the Irish.

Josh: Lefty O'Doul was French.

Kevin: But he wore a big green suit.

Josh: That's just good marketing.

WE'RE GONNA NEED A BIGGER BOAT

McCovey Cove and the frequency of balls hit into the water create a rare outside-the-ballpark, water-related experience in San Francisco. Boats, rafts, jet skis, canoes, kayaks, and anything that keeps people above the water show up whenever there is a home game. From well before the game begins until long after it's over, ball hawks and watersport enthusiasts crowd the Cove to enjoy the wet and wildest tailgate in the majors. Can't get tickets? Why not rent whatever form of watercraft you can captain and head to the spot where the other ticketless super fans gather?

THE HOME RUN KING?

The only marker you will find at AT&T noting the crowning achievement of Barry Bonds is a small plaque in center field mentioning the accomplishment. Babe Ruth, Henry Aaron, and Willie Mays are also mentioned. It's about as understated a tribute as you'll find anywhere, about anything. As we've said, the Giants have taken down the super-sized images of Bonds and his chase of history that once adorned the ballpark.

"I LEFT MY HEART . . ."

You know the rest. Win, lose, or rainout, the Giants play Tony Bennett's classic, "I Left My Heart in San Francisco" at the end of each game. It's a slower song than most ballpark finales, but in this easy-to-love city, it's a fitting choice.

Josh: Have you switched to wine?

Kevin: Yeah, so?

Josh: Never thought I'd see the day.

Kevin: When in Rome, my friend.

EIGHTH INNING SING-ALONG

To rally the crowd when the team is down, as well as to celebrate a lead, the Giants play "Lights" by hometown heroes Journey during the eighth inning. Interestingly, the Dodgers play Journey's "Don't Stop Believin'" as their sing-along. Journey lead singer (and Giant fan) Steve Perry asked them to stop, but as of yet, their tradition continues.

FEELS LIKE A HITCHCOCK FILM

A ballpark built so close to the Bay has its disadvantage as well. It seems the sea gulls know just about how long ballgames run, as hundreds gather in the later innings and circle over-head menacingly. Our game went into extra innings, so these vultures had to wait to dive down into the seats to get their nightly morsels of Garlic Fries and spilled BBQ sauce from Baby Bull sandwiches. So these winged stomachs lined up on the roof, perched, awaiting our departure.

Kevin: I'm afraid of birds.

Josh: Grow a spine, Tippi Hedren.

LOU SEAL

Honoring the San Francisco Seals of the Pacific Coast League is mascot Lou Seal. Clever name, but it's technically short for Luigi Francisco Seal. Lou signed with the Giants in 1996 and has been performing better than average in the "mascot acting goofy" department ever since.

Though we love Lou, we can't help but wonder why "Crazy Crab" was de-shelled as the Giants mascot. The crustacean that Giants fans loved to hate, Crazy Crab is perhaps our favorite mascot of all time. So despised was the pink and orange Nerf crab that booing and heckling became a sport. Crazy Crab eventually was limited to only appearing once a game, and he taunted the fans into hurling abuse at him . . . like they needed any encouragement. Though Crazy Crab was cracked and steamed long before Candlestick's demise, he was so un-popularly popular, that he was brought out at the final game played at the Stick, and also at a game at AT&T in 2008. Maybe it's nostalgia, but now, it seems, Crazy Crab is poised to make something of a comeback. There are signs of him in the ballpark, including the crab sandwich stand named in his honor. And there are websites with real petitions lobbying for the permanent return of the Crab. Don't believe us? Check out www.rehabthecrab.com/.

RALLY PUMPKIN (SUPER-FAN)

This rotund fellow combines everything we love about baseball: pumpkins, dancing, and Halloween. Seriously, though, Rally Pumpkin, aka "Jingles," shows up in the seventh inning when the Giants are down, wearing an orange beret,

Sports in the City

The Joe DiMaggio Trail

Another local son that made good and left his heart in San Fran was none other than the Yankee Clipper. Head to the historically Italian North Beach section of town and find The North Beach Playground and Pool (800 block of Columbus Street) to see where a youthful Joltin' Joe played his inner city ball on the pavement. Later in life, DiMaggio would return often to the neighborhood in North Beach to hang out at Bimbo's nightclub (1025 Columbus Ave.). He even took Marilyn Monroe there on occasion.

For folks who can't get enough Joe, he was born in Martinez, which is about an hour from San Francisco depending on traffic. The Martinez Museum has a modest amount of DiMaggio items on display. On display at the Martinez Marina Park is the 22-foot long Chris-Craft sports boat DiMaggio received as a gift from the Yankees. He donated the boat to the city, after he and Marilyn had made good use of it on the Bay.

orange shorts, and an orange shirt with differing messages airbrushed across his ample chest and back. Rally Pumpkin even has his own website: http://rallypumpkin.com/. Boy, being a super-fan sure has changed since we first published this book.

BRYAN STOW (SUPER-FAN)

It's worth mentioning that Bryan Stow did not become a super-fan by choice, but by circumstance. Stow was beaten into a coma outside Dodger Stadium for wearing his Giants' gear to a game in Los Angeles. During the game, Stow texted his family that he feared for his safety, and sadly he was proven correct. What more can you say about this super fan than that he took a beating for the team he loves (albeit unwillingly), and Giants' fans have rallied around him. We hope and pray for the best for Mr. Stow and his family.

While We Were in San Francisco
Our First Great American Baseball Road Trip Came to an End

San Francisco was the last stop on our illustrious first baseball road trip, and we both were exhausted. It was the second of our two games at AT&T (then called Pac Bell), and though thoroughly tired, we were more than a bit saddened by our adventure coming to an end. We sat watching batting practice from behind the fence on the promenade outside the park.

"Well, this is it," said Josh. "We head back tomorrow."

"Yep," said Kevin, mournfully. "It's been a good run."

"I feel bad that you never got a ball," said Josh, who had tallied eight free baseballs on the trip, either caught in the stands, tossed to him by players, or stolen from small children.

"That's okay," said Kevin. "You got my share. And you got to see plenty of the country."

"True," said Josh. "It's been quite a trip."

"I feel bad we never got to go to Vesuvio," Kevin said referring to a bar in North Beach where Jack Kerouac, beatnik godfather and one of his favorite writers, used to hang out. "We should go there now. City Lights bookstore is right across the alley. We've got time to get there and back before the game."

"Ahh," said Josh. "I'd rather watch BP."

"We watched BP from this same spot yesterday," Kevin protested. "And Kerouac was the inspiration for all mythic road trippers that have followed. We're writers now . . . we have to go."

"So what?" said Josh. "I never miss BP."

"So what?" screamed Kevin. "So what? So Kerouac was from Massachusetts just like you. And he wrote about America just like you. And who knows if you'll ever be in San Francisco again. It seems to me you'd be curious, at least."

"I guess I'm just more of a baseball fan, than a road trip fan," said Josh. Both of us were keeping our eyes on the hitters.

"You know," said Kevin, exasperated, "we've traveled all this way together, through thick and thin, good times and bad. I'd think you'd want to broaden your horizons just a little bit. There's more to life than baseball, you know." Just as the words left Kevin's mouth a mammoth crack of the bat rang out, and we instinctively left the fenced in viewing area for the promenade.

"It's coming," cried Josh.

And clear the wall it did. The monster shot came splashing down into McCovey Cove between two guys in a rubber raft and a woman in a canoe. Both feverishly paddled toward the water plunge where the ball had submerged. While Josh hesitated, Kevin dived in like he was going after a drowning child.

The ball surfaced first, nearly popping back out of the water with its return force. The canoe was a bit closer, but the two guys in the raft had their paddles twirling like eggbeaters. It was a melee, and the ball was lost in the froth.

Kevin surfaced, and swam away from the boats and the flailing paddles, which were now close enough to be whacking one another. With some help from Josh, he pulled himself onto the dock and promenade with the ball in his hand.

"So," said Josh, as his waterlogged friend dripped Bay water all over the promenade, "baseball isn't everything, huh?"

After the game, with the twinkling lights of the Bay before us and the golden voice of Tony Bennett crooning "I Left My Heart in San Francisco" over the P.A. system, Kevin could do nothing but grin (and shiver as he had all game long) as he looked at his prize. "I guess you were right," he said. "It was a good idea to stick around."

"It's what Kerouac would have done," joked Josh.

"Well said," Kevin added. We weren't sure if we would ever be coming back to this ballpark. But we'd lived the experience to the fullest. Of that, there was no doubt.

The moral to the story: This life we share is meant to be experienced. Though we have written a book (twice now) detailing some of the great adventures to be had on the mythical road to baseball nirvana, we don't have the capacity to list everything. No one does. America is an enormous country, just waiting to be explored and rediscovered. And a road trip of any merit should be guided by a book or another person only in part. The rest should be up to you, the road tripper, to get on out there and see all that's new, if only to you. So, gather your pals and get out on the road. Experience America for yourself.

Baseball is so woven into the fabric of American culture and life that the two cannot be separated. Aside from big league ball, there are more than a hundred minor league parks to see, thousands of city teams, Little League teams, club teams, college and high school teams. Our country is dotted with beautiful diamonds of green grass and brown dirt, even in the smallest of towns. Some teams are lucky enough to play their games in ballparks of great beauty and history. Others play on quaint little sandlots that only have holes where the bases ought to be. But in our estimation, all ballparks are beautiful, if only for the simple reason that baseball is played on them.

Happy travels!

ACKNOWLEDGMENTS

Josh would like to thank his wife, Heather, for her patience and encouragement; his son, Spencer, for being the best alarm clock a guy could ever want and a pretty awesome kid, too; his father, Richard, for throwing countless "sponge balls" to him against the backyard chimney; his mother, Cathy, for instilling in him a passion for reading; and his brother, Jamie, for always being his first and best proofreader. Josh also thanks his in-laws, Judy and Ed Gurrie, for being such enthusiastic promoters of his books, and Butch Razoyk and Lynn Pastor, for often reminding him that it takes patience and a lot of faith in oneself to succeed in any business.

Kevin would like to thank his wife, Meghan, whose sacrifices border on the miraculous; his daughters Maeve and Rory for inspiring all things wonderful in his life; his brother, Sean, for his research assistance and touring of Southern California, and for helping him to build their first baseball field together in the yard, despite living on a hill; his sister, Colleen, for being a wonderful big sister, a devoted mother, an excellent teacher, a passionate reader, and a fellow non-Yankee fan; his mother, Vickie, for her love of the Dodgers in the face of marrying into a family of Yankee fans; his father, Thomas, for crouching in the catcher's position three entire summers to shag misguided fastballs; to Paul and Matthew Schmitz, brother geniuses of baseball, high and low culture, and everything that makes life worth living; to Paul Lukinich, a friend from the good old days, and to Jordan Parhad and his lovely wife, Elisa, whose dual fountains of creativity never cease to inspire.

We extend special thanks to Pam Painter for believing in our project way back when we were just two grad students with a good idea but no real idea of how to put a book proposal together and find a publisher. We also thank Colleen Mohyde, our literary agent at the Doe Coover Agency; George Donahue, our first editor at Lyons; and Keith Wallman, our current editor at Lyons.

For couches to sleep on and hot meals along the road, we wish to thank James McCarthy III, Chris Razoyk, Louis Galvan, Aaron Fournier, Kevin and Kristen Maguire, Joe and Jane Hernandez, Kevin Larsen, Rob and Maureen Vischer, Dave and Kate Hayden, Michael and Judy Coughlin, Heidi and Jason Torok, Clarissa Sansone, Brian Coughlin, Trish and Paul Iovino, Michael Rowe, the Coughlins (John, Alexy, Kieran, and Patrick), Krysia and Ricardo Vila-Roger, Curt and Janna Mitchke, John and Rosie Balding, Chris and Daisy Balding, Linda, Erin, and Jeremy Davis, John and Tracy Lewis, Kathryn Halaiko, Aaron Kaufmann, Joe and Carol Bird, and Anne Schmitz.

For help with content and for joining in on our little adventure we would like to thank Rich Hoffman, Joe Bird, Chris Stagno, Matt Jordan, Shilad Sen, Thad Henninger, Gary DiPiazza, Lyle Applebaum, Earl McDaniel, Nathan Thompson, Jessie Wine, Leo Panetta, Mark Alberti, Michael Hernandez, Richie Platzman, John Murphy, Rebecca Murphy, Douglas Hammer, Jim Kauss, Stuart Chapman, Randy Begoya, Doug Kierdorff, Jeff Schaffer, Sean and Chrissy Dooley, Mark "the Cruiser" Diver, Richard Cassinthatcher IV, Bob and Lauren Boland, Lyle and Sarah Overbay, Tim and Kyle Malone, James Sander, "the Reverend" Hubie Dolan, Tim Harrington, Paul Lukinich, Ken Betzler, Jay Knapp, Daryl Gee, Tom White, and the entire Gonzaga Gang—Go Zags!

Thanks also go out to the many Major League teams that provided us with complimentary seats and/or photographs of their ballpark.

APPENDIX: PLANNING YOUR TRIPS

All you need to begin charting your next baseball adventure is a copy of our book, a copy of the Major League Baseball schedule, and a general idea of how much vacation time you have coming your way. Oh, yeah, having a few bucks in your pocket and a GPS don't hurt either.

We thought we'd provide four examples of ways in which you might make the most of your time on the road by incorporating a special theme or four to your trip. We have provided one sample itinerary for select ballparks of the Northeast, the South, the Midwest, and the West. The shortest of these is the Northeast trip, which covers five Major League parks in five days, while the longest is the West Coast trip, which covers eight big league parks and a bunch of minor league ones in fifteen days. The Northeast trip combines a focus on big eating with your ballpark exploration. The South trip includes visits to baseball museums along the way. The Midwest trip includes stopovers at historic baseball diamonds. And the West trip includes detours to Pacific Coast League parks.

Remember, these themes are just examples of ways in which you might add a special wrinkle to your travels. And they're interchangeable. If you'd like to visit the minor league ballparks of the Northeast, or you'd like to eat your way across the Midwest, there's no reason why you shouldn't. We encourage you to shape your own adventures according to your own personal tastes and interests. Of course, you're free to follow in our footsteps precisely if you'd like.

Enjoy your travels. And please e-mail us with feedback, stories, and photos from the road. You can contact us at pahigian35@yahoo.com and ktoconnell@hotmail.com.

Sample Itinerary 1
The Babe Ruth Big Eating Tour
Days: Five
Cities: Four
Ballparks: Five
Oriole Park at Camden Yards, Baltimore, Maryland
Citizens Bank Park, Philadelphia, Pennsylvania
Yankee Stadium, The Bronx, New York
Citi Field, Queens, New York
Fenway Park, Boston, Massachusetts

No celebrity personified the indulgence and decadence of the Roaring Twenties quite so much as Babe Ruth. And no American sports figure in the past or present defined his generation and reinvented his sport the way the Bambino did. Perhaps the only thing more famous than the iconic Sultan of Swat's prodigious long balls was his insatiable appetite—for food, drink, and tawdry women. As such, this quick-hitting roadie through the Northeast delivers food, drink, and Bambino-related attractions in abundance. As for the saucy women, well, they don't fall under our area of expertise.

The trail begins in Baltimore where the Babe was born, travels north through Philadelphia, then on to New York City, where Ruth obliterated slugging record after slugging record. It finishes in Beantown, where the Babe began and ended his Major League career.

BEFORE HITTING THE ROAD
Prior to this sojourn we recommend reading Robert Creamer's *Babe: The Legend Comes to Life,* which does a superb job of demystifying the complex man who was George Herman Ruth. Another interesting book is John Robertson's *The Babe Chases 60: That Fabulous 1927 Season, Home Run by Home Run,* which provides a blow-by-blow account of Ruth's legendary record-shattering year. Finally, we recommend Leigh Montville's *The Big Bam: The Life and Times of Babe Ruth,* which is as exhaustive a biography on Ruth as you'll ever find. For pre-trip viewing, we recommend *The Babe Ruth Story* (1948), which is widely considered the worst baseball movie ever made. For precisely that reason, you will enjoy it, especially after having read Creamer's book on the Babe. This movie's hilarity begins with forty-two-year-old actor William Bendix playing the Babe as a teenager, then offers an outlandish account of the saint-like Babe's heroism. During the film, Ruth draws the wrath of his manager after missing a game to take an injured puppy to the hospital. Later, he hits a home run that causes a crippled boy to rise from his wheelchair in awe, even though doctors had told him he'd never walk again. The movie is chock-full of ridiculously sentimental moments. Trust us, this one's so bad, it's worth watching, especially if you know a little beforehand about the Babe. The second film we recommend is *The Babe* (1991) starring John Goodman. The film succeeds by comparison in depicting Ruth as a human being, afflicted by human wants, needs, insecurities, and vulnerabilities. It also delves into Ruth's personal life, shedding light on the Babe's first marriage and his relationships with teammates.

THE ROAD TRIP
DAY ONE: BALTIMORE

In 1895 George Herman Ruth was born in Baltimore, two blocks from where Oriole Park at Camden Yards stands. He spent his early childhood in a saloon on Emory Street that was owned and operated by his family. Then, in 1902, he was sent to St. Mary's Industrial School for Boys on the outskirts of Baltimore. While the Babe endured this lonely childhood, his parents birthed seven other children, yet only one survived infancy.

In February 1914, Jack Dunn, the owner of the minor league Baltimore Orioles, assumed legal guardianship of the Bambino in order to sign him to a professional contract. But when the Orioles encountered financial difficulties, Dunn was forced to sell Ruth to the Red Sox. Later that year, ten months after leaving St. Mary's, Ruth started his first big league game as a pitcher for the Red Sox.

Afternoon: Visit The Babe Ruth Birthplace and Museum located a few blocks from Camden Yards at 216 Emory St. The attractions include a 714 Exhibit, which chronicles the Babe's homers. For more information, visit www.baberuthmuseum.com.

Game time: Enjoy some barbecue on the Babe Ruth Plaza, located just inside the Oriole Park turnstiles on Eutaw Street. The plaza is a great place to snag a batting practice homer. Just bring a glove, because the competition can be fierce.

Late-night: While the crab-cake sandwiches inside the park are very good, we recommend saving some of your appetite for after the game. Visit Bohager's Bar and Grill at 701 South Eden St., where the Crab Deck features Maryland blues in heaping portions. Then head to the Downtown Sports Exchange at 200 West Pratt St., to catch the West Coast games and enjoy a nightcap.

DAY TWO: PHILADELPHIA

Wearing a Boston Braves uniform, the Babe played the very last game of his career at Philadelphia's Baker Bowl, on May 30, 1935. But don't worry: That doesn't mean the Phillies' current park has to be the last stop on your trip. We recommend getting a good night's rest in Baltimore, then making your way to the City of Brotherly Love in midafternoon. This will allow you to miss the morning rush on Interstate 95 North. Baltimore and Philly are only about a hundred miles apart, so expect a two-hour drive.

Afternoon: Ditch the car in a public parking lot and take a walk on famous South Street. If you're interested, check out the Liberty Bell Pavilion, Betsy Ross House, and Independence Hall on 5th and 6th Streets.

Game time: Visit Ashburn Alley, where plaques and statues honor former Phillies and Athletics heroes like Richie Ashburn, Gabby Cravath, Billy Hamilton, Steve Carlton, and Mike Schmidt. Treat yourself to a snack at Bull's Barbecue, which is run by former Phillies slugger Greg "Bull" Luzinski, or at Harry the K's, which features the massive sandwich known as the Schmitter.

Late-night: Visit cheesesteak central. Philly invented the cheesesteak, so don't miss out on this tasty regional specialty. After the bars close, head to the intersection of Passyunk Avenue and 9th Street where Geno's Steaks and Pat's Steaks sit on adjacent corners. Josh prefers a Pat's hoagie with provolone, while Kevin favors a Geno's sandwich topped with gooey orange Whiz. Either way you can't go wrong—well actually, you can. These joints aren't located in the city's best neighborhood, so consider taking a cab across town and having the cabby wait for you while you get your treat. Fainthearted types can visit Jim's Steaks on the corner of 4th Street and South Street where the steaks are almost as good and the atmosphere is more tourist-friendly.

DAY THREE: NEW YORK

The New York beat reporters loved to play up Babe Ruth's big appetite, larger-than-life persona, and gargantuan heart. This is where the Babe earned such monikers as "the Sultan of Swat," "the King of Swing," and "the Bambino," along the way to becoming the most widely recognized human being on the planet. This is where he posed with a crown on his head for the famous *Life* magazine cover. This is where he allegedly ate sixteen hot dogs right before a game, homered in his first at-bat . . . and then belched in triumph as he circled the bases.

You'll want to arrive in the Big Apple early, and with your appetite whetted. Philadelphia and New York are about ninety miles apart, but driving in the city can be a nightmare. We recommend staying at a hotel in Jersey City or Newark and taking the Path Train to Manhattan, then the subway to the Bronx.

Afternoon: Stretch your stomach with an early lunch at Mickey Mantle's Restaurant, located at 42 Central Park South. The place is full of memorabilia and serves an impressive menu of upscale pub food.

After lunch, stroll around Central Park, then hop on the 4 Express train, which will take you to the Bronx. Before heading into the stadium that was modeled after the original "House that Ruth Built," duck into Billy's Sports Bar (856 River Ave.) to check out the mural of Babe Ruth.

Next, check out Babe Ruth Plaza, located between Gates 4 and 6 of Yankee Stadium, where Ruth's accomplishments are celebrated with porcelain images and storyboards displayed on light posts.

Finally, if time allows, take the Yankees' Classic Tour, a behind-the-scenes walk through new Yankee Stadium that includes a stop at the Yankees Museum. For more information, visit: http://newyork.yankees.mlb.com/nyy/ballpark/stadium_tours.jsp.

Game time: It is *essential* that you enter Yankee Stadium right when the gates open. This way you'll have time to visit Monument Park, which only remains accessible to fans until forty-five minutes before the scheduled first pitch. Here you'll find the Bambino's retired number 3, his plaque, and his monument. Have the camera ready and pose with the Babe!

Late-night: Take the 4 train back into Manhattan and treat yourself at the tavern of your choice. The bars stay open until 4:00 a.m. and you're not driving very far tomorrow so being a bit bleary-eyed shouldn't cause you too much trouble.

DAY FOUR: NEW YORK

You've got another game to catch in New York . . . after you visit another Ruth attraction, of course.

Afternoon: Take a drive on Route 87 North to nearby Hawthorne, New York. At the Gate of Heaven Cemetery you'll find Ruth's gravesite in Section 25, Plot 1115, Grave 3. This is a more popular tourist attraction than you'd think. As you'll see, his large stone is usually adorned by Yankee Stadium ticket stubs, hot dog wrappers, and napkins, not to mention the beer cans that pilgrims often leave behind.

Game time: Take the 6 train from Manhattan to Queens and catch a Mets game at Citi Field.

Late-night: Still tired from last night? If so, hit the rack early and rest up for tomorrow. If not, the night is young, and this is the city that never sleeps.

DAY FIVE: BOSTON

Boston is where the Bambino's career began. After pitching the Red Sox to a World Championship in 1918 when he won two games and posted a 1.06 ERA in October, Ruth tried his hand at hitting the next season and bashed a then-league-record twenty-nine dingers in part-time play. A season later, the Sox sold him to the Yankees, where he became a full-time outfielder. The rest, as they say, is history. But it's a little-known fact that Ruth returned to Beantown in 1935 to finish his career with the National League Boston Braves.

Two hundred and ten miles of highway lie between New York and Boston. If you depart NYC by 8:00 a.m., you should arrive in Boston by lunchtime.

Afternoon: Visit the New England Sports Museum located inside Boston's Fleet Center, home to the NHL's Bruins and NBA's Celtics. The Fleet Center is easily accessible by the MBTA's Green and Orange Lines, using the North Station stop. The NESM offers an extensive baseball exhibit, including plenty of Bambino memorabilia. For information, visit: www.tdgarden.com/sportsmuseum/default.asp.

For lunch, walk a few blocks to Boston's famous North End, a big Italian neighborhood that makes New York's Little Italy look like a food court. We recommend La Famiglia Giorgio (112 Salem St.) or Regina Pizzeria (11½ Thacher St.).

After lunch, hop back on the Green Line, take it to the Kenmore or Fenway stop and you'll be in the Fenway district. If the ballpark gates haven't opened yet, stand behind the Green Monster on festive Lansdowne Street to see if you can snag a batting practice homer. Or perhaps you'd prefer to sit down and have a pint of Bambino Ale at Boston Beerworks (61 Brookline Ave.). Tip one back for the Babe!

Game time: This is another park you'll want to enter early. Walk around during batting practice and soak up the history. Touch the Green Monster in left, walk down to field level in right and try to imagine how the Babe must have felt a hundred years ago standing on the mound in brand-new Fenway. Though you might still be full from lunch, cram down a Fenway Frank.

Late-night: After the game, buy a sausage sandwich from one of the street vendors outside. Stand off to the side and savor it as the crowd marches past. You did it: five parks in five days!

Sample Itinerary 2
The Southern Museum Tour
Days: Eight
Cities: Seven
Ballparks: Seven
Marlins Park, Miami, Florida
Tropicana Field, St. Petersburg, Florida
Turner Field, Atlanta, Georgia
Busch Stadium, St. Louis, Missouri
Kauffman Stadium, Kansas City, Missouri
Rangers Ballpark, Arlington, Texas
Minute Maid Field, Houston, Texas

Museums: Seven
Ted Williams Museum, St. Petersburg, Florida
Braves Museum and Hall of Fame, Atlanta, Georgia
Ty Cobb Museum, Royston, Georgia
Negro Leagues Museum, Kansas City, Missouri
American Jazz Museum, Kansas City, Missouri
Royals Hall of Fame, Kansas City, Missouri
Rangers Museum, Arlington, Texas

The Deep South houses a sampling of post-1960s baseball stadiums. From a retractable roof stadium to ballparks in the retro-classic style, the South truly has it all. Aside from offering baseball wanderers a diverse array of yards, Dixie also provides an assortment of opportunities for fans to brush up on their hardball knowledge through visits to baseball museums. So whether or not you've already made your first pilgrimage to the granddaddy of all baseball history halls in Cooperstown, build a few extra days into your tour of the South. This is a great April trip for fans like Josh and Kevin who live in cold-weather climates.

BEFORE HITTING THE ROAD
In the months leading up to your trip, put Ken Burns' epic documentary *Baseball* (1994) in your Netflix queue. We know, you've probably seen it before, or at least parts of it. But even so, watching this nine-plus–volume diary of the game's past—from start to finish—is a great way to spend a chilly week in February or rainy week in March as you await the season. We also recommend that you read *The Glory of Their Times* by Lawrence Ritter, who interviewed more than two dozen Dead Ball Era stars prior to their passing to preserve their amazing memories of the game in its infancy.

THE ROAD TRIP
DAY ONE: MIAMI
There is plenty of baseball history in South Florida—much of it related to the Grapefruit League spring circuit. And now there's a new ballpark for the Marlins, their fans, and road trippers like you to enjoy.
Game time: The Marlins don't have a multitude of baseball memories to celebrate, but they do have two World Series titles and counting to their credit. And that's a lot more than Kevin's Mariners have.

DAY TWO: ST. PETERSBURG
As far as domes go, Tampa Bay's Tropicana Field is one of the more aesthetically interesting ones. But it's still a dome.
Afternoon: Head to the scenic St. Petersburg waterfront and check out venerable Al Lang Field, former spring home of the New York Yankees and Rays, among other teams. Then follow the historical markers of Baseball Boulevard along the one-mile walkway that leads to the Trop.
Game time: Pining for that old-time ballpark atmosphere? A well-done mural that covers much of the first and second levels of the concourses behind the stands will remind you of all you're missing at Tropicana Field. Take a long look, and then say a prayer that no batted balls will strike the catwalks while you're in town.

When the game hits a lull, head out to the center-field concourse where the Ted Williams Museum treats fans to items related to Ted's childhood, military days, fishing exploits, and prolific baseball career. What? You thought the Splendid Splinter was a Red Sox icon? Well, we did too. But Williams retired to Florida after his career and loved fishing in the Keys almost as much as he loved slashing line drives. In his final years, he ran the Museum in Hernando, Florida up north. Then, when he passed, the Rays were generous enough to free up some concourse space for it.

DAY THREE: ATLANTA
A beautiful ballpark of the classical ilk, Turner Field provides a great outdoor venue for hardball, especially in April and May before the famously oppressive Hotlanta weather becomes too unbearable.
Braves Museum and Hall of Fame: Arrive at Turner at least an hour early so you'll have time to visit the Braves Museum and Hall of Fame, which is accessible from outside the park as well as from within. Check out the old dugout benches and bat racks from Atlanta-Fulton County Stadium and the old railroad car like the kind the players used to ride.
Game time: On your way into the game walk through the Green Parking Lot where a large portion of the otherwise demolished County Stadium outfield fence still stands intact in tribute to Hank Aaron. This is where history happened: number 715. The ball cleared the wall and a new home run champion was crowned.

DAY FOUR: ATLANTA TO ST. LOUIS
Before heading to the Gateway City, make a detour to the Ty Cobb Museum, located in Royston, northeast of Atlanta. Despite his reputation for being a real creep, Cobb was actually very generous to the people of his hometown. He funded construction of a hospital in his later years. Appropriately then, this small museum that pays tribute to his life is located inside the Joe A. Adams Professional Building of the

Ty Cobb Healthcare System. The Ty Cobb Museum (461 Cook St., Royston) houses everything from Cobb's Shriners fez to his false teeth, as well as a fair share of baseball mementos.

Just a mile away on Highway 17, Rose Hill Cemetery is home to Cobb's mausoleum, so be sure to pay your respects on the way out of town.

DAY FIVE: ST. LOUIS

St. Louis is a great baseball town, and the Cardinals franchise is steeped in history. But the Cardinals closed their Museum in 2008. A new Ballpark Village is scheduled to open in 2013, in the street surrounding new Busch Stadium, including the relocated Museum. So stay tuned!

DAY SIX: KANSAS CITY

Out of the unconscionable exclusion of African Americans from the American and National Leagues grew a thriving culture of baseball in the Negro Leagues. Although these leagues were separate from the white Major Leagues, they made many contributions to the evolution of the game. The first night game, for example, was a Negro Leagues affair.

Today, in order that the Negro Leagues won't ever be forgotten, the Negro Leagues Museum (1616 E. 18th St., Kansas City, Missouri) offers a half-day worth of exhibits for fans to review. The highlight is a mock field in the center of the museum where stars like Josh Gibson, Rube Foster, Satchel Paige, and Buck O'Neil appear in the person of bronze statues, placed at their familiar positions on the field.

The American Jazz Museum is located in the same building as the Negro Leagues one. Celebrating Louie Armstrong, Ella Fitzgerald, Kansas City's own Charlie Parker, and others, it offers a wonderfully interactive tour that allows visitors to experience the music of Americana. Clearly, during a defining moment in American history this once vibrant community at 18th and Vine Street lived for jazz and baseball.

Game time: Inside Kauffman Stadium the Royals maintain a team Hall of Fame on the left-field concourse. The exhibits celebrate legendary Royals like George Brett and Frank White and the 1985 World Series trophy is on display.

DAY SEVEN: ARLINGTON

While the Texas Rangers may not have a World Series trophy of their own to display yet, they do have one beauty of a ballpark. For a while they also had the largest, most impressive collection of baseball memorabilia south of Cooperstown.

But the three-floor Legends of the Game Museum has been reduced to its current state as a small Rangers Museum only.

Game time: The lone player statue inside the ballpark is of Nolan Ryan, who won just fifty-one games while a member of the Rangers. But look at it this way: Elvis Andrus and Josh Hamilton are out on the field making history in the present. Someday there may well be statues of the pair near the one of the grizzled Texas flamethrower and you'll be able to say you saw them in their prime.

DAY EIGHT: HOUSTON

Last stop, Houston. Road-weary and bloated with hot dogs and baseball history, you deserve a day to relax. And you can, because there's no hardball museum to visit in Houston. Take a drive to the old Astrodome before the game and then treat yourself to some delicious Mexican food.

Game time: On the way into Minute Maid Park, stop by the plaza on the Crawford Street side of the field and say hello to the larger-than-life statues of former Astros Jeff Bagwell and Craig Biggio. The two play mock-catch on a miniature infield. Inside the park, take a stroll along Home Run Alley, which runs behind the stands in left. Here, bats and gloves of former Astros are on display.

Sit back and enjoy the game. Your trip is nearing its end. Hopefully you'll return home refreshed and ready to test your friends' and coworkers' baseball knowledge with trivia you gathered while touring the ballparks and museums of the South.

Sample Itinerary 3
The Ballparks, Ballparks, and More Ballparks Tour of the Midwest

Days: Ten
Cities: Seven
Ballparks: Nineteen (Eight current MLB parks)
PNC Park, Pittsburgh, Pennsylvania
Forbes Field site, Pittsburgh, Pennsylvania
Great American Ballpark, Cincinnati, Ohio
Crosley Field replica, Blue Ash, Ohio
Riverfront Stadium replica, Blue Ash, Ohio
Progressive Field, Cleveland, Ohio
League Park site, Cleveland, Ohio
Wrigley Field, Chicago, Illinois
U.S. Cellular Field, Chicago, Illinois
Comiskey Park site, Chicago, Illinois
Comerica Park, Detroit, Michigan

Tiger Stadium site, Detroit, Michigan
Miller Park, Milwaukee, Wisconsin
Helfaer Field, Milwaukee, Wisconsin
Field of Dreams, Dyersville, Iowa
Target Field, Minneapolis, Minnesota
Metrodome, Minneapolis, Minnesota
Metropolitan Stadium site, Bloomington, Minnesota
Midway Stadium, St. Paul, Minnesota

Aside from offering an assortment of top-notch baseball diamonds currently in use by MLB teams, the cities of the Midwest also house more than their share of old-time ball-park relics, novelty parks, and minor league parks. So build an extra day or two into your tour to accommodate some of the pit stops just off the beaten track in the Heartland.

BEFORE HITTING THE ROAD

Even though you've seen it before and have probably soured on all things Costner ever since that legendary *Waterworld* flop, you should rent *Field of Dreams,* pop some corn, and turn down the lights. Pay attention to the field, farmhouse, ghost players, and even the background actors or "extras." We'll explain why later. If time allows, you might also want to read the book upon which the movie was based: W. P. Kinsella's *Shoeless Joe* is a quick read that contains a few twists that aren't in the movie. We think you'll like it.

Next, rent *61** and *Major League,* paying special attention to the ballparks in which the two movies were filmed. See if you can guess which parks they used (hint: *61** was not filmed at Yankee Stadium and *Major League* was not filmed at Cleveland's Municipal Stadium).

Finally, warm up your shoulder with a few hours of long toss in the days before your trip, and be sure to pack your mitt and a ball.

THE ROAD TRIP
DAY ONE: PITTSBURGH

After enjoying the old-time flavor of Forbes Field for more than sixty years (1909–1970), the Pirates and their fans suddenly found themselves in Three Rivers Stadium, a monolithic cookie-cutter, where they would remain for three decades. For a while the team maintained its winning ways in the new stadium, but eventually the Pirates sprang a leak and fans started jumping ship. Today, old-time hardball has returned to the 'Burgh in the form of a beautiful ballpark that provides striking views of the game and downtown skyline.

Afternoon: Visit the remnants of Forbes Field on the University of Pittsburgh campus. You'll find the brick outfield wall, covered in ivy, the flagpole that once stood in play, and even the original home plate, which resides under glass in the lobby of a nearby academic building.

Game time: On your way to the game, linger for a moment as you walk across the Roberto Clemente Bridge and reflect upon how far Pittsburgh has come since its Three Rivers days. Be sure to get a ticket behind the plate or on the third-base side, to allow for a view of the sun setting on the river and city beyond the outfield fence.

DAY TWO: CINCINNATI

Another day, another scenic retro park located on the banks of a river. What a life! As was the case in Pittsburgh, Cincinnati once housed a regal old-time yard—Crosley Field—before building a cookie-cutter—Riverfront Stadium—and then finally building a retro park—Great American Ballpark. Notice a theme starting to develop on this trip? By the end of the day you should. You'll be sampling the three predominant ballpark types of the last century: classical era, cookie-cutter/dome era, and retro era.

Afternoon: While it's not possible to actually visit the recently imploded Riverfront Stadium, home to the Reds from 1971 to 2002, or the long-gone Crosley Field (1912–1970), there is hope yet for ballpark wanderers. On the ride from the 'Burgh to Cincy, make a pit stop in Blue Ash, Ohio, where you'll find adjacent replica ball fields that the Reds use for old-timers' games. One field mirrors the exact field dimensions of Riverfront Stadium, and the other, the dimensions of Crosley Field. A replica of the Crosley scoreboard stands in the new Crosley outfield, and there's even an outfield embankment like the one in the original park. Check out the multitude of plaques lining the dugouts that honor Reds greats, and then bust out your glove and take to the field of your choice for a game of catch.

Game time: Before heading through the gates, visit Crosley Terrace outside, where statues honor such Crosley Era stars as Frank Robinson, Ted Kluszewski, Ernie Lombardi and Joe Nuxhall engaged in simulated game-action. Afterwards, follow the same protocol as in Pittsburgh. Settle into a seat between the bases at Great American and enjoy a view of the river.

DAY THREE: CLEVELAND

Different town, same story. After enjoying countless games during baseball's early years in League Park (1891–1946), Cleveland built the monstrous and multipurpose Municipal Stadium (1932–1993) before unveiling in 1994 the ballpark originally known as Jacobs Field, a baseball-only facility that re-embraces the warm and cozy elements of the classical ballpark era. It's since been renamed, of course, in honor of an insurance company. Such is life in our modern times.

Afternoon: Pay a visit to the crumbling, but resilient remnants of League Park. A youth field sits on the old stadium grounds, but a great deal of the old park remains around it. The actual ticket booths are intact, as is a very large portion of the intricate facade along the left-field side. After snapping a few photos, whip out your glove, head onto the diamond and make like Nap Lajoie!

Game time: Pay a visit to the Bob Feller statue on the way into Progressive Field. Then grab a Panini sandwich and enjoy the game.

DAY FOUR: DETROIT

When it comes to ballpark evolution, Detroit charted a different course than the first three cities on this trip. Motown wisely chose not to bite on the multipurpose movement that overtook much of the Midwest, opting instead to hold onto its old-time gem for as long as possible. Tiger Stadium served the team well for the better part of a century (1912–1999) before giving way to Comerica Park, which despite some imperfections provides a festive atmosphere for a game in an extremely open-air setting.

Afternoon: Take a drive past the old Tiger Stadium site, where today not much remains other than the footprint of the old field at the corner of Michigan and Trumbull. Eventually some developer will build condos or a hotel or mall on this site, but for now it's just growing dandelions. As for the site's pop-culture significance … The Roger Maris-/Mickey Mantle-focused drama *61 was filmed at Detroit's famous "Corner," as Tiger Stadium stood in for a certain ballpark in the Bronx.

DAY FIVE: CHICAGO

On the North Side of Chi-town you'll find the best of the old-time parks incarnate in Wrigley Field, while on the South Side you'll find one of the least-inspired but well-retrofitted new parks in U.S. Cellular Field. What the latter lacks in intimacy is more than made up for by the Friendly Confines of Wrigley. Make no mistake, your three-games-in-two-days visit to the Windy City will be a blast.

Ernie Banks was right when he said, "It's a nice day, let's play two." You may not have the option of playing two, but you can watch two games in one day if you schedule your visit to Chicago during a time when the White Sox and Cubs are both at home.

Game time: Welcome to Wrigleyville. Let the fun begin. Say hello to Cubs super-fan Ronnie Woo Woo, drink a few cans of Old Style at Murphy's Bleachers, then watch a game from the Bleachers. As far as ballgame experiences go, this one is second to none.

Between Games: Ride the "L" south. Your hardball dream day is only half over.

Game time: Before entering The Cell, check out the foul lines of old Comiskey, painted in white, on the asphalt of the new stadium's parking lot. Then be sure to get a seat in the ballpark's lower level. If it's a hot and humid night, take a pregame stroll to the outdoor shower on the left-field concourse.

DAY SIX: CHICAGO

One game at Wrigley wasn't enough. You're in town and the sun's shining. The Cubbies are playing an afternoon game. So treat yourself.

Morning: Bring your mitt and shag BP homers with the crew on Waveland Avenue behind the left-field bleachers.

Game time: Same drill as yesterday. Only don't get quite so drunk. You have some driving to do, either tonight or tomorrow morning.

DAY SEVEN: MILWAUKEE

The friendly folks in Brew City didn't have a Major League team back in the classical ballpark era. So when the erstwhile Boston Braves came to town Milwaukee unveiled mulipurpose County Stadium (1953–2000), which later served as home to the Brewers. Then, in 2001, the Sons of Selig unveiled a gigantic retractable dome. Miller Park provides some terrific lower-level seats and some terrible Uecker seats upstairs.

Afternoon: Did somebody say "tailgate?" This is as good as it gets when it comes to pregame gorging. Arrive at the parking lot early and bring your grill. Bratwurst and dilly beans are on the menu. After eating and drinking yourself silly, take a stroll across the parking lot to Helfaer Field, a youth diamond laid at the approximate location of where County Stadium once stood. Play catch on the field, and then check out the plaques on the concourse to learn more about County Stadium. Remember the movie *Major League?* It was filmed at County Stadium, which stood in for Cleveland's Muni.

Game time: We can't stress enough the importance of getting a seat on the first or second level, preferably between the bases. The disparity between the good seats and bad seats is greater here than at almost any other park.

DAY EIGHT: DYERSVILLE, IOWA/DRIVING DAY

You won't be seeing a game today, or maybe you will. On the ride from Milwaukee to Minneapolis, swing a few miles out of the way and make for Dyersville, to visit the Field of Dreams Movie Site. Toss a ball around the field, say hello to Don Lansing, who lives in the old white farmhouse from the movie and who appeared in several scenes as an extra. Then settle into the first-base bleachers. Watch the ghost players glide effortlessly toward the cornrows to make spectacular catches. Listen for the crack of the bat or the pop of a pitch hitting the catcher's mitt.

DAY NINE: MINNEAPOLIS

If you're interested in ballpark evolution, consider Minneapolis a must-visit on your tour of the Midwest. The Metrodome still stands, even though the Twins have moved on to greener pastures. So do a lap around the Met, which opened in 1982 to replace Metropolitan Stadium—a converted minor league park that housed the Twins from 1961 to 1981.

Afternoon: From the Field of Dreams to the Field of Screams. That's right, where Metropolitan Stadium once stood visitors now find the Mall of America's indoor amusement park. The massive mall is in Bloomington, Minnesota. Today, the original home plate and a bleacher seat that Harmon Killebrew once hit with a mammoth home run are all that remain.

Game time: Not only did Target Field return the Twins and their fans to baseball in the great outdoors, but it did so in style when it opened in 2010. After years in the Homer Dome, it's easy to see why Twins fans fell in love with this place immediately. It's cozy and offers great site lines. Be sure to check out the statues of Killebrew, Rod Carew, and Kirby Puckett outside.

DAY TEN: ST. PAUL

Although you've already enjoyed plenty of big league ball on this trip, we recommend a game at zany Midway Stadium, home to the independent league St. Paul Saints.

Afternoon: Tailgating is popular among Saints fans, but arrive early as lot space is limited.

Game time: Keep an eye out for actor Bill Murray who is a part-owner of the Saints. He sometimes shows up to coach third base. And be on the lookout for the potbellied pig that delivers balls to the home plate ump, and all kinds of other unexpected wonders. Have a few brats and a few brews. This is the indy minors, so have fun. Besides, you just saw eighteen ballparks in 10 days, so you ought to feel pretty good about yourself!

Sample Itinerary 4
West Coast Major/Minor League Tour

Days: Fifteen
Cities: Fifteen
Ballparks: Seventeen (Eight MLB parks)
Coors Field, Denver, Colorado
Security Service Field, Colorado Springs, Colorado
Isotopes Park, Albuquerque, New Mexico
Chase Field, Phoenix, Arizona
Aces Ballpark, Reno, Nevada
Cashman Field, Las Vegas, Nevada
Petco Park, San Diego, California
Dodger Stadium, Los Angeles, California
Angel Stadium of Anaheim, Anaheim, California
Chukchansi Park, Fresno, California
AT&T Park, San Francisco, California
The O.co Coliseum, Oakland, California
Raley Field, Sacramento, California
Cheney Stadium, Tacoma, Washington
Safeco Field, Seattle, Washington

If you've got a tank full of gas and the better part of a month to blow, this is the trip for you. Fans of bush league ball and students of the game's history will also dig this trip. To the uninformed observer, baseball may seem like a new phenomenon in many West Coast cities, but nothing could be further from the truth. The Pacific Coast League dates back to 1903. That's right, it's nearly as old as the American League, and at one point—before the Giants and Dodgers jumped town for the West Coast—it was considered by many to be a third Major League. Ted Williams and Joe DiMaggio were well-known entities on the West Coast, starring in the PCL before becoming household names in the rest of the country. Today sixteen of the thirty big league teams have affiliates in the Triple-A PCL. The teams of the PCL play in some of the largest minor league yards, with most of those ballparks holding a capacity of nearly ten thousand. And they need all the seats they can squeeze in. The league has a rabid following.

BEFORE HITTING THE ROAD

We highly recommend Dick Dobbins's superbly researched book, *The Grand Minor League: An Oral History of the Old Pacific Coast League*.

THE ROAD TRIP
DAY ONE: DENVER

Watching baseball at Coors Field doesn't require an oxygen mask. But it might come in handy if you sit above the "mile high" marker in the upper deck. Seriously, though, just be sure to avoid the Rocky Mountain Oysters.

DAY TWO: COLORADO SPRINGS

There isn't much of a drive between Denver and Colorado Springs, but the ride is nonetheless breathtaking here in Wile E. Coyote country. Be sure to visit Pike's Peak or one of the many other viewing areas. The Sky Sox play just sixty miles south of their parent club, the Rockies.

DAY THREE: ALBUQUERQUE

That's right, this PCL affiliate is named the Albuquerque Isotopes. Homer Simpson fans will be disappointed, however, to learn that the mascot is named Orbit and not Hungry, Hungry Homer. There are, however, statues of Homer and Marge on the ballpark concourse.

DAY FOUR: PHOENIX

Still sunburned from yesterday's game? Don't despair. Chase Field has a roof and the folks in Arizona aren't afraid to use it. Buy some "frozen water" on the way into the park, then wait for the roof to open just before first pitch, as is the local custom.

DAY FIVE: LAS VEGAS

There isn't much else going on in this sleepy desert outpost, so why not catch a game at Cashman Field? The ballpark is surrounded by palm and olive trees, while a desert mountain range rises to the northeast. All right, we know you're not driving to Las Vegas to see the palm trees. But the home of the LV 51s is worth a visit, if only to see the ghoulish space alien mascot of this team named after Area 51.

DAY SIX: ACES BALLPARK: RENO

Expect to see plenty of triples at this spacious yard that opened in 2009 after Reno lured the former Tucson Sidewinders out of Arizona.

DAY SEVEN: SAN DIEGO

Pay a visit to sunny Petco Park. Although the view might not be the best the park has to offer, if you want to catch some rays, opt for a cheapie seat out at the right-field beach.

DAY EIGHT: LOS ANGELES

Dodger Stadium has seen more hardball history than all of the other MLB ballparks in the West combined. Think Blue!

DAY NINE: ANAHEIM

The Big A has improved by leaps and bounds since the football seats were carted away. Enjoy the view of the San Bernardino Mountains, smog permitting.

DAY TEN: FRESNO

We have a feeling you'll like the Grizzlies' Chukchansi Park. It's located downtown and features stunning views of the Sierra Mountains.

DAY ELEVEN: SAN FRANCISCO

It doesn't happen as often as it used to, but you just might see a slugger put one in the drink while you're in town.

DAY TWELVE: OAKLAND

Be certain to make note of the announced attendance for your A's game at the Coliseum. Or take the bull by the horns and count the fans yourself before the announcement comes.

DAY THIRTEEN: SACRAMENTO

The River Cats typically average more than ten thousand fans per game and have led the minors in attendance on several occasions. If only their big league parent club—the A's—could do so well.

DAY FOURTEEN: TACOMA

Tacoma is home to the Rainiers. No, it's not rainier in Tacoma than in the team's big league city, Seattle. The Tacoma squad's name serves a dual purpose. First, the Rainier name honors the Seattle Rainiers, who played PCL ball in the Emerald City long before the M's came to town. That team was named after owner Emil Sick's Rainier Beer. Second, the Rainier Brewery was named after Mount Rainier, which looms even larger in the city of Tacoma than it does in Seattle. Set in the Snake Lake area, Tacoma's Cheney Stadium dates from 1960 but was fully renovated prior to the 2011 season.

DAY FIFTEEN: SEATTLE

Don't worry if it rains. The fans are all "safe" here.

Enjoy the game and have a pint of Pyramid Ale for us. A long and winding journey has reached its end.

SELECTED BIBLIOGRAPHY

Our task was made more feasible thanks to the following books, magazines, newspapers, and websites that we used as reference sources:

Periodicals

Baseball Weekly/Sports Weekly, 1993–2003.
The Boston Globe, 1925–2011.
The New York Times, 1979–2011.
The San Diego Union, 2003.
Sports Illustrated, 1988–2011.
The Sporting News, 2000–2011.
USA Today, 1998–2011.

Books

Adair, Robert K. *The Physics of Baseball,* 3rd ed. New York: Harper Collins, 2002.

Adams, Bruce, and Margaret Engel. *Fodor's Baseball Vacations: Great Family Trips to Minor League and Classic Major League Ballparks Across America.* 3rd ed. New York: Fodors Travel Publishing, 2002.

Ahuja, Jay. *Fields of Dreams.* New York: Citadel Press, 2001.

Angell, Roger. *The Summer Game.* New York: Viking Press, 1972.

Bouton, Jim. *Ball Four.* New York: Macmillan General Reference, 1990.

Bukowski, Douglas. *Baseball Palace of the World: The Last Year of Comiskey Park.* Chicago: Lyceum Books, 1992.

Cramer, Richard Ben. *Joe DiMaggio: The Hero's Life.* New York: Simon & Schuster, 2000.

Darnell, Tim. *The Crackers: Early Days of Atlanta Baseball.* Athens, Georgia: Hill Street Press, 1999.

Dobbins, Dick. *The Grand Minor League: An Oral History of the Old Pacific Coast League.* San Francisco: Woodford Publishing, 1999.

Field of Schemes: How the Great Stadium Swindle Turns Public Money into Private Profit. Cagan, De Mause, eds. Monroe, Maine: Common Courage Press, 1998.

Goodwin, Doris Kearns. *Wait Till Next Year.* New York: Touchtone Books, 1998.

Halberstam, David. *Summer of '49.* New York: Avon Books, 1989.

James, Bill. *The New Bill James Historical Baseball Abstract.* New York: Free Press, 2001.

Johnson, Rody. *The Rise and Fall of Dodgertown: 60 Years of Baseball in Vero Beach.* Gainesville, Florida: University Press of Florida, 2008.

Kahn, Roger. *The Boys of Summer.* New York: Harper Perennial, 1998.

———. *The Era: 1947–1957, When the Yankees, the Giants, and the Dodgers Ruled the World.* Lincoln, Nebraska: University of Nebraska Press, 2002.

Leventhal, Josh. *Take Me Out to the Ballpark.* New York: Black Dog and Leventhal Publishers, Inc., 2000.

Lewis, Michael. *Moneyball: The Art of Winning an Unfair Game.* New York: W. W. Norton & Co., 2003.

Lyle, Sparky. *The Bronx Zoo.* New York: Crown Publishers, 1979.

Mandel, Mike. *SF Giants: An Oral History.* Santa Cruz, California: Mike Mandel, 1979.

Mock, Joe. *Joe Mock's Ballpark Guide.* Grand Slam Enterprises, 2001.

O'Neal, Bill. *The Pacific Coast League: 1903–1988.* Austin, Texas: Eakin Publications, 1990.

O'Neil, Buck. *I Was Right On Time.* New York: Simon & Schuster, 1996.

Pahigian, Joshua. *101 Baseball Places to See Before You Strike Out.* Guilford, Connecticut: The Lyons Press, 2008.

———. *Spring Training Handbook.* Jefferson, North Carolina: McFarland and Company, 2005.

Palmer, Pete and John Thorn. *Total Baseball,* 6th ed., New York: Total Sports, 1999.

Peterson, Robert. *Only the Ball Was White: A History of Legendary Black Players and All-Black Teams.* New York: McGraw-Hill, 1984.

Rielly, Edward J. *Baseball: An Encyclopedia of Popular Culture.* Lincoln, Nebraska: University of Nebraska Press, 2005.

Riley, James A. *The Biographic Encyclopedia of the Negro Baseball Leagues.* New York: Carroll and Graf Publishers, 2002.

Ritter, Lawrence. *The Glory of Their Times: The Story of the Early Days of Baseball by the Men Who Played It.* New York: Macmillan, 1966.

———. *Lost Ballparks: A Celebration of Baseball's Legendary Fields.* New York: Penguin, 1994.

Ritter, Lawrence, and Donald Honig. *The 100 Greatest Baseball Players of All Time.* New York: Crown Publishers, Inc., 1981.

Rosen, Ira. *Blue Skies, Green Fields.* New York: Clarkson N. Potter, 2001.

Shatzin, Mike, and Jim Charlton. *The Baseball Fan's Guide to Spring Training.* Reading, Massachusetts: Addison-Wesley Publishing Company, Inc., 1988.

Shaughnessy, Dan. *Curse of the Bambino.* New York: Dutton, 1990.

Shaughnessy, Dan, and Stan Grossfeld. *Spring Training: Baseball's Early Season.* Boston: Houghton Mifflin Company, 2003.

Smith, Ron. *The Ballpark Book.* St. Louis: The Sporting News, 2000.

Sotheby's: The Barry Halper Collection of Baseball Memorabilia, Japan: Barry Halper Enterprises, 1999.

The Stadium: Architecture of Mass Sport. Provoost, Michelle, ed. Netherlands: NAI Publishers, 2000.

Stump, Al. *Cobb: A Biography.* Chapel Hill, North Carolina: Algonquin Books of Chapel Hill, 1994.

Sullivan, Neil J. *The Dodgers Move West.* New York: Oxford University Press, 1987.

Thornley, Stew. *Land of the Giants: New York's Polo Grounds.* Philadelphia: Temple University Press, 2000.

The Ultimate Baseball Book. Okrent, Lewine, eds. Boston: Houghton Mifflin Company, 2000.

Vancil, Mark. *The New York Yankees: New York Yankees—100 Years—The Official Retrospective,* Ballantine Books, 2003.

Veeck, Bill, with Ed Linn. *Veeck, as in Wreck.* New York: Putnam, 1962.

Von Goeben, Robert. *Ballparks.* New York: Metro Books, 2000.

Westcott, Rich. *Philadelphia's Old Ballparks.* Philadelphia: Temple University Press, 1996.

Wood, Bob. *Dodger Dogs to Fenway Franks.* New York: McGraw-Hill Publishing Co., 1988.

Websites

www.ballparkdigest.com
www.ballparks.com
www.ballparksofbaseball.com
www.baseball-almanac.com
www.baseballcube.com
www.baseballlibrary.com
www.baseball-reference.com
www.espn.com
www.mlb.com
www.nationalpastime.com
www.planeta.com

Videos/DVDs

Burns, Ken. *Baseball: A Film by Ken Burns.* PBS Home Video, 1997.

When It Was a Game—Triple Play Collection. Warner Home Video, 2001.

ABOUT THE AUTHORS

Josh Pahigian

Photo by Heather Pahigian

Josh Pahigian swore off baseball for the first time at age twelve when the ball went through Bill Buckner's legs in the 1986 World Series. He rejoined Red Sox Nation the following March, but retained his Red Sox fatalism until October 2004, when suddenly a weight was lifted from his shoulders, his head emerged from a post-adolescent fog that had lasted about a decade too long, and a whole bunch of other clichés came crashing down. He looks at life a lot more optimistically now that his Red Sox have won two World Championships in his lifetime.

Besides co-authoring this book, Josh has published six other books—including *101 Baseball Places to See Before You Strike Out* and *The Ultimate Minor League Baseball Road Trip*, both with Lyons Press. Josh has also written for several print and web-based periodicals, including ESPN.com. In addition, his short stories have appeared in national and international literary journals and magazines, in English and in translation in Armenian.

Josh lives in Buxton, Maine, with his wife, Heather, and son, Spencer. He holds degrees from the College of the Holy Cross and Emerson College. He teaches part-time at the University of New England.

Kevin O'Connell is a West Coast sports fan living in the East, which means he's an incurable insomniac, up all hours of the night watching his beloved Seattle Mariners and Gonzaga Bulldogs. One day he hopes one of these two teams will find their way into a championship game—and perhaps even win it. Until then, he watches and practices Zen-like patience.

Along with co-authoring both versions of this book, he also collaborated on *Why I Hate the Yankees,* a satirical and critical look at America's most successful sports franchise. He's the writer of articles for magazine, newspaper, and web publications, including ESPN Travel. Kevin is the screenwriter of the short film *Houses and Rooms,* which premiered at the Seattle International Film Festival.

Kevin lives with his wife, Meghan, and his daughters, Maeve and Rory, in Pittsburgh, Pennsylvania. He holds degrees from Emerson College and Gonzaga University.

Both authors are interested in receiving reader feedback. Get in touch with them via e-mail at pahigian35@yahoo.com or ktoconnell@hotmail.com.

Kevin O'Connell

Photo by Meghan Coughlin

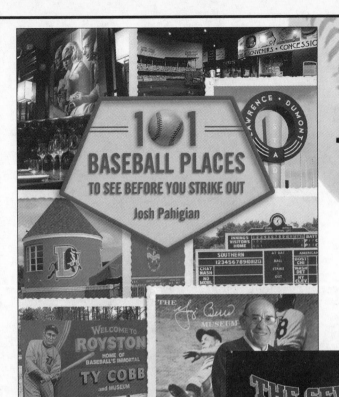

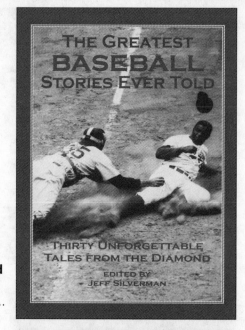

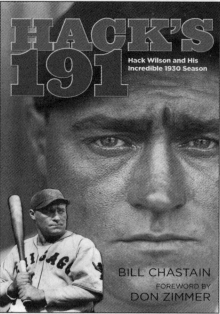

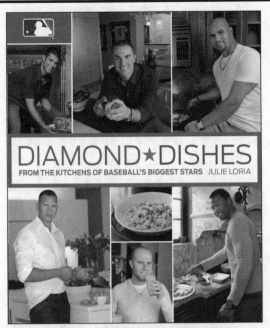
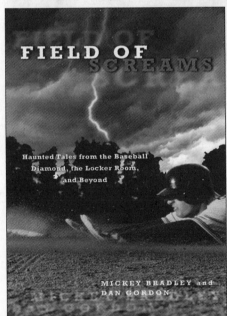

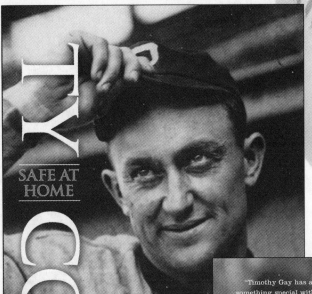

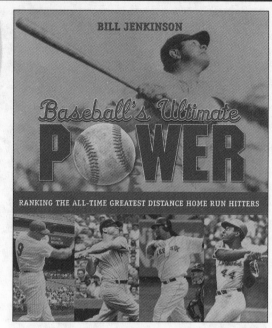
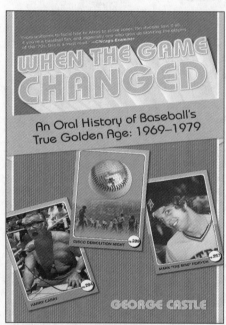